ENCYCLOPÆDIA AMERICANA.

A

POPULAR DICTIONARY

OF

ARTS, SCIENCES, LITERATURE, HISTORY, POLITICS AND BIOGRAPHY,

A NEW EDITION;

INCLUDING

A COPIOUS COLLECTION OF ORIGINAL ARTICLES

IN

AMERICAN BIOGRAPHY;

ON

THE BASIS OF THE SEVENTH EDITION OF THE GERMAN

CONVERSATIONS-LEXICON.

EDITED BY

FRANCIS LIEBER,

ASSISTED BY

E. WIGGLESWORTH AND T. G. BRADFORD.

VOL. XI.

I0836595

BOSTON:
B. B. MUSSEY & CO.
1851.

Entered, according to the Act of Congress, in the year 1831, by
Carey and Lea,
In the Clerk's office of the District Court of the Eastern District of Pennsylvania.

Printed by T. K. & P. G. Collins.

ENCYCLOPÆDIA AMERICANA.

REVELATION. Besides the exhibitions of divine agency in the works of nature, and the inward disclosures of divinity in the human mind, we find among almost all nations traditions of an immediate revelation of the will of God, communicated by words or works of supernatural significance or power. The nations of antiquity traced the origin of their religions, and even of their civilization, to the instructions of the gods, who, in their opinion, taught their ancestors as men teach children. As a child, without the assistance of others, would be incapable of acquiring knowledge, so the human race, in its infancy, could not have made the first step in the arts and sciences without a guide; and even if external nature, in its various objects and phenomena, were a sufficient guide to that kind of knowledge and skill which is necessary to provide for the bodily wants of man, can it be supposed that this nature could set in action his moral faculties, and open to his view the world of spiritual being? To reason, which derives its knowledge from sensual experience, the world is a riddle: the solution of this riddle—a knowledge of God and his relation to the world—could have been given only by God himself. Whatever knowledge man possesses of this subject must have been received directly, by oral communication, from the Deity, without which he could never, or at least not so soon nor so surely, have acquired it. In this revelation of himself, God adapted his communications to the comprehension of the beings for whose instruction it was intended; and we may distinguish three periods in this education of the human race in divine things. The earliest revelations, made in the patriarchal age, were common to the progenitors of all people; and their light shines through the darkness of all the heathen mythologies, which, on closer examination, plainly appear to have been built up on the simple religious notions of the primitive age, confirming the declaration of Scripture, that God has never left himself without a witness in the world. These earlier notions were preserved pure, and gradually enlarged, during the Mosaic period, by successive revelations to chosen individuals, with whom the Bible makes us acquainted under the name of prophets, from Moses to Malachi. God finally completed his revelations through Christ. Thus has revelation educated the human race from infancy to manhood, and man, dismissed from this school eighteen centuries ago, has now only to make the light, thus received, known and healing to all. The evidences of this divine plan of the education of the human race, proclaimed and accomplished in the Bible, are exhibited in the history of the world. (See *Christianity.*)

REVELATION. (See *Apocalypse.*)

REVENUE. For the revenue of the different states of Europe and America, see the articles on the respective countries; also the *Table of European States.* (The early copies of this work have an improved form of this table after the index of vol. v.) See also the article *Taxes.*

REVERBERATION, in physics; the act of a body repelling or reflecting another after its impinging on it. *Echoes* are occasioned by the reverberation of sounds from arched surfaces.—In glass furnaces, the flame *reverberates*, or bends back again, to burn the matter on all sides.—In chemistry, *reverberation* denotes a circulation of flame, or its return from the top to the bottom of the furnace, to produce an intense heat, when calcination is required.

REVEREND; a title of respect given to

ecclesiastics. The religious, in Catholic countries, are styled *reverend fathers*, and the abbesses, prioresses, &c., *reverend mothers*. In England, bishops are *right reverend*, archbishops *most reverend*, and the lower clergy *reverend*

REVERSION; the residue of an estate left in the grantor, to commence in possession after the determination of the particular estate granted. The estate returns to the grantor or his heirs after the grant is over.

REVIEWS. The French were the first to establish critical journals. The *Bibliographia Parisina* of Jacob (1645) was merely a yearly catalogue of new books, without remarks of any kind; but it is said to have suggested the idea of the *Journal des Savans*, a weekly journal, instituted in 1665, by M. de Sallo, which contained analyses and critical judgments of new works. It was afterwards edited by the abbés Gallois and De la Roque, and president Cousin. From 1715 to 1792, it was conducted by a society of scholars, and appeared in monthly numbers. In 1792, it was discontinued, and revived, in 1816, under the patronage of the crown. The collaborators since its revival have been De Sacy, Langlès, Raynouard, Raoul-Rochette, Rémusat, Dacier, Quatremère de Quincy, Letronne, Biot, Cuvier, &c. The collection from 1665 to 1792 forms 111 vols., 4to., reprinted Amsterdam (1684 seq.), 381 vols., 12mo. The *Mercure de France*, begun in 1672, under the title of *Mercure Galant*, and still continued, was originally designed for the amusement of the court, and men of the world, and was very miscellaneous in its contents. The editorship, which was bestowed as an act of court favor, was sometimes in good hands, as, for example, Marmontel's. The *Année littéraire* (1754—76) acquired celebrity under the management of Fréron. (q. v.) The *Journal étranger* (1754—62) and the *Journal encyclopédique* (1756—91) contained dissertations and papers of various kinds, as well as reviews. The *Revue* (originally *Décade*) *philosophique, littéraire et politique* (1794—1807), was for a time edited by Ginguené, and was distinguished for consistency of principle during a succession of most agitated periods. Millin's *Annales* (originally *Magazin*) *encyclopédiques* (1795—1818), together with critical reviews, contains a valuable mass of original essays, and a great variety of interesting intelligence relating to all countries. It has been succeeded by the *Revue encyclopédique*, which still appears in monthly numbers, on a similar but more extended plan. The *Revue* was edited till the close of 1831 by Jullien (q. v.), and is now conducted by M. Hippolyte Carnot. The *Bulletin universel* (q. v.), conducted by baron Ferussac, has appeared since 1824, and contains, as its name imports, information on every subject in literature, science, and the arts. The *Revue Française* was established in 1828, and has been conducted with great ability in the hands of Guizot (q. v.) and the duke de Broglie. The *Revue Britannique* (1825), *Revue Germanique* (1829), and *Revue Européenne* (1831), are monthly journals, devoted, as their titles indicate, to foreign literature. In most of the French journals, the names of the authors are attached to each article.—The freedom of the press in Holland led to the establishment, in that country, by learned foreigners, of some of the most valuable critical journals, which have appeared any where. Acute criticism, extensive erudition, and charm of style, are united in a remarkable degree in the *Nouvelles de la République des Lettres*, edited from 1684 to 1687 by Bayle, and continued by other hands; the *Histoire des Ouvrages des Savans*, by Basnage (1687—1709); and the several journals conducted by Leclerc (*Bibliothèque universelle*, 1686—93, 23 vols.; *Bibliothèque Choisie*, 1703—13, 27 vols.; and *Bibliothèque ancienne et moderne*, 1714—27, 28 vols.). Besides these are distinguished the *Journal littéraire* (1713—37), *Bibliothèque raisonnée* (1728—51), and *Bibliothèque nouvelle* (1738—44). Among the Dutch literary journals, conducted by native scholars, the principal are *De Boekzaal van Europe* (from 1692, under different titles); *Het Republyk de Geleerden* (1710—48); *Allgemeene Konst-en Letter-Bode* (since 1788, which is most highly esteemed in Holland); *De Recensent ook der Recensenten;* the *Vaderlandsche Bibliothek* (1790), &c.—The Italian journals of criticism are characterized by the completeness of their analyses of works: the principal are the *Giornale de' Letterati d'Italia* (Venice, 1710—33), edited at first by Apostolo Zeno, and rich in materials of literary history; the *Biblioteca Italiana* (Milan, 1816 seq.), edited until 1826 by Acerbi, and since by Gironi, Carlini, and Fumagalli, and distinguished for acuteness of criticism and freedom of judgment; the *Novelle Letterarie* (Florence, 1740), conducted for some time by the learned Lami; the *Antologia di Firenze*, which contains also original essays; the *Effemeridi Letterarie*, and the *Giornale Arcadico* (1819 seq.), both at Rome, and the *Giornale enciclope-*

lico (Naples, 1806), chiefly a selection from other journals. The *Giornale de' Letterati* (Pisa, 1771 seq.) was for a time edited by the celebrated biographer Fabbroni, and is one of the best Italian periodicals.—The principal literary journals of Spain are the *Diario de los Literatos de España* (1737—43, 4 vols.), and the *Memorial litterario de Madrid* (1784—1807), which contain little more than an account of the contents of books. In 1831, a journal in Spanish was undertaken at Havana, under the title of *Revista Bimestre Cubana*, by Mariano Cubi i Soler.—Germany has been most fruitful in critical journals, which are more severely literary and learned than the English productions of the same kind. The earliest critical periodical is the well-known *Acta Eruditorum* (Leipsic, 1682—1776), established by Otto Mencke, and containing, besides reviews, original treatises. Thomasius's *Monatsgespräche* (1688—90), and Tenzel's *Monatliche Unterredungen* (1689, continued under the title *Curieuse Bibliothek*), are among the earlier German journals of criticism. The *Neuen Zeitungen von gelehrten Sachen* (Leipsic, under different titles, 1715—97) gives an abstract of all native and foreign journals up to 1740. The *Göttinger gelehrten Anzeigen* (Göttingen, 1739, under different titles) was edited by Haller and Heyne, and contains contributions from Michaelis, Eichhorn, Blumenbach, Hugo, Spittler, Heeren, &c. The *Briefe, die neueste Literatur betreffend* (Berlin, 1759—65), by Lessing, Mendelssohn, Nicolai, &c., and the *Allgemeine Deutsche Bibliothek* (Berlin, 1766—96, 118 vols., *Neue Allg. Deutsche Bib.* 1793—1806, 107 vols.), form a new period in German literature. The *Allgemeine Literaturzeitung* (Jena, 1785, transferred to Halle in 1804, edited by Schütz and Hufeland) took a yet wider range and a higher tone. On its removal to Halle, Eichhorn undertook the *Neue Jenaische Allgem. Litteraturzeitung* (Jena, 1804). The *Leipziger Literaturzeitung* (since 1800, under several titles), and the *Erlanger Literaturzeitung* (1746—1810), are of inferior value. The *Heidelberger Jahrbücher der Literatur* (1808), and the *Wiener Jahrbücher der Literatur* (1818), have enjoyed considerable reputation. The *Hermes* (Leipsic, 1819, discontinued 1831, 35 vols.) was distinguished for its elevated tone, and depth and variety of erudition.—In England, the Gentleman's Magazine (1731), which at first consisted merely of selections from newspapers, curious intelligence, &c., is venerable for its age; it still appears, after the lapse of a century, under the editorship of Sylvanus Urban (the original Urban was, as is well known, the bookseller Cave), and has acquired celebrity by the early connexion of Dr. Johnson with its publisher. There is an index extending from 1731 to 1786, and a second from 1787 to 1818 (2 vols., 1829), with a historical preface by Nichols. The Monthly Review (1749) was the first critical journal established in England; it was followed by the Critical Review (1756). The British Critic (1793) has appeared since 1827 in quarterly numbers, under the title of the Theological Review, and is the organ of the church party. A new era of periodical criticism, in Great Britain, began with the Edinburgh Review (q. v.), which took a wider range and a loftier tone, both in politics and literature, than had been assumed by any of its predecessors. The London Quarterly Review was established, under the management of Gifford, in 1809, and has supported tory and high church principles. In 1825, it passed into the hands of H. N. Coleridge, and is at present edited by Mr. Lockhart. The principal contributors to this journal have been Gifford, Southey, Scott, Croker, &c. These two Reviews are republished in the U. States; and there have recently been announced, as preparing for publication, Selections from the Edinburgh Review, with a Preliminary Dissertation and Notes by Maurice Cross, and Essays, moral, political and literary, selected from the Quarterly Review, with an Introduction by Mr. Lockhart. The Westminster Review (established in 1824) is the advocate of radical reform in church, state and legislation, and was established by the disciples of Jeremy Bentham (q. v.), whose principles in law and morals it supports. The Foreign Quarterly Review (established in 1827) is devoted to foreign literatures. Blackwood's Edinburgh Magazine (1817, edited by Wilson), though but partially occupied with critical matter, contains many able criticisms. Its politics are high tory. Tait's Edinburgh Magazine has recently been started (April, 1832), professedly to defend opposite principles in politics, and to assume a higher tone in literature than has been usually adopted by these smaller periodicals. The other English magazines are chiefly filled with matter of local or temporary importance. We must not, however, forget to mention the Retrospective Review (14 vols., ending in 1827), devoted to notices of old works, and the celebrated Anti-Jacobin Review (chiefly political,

1798—1801).—In the U. States, the principal journals of this kind are the North American Review, and the American Quarterly Review. The former was established at Boston, in 1815, by William Tudor, and at first consisted of essays, selections, poetical effusions, &c., with but little criticism. It was afterwards under the editorship of Mr. Channing, now professor of rhetoric in Harvard college, and assumed more the character of a critical journal. In 1820, it passed into the hands of Mr. Edward Everett, and in 1825 into those of Mr. Jared Sparks, from whom it was transferred, in 1830, to the present editor, Mr. Alexander H. Everett. A general index of the twenty-five first volumes was published in 1830. The work contains a mass of valuable information in regard to American politics, law, history, &c. The American Quarterly Review (Philadelphia, 1827) is edited by Mr. Robert Walsh. The Southern Review (Charleston, 1828), which was very ably conducted by the late Mr. Elliott (q. v.) and Mr. Legare, was discontinued with the close of the eighth volume (1832).

Revise, among printers; a second or third proof of a sheet to be printed; taken off in order to be compared with the last proof, to see whether all the mistakes marked in it are actually corrected.

Revolution, and Insurrection. We shall not here go into the question of the great changes wrought in the condition of society by political revolutions, which seem necessary to its progress, but shall confine ourselves to a few remarks on the right of insurrection against established governments. There has been much speculation on the subject whether citizens, under any circumstances, are allowed to take up arms against established authorities, and, if so, under what circumstances, &c. Without being able to enter here into all the arguments on this subject, the question may be briefly considered thus: If governments are instituted merely for the benefit of the people, it is clear that, if they have failed to answer their end, and will not submit to such changes as the people consider necessary, the people have the right, nay, are even under obligation, to overturn the existing system by force, on the general principle that all rights may be maintained by force when other means fail. The principle is so evident that it would never have been disputed, had it not been for monarchs and their supporters, who dreaded its application. In extreme cases, it is admitted by all. None, for instance, would have denied the Arabs in Egypt, or the Berbers in Barbary, the right to rise against what was called their government—a band of cruel and rapacious robbers. But at what point does this right of insurrection begin? This point it is impossible to fix in the abstract. A treatise not confined to narrow limits, like this article, might make a full statement of cases imaginary or real, and point out what was demanded in each; might hold up to view the evils of a bad government on one side, and of civil war on the other, and endeavor to show under what circumstances it was better to endure the one or to hazard the other; but it could not lay down any general rule but the vague one already given. The character of insurrections, which, while they present some of the brightest and some of the foulest spots in history, always derange the frame-work of society, is such, that they will not, generally speaking, be lightly entered into. Fanatics may sometimes take up arms from slight causes; but, generally speaking, that principle in human nature which leads men to endure the evils of established systems as long as they are endurable, will be a sufficient security against the abuse of the indefinite rule which we have stated. But while we maintain the right of insurrection, under certain circumstances, from the inalienable rights of mankind, we also admit that it can never be lawful in the technical sense of the word, because it is a violation of all rules of positive law. All the rights which a citizen, as such, enjoys, emanate from the idea of the state; and the object of an insurrection is the destruction, at least for the time, of that order which lies at the basis of the state, by the substitution of force for law. The right of a citizen, as such, to rebel, is a contradiction in terms, as it implies that the state authorizes its own destruction. An insurrection becomes lawful, in the technical sense of the word, only when it has become a revolution, and has established a new order in the place of the old. We speak, of course, of insurrections against established governments. An insurrection to overthrow an usurpation is of a totally different character, as its object is the restoration of the established order, which has been arbitrarily interrupted. While, therefore, the right of insurrection is inherent in man, it can never be rationally admitted as a principle of any constitution of government; and it was equally unphilosophical and inexpedient for one of the early French constitutions to give the right of opposing by force the exercise of unlawful power; but, from the constitution of human society, it hardly seems possible to avoid the occurrence of forcible changes in political systems. Nothing in this world can last forever; institutions established centuries ago, to answer the demands of a state of things which has long ceased to exist, frequently become extremely oppressive, from their inconsistency with the new tendencies which have sprung up in society. Sometimes the evil may be remedied without bloodshed; sometimes happy accidents facilitate a change; at other times, however, the old order of things assumes a tone of decided hostility to the new tendencies; and this is what must be expected in a large proportion of cases. Then it is that revolutions break out, and eventually establish a new order, from which new rights and laws emanate. While, therefore, the philosopher and historian acknowledge the necessity, and even obligation, of insurrections, they will, nevertheless, not fail to utter a solemn admonition against resorting rashly to this extreme remedy for violated right. There is a solidity, an authority, a completeness, in a political system which has acquired maturity by slow degrees and long struggles, that can never belong to any new system suddenly substituted in its stead. There can be no security for permanent liberty till the civic element has become developed, and men have become attached to a given system of social connexions. The common principle, therefore, of weighing the evil to be risked against the good to be gained, by a political revolution, needs to be strongly impressed upon every people in a state of political excitement.

Revolutionary Tribunal. (See *Terrorism.*)

Reynard the Fox. (See *Renard.*)

Reynolds, sir Joshua, an eminent English painter, was born at Plympton, in Devonshire, in 1723, being the tenth child of the master of the grammar-school of that town. He early discovered a predilection for the art of drawing, which induced his father to place him, at the age of seventeen, with Hudson, the most famous portrait painter in London, with whom he remained three years, and then, upon some disagreement, returned into Devonshire. He passed some time without any determinate plan, and, from 1746 to 1749, pursued his profession in Devonshire and London, and acquired numerous friends and patrons. Among the latter was captain (afterwards lord) Keppel, whom he accompanied on a cruise in the Mediterranean. He then proceeded to Rome, in which capital and other parts of Italy he spent three years. On his return to London, he painted a full-length portrait of captain Keppel, which was very much admired, and at once placed him at the head of the English portrait-painters. Rejecting the stiff, unvaried and unmeaning attitudes of former artists, he gave to his figures air and action adapted to their characters, and thereby displayed something of the dignity and invention of history. Although he never attained to perfect correctness in the naked figure, he has seldom been excelled in the ease and elegance of his faces, and the beauty and adaptation of his fancy draperies. His coloring may be said to be at once his excellence and his defect. Combining, in a high degree, the qualities of richness, brilliancy and freshness, he was often led to try modes which, probably from want of a due knowledge in chemistry and the mechanism of colors, frequently failed, and left his pictures, after a while, in a faded state. He rapidly acquired opulence; and, being universally regarded as at the head of his profession, he kept a splendid table, which was frequented by the best company in the kingdom, in respect to talents, learning and distinction. On the institution of the royal academy, in 1769, he was unanimously elected president; on which occasion the king conferred upon him the honor of knighthood. Although it was no prescribed part of his duty to read lectures, yet his zeal for the advancement of the fine arts induced him to deliver annual or biennial discourses before the academy on the principles and practice of painting. Of these he pronounced fifteen, from 1769 to 1790, which were published in two sets, and form a standard work. In 1781 and 1783, he made tours in Holland and Flanders, and wrote an account of his journey, which consists only of short notes of the pictures which he saw, with an elaborate character of Rubens. He was a member of the celebrated club which contained the names of Johnson, Garrick, Burke, and others of the first rank of literary eminence, and seems to have been universally beloved and respected by his associates. He is the favorite character in Goldsmith's poem of Retaliation; and Johnson characterized him as one whom he should find the most difficulty how to abuse. In 1784, he succeeded Ramsay as portrait-painter to the king, and continued to follow his profession, of which he was enthusiastically fond, until he lost the sight of one of his eyes. He, however, retained his equable spirits until threatened, in 1791, with the loss of his other eye, the apprehension of which, added to his habitual deafness, exceedingly depressed him. He died in 1792, in his sixtieth year, unmarried, and was interred in St. Paul's cathedral. Sir Joshua Reynolds, although there was scarcely a year in which his pencil did not produce some work of the historical kind, ranks chiefly in the class of portrait-painters. His Ugolino, and his Death of Cardinal Beaufort, are, however, deemed, in grandeur of composition and force of expression, among the first performances of the English school. But, on the whole, his powers of invention were inadequate to the higher flights of historic painting, although inexhaustible in portrait, to which he gave the most delightful variety. His character as a colorist has been already mentioned; and, though not a thorough master in drawing, he gave much grace to the turn of his figures, and dignity to the airs of his heads. As a writer, he obtained reputation by his Discourses, which are elegant and agreeable compositions, although sometimes vague and inconsistent. He also added notes to Dufresnoy's Art of Painting, and gave three papers on painting to the Idler. The Literary Works of Sir Joshua Reynolds were edited by Mr. Malone, in two volumes quarto, in 1797, with a life of the author. Farington and Northcote have written Memoirs of his life.

Rhabdomancy is the power considered by some as existing in particular individuals, partly natural and partly acquired, of discovering things hid in the bowels of the earth, especially metals, ores, and bodies of water, by a change in their perceptions; and likewise the art of aiding the discovery of these substances by the use of certain instruments, for example, the divining rod. That rhabdomancy, generally speaking, is little more than self-delusion, or intentional deception, is now the opinion of most natural philosophers and physiologists; still it has some champions. According to Ritter and Amoretti's accounts (see *Physical and Historical Inquiries into Rhabdomancy*, &c., in German, by Carlo Amoretti, from the Italian, with *Supplementary Treatises* by Ritter, Berlin, 1809, and Amoretti's *Elementi di Elettrometria Animale*, Milan, 1816), an acceleration or retardation of the pulse, and a sensation of cold or heat in different parts of the body, often so great as to affect the thermometer, take place in certain persons when they are in the vicinity of subterranean bodies of water or ore, &c.; also peculiar sensations of taste, spasmodic contractions of particular parts, convulsions often equal to electric shocks, giddiness, sickness, disquietude, solicitude, &c. Rhabdomancy was known even to the ancients. "From the most remote periods," says Kieser, in his System of Tellurism (in German, first volume), "indications are found of an art of discovering veins of ore and water concealed in the bowels of the earth, by a direct perception of their existence." The story of Lynceus is connected with this notion. Snorro Sturleson (*Heimskringla, eller Snorro Sturleson's Nordländske Konunga Sagor*, Stockholm, 1697, folio, p. 1, c. vii) relates that Odin knew where gold, silver and ore lay hidden under the surface of the earth. Del Rio (Martin del Rio, *Disquisitionum Magicarum Libri sex*—Six Books of Magical Disquisitions—Cologne, 1633, quarto,) relates that there were some Spaniards, called *Zahuris*, who saw things concealed under the surface of the earth, such as veins of water and ores, and also dead bodies, &c. The instruments of rhabdomancy are known under the names of the *sidereal pendulum*, the *bipolar cylinder*, and the *divining rod*. The magnetic pendulum consists of a small ball, of almost any substance (for example, metal, sulphur, wood, sealing-wax, glass, &c.), which is suspended from an untwisted string, such as the human hair, unspun silk, &c. In using this, the string of the pendulum is held fast between two fingers, and remains suspended over the sidereal substance (as, for example, a plate of metal, or a cup filled with water and salt), without motion. If, now (say the advocates of rhabdomancy), the person who holds the pendulum possesses, in any degree, the magnetic susceptibility (the rhabdomantic quality), the pendulum will move in a circular orbit, with some differences, according to circumstances. These circumstances are the substance of the pendulum and of the objects under it, the distance of the pendulum from these objects, and the nature of the person who holds the pendulum, and of those who come in contact with him, &c. The principal difference of the motion of the pendulum is, that it moves, in some cases, from left to right, that is, with the sun; in others, from right to left, or against the sun. That the mechanical motion of the fingers does not produce the vibration of the pendulum, at least in many cases, appears from accurate observation of many experiments of this kind; and this circumstance is, moreover, remarkable, that the vibrations do not ensue unless the hand of a living person comes in immediate contact with the string. The bipolar cylinder consists of a body having two poles, and easily moved, as, for instance, a magnetic needle, or a cylindrical bar, of two different metals; any light cylindrical body, such as a quill with the feathers on, will serve. The diviner holds the cylinder in a perpendicular direction, between his thumb and forefinger, while with his other hand he touches some magnetic body, as, for instance, a metal. Under these circumstances, a slow, revolving motion of the cylinder takes place between the fingers, which likewise, as in the case of the pendulum, sometimes moves in a forward and sometimes in a retrograde direction, according to circumstances. (For the divining rod, see the article under that head.) The two ends of this rod are held in the hand, so that its curvature is inclined outwards. If the person who holds the rod possesses the powers of rhabdomancy, and touches the metallic or any other magnetic substance, or comes near them, a slow, rotatory motion of the rod ensues in different directions, according to particular circumstances; and, as in the other cases, no motion takes place without a direct or indirect contact with a living person. In the south of France, and in Switzerland, this art is frequently made use of under the name of *metalloscope* (the art of feeling or discovering metals), and of *hydroscope* (the art of feeling or discovering water). In the practice of this art, the direction, duration, and other circumstances, of the motion of the instruments, determine the quality, quantity, distance and situation of the subterranean substances, or the different sensations of different rhabdomantists, are taken into account.

Rhadamanthus was the brother of Minos, the first lawgiver of Crete and the Grecian world. According to another tradition, Rhadamanthus himself laid the foundation of the Cretan code of laws, which his brother Minos only completed. He, probably, belonged to the family of Dorus (a descendant of Deucalion), whose son Tectamus, or Teutamus, went to Crete with his son Asterius (who was, probably, the father of Rhadamanthus and Minos), in that time of general emigration in Greece. Rhadamanthus, and Minos and Æacus, the progenitors of Achilles, were the three judges, who administered justice to the dead at the entrance of the kingdom of spirits, near the throne of Pluto, continuing the occupation in which they had spent their earthly existence; for it was then the common opinion of the Greeks that the spirit, which arrived in the dark kingdom of Tartarus, strove to continue the business of life. The whole notion of Tartarus, however, in this view, was rather a philosophical allegory than a true mythus.

Rhætia included the two countries of Rhætia Proper and Vindelicia, which were afterwards separated under the names of *Rhætia Prima* and *Secunda* (First and Second Rhætia). The former, or Rhætia Proper (*Rhætia Propria*), extended from the Rhine to the Norican Alps, and from Italy to the borders of Vindelicia. It contained the rivers Rhine (*Rhenus*), Inn (*Ænus*), Adige (*Athesis*), and many smaller ones, and included the modern Vorarlberg and Tyrol, with a part of the country of the Grisons. At an earlier period, the Etrurians, under their leader Rhætus, took possession of this mountainous region; but, being afterwards driven out by the increasing power of the Gauls, they went to Italy, where they played a conspicuous part in its early civilization. Justin, Pliny and Stephen the Byzantine, therefore, called the Rhætians an Etrurian race. (See *Etruria.*) Among the Gauls who subsequently occupied this country, the Brenni are more distinguished by name than by importance. The Romans planted colonies here as in the other provinces; among which Tridentum (*Trent*), Bellunum (*Belluno*), Bauzanum (*Bolzano*), Bilitio (*Bellinzona*), Clavenna (*Chiavenna*), and Curia (*Coire*), were the principal. Several of these cities, however, were only indebted to the Romans for their extension and embellishment. The Rhætians repeatedly laid waste the Roman territories, in conjunction with the Gauls, and Augustus, therefore, sent his step-son Drusus against them. The latter defeated them (16 B. C.) near Trent; but as this victory was not decisive, he undertook, with his brother Tiberius, a second campaign, in which Tiberius attacked the Vindelici from lake Constance, while Drusus advanced against the Rhætians by land. In this expedition, the Romans were victorious, and both countries were made Roman provinces. Rhætia Transdanubiana, the country on the left bank of the Danube, was well known to the Romans, but never conquered by them. After the fall of the Roman pow er the Alemanni and Suevi occupied these provinces.

Rhætian Alps. (See *Alps.*)

Rhamazan, or Ramadan; the ninth month in the Turkish year. As the Mohammedans reckon by lunar time, it begins each year eleven days later than in the preceding year, so that in thirty-three years it occurs successively in all the seasons. In this month the Mohammedans have their great fast daily, from sunrise to sunset. This fast and the Bairam (q. v.) feast, which immediately follows it, are the two principal Mohammedan festivals.

Rhapsody (from the *Greek*) was originally a series of poetical effusions, which, though separate, yet had still a connexion with each other, as, for example, the poems of Homer. (q. v.) Those wandering minstrels among the ancient Greeks, who sang the poems of Homer (these were also called *Homerides*), or their own composition, were called *rhapsodists.* They derived their name, according to some, from the staff which they carried in their hand; according to Pindar, however, they were thus named from their connecting together many detached pieces of poetry. At present, we understand by *rhapsody*, a collection of poetical effusions, descriptions, &c., strung together, without any necessary connexion.

Rhea. The older deities of the Greek mythology are enveloped in such a mist, that we often find the mythuses of different ages and people combined together, as is the case with the mythological accounts of Rhea and Cybele. (q. v.) Rhea was a Titanide, and of Grecian origin, while Cybele was of Phrygian derivation; they were first confounded, probably, in Crete, on account of the similarity of their attributes. Still the evidences of their independent origin are visible; and, although we are acquainted with the mythus of Cybele only through that of Rhea, yet the latter was finally swallowed up by the former. Rhea, one of the most distinguished of the Titanides (see *Titan*), was the sister and wife of Saturn, and with him a symbol of the first creation. Rhea, the Flowing (from ῥεειν to flow), is the symbol of the struggle between chaos and order. The former is yet superior; by the side of Rhea is Saturn, jealous of the new forms, and annihilating them at the moment of their creation—the symbol of all-devouring time. But in the end, order must prevail; the decisive moment has arrived; by the advice of Gaia, her mother, Rhea gives a stone, instead of her infant, to her husband Saturn, who, terrified by ancient prophecy (see *Saturn*), had swallowed his children at the moment of birth She thus saves from destruction three sons and three daughters, Jupiter, Vesta, Ceres, Juno, Neptune and Pluto, the new inhabitants of Olympus, and overthrows her own power. She continued to retain the power of prophecy; and some traces of her were preserved in the mysteries, in which, however, she was confounded with Cybele. As the preserver of the future sovereign of gods and men, she was the symbol of the productive power of nature, the preserving and life-giving principle of the world. Her attributes, as the tamer of lions, which are harnessed to her chariot, and as the companion of Bacchus, and her crown of turrets, point to the same symbol. Her worship was the rudest form of natural religion, and was attended with the greatest excesses of licentiousness and cruelty.

Rhea, Sylvia, lived about 800 B. C., and was the daughter of Numitor, king of Alba, in Italy. Although a vestal virgin, from the embrace of Mars, she brought forth twins, Romulus and Remus, the founders of Rome.

Rheims, or Reims (Remi); a city of France, department of the Marne, ninety miles north-east of Paris; lat. 49° 14′ north; lon. 4° 2′ east; population 38,000. Rheims is a very old town: the streets are, in general, broad and regular, the houses well built, and there are numerous large gardens. It contains some remarkable public buildings, among which are the *hôtel de ville*, finished in 1825; a magnificent cathedral of the twelfth century, one of the finest monuments of the kind in France, with a portal of great beauty; and the church of St. Remy, in which was preserved the holy oil used in the consecration of the kings. (See *Ampulla.*) The coronation of the French kings from the time of Philip Augustus (1179) to Charles X (1825), with the exception of Henry IV, crowned at Chartres, Napoleon, crowned at Paris, and Louis XVIII, who was not crowned at all, took place in the cathedral of Rheims (see *Coronation*); but this expensive ceremony was abolished in 1830. This town was the scene of some hard fighting between the French and Russians, in 1814. The latter took possession of Rheims, March 12, but were driven out by Napoleon, then on his march from Laon, on the 13th, with the loss of their general, St. Priest, and 2000 men. (See *Châtillon, Congress of.*)

Rheingau; a part of the duchy of Nassau, along the right bank of the Rhine, about five leagues long. It is well peopled, and produces some of the choicest Rhenish wines. (q. v.) *Gau* is a German word, signifying *district.*

Rhenish Confederation. (See *Confederation of the Rhine.*)

Rhenish or Rhinland Foot; equal to 1.023 English, or 24 Rhenish equal to 25 English. (See *Measures*, vol. viii, page 366.)

Rhenish Wines; the finest wines of Germany. The vines on the Rhine were planted in the third century, under the emperor Probus. According to a still existing tradition, Charlemagne transplanted the first vine in the Rheingau (q. v.) from Orleans. The Rheingau is the true country of the Rhenish wines. The best are those of Assmannshausen (chiefly red), Rüdesheim, Rottländer, Hinterhäuser, Geissenheim, Johannisberg (q. v.), the best of all, of which a bottle of the first quality, in ordinary seasons, costs, on the spot, from four to five florins, and Hattenheim (called *Markebrunner*). Besides the wines of the Rheingau, the following are good Rhenish wines: on the left bank, the Nierensteiner, Liebfrauenmilch (translated, Our Lady's Milk), a mild wine growing near Worms, Laubenheimer, Bacheracher; on the right bank, Hochheimer. Among these wines, the Laubenheimer and Assmannshäuser are the most agreeable; the Hochheimer, Johannisberger and Geissenheimer, the most aromatic; the Nierensteiner, Markebrunner, Bacheracher and Rüdesheimer, the strongest and most fiery. Among the best vintages are those of 1748, 1760, 1762, 1766, 1776, 1779, 1780, 1781, and more particularly those of 1783 and 1811; also that of 1822. Rhenish wines improve much with age, and continue improving longer than any other wines. Some wine-cellars, as that of the city of Bremen, have Rhenish wine above 150 years old. (See also *Hock*, and *Moselle Wines.*)

Rhetoric is the art of clothing the thoughts in the most agreeable and suitable form, to produce persuasion, to excite the feelings, to communicate pleasure. Speech is addressed to the understanding, the will and the taste; it treats of the true, the beautiful and the good; and is, therefore, didactic, critical, and pathetic or practical. These different objects are often united in the same work, which, therefore, partakes of all the three characters above mentioned, but, at the same time, one or the other character so far prevails as to give a predominant temper to the whole. In a narrower sense, *rhetoric* is the art of persuasive speaking, or the art of the orator, which teaches the composition and delivery of discourses intended to move the feelings or sway the will of others. These productions of the rhetorical art are designed to be pronounced, in the presence of hearers, with appropriate gesture and declamation; and they often, therefore, require a different style of composition and arrangement from those works which are intended for readers, or simply to be read and not oratorically declaimed, and which are embraced in the jurisdiction of rhetoric in its widest sense. The Romans distinguished three kinds of eloquence—the demonstrative, occupied with praise or blame, and addressed to the judgment; the deliberative, which acts upon the will and the inclinations by persuasion or dissuasion; and the judicial or forensic, which is used in defending or attacking. The Greeks divided discourses according to their contents as relating to precepts (λογους), manners (ἠθη), and feelings (παθη), and as, therefore, calculated to instruct, to please, and to move—a division easily reconcilable with the former. The Romans had, also, a corresponding division into the *genus dicendi tenue, mediocre* and *sublime.* Another division of eloquence, founded on the subject to which it relates, is into academical, sacred (pulpit eloquence) and political. The two latter only allow of the lofty flights of eloquence. In the wider sense, as above explained, rhetoric treats of prose composition in general, whether in the form of historical works, philosophical dissertations, practical precepts, dialogues, or letters, and, therefore, includes the consideration of all the qualities of prose composition, purity of style, structure of sentences, figures of speech, &c.; in short of whatever relates to clearness, preciseness, elegance and strength of expression In the narrower sense of rhetoric, as the art of persuasive speaking, it treats of the invention and disposition of the matter. The latter includes the arrangement of the parts, which are the exordium or introduction, narration (when necessary), proposition and division, proof or refutation, and conclusion or peroration, and the elocution, which relates to the style, and requires elegance, purity and precision. The delivery, or pronunciation, also falls here. Aristotle, Cicero and Quintilian are the principal writers on rhetoric among the ancients; and the most valuable English works on this subject, are Campbell's Philosophy of Rhetoric, Blair's Lectures on Rhetoric, and the Elements of Rhetoric by Whately (now archbishop of Dublin).

RHETORICIANS and GRAMMARIANS. 1st. Those who were skilled in language were called, by the ancient Greeks and Romans, *grammarians*, or *philologists*. Their studies embraced every kind of literary productions (γραμμα, writing), and whatever might be necessary to illustrate and explain them. But the grammarians, who were called also, at first, *critics*, and by the Romans *literati*, occupied themselves chiefly with the explanation and criticism of the earlier poets. They were distinguished from the grammatists (*grammatistæ, literatores*) by deeper and more extensive erudition: the grammatists treating mainly of the elements and rudiments of knowledge. We find the first examples of scientific researches into language among the *sophists*, who, in the age of Pericles, practised themselves in their schools, in the explanation of the poets, and particularly Homer, for the purpose of cultivating the taste, and exercising the critical powers; and their ingenuity was principally occupied upon difficulties of their own raising. By this practice, they taught their pupils to examine the laws of language accurately, and observe them carefully. Some of the scholars of Socrates, especially Plato, also distinguished themselves by their illustrations of the poets. Aristotle, who is called the founder of criticism and grammar, made a revision of the Homeric poems for Alexander the Great, and attempted to purify them from interpolations. Before him, however, Pisistratus is related to have arranged the poems of Homer (q. v.), in the order in which they now stand, and Cynæthus of Chios, Antimachus of Colophon, Theagenes of Rhegium, and some others, had occupied themselves with the interpretation of Homer. But although some individuals had turned their attention particularly to the explanation, or the emendation, of the ancient authors, the science of language and criticism was carried to much greater perfection by the Alexandrian scholars. After Alexandria had become the seat of science, the rules of the Greek language, the laws of the interpretation of authors, and the explanation of mythology, the rules for the determination of the various readings, and the particular merits of separate passages, or whole books, became subjects of study. The age of the Alexandrian grammarians (see *Alexandrian School*) is, therefore, the first period in the history of the ancient grammarians: they decided the relative rank of the authors who were to be considered as models of taste, revised some of their works, illustrated them with various researches, unravelled and explained mythology, composed lexicons upon individuals or upon bodies of authors, collected the rules of grammar, and judged the faults and merits of writings, which is the province of the higher criticism. To refer to remarks of different kinds upon the margins of the books, the grammarians made use of critical marks and signs. Different signs were used for different authors. Among the grammarians of this age, Didymus of Alexandria, who lived in the time of Augustus, deserves to be mentioned as a critic: he was surnamed ὁ χαλκεντερος (Ironsides), because he wrote 4000 books. The second period embraces the period of the New Platonists, who considered these objects of inquiry important enough to occupy their attention. The critics and grammarians of this age generally turned their attention more to the thoughts of authors and the contents of their works, than to the explanation of words or the laws of language. In all of them, the spirit of their scientific system, founded upon religion, is apparent; few of them penetrated the peculiar character of Grecian antiquity. This period commences with Plutarch of Chæronea (A. D. 100), to whom some critical and grammatical writings are attributed, which are, however, unworthy of him. The third period embraces those grammarians, mostly monks, who diligently compiled from the ancient authors, collected dictionaries from different writings, gave rules for preserving the purity of the Attic dialect from individual authors, or made annotations on the margins of manuscripts. Many grammatical works of this age are yet extant, in judging of the intrinsic value and utility of which, not only the qualifications of their authors, but more particularly the purity of the sources whence they drew, must be taken into consideration. This period includes those Greeks, who, fleeing from their country, first revived a taste for the study of Greek in Italy, at the end of the fourteenth, and particularly in the fifteenth century. Some collections of the Greek grammarians were made in the fifteenth and sixteenth centuries, among which the *Cornucopia et Hortus Adonidis* (Venice, 1496, folio), and Alexander Heladius's Gleanings of the Greek language, are worthy of notice. Neither Grecian literature, in general, nor grammatical studies, were cultivated by the earlier Romans; they were looked upon by the multitude as a waste of time, and by patriots, as hurtful to morals, while the state was yet rude and warlike, and the want of a more refined taste was not yet felt. But acquaintance with the Greeks attracted the attention of many to this subject, and some of the most distinguished men—Scipio Africanus and Caius Lælius, for example—encouraged the cultivation of Grecian learning. The first Roman teachers of grammar, Livius Andronicus and Ennius (B. C. 236—166), who were in part of Grecian descent, and wrote both in prose and poetry, made translations from some Greek authors. A general taste for philological learning, and the auxiliary sciences, among the Romans, was promoted by the mission of the Greek critic and grammarian Crates of Mallus, a contemporary of Aristarchus, to the Roman senate, as ambassador of king Attalus Philadelphus, soon after the death of Ennius (B. C. 170): during his long residence there, he delivered lectures from time to time, and his lessons awakened, among the Romans, a disposition to imitate the example of the Greeks. As Grecian science became the standard to which the Romans attempted to conform, the latter preserved, in its full extent, the Grecian idea of the science of language, and the Roman dialect of the Latin language became, under the influence of the Grecian, the language of books, and of the cultivated classes. The grammatical studies became so popular, that the most distinguished men wrote upon them; and there always continued to be schools of reputation in Rome. The teachers received very high prices for tuition; and Marcus Scaurus gave about 16,000 dollars for a learned slave, Lutatius Daphnis, and soon after set him at liberty; and Lucius Apuleius received a salary of nearly 10,000 dollars a year, from a rich Roman knight, for his lessons. The study of grammar was likewise diligently prosecuted in the provinces, and some of the most distinguished teachers were in Gaul. With the increase of literary works in the Roman language, increasing attention was paid to the primitive Latin tongue, and to Roman literature and antiquity. Suetonius devoted a particular treatise to the oldest Latin grammarians, in which he gives accounts of their lives and writings. The extant writings of the later Latin grammarians are to be found in the collection of Elias Putsch (Hanau, 1605, 4to.). Vespasian and Adrian confirmed to the grammarians the privilege of exemption from civil services and burdens. Private citizens also took an interest in the schools, and supported them at their own expense. As, in the earliest times, instruction in grammar and music was given by the same person, the ancient grammarians also gave lessons in rhetoric; and many are distinguished as authors in both departments. Even after the sciences had become distinct, the grammarians still continued to teach some of the elementary branches of rhetoric, and, in earlier times, orators passed directly from the school of a grammarian to take part in judicial proceedings.—2d. Instructers in eloquence were called *rhetoricians* among the Greeks; and they also bore the same name, or that of professors (*professores*), among the early Romans. The invention of rhetoric is ascribed by the Ægyptians and poets to Thoth, Hermes, or Mercury, as, in ancient times, the mental powers and operations, in general, were looked upon as something divine. Pittheus, the uncle of Theseus, is said to have first taught this art at Trœzene, in the temple of the Muses, and to have composed a treatise upon it; but this, at so early a time, is incredible. Some consider Empedocles (B. C. 444) as the inventor of rhetoric, of which he may have laid the first foundation; others, Corax and Tisias of Sicily, who first reduced the rules of rhetoric to writing, when, in consequence of a revolution there, many disputes arose concerning property, and the want of a style of speaking suitable for courts of justice was much felt. Some ascribe the invention of rhetoric to Gorgias of Leontium, in Sicily, a pupil of Empedocles, as he was the first who made use of the artificial figures and forms of speech. Others have recognised Aristotle as the inventor of rhetoric, who, in fact, first gave it a scientific form. We find two sects of rhetoricians mentioned, the Apollodorians and Theodorians, so called from Apollodorus of Pergamus, who was the teacher of the emperor Augustus at Apollonia, and from Theodorus, to whose lessons the emperor Tiberius is said to have attended at Rhodes. The object of Grecian rhetoric was to represent every thing so as to give it the appearance of plausibility and truth. Before Aristotle, the sophists, the successors of Zeno, the Eleatic, in dialectics, were teachers of eloquence: arrogant, vain, avaricious, and selfish, they endeavored to win admiration by their dexterity in speaking on all questions, even without preparation, and to gain influence by the acts of persuasion, at a time when wealth, luxury, licentiousness, and the splendor of political eloquence, which (particularly in Athens, where it was favored by democratic institutions, and had arrived at its full maturity) invited to such a study (in the 84th Olympiad, or B. C. 440). As art naturally precedes science, the practice of eloquence is of earlier origin than the rules of rhetoric. The rhetoricians drew their rules and examples from the master-works of the orators, whose name (ῥητορες) was afterwards applied to them. But this mode of proceeding was changed about the time of the Ptolemies, when two ingenious and learned critics, Aristophanes and Aristarchus, taught in Alexandria. They selected ten Attic orators (whose lives are given in a work ascribed to Plutarch) as models of imitation, whose works they analyzed, and from them derived their principles. But while the art of oratory was older than the science of rhetoric, the latter long survived the former, continuing its instructions even to the time of Theodosius the Great. Eloquence flourished at Athens only 150 years, and perished, with every thing noble and great, on the overthrow of liberty, under whose patronage it had flourished, and whom it in turn defended. It was carried to Asia Minor, Rhodes, where Æschines introduced it at the time of his banishment, and other islands, but, in these wanderings, lost its original charms, and was corrupted by foreign manners. Thus arose the distinction of the Attic, Asiatic and Rhodian orators. A sparing use of ornament, combined with a judicious abstinence from striking contrasts, characterized the Attic style. The Asiatic eloquence indulged in a greater fulness of expression, and a free use of rhetorical ornaments. The Asiatic orators, particularly those of Lycia and Caria, were addicted to a sort of rhythmical close of their sentences. The Rhodian eloquence is said to have preserved a medium between these two. Eloquence was finally transplanted to Rome by Greek teachers, where it shone with a new splendor; and Cicero appeared as the greatest public orator of his country. But here, also, after arriving at the highest perfection, it began gradually to decline; for, when freedom of speech was restrained, public eloquence ceased to be esteemed. The old sophists certainly did an important service by the establishment of schools of oratory: at one time, they were the only public teachers of rhetoric, and they encouraged the youth to aim at the glory of eloquence, both by instruction and practice, and by their own example, as declaimers (*declamatores*). The sophists were distinguished by a purple gown, which was a sort of official dress. At Athens, no one, and particularly no foreigner, was allowed to assume this dress without the consent of the fraternity of the sophists, and without having been admitted into the order: the Roman emperors also prohibited those who were not regularly qualified from teaching declamation. Besides other secret usages in the Greek ceremony of admission, the candidates were led to a public bath. After the bath, the person received the mantle, by the authority of the president of the department of eloquence, to whom he paid a large fee for this permission. With the mantle, the initiated person received the dignity and name of a sophist. They, who in this manner had obtained the rank of a rhetorician, spent their time in teaching oratory, and engaged in various rhetorical exercises with their scholars. The principal design of rhetorical instruction was to prepare the scholars for conducting legal processes, in which every thing was transacted orally. Those who, in the rhetorical schools, practised themselves in speaking upon supposed cases, and their pupils, were called *scholastics;* but this name was finally brought into contempt. The rhetorical instruction of the sophists consisted chiefly in arts of deception, in the means of blinding one's adversary, and ensnaring him by sophistical subtleties and quibbles. They required a large fee, which was paid beforehand. In later times, the Grecian and Latin rhetoricians were paid by the Roman emperors (first under Vespasian). The rhetoricians also wrote speeches for others. Antiphon was the first who composed forensic speeches for the use of others. With an oration of Lysias, Iphicrates very often gained the advantage over his adversary. Anytus, by a speech prepared for him by the sophist Polycrates, obtained the condemnation of Socrates, who disdained to use one written for him by Lysias. Dinarchus became rich by composing orations for others. The prices paid for them were high, and many writers obtained so much celebrity as to be constantly occupied in this way. At length this traffic fell into merited contempt, and many great men avoided leaving written speeches, from fear of being reproached as sophists.

Rheumatism; a disease attended with sharp pains, which has so much resemblance to the gout, that some physicians have considered it as not an entirely distinct disease; although they are by no means to be confounded. (See *Gout*.) Rheumatism is distinguished into *acute* and *chronic*. The former is of short continuance, and either shifting to different parts of the body or confined to a particular part: in the latter case, it has a tendency to pass into the chronic, unless properly attended to: it is often attended with fever, or sometimes comes on in the train of a fever. This combination of rheumatism with fever is called *rheumatic* fever, which is considered by physicians a distinct species. Chronic rheumatism is attended with pains in the head, shoulders, knees, and other large joints, which, at times, are confined to one particular part, and at others shift from one joint to another, without occasioning any fever; and in this manner the complaint continues often for a considerable time, and at length goes off. No danger is attendant on chronic rheumatism; but a person having been once attacked with it, is ever afterwards more or less liable to returns of it. Neither is the acute rheumatism frequently accompanied with much danger. The acute is preceded by shivering, heat, thirst, and frequent pulse; after which the pain commences, and soon fixes on the joints. The chronic rheumatism is distinguished by pain in the joints, without fever, and is divided into three species; *lumbago*, affecting the loins; *sciatica*, affecting the hip; and *arthrodynia*, or pains in the joints. The acute rheumatism mostly terminates in one of these species. Rheumatism may arise at all times of the year, when there are frequent vicissitudes of the weather from heat to cold, but the spring and autumn are the seasons in which it is most prevalent; and it attacks persons of all ages; but very young people are less subject to it than adults. Obstructed perspiration, occasioned either by wearing wet clothes, lying in damp linen, or damp rooms, or by being exposed to cool air when the body has been much heated by exercise, is the cause which usually produces rheumatism. Those who are much afflicted with this complaint, are very apt to be sensible of the approach of wet weather, by finding wandering pains about them at that period. Rheumatism usually attacks only the external muscular parts, but has sometimes been known to affect the internal parts, especially the serous membranes, the *pleura*, the *peritonæum*, the *dura mater*.

Rhigas, Constantine, the Tyrtæus of modern Greece, the first mover of the war for Grecian independence, was born about 1753, at Velestini, a small city of Thessaly, and was early distinguished for talent. As he was not rich enough to devote himself to literature, he engaged in commerce, went to Bucharest, and remained there until 1790. He made himself intimately acquainted with the literature of ancient Greece. Latin, French, Italian and German were familiar to him: he wrote Greek and French, and was a poet and a proficient in music. He formed the bold plan of freeing Greece from the Ottoman Porte by means of a great secret association, and succeeded even in bringing powerful Turks into his conspiracy; among others, the celebrated Passwan Oglou. He then went to Vienna, where many rich merchants and some learned men of his nation resided. From this place he held a secret correspondence with the most important confederates in Greece, and in other parts of Europe. At the same time, he published a Greek journal, translated the Travels of the Younger Anacharsis, and wrote a treatise upon tactics. His patriotic songs, in his native language, were calculated to inflame the imagination of the Greek youth, and to embitter them against the Mussulmans. He likewise prepared a map of all Greece, with the ancient and modern names of places, in twelve sheets, which was printed at the expense of his countrymen in Vienna. He perished at the age of forty-five, having been arrested in Trieste. The signatures of all the confederates were contained in a document which he always carried about with him. This he destroyed in the night, and swallowed the names of his countrymen. With several other prisoners he was conducted to Vienna. Rhigas and three others of those arrested were sent back in chains to Belgrade, in May, 1798, and, according to some accounts, beheaded, and cast into the Danube. According to other accounts, Rhigas was sawed asunder between two boards.

Rhine (in German, *Rhein*; in Dutch, *Rhyn*, or *Ryn*); in magnitude the fourth river of Europe, and one of the noblest rivers in the world. There are rivers whose course is longer, and whose volume of water is greater, but none which unites almost every thing that can render an earthly object magnificent and charming, in the same degree as the Rhine. As it flows down from the distant ridges of the Alps, through fertile regions into the open sea, so it comes down from remote antiquity, associated in every age with momentous events in the history of the neighboring nations. A river which presents so many historical recollections of Roman conquests and defeats, of the chivalric exploits of the feudal period, of the wars and negotiations of modern times, of the coronations of emperors whose bones repose by its side; on whose borders stand the two grandest monuments of the noble architecture of the middle ages; whose banks present every variety of wild and picturesque rocks, thick forests, fertile plains, vineyards sometimes gently sloping, sometimes perched among lofty crags, where industry has won a domain among the fortresses of nature; whose banks are ornamented with populous cities, flourishing towns and villages, castles and ruins, with which a thousand legends are connected, beautiful and romantic roads, and salutary mineral springs; a river whose waters offer choice fish, as its banks offer the choicest wines; which, in its course of 900 miles, affords 630 miles of uninterrupted navigation, from Bâsle to the sea, and enables the inhabitants of its banks to exchange the rich and various products of its shores; whose cities, famous for commerce, science, and works of strength, which furnish protection to Germany, are also famous as the seats of Roman colonies, and of ecclesiastical councils, and are associated with many of the most important events recorded in history;—such a river it is not surprising that the Germans regard with a kind of reverence, and frequently call in poetry *father Rhine*, or *king Rhine.* (See Byron's verses on the Rhine, in *Childe Harold*, canto iii, stanzas 55—61.) Since the French revolution, the Rhine has been frequently called in France the natural boundary between France and Germany: with equal reason the Elbe might be called so, and perhaps would have been called so, had the French empire continued, as it had extended already to that river at one point.* The Rhine rises in the Swiss canton of the Grisons (q. v.), from three chief sources. The first comes from the mountain called Crispalt, north-east of the St. Gothard, and unites at Dissentis with the second, which comes from the Lucmanian mountain: both unite with the third, which comes from a glacier in the mountain of Adula, about twenty leagues distant from Reichenau, the point of confluence of all three. The river here takes the name of *Rhine*, and is 230 feet wide. It passes through the Bodensee (lake of Constance, q. v.). From Reichenau to Bâsle it is navigable at intervals, sometimes only by rafts. Before it falls into the lake of Constance, it forms the cataract of Schaffhausen, in the canton of Zürich, where the river is closely compressed by rocks, and falls with great fury eighty feet. After having traversed or touched several cantons of Switzerland, also Austria, Baden, France, Bavaria, Hessia, Nassau, Prussia and the Netherlands, it divides into several branches. Hardly has it entered Holland (at Emmerich), when it sends off to the left a considerable branch, the Waal, which joins the Meuse at Woudrichem. Somewhat lower down, a little above Arnheim, on the right, a branch is formed which occupies the bed of a canal constructed by Drusus; this is the New-Yssel, which, after having joined the Old-Yssel, at Doesburg, takes the name of Yssel, or Over-Yssel, and empties into the Zuyder-Zee. Arrived at Wyk-by-Duurstede, twenty-seven miles east of Arnheim, the Rhine divides into two branches; one of which, the chief continuation of the river, is called Lech, and joins the Meuse: it forms on its right the Neder-Yssel, which also joins the Meuse; the other branch, formerly the most considerable, but now small, is now called the Crooked Rhine (*Kromme-Rhyn*), and takes its course to Utrecht, where again it splits: the north-west branch is called Vecht, and empties into the Zuyder-Zee; the other, western branch, called Old Rhine (*Oude-Rhyn*) empties into the North sea, two leagues from Leyden. It formerly disappeared in the downs of Katwyk, formed in 860; but it has been conducted by a canal from Leyden to the sea. The most important rivers which flow into it are, the Aar, Kinzig, Murg, Neckar, Maine, Nahe, Lahn, Moselle, Erft, Ruhr, Lippe: the most important places on the banks are Constance, Schaffhausen, Bâsle, Spire, Manheim, Worms, Mentz, Bingen, Coblentz, Bonn, Cologne, Dusseldorf, Wesel, Emmerich, Arnheim, Utrecht, Leyden. The whole basin of the Rhine is about 180 leagues long, and 100 leagues wide, where it is the widest, and comprises about 10,000 square leagues. The canal of the Rhone and Rhine unites these two rivers by means of the Saône the great canal of the North uniting the Rhine with the Meuse and the Nethe, and thus with the Scheldt. In the article *Danube*, we have spoken of the projected

* Rivers are, generally speaking, poor means of political separation, because they are, in fact, means of connexion rather than of separation. Mountains and languages furnish far more effectual lines of demarkation. The only reason why rivers have often been taken as frontiers is, because they are lines drawn by nature, which can be easily designated in treaties.

canal which was to unite the Danube and the Rhine, the Black sea and the Northern ocean. The Rhine furnishes excellent salmon (called *Lachse* when they ascend the river in spring, coming from the sea, and *Salmen* when they descend in autumn to the sea), sturgeons, lampreys, pikes, and excellent carps. From Strasburg to Spire, the Rhine is about 1100 feet wide; at some parts of the Rheingau, it is 1800; at Cologne, 1300. At Schenkenschanz, where it enters the Netherlands, it is 2150 feet wide. Its depth from Bâsle to Strasburg is between ten and twelve feet; at Mentz, twenty-four; at Dusseldorf, fifty. When the snow melts in Switzerland, the Rhine rises from twelve to thirteen feet above its common level. The mean descent of the river is about seven feet a mile; its current runs about 288 feet in a minute, or about three and a third miles per hour. Vessels of from 300 to 450 tons go up the river to Cologne, those of 125 to 200 to Mentz, those of 100 to 125 to Strasburg. Steam-boats and "water diligences" render communication easy. The congress of Vienna, in 1815, declared the navigation of all the German rivers free; but this ordinance has not been carried into effect as regards the Danube (q. v.), and it was not till after fifteen years' negotiation between the various powers, and after 563 protocols had been drawn up on the subject that the navigation of the Rhine was made free, in the year 1831. Three books contain every thing necessary for a journey along the Rhine: one, by Lange, comprehends the journey from Mentz to Dusseldorf, the most romantic part south of Basle; another, by Aloys Schreiber, comprehends the whole course of the Rhine, with excursions into neighboring parts; the third is by Ch. A. Fischer—Newest Guide from Mayence to Cologne (Frankfort, 1827). There exist excellent representations of the scenery of the Rhine, semi-perspective and semi-topographic, very ingenious productions, which afford the traveller the highest gratification.—See, also, the *Panorama of the Rhine, from Mayence to Cologne*, by Delkeskamp (Dresd. and Frankf., 1825, in 80 engravings), also Primavesi's *Course of the Rhine from its Sources to its Mouth, drawn from Nature* (1818), and Historico-Statistical Panorama of the Rhine, from Bingen to Coblentz, by Dahl (Heidelberg, 1820). Aloys Schreiber's book contains a catalogue of all the works on the Rhine or relating to it.

Rhine; one of the eight circles of Bavaria, commonly called *Rheinbaiern*, separated from the rest of the kingdom, on the left bank of the Rhine. It is chiefly composed of the former French department Mont-Tonnere. The Mont-Tonnere, 2100 feet high, is the summit of the Vosges (q. v.), which traverse the circle. Inhabitants, 517,081; square miles, about 3000.

Rhine, Departments of the Upper and Lower. (See *Department*.)

Rhine, Confederation of. (See *Confederation of the Rhine*.)

Rhine, Lower (in German, *Niederrhein*), a Prussian province, with the title of a grand-duchy, formed by the congress of Vienna, in 1815, containing 1,127,297 inhabitants and 6100 square miles, embraces both banks of the Rhine, and is bounded by the Prussian provinces of Juliers-Cleves-Berg and Westphalia, by Nassau, Hesse-Darmstadt, France, the Netherlands, and several smaller territories. The Hundsrück (q. v.) traverses the province of the Lower Rhine between the rivers Nahe and Moselle, and joins the Vosges. The Eiffel and the High Veen are ridges of hills coming from the Ardennes. The province furnishes game, fish, grain, fruits, flax, hemp, wine, wood, silver, iron, copper, lead, calamine, marble, slate, sand and mill stones, basalt, tufa, porphyry alum, sulphur, coals, and mineral waters. In some parts much manufacturing industry exists. Much cloth is made in and near Aix-la-Chapelle. The other manufactures are linen, silks, leather, iron and steel wares. The inhabitants are mostly Catholics; in the southern part French is spoken in some places. The province is divided into three governments—Aix-la-Chapelle, Treves, and Coblentz. Aix-la-Chapelle (q. v.) is the chief place. The province comprehends the chief part of the ancient archbishopric of Treves, the abbeys of Prüm, Cornely-Munster, Malmedy, part of the old archbishopric of Cologne, of the duchy of Luxemburg and Juliers, &c.

Rhinoceros. This is a large animal, belonging to the order of *pachydermata*, having each foot divided into three toes, and furnished with one or more horns on the snout. There are several species, the best known of which are the Indian, or one-horned, and the African, or two-horned.—*One-horned rhinoceros*. This species is a native of India, particularly of that part beyond the Ganges. It is a clumsy and deformed looking animal: a single black horn, placed near the end of the nose, makes its specific character. The upper lip is very large, and overhangs the lower: it is furnished with strong muscles, and is employed by the animal somewhat as the elephant uses his trunk. The ears are large, erect and pointed. The skin is naked, rough, and extremely thick; about the neck it is gathered into large folds; a fold also extends between the shoulders and fore legs, and another from the hinder part of the back to the thighs. The tail is slender, flat at the end, and furnished at the sides with very stiff, black hairs. The legs are very short. This animal was well known to the ancients, and was introduced into the games of the circus by Pompey; in all probability it is the *reem* (unicorn) of the Bible. From the time of the fall of the Roman empire, however, it was lost sight of so completely, that, prior to the sixteenth century, naturalists were of opinion, that it had never existed, or, if so, that it was extinct. When the Portuguese, however, doubled the cape of Good Hope, and opened the way to India, these animals again became known, and many were introduced into Europe. The first that appeared in England was in 1684. The rhinoceros lives in shady forests adjoining rivers, or in the swampy jungles with which its native country abounds. Though possessed of great strength, and more than a match for either the tiger or the elephant, it is quiet and inoffensive unless provoked. The female produces one at a birth. The growth of the young is very gradual, as, at the age of two years, it scarcely attains half its height. The sight of the rhinoceros is by no means acute, but, on the contrary, its senses of smelling and hearing are very vivid. Its chief food is canes and shrubs. It was for a long time supposed that the tongue was hard and exceedingly rough; but recent observations have shown that it does not present these peculiarities. The flesh somewhat resembles pork in taste, though of a coarser grain and stronger taste.—*Two-horned rhinoceros.* This species is a native of Africa, and resembles the preceding in many particulars, but differs in being provided with an additional horn, of a smaller size, situated nearer the forehead; the skin also is not thrown into the folds so remarkable in the Indian species; at least, this is the account given by Sparrman, whilst Bruce represents it as having them. The two-horned rhinoceros was better known to the ancients than the last-mentioned kind, and is represented on many of their coins, especially those of Domitian. The rhinoceros is greatly inferior to the elephant in docility, and has never been made sociable to man. The skin is used for whips and walking-canes, and of the horns drinking-cups were made, which were highly esteemed by the East Indians, as they imagined that if poison were put into them, the liquor would ferment till it ran out of the vessel. Martial informs us, that Roman ladies used these horns as cases to hold their essence bottles and oils. The skin of the rhinoceros is also used by the Javanese for shields.

Rhinoplastic (from ῥιν, the nose, and πλαστικη, the art of forming). The art of restoring the nose, when lost by disease or external injury, was early practised, in India, by the Bramins, and is even now practised by the descendants of this caste, the Coomas, by means of a piece of skin cut from the forehead. In 1442, Branca, a Sicilian physician, operated by means of a piece of skin cut from the arm of the individual; and, after him, this method was preserved in the family of the Bajani as a secret, until Caspar Tagliacozzi (born in 1546, died in 1599) practised it in Bologna, and made it public in 1597. He pursued the method of taking the skin from the arm. This method was last practised by Molinetti, in the beginning of the seventeenth century. In 1816, Gräfe, a German physician, attempted the formation of the nose from the skin of the arm upon a young soldier who had lost his nose by a sabre cut. The method differed but little from that of Tagliacozzi.—See Gräfe's *Rhinoplastic* (Berlin, 1818, quarto).

Rhode Island, one of the U. States, includes what was formerly known by the name of *Rhode Island and Providence Plantations;* it originally consisted of two plantations, or provinces. This state is bounded north and east by Massachusetts, south by the Atlantic ocean, and west by Connecticut; length 49 miles; breadth 29; square miles 1350; population in 1810, 76,931; in 1820, 83,059, including 48 slaves; in 1830, 97,212, including 14 slaves; lat. 41° 22′ to 42° 3′ N.; lon. 71° 6′ to 71° 38′ W. In the north-west part of the state, the country is hilly and rocky, but in other parts it is mostly level. The soil is better adapted to grazing than tillage, except on the island of Rhode Island, which has an excellent soil, adapted to the growth of every thing that is suited to its climate. A considerable part of the state has a thin soil, and affords small crops of New England productions; but the country near Narraganset bay is generally very fertile. Great numbers of cattle and sheep are produced on the islands, and on the margin of the bay; and butter and cheese, cider, many kinds of fruit, corn, rye, barley, and oats, are produced in abundance. The rivers and bays afford a great variety of excellent fish. Iron in abundance, small quantities of copper, limestone, and a mine of anthracite, are the minerals and fossils that have hitherto been found. The rivers are the Pawtucket, Providence, and Pawtuxet. Narraganset bay extends from south to north through nearly the whole length of the state, and embosoms Rhode Island, Connecticut, Prudence, Patience, Hope, Dyer's, and Hog islands. Block island, in the Atlantic, south of the state, is the most southerly land belonging to it. The exports of Rhode Island consist principally of flax-seed, lumber, horses, cattle, beef, pork, fish, poultry, and cotton and linen goods. Its manufactures have greatly increased within the last ten years, and add greatly to its wealth. The value of its exports of domestic produce, during the year ending September 30, 1829, was $337,468. Its tonnage in 1828 was 43,406. Since these periods, the commerce of the state has rapidly increased. The commercial and manufacturing interests of Rhode Island are principally centred in Providence. This has become one of the most important cities of New England, and contains now about one fifth of the population of the state. Newport is somewhat less than half the size of Providence, and the other towns are not large. The general assembly of Rhode Island meets four times in a year: at Newport on the first Wednesday of May, which is the commencement of the political year, and again at the same place in June; in October, it meets alternately at Providence and South Kingston; and in January at East Greenwich, Bristol, or Providence. Brown university is situated at Providence. At the same place there is a seminary styled the *Friends' boarding-school*, and there are eight or ten academies in the state. (See *Providence*.) The state now pays $10,000 annually for the support of free schools; and this sum is divided among the several towns, according to their population. This, however, affords but imperfect means for the education of the poorer classes of society. In 1831, the Baptists in Rhode Island had sixteen churches, twelve ministers, 2600 communicants; the Methodists ten preachers, 1,100 members; the Congregationalists ten churches, ten ministers, 1000 communicants; the Unitarians two societies, two ministers; the Sabbatarians about 1000 communicants; the Six-Principle Baptists about eight churches and 800 communicants. There are many Friends, and some of other denominations. The settlement of Rhode Island was commenced, at Providence, in 1636, by the celebrated Roger Williams, a minister, who was banished from Massachusetts on account of his religious opinions. (For further information respecting the history, see *Providence*, and *New England*.)

Rhode Island; an island situated in Narraganset bay; lat. 41° 25′ N.; lon. 71° 20′ W. The state of Rhode Island takes its name from this island. It is about fifteen miles from north to south, and three and a half wide, and is divided into three townships, Newport, Portsmouth and Middletown. It is a noted resort for invalids from southern climates. The island is very fertile, pleasant, and healthful; and many travellers call it the *Eden of America*. It suffered greatly by the war of the revolution, but has been, in a considerable degree, restored to its former beauty and value. About 40,000 sheep are fed on the island, besides neat cattle and horses. There is a coal-mine on the north part of the island, but the coal is not, at present, much esteemed.

Rhodes ('Ροδος, from ροδον, a rose, or from ροδος, noise of waters); an island in the Grecian archipelago, lying between Crete (Candia) and Cyprus, ten miles from the southern coast of Asia Minor; thirty-six miles in length, and fourteen in breadth; 450 square miles. Rhodes was, in ancient times, sacred to the sun, and was celebrated for its serene sky, its soft climate, fertile soil, and fine fruits. The republic of Rhodes was an important naval power, and planted colonies in Sicily, Italy and Spain. The beauty and size of its works of art were admired in all Greece, and it was much visited by the Romans on account of them. The commercial laws of the Rhodians were adopted, as the basis of marine law, on all the coasts of the Mediterranean, and some fragments of them still retain their authority. (See *Commercial Law*.) This rich and powerful republic took an important part in several of the Roman wars, and was first made a Roman province in the reign of Vespasian. In 1309, after the loss of Palestine, the knights of St. John occupied the island, and were thence called the *knights of Rhodes*. In 1480, they repelled an attack of the Turks, but, in 1522, were obliged to surrender the island to Soliman II. (See *John, Knights of St.*) The population is differently estimated, by Savary at 36,500, of which about one third are

Greeks, with an archbishop. The island is governed by a pacha, who is under the capudan pacha or high-admiral and governor of the islands of the Archipelago. The revenue of the sultan from the island is estimated at 90,000 piasters. The productions are corn, wine, oil, cotton, fruits, wax, honey, &c. The capital, Rhodes (lon. 28° 12′ E.; lat. 36° 26′ N.), has a population of 6000 Turks. The suburb Neachorio is inhabited by 3000 Greeks, who are not permitted to reside within the city. The town is surrounded by three walls and a double ditch, and is considered by the Turks as impregnable. It has two fine harbors, separated only by a mole. The celebrated colossus probably stood here. (See *Colossus*.)

RHODIUM; a new metal, discovered among the grains of crude platina by doctor Wollaston. Its specific gravity is 11. It readily alloys with every other metal, except mercury. One sixth of it does not perceptibly alter the appearance of gold, but only renders it more fusible. When pure, it is brittle, and requires a much higher temperature for its fusion than any other metal, unless it be iridium. It is insoluble in all acids. Doctor Wollaston made silver pens, tipped with rhodium, which, from its great hardness, were not liable to be injured by use.

RHODODENDRON MAXIMUM, or DWARF ROSE BAY; one of the most ornamental shrubs of North America. It is generally about ten feet high, but sometimes reaches to twenty or twenty-five, with a trunk four or five inches in diameter. The leaves are large, oval, oblong, coriaceous, smooth and shining; the flowers large, rose-colored, with yellow dots on the inside, and are disposed in an elegant terminal cluster. It is most abundant about the Alleghany mountains, where it sometimes forms impenetrable thickets, presenting a magnificent appearance when in flower. The wood is hard, compact, and fine-grained, but inferior, in these respects, to that of the mountain-laurel, and has not hitherto been applied to any useful purposes. Two other species of rhododendron inhabit the more southern parts of the Alleghanies. The species of rhododendron are shrubs, with alternate, entire, evergreen leaves, and ornamental flowers, usually disposed in terminal corymbs. About eighteen species are known, which inhabit the cold and temperate parts of the northern hemisphere, and especially mountainous districts. One, the *R. Lapponicum*, grows as far north as civilized man has penetrated, and, in common with other arctic plants, is found, within the U. States, only on the summits of the White mountains of New Hampshire. An Oriental species, sometimes seen in our green-houses, resembling the *R. maximum*, but with brilliant scarlet flowers, hardly yields in magnificence to any production of the vegetable creation. All the species are cultivated in gardens on account of the beauty of their flowers.

RHONE (Rhodanus); a great river in the south of Europe, which rises in the central and highest part of Switzerland, at the foot of mount Furca, only five miles from the source of the Rhine. It flows in a western direction through a long and wide valley of the Swiss canton of the Valais, and, being swelled by a number of mountain streams, it passes through the lake of Geneva. Flowing southward, and being joined by the Saône and other streams, such as the Isère, the Drôme, the Ardeche, and the Durance, it discharges itself, after a course of nearly 500 miles, by three mouths, into the part of the Mediterranean called the gulf of Lyons, where its branches form the island of Camargue. The principal cities on the Rhone are Geneva, Lyons, Vienne, Avignon, Beaucaire and Arles. It is the most rapid river of Europe. The navigation down the stream is easy, but the upward can be performed only by draught or steam. (See *Canals*.) It carries down large quantities of earth, which it deposits at its mouth. Below Lacluse, the river plunges, with great noise, into a cavity of the rocks, and disappears for the distance of sixty paces. Several miles below this place, at a point called Malpertuis, it again almost entirely disappears under the rocks.

RHÖNGEBIRGE; a range of mountains in Germany, extending from Kaltennordheim to beyond Bischofsheim, about 30 miles in length; it traverses the northwest of Bavaria, and part of Hesse Cassel, approaching the Thuringian forest on the north, and the Spessart towards the south. The highest summit is the Kreutzberg, 2800 feet high.

RHUBARB (*rheum*); a genus of plants, mostly inhabiting the interior of Asia. It belongs to the family *polygoneæ*, together with the docks, which it somewhat resembles. It is one of the few genera which have nine stamens, the *enneandria* of Linnæus. The roots and leaves are remarkably large, and the flowers inconspicuous, but disposed in very ample panicles. The seeds are provided, at the angles, with a membranous wing. The roots of all are mildly purgative, com-dined with tonic and strengthening properties; that of the officinal rhubarb (*R. valmatum*) is considered the most efficacious, but there is no great difference in this respect. The officinal or true rhubarb grows wild along the frontiers of China, near the great wall, upon a chain of mountains which stretches from the Chinese town Sini to lake Kokonor, near Thibet. It is easily distinguished by having the leaves divided into acute lobes; the roots are very large, yellow and branching; the stem is of moderate height, cylindrical, smooth and striated, provided at base with a great number of large petiolate leaves; these are divided into five or seven lanceolate, acute segments, each of which is again subdivided, and are green and rough above, a little whitish and pubescent beneath, and traversed with large yellowish nerves; their leaf-stalks are very long, and grooved; the flowers are small, yellowish-white, and are disposed in numerous upright panicles; the seeds are blackish-brown and triangular. It is usual with the Chinese, when the roots have been taken from the ground, cleaned and pared, to cut them in slices and lay them upon long tables, taking care to turn them three or four times a day, experience having taught that if exposed to a free current of air, they become light, and lose a portion of their strength. After the fourth day, they are perforated and strung upon cords, in such a way as not to touch each other, and are suspended to dry in the shade, either upon trees or in tents. In about two months, the roots have lost seven eighths of their weight, and are fit for market. Winter is the proper season for taking up the roots. Formerly rhubarb was brought from China, through Tartary, to Ormuz and Aleppo, thence to Alexandria, and even to Vienna. This was called *Turkey* rhubarb. Now it is brought by sea from Canton and Ormuz. All the rhubarb of commerce is obtained from the chain of mountains above mentioned. It is only within a few years that the officinal rhubarb has been successfully cultivated on a large scale in Europe. It is most readily multiplied by planting pieces of the root containing eyes, thirty or more of which are afforded by a root four or five years old: half an inch of the root is sufficient to ensure the shooting of these eyes. They are planted a little before the opening of the spring, after leaving them exposed to the air for a day, in order that cicatrices may be formed: they should be placed in quincunx order, about six feet apart, as the leaves occupy a very great space; but as, for the two first years, they do not fill this space, some other crop may be raised between them. It is an injudicious practice to cut away the leaves, and hinders the growth of the roots; but to cut or break the stems, about a foot from the ground, is very often advantageous. The plant may remain in the ground all winter, but during severe frosts should be covered with straw or dry leaves. A deep soil, and one where sand does not predominate, seems best adapted to its culture; but it succeeds in every soil that is not arid or watery; neither does it fear shade or a northern exposure; in dry weather, watering is advantageous, but long rains are very injurious. The roots are taken from the ground only after the fourth or fifth year, but sooner in a dry and warm soil than in a moist and cool one; when taken up too soon, their substance is soft, and will lose eleven twelfths of its weight in drying; on the other hand, if left too long in the earth, the roots become hollow, or even rot in the centre. The time for removing them is in the autumn, after the leaves are perfectly dry. The stocks live ten or twelve years in a good soil, and only half as long in one which is less adapted to them. The rhubarb of commerce is brownish-yellow externally, saffron-yellow within, and variegated with white and reddish streaks. The odor is disagreeable, and the taste bitter, astringent, slightly acrid, and nauseous. Its properties are, at the same time, tonic and purgative. It is administered in powder, in mixtures, or formed into pills, or the root may be chewed in substance. The value of the annual import of this article into Great Britain is said to exceed $1,000,000. The bark of rhubarb has been used for tinctures, and is found, in every respect, as efficacious as the best part of the roots, and the seeds possess nearly the same qualities. The leaves impart an agreeable acidity, somewhat similar to that of sorrel; and a marmalade is made from the fresh stalks, by stripping off the bark, and boiling the pulp with an equal quantity of sugar. The common garden rhubarb (*R. rhaponticum*) has obtuse, smooth leaves, with hairy veins beneath. It was first brought into Europe about the year 1610, and is chiefly in request for the stalks of the leaves, which, when young, are used for pies and tarts. The root has occasionally been sold for the rhubarb of commerce, and for a long time was supposed to be identical with it. The *rheum ribes* is remarkable for having the seeds enveloped in a succulent and reddish pulp. It grows on the mountains of Syria and Persia, and is, besides, cultivated on an extensive scale in those countries, on account of the agreeably acid flavor of the leaves, leaf-stalks and young stems. These are sold constantly in the markets, and are eaten either in a crude state, with salt or vinegar, or are preserved in wine, or with sugar.

RHUMB, in navigation; a vertical circle of any given place, or the intersection of such a circle with the horizon; in which last sense *rhumb* is the same as a point of the compass.

Rhumb-line; a line prolonged from any point of the compass, on a nautical chart, except from the four cardinal points.

RHUNKEN. (See *Ruhnkenius.*)

RHUS. (See *Sumac.*)

RHYME, in poetry; the correspondence of sounds in the terminating words or syllables of verses. The vowel and the final articulations or consonants should be the same, or nearly the same, in sound. The initial consonants may be different. Languages which have not, like the English, a great variety of shades between the Italian sounds of *a*, *e*, *i*, *o*, *u*, admit only pure rhymes; that is to say, the corresponding syllables must have exactly the same vowel sound. English verse is much less restrained; and we find in the best English poets rhymes which strike a foreign ear as very impure. In some instances, such as *sky* and *liberty*, *hand* and *command*, *gone* and *alone*, the correspondence in the letters makes what might be called a rhyme to the eye, which supplies, in some measure, the want of correspondence in sound. In other instances, however, this is not the case, as in *revenge* and *change*, *remote* and *thought;* and the liberty of making rhymes of syllables corresponding in sound, though different in spelling, is greater in English than in most other languages; as *water* and *mortar*, *warm* and *storm*. If the rhyme is only in the last syllables, as in *forgave* and *behave*, it is called a *male* rhyme; if in the two last syllables, as *bitter* and *glitter*, it is called a *female* rhyme. Sometimes the three last syllables rhyme, as *callosity* and *reciprocity*, or the Italian *diacine* and *duracine*, or *tavola* and *favola* (the *verso sdrucciolo*). This last sort of rhymes is principally used in pieces of a comic or conversational character. Rhymes which extend to more than three syllables are almost confined to the Arabians and Persians, in their short odes (*gazelles*), in which the same rhyme, carried through the whole poem, extends sometimes to four and more syllables. Some languages incline more to the male rhyme, as the English, on account of its superabundance of monosyllables; others, as the Spanish and Italian, more to the female: the German and French possess an almost equal store of both; hence in these two languages we find them generally interchanged regularly; yet there are numerous poems in these languages, written exclusively in male or female rhymes. Of the four continental idioms just mentioned, the German, from its abundance of consonants, has the greatest variety of final syllables, and therefore the smallest collection of rhymes for any given termination. It has, however, to compensate for this deficiency, a regular prosody, arising from the possession of long and short syllables. The modern use of rhyme was not known to the ancients. We meet, indeed, with some rhymed verses in Ovid, in which the rhyme was evidently intentional; but the object was not to distinguish the verses, but to give impressiveness to the sense, as Shakspeare often introduces a rhymed couplet, for the same purpose, in blank verse. In the Latin poems of the fathers of the church of the fourth century, rhymes are more frequently used. The rhyme is harmony, music, and therefore is addressed directly to the feelings, and thus partakes essentially of the character of modern art, whilst the metrical forms of antiquity are in the spirit of that plastic age. (See *Classic*, *Plastic*, and *Romantic.*) The Goths introduced rhyme from the East into the northern languages. The most ancient relics of Scandinavian poetry are not in rhyme, but are distinguished by alliteration (q. v.). These circumstances gave rise to the opinion that rhyme originated with the Arabians, who came into contact with the Europeans of the south as early as the eighth century. Schlegel, in his *Observations sur la Littérature Provençale*, however, denies this. Joseph von Hammer, on the other hand, is a decided believer in the influence of the Arabians on the provençal poetry in respect to the structure of rhymed couplets and the forms of rhyme in the southern poetry; which seems undeniable, though it is not necessary to derive rhyme itself from the Arabians. The oldest forms of rhymed verse are the couplet and the continuation of one and the same rhyme through a whole piece. The Troubadours (q. v.) first attempted a variety of artificial combinations of rhyme in the sonnet, canzone, &c., and the Span iards and Italians, with their musical languages and delicacy of ear, perfected the forms of involved rhyme. The Italians, however, at a later period, carried the artificial intricacies of rhyme to great excess. Rhyme, well managed, is one of the most pleasing of all inventions for entertaining the mind, constantly raising expectation, and as often satisfying it. The ear anticipates the sound, without knowing what the sound will express; and how various are the forms of grace and majesty of which it is susceptible! Yet it has misled many persons to think they were composing poetry, whilst they were only rhyming; and were it not for rhyme, we might have been saved from a flood of insipid verse, which has so long overspread the field of literature. (See *Sonnet.*)

Rhythm. (See *Appendix*, end of this volume.)

Rial, Real; a Spanish coin. (For the *real de plata* (silver rial), see *Coins.*) The *real de vellon* (copper rial) is equal to $4\frac{85}{100}$cts.

Rialto. (See *Venice.*)

Rib. The ribs are long curved bones, placed in an oblique direction at the sides of the chest. Their number is generally twelve on each side; but, in some subjects, it has been found to be thirteen, and in others, though more rarely, only eleven. They are distinguished into *true* and *false* ribs. The seven upper ribs, which are articulated to the sternum, are called *true* ribs, and the five lower ones, which are not immediately attached to that bone, are called *false* ribs. The use of the ribs is to give form to the thorax, and to cover and defend the lungs; also to assist in breathing; for they are joined to the vertebræ by regular hinges, which allow of short motions, and to the sternum by cartilages, which yield to the motion of the ribs, and return again when the muscles cease to act. (See *Respiration.*)

Ribera, Giuseppe. (See *Spagnoletto.*)

Ricardo, David, a celebrated writer on finance and statistics, was of a Jewish family, and was born in London in 1772. His father was a stock broker, and the son was intended for the same profession. His character for probity, industry and talent early procured him means of support; and, becoming a member of the stock exchange, he accumulated immense property. In 1810, he appeared as a writer in the Morning Chronicle, on the subject of the depreciation of the national currency; and he afterwards embodied his ideas in a distinct work, the reasonings of which were adopted in the Report of the Bullion Committee of the house of commons. He next published an Essay on Rent, in which he advocated the principles of Malthus concerning population. His most important production is his treatise on Political Economy and Taxation, which affords a luminous exposition of the origin and fluctuations of national wealth and expenditure. In 1819, Mr. Ricardo obtained a seat in parliament for the Irish borough of Portarlington, and as a senator attracted the respect and esteem of all parties. He died in September, 1823. Mr. Ricardo is said to have been a Unitarian, though he usually attended the service of the established church after renouncing Judaism.

Ricci, Lorenzo, the last general of the Jesuits previously to their suppression by pope Clement XIII, was born at Florence in 1703, entered the order at the age of fifteen, and, after having been professor of rhetoric and philosophy at Sienna, he became spiritual director at the Roman college, and secretary of his order. In 1758, he succeeded to the office of general on the death of Centurioni. Resisting the suppression of the Jesuits, he was sent to the castle of St. Angelo, where he died in 1775. (See *Jesuits.*)—See his life, by Caraccioli.

Ricci, Scipio, bishop of Pistoia and Prato, nephew of the preceding, was born at Florence, in 1741. Being favored by the grand-duke of Tuscany, Leopold, he opened, at Pistoia, in 1786, a synod, with a view to the propagation of some new religious doctrines; by which he incurred the displeasure of the pope, and was obliged to resign his see. In 1799, he was imprisoned for declaring in favor of the decrees of the constituent assembly, which had been formed under the influence of the French. Being set at liberty, he signed, in 1805, a formula of adhesion to the bulls which he had objected to, and became reconciled to the holy see. He died in 1810. In 1824, appeared the *Vie et Mémoires de Scipion Ricci*, by M. de Potter (translated into English by T. Roscoe, 2 vols., 1829).

Riccoboni, Lodovico, born at Modena in 1677, manifested an early passion for the theatre; and, having become the director of a theatrical company at the age of twenty-two years, he endeavored to reform the Italian theatre, by substituting regular pieces for the miserable farces which then had possession of the stage in Italy. (See *Drama*, and *Italian Theatre.*) Wearied with the opposition made to his efforts by the perverse taste of his countrymen, he went to Paris with his company, and associated himself with Dominique and Romagnesi, with great success. In 1729, the duke of Parma appointed him inspector of the theatres in his dominions; but, in 1731, he returned to Paris, where he devoted his last years to literature, and died in 1753. He was the author of numerous comedies, and translated several pieces from the French. We have also by him an *Histoire du Théâtre Italien.* His wife Helen (born 1686) distinguished herself on the stage, and by her poetical compositions, which procured her admission into several Italian academies. Their son Francesco, born at Mantua in 1707, died at Paris in 1772, was more successful as a dramatic writer than as an actor. Besides his comedies, which were very popular, he wrote a work entitled *L'Art du Théâtre* (Paris, 1750). His wife, born at Paris in 1714, is esteemed one of the best French novelists. She suffered much from the neglect of her husband, and died in poverty, in 1792. Her complete works have been several times published (best edition, Paris, 1818, 6 vols., 8vo.).

Rice (*oryza sativa*). This important article of food is now cultivated in all the warmer parts of the globe. It was long known in the East before it was introduced into Egypt and Greece. Pliny, Dioscorides and Theophrastus mention it as being brought from India; but it was little cultivated in their time upon the borders of the Mediterranean. It was introduced into Carolina about the year 1697, and is now cultivated extensively in many parts of the south of Europe. In Britain, the chief supply of rice is from Carolina; and this is considered far superior to the India rice, which is small, meagre, and the grains frequently broken. Immense districts of country would have remained desolate and irreclaimable, if nature had not granted to a simple grass the property of growing exclusively in inundated and marshy grounds. It has altered the face of the globe and the destiny of nations; for there can be no doubt that it is to this grain that the Chinese and Hindoos owe their early civilization. An immense population in those and the surrounding countries is now dependent on the rice crops; and when these fail, thousands perish of hunger. The culm of the rice is from one to six feet high, annual, erect, simple, round, and jointed; the leaves are large, firm, and pointed, arising from very long, cylindrical, and finely striated sheaths; the flowers are disposed in a large and beautiful panicle, somewhat resembling that of the oat. The seeds are white and oblong, but vary in size and form in the numerous varieties. It is important to be acquainted with these varieties, in order to choose which are best suited to certain soils or localities; some are preferable on account of the size and excellence of the grains; others, from their great bearing, or the time of ripening; others, again, from their more or less delicacy with respect to cold, drought, &c. The Hindoos, Chinese, Malays, and the inhabitants of the neighboring islands have paid most attention to the cultivation of these varieties. One species only of rice is known. Rice can be profitably cultivated only in warm climates; and here it is said to yield six times as much as the same space of wheat lands. The Chinese obtain two crops a year from the same ground, and cultivate it in this way from generation to generation on the same soil, and without any other manure than the mud deposited by the water of the river used in overflowing it. After the waters of the inundation have withdrawn, a few days are allowed for the mud to become partially dry; then a small spot is enclosed by an embankment, lightly ploughed and harrowed, and the grain, previously steeped in dung diluted with animal water, is then sown very thickly on it. A thin sheet of water is immediately brought over it, either by a stream or the chain-pump. In the mean time, other spaces are preparing for being planted in a similar manner. When the plants are six or seven inches high, they are transplanted in furrows made by the plough, so as to stand about a foot apart every way: water is then brought over them, and kept on till the crop begins to ripen, when it is withheld; so that when the harvest arrives the field is quite dry. It is reaped with a sickle, threshed with a flail, or the treading of cattle, and the husk is taken off by beating it in a stone mortar, or passing it between flat stones, as in a common meal mill. The first crop being cut in May, a second is immediately prepared for, by burning the stubble, and this second crop ripens in October or November. After removal, the stubble is ploughed in, which is the only vegetable manure such lands can be said to receive. In Japan, Ceylon, and Java, aquatic rice is cultivated nearly in the same manner. A rice plantation requires constant attention. The proprietor must make daily visits, in order to see that the various aqueducts, flood-gates and embankments of the different compart ments are all in order, and that the water constantly remains at the same height. The maturity of the grain is ascertained by the yellowness of the straw, and it is harvested much in the same manner as other grains, with this difference, that in certain districts the tops only are cut. Rice, when stowed in the granary, is subject to the depredations of a small curculio; but it is found that this insect attacks it only when enveloped in the husks. Aquatic rice is cultivated by the Chinese, even in the midst of rivers and lakes, by means of rafts made of bamboo and covered with earth. Mountain rice is cultivated on the mountains of the eastern islands and of Cochin-China, much in the same way as our barley; but it is to be observed, that it is planted at the commencement of the rainy, and reaped at the beginning of the dry season, and also that these mountains receive from the atmosphere a much greater proportion of moisture than lower districts. There is a kind of rice hardy enough to grow on the edge of the Himalaya snows, and which may probably, at some future time, prove a valuable acquisition to the European cultivator. Rice is even cultivated in the south of Germany, and, from long culture in a comparatively cold country, has acquired a remarkable degree of hardiness and adaptation to the climate—a circumstance which has frequently been alluded to as an encouragement to the acclimating of exotics: it is found that rice seeds direct from India will not ripen in Germany at all, and even Italian or Spanish seeds are much less early and hardy than those ripened on the spot. A crop has been obtained in England, on the banks of the Thames. In some parts of the East. rice is freed from the husks by immersion in hot water, by which the grains are slighuy swelled, and burst the envelopes. As an article of diet, rice has been extolled as superior to almost any other vegetable. Large quantities are annually imported into Europe, and it is highly esteemed in puddings and numerous other culinary preparations. On account of its being destitute of gluten, it cannot be made into bread, like wheat. Indeed, on account of its excellence and cheapness, it claims attention as a general article of sustenance for the poorer classes of society; as it is well known that a quarter of a pound of rice, slowly boiled, will yield more than a pound of solid and nutritive food. However, it has been found that, in Europe, the poor constantly reject the use of rice when potatoes are to be had; and, in truth, it does not seem to be so well adapted to European constitutions as that root. The inhabitants of the East obtain from rice a vinous liquor, more intoxicating than the strongest wine; and an ardent spirit, called *rak*, or *arrack*, is also partly made from it. The latter is chiefly manufactured at Batavia, and at Goa, on the coast of Malabar, and is said to be distilled from a mixture of the infusion of rice and of the juice of the cocoa-nut tree. The general appellation of rice throughout the East Indies is *paddy*.

Rice-Bunting, or Bob-o-Link (*icterus agripennis*, Bonap.; *emberiza oryzivora*, Wilson); specific characters, tail-feathers very acute; adult male in spring dress, black; the hind head, yellowish-white; scapulars, rump and tail coverts, white, tinged with ash; female young, and male in early autumn and winter dress, varied with brownish-black and brownish-yellow, beneath dull yellow; the male with much more yellow. This bird migrates over the continent of America from Labrador to Mexico, and over the Great Antilles, appearing in the southern extremity of the U. States about the middle of March or beginning of April. About the first of May, the bob-o-links reach Massachusetts. The rearing of their young takes place north of the fortieth degree of latitude. Their food is insects and worms, and the seeds of the grassy meadows. In the autumn, they sometimes attack the crops of oats and barley. The song of the male continues, with little interruption, as long as the female is sitting, and is singular and pleasant; it consists of a jingling medley of short, variable notes, confused, rapid and continuous. The relish for song and merriment is confined to the male, and diminishes as the period of incubation advances. The male generally loses his musical talent about the end of the first week in July, from which time, or somewhat earlier, his plumage begins to lose its gay colors, and to assume the humble hue of that of the female. About the middle of August, they enter New York and Pennsylvania, in vast foraging parties, on their way to the south. There, along the shores of the large rivers lined with floating fields of wild rice, they find abundant subsistence, grow fat, and their flesh becomes little inferior in flavor to that of the European ortolan; on which account the reed or rice birds, as they are then called, are shot in great numbers. When the cool nights in October commence, they move still farther south, till they reach the islands of Cuba and Jamaica.

Rice Glue. (See *Cements.*)

Richard I, king of England, surnamed Cœur de Lion, second son of Henry II, by Eleanor of Guienne, was born in 1157. In 1173, he was induced by his mother to unite with his brothers, Henry and Geoffry, and other confederates, in a rebellion against his father, which, however, that active prince soon quelled. This conduct he repeated on more than one occasion, until, in 1189, he openly joined the king of France, and, in the war which ensued, pursued the unhappy Henry from place to place, who, being at the same time deserted by his youngest son, died, worn out with chagrin and affliction, at Chinon, cursing his undutiful and ungrateful children with his latest breath. (See *Henry II.*) On this event, Richard succeeded to the throne of England, and, visiting his father's corpse the day after his decease, expressed great remorse at his own conduct. Having settled his affairs in France, he sailed to England, and was crowned at Westminster. He prudently gave his confidence to his father's ministers, and discountenanced all who had abetted his own rebellion. He had taken the cross previously to his accession, and now bent all his views to the gratification of his martial ardor in the fields of the East. He raised money by the sale of the crown property and offices, and by every other means he could devise, including the remission of a large sum of the vassalage imposed by his father upon Scotland. He then sought an interview with Philip of France, who had also taken the cross, in which mutual conditions respecting their joint operations were agreed upon. A great number of English barons and others took the cross on this occasion, to which enterprise a massacre of the Jews, in several of the principal towns of the kingdom, formed a prelude. At midsummer, 1190, Richard and Philip united 100,000 of their bravest subjects on the plains of Vezelai. Richard then proceeded to embark at Marseilles, and the two kings met at Messina, where they spent the winter. Here Richard was joined by Berengaria, daughter of Sanchez, king of Navarre, his intended wife; but, without staying to celebrate his nuptials, he put to sea with his fleet, which was soon after dispersed by a storm. The king got into Crete; but those of his ships which had his bride and his sister, the queen of Sicily, on board, were driven into Cyprus, where the king of that island imprisoned the crew, and refused to deliver up the princesses. In revenge for this insult, Richard landed his army, and obliged the king to surrender himself and his sovereignty. In Cyprus, he consummated his nuptials, and then embarked for Palestine. At this period, the siege of Acre was carrying on by the remnant of the army of the emperor Frederic, and other Christian adventurers, and defended by a Saracen garrison, supported by the celebrated Saladin. (q. v.) The arrival of the two kings infused new vigor into the besiegers, and the place surrendered in July, 1191. This advantage was, however, succeeded by mutual jealousies, more especially excited by a contest for the crown of Jerusalem, between Lusignan and Conrad of Montferrat; the former being supported by Richard, and the latter by the king of France. At length, disgusted with a warfare in which he only acted a secondary character, the latter returned to Europe, leaving 10,000 men with Richard. A general engagement took place, in which Richard, by the greatest bravery and military skill, gained a complete victory, which was followed by the possession of Joppa, Ascalon, and other places. Richard advanced within sight of Jerusalem; but, the greater part of the auxiliaries refusing to concur in the siege, he retired to Ascalon, and, perceiving his difficulties increase, concluded a truce with Saladin, on condition that Acre, Joppa, and the other seaports of Palestine, should remain in the hands of the Christians, who were also to enjoy full liberty of performing pilgrimages to Jerusalem. Richard now prepared to return to England, but previously concurred in the election of Conrad (almost immediately after assassinated) to the nominal sway of Jerusalem, and bestowed his conquered kingdom of Cyprus upon Lusignan. He embarked at Acre in October, 1192, and sailed for the Adriatic; but was wrecked near Aquileia. Taking the disguise of a pilgrim, he pursued his way through Germany, until, being discovered near Vienna, he was arrested by the order of Leopold, duke of Austria, who, having received an affront from him in Palestine, seized this opportunity to gratify his avarice and revenge. The emperor, Henry VI, who had also a quarrel with Richard, for his alliance with Tancred, the usurper of the crown of Sicily, hearing of his captivity, demanded him from Leopold who gave him up, on the stipulation of a portion of his ransom. While Richard was imprisoned, his brother John (q. v.)

had taken up arms in England, in concert with the king of France. Richard bore his misfortunes with courage, and when the emperor charged him, before the diet of Worms, with various imaginary offences, he refuted these accusations with so much spirit, that the assembly loudly exclaimed against his detention. At length a treaty was concluded for his liberation, on the payment of a ransom of 150,000 marks, which being raised in England, Richard obtained his liberty. Richard embarked at the mouth of the Scheldt, and safely reached England in March, 1194, to the great joy of his subjects. After being re-crowned in England, he landed in France in May, 1194, where he was met by his brother John, who threw himself at his feet, and, under the mediation of his mother, entreated forgiveness. "I forgive him," said Richard, "and I hope I shall as easily forget his injuries as he will my pardon." In the ensuing war with Philip, Richard gained some advantages; but a truce soon suspended their hostilities. Leopold, having received an accidental hurt which proved mortal, expressed remorse for his treatment of Richard, and gave up all claim to the remainder of his ransom. The emperor also offered to remit the remainder of his debt, provided he would join him in an offensive alliance against France, which was readily agreed to. England, during this period of useless contention, partly through the rapacity of government, and partly through unpropitious seasons, productive of famine and pestilence, was in a state of great depression. A lasting accommodation with France was in agitation, preparatory to another crusade, when the life and reign of Richard were suddenly brought to a close. A considerable treasure having been found in the land of the viscount of Limoges, he sent part of it to Richard as his feudal sovereign. The latter, however, demanded the whole; which being refused, he invested the castle of Chalus, where the treasure was concealed, and, having refused terms of surrender to the garrison, in the openly expressed determination of hanging the whole of them, was wounded by a shot from the crossbow of one Bertrand de Gourdon. The assault was, however, successfully made, and all the garrison hanged, with the exception of Gourdon, who was reserved for a more cruel death. Richard, apprized that his wound was mortal, asked him what had induced him to attempt his life. The man replied, "You killed my father and my brother with your own hand, and designed to put me to an ignominious death." The prospect of death had inspired Richard with sentiments of moderation and justice, and he ordered Gourdon to be set at liberty, and allowed a sum of money; but the savage Marcadée, who commanded the Brabançons, which the king had hired for the expedition, caused the unhappy man to be flayed alive. Richard died of his wound on the 6th of April, 1199, in the forty-second year of his age, and tenth of his reign, leaving no issue. The character of this king was strongly marked. He was the bravest among the brave, often frank and liberal, and not devoid of generosity. At the same time, he was haughty, violent, unjust, rapacious, and sanguinary; and, to use the expression of Gibbon, united the ferocity of a gladiator to the cruelty of a tyrant. His talents were considerable, both in the cabinet and in the field, and he was shrewd in observation, eloquent, and very happy at sarcasm. He was also a poet; and some of his reputed compositions are preserved among those of the Troubadours. On the whole, a sort of romantic interest is attached to the character and exploits of this prince, which, in the eye of reason, they little merit, as the career of Richard produced calamities poorly atoned for by the military reputation which alone attended it.

RICHARD II, king of England, son of Edward the Black Prince, and grandson of Edward III, was born in 1366. He succeeded the latter in 1377, in his eleventh year, the chief authority of the state being in the hands of his three uncles, John of Gaunt, duke of Lancaster, Edmund, earl of Cambridge, afterwards duke of York, and Thomas of Woodstock, subsequently duke of Gloucester. The earlier years of the king's minority passed in wars with France and Scotland, the expense of which led to exactions that produced the insurrection headed by Wat Tyler. Its termination in the death of its chief leader in Smithfield, by the hand of the lord mayor of London, in the presence of the young king, afforded the latter an opportunity to exhibit a degree of address and presence of mind, which, in a youth of fifteen, was very remarkable. Whilst the rioters stood astonished at the fall of their leader, the young king calmly rode up to them, and, declaring that he would be their leader, drew them off, almost involuntarily, into the neighboring fields. In the mean time, an armed force was collected by the lord mayor and others, at the sight of which the rioters fell on their knees and demanded pardon, which was granted them on the condition of their immediate dispersion. Similar insurrections took place in various parts of the kingdom, all of which were, however, put down, and Richard, now master of an army of 40,000 men, collected by a general summons to all the retainers of the crown, found himself strong enough to punish the ringleaders with great severity, and to revoke all the charters and manumissions which he had granted, as extorted and illegal. The promise of conduct and capacity which he displayed on this emergency was but ill answered in the sequel; and he very early showed a predilection for weak and dissolute company, and the vicious indulgences so common to youthful royalty. In his sixteenth year, he married Anne, daughter of the emperor Charles IV, and, soon after, was so injudicious as to take the great seal from Scroop, for refusing to sanction certain extravagant grants of lands to his courtiers. Wars with France and Scotland, and the ambitious intrigues of the duke of Lancaster, disquieted some succeeding years. The favorites of Richard were Michael de la Pole, earl of Suffolk and chancellor, and Robert de Vere, earl of Oxford, the latter of whom he created duke of Ireland, with entire sovereignty in that island for life. The duke of Lancaster, being then absent, prosecuting his claim to the crown of Castile, the king's younger uncle, the duke of Gloucester, a prince of popular manners, and unprincipled ambition, became the leader of a formidable opposition, which procured an impeachment of the chancellor, and influenced the parliament so far that it proceeded to strip the king of all authority, and obliged him to sign a commission appointing a council of regency for a year. Being now in his twenty-first year, this measure was very galling to Richard, who, in concert with the duke of Ireland, found means to assemble a council of his friends at Nottingham, where the judges unanimously declared against the legality of the extorted commission. Gloucester, at these proceedings, mustered an army in the vicinity of London, which being ineffectually opposed by a body of forces under the duke of Ireland, several of the king's friends were executed, and the judges who had given their opinion in his favor, were all found guilty of high treason, and sentenced to imprisonment for life in Ireland. A reaction was soon produced by the tyranny of the ascendant party; so that, in 1389, Richard was encouraged to enter the council, and, in a resolute tone, to declare that he was of full age to take the government into his own hands; and, no opposition being ventured upon, he proceeded to turn out the duke of Gloucester and all his adherents. This act he rendered palatable to the nation by publishing a general amnesty, and remitting the grants of money made by the late parliament. Several years of internal tranquillity ensued, which was promoted by the return of the duke of Lancaster, who formed a counterbalance to the influence of the duke of Gloucester; and Richard prudently kept on the best terms with him. By his fondness for low company, by spending his time in conviviality, and amusement with jesters, and persons of mean station and light behavior, the king forfeited the respect of his subjects, while his weak attachment to his favorites placed all things at their disposal, and made a mere cipher of himself. Encouraged by these follies, the duke of Gloucester once more began to exercise his sinister influence, and, the most criminal designs being imputed to him, Richard caused him and his two chief supporters, the earls of Arundel and Warwick, to be arrested. The earl of Arundel was executed, and the earl of Warwick condemned to perpetual banishment. The duke of Gloucester had been sent over to Calais for safe custody, and was there suffocated. A quarrel between the duke of Hereford, son of John of Gaunt, and the duke of Norfolk, was the incidental cause of the revolution which terminated this unsettled reign. The king banished both the dukes—Norfolk for life, and Hereford for ten, afterwards reduced to six years. It was, however, declared that each of them should be duly entitled to any inheritance which might fall to them during their absence; but, on the death of John of Gaunt, in 1399, the unprincipled Richard seized his property as forfeited to the crown. The king having embarked for Ireland, to revenge the death of his cousin, the earl of March, who had been killed in a skirmish with the natives, Henry of Bolingbroke, as the duke of Hereford was now called, made use of this opportunity to land in Yorkshire, with a small body of forces, and, being joined by the earls of Northumberland and Westmoreland, and other influential leaders, proceeded southward, at the head of 60,000 men, nominally to recover his duchy of Lancaster. When Richard, upon this intelligence, landed at Milford haven, he found himself so much deserted, that he withdrew to North Wales, with a design to escape to France. He was, however, decoyed to a conference with Henry, seized by an armed force, and led by his successful rival to London. As they entered the capital, Henry was hailed with the loudest acclamations, and the unfortunate Richard treated with neglect and even contumely. His deposition was now resolved upon, to be preceded by a forced resignation of the crown. Thirty-five articles of accusation were accordingly drawn up against him, of which several were exaggerated, false and frivolous, but others contained real instances of tyranny and misgovernment; and king Richard was solemnly deposed Sept. 30, 1399. Henry then claimed the crown, which was awarded to him. (See *Henry IV.*) Richard was committed, for safe custody, to the castle of Pomfret. Of the manner of his death no certain account has been given; but a popular notion prevailed, that his keeper and guards killed him with halberds. It is more probable that starvation or poison was had recourse to, for his body, when exposed, exhibited no marks of violence. He died in the thirty-fourth year of his age, and twenty-third of his reign.

Richard III, king of England, born in 1450, was the youngest son of Richard duke of York. On the accession of his brother, Edward IV, he was created duke of Gloucester, and, during the early part of Edward's reign, served him with great courage and fidelity. He partook of the ferocity which was ever a dark feature in the character of the Plantagenets; and is said to have personally aided in the murder of Edward prince of Wales, after the battle of Tewksbury, and to have been the author, if not the perpetrator, of the murder of Henry VI (q. v.) in the Tower. This bloody disposition was, however, united in him with deep policy and dissimulation, which rendered him still more dangerous. He married, in 1473, Anne, who had been betrothed to the murdered prince of Wales, joint heiress of the earl of Warwick, whose other daughter was united to the duke of Clarence. Quarrels arose between the brothers on the division of the inheritance of their wives; and Richard, who found his elder brother an obstacle to his views of aggrandizement, combined in the accusations against that weak and versatile prince, which brought him to destruction. On the death of Edward, in 1483, the duke of Gloucester was appointed protector of the kingdom; and he immediately caused his nephew, the young Edward V, to be declared king, and took an oath of fealty to him. The two ascendant factions, that of the queen's relatives, headed by her brother, earl Rivers, and that of the more ancient nobility, who were led by the duke of Buckingham and lord Hastings, courted the favor of the protector, who dissembled with each, while he was secretly pursuing the schemes of his own dark ambition. His first object was to get rid of those who were connected with the young king by blood; and, after spending a convivial evening with Rivers, Grey, and sir Thomas Vaughan, he had them arrested the next morning, and conveyed to Pomfret, where they were soon after executed without trial. Alarmed at the arrest of her relatives, the queen dowager took refuge in the sanctuary at Westminster, with her younger son, the duke of York, and her daughter. As it was necessary, for the protector's purposes, to get both his nephews into his hands, he persuaded two prelates to urge the queen to deliver the duke of York into his hands, upon the most solemn assurances of safety. Lord Hastings, although opposed to the queen's relatives, being the steady friend of her children, was next arrested, while sitting in council, and led to immediate execution. After this bold and bloody commencement, he proceeded in an attempt to establish the illegitimacy of Edward's children, on the pretence of a previous marriage with the lady Eleanor Talbot, daughter of the earl of Shrewsbury, and scrupled not to countenance an attack on the character of his own mother, who was affirmed to have given other fathers to Edward and Clarence, and to have been true to her husband only in the birth of Richard. All these pleas were dwelt upon in a sermon preached at St. Paul's cross. The duke of Buckingham afterwards, in a speech before the corporation and citizens of London, enlarged upon the title and virtues of the protector, and then ventured to ask them whether they chose the duke of Gloucester for king. On their silence, he repeated the question, and a few prepared voices exclaimed, "God save king Richard!" This was then accepted as the public voice, and Bucking ham, with the lord mayor, repaired to the protector with a tender of the crown. He at first affected alarm and suspicion, and then pretended loyalty to his nephew, and unwillingness to take such a burden upon himself, but finally acceded; and he was proclaimed king on the 27th of June, 1483, the mock election being secured by bodies of armed men, brought to the metropolis by himself and Buckingham. The deposed king and his brother were never more heard of, and, according to general belief, they were smothered in the Tower of London, by order of their uncle. (See *Edward V.*) The new reign commenced with rewards to those who had been instrumental to the change, and with endeavors to obtain popularity. Richard, with a splendid retinue, made a progress through several provincial towns, and was crowned a second time at York, on which occasion he created his only son prince of Wales. But hatred and abhorrence of Richard soon became the general sentiment of the nation, and all men's eyes were turned towards Henry, earl of Richmond, maternally descended from the Somerset branch of the house of Lancaster. Buckingham, not thinking himself adequately rewarded, entered into a conspiracy against him, with other malcontents in the south and west of England, but was suddenly deserted by his followers, betrayed into the hands of authority, and executed without trial. About the same time, the earl of Richmond, who had embarked with a fleet from St. Malo, encountered a violent storm, and was obliged to return. The death of his son, the prince of Wales, was a severe stroke to Richard; and such was the odium attached to his character, that the death of his wife, which followed soon after, was, without the least evidence, attributed to poison. He immediately determined to marry his niece Elizabeth, the daughter of his brother Edward, and legitimate heiress of the crown, in order to prevent her union with Richmond. In August, 1485, Richmond landed with a small army at Milford haven. Richard, not knowing in what quarter to expect him, was thrown into much perplexity, which was aggravated by his suspicion of the fidelity of his nobles, and especially the Stanleys, the chief of whom had become the second husband of Margaret, the earl of Richmond's mother. When informed of the advance of his rival, he, however, took the field with great expedition, and met him with an army of 15,000 men at Bosworth, in Leicestershire. Richmond had only 6000 men, but relied on the secret assurances of aid from Stanley, who commanded a separate force of 7000. The battle was fought on the 23d of August, 1485; and, in the midst of it, Stanley, by falling on the flank of the royal army, secured the victory to Richmond. (See *Henry VII.*) Richard, finding his situation desperate, rushed against his competitor, slew his standard-bearer, and was on the point of encountering Richmond himself, when he sunk under the number of his assailants. The body of Richard was found in the field stripped naked, in which condition it was carried across a horse to Leicester, and interred in the Grey Friars' churchyard. Thus fell this odious prince, in his thirty-fifth year, after possessing the crown, which he had acquired by so many crimes, for two years and two months. Richard possessed courage, capacity, eloquence, and most of the talents which would have adorned a lawful throne. Many of his bad qualities have probably been exaggerated, but undeniable facts prove his cruelty, dissimulation, treachery, and relentless ambition. Gibbon has answered the Historic Doubts of Walpole concerning the reign and character of Richard Richard III has been represented as of small stature, deformed, and of a forbidding aspect; but there is some testimony to prove that his personal, like his mental, defects, have been magnified by the general detestation of his character.

Richardson, Samuel, a distinguished English novelist, was born in 1689, in Derbyshire, and received only a common school education. He early discovered a talent for story-telling and letter-writing, and, at the age of thirteen, was the confidant of three young women in their love secrets, and employed by them in their amatory correspondence. At the usual age, he was bound apprentice to Mr. John Wilde, a printer of Stationer's hall, London, and, after the expiration of his apprenticeship, passed five or six years as a foreman in a printing-office, until at length he set up for himself. His habits of diligence, accuracy, and honorable dealing, acquired him an extensive business; and, beginning to thrive in the world, he married the daughter of his former master. His Pamela, the first work which gave him distinction as a writer, was published in 1741. The first two volumes were completed in two months; and so great was its popularity, that it ran through five editions in one year, and was even recommended from the pulpit. The novelty of his plan, with many passages of great beauty, and interesting traits of character, may account for much of this reception; but, even at that time, critics existed who entertained those opinions of its imperfections, and doubts of its salutary tendency, which have since become almost general. He was led, by a spurious continuation, to add two volumes to his Pamela, which are inferior to the former; but, in 1748, the appearance of the first two volumes of his Clarissa fully established his literary reputation; and its pathos, its variety of character, and minute developement of the movements of the human heart, will cause it ever to be regarded as a noble monument of its author's genius. The History of Sir Charles Grandison appeared in 1753. The interest taken in this work was not equal to that produced by the former, although perhaps exhibiting more compass and invention; but the character of the hero is in some degree repulsive, and the prolixity of the author began to engender satiety. The character of Clementina is a masterly example of delicate delineation. This work was, as well as the preceding, translated into foreign languages, and received with great applause. In all the productions of Richardson, the style is inelegant, gossipping and verbose, and he seldom knows when to leave off. In 1754, he rose to be master of the Stationers' company; and, in 1760, purchased a moiety of the patent of law printer to the king. As he grew rich, he indulged himself with a country residence at Parson's-green, Middlesex, where he lived, surrounded with a circle of affectionate admirers, particularly females, to whom it was his delight to read his work in the progress of composition. In mixed company, he was rather silent and reserved. Nothing could exceed his piety, moral worth, and general benevolence. He died of an apoplexy, in 1761, at the age of seventy-two, and was buried in the church of St. Bride, in Fleet street. His correspondence was published in 1804, in 6 vols., 8vo., with a life, by Mrs. Barbauld.

Richelieu, Armand Jean du Plessis, cardinal, duke de, one of the greatest statesmen of France, was born at Paris, in 1585, and at the age of twenty-two years was made bishop of Luçon. His country had already been restored from its long troubles to tranquillity, prosperity, and order, by Henry IV (q. v.) and his great minister Sully. (q. v.) In 1616, the queen-mother, Mary of Medici, into whose favor Richelieu had insinuated himself, made him her grand almoner and one of the secretaries of state. On the disgrace of the queen (see *Mary of Medici*), he continued attached to her cause, and effected a reconciliation between her and her son Louis XIII (1619), which, however, was soon interrupted by her intrigues against the constable Luynes, the favorite of the king. Richelieu, who was thus placed between the two contending parties, loved by neither, but considered by both as a useful instrument, had a difficult part to act, and it required all his prudence to enable him to keep his position. In 1622, he obtained the cardinal's hat, through the influence of Mary, and, in 1624, entered the council of state, and was soon at the head of affairs. The premier now felt himself in a condition to drop the mask which he had hitherto worn, and Mary too late regretted the protection she had extended to him. The adherence of this princess to the political system of the house of Hapsburg was injurious to the interests of France. Almost all the French princes had kept up a constant opposition to that powerful family, and no sooner was Richelieu seated in his high post, than he began systematically to extend the power of the crown by overthrowing the privileges of the great vassals, and to increase the influence of the French monarchy by undermining that of the Hapsburgs, both beyond the Pyrenees and in Germany. Louis XIII, who was sensible of the energy of his minister, favored his plans, while he always showed a dislike for the man, whom he would gladly have destroyed, had he been able to govern without him. The Reformed (Huguenots) in France had for a long time resisted the royal power; and bloody insurrections, in several preceding reigns, had arisen from their struggles with the spiritual and temporal authorities, in defence of their civil rights and freedom of conscience. The wisdom and mildness of Henry IV had assuaged the excitement of the contending parties, but his reign was too short to extinguish the fires which still glowed beneath the embers. The struggle for religious freedom was too often, indeed, made a pretext, by the nobles, and even the princes of the blood royal, to cloak and further their own ambitious designs; and both religious parties, Catholics as well as Protestants, had thus alternately served as a check upon the despotic exercise of the royal power. Richelieu, therefore, resolved to crush the weaker by the aid of the stronger party, and thus to deprive those, who should be disposed to resist his schemes, of their main prop By the edict of Nantes, the Huguenots had been placed on nearly the same footing with the other subjects of the kingdom: there were some provinces in which they had the ascendency, and their armed force was sufficient to shake the throne, should they be excited to rise against it. Their rallying point was Rochelle; and Richelieu neglected no means to make himself master of that city. In the celebrated siege of Rochelle, he commanded the army in person. The attack and defence of the place are considered as affording models of perseverance, valor, and military skill. Rochelle, supported by England, from which it continually received supplies, held out for a long time against all the efforts of the cardinal; and the hope of reducing it was already nearly abandoned, when Richelieu, by the erection of an immense mole, cut off the communication by sea, and finally compelled it to surrender by famine (1629). The second step of Richelieu was the removal of the queen-mother from court. That princess endeavored to effect the fall of the minister: she had already gained over the king to her purpose, in a secret interview, when Richelieu entered the cabinet: the queen overwhelmed him with reproaches. He continued calm, had recourse to prayers and tears, and finally requested the king's permission to leave the court. The preparations were already made for his departure; but the king, who was not less offended by the violence of the queen, than pleased by the respectful demeanor of the cardinal, asked the advice of his favorite, St. Simon. The latter represented to him the services of Richelieu, and the impossibility of dispensing with his aid. Louis, therefore, ordered him to Versailles, and assigned him apartments in the palace directly below his own. This day (November 10, 1630), on which the hopes of the queen and of the cardinal's enemies were disappointed, was called the "day of the dupes" (*la journée des dupes*). As the queen continued to declare herself irreconcilable with Richelieu, the cardinal prevailed upon the king to banish her (1631) to Compiegne, removed her friends from place, and threw some of them into the Bastile. This step, and the almost total annihilation of the privileges of the parliaments and the clergy, excited all classes against the despotic administration of the cardinal, and the discontents broke out in numerous risings and conspiracies, which, however, were not only suppressed by the prudence and vigor of his measures, but also contributed to the furtherance of his plan, and gradually rendered the royal power entirely absolute. In 1632, the royal arms, directed by Richelieu, suppressed the rebellion of the dukes of Orleans and Montmorency, the adherents of the banished queen, and Montmorency perished on the scaffold, although the royal family itself interceded in his behalf. Equally unsuccessful were the attempts of the dukes of Lorraine, Guise, Bouillon, &c.; even those whom the king privately favored were obliged to yield to the all-powerful minister, and paid with their lives for their rashness in venturing to oppose him, as in the instance of Cinq-mars, who, a short time before Richelieu's death, had entered into a conspiracy against him, which the king was, not without reason, believed to have favored. While the minister was thus extending the power of the crown at home, he did not neglect the aggrandizement of the monarchy abroad. The thirty years' war gave him an opportunity of effecting this object. The same man who persecuted, with the greatest severity, the Protestants in France, employed all the arts of negotiation, and even force of arms, to protect the same sect in Germany, for the purpose of humbling the house of Austria. The king of Sweden, the great bulwark of religious liberty in Germany, received aid of every kind from Richelieu, as long as he was not in danger of becoming formidable to France; but when the brilliant victories of Gustavus Adolphus gave the cardinal reason to consider his power as more dangerous than that of Austria, he abandoned that prince in the midst of his successes. The war which he undertook against Spain, and which continued till 1659, put France in possession of Catalonia and Roussillon, and the separation of Portugal from Spain was effected by his assistance. He also endeavored to weakened the Austrian influence in Italy, and procured the transfer of the duchy of Mantua to the duke of Nevers. In general, however objectionable may have been his character as a man, the duke de Richelieu must be allowed to have deserved the character of a great statesman: he cannot be denied the glory of having raised the power of the sovereign in France to its highest pitch; but he was proud, arrogant, vindictive and unprincipled. The protection which he gave to letters and art (in the establishment of the French Academy, 1635, and of the *Jardin des Plantes*, for example) cannot reconcile us to his faults. (See *Corneille*.) Richelieu died December 4, 1642, after having indicated Mazarin as his successor. Louis XIII died a few months after him; but in the long reign of Louis XIV (q. v.), the effects of Richelieu's policy became visible. See *Maximes d'État ou Testament politique du Cardinal de Richelieu* (Paris, 1764), Leclerc's *Vie de Richelieu*, and Jay's *Histoire du Ministère de Richelieu* (1815).

Richelieu, Louis François Armand du Plessis, duke de, marshal of France, member of the French academy, and of the academy of sciences, was born at Paris in 1696. His handsome person, his vivacity, and his wit, early made him a favorite at court, and particularly with the duchess of Burgundy (1711). His childish follies were made a handle of by malice, and the *jolie poupée*, as he was called at court, was thrown into the Bastile. After his release, he was made aid of marshal Villars, who was pleased with his liveliness, and his free and reckless manners. He was distinguished, even at the court of the regent, for his amours and affairs of honor, and was twice confined in the Bastile. In the twenty-fourth year of his age, the French academy chose him one of its members, although he had never written any thing beyond a *billet doux*, and was entirely ignorant of orthography. Fontenelle, Campistron, and Destouches, each, prepared for him an inaugural discourse, from each of which he selected such parts as he liked, to form a whole. He distinguished himself at the siege of Philipsburg (1734), and in the battle of Fontenoy (1745), by his courage and presence of mind. On the occasion of the marriage of the dauphin with the princess of Saxony, he was sent as ambassador to the court of Dresden, where he made the most extraordinary display of pomp. Nothing, however, could equal the magnificence of his entry into Vienna, as ambassador to that court, when the horses of his retinue were shod with silver, in such a manner that the shoes should fall off, to be picked up by the populace. In 1756, he was created marshal, and commanded at the siege of Mahon, which was occupied by the English. After the capture of that place (June 28, 1756), he received the command of the French army in Germany. But the marshal had offended Mad. de Pompadour, by rejecting her proposal of a match between his son and her daughter; and after the convention of Closter Seven (1757), he was recalled. He had enriched himself while in Germany, where he had also indulged his soldiers in license and plunder, by his exactions. It should always be remembered to his credit, that he dissuaded Louis XV from persecuting the Protestants. His example contributed greatly to extend the prevalence of licentiousness in France, since he was the dictator of fashion. He continued to prosecute affairs of gallantry even in his old age, and was married, the third time, at the age of eighty-four years. The *Mémoires du Maréchal de Richelieu* were written, under his direction, by Soulavie. He died August 3, 1788, ninety-three years old; and two days before his death, a lady having observed to him that his face still retained its beauty, he replied, "Madame, you take my face for your mirror." Marshal Richelieu had the courage, the fortune and the talents of a great general, the sagacity, prudence and penetration of a great statesman; but, with these and many amiable qualities, he chose to be nothing but a common courtier.

Richelieu, Armand Emanuel du Plessis, duke de, minister of state under Louis XVIII, grandson of the preceding, was born at Paris in 1766, and, after studying in the college of Plessis, travelled in Italy, whence he returned, at the commencement of the revolution, in 1789. He soon after obtained permission from the king to go to Vienna, where he was well received by the emperor Joseph II; but he soon quitted that capital with the young prince de Ligne, and entered into the service of Catharine II, then at war with the Turks. He distinguished himself at the taking of Ismail by Suwarrow, and was rewarded with the rank of major-general. In 1794, he was with Louis XVIII in England, whence he returned to Russia; but, not being well treated by the emperor Paul, he quitted that country, and, after the peace of 1801, revisited France, where Bonaparte in vain attempted to attach him to his service. He went again to St. Petersburg, and, at the commencement of 1803, was nominated civil and military governor of Odessa, a Russian colony on the Black sea, which flourished greatly under his superintendence. On the restoration of Louis XVIII, the duke de Richelieu took his seat in the chamber of peers, and resumed his functions as first gentleman of the bed-chamber. In March, 1815, he accompanied the king to Ghent, and, returning with him to Paris, after the battle of Waterloo, he was appointed president of the council of ministers, and placed at the head of the foreign department. He presided at the installation of the four academies in April, 1818, and in September following he was made president of the French academy. In the same month, he ap peared at the congress of Aix-la-Chapelle. He subsequently resigned his office as minister of state (see *Decazes*, and *Louis XVIII*); but on the assassination of the duke of Berry, in 1820, he again became president of the council. He fruitlessly opposed the establishment of the censorship of the press, and, finding he had lost his influence, he again retired from office (see *Villèle*), and died soon after, in May, 1822.

RICHMOND; a city, port of entry, and metropolis of Virginia, in Henrico county, on the north side of James river, between fifty and sixty miles above City Point, and 150 miles above the mouth of the river. It is at the head of tide-water, just below the falls, and opposite to Manchester, with which it is connected by bridges; 25 miles north of Petersburg, 123 south by west of Washington; lat. 37° 32′ N.; lon. 77° 21′ W.; population, in 1820, 12,046; in 1830, 16,060, including 6345 slaves, and 1900 free blacks. The situation of Richmond is highly picturesque and healthful, and it is a flourishing commercial city. Most of the houses are of brick, and many of them are elegant. Its public buildings are very commodious, and in good style, and it has considerable manufactures. The falls extend nearly six miles, in which the river descends eighty feet. A canal passes around these falls, and the river is navigable for batteaux 220 miles above them. The city is thus connected with a very extensive back country that is highly productive of wheat, corn, hemp, tobacco and coal. Vessels drawing ten feet of water come to Rockets, just below the city, and those drawing fifteen feet ascend to Warwick, five miles below Richmond. The inland, coasting and foreign trade of Richmond are extensive, and increasing; and the city possesses great advantages as a healthy and pleasant place of residence. It has good schools, and convenient houses of worship for many religious denominations. The Virginia armory is an extensive establishment, and capable of supplying the state with arms. The penitentiary is under good regulations. The new court-house is a very spacious and elegant building. The capitol has a very commanding situation on Shockoe hill. In 1811, December 26, the theatre at Richmond took fire during an exhibition, and seventy-two persons lost their lives in the conflagration. An elegant episcopal church, of brick, called the *Monumental church*, has since been erected on the spot, with a monument in front, commemorative of the melancholy event.

RICHMOND; a village of England, county of Surrey, on an eminence on the south bank of the Thames, of great celebrity for the beauty of its scenery, and for having been, during several centuries, the seat of a royal palace now demolished. George III frequently resided here, in the early part of his reign; and an observatory was erected here from designs by sir William Chambers. Part of the park is occupied by the royal gardens. The new, or great park, formed by Charles I, is well stocked with deer; it is enclosed by a brick wall eight miles in compass. The rich scenery of Richmond and its vicinity have been the theme of general admiration, and have attracted a number of families of distinction, whose seats render the village and neighborhood remarkably gay and splendid. The village extends about a mile up the hill from the Thames, skirted and intermingled with agreeable gardens. The view from Richmond hill is particularly celebrated. Among the monuments in the church is one to Thomson, who resided here. Population, in 1821, 5994; nine miles south-west of London.

RICHTER, Jean Paul Frederic, a German writer of the first rank in belles-lettres, was born, March 21, 1763, at Wunsiedel, in the Fichtelgebirge, and died November 14, 1825, at Baireuth. His father was, at the time of his birth, rector at Wunsiedel, at a later period pastor at Schwarzbach on the Saale. In 1780, Richter entered the university of Leipsic, in order to study theology, but soon changed his plan, and devoted himself to belles-lettres. As early as 1798, he was known as a distinguished writer at Leipsic. He went to Weimar, Berlin, Meiningen, &c., and settled at Baireuth, having been made counsellor of legation by the duke of Saxe-Hildburghausen, and having received from the prince primate (Dalberg) a pension, which the king of Bavaria continued after Baireuth had fallen to him. He seldom left his home, and only to make short journeys to the Rhine, Berlin, Dresden, &c. He had married during his early stay at Berlin, and had two daughters. Secured by his pension from want; happy in his domestic relations; blessed with numerous friends, and an almost childlike amiableness, which enjoyed to the last the pleasures of nature, as if they had been always new; having millions of admirers; unambitious of vain distinctions, or objects beyond his reach; with a heart susceptible of the noblest emotions; believing in man's goodness, and firmly relying on the immortality of the soul—he mav be said to have been one of the happiest men that ever trod this earth. His death corresponded with his life; he calmly fell asleep. It would be difficult to give a distinct idea of Jean Paul's works (this was the name under which he wrote) in a brief sketch like ours. Jean Paul is a humorous writer, but his humor is of a peculiar sort. The want of a public life obliges the Germans to live much in reflection, the effect of which is visible in almost all their writings, and has left its traces in those of Jean Paul. His humor is deeply reflecting and philosophic, at the same time often truly comic. He frequently rises to the highest regions, where he can speak only in bold metaphors; and, before we are aware, we hear his inspiring tones die away like those of a lark, when the bird has come again to the ground. If it can be said of any man's writings that they are poetry in a prose form, it is true of many passages in Jean Paul's works. His writings are generally in the form of novels, but they have little of the character of what we generally understand by novels. He seems to have liked particularly to analyze emotions, to dissect individual character in every station, even the humblest. He does not exhibit man under those general influences which operate on large masses of men, but deals almost exclusively with the individual considered as such. He very frequently recurs to the immortality of the soul. In his writings, as in his life, he appears amiable in the highest degree. His works are the following:—Greenland Processes (Berlin, 1783); Selection from the Papers of the Devil (1788); the Invisible Lodge (1793); Hesperus (1795); Quintus Fixlein (1796; and 1800); Biographical Entertainments under the Skull of a Giantess (1796); Flower, Fruit and Thorn Pieces (1796); the *Jubelsenior* (1797); the Valley of Campan, with a Satirical Appendix (1797); Palingenesies (1798); Letters, and Future Course of Life (1799); Titan (1800—1805); *Die Flegeljahre** (1803—1805); Katzenberger's Journey to the Watering Place (1809); the Field Preacher Schmelzle's Journey to Flötz (1809), &c. In 1804, he produced his first philosophical work of importance, his Introduction (*Vorschule*) to Æsthetics (2d ed. 1809), to which he added, in his last years, a *Nachschule*, with an Appendix, containing Reviews (Breslau, 1825). It is full of original and discriminating views, yet hardly a philosophically systematic work. In 1807, he published his *Levana*, a work on education, full of intelligent views. We must mention, also, his *Fibel* (Spelling-book); Peace Sermon (1809); Change of Throne between Mars and Phœbus in 1814; Political Sermons in Lent (1817); several essays, for instance, in his Museum (1814), and *Herbstbluminen* (1810—1820). In 1820 appeared his Comet, or Nic. Markgraf, a comic work. Shortly before his death, he began a new edition of his complete works. After his death, appeared his unfinished work Selina, or on Immortality. From memorandums left by him, a work was prepared, after his death, called *Truths from Jean Paul's Life* (3 vols., Breslau, 1826—28.)

* *Flegel* is the German for *clown, rude fellow;* and *Flegeljahre* (clown-years) signifies, in German, the period of transition from boyhood to manhood, when the character is unformed, and the manners embarrassed, awkward, and often rude.

Ricinus Communis. The *palma christi*, or castor oil plant, in Barbary, its native climate, often becomes a pretty stout tree, twenty or twenty-five feet in height; but, as cultivated with us, is an annual, herbaceous plant, not rising above six or eight; if, however, it be sheltered in a green-house, the stem persists, and becomes woody. The leaves are large, alternate, divided into six lobes, and peltate, or having the stalk inserted into the centre of the leaf. The flowers are disposed in long, branching spikes, the male occupying the inferior portion, which is contrary to the usual arrangement in monœcious plants. The fruit consists of three united, prickly capsules, each containing a large, smooth, shining, oblong, variegated seed. These seeds contain a virulent acrid and nauseous principle, which seems to reside exclusively in the germ. Hence it happens that, when eaten entire, two or three seeds will produce dangerous and even fatal effects, while the oil that is obtained from them in large quantities is mild, insipid, emollient, and gently purgative. This oil is procured by a moderate pressure, for the germ fortunately retains its oil with more pertinacity than the remainder of the seed; or by plunging the seeds in warm water, when the mild oil rises to the surface. The use of castor oil as a purgative is familiar to every one, and has been known from remote antiquity. In some countries, it is burnt in lamps, or is even employed with lime to make a cement, which with age becomes as hard as stone. The castor oil plant is now cultivated, to some extent, in New Jersey, Virginia, &c. for commercial purposes.

Rickets (*rhachitis*), or English Dis

EASE; a modification of the scrofula, which commonly appears after the age of nine months and before that of two years, attacking principally the bones. The disease is known by a large head, prominent forehead, projecting breast bone, flattened ribs, big belly, and emaciated limbs, with great debility. The bones and spine of the back are variously distorted. Nature frequently restores the general health, and leaves the limbs distorted. In the treatment of rickets, besides attention to the regimen, those means are employed by which the system is invigorated. Tonic medicines, the cold bath, &c., are beneficial. The child should be kept clean and dry, regularly exercised, and allowed to enjoy pure air. The food should be nutritious, and easy of digestion. The rickets sometimes manifests itself in adults, and often proves fatal in a short time.

RICOCHET. (See *Range.*)

RIDGE ROAD, or ALLUVIAL WAY; a remarkable ridge along the south shore of lake Ontario, in New York. It extends from Rochester on the Genesee, to Lewiston on the river Niagara, eighty-seven miles. It is composed of common beach sand and gravel stones worn smooth, and these are intermixed with small shells. Its general width is from four to eight rods, and it is raised in the middle with a handsome crowning arch, from six to ten feet. Its general surface preserves a very uniform level, being raised to meet the unevenness of the ground which it covers. At the rivers Genesee and Niagara, its elevation is about 120 or 130 feet; and this is its elevation above lake Ontario, from which it is distant from six to ten miles. There is a regular and gradual descent from the road to the lake. There seems to be no way of accounting for this ridge, without supposing that the surface of lake Ontario was 130 feet higher at some former period than it is at present; and, if this be admitted, we are led to inquire whether Erie and Ontario did not constitute one lake. But it is replied, that there is a similar ridge on the south side of lake Erie, for 120 miles. The ridge road of New York is one of the best roads in the state. (See *New York.*)

RIDING. (See *Horsemanship*, and *Manege.*)

RIDING AT ANCHOR. (See *Anchor.*)

RIDINGS (corrupted from *trithing*); the three jurisdictions into which the county of Yorkshire, in England, is divided, on account of its extent. They are called the *North*, *East* and *West* Ridings.

RIDLEY, Nicholas, bishop of London in the reigns of Edward VI and his successor Mary, was born about the commencement of the sixteenth century, and educated at Cambridge. He travelled on the continent, and, during a three years' absence from his native country, became acquainted with several of the early reformers, whose doctrines he afterwards warmly espoused. Returning to Cambridge, he filled the office of proctor to the university, and as such protested against the claims of the papal see to the supreme ecclesiastical jurisdiction in the realm. He was also chosen public orator, and, through the patronage of archbishop Cranmer (q. v.), became one of the king's chaplains; and, in the second year of Edward VI, he was elevated to the see of Rochester. Three years after, on the deprivation of Bonner, Ridley was made bishop of London, and distinguished himself by his tempered zeal in favor of the Protestant church, and especially by his liberality and kindness towards the family of his predecessor. On the death of Edward, a dread of the succession of a Roman Catholic sovereign induced him to listen to those who made an attempt to secure the Protestant ascendency, by placing the lady Jane Grey upon the throne. The defeat of this scheme, the active part he had taken in the establishment of the new discipline, and the construction of the liturgy, together with his intimate connexion with Cranmer, marked Ridley out as one of the most prominent victims of papal authority. The form of a trial was, indeed, granted him: a deputation of popish bishops was appointed to hold a formal disputation on the controverted points with him at Oxford, and he was condemned, as a recusant and obstinate heretic, to the stake. This sentence he underwent with the greatest fortitude, in company with his friend and fellow-sufferer Latimer (q. v.), Oct. 15, 1555, in Oxford. His life has been written by the reverend doctor Ridley, prebendary of Salisbury.

RIDOTTO; a masquerade, attended with music and dancing, and other amusements. A *ridotto* commonly takes place on fast-eve, in those places where the carnival is celebrated.—*Ridotto*, in Venice, is also the name of a public place, where, during the carnival, games of hazard, particularly faro, are played. Formerly, none but a Venetian noble could have a bank in the *ridotto*; and particular privileges were granted to him as banker. On each side stood a lady in a mask, to give him warning of any thing to his disadvansage. No persons but nobles were permitted to play, unless in a mask.

Ried, Treaty at, Oct. 8, 1813. (See *Bavaria.*)

Riedesel, Frederica Charlotte Louisa, baroness, the daughter of the Prussian minister of state Massow, was born at Brandenburg in 1746. At the age of sixteen, she was married to lieutenant-colonel Riedesel, who commanded the Brunswick troops employed in the English service in America in 1777. Madame Riedesel, who accompanied her husband, wrote an interesting account of her adventures, published by her son-in-law, the count de Reuss, under the title of Voyage to America, or Letters of Madame von Riedesel (translated into English, New York, 1827). She returned to Europe in 1783; and having lost her husband (who had been made a general) in 1800, she fixed her residence at Berlin, where she died in 1808.

Riego y Nuñez, Rafael del, a Spanish patriot, born of a noble family, in the province of Asturias, in 1785. After having been liberally educated, he entered the army, and served during the invasion of Spain by Bonaparte. He was taken prisoner; and, on his liberation, the constitutional general Abisbal gave him a staff appointment; and when that chief betrayed the cause of independence, Riego retired from the service in disgust, and for a time led a private life. In the beginning of 1820, at the head of a battalion, he proclaimed the Spanish constitution, and, traversing a large extent of country, shut himself up in a fortress, with the small number of troops who had the patriotism and courage to follow his example. Being threatened by a powerful army, and aware of the danger of delay, he sallied forth from the isle of Leon with a few hundred brave men, made his way through the forces that opposed his passage, visited several large towns, intimidated the authorities, fought obstinately, lost the greater part of his troops, and retired to the mountains with the determination to defend himself to the last extremity, rather than submit to the mercy of his enemies. But the spirit of freedom which he had excited was not extinguished; the provinces ranged themselves under the banners of independence, and Riego received the homage of national gratitude. His popularity excited the jealousy of those in power, and he was calumniated as a promoter of anarchy and disorder: his army was dissolved, and he was proscribed. But he preserved the confidence of the people, and was appointed a deputy to the cortes of 1822, of which assembly he became the president, and in this arduous station displayed prudence and firmness, with a conciliatory disposition that did him honor. When king Ferdinand refused to maintain the constitution which he had sworn to observe, Riego again appeared in arms to assert the liberty of his country; but it was destined to fall before foreign foes. He was taken prisoner after the surrender of Cadiz to the French, under the duke d'Angouleme, and, being conveyed to Madrid, was executed as a traitor, Nov. 7, 1823. His widow, who sought refuge in England, died at Chelsea, June 19, 1824.—See the *Memoirs of the Life of Riego*, by the canon Riego (London, 1824), and Mathew's *Narrative*, &c.

Rienzi, Nicholas Gabrini de; a native of Rome, who, in the fourteenth century, became celebrated by his attempts to restore the Roman republic. Although the son of one of the lowest order of tavern keepers, he received a literary education, and early distinguished himself by his talents, parts, and elevated sentiments. The glory of ancient Rome excited his enthusiasm, and he came to be regarded by the common people as an extraordinary person, destined to rescue them from the tyranny of the aristocracy, which, on the removal of the popes to Avignon, had become in the highest degree insolent and oppressive. He obtained the post of public scribe or notary, and in 1346 was joined in a deputation to pope Clement VI, at Avignon, to exhort him to bring back the papal court to its original seat. He acted on this occasion with so much energy and eloquence, that the pope created him an apostolic notary, which office, on his return, he executed with strict probity. He let no opportunity escape to excite the discontent of the people, by haranguing against the nobility and the defects of the public administration. Having prepared men's minds for a change, and engaged persons of all orders in his designs, in the month of April, 1347, during the absence of the governor of Rome, Stephen Colonna, he summoned a secret assembly upon mount Aventine, before which he made an energetic speech, and induced them all to subscribe an oath for the establishment of a plan of government, which he entitled the *good estate.* He had even the address to gain over the pope's vicar, and, in a second assembly in the capitol, produced fifteen articles as the basis of the good estate, which were unanimously approved; and the people conferred upon him the title of *tribune*, with the power of life and death, and all the other attributes of sovereignty. The governor, Colonna, upon his return, threatened him with punishment, but was himself constrained to quit the city; and Rienzi banished several of the noble families, after capitally punishing such as were convicted of oppression and injustice. In the first exercise of his authority, he conducted himself with a strict regard to justice and the public good; and even the pope was induced to sanction his power. The reputation of the new tribune extended throughout Italy, and his friendship was even solicited by the king of Hungary and the emperor Louis. Petrarch was highly interested in his proceedings; and there are extant several eloquent letters, in which that poet exhorts him to persevere in his glorious undertakings. But the intoxication of supreme power began to betray him into extravagances. He caused himself to be created a knight, with a mixture of religious and military ceremonies, and cited the two rival emperors, Charles and Louis, to appear before him to justify their pretensions. He also dismissed the pope's legate, and, reducing the nobles into complete humiliation, commenced a reign of terror. But at length, finding that he had lost the affection and confidence of the people, he withdrew, in 1348, from Rome, and remained in Naples until 1350, when he took advantage of the jubilee to return secretly to Rome; but being discovered, he withdrew to Prague. Thence he came into the hands of pope Clement at Avignon, who confined him three years, and appointed a commission to try him; his successor, Innocent VI, released Rienzi, and sent him to Rome to oppose another popular demagogue, named Boroncelli. The Romans received him with great demonstrations of joy, and he recovered his former authority; but after a turbulent administration of a few months, the nobles excited another sedition against him, in which he was massacred in October, 1354. His last brief career had been marked with great cruelty, which excited the populace to treat his remains with indignity. Rienzi, who possessed a union of fanaticism and artifice, was more energetic in speech and council than in action, and failed in courage and presence of mind in great emergencies.

Ries, Ferdinand, a distinguished pianoforte player and composer, was born in Bonn, on the Rhine. Beethoven was his teacher, and under his direction he appeared before the public in Vienna, in 1804 and 1805. After several journeys, he settled in London, as teacher and composer. In 1817, he also became director of the philharmonic concert. In 1825, he retired to Bonn. His productions are very numerous.

Riesengebirge (the Giants' mountains); part of the Sudetic chain, separating Silesia from Bohemia and Moravia, till it joins the Carpathians; but the term is properly applied to that part of this range which lies between the sources of the Neisse and the Bober. It contains the loftiest mountains of the north or central part of Germany. Some of the principal summits are Schneekoppe, 5270 feet high; Great Sturmhaube, 5030 feet high; and Lesser Sturmhaube, nearly as high. The valleys of the Riesengebirge present many picturesque scenes. (See *Sudetic Mountains.*)

Rifacimento (*Italian*, a remaking, or reëstablishment) is now often used in English. One of its most common applications is to the process of recasting literary works, so as to adapt them to a changed state of circumstances; as when a work written in one age or country is modified to suit the circumstances of another. The German word *Umarbeitung* is still more expressive.

Rifle; a fire-arm which has the inside of its barrel cut with from three to nine or ten spiral grooves, so as to make it resemble a female screw, varying from a common screw only in this, that its grooves or rifles are less deflected and approach more to a right line; it being now usual for the grooves with which the best rifled barrels are cut, to take about one whole turn in a length of thirty inches. The number of these grooves differ according to the size of the barrel and the fancy of the workman; and their depth and width are not regulated by any invariable rule. The period of their invention cannot be precisely determined. In 1381, the city of Augsburg promised, in the war of the free imperial cities against the nobility in Franconia, Suabia and Bavaria, to send thirty rifles (*busses, büchsen*) to the army. In 1498, fire-arms with rifled barrels were used at a public shooting-match in Leipsic.

Riga; a fortified city in the Russian government of the same name (see *Livonia*), lying on the Duna, or Dwina, seven miles above its entrance into the gulf of Riga; lat. 56° 57′ N.; lon. 24° 5′ E. The suburbs, which were almost entirely destroyed in 1812 (see *Russian-German War*), have since been rebuilt with broad, handsome streets, and numerous public walks and squares. The city has also received many additions and ornaments of late. The population, which, in 1821, amounted to 41,500, was, in 1828, 55,547, principally Lutherans. In 1829, 1403 vessels entered the port of Riga; the exports for the same year amounted to 47,888,000 roubles. The commerce is principally carried on by English merchants. There are numerous public institutions and buildings here, among the latter of which are the magnificent town-house, an imperial palace, the old castle, &c. The inhabitants are chiefly Germans, or of German origin. Next to Petersburg, Riga is the most important commercial place in the empire, and has large naval establishments. Corn, flax and hemp are the chief articles of export. Riga was founded in 1200, by bishop Albert, and, until the middle of the sixteenth century, belonged to the Teutonic knights. In 1710, it was taken possession of by Russia.

Rigadoon; a lively kind of dance, performed in figure by a man and woman, and the tune of which is always written in triple time. The rigadoon was borrowed originally from Provence. The word is formed from the French word *rigaudon*, signifying the same thing.

Rigging; a general name given to all the ropes employed to support the masts, and to extend or reduce the sails, or arrange them to the disposition of the wind.—*Standing rigging* is that which is used to sustain the masts, and remains in a fixed position; as the shrouds, stays, and back-stays.—*Running rigging* is that which is fitted to arrange the sails by passing through various blocks, in different places about the masts, yards, shrouds, &c., as the braces, sheets, halliards, clew-lines, &c., &c.

Righi, or Rigi (*Mons regius*, or *Regina montium*); an isolated mountain in the canton of Schweitz, between the lakes of Zug, Lucerne and Lowertz, 6000 feet high. The view from the summit is remarkably fine, and attracts great numbers of travellers; it embraces the whole of the north and east of Switzerland, far into Swabia, the Jura, the Alps to the Jungfrau, and fourteen lakes. Füssli (see *Fuseli*) and Meyer published the finest views in the Sketches on the Righi (Zurich, 1807).

Right and Left Bank of a River. That bank which is on the right of a person looking down the river is called the *right* bank; the other the *left*.

Right, Petition of. (See *Petition of Right*.)

Rights, Bill of. (See *Bill of Rights*.)

Rights, Declaration of. (See *Bill of Rights*.)

Rimini (Ariminum); a city in the States of the Church, on the Marecchia, near its entrance into the gulf of Venice; lat. 44° 4′ N.; lon. 12° 34′ E. There is a harbor at the mouth of the Marecchia, which, however, is choked up by sand and stones, brought down by the river. The sea has receded more than two miles from the ancient light-house, which is now surrounded by gardens. The river is crossed by a handsome marble bridge, of five arches, built by Tiberius, at the point where the Flaminian and Æmilian ways met, and is the finest monument of antiquity of the kind Before one of the gates is an ancient triumphal arch, erected in honor of Augustus. The cathedral erected on the ruins of the temple of Castor and Pollux is, like several of the other churches, built of the marble taken from the ruins of the old port. The church of S. Francesco, built in the middle of the fifteenth century, is celebrated for its noble and splendid style of architecture. It was erected by Pandolfo Malatesta, whose family governed Rimini for a long period, in the middle ages, and adorned the city with many public buildings. In the *Piazza del Commune* is a handsome fountain, and a bronze statue of pope Paul V; in the market-place is shown a pedestal, from which it is pretended that Cæsar harangued his troops before passing the Rubicon. Rimini contains some other fine remains of antiquity. March 25, 1831, it was occupied by Austrian troops, after having been some time defended by Italian patriots.

Ring. (For the pope's ring, see *Fisherman's Ring*; for the bishop's, see *Investiture*, also *Kiss*; for Saturn's ring, see *Planet*, and *Saturn*. See also *Fairy Circle*.)

Rio bravo del Norte. (See *Norte*.)

Rio de Janeiro, or S. Sebastiaõ (often called simply *Rio*); capital city of Brazil, on the western shore of the bay of the same name, which makes up from the Atlantic ocean; lat. 22° 54′ S.; lon. 43° 15′ W.; population in 1820, estimated at 135,000, and by Walsh, in 1830, at 150,000. Before the arrival of the Portuguese court, in 1808 (see *John VI*), the population was about 50,000, and occupied only that part of the city now called the *old city*. The streets of the new city are broad and straight, and the houses in both sections are mostly built in the same style, of granite, and three stories high. The public places are not remarkable for beauty, but most of them have fountains supplied with water by a very handsome aqueduct.

The imperial palace, formerly the residence of the viceroys, is built in an ordinary style, and was enlarged, after the arrival of the court, by connecting it with the Carmelite monastery. The mint, the custom-house, the arsenal, and the exchange, are handsome buildings. The churches and convents (five) present nothing deserving of notice. The public gardens are prettily laid out, and enjoy a fine prospect. Music is a favorite amusement of the people, and is cultivated with success by all classes. The manufacturing industry is inconsiderable; but Rio is the great mart of Brazilian commerce; the harbor is one of the finest and safest in the world. All the ports between Bahia on the north and Montevideo on the south send their merchandise to Rio for exportation or consumption. The internal commerce with the inland provinces is also extensive, particularly in mineral riches. Sugar, coffee, cotton, tobacco, hides, tallow, furs, molasses, indigo, fustic, cocoanuts, diamonds, topaz, and other precious stones, are among the exports. (See *Brazil.*) The climate is warm and humid; and, on account of the marshes which surround the city, and the filth of the streets, the vultures being the only scavengers, the city is often an unhealthy residence for strangers; but, by adopting the Brazilian mode of living, avoiding exposure in the sun, night dews, abstaining from spirituous liquors, and using vegetable diet, the danger is averted. The population consists of a singular mixture of colors and nations; about two thirds are negroes, mulattoes, &c.; and among the whites are seen French, Germans, English, Italians, Dutch, and North Americans. The environs are charming, and vegetation never ceases. The place derives its name signifying *river of January*, from the mistake of the first discoverer of the bay, who conceived it to be the mouth of a large river. It was founded by the Portuguese in 1565, and in 1763 was made the capital of Brazil. It was the residence of the Portuguese court from 1808 to 1821, and, in 1822, became the capital of the independent empire of Brazil. (See *Pedro I.*) In 1831 (April 7), it was the theatre of a revolution, in which 6000 armed citizens were joined by the troops of the line in their opposition to the government, and in consequence of which dom Pedro abdicated the throne in favor of his son, Pedro II.—See Walsh's *Notices of Brazil* (London, 1830).

Rio Grande. (See *Plata, La.*)

Riots are disturbances of the public peace, attended with circumstances of tumult and commotion, as where an assembly destroys, or in any manner damages, seizes, or invades the property either of individuals or the public, or does any injury to the persons of individuals, or invades, seeks, or pursues them, with intent to confine them, or put them in fear, or violently constrains any one to act contrary to his interest, duty, or inclination. Where three or more persons assemble on their own authority to disturb the public peace, whether in a house or highway, with intent mutually to assist each other against any who shall oppose them in the execution of some enterprise of a private nature, and they afterwards actually execute the same, in a violent and turbulent manner, to the terror of the people, whether the act be lawful or not, they incur the guilt of a riot. All who are actually engaged in a riot are considered, in law, as equally guilty of the offence; but the circumstances of each are to be considered in assigning his punishment. A riot will not be justified by an apparently useful and laudable object, as to put down a house of ill fame or a common gaming house, or to remove other great and confessed nuisances. The law of Massachusetts of 1786 (ch. 38) enacts, that where any persons, to the number of twelve or more, armed with clubs or other weapons, or where any number of persons, consisting of thirty or more, shall be unlawfully riotously or tumultuously assembled, any justice of the peace, sheriff or deputy-sheriff of the county, or constable of the town, shall make open proclamation among the rioters, or as near to them as he can come, and charge all persons so assembled immediately to disperse themselves, and peaceably to depart to their homes, under penalty of the pains inflicted by said act. If any persons so unlawfully assembled do not disperse themselves within one hour after proclamation made, or attempted to be made, it is lawful for any officer to command sufficient aid to seize such offenders, and to require an armed force if the rioters appear armed. Should any of the latter be killed or wounded by reason of their resistance, the magistrate or officer will be held guiltless; but if the magistrate or officer or any of his assistants, should be killed in their endeavors to restore the peace and to arrest the offenders, it would be murder in all those who were guilty of the riot. Similar provisions exist in other states of the Union, as well as in England.

Ripperda, John William, baron of,

born in 1680, of a noble family in Groningen, was educated under the Jesuits of Cologne, but, on marrying a Protestant lady, conformed to her religion. He rose to the rank of colonel in the Dutch service, and in 1715 was sent on a mission to Philip V of Spain, when he returned to the Catholic religion, and settled at Madrid; and the king finally made him duke of Ripperda, and his prime minister; but, from his inefficiency, incurring the displeasure of the king, he was dismissed, and confined in the castle of Segovia, whence he escaped and went to England, where he remained until 1730, when he crossed over to the Hague, and resumed the Protestant religion. But his restless and ambitious disposition would not allow him to remain tranquil, and in 1731 he went to Morocco, where he was favorably received by Muley Abdalla, and declaring himself a convert to the Mohammedan religion, and taking the name of Osman, he obtained the chief command of the Moorish army at the siege of Ceuta. On the defeat of the Moors, he fell under the displeasure of the emperor, and for a time he lived in retirement. He then formed a new project for the consolidation of different religions, particularly the Jewish and Mohammedan; and it is said that he even made some converts. He finally retired to Tetuan; but his projecting spirit animated him to the last, and he advanced considerable sums to Theodore, baron Neuhof, to assist his attempts on the crown of Corsica. His death took place in 1737. See Moore's *Life of the Duke of Ripperda* (1806).

Rip-raps. (See *Dover, Straits of.*)

Ripuaria, Lex. The *Loi des Ripuaires* was a collection of laws like the Salic law for the Franks. The latter is supposed to have been the code of those Franks who lived between the Meuse and Loire, and the Ripuarian law that of those who lived between the Meuse and the Rhine. It was drawn up under king Theodoric, at Châlons-sur-Marne. Its spirit is barbarous, like that of the Salic law.—*Ripuarii* was a collective name given by the Romans to all the various tribes of Franks who inhabited the country from the river Lahne to the Lippe, along the Rhine.

Ritornello (*Italian*), in music; a passage which is played whilst the principal voice pauses; it often signifies the introduction to an air or any musical piece. This *ritornello* is often repeated after the singing voice has concluded; hence the name. In Italian operas, the *ritornelli* are often unduly prolonged.—*Ritornelli* are also popular songs of three lines each, sung in the Italian mountains, which are also used by the *improvvisatori*. The metre and number of the syllables are not subject to rule. The first line, however, is generally the shortest.

Rittenhouse, David, a distinguished American astronomer, was born near Germantown, Pennsylvania, April 8, 1732. During his early years, he was employed on his father's farm; yet, even there, his peculiar genius manifested itself. His younger brother used to say, that while David was employed in the fields, he repeatedly observed the fences, and even the plough with which he had been working, marked over with mathematical figures. The construction of a wooden clock exhibited the first evidence of his mechanical talents. He was then but seventeen years of age, and had never received any instruction, either in mathematics or mechanics. The delicacy of his constitution, and the irresistible bent of his genius, soon after induced his parents to allow of his giving up husbandry, and to procure for him the tools of a clock and mathematical instrument maker. From the age of eighteen to twenty-five, he applied himself with the greatest assiduity, both to his trade and to his studies. Engaged throughout the day in the former, it was only the time commonly assigned to rest, or, to use his own expression, his *idle hours*, that he could devote to the latter. Yet, with so little time at his command, with but two or three books, and without the least instruction, he acquired so considerable a knowledge of the mathematical sciences, as to be able to read the *Principia* of Newton. It is even asserted, that he discovered the method of fluxions, and that he did not know, until some years afterwards, that Newton and Leibnitz had contested the honor of an invention of which he deemed himself the author. It was during this double employment of his time in labor and in study, that Mr. Rittenhouse planned and executed an instrument, in which his mathematical knowledge, and his mechanical skill, were equally required. This instrument was the *orrery*. Machines, intended to give to the student of astronomy a general conception of the relative motions of the heavenly bodies, had been constructed before; but the object of Mr. Rittenhouse was, to construct an instrument, by means of which he could exhibit, with accuracy, the positions of the planets and their satellites at any given period of the world, past, present, or future. It was, in fact, to make a kind of perpetual astronomical almanac, in which the results, instead of being given in tables, were to be actually exhibited to the eye. In this attempt he succeeded. Two of these orreries were made by his own hands. One belongs to the university of Pennsylvania; the other to the college of Princeton. In 1769, Mr. Rittenhouse was named one of the committee, appointed by the American philosophical society, to observe the transit of Venus over the sun's disk, which happened June 3 of that year. A temporary observatory was directed to be built for the purpose, near his residence. In silence, and trembling anxiety, Mr. Rittenhouse and his friends waited for the predicted moment of observation; it came, and brought with it all that had been wished for and expected by those who saw it. In our philosopher, it excited, in the instant of one of the contacts of the planet with the sun, an emotion of delight so exquisite and powerful as to induce fainting. The reputation which Mr. Rittenhouse had now so justly acquired, as an astronomer, attracted the attention of the government, and he was employed in several geodesic operations of great public importance. In 1779, he was appointed by the legislature of Pennsylvania, one of the commissioners for adjusting a territorial dispute between that state and Virginia; and the success of this commission is ascribed, in a great degree, to his skill and prudence. In 1786, he was employed in fixing the northern line, which divides Pennsylvania from New York. In 1769, he was employed in settling the limits between New York and New Jersey; and, in 1787, he was called upon to assist in fixing a boundary line between the states of Massachusetts and New York. Mr. Rittenhouse was elected a member of the American academy of arts and sciences, at Boston, in 1782, and of the royal society of London, in 1795. In 1791, he was chosen the successor of doctor Franklin, in the presidency of the American philosophical society. All his philosophical communications were made through the medium of the Transactions of this society, and the list of his papers, printed in the three first volumes, shows his zeal for science and the fertility of his genius. In 1777, doctor Rittenhouse was appointed treasurer of Pennsylvania, in which office he continued until 1789. In 1792, he was appointed, by the general government, director of the mint of the U. States. The mechanical skill of doctor Rittenhouse rendered him a highly useful officer. In 1795, he was obliged to resign in consequence of the state of his health. His constitution, naturally feeble, had been rendered still more so by sedentary labor and midnight studies, and on the twenty-sixth of June, 1796, he died. His last illness was short and painful, but his patience and benevolence did not forsake him. Upon being told that some of his friends had called at his door to inquire how he was, he asked why they were not invited into his chamber to see him. "Because," said his wife, "you are too weak to speak to them." "Yes," said he, "that is true, but still I could have pressed their hands." In private life, doctor Rittenhouse exhibited all those mild and amiable virtues by which it is adorned. As a husband, a father, and a friend, he was a model of excellence. Immediately after his decease, the American philosophical society decreed him the honor of a public eulogium; and this duty was executed in the ablest manner by doctor Rush. In 1813, a large volume of memoirs of his life was published by his relative, William Barton, esquire, of Lancaster, the materials for which were derived from the work just mentioned.

Ritter, John William, a distinguished natural philosopher, was born in 1776, at Samitz, near Hainau, in Silesia, and died, in 1810, in Munich. He distinguished himself by the study of galvanism; but excessive labor, exhausting experiments, a bad wife, and consequent intemperance, brought him early to the grave. His works, which are of uncommon importance, as far as galvanism is concerned, are, Contributions to the better understanding of Galvanism (Jena, 1801, 2 vols.); Proof that a continual Galvanism accompanies the Process of Life (Weimar, 1798); Physico-Chemical Treatises (Leipsic, 1806, 3 vols.); Fragments of the Papers of a young Philosopher (Heidelberg, 1810, 2 vols.); all in German. He contributed many articles to Gilbert's Annals of Physics, and Voigt's Magazine of Natural Science.

Ritzebüttel; a bailiwick under the jurisdiction of Hamburg (q. v.), between the mouths of the Elbe and Weser, with 3900 inhabitants. Its chief place is Ritzebüttel, a borough, one mile south from Cuxhaven (q. v.); lat. N. 53° 52′ 8″; lon. E. 8° 41′ 10″. It has 1500 inhabitants. Travellers wait here to embark at Cuxhaven.

Rivers are to be traced to springs, or to the gradual meltings of the ice and snow which perpetually cover the summits of all the most elevated ranges of mountains upon the globe. The union of various springs, or of these meltings, forms rivulets: these last follow the declivity of the ground, and commonly fall, at different stages, into one great channel, called a *river*, which, at last, discharges its waters into the sea, or some great inland lake. The declivities along which descend the various streams that flow into one particular river are called its *basin*—a term, therefore, which includes the whole extent of country from which the waters of the river are drawn. As mountainous regions abound in springs, we find that most rivers, more especially those of the first class, commence from a chain of mountains; each side of a chain also has its springs, and the rivers which originate on one side flow in the opposite direction to those which rise on the other. As it is the property of water to follow the most rapid descent that comes in its way, the courses of streams point out the various declivities of the earth's surface, and the line from which large rivers flow in contrary directions (German *Wasserscheide*), generally marks the highest parts of the earth. In European Russia, where the rivers are very extensive, there is, however, a singular exception to this rule, the line which separates the sources of those rivers being very little above the level of the Baltic, or of the Black sea. It has been observed, by some writers, that the extent of a river is in proportion to the height of the range of mountains from which it descends. This is, in a certain degree, true, because the greater the bulk of the mountains, the more numerous the springs and torrents which they furnish; but the relation between the extent of a river and the surface of its basin is much closer and more invariable. Even this is not sufficiently comprehensive; for it is evident that the size of a river depends upon three circumstances—the surface of its basin; the abundance, or otherwise, of that surface in springs; and the degree of humidity possessed by the climate of the region from which it draws its supplies. As many springs, however, are formed by the rains, the second of these circumstances will, in some measure, vary with the last. By an attention to these remarks, the causes of the great size of the South American rivers will be apparent. The peculiar position of the Andes, with respect to the plain of that continent; the fact, that by very far the largest proportion of its running waters are drained off in one general direction (towards the Atlantic); the multiplicity of streams that intersect the country; and the humidity of the climate—all contribute to that result. The Andes being placed so near the coast of the Pacific, the rivers which flow from them into that ocean are small; while those which flow on the other side, having such an immense space to traverse, are swelled into a most majestic volume before they reach the Atlantic. The physical circumstances of the old continent are unfavorable to the accumulation of such vast bodies of water as the rivers of South America. Europe is not of sufficient extent; Africa is oppressed by a scorching climate, and abounds in sandy deserts; in Asia, the atmosphere generally is not so moist, while the more central position, for the most part, of the great mountainous range of that continent, and the existence of capacious inland lakes, which are the final receptacles of the streams that fall into them, are the causes why the waters are more equally drained off in different directions than in the New World. When water, by following a descent, has once received an impulse, the pressure of the particles behind upon those before will be sufficient to keep the stream in motion, even when there is no longer a declivity in the ground. The only effect is, that in passing along a level, the course of the stream becomes gradually slower—an effect which may be perceived, more or less, in all running waters that originate in mountainous or hilly tracts, and afterwards traverse the plains. The declivity of many great rivers is much less than might at first be supposed. The Maranon, or Amazons, has a descent of only ten and a half feet in 200 leagues of its course, that is, one twenty-seventh part of an inch for every thousand feet of that distance. The Loire, in France, between Pouilly and Briare, falls one foot in 7500 but between Briare and Orleans, only one foot in 13,596. Even the rapid Rhine has not a descent of more than four feet in a mile, between Schaffhausen and Strasburg, and of two feet between the latter place and Schenckenschantz. When rivers flow through a mountainous and rugged country, they frequently fall over precipices, and form *cataracts* (q. v.), in some cases, several hundred feet in depth. The most celebrated falls in the world are those of the Niagara, in North America. In the tropical regions, most of the rivers are subject to periodical overflowings of their banks, in consequence of the rains which annually fall in such abundance, in those countries, during the wet season. The overflow of the Nile was considered by the ancients, who were ignorant of its cause, as one of the greatest mysteries of nature; because, in Egypt, where the overflow takes place, no rain ever falls. The apparent mystery is easily explained, by the circumstance of the rains descending upon the mountains in the interior of Africa, where the Nile rises. The consequent accumulation of the waters among the high grounds, gradually swells the river along its whole extent, and, in about two months from the commencement of the rains, occasions those yearly inundations, without which Egypt would be no better than a desert. The disappearance of some rivers, for a certain distance, under ground, is accounted for with equal facility. When a river is impeded in its course by a bank of solid rock, and finds beneath it a bed of a softer soil, the waters wear away the latter, and thus make for themselves a subterraneous passage. In this way are explained the sinking of the Rhone, between Seyssel and L'Ecluse, and the formation, in Virginia, of the magnificent rock bridge which overhangs the course of the Cedar creek. In Spain, the phenomenon exhibited by the Guadiana, which has its waters dispersed in sandy and marshy grounds, whence they afterwards emerge in greater abundance, is to be referred to the absorbing power of the soil. Rivers, in their junction with the sea, present several appearances worthy of notice. The opposition which takes place between the tide and their own currents, occasions, in many instances, the collection at their mouths of banks of sand or mud, called *bars*, on account of the obstruction which they offer to navigation. Some streams rush with such force into the sea, that it is possible, for some distance, to distinguish their waters from those of the sea. The shock arising from the collision of the current of the majestic Amazons with the tide of the Atlantic is of the most tremendous description. (See *Mascaret.*) Many of the largest rivers mingle with the sea by means of a single outlet, while others (for instance, the Nile, the Ganges, the Volga, the Rhine, and the Orinoco), before their termination, divide into several branches.* This circumstance will depend upon the nature of the soil of the country through which a river runs; but it also frequently results from the velocity of the stream being so much diminished in its latter stage, that even a slight obstacle in the ground has power to change its course, and a number of channels are thus produced. Another cause may be assigned for the division into branches of those rivers which, in tropical countries, periodically inundate the plains; the superfluous waters which, at those periods, spread over the country, find various outlets, which are afterwards rendered permanent by the deepening of the channels by each successive flood. In some of the sandy plains of the torrid zone, the rivers divide into branches, and, from the nature of the soil and the heat of the climate, they are absorbed and evaporated, and thus never reach the sea. (See the articles *Amazons*, *Plata*, *Mississippi*, *Missouri*, *Lawrence, St.*, *Danube*, *Rhine*, *Nile*, *Niger*, *Ganges*, &c.)

Rivers, Navigable, form one of the most important items of the productive capacity of a country; and a view of the navigable rivers of all the different countries, taken from good authorities, would be a most interesting document for the political economist, but would much exceed the limits of the present work; so that we are obliged to confine ourselves to a brief sketch of the navigable rivers of North America. The canals have been treated of under the heads of *Canal*, and *Inland Navigation*. (For the rivers of other countries, see the respective articles.) The most natural way of treating the subject would be according to the basins of the largest rivers. Mr. Darby, in his View of the United States (Philadelphia, 1828), gives an interesting account of these basins. North America empties its waters into the sea, through many rivers, the largest of which, on the eastern side, are the Mississippi and St. Lawrence; on the western, the Columbia or Oregon; and on the northern, Mackenzie's river. (For further information respecting the origin of these rivers, their connexion with others, and with lakes, see our article *North America;* for the Mississippi and its navigation, see *Mississippi.*) Its principal tributary stream is the Missouri. (q. v.) Owing to the secondary character of the country, the numerous branches of these rivers are generally navigable, and afford a passage from almost every part of the Western States and the vast regions at the base of the Rocky mountains (q. v.) to the gulf of Mexico and the ocean, at least during the season of high water, from the spring to the middle of summer. The current of the principal rivers is so rapid,

* The triangular space formed by a river pouring itself into the sea by various mouths, is called a *Delta*, from its resemblance to the shape of the fourth letter (Δ) of the Greek alphabet.

that although they are deep enough to admit vessels of considerable size, the navigation is chiefly carried on by means of steam-boats. The Arkansas river is the next branch to the Missouri in size. (See end of the article *Arkansas.*) The Canadian, a branch of the Arkansas, 1000 miles in length, is navigable 100 miles. The Red river is navigable 500 miles from its junction with the Mississippi. (See *Red River.*) The tributaries of the Missouri are usually blocked up at their mouths, after the floods in July, until the next spring, with mud brought down by the Missouri. The Platte (q. v.) is fordable in almost every part, and navigable only for canoes made of skins. The Yellowstone (q. v.) is navigable through the greater part of its course. Other important branches of the Missouri are the Kansas (q. v.) and Osage (q. v.), navigable for boats 600 miles. The chief branches of the Mississippi above the Missouri are the Illinois (q. v.), River de Moines, Rock river, St. Peter's, and Wisconsin, each of which may be considered as affording 400 to 500 miles of navigation. The White river, 1300 miles long, joins the Mississippi 51 miles above the Arkansas, and is said to be navigable for boats 1200 miles. On the eastern side, the largest branch of the Mississippi is the Ohio. (q.v.) Its branches are the Alleghany (q. v.), Monongahela(q. v.), Muskingum, Scioto(q. v.), Big Beaver, Hockhocking (q. v.), Great Miami (q. v.), Wabash (q. v.), Great Kenhawa (q. v.), Big Sandy, Kentucky (q. v.), Green river (q. v.), Cumberland (q. v.), and Tennesee. (q. v.) They are all navigable for several hundred miles. Among the rivers emptying into the gulf of Mexico, are also the Appalachicola (q. v.), in Florida; Mobile (q. v.), formed by the junction of the Alabama (q. v.) and Tombigbee. (q. v.) The Cahawba falls into the Mobile. All are navigable for a considerable extent. Between Mobile bay and New Orleans, there is an interesting inland navigation through lake Ponchartrain (q. v.), the Rigolets, lake Borgne (q. v.), Pass au Chretien, and Pass au Heron. This is formed by a chain of islands, and is not navigable for vessels drawing more than five feet. Pearl river joins the Rigolets. Its navigation is much impeded by shallows and timber. Sabine river, forming the eastern boundary of Texas, is navigable about 280 miles, but has only three feet water on the bar at its mouth. The Atchafalaya, Teche and Courte, unite to form a river of great importance west of the Mississippi. It flows into the bay of Atchafalaya. The Atchafalaya is navigable for rafts. La Fourche, an outlet of the Mississippi, admits vessels drawing four to five feet to within thirty miles of its efflux. (For the Rio del Norte, see *Norte, Rio del.*) The Rio Huasaculco and Alvarado, both south-east of Vera Cruz, are calculated to facilitate the communication with Guatimala. The St. Jago might form a communication to Port St. Blas or the Pacific. The river Atrato, which falls into the gulf of Darien, south-east of Panama, is united by a little canal, for boats in the rainy season, with Rio San Juan, a brook which empties into the Pacific. The Colorado, about 1000 miles long, empties into the gulf of California. (For lake Nicaragua, 120 miles long, 41 wide, see *Nicaragua.*) The Columbia or Oregon has three great tributaries, the Multnomah (q. v.), Lewis's river (q. v.), and Clarke's river. Vessels of 300 tons may ascend to the mouth of the Multnomah, 125 miles, and sloops to the head of tide water, 60 miles farther. (For more information respecting this river, see the article on it: for Mackenzie's river, see the article.) Coppermine river is scarcely navigable by canoes near its opening into the Polar sea. Churchill river, which empties into Hudson's bay, but is connected by means of lakes with the river Athapescow, would form an invaluable communication, were the climate less rigorous. The Saskashawin is formed by two considerable rivers that come from the foot of the western mountains, and falls into lake Winipeg. (q. v.) This lake receives the great river Assiniboins (q. v.), from the south side after the junction of that stream with Red river, and discharges itself into Hudson's bay by the Nelson and Severn rivers. (For the St. Lawrence, see *Lawrence, St.*) This river affords, even in winter, means of easy communication by sledges. The common route of fur traders, in their bark canoes, is from the St. Lawrence, through the Ottawa or Grand river, and thence by a short portage to lake Nipissing, and down the French river into lake Huron. From lake Huron they proceed, through the straits of St. Mary and lake Superior, to the Grand Portage, nine miles in length, which brings them to the great northern chain of lakes, beginning with the lake of the Woods, at the distance of 1100 miles from the place of their departure. Ottawa river flows into the St. Lawrence above Montreal. Its course is interrupted by rapids and falls; but fur traders overcome these difficulties with their canoes. St. John's flows through New Brunswick, and runs into the bay of Fundy. For boats it is navigable 200 miles; for sloops of fifty tons, 80 miles. Its tributaries are the St. Francis (q. v.), Aroostook, Madawaska. As a navigable channel, it is superior to any north-east of the Hudson. The numerous rivers on the eastern declivity of the Apalachian chain afford the advantages of a good inland navigation to most parts of the Atlantic states. In all those streams which flow through the alluvial region from the Mississippi to the Roanoke, the tide waters of the ocean terminate at some distance from the foot of the mountains, varying from 30 to 120 miles. From the Roanoke to the Hudson, they extend through the alluvial region to the base of the primitive hills; but in no rivers south of the Hudson do they pass beyond the alluvial region. As far as the tide flows, the streams are generally navigable for sloops. In passing from the hilly and primitive to the flat and alluvial region, the streams are almost uniformly precipitated over ledges of rocks, by rapids, which obstruct their navigation. Indeed, the line of alluvion marks the line of navigation from the sea, which passes through Milledgeville on the Altamaha, Augusta on the Savannah, Columbia and Camden on the Santee, Richmond on the James, Fredericksburg on the Rappahannock, Georgetown on the Potomac, and Trenton on the Delaware. (See the articles on these rivers, and our article *North America*, division *Geology of*.) Above the rapids, navigation is performed entirely by boats propelled by oars or poles, or drawn up by ropes, or by means of the bushes growing on their banks. (For the Savannah river, see the article.) The rivers of South Carolina are navigable nearly through the alluvial region, and there are some good harbors at their mouths. The coast of North Carolina is bordered with a range of low, sandy islands, enclosing a chain of sounds. Their entrances are generally obstructed by bars, which vessels of considerable size cannot pass. But the streams are navigable for sloops some distance into the interior. The Chesapeake bay is, of itself, an inland sea of considerable size, and, with the numerous streams and inlets on its borders, forms an important channel to the ocean for a large extent of country, including the whole of Maryland and the eastern declivity of Virginia, and extending through the middle section of Pennsylvania, nearly to the small lakes of New York. (See *Chesapeake*, *James River*, *Potomac*, *Susquehannah*. For the Delaware bay and river, see *Delaware*.) New Jersey has the Raritan (q. v.); and the Passaic (q. v.) and Hackinsack afford a short inland navigation. The Hudson is the only river in the U. States where the tide passes through the alluvial, primitive and transition formations. It is navigable for ships to the city of Hudson, and sloops of considerable burden pass through all the formations, to the falls of the secondary country, above Troy, which is 165 miles from the ocean. (See *Hudson*.) In the rivers of the U. States east of the Hudson, the tide extends only a small distance, and the navigation is obstructed by the falls and rapids, which are common in primitive countries. The Connecticut is navigable for vessels of considerable size fifty miles, to Hartford. (See *Connecticut*.) The Merrimac (q. v.) of New Hampshire is much obstructed by rapids. The rivers of Maine are generally obstructed. The Penobscot (q. v.), the St. John's, already mentioned, and the western branch of the Kennebec (q. v.), afford a boat navigation nearly to their sources. The heads of these rivers approach within no great distance of the waters of the St. Lawrence; and the portage from the head of the Kennebec to that of Chaudiere river is only five miles. The waters of the St. Lawrence or the great lakes have two natural communications with the branches of the Mississippi at particular seasons. The Fox river, which flows into the branch of lake Michigan called Green Bay, rises near the Wisconsin branch of the Mississippi, and afterwards flows within a mile and a half of its channel, separated from it only by a short portage over a prairie.

Rivoli; a village in the Lombardo-Venetian kingdom, five leagues north-west of Verona, between lake Garda and the right bank of the Adige, near the imperial road leading from Trent to Verona, with 535 inhabitants, famous for a bloody battle between Bonaparte and the Austrians, on Jan. 14 and 15, 1797, which decided the fate of Italy. After the Austrian general Alvinzi had been forced back to Verona, Napoleon turned and followed general Provera, beat him on the 15th at La Favorite, and made 6000 prisoners. On these two days, the French took above 20,000 prisoners and 46 cannons. Thus the fourth Austrian army in Italy was almost entirely destroyed. The fall of Mantua was a consequence. Masséna (q. v.) distinguished himself greatly on this occasion, and Napoleon subsequently made him duke of Rivoli. Napoleon gives a description of the battle in his *Mémoires* (t. iv, p. 331 et seq.)

RIVOLI, DUKE OF. (See *Masséna.*)

RIX DOLLAR; a silver coin in different countries on the continent, and of different values. (See *Coins.*)

RIZZIO, or RICCI, David; the son of a professor of music and dancing at Turin, where the subject of this article was born, in the earlier part of the sixteenth century. His musical abilities procured him notice at the court of Savoy, while his talents as a linguist caused him to be selected by the ambassador from the grand-duke to Mary queen of Scots, as a part of his suite. In 1564, he first made his appearance at Holy Rood house, where he soon became so great a favorite with the queen, that he was appointed her secretary for foreign languages. (See *Mary Stuart.*) The distinction with which he was treated by his mistress, soon excited the envy of the nobles, and the jealousy of Darnley; the hatred of the former being increased as much by the religion as by the arrogant deportment of the new favorite, while the suspicions of the latter were excited by his address and accomplishments. A conspiracy, with the king at its head, was formed for his destruction, and before he had enjoyed two years of court favor, the lord Ruthven, and others of his party, were introduced by Darnley into the queen's apartment, where they despatched the object of their revenge by fifty-six stabs, in the presence of his mistress, in 1566. Popular tradition assigns to Rizzio the amelioration of the Scottish style of music. His skill in the performance of the national melodies on his favorite instrument, the lute, tended not a little to their general improvement and popularity with the higher classes; but it is evident that the style of Scottish music was determined long before the time of Mary; and many of the airs which have been ascribed to Rizzio are easily traced to more distant periods.

ROADS. Roads intended for the passage of wheel carriages are made more level, and of harder materials, than the rest of the ground. In roads the travel on which does not authorize great expense, natural materials alone are employed, of which the best are hard gravel and very small stones. The surface of roads should be nearly flat, with gutters at the sides, to facilitate the running off of water. If the surface is made too convex, it throws the weight of the load unequally upon one wheel, and also that of the horses on one side, whenever the carriage takes the side of the road. Hence drivers prefer to take the middle or top of the road, and, by pursuing the same track, occasion deep ruts. The prevention of ruts is best effected by flat and solid roads, and by the use of broad wheels. It would also be further effected if a greater variety could be introduced in the width of carriages. Embankments at the sides, to keep the earth from sliding down, may be made by piling sods upon each other like bricks, with the grassy surface at right angles with the surface of the bank. But stone walls are preferable for this purpose, when the material can be readily obtained. —*Pavements.* Pavements are stone coverings of the ground, chiefly employed in populous cities and the most frequented roads. Among us, they are made of pebbles of a roundish form, gathered from the sea-beach. They should consist of the hardest kinds of stone, such as granite, sienite, &c. If flat stones are used, they require to be artificially roughened, to give secure foothold to horses. In Milan, and some other places, tracks for wheels are made of smooth stones, while the rest of the way is paved with small or rough stones. (See *Pavements.*) The advantage of a good pavement consists not only in its durability, but in the facility with which transportation on it is effected. Horses draw more easily on a pavement than on a common road, because no part of their power is lost in changing the form of the surface. The disadvantages of pavements consist in their noise, and in the wear which they occasion of the shoes of horses and tires of wheels. They should never be made of pebbles so large as to produce much jolting by the breadth of the interstices.*—*McAdam Roads.* The system of road-making which takes its name from Mr. McAdam combines the advantages of the pavement and gravel road. The McAdam roads are made entirely of hard stones, such as granite, flint, &c., broken up with hammers into small pieces, not exceeding an inch in diameter. These fragments are spread upon the ground to the depth of from six to ten inches. At first the roads thus made are heavy and laborious to pass, but in time the stones become consolidated, and form a mass of great hardness, smoothness and

* Mr. Telford has constructed, in England, a kind of paved road, in which the foundation consists of a pavement of rough stones and fragments, having their points upward. These are covered with very small stone fragments and gravel, for the depth of four inches, the whole of which, when rammed down and consolidated forms a hard, smooth and durable road.

permanency. The stones become partly pulverized by the action of carriage wheels, and partly imbedded in the earth beneath them. The consolidation seems to be owing to the angular shape of the fragments, which prevents them from rolling in their beds, after the interstices between them are filled. Mr. McAdam advises that no other material should be added to the broken stones, apparently with a view to prevent the use of clay and chalk, which abound in England. It appears, however, that a little clean gravel spread upon the stones, causes them to consolidate more quickly, and has the good effect of excluding the light street-dirt, which otherwise never fails to become incorporated, in large quantities, among the stones.

Roanoke, a river of North Carolina, is formed by the union of the Staunton and Dan, the former of which rises in Virginia, and the latter in North Carolina. It flows into Albemarle sound, lat. 35° 58′ N., and is navigable for vessels of considerable burden 40 or 50 miles, for large boats, 70 miles, and for boats of five tons, 270 miles. Improvements have been made, by constructing canals around the falls, and opening a water communication between Norfolk and the interior of North Carolina. The soil on the borders of the Roanoke is very productive.

Roasting Jack. (See *Jack.*)

Robbery; a felonious and forcible taking away another man's goods or money from his person, presence or estate, by such acts as put him in fear, &c. The previous putting in fear is the criterion which distinguishes robbery from other larcenies; yet this does not imply any great degree of affright in the person robbed: it is sufficient that so much force or threatening, by word or gesture, is used, as might create an apprehension of danger, so as to lead a man to part with his property against his consent. If a man be knocked down without previous warning, and stripped of his property while senseless, though, strictly speaking, he cannot be said to be put in fear, yet this is undoubtedly a robbery; or if a person with a sword drawn beg alms, and money is given him through apprehension of violence, this is a robbery. If a thief, having once taken a purse, returns it, still it is a robbery. Highway robbery, or the forcible taking of property from travellers, in many countries, is a capital offence, and, in all civilized countries, is severely punished.

Robert I. (See *Bruce, Robert.*)

Robertson, William, the celebrated historian, was born at Borthwick, Scotland, where his father was minister, in 1721. In 1733, his father removed to Edinburgh, as minister of the Grey Friars in that city. After the completion of his course in the theological class of Edinburgh, Robertson obtained a license to preach, in 1741, and, in 1743, was presented to the living of Gladsmuir, in East Lothian. He soon began to be distinguished by his eloquence and good taste as a preacher, and became known as a powerful speaker in the general assembly of the church of Scotland, in which he obtained an ascendency by his eloquence and great talents for public business, which, exerted on the side of authority, gave him, for a long time, the lead in the ecclesiastical politics of Scotland. His History of Scotland, during the Reigns of Queen Mary and King James VI, appeared in 1759 (2 vols., 4to.), and was received with general applause. In this praise no one more heartily concurred than Hume, between whom and doctor Robertson, notwithstanding religious and political differences, an intimate friendship was maintained through life. The distinction acquired by this work, which reached a fourteenth edition before his death, led to the author's nomination to be chaplain of Stirling castle in 1759, of the king's chaplains in 1761, and principal of the university of Edinburgh in 1762. Two years after, he was made historiographer royal of Scotland, with a salary of £200 per annum. As head of a flourishing seat of education, he was attentive to all his duties, and coöperated with the greatest liberality in all the improvements which have raised Edinburgh to its present celebrity. His History of the Reign of Charles V appeared in 1769 (3 vols., 4to.), and his History of America in 1777 (2 vols., 4to.). His latest work appeared in 1791, under the title of an Historical Disquisition concerning the Knowledge which the Ancients had of India, and the Progress of Trade with that Country prior to the Discovery of the Cape of Good Hope (4to.). Doctor Robertson died in 1793. As a historian, he is admired for skilful and luminous arrangement, distinctness of narrative, and highly graphical description. His style is pure, dignified, and perspicuous. (See the Account of his Life and Writings by Dugald Stewart.)

Robespierre, Maximilian Isidore, was born at Arras, in French Flanders, in 1759, and was the eldest son of an advocate of the superior council of Artois.

His father dying when he was young, he was indebted for his education to the bishop of Arras, who gave him an exhibition at the college of Louis le Grand, at Paris. He completed his youthful studies in a manner creditable to his talents and application, and, at this period, is said to have derived an attachment to republicanism from the lessons of one of his tutors, M. Hérivaux, who was an enthusiastic admirer of the heroes of ancient Greece and Rome. In 1775, when Louis XVI, after his accession to the crown, made his entry into Paris, Robespierre was deputed by his fellow students to present their homage to the new sovereign. Having adopted the law as a profession, he became an advocate of the council of Artois. Previously to the revolution, he was advantageously known, both on account of his professional abilities, and the liberal and enlightened spirit which he exhibited in his conduct and writings. In 1789, he was elected a deputy from the *tiers état* of the province of Artois to the states-general. In that assembly, he advocated the liberty of the press, and other popular topics of discussion; but his eloquence did not attract much attention, and he attached himself, in the first instance, so closely to Mirabeau, that he acquired the epithet of *Le Singe de Mirabeau*. At this time, however, he frequented the Jacobin assemblies and clubs of the lower orders, over whom he gained an ascendency, of which he afterwards availed himself to make his way to despotic power. In January, 1791, he spoke repeatedly on criminal legislation; and he subsequently displayed so much moderation in discussions relative to the emigrants and the priests, as led to suspicions that he was actuated by some secret motives. In a speech on the 30th of May, he recommended the abolition of capital punishments. He is said to have been much alarmed at the flight of the king from Paris, and equally rejoiced at his forced return from Varennes; and, from that period, he seems to have used all his influence in overturning the monarchy. His projects now gradually became developed; and, at the tumultuary meeting in the Champ de Mars, July 17, an altar, with the inscription, *A celui qui a bien merité de la Patrie*, and below it the name of *Robespierre*, testified his high favor with the people. The closing of the constituent assembly, Sept. 30, afforded him another triumph, when the mob presented him with a garland of oak leaves, and, taking the horses from his carriage, drew him through the streets, exclaiming, "Behold the friend of the people, the great defender of liberty!" It does not appear that he actively interfered in the riot of Aug. 10, 1792, or in the massacres which took place in the prisons of Paris, in the beginning of September; but he was connected with Marat and Danton, of whose crimes, and those of their associates, he had sufficient address to reap the fruits, and, like other tyrants, at length made his instruments his victims. After the execution of the king, in promoting which the Brissotins, or Girondists (q. v.), coöperated with Robespierre and the Jacobins (q. v.), the former were sacrificed to the ascendency of the latter. The Hebertists (see *Hébert*), who had joined in this work of destruction, were the next victims to the jealousy of the dictator, who had no sooner sent them to the scaffold, with the assistance of Danton and his friends, than he adopted measures for the ruin of that popular demagogue, whom he dreaded as his most dangerous rival. His next measure was to throw the imputation of atheism and irreligion on those whom he had destroyed, and to establish a species of religious worship. Barrère, by his direction, promulgated his new system of worship, and, June 8, 1794, Robespierre in person celebrated what he termed "the feast of the Supreme Being." His power seemed now to be completely established, and the reign of terror was at its height; but his cruel tyranny and mysterious denunciations had alarmed many of those who had been most intimately connected with him, and a conspiracy was formed for his destruction. (See *Terrorism*.) At this critical juncture, far from acting with the decision which previously marked his conduct, he waited for the attack of his enemies, and secluded himself from the public for more than a month, during which period he is said to have been employed in preparing an elaborate defence of his conduct, to be delivered in the national convention, where he made his appearance for that purpose July 26 (8th Thermidor), 1794. He was indirectly attacked by Bourdon de l'Oise; after which Vadier, Cambon, Billaud-Varennes, and several other members, spoke against him. He now perceived the extent of his danger; and the ensuing night was passed in consultation with St. Just, and others of his most intimate partisans; but then deliberations led to no decisive results. The next day, when they appeared in the convention, Tallien and Billaud openly accused Robespierre of despotism. A tumult ensued, and, amidst cries of *A bas le tyran!* he in vain endeavored to obtain a hearing. At length a decree of arrest was carried against him; and his brother, and his friends St. Just, Couthon, and Le Bas, were included in it. Robespierre was sent to the Luxembourg prison; but, in the night, he was set free by the keeper, and was conducted to the hall of the commune of Paris, where Henriot, commander of the national guard, Fleuriot, the mayor of Paris, and others of his creatures, had assembled forces for his defence. This was the critical moment; but neither Henriot, nor Robespierre himself, had spirit sufficient to head the mob and lead it against the convention. While they deliberated, their opponents proceeded to action. Barras and others having been appointed commissioners to direct the armed force of the metropolis, they, without difficulty, secured the persons of the fallen tyrant and his associates, who were all guillotined the next day, July 28, 1794. Robespierre endeavored in vain to escape a public execution, by shooting himself with a pistol at the moment of his seizure; but he only fractured his lower jaw, and thus subjected himself to protracted suffering, which excited no compassion. Of the wretches who disgraced the revolution, Robespierre was the most notorious, but not the most infamous. He did not court the dregs of the people, like Marat; he amassed no money. He was politically insane, and was not, moreover, the author of all the enormities with which he has been charged. Among his colleagues of the committees, and especially those who were sent into the departments, many exercised cruelties which far exceeded their instructions. Those who contributed most to his overthrow, and were loudest in their accusations against him, had profited by his crimes, in which they were deeply involved; and, like the scape-goat of the Jews, he was charged with the sins of the whole nation, or rather of the Jacobin government. In the Memorial from St. Helena, Napoleon is stated to have said that Robespierre displayed in his conduct more extensive and enlightened views than have been generally ascribed to him; and that he intended to reëstablish order, after he had overturned the contending factions; but, not being powerful enough to arrest the progress of the revolution, he suffered himself to be carried away by the torrent, as was the case with all before Napoleon himself, who engaged in a similar attempt. As a proof of this, the emperor asserted that when with the army at Nice, he had seen in the hands of the brother of Maximilian Robespierre letters, in which he expressed an intention to put an end to the reign of terror. On the whole, it is reasonable to conclude that something like principle and genuine enthusiasm guided this hateful and unhappy man in the first instance; but, wholly unable to govern the elements of wild disorder afloat around him, the characteristic cruelty of perplexed cowardice at length became his only instrument, either of action or self-defence. However stimulated, his career exhibits one of the most signal instances of cruelty upon record. Among the published works of Robespierre are, *Plaidoyer pour le Sieur Vissery*, in favor of the right of setting up electrical conductors against lightning (1783, 8vo.); *Discours couronné par la Soc. Roy. de Metz sur les Peines infamantes* (1785, 8vo.); *Éloge de Gresset*, in which the author displays an attachment to monarchical government and religious institutions; *Éloge de Prés. Dupaty;* and a political journal, called *Le Défenseur de la Constitution.* The *Mémoires* of Riouffe, and the *Papiers trouvés chez Robespierre*, &c., contain much curious information concerning him.*

ROBIN, AMERICAN, or MIGRATING THRUSH (*turdus migratorius*, Lin.); specific character, dark ash-color; beneath rufous; head and tail black; the two exterior feathers of the latter white at the inner tip. The robin is found in summer throughout North America, from the desolate regions of Hudson's bay, in the fifty-third degree, to the table-land of Mexico. These birds retire from higher latitudes only as their food begins to fail, and they make their appearance in Massachusetts, feeding on winter berries, till driven to the south by inundating snows. At this season, they are numerous in the Southern States. Even in the vicinity of Boston, flocks of robins are sometimes seen assembling round the open springs in the depth of winter. Towards the close of January, the robin, in South Carolina, still tunes his song, and about the second week of March begins to appear in the Middle States. By the 10th of that month, they may also be heard in Massachusetts. Their nests are often seen on the horizontal branch of an apple-tree, or in a bush or tree in the woods, and so large as seldom to be wholly concealed. The eggs, about five, are of a

* The sister of Robespierre still enjoys a pension from the French government.

bluish-green, and without spots. To avoid the attacks of the cuckoo, the robin, says Mr. Nuttall (see his *Ornithology*, from which these remarks are taken), has been known to build his nest within a few yards of the blacksmith's anvil, and even in the stern timbers of an unfinished vessel, in which men were constantly at work, and to take the materials of his nest from the pine shavings on the carpenter's bench. They raise several broods in a season. They seem content in a cage, sing well, and readily learn lively parts of tunes, and have even been taught "Old Hundred." They also, in this situation, imitate the notes of most of the birds about them.

Robin Goodfellow. (See *Browny.*)

Robin Hood. (See *Hood, Robin.*)

Robinia. (See *Locust.*)

Robinson, John, minister of the English church in Holland, to which the first settlers of New England belonged, was born in Great Britain, in 1575, and educated at Cambridge. He for some time held a benefice in the established church, but, in 1602, became pastor of a dissenting congregation in the north of England, and, in consequence of persecution, went with them to Holland in 1608. After a short residence at Amsterdam, they removed to Leyden. His talents and reputation were such, that he held a public disputation with Episcopius in 1613. A part of his church emigrated to Plymouth in 1620, and it was his intention to follow them with the remainder; but his sudden death, March 1, 1625, prevented. He was distinguished for learning, liberality and piety.

Robinson, Robert, an eminent dissenting divine, was born in Norfolk, in 1735, and educated at a grammar-school in his native county; but, owing to the loss of his father, and the humble circumstances of his mother, he was apprenticed, at the age of fourteen, to a hair-dresser in London. Having attached himself to George Whitefield, he became a preacher among the Calvinistic Methodists, but subsequently relinquished his connexion with the Methodists, and established an independent congregation at Norwich, over which he presided. He was afterwards chosen pastor to a small Anabaptist congregation at Cambridge, and retained this situation during the remainder of his life. In 1773, he removed to Chesterton, near Cambridge, where he engaged in trade as a farmer, corn-dealer and coal-merchant. His learning and abilities procured him much respect from the members of the university, and other persons belonging to the established church; and he received offers of promotion if he would become a conformist, which he declined. In 1774, he published a translation of the sermons of Saurin, with memoirs of the reformation in France, and the life of Saurin. In 1776, was published his Plea for the Divinity of Jesus Christ, &c. Among his other works are his Plan of Lectures on Non-conformity; the General Doctrine of Toleration; Slavery inconsistent with Christianity; and Sixteen Discourses, which had been delivered extempore to illiterate audiences in the vicinity of Cambridge. These were very liberal on doctrinal points; and his tendency to Unitarian principles soon became known, although he still continued his ministerial labors at Cambridge. He died in 1790, in the fifty-fifth year of his age

Robinson, Frederic. (See *Goderich, Lord.*)

Robinson Crusoe. This celebrated romance, written by the well-known Defoe (q. v.), was published in 1719, under the title of the Life and surprising Adventures of Robinson Crusoe, of York, Mariner, who lived eight and twenty Years all alone, &c., written by himself. The favorable reception this attempt met with induced the author to pursue the subject, and, a few months later, appeared the Further Adventures of Robinson Crusoe, being the second and last Part of his Life, &c. It was with difficulty that the author could at first get any of the trade to undertake the publication of this work, which has since appeared under an almost endless variety of forms, and in almost all languages, and has been the delight of childhood no less than the amusement of those of mature years. "Was there ever any thing written by mere man," says doctor Johnson, "that was wished longer by its readers, excepting Don Quixote, Robinson Crusoe, and the Pilgrim's Progress?" "There is one book," says Rousseau, "which shall long form the whole library of Emile, and which shall preserve a high rank to the last: it is not Aristotle, nor Pliny, nor Buffon: it is Robinson Crusoe." Its fine sentiments, its pure morality, its practical good sense, and its religious character, united with its simplicity, truth of description, and natural and lively delineations of the passions, combine to give it the charm of fiction and the air and weight of reality. A third part, intended as a vehicle for fuller moral and religious instruction, appeared under the title Serious

Reflections during the Life and surprising Adventures of Robinson Crusoe, by himself (1722). The work was immediately translated into French, and, soon after, into other languages; and various imitations appeared, both in English and in other languages. The *rifacimento* of Campe, in German, is much used on the continent (translated into Spanish, French, Italian, Latin, &c.), and has been turned into English. The best English editions are those of Chalmers, with a life of Defoe (1790, 2 vols., 8vo.); the academic edition of Mawman (1815), with geographical and nautical notes; and the edition of Cadell and Davies (1820, 2 vols.), with engravings by Heath. The story of Defoe's fraudulently using the papers of a Scotch mariner, by the name of Selkirk, in the composition of his book, is without foundation. He took the hint, doubtless, from Selkirk's adventures, as Shakspeare borrowed Hamlet, Macbeth, or Romeo and Juliet, from Scotch and Danish chronicles or Italian ballads. The real story of Selkirk is as follows: He was a Scottish sailor, who passed some years alone on the island of Juan Fernandez, and was a native of Largo, in Fifeshire. In 1703, he sailed as master in the Cinque Ports privateer, under captain Stradling. In consequence of some difference with his commander, he went ashore at Juan Fernandez, and remained in his solitude till he was taken away by captain Woods Rogers, in January, 1709. Some account of his residence was published by Steele in the Englishman (No. 26), and in Rogers's Voyage round the World (1712); but there is no reason to believe that he had any papers, or journal of any sort.—See Howell's *Life and Adventures of Alexander Selkirk* (Edinburgh, 1829); and Wilson's *Life of Defoe* (3 vols., 8vo., 1830).

Rob-Roy (that is, *Robert the Red*); a celebrated Highland chief, whose true name was Robert Macgregor, but who assumed that of Campbell, on account of the outlawry of the clan Macgregor by the Scotch parliament, in 1662. He was born about 1660. His mother was a Campbell of Glenlyon, and his wife, Helen, a Campbell of Glenfalloch. Like other Highland gentlemen, Rob-Roy was a drover previous to the rebellion of 1715, in which he joined the adherents of the pretender. (See *Stuart, James Edward.*) On the suppression of the rebellion, the duke of Montrose, with whom Rob-Roy had previously had a quarrel, took the opportunity to deprive him of his estates; and the latter began to indemnify himself by a war of reprisals upon the property of the duke. An English garrison was stationed at Inversnaid, near Aberfoyle, the *clachan* (residence) of Rob-Roy; but his activity and courage saved him from the hands of his enemies, from whom he continued for some time to levy black-mail. He died in 1743. (See *Highlands.*) His fortunes and those of his clan form the subjects of Rob-Roy and the Legend of Montrose.

Rocambole (*allium scorodoprasum*); a species of onion, having bulbs resembling those of the garlic; but the cloves are smaller. It is cultivated for the same purposes, and is considered as having a more delicate flavor.

Rochambeau, Jean Baptiste Donatien de Vimeur, comte de, marshal of France, born at Vendome, in 1725, entered the army at the age of sixteen, and served in Germany under marshal Broglio. In 1746, he became aid-de-camp to Louis Philip, duke of Orleans; and afterwards, obtaining the command of the regiment of La Marche, distinguished himself at the battle of Lafeldt, where he was wounded; obtained fresh laurels at Creveldt, Minden, Corbach and Clostercamp; and, having been made lieutenant-general, was, in 1780, sent with an army of 6000 men to the assistance of the U. States of America. Having embarked in Rhode Island, he acted in concert with Washington, first against Clinton, in New York, and then against Cornwallis, rendering important services at the siege of Yorktown (q. v.), which were rewarded by a present of two cannons taken from lord Cornwallis. After the revolution, Rochambeau was raised to the rank of a marshal by Louis XVI, and he was appointed to the command of the army of the north. He was soon superseded by more active officers, and, being calumniated by the popular journalists, he addressed to the legislative assembly a vindication of his conduct. A decree of approbation was consequently passed in May, 1792, and he retired to his estate, near Vendome, with a determination to interfere no more with public affairs. He was subsequently arrested, and narrowly escaped suffering death under the tyranny of Robespierre. In 1803, he was presented to Bonaparte, who, in the year following, gave him a pension, and the cross of grand officer of the legion of honor. His death took place in 1807. His *Mémoires* were published in 1809 (8vo.). Robin's *Voyage dans l'Amérique Septentrionale* (1782) contains some important details concerning Rochambeau's campaign in the United States.

ROCHECHOUART. (See *Montespan.*)

ROCHEFOUCAULD, François, duke de la, prince of Marsillac, a wit and nobleman of the reign of Louis XIV, was born in 1613. He distinguished himself as the most brilliant nobleman about the court, and by his share in the good graces of the celebrated duchess of Longueville, was involved in the civil war of the Fronde. He signalized his courage at the battle of St. Antoine in Paris, and received a shot which for some time deprived him of sight. At a more advanced period, his house was the resort of the best company at Paris, including Boileau, Racine, and the mesdames Sévigné and La Fayette. He died in 1680, in his sixty-eighth year. This nobleman wrote *Mémoires de la Régence d'Anne d'Autriche* (2 vols., 12mo., 1713), a spirited and faithful representation of that period; but he is chiefly famous for a work, entitled *Réflexions et Maximes*, founded on the principle that self-love is the foundation of all our actions.

ROCHEFOUCAULD-LIANCOURT, François Alexandre Frédéric, duke de la, born in 1747, was a member of the constituent assembly in 1789, after the dissolution of which he took the military command at Rouen, in his capacity of lieutenant-general (1792). After the 10th of August, the duke de Liancourt, as he was then styled, left France, and resided for eighteen months in England. He then travelled through the U. States, whence he returned in 1798, and, after the 18th Brumaire, returned to France, where he devoted himself to the promotion of the useful arts and to benevolent offices. It was through his influence that vaccination was introduced into France. After the restoration, he was created a peer, but, on account of the liberality of his sentiments, was, in 1823 and 1824, excluded from the council of state, and removed from the several boards of which he was a member; among others, of that for the encouragement of vaccination. This venerable philanthropist and patriot, whose last years were persecuted by the intemperate zeal of political bigotry, died at Paris, in 1827, at the age of eighty-one years. His life, by his son, was published the same year. His principal work is his *Voyage dans les États-Unis* (8 vols., 8vo.).

ROCHEJAQUELEIN, Henri de la, the hero of Vendée, born at Chatillon, in Poitou, in 1772. The peasants of the neighborhood having risen in the royal cause (1792), he placed himself at their head, and led them against the republican troops, after a short harangue;—*Allons chercher l'ennemi; si je recule, tuez-moi; si j'avance, suivez-moi; si je meurs, vengez-moi.* After gaining sixteen victories in ten months, he fell, at the age of twenty-two years (March 4, 1794) in a single combat with one of the republican soldiers. Marie Louise, marchioness de la Rochejaquelein, wife of his elder brother, who fell in Vendée in 1815, has written Memoirs of the War in the Vendée.

ROCHELLE, LA; a commercial city of France, in the department of the Lower Charente, on the Atlantic ocean, 100 miles north-west of Bordeaux; lat. 46° 9′ N.; lon. 1° 9′ W.; population, 17,500. It is well built, and strongly fortified (by Vauban), and contains many handsome squares and fountains. The harbor is safe and commodious, but is accessible for large vessels only at high water. The *Place d'armes*, or *du château*, is one of the finest in France. Glass, stone-ware and refined sugar are the principal articles manufactured, and it has a considerable commerce. Rochelle is chiefly remarkable as the stronghold of the French Protestants (see *Huguenots*) in the times of the house of Valois, and of the first Bourbons. In 1627, it was besieged by Richelieu (q. v.), and was reduced by famine, after a heroic defence, in which 15,000 of the besieged perished. A great number of the inhabitants fled to North America.

ROCHELLE SALT. (See *Tartaric Acid.*)

ROCHESTER, John Wilmot, earl of, a witty and profligate nobleman of the court of Charles II, was born in 1648, and, on the death of his father, succeeded him in his titles and estates, the latter of which his extravagance soon dissipated. Having gone through the usual course of academical study at Oxford, he made a tour through France and Italy, and then served in the fleet under lord Sandwich. On his return to England, he rushed into the full vortex of dissipation, and became the personal friend and favorite of his sovereign, who is said to have encouraged and shared many of his exploits. The levity of his disposition frequently brought him into disgrace, and he was more than once forbidden the royal presence: his companionable qualities, however, which made him necessary to the amusement of his master, prevented his occasional exile from being ever of long continuance. His constitution at length gave way under such excesses; and, at the age of thirty he was visited with all the debility of old age. He lingered for some time in this condition, and died, professing great penitence for his misspent life, July 26, 1680. His poetical works, some of which are of the most disgusting description, have been frequently printed. A few of his poems are of a better description, especially his poem on Nothing, and his lampoon upon sir Carr Scroope, which exhibit some vigor, with careless versification. His satire on Man is little more than a translation from Boileau. (See his Life by bishop Burnet, and Johnson's *Lives of the Poets*.)

ROCHESTER, in the western part of New York; lat. 43° 15′ north; lon. 77° 51′ west, on both sides of Genesee river; seven miles from lake Ontario; two from steam-boat navigation; 217 west of Albany; 75 east of Buffalo;—shortest mail routes, and, by canal, 269 west of Albany; 94 east of Buffalo.—*Corporate limits.* Two square miles, including parts of the towns of Gates and Brighton. Population, with suburbs, in 1815, 331; in 1820, 1502; in 1825, 4274; in 1826, 7669; in 1828, 10,818; in 1832, 12,000 souls, chiefly from New England. The public buildings are a court-house, gaol, two markets, ten churches, and one high-school edifice.—*Public works.* Canal aqueduct of stone, 804 feet long, on eleven arches, iron railed; three mill-dams with side courses; three bridges over the river, and fourteen over the canal; three miles of stone sewers under the streets, of three by one and a half feet in the clear, in some of which, water flows from the canal, affording, at suitable points, reservoirs for fire-engines; pebble stone pavements on several streets; about ten miles of brick and stone flagging upon side-walks; about sixty public streets and twenty public alleys, the principal ones lighted at public expense; and harbor-piers are constructing by the U. States.—The *religious societies* are twelve, and there are seventeen benevolent societies.—The *literary institutions* are the Franklin institute, the Rochester Athenæum; the Rochester institute for general education; the Rochester institute for practical education; two high schools; two public charity infant schools; two seminaries for young ladies; several district schools, and many private schools and instructers in foreign languages and in gymnastics.—The *moneyed incorporations* are—the bank of Rochester, capital $250,000; the bank of Monroe, capital $300,000; the Rochester savings bank.—The *newspapers*, one daily, and five weekly.—The *post-office receipts*, annually, are exceeded in amount in the state of New York only by those of New York and Albany; and the canal toll-office receipts, only by those of Albany.—The *manufactories* are sixteen flour mills (thirteen stone and three wood), containing sixty-eight runs of stone, capable of making 350,000 barrels per annum, though actually having made, in 1831, only 252,000, shipped to New York and Montreal; four woollen factories; two cotton; three marble; one pail and tub; one shoe-last; two tobacco; one nail; three scythe, axe and edge-tool; six tin and sheet iron; three soap and candle; three morocco; two plough; two comb; one looking-glass; one window sash; one barrel; two stone and earthen ware; one starch; one glove factory and three clothieries; one brass foundery; seven machine shops; three gunsmith; two iron turners; two braziers; four chairmakers; six cabinet; four hatters; six saddlers; fifteen coopers; seventeen blacksmiths; six goldsmiths; three coppersmiths' shops.—*Canal commerce.* Six lines of canal craft, numbering 160 boats, of forty tons each, towed by 800 horses, built, equipped and owned principally at this place, make it the seat of the transportation business, boat-building, and trades connected with it, giving employment to five extensive boat-building establishments, of between twenty and forty men each, besides joiners, smiths, &c. The superior white oak and pine lumber here, with its central location at the turning point of water conveyance between the west, New York and Montreal, confer these peculiar advantages.—*Lake trade.* At the port of Genesee, the outlet of the foreign trade, and the entrepot of Rochester, the aggregate tonnage, entering and clearing, both domestic and foreign, in 1831, amounted to 19,868 tons; value of exports in the same period, $234,792,37; of imports, $1655,63, as appears from the collector's returns. Several weekly packets ply between it and the Canadian ports, and three steam-boats. There are more than one hundred vessels, of all descriptions, on the lake, and about fifteen steam-boats.—*River.* The river Genesee is navigable fifty miles, and, at high water, ninety miles above Rochester, bringing to it the produce of a fertile south and south-west country, of about 2000 square miles in extent. It passes rapidly through the village, and is there walled on each side with hammer-dressed stone, a distance of about three fourths of a mile, to the height of from ten to twenty feet, according to the depth and inequalities of the base. From the village towards the lake, in the course of two miles, the river descends over falls of 10, 20, 96 and 104 feet, and, at low water, flows in the quantity of 20,000 cubic feet per minute, equal to the power of 12,800 horses, or 640 steam-engines of twenty horse power each. The natural advantages of Rochester, in the fertility of its interior and immense water power, with water communications in every direction, make it the commercial emporium of Western New York.

Rock Salt. (See *Salt.*)

Rocket (*eruca sativa*, or the *brassica eruca* of Linnæus); a cruciferous plant, allied to the turnip and cabbage, growing wild in many parts of Europe. It has a strong, disagreeable odor, an acrid and pungent taste, but is, notwithstanding, much esteemed by some, and especially by the Italians, who use it in their salads. Its medicinal properties are antiscorbutic, and very stimulant. The stem is about a foot and a half high, rough, with soft hairs, and bearing long, pinnated leaves; the flowers are whitish or pale yellow, with violet veins, and are disposed in racemes. This plant is almost unknown in the U. States. The term *rocket* is also applied to the different species of *hesperis*—cruciferous plants with purple flowers, often cultivated for ornament in gardens.

Rocket, Sky. (See *Pyrotechny.*)

Rockets, Congreve. (See *Congreve, Sir William.*)

Rockingham (Charles Watson Wentworth), marquis of, born in 1730, succeeded his father in his titles and estates in 1750, and, in 1765, became first lord of the treasury (prime minister). American affairs formed, at that time, a leading subject of discussion; and Rockingham took the middle way of repealing the stamp-act, and declaring the right of Great Britain to tax the colonies. He was therefore deserted by some of his supporters (among others, by Chatham), and retired from the ministry in 1766. He afterwards acted in concert with Chatham, in opposition to the North ministry, on the fall of which, in 1782, he was again placed at the head of the treasury, but died in the same year, and was succeeded by lord Shelburne. (See *Lansdowne.*)

Rocks. (See *Geology.*)

Rocky Mountains, in the western part of North America, extend from lat. about 70° north to Mexico, where the chain is continued by the Cordilleras. Their distance from the Pacific ocean is about the same as that of the Alleghanies from the Atlantic; but the extent, and breadth, and height of the Rocky mountains are much greater than those of the Alleghanies. They are of decidedly primitive formation; but they have not been so well explored as to enable us to give any scientific statements in relation to them. In latitude 47°, they are so elevated as to be covered with ice and snow in July. Some of the peaks are supposed to be twelve or thirteen thousand feet high, and the range generally is considerably higher than any other in North America, except that of the Cordilleras. The numerous peaks are not named, and have not been measured We know not with certainty that any of them are volcanic. The trappers, who are almost the only white people that visit them, frequently relate that they have heard explosions, which were supposed to be from volcanoes. Pumice stones, of a reddish color, and remarkably perfect, frequently descend the Missouri. These are said by some to be formed from burning coal-mines; but it is more probable that they proceed from volcanoes. These mountains generally appear black, rugged, and precipitous, though their aspect is not uniform. The great rivers that are discharged from their eastern and western declivities wind far among the mountains, the Arkansas on the east, and the Oregon, or Columbia, on the west, more than a hundred leagues, before they escape to the plains. In following the beds of such streams, travellers pass through the range without any considerable ascent or obstruction. Following the Platte, which is one of the principal southern branches of the Missouri, the traveller finds a road even to lake Buenaventura, on the Pacific plains, that needs little labor to adapt it to the passage of horses and wagons. Such is the testimony of numerous traders, who cannot be supposed to be deceived, nor to intend deception. The southern part of this range is called the *Masserne mountains.* They give rise to the Rio Colorado, which flows into the Pacific, the Rio del Norte of Mexico, the Yellowstone of the Missouri, and the Arkansas and Red, which flow into the Mississippi. A single peak of this range is seen, as a landmark, for an immense distance on the plains of Arkansas and Texas. This is called *mount Pike*, and has been variously estimated at from seven to ten thousand feet in height. Many accounts have been given of the appearance of silver and other metals in the Rocky mountains, but we have not yet been favored with any important specimens.

Rocroy; a town of France, 15 miles

north-west of Mézières, 110 north-east of Paris, celebrated for the victory gained by the duke d'Enghien (afterwards the great Condé), over the Spaniards, who were besieging the city, May 19, 1643. (See *Condé.*)

Rode, Pierre, one of the greatest living violin players, was born at Bordeaux, in 1774, and is a pupil of Viotti. In 1801, he was made a professor in the conservatory of Paris. In 1802, Napoleon appointed him first violinist and master of his chapel; but he did not remain long in this office. In 1803, he made his second journey to Germany; in 1804, the emperor Alexander gave him an appointment at St. Petersburg; in 1809, he returned to France; and, in 1812, lived for some time in Berlin. He now lives in France. Much to the regret of the lovers of music, his fortune prevents him from performing in public.

Rodney, Cæsar, a signer of the Declaration of Independence, was born at Dover, Delaware, about the year 1730. His father came over to this country with William Penn, and, after a short residence in Philadelphia, settled in Kent, a county upon the Delaware. His eldest son, the subject of this sketch, inherited from him a large landed estate, in consequence of the system of entail then in use. At the age of twenty-eight years, Cæsar Rodney was appointed high-sheriff, and, on the expiration of his term of service, was created a justice of the peace, and a judge of the lower courts. In 1762, and perhaps even earlier, he represented his county in the provincial legislature, by which, in 1765, he was sent, in conjunction with Mr. M'Kean and Mr. Kollock, to the congress that met at New York for the purpose of consulting upon the measures to be adopted in consequence of the stamp act, and other oppressive acts of the British government. In 1769, he was elected speaker of the house of representatives, and continued to occupy the chair for several years. About the same time, he was appointed chairman of the committee of correspondence with the other colonies; and when, in 1774, the combined efforts of the various committees had brought about the measure of a general congress, he was chosen one of the delegates to it from his native province. He was re-elected in the following year, and also made a brigadier-general in the colony. At the time when the question of independence was brought before congress, Mr. Rodney was on a tour through the southern part of Delaware, for the purpose of quieting the discontent prevalent in that quarter of the country, and preparing the minds of the people for a change of their government. His two colleagues, Mr. M'Kean and Mr. Read, were divided upon the subject, the former being favorable, the latter opposed to a declaration of independence. Mr. M'Kean, being acquainted with the views of Mr. Rodney, despatched an express, at his private expense, to inform him of the delicate posture of affairs, and urge him to hasten his return to Philadelphia. He did so immediately, and, by great exertion, arrived just as the members were entering the house for the final discussion. He entered the hall with his spurs on his boots, and soon afterwards the great question was put. By his vote in the affirmative, he secured that union among the colonies in the matter which was all-important. In the autumn of 1776, a convention was called in Delaware for the purpose of framing a new constitution, and appointing delegates to the succeeding congress. In this assembly, a majority was opposed to Mr. Rodney, who failed, in consequence, in obtaining a reëlection. This circumstance was principally attributable to the royalists, who abounded especially in the lower counties. Mr. Rodney, however, still continued a member of the council of safety, and of the council of inspection, the functions of both of which offices he assiduously discharged, being particularly active in collecting supplies for the troops of the state, then with Washington in New Jersey. In 1777, he repaired in person to the camp near Princeton, where he remained for nearly two months, engaged in laborious services. In the autumn of the same year, he was again chosen a member of congress; but, before taking his seat, he was chosen president of his state. In this station he remained for four years, during which he had frequent communications from Washington relative to the distressed condition of the army, and exerted his utmost ability in affording aid. In 1782, he was compelled to retire by the delicate state of his health. He died in 1783.—Mr. Rodney was a man of pure integrity and patriotism; he was remarkable for good humor and vivacity, as well as for the disinterestedness and generosity of his character.

Rodney, George Brydges, baron Rodney; a naval commander, born in 1717. His father, a captain in the royal navy, educated his son for the same profession. The latter first obtained a ship in 1742, and, in 1749, went to Newfoundland as governor

In 1759, having been promoted to the rank of admiral, he commanded the expedition destined for the bombardment of Havre, which he executed with success. In 1761, he sailed to the West Indies, where he distinguished himself in the reduction of Martinique, and, on his return, was rewarded with a baronetcy. A contested election for Northampton (1768) impaired his finances, and he found it necessary to retire to the continent. The French government made some overtures to him, which would have recruited his fortune. These he rejected; and, the fact having transpired, he was placed in command of a squadron destined for the Mediterranean. In 1780, he fell in with admiral Langara's fleet, off cape St. Vincent, and completely defeated it. In 1781, he sailed for the West Indies; and, April 12, 1782, obtained a decisive victory over the French fleet, under De Grasse, capturing five and sinking one of his largest vessels. A barony, and a pension of £2000, were bestowed upon him for his services; and on his decease, in 1792, a monument was voted to his memory, at the national expense, in St. Paul's. Lord Rodney is described by some writers as the first who practised the system of breaking through the centre of the enemy's line. (See *Clerk.*)

Rodolph I, emperor of Germany, founder of the imperial house of Austria, was born in 1218, being the eldest son of Albert IV, count of Hapsburg, and landgrave of Alsace. He was brought up in the court and camp of the emperor Frederic II; and, on the death of his father, succeeded to territories of a very moderate extent, which, in the spirit of the times, he sought to augment by military enterprises. In 1245, he married a daughter of the count of Homburg, by whom he acquired an accession of territory; and, some years after, served under Ottocar, king of Bohemia, against the pagan Prussians. Several years of active warfare ensued, in which he much distinguished himself by his prudence, valor, and the spirit of justice with which he protected the inhabitants of the towns from their baronial oppressors. In 1273, as he was encamped before the walls of Bàsle, he received the unexpected intelligence that he was elected king of the Romans, and emperor, in preference to Alphonso, king of Castile, and Ottocar, king of Bohemia Rodolph, then in his fifty-fifth year, willingly accepted the proffered elevation, and, being crowned at Aix-la-Chapelle, immediately strengthened himself by marrying two of his daughters to the count palatine of Bavaria and the duke of Saxony. He also took measures to ingratiate himself with pope Gregory X, who induced the king of Castile to withdraw his pretensions. The king of Bohemia, however, at that time one of the most powerful princes in Europe, persisted in his opposition, and a war ensued, in which he was defeated, and compelled to sue for peace, and agree to pay homage. Stung by this disgrace, the Bohemian king broke the treaty in 1277, and the following year Ottocar was again defeated and slain. By the treaty with his successor, which followed, Rodolph was to hold Moravia for five years, and retain the Austrian provinces which had been previously yielded by Ottocar, and the securing of which to his family was henceforward his primary object. After some abortive attempts to restore the influence of the empire in Tuscany, he contented himself with drawing large sums from Lucca and other cities, for the confirmation and extension of their privileges. No foreign foe remaining, he assiduously employed himself to restore peace and order to Germany, and wisely put down the private fortresses, which served as a retreat to banditti and to ferocious nobles. For these and other eminent services in the same spirit, he obtained the title of "a living law," and was regarded as a second founder of the German empire. He subsequently engaged in war with the counts of Savoy and of Burgundy, and delivered the young king of Bohemia from the captivity to which he had been subjected by the regent Otho, and married him to one of his daughters. The final object of the emperor was to secure the imperial succession to his son Albert; but the electors, jealous of the rapid rise of the family, could not be made to concur, and Rodolph felt the disappointment severely. He had, however, laid a permanent foundation for the prosperity of his race; and, after a reign of nineteen years, expired in July, 1291, in the seventy-third year of his age. There is scarcely an excellency, either of body or mind, which the biographers of the house of Austria have not attributed to its founder; and he appears to have merited no small portion of their panegyric. Few princes have surpassed him in energy of character and in civil and military talents. He was personally brave, almost to rashness, indefatigable, simple and unaffected in his manners, affable, and magnanimous. In the beginning of his career, he seems to have shared in the usual license of the period, in pursuit of aggrandizement; but, as an emperor, he has been considered, for the most part, as equitable and just as he was brave and intelligent.

RŒDERER, Pierre Louis, count, born at Metz, in 1754, was counsellor of the parliament of Metz before the revolution. In 1789, he was chosen deputy to the constituent assembly. A high reputation for talents preceded him, which was justified by the eloquence of his speeches on the most important questions He was a constitutional royalist, yet made such frequent concessions to the republican party that they reckoned him among their number. He was appointed a member of the committee of finance, of which he became the usual reporter, or chairman. In the manner in which M. Rœderer developed his system of finances, and the ability with which he defended his reports, his talent was especially displayed. When the schism arose in the Jacobin club, M. Rœderer joined the Feuillants, but speedily returned to the former. After the close of the session of the constituent assembly, he was appointed *procureur-syndic* of the department of the Seine. On the morning of the 10th of August, accompanied by the directory of the department, he repaired to the palace, and represented to the king and queen that the danger was far beyond any thing they had conceived, and that the royal family incurred the danger of being destroyed within the palace, if the king did not repair to the national assembly for protection. Soon after the events of that day, he was accused by the revolutionists, and seals were put upon his papers. He withdrew himself from danger, and did not reappear till after the 9th of Thermidor. In 1799, when Bonaparte returned from Egypt, M. Rœderer succeeded in forming political ties between him and Sieyes; and he was also among those who most aided in preparing the revolution of the 18th of Brumaire. Called to the senate at its first formation, he declined to take a seat there, but was made counsellor of state. There he occupied himself with the framing of a number of laws, which he presented to the legislative assembly; and he was principally charged with the establishment of the prefectures. He was the chief instrument of concluding the treaty which put an end to the misunderstandings between France and the U. States. In 1802, he presented to the legislative assembly the project of the order of the legion of honor, of which he was named commandant. In 1803, he took a seat in the senate, and was one of the members appointed to confer with the Swiss deputies assembled at Paris upon the means of giving a new constitution to their country. Shortly after, he was made count. He took a large share in the whole organization of the kingdom of Naples under Joseph Bonaparte. (See *Joseph Napoleon.*) On the return of the Bourbons, M. Rœderer disappeared from the political world. He is the author of several historical works of much value.

RŒMER; the name of the town-house in Frankfort on the Maine, in which the deliberations on the election of the German emperor were held. The newly crowned emperor here received homage. In one large room of the Rőmer are the pictures of all the emperors from Charlemagne to Francis II; and it is a curious fact, that the walls had been so filled as to leave room but for one picture more, when the portrait of Francis II, with whom the German empire expired, was added to the series. The name of the house comes from the family Rőmer which sold it, in 1405, to the city.

ROGER or ROGIER VAN DER VEYDE, one of the most eminent painters of the Old Netherlandish school, was born at Brussels, and died in 1529. In the hall of his native city are four allegorical pictures by him. A celebrated Descent from the Cross, executed by him, was sent to Spain; another is in Aix-la-Chapelle. Roger was also distinguished as a painter on glass.

ROGER DE HOVEDEN. (See *Hoveden, Roger de.*)

ROGERS, Woods, an English circum navigator, belonged to the royal navy in 1708, when he was invited by the merchants of Bristol to take the command of an expedition to the South sea. He set sail with two vessels, the Duke and the Duchess, taking out Dampier as a pilot. Passing to the south of Terra del Fuego, in January, 1709, they entered the Pacific ocean, and, February 1, arrived at the isle of Juan Fernandez, where they found Alexander Selkirk (see *Robinson Crusoe*), and, having visited the coast of California, crossed the Pacific, and returned to England in October, 1711. Captain Rogers was afterwards employed with a squadron to extirpate the pirates who infested the West Indies. He died in 1732. His Voyage round the World was published in 1712.

ROGERS, Samuel; a distinguished living poet. His father was a banker in London. Mr. Rogers is also a banker, and master of an ample fortune, which he has always been content to enjoy in pri vate life. His first appearance as an author was in 1787, when he published an Ode to Superstition, with other Poems. After an interval of five years, this was succeeded by the Pleasures of Memory, which fixed his reputation as a poet. His Epistle to a Friend, with other Poems, appeared in 1798, and the Vision of Columbus in 1814. Since then he has sent from the press Jacqueline, a Tale, which accompanied lord Byron's Lara (1814); Human Life, a Poem (1819); and Italy, a Poem (1822). The power of touching the finer feelings, and of describing visual and mental objects with truth and effect, a graceful style, a happy choice of expression, and a melodious flow of verse, are the principal characteristics of the poetry of Mr. Rogers. Without being an imitator of Goldsmith, he belongs to the school of that poet. Byron says of him, "We are all wrong except Rogers, Crabbe and Campbell." (See *Moore.*)

Rogier. (See *Roger.*)

Rohan, Louis René Edouard, prince de, cardinal-bishop of Strasburg, born in 1734, was at first known under the title of *prince Louis*. The dissipation in which the young ecclesiastic indulged, did not prevent him from attending to study, nor from forming ambitious projects. In 1772, he went as ambassador to the court of Vienna. He derives his notoriety, however, chiefly from the affair of the necklace. (See *Marie Antoinette*, and *Lamotte.*) He was then grand almoner of France, and, being thrown into the Bastile, continued in prison more than a year, when he was acquitted and released by the parliament of Paris (August, 1786). He was afterwards a member of the constituent assembly, but, on account of his opposition to the revolutionary principles, was obliged to retire to Germany, where he died in 1803. (See the *Mémoires* of Georgel, Campan, &c., and the *Recueil des Pièces concernant l'Affaire du Collier.*)

Roland, Jean Marie Baptiste de la Platière, born in 1734, was, previous to the revolution, engaged in manufactures. Being sent to Paris by the city of Lyons, on official business before the national assembly (1791), he became connected with Brissot and other popular leaders, through whose influence he was appointed minister of the interior in 1792: his principles, however, were so far from being agreeable to the king, that he was dismissed after a few months; but, after the 10th of August (see *Louis XVI*), he was recalled to the ministry, and continued to hold his place until the proscription of the Girondists (q. v.) compelled him to leave Paris. On receiving, at Rouen, the news of the death of his wife, he killed himself with a sword-cane. Roland was the author of the Dictionary of Manufactures (3 vols., 4to.), forming part of Panckoucke's *Encyclopédie Méthodique*, and of several other works. His wife, *Manon Jeanne*, was born at Paris, in 1754, and was the daughter of an engraver. She was remarkable for her beauty, and received an excellent education. The study of Greek and Roman history early inflamed her imagination, and gave her a tendency to republican sentiments. After her marriage, in 1779, madame Roland took part in the studies and tasks of her husband, and accompanied him to Switzerland and England. The revolution found in her a ready convert to its principles; and, on the appointment of her husband to the ministry, she participated in his official duties, writing and preparing many papers, and taking a share in the political councils of the leaders of the Girondist party. (See *Girondists.*) On the fall of her husband, she was arrested. She conducted with great firmness during the trial, and at the time of her execution, "Oh Liberty, what crimes are committed in thy name!" was her exclamation, when she arrived at the scaffold (November 8, 1793). Madame Roland had laid aside the modesty and softness of her sex, and had adopted deistical notions in religion. While in prison, she wrote Memoirs of her Life, which have since been published, with her other writings relating to the events of the revolution. The most complete edition is that forming part of the memoirs relating to the French revolution, under the title *Mémoires de Madame Roland, avec une Notice sur sa Vie*, with notes (1820). (See *Memoirs.*)

Roland, or Orlando; a celebrated hero of the Romances of Chivalry, and one of the paladins (q. v.) of Charlemagne, of whom he is represented as the nephew. His character is that of a brave, unsuspicious, and loyal warrior, but somewhat simple in his disposition. According to the romances, he fell, on the retreat of Charlemagne from Spain, in the Roncesvalles (Roncevaux), a pass of the Pyrenees, with the flower of the Frankish chivalry. His adventures are contained in the fabulous Chronicle of Turpin (*De Vita Caroli Magni et Rolandi*), and the old French romances relating to Charlemagne and his paladins. (See *Romance.*) The celebrated romantic epics of Boiardo (*Orlando Innamorato*) and Ariosto (*Orlando Furioso*) relate to him and his exploits.

Roland's or Ruland's Columns are stone statues of a man in armor, generally rudely formed, and found in twenty-eight German cities. According to tradition, they were erected in honor of Charlemagne's paladin (q. v.) Roland; but, if ever this hero existed (see *Roland*), the Germans, particularly the Saxons, in whose former territory they are found, would probably have been the last to erect statues to him. Besides, they are evidently of a later age: probably they were the same with the *Weichbild*, the symbol of incorporated towns, possessing jurisdiction over their own members; and thus the name has been considered a corruption of *Rügelandssäulen* (Rügeland's columns), from *Rüge*, which was equivalent, formerly, to *court of justice*. See Türk *De Statuis Rolandinis* (Rostock, 1824).

Roller (*coracias*); a genus of birds allied to the crows and jays, found in Europe, Asia, Africa, and the hot climates of America. They are more wild and untractable than their congeneres, and do not appear to possess the imitative faculty of the jay or magpie, as all attempts to teach them to speak have been unsuccessful. The plumage of almost all the species is very beautiful, being in general an assemblage of blue and green, mixed with white, and heightened by the contrast of more obscure and less vivid colors. The rollers are very shy, inhabiting the thickest and most unfrequented woods, though, like the crows, they are frequently seen in newly ploughed fields, searching for worms and larvæ. They are not carnivorous, except in cases of necessity, and their flesh is said to be palatable.

Rollin, Charles, a historian, was born at Paris in 1661. His father was a cutler, who intended him for the same business; but his talents obtained the notice of a learned Benedictine, who procured him a place in the college of Du Plessis, by which he was enabled to gratify his inclination for learning. After going through a course of theology at the Sorbonne, he received the tonsure. In 1688, he obtained the chair of eloquence in the royal college, of which he became rector in 1694; reformed the academical course in many particulars, and revived the study of the Greek language. In 1698, he was chosen coadjutor or head of the college of Beauvais, which was also much benefited by his attention. In 1720, he was again chosen rector of the university of Paris; but was displaced in consequence of his connexion with the Jansenists. His productions are *Traité des Études* (1726); *Histoire Ancienne* (13 vols., 1730 and 1738); and Roman History (5 vols.), to the war against the Cimbri (completed by Crevier, 16 vols., 12mo.). He died in 1741. Rollin's writings are distinguished for purity and elegance of style, but they are diffuse and prolix, and his historical works are deficient in critical sagacity. There is an edition of his works in 30 vols., 8vo. (Paris, 1827), with notes on the historical part by Guizot.

Romagna; formerly a province of the States of the Church, bordering on the Adriatic, forty-five miles in length by thirty in breadth. The delegations of Forli and Ravenna have been formed from it.

Romaic. (See *Greece*, division *Modern Greek Language and Literature*.)

Romana, marquis de la; general in the war of the Spaniards against Napoleon. Preparatory to his plans against the Bourbons in Spain, the French emperor had drawn to Germany, in 1807, a body of from ten to twelve thousand Spanish troops, at the head of which was general Romana, who, taking advantage of his station on the island of Funen, entered into a secret correspondence, with the commander of the English fleet established there, obtained English transports, and, with all his forces, excepting a few divisions, who could not be brought up quick enough, embarked, between the seventeenth and twentieth August, 1808, at Nyborg and Svenborg, and arrived at Corunna. From this time, Romana was incessantly employed in exciting the Spaniards. He was the first to suggest the idea of arming the peasantry and forming the Guerillas. (q. v.) In this way as well as by his personal services in the field, Romana had an important part in maintaining the independence of Spain. He died in 1811.

Roman Catholic Church; that society of Christians which acknowledges the bishop of Rome as its visible head, in contradistinction to the Greek church, which likewise calls itself a *catholic*, that is, a *universal* church, but disowns the Roman pope. The Roman Catholic church exercised a spiritual supremacy over all Europe, with the exception of Russia and Turkey, until the time of the reformation. It has more followers than all the Protestant sects united; and its exertions have gradually brought nearly 2,000,000 of the adherents of the Greek ritual in Europe under the spiritual dominion of the pope. (See the article *United Greeks*.)

I. *The Foundation of the Catholic Faith.* Christianity is a revelation, a positive historical religion. Both Protestants and Catholics believe in the reality of Christ's revelation; and the first and fundamental difference between them is, that the former considers the Bible the only repository of this divine revelation, while the Catholic acknowledges, in addition to this, the authority of tradition, or (which amounts to the same thing) considers the Christian revelation as handed down by tradition, of which the Bible, according to his belief, makes a part, just as a code of laws constitutes a part only of the whole law of a land; and its deficiencies are supplied by the traditional law preserved among the people, without which no code could exist. The Catholic considers tradition as the very life of his church, and the whole of his religion as depending upon a correct understanding of it; for which reason we give the following exposition, the production of a Catholic writer, without comment. —Mankind commenced with goodness, but error and evil soon sprang up. The Son of the eternal Father came, took away guilt, and established Christianity. The Son, the Holy Spirit, and the apostles of the Son, taught it, and the believers handed it down from generation to generation. Various portions of that which the apostles taught and delivered as what they had received from their Lord, and seen of him, were committed to writing; and such writings became a part of the revelation. The revelation brought by the Son was not a written code, but the living Word. The Son did not write a single letter. The apostles were not commanded to commit doctrines to paper, but to go into all the world and to preach the gospel. (*Matt.* x. 7.) There was a rule of faith which, for a long time before the New Testament was written, was the spiritual property of the church. In the course of centuries, the Epistles of the apostles were collected, and, several centuries after the origin of Christianity, these, together with the Gospels, which were also authenticated by tradition, were formed into the *canon* (q. v.), which constitutes the body or entire collection of those writings which have been transmitted to us as divine: thus none of the fathers thought of confining the sources of the religious knowledge of the church to them exclusively. Irenæus says, "Every one who would know the truth is at liberty to *examine the tradition of the apostles, which has been proclaimed through all the world*; and we might also refer to the authority of all those bishops who have been appointed in the church by the apostles and their successors, even to our times. If the apostles had left behind no writings, should we not have been obliged to follow the tradition preserved by those to whose care the apostles intrusted the church? Many barbarous nations which believe in Christ, and upon whose hearts the doctrines of salvation have been impressed by the Holy Spirit without the aid of writing, do so, and carefully preserve the old tradition." Clement of Alexandria speaks of his teachers thus: "They preserved the true tradition of the doctrines of salvation, and, by the help of God, handed it down to us from Peter, James, John and Paul, the holy apostles (like children who transmit the inheritance of their father), in order to deposit the seeds of apostolical doctrine preserved by their predecessors." Basilius: "Some of the dogmas and public instructions preserved in the church, we have learned from the Sacred Scriptures; others we have received as mysteries handed down to us by the tradition of the apostles. Both have equal validity in religion, and no man will gainsay them, who is in the least conversant with the order of things established in the church. I consider it as apostolical to adhere, also, to the unwritten traditions." Chrysostom says, "Thence it appears that the apostles did not teach every thing by epistles, but that they also taught without writing. But the unwritten instructions are as worthy of belief as the written. Let us, therefore, hold the tradition of the church as worthy of belief." Other fathers of the church have expressed themselves alike decisively; and even the Protestant Semler says, "Nothing but ignorance of history has confounded the Christian religion with the Bible, as if there were no Christianity when there was yet no Bible; or as if, on that account, those Christians who, of four Gospels, knew only one, and of so many Epistles knew only a few, had been less truly pious. Previous to the fourth century, no such thing as a complete New Testament had been thought of; and yet there were always genuine disciples of Christ." That which was written is, therefore, according to the Catholic view, only a part of the tradition, and not the tradition itself. The knowledge of the Catholic church is of a historical character, not speculative. The Catholic believes that his tradition rests on the same grounds as the faith of the Protestant in the Bible, because it is tradition originally which assures the Protestant of the genuineness of the Bible.

The consistent Catholic, therefore, endeavors to ascertain accurately this tradition; i. e. to guard the purity of his faith. The first means for the attainment of this object was the authority of the Sacred Scriptures. They obtain authority as the embodying of tradition; necessarily subjected, however, to the judgment and the exposition of the church, on which, indeed, all tradition, and even Scripture, is, according to him, dependent. By this authority of the Bible, the falsification of traditions has been, in a great measure, prevented. In the controversies concerning tradition, and concerning the accounts and the meaning of the Bible, the belief of the church always decided. The actual belief of the church universal is, necessarily, the Catholic's last appeal; but what this is may be the subject of controversy. There is, in this case, no better remedy than to assemble the church, and let her express herself as is done in councils. The Catholic doubts not that the same Holy Spirit which is promised to the church, even till the end of time, will assist the church, when assembled, in rightly expressing her faith. The council creates no articles of faith. The whole church is unable to do this. The council merely expresses what the church believes, and declares that the church has preserved such a truth. The church, in the possession of a revelation handed down by tradition, must declare herself infallible. The established religious faith necessarily excludes a conviction of the possibility of the truth of the opposite opinion. If, therefore, the revelation, the tradition, is in itself infallible (as the Protestant holds the Bible to be infallible), should the church, which expresses this tradition, be less infallible? The church explains the Bible in accordance with tradition, of which it is a part and a copy. What the council expresses as a doctrine of faith is a canon. A canon is that which, according to the judgment of the church, is expressed in the Bible, and has always, and every where, and by all, been believed (*semper et ubique et ab omnibus creditum*). Whenever the church finds one of these requisitions wanting, it establishes no canon. In this way the Bible and tradition are intimately blended. If it is asked, Why does the church consider those historical truths which have been handed down by tradition, and attested by the church assembled, as real truths? the answer of the Catholic is, Because her institution is of divine origin, and because a revelation has been delivered to her. Reason here objects, that the conclusion is obtained by arguing in a circle. The Catholic replies, that the objection is made because reason is desirous of having that proved which, resting on itself, is capable of no proof, and which, if it might have been proved and confirmed by evidence external to itself, would fall to pieces, because it would then be necessary to place reason above revelation. How can the church be censured for laying claim to infallibility, for rejecting the criticism of reason? If Christianity is a revelation, faith can be grounded only upon the testimony of the church (which, by means of tradition, hands down revelation, the sacred books, and regulations), and not upon the free investigation of reason, which protests against authority. That one council should, with respect to doctrine, contradict another, is an event which is, and must be, inconceivable to the Catholic. This is the fundamental view of Catholicism. There can, therefore, be only one infallible church.

II. *The Doctrines of Catholicism.** The Catholic church is the community of saints, which has one faith, one charity, one hope. It believes in the doctrine of the Trinity, the redemption, &c. It believes in free will, immortality, and the moral law. The church is to restore the kingdom of God. The first man was created immediately by God, free from sin, adorned with innocence and holiness, and possessed of a claim to eternal life. This first man sinned, and thereby lost his innocence, holiness, and claim to eternal life. By his sins, all his posterity became sinners before God, and, therefore, in like manner, lost eternal life. In this state of moral corruption, man was not to remain. Called to the kingdom of God, he must become holy and perfect, as God himself is holy and perfect. Revelation assists him in the attainment of this high destination; first, by informing him of what it is necessary for him to know (by enlightening mankind), and, secondly, by an extraordinary internal sanctification (by the consecration of mankind). But man actually attains to his high destination by faith in these doctrines and this sanctification, and by a course of life uninterruptedly continued and regulated accordingly. The Catholic believes in the immortality of the soul, and that it will hereafter be clothed with its body, which God will raise in perfection; further, that the condition of man in a future state will

* We continue to give the statement of the Catholic writer.

vary according as he has done good or evil. The wicked are for ever deprived of the sight of God. How those images in the sacred books, which represent this state to the senses, are to be understood, is not decided by the church. The good enjoy God for ever, and are blessed. The state of the good and the wicked commences immediately after death. A middle state is admitted for those souls which were not entirely estranged from the Eternal, which, therefore, in the other world, still have a hope of ultimately becoming united with the Creator. (See *Purgatory.*) The happy spirits, in the church triumphant, have not ceased to be connected with their brethren in the church militant. A band of love unites both worlds. (See *Saints.*) Every one is rewarded according to those works which he has freely performed, although, at the same time, he has followed the influences of grace; but, as the Eternal foreknows the actions of men, so he foreknows, likewise, who will attain to happiness. (Controversy concerning predestination, decided by the council of Trent, session VI, canons 12, 15, 17.) A religious mind conceives the world to be entirely dependent upon God, and so revelation represents it. According to this, the world was created by God. Whether the Mosaic cosmogony is to be literally understood, the church has by no means decided. God preserves and governs the world. Hereafter, the world is to be destroyed. Man having been thus instructed by the church respecting divine things, men and the world, it is necessary, in the second place, that he should be sanctified and consecrated by her. "The Christian standard demands not only an enlightened man, but one who is adorned with holiness; a man who is repelled from God by no polluting stain, but is drawn towards him by a pure nature. It requires a man who comes into connexion with God, not merely by a purely moral intercourse, in a spiritual way, but who, surrounded by the light of God himself, sees and enjoys him, and is exalted above sin, suffering and death." The Founder of our religion, therefore, in the first place, made a universal atonement for mankind; secondly, ordained means for their purification and sanctification, according to their various necessities. The Savior, by his death, procured the pardon of sin for all men, justified them, and put it into their power to make themselves partakers of his elevation. Now the particular means for the purification and the sanctification of men are the seven sacraments. (q. v.) These sacraments are the essence of the Catholic mysteries. Without mysteries, man is cold and insensible. The Catholic mysteries, however, differ from the Protestant in this, that the former have a more universal and more settled character, while the latter are suffered to take their tone from the feelings of individuals. The centre of the Catholic mysteries is the sacrament of the Lord's supper, whereby believers join in real communion with the Lord. For all conditions and wants, she has made provision, and in her bosom has prepared a suitable asylum for every one. A man would greatly err, however, if he should believe that the church favored mysteries, and attached herself to the arts, merely for the purpose of attracting adherents, and concealing internal defects. She needs it not. She offers words of life. Her system of belief is pure and consistent, and her morality is also pure. Indeed, the peculiar faith of the Catholic church has so often been disfigured by Protestants, that it is not strange that even the well-educated Protestant pities the honest Catholic, on account of the doctrines and ordinances falsely attributed to the Catholic church.

III. *The ecclesiastical Constitution of Catholicism, or the Catholic Church.* [It would be impossible even to mention all the objections which have been started against the organization of the Catholic church in the present work; but its historical importance makes it necessary to be known; and it is but fair to let the Catholics give their own statement on this subject. We therefore proceed with the Catholic article.] It was the design of Christ to establish a church, and certainly one which should endure. The object of the church is, through Christ, to reconcile fallen humanity with God. The church, which is to accomplish this object, is a spiritual and visible society. As a spiritual society, it stands in relation to Christ. As such, it is the union, the community, of all her living members with God the Father, through one Christ, in one Spirit of love. The apostle Paul represents these ideas particularly under two forms—under the form of a body, and that of a building. 1. He represents it under the form of a body. (*Eph.* iv; 1 *Cor* xii, 4—30, xiii, 1—13, xiv, 1—40.) According to this, the church is a spiritual organization under one Head, Christ, in which no member is to remain isolated from the body, but each must necessarily make common cause with the rest, to accomplish the objects of the Spirit. 2. He represents it to us under the form of a house, a palace, a temple, a divine building. (*Eph.* ii, 19—22; 1 *Tim.* iii, 15.) Further, the church is not merely a spiritual, but a visible, society, since it exists upon earth as a society of visible combatants, engaged in warfare; and also, according to the figures of the apostle, is compared to a body, a temple, a palace, a house of God; and, finally, since Christ, though he operates invisibly by his Spirit, must also operate through visible organs, however named, whether apostles, teachers or pastors. The visible church of Christ, contemplated as the visible body of Christ, is necessarily a union, a combination, a community, of all the members under one visible head, which has no other object than to effect and maintain a union with Christ, and, through Christ, with God the Father. This visible union of all the members in the visible church of Christ, can be effected only by the close connexion of individual churches with their immediate pastors, and of these with their superior pastors, who must also be connected with the centre of union, and thus maintain a connexion with Christ, the invisible Head, and, through Christ, with the Father. This intimate connexion with the centre of union necessarily presupposes that the visible head of all the church is in possession of the preëminence in authority and jurisdiction. This primacy, according to all the traditions of the apostles, rests in the person of the Roman bishop, as the successor of St. Peter, whom Christ made the rock of his church, that is, the immovable centre of his visible church. (*Matt.* xvi, 16.) The union of the church, by the connexion of individual churches with their pastors, and of these with their superior pastors, and of these last with the supreme pastor and head of the church, presupposes a hierarchy. This hierarchy is spiritual; spiritual in its origin, tendency, and mode of operation, though its actions must be visible. It is not, however, to be believed, because the Catholic church is a hierarchy, that she has any other head than Christ. He who is the Foundation of the world, is also the sure and proper foundation of the Catholic faith. The connexion which Christians have with the visible centre of union has for its highest object a connexion with Christ, the invisible Centre of union. To the Catholic, Christ is all in all. (*Col.* iii, 2.) For him there is salvation only in Christ. From Christ he derives all his gifts.—We shall now give a more particular explanation of the points of difference between this and other ecclesiastical systems. The church could not be one with the state. Religion was to be preached to all nations, and spread to the farthest boundaries of the world. States are subject to the vicissitudes of time. They may be, and indeed have been, hostile to religion. It was on this account that Christ said, "My kingdom is not of this world." The church, therefore, cannot recognise princes as bishops, as the Lutheran church does. She can, in general, allow them no influence in the management of church affairs; and where states have arrogated to themselves such influence, a reaction has soon followed, which has often passed as far to the opposite extreme. The regulation of the church could, also, not be made dependent on the religious communities. It is impossible for learners to define what instructions they ought to receive. Faith, in the church, does not originate with the low and pass to the high, but it originates with the high and passes to the low; not through the investigations of the communities, but through the instruction and the doctrines of salvation communicated by the apostles and bishops. The apostle Paul says, in the First Epistle to the Corinthians, that he was commissioned as an apostle by God, and by no means that he was ordained by Christian communities, which he, in fact, was just establishing. The apostles only, not Christian communities, were commanded to go into the world, and to teach all people. The former only, not the latter, were promised assistance. The Sacred Scriptures were by no means sufficient to preserve the true doctrine unchanged There was need of the living Word, of the ministry, and of the assistance of the Spirit. "Know this first," says 2 Peter, i, 20, "that no prophecy of the Scripture is of any private interpretation." The apostles exercised the power of the church. They held their first council at Jerusalem. "It has pleased the Holy Spirit and us," said they, when they sent their decrees to Christian communities. This power, however, was no prerogative of the apostles individually, but a power which they possessed by virtue of their office, and which was to be extended to their successors, and that of necessity. This is proved, not only by the express assertion of Jesus, who says, in Matthew xvi, 18, that he will build his church upon a rock, and the gates of hell shall not prevail against it; and, in another place, promises to remain with them, even to the end of the world, by means of his Comforter (evidently referring to the power which preserves and governs the church); but it also naturally follows, from the plan of Christ, to establish a church universal, which would necessarily require the extension of this power to the successors of the apostles. The apostles, therefore, actually established bishops in every place; and, after their death, these bishops conducted the church, which continued to remain one and the same, until, in modern times, it entered into the heads of the reformers, to attack its constitution: hence the Catholic church has been preserved from the fate of Protestant churches, which, for want of such a constitution, have been lost in isolated communities. The bishops and successors of the apostles now form an association like that of the apostles. "There is one bishopric," says Cyprian (*De Unitate Ecclesiæ*), "of which a part is held by each individual bishop, who is also a partaker of the whole in common with his brethren" (*Episcopatus unus est, cujus a singulis in solidum pars tenetur*). Therefore, as the rays of the sun are many, but there is only one light; and as the branches of a tree are many, but make only one tree, fastened to the ground by a strong root; and as from one fountain many brooks may flow, and yet remain one at their source; so the church, which, by means of her prolific increase, extends herself in great numbers, far around, is also one. Every bishop is not merely a bishop of the world, but also of his own diocese. He is not an *œcumenical* or *universal bishop*, as John the Faster, of Constantinople, maintained of himself—a title which even Gregory declined. The diocese of the bishop originally consisted of the Christian community of a city. From this place, the bishop spread Christianity, and organized new Christian communities, to which he gave pastors, as his delegates, to discharge a part of his official duties. These pastors, and the presbytery of the capital, formed the bishop's very influential council. They gave their opinions in the synod of the diocese; and the presbytery of the capital, afterwards called the *cathedral chapter*, was the representative of those pastors who did not assemble. The bishop only had *episcopal* power, properly so called. Pastors and presbyters were only an emanation from him. That bishops and priests, however, did not, as the Protestant systems of presbyterianism maintain, constitute only one order under different names, follows, not only from tradition, but, with uncommon clearness, from the genuine epistles of St. Ignatius, who lived about 107, and was a pupil of the apostles. In these, the bishop, as one ordained by God, is always distinguished from the assembly of priests. That, moreover, the order of priests was generally distinguished from the laity, by consecration, and by a divine mission, from the commencement of the church, follows from tradition, and also from the epistles of Paul to Timothy and Titus, and several other of his epistles. (Concerning the relation of the pope to bishops, and to the church in general, see *Pope*.) It will be sufficient to observe, here, that the church forms a kind of confederacy, in order to maintain her union, through the bishop at Rome, as successor to the chief of the apostles—through him whom Cyprian has called the *centrum unitatis* of the church; that the pope, by divine appointment, is the organ of the church; and that, at the assemblies of the church, he presides as first among equals (*primus inter pares*). Archbishops, patriarchs, &c., are not essential parts of the hierarchy, but have only become incidentally attached to it.

Roman Cements. (See *Cements*.)

Roman King. (See *German Empire*.)

Roman Law. (See *Civil Law*.)

Roman Literature. (See *Rome*.)

Romance (so called from the *Romance* or *Romanic* language); a fictitious narrative in prose or verse, the interest of which turns upon marvellous and uncommon incidents. The name is derived from the circumstance of the romantic compositions of this kind having been written in the vulgar tongues, which were derived from the Roman, at a period when Latin was still the language of literature, law, &c. We have already given some general views of the origin and character of romantic fiction under the head of *Novels*. The modern European romance was at first metrical in its form, and founded on historical, or what was thought to be historical, tradition. The transition from the rhymed chronicles, which we find in the early periods of modern European history, to the metrical romance, was easy, and much of the material of the latter was derived, with suitable embellishments, from the former. The Anglo-Norman romance *Le Brut* (1515), written by Wace, was founded on the chronicle of Geoffrey of Monmouth. The *Roman de Rose*, by the same author, is a fabulous history of the Norman dukes

In the end of the twelfth and beginning of the thirteenth centuries, great numbers of French metrical romances were written in England and Normandy, principally on the subject of Arthur and his knights of the round table, or on classical subjects, such as the Trojan war. The metrical romance was followed by the prose romance, which was founded on the same cycles of events and characters, but with great additions of adventures, machinery, &c. The prose romances were written chiefly during the thirteenth, fourteenth and fifteenth centuries, and were at first mere versions of the metrical romances. They assumed the tone of history, and pretended to the character of presenting historical facts. They may be divided into romances of chivalry, spiritual or religious romances, comic, political, pastoral, and heroic romances. The romances of chivalry, considered in reference to the personages of whom they treat, form four classes:—1. Those relating to Arthur and the knights of the round table, and their exploits against the Saxons: among these are Merlin, Sangreal, Lancelot du Lac, Artus, &c. 2. Those connected with Charlemagne and his paladins, in which the enemy against whom the heroes contend are the Saracens: these are Guerin de Monglave, Huon de Bordeaux, &c.; the latter are founded on the fabulous chronicle of Turpin, from which are borrowed the expedition of Charlemagne into Spain, the battle of Roncesvalles, &c.; the former are derived, in a great measure, from the chronicle of Geoffrey of Monmouth. 3. The Spanish and Portuguese romances contain chiefly the adventures of two imaginary families of heroes, Amadis and Palmerin: their opponents are the Turks, and the scene is often in Constantinople. (See *Amadis.*) 4. The classical romances represent the mythological or historical heroes of antiquity in the guise of romantic fiction; thus we have the *Livre de Jason*, *Vie de Hercule*, *Alexandre*, &c., in which those heroes are completely metamorphosed into modern knights. The romances of chivalry are of Anglo-Norman origin, and, though naturalized in the Spanish peninsula, did not obtain that popularity and, influence in Germany, Southern France (see *Provençal Poets*) and Italy, which they enjoyed in England, Northern France and the peninsula. Italy adopted, indeed, at a later period, the tales of Charlemagne and his peers, which form the subjects of the romantic epics of Boiardo (*Orlando Innamorato*), Pulci (*Morgante Maggiore*), and Ariosto (*Orlando Furioso*); and thus the fictitious narratives originally composed in metre, and then re-written in prose, were decorated anew with the honors of verse. (See *Italian Literature*, division *Poetry.*) The spiritual romance differed from the chivalrous in recording the deaths of martyrs and the miracles of saints, but, in point of style and composition, was not essentially different from it. Among the works of this class are the Golden Legend, the *Contes Devots* of the French, and one of the most remarkable works of fiction, the Pilgrim's Progress. (See *Bunyan.*) The comic romance was the production of a later age, when the spirit of chivalry had become extinct, and new forms of society succeeded. Rabelais, Cervantes (whose Don Quixote was the death-blow of the romances of chivalry), Mendoza (q. v.), author of *Lazarillo de Tormes*, the first romance in the style called *gusto picaresco*, Scarron (*Roman Comique*), were the principal writers of this kind of romantic composition. The political romance also forms a class by itself, to which the *Cyropedia* of Xenophon (q. v.) may be considered to belong; Barclay's *Argenis*, *Telemachus* (see *Fenelon*), and *Sethos*, are the principal works of this class. In the time of Cervantes, the pastoral romance, founded upon the Diana of Montemayor (q. v.), was prevailing to such an extent as to attract his satire. In imitation of it, D'Urfé wrote his well-known *Astrée*, which gave rise to the heroic romance of the seventeenth century. Gomberville, Calprenède and madame Scudéri composed these insipid and interminable folios, in which the heroines are all models of beauty and perfection, and the heroes live through their long-winded pages for love alone. (See, on the subject of romance in general, Dunlop's *History of Romantic Fiction;* Ellis's *Specimens of Early English Fiction;* Panizzi's *Essay on the Romantic Narrative Poetry of the Italians*, prefixed to his edition of Boiardo and Arisosto (London, 1830). See also the article *Romantic*, and the works there referred to.)

ROMANIA, RUMELIA, or RUM-ILI. This name (signifying the *country of the Romans*) is applied by the Turks to the greater part of the Turkish empire in Europe, and by European writers to that part lying south of the Balkan, comprising the ancient Macedonia, Thrace and (previous to the Greek revolution) Greece (See *Turkey in Europe.*)

ROMANIC LANGUAGES, or ROMANCE. In the countries belonging to the Western

Roman empire, where Latin had been introduced, new dialects were formed at the time of the decline and fall of the empire, from the mixture of Latin with the languages of the barbarians, by whom the countries had been overrun. These were called *Romanic* idioms, or *Romance*. In all of them Latin was the basis and chief ingredient, and from them have sprung the languages now prevalent in the South of Europe—the Italian, French, Spanish, Portuguese, and the Rhætian, or Romanic in the narrower sense. Raynouard believes in an original Romanic language, which served as a common stock to the above dialects; but A. W. von Schlegel denies this, and has investigated the matter in his *Élémens de la Grammaire de la Langue Romane avant l'An* 1000 (Paris, 1816). A further corruption of the Italian gave rise to the *lingua Franca*. (q. v.)

Romano, Giulio. (See *Giulio Romano*.)

Romantic, in æsthetics, is used as contradistinguished to *antique*, or *classic*. (See these two articles.) Christianity turned men's thoughts from the external world, and the present condition of man, which had engrossed the attention of antiquity, to his spiritual nature and future destiny; and all the works of imagination soon testified of the change. An unbounded world of imaginary beings, good and bad, beautiful and deformed, human, animal, angelic and demoniac, was created. The effect was increased by the mixture of the northern element with that of the south; for the northern mythology (q. v.) was full of supernatural, shadowy beings. A further consequence of Christianity was the giving of increased importance to the individual. The love and hatred, success and sufferings, of individual men assumed a more prominent place than had been allowed them in antiquity; the sense of personal dignity was heightened, and the longing for something better than the present world can afford, became more intense. These circumstances furnished the chief elements of romantic poetry—the poetry of the middle ages. The Greek lived in what is and was, the Christian in what is to come. So much is the spirit of romantic poetry connected with Christianity, that Jean Paul says, in his *Vorschule zur Æsthetik:* "The origin and character of the whole modern poetry is so easily to be derived from Christianity, that the romantic might be called with equal propriety the *Christian* poetry." And so much is romantic poetry impressed with the longing for something beyond the existing world, that Viennet, in his *Epître aux Muses sur les Romantiques* (Paris, 1824), says:—

C'est la mélancolie et la mysticité,
C'est l'affectation de la naïveté; W
C'est un monde idéal qu'on voit dans les nuages
Tout, jusqu'au sentiment, n'y parle qu'en images.
C'est un je ne sais quoi dont on est transporté;
Et moins on le comprend, plus on est enchanté.

Romantic poetry first grew up in the south of Europe, as its name would naturally lead us to suppose (see *Romanic Languages*), and was imbued with the spirit of chivalry, which also had its origin there. Hence the reason why love holds so prominent a place in romantic poetry. The reader will find some remarks applicable to this subject in the article *Chivalry*, where we have attempted to trace the causes of this singular institution. The age of chivalry has passed; the chivalrous spirit has taken a different direction (Humboldt, Parry, Caillié, are our knight-errants); but the causes which produced the romantic poetry are by no means all extinct; and the poetry of our time has much more resemblance to that of the middle ages than to the Greek. The same circumstances which gave its character to the poetry of the middle ages, had a corresponding influence on the fine arts in general, and music, painting and architecture were imbued with a peculiar spirit. The magnificent Gothic cathedrals which still remain, bear witness to the aspirations which Christianity awakened, and the solemnity which it inspired. The term *romantic*, therefore, is frequently applied to modern art in general, as contradistinguished to the antique *classic* or *plastic*. (q. v.)—See the article *Middle Ages*, also the excellent work of Bouterwek, *History of Arts, Sciences*, &c.; Jean Paul's *Vorschule;* an *Essay on the Romantic Narrative Poetry of the Italians*, in Panezzi's edition of Bojardo and Ariosto, vol. i. (London, 1830), and *Storia ed Analisi degli antichi Romanzi di Cavalleria e dei Poemi Romanzeschi d'Italia con Dissertazioni sull' Origine, sugl' Instituti, sulle Ceremonie de' Cavalieri, sulle Corti d'Amore*, &c., by Giulio Ferrario (Milan, 4 vols., 1828); the last of the four volumes is a *Bibliografia dei Romanzi*, &c. *d'Italia*. See, also, our articles on the *Portuguese*, *Spanish*, and *French Literatures*.

Romanzoff, Peter Alexandrowitsch, count, a Russian general and field-marshal, born about 1730, was descended from an illustrious family, and, having entered into the army when very young, his courage and abilities soon procured him promotion. He commanded at the taking of Colberg in 1761; and in the following year the death of Peter III prevented the invasion of Holstein, which he was about to undertake at the head of 40,000 men. Catharine II made peace with the Danes, and, in 1769, employed Romanzoff against the Turks. He succeeded prince A. Galitzin, as commander-in-chief, in 1770, and obtained many advantages over the enemy in that and the following years, previously to the treaty into which he forced the grand vizier to enter, in his camp at Kainardgi, in July, 1774. He soon after set out for his government of the Ukraine. Romanzoff served against the Turks in the war which began in 1787. He died in December, 1796.

ROMANZOFF, Nich. (See *Rumjanzoff.*)

ROMBERG, Bernard and Andrew; two distinguished German musicians, sons of two brothers, who were likewise known in their time. The former is the first violoncello player now living, and was born in 1770: the latter, chiefly known as a performer on the violin and a composer, was born in 1767, both in the territory of Münster. Both appeared as early as their seventh year in concerts. After many journeys and various appointments, they met in Paris, 1800, where they composed jointly for the *théâtre Feydeau* the opera *Don Mendoza.* In 1801, Bernard was appointed professor of the violoncello in the Paris conservatory. In 1805, he received an appointment in the royal chapel at Berlin, which he subsequently resigned. He now lives in Berlin.—*Andrew* settled in Hamburg, and has produced many beautiful compositions, and in his instrumental pieces resembles Haydn. He died at Gotha, in 1821.

ROME (Roma), the *eternal city,* as it is often called, with which almost every thing great and memorable that has happened in Europe for 2500 years has been connected, and which, first with the sword, and afterwards with the more powerful arms of religious faith, ruled a large portion of the European world for centuries, and saw people of all climes bend before its majesty, is now only the shadow of its former greatness. Ancient Rome was situated nearly on the site of the modern city, in Latium, on several hills (whence the poetical appellation of the *seven-hilled city*), on both sides of the river Tiber, not far from the Mediterranean sea; but the principal part of the city lay upon the eastern side of the river. Here was situated the Pincian mount, and on the river lay the Campus Martius, the Capitoline hill, the Roman forum, and mount Aventine. The Quirinal, Palatine, and Cœlian hills, formed a second range eastward of the preceding, extending from north to south; the Viminal and Esquiline a third. On the other side of the Tiber lay the Vatican mount and Janiculum. This region was inhabited before the foundation of Rome. The city of Pallantium, built by some Greek colonists on the Capitoline mount, was perhaps still in existence when Romulus and Remus led a colony thither from Alba Longa; so that this city was only extended, and Rome Proper was not entirely new. The new city probably derived its name, not from its founder (who was, perhaps, called *Romulus* from it), but from the river, which, as Servius informs us, was anciently called *Rumon.* The derivation from the Greek ῥωμη (strength) is an absurdity, and of late origin. Two different epochs are assigned for the foundation of Rome. According to Cato it was built 752, according to Varro, 754 years before Christ. The latter date is generally adopted. The founding of the city commenced with ceremonies borrowed from the Etrurians. Romulus traced a square furrow round the Palatine hill with a plough drawn by two white cattle, and caused a wall of earth to be thrown up in the direction of the furrow. The interior was filled with huts.—The history of Rome is divided into three periods, in the first of which Rome was a kingdom, in the second a republic, and in the third an empire.—I. From the foundation of the city to the year 245, Rome was a monarchy. Romulus was chosen the first king of the new city. He adopted the Etrurian emblems of royalty—twelve lictors (q. v.); but his power, and that of his successors, was so circumscribed, that Rome was, even then, in reality, a free state. A sort of municipal constitution was formed, probably after the model of that of the mother city. The principal points of this constitution are the creation and constitution of the senate; the origin and permanent establishment of the patricians, or hereditary nobility; the division of the people into classes, and the different kinds of popular assemblies (*comitia*) founded thereupon; the religious institutions; and, finally, the domestic relations of clientship, marriage, and particularly of the power of a father. Romulus, the leader of the colony (from A. U. 1 to 37), increased the number of the citizens by the establishment of an asylum, and by the incorporation of a part of the Sabines

Numa Pompilius (39—82) founded the Roman state-religion; Tullus Hostilius (82—114) conquered Alba, and laid the foundation for the supremacy of Rome over Latium; Ancus Martius (114—138) built Ostium; Tarquinius Priscus (138—176) carried on a war with the Etrurian confederacy; Servius Tullius (176—220), the ablest of the kings, placed Rome at the head of the Latin confederacy, and divided the nation, according to property, into six classes, upon which the *comitia centuriata* and the census were founded; the seventh and last king, Tarquin the Proud (220—245), aspired to absolute power, and was expelled on account of his tyranny. The constitution was then remodelled (509 B. C.). (See *Romulus*, *Numa*, and *Tarquinius*.) Even at this period, we can perceive in the Romans a manly, free, bold and ambitious people. Agriculture and war were their chief occupations. In private life, simplicity of manners and pleasures prevailed.—II. Rome as a republic, from 245 to 727 A. U.—*First period.* The royal power, with the same indefiniteness as it had been exercised by the kings, was committed to two consuls, chosen annually. At the commencement of the new government, Rome had to sustain a contest with the Etrurians and Latins for its freedom. The oppressions of the patricians, who arrogated the whole power to themselves, exasperated the plebeians, and produced, in the year 261, the establishment of tribunes of the people (*tribuni plebis*), who were to protect their rights and liberties against the encroachments of the nobility. A protracted contest arose between the patricians and the guardians of the plebeians, the principal points of which were as follows:—(*a.*) The tribunes, in their accusation of Coriolanus, claimed the right of bringing individual patricians before the tribunal of the people, and thus gave rise to the *comitia tributa*, so fatal to the nobility; (*b.*) they demanded that the lands taken from the neighboring states should be distributed among the poorer people, and thus gave rise to the contests relative to the agrarian laws (*leges agrariæ*); (*c.*) the tribune Publius Volero extended the prerogatives of the *comitia tributa*, and gave them the choice of the tribunes; (*d.*) the tribune Caius Terentius Arsa endeavored to circumscribe the consular power by the formation of a code of laws. (See *Twelve Tables*, and *Appius Claudius*.) Although the new laws defined the legal relations of all citizens, yet the government of the state remained in the hands of the aristocracy, which was kept totally distinct from the plebeians by the prohibition of intermarriage. This prohibition gave rise to new contests, which ended in its abolition. The plebeians likewise obtained, eighty years after, a participation in the honors of the consulship. During these disputes, the office of censor was established. Meanwhile, Rome was constantly engaged in petty wars and quarrels with the neighboring states. That the population might not diminish, freedmen, and even prisoners of war, were admitted into the number of citizens. Rome became altogether a military state; pay was introduced into the Roman armies, which rendered it necessary to impose higher taxes. The city was, at this time, reduced to the brink of destruction by the Senonian Gauls, who captured and reduced it to ashes (A. U. 365). Camillus (q. v.), however, the savior of Rome, restored it from its ruins. The first plebeian consul was elected in the year 388, and the plebeians soon participated in all offices—in the dictatorship, in 398; in the censorship, in 403; in the pretorship, in 417; and in the priesthood, in 454 (300 B. C.). A complete political equality of patricians and plebeians existed at the end of this period; internal contests ceased, and, in the same proportion, the power of the state abroad increased, and the splendid period of conquests began. During this period, the manners of the Romans were characterized by the ancient simplicity and rudeness: science and the fine arts were as yet unknown to them; but useful arts, commerce (a treaty of commerce was concluded with the Carthaginians in 409), navigation, and mechanic arts, were cultivated. Agriculture was still the chief source of national wealth.—The first years of the *second period* were yet marked by contests between the plebeians and patricians. Rome was also visited by the plague, which gave rise to the introduction of theatrical shows from Etruria. The Romans now gained several victories over the Gauls, in which Titus Manlius Torquatus (see *Manlius*) rendered himself conspicuous. Two laws settled the rate of interest in favor of debtors. From an alliance which had been concluded a few years before with the Samnites (q. v.), a formidable war between the two nations broke out in 411, which lasted till 464, opened the way for the subjugation of all Italy, and laid the foundation of the future greatness of Rome. This war was the heroic age of the Romans; it taught them tactics; it settled their relations with their neighbors, the Latins and Etrurians, the former being completely reduced, and the latter repeatedly humbled; and brought the Romans sometimes into friendly and sometimes into hostile contact with the distant Lucanians, Apulians and Umbrians. In this period, the principles of their policy towards conquered nations were also developed. After the subjugation of the Samnites, the Romans attempted to secure their authority in Lower Italy, in consequence of which the Tarentines called to their aid (A. U. 473) Pyrrhus (q. v.), king of Epirus, who, notwithstanding his knowledge of the Macedonian art of war, was finally worsted, and obliged (479) to evacuate Italy. Tarentum fell into the hands of the Romans in 482, and soon after all Lower Italy. The fame of Rome extended even to Egypt, the king of which, in 481, sent an embassy to seek for the friendship of the Romans. Authority was maintained among the conquered people chiefly by the establishment of colonies of Roman citizens, who served as garrisons in those cities in which they were placed. Each colony had its own constitution, similar to that of Rome. This colonial system gradually embraced all Italy. For convenience of communication, great military roads were laid out in different directions. Some of the Italian cities and people enjoyed all the rights of Roman citizens (*municipia*); others had the rights of colonies (*jus coloniarum*); the others were either allies (*socii*) or subjects (*dedititii*). The latter were governed by prefects sent from Rome. Rome had already a navy, and the office of *duumviri navales* was instituted for the general management of naval affairs. The judiciary was improved by the appointment of the pretors (q. v.), and the police by that of *curule ædiles* and the *triumviri capitales*. Learning and the arts now began to appear. Fabius Pictor introduced the art of painting into Rome, Lucius Papirius Cursor brought (461) the first dial; and Spurius Carvilius caused a statue of Jupiter to be cast. With the worship of Æsculapius the science of medicine came to Rome; the works of Appius, and the temple of Concord by Camillus, prove the progress of architecture. But by the side of noble specimens of morality, temperance, integrity and patriotism, individual examples of luxury, effeminacy and degeneracy already began to appear.—In the *third period*, Rome made the first advances to the dominion of the world. She maintained, in three wars, a desperate struggle with Carthage, and destroyed her rival. (See *Carthage, Hannibal, Fabius, Scipio, Masinissa*, &c.) The first war with Carthage was made for the possession of Sicily and the dominion of the sea; it lasted twenty-three years (from 489 to 511 of the building of the city), and ended with the expulsion of the Carthaginians from Sicily. Rome, made arrogant by success, then deprived them of the island of Sardinia, in the time of peace (517). She next humbled the piratical Illyrians, on the Adriatic sea, and thus appeared as the friend of Greece. Corcyra, Apollonia, and other Greek cities, put themselves under the protection of Rome; the Achæans, Ætolians and Athenians emulated each other in expressions of gratitude. While Carthage endeavored to indemnify herself in Spain for her former losses, and was compelled by the Romans to promise not to pass the Iberus (Ebro), a bloody war broke out with the Cisalpine Gauls, which continued for six years, and resulted in the foundation of the Roman dominion in the north of Italy (about 222 B. C.). Then began the second Punic war. Hannibal commenced the attack, and made Italy the theatre of the war. It continued from 536 to 553. After many bloody battles, Carthage was subdued; but Rome, notwithstanding her great loss of men and the devastation of Italy, came out of the war more powerful than she had entered it, with an acquisition of foreign territory and the dominion of the sea. Without any change of the form of the constitution, the senate had now acquired an almost absolute power. The ambition of universal dominion already inspired the nation. At the end of the second Punic war, Sicily, Sardinia, Corsica, and a part of Spain, and Cisalpine Gaul, were Roman provinces; Carthage was entirely dependent upon Rome. On the other hand, the kingdom of Macedonia in the East, with the Grecian republics, composed a political system, very complicated in itself, but first brought into connexion with Rome after the Illyrian war, and the connexion of Philip II with Hannibal. Of the three powers of the first rank,—Syria, Macedonia and Egypt,—the two first were allied against the latter, which was on friendly terms with Rome. The powers of the second rank—the Ætolian league, the kings of Pergamus, the republic of Rhodes, and other smaller states, such as Athens—were already allies of Rome, and had been leagued with her against Philip (543); the Achæan confederacy, on the contrary, was attached to the Macedonian interest. Hardly was the peace made with Carthage, when the war broke out with Philip of Macedonia. In the beginning of this war, the Romans were unfortunate, till Titus Quinctius Flaminius, by his policy and military talents, laid the foundation for the power of Rome in the East. By the decisive battle of Cynocephale (557), Philip lost his naval superiority and his influence over Greece, whose dependence upon Rome was secured by Quinctius granting her freedom. Roman deputies, such as retained Carthage and Numidia in subjection, exercised a supervision in Greece and Macedonia, and interfered in the domestic policy of these states. To the Greeks, particularly to the proud Ætolians, this was the more intolerable, as the Roman army remained in their country three years. The peace with Philip contained the seeds of a greater war with Antiochus, from whom Rome demanded the Grecian cities which Philip had possessed in Asia, and which Antiochus had now occupied. The difficulties began in 558, when Antiochus took possession of the Thracian Chersonese: they were increased by Hannibal's flight to the court of that prince (559), and soon broke out into a formal war, in the conduct of which Antiochus and Hannibal did not agree, the former being unwilling to adopt decisive measures. Antiochus, defeated by sea and land, found himself, after the battle of Magnesia (564), forced to conclude a peace, which obliged him to retire behind the Taurus, and made him altogether dependent upon Rome. At the same time, bloody wars were carried on in Spain and Upper Italy. In 569, the troubles with Philip broke out anew, because he had made some small conquests; but the negotiations which were entered into with his son Demetrius, and the death of Philip (which took place in 575), delayed the war till 582. The war with Perseus of Macedon (q. v.), the son of Philip, terminated in the total subjection of the kingdom by the victory of Paulus Æmilius, at Pydna. The conquest of Egypt, by Antiochus Epiphanes, was prevented by the decision of Popilius, the Roman ambassador. After the conquest of Macedonia, Rome openly pursued her plan of universal dominion, and spared no means for attaining it. The division of Egypt was accomplished, and the protection of Syria assumed, which country was thenceforth rendered defenceless. After unparalleled oppressions, Carthage was now to be destroyed. This was accomplished in the third Punic war, which lasted from 604 to 608, when the proud Carthage was conquered (146 B. C.). At the same time, a new war was carried on in Macedonia, against Andriscus, who had placed himself at the head of the disaffected, but who, in 606, submitted to Metellus. Then commenced the Achæan war, the object of which was the dissolution of the Achæan league. Mummius terminated this war in 608 (146 B. C.), by the destruction of Corinth; Greece and Macedonia were reduced to Roman provinces. Thus had Rome, within the space of 118 years, made herself mistress of the world. The Roman tactics had now become so perfect, that no phalanx could withstand the legions. But the Romans were, as yet, unskilled in naval warfare, and the younger Africanus was the first who carried the art of conducting a siege to some perfection. Out of Italy, Rome occupied, under the name of provinces, Hither and Thither Spain (neither of which was entirely reduced), Africa (the territory of Carthage), Sicily, Sardinia, Corsica, Liguria, Cisalpine Gaul, Macedonia and Achaia. Not only individual opulence, but the public revenue, was greatly increased. The finances of Rome were conducted with the strictest regularity. With the wealth, the cultivation and refinement of the Romans also increased. Their first poets appeared, and the first regular dramas were now exhibited in Rome. Learning flourished after the wars in Greece and Asia. Lucilius wrote satires, and Fabius Pictor and Cato composed the annals of Roman history. The language was developed. The calculation of solar and lunar eclipses, and the construction of water-clocks and of more accurate sun-dials, became known to the Romans. In the fine arts the Romans were, as yet, barbarians. After the second Punic war, the ancient purity and simplicity of manners gradually declined. At funerals, the cruel combats of gladiators were exhibited; immense sums were spent in public shows; and licentiousness began to prevail. Even in this period, laws were enacted against luxury, and the shameless *bacchanalia* were prohibited in 568 —*Fourth period.* The wars in Spain, particularly against the Celtiberians and Lusitanians, were prosecuted with vigor. In the peasant Viriathus, the Romans found a formidable enemy. The rapacity of the proconsul Licinius Lucullus (603), and of the pretor Sulpicius Galba (604), caused the war to break out with renewed fury, under the conduct of Viriathus. After his assassination (614), Lusitania was reduced; but, on the other hand, the Numantines compelled the consul Mancinus to a disadvantageous treaty. (See *Numantia.*) Scipio terminated this war in 621; but Northern Spain still remained unsubdued. In the same year, the Romans received from Attalus the kingdom of Pergamus, in Asia, by bequest, and maintained their claims to it against Aristonicus. With this acquisition, foreign wars ceased for a time; but Rome was agitated with internal commotions, which finally broke out into bloody civil wars. The unlimited power of the senate had created a hateful family aristocracy, which the tribunes of the people resisted, and which produced contests between the aristocratic and democratic parties more fatal than the former disputes between the patricians and plebeians. The contest began with Tiberius Gracchus (q. v.), who, for the relief of the lower orders of the people, demanded a juster distribution of the public lands. He was killed in an insurrection of the people; but the agrarian law remained in full force, and the disturbances still continued. Although the return of Scipio Æmilianus gave new strength to the aristocracy, yet the general insurrection of slaves in Sicily (620—623) was favorable to the democratic party. The tribunes of the people obtained a voice and a seat in the senate: they also endeavored to make their reëlection legal. The disturbances were quieted for a time by removing the chiefs of the popular party, under honorable pretences. During these events, the foundation of the Roman power in Transalpine Gaul was laid by Marcus Fulvius Flaccus, in 626, and as early as 632 the southern part was made a Roman province. In 631, Caius Gracchus was chosen tribune of the people; he renewed the agrarian laws with severer provisions, and gave rise to more dangerous excitements than his brother Tiberius. He endeavored to make the equestrian order a counterpoise to the power of the senate, and attempted to strengthen his party by the admission of the whole population of Italy to the rights of Roman citizens; but the senate succeeded in depriving him of the favor of the people, and in effecting his ruin. In 633, he was killed in a riot, and the aristocracy took advantage of their victory to abolish the agrarian laws. On the other hand, difficulties arose with the Italian allies, who demanded the privileges of citizenship, and the breaking out of the war was prevented merely by accident. These factions had an injurious effect upon morals, which neither the strictness of the censorship, nor the sumptuary laws, nor the laws against celibacy (which were already become necessary), could control. Rapacity was the prevailing vice of the great, and licentiousness that of the multitude. The enormous wealth of the public treasury produced public luxury, which was soon followed by private luxury, that found ample means for its gratification in the extortions of the governors, and in the presents of foreign princes. The influence of bribery was particularly apparent in the war against Jugurtha (636—648), which was even protracted by it. The end of this bloody war opened to a plebeian, Caius Marius, the way to the highest dignities of the state, by which the aristocracy received a severe blow. He succeeded in overturning the constitution, while the war with the Cimbri, during a new servile war in Sicily, rendered him indispensable to the state. He was consul four years successively. At length, in 654, the storm burst over him, and, after a long struggle, he retired to Asia. (See *Marius.*) From 656 to 663, quiet prevailed, and the provinces enjoyed a short rest. The power of the equestrian order became a new source of abuses. It held the senate in dependence, and could easily oppose all reforms in the provinces, since it had not only the control of the judiciary, but farmed the revenues of the state. The contest which arose between the knights and the senate concerning the judicial power, was ruinous to the state. The knights were deprived of a part of their judicial power by Lucius Drusus, the tribune; but the manner in which this was effected kindled the dangerous social war. He proposed to admit the allies to the rights of citizenship, but his proposition excited so much dissatisfaction that he was murdered. The people of Italy, from the Liris to the Adriatic, now took up arms with the design of throwing off the Roman yoke. The danger was great. The *fasces* were committed to Lucius Julius Cæsar and Publius Rutilius Lupus, and under these consuls were formed the greatest generals of the time—Cn. Pompeius, C. Marius, Cæpio, C. Perpenna, Valerius Messala, Cornelius Sylla, T. Didius, P. Lentulus, P. Licinius, and M. Marcellus. But there were also men of distinguished talents on the other side; and, after the war had been carried on from 653 to 656, with various success and the greatest fury, it was terminated only by conceding the claims of the allies; and Rome thus ceased to be regarded as the exclusive head of the state. The devastations of Mithridates (q. v.), and the disputes between Sylla and Marius, made this concession necessary. The quarrel between these two distinguished Romans commenced at the beginning of the first Pontic war. (See *Marius*, and *Sylla.*) The senate having given the chief command to Sylla, Marius united himself (656) with the tribune Sulpicius, for the purpose of displacing him from this office. But Sylla, at the head of his army, drove Marius from Rome, restored the dignity of the senate, and hastened to his province, after he had, in order to gain the people, raised his adversary, Cinna, to the consulship. The consequence was, that, during this war (656—659), a new anarchy prevailed in Rome, which became still more terrible after the death of Marius. In 671, the banished Sylla returned to Rome: a terrible civil war was the result, which was ended, in 673, by Sylla's elevation to the dictatorship. Sylla endeavored to overthrow the democratic party. The attempt of Æmilius Lepidus to oppose him was without success. The war which broke out in Spain, under Sertorius, a leader of the democratic party, was more serious, and was concluded, in 682, by his assassination. At the same time, the frightful war of the gladiators and slaves broke out in Italy, and a new and more dangerous war began with Mithridates in Asia. The pirates were so powerful at this time, that they rendered the seas unsafe with their fleets, and threatened Rome with a famine. Pompey (q. v.) saved the state, however, by conquering first the pirates, and afterwards Mithridates. Asia Minor, Syria and Crete were made Roman provinces; Armenia, Cappadocia, the Bosphorus and Judea became wholly dependent upon Rome, and the Thracian power was broken. No foreign enemy could any longer be dangerous to Rome; but new commotions were constantly agitating her. Some attempts to overturn the constitution of Sylla were indeed frustrated; but, even in 679, Opimius carried a law providing that the tribunes should not be excluded from higher offices, and that the judicial tribunals should be restored to the knights; and Pompey and Crassus, during their consulship in 684, nearly annihilated it by completely restoring the tribunitial power. By this victory of the democratic party, a kind of oligarchy was established, and powerful individuals obtained the direction of affairs. The conspiracy of Catiline (see *Catiline*) had for its object the overthrow of the existing powers, and the elevation of a party from the dregs of the people. Cicero defeated it, and restored internal tranquillity. Nevertheless, the state continued to decline; luxury, introduced by the immense wealth of Asia, had destroyed all the remains of ancient virtue. Selfishness and ambition were the ruling passions of the great. Pompey, who had now returned from Asia, found in the severe Cato a superior, and attached himself to the popular party, in order to prosecute his designs with their assistance Cæsar's return from Lusitania (694) gave affairs a different turn. He formed with Pompey and Crassus the first triumvirate (q. v.), as it was called, and succeeded (695) to the consulship, which prepared the way for his assumption of the dictatorship. He obtained the province of Gaul for five years, and thus gained an opportunity of making conquests and forming an army. The chiefs of the senate, Cicero and Cato, were banished by the tribune Clodius before his departure; but the triumvirate caused Cicero to be recalled by the tribune Milo, without being able to destroy the power of Clodius. Cæsar accomplished, during his administration in Gaul, the subjugation of that country (696—704). The contest which arose during his absence between himself, Pompey, and Crassus, was settled in 698 by the treaty of Lucca, by which Cæsar obtained his province for five years more, and Pompey and Crassus the consulate for the succeeding year, after which the former was to have Spain and Africa, and the latter Syria, as their respective provinces. In spite of Cato's opposition, this plan was effected; but when Crassus fell, on his expedition against the Parthians, and Pompey, instead of departing to his province, remained at the head of the republic as sole consul, with almost dictatorial power, a civil war was unavoidable. (See *Cæsar*, and *Pompey.*) Instead of obeying the decree of the senate, Cæsar passed the Rubicon, and compelled Pompey to fly from Rome. The civil war broke out, and was ended in 706 at Pharsalia. Cæsar now became dictator, with the most extensive power. His first object was the entire reduction of the party of Pompey, and the restoration of order to Italy. He was assassinated in 710; but his adversaries could not preserve the republic. In 711, a new triumvirate was formed between Octavius, Antony and Lepidus; the object of which was the annihilation of the republican party. For the manner in which they pursued this object, by proscriptions and violence, and for their subsequent divisions, until the battle of Actium rendered Octavius master of the Roman empire, see the articles *Antony*, and *Augustus*. Rome now ceased to be a republic. The principal changes which the Roman constitution underwent during this period, have already been related. Bribery and private interest governed the assemblies of the people; interest and ambition actuated the public officers. The equestrian order now gained great power and immense riches. Marius extended the military system, but discipline was destroyed. The armies fought for their generals rather than for the state. They obeyed whoever paid them. But literature made great progress. To this period belong the poets M. Pacuvius, C. Lucilius, Plautus, Terence, Lucretius and Catullus; the historians Calpurnius Piso, Porcius Cato, Rutilius Rufus, Claudius Quadrigarius, and particularly Cæsar, Sallust, Cornelius Nepos, Hirtius Pansa, &c.; Cicero, the orator and philosopher, and Terentius Varro, the learned grammarian, who likewise wrote upon agriculture. At the close of this period began the golden age of Roman literature and art. The Greeks were imitated with taste and success. Not only the Roman youths went to Greece to complete their education, but learned Grecians flocked to Rome, and were employed in education and instruction. The language reached its highest perfection, and the theatre exhibited its masterpieces. Of the philosophical sects of Greece, the schools of Epicurus and Zeno met with the greatest success. Grecian artists elevated the standard of the arts, and Rome was filled with splendid buildings and the master works of sculpture. In the time of Cæsar and Pompey, the Grecian artists Arcesilaus, Pasiteles, Zopyrus, Criton, Nicolaus Strongylion, and the great lapidary Dioscorides, resided at Rome. But the corruption of morals increased with the increase of luxury; the greatest part of the people, especially of the nobility, was sunk in debaucheries and vices of every description. Laws were of little avail; agriculture and the mechanic arts were left entirely to slaves, who were treated in the most cruel manner. The common people lived, in spite of their poverty, in idleness, and were ready to devote themselves to those who would give them largesses. Every thing was to be obtained by gold.—III. We are next to consider Rome with a monarchical government, under the Cæsars, from the foundation to the division of the empire, from the year of the city 727 to 1148 (or 395 A. D.). This period forms four divisions:—1. Octavius returned to Rome as a conqueror in 725, and for forty-three years remained at the head of the government. He was the first sovereign in Rome without adopting this title. Satisfied with the surname of Augustus (q. v.), which was given him in 727, he ruled with mildness, retaining the republican forms of government. He united in his own person the offices of consul, tribune, imperator and proconsul in all the provinces, and finally that of "*magister morum*" and *pontifex maximus*. To avoid the appearance of usurpation, he caused the supreme power to be confirmed to him from time to time. The senate acted the part of a council of state. The republican magistracies were retained, but their power was lost: on the other hand, the prefects of the city and of provisions became the most important officers, because upon them depended the public tranquillity. A city militia (*cohortes urbanæ*) and a body-guard (*cohortes prætorianæ*) were formed. The governors of the provinces were paid and limited in their power. Improvements were introduced in the financial system. The distinction between the public treasury and private purse of the emperor, naturally existed at first; but afterwards both were united. The boundaries of the empire were extended, particularly by the addition of Egypt (724), Pannonia (719), Mœsia (725), Rhætia, Vindelicia and Noricum (739), and by the complete subjugation of Northern Spain and Western Gaul (729). On the other hand, the Romans were unsuccessful against the Germans. The successor of Augustus was his step-son Tiberius (q. v.), from 767 to 790. Under him despotism was established by the tribunals of majesty (*judicia majestatis*). The servility and timidity of the senate in this matter was as criminal as the tyrannical character of the prince, who suffered himself to be guided from 776 to 784 by the monster Sejanus. His successors were Caligula (until 794) and Claudius (until 807); the former a mad tyrant, and the latter a dotard. The conquests in Britain began (796) under Claudius, and Mauritania (795), Lycia (796), Judæa (797), and Thrace (800), were declared provinces. His successor, Nero (from 807 to 821), a hypocritical tyrant, addicted to debauch and cruelty, was the last emperor of the family of Augustus. Under him the greatest part of Britain was made a Roman province, and war was successfully carried on in Armenia and against the Jews. During the disturbances which followed Nero's death, in less than two years, three persons made themselves masters of the throne by force—Galba, Otho and Vitellius. (See the articles.) This period, particularly the reign of Augustus, was the golden age of literature and the arts. Instead of politics, the distinguished men of the empire were engaged in science, and especially in polite literature: they also protected and patronised men of letters: such patrons, for example, were Mæcenas and Agrippa. Augustus and Asinius Pollio founded public libraries. In poetry, the names of Virgil, Ovid, Cornelius Gallus, Cornelius Severus, Tibullus, Propertius, Gratius Faliscus, Manilius, Horace and Phædrus are distinguished; and there were a multitude of epigrammatists. Livy and Dionysius of Halicarnassus wrote their valuable histories. Eloquence necessarily declined, but philosophy and mathematics found both admirers and cultivators. Vitruvius was celebrated on account of his knowledge of architecture, and Hyginus on account of his *Astronomicon*. As a grammarian, M. Verrius Flaccus deserves to be mentioned: geography had a Strabo, and jurisprudence Q. Antistius Labeo, C. Anteius Capito and C. Trebatius Testa. Architecture, sculpture and glyptics also flourished. After the death of Augustus, literature declined, and the style and language degenerated. M. Annæus Lucan, Valerius Flaccus and Persius Flaccus distinguished themselves, however, as poets; Velleius Paterculus, Diodorus Siculus and Valerius Maximus as historians; M. and L. Annæus Seneca as rhetoricians and philosophers; and Aurelius Cornelius Celsus as a physician. Asconius Pedianus wrote commentaries on the writings of Cicero; and in jurisprudence Masurius Sabinus, M. Cocceius Nerva, Cassius Longinus and Sempronius Proculus were eminent. The arts declined; the corruption of manners was increased by debauchery and unnatural passion; foreigners and freedmen were the confidants of the emperor; the soldiers formed a distinct order, and served not the state, but the despots whom they rendered dependent upon themselves.—2. After the fall of Vitellius, Flavius Vespasianus (823) ascended the throne. He restored the empire by introducing order into the finances, promoting public education, reviving discipline, and abolishing the tribunals of majesty. Under his government, the war with Civilis the Batavian broke out, and the conquest of Britain by Agricola was completed. Vespasian reigned till 832, his excellent son Titus till 834, and the brother and successor of the latter, Domitian, a perfect tyrant, until 849. Under his reign arose the war with Decebalus, the king of the Dacians, who stirred up the wars of the Marcomanni, Quadi and Jazyges, from 839 to 843, which proved so unfortunate to the Romans. He was murdered, and was followed by several celebrated sovereigns. Nerva (until 851) abolished the reign of terror, diminished the taxes, and encouraged industry; Trajan (until 870) restored, as far as possible, a free constitution, and enlarged the empire by fortunate wars against the Dacians, Armenians and Parthians; and Adrian (to 891) improved the internal condition of the empire, and the discipline of the soldiery. Rome was happy under the peaceful government of Antoninus Pius (until 914); under that of Marcus Aurelius, or Antoninus, the philosopher (until 933), great disasters and bloody wars with the Catti, Parthians, and especially the Marcomanni, disturbed the empire; but his wisdom healed all wounds. With him (180, A. D.) ended the prosperity of Rome. The constitution of the state was now a limited monarchy founded upon civil freedom. The offices of state became in part mere titles of honor; and, on the other hand, a great number of court offices were instituted, which were continually usurping power. Italy was divided into four provinces, which were governed by men of consular rank. The *edictum perpetuum* effected great changes in the administration of justice, and the imperial commands were continually encroaching upon the decrees of the senate. In the military department, likewise, great alterations had taken place, particularly a different division of the troops. Literature, particularly poetry and eloquence, were on the decline; but the emperors endeavored to promote learning, by the collection of libraries, by the erection of public halls, and by supporting instructers. The poets of this period are Silius Italicus, Papinius Statius, Juvenal and Martial; the historians are Tacitus, Appian, Florus, Justin, Curtius, Arrian, Suetonius and Plutarch; the principal orator was Pliny the younger; Epictetus and Marcus Aurelius were distinguished as Stoic philosophers and besides these there were many New Platonists; Galen and Scribonius Largus were the chief physicians. Frontinus wrote upon hydraulic architecture. Pliny the elder upon the productions of nature and art, Columella upon agriculture and gardening, and Polyænus and Frontinus upon military stratagems; Gellius was celebrated for his knowledge of antiquity; in geography Ptolemy and Antoninus, author of a journal of travels to Britain, were eminent; and Quinctilian was distinguished in rhetoric: Salvius Julianus, Aburnus Valens, Sextus Cæcilius Africanus, Terentius Clemens, Vinidius Verus, and Junius Mauritianus, were celebrated jurists; and Sextus Pomponius, C. Velusius Mæcianus, Q. Cervidius Scævola, and Ulpius Marcellus, were yet more distinguished authors on the subject of jurisprudence.—3. From this time the decline of the Roman empire was constantly accelerated. Commodus, the son of Marcus Aurelius (from 933 to 945) was a monster. He purchased peace of the Marcomanni, and his generals fought successfully in Dacia and Britain. Great commotions followed his death. Pertinax reigned only two months, and Marcus Didius Julianus, who purchased the empire, as the highest bidder, for an equal period; the army in Illyria then chose Septimius Severus emperor, and the one in Syria, Pescenninus Niger. The former maintained his claims, and reigned till 965. He kept in check the Parthians and Britons. Caracalla (till 970) was a tyrant; his murderer, Macrinus, succeeded, and reigned till 971; Heliogabalus, a shameless voluptuary, till 975; and Alexander Severus, an excellent prince, till 988. After the latter, his murderer, Maximin the Thracian (till 991), exercised a military despotism. While he was carrying on the war in Germany with success, the senate chose the elder Gordian emperor, and, after the death of Gordian, Maximus Pupienus and Clodius Balbinus. The pretorians murdered them, and raised the younger Gordian to the throne; and he reigned until 997, and Marcus Julius Philippus till 1002. Then succeeded Trajanus Decius (slain by the Goths, 1004); Trebonianus Gallus (till 1006); Æmilius Æmilianus (three months); Pulius Licinius Valerianus (1011); Publius Licinius Gallianus (until 1021), under whom almost all the governors raised themselves to the rank of emperors, and the Germans and Persians triumphed over the Romans; M. Aurelius Claudius (until 1023), who overthrew the Alemanni and Goths; Domitius Aurelianus (until 1028), who recovered all the lost countries, took Zenobia prisoner, and voluntarily evacuated Dacia; M. Claudius Tacitus (until 1029); Probus (until 1035), a warlike and prudent prince; M. Aurelius Carus (until 1036); and Marcus Aurelius Numerianus (until 1037), an accomplished and gentle prince: Dioclesian succeeded him (until 1058); he appointed M. Valerius Maximian his colleague, and united Caius Galerius, Maximian associating Flavius Constantius Chlorus, in the empire, as assistants: they distributed the empire among themselves, without dividing it, and not only resisted the barbarians, but extended the empire in the East to the Tigris: the two emperors retired from the government (1058), and Galerius succeeded in the East, and Constantius in the West. Galerius appointed two assistants (Cæsars), Flavius Severus and Maximin. Constantius died in 1059, and left his dominions to his son Constantine, who, in 1076, succeeded to the whole empire, by a series of perfidious artifices. In this period, the constitution remained nominally the same, but a military despotism controlled every thing. The soldiery made and unmade emperors. In the administration of justice, the emperors decided by their constitutions, so called. The corruption of manners, the weakness of the empire, oppressive taxes, the poverty of the people, the tyranny of the rulers, and the encroachments of the barbarians, continually increased. Literature and taste declined; language and style degenerated. Some individuals studied the ancients, and took them for models. Among the poets, Terentianus Maurus and Nemesianus are worthy of notice; among the historians, Dio Cassius and Herodian are of acknowledged merit; and the *Scriptores Historiæ Augustæ*, Spartianus, Capitolinus, Trebellius Pollio, Vopiscus, Lampridius, and Vulcatius Gallicanus, must be mentioned. Apuleius wrote romances, and Ælian compiled anecdotes. Mamertinus, Nagarius, Magnus Ausonius, &c., panegyrists of the emperors, and Latinus Drepanius, Eumenius and Pacatus composed rhetorical works. Latinus Solinus the grammarian wrote an abridgment of Pliny's Natural History, under the title of *Polyhistor;* Serenus Samonicus a didactic poem upon medicine; Palladius a work upon agriculture; and Censorinus the grammarian a learned chronological work *De Die natali*. Papinian, Ulpian, Julius Paulus and Herennius Modestinus were eminent jurists. Art was extinct. The Christian religion was already widely extended.—4. Constantine the Great (reigned until 1099) embraced Christianity, in 1064, from political motives, and it thus became the predominant religion. The imperial residence was removed to Constantinople: the empire was divided anew, and the civil and military power were separated. After the death of Constantine, his three sons, Constantine, Constantius and Constans, divided the empire, until Constantius, in 1106, united the whole, after a war of twelve years' duration. He reigned first with the Cæsar Constantius Gallus, and afterwards with the Cæsar Julian, until 1114, maintaining constant wars with the barbarians. His successor was Julian (until 1116), an able and virtuous prince, called the *Apostate*, because he relapsed into heathenism. After him, Jovian reigned until 1117, Valentinian I, in the West, until 1128, Valens, in the East, until 1131, in whose reign the Huns entered Europe; Gratian and Valentinian II succeeded in the West; the former reigned until 1136, the latter until 1145, and Theodosius until 1147 in the East, and until 1148 over the whole empire. He divided the empire (395 A. D.), which henceforth remained separated, into the Eastern and Western Roman empires. (See the history of the former under the head *Byzantine Empire*, and of the latter under *Western Empire*.) To this period belong the following authors: Claudian the poet, Ammianus Marcellinus, Aurelius Victor, Eutropius, and Zosimus, historians. Symmachus was celebrated as a rhetorician, and Themistius as a sophist. Vegetius wrote upon the science of war, and Macrobius was a successful follower of Varro and Gellius. Victor and Sextus Rufus wrote upon the topography of Rome. From this time the Roman language continually degenerated by the intermixture of barbarous words, and the corruption of taste, until at length it wholly disappeared in the Romanic languages, and all learning perished. For the earlier periods of Roman history, see Niebuhr's *Roman History*, Ferguson's *History of the Roman Republic*, Wacksmuth's *Early History of Rome* (in German, 1819). For the history of the empire, see the works of Tillemont, Crevier, Gibbon, and that of Hübler (3 vols., Freyburg, 1803).

Ancient Rome, although visited for a thousand years by various calamities, is still the most majestic of cities. The charm of beauty and dignity still lingers around the ruins of ancient, as well as the splendid structures of modern Rome, and brilliant recollections of every age are connected with the monuments which meet the passing traveller at every step. The characteristics of ancient and modern times are no where so distinctly contrasted as within the walls of Rome. Ancient Rome was built upon several hills, which are now scarcely discoverable, on account of the vast quantities of rubbish with which the valleys are filled. (See the preceding historical sketch.) The eastern bank of the Tiber was so low as to subject the city to frequent inundations. The extent and population were very different at different times. We speak here of the most flourishing period. Vopiscus, in his life of Aurelian, relates that the circumference of the city, after its last enlargement by that emperor, was 50,000 paces, for which we must probably read 15,000, as Pliny estimates the circumference, just before the reign of Aurelian, at 13,000 paces, and the accounts of modern travellers agree with this statement. The inhabitants at that time may have amounted to about 3,000,000. The number of inhabitants enjoying the rights of citizenship was never more than 300,000. Romulus surrounded the city with a wall, or rather with an earthen mound. Of the four gates which he built—the Porta Carmentalis, the Pandana or the Saturnia, the Roman gate, and the Mugionia—the Carmentalis alone remains. The wall ran from mount Palatine, at the foot of mount Aventine, to the Tiber; one part of it then extended between the Tiber and the Capitoline hill, and on the other side separated the Palatine from the Cœlian, Esquiline, Viminal, and Quirinal hills, and finally terminated at the capitol. The second, or the Servian wall, was much more extensive, and embraced all the above mentioned hills, on the southern and eastern sides; ran round under mount Aventine to the Tiber; thence passed to the west side of the river, where, being continued in the form of a triangle, as far as the summit of Janiculum, it separated this from the other hills; and then, proceeding to the southern end of the island of the Tiber in a direct course, embraced the whole body of the buildings beyond the river. On the north side of the city, the old walls of Romulus were mostly preserved; but the old wall terminated at the summit of Quirinalis, while the Servian extended to its easternmost extremity, and then ran round the other hills towards the east. The Pincian hill, Campus Martius, and the Vatican hill, therefore, lay entirely outside of it. The third, or Aurelian wall, likewise included all these parts. It ran from the northeastern extremity of Quirinalis, northwardly; embraced the Campus Martius, which it separated from the Pincian hill; extended beyond the latter to the river; enclosed, beyond the river, the Vatican, in a large bend; and then joined the old wall, which reached to the summit of Janiculum; so that the island of the Tiber was now contained within the limits of the city. In so large a circuit the number of gates must have been considerable. Pliny enumerates thirty-seven, of which several yet remain, but under different names. Ancient Rome had several bridges, of which some are still passable. The lowest and oldest bridge was the Pons Sublicius, which led from mount Aventine into the valley below Janiculum, and is no longer standing. The second led from the forum to Janiculum, and was called Pons Senatorius, because the solemn procession of the senate passed over it, when the Sybilline books were to be carried from Janiculum. It was the first stone bridge in Rome, and still exists in ruins under the name of Mary's bridge (Ponte Rotto.) Two bridges led to the island in the Tiber, one from the east, and the other from the west side; the former was called Pons Fabricius (now Ponte di Quattro Capi), and the latter Pons Cestius (now Bartholomew's bridge). A fourth bridge, Pons Janiculensis (now Ponte Sisto), led from the Campus Martius, near the theatre of Marcellus, to Janiculum. The ruins of the fifth, Pons Vaticanus, or Triumphalis, may be seen near the hospital of S. Spirito, and led from the Campus Martius to the Vatican. The Ælian bridge (Pons Ælius; now the beautiful bridge of St. Angelo) led to the Moles Adriani. Beyond the wall, and above the Pincian hill, was the seventh bridge, Pons Milvius, (now Ponte Molle), built by Æmilius Scaurus, after the time of Sylla. The streets of Rome, even after the city was rebuilt under Nero, were very irregular. The public squares, of which there were a great number, were distinguished into *areæ*, squares in front of the palaces and temples; *campi*, open places, covered with grass, which served for popular assemblies, public processions, for the exercise of the youth in arms, and for the burning of the dead bodies; and *fora*, which were paved, and served either for the assembling of the people, for the transaction of public affairs, or for the sale of goods, or for ornament. Among the latter, the Forum Romanum (see *Forum*), and Campus Martius (q. v.), were the most celebrated. The earliest division of Rome was made by Servius Tullius; he divided it into four quarters, which he called Tribus urbanæ; they were the Tribus Suburbana, Collina, Esquilina and Palatina. This division continued till the reign of Augustus, who divided the city into fourteen regions, according to which ancient Rome is generally described: 1st. Porta Capena; 2d. Cœli Montium; 3d. Isis et Serapis, or Moneta; 4th. Via Sacra, afterwards Templum Pacis; 5th. Esquilina cum colle et turri Viminali; 6th. Alta Semita; 7th. Via Lata; 8th. Forum Romanum; 9th. Circus Flaminius; 10th. Palatium; 11th. Circus Maximus; 12th. Piscina Publica; 13th. Aventinus; 14th. Trans Tiberim. The temples, theatres, amphitheatres, circuses, naumachiæ, porticoes, basilicæ, baths, gardens, triumphal arches, columns, sewers, aqueducts, sepulchres, &c., are the principal public buildings and monuments. For the capitol, the citadel, and principal temple of Rome, consecrated to Jupiter Capitolinus, and the Pantheon, see the articles. Next to these, the following were the most remarkable: the temple of Æsculapius, in the island of the Tiber, which was consecrated to that god, now the church of St. Bartholomew; the temple of Antoninus and Faustina, in the Via Sacra, now the church of S. Lorenzo in Miranda; the magnificent temple of Apollo, which Augustus built of white marble, on the Palatine, in which were preserved the Sybilline books (it contained, besides many other curiosities, a splendid library, and served as a place of resort to the poets, who here recited their works); the temple of the Cæsars (Templum Cæsarum), which contained the statues of the Cæsars, the heads of all which were struck off at once by lightning; the temple of the Dioscuri, in the Forum Romanum, under the Palatine hill, opposite the church of Sta. Maria Liberatrice, built in honor of the two youths, who, in the battle of the lake Regillus, assisted the Romans in gaining the victory, and were supposed to be Castor and Pollux; the temple of the goddess Seia, under the Palatine, built by Servius Tullius, which Nero enclosed in his golden palace, and caused to be covered with transparent Cappadocian marble; the temple of the confederacy, under the name of *Templum Dianæ commune*, which the Latin cities built in union, by the persuasion of Servius Tullius, and upon a monument in which were inscribed the articles of the confederation (this temple was situated upon the Aventine hill, near the church of Sta. Prisca); the temple of Janus, upon the island of the Tiber, near the modern Sistine bridge, one of the most beautiful of ancient Rome; the temple of the Flavian family, in which Domitian was buried, still standing on the Piazza Grimana; the temple of Hercules and the Muses, built in the ninth region by Fulvius Nobilior, who placed here the images of the Muses, brought by him from Ambracia; the temple of Honor and Virtue, in the first region, built by Marcus Marcellus, and ornamented by the Marcelli with the monuments of their family; the temple of Jupiter Stator, on the declivity of the Palatine hill, and vowed by Romulus on an occasion when his soldiers began to flee; the temple of Jupiter Tonans, built by Augustus with much splendor on the slope of the Capitoline hill; the beautiful temple of the Lycaonian hill, on the island of the Tiber, which thence received the name of Lycaonia; two temples of Isis and of Serapis; the temple of Juno Moneta, built upon the spot where the house of Manlius was torn down, on the fortifications of the Capitoline hill, because the awakening of the garrison on the attack of the Gauls, was attributed to this goddess; the temple of Liberty, built by Gracchus in the thirteenth region, and restored by Asinius Pollio, who there established the first public library; the temple of Mars, on the east side of the Appian Way, before the Porta Capena, in the first region, in which the senate gave audience to generals who claimed the honor of a triumph, and likewise to foreign ambassadors (the church delle Palme stands upon its ruins); the temple of Mars Ultor, built by Augustus with great splendor, when he recovered the eagles of the legions that had been conquered by the Parthians; the splendid temple of Minerva, which Domitian built in the forum of Nerva; another temple of the same goddess, which Pompey built in the Campus Martius, and which Augustus covered with bronze; the temple of Peace, once the richest and most beautiful temple in Rome, built by Vespasian, in the Via Sacra, in the fourth region, which contained the treasures of the temple of Jerusalem, a splendid library, and other curiosities, but was burnt under the reign of Commodus; the temple of the goddess Salus, which was painted by Fabius Pictor, the first Roman painter; the temple of Saturn, built by Tarquin the younger, which was afterwards used for the treasury and the archives of Rome; the temple of the Sun, which Aurelian erected at an enormous expense, and of which some ruins still exist; several temples of Venus, and among them, particularly, the magnificent temple of Venus Genitrix, which Cæsar caused to be built to her as the origin of his family, and the temple of Venus and Roma, of which Adrian himself designed the model; the temple of Vesta, one of the oldest and most remarkable, built by Numa on the southern summit of the Palatine: in it were contained the *ancilia*, or sacred shields, and the palladium, sacred fire, &c. Of the palaces, the imperial was the most distinguished. It was built by Augustus upon the Palatine hill, and gave the name to the tenth region of the city. The front was on the Via Sacra, and before it were planted oaks. Within the palace lay the temple of Vesta, and also that of Apollo, which Augustus endeavored to make the chief temple in Rome. The succeeding emperors extended and beautified this palace. Nero burnt it, but rebuilt it, of such extent that it not only embraced all the Palatine hill, but also the plain between that and the Cœlian and Esquiline, and even a part of these hills, in its limits. He ornamented it so richly with precious stones, gold, silver, statues, paintings, and treasures of every description, that it justly received the name of *domus aurea* (golden house). The following emperors not only stripped it of its ornaments, but Vespasian and Titus caused some parts of it to be pulled down. Domitian afterwards restored the main building. In the reign of Commodus, a great part of it was burnt; but it was restored by him and his successors. In the time of Theodoric, it needed still further repairs; but this huge edifice subsequently became a ruin, and on its site now stand the Farnese palace and gardens, and the Villa Spada. Among the theatres, those of Pompey, Cornelius Balbus, and Marcellus, were the most celebrated. Pompey built that which bore his name, after his return from Greece, and adorned it with the most beautiful Grecian statues. An aqueduct brought water into every part of it. In order to protect it from destruction, he built within its precincts a splendid temple to Venus Victrix. It was capable of containing 40,000 persons. Caligula first finished it, but Tiberius had previously restored the scenes: Claudius, still later, did the same thing, and the Gothic king Theodoric caused it to be repaired. A few remains of it are yet to be distinguished near the palace Ursini. The theatre of Balbus, the favorite of Augustus, was situated in the Campus Martius. The theatre of Marcellus was built by Augustus in memory of his nephew Marcellus. It accommodated 22,000 spectators, and was repaired by Vespasian. Some beautiful ruins of it are still to be seen. Among the amphitheatres, that of Titus was the most remarkable. (See *Coliseum*; and for the circus maximus and the circus of Caracalla, see *Circus*.) Among the remaining circuses, the following deserve to be mentioned: the circus Agonalis, in the ninth region; the circus Aurelius, in the gardens of Heliogabalus, in the fifth; the circus Flaminius, in the ninth, one of the largest and most remarkable, upon the ruins of which the church of St. Caterina de' Funari and the palace Maffei now stand; the circus of Flora in the sixth region, upon the same spot which the Piazza Grimana now occupies, where the licentious *Floralia* were celebrated; lastly, the circus of Nero, in the fourteenth region, near the modern church of St. Peter; and the circus of Sallust, the ruins of which are still visible near the Colline gate. Without stopping to describe the Naumachiæ (q. v.), we will proceed to the porticoes or colonnades. Among these are the Porticus Argonautarum, also called Porticus Neptuni, Agrippæ, or Vipsanii, which Marcus Vipsanius Agrippa built in 729, and adorned with paintings, representing the history of the Argonauts: it was situated in the Campus Martius, surrounded by a laurel grove, and the marble pillars, still visible in the Piazza di Pietra, probably belonged to it; the splendid portico of Europa, in the Campus Martius, supposed to have been built by Augustus, and containing the history of Europa; the Porticus Hecatonstylon, in the ninth region, so called from its having 100 pillars; the portico of Livia, in the third region, built by Augustus, and demolished by Nero; the portico of Metellus, founded by Metellus Macedonicus, between the temple of Apollo, built by him; and that of Juno, in the ninth region, and ornamented with statues, brought by him from Macedonia; the Porticus Milliarensis, or of the thousand columns, the ruins of which are yet to be seen in the gardens of the duke of Muti; the portico of Octavia, built by Augustus; and the portico of Pola, built by Marcus Vipsanius Agrippa; the portico of Pompey, called the Corinthian, from its pillars being of that order of architecture; Pompey built it near his theatre, and ornamented it with golden tapestry: finally, the portico of the sun (*Porticus Solis*), which was built by Aurelian. Among the Basilicæ (q. v.), one of the most beautiful was the Æmilian, on the northerly side of the Forum Romanum, built by Paulus Æmilius. We will also mention the Basilica Caii, or Lucii, on the Esquiline hill, the splendid Basilica Julia, on the southern side of the Forum Romanum, built by Julius Cæsar, and the Basilica Portia, which was the oldest, and was built by Cato the Censor. Of the public baths, some of which equalled in extent large palaces, and were ornamented with still greater splendor, there have been enumerated about 22 warm, and 856 cold, besides 880 private baths. Mæcenas and Agrippa founded the first public baths, which were afterwards surpassed by those of Caracalla, and these, in their turn, by those of Dioclesian, vestiges of which remain till this day. Rome was likewise rich in magnificent gardens. The gardens of Lucullus, in the ninth region, hold the first rank; after these, the gardens of Asinius Pollio, Julius Cæsar, Mæcenas, Heliogabalus, &c. Of the triumphal arches, the most celebrated are, that of Constantine, the ruins of which are yet seen; that of Drusus, in the Appian Way, of which the modern gate of St. Sebastian is said to have been built; that of Gallienus, and those of Severus and Titus, which are yet in good preservation; the former in the Forum, and the latter in the Vicus Sandalarius. Among the columns, the most beautiful was Trajan's pillar, 118 feet in height, still standing. Instead of the statue of that emperor, which it formerly bore, Sixtus V placed upon it a statue of St. Peter, in bronze, twenty-three feet in height. The bass-reliefs, with which it is ornamented, represent the exploits of Trajan, and contain about 2500 half and whole human figures. A flight of stairs, within the pillar, leads to its summit. The *columna rostrata*, which Duillius erected in commemoration of his victory over the Carthaginian fleet, and the pillars of Antoninus and Aurelian, are still standing. The sewers (*cloacæ*), by means of which the filth and superfluous water of the city were conveyed into the Tiber, are among the most remarkable architectural works of ancient Rome; they are subterranean canals, of from ten to sixteen feet in height, and from twelve to fourteen in width, and, although constructed in the earliest ages of the city, are of such an indestructible solidity, that several earthquakes have but slightly injured them; and some parts of them are in perfect preservation. (Concerning the aqueducts of Rome, of which about twenty have been enumerated, see *Aqueduct.*) Among the magnificent sepulchral monuments, the mausoleum of Augustus and the Septizonium of Septimius Severus surpassed all others in splendor. This city was also rich in splendid private buildings, and in the treasures of art, with which not only the public places and streets, but likewise the residences and gardens of the principal citizens, were ornamented, and of which but comparatively few vestiges have survived the ravages of time. See Burton's *Antiquities of*

Rome (Oxford, 1821); Nardini's *Roma Antica* (Nibby's edition, with annotations, plans, &c., Rome, 1820, 4 vols., 8vo.); Venuti's *Descrizione topographica delle Antichità di Roma* (3d edition, with Piali's notes, Rome, 1824, 2 vols. quarto, with 72 engravings).

Modern Rome; the capital of the States of the Church, the residence of the pope, and for centuries the capital of Christendom, at present the capital of the world of the arts (41° 53′ 45″ N. lat.; 12° 28′ E. lon). It is about thirteen miles in circuit, and is divided by the Tiber into two parts. The churches, palaces, villas, squares, streets, fountains, aqueducts, antiquities, ruins,—in short, every thing proclaims the ancient majesty and present greatness of the city. Among the churches, St. Peter's is the most conspicuous, and is, perhaps, the most beautiful building in the world. Bramante began it; Sangallo and Peruzzi succeeded him; but Michael Angelo, who erected its immense dome, which is 450 feet high to the top of the cross, designed the greatest part. Many other architects were afterwards employed upon it; Maderno finished the front and the two towers. The erection of this edifice, from 1506 to 1614, cost 45,000,000 Roman crowns. Before we arrive at this beautiful temple, the eye is attracted by the beautiful square in front of it, surrounded by a magnificent colonnade by Bernini, and ornamented by an Ægyptian obelisk, together with two splendid fountains. Upon entering the vestibule, Giotto's mosaic, la Navicella, is seen. Under the portico, opposite the great door, is Bernini's great bass-relief representing Christ commanding Peter to feed his sheep; and at the ends of the portico are the equestrian statues of Constantine by Bernini, and of Charlemagne by Cornachini. The union of these master works has an indescribable effect. The harmony and proportion which prevail in the interior of this august temple are such, that, immense as it is, the eye distinguishes all the parts without confusion or difficulty. When each object is minutely examined, we are astonished at its magnitude, so much more considerable than appears at first sight. The immense canopy of the high altar, supported by four bronze pillars of 120 feet in height, particularly attracts the attention. The dome is the boldest work of modern architecture. The cross thereon is 450 feet above the pavement. The lantern affords the most beautiful prospect of the city and the surrounding country. The splendid mosaics, tombs, paintings, frescoes, works in marble, gilded bronze and stucco, the new sacristy, a beautiful piece of architecture, but not in unison with the rest, deserve separate consideration. The two most beautiful churches in Rome next to St. Peter's are the St. John's of the Lateran, and the Santa Maria Maggiore. The former, built by Constantine the Great, is the parochial church of the pope; it therefore takes precedence of all others, and is called *Omnium urbis et orbis ecclesiarum mater et caput* (the head and mother of all churches of the city and the world). In it is celebrated the coronation of the popes. It contains several pillars of granite, *verde antico*, and gilt bronze; the twelve apostles by Rusconi and Legros; and the beautiful chapel of Corsini, which is unequalled in its proportions, built by Alexander Galilei. The altar-piece is a mosaic from a painting of Guido, and the beautiful porphyry sarcophagus, which is under the statue of Clement XII, was found in the Pantheon, and is supposed to have contained the ashes of M. Agrippa. The nave of the church of Santa Maria Maggiore is supported by forty Ionic pillars of Grecian marble, which were taken from a temple of Juno Lucina: the ceiling was gilded with the first gold brought from Peru. We are here struck with admiration at the mosaics; the high altar, consisting of an antique porphyry sarcophagus; the chapel of Sixtus V, built from the designs of Fontana, and richly ornamented; the chapel of Paul V, adorned with marble and precious stones; the chapel of Sforza, by Michael Angelo; and the sepulchres of Guglielmo della Porta and Algardi. In the square before the front is a Corinthian column, which is considered a masterpiece of its kind. The largest church in Rome next to St. Peter's was the Basilica di San Paolo fuori delle Mura, on the road to Ostia, burnt a few years since. (See *Paul, Churches of St.*) The church of S. Lorenzo, without the city, possesses some rare monuments of antiquity. The church of San Pietro in Vincola contains the celebrated statue of Moses, by Michael Angelo. The church of St. Agnes, in the place Navona, begun by Rainaldi and completed by Borromini, is one of the most highly ornamented, particularly with modern sculpture. Here is the admirable relief of Algardi, representing St. Agnes deprived of her clothes, and covered only with her hair. The Basilica of St. Sebastian, before the Porta Capena, contains the statue of the dying saint, by Giorgetti, a pupil of Algardi, and the master of Bernini. Under these churches are the catacombs, which formerly served as places of burial. In the church of St. Agnes, before the Porta Pia, among many other beautiful columns, are four of porphyry, belonging to the high altar and considered the most beautiful in Rome. In a small chapel is a bust of the Savior by Michael Angelo, a masterpiece. In the church of St. Augustine, there is a picture by Raphael, representing the prophet Isaiah, and an Ascension, by Lanfranco. The monastery has a rich library, called the Angelica, and increased by the library of cardinal Passionei. The following churches also deserve to be mentioned, on account of their architecture and works of art; the churches of St. Ignatius, St. Cecilia, S. Andrea della Valle, S. Andrea del Noviziato, the Pantheon (also called la Rotonda), in which Raphael, Annibal Caracci, Mengs, &c., are interred. All the 364 churches of Rome contain monuments of art or antiquity. Among the palaces, the principal is the Vatican, an immense pile, in which the most valuable monuments of antiquity, and the works of the greatest modern masters, are preserved. Here are the museum Pio-Clementinum, established by Clement XIV, and enlarged by Pius VI, and the celebrated library of the Vatican. (q. v.) The treasures carried away by the French have been restored. Among the paintings of this palace, the most beautiful are Raphael's frescoes in the *stanze* and the *logge*. The principal oil paintings are in the *appartamento* Borgia, which also contains the Transfiguration, by Raphael. In the Sixtine chapel is the Last Judgment of Michael Angelo. The popes have chosen the palace of Monte Cavallo, or the Quirinal palace, with its extensive and beautiful gardens, for their usual residence, on account of its healthy air and fine prospect. The Lateran palace, which Sixtus V had rebuilt, by Fontana, was changed, in 1693, into an alms-house. Besides these, the following are celebrated: the palace della Cancelleria, the palace de' Conservatori, the palace of St. Mark, the buildings of the academy, &c. Among the private palaces, the Barberini is the largest; it was built by Bernini, in a beautiful style. Here are the Magdalen of Guido, one of the finest works of Caravaggio, the paintings of the great hall, a masterpiece of Peter of Cortona, and other valuable paintings. Of works of sculpture, the Sleeping Fawn, now in Munich, was formerly here; the masterly group representing Atalante and Meleager, a Juno, a sick Satyr, by Bernini, the bust of cardinal Barberini, by the same artist, and the busts of Marius, Sylla and Scipio Africanus, are in this palace. The library is calculated to contain 60 000 printed books and 9000 manuscripts; a cabinet of medals, bronzes, and precious stones, is also connected with the library. The Borghese palace, erected by Bramante, is extensive, and in a beautiful style; the colonnade of the court is splendid This palace contains a large collection of paintings, rare works of sculpture, valuable tables, and utensils of rich workmanship, of red porphyry, alabaster, and other materials. The upper hall is unrivalled; the great landscapes of Vernet, with which it is adorned, are so true to nature, that, upon entering, one imagines himself transported into real scenes. The palace Albani, the situation of which is remarkably fine, possesses a valuable library, a great number of paintings, and a collection of designs by Caracci, Polydoro, Lanfranco, Spagnoletto, Cignani, and others. The palace Altieri, one of the largest in Rome, is in a simple style of architecture, and contains rare manuscripts, medals, paintings, &c., and valuable furniture. In the palace Colonna there is a rich collection of paintings by the first masters; all the rooms are decorated with them, and particularly the gallery, which is one of the finest in Europe. In the gardens are the ruins of the baths of Constantine and those of the temple of Sol. The Aldobrandini (q. v.) palace contains the finest monument of ancient painting—the Aldobrandine Wedding, a fresco purchased by Pius VII, in 1818, in which the design is admirable. The great Farnese palace, begun from designs of Sangallo, and completed under the direction of Michael Angelo, is celebrated both for its beauty and its treasures of art. The Caracci and Domenichino have immortalized themselves by their frescoes in its gallery. The Farnese Hercules, the masterly Flora, and the urn of Cæcilia Metella, formerly adorned the court; and in the palace itself was the beautiful group of the Farnese bull. But when the king of Naples inherited the Farnese estate, these statues, with other works of art, were carried to Naples, where they now adorn the palace degli Studj. Not far off is the palace Corsini, where queen Christina lived and died in 1689. It contains a valuable library and gallery. The palace Giustiniani also had a gallery adorned with numerous valuable statues and works of sculpture; its principal ornaments were the celebrated statue of Minerva, the finest of that goddess now known, and the bass-relief of Amathea suckling Jupiter. These treasures were nominally bought by Napoleon, and are now in Paris. The paintings are chiefly in the possession of the king of Prussia. In the palace Spada is the statue of Pompey, at the foot of which Cæsar fell under the daggers of his murderers. We have yet to mention the palace Costaguti, on account of its fine frescoes; Chigi, for its beautiful architecture, its paintings and library; Mattei, for its numerous statues, reliefs and ancient inscriptions; the palace of Pamfili, built by Borromini, for its splendid paintings and internal magnificence; that of Pamfili in the square of Navona, with a library and gallery; Rospigliosi, upon the Quirinal hill, &c. Among the palaces of Rome, which bear the name of *villas*, is the Villa Medici, on the Pincian mount, on which were formerly situated the splendid gardens of Lucullus: it once contained a vast number of masterpieces of every kind; but the grand-dukes Leopold and Ferdinand have removed the finest works (among them, the group of Niobe, by Scopas) to Florence. This palace, however, is yet very worthy of being visited. Under the portico of the Villa Negroni are the two fine statues of Sylla and Marius, seated on the *sella curulis*. In the extensive garden, which is three miles in circuit, some beautiful fresco paintings have been found in the ruins of some of the houses. The Villa Mattei, on the Cœlian mount, contains a splendid collection of statues. The Villa Ludovisi, on the Pincian mount, not far from the ruins of the circus and the gardens of Sallust, is one and a half miles in circuit, and contains valuable monuments of art, particularly the Aurora of Guercino, an ancient group of the senator Papirius and his mother (or rather of Phædra and Hippolytus), another of Arria and Pætus, and Bernini's rape of Proserpine. The Villa Borghese, near Rome, has a fine, but an unhealthy situation. The greatest part of the city, and the environs as far as Frascati and Tivoli, are visible from it. It has a garden, with a park three miles in circuit. This palace was ornamented in its interior, and furnished with so much richness and elegance, that it might have been considered the first edifice in Rome, next to the capitol, particularly for its fine collection of statues. The most remarkable among them were the Fighting Gladiator; Silenus and a Faun; Seneca, in black marble, or rather a slave at the baths; Camillus; the Hermaphrodite; the Centaur and Cupid; two Fauns playing on the flute; Ceres; an Ægyptian; a statue of the younger Nero; the busts of Lucius Verus, Alexander, Faustina and Verus; various relievos; among which was one representing Curtius; an urn, on which were represented the festival of Bacchus; another supported by the Graces; two horns of plenty, &c. The greatest part of these has not been restored from Paris. The exterior is ornamented with ancient reliefs. The Villa Pamfili, before the Porta di San Pancrazio, also called Belrespiro, has an agreeable situation, and is seven miles in circumference. The architecture is by Algardi, but has been censured by connoisseurs. In the interior there are some fine specimens of sculpture. Full descriptions of this and of the Villa Borghese have been published. The Villa Albani, upon an eminence which commands Tivoli and the Sabina, is a temple of taste and splendor. The cardinal Alexander Albani expended immense sums upon it, and, during the space of fifty years, collected a splendid cabinet. The ceiling of the gallery was painted by Mengs, and is a model of elegance. The Villa Lante and the Villa Corsini deserve to be mentioned on account of their fine prospects. The Villa Doria (formerly Algiati), in which Raphael lived, contains three fresco paintings of this great master. The Villa Farnese contains the remains of the palace of the Roman emperors. The capitol (q. v.) contains so many and such magnificent objects of every description, that it is impossible to enumerate them here. We must be satisfied with mentioning the equestrian statue of Marcus Aurelius, before the palace; the Captive Kings, in the court; the *columna rostrata;* and within, the colossal statue of Pyrrhus; the tomb of Severus; the Centaurs, of basalt; the beautiful alabaster pillars; the masterpiece in mosaic, which once belonged to cardinal Furietti, representing three doves on the edge of a vessel filled with water, which is described by Pliny. The fountains are among the principal ornaments of the squares in Rome. The fountain in the Piazza Navona, the most splendid of them all, has been particularly admired; it is surmounted by an obelisk, and ornamented by four colossal statues, which represent the four principal rivers in the world. The fountain of Paul V, near the church di San Pietro in Montorio, is in bad taste, but furnishes such a body of water, that several mills are carried by it. The fountain di Termini is adorned with three reliefs, representing Moses striking water from the rock, and with a colossal statue of that prophet, with two Ægyptian lions in basalt. The splendid fountain of Trevi supplies the best water, which it receives through an ancient aqueduct. Among the streets, the Strada Felice and the Strada Pia, which cross each other, are the most remarkable; among the bridges, that of St. Angelo (formerly Pons Ælius), 300 feet in length; and among the gates, the Porta del Popolo (formerly Porta Flaminia). Of ancient monuments, the following yet remain: the Pantheon, the Coliseum, the column of Trajan, that of Antonine, the amphitheatre of Vespasian; the mausoleum of Augustus, the mausoleum of Adrian (now the fortress of St. Angelo); the triumphal arches of Severus, Titus, Constantine, Janus, Nero and Drusus; the ruins of the temple of Jupiter Stator, of Jupiter Tonans, of Concordia, of Pax, of Antoninus and Faustina, of the sun and moon, of Romulus, of Romulus and Remus, of Pallas, of Fortuna Virilis, of Fortuna Muliebris, of Virtue, of Bacchus, of Vesta, of Minerva Medica, and of Venus and Cupid; the remains of the baths of Dioclesian, of Caracalla and Titus, &c.; the ruins of the theatre of Pompey, near the Curia Pompeii, where Cæsar was murdered, and those of the theatre of Marcellus; the ruins of the old forum (now called Campo Vaccino); the remains of the old bridges; the circus maximus; the circus of Caracalla; the house of Cicero; the Curia Hostilia; the trophies of Marius; the portico of Philip and Octavius; the country house and tower of Mæcenas; the Claudian aqueduct; the monuments of the family of Aruns, of the Scipios, of Metella (called Capo di Bove); the prison of Jugurtha (Carcere Mamertino), in which St. Peter was imprisoned; the monument of Caius Cestius, which is entirely uninjured, in form of a pyramid, near which the Protestants are buried; the Cloaca Maxima, built by Tarquin, &c. Besides the obelisk near the Porta del Popolo, that raised in the pontificate of Pius VI, on mount Cavallo, is deserving of notice. The principal collections of literature and the arts have already been noticed; but the Museo Kircheliano deserves to be particularly mentioned: there are, besides, many private collections and monastic libraries, which contain many valuable works. Such treasures, especially in the arts, make Rome the great school of painters, statuaries and architects, and a place of pilgrimage to all lovers of the arts; and there are here innumerable *studj* of painting and sculpture. Roman art seems to have received a new impulse. The academy of San Luca was established solely for the art of painting; and there are also many literary institutions in the city. The principal college of the university, erected by the popes Innocent IV (1245), Boniface VIII (1303), and Clement VI (1311), is called *della Sapienza*, from its motto, *Initium sapientiæ timor Domini.* It is a splendid building, in which there are eight professors in theology, six in law, eight in medicine, five in philosophy, one in the fine arts, and four in the Hebrew, Greek, Syriac and Arabic languages. Of the other colleges, in which instruction is given in the sciences and in languages, the Collegium de propaganda Fide is particularly remarkable for its rich library and its printing-office, which is worthy of being visited, and which contains works in thirty ancient and modern languages: besides these are the Collegium Clementinum, the Collegium Romanum and the Collegium Nazarenum, institutions for instruction in the Oriental languages, the Hungarian and the German college, &c. Among the academies and learned societies in Rome, the most important are the academies of Roman history, of geography, of ecclesiastical history, of Roman antiquities, of the Arcadians, &c. The two principal theatres are those of Alberti and Argentina, in which operas and ballets are exhibited; the theatres della Valle and di Capranica are of the second rank, in which comic operas, comedies, and sometimes tragedies, are performed. La Paze and La Palla Corda are of the lowest rank, in which the opera buffa and farces are acted for the amusement of the populace. But they are opened only for a short time during the year. The festivals in Rome most worthy of notice are the grand procession on Corpus Christi day, and the ceremonies of Passion week in the Sistine chapel, where is performed the immortal Miserere of Leo Allegri; the illumination of the cross on St. Peter's, the illumination of the Pauline chapel, &c.; besides these, there are the illumination of the immense dome of St. Peter's, upon the day of that saint, the great fire works, or the Girandola of 4500 rockets, which are discharged from the castle of St. Angelo, upon the anniversary of the pope's coronation, and which produce an indescribable effect, on account of the vicinity of the river, in whose waters the lights are reflected. (For the *Carnival*, see the article.) The climate of Rome from July until October is unhealthy, and the foreigner is then exposed to dangerous fevers. This *aria cattiva* renders whole quarters of the city uninhabitable during these months. It appears to extend gradually, and to be about to take full possession of the eternal city. (See *Campagna di Roma*, *Malaria*, and *Pontine Marshes*.) The south wind, known by the name of *sirocco*, affects the elasticity of the muscles without being dangerous. Consumption has in Rome a malignant character, communicating itself to the healthy by means of articles of clothing and furniture, and spreading among occupants of the same house with the diseased person, even without such adventitious aid. It is even communicated by books. The water is different in different parts of the city. The fountain of Trevi furnishes the most wholesome water; that from the *thermæ* of Dioclesian and the fountain of Gianicola is unwholesome, and banished from all tables. In Rome, the hours are counted up to 24, as is the case in many of the other Italian cities. The most frequented promenade is the Corso. From 22 to 24 o'clock (5 to 7), it is filled with pedestrians and equipages. In 1824, Rome contained 136,300 inhabitants; 35,900 houses; 346 churches, 81 of them parish churches; 30 monasteries, and upwards of 120 palaces. In 1830, the population was 144,542, among which were 35 bishops and archbishops, 1490 priests, 1983 monks, 2390 nuns, and 10,000 Jews residing on the left bank of the Tiber, in a quarter called Ghetto. The view of the majestic ruins; the solemn grandeur of the churches and palaces; the recollections of the past; the religious customs; the magic and almost melancholy tranquillity in the splendid villas; the enjoyment of the endless treasures of art,—all this raises the mind to a high state of excitement.—See Fea's *Descrizione*; the splendid *Vedute di Roma*, by Piranesi (2 vols., folio, 138 plates); *Description of Rome*, by Platner, Bunsen and Gerhard, with a Sketch of the History of the old, and of the Restoration of the new City, by Niebuhr, with plans and views, in two volumes (in German); *Rome in the 19th Century*. For other works on the subject, see the article *Italy, Travels in*.

Roman Æra, and Calendar. (See *Calendar*, and *Epoch*.)

Roman Language. The old Latin and the Roman languages are different. From the first—traces of which are yet to be found in the laws of the twelve tables, and which became obsolete so early that, in the time of Cicero, the hymns of the Salii (priests of Mars) were unintelligible—the Roman language was formed, posterior to the adoption of the laws of the twelve tables, not without being influenced by the Greek. It was divided into the *sermo urbanus*, *rusticus*, and *peregrinus*. The first of these dialects was spoken in Rome itself, the second in the country, and the third generally in the provinces. If we possessed the *Origines* of the elder Cato, we should be able to decide with certainty who were the earliest inhabitants of Italy, and what was the origin of the native Latin language. We are able only to discover from the scattered and disconnected accounts of the ancients that the Œnotrii (who were probably of Arcadian, or, rather of Pelasgian origin), the Ausonii (among these are included the Osci and Volsci), the Sabelli or Sabines, the Tyrhenii (Etrurians and Tuscans, from whom originated the augury and the priesthood of the Romans), and, lastly, the Umbri, are to be considered as the principal aborigines of Italy, to whom the old Latins, or the *abgrigines*, as they were called, joined themselves. With these the Trojans under Æneas were incorporated; but the number of these was too small to have any decisive influence upon the Latin language, although these foreigners at length obtained dominion over the whole country. The Greek colonies are more important in this view, viz. the Achaians, Locrians and Dorians, who inhabited Middle and Lower Italy, and extended their customs, and even the common use of their language, beyond their own settlements in this country. The Latin must, therefore, necessarily have been much influenced by the language of these colonies. Besides the old Italian language, we read of the Etrurian, the Oscian, and the Volscian, which, perhaps, were only different dialects. The Oscian maintained itself still later among the Atellani. After the conquest of the south of Italy and Sicily, of Macedonia and Achaia, the Greek language must have been better known to the Romans; and thus the influence of the Greek language upon the formation of the Roman came to be of more importance. We likewise find, in the derivation of many words, as well as in the syntax of this language, frequent traces of Greek origin; and, indeed the oldest Roman authors (for example Plautus, Terence, Lucretius, and even Catullus) make use of many Greek idioms. The Romanic languages (see *Romanic*) are formed, for the most part, from the dialect of the country and the provinces.

Roman Literature. The history of

Roman literature is generally divided into four periods:—1. from the earliest times till Cicero; 2. till the death of Augustus, usually called the *golden age*, to which, however, some earlier writers are considered to belong; 3. till the death of Trajan, called the *silver age;* 4. till the subjugation of Rome by the Goths, called the *brazen age*. Poetry, in this language, as in all others, preceded prose; but Roman prose was not of native growth; it was an exotic, to which Greek models first gave birth, and which rhetoric and the schools afterwards improved (see *Rhetoricians*); for native poetry in Rome was blighted in the bud by Grecian influence. To this belong the Saturnian songs. Among the first essays in poetry were the *Atellanæ Fabulæ* (q. v.), and the succeeding attempts were likewise, with few exceptions, dramatic. Livius Andronicus, a Greek captive of Tarentum, first gave the Odyssey to the Romans, about 500 years after the foundation of the city, and made them acquainted with the dramatical riches of the Greeks by means of Latin translations, or imitations of Greek tragedies and comedies. He was followed by Nævius, who wrote a historical poem on the first Punic war, the two tragic writers Pacuvius and Attius, and by Ennius (q. v.), the first epic poet, and the founder of Roman poetry, whom Cicero and Virgil esteemed very highly. Ennius introduced the Greek hexameters, and wrote the Roman annals, in eighteen books, &c. Contemporary with him was Plautus, of whose pieces twenty-one are now extant. His power was greatest in low comedy; he possessed humor, wit, and a genuine comic language. Next follow Cæcilius, of whose works we are acquainted with the titles and fragments of forty-five pieces, and Terence, a successful imitator of Menander and others, who was distinguished by the truth and delicacy of his dialogue, his finished style, and the regular disposition of his Greek character pieces. These three comic writers took the new comedy of the Greeks as their model (*comœdia palliata*). On the other hand, Afranius, with a few others, introduced Roman manners upon the stage (*comœdia togata*). Soon after him, Lucilius (q. v.) discovered a talent for satire, of which he was the father among the Romans. The Romans, after this period, had no distinguished dramatic writers; their pieces were mostly translations or imitations of Grecian works. Of the *mimæ* (comic monodramas) of Laberius and Syrus, we know too little to assign them a definite place; but they are celebrated. The later tragic writers, likewise, of the Augustan age, Asinius Pollio, Varius with his Thyestes, and Ovid with his Medea, are praised; but it is easy to imagine the causes which must have contributed to prevent tragedy from flourishing on the Roman stage. We need only to remember the kings led in triumph, and left to perish in prison, the gladiatorial games, and the combats of wild beasts. Among a people who took delight in such scenes, we could not expect to find a relish for the tamer excitement and moral influence of tragic spectacles. The only specimen of the tragic poetry of a later age which is preserved to us, is the ten tragedies under the name of Annæus Seneca, but which are, not without reason, ascribed to several authors. They are rude declamations, without nature or truth, which originated from the schools of the rhetoricians; and their bombast could please only the most uncultivated minds. Lucretius, who took a new path among the earlier poets of Rome, wrote a philosophical poem, in six books, concerning the nature of things, after the system of Epicurus, which he adorned with a true poetic coloring. He took a different course from many scientific poets among the Greeks, and is an animated delineator of nature, full of strength and originality, but not without harshness and obscurity. Catullus was distinguished in a different department—in lyric poetry, in elegy, and in epigrams. He had much real wit and delicacy of feeling, but, like most of the amorous and satirical poets of the ancients, paid too little regard to decency of expression, which is easily explained by the relative condition of the two sexes at that time. Much purer and more graceful are the works of Tibullus, to whom we may, with Quinctilian, adjudge the first rank among elegiac poets. With the age of Augustus, and the loss of liberty, a new spirit appeared in Roman literature. Augustus himself and Mæcenas were the patrons of poetic talent. The first of the poets thus patronised is Virgil, who, in his Æneid, represents the landing of Æneas and the foundation of his dominion in Latium. Although the poet himself directed this work to be destroyed, on account of its imperfect state, it is a noble monument of his wish to create for his contemporaries a new Iliad; and, though he has fallen short of his model, he cannot be denied the praise of patriotic feeling, refined taste, and highly poetical language. More perfect, of its kind, is his poem on agriculture (Georgica), which, in the form of a didactic poem, and in a highly finished style, exhibits his views and feelings respecting rural life. His earlier Eclogues, or pastorals, manifest the same love for nature and a country life. If we recognise in Virgil the first epic and didactic poet of the Romans, Horace is the favorite of the lyric muse, and the priest of the muses, although one cannot judge with certainty concerning his originality, after the loss of his Grecian models; yet his odes are often founded upon national subjects, and then he discovers strong feelings, expressed in a manner becoming a Roman. Many of his odes are patriotic, and others breathe a most charming grace. This poet is also eminent in satire, a species of writing original with the Romans, and which appears to have had a decisive influence on the character of their literature. In most of his epodes and epistles, he touches, with a playful ease and great versatility, upon the ridiculous rather than the criminal, although the latter was not altogether excluded from his satire. In the Augustan age, Propertius and Ovid are among the elegiac poets whom we still possess. In Propertius, a certain dignity appears in the midst of his habitual sensuality, although he was often forced in his thoughts and expressions. The most fruitful poetic talent, and the greatest ease of versification, cannot be denied to Ovid (q.v.); he only indulged too much in his fertility of invention, and was often unmanly in his elegiac complaints. The most characteristic of his poems are the *Fasti*, or the poetical description of the Roman festivals, and their origin; the least pleasing are, perhaps, his *Heroides*, or heroic epistles, of which he is the inventor. They are too monotonous, and too much filled with amorous complaints, to have either dignity or truth; they are rather to be considered as rhetorical exercises. Of the other poets belonging to this age there is little to be said. Some esteemed elegiac writers, such as Pedo Albinovanus and Cornelius Gallus, are almost entirely lost to us. A poem upon Ætna, attributed to Cornelius Severus, who is praised by Quinctilian, has little inventive power; and the didactic poem of Gratius Faliscus upon the chase (*Cynegeticon*), and that of Manlius upon astronomy, some passages excepted, are more valued for their materials than their manner, which, though inferior, resembles the productions of the Alexandrian school of Greek poetry.—The third age, after the death of Augustus, begins with Phædrus, an imitator of Æsop, who has more merit, in regard to style, than invention and manner. The degeneracy of Roman poetry is displayed in the harsh and obscure Persius. He and the later Juvenal expressed their indignation at the corruption of the age with unrestrained severity, but have more moral than poetical value. In the principal writers of the later poetry—Lucan, who returned to the historical epic in his versification of the civil war between Cæsar and Pompey, and the bombastic Statius, who wrote the Thebaid and the beginning of the Achilleis, in verse, to say nothing of the minor poets—we find a universal barrenness of invention, and a coldness, which vainly endeavors to kindle itself and its hearers by the fire of rhetoric. These poets had long since lost all poetic feeling, and even the love of republican freedom. With such a corrupt taste as that of the Romans, poets like the pompous Statius, or the wanton epigrammatist Martial, to whom we cannot deny wit and fertility of invention, could alone be successful. Lucan, however, with all his defects of plan and unworthy adulation, sometimes exhibits great elevation of sentiment, vigor of expression, and a happy delineation of character. Valerius Flaccus, who described the Argonautic expedition in verse, in imitation of Apollonius Rhodius, endeavored to shine by his learning, rather than by his originality and freshness of coloring, and Silius Italicus, a great admirer of Virgil, who selected the second Punic war, as the subject of a heroic poem, is merely a historic poet. In the fourth period, Roman literature sunk to a still lower state. The twenty-four fables of Arvienus, or Arvianus, are in a stiff and forced style; on the other hand, the poem of Nemesianus, on the pleasures of the chase, and the seven eclogues of Calpurnius, have some pretensions to purity and ease of style. Ausonius, in his epigrams and idyls (so called), and particularly in his poems on the Moselle, forms as it were the line of division between the ancient and the modern world; Claudian appears almost a miracle in this brazen age. Although not free from rhetorical and epigrammatical excrescences, and, from the desire of displaying his learning, he is still far above his age, and often approaches to a graceful style. We conclude this part of the subject with Rutilius Numantianus, whose voyage to Gaul, in elegiac measure, is not without merit, and with two Christian poets, Prudentius and Sedulius, in whose writings we find hardly any thing but modern features and the first germs of the church songs. In the Roman prose literature, which is, on the whole, of a higher character than the poetical, eloquence, history, philosophy and jurisprudence are the principal departments. After the Romans had entered Greece as conquerors, and began to pay more attention to learning, and particularly after they became sensible of the political importance of eloquence, the Greeks were necessary to their conquerors, as teachers of rhetoric, and of the Greek language and literature, although in this period they were twice banished from Rome. (See *Rhetoricians*, and *Grammarians*.) Theoretical instruction was connected with the practice of declamations, as a preparation for public speaking, as forensic eloquence was always the object of ambition during the republic. Of their orators we know many merely by name and by the reputation which they enjoyed. To this class belong Cornelius Cethegus, Tiberius Gracchus, Cotta, Sulpicius, but particularly Licinius Crassus, Antonius, Hortensius, and even Cæsar himself. Cicero not only acquired the most splendid fame in eloquence, the finest models of which we possess in the fifty-nine orations of his yet extant, but also appears as a teacher in his rhetorical works, and in general had a most important part in founding Roman prose literature. In the age of Augustus, after the death of the last champion of Roman liberty, free eloquence necessarily became silent; yet the works of this, and even of later periods, were more or less imbued with the old spirit. The panegyric of Pliny the younger upon Trajan may be considered as the last note of Roman eloquence: the author was distinguished in Rome as a forensic orator. We can best judge of the fallen state of eloquence by examining the works of Fronto, and later orators (the panegyrists), in imitation of Pliny. Quinctilian, a contemporary of Pliny, is to be regarded as the last stay of rhetoric, both by instruction and his own example. We have under his name 19 greater and 145 smaller declamations. But his merit is greater as a rhetorician and grammarian. In his twelve books *De Institutione oratoria*, he explains the characteristics of the best models, and at the same time lays down the best rules. Cicero, Cæsar, and Terentius Varro, in the most flourishing ages of Roman literature, had, by their grammatical writings, contributed to promote a scientific study of the language, and to give it thereby a settled form. Varro, the most learned philologist and antiquarian of his age wrote a work upon the Latin language in twenty-four books, of which only six remain entire. In a rhetorical view, the declamations (*controversiæ* and *suasoriæ*) of Marcus Seneca, and particularly the valuable dialogue On the Causes of the Decline of Eloquence, which has been attributed by most authors to Quinctilian, must be named. Later grammarians, or teachers of language and literature of the age of the Antonines, are Aulus Gellius, Censorinus, Nonius Marcellus, Pomponius Festus, Macrobius, Donatus and Priscianus, who are valuable for their grammatical information, their commentaries upon more ancient authors, and their preservation of fragments of them. The first historical writings were merely details of events, preserved in the annals of the high priest (*pontifex maximus*), upon a tablet in his house, and the catalogue of the consuls, with a notice of the most remarkable events, recorded in the temple of Juno Moneta (*libri lintei*). Fabius Pictor, Albinus Posthumius, the elder Cato, Cœlius Fannius, Valerius of Antium, and some others, were the first historians among the Romans, but without any pretensions to skill in the historical art. Great authors first appeared in the most splendid age of Rome. The spirit, the beautiful simplicity and the judicious style of Julius Cæsar, in his Commentaries on the Gallic and Civil Wars, carried on by himself, have always been admired. The style of Sallust is sometimes forced, but he displays great care in his narrative and in his delineation of character, with such richness of thought and depth of observation,that he may not disadvantageously be compared with his model Thucydides. If we except the lost universal history of Trogus Pompeius, Livy embraces the widest field among the Roman historians, and deserves to be called perfect in narration and style, although some have attributed to him a certain Patavinity (the provincial dialect of his native city, Patavium). His history begins with the arrival of Æneas in Italy, and reaches to the year of Rome 744; but a few books only are extant. Cornelius Nepos stands next to these models of historical writing, with his lives of distinguished generals, at least for purity of style. It is to be lamented that his principal historical work is lost. Under the oppression of despotism, even history, which had hitherto been so well sustained by the Romans, degenerated: this appears from the forced and declamatory style of Velleius, from whom we possess a short sketch of Roman history, in which he indulges in the grossest flattery. Florus is still more to be condemned: he wrote an abridgment of Roman history; but his style is bombastic, and his adulation disgraceful. Valerius Maximus, in his memoirs of memorable men, is a mere compiler and collector of anecdotes. Suetonius, besides his rhetorical and grammatical works, wrote the lives of the emperors, which are interesting from their contents. Tacitus elevated himself above a degenerate age by his truly Roman spirit, his depth of thought, and power of expression, which has been often imitated, but seldom with success. It may be said, with truth, that in him the poet, the philosopher and the historian are united. After Trajan, we meet no great authors; but Greek literature again asserted its claims, and Roman history was treated of by Greek authors. It is perhaps owing to Justin's abridgment, that we have lost the general history of Trogus Pompeius, in forty-four books. So great was the ignorance of Roman history under the later emperors, that Eutropius was ordered by the emperor Valens to write a short sketch of it. Of Aurelius Victor little need be said, and we cannot greatly lament the loss of his principal work upon the origin of the Roman people, which extended only through one year after the foundation of Rome. Ammianus Marcellinus is of superior merit, and, although his style is somewhat barbarous, contains interesting views, and displays a sound judgment. The six authors of the imperial history (*Scriptores Historiæ Augustæ*), Spartianus, Capitolinus, Trebellius, Vopiscus, Gallicanus, and Lampridius, deserve little praise. The Romans distinguished themselves in philosophy only by spreading the doctrines of the Greek philosophers in a popular language; and the most eminent statesmen, in the most flourishing periods of Rome, were friends and admirers of philosophy. Among the earlier Romans, Lælius, Scipio Africanus the younger, and Lucullus, deserve to be mentioned in this view. Of the lofty spirit of Lucrétius, although he embraced an odious system, and the principles of Horace, who called Epicureanism an *insane wisdom*, we have already spoken; but Cicero, by the introduction of the more elevated moral philosophy of the Greeks, rendered the most important service to the intellectual cultivation of his countrymen. He did not wander in the labyrinths of speculation, but he clung to philosophy in prosperity and adversity, and taught it in a classical language. Originally a follower of Plato, he often adopted the ethical lessons of the Stoics, or, when their excessive austerity repelled him, embraced those of Aristotle. The doctrines of Epicurus he rejected as injurious to men, and especially in their relations of citizens. His works also afford much information in regard to the history of ancient philosophy; for example, his Tusculan questions. Philosophy, although sometimes persecuted by the emperors, as it had been earlier by Cato the elder, always found admirers at Rome, and almost every school had its adherents there; but it was more the subject of conversation, in the schools and in the world, than of writings. The old academy and the school of Epicurus were at first the most popular; but oppression turned men to Stoicism, which, with its pompous apothegms, influenced some of the poets also, as Lucan, for example. The philosopher Annæus Seneca, in the age of Nero, of whom, besides other works, we possess twelve philosophical treatises, is distinguished for his artificial subtleties and glittering antitheses; but his writings contain many excellent thoughts, finely expressed. In the fourth period of Roman literature, we shall only mention Apuleius. The most known of his productions is the Golden Ass. He was of the sect of the New Platonists; and, even in the pleasing tale of Psyche, we find traces of the Platonic philosophy. The epistolary style is connected with eloquence, and Roman literature contains some collections of epistles worthy of imitation. The letters of Cicero are mostly addressed to the greatest men of his age, on passing events, and are written with purity, and elegance, and simplicity They contain authentic materials for the history of the time, and are the last memorials of the republic. The letters of Pliny the younger are written with taste and elegance, and give us a pleasing picture of their author; but they are too artificial, and appear to owe their existence less to any real occasion for writing than to the wish of appearing as an author. The twenty-four letters of Annæus Seneca to Lucilius relate chiefly to the philosophical system of the Stoics, and are more worthy of attention for their matter, than their manner, which partakes of the common faults of his style. We have yet to notice the letters of Symmachus, about the end of the fourth century, and those of the still later

Apollinarius Sidonius, who was also known as a poet. The former are not unsuccessful imitations of Pliny the younger; the latter are marked by the faults of their age, but are interesting for their contents. With the poets are connected the mythological authors of the Romans. The Roman worship was in a great measure similar to that of the Greeks, but by no means entirely the same, as many have supposed: the heroic mythology of the Greeks was introduced into Rome by the poets, although it had no connexion with the national traditions. The Roman mythological writers, therefore, derived their knowledge mostly from Greek sources, and have little that is peculiar or original. The domestic religion of the Romans is to be learned from their antiquarian and historical authors. Hyginus, whose age we cannot accurately determine, left a collection of 277 mythological stories, which are, perhaps, the outlines of ancient tragedies. A poetical astronomy of the same author illustrates the constellations celebrated in poetry. The age of Fulgentius, by whom we have three books of mythological fables, is equally uncertain. Petronius, a contemporary of Nero, may most properly be mentioned here, as he is connected with the poets by his *Satyricon*, in which he describes the corruption of his age with wit and vivacity, and by his poetical pieces interspersed through that work. In mathematics, the Greeks had laid the foundation for a scientific geometry and astronomy, and medicine opened a wide field for their inventive spirit. In all these departments, the Romans were not much distinguished. Among the mathematical authors, Vitruvius is the first, both in time and merit. He was also an architect; and his work on architecture is still highly esteemed. Frontinus wrote upon aqueducts, Vegetius upon the military art (the application of mathematics to the art of war could not fail to find favor among the Romans); and after him Firmicus Maternus wrote a Mathesis; but this is, in reality, a treatise on astrology, as was also the work of Julius Obsequens on prodigies. Pomponius Mela and Vibius Sequester are worthy of being mentioned as geographers. The latter gives a list of the names of rivers, seas, mountains, forests, &c. Tacitus, by his description of ancient Germany, may be included under this head. Physicians were first esteemed among the Romans after the time of Cæsar and Augustus; and the eight books of Celsus on medicine, which form only a part of a large encyclopædia, are very important, both on account of their contents and their style. Æmilius Macer and Aulus Apuleius (not the Apuleius before mentioned) wrote concerning the qualities of plants. We also possess some unimportant treatises on medicine by Scribonius Largus and Marcellus Empiricus; and there is still extant a poem on the subject of this science by Serenus Sammoniacus, a favorite of the emperor Severus. Several agricultural works of the Romans are entirely lost to us. There is still extant a work on agriculture, which bears the name of Cato the elder; and the three books of the learned Varro on husbandry are very important and instructive. The works of Columella and Palladius on agriculture, are partly written in verse, and deserve commendation. A miserably written work on the art of cookery is ascribed to the notorious *gourmand* Apicius.—Among the polyhistors is Pliny the elder, who wrote a work on natural history, in which he at the same time treated of cosmography and geography, medicine and the arts, with great erudition, but yet in a stiff style. He has given us an example of what the Romans might have done with their great advantages, for the extension of human knowledge. Solinus made an abridgment of this work. Finally Marcianus Capella, in the fifth century, wrote, in barbarous language, a sort of encyclopædia, under the name of *Satyricon* (on account of the variety of its contents), in which he treated of several of the sciences, with their most important principles. On a review of Roman literature, we find, that it continued to flourish only for a short time, from Cicero till the death of Trajan, that the prose reached a higher degree of excellence than poetry, in which various departments obtained various success, and that, notwithstanding the merits of the Romans in art and literature, the Greeks excelled them. Perhaps their literature, at least the poetry, would have attained a greater elevation, if they had imitated less, and sought for original ideas in domestic scenes.—See Manso, *On the Characteristics of Roman Literature* (in German, Breslau, 1818); Cavriana, *Delle Scienze, Lettere ed Arti dei Romani dalla Fondazione di Roma fino al Augusto*, Mantua, 1822, 2 vols.); Dunlop's *History of Roman Literature* (3 vols., 1828). In jurisprudence alone did Roman literature acquire an entirely peculiar character, and an elevation which it has maintained down to the latest times, and which has enabled it to exert a powerful influence on all the refined nations of modern Europe. (See *Civil Law.*)

ROMAN SCHOOL. (See *Italy;* division, *Italian Art.*)

ROMILLY, sir Samuel, an eminent lawyer, the son of a jeweller, of French extraction, was born in London, in 1757. He received a private education, and was placed in the office of a solicitor, which he quitted to study for the bar, to which he was called in 1783. For some years his practice was chiefly confined to draughts in equity; but he gradually rose to distinction in the court of chancery, in which he ultimately took the lead, being equally distinguished by his profound legal information, and logical and forcible eloquence. His general politics agreeing with those of the whigs, he was, during the short administration of Mr. Fox and lord Grenville (1806), appointed solicitor-general, and knighted. When his party went out of office, he remained in parliament, where he became distinguished by his talent in debate, and particularly by the eloquence with which he pleaded the necessity of a revision of the criminal code, with a view to the limitation of capital punishment, and a more appropriate regulation of the scale of penalties. On this subject he also composed a very able pamphlet—Observations on the Criminal Law of England (1810)—and to his exertions may be traced the final determination of the executive to the reforms and condensation of the various acts in regard to crime, which have since taken place under the superintendence of sir R. Peel. Sir Samuel Romilly also published Objections to the Creation of a Vice-chancellor (1812); and was in the height of popularity and reputation, when a nervous disorder, produced by grief at the death of his wife, to whom he was devotedly attached, deprived him of reason, and, in a fit of temporary frenzy, he terminated his useful and philanthropic existence, November 2, 1818. A collection of his speeches, with a Memoir of his Life, by H. Peters, was published in 1820. B. Constant published his *Éloge* (Paris, 1819).

ROMULUS was the founder and first king of Rome. According to tradition, his mother was Rhea Sylvia, a daughter of Numitor, king of Alba, and one of the priestesses of Vesta, who were employed in preserving the fire sacred to this goddess, and were bound to spend their lives in strict chastity. She was devoted to the service of Vesta, by her uncle Amulius, who had deprived her father of his throne, and wished to prevent her from having posterity who might dispossess him of his usurped crown. But the royal maid forgot her vow of chastity, and male twins were the fruit of her clandestine amour. In order to escape the horrible punishment denounced by the law against those vestals who violated their vows, Rhea Sylvia gave out that Mars, the god of war, was the father of her children. This artifice saved the mother, and a fortunate accident her children, who were exposed by command of Amulius in a wild and desert country on the banks of the Tiber. Here a she wolf is said to have found them, and to have suckled them until chance brought thither a countryman, Faustulus by name, who took them home and educated them. With him Romulus and Remus spent their youth, exercising themselves in the chase, and sometimes in rapine. The younger, Remus, was taken prisoner by the servants of Amulius, and his courageous brother collected a small band of enterprising companions, with whom he not only freed his brother, but likewise deprived Amulius of his usurped throne, and reinstated his old grandfather Numitor in his dominions. After the termination of this exploit, Romulus, in connexion with his brother, resolved to build a city. The gods, it is said, during a solemn sacrifice, pointed out the proper site, by the flight of seven eagles. Thus was Rome founded in the year 752 (according to others 754) B. C. The unanimity which had heretofore prevailed between the two brothers, ended with this enterprise: either from ambition or a sudden burst of anger, Romulus imbrued his hands in his brother's blood. According to another tradition, Remus fled from the anger of his brother beyond the Alps, and founded Rheims. The small numbers of friends who had followed Romulus were by no means sufficient to people his city; he saw himself, therefore, compelled to make it a place of refuge for every houseless exile. Men enough were thereby gained, but the Roman citizens soon wanted women, and their proposals for the daughters of the neighboring cities were rejected by the fathers of the maidens, who looked with an envious eye on the increase of this city. On this account Romulus instituted a religious festival, to which he invited the Sabines (see the article *Sabines*), with their wives and daughters. They came; but, in the midst of the festival, the unarmed strangers were suddenly attacked, and deprived of their wives and daughters, and every Roman hastened to provide himself with a female companion. The two states thus became engaged in war; but the entreaties of the ravished females, who threw themselves between the contending parties, at length effected a peace, and Rome gained by her union with the Sabines an important addition. Many successful wars, which always ended in additions of population and territory to the infant state, confirmed and extended its power. Romulus was strict and arbitrary; too much so, perhaps, for his subjects; and his sudden disappearance naturally excited the conjecture that he fell by the hand of a malcontent. According to tradition, he ascended to heaven into the company of the gods, after he had completed the work of founding the eternal city; and, until the introduction of Christianity, Rome worshipped its founder in temples expressly dedicated to him. It is likewise possible that he was struck by lightning; for his disappearance is said to have happened during a thunderstorm, while he was without the city, near the marshes of Caprea, reviewing his army. Romulus reigned about thirty-seven years, and was about fifty years of age; and the rude, but, considering the time and circumstances, the appropriate laws and ordinances, which he gave his people, bear witness of his capacity as a ruler. When Romulus died, Rome, according to a census which he caused to be made a short time before his death, is said to have contained between 3000 and 4000 men capable of bearing arms. (See *Rome.*)

Roncesvalles (French *Roncevaux*); a valley in Navarre, between Pampeluna and St. Jean de Port, where, according to tradition, the rear of Charlemagne's army was defeated by the Arabs, in 778, and the brave Roland (q. v.) killed. The battle forms an essential part in the fabulous cyclus of Charlemagne. The chief place of the valley, called also Roncesvalles, is traversed by the (so called) gates of Roland, leading over the Pyrenees to France; and in the church of the little place, fabulous antiquities bearing the name of Roland are shown. The French, under Moncey, here defeated the Spaniards in 1794; and Soult took a strong position here in 1813, from which Wellington drove him.

Rondo (*Italian*), or Rondeau (*French*); a composition, vocal or instrumental, generally consisting of three strains, the first of which closes in the original key, while each of the others is so constructed, in point of modulation, as to reconduct the ear, in an easy and natural manner, to the first strain. The *rondo* takes its name from the circumstance of the melody *going round*, after both the second and third strain, to the first strain, with which it finally closes.

Ronsard, Pierre de, an early French poet, who contributed to the improvement of the language and literature of his country, was born of a noble family of Vendome, in 1524. Having finished his education, he resided some time at the court of James V of Scotland, and, on his return from his travels, was employed in a diplomatic capacity in Germany. At the Floral games, at Toulouse, he triumphed over his competitors, and received a silver statue of Minerva, which he presented to Henry II. He was greatly esteemed by that prince, and by his successors, Francis II and Charles IX. He distinguished himself in the wars against the Huguenots; obtained the abbey of Bellozane; and was also prior of St. Cosme, near Tours, where he died in 1585. His writings, consisting of sonnets, madrigals, eclogues, lyric pieces, elegies, and satires, and an epic poem, *La Franciade*, are of little merit. (See *France, Literature of*, division *Poetry*, pp. 264 and 265.)

Roof. (See *Architecture*, vol. i. page 337.)

Rooke, sir George, an English admiral, descended of an ancient family, in the county of Kent, was born in 1650. His strong predilection for a seafaring life induced him to enter the royal navy at an early age, in which he rose to the highest situations. His conduct in several naval expeditions under king William and queen Anne placed his name high in his profession; especially the gallantry which he displayed in the destruction of the French and Spanish fleets in Vigo bay, 1702, and the capture of Gibraltar, in 1704. Sir George occupied a seat, during several parliaments, for Portsmouth, and another at the council-board of the lord high admiral, prince George of Denmark. His votes on several occasions, particularly one in favor of Harley as speaker of the house of commons, in 1701, obscured his merits in the eyes of the court party; the value of his services was depreciated, and his good fortune ascribed to accident. He at length retired in disgust from the service to his family seat in Kent, where he died in 1709. (See Campbell's *Lives of the Admirals.*)

Root, in arithmetic and algebra, denotes any number or quantity, which, by successive multiplications into itself, produces powers. (See *Power.*) Thus 2 is a root of 4, 8, 16, because $2 \times 2 = 4$ $2 \times 2 \times 2 = 8$; $2 \times 2 \times 2 \times 2 = 16$. The power is named from the number of the factors, and the root is named from the power. Thus if a quantity be multiplied once by itself, the product is called the second power, or square, and the quantity itself the square root, or the second root of the product; if multiplied twice, we have the third power, or cube, and the quantity is the cube root, or third root; and so on: the fourth root is the biquadrate. Beyond this the roots are commonly called the fifth, sixth, &c. roots. The algebraic sign of root is $\surd$, and the fourth root of sixteen, equal to two, is written thus: $\sqrt[4]{16} = 2$. The same is the case with algebraic magnitudes: as, $\sqrt[2]{(a^2 + 2\,ab + b^2)} = a + b$. To extract the given root of mathematical expressions, is one of the most important of mathematical operations.

Root Husbandry. (See the article *Agriculture.*)

Root, of plants. (See *Plant.*)

Rope, in mechanics. (See *Mechanics.*)

Ropiness; a frequent disease of wines, which have undergone an incomplete fermentation; or of sweet wines that have been bottled too soon. It shows itself by a milky or flaky sediment, and an oily appearance of the liquor when poured out. It arises from a partial combination of the mucilaginous, extractive, and saccharine principles of the wine.

Rosa, Mount (Mons Sylvius); the highest summit of the Swiss Alps, separating the Valais from Italy (lat. 45° 55′ N.). (See *Alps.*) According to the latest measurements, it is about 15,535 feet high, being from 200 to 250 feet lower than Mont Blanc. (q. v.) From the ever-blooming gardens of the Borromean isles, the traveller arrives in nine hours at Macugnaga, at the foot of the glaciers (q. v.) of mount Rosa. The valleys on the east and south are inhabited by people of German origin. Those on the west are uninhabited. Mount Rosa derives its name from its consisting of a number of lofty peaks, rising from a centre somewhat like the leaves of a rose. Jos. Zumstein made five journeys (1819—1822) to the summit. In 1820, he passed the night in a cleft in the ice twelve fathoms deep, to be able to reach the summit the next day. The group seems to consist, particularly in its upper half, of mica slate, which alternates occasionally with gneiss. It contains gold, silver, copper, and iron mines. Granite, in large masses, is found only at the foot of the mountain. Winter and summer rye ripen here at the height of from 5500 to 6000 feet; the grape, as high as 3090 feet (on the northern side 2200 feet); a covering of green turf is found as high as 9639 feet; the *pyrethrum Alpinum* and *Phyteuma pauciflorum* grow 11340 feet above the sea, on rocks free from ice. Between the north and south side there is a difference in the limit of vegetation of almost 1000 feet. The limit of perpetual snow is, on the south side, 9500 feet; the limit of trees, 7000 feet.—See *Der Monte Rosa, eine topographische und naturhistorische Skizze nebst einem Anhange der von Herrn Zumstein gemachten Reisen zur Ersteigung seiner Gipfel* (Vienna, 1824).

Rosa, Salvator; a celebrated painter, distinguished likewise as a musician and a poet. He was the son of an architect and surveyor, and was born at the village of Renella, in the kingdom of Naples, in 1615. He was intended for the church; but leaving, of his own accord, the seminary in which he had been placed for education, at the age of sixteen, he devoted himself to the study of music, and with such success that he became a skilful composer. His eldest sister having married Francesco Francanzani, a painter of considerable talent, Salvator, from frequenting his work-room, acquired a predilection for the art, in which he afterwards excelled. He at first amused himself with copying whatever pleased his fancy in the paintings of his brother-in-law; and his latent genius being thus awakened, his sketches were so much admired, that he was easily persuaded to adopt painting as a profession. But his taste was formed more from the study of nature among the wilds of the Apennines than from the lessons of other artists; and he delighted in delineating scenes of gloomy grandeur and terrible magnificence, to which the boldness of his conceptions, and the fidelity of his representations, communicate a peculiar degree of interest. He worked for some time at Naples in obscurity, till, one of his pictures being observed by the famous painter Lanfranco, he generously recommended Salvator to notice, and procured him effectual patronage and support. He removed to Rome, where he established his reputation, and raised himself to celebrity and independence. He afterwards went to Florence, where he was patronised and employed by the grand-duke and other members of the family of Medici. At length returning to Rome, he painted many pictures for the churches in that city, where he died in 1673. His satires and other poetical productions have been often printed under the title of *Rime di Salvatore Rosa, Pittore e Poeta Napolitano.* On account of his caustic wit, he was excluded from the Roman academy. Some time after, the academy having refused admission to another artist, who practised surgery as well as painting, Salvator Rosa observed that it was very injudicious in them, as the academy greatly needed a surgeon to replace the legs and arms that the members daily dislocated.

ROSARY, among the Catholics, consists of a string with a number of small beads of different sizes, which they use in saying over their prayers. It was introduced, according to some, by Dominicus de Guzman, the founder of the Dominican friars, in the first half of the thirteenth century. There are always in the rosary five or fifteen divisions, each containing ten small beads and one large one: for each of the smaller beads an Ave Maria, and for each of the larger a Paternoster (q. v.) is repeated. The Benedictine monks, however, as early as the sixth century, are said to have repeated their prayers, while at their work, according to a series of small beads, which were fastened upon a string. In honor of the victory obtained over the Turks at Lepanto (Oct. 7, 1571), pope Gregory XIII, in 1573, instituted the festival of the rosary, which is annually solemnized on the first Sunday of October. Pope Clement XI extended this festival through all the Catholic part of Western Europe, in honor of the victory gained over the Turks at Peterwardein, Aug. 5, 1716. The Asiatic worshippers of the grand lama, and the Mohammedans, make use of a similar string, provided with beads, for saying their prayers. The string of the Mohammedans has ninety-nine small beads, which they, in their prayers, drop through their fingers, one after the other, while they recount the ninety-nine qualities of the Deity, mentioned in the first part of the Koran. Their beads are generally made of holy earth, from Mecca or Medina.

ROSCELLINUS. (See *Nominalists.*)

ROSCOE, William, was born in 1752. His parents were in an humble sphere of life, and could only afford him a common school education; and even this was interrupted. At an early age, he was articled to an attorney in Liverpool; and this obliged him to study the Latin language; but he did not confine himself to what was necessary to his profession, and by dint of hard study, he read and made himself master of the most distinguished Latin classics. In this he was assisted by a friend. He next studied the Italian and French languages, and in the former he became uncommonly proficient. He still found time to attend to his business, and to peruse the English poets. At the age of sixteen, he commenced poet, and composed Mount Pleasant, a descriptive poem. Having finished his clerkship, he was taken into partnership, by Mr. Aspinall, an attorney of considerable practice; and he carried on the whole of the business, to which he paid a strict attention. During this period he contracted a friendship with doctor Enfield and doctor Aikin. Painting and statuary were also objects of his attention, and, in 1773, he read, at the society in Liverpool, an ode on those subjects, and also sometimes read lectures there. When the question of the slave-trade was brought before the public, Mr. Roscoe took a warm part in favor of the abolition, and most cordially joined Mr. Clarkson in his endeavors. He also wrote a reply to a Spanish Jesuit on that subject. His Scriptural Refutation of a Pamphlet on the Licitness of the Slave-Trade, and his Wrongs of Africa, appeared in 1788; and, in 1795, he brought out the work which has gained him so much celebrity—the Life of Lorenzo de' Medici (2 vols., 4to., 1795). About the year 1797, Mr. Roscoe retired from the practice of an attorney, and entered himself as a student of Gray's Inn, with a view to the bar. During this period, he had leisure for other studies, and published the Nurse, a poem, from the Italian, and wrote the Life and Pontificate of Leo X (4 vols., 1805). Though the Life of Leo is not equal to his Lorenzo, it is a composition which displays talent and extensive research. Mr. Roscoe being attached to the whig party, they supported him as a candidate to represent Liverpool, and he was successful, but at the next election was thrown out. He had, some time before, entered into business at Liverpool as a banker, but was unsuccessful. He died in June, 1831. Mr. Roscoe was the author of several political pamphlets, and the great mover and supporter of several public works in Liverpool. To the botanic garden and to the Atheneum he lent much effective assistance. His Life and Correspondence has been recently announced.

ROSCOMMON, Wentworth Dillon, earl of, was born in Ireland, in 1633, and was educated at Caen, in Normandy. Returning to England on the restoration, he plunged into the dissipation of the dissolute court, ruined his estate by gaming, became involved in quarrels, and found it necessary to go to Ireland. Here he pursued nearly the same course, and soon after returned to England. From this time he began to act with more discretion, and became distinguished among the wits of the day. On the accession of James II (q. v.), he went to Italy, and died at Rome in 1684. His principal production is the poetical Essay on translated Verse. Johnson calls him the most correct writer of English verse before Dryden.

Rose. The rose has always been the favorite flower among civilized nations. The beauty of its foliage, the elegance of its form, the large size and agreeable tints of the flowers, together with their delicious fragrance, have all conspired to acquire for it the distinction of the queen of flowers. The species of rose are numerous, especially on the Eastern continent, and are extremely difficult to distinguish. All seem to be exclusively confined to the temperate and cold parts of the northern hemisphere. About half a dozen are found in the U. States. They are spiny shrubs, with pinnated leaves, provided with stipules at their base; the flowers are very large, and are disposed, in a greater or less number, at the summit of the branches, or upon lateral branchlets; the calyx is enlarged below, and contracted at its orifice, where it divides into five lanceolate segments; the corolla consists of five heart-shaped petals, and the stamens are numerous; the seeds are very numerous, covered with a sort of down, and are attached to the interior of the tube of the calyx, which, after flowering, takes the form of a fleshy globular or ovoid berry. The rose has given its name to a distinct family of plants, the *rosaceæ*, comprehending the apple, peach, cherry, raspberry, strawberry, &c. Roses in general are not delicate with respect to the nature of the soil, but flourish in almost every kind. Their easy culture has distributed them into almost every garden. The color is, in different species and varieties, red, white, yellow, purple, or striped, either simple or in almost numberless shades and mixtures; the flowers are single, semidouble and double. Many hundred varieties are enumerated in the European catalogues, and new ones are produced annually: some of them are quite black. New varieties are obtained from seed, but the usual mode of propagation is by layers. All will grow by cuttings, and some freely, but this mode is seldom resorted to. For preserving delicate varieties, the best mode seems decidedly that of budding on hardier sorts. To produce strong flowers, requires some attention in pruning: old wood should be yearly cut out, and the young shoots thinned and shortened according to their strength, and whether number or magnitude of flowers be desired. Where very large roses are wanted, all the buds except that on the extreme point of each shoot should be pinched off as soon as they make their appearance, and the plant liberally supplied with water. Some roses are cultivated on a large scale for commercial purposes, for distilling rose water, and for making ottar or essential oil of roses. Six pounds of rose petals will impregnate, by distillation, a gallon of water strongly with their odor; but a hundred pounds scarcely affords half an ounce of ottar. (See *Ottar of Roses.*) Perfumers, distillers and confectioners make great use of the perfume of the rose. A conserve and a sirup, which are used in medicine, are also prepared from their petals: these last, if bruised and reduced to a paste, moulded and dried, will preserve their fragrance for many years. In the north of Europe, the berries of the rose, with the addition of sugar, are sometimes employed in the preparation of domestic wines; and the pulp, in a dried state, affords a grateful ingredient in sauces. The leaves of every kind of rose have been recommended as a substitute for tea; and in Europe are employed in currying the finer kinds of leather.

Rose Acacia (*robinia hispida*); a highly ornamental, flowering shrub, inhabiting the southern parts of the Alleghany mountains, and now frequently seen in gardens, in Europe, as well as in the U. States. It is a species of locust, and the flowers resemble those of the common locust, but are very large, and rose-colored. Their beauty is enhanced by the brown, bristly covering of the stalks and calyx; they somewhat resemble the moss rose, in this respect. The stem is very hispid. (See *Locust.*)

Rose Feasts. At Salency (a village near Noyon, in the ci-devant Picardy, now department of the Oise), a festival, of a peculiar kind, is celebrated June 8. A girl is selected (formerly by the seigneur, at present probably by the justice of the peace) from three most distinguished for female virtues. Her name is even pronounced from the pulpit, that objections may be made to her. She is afterwards conducted in procession to the church, where she hears the vesper service, kneeling in a place of honor. After this, she used to open a ball in the evening with the seigneur. She receives a present. The girl is called *la rosière*, because she is adorned with roses. The feast was imitated in several other places (e. g. at Surène, near Paris). Though the effect has been good, it is undoubtedly exaggerated by some travellers. The eighth of June is the day of St. Medard, bishop of Noyon (475 to 545), and tradition says he established the festival, but the Bollandists (q. v.) mention nothing of this fact. It is more probable that its foundation dates from the time of Louis XIII. From him comes the silver clasp, which holds the wreath of roses together; and to his time probably belongs the picture of the first rose feast in the church of Salency.

Rose of Jericho (*anastatica hierichuntia*); a cruciferous plant, growing in the arid wastes of Arabia and Palestine, which possesses the curious property of recovering its original form, however dry it may be, upon immersion in water. The generic name has been applied to it from this circumstance, and, in the Greek, signifies *resurrection*. It is a small, annual, herbaceous plant, three or four inches high, with minute white flowers, which are succeeded by a little pod, divided into two cells, each containing one or two seeds. When the seeds are ripe, the leaves fall off, the branches curl inwards, and interlace, forming a rounded pellet about as large as the fist, which is torn up and rolled over the sands by the autumnal winds. In this state, if moistened, it gradually unrolls its branches, and contracts again into a ball as it becomes dry. This circumstance has often been taken advantage of to impose on credulous persons.

Rose Wood (*amyris balsamifera*); a small West Indian tree, the wood of which forms an important article of commerce, and is much used by cabinet-makers for the covering or veneering of tables and other furniture. Its grain is of a dark color, and very beautiful. The tree yields an odoriferous balsam, much esteemed as a medicine in various diseases, and as an external application. A species of amyris grows wild in East Florida; but it is little known.

Rosemary (*rosemarinus officinalis*); a shrubby, aromatic plant, growing wild in the southern parts of Europe. It belongs to the *labiatæ*, and has but two stamens. The stem is three or four feet high, bearing opposite linear and sessile leaves, which are smooth and shining above, and whitish and cottony on their inferior surface; the flowers are pale-blue, or almost ash-colored, and disposed in little racemes, which arise from the axils of the leaves towards the extremities of the branches: they expand in April and May. All parts of the plant have a strong and penetrating odor. The leaves are used in Italy for seasoning certain dishes. Rosemary is tonic and stimulant, and formerly enjoyed considerable repute as a medicine, but is now rarely employed. It yields, by distillation, a light, pale, essential oil, of great fragrance. It is less used in medicine than as an aromatic, and is the principal ingredient in Hungary water.—A second species of rosemary is found towards the southern extreme of South America.

Rosenmüller, John George, a celebrated German theologian (born in 1736, died in 1815), was professor of theology at Erlangen and Leipsic, and distinguished himself as a preacher, and by his activity in the cause of education. Of his numerous works, we shall mention only his *Scholia in N. Testament.*, and his *Hist. Interpretationis Librorum Sacrorum* (5 vols., 1795—1814).—His son *Ernest Frederic Charles*, a distinguished Orientalist, born in 1768, was educated at Leipsic, where he heard the lectures of Morus, Platner, Beck, &c. In 1795, he was extraordinary professor of Arabic, and, in 1813, ordinary professor of Oriental literature. Among his works are his valuable *Scholia in Vet. Testamentum; Scholia in Nov Testamentum*; the East, in Ancient and Modern Times (6 vols., 1818—20); Manual of Biblical Antiquities, and Manual of Biblical Criticism and Exegesis (4 vols., in German). These works contain a great mass of valuable matter, critical, exegetical, geographical, and historical. Rosenmüller has also rendered important services to Oriental literature by his *Institutiones Linguæ Arabicæ* (1818); *Arabum Adagia; Analecta Arabica* (1826, 2 vols.), &c.—A second son, *John Christopher* (born 1771, died 1820), was an eminent anatomist, and (1802) professor of anatomy and surgery at Leipsic. Besides some writings on subjects of natural history, he was the author of Anatomico-Surgical Delineations (German and Latin, 1804—12 3 parts), Manual of Anatomy, and of several articles in Pierer's Medical Dictionary, and other periodicals, and of various other literary works.

Roses, War of the, from the reign of Henry VI (1452) to that of Henry VII (1486). (See *Great Britain*; also *Edward IV* and *V*, *Richard III*, and *Henry VI* and *VII*.)

Rosetta; a city of Egypt, near the mouth of that branch of the Nile anciently called the *Bolbitic*, now commonly called the *canal of Rosetta* (see *Nile*); lat. 31° 24′ N.; lon. 30° 28′ E.; population, 13,500, principally Copts. Rosetta is thought to have been built by the caliphs, in the ninth century. It is important as a depot of goods brought down the river, and forms the medium of communication between Alexandria and Cairo. The city is more neatly built than the other Egyptian cities, and is particularly distinguished for the beauty and luxuriant vegetation of its environs. The streets are not, however, broad; and, as the houses are of several stories, each projecting over that beneath, they nearly meet at the top, which promotes coolness, but gives a gloomy appearance to the place. The celebrated Rosetta stone was found here during the French campaign in Egypt. (See *Hieroglyphics*.)

Rosetta Stone.—See *Hieroglyphics* (p. 314); also the work of the marquis Spineto on Hieroglyphics, mentioned in that article. In his work, a full account is given of the discovery of the art of deciphering the hieroglyphics, for which this stone furnished the first means. There is also (p. 58) a translation of the curious decree, which is partly reprinted in Stuart's Translation of Greppo's Essay on the Hieroglyphic System.

Rosicrucians; members of a society the existence of which became known, unexpectedly, at the beginning of the seventeenth century. Its object was, ostensibly, the reformation of state, church, and individuals; but closer examination showed that the discovery of the philosopher's stone was the true object of the fully initiated. A certain Christian Rosenkreuz, who was said to have lived long among the Bramins, in Egypt, &c., was pretended to have founded the order, in the fourteenth century; but the real founder is believed to have been Andreä, a German scholar, of the beginning of the sixteenth century, whose object, as is thought, was to purify religion, which had been degraded by scholastic philosophy. Others think that he only gave a new character to a society founded before him, by Agrippa von Nettesheim. Krause (mentioned in the article *Masonry, Free*) says that Andreä occupied himself from early youth with the plan of a secret society for the improvement of mankind. In 1614, he published his famous Reformation of the whole wide World, and *Fama Fraternitatis*. Christian enthusiasts and alchemists considered the society poetically described in those books as one really existing; and thus Andreä became the author of the later Rosicrucian fraternities, which extended over Europe, and were even brought into connexion with free-masonry. (q. v.) After a number of books had been written on the Rosicrucian system, and the whole exploded, the interest in the Rosicrucians was revived, in the latter half of the eighteenth century, in consequence of the abolition of the order of Jesuits, and the stories of their secret machinations, as well as of the frauds of Cagliostro (q. v.) and other notorious impostors.

Rosière, La. (See *Rose Feasts*.)

Rosin. (See *Resin*.)

Roskolnicians, also Raskolnicians; schismatics of the Russian Greek church. They call themselves *Starowerzi* (i. e. following the old faith), or *Isbraniki* (i. e. elected). They suffered much persecution under Peter the Great. Catharine II gave them religious liberty. Many tribes of Cossacks and a great part of the inhabitants of Siberia belong to this sect.

Rosoglio, or Rosoli; originally sometimes used as a generic term for the creams, or superfine liqueurs (see *Liqueurs*), but is more generally applied to a certain species of these.

Rosoli. (See *Rosoglio*.)

Ross. (See *North Polar Expeditions*.)

Ross, George, a signer of the Declaration of Independence, was born, in 1730, at Newcastle, Delaware, where his father was the pastor of the episcopal church. He commenced the study of the law in Philadelphia, at the age of eighteen, and, when admitted to the bar, established himself in Lancaster, Pennsylvania. In 1768, Mr. Ross was chosen a representative in the assembly of Pennsylvania, and retained his seat in that body until 1774, when he was elected one of the delegates to the first general congress at Philadelphia. At the time of his election, he was also appointed to report to the assembly of the province a set of instructions to regulate the conduct of himself and his associates. In 1777, indisposition caused Mr. Ross to resign his place in congress; on which occasion the inhabitants of Lancaster voted him a piece of plate, to be paid for out of the county stock. Mr. Ross, however, thought it his duty to decline the present. On the dissolution of the proprietary government in Pennsylvania, a general convention was assembled, in which Mr. Ross was ap pointed to assist in preparing a declaration of rights on behalf of the state, in forming rules of order for the convention, and in defining and settling what should be considered high treason and misprision of treason against the state, and what punishment should be inflicted for those offences. In April, 1779, Mr. Ross was appointed a judge of the court of admiralty for the state of Pennsylvania; but, in the ensuing July, a sudden and violent attack of the gout terminated his life in the fiftieth year of his age.

Ross, Man of. (See *Kyrle.*) The village of Ross is in Herefordshire, twelve miles south-east of Hereford, and a hundred and fifteen north-west of London.

Rossbach; a village, in the Prussian province of Saxony, between Naumburg and Merseburg, famous for the decisive victory which Frederic the Great obtained there over the imperial and French troops under marshal Soubise, Nov. 5, 1757.

Rossberg; a mountain in Switzerland, near the east bank of lake Zug, and not far from Righi. (q. v.) In 1806, in consequence of a long continuance of heavy rain, a large mass detached itself, and covered with desolation the valley of Goldau. Part of it reached lake Lowerz, which rose above its banks. Above a hundred lives were lost by this disaster.

Rossini, Gioachimo; the most popular of the living operatic composers of Italy, whose works have been received with equal applause on both sides of the Atlantic. In his seventeenth year, according to an Italian journal, Rossini began to unfold his musical talents, and in his thirtieth year he had already numbered above thirty brilliant triumphs. The annals of music hardly contain another such instance of rapid success. Rossini was born at Pesaro, a small town of Romagna, in 1792: his father was a strolling musician, his mother an under singer at the inferior theatres. While a child, he sang on the stage at Bologna with his mother, but received no regular musical education, relying principally upon his acquaintance with the works of recent composers, Haydn, Mozart, Cherubini, Spontini, and his own talents for singing. He began to compose at an early age, wrote an overture and a cantata (*Il Pianto d'Armonia*) in 1808, and became the director of a musical society. In 1812, his first opera was performed at the theatre Della Valle in Rome. His next productions were the following, written in the order in which they are given: *L'Inganno felice* (1812); *Ciro in Babilonia*, an oratorio; *La Pietra di Paragone*, a buffa, with which he made his debut in Milan and Ciampiale. His *Tancredi*, which was brought forward at Venice in 1813, with brilliant success, attracted the greatest attention. From that time his works were called for by all the Italian theatres; and, by his rapidity of execution, he contrived, though often to the injury of his reputation, to answer all the demands made upon him. It is well known that the same overture sometimes serves for several operas, both comic and tragic. His next pieces were *Aureliano in Palmira*; the buffa piece, *Il Turco in Italia*; *Elizabetta* (1815); *Il Barbiere di Seviglia*; *Otello* (1816); *Cenerentola*; *La Gazza ladra*; *Armida* (1817); *Moïse*; *Riccardo e Zoraide* (1818); *Odoardo e Cristina*; *La Donna del Lago*; *Bianco e Falliero* (1819); *Matilda di Chabran*, or *Corradino* (1821); *Zelmira* (1822); *Semiramide* (1823). In 1822, Rossini went to Vienna, and the next year to London. In 1824, he was at Paris, but produced little, and soon visited the northern parts of Germany. (See *Italy*, division *Italian Music.*)

Rosstrappe (*horse's hoof-mark*); one of the finest spots in the Hartz mountains, near the village Thale, on the river Bode, above which the rocks rise 830 feet. One of these, a rugged and precipitous peak, has on its top an indentation like the print of the hoof of a gigantic horse, which gives its name to the neighboring district.

Rostock; a seaport of the Baltic, in Mecklenburg-Schwerin, with 19,024 inhabitants, among whom no Jew is suffered. It was a member of the Hansa (q. v.) from the earliest time of this league to 1630, when the greater league was dissolved. Its former importance was great. Its university was founded in 1419; it has twenty-three *professores ordinarii*, but is one of the less important universities of Germany. No subject of Mecklenburg-Schwerin can have an appointment in that country under the government, without having studied for some time in Rostock. There are generally but about a hundred and fifty students there. The library has about 80,000 vols. Lat. N. 54° 0′ 1″; lon. E. 12° 12′ 16″. It is the largest city of the grand-duchy. In 1824, four hundred and eighty-six vessels entered this port, and five hundred and seventeen cleared out.

Rostopschin, Feodor, count, was born in 1760, of an ancient Russian family. He entered the imperial guards as a lieutenant, and afterwards travelled into foreign countries. He was afterwards highly promoted under Paul I, and loaded with orders, but afterwards dismissed in disgrace. Under Alexander, he obtained the important post of governor of Moscow, and exercised an important influence over the campaign of 1812, even if the assertion of the French, that the burning of the city was his work, should be untrue. He himself decidedly denied this charge in his *Vérité sur l'Incendie de Moscow* (Paris, 1824). It is certain, however, that he caused his villa near Moscow to be burnt, and took measures for the destruction of the magazines in that city. Buturlin calls him the author of the conflagration, and the public voice in Russia coincides with this opinion. In 1814, he accompanied the emperor Alexander to the congress at Vienna. He afterwards travelled, and spent several years in Paris, where he became acquainted with some of the most distinguished families, and united his daughter in marriage to a grandson of the celebrated count Ségur (French ambassador to the court of Catharine II). He returned to Russia, and died in Moscow, at the commencement of the year 1826.

Rostra (incorrectly *rostrum*); a tribunal (*suggestus*) in the forum in Rome, whence the orators used to harangue the people, so called from the beaks (*rostra*) of the ships taken from the Antiates, with which it was adorned.

Rot, Dry. (See *Dry Rot.*)

Rota or Ruota Romana; the highest papal court of appeal, whose jurisdiction extends over all Catholic Christendom, and which decides not only spiritual controversies, but all questions concerning ecclesiastical benefices of a value above five hundred *scudi;* and the decisions thereof have the highest authority, derived from the doctrine of the pope's infallibility. The *rota Romana* has a collegiate constitution, and consists of twelve prelates, of whom three must be Romans, one a German, one a Frenchman, and one a Spaniard. They collectively bear the title of *auditori della rota*, or auditors of the holy apostolical palace, because their sessions are held semi-weekly in the palace of the pope. The name of this court is derived, perhaps, from the circumstance that the floor of their hall is overlaid with marble slabs in the form of wheels (*rotæ*): according to some, it is so named because, in ancient Rome, a round public building stood upon the place where this tribunal was first established. Other supreme courts, as, for example, at Genoa, have borne the same name. This court ceased with the papal government, but is now reëstablished. (See *Curia, Papal.*)

Rotation. The motion of the different parts of a solid body about an axis is called *rotation*, being thus distinguished from the progressive motion of a body about some distant point or centre; thus the diurnal motion of the earth is a motion of rotation, but its annual motion one of revolution.

Rotation of Crops. Some sorts of crops exhaust the soils on which they grow, much less than others, as is the case with many of what are called *green* crops, when compared with the white or corn kind; so that it is highly advantageous to alternate them. Moreover, certain sorts of green crops are well suited, by the shade of their leaves and the kind of culture which they require while growing, for keeping the ground clean from weeds, and in a mellow and suitable state for the reception of the more valuable sorts of grain crops. All the culmiferous plants injure the ground in a high degree, which probably depends upon their having but few, and those small, leaves, so that they are obliged to draw their nourishment chiefly from the soil; also from their seeds ripening all at the same time, and the plants ceasing to grow when they begin to ripen, so that the roots cease to penetrate into the ground, and, of course, to move or loosen it. The green crops, and those of the root kind, being opposite to the white in each of the respects just mentioned, serve, generally speaking, when alternated with them, to counteract their injurious effects. The alternation of crops is a matter of vast importance in agriculture, and one in which great improvements have been made within the last century.

Roth; German for *red*, and found in many geographical names, as *Rothweil* (red village).

Rothschild. This celebrated European house has raised itself from an humble sphere to an unexampled degree of wealth and importance by judicious enterprise, a sagacious and systematic series of operations, which thousands of others had the same opportunities to take advantage of, a reputation for fair dealing, and a correct estimate of men and events. The father of the five brothers now living, Mayer Anselm, was born at Frankfort on the Maine, in 1743, and died in 1812. His parents died when he was but eleven years old, and he was, as is common with poor Jews in Germany, educated for a teacher. This occupation not suiting his taste, Rothschild engaged in trading, in a small way, and was not long after employed in a banking house in Hanover; and in a few years his industry and frugality made him master of a small capital. Returning to Frankfort, he married, and established the banking house, which is still in existence. His activity, intelligence and integrity in a short time procured him a continually increasing credit particularly after his nomination as agent to the landgrave of Hesse, in 1801. In 1802, 1803 and 1804, his affairs continued to prosper so much, that at this period he was able to contract for a Danish loan of four million dollars. The house now consists of his five sons; Anselm, born in 1773, the head of the house, resides at Frankfort; Solomon, born in 1774, resides alternately at Berlin and Vienna, principally at the latter place; Nathan, born in 1777, has lived in London since 1798; Charles, born in 1788, is at Naples; and James, born in 1792, at Paris. In 1813 occurred those political events which raised the house of Rothschild to the position it has since occupied in the commercial and financial concerns of the world. In a period of twelve years, about 500 million dollars were raised by the house for different powers, by way of loan or subsidy, which were distributed in nearly the following proportion: for England two hundred millions, for Austria fifty millions, for Prussia forty millions, for France eighty millions, for Naples fifty millions, for Russia twenty-five millions, for several German courts four millions, for Brazil twelve millions, exclusive of various other large sums. The remarkable success of the Rothschilds, setting aside the great opportunities which they have enjoyed from favorable circumstances, may be attributed to their strict adherence to two fundamental maxims. The first of these, in compliance with the dying injunctions of their father, is their conducting all their operations entirely in common. Every proposition of magnitude made to one of them is submitted to the deliberations of all; no project is adopted until thus fully discussed, and it is then executed by united efforts. A second principle is, not to aim at exorbitant profits, to set definite limits to every operation, and, so far as human prudence and oversight can do, to render it independent of accidental influences: in this maxim lies one of the main secrets of their strength. The reasonableness of their terms, the punctuality with which they execute their contracts, the simplicity and clearness of their plans, and their judicious manner of carrying them into effect, fortify their credit. A constant exchange of couriers is kept up between them, who are frequently in advance of those of the government. Several princes have publicly acknowledged their obligations by conferring nobility and other honors upon the different members of the family. In the latter part of 1831, the Rothschilds contracted for a loan of 15 million francs for the court of Rome, which may be increased to 25 millions.

Rotrou, Jean, a French tragic poet, born at Dreux, in 1609, was the most distinguished dramatic writer among the predecessors of Corneille. (q. v.) Of his thirty-six tragedies, tragi-comedies and comedies, only one—the tragedy of Venceslas (as revised by Marmontel)—keeps the stage; the plot of this piece is borrowed from the Spanish of Roxas. Rotrou endeavored to elevate the tone of the drama by giving it a moral purpose, and his heroes and heroines are made to utter Christian sentiments. Richelieu, who granted him a pension, could not prevail upon him to assist in decrying the *Cid* of Corneille. In 1650, Rotrou fell a victim to a pestilential disease, to which he nobly exposed himself in the discharge of his official duties, as one of the principal magistrates of his native place. His *Œuvres* appeared at Paris in 1820, in 5 vols. (See *France, Literature of*, division *Dramatic Poetry*.)

Rotteck, Charles von, a distinguished German historian, professor at the Catholic university of Freiburg, in Baden, was born in Freiburg, in 1775. In 1798, he was appointed professor of universal history. In 1818, he exchanged the chair of history for that of natural law and politics. He is a member of the academy of sciences in Munich. Rotteck is distinguished from almost all other German historians, by the circumstance that his works, in addition to deep research and critical acuteness, display a civic spirit, if we may call it so. Though born in a country where civil liberty was so little understood in the time of his education, he has, nevertheless, learned to understand it, and to trace its developement in history. His chief work is his Universal History, the ninth volume of which appeared in 1826. The sixth edition is probably published by this time. As a recommendation of this work, we would mention that the subscription for an abridgment of it was prohibited in Prussia in 1831. His work on Standing Armies and a National Militia was translated into English and French, and Benjamin Constant translated his Ideas on Representative Estates. Rotteck has been likewise active as a representative in the chamber of Baden. Besides his more extended works, he has written several important articles in periodicals and encyclopedias, and Manual of Natural Law and Politics. He would have found a noble field, had he been born in a country where the activities of men were unchecked by arbitrary institutions, or at a time of a warm struggle for freedom in his own country.

ROTTEN BOROUGHS. (See *Great Britain*, division *English Constitution*, p. 610, and *Parliamentary Reform*, at the close of the last volume of this work.)

ROTTERDAM; a city of the Netherlands, province of South Holland, on the right bank of the Meuse, which is here above a mile in width, twenty miles from its mouth; lat. 51° 55′ N.; lon. 4° 28′ E.; twelve miles south-east of the Hague, thirty-three south-west of Amsterdam. Rotterdam is the second city in the Dutch provinces, for commerce and wealth, and contains 63,093 inhabitants. The form of Rotterdam is triangular, its longest side (above a mile and a half in extent) stretching along the bank of the Meuse. The town is surrounded by a moat, and entered by six gates towards the land, and four towards the water. It is traversed by the Rotte, a broad canal, which here joins the Meuse. Rotterdam is intersected, even more than other towns in Holland, by canals, which divide the half of the town, near the river, into several insulated spots, connected by drawbridges. These canals are almost all bordered with trees. The row called the Boomtjes is the finest in the city, as well in regard to buildings as for its pleasant prospect across the Meuse. Next to the Boomtjes comes the Haring-vliet. The other streets are, in general, long, but narrow. The houses of Rotterdam are rather convenient than elegant: their height is of four, five or six stories. Of the public buildings of Rotterdam, the principal are the exchange, finished in 1736, the great church of St. Lawrence, from the top of which there is a most extensive prospect. After these come several other churches, the whole number of which is fifteen, the town-house (an old edifice), the admiralty, the academy, the theatre, the extensive buildings of the East India company, a number of large ware-houses, and a few manufactories. Rotterdam has an active transit trade; the manufactures are not extensive; sugar refineries and distilleries furnish the chief articles of industry. There are several learned societies. It is the birth-place of the celebrated Erasmus. Rotterdam received the title and privileges of a city in 1270. Its commerce suffered severely from the French revolution; and, in 1825, an inundation of the Meuse did great damage to the city. (See *Netherlands*.)

ROTUNDA (*rotonda*); every building round within and without, as the Pantheon, in Rome.

ROUBILLIAC, Louis Francis, a sculptor, was a native of Lyons, in France, who settled in England, in the reign of George I; and, in the absolute dearth of native talent which prevailed at that period, he long stood at the head of his profession. He executed a statue of Händel for Vauxhall gardens, and another of sir Isaac Newton, erected at Trinity college, Cambridge; but was chiefly employed on sepulchral monuments. He wrote satires in his native language. He died, in London, in 1762.

ROUBLE; a Russian coin. (For the silver rouble, see *Coin*, division *Russian*; for the paper rouble, see *Assignation*.) By the official valuation of the paper rouble, in the payment of taxes, a few years since, one silver rouble was equal to three roubles sixty copecks paper.

ROUCOU. (See *Annotto*.)

ROUÉ. This term is applied to a person, in the fashionable world, who is devoted to a life of pleasure and sensuality, and regardless of the restraints of moral principle. Philip, duke of Orleans, who, during the minority of Louis XV, was regent of France, and had a low opinion of men in general, and his friends in particular, applied the name of *roués* to his favorites and boon companions, to signify that they were fit to be broken on the wheel.

ROUEN (Rothomagus); a city of France, formerly capital of the province of Normandy, at present of the department of the Lower Seine, on the right bank of the river Seine, eighty-six miles north-west of Paris, forty-five south-east of Havre. The population, by the official enumeration of 1827, was 90,000: it is now estimated to exceed 100,000. Rouen is an archiepiscopal see, and the seat of various judicial and administrative authorities, and is one of the richest commercial cities of France. The Seine is crossed by a bridge of boats, which is paved, and rises and falls with the tide, and a new stone bridge, recently erected. The city is not prettily built, the streets being mostly narrow and dark, and the houses chiefly of wood. The quays along the river are handsome. The principal public buildings are the great cathedral, the church of the ancient abbey of St. Ouen, remarkable for its lofty tower, the *palais de justice*, and the theatre. In the market-place *aux veaux* is a statue of the maid of Orleans, who was burnt here by the English, in 1430. Rouen has several literary and scientific institutions and societies, and seminaries of education, a public library, a mint, fourteen churches, several hospitals, &c. The transit trade of Rouen is considerable. The city is seventy miles from the sea, including the windings of the river, and, with the aid of the tide, vessels of 150 or 200 tons come up to the quays. It is more important as a manufacturing place, having manufactures of cotton, linen, woollen, iron ware, paper, hats, pottery, sugar-refineries, &c. Dyeing is also extensively carried on.

Rouget de l'Isle. (See *Marseillaise Hymn.*)

Roum (i. e. the *kingdom of the Romans*); a name given to Natolia by Solyman, sultan of the Turks, when he invaded and became master of it, in the eleventh century. It is now chiefly applied to a part of Asiatic Turkey, extending from the Mediterranean to the Black sea, east of Caramania and Natolia, and west of Armenia and the government of Diarbekir, including the governments of Sivas, Adana and Marasch. (See *Turkey in Asia.*)

Roumelia. (See *Romania.*)

Round Robin (corruption of *ruban rond*, a round ribbon) was used, originally, by the French officers when signing a remonstrance. They wrote their names in a circular form, so that no one should be obliged to head the list.

Round Table. If we may believe tradition, towards the end of the fifth century, there reigned in Britain a Christian king, the British Uther-Pendragon, who had a most powerful and not less wise and benevolent enchanter, Merlin, for a counsellor. Merlin advised him to assemble all his knights, who were distinguished for piety, courage, and fidelity towards him, at feasts about a round table. It was calculated to receive fifty knights, and was to be occupied, for the present, only by forty-nine, one place remaining empty for an occupant yet unborn. This was Arthur, or Artus, son of the king by Igerna, whom the king, by the magic power of Merlin, was permitted to enjoy under the form of her husband Merlin had exacted a promise that the education of the prince should be intrustedto him; and he accordingly instructed him in every thing becoming a brave, virtuous and accomplished knight. Arthur, therefore, at a later period, occupied the empty seat at the round table, which, under him, became the resort of all valiant, pious and noble knights. (See *Merlin*, and *Arthur.*) This table, admission to which became the reward of the greatest virtues and feats of arms, afforded materials for the romantic poets of the Anglo-Normans, forming a distinct cycle of characters and adventures. (See *Romance*, and *Chivalry.*) According to another account, Arthur himself established the round table at York. Von Hammer thinks the fiction is of Eastern origin. The adventures of the knights of the round table are founded on the legend of the Sangreal, or Sangraal, which is probably a corruption of the Latin *sanguis realis*, or the French *saing real* (true blood). According to this legend, Joseph of Arimathea received into the cup from which Jesus drank at the last supper the blood which flowed from his side on the cross. By means of this cup, called *graal*, Joseph performed the most astonishing miracles, in different countries, particularly in Britain—a power which was also possessed by his descendants, who inherited the cup. In the course of time, however, it was lost; and, for the purpose of recovering it, Pendragon, father of Arthur, founded the order of the round table, the knights of which bound themselves to wander over the whole world in search of the sangraal. This legend was probably blended with the British traditions of king Arthur by the Trouvéres, or Anglo-Norman poets. Among the romances of the round table, are Tristan de Leonnois, Lancelot du Lac (see *Lancelot*), Perceforest, Sangraal, &c.

Rousseau, Jean Baptiste, an eminent French lyric poet, born at Paris, in 1671, was the son of a shoemaker, but received a good education, and, at an early period, displayed a strong taste for poetry. In 1688, he obtained a situation in the service of the French ambassador at Copenhagen, and subsequently accompanied marshal Tallard to England, as his secretary. He wrote several pieces for the theatre, on the success of one of which, having, according to the Parisian custom, appeared on the stage to receive the congratulations of the audience, he is said to have had the ingratitude to disown his father, when the old man, rejoicing at his son's triumph, came forward to speak to him, before the friends who surrounded him. In 1701, he was admitted into the academy of inscriptions and belles-lettres, and his lyric compositions procured him high reputation among the French literati; but his turn for satire, and his quarrelsome temper, at length involved him in disgrace. Some abusive and indecent verses were circulated at Paris, which Rousseau was accused of having written, but which he disclaimed, and professed to have discovered the author in the person of his enemy, Saurin. To relieve himself from the obloquy under which he labored, he commenced a prosecution of that academician, for composing the defamatory couplets in question, and having failed in substantiating the allegation, he was exiled from France in 1712. He went to Switzerland, and afterwards resided at Vienna, under the patronage of prince Eugene. The latter part of his life was spent in the Netherlands, where he obtained a pension from the duke of Aremberg, which he resigned on having forfeited the favor of that nobleman. His death took place at Brussels, in 1741. An edition of his works was published under his own inspection, by Tonson (London, 1723, 2 vols., 4to.); and since his death they have been often printed, in various forms. The best edition is that of Amar, with a commentary and life of the author (5 vols. Paris, 1820). The same editor has also published his *Œuvres Poétiques*, with a commentary (2 vols., 1824). Rousseau's works are—1. Four books of Odes, the first book containing odes from the Psalms: purity and elegance of expression are here combined with beauty and dignity of versification; but the lyric enthusiasm is often wanting; 2. cantatas, of which he was the creator, and in which he is very distinguished; 3. epistles in verse, the least pleasing of his works, but highly popular in their day, on account of their satirical allusions; 4. allegories, forced and monotonous; 5. epigrams, which, next to his odes and cantatas, are the best of his works, and, with some exceptions, are witty, finely turned, and well expressed; 6. four comedies in verse, and two in prose; 7. his operas have no merit.

Rousseau, Jean Jacques, born at Geneva, in 1712, was the son of a watch-maker. His mother died in bringing him into the world, and he therefore calls his birth his first misfortune. In his Confessions, he tells us that at the age of seven he was very devout; that at this time he was a great reader of romances; and at the age of eight knew Plutarch's Lives by heart. He also became acquainted with Tacitus and Grotius, which lay about in his father's shop, while quite a boy, and his musical taste was displayed at the same early age. In his tenth year, he was placed with a clergyman in the country, and in his fourteenth was articled to an engraver, whose severity disgusted him with his situation. He therefore ran away from his master, and, after wandering about for some time in Savoy, became a convert to the Catholic religion, to save himself from starvation. Being placed in a monastery to receive the necessary instruction, the young convert soon made his escape, and, after a series of adventures, was recommended, by a clergyman, to the notice of madame de Warens, in Annecy, who caused him to be instructed in science and music, and treated him with the greatest affection. At the age of twenty, Rousseau went to France, with the expectation of being able to maintain himself by giving lessons in music. In Besançon, he sang at some concerts with success, and received the promise of a place; but after teaching music some time at Chamberry, he went, on account of ill health, to Montpellier. Here, finding the sea air not to agree with him, he returned to his benefactress, and remained with her until 1742, when he received the place of secretary to the French ambassador in Venice. After remaining there a year and a half, he went to Paris, and made his living by copying music, employing his leisure hours in the study of natural science. In 1750, he gained the prize offered by the academy of Dijon, on the question, whether the revival of learning has contributed to the improvement of morals, taking the negative side of the question, it is said, at the suggestion of Diderot. He soon after brought out his *Devin du Village*, a comic opera, of which he had himself composed the music. This piece was received with general favor, and the author was almost worshipped by the French; but the appearance of his celebrated Letter on French Music (1753), in which he pointed out its defects, excited a general storm. Singers and connoisseurs, who could not wield the pen, contributed to spread calumnies, pasquinades and caricatures against the author, who retired to Geneva. By his change of religion he had lost the rights of a citizen. He now again embraced Protestantism, and was formally reinstated in the privileges of a free citizen of Geneva. From Geneva, Rousseau went to Chamberry, where he wrote his essay *Sur l'Inégalité parmi les Hommes*. This work excited still more sensation than his prize essay. In it he compares the wild and civilized man, represents the former as the state of nature and innocence, and treats the idea of property, and the wealth and inequality of condition to which it gives rise, as the source of misery and corruption among men. He now returned to Paris, and, fixing himself at Montmorency (q. v.), wrote his Social Compact, his New Eloisa, and his Emilius—works which had a powerful influence on his age. His political treatises, particularly the essays on the social compact, and the inequality of conditions, were the sources of many of the speculative errors of the French revolution. His New Eloisa produced a very different, but equally strong sensation in France, where love merely fluttered around the toilet, and in those countries where female virtue was looked upon with respect. His celebrated work on education, *Émile, ou de l'Éducation* (1762), was originally written for the use of a mother. It was condemned by parliament to be burnt on account of its religious views, and he himself was sentenced to imprisonment. He wished to retire to Geneva; but he was also threatened with imprisonment there, and his book was burnt by the common hangman. He therefore took refuge in Moitiers-Travers, a small village of Neufchâtel, where he again found himself among Protestants, the simplicity of whose worship was agreeable to him. The Geneva clergy assailing him from their pulpits, he wrote his celebrated Letters from the Mountains, in reply to their calumnies. This work, with his Letter to the Archbishop of Paris, and his *Dictionnaire Physique Portatif*, were publicly burnt in Paris, in 1765. New troubles drove him from Moitiers, and he resided two months on Peter's island, in the lake of Bienne. His residence here produced his *Botaniste sans Maître*. Neither was he long tolerated here; but the canton of Berne ordered him to quit the country without delay in the severest season of the year. On reaching Paris, he became the object of ridicule to the philosophers, but was kindly received by Hume, whom he accompanied to England; but, yielding to his unfounded suspicions of his friends in England, towards whom he conducted with the most perverse ingratitude, he left the country, and returned to Paris in 1767. (See Hume's *Private Correspondence*, London, 1820.) In 1768 he published his Musical Dictionary, and soon after appeared his melo drama of Pygmalion. As he grew older his dislike of society increased, and he retired in May, 1778, to Ermenonville (q. v.), near Paris, where he died of apoplexy, July 2 of the same year, at the age of sixty-six years. He was buried in the isle of poplars, where a monument is erected to his memory. The principal traits of his character were an enthusiastic passion for love and freedom, a spirit of paradox, an inflexible obstinacy, and a warm zeal for the good of men, combined with a gloomy hypochondria. His works were published at Paris, 10 vols., 1764, and have often been republished. The best edition is that of 1824, seq., 20 vols., with the notes of Musset-Pathay, who is the author of an excellent work—*Histoire de la Vie et des Ouvrages de J. J. Rousseau* (1 vol., Paris, 1827). Theresa Levasseur became his companion in 1745; in 1768 Rousseau married her. His children by her had all been placed in the foundling hospital. She was faithful to him, and knew how to gratify his humors, but had no other merit. In 1791, a *fête champètre* was established at Montmorency, in honor of Rousseau, and his bones were deposited, in 1794, in the Pantheon.

Roussillon; before the French revolution, a province of France, once belonging to Spain, bounded north by Languedoc east by the Mediterranean, south by Catalonia, and west by the Pyrenees; about eighteen leagues in length, and twelve in breadth. The land is fertile in general. The principal rivers are the Tet and Tech. Perpignan (q. v.) is the capital. It now forms the department of the Eastern Pyrenees. The counts of Roussillon governed this district for a long time. The last count bequeathed it to Alphonso of Arragon, in 1178. In 1462, it was ceded to Louis XI of France; but in 1493 it was restored to the kings of Arragon, and in 1659 was finally annexed to France by the treaty of the Pyrenees. (See *Pyrenees, Peace of.*)

Roussillon Wines; in general, the wines of the province of this name. The best for export are those of Baix, Tormilla, Salces, Rivesaltes, Spira, Collioure, Bagnols, Parcous, and St. André. The red sorts are thick, of a beautiful color, and used chiefly to improve other wines. A particular sort is called Grenache, and is, at first, similar to the Alicant wine, dark red, but grows paler with age, and in the sixth or seventh year is similar to the famous Cape wine. Of the white Roussillon wines, the Maccabeo is the most costly

Roveredo (in German, *Rovereith*); a well built town in Tyrol, in the valley of the Adige, on the road from Trent to Peschiera, with about 12,000 inhabitants who chiefly live by spinning, dyeing, and selling silk, particularly sewing silk; lat. 45° 55′ 36″ N.; lon. 11° 0′ 43″ E. The place is of military importance, as is proved by several battles which have been fought there. Masséna obtained a victory at this place over a part of the army of Wurmser, September 3 and 4, 1796. The loss of the Austrians was estimated at 5000 men and 25 cannons.

ROVIGO; a town on a branch of the Adige, in the Lombardo-Venetian kingdom, with 1000 inhabitants, from which Napoleon gave the title of duke to his minister of police, Savary. (q. v.)

ROWE, Nicholas, an English dramatic poet, born in 1673, at Little Berkford, Bedfordshire, was the son of John Rowe, a serjeant-at-law. He studied at Westminster, as king's scholar, under the celebrated Dr. Busby, and at the age of sixteen was entered a student at the Middle Temple; but on the death of his father, he gave up the law, and turned his chief attention to polite literature. At the age of twenty-four, he produced his tragedy of the Ambitious Stepmother; Tamerlane followed, which was intended as a compliment to king William, who was figured under the conquering Tartar; while Louis XIV, with almost equal want of versimilitude, ranked as the Turkish Bajazet. It was, however, a successful piece; and indeed, with little nature, contains many elevated and manly sentiments. His next dramatic performance was the Fair Penitent, re-modelled from the Fatal Dowry of Massinger. In 1706, he wrote the Biter, a comedy, which being altogether a failure, he was prudent enough to keep to his own line, and, from that time to 1715, produced his Ulysses, Royal Convert, Jane Shore, and Lady Jane Grey. When the duke of Queensbury was made secretary of state, he appointed Mr. Rowe his under-secretary. This post he lost by the death of his patron; and, on the accession of George I, he was made poet-laureate, and also obtained several posts, the emoluments of which, aided by his paternal fortune, enabled him to live respectably. He died in 1718, in his forty-fifth year, and was buried in Westminster abbey, where his widow erected a monument to his memory. Rowe was respectable, and possessed agreeable talents for society. His dramatic fables are generally interesting, and the situations striking; his style singularly sweet and poetical; his pieces forcibly arrest attention, although they but slightly affect the heart. As an original poet, Rowe appears to advantage in a few tender and pathetic ballads; but as a translator, he assumes a higher character, as in his version of Lucan's Pharsalia, published after his death, which, although too diffuse, was highly praised by Johnson. The poetical works of Rowe were published collectively, in 3 vols., 12mo., 1719.

ROWE, Elizabeth, a lady distinguished for her piety and literary talents, was the daughter of Mr. Singer, a dissenting minister of Ilchester, where she was born in 1674. She became accomplished in music and painting at a tender age, and even attempted versification in her twelfth year. In 1696, she published a volume of Poems on several Occasions, by Philomela. The charms of her person and conversation procured her many admirers, among whom she chose Mr. Rowe, the son of a dissenting minister, whom she lost a few years after marriage, by a consumption, at the early age of twenty-eight. On this event she retired to Frome, where she produced the greatest part of her works, the most popular of which was her Friendship in Death, or Twenty Letters from the Dead to the Living—a work of a lively imagination, strongly imbued with devotional feeling. This production, which was published in 1728, was followed, in 1729 and 1731, by Letters, moral and entertaining, in Prose and Verse. In 1736, she published a History of Joseph, a poem, which she had composed in early life. After her death (1736), doctor Isaac Watts published her Devout Exercises of the Heart; and in 1739 her Miscellaneous Works, in Prose and Verse, appeared in 2 vols., 8vo., with an account of her life and writings prefixed.

ROXANA. (See *Alexander*.)

ROXBURGH, duke of, was a celebrated bibliomanist. His library of 9353 works, which was particularly rich in old romances of chivalry, and in early English poetry, was sold by public auction in London, in 1812. The catalogue was made out by G. and W. Nicol. The prices paid for some works were enormous. A copy of the first edition of Boccaccio (Venice, in 1471, folio) was bought by the marquis of Blandford (duke of Marlborough), for 2260 pounds sterling; a copy of the first work printed by Caxton, with a date, Recuyell of the Historyes of Troye (1471, folio), was sold for 1000 guineas; and a copy of the first edition of Shakspeare (1623, folio) for 100 guineas. The Roxburgh club, formed in commemoration of this triumph of bibliomany, celebrates its anniversary (June 17), on that of the sale of the Boccaccio. Every year, one of the members is required to be at the expense of an impression of some rare book, of which only copies enough for the club are struck off.

Roxolana. (See *Solyman* II.)

Roy, Rammohun. (See *Rammohun Roy*.)

Royalists. In France, after the revolution of 1792, this name was given to the adherents of the Bourbons ; and from the restoration, in 1814, down to the revolution of 1830, it served to designate those who were in favor of the old system of things, and opposed to liberal principles. Those of the former royalists who continue to adhere to, and in fact are often active for the elder line of the Bourbons, are now generally called *Carlists* (from Charles X). Those royalists who carried farthest the doctrine of legitimacy (q. v.), the touchstone of this party, are called *ultras*, without addition, though this term might be, and in some cases actually is, applied to the ultra-liberals.

Royer-Collard, Pierre Paul, one of the most profound orators in the left centre (see *Centre*) of the French chamber of deputies, born in 1763, at Sompuis, near Vitry le François, in 1789 was chosen advocate of the parliament of Paris. He was elected a member of the common council of Paris, being considered a friend of legal freedom. With the tenth of August his membership ceased. He passed safely through the bloody period of 1793 and 1794, and in May, 1797, was chosen a member of the council of five hundred, from the department of Marne ; but three months later, on the 18th of Fructidor, he was expelled, because he was opposed to the oath required of the clergy. He afterwards, together with the marquis of Clermont-Gallerande, the abbé Montesquiou, and M. Becquey, was one of the counsellors of the king in France, until Louis XVIII fled to England, when this body was dissolved. Royer-Collard now lived devoted to the sciences, and, in 1811, was made dean of the philosophical faculty, and professor of the history of modern philosophy. Here, for two years, he displayed the talents of a Pascal. So profound was he in theory, so convincing was his logic, and so animated and eloquent his delivery ! Victor Cousin was his scholar. He likewise exhibited the rare talent of philosophical eloquence as a political orator in the chamber, where his calm and firm character gave something of the sublime to his independent thought. Royer-Collard adhered, as appears from his Discourses (*Discours*), printed in December, 1813, to the Scotch school of philosophy. In 1814, Louis XVIII appointed him director-general of the press and the book trade, and afterwards state counsellor and knight of the legion of honor. When Napoleon returned, in 1815, he resigned all his political offices, and remained only a professor. After the second restoration, he was again called into the council of state, and appointed president of the department of education. Here he effected much good, especially in the normal school, which is now abolished ; he likewise defended all he could against the effects of party hatred. In the session of the chamber, in 1815, he voted with the minority for the charter, and for the constitutional mode of election. In the following sessions he maintained that the chamber of deputies is not bound by the opinions of its constituents, being merely an elective, and not a representative body, and was often proposed as a candidate for the presidency. In the session of 1817, he was considered as the head of the few deputies who were called *doctrinaires*. (q. v.) After 1819, he was no longer at the head of the department of public education, probably because his views did not coincide with those of the ministry ; for he opposed with all his ability the laws of exception (see *Laws of Exception*); the new mode of election ; the grant of the 100,000,000 francs for the Spanish war, and similar measures, until the dissolution of the chamber in 1823. Being again elected from the department of Marne, for the session of 1824, he voted against septennial elections, and, in 1825, against the laws respecting sacrilege. In 1827, he was chosen a member of the French academy in place of La Place. In February, 1828, he was chosen president of the chamber of deputies, and rechosen in 1829 and 1830.

Rozier, Pilatre de. (See *Aëronautics*.)

Rubble Walls. (See *Architecture*, vol. i, page 335.)

Rubens, Peter Paul, the most eminent painter of the Flemish school, was the son of a doctor of laws and a sheriff of Antwerp, who, during the troubles of the Low Countries, retired to Cologne, where his celebrated son was born in 1577. The family subsequently returned to Antwerp, where the subject of this article received a literary education, and early displayed a talent for design, which induced his mother, then a widow, to place him with the painter Van Oort, whom he left for the school of Otto Venius. His talent having made him known to the archduke Albert, governor of the Netherlands, that prince employed him on several pictures, and recommended him to the duke of Mantua, at whose court he remained six years, studying the works of Giulio Romano, and other great artists, and paying particular attention to the coloring of the Venetian school. In the interval he also visited Madrid, on a commission for the duke, where he saw some of the finest works of Titian and other masters. On leaving Mantua, he visited Rome and other cities of Italy, copying some of the best pictures, and perfecting himself in every branch of his profession. After a residence of seven years in Italy, he returned to Antwerp, being recalled by the illness of his mother, who died before his arrival. This event induced him to retire to the abbey of St. Michael, where he gave himself up for a time to solitary study. His reputation now stood so high, that he was called to the court of the archduke, and pensioned; soon after which, he married his first wife, and lived in a style of great magnificence, which excited much envy among inferior artists, who sought to lower his reputation by attributing the best parts of his pictures to his numerous pupils. These calumnies he treated with disregard, and, aware of the source of much of the ill-will, relieved the necessities of some of his principal decriers. For the cathedral at Antwerp he painted that great masterpiece, the Descent from the Cross; for the Jacobites the Four Evangelists; and he continued to execute many great works with surprising facility, until, in 1620, he was employed by Mary de' Medici to adorn the gallery of the Luxembourg, for which he painted a well-known series of magnificent pictures, allegorically exhibiting the principal events in the life of that princess. Such was the opinion of his general talents, that he was chosen, at the recommendation of the archduchess Isabella, to be the private negotiator of a peace between Spain and England; for which purpose he visited Madrid in 1628, where he was treated with great distinction. He painted for Philip IV, and his minister Olivarez, twelve or fourteen of his most celebrated pictures, in the short space of nine months; and, in 1629, he returned to Flanders with a secret commission, and proceeded to England. Although not received openly as a minister, Charles I, who was both a patron and judge of the fine arts, was much gratified by his visit; and, during his stay in England, where he succeeded in his negotiation, he was engaged to paint the ceiling of the banqueting-house at Whitehall. He also executed several other pictures for the English nobility, some of which are to be found at Blenheim, Wilton, Easton, &c. He remained in England about a year, during which time he received the honor of knighthood, and then returned to Flanders, where he married the beautiful Helen Formann, his second wife, and was nominated secretary to the council for the Low Countries. He maintained a highly dignified station through the rest of his life, which was one of continued prosperity, until his death at Antwerp, in 1640, in the sixty third year of his age. Rubens, beyond all comparison, was the most rapid of the great masters; and so many pictures bear his name, it is impossible not to credit a part of what was asserted in his own days, that the greater portion of many of them was performed by his pupils. His great characteristics are freedom, animation, and striking brilliancy and disposition of coloring, the favorite tone of which is that of a gay magnificence, from which, whatever the subject, he never deviated. Besides the excellence of his general powers, he saw all the objects of nature with a painter's eye, and instantly caught the predominating feature by which the object is known and distinguished; and as soon as seen, he executed it with a facility that was astonishing. According to sir Joshua Reynolds, he was the greatest master of the mechanical part of his art that ever existed. His chief defects consist in inelegance and incorrectness of form, a want of grace in his female figures, and in the representation of youth in general, and an almost total absence of sublime or poetical conception of character. The works of Rubens are found in churches, palaces and galleries throughout Europe; for every branch of the art was cultivated by him,—history, landscape, portrait, and even common life. His celebrated Rape of the Sabines is in the national gallery of Great Britain The number of engravings from the designs of Rubens exceed three hundred. This great painter, who was no mean scholar, wrote some treatises on his art in very good Latin. (See sir Joshua Reynolds's *Works*; Walpole's *Anec*; Fuseli's *Lectures*.)

Rübezahl. (See *Ruebezahl*.)

Rubicon; a river of Italy, anciently forming the boundary between Gaul and Italy. Cæsar, by passing this river with his troops, and thus leaving the province assigned him, made war on the republic. (See *Cæsar*.)

Rubric, in the canon law, signifies a title or article in certain ancient law books; thus called because written, as the titles of the chapters of our ancient Bibles are, in red letters.—*Rubrics* also denote the rules and directions given at the beginning and in the course of the liturgy, for the order and manner in which the several parts of the office are to be performed. There are general rubrics, special rubrics, a rubric for the communion, &c. In the Romish missal and breviary are rubrics for matins, for lauds, for translations, for beatifications, &c.

Ruby, Oriental. (See *Corundum.*)

Rudder. (See *Helm.*)

Rüdesheimer. (See *Rhenish Wines.*)

Rue (*ruta graveolens*); a strong-scented plant, cultivated in gardens, but more frequently in Europe than in the U. States. We have hardly a native plant with which it can be compared in appearance. The root is perennial, woody; the stems, branching almost from the base, about two feet high, bearing alternate petiolate and very much divided leaves; the flowers are yellow, and disposed in corymbs at the summit of the branches; the calyx is persistent, and divided into four or five segments; the corolla consists of as many oval petals, and is longer than the calyx; the stamens are eight or ten, and the style single. The odor of rue is very strong and disagreeable, and the taste acrid and bitter. It has been celebrated as a medicinal plant from high antiquity, and a great variety of virtues have been attributed to it, but is now comparatively little used, being chiefly employed in cases of hysteria and flatulent colic. Notwithstanding its disagreeable taste and odor, the leaves were employed for culinary purposes by the ancient Romans, and even now enter into the composition of certain dishes, and especially of salads, in some parts of Italy and Germany. About twenty species of rue are known, all natives of the eastern continent.

Ruebezahl; the name of a mountain spirit, sometimes friendly, sometimes mischievous, dwelling in the Riesengebirge, in Silesia. Rübezahl corresponds to our Robin-Goodfellow. He has become, of late, the hero of some operas. (See *Browny*, and *Elf.*)

Ruff (*machetes pugnax*). A species of the shore birds, alike curious in the disposition of its plumage and for its pugnacious character. It is about a foot in length, with a bill an inch long. The plumage varies so much in color, in different individuals, that many imaginary species have been formed. It derives its common name from the disposition of the long feathers of the neck, which stand out like the ruff formerly worn: it is, however, only the male that is furnished with this appendage, which he does not gain till the second year, before which period he closely resembles the female. They are birds of passage, appearing at certain seasons of the year, in great numbers, in the north of Europe. They are generally taken in large nets, resembling those used in this country for the capture of the wild pigeon. When fattened, they are dressed like the woodcock, without withdrawing their intestines or their contents, which are considered by the connoisseurs as affording the most delicate kind of seasoning for these birds. The males are much more numerous than the females, and during the pairing season have numerous and severe conflicts for the possession of their mates. These combats are thus described by Pennant and other writers:—The male chooses a stand on some dry bank near the water, round which he runs so often as to make a bare circular path; the moment a female appears in sight, all the males within a certain distance commence a general fight, placing their bills to the ground, spreading their ruff, and using the same action as the common cock. This pugnacious disposition is so strong, that, when they are kept for the purpose of fattening, their place of confinement is obliged to be dark, as, the moment any light is admitted, they attack each other with such fury, and fight with so much inveteracy, as to occasion a great slaughter. The female lays four eggs, forming her nest in a tuft of grass, and incubates about a month.

Rugen; the largest island in the Baltic, belonging to Germany, about a mile from the continent, containing 360 square miles, and 28,000 inhabitants. It belongs to the government of Stralsund, in the Prussian province of Pomerania. (q. v.) Its northern coast consists chiefly of precipitous chalk rocks, and the whole island is rich in romantic scenery, for which reason it is much resorted to by travellers. The capital is Bergen, with 2200 inhabitants. The Stubbenkammer, the north-eastern promontory, rises 543 feet above the sea. Not far from it is the Stubbenitz, a beautiful beech wood, probably the place where, according to Tacitus, the ancient Rugians worshipped the goddess Hertha. Arcona (lat. N. 54° 38′ 40″; lon. E. 13° 25′ 35″) is the most northern point of Germany proper. Rugen came under the Prussian government in 1815, with the rest of Swedish Pomerania. The Rugians are a hardy race of fishers and husbandmen. The inhabitants of the peninsula of Mőnkguth are very tall.—See J. J. Grűmbke's account of the island (in German; Berlin, 1819, 2 vols.).

Rugendas, George Philip, one of the most famous battle painters, was born at Augsburg, in 1666. After six years' study, his right hand became disabled by a fistula. He continued to work with the left. He painted and engraved much. His pictures are full of spirit and ease; there is an endless variety in the attitudes of his horses. Among his engravings, all labored with uncommon care, are distinguished six large ones, representing the siege of Augsburg, of which he was a witness. He died at that city, in 1742. His sons George Philip (died 1774) and Christian (died in 1781) are also known as engravers.

Ruhe, the German for *rest*, used as an affix to several geographical names; for instance, *Carlsruhe* (rest of Charles; place of repose for Charles).

Ruhnkenius, David (properly *Ruhnken*), professor of history and eloquence in the university of Leyden, one of the most celebrated classical scholars of his time, and especially distinguished for his simple, beautiful, classic Latin style, was born in 1723, at Stolpe, in Hither Pomerania. His opulent parents designed him for study, and sent him at first to Kőnigsberg, where he made himself acquainted with classic authors of antiquity, and also practised music and other of the fine arts. In his eighteenth year, he went to Wittenberg, and studied with eagerness the philosophy of Wolf Two years after, he went to Leyden, to enjoy the instructions of the celebrated Hemsterhuys in the Greek language. There he spent six years, and devoted himself to the whole circle of the humane studies, under the guidance of his great teacher. The first fruits of his application were two *Epistolæ criticæ* (1749 and 1751); the subject of the first of which was the hymns of Homer, Hesiod, and the Greek anthology; of the second, Callimachus, Apollonius and Orpheus. It was now his wish to obtain a philosophical professorship in some Dutch university; but, having no prospect of such an appointment, he resumed, at Hemsterhuys' advice, the study of the Roman law, which he had begun in Wittenberg. But without being diverted from Greek literature, he undertook an edition of Plato. For this end, he procured from the library of San germann, at Paris, a transcript of the only existing copy of Timæus's Lexicon of Plato, and published it, with a commentary (Leyden, 1756 and 1789). So much critical and grammatical erudition can rarely be found condensed into so narrow a space. This work was sufficient to give Ruhnken a rank among the first philologists of his times. As he had become fond of his easy life in Holland, he declined several honorable offers of professorships in foreign countries, and devoted his leisure to a literary tour, with the intention of consulting the principal libraries of Europe. For a year, he labored amid the treasures of the royal library of Paris, where, with unwearied industry, he transcribed and collated manuscripts, and made excerpts from them. Hemsterhuys had, meanwhile, found opportunity, as he was now oppressed with age and sickness, to get Ruhnken appointed assistant lecturer on the Greek language; and, on the death of Ouderdorp, he was appointed professor of history and eloquence. Of his numerous works, among which are his Memoir of Hemsterhuys, his edition of Muretus, the most distinguished is his *Velleius Paterculus* (Leyden, 1779)—a true model for the treatment of Latin classics. In 1780, he published a hymn of Homer to Ceres, which Mathäi had discovered in Moscow, and communicated to him in a letter. In his intended edition of Plato he had only finished the *scholia*, when death put an end to his activity, in 1798. His life has been written in a masterly manner by his scholar Daniel Wyttenbach.

Rule of Three, in arithmetic, called by some authors the *golden rule*, is an application of the doctrine of proportion to arithmetical purposes, and is divided into two cases, *simple* and *compound;* now frequently termed *simple* and *compound proportion.*—*Simple rule of three*, or *simple proportion*, is when, from three given quantities, a fourth is required to be found, that shall have the same proportion to the given quantity of the same name, as one of the other quantities has to that of the same name with itself. This rule is, by some authors, divided into two cases; viz. the *rule of three direct*, and the *rule of three inverse;* but this distinction is unnecessary, and the two cases are now generally given under one head by the best modern authors; but as they are still retained by others, it will not be amiss to point out the distinction. The *rule of three direct*, is when more requires more, or less requires less, as in this example: "If three men will perform a piece of work, as, for instance, dig a trench forty-eigh yards long, in a certain time, how many yards will twelve men dig in the same time?" where it is obvious, that the more men there are employed, the more work will they perform, and therefore, in this instance, more requires more. Again, "If six men dig forty-eight yards in a given time, how much will three men dig in the same time?" Here less requires less, for the less men there are employed, the less will be the work that is performed by them; and all questions that are in this class are said to be in the rule of three direct.—The *rule of three inverse*, is when more requires less, or less requires more; as in this case—"If six men dig a certain quantity of trench in fourteen hours, how many hours will it require for twelve men to big the same quantity?" or thus, "If six men perform a piece of work in seven hours, how long will three men be in performing the same work?" These cases are both in the inverse rule; for in the first more requires less, that is, twelve men being more than six, they will require less time to perform the same work; and in the latter, the number of men being less, they will require a longer time. All questions of this class are said to belong to the rule of three inverse. These two cases, however, as we before observed, may be brought under one general rule, as follows:—*Rule*. Of the three given terms, set down that which is of the same kind with the answer towards the right hand; and then consider, from the nature of the question, whether the answer will be more or less than this term. Then, if the answer is to be greater, place the less of the other two terms on the left, and the remaining term in the middle; but if it is to be less, place the greater of these two terms on the left, and the less in the middle; and in both cases, multiply the second and third terms together, and divide the product by the first term for the answer, which will always be of the same denomination as the third term.—*Note* 1. If the first and second terms consist of different denominations, reduce them both to the same; and if the third term be a compound number, it is generally more convenient to reduce it to the lowest denomination contained in it.—*Note* 2. The same rule is applicable whether the given quantities be integral, fractional or decimal.

Rules of Legislative Bodies. (For those of the U. States, see the article *Congress*; also Jefferson's *Manual of Parliamentary Practice*. For those of England, see the article *Parliament*; also the *Precedents of Proceedings in the House of Commons*, 4th ed., 1818, 4 vols., 4to, by Hatsel.) The French chamber of deputies, June 23, 1814, received a full system of rules of ninety-four articles. But there is hardly a session in which the course of the deliberations is not interrupted by violent exclamations, and the hubbub of the majority. In their leading features, the French rules are the same with the English and American. Some of the principal peculiarities are, that, for preliminary investigations, the whole chamber is divided, by lot, into nine committees (*bureaux*), of which the chairmen, or *reporters*, as they are called, in every case form a committee of nine members, which appoints one of their number to report to the chamber. Private petitions are either wholly rejected (*la chambre passe à l'ordre du jour*), or delivered to the ministers for consideration. It may, however, happen that they give rise to serious discussions in the chamber. Motions must be put in writing, read, and a day fixed for their discussion. Such a motion, moreover, must, as in other parliamentary bodies, be seconded; and its discussion may be prevented by a call for the previous question. If the further discussion is resolved on, all who wish to speak give in their names to the clerk, and, after the report of the committee, the speakers are heard, in turn, from the tribune. The members do not speak in their places, but from a sort of pulpit. No deputy can speak twice on the same subject. Most of the speeches are still read, and few of the members are able to speak without preparation. The chamber commonly votes by the members on one side of a question rising, and the others remaining seated, and the secretary decides on which side is the majority. But on the passage of laws, the main vote is always taken by balls (*scrutin secret*), in which all the members are called by name (*appel nominal*), every one receives a black and a white ball, and votes by casting one of them in an urn. The chamber of peers, on the contrary, votes by written yeas and nays. Propositions from the king may be submitted to the chambers by the ministers (who, by virtue of their office, have a seat and voice in both chambers), or by special commissioners.

Rum; the distilled liquor obtained from the fermented juice of the sugar-cane or molasses. The following is the process employed in Jamaica: The materials for fermentation are molasses, scummings of the hot cane-juice, or sometimes raw cane-liquor, lees, or *dunder* (as it is called), and water. The dunder answers the purpose of yeast, and is usually prepared by a separate fermentation of cane, sweets and water. The materials being mixed in due proportions (which are about equal parts of scummings, dunder and water), the fermentation (q. v.) soon begins, and in twenty-four hours the liquor is fit for the first charge of molasses, which is added in the proportion of three gallons for every hundred gallons of the liquor. Another charge is added in a day or two, or afterwards. The heat in fermentation should not exceed 90° or 94°. The fermentation falls in six or eight days, and the liquor grows fine and fit for distillation. (q. v.) In about two hours after lighting the fire, the spirit begins to run (in a still of 1200 gallons); and it is collected as long as it is inflammable. The first spirit is called, in the country, *low wines;* and it is rectified, in a smaller still, to the Jamaica proof, which is that in which olive oil will sink. The spirit called *New England rum* is prepared from molasses, and largely exported.

Rumelia, or Rum-Ili. (See *Romania.*)

Rumford, Count, so called from the title conferred on him by the elector of Bavaria, was born in Woburn, New England, in 1752. His name was Benjamin Thompson. He acquired, when young, a knowledge of natural philosophy, by the aid of the professor of that science in the college of Cambridge. He then employed himself as a teacher, till he was raised to independence by an advantageous marriage, when he became a major in the militia of his native province; and when the war took place between Great Britain and her colonies, his local knowledge enabled him to render services of importance to the English commanders. He went to England, and, as the reward of his services, obtained a situation in the foreign office, under lord George Germaine. Towards the close of the war, he was sent to New York, where he raised a regiment of dragoons, of which he was appointed colonel, and thus became entitled to half-pay. Returning to England in 1784, he received the honor of knighthood, and was for some time one of the under secretaries of state. Soon after, he went to the continent, and, through the recommendation of the prince of Deux-Ponts (afterwards king of Bavaria), entered into the service of the reigning elector-palatine and duke of Bavaria, when he effected many important and useful reforms in both the civil and military departmen of the state. Among these was a scheme for the suppression of mendicity, whicl he carried into execution at Munich anu other parts of the Bavarian territories, providing labor for able-bodied paupers, and exciting a spirit of industry among the lower orders of the people in general. As the reward of his success in this and other undertakings, he received from the sovereign of Bavaria various orders of knighthood, was made a lieutenant-general, and created count Rumford. He left Bavaria in 1799, and returned to England, where he employed himself in making experiments on the nature and application of heat, and on other subjects of economical and philosophical research. He likewise suggested the plan, and assisted in the foundation, of the royal institution, which led to other establishments of a similar description. In 1802, he removed to Paris, where he took up his residence; and, his wife being dead, he married the widow of the celebrated Lavoisier; but the union proved unfortunate, and a separation ere long took place. Count Rumford then retired to a country house at Auteuil, about four miles from Paris, and there devoted his time to the embellishment of his domain, and to the cultivation of chemistry and experimental philosophy. Though he disliked both the character and politics of the French, he preferred the climate of their country to every other; and he therefore procured permission from the king of Bavaria to continue in France, and retain the pension of 1200 pounds a year, granted him by that prince. He died in August, 1814, leaving by his first wife a daughter, who resided at Boston, in the U. States. Count Rumford was by no means a man of learning, his literary acquirements being confined to the English, French and German languages; but he was familiar with the discoveries and improvements of modern science, and the industry and perseverence with which he pursued his inquiries enabled him to make some considerable additions to our knowledge of chemistry and practical philosophy. Besides a great number of papers in various scientific journals, he published four volumes of Essays, experimental, political, economical, and philosophical.

Ruminant, in natural history, is applied to an animal that chews over again what it has eaten before. This is popularly called *chewing the cud.*

RUMJANZOFF, Nicholas Petrowitsch, count, chancellor of the Russian empire, was the son of the field-marshal Peter Rumjanzoff, or Romanzoff (q. v.), distinguished in the reign of Catharine by his victories over the Turks. He began his career about 1785, as Russian ambassador at Frankfort on the Maine. He was afterwards minister of commerce, and did much to promote the internal and foreign trade of Russia. In 1807, he became minister of foreign affairs, and, soon after, chancellor of the empire. He accompanied the emperor, in 1808, to Erfurt; and, in 1809, concluded peace with Sweden. During the campaign of 1813—14, he remained in Petersburg, at the head of the department of foreign affairs, which, however, were directed, in the imperial camp, by the emperor himself. After the return of the emperor, he resigned the port-folio to count Nesselrode. From this time, count Rumjanzoff, who had almost totally lost his hearing, lived retired from public affairs, and devoted his great riches to patriotic and scientific undertakings. He promoted greatly the introduction of the system of mutual instruction. Kotzebue's voyage round the world was executed, and the description of it printed, at his expense. The Russian *codex diplomaticus* has been printed, at his expense, at Moscow, since 1813. For professor Hase of Paris he defrayed the expenses of an edition of Leo Diaconus, and to the imperial academy of science he gave 25,000 roubles, to be spent in printing old Russian annals and chronicles. He also caused a monument of much importance, as connected with the history of art in the middle ages, the Chersonese gates of the cathedral at Novgorod (containing forty-six biblical and historical scenes), to be described by Adelung (q. v.), and the work to be printed at his expense. In 1820, he established on his domains (containing one town, ninety villages, and 30,000 souls), at Homel (in the government of Mohilew), a charitable school. He collected from sixty to two hundred of the vagrant and mendicant children of bond-peasants in a wing of his castle, where they were clothed, fed, taught on the system of mutual instruction, and exercised in some trade. To Rumjanzoff, also, we are indebted for the first edition, in the Tartar language, of Abulgasi's History of the Mongols and Tartars (Kasan, 1825). The count died at St. Petersburg, in January, 1826, in the seventy-third year of his age, without children. Among other things, he left a valuable collection of Oriental coins.

RUNIC ALPHABET and WANDS. This alphabet, peculiar to the ancient northern tribes of Europe (Germans and Scandinavians), is considered, by some scholars, to have existed before the Christian era, by others, to have originated later. The similarity of a few Runic characters to corresponding Roman ones, proves nothing, as it prevails with but a few of them; moreover, the Runic alphabet has but sixteen characters: this limited number is hardly reconcilable with the idea of the Scandinavians having borrowed it from the Romans. Rude nations want many, rather than few, characters for their undefined sounds. Yet could the northern tribes, immersed as they were in ignorance, have invented their own alphabet? Frederic von Schlegel advances the hypothesis, that the Phœnicians, navigating in early antiquity to the coasts of the Baltic, might have carried the art of writing to those northern regions, and that the Runic grew out of the Phœnician characters, and was preserved by the priests, together with several magic arts. The similarity of a few of the Runic signs to those of the Romans, might be explained by the fact, that the Romans themselves received their characters from an Eastern source. The fact, that in Spain and other countries in the south-west of Europe, remains of the Runic and Runic stones (tomb-stones, land-marks, &c.) are met with, is to be explained from the influx of the tribes of ancient Germany and Scandinavia into those countries at the time of the general migration of nations. W. C. Grimm, in his *Ueber Deutsche Runen* (Göttingen, 1821), endeavors to show that the Germans had, probably, in ante-historic times, characters of more than accidental similarity to those of the Greek and other alphabets, and that the German Runic, properly so called (that of the Saxons of the northern Elbe), is between the ancient northern (Scandinavian) Runic and the Anglo-Saxon; so that the German Runic originated from the former, and produced the latter. The word *rune* he derives, as Mone does, from *runen* (i. e. to make a slight incision or scratch): others derive it from the German *raunen* (i. e. whisper); hence *runic*, as designating a secret, mysterious writing, belonging to the priests. According to Dahlmann and Kopp, the northern Runes are of later origin than is generally supposed. The Runic *codices* are proved to be of less antiquity than some written in common characters.

Langebeck found, in 1753, that none of the numerous Runic writings in Gothland reached back farther than the year 1200 of our era; the latest were of the year 1449. (See Brynjulf's work on the Runes, and Rasmus Nyerup's works.) —*Runic wands* were willow wands, inscribed with mysterious characters, and used by the heathen tribes of the north of Europe, in the performance of magic ceremonies. Such wands were also employed by the ancient inhabitants of Sweden and Norway, to note the succession of time. To this day, the peasants of those countries use similar wands instead of an almanac; and in Germany sticks are used in keeping the ordinary accounts between families and the persons from whom they receive their daily supplies; for instance, the family and the baker each have a stick, and the two are put together, and a notch made in them with a file, when bread is delivered; thus each has a check on the other.

Runnymede, in England; the celebrated meadow where the conference was held, June 15, 1215, between John and the English barons, in which the former was compelled to sign *Magna Charta* (q. v.), and the *Charta de Foresta.* (See *John.*) It is five miles east of Windsor, in Surrey, and is now divided into several enclosures.

Rupert or Robert of Bavaria, prince, the third son of Frederic V, elector palatine and titular king of Bohemia, by the princess Elizabeth of England, daughter of James I, was born in 1619, and, becoming an exile through the misfortunes of his father, at the commencement of the civil war in England, he offered his services to his uncle, Charles I, and had the command of a corps of cavalry, at the head of which he distinguished himself at the battle of Edgehill, in 1642, and at Chalgrave Field, in 1643. Soon after, he took Bristol, and obliged the enemy to raise the sieges of Newark and of York. He displayed his courage at Marston Moor and at Naseby; but his impetuosity and imprudence contributed to the disastrous result of those engagements. He afterwards shut himself up in Bristol; but, having surrendered that place, after a short siege, to Fairfax, his conduct so much displeased the king, that he dismissed the prince from his service. He then went abroad, and, after the death of Charles I, he was made commander of that part of the fleet which adhered to Charles II, in 1648. Prince Rupert for some time carried on a predatory warfare against the English, and at length sailed to France, and joined Charles II at the court of Versailles. His time was chiefly devoted to scientific studies, till the restoration, when he returned to England. In 1666, he was appointed, in conjunction with Monk (q. v.) to the command of a fleet against the Dutch; and, in the next war with Holland, in 1673, was made admiral of the fleet. In 1679, he was nominated a member of the new privy council; but from that period he interfered but little in public affairs, leading a retired life, and spent much of his time at Windsor castle, of which he was governor. Many useful inventions resulted from his studies, among which are the invention of prince's metal, and the discovery of the method of engraving in mezzo-tinto. The prince died in London, 1682.

Rupert's Drops, or Glass Tears. (See *Annealing.*)

Ruppin, Count. Under this name the king of Prussia travels incognito. Ruppin is a small town in Brandenburg.

Rupture. (See *Hernia.*)

Rural War. (See *Peasants' War.*)

Ruscsuck, also Rustschuk, in Bulgaria, in the sangiacat of Nicopolis, is situated on the right bank of the Danube, at the confluence of the Lom, and almost opposite Giorgiev. The city, formerly an important fortress, has extensive works and a castle. It is the see of an archbishop, and has 30,000 inhabitants; partly Turks, partly Greeks, Armenians, Gypsies and Jews; and carries on an active trade, manufactures silk, wool, cotton, leather, tobacco, &c. Ruscsuck is of the highest importance in a military point of view, as the wars between Russia and the Porte, in 1809, 1810, and 1811, have proved.

Rush. This term is, strictly speaking, applied to the different species of *juncus*, sedge-like plants, chiefly growing in marshes, with inconspicuous greenish flowers, though belonging to the class *hexandria* of Linnæus. The *J. effusus*, or soft rush, is a common plant, in low grounds, in the more northern parts of the eastern and western continents, and is rendered conspicuous by its tufts of long awl-shaped leaves and stems, somewhat resembling the spines of a porcupine. The flowers are in loose, lateral panicles. The leaves and stems are used for making mats, baskets, and children's ornaments, and their pith is used for wicks to burn in lamps. The species of *juncus* are herbaceous plants, inhabiting the northern hemisphere, with fibrous and usually perennial roots; their leaves are cylindrical or a little compressed, often containing transverse internal partitions, which give them a jointed appearance; their flowers are small, greenish or brownish, terminal or lateral, and generally disposed in panicles or corymbs. We have several species in the U. States, the most remarkable of which is the *J. militaris* of Bigelow, a strictly aquatic plant, attaining large dimensions, and the largest of the American species. The different species of *scirpus*, or club-rush, are also common in marshes. They are distinguished by having their flowers disposed in little solid oval spikelets; in some species, terminal and solitary; in others, forming wide-spreading panicles. The bull-rush (*S. lacustris*) is aquatic, growing in deep water throughout the northern hemisphere. It is used for the bottoms of chairs, and, for the finer sort, is cut when a year old. Cottages are sometimes thatched, and pack-saddles stuffed with it. The Chinese cultivate the *S. tuberosus*, or water chestnut, in tanks, the bottoms of which are manured and exposed for a time to dry in the sun. The tubers of the roots are eaten either boiled or raw, and are esteemed both as food and medicine. This plant has not yet been introduced into Europe.

Rush, Benjamin, M. D., was born on the 24th December, 1745 (old style), near Philadelphia, and, in 1759, entered the college of Princeton, where he graduated, in 1760, before he had completed his fifteenth year. The next six years of his life were devoted to the study of medicine. During his novitiate, he translated the aphorisms of Hippocrates into English, and also began to keep a note-book of remarkable occurrences, which he continued through life. From a part of this record, written in the seventeenth year of the author's age, we derive the only account of the yellow fever of 1762, in Philadelphia. In 1766, he went to Edinburgh to study at the university in that city, and took his degree of M. D. there in 1768. The next winter he spent in London; in the spring, he went to France; in the autumn, he returned to Philadelphia, and commenced the practice of his profession. In 1769, he was elected professor of chemistry in the college of Philadelphia, and when, in 1791, the college was merged in the university of Pennsylvania, he was appointed professor of the institutes and practice of medicine, and of clinical practice. In the previous year, he had begun to publish his new principles of medicine, depending chiefly for the cure of diseases upon bleeding and cathartics; and these were more or less developed by him in his successive annual courses of lectures, for the subsequent twenty-three years of his life. In the year 1793, when Philadelphia was desolated by the yellow fever to an extent almost equal to that of the ravages of the plague in the old world, the theories and the active strength of doctor Rush's genius were put to the test. All the physicians, for some time after the commencement of this disease, were unsuccessful in its treatment. Doctor Rush adopted a new mode of treatment, to which he was led by a manuscript of doctor Mitchell, of Virginia, respecting the yellow fever which prevailed there in 1741. His success was great, and naturally brought him a great increase of practice. He had scarcely a moment of repose. Whilst at his meals, his house was filled with persons, chiefly the poor, waiting for his advice; every day he was obliged to refuse numerous applications, and in riding through the streets he was often forced to tear himself away from persons who attempted to stop him, and to drive his chair as speedily as possible out of the reach of their cries. His incessant labors of body and mind, by night and day, nearly cost him his life; but, by timely and proper treatment, he was rescued from the grave. This was the most eventful year of his life, and in it he laid the foundation of a reputation inferior to few in the annals of medicine. Doctor Rush did not confine his attention exclusively to the practice of his profession, but took an active and zealous part in political affairs. He was an ardent friend of liberty, and was one of the signers of the Declaration of Independence. In 1777, he was appointed physician-general of the military hospital in the middle department; some time after which, he published his observations on our hospitals, army diseases, and the effects of the revolution on the army and people. In 1787, he was a member of the convention of Pennsylvania for the adoption of the federal constitution, which received his warmest approbation. During the last fourteen years of his life, he was treasurer of the U. States' mint. Doctor Rush took a deep interest also in the many private associations for the advancement of human happiness with which Pennsylvania abounds. He was an honorary member of many of the literary institutions, both of this country and of Europe. In 1805, he received a medal from the king of Prussia, for his replies to certain questions respecting the yellow fever. On a similar account, he was presented with a gold medal, in 1807, from the queen of Etruria;

and, in 1811, the emperor of Russia sent him a diamond ring, as a testimony of his respect for his medical character. The life of this great and good man was terminated April 19, 1813, in the sixty-eighth year of his age. Notwithstanding his great labors as a lecturer and practitioner, he was a voluminous writer, having, during forty-nine years, from the nineteenth year of his age to within a short period of his death, been constant in the employment of the pen. His printed works consist of seven volumes, six of which treat of medical subjects, and the other is a collection of essays—literary, moral and philosophical. He also wrote various political essays, which were published in the papers of the time. From the result of his individual experience and observation, he established more principles, and added more facts to the science of medicine, than all who preceded him in his native country. He possessed a lively imagination, a retentive memory, and a discriminating judgment, together with the power of intense application. He was, moreover, philanthropic, kind and religious.

Rushworth, John, an industrious collector of historical matter, born in 1607, was, for some time, a student at Oxford, which he quitted for Lincoln's-inn, where he remained until he was called to the bar. He was, however, more attached to politics than to law, and made it his business to attend parliament, the star-chamber, and other courts, when important business was transacting, in order to take notes of what he saw and heard. In 1640, he was assistant clerk of the house of commons; and when sir Thomas Fairfax became general of the parliamentary forces, he was appointed his secretary. He was a member of parliament in 1658, and, in 1660, he was reëlected for Berwick in the healing parliament. In 1667, he was made secretary to sir Orlando Bridges, keeper of the great seal, but, after the decease of that lawyer, was arrested for debt, and committed to the king's bench prison, where he died in 1690. His Historical Collection of private Passages in State, weighty Matters in Law, and remarkable Proceedings in Parliament, was published at different times, in folio, until it amounted to eight volumes, including the trial of the earl of Strafford, published in 1680. The first seven volumes of these were reprinted uniformly in 1721.

Russell, lord William, third son of the first duke of Bedford, and a distinguished supporter of liberty, was born about 1641. He was educated in the principles of constitutional freedom espoused by his father and yielded to the vortex of dissipation introduced by the restoration, until his marriage with Rachel, second daughter and co-heiress of the earl of Southampton (then widow of lord Vaughan), which wholly reclaimed him. He represented the county of Bedford in four parliaments, and, being highly esteemed for patriotism and independence, was regarded as one of the heads of the whig party. When Charles II, exasperated at the court of France for withdrawing his pension, appeared desirous of joining the continental confederacy against Louis XIV, a French war being generally popular in England, the parliament voted a large supply of men and money. The whigs, aware of the king's character, dreading to give him an army, which might as probably be employed against liberty at home as against France, opposed the measure. This movement being acceptable to the French king, an intrigue commenced between the leading whigs and Barillon, the French ambassador, the consequence of which was the receipt, on the part of some of them, of pecuniary assistance, in order to thwart the intended war. From that minister's private despatches, sir John Dalrymple, in his Memoirs of Great Britain, has published a list of those persons; but lords Russell and Holland are specified as refusing to receive money on this account. (See *Sidney, Algernon.*) In 1679, when Charles II found it necessary to ingratiate himself with the whigs, lord Russell was appointed one of the members of the privy council. He soon, however, found that his party was not in the king's confidence, and the recall of the duke of York, without their concurrence, induced him to resign. Although his temper was mild and moderate, his fear of a Catholic succession induced him to take decisive steps in the promotion of the exclusion of the duke of York. In June, 1680, he went publicly to Westminster-hall, and, at the court of king's bench, presented the duke as a recusant; and, on the November following, carried up the exclusion bill to the house of lords, at the head of two hundred members of parliament. The king dissolved the parliament, and resolved thenceforward to govern without one; and arbitrary principles were openly avowed by the partisans of the court. Alarmed at the state of things, many of the whig leaders favored strong expedients, in the way of counteraction, and a plan of insurrection was formed for a simultaneous rising in England and Scotland. Among these leaders, including the dukes of Monmouth and Argyle, the lords Russell, Essex and Howard, Algernon Sidney and Hampden, different views prevailed; but lord Russell looked only to the exclusion of the duke of York. While these plans were ripening, a subaltern plot was laid by some inferior conspirators, for assassinating the king on his return from Newmarket, at a farm called the *Ryehouse*, which gave a name to the conspiracy. Although this plan was not connected with the scheme of the insurrection, the detection of the one led to that of the other, and lord Russell was, in consequence, committed to the Tower. After some of the Ryehouse conspirators had been executed, advantage was taken of the national feeling, to bring him to trial, in July, 1683; and pains being taken to pack a jury of partisans, he was, after very little deliberation, brought in guilty of high treason. "It was proved," says Hume, "that the insurrection had been deliberated on by the prisoner; the surprisal of the guards deliberated, but not fully resolved upon; and that an assassination of the king had not been once mentioned or imagined by him." The law was, on this occasion, stretched to the prisoner's destruction, and his condemnation was deemed illegal by judge Atkins and many other authorities, not to dwell on the act which on this ground reversed his attainder. Once condemned, such a victim was too agreeable to the court, and to the vindictive feelings of the duke of York, to meet with mercy; and the offer of a large sum of money from his father, whose only son he had now become, to the duchess of Portsmouth, and the pathetic solicitations of his wife, proved in vain, and he obtained remission only of the more ignominious parts of his sentence. He was too firm to be induced by the divines, who attended him, to subscribe to the doctrine of non-resistance, then the favorite court tenet of the day; and it is to be regretted that he was induced to write a petitionary letter to the duke of York, promising to forbear all future opposition, and to live abroad, should his life be spared. It is presumed that this letter was written in compliance with the solicitations of his friends, for he nobly refused the generous offer of lord Cavendish to favor his escape by exchanging clothes; and, with equal generosity, declined the proposal of the duke of Monmouth (q. v.) to deliver himself up, if he thought the step would be serviceable to him. Conjugal affection was the feeling that clung closest to his heart; and when he had taken the last farewell of his wife, he exclaimed, that the bitterness of death was past. He was beheaded in Lincoln's-inn fields, July 21, 1683, in the forty-second year of his age. To the character of this regretted nobleman for probity, sincerity, and private worth, even the enemies to his public principles have borne ample testimony. Of his talents, Burnet observes, that he was of a slow but sound understanding.—Lady *Rachel Russell*, his wife, by the affectionate zeal with which she assisted her husband, and the magnanimity with which she bore his loss, obtained the respect and admiration of the world. Upon his trial, she accompanied him into court; and when he was refused counsel, and allowed only an amanuensis, she stood forth as that assistant, and excited the respect and sympathy of all who beheld her. After his death, she wrote a touching letter to the king, in which she asserted that the paper delivered by him to the sheriff, declaratory of his innocence, was his own composition, and not, as charged by the court, dictated by any other person. She spent the remainder of her life in the exercise of pious and social duties. A collection of her letters was published in 1775 (4to.). Lord John Russell has written a life of lord William Russell. This exemplary woman died in 1723, aged eighty-seven.

Russell, lord John, is the third son of the duke of Bedford, and was born in 1792. He completed his education at Cambridge, and entered parliament in 1818, as member for Huntingdonshire, which he continued to represent till 1826, when he lost his seat for that county, on account of his views of the Catholic relief question. He was then returned for the borough of Bandon, in Ireland, and is at present member for Devonshire. Lord John Russell, though not distinguished for brilliant or commanding talents, has held a respectable standing in parliament by his attention to business. Immediately after taking his seat, he brought forward a motion for parliamentary reform, pointing out in his speech the abuses of the rotten and close boroughs, and recommending the grant of the elective franchise to the large towns. The only result of this attempt was the disfranchising of the borough of Grampound, the franchise of which was transferred to the county of York. During the succeeding years, lord J. Russell brought forward a series of motions for reform, which were all negatived.

His Bill for the Disfranchisement of Penryn (1828) passed the commons, but was rejected by the lords. In the session of 1828, he brought in a bill for the repeal of the corporation and test acts, which was passed into an act. On the formation of the new whig ministry (Dec. 30, 1830), he was made paymaster of the forces, and, as such, has since been admitted into the cabinet, and brought in the ministerial reform bill. (See *Parliamentary Reform*, at the end of the last volume.)

RUSSIA. The Russian empire stretches over half Europe, and the whole of Northern Asia, from the Baltic to the Pacific, and includes vast territories on the northwestern coast of North America. It lies between lat. 38° and 79° N., and lon. 19° E. and 130° W., extending through 211 degrees of longitude. It is bounded N. by the Northern or Icy ocean; W. by Norway, Sweden, the Baltic sea, Austria and Prussia; S. by Turkey, the Black sea, Persia, the Caspian sea, Independent Tartary, China, and the U. States of North America; and E. by the British possessions in North America. The total superficial area is estimated at 8,000,000 square miles, of which about 1,500,000 are situated in Europe, and 5,600,000 in Asia. The southern boundary of the American possessions of Russia was fixed by the convention of 1824, between Russia and the U. States, at 54° 40′ N. lat. The Russian dominions compose about one seventh of the habitable globe. European Russia is for the most part level, but in the southern parts the face of the country is somewhat uneven. Between the Black and Caspian seas is the Caucasus (q. v.); in the south-west are branches of the Carpathian mountains (q. v.), and in the north-west the elevated plain of the Wolchonski forest. In the east is the Ural (q. v.) chain, dividing Europe from Asia, and terminating at the Frozen ocean. Several branches of this chain shoot off into Asiatic Russia, among which are the Schooget, with its salt mines, the Sok mountains, the Little Altai, the Baikal mountains, the Apple and Stanwowoi mountains, which form the Chinese and Russian boundary, and extend to the Tchutschian peninsula. The south-western part of Russia consists of steppes (q. v.), which are either uninhabited, or furnish pasture-grounds to nomadic tribes. The climate is various. In the south, the winters are short and mild, the spring early, the summers long and hot, with little rain, and a late autumn. In central Russia, the winters are longer and more severe, particularly in the eastern parts, and the summers shorter; in the north, quicksilver freezes so as to be malleable even in a warm room, and the waters are frozen from October to the end of May. In central Russia corn is raised in considerable quantities, but in the northern parts the crops are small and uncertain. Washed by the Frozen ocean, which forms the White sea and the basins of the Obi, Yenissey and Lena, on the north; by the Pacific ocean, with Beering's and Cook's straits, and the gulfs or bays of Anadyr and Kamtschatka or Okotsk, on the east; by the Black sea on the south; and by the Baltic, with the gulfs of Bothnia, Finland and Riga on the west,—Russia has two great declivities, the one towards the north-east and north-west, and the other towards the south. Down these flow the Dwina, with the Jug and the Suchowna, the Petchora, the Obi, the Yenissey and the Lena, in the north; the Duna, the Niemen, and the Neva, in the north-west; and the Don, the Dnieper, the Cuban, the Volga and the Ural, in the south. Besides numerous salt springs and small lakes, Russia contains fourteen large bodies of water, among which are the Caspian sea, lakes Ladoga, Onega and Peipus, lake Sak, in the Crimea, and lakes Baikal, Aral and Altin. Artificial water communications are constantly increasing on a systematic plan. The canals of Vishney-Volotchok, connecting Petersburg with Astrachan, the Novgorod canal, the Beresina canal, connecting the Baltic and Black seas, and the Ladoga canal, by which the navigation of the tempestuous Ladoga is avoided, are among the most important. A system of water communication extends through Siberia, from the Chinese wall to Petersburg, Archangel and Riga, so that European wares can be procured at moderate prices in Kolyvan, Tomsk and Irkutsk. Russia raises much more corn than it consumes. Fruits and wine are produced in abundance. The forest also yields important articles of export, besides supplying the consumption: mulberry trees have been planted to a great extent. The raising of cattle, horses and sheep, the keeping of bees (600,000 pounds of wax and honey can be annually exported), and silk-worms (furnishing 16,000 pounds of silk yearly), are profitable occupations. Camels, buffaloes, and wild animals of all sorts, are also numerous. The annual product of the fisheries is reckoned at 15,000,000 roubles. Gold (from the Beresov mines), silver (from the Kolyvan and Nertchinski mines), platina, copper, iron, zinc, quicksilver, alum and salt (to the yearly amount of 500,000,000 pounds), are among the mineral productions. The total value of the natural productions of the empire is estimated to exceed 40,000,000 roubles. The population of Russia, including Poland and Finland, is 57,000,000, of nine different races:—1. Sclavonians, 44,000,000, including the Russians (42,000,000, among whom are the Cossacks, about 600,000 capable of bearing arms) and the Poles; 2. Finns, who are scattered over the country, from Tornea and the Niemen to the Obi (3,000,000); 3. Tartars, from the Dniester to the Caucasus (2,000,000), mostly under their own government, without agriculture or fire-arms; 4. Georgians and Circassians (2,000,000); 5. Samoiedes; 6. Mantchoos; 7. Mongols, to whom belong the Calmucks; 8. eastern tribes (including Tchutsches, Kuriles and Aleutians); 9. Jews, particularly in the Polish provinces. Besides these races, there are natives of almost all countries of Europe and Asia, as Greeks, Arabs, Hindoos, Gypsies, French, English and Danes. There are among these Russian subjects eighty tribes, differing in language, religion and manners, from the rudest state of barbarism to the highest degree of European civilization. The population is divided into four classes, the nobility, clergy, common people or freemen, and peasants or serfs. In 1811, the number of persons subject to do military duty was as follows: 643,135 persons engaged in trade; 6,389,279 crown peasants; 10,113,177 peasants belonging to individuals; 1,077,636 appanage peasants; 112,453 freemen; in all, 18,335,730 men. We find manufactures of leather, tallow, candles, soap, felt, coarse linen, mats of the bark of the linden tree, hardware, and the art of dyeing, among the Russians before the time of Peter the Great; but since his reign these have been carried to much greater perfection, and many new manufactures have been introduced. In 1815, Russia contained 3253 manufacturing establishments; 23 of these deliver to the government annually cloth of 700,000 roubles in value, and there are, besides, 181 private establishments. Drugs are prepared in forty-five laboratories; and there are distilleries of brandy, of which 120,000,000 gallons are consumed in the country. Ship building is carried on in the large villages on the Wolga and in the seaports. On the Wolga, boats are built without iron, which are eventually used in Petersburg, Astrachan and other cities for fuel. The fabrication of fire-arms is the most important branch of metallic manufactures; in Tula alone 17,000 muskets, 6500 pair of pistols, and 16,000 side-arms, are made by about 6000 workmen. The board of manufactures, in Moscow and Petersburg, has the superintendence over all the branches of manufacturing industry. The commerce is carried on partly by land and partly by sea. The inland commerce is neither impeded by tolls nor staples, but is facilitated by navigable rivers, lakes, canals, the snow in winter, and the great fairs, especially at Novgorod. Goods may be exported from any port or frontier place, but can be imported only into Petersburg, Riga and Odessa. The foreign land trade in Asia is with China, Persia, Bucharia, and the Caucasian countries, and in Europe with Turkey, Galicia, Prussia, Silesia and Saxony. This branch of trade is chiefly in the hands of Armenians, Bucharians and Jews, while the maritime is chiefly carried on by the English. Since 1815, the yearly value of the imports by sea has amounted to 28,000,000 roubles, and that of the exports to 45,000,000. The shares of the American commercial company, and of that of the White sea, command good prices. The board of commerce in Petersburg is the supreme tribunal in all commercial matters. In 1770, a bank was established, whose paper is at par, and has afforded great facilities to the inland trade. The government is an unlimited monarchy; the emperor is autocrat of all the Russias; the state is indivisible; the ruler cannot be, at the same time, ruler of any other country (since 1815, however, he has been king of Poland), and must be of the Greek religion. In 1797, the succession was settled in the male line, by the rules of primogeniture, and, in failure of males, in the female line. All the princes of the blood are called grand-princes. By the ukase of March 20, 1820, it was declared that only the children of a marriage acknowledged by the emperor are capable of succeeding to the throne. The highest councils are, 1. the imperial council, under the presidency of the emperor, erected Jan. 1, 1810, with four departments—that of legislation (the supreme tribunal in civil and ecclesiastical suits), that of war, that of civil and ecclesiastical affairs, and that of finance; 2. the senate, for home affairs (a deliberative body, consisting of eight departments, three of which have their seat in Moscow); 3. the holy synod; 4. the ministry of state. The ministers have a seat and voice in the imperial council and in the senate. The ministry is divided into three sections—that of foreign affairs, war, the marine, the home department, ecclesiastical affairs, education and finance; that of the imperial treasury; and that of the public accounts, roads and canals, and justice. The whole state is divided into fifty-one governments and several provinces; of these, forty are in Europe, exclusive of the Cossacks of the Don, the Cossacks of the Black sea, and the kingdom of Poland. (q.v.) The revenue, including that of Poland, amounted, before the recent disturbances, to $55,000,000; the public debt, in 1824, was $170,000,000. The bank paper, which, since 1817, has been in a course of redemption, was about $150,000,000. The army, in 1822, consisted of more than 1,000,000 men, among whom 613,000 were infantry, 118,000 cavalry, 47,000 artillery, 105,000 irregular cavalry, 77,000 in garrison, 27,000 supernumeraries, and 50,000 forming the Polish army. In 1827, the number of troops was 649,300, exclusive of 20,000 officers, which, in 1828, was increased, on account of the Turkish war, to 870,000. (See *Military Colonies.*) The navy has its principal station on the Baltic; it consists, according to the most probable accounts, of 32 ships of the line, 25 frigates, 20 corvettes and brigs, 87 smaller vessels, 25 floating batteries, and 121 gun-boats, with 6000 cannon and 33,000 men. The principal naval station, on the Baltic sea, is Cronstadt, and, on the Black sea, Sebastopol. There are some ships on the Caspian. No country in Europe supports its military forces so cheaply as Russia. The prevailing religion is that of the Greek church, with a full toleration of all religions; all Christian sects enjoy equal privileges. The supreme direction of the affairs of the Greek church is intrusted to the holy synod at Petersburg; subordinate to this are 20 arch-priests, with the same number of consistories, and 68,000 secular clergy; there are 480 male and 80 female convents, with 7300 monks and 1300 nuns, all of the rule of St. Basil. (See *Greek Church.*) Those who adhere to the old Greek church are called *Roskolnicians.* (q. v.) There are about 40,350,000 members of the Greek church (including 570,000 Roskolnicians); 6,000,000 Catholics and united Greeks; 2,400,000 Lutherans; 83,000 Calvinists; 9200 Herrnhutters; 6000 Mennonites; 100,000 Armenians; 3,100,000 Mahometans; 500,000 Jews; 300,000 worshippers of the grand lama; and 600,000 fetichists. For all branches of education, Russia has numerous and excellent institutions, among which are the eight universities of Moscow, Helsingfors, Wilna, Dorpat, Petersburg, Charkow, Kazan and Warsaw. In 1829, the number of students was 3647. There are, also, a number of primary and intermediate schools; in 1824, the whole number was 1411, with 69,269 scholars, besides 344 schools maintained by the Greek clergy for the lower classes, with 45,851 pupils. The Petersburg Bible society, instituted by the emperor Alexander, had, in 1818, 128 branches, and has printed the Bible in 29 languages. One hundred and fifty years ago, there were only two printing establishments in Russia; there are now sixty-one. The population of Russia is composed of four different classes, as has already been mentioned. The boors or peasants are the property of the crown or of individuals; they amount to about 35,000,000, and are in a state of great poverty. They are sometimes emancipated by their owners, and are sometimes permitted to purchase their freedom. The noble families are about 150,000, comprising 750,000 individuals, and enjoy some privileges and exemptions. The freemen, not nobles nor clergymen, are divided into six classes—the inhabitants of cities, the three guilds (capitalists, according to their income tax), the trades, foreigners or strangers, the notable citizens (*savans*, artists, bankers), and the colonists. In regard to rank, these classes form fourteen gradations; and all who can claim either of the eight highest are considered as noble. Russia has six orders, of all of which the emperor is grand-master. The order of St. Andrew, the oldest and most distinguished, was founded by Peter I, Nov. 30, 1698, as a military order of merit, for those generals who had distinguished themselves in the Turkish war. The female order of St. Catharine, was founded by Peter I, Nov. 24, 1714, in honor of his wife, Catharine, who had rescued him from his difficult situation on the Pruth. The Alexander Newsky order was instituted by Peter I; but the arrangements were completed by Catharine I, Aug. 30, 1725. The military order of St. George was revived by Alexander in 1801. The order of St. Wladimir, for civil and military merit, instituted by Catharine II, (1782), was revived by Alexander (1801). The order of St. Anne is an order of merit for all ranks, and even foreigners. The spiritual order of St. John, instituted by Paul in 1797, has a Greek priory, with 128,000 roubles income, and a Catholic priory, with 84,000 roubles income. The present reigning house of Holstein-Gottorp was preceded by that of Romanoff, the first prince of which, Michael Feodorowitsch, ascended the throne in 1613, and died in 1645. His successors were Alexis Michailowitsch, died 1676; Feodor Alexiewitsch, died 1632; Ivan Alexiewitsch, and Peter I, Alexiewitsch, the former till 1688; the latter assumed the title of emperor in 1721, died 1725; Catharine, empress, died 1727; Peter II, died 1730; Anna, died 1741; Ivan III, deposed 1740; Elizabeth, died 1762:—House of Holstein-Gottorp: Peter III, deposed 1762; Catharine II, the Great, died 1795; Paul I, died 1801; Alexander, died 1825. Nicholas I, Paulowitsch, born July 7, 1796, married, July 13, 1817, the Prussian princess Charlotte, (born July 13, 1798), succeeded his brother Alexander, after the renunciation of the throne by his elder brother Constantine Cæsarowitsch, in Dec. 1825. The heir apparent is Alexander Nicholaiewitsch, born April 29, 1818; the other children of the emperor are, Maria, born 1819; Olga, born 1822; Alexandra, born 1825; Constantine Nicolaiewitsch, born 1827. The emperor has one brother, Michael, born 1798, and two sisters, Maria, wife of the duke of Saxe-Weimar, and Anna, (born 1795), wife of the prince of Orange. The sons and daughters of the imperial house have the title of grand-princes, and grand-princesses of Russia, with the style of imperial highness. (See *Statistique de la Russie*, by Schnitzler, Paris, 1829.)—After these statistical sketches, let us now throw a glance at what has been effected by the government, for the most important public interests, during the last 15 years. Civilization has made rapid progress during this period; the peasants, in general, have acquired some legal protections against the caprice of their masters, and the great work of emancipation has been effected in the Baltic provinces. In 1818, the nobility of Courland abolished villenage, and in 1819 the Livonian nobles made a provision for its gradual extinction, by which all peasants born after that year were declared to be born free, and all bondage was to cease after 1826. In 1823, the emperor directed the imperial council to take measures for preventing the sale of the peasants, independently of that of the land to which they are attached. In the military colonies, there are no serfs. The settlement of foreign colonists in Russia has been encouraged, and the German and Swiss have emigrated in great numbers to the southern parts of Russia. The government has also made grants of wild lands, in the southern districts, to military veterans, and, by a ukase of 1822, the crown peasants of the provinces, in which the land is poor, are permitted to settle on the fertile lands in Siberia. Some of the nomadic tribes have begun to practise agriculture, and receive assistance from the government, which requires them, however, to embrace Christianity. The Jews have been encouraged to turn their attention to agricultural and mechanical industry; and agricultural societies and schools have been established. In 1820, the number of sheep in Russia was estimated at more than sixty millions; and the wool exported from Odessa was considered equal to the best Spanish. The army is clothed in domestic woollens. The discovery of gold and platina in the Ural mountains (see *Ural*), in 1821 and 1823, is of the highest importance, and government has done much to promote the science of mining, and the establishment of salt works. The cultivation of the grape has been introduced, with the happiest results, in Siberia. The subject of education has also received the attention of government: the management of this department belongs to the ministry for ecclesiastical affairs. In 1823, besides the seven universities, there were eighteen institutions for the promotion of science and the arts, and in 1824, observatories were erected at Nicolaieff, on the Black sea, and at Moscow. There are also gymnasia, provincial schools, and schools for the instruction of the lower classes on the Lancasterian plan. The different religious denominations have good theological institutions, and the Bible has been widely disseminated, in different languages, among the people. Some distinguished patrons of science, as well as the government itself, have caused scientific voyages and journeys to be prosecuted at their own expense. (See *Kotzebue*, *Krusenstern*, *Romanzoff*, and *North Polar Expeditions*.) The legislative committee, by order of the emperor, published the Institutions and Pandects of the Russian law, in 1819—23, in twenty-two volumes. A complete collection of the Russian laws and legal decisions has been published since 1821 and there is also a collection of the criminal laws, in sixteen volumes (1753—1826) and a collection of the laws relating to the taxes, the public accounts, the investi gation of the condition of the population, &c. (21st vol., 1827). Among the particular laws, the ukase of 1822, abolishing the practice of branding, after the punishment of the knout, deserves mention.

Russian Bath. (See *Bath*, vol. i, page 610.)

Russia, History of.—1. *Early History.* A number of nomadic tribes, reaching to the confines of the Roman Empire, were comprehended under the name of Scythians and Sarmatians. They inhabited the countries between the Don and Dnieper, described by Herodotus. Strabo and Tacitus mention, also, the Roxolani as a Sarmatian tribe. In the second century of the vulgar era, the Goths came from the north into the countries between the Don and the Danube. From the fifth century, the Alans, Huns, Avars and Bulgarians followed each other in this region. The Slavi, a Sarmatian tribe, retired more to the west and north; the Chazars, pressed by the Avars, entered, in the sixth century, into the countries between the Wolga and the Don, pressed forwards by degrees to the Danube, conquered the Crimea, and thus came into close contact with the Byzantines. (The empress Irene was a Chazarian princess.) The Petchenegues, who were of a kindred stock with the Chazars, and dwelt along the Caspian sea, moved towards the west, and pressed the Hungarians to Pannonia, whilst they occupied the countries between the Don and the Aluta. In the north of Russia dwelt the Tschuds (Finns and Esthonians), Finnish tribes. All these tribes were wandering herdsmen and hunters. At a later period only, a part of them acquired some degree of civilization by entering the provinces of the Roman empire, coming into contact with the Byzantines, and embracing Christianity. The Sclavonic tribes showed earliest the germs of civilization. They passed, in the fifth and sixth centuries, from the northern part of the Danube down the Vistula, and up the Dnieper. They built the two cities Novgorod (*novus hortus**) and Kiev, which, at a later period, became powerful by means of their commerce, but, at the beginning, suffered greatly from the Chazars. Novgorod also suffered from the Varagians, a piratic tribe on the Baltic, and therefore sent to beg their protection, offering to submit to their sovereignty in return. Induced by this offer, many of this tribe went, in the year 862 (according to Nestor, from the other side of the sea†), under the conduct of the brothers Ruric, Sineus and Truwor, their chieftains, and founded three principalities in the neighborhood of the city of Novgorod. After the death of his brothers, Ruric ruled alone, and united his countrymen and the Slavi into one people—the Russians. The new state, with a military organization, embraced Northern Russia, and was known under the name of Holmgard, Gardarike, and Ostrogard. Ruric died in 879. His son Ighor, under his guardian Oleg (Olaf), conquered Kiev, and made it his capital. Ighor's widow and successor embraced Christianity in 955, in Constantinople. Hence the introduction of the Greek ritual into Russia. The grandson of Ighor, Wladimir I of Novgorod, the Saint, or the Great, united the whole of Ighor's dominions in 980. He made extensive conquests, married the Greek princess Anna, was baptized, at Cherson, in 987, and died in 1015, having endeavored to give his people a higher degree of civilization. He divided his dominions among his twelve sons: according to the Slavonic custom, the various territories inherited by his sons were to remain under the grand principality of Kiev; but bloody family wars ensued for the dignity of grand-prince. Wladimir II, remotely connected with this line, was elected grand-prince by the people of Kiev, in 1114. Alexius Comnenus, the Byzantine emperor, acknowledged him as czar. His son George built Moscow in 1147. The surrounding nations took advantage of the internal dissensions of the country to invade it. The most dangerous of these

* The Russian language uses, as is known, *g* instead of *h* (hospodar, gospodar).

† The ancient inhabitants of Scandinavia received different names in the different countries in which they settled. In England, they were called *Danes*; in France, *Normans*; in Russia, *Waragians*, or *Varagians* (translated *wandering hunters, adventurers*). The Tschuds, in the Finnish dialect, called them *Ruotsi, Rutzi* (i. e. foreigners, adventurers); hence *Rohs*, and now *Russians*. This appellation was used, even before the time of Ruric, by the Byzantines, though not before the beginning of the ninth century. According to Nestor, the term *Russians* became general only after the Varjagi had made themselves, through Ruric, the ruling caste among the Slavi. Nestor calls Ruric and his brothers *Njemtzi* (i. e. Germans); Thunmann and Schlözer consider them to be Scandinavians (Normans); Ewers calls them, without ground, *Chazars*. Ruric and his followers probably came from Vagria, from the then known port Aldeigaborg, now Aldenburg, or Oldenburg. They were, perhaps, Frisians, or Jutes. The first place which Ruric founded near Novgorod, and fortified, was called by him *Aldeigaborg*, from which, to this day, lake Ladoga (formerly Aldoga) has its name.

neighbors were the Mongols (from 1223). After a devastating war of fifteen years, and when the grand-prince George II had fallen in battle at Sita, in 1238, against the khan Batu, the Mongols (q. v.) occupied all Russia, Novgorod only being excepted by treaty. In respect to civilization, the Russians were then in a low condition, owing to the variety of tribes of which they were composed, and their military organization. Commerce was chiefly in the hands of German merchants, who, since 1200, had entered the country with the missionaries from the Dwina. Novgorod and Kiev were the chief commercial cities. Events were recorded in monkish chronicles (yet in the language of the country), of which, since Nestor (who died about 1113), a long series is extant. Whilst the Mongols oppressed the Russians, the Livonians, Teutonic knights, and Swedes, attacked them on the other side. An annual tribute was paid to the Mongols, and nothing was to be undertaken which should appear dangerous to the latter; yet, even in this condition, the Russian princes carried on some successful wars. Alexander defeated the Swedes, in 1241, on the Neva, and received the surname of Newsky. (See *Alexander Newsky.*) His youngest son, Daniel, came to the throne fourteen years after Alexander's death, lived in Moscow, and, in 1296, first assumed the title of grand-prince of Moscow. The Russians struggled against the Tartars, and even defeated them, in 1360, but were obliged, nevertheless, to return to the condition of tributaries.—II. *Middle Period.* Iwan I (Wasiliewitsch the Great, who reigned from 1462 to 1505) succeeded, after a struggle which continued from 1477 to 1481, in freeing Russia from the Tartars. The conquests of Timour, and partitions of the Tartar territory, had weakened the power of the Mongols. In this period, the Cossacks arose. The Poles and Lithuanians had conquered the whole of Western Russia to Kiev, and subjected the vanquished people to religious persecution, as well as political oppression. On the east, the Tartars of the Crimea bore hard upon Russia. The discontented therefore retired into the fertile but uninhabited Ukraine, and adopted a military organization, under the control of atamans (hetmans). The wife of Iwan I (Zoë, a Greek princess, through whom the double-headed eagle came into the Russian arms) did much good in Russia. Iwan made the indivisibility of the realm a fundamental law; he introduced fire-arms into Russia, and made Kasan dependent upon her. His son Wasilei had many conflicts with the Poles. The German emperor Maximilian endeavored to make peace between them, in order to institute a sacred league of Christian princes against the Turks, and sent baron von Herberstein (q. v.) to the czar. Pope Clement VII strove to win the czar over to the Roman Catholic church, and offered him the royal title; but Poland did not enter into the pope's plan. In the promotion of civilization, Iwan Wasiliewitsch II surpassed all his predecessors. German artists and learned men went, by the way of Lübeck, to Russia; printing-offices were established; commerce was promoted by a treaty with Elizabeth of England, in 1553, as the English had just found the way by sea to Archangel. Iwan established a standing army, the Strjelzi, or Strelitzes (shooters); conquered Kasan in 1552, the kingdom of Astrachan in 1554, and strove to drive the Teutonic knights from Livonia; but Denmark, Poland and Sweden attacked him, and a conspiracy in the interior broke out. In this embarrassment, he implored the emperor Rodolph II and pope Gregory XIII to interfere; and the nuncio of the latter brought about the peace of Zapolia between Iwan II and Stephen Bathory, king of Poland, in 1582, by which Livonia was ceded to Poland. Towards the end of Iwan's reign, the Cossack Yermak discovered Siberia (about 1578). Iwan died in 1584. Feodor, his successor, conquered Siberia entirely in 1587, and surrendered Esthonia to Sweden in 1595. Feodor, the last of Ruric's descendants, died in 1598; and Russia was shaken by internal convulsions and external wars, which greatly retarded her progress in civilization. The war of the Polish party with the party of the pseudo-Demetrius* was not ended until Michael Fedorowitsch ascended the throne in 1613; after which a treaty of peace was concluded at Stolbowa, with Sweden, in 1617, and at Divelina, with Poland, in 1618.—III. *Modern History.* The Russians elected Michael, a son of Philaret, metropolitan of Rostoff, and, at a later period, patriarch (Philaret's original name was Feodor Nikitowitsch Romanoff), in 1613, czar, with unlimited and hereditary power. After having overcome many obstacles, he reigned in com-

* The genuine Demetrius, younger son of Iwan II, and brother to Feodor, is said to have been murdered by the usurper Boris; but modern inquiries have thrown much doubt on this subject. The murdered Demetrius is a saint in Russia.

parative tranquillity, till 1645. Under his son Alexei, the last pseudo-Demetrius was beheaded, in 1653. In this period, also, begin the wars with the Turks (neighbors of the Russians since 1472), on account of the Ukraine, in 1671. Alexei (died in 1676), and his son, Feodor III (died in 1682), did much for the industry, commerce, internal organization, legislation, &c. of the empire. The former established the first posts in Russia, and humbled the patriarchs; whilst the latter put an end to the claims of the nobility to the higher offices, by burning their pedigrees. He appointed his half-brother, Peter, his successor, passing over the weak Iwan. After 1689, Peter ruled alone, having put Sophia, sister to Feodor, in a convent, and having received from Iwan a surrender of his claims to the government. Russia now extended from Archangel to Azoph; but was as yet separated from the Baltic. The inhabitants of this vast territory formed one nation, united by the ties of language and religion. Peter made the Russians Europeans, as Philip had made the Macedonians Greeks. (See the article *Peter I.*) By the acquisition of the coasts of the Baltic, Russia entered into the series of European powers. At Pultawa, July 8, 1709, the supremacy of Sweden in the north was destroyed; and, in 1721, Sweden, exhausted by a struggle of 20 years, concluded the peace of Nystadt, under hard conditions. (See *Northern War.*) Peter's views respecting Persia, the Porte, and Poland, were realized by his successors.—His wife, Catharine I (q. v.), reigned from 1725 to 1727, under Menschikoff's influence, only occupied with the concerns of the interior. Under Peter II, her successor, who died in 1730, the Dolgorucky, who had overthrown Menschikoff, found so much to occupy them in the domestic affairs of the country, that they did not pay much attention to the foreign relations. When Anna (q. v.), niece of Peter I, and, from 1711, widow of Frederic, duke of Courland, ascended the throne, the nobles endeavored to limit the power of the sovereign; but their plans were frustrated, and a cabinet composed of foreigners was the consequence. Münnich and Ostermann, of Peter's school, turned their thoughts to foreign aggrandizement.—Russia established her influence over Poland, by putting Augustus III on the throne. Münnich took Azoph and Oczakow by storm; the victory of Stewutschan, in 1739, threw Choczim and Moldavia into the Russian power—advantages, however, which were lost, in consequence of the unfortunate campaign of the Austrians, and the peace of Belgrade, in 1739. Russia, nevertheless, had acquired, by these conquests, much influence among the powers of Europe; and her armies were vastly improved. Anna died in 1740, and Iwan III, two months old, was placed on the throne, under Biron's guardianship: but, Dec. 6, 1741, the princess Elisabeth, youngest daughter of Peter the Great, ascended the throne, and imprisoned Iwan III (grandson of the sister of Anna). Elisabeth, (q. v.), who was notorious for gross and open licentiousness, sent the chancellor Ostermann and field-marshal Münnich to Siberia. The German language had, till then, prevailed at court and in the chief schools; but the French now gradually gained the ascendency. France had instigated Sweden to a war with Russia, during the Austrian war of succession, in order to prevent Russia from affording aid to Maria Theresa of Austria; but the conquest of Finland caused the peace of Abo (q. v.), Aug. 17, 1743. The act of succession of prince Adolphus Frederic of Holstein-Gottorp confirmed the influence of Russia over Sweden. In favor of this prince, his cousin Charles Peter Ulrich, of Holstein-Gottorp, resigned his claims upon the Swedish throne, and was declared by his aunt, the empress Elisabeth, in 1743, her successor in that of Russia. Lestocq (q. v.) was banished, and Bestucheff, taking charge of the foreign relations, changed the foreign policy of the country, so that, in 1747, Elisabeth renewed her alliance with Austria and England, and sent an army to Germany against France, by which means she contributed to bring about the peace of Aix-la-Chapelle. (q. v.) In 1754, Russia assisted Austria against Prussia, in the seven years' war. Elisabeth died Jan. 5, 1762, and her successor, Peter III (q. v.), the admirer and friend of Frederic the Great, immediately concluded a peace and alliance with him. But Catharine II deprived her husband of his throne and life, July 9, 1762, and confirmed only the peace with Frederic, and not the alliance. With the reign of this able, artful and licentious woman begins a new era in Russian history. (For an account of her life, see *Catharine II.*) As soon as she had relieved the country from an exhausting war, she invited all kinds of colonists into it, and collected around her distinguished foreigners to assist her plans; schools, laws, commerce, industry,—every thing received a new impulse. The revenue rose from thirty millions of roubles to sixty millions; the army was increased to 450,000 men; the navy to forty-five vessels of the line. She caused, in 1764, Stanislaus Poniatowski, who had been one of her lovers, to be elected king of Poland; and foreign laws were forced upon the people; but their despair produced, on a sudden, the general confederacy at Bar, and Poland resisted Catharine for six years. She was victorious by land and sea against the Porte (1770), and would have been able to humble Poland, had not the breaking out of the plague in Moscow, the insurrection of a common Cossack, Pugatscheff (q. v.), and the revolutions in Sweden, given so much employment to her forces. At length, the partition of Poland took place (Aug. 5, 1772), and Russia received that part of Poland which lies between the Duna, the Dnieper, and Drutsch. (See *Poland.*) Besides this, the influence of Russia upon that unhappy country was confirmed by the establishment of a permanent council, the guarantee of an elective kingdom, and the *liberum veto*. July 22, 1774, she concluded peace with the Turks, by which she acquired Kinburn, Azoph, part of the Crimea, and Kabarda: all the other conquests were restored. In 1776, she divided the empire into governments. In 1780, she instituted the alliance, called the *armed neutrality*, between Russia, the German emperor, Prussia and Portugal, against the naval power of the English. In 1778, she had taken a new lover, Potemkin (q. v.), who directed the Russian policy until 1791, when he died. With him she planned the expulsion of the Turks from Europe, and the reëstablishment of the Byzantine empire; but political considerations prevented the execution of this idea at the time it was projected; and when it was resumed, ten years later, it succeeded but very partially. In 1783, Russia took possession of Little Tartary; thus she held the key to the Ottoman empire. The favor of Prussia had been won by the first partition of Poland, that of Austria by the project of an exchange of Bavaria. Austria, in fact, was even connected with Russia by an alliance against Turkey, so that the idea of expelling the Turks was not a mere chimera. The war with the Porte began. The attempt of the Turks to reconquer the Crimea was frustrated; their fleet was defeated, in 1788, at the mouths of the Dnieper. Oczakow was taken by a bloody assault; but again the Austrians were unsuccessful. Joseph II lost, at Lugos, September 20, 1788, his health and military reputation. Yet the Austrian and Russian armies were subsequently victorious; but, in 1790, Austria retired from the theatre of war, after the convention of Reichenbach; and when Gustavus III of Sweden had invaded Finland, Catharine became inclined to peace. The Turks did not take advantage of the propitious moment. The peace of Werela, in 1790, put an end to the war with Sweden, after several naval battles, advantageous to the latter. Austria concluded peace with Turkey at Sistova, in 1791; Russia at Jassy, January 9, 1792, by which only Oczakow, with its territory, was taken from the Porte, and the Dniester became the frontier of Russia towards Moldavia and Bessarabia. During this war, Prussia had prevented Poland from joining Russia against the Turks; and the Prussian party in Poland, with Ignatius Potocki at their head, gave a new constitution to the country, May 3, 1791. Felix Potocki, at the head of the Russian party, formed, in 1792, the confederation of Targowitz, for the support of the old constitution. But Prussia, at war with France, feared a war with Russia, and, breaking her word given to the Poles, marched an army into Poland. The second partition of this ill-fated country took place at Grodno, August 17, 1793 (see *Poland*), by which Russia acquired 13,609 square miles (the greater part of Lithuania, with Wilna, of Volhynia, and the rest of Podolia). The wreck of the republic was annexed to Russia by the act of union. In 1794, Kosciusko (q. v.) and Madalinski rose for the deliverance of their country. In the same year, the republic was entirely dissolved. In this last partition, Austria also took a share. October 24, 1795, the boundary treaty between Russia and Prussia was concluded, and finally settled January 26, 1797. Courland (q. v.) was taken by Russia as a Polish fief. Catharine died November 17, 1796, having added to the empire of Russia 210,000 square miles of fertile land. She had not taken an active part against the French revolution, though she had concluded an alliance with England and Austria; but her only son, Paul I (q. v.), united with Naples, Turkey, Austria and England, whilst Bonaparte was in Egypt. Suwaroff, commander of the united Austrians and Russians in Italy, was victorious at Cassano, April 27, 1799, on the Trebia, July 17, and at Novi, August 15; but political considerations obliged him to march back, and Masséna having been victorious over Korsakoff in

Switzerland, he was compelled to retire to Upper Germany. The alliance between Russia and Austria was broken, as was also that of Russia with England. Paul was embittered against England for occupying Malta; yet the naval war was continued jointly. The Russians and Turks occupied Corfu. In 1800, the republic of the Seven Islands was established under the guarantee of the Porte and Russia, and was occupied by troops of the latter until 1807—a circumstance which very much increased the Russian influence in the Mediterranean. Paul renewed the plan of an armed neutrality in the north, in consequence of which the battle of Copenhagen took place, April 2, 1801; but the emperor had died nine days previous, and his successor declared himself for peace and for England. Under Alexander's mediation, the peace of Luneville (q. v.) was concluded. He then devoted himself to the internal improvement, appointed a committee, under prince Lapuchin, for the revision of the laws, constituted the senate as a kind of intermediate body between the monarch and the people, and gradually mitigated the rigor of bondage, especially in the crown-villages and the German provinces. The police, especially that of the health department, was greatly improved; about 2000 physicians were paid by government; vaccination was introduced. Agriculture was much improved under him, and some nomadic tribes, as well as the Nogay Tartars, devoted themselves to husbandry. Science was fostered. Krusenstern circumnavigated the world. In Charkow and Kasan, universities and schools were established. But Alexander soon became engaged in the desolating conflicts of Europe with France; at first in 1805, in favor of Austria, until the unfortunate battle of Austerlitz; in the next year in connexion with Prussia. Again unsuccessful, Russia concluded peace with France at Tilsit, in 1807; received a part of Poland (Bialystock), and ceded Jever; evacuated Cattaro and Corfu; broke off all connexion with England; and declared war against Sweden, the only ally of Britain. In the same year (1809), the peace of Fredricshamm made Finland and East Bothnia, with Tornea and the Aland islands, a Russian province. In the war between Austria and France, in 1809, Russia took but little share, but continued with vigor the war with the Porte and with Persia. By the peace of Vienna she received a part of East Galicia, which, however, was restored at the congress of Vienna. When, at length, Russia objected to the extension of France to the river Trave, on account of the emperor's connexion with the duke of Oldenburg, and could not, in her commercial system, accede to the views of Napoleon, the war of 1812 began, which, in the sequel, involved all the powers of Europe, and caused the overthrow of Napoleon in 1815. (See *Russian-German War.*) Russia, it is true, had suffered immensely by this devastating war; but it emerged as a power of preëminent importance, and strengthened by the addition of Poland (q. v.) to its immense territory. This influence seemed, during the reign of Alexander, continually to increase by means of the holy alliance (q. v.), founded and supported by him. At Vienna, in 1815, at Aix-la-Chapelle, in 1818, at Troppau, Laybach, Verona (see *Congress*), this influence was manifested, and the French cabinet was for a considerable time divided into an English and a Russian party. During the struggle with Napoleon, Russia discontinued its hostilities with Persia and the Porte. The peace of Bucharest, May 28, 1812, with the latter, gave her Moldavia as far as the Pruth, Bessarabia, and the chief mouths of the Danube: the peace of Tiflis, in 1813, with the former gained her all the territory west of the Caspian sea, between the Kur and the Araxes, Georgia having been united before with Russia, in 1801; and, on the east coast as far as the gulf of Balkan, with the exclusive navigation of the Caspian sea. Particularly since the congress of Aix-la-Chapelle, Russia may be considered as having found that her influence over Europe would be best promoted by the continuance of peace, which would enable her to develope those resources which make a country formidable in war. Alexander labored with great sagacity to develope the military power as well as the productive capacity of his empire, and at the same time interfered in the affairs of Italy and Spain, and exerted a great control over France and Germany, the less supportable as it was founded on the predominance of force over intelligence. He reorganized almost the whole interior of the empire. (See *Alexander I.*) After the death of this emperor, December 1, 1825, his brother Nicholas ascended the throne, Constantine Cæsarowitsch having renounced his right. (See *Constantine*, and *Nicholas I.*) A conspiracy, mentioned already in the article *Alexander*, broke out December 26, 1825, when the regiments of the guard, who had taken the oath to Constantine immediately after Alexander's death, were to take the oath to Nicholas. Two companies refused, and a tumult ensued, which continued for one day, and was suppressed at last by the mingled firmness and moderation of Nicholas. The investigation of this matter brought to light a conspiracy which had existed already for years, founded, as it would appear, partly on crude political ideas, partly on the offended pride of the old Russian nobility. The committee of investigation published a report May 30 (June 11), 1826. The most guilty, some high officers, were hanged, others sent to Siberia, and others pardoned. The foreign relations of Russia with China have remained unaltered since the treaty of eternal amity between the two countries, concluded in 1727. This treaty provides for the residence of a Russian mission (a mission of young men who study Chinese) in Pekin, by means of which the Russians always maintain a communication with the capital of China. According to the peace of Gulistan, October 12, 1813, ratified at Tiflis, September 15, 1814, Russia received, besides the territory along the Caspian and the exclusive navigation of that sea with ships of war, the right of trade in Persia, in consideration of paying a duty of five per cent., and engaged to support that prince, whom the reigning sovereign should designate for his successor, and not to suffer any interference of a foreign power in the internal affairs of Persia. General Jermoloff at the same time made war upon the mountaineers of the Caucasus, who make a business of robbery. Most of them had submitted in 1823, and, in the same year, seven khans of the Kirguises and Calmucks had passed from the Chinese sovereignty voluntarily under the Russian. About this time the Persian shah had appointed his son Abbas-Mirza his successor, when the settling of the new boundaries caused disputes, which were not settled at the time of Alexander's death. Nicholas sent prince Menschikoff to the court of Teheran, to propose an exchange of the province in question; but the warlike Abbas-Mirza thought the moment propitious for attacking Russia, and marched, August, 1826, over the frontier, called the Mussulman subjects of Russia to arms, and advanced as far as Elizabethpol; but, September 14, the Persian army was defeated, and September 25, general Paskewitsch overcame the Persian crown-prince at Elizabethpol, and freed the Russian territory. September 28, Russia declared war against Persia. Paskewitsch, being appointed commander-in-chief, passed the Araxes, took, April 27, the celebrated Armenian monastery, Etschmiasin, October 3, the fortress Sardor Adad, and, October 19, the fortress of Erivan, the bulwark of Persia against Russia. The Russians now entered ancient Media without opposition, and forced the shah to sue for peace. November 5, 1827, the preliminaries were signed, according to which Persia ceded the khanships of Erivan, on both sides of the Araxes, and the khanship of Nakitschevan, paid the expenses of the war, and the losses caused by the invasion. In the article *Ottoman Empire* (vol. ix, p. 460), we have touched upon the relations between the Porte and Russia, during the years 1826 and 1827. (For the part of Russia, in the mediation between Turkey and the Greek insurgents, and in the battle at Navarino, see the end of our article *Greece, Revolution of Modern.*) The patience of Russia was now exhausted by the conduct of the Porte. February 27, 1828, the Russian minister Nesselrode declared to France and Great Britain, that his sovereign must have satisfaction for the violation of the treaty of Ackermann, and for the hatti sheriff of December 20, 1827, which the Porte had addressed to all the pachas, and which contained many offensive charges against Russia. March 14, the emperor Nicholas issued a declaration of war against the Porte. The Russian forces passed the Pruth, May 7, to the number of 115,000 men, including persons of all descriptions, attached to the camp. Count Diebitsch, to whom the plan of the campaign was ascribed, was chief of the emperor's staff which, on May 19, arrived before Brailow. Count Wittgenstein was commander-in-chief. Jassy was occupied May 7, Bucharest May 12, and Brailow invested on the 11th. June 11, the third division of the Russian army, in which was the emperor's head-quarters, crossed the Danube. June 15, an attempt was made to carry Brailow by storm, but without success; it capitulated, however, on the 19th. The Russians had now the lower Danube in their power, which secured the connexion of the army with Russia. The divisions advanced singly. After the battles of the 7th and 20th of July, the Turks retired into the fortified mountain position of Choumla, which was the centre of their operations. The Turkish army, under Hussein Pacha, here consisted of more than 40,000 men. Varna, fortified by nature and art, and defended by the favorite of the sultan, the capudan pacha, and the warlike Jussuf Pacha of Seres, formed the right wing of the Turkish position. Around these gates of Constantinople (as they are called), Varna and Choumla, the hottest conflict ensued. The principal army, 45,000 men strong, under field-marshal Wittgenstein, with whom the emperor had his head-quarters, approached Choumla, whilst lieutenant-general Roth besieged Silistria, and lieutenant-general count Suchtelen watched Varna. The grand vizier would not give battle at Choumla, but confined himself to the defence of the place. The Russians took possession at last of the key of the Balkan, Prawodi, from which a strong division of the army might have pressed forward to Aidos; but they did not dare to leave Choumla and Varna in their rear, and some battalions, who had proceeded too far, suffered loss near Eski Stambol, and an intrenchment was taken by the Turks. In proportion to the difficulty of carrying on the siege, in a vast and almost uninhabitable country like Bulgaria, under the fatal influence of the climate, were the efforts of the Russians to get possession at least of Varna. After this place had been invested on the land side by prince Menschikoff, and on the sea side by the fleet from the Black sea, returning from Anapa, under admiral Greig, breaches were made. Omer Vriones advanced to its relief, but was driven back by prince Eugene of Würtemberg; a body of troops forced their way into the bastion, October 7, and entered the city, which they soon left again. Terrified by this, the enemy gave up all further resistance, and Jussuf Pacha came himself to the Russian camp to negotiate. The capudan pacha retired into the citadel. The Russians took possession of all the bastions of the fortress, October 11, after two months' siege, without any conditions on the part of the inhabitants. The capudan pacha had liberty to retire with 300 men. Jussuf Pacha of Seres went over to the Russians with several Turkish troops, and repaired to Odessa. After this conquest, the Russians drew back from Choumla, October 15. The siege of Silistria did not take place till the last of September. Winter came on unusually early, and diseases became prevalent; a scarcity of food and provender existed, so that the siege was raised on November 10th. The campaign in Asia was successful; prince Menschikoff, on the 22d of June, had taken the fortress of Anapa, on the Black sea, which was dangerous for the provinces of Russia beyond the Caucasus, in consequence of which the predatory population of the neighboring mountains submitted to the Russians. The Russian army under count Paskewitsch forced their way from Caucasus and Ararat into Asiatic Turkey, and took by storm, July 5, the strong fortress of Kars, the central point of Turkish Armenia, together with the enemies' camp. Whilst the Russian fleet on the Black sea destroyed a Turkish flotilla, August 8, and the batteries of Iniada, on the coast, near Constantinople, and supported the attack on Varna, Paskewitsch took the fortresses of Achalkalaki, Gertwiss, and, July 26, Poti, which being situated at the mouth of the Phasis, secured the possession of Mingrelia and Imiretia. The Turks, indeed, wished to press forward from Arsrum, (Erzerum), and for this purpose placed an army of 30,000 men near Akhalzich. But Paskewitsch crossed an almost impassable mountain, and beat the enemy at Kura, and, on the 21st, the principal body of his forces, after which he took Akhalzich by storm (on the 25th). The citadel capitulated. Several strong fortresses fell into the Russian power up to the 21st of September, so that the whole pachalic of Bajasid, as far as the banks of the Euphrates, was conquered. The campaign in Europe corresponded less to the general expectation. The numbers of the army were not so complete as had been calculated, and the supplies were deficient. The loss of the horses could not be immediately repaired. The prevalent diseases had greatly weakened the army. At last, a severe winter came on, and put an end to the campaign in both countries. Its results, however, were important. In Europe and Asia, Russia had taken possession of two Turkish principalities, and three pachalics, fourteen fortresses and three castles, besides commanding a long line of country, and four passages over the Danube. The Russian emperor had repeated, during and after the campaign, as well as before it, to the British ambassador-extraordinary, lord Heytesbury, his inclination for peace with the Porte, on the terms of indemnification for the expenses of the war, and security against future injuries and violations of treaties; but the Porte had rejected all mediation on the basis of the London treaty, and refused to send envoys to negotiate with the ambassadors of the three powers, and the commissioners of the Greeks. On the contrary, Mahmoud had announced a new campaign, with the words, "Honor and independence are worth more than life." Hitherto the negotiations had been carried on in Constantinople, with the reis effendi, by the minister of the Netherlands. He had delivered to the reis effendi the manifesto of France, Great Britain and Russia, of August 11, 1828, which made known to the Porte the motive and object of the French expedition against the Morea. The Prussian ambassador, Canitz, likewise advised the Porte to yield, but, till January, 1829, without success. The sultan had even banished to Asia many of the friends of peace among the ulemas, on account of their sentiments. Still he showed, on several occasions, an unexpected regard for the laws of nations. He did not close the Bosphorus against the trade of neutrals with Russia until the 13th of September; the Russian prisoners were well treated; the Russians settled in Constantinople were protected, and the irritated Turks were kept in unusual restraint. On the other hand, Jussuf Pacha of Seres, for surrendering Varna, which had till then resisted all attacks, was banished, and his estates confiscated. The grand vizier, Mehmed Selim, was deposed for his delay in relieving that fortress, and banished to Gallipoli. At length a strong body of cavalry from Asia, under the command of the brave Tshapan Oglu, joined the forces, to open the campaign of 1829. February 21, 1829, general Diebitsch* was appointed commander-in-chief of the Russian forces; but even previous to that event, and in the midst of winter, the Russian forces had not been reduced entirely to inaction. The fortresses of Kale and Tourno, on the Danube, were taken at the end of January, with eighty-seven pieces of cannon, while the thermometer of Fahrenheit was at zero. February 18, a flotilla of thirty Turkish vessels, frozen up near Nicopoli, was destroyed. February 25, the fortress of Sizeboli, beyond the gulf of Bourgas, east of the Balkan, was taken by a Russian fleet. The garrison, consisting of about 16,000 Albanians, retreated, and joined the main body under Hussein Pacha. But it was in Asiatic Turkey that the serious operations of the campaign commenced. On the night of March 3d, a Turkish force of more than 20,000 men made an attack on Akhalzich. General Paskewitsch immediately sent a reinforcement to the relief of the place, and on the 16th the besieging force retreated. June 14th, a body of Turks, who had been drawn down, by the movements of the Russians, from the mountains of Adjar, were attacked in their intrenched camp by generals Mouravieff and Bourtsoff. The camp was carried by assault, and large stores of provisions and ammunitions, nearly 400 prisoners, &c., were taken. An army of 50,000 men had been collected by the seraskier of Erzerum, and divided into two corps, one commanded by the pacha of three tails, Hagki, an officer of high renown in Asiatic Turkey, who, with 20,000 men, was stationed at the passes of the mountains of Saganlon; the other, of 30,000 men, under the seraskier of Erzerum himself. These two corps, by the manœuvres of general Paskewitsch, were separated from each other, and successively totally defeated, at the beginning of July. July 3, Paskewitsch took possession of Erzerum, the centre of the Turkish power in Asia. The seraskier, commander-in-chief of the whole Turkish army, and governor of all Asiatic Turkey, was taken prisoner, together with four principal pachas, and 150 pieces of cannon. The sharpest contest of the Asiatic campaign was occasioned by the attempt of the pacha of Van to rescue from the Russians the fortress of Bajasid. The attack was made with 7000 infantry and 5000 cavalry, aided by the fire from a battery, on a range of rocks, which swept the Russian troops on the flank and rear, and the fire of musquetry from the inhabitants of the Tartar quarter of the place. After thirty-two hours of incessant fighting, the Turks retreated. The career of Paskewitsch in this campaign had been one of continual success; and such had been his preceding campaign in Persia. In the European provinces, the campaign commenced by the renewal of the siege of Silistria, under the immediate direction of Diebitsch. May 17, a detachment of the Russian army, posted near the village of Eski Arnaoutlar, was attacked by the Turkish army commanded by the grand vizier from Choumla, at three in the morning. The battle lasted till eight in the evening, when the Turks retired. June 11, the battle of Koulevtcha, or Prawodi, took place between the army of Diebitsch and that of the grand vizier. It was contested with obstinacy, and the victory displayed rather the superiority of European tactics than of courage. June 30, Silistria surrendered, and the garrison of 10,000 men

* Diebitsch was the son of a Silesian officer in the Prussian, and afterwards in the Russian service. In 1813, he was lieutenant-general and quartermaster-general, and, subsequently, adjutant-general to Alexander. In the battle of Austerlitz he was wounded in the hand; at Dresden he received a severe contusion, and had two horses shot under him; and he distinguished himself in the actions of Eylau and Friedland.

became prisoners of war; 22C pieces of cannon, 80 standards, and the whole Turkish flotilla, fell into the hands of the Russians. Immediately after the surrender of Silistria, Diebitsch commenced his preparations for the passage of the river Kamtchik and the Balkan mountain. He left his camp before Choumla July 17. July 22, the Russians had made such progress, that the general headquarters of the army were removed to Erketch, on the summit of the Balkan, after considerable opposition from the Turks, at the passage of the Kamtchik. Mezembri was occupied on the 23d, and fifteen pieces of cannon, and large quantities of warlike stores, taken. Arriving on the shores of the Euxine, the progress of the army was aided by the coöperation of the fleet under admiral Greig, consisting of three ships of the line, three frigates, and some smaller vessels. After the successive occupation of sundry villages from day to day, the last resistance on the part of the Turks before the Russians reached Adrianople, was made at Slivno, or Selimno, said to be next in importance to Adrianople, among the cities of the Ottoman empire. The Turks abandoned the city August 12, after a very feeble resistance. From this time the Russians encountered hardly any difficulties, before reaching Adrianople, except such as arose from the excessive heat of the weather, the rocky ground, and bad state of the roads. On the 19th, the Russians approached Adrianople, which was occupied the next day without opposition. Negotiations now commenced, and, September 14, a treaty of peace was signed, the principal points of which were the cessation of hostilities; the restoration by Russia of the principalities of Walachia and Moldavia, and of all the towns occupied by the Russians in Bulgaria and Rumelia; the settlement of the boundaries between the two powers in Europe and Asia; the provisions for the religious liberty, independent administration and free trade of the people of Moldavia and Walachia; freedom of commerce to Russian subjects throughout the Ottoman empire, as secured by former treaties; free commerce and navigation of the Black sea to all nations at peace with the Porte; the stipulation of the Porte to pay 1,500,000 ducats of Holland to Russia within eighteen months, as an indemnification for losses of Russian subjects, and a further sum, such as should be agreed on, as an indemnity for the expenses of the war; the accession of the Porte to the arrangements of Russia, Great Britain and France, respecting Greece. By a subsequent separate act, the indemnities mentioned as stipulated were agreed to be paid by instalments, the first in four increasing payments at short intervals; the second in ten annual instalments. On the first payment of the portion of the smaller sum, the Russian forces were to retire from Adrianople; on the second, to recede beyond the Balkan; on the third, to repass the Danube; and on the fourth payment, to evacuate the Turkish territory. Thus the emperor Nicholas, according to the pledge which he had given to his allies at the commencement of the war, stopped short in the career of conquest, when he had obtained the objects for which the war was professedly undertaken.—The beginning of the insurrection in Poland has been given in the article *Poland*. The following is a short account of the struggle which ensued.* When the diet of Poland met, Dec. 18, 1830, at Warsaw, general Chlopicki resigned the dictatorship; on the 20th, indeed, he was reinstated in the office, but he finally resigned, January 19, 1831. Whilst Poland was preparing for the unequal conflict with great enthusiasm, at least among the better educated classes, the Jews not excepted, the emperor Nicholas, December 17 (24), 1830, issued a proclamation to the Poles, calling upon them to submit to their legitimate government. January 21 prince Radzivil was elected commander-in-chief of the Polish army, and on the 24th, the termination of the Russian dynasty in Poland was declared. Marshal Diebitsch, who had so successfully conducted the war with the Turks, entered Poland at the head of a large army. He advanced as far as Warsaw, and was victorious over the Poles near the walls of their capital, February 25, 1831 (the loss of the Poles is stated to have been 5500; that of their enemies 4500); but when prince Radzivil resigned the command on the 28th, and Skrzynecki, then only a colonel, was appointed in his place, the Polish cause gained strength. This brave officer, though finally unsuccessful, like the heroic Kosciusko, proved that he deserved a better fate. March 31, he was victorious over the Russians near Praga, in a night attack. He advanced cautiously, and, favored by the darkness of the night, reached their cantonments without

* As our only information on this sad subject is derived from the newspapers, and works compiled from such sources, we have thought it best to confine ourselves to narrow limits.

being perceived. The advanced guard of general Geismar, consisting of 8000 or 10,000 men, was first attacked, and almost wholly destroyed: the Poles took 4000 prisoners and 1600 pieces of cannon. Immediately afterwards, he attacked general Rosen, who was posted with 20,000 men at Dempe Wielski, and obliged him to retreat with the loss of 2000 prisoners and nine pieces of cannon. Another important victory was afterwards gained near Zelechow, where 12,000 Russians were killed, wounded or taken, with twelve pieces of cannon. During this action, the Lithuanians and Volhynians, who served in the Russian army, turned their arms against the Russians, and materially contributed to the success of the Poles. The peasants in various quarters of Poland now took an active part in the war, and hastened, with whatever weapons they could obtain, to the army. Insurrections broke out in Lithuania, Volhynia, Kowno, the Ukraine, Wilna, and even in ancient Poland, as far as Smolensk. On the other hand, general Dwernicki, who had been sent to make a demonstration in the rear of the Russians, and who had been victorious over them, was at last compelled to pass into the Austrian dominions, where he surrendered to the authorities of that country, April 27, with 5000 Poles. He is said to have been treated humanely. Skrzynecki, after having had several unsuccessful encounters with the Russians, and having avoided a decisive engagement with an enemy superior in strength, at last fought the battle of Ostrolenka, May 26. The Russian army is said to have amounted to 55,000, and the Polish to 20,000. The Russians were victorious. The same day the Polish general Chlapovski was victorious over the Russians, under Sacken, at Mariampol. The ardor of the people still continued, and hopes were entertained in every country that the manly resistance of the Poles would induce the powerful cabinets to interfere; but, unfortunately, Prussia and Austria, being themselves in possession of a part of the spoils of Poland, did all in their power to prevent interference, whilst England and France were too much occupied at home to render essential aid. June 19, count Diebitsch suddenly died of the cholera morbus, which the Russian army had carried to Poland, at Klechewo, having been superseded, on the 16th of the same month, by general Paskewitsch, whose campaign in Asia has been already mentioned. The military operations were now prosecuted with new vigor, and the emperor, who, in a manifesto addressed to the Russians, had called them the legitimate masters of the Poles, was ready to make every sacrifice to regain the Polish throne. The Poles were successful, July 14, under general Chrzanski, five miles from Warsaw, against the Russians; but, owing to causes which have not yet been satisfactorily explained, a change of government took place in Warsaw, and general Skrzynecki was superseded by Dembinski as commander-in-chief. The behavior of the former seems to have been throughout exemplary, and such was his deportment on his discharge from the supreme command. The skill and valor of generals Roziski and Czartoryski were no longer of any avail. A conspiracy of the Russian prisoners in Warsaw was discovered and punished. Krukowiecki was appointed Polish dictator. Paskewitsch made preparations for the taking of the city, in which he succeeded September 7, at six o'clock, when the capital surrendered by capitulation, after a most sanguinary conflict of two days' duration, during which the Polish soldiers behaved heroically, whilst it is not yet sufficiently explained, whether the authorities did their duty. The Polish army, followed by the diet and the members of government, retired through Praga, on the night of the 7th, and, early on the 8th, the Russians entered Warsaw.* The Polish army remained for a short time at Modlin; but the country was soon obliged to submit entirely to the Russian forces, with which the grand-prince Michael, brother to the emperor Nicholas, had entered Warsaw. He organized a provisory government, of which, at first, he himself, and soon after, general Paskewitsch, was the head. This general

* The St.Petersburg papers of October, in the official account of the taking of Warsaw, say that 132 pieces of cannon, 2,000,000 of cartridges, a vast quantity of military stores of every description, and immense magazines of provisions, fell into the hands of the Russians; that 3000 prisoners were taken, among whom were 60 staff and superior officers; that many more must have perished during the attack, by the burning of the buildings, and the destructive fire of the artillery, which, during the two days, expended 29,000 cartridges; that, besides the above-mentioned prisoners, above 4000 soldiers of the Polish army, 1200 generals and officers, had quitted the Polish service, and joined the Russians; that the whole loss of the Russian army was 3000 killed, including 63 officers, and 7500 wounded, including 445 officers. The public will probably soon receive an account of the whole revolution, from the Polish refugees in France. A work on this subject has been advertised in Boston, as preparing for the press, by major Hordinsky, a Polish officer.

was made prince Warszawski (the Warsovian) as a reward for his services. A sort of amnesty was proclaimed; but the corps of generals Romarino, Kamniski and Rubinski were prohibited from returning to Poland, because they continued in arms after the capitulation of Warsaw, in contempt of the orders of the Polish commander-in-chief. Many distinguished Poles were sent into the interior of Russia or to Siberia; many of all ranks emigrated, chiefly to France. They were every where, in Germany and France, enthusiastically received by the people, and in the latter country were also aided by the government. General Skrzynecki is said to live in Austria, and to be honorably treated. Though the kingdom of Poland, it seems, is not to be entirely incorporated with Russia, like those portions which were torn from it by the partitions, yet the intention of the Russian government appears to be to deprive it entirely of a general diet, and to establish provincial chambers. Thus that gigantic power, which, even under an enlightened monarch, is, from the very form of its government, hostile to the constitutional principle, developing itself so rapidly in the west of Europe, and which unites the force both of barbarism and civilization, has come close upon western Europe, and exercises, at least for the present, a powerful influence upon it; as is evinced—if an example among so many were necessary—in the Belgic question. However distant the time may be, Europe will not be safe until Poland is reëstablished; without which, Austria and Prussia, particularly the latter, must remain bound to Russia.

Russian-German War, 1812—1815. Between France and Russia a coldness had arisen since 1809, although the meeting of the monarchs of the two countries at Erfurt, in 1808 (especially when the geographical situation of their states was considered), seemed to give assurance of a lasting peace. The slight share which the tardy army of Russian auxiliaries took in the war against Austria, showed that its commander had received injunctions to be circumspect in his proceedings. At the same time, all the Russian harbors were opened to the English, provided they displayed the American flag, while French goods were strictly prohibited. This induced Napoleon, in order to enforce his commercial prohibitions against England, to make himself master of the northern sea-board of Germany, and incorporate the country of the duke of Oldenburg, a near relation of Alexander with France. Against this proceeding, Russia made an energetic protest; and, as early as 1811, five Russian divisions assumed a position opposite Warsaw. On the other hand, Napoleon caused the fortresses on the Vistula and Oder to be declared in a state of siege, sent thither large masses of troops, and occupied Swedish Pomerania, because Charles XIII of Sweden declined a closer connexion with France. (The causes of the war between France and Russia are further treated of in the article *Napoleon*, Appendix of vol. x.) The Russians adopted the plan of offensive operations; and it had been resolved to treat the approach of the French to the Oder as a declaration of war, to let the Russian army enter Prussia, ascertain the sentiments of this state, and commence hostilities. But political considerations, especially the situation of Prussia, urged the abandonment of this plan. On the French side, the visit of so many princes and kings, and even of the Austrian emperor, to Dresden, gave intimations of some great project, although Napoleon's departure from Paris, according to the *Moniteur*, had no object but a review of the army of the Vistula. Perhaps he might still hope to avert the gigantic struggle, without departing from his purposes; at least for this object the count de Narbonne proceeded to the camp of Alexander, at Wilna, and offers of peaceable arrangements were made. For the contest in the Peninsula, which daily became more obstinate, and consumed a large amount of men and money, might well appear to him an obstacle in the way of a struggle with Russia; but he calculated that his army, amounting nearly to one million, all of which he had rendered perfectly disposable by the institution of a new national guard of 80,000 men, would be sufficient for the conflict in both quarters; and he also relied upon a great mass of auxiliary forces, chiefly promised by the confederation of the Rhine (100,000 men), and, finally, on the alliance with Prussia and Austria, which covered him on both flanks, secured his retreat, and both together furnished 60,000 men. When, therefore, Napoleon's ambassador, the object of his mission unattained, returned to Dresden, half a million soldiers (French, Germans, Italians, Poles, Swiss, Spaniards, and Portuguese), with more than 1200 cannon, were put in motion, about the end of July, to attack the Russians on the other side of the Niemen and the Vistula. The Russians, in three divisions, occupied a line including Kiev and Smolensk to Riga. The first western army (127,000 men), in Lithuania and Courland, was commanded by Barclay de Tolly, who had till then been minister of war, under whom was Wittgenstein; the other western army (48,000 strong), between Smolensk and Kiev, was commanded by prince Bagration. General Doctoroff led a third body of forces, which served to keep up the communication between the other two. Goods and records had long before been generally conveyed into the interior. Riga, Smolensk, &c., were fortified, and an entrenched camp established on the Dwina. Napoleon, already near the Russian frontier, made another diplomatic attempt, and sent count Lauriston, who had formerly been ambassador at Petersburg, to the emperor Alexander; but their views were too much at variance, and Napoleon said, in his usual tone, "The conquered assume the style of the conqueror; fate overcomes them; let their destiny be fulfilled." June 24, his main forces passed the Niemen, while the rest crossed the Vistula farther down. As the passage took place near the influx of the Wilna,* and this river, which flowed on their left flank, was also crossed, the Russians were surrounded as far as the Dwina, entirely separated from the second western army, and compelled either to risk a decisive battle with divided forces, or to make a speedy retreat. They chose the latter, and sacrificed their great magazines, which were to have given subsistence to their right wing. Wilna, which had been Alexander's head-quarters, now became the head-quarters of Napoleon, who here organized (an important secondary object of this war) the restoration of Poland. Napoleon made a considerable stay in Wilna, partly for that purpose, partly for the sake of obtaining information of the operations of the right wing under Poniatowski, Schwartzenberg, and Regnier, over whom the king of Westphalia was commander-in-chief. He had received orders to keep the second western army still separate from the first, from which it had been divided by the march to Wilna, and to prevent any junction farther in the rear. These orders marshal Davoust, who joined on the left the flank of the king of Westphalia, executed so fully, that the corps of general Doctoroff was separated from the forces of Bagration, as well as from the western army of Barclay de Tolly, and almost surrounded, when a rain of thirty-six hours made the roads impassable, and the sudden change to cold from intolerable heat, killed, by thousands, the horses of the French, exhausted by wants of all kinds, so that Doctoroff escaped with moderate loss. The cau-

* The first Russian western army was stationed along the Niemen as far as Grodno, and comprised six corps of infantry and two of cavalry. The second western army was in the vicinity of Slonim, consisting of four battalions of infantry and one of cavalry. The communication between them was kept up by the hetman Platoff, with 10,000 Cossacks, at Bialystock. The army of Volhynia, under Tormassoff, at Lutzk, was composed of two divisions of infantry, and one of cavalry, containing together about 20,000 men. In Courland, Riga was protected by general Essen with about 10,000 men. One reserve was formed by general Miloradowitsch in Novgorod, another by general Œrtel in Smolensk. There were, moreover, 16,000 men, under Steinheil, in Finland, which, subsequently, with the 25th division of infantry from Petersburg, reinforced the corps of Wittgenstein. In September, Kutusoff's army of 85,000 men, which had been till then employed against the Turks, first united itself with the forces of Tormassoff. Soon after the invasion commenced, militia companies were formed in Moscow, Petersburg, and other places, for supplying the army. Some of these companies fought at Borodino, and several divisions of them accompanied the army in Germany, in 1813. The Russian plan of the campaign was, by retreating, to avoid a decisive battle, until the enemy should be remote from all his resources, and weakened by marches through a desolate region, and the Russian army should be so considerably strengthened by the accession of all the forces that might be, meanwhile, raised, as to have a decided superiority. The bodies of troops detached on the two wings, were to prevent the enemy from spreading out his forces, and to coöperate in his destruction, if he should be defeated. Calculation was also made of the possible arrival of the Moldavian army after the conclusion of peace with the Porte. Particular circumstances, however, gave rise to many errors in the execution of this plan. Napoleon's scheme, on the contrary, was, to use every effort to compel the Russians to battle, to destroy them after the defeat, and, pressing forward with haste to the capital, to proffer peace. Collateral corps were, meanwhile, to cover his line of communication with Germany, weaken the resources of the enemy, and lead them to take false steps. But the French commander, long accustomed to success, committed the mistake of attempting to carry on the war in Russia, as in Lombardy, without magazines: he overlooked the fact that he ruled the conquered country only in a comparatively small extent, and must, therefore, leave the enemy in possession of his resources: he entirely mistook the character of his enemy. He, nevertheless, made good use of the chief error of the Russians—the wide interval between the two western armies—by crossing the Niemen at Kowno, and advancing with rapidity to Wilna. Murat hereupon pursued the western army, which retired to the entrenched camp at Drissa. Macdonald drove general Essen back towards Mittaw, and Oudinot, Wittgenstein to Wilkomirz. Two divisions under Kamensky were separated from the second western army, and joined the corps in Volhynia.

tion, boldness and courage of prince Bagration, with the want of military penetration on the part of the king of Westphalia, likewise frustrated the plans against him. He even succeeded in surprising, on his retreat, the Poles in Romanoff, and destroying a corps of 6000 men, and in stationing in Volhynia general Tormassoff, who not only perpetually confronted the extreme right wing of the French, but, by a bold attack on its flank, took prisoners a whole brigade of Saxons, in Kobryn, July 27. At Mohilew, he finally succeeded in throwing himself, with all his forces, on marshal Davoust, who defended himself with ability, but would not have escaped without the greatest loss, had not Bagration been every minute in fear of an attack from the king of Westphalia on his flank. When the news of these events had reached Wilna, Napoleon hastened to his troops, which already stood on the Dwina, where they were watching the Russians in their large entrenched camp, and had suffered considerable loss from their sallies. A bridge of boats gave the Russians the advantage of stationing their main forces on whichever bank of the Dwina they pleased. The camp was extremely strong, both by nature and art, since the eminences of the right bank commanded the left. Napoleon, however, ordered a detachment to go round the camp by the road to Poloczk; and, as the previous consequences of his judicious division of the Russian line had not yet been repaired, that is, the two Russian western armies had not yet formed a junction, the Russians had no alternative but to let half their forces be destroyed or to leave their camp and hasten to the Dnieper, where Bagration hoped to join them. Prince Wittgenstein alone maintained his situation, in order to cover the road to Petersburg, and to prevent the investing of Riga. The main army of the French, with the exception of three corps under Reggio, Macdonald and St. Cyr, which blockaded Riga, and endeavored to take possession of the road to Petersburg (which gave rise to a number of bloody indecisive battles), now went, part across the Dwina, part along the river as far as the heights of Wolgonsk, in pursuit of the Russian army, whose rear-guard frequently fought considerable battles with the pursuers, and, from the 25th to the 27th July, contested every foot of ground at and behind Ostrowno. But marshal Davoust, pressing forward between the armies of Bagration and Barclay de Tolly, and thus keeping them apart, finally compelled them to quit the field and retire to Smolensk. Heat, and want of all kinds, had, meanwhile, operated so detrimentally on the French army, that it was obliged to halt at this point for ten days, during which the two Russian armies finally formed a junction under the walls of Smolensk. They immediately began to act on the offensive.* With 12,000 cavalry they attacked general Sebastiani (August 8), and drove him back, with loss, a mile and a half. On the 17th, the main body put itself in motion to encounter the French army, which had advanced, on the 10th, to compel, if possible, a general battle. When Napoleon saw his attempts to surround the right wing of the Russians defeated, he ordered his right wing, under Poniatowski, to hasten, by way of Ortza, by rapid marches, to cut off the Russians from Moscow. On the other hand, Bagration hastened to defend this road, and Barclay de Tolly sought to retard the enemy as much as possible. Smolensk, an old place, formerly strongly fortified, and the whole position on the Dnieper, greatly favored his plan; and not till the midnight of the 17th, after a loss of many thousands, did the French succeed in taking this bulwark, reduced, for the most part, to a ruin. The French army was now in possession of the road to Moscow, and formed a triangle, with the left angle before Riga, with the right on the Bug, and with the foremost at Smolensk, on the Dnieper. On the left, and in the rear, it was tolerably based, but very badly on the right flank, where the division of Tormassoff was continually making attacks. August 19, Napoleon left Smolensk, in pursuit of the Russians, whose rear encountered, at Volontina, the French van under marshal Ney. The duke of Abrantes, who had superseded the king of Westphalia, had already come up in the rear of this body, when part of the main army of the Russians hastened to its succor; and by this means it succeeded in leaving, though with great loss, the narrow defile, 30 miles in length. The Russian army retired, in haste, burning all the towns through which it passed. With equal haste, the troops of Napoleon followed, suffering more and more from want and

* According to Russian accounts, the first army alone was in the battle of Smolensk, as the second immediately after the junction, had proceeded by rapid marches to Dogorobusch, and covered in its rear the road to Moscow. After the battle, the two armies again united, notwithstanding the exertions of the enemy.

the climate. Meanwhile, Barclay de Tolly had to resign the chief command to Kutusoff, who had reaped new laurels in the Turkish war just ended. Reinforced by militia and reserves, he resolved to await the enemy seventy miles from Moscow, in a strong position, which was entrenched as well as time permitted. September 5, the French encamped opposite him, and, on the evening of the same day, one of the outworks of the Russian camp was taken, after the most dreadful slaughter; and at sunset of the 7th began the most bloody battle of this war, in which the one party fought to put an end to all their privations and sufferings, the other to defend their country and preserve its capital. (See *Moskwa, Battle of the.*) The Russians lost 25,000 men; the French themselves estimated their own loss at 10,000; the number of wounded cannot be ascertained. Although the Russians were broken in their centre by the perseverance of Ney and the viceroy, on the right and left they remained masters of the field of battle; and, without any great loss of artillery, and still less of prisoners, they were able to retire to Moscow, whither Napoleon's army, after two days' repose, followed in two divisions, of which the first was designed to attack the Russians in the flank. Kutusoff did not dare to risk a battle before the gates of Moscow. He marched through, and abandoned it to the flames and the French, who, September 14, entered the desolate city. Moscow (q. v.) was devoted to destruction, and all the hopes built on the possession of it disappointed. Kutusoff, by a lateral march to the south, stationed himself at Kaluga, and threatened every minute to interrupt the communication of the French with their base on the Vistula. His Cossacks pressed forward to Smolensk. Werega, situated south of Moscow, constituting, as it were, a post for the protection of the French, was surprised by him, September 29. Nothing could save the French army but a speedy retreat or peace. Of the latter Napoleon entertained the more hope, as he was too proud for the former. Every day heightened the sufferings of his army, the provisions having been wasted, and foraging becoming continually more dangerous, from the conflux of Russian peasants and Cossacks. After Kutusoff had been reinforced from all quarters, by Cossacks and by militia, the summoning of which Alexander had himself superintended in summer, and the French army had been diminished in equal proportion (their loss in Moscow, by famine, assassination, the assaults of marauders, &c., was rated at 40,000 men), he suddenly threw aside the mask of pacific negotiations, and (October 8) caused a strong body, under general Bennigsen, to surprise, at Tarutino, the unexpecting French, commanded by Murat and Sebastiani, and drove them back with great loss. From necessity, Napoleon now did what he should have done four weeks before: October 19, he evacuated Moscow. By his original direction towards Kaluga, he gained, indeed, a march of Kutusoff; but, after the engagement at Malo-Yaroslawetz (October 24), after which the Russians drew back, Napoleon was either deceived respecting this circumstance, or not sufficiently informed; and his army, confined to the high road to Smolensk, also drew back, which was the principal cause of its destruction. For, every moment, the want of cavalry became more perceptible, while the Russians, with theirs, could multiply attack on attack. The French columns, consequently, had to march continually in denser order: in addition to this, the country was a desert, and want of all kinds had already dissolved the bonds of obedience, while the severity of the winter now covered the roads with ice and snow, destroying men and horses by thousands; and the Russians attacked in continually increasing numbers. After a thousand sacrifices, Smolensk was reached (November 12). But in vain had the remnants of the army hoped to find there repose, nourishment, clothing. The peace with the Porte had permitted the Moldavian-Russian army, under admiral Tschitschakoff, to put itself in Napoleon's line of communication. Leaving some forces behind, to employ the Austrians and Saxons in Volhynia, he proceeded with the rest of the army to the Beresina, where he tried to form a junction with Wittgenstein on the Dwina, in order to cut off Napoleon altogether.* The

* Here the two wings of the Russians could attack with decided effect; for Wittgenstein, after being joined by the Finland corps, had defeated, on the Drissa, the troops left at Poloczk by Napoleon, with such loss, Oct. 18, that they had to retire across the Dwina. They, nevertheless, succeeded in uniting their forces at Czasnicki, Oct. 30, with the ninth corps, and, Oct. 15, repelling Wittgenstein's attack at Smoliani. But, instead of pursuing his foe on the march to Ratalieczi, Wittgenstein now turned against Baran, by doing which he abandoned the corps of Tschitschakoff, on the Beresina, to its fate. During this contest on the Drissa, the army of Volhynia was defeated, Aug. 12, by the combined Austrian and Saxon force on the Poddobna, and driven back to Lutzk,

French army was, by this means, obliged to leave Smolensk on the 13th, and, with the loss of two whole battalions, under Davoust and Ney, at a temperature of 5° above Fahrenheit's zero to 8° below it, with no food but the flesh of the horses, perishing by thousands, hastened to anticipate the enemy, who were pressing forward from the north and south. This Kutusoff might, perhaps, have frustrated; but after the battle (November 18) at Krasnoi, from causes as yet unknown, he relinquished the pursuit, and Napoleon had the good fortune to be met by fresh troops from the Dwina, who compensated, at least in some degree, for the entire loss of his cavalry; and, reinforced by these, under the command of Belluno, Reggio and Dombrowski, he succeeded in deceiving admiral Tschitschakoff respecting the true point of passage over the Beresina, at Semlin, above Borissoff. There, on the 27th and following days, the passage took place, with a loss of 20,000 men and a great part of the baggage and artillery. But the road to Wilna, which was entered, was very long, and the cold, which increased every day, together with the most horrible want, carried disorder, misery and despair to the highest pitch. December 3, Napoleon issued his twenty-ninth bulletin from Molodetschno; and, on the 4th, at Smorgonie, he intrusted the command of the army to the king of Naples, and hastened himself, under the strictest incognito, by way of Warsaw and Dresden, to Paris. Marshals, officers of high and low rank, followed the example of the emperor. No company kept long together. The sole object of all was to save life, and, if possible, the booty taken from strangers or their comrades. In Wilna, the last remains were attacked by surprise, and driven to the Niemen, behind which they dispersed in all directions, carrying pestilence wherever they went. Of the whole army which crossed the Niemen in June, the Prussian almost alone returned, which had saved itself by a capitulation (at Tauroggen, December 30), and remained in arms, under York, in Prussia. The Austrians and Saxons, driven back to Warsaw, also returned to their frontiers. The capitulation of the Prussian general York was the signal of the awakening of the Prussian people, who, for five years, had been humbled by the French. January 22, the king went from Potsdam to Breslau, and (Feb. 3, 1813) summoned all capable of bearing arms to battle for their country. He did not yet designate his object, but his people understood him, and, with unparalleled enthusiasm, thousands poured forth to the places of rendezvous, from every section of the country; thousands too old for battle contributed their savings. In vain had the French, with the aid of their last reserves, and of troops thrown together in haste, made efforts to remain on the Pregel, on the Vistula, and on the Oder. The Russians advanced slowly indeed, but every where with overwhelming power; and the viceroy of Italy, on whom Napoleon had devolved the chief command, could do nothing but retire behind the Elbe with the least possible loss. March 8, after the last battle, he crossed the river to Magdeburg. Prussia now declared war against France, and concluded an alliance with Russia. Shortly afterwards, Kutusoff's proclamation at Kalisch announced the dissolution of the confederation of the Rhine, March 25th. Meanwhile, Napoleon had formed in France a new army, which passed the Rhine at the end of March. But Austria was neutral, the confederation of the Rhine without strength and without will, the popular insurrection almost universal in northern Germany; along the Elbe and to the Weser, time alone was needed to arm the people, who were here more enraged than in many other German countries, because they were more immediately and severely oppressed by French dominion. Napoleon appreciated the danger, and hastened to despatch the most necessary forces to the points most threatened. Happily for him, the Russians and Prussians were not in a state to derive the full advantage from the favorable situation of things. The forces of

behind the Styr. But being reinforced to double its former strength by the army of the Danube, it soon compelled that body to retreat; and its commander, admiral Tschitschakoff, leaving general Sacken with 25,000 men at Brzesc, marched thence, Oct. 27, in the direction of Minsk, in the rear of the main army of the French. The two bodies attempted to prevent him, but were themselves incessantly pursued by Sacken; and after they had beaten him at Wolkowisk on the 16th Nov., and driven him behind Brzesc, Tschitschakoff, who had already apprized Wittgenstein of his march, through colonel Czenitschef, succeeded in entering Minsk, Nov. 16, where he rested three days, captured Borissoff on the 21st, but left it again on the 23d, and on the 26th displayed his forces opposite the enemy on the Beresina. The Russian army on this day was still on the banks of the Dnieper. Wittgenstein should now have joined Tschitschakoff, but, instead of so doing, he pursued, on the 27th, the division Partonneaux of the ninth corps, and captured it; but, meanwhile, Napoleon had effected, though with great loss, a passage over the Beresina, which Tschitschakoff could oppose, but not prevent.

the Russians were almost exhausted; those of the Prussians had first to be formed; the blockade of the fortresses on the Oder and Vistula occupied many troops. Kutusoff manifested little zeal for the emancipation of Germany, and wished it to be attempted, not from Saxony, but on the Lower Elbe; time was lost in negotiations with the king of Saxony during which Kutusoff fell sick, and died, at Buntzlau, April 28. The viceroy was thus enabled to unite the remnants of the army under the walls of Magdeburg, and even advance against Berlin, by this means occasioning the indecisive engagement at Leitzkau or Möckern, April 5, while Vandamme and Davoust, between the Weser and Lower Elbe, put down the popular fermentation with iron hand, and threatened the city of Hamburg, which had most spiritedly shaken off their yoke; when the whole right bank of the Elbe was cleared of the French by the bold Tettenborn. The allied army, hardly 70,000 strong, now had in front an army of the French of almost twice their strength. Napoleon united his forces with those of the viceroy, who marched in a southerly direction along the Saale, and crossed this river at Wettin, while Napoleon passed it at Jena. May 1, he advanced upon the Elbe. The Prussians and Russians saw themselves in danger of being cut off from the river by a march from Merseburg by way of Leipsic, and resolved to give battle. The engagement was commenced at Grossgörschen, not far from Lützen (q. v.), about noon of May 2, and had no object but to surround Napoleon, who was pressing on to Leipsic, with the left wing, cut him off from the Saale, and with the right attack his flank. But this was well protected by detachments posted in the villages of Grossgörschen, Kaja, &c. Unexpected as was the attack, the French resisted it with bravery. Napoleon's main body, divided into large squares, either repelled all attacks, or soon recovered their lost advantages. The engagement in the villages thus lasted, with terrible slaughter, till dusk, when the corps of Lauriston, forming Napoleon's vanguard on the way to Leipsic, came up to attack the allies in the right flank. This compelled them to retreat to their old position, which, not being pursued by Napoleon, they left, May 3, retiring to the Upper Elbe, without loss of artillery, but with great loss in killed and wounded (about 15,000), which was, however, at least equalled by the loss of the French. Napoleon followed the allies with the infantry, but from want of cavalry, which was still behind, could do them but little damage. May 8, he was already master of Saxony and the Elbe, Dresden having been evacuated, Torgau having been opened by general Thielemann, and the siege of Wittenberg having been raised. The king of Saxony now had to return from Prague, and Napoleon proceeded to Lusatia, where the allies, reinforced by a body of 17,000 men under Barclay de Tolly, awaited him at Bautzen, behind the Spree, in a strong position. But Napoleon had also received new forces from the confederation of the Rhine and from France; and thus began, May 19, the prelude to a second great battle, which was fought on the 20th and 21st, at and near Bautzen, and, the right wing of the allies having been surrounded, terminated to their disadvantage, so that the Prussians and Russians drew back towards Schweidnitz, in Silesia, and the French advanced to Breslau, though with several losses, especially at Görlitz, where Duroc and two other generals fell, and at Hanau. A truce, which was concluded June 4, under Austrian mediation, at the village of Pläswitz (in the circle of Strigau), allowed the French to remain masters of the Oder as far as its entrance into the Saxon territory, and of the whole Elbe to its outlet, while it also allowed the allies to procure reinforcements, to await the arrival of the crown-prince of Sweden, who took an active part against Napoleon, and to give Austria time either to complete its preparations and join the allies, or to negotiate a peace, which was to be discussed in a congress to be held at Prague. This truce was peculiarly disadvantageous to Napoleon. He derived no advantage from it, except that a number of bold partisans, who swarmed in his rear, had to retire over the Elbe till June 12, and that he could maintain Hamburg, which, supported by so many friends,—Danes, Swedes, Prussians, Russians, Englishmen,—and finally abandoned by all, had been already occupied by the French, June 2, through Danish mediation. The congress of Prague began its session at a late period, and led to nothing. Russia and Prussia made such conditions as were required by national honor and independence; the mediation of Austria, and the neutrality which she had observed, Napoleon regarded as infidelity to the alliance of the previous year. Austria evidently took part in the negotiations at Prague, without a sincere wish for peace. August 17, the war began more fearfully than ever. The participation of Austria in the war Napoleon had anticipated after the battle of Lützen, and he had, for that cause, sent the viceroy with officers and subalterns to Italy, to collect an army. For the same reason, Bavaria had to draw out its forces on the Inn. They were joined by a corps of chosen men, chiefly cavalry, which had come from Spain. But the main bodies on the side of Napoleon were stationed on the Upper and Middle Elbe and at Hamburg; those on the side of the allies, in Bohemia and Silesia, with the exception of the great corps which covered Berlin, and protected the Lower Oder against Davoust. The allies had agreed, especially since the convention at Trachenberg, on the 9th, 10th and 11th July, to surround Napoleon's flank, from Bohemia, his right in particular, and to cut him off from his base of operations. For that purpose, Blücher immediately drew back as Napoleon advanced against him, while the main army, under the command of prince Schwartzenberg, entered Saxony; and Dresden, which had been fortified at the time of the truce, had begun to cherish hopes, when Napoleon's main forces arrived from Lusatia by forced marches, and not only repulsed the assault on Dresden (q. v.), but also (August 27) inflicted on the allies a defeat, which, as they were cut off from the main roads to Bohemia, and all the by-roads were destroyed, would have caused the annihilation of the whole army, if from that moment Napoleon's star had not set for ever. The victor at Dresden, on the 26th and 27th August, where Moreau (q. v.) was mortally wounded, was stayed in his progress by the defeat of Vandamme, at Culm, August 30; by the simultaneous overthrow of his army in Silesia, under Macdonald; by the hard-fought battles at Gross-Beeren, August 23, at Belzig, August 27; and by the defeat which Ney suffered at Dennewitz, September 6. In addition to these misfortunes, want of all kinds prevailed in exhausted Saxony, and lamentations in the hospitals, where thousands perished of dysenteries and fevers. At last, by some rapid, well-covered marches, Blücher formed a junction on the Elbe with the crown-prince of Sweden, while he surprised a French corps under count Bertrand, watching the passage at Wartenburg, and took up a position between the Muldau and Elbe. As soon as he was advised of this, Napoleon started from Dresden, October 7, in the hopes of overpowering them both separately. But they had already crossed the Muldau to the Saale. The great Bohemian army had also advanced on his right flank. These and Blücher's flying corps met in his rear, and general Thielemann, who had exchanged the Saxon service for the Russian, took whole troops of French fugitives, and fought several battles between the Elster and the Saale, almost all of which resulted to the disadvantage of the French. On the opposite side, the bold Czernitschef pressed forward so rapidly with his Cossacks to Cassel, that he was able, October 1, to declare the kingdom of Westphalia dissolved. After some movements on the right bank of the Elbe, which seemed to threaten Berlin, Napoleon proceeded with his main army to the plains of Leipsic, at which he arrived with the guards October 14, when Schwartzenberg had already commenced against the king of Naples, who had commanded the left wing of Napoleon from Dresden, a reconnoisance, which resulted in a smart skirmish of the cavalry at Liebertwolkwitz. Meanwhile, Augereau had brought up an excellent *corps de reserve:* his army had also been reinforced at Erfurt by 14,000 newly organized fugitives; and, as he probably thought, that he had deceived the crown-prince and Blücher by movements made the other side of Wittenberg, and that he had gained so much time, that he could meet the great Bohemian army alone in a decisive engagement, he did not delay to encounter it in the spacious plain near Leipsic, between the Pleisse, Elster and Parthe. About nine o'clock in the morning of October 16, the engagement commenced to the south of Leipsic. Napoleon had rested his right wing, under Poniatowski, on the Pleisse, and strongly garrisoned all the villages from Konnewitz to the river. His centre was stationed at Wachau. The left wing was supported by the heights of the Parthe. Prince Schwartzenberg sought to turn the right wing; but all his efforts were vain, because Napoleon made such progress in the centre, that all the reserves destined for that manœuvre had to be used for the reinforcement of the centre. After destructive attacks on both sides, Napoleon had gained some ground in the centre and on the left wing. Count Bertrand repelled an attempt of the Bohemian army to gain possession of the defile of Lindenau, and, at the same time, of Napoleon's whole line of retreat, perhaps of the city of Leipsic itself. But the duke of Ragusa was very unfortunate at Möckern, where he occupied a wide line to the north of Leipsic, and was unexpectedly attacked by general Blücher with the greatest impetuosity, totally defeated, after an obstinate resistance, on his left wing, and driven back, in disorder, to Gohlis. On the 17th, Napoleon negotiated, through count Meerveldt, who had been taken prisoner, for liberty to retire undisturbed, and for an armistice, both of which proposals were the less listened to, because the allies could now conduct their operations with a mutual understanding, the crown-prince of Sweden having joined Blücher with upwards of 60,000 men, and general Bennigsen, with almost an equal number, being every minute expected from Grimma. October 18, therefore, a fearful conflict took place at Leipsic. The French fought with desperation, to save their honor and secure their retreat, which had been commenced at day-break. Their centre and their right wing, from Probstheyda to Konnewitz, remained firm. The left, supported in Schönfeld on the Parthe, was defeated rather by the defection of the Saxons and Würtembergers, than from want of bravery; and nothing but the inexplicable carelessness of Napoleon on the 19th October converted the regular retreat, at last, into a flight, and a general overthrow of the rear. (See *Leipsic*.) This battle emancipated Germany. Bavaria had already (October 8) renounced the confederation of the Rhine, and united with Austria. All the German princes followed this example, with the exception of the king of Saxony (prevented by his imprisonment in Leipsic), Jerome of Westphalia, and the prince-primate. After the loss of many thousands, in prisoners and disabled, Napoleon, assailed or harassed in every quarter, was obliged, in order to gain the Rhine, to sustain a bloody conflict (October 31) with the Bavarians and Austrians stationed at Hanau. (q. v.) The allies made a halt on the Rhine, in order to unite the forces of liberated Germany with those furnished by England and Holland, which was now working its own emancipation. The number of troops collected against Napoleon in 1814 amounted to 1,208,000. The only remaining vestiges of Napoleon's power were the fortresses on the Vistula, Oder, Elbe, &c., in which, however, his best troops, cut off from all succor, finally perished, from want and suffering, or were forced to surrender. Even the Danes, who had been forced to form the closest union with Napoleon, in consequence of the hard terms proffered them by England and Sweden in the spring of 1813, were obliged to concede to the crown-prince of Sweden, in the peace of Kiel (Jan. 14, 1814), all that they had formerly refused. The Rhine having been passed subsequently to Jan. 1, 1814, at Caub, Manheim, Rastadt, Ehrenbreitstein, and Düsseldorf, it was easy to see that Napoleon would be eventually overpowered, because in France many had fallen from him since fortune forsook him, and the old aristocracy raised their heads again, whilst the people at large were exhausted by war. Immediately after his arrival, he had indeed set every spring in motion, in order to repeat, once more, the unexampled exertions which had been made in 1811 and 1813. But affairs in Spain had taken a most unfavorable turn. Marshal Jourdan had been totally defeated by Wellington, at Vittoria (June 21, 1813), and had been forced back to the Pyrenees, with the loss of his artillery; and, subsequently, Soult and Suchet had with difficulty kept the enemy from the soil of France itself, and it was consequently necessary to send thither new forces. For the first time, therefore, the senate ventured, though timidly, to represent the misery of France, when repeated decrees of Napoleon ordered the levy of nearly half a million new conscripts of 1807—1814, the organization of cohorts of national guards, and the formation of four armies of reserve. Still stronger terms did the deputies Lainé and Raynouard use in the legislative body; and, in consequence of the general indignation at the enormous expenditure of human life, great difficulties now presented themselves, when the demands of self-defence were imperative, in the way of collecting the myriads which were necessary, and to provide them with artillery, horses, and other requisites. Beyond the Rhine, therefore, from Switzerland to Holland, which was for the most part voluntarily evacuated by the French, the allies found but little resistance. Almost without loss of blood, they were able to gain possession of mount Jura, to put their left wing in communication with the Austrian army of Italy (which, commanded by general Hiller, had threatened, from Tyrol, to cut off the viceroy, and had obliged him to retreat to the Adige), to make themselves masters of all the passes to Italy, of the city of Geneva, of the roads over the Simplon and Bernard, and, as early as the 9th January, to occupy a new line, covered on the left by the Seine, on the right by the Meuse, in Alsace, Lorraine, Deux-Ponts, &c., with the exception of the invested fortresses. Napoleon had issued a proclamation for a kind of general rising of the people, or a levy in mass. This measure, which did wonders in the revolution, had, in this instance, but little effect among the suffering people. In a few quarters only, and not till the excesses of the enemy, exasperated by national hatred, had occasioned excitement, did the call produce some effect, but could give no new direction to the course of affairs. The allies, continuing to advance, occupied the Saar, the Moselle, the passes of Ardennes, almost without a blow. In no instance had a French general strength enough to maintain the most important points against the overwhelming force of the invaders; and it was hoped, by the middle of February, to reach Paris in safety, when Napoleon, who left it on the 25th January, and went to join his army (assembled, after infinite trouble, on the Aube), fought, from January 27 to February 3, a number of battles, which, with that at Brienne, on February 1, form one of the most striking exhibitions in military history. Napoleon put forth all his skill. He lost the battle of Brienne, after his army of 70,000 men had made the most desperate resistance, which, regardless of danger, he superintended every where, and left behind 73 cannon and 12,000 prisoners, to retire, as it seemed, beyond Troyes. Meanwhile, the eagerness of the allies to improve the first victory on the soil of France, gave rise to a separation of their forces, of which Napoleon took advantage judiciously and boldly. Having received on wagons new troops from the army of Spain, he proceeded, with rapidity, from the Seine to the Lower Marne, along which the army of Blücher was marching, in security, to Paris. He broke through its centre, and destroyed, at Champeaubert (February 10), the column of general Olsusieff. Without the aid of general York, general Sacken would have met with a similar fate the next day, at Montmirail. In like manner (February 14), Napoleon repulsed, with considerable loss, at Vauchamp and Etoges, the columns led by the field-marshal himself. With great exertions, a union was, at last, effected with Blücher's reserves. Schwartzenberg and Wrede were then, with the Würtemberg troops, beyond the Seine; for Napoleon had been deemed sufficiently enfeebled to allow them to proceed towards Paris in two large columns, one on the Seine, the other on the Marne. This idea had been, in part, recommended by the barrenness of Champagne. The great triangle between the Seine and Marne consequently separated them, for in it stood Napoleon's army. To make a lateral movement, it was necessary to cross the Seine, over which there were only two points of passage, at Nogent (strongly fortified) and at Bray, without a bridge, but in sight of a weak French reconnoitring party. Napoleon now hoped to gain important advantages over the army of Schwartzenberg. Wrede, united with Wittgenstein's corps, had to return across the Seine (February 17). On the 18th, Napoleon attacked the Würtembergers, at Montereau, at the confluence of the Yonne and Seine; but they retired, though with loss, to the left bank of the Seine. Schwartzenberg now hastened back, and passed the Seine at Troyes, to renew his communication with Blücher. Constantly hard pressed, the allies had to continue retiring; and the situation of affairs was so uncertain that, in the head-quarters of the monarchs themselves, a diversity of opinions prevailed, which had an influence on the congress of Chatillon. (q. v.) But in this very crisis, which inspired Napoleon with such hopes that he raised his demands higher at Chatillon than he had done since the battle of Leipsic, a new turn was given to affairs. The allies concluded the treaty of Chaumont. (q. v.) After the indecisive battle of Bar sur Aube (February 27), Napoleon marched against Blücher, who was approaching the northern army, the van of which had already taken Soissons, but had lost it again. But in a lucky moment, Soissons capitulated (March 2), and Blücher formed a junction with the northern army, under Bülow, who had taken several fortresses in the Low Countries and Picardy, especially La Fere (February 26), with a great quantity of stores, by means of general Thümen. The duke of Weimar, who arrived with 30,000 Saxons and other troops, had blockaded the unconquered places. On the extreme left wing, also, of the allied army, from Geneva, the most decided advantages were gained. The count of Bubna here, likewise, had been obliged to contend, till February 25, with obstacles of all kinds Marshal Augereau, inspirited by some reinforcements from Spain, had received from Napoleon orders to advance on this side, and repulse the left flank of the allies. All the Austrian wounded were taken to Berne, and Geneva was considered in great danger; but when the prince of Homburg and count Bianchi came up with considerable reinforcements, Auge reau lost his former advantages as rapidly as he had gained them. Napoleon now saw himself in danger of being surrounded on both flanks, and confined between the Seine and Marne. He therefore (March 9) attacked Blücher's army at Craone, and, on the 10th, gave battle at Laon, and was defeated. He now returned across the Aisne and Marne, took Rheims, and threw himself with impetuosity on Schwartzenberg, at Arcis sur Aube; but, repulsed on the 20th and 21st, with loss, he resumed his former plan, to approach the Rhine in the rear of the allies, supported by the fortresses of the Moselle, exhort the people to a general rising, unite with Augereau, and intercept the retreat of the allies. But the allies, merely keeping watch on him, made a rapid march to Paris (q. v.); for marshal Augereau had already been driven back to Lyons, which capitulated March 21. After the victory over Soult at Orthes, February 27, the English had gained possession of the city of Bordeaux, and driven back marshal Soult to Toulouse. Finally, advices were received at head-quarters, from Paris itself, disclosing the existence of an anti-Napoleon party, and describing the conquest of the city as easy, it being defended solely by the national guards. The battle of March 30 gave them access to the capital of France. Napoleon's family had already fled from the city. Alexander now declared that he would never treat with the emperor or his family. April 1, a provisional government was organized by Talleyrand, which declared Napoleon deposed, and transferred the crown to the Bourbons. Napoleon hastened back too late for the preservation of Paris. He approached only as near as Fontainebleau. Here the fragments of the troops which had left Paris, according to the capitulation, were reunited; but Marmont, with his corps, abandoned the emperor April 4. After many negotiations, Napoleon abdicated the throne, stipulating only for the imperial title, the island of Elba, with entire sovereignty, two millions of francs, &c., all of which were granted him. April 9, an armistice was concluded with all the French commanders. Most of the fortresses situated without the boundaries of ancient France, opened their gates; the others, situated within it, acknowledged Louis XVIII willingly or unwillingly. Davoust, in Hamburg, hesitated the longest: he did not depart till May 29. At the same time, the taking of Paris decided the fate of Italy. In this country, partly through the excellent precautions of the viceroy, partly through the equivocal conduct of Murat, king of Naples, who had left the party of Napoleon, and, favored by Austria, embraced that of the allies, without doing any thing in good earnest for them, the war had not taken a decisive course. Since the battle which the viceroy had fought with the Austrian general on the Mincio, he maintained his position on this river, with an army of 30,000 men, at most, against the same number of Neapolitans and 50,000 Austrians. The accounts from Paris gave here, also, a new direction to affairs. April 16, a truce was concluded, which allowed the French troops to depart for France, and compelled the Italian to remain. But an insurrection in Milan made a change in regard to the condition, that the fate of Italy should be decided in Paris; and prince Eugene resigned his command of the troops to the Austrian general Bellegarde (who had taken Hiller's place), and went, by way of Verona, to Munich. Meanwhile, the count of Artois had entered Paris, as the representative of Louis XVIII. April 23, he concluded a general truce with the allied monarchs, and a preliminary treaty respecting the future conditions of peace. Louis XVIII entered Paris himself, May 3. On the 5th, Schwartzenberg resigned the chief command, and the armies retired with rapidity to the Rhine, though peace was not signed till May 30. (See *France, since* 1814.) On the whole, on account of the great expectations excited by the hatred against France, the joy at this peace was very slight, although it had taken from France upwards of one hundred fortified places, and twenty-five millions of souls.

The tranquillity of Europe was soon again disturbed. In France, Louis XVIII did not succeed in winning the love of the people, to which he had so long been a stranger. Napoleon, therefore, escaped from Elba, and reascended the French throne March 20, 1815. (See *Napoleon.*) The monarchs being determined to support the Bourbons, the flames of war were again kindled. About 770,000 soldiers were gathered from Germany, Russia, Belgium (which was united into one kingdom with Holland), England, and Denmark. Napoleon, on his side, was not idle. From all France, he had convened in Paris, to a great *champ de Mai*, in the beginning of June, 4000 deputies, who swore fidelity to the new constitution and to him. From the 20th March, he, Carnot, Davoust, and others, had done every thing to put the army in a respectable state. Their efforts were very much aided by the enthusiasm of the old soldiers, who had, meanwhile, returned home from imprisonment. The Austrian emperor was threatened by a storm in Italy, which seemed to be connected with that in France. Murat, king of Naples, had been obliged to undergo, at the congress of Vienna, a contest with the Bourbon courts; so much the harder, as England was under obligations to the former king of Naples, and, moreover, understood Murat's equivocal behavior the year before, and therefore declared, in express terms, that he could not remain king. Austria alone, the more faithful to her engagements with him because it was less for her advantage to have a Bourbon for a neighbor, in the south of Italy, spoke in his favor; but either gave up his cause at last, or, at least, Murat thought himself abandoned by her, or believed that the landing of Napoleon would afford him means, during the prevailing fermentation in Italy, to make himself master of the whole peninsula; so that, on the 4th of April, without declaration of war, he attacked Rome and the Austrian line of troops with 50 to 60,000 men. The Austrians, hardly 12,000 men strong, under general Bianchi, retreated, fighting, behind the Po, where they maintained themselves till the troops sent thither in wagons had arrived; after which, general Frimont, who commanded them, advanced again so quickly, and so skilfully, that, twenty days after, Murat was in the most desperate situation; and his dispirited troops by degrees dispersed, and would not stand an attack. Surrounded, and cut off from the best roads, he saw himself forced to retreat continually through by-paths, where artillery and baggage were lost. An attempt to save himself by a truce, failed, from the firmness of the Austrian general; another, at Tolentino, May 1—3, to improve his situation by arms, was frustrated by the valor of his enemy; and, in consequence of this last vain attack, made with desperation, and much personal exposure, his army totally dispersed, and he himself fled to France.—His wife was taken to Austria. The wreck of the army, 5000 strong, laid down their arms behind the river Volturno, May 20. Half the Austrian army, on account of the unexpectedly slight resistance which they had met with, had proceeded to Upper Italy, in order, from thence to enter France, over the Alps. But orders from Vienna delayed the invasion, that the Russians might have time to come up. Half of June had consequently elapsed, when the attack was made on the side of Napoleon, equally impetuously and unexpectedly. Immediately after the *champ de Mai*, he left Paris for the army of 150,000 select troops, stationed on the northern boundary, taking with him the guards assembled at Lyons, and, with them, attacked, at day-break, June 15, more than 200,000 Englishmen and Prussians, who were encamped along the Dyle and Sambre, under the command of Blücher and Wellington. Without giving them time to unite, he drove the Prussians back behind Fleurus, and defeated them at Ligny, June 16; while Ney attempted to retard, at Quatre Bras, the English, who were hastening on the Brussels road, and prevent their junction with Blücher. In the battle that took place there, in which the duke of Brunswick fell, Ney was unable entirely to accomplish Napoleon's object; but neither could Wellington come to the succor of the Prussians, who were, therefore, obliged to make a retreat, in which they were favored by the darkness of the night. The next day, Napoleon detached two of his *corps d'armée* to pursue the Prussians, who were retreating to Wavre: with the rest of the army, he advanced, on the Brussels road, to crush the English, as he thought he had crushed the Prussians. Wellington had, meanwhile, assumed a position before the great forest of Soigny, on an elevated plain, which formed a natural fortress. (See *Waterloo, Battle of*.) On the 18th, Napoleon attacked this position, in the conviction that the English would not make a long resistance. But all his attacks were unsuccessful, and the more he wasted his forces in vain, the more terrible was his defeat, when, towards evening, the army of the Prussians, beaten on the 16th, but only the more eager for battle, coming up from Wavre in two divisions, fell upon the right wing and the rear of the French army, through the defile of St. Lambert. Wellington, now making a general movement forward, in one hour the whole French army was dispersed, and Napoleon himself carried along with the fugitives. Blücher ordered all the cavalry to pursue the fugitives, in the moonlight night. All the artillery and baggage was lost; no point of retreat was specified; they who had hoped to be in Brussels in the morning, wandered about on the Sambre, in the most melancholy condition. Not a single *corps d'armée* opposing the conquerors, the fortified places situated in their route were taken or surrounded. Deputies from Paris, suing for a truce, and announcing Napoleon's abdication, were not heard. The allies advanced, taking advantage of the first consternation. June 27, they were already masters of the main roads leading to Paris, and expected to gain possession of the capital without a stroke of the sword. But the two French generals Vandamme and Grouchy, who had pursued the Prussians, after the battle on the 16th, and had driven general Thielemann from Wavre, at the very moment when Napoleon's army was dispersed, made such a rapid and judicious retreat, that, to the surprise both of friend and foe, they arrived, with moderate loss, under the walls of Paris at the same time with Blücher and Wellington. Paris was better fortified than in 1814; but, as the fortifications were surrounded, the city was in danger of being stormed on its weakest side. Grouchy and Vandamme were the less able to encounter the allies, as every day brought accessions to the forces of the Prussians and English; a truce was, therefore, made, and Paris evacuated. (See *Paris.*) All the troops retired behind the Loire, with their baggage, artillery, &c., and on the 6th the city was surrendered. Thus the war was essentially decided by the battle of Waterloo. While the Russians, Bavarians, Würtembergers, and Austrians, were coming up from all sides, the French forces stationed in different quarters were too inconsiderable to do any thing but shed their blood in vain, notwithstanding the brave resistance of Rapp under the walls of Strasburg, of Suchet before Lyons, and notwithstanding popular insurrections in several parts of Alsatia and Lorraine. Armistices put an end, by degrees, to the war in these quarters the more speedily, because Louis XVIII had already made his entry into Paris, July 9. Immediately after his return, Napoleon had abdicated. He hoped, perhaps, by that means, to appease the storm, and departed for Rochefort, where he finally, July 15, surrendered to the English. In Paris, a diversity of opinions prevailed in the chambers of peers and representatives. Their attention was occupied, while the conquerors advanced, with the subjects of a republic, of Napoleon II, and a new constitution; till Fouché, who stood at the head of the provisional government, closed their halls, and Louis reascended the throne, strongly as such a proceeding was deprecated by the voice of the people in the chambers and in the army. This restoration had much influence on the event of the war. The princes had received Louis as their ally. In their declarations, they had spoken merely against Napoleon, not against the French people. The more active a part the people had taken against them, and the more strongly they still expressed themselves, in some places, against the Bourbons, so much the more cautiously had they to act, in order to maintain the Bourbons on the throne (contrary to the former opinion of the prince regent), against the will of the French people. France was, therefore, still overwhelmed with troops, and the ministers of the allies were engaged with those of Louis in the adjustment of political relations; but up to September 29, the parties were so far from agreeing, that the former all took their departure. Not till new ministers had been appointed, a few days after, by Louis XVIII, were the preliminaries of peace signed (October 2): these were confirmed in the definitive treaty of November 20, which, 1. fixed the boundaries of France as they were in 1790; but, 2. took from it the fortresses of Landau, Saarlouis, Philippeville, Marienburg, Versoix, with a certain circuit of territory about each, to be subsequently defined; 3. provided that Huningen should be dismantled; 4. fixed an indemnity of 700,000,000 francs for the expenses of the war, payable in five years; 5. provided that a line from Condé, through Bouchain, to Bitsch, should be occupied, for the same time, by the allies, with 150,000 men, at the expense of France; and, 6. secured the demands of all private persons on France, with the exception of the bank of Hamburg, emptied by Davoust in 1813. This was the actual termination of the war; for, till then, the northern fortresses of France had been besieged, at least by the Prussians, and for the most part conquered. By a separate agreement, half voluntary, half forced, the restoration was granted of all the works of art, of Italy, Germany, &c., accumulated in Paris since 1792. Respecting Napoleon, the allies agreed that he should live at St. Helena, at the expense of England, as a prisoner of war, but with all the alleviations of which such a situation could admit. His whole family was banished from France, under penalty of death, and the members of it were obliged to have passports from the great powers. The banishment of the Bonapartes was again pronounced in 1831, together with that of the elder line of the Bourbons. Murat, impelled by an unhappy error, and deceived by the Neapolitan police, made an attempt to recover his kingdom, and, October 13, died the death of a criminal, at Pizzo, in Calabria. (See *Murat.*) (See the *Histoire de l'Expédition de Russie*, with an atlas, 3d edition, Paris, 1825, 3 vols., by the French colonel of artillery, marquis de Cham bray. The Russian colonel Butturlin's *Hist. milit. de la Campagne de Russie en* 1812, Paris, 1824, 2 vols., with plans, was used by Chambray, in the new edition of his work. See, also, the marquess of Londonderry's *Narrative of the War in Germany and France, in* 1813 *and* 1814; and Ségur's *Histoire de Napoleon et de la Grande Armée pendant l'Année* 1812 (Paris, 1825, 2 vols.).

Russian Language and Literature.—Under this head we must distinguish two languages: 1. The Russian language, originally the dialect of the Sclavi, who founded the empire. It underwent, as did the empire itself, various changes. Thus it has, by degrees, incorporated into itself much of the Scandinavian, Mongolian, Tartar (1225 to 1477), and German, also the Polish and French languages. The improvement of this forcible and harmonious idiom is not, however, concluded, but is continually advancing by means of the national literature.—2. The Sclavonian language, or that of the Sclavonian Bible. It was fixed by the translation of the Holy Scriptures, and so settled that it has since experienced but few alterations. It is the language of the Bible, of the old chronicles, as, for instance, Nestor's, about 1100, of the ecclesiastical laws, of some of the pastoral instructions, and of the prayers in the liturgy.—A mixed language arose from the combination of these two already mentioned, which is used in sermons, in rhetorical prose, and in the higher species of poetry. Its principal ingredient is the Sclavian language; but it has borrowed those words and phrases from the Sclavonian, which, being used for the expression of biblical ideas and images, have thereby acquired more strength and dignity. The Sclavonian, however, prevails in sermons, and the Russian in oratorical prose, and in the more elevated kinds of poetry.—*History of the Russian Language.* The first period, which was the longest, and most destitute of literary productions, extends from the foundation of the empire to Lomonosoff, who first introduced a permanent change into the Russian language. Important, as contributing to fix the written language, was the introduction of a current written character, whereby the unwieldy letters before used, and introduced by Cyril, were superseded (see *Cyril*), for the full expression of the tones, which are peculiar to the Sclavian language, and for which the Greek letters were neither suitable nor sufficient. Cyril had borrowed some characters from the Asiatic alphabets, the form of which was an impediment to a people not fond of writing. About the end of the seventeenth century, Elias Kopiewitsch improved it, and brought the letters to their present form, for the embellishment of which so much has been done in the last ten years, that the Russian characters may compare in beauty of form with those of any European language. The history of the Sclavian press has, in modern times, attracted much attention, and a copy of a work printed in 1475 has been found. A Sclavonian psalter was printed at Cracow, 1481. The psalter of Kiev (1551) is the oldest work printed in Russia itself. Cracow was the cradle of Sclavonian typography. The oldest monuments of the language are, Oleg's treaty of peace and commerce of the year 912; Igor's treaty with the Greek emperor (945); the municipal charter of Novgorod (1019): but the most important memorials are the Russian laws in the time of Jaroslaff (who died in 1054); the expedition of Igor, a heroic poem of the twelfth century; popular songs, and the poems of the prince Cantemir, in the reign of the empress Anna. This predecessor of Lomonosoff possessed true talent, had received a European education, and was well acquainted with the classics. His poems consist of satires and epistles, in which, in imitation of Horace and Boileau, he described in true colors the manners and faults of his times. The spirit of his poems is modern, the form antique, but his verse is rhymed. He likewise translated into Russian Fontenelle's Dialogues on the Plurality of Worlds; but the language was as yet too little refined to preserve the beauty of the original. This period shows only individual monuments of a written language in the first stages of improvement. Peter the Great had, unintentionally, given it a retrograde direction, when he introduced many foreign expressions, in place of a great number of existing technical terms, which thus became disused, so that the language itself became poorer, and was disfigured. The second period extends from Lomonosoff to Karamsin. Lomonosoff (q. v.), a man of genius, created the language of Russian poetry, by the introduction partly of poetical expressions and partly of new forms, which he borrowed principally from the German literature, and which served his successors as models. His example likewise shows how the Russian language can be enriched and ennobled by expressions and phrases from the Sclavonic. He first developed its grammatical structure, and contributed also to form its prose. His odes relate to the circumstances of the day; we find in them little poetry, but much rhetorical richness. In his tragedies, the lyric tone prevails, and dramatic power is sought for in them in vain. In epic poetry, his Peter the Great was a first attempt; there are individual passages, indeed, of great merit; but the poem, as a whole, is devoid of interest. His imitations of the Psalms are rich in poetical expression. His epistle on the utility of verse shows his great command of the language. Sumarokoff, an author celebrated in his time, is too diffuse upon every subject. His fertility in tragedy and comedy, in satires, epistles, elegies, eclogues, fables, epigrams and songs, gave him reputation; but in no department can he be considered a model. Keraskoff has produced two large epics upon the conquest of Kasan, and upon Wladimir the Great, besides tragedies, odes and epistles. His language is beautiful, and far more smooth than that of Lomonosoff, but his talents are much less conspicuous. He was considered in his time as the Homer of Russia; but he is now forgotten.—Maykoff acquired a reputation by two burlesque poems, which were, however, not the less worthless on that account.—Kniäshjinin imitated the French in his tragedies and comedies, too closely indeed, but not without talent. Some comedies, in which he has interwoven many of the follies of the times in which he lived, have maintained themselves upon the stage till the present time. He very much excelled Sumarokoff; and some of his scenes, even now, are read with pleasure, although the language has proceeded so far in improvement.—Kostroff deserves mention on account of his translation of the first books of the Iliad into Alexandrine verse, and of Ossian into prose. His language is not without force.—Bobroff, a wild genius, has left behind him a number of bombastic odes, and a descriptive poem, *Tauria*, a chaos, but which contains here and there some brilliant passages.—Bogdanowitsch (q. v.), author of a poem called *Psyche*, in imitation of La Fontaine, is *naïf*, and full of grace and originality, but diffuse, and deficient in taste.—Oseroff belongs, if his language is considered, to this period, although his poems appeared in that which followed. The plan of his tragedies is French, the language neither pure nor beautiful, but the expression is often forcible, and the description of the passions natural; some scenes are really tragic; some of his characters are well delineated and supported.—Petroff was a true poet, but his language is rude; he had many ideas and striking images. He celebrated the victories of Catharine the Great in his odes. His heroes were Potemkin and Románzoff. His translation of the Æneid into Alexandrine verse is very unpolished in its language, but is full of power.—Lomonosoff also commences the series of prose writers of this period. His eulogies upon Peter the Great and Elizabeth contain few ideas, but much rhetorical ornament. Both of these writings are entirely different from those of his predecessors. They have very much improved the language, but still have not given it a permanent form. The same may be said of his scientific treatises upon electricity and metallurgy, of his Essay towards a Russian grammar, and of his Rhetoric, which contains many fragments translated from the ancients.—Weissen (Wisin) wrote two comedies in prose, full of genuine humor, which describe in true colors some of the absurdities of the age; both of these have maintained themselves upon the stage. He also wrote two very original satires, and some translations from Montaigne and Terrasson.—Muravieff, the tutor of the emperor Alexander, composed for his noble pupil several treatises upon Russian history, some dialogues of the dead, and some fragments, in the manner of the English Spectator, under the title of the *Suburban*. His style is not wholly pure, neither has he a great command of language: it is evident that he has formed his style from the imitation of French writers; but he is full of ideas, and particularly rich in imagery. When we read his works, we feel that his mind is conversant with all the beauty contained in ancient and modern literature. A good heart, a pure mind, and a love of virtue, are conspicuous in every thing that he has written. He was in advance of his age. But he had little effect upon his contemporaries, as he permitted but few of his writings to be printed, and his works did not appear till long after his death. In general, it may be said, that during this period the genius of Lomonosoff awakened a taste for literature in his nation. People eagerly read every thing that was printed, particularly poetical productions. In Sumarokoff they saw a great tragic writer, and in the poem of Keraskoff, with all its defects, an Iliad. They felt the beautiful, but did not know how to distinguish it from what was miserable. Taste was in the cradle, and criticism still unborn. We may consider this age as the awakening period of genius and poetry. In the last half of it, a man of genius made his appearance, who belonged to no school, of an original and peculiar mind, without high cultivation, but unique in his kind, and the true representative of Russian poetry. This man was Derschawin. (q. v.) He celebrated the glory of the Russian arms during the reign of Catharine, as did Lomonosoff and Petroff; but while these were only eulogists of their sovereign and her generals, Derschawin celebrated them in the true spirit of a poet. He remained a philosopher even at the foot of the throne: his own character appears in whatever he said of others: he awakened great and patriotic feelings, and at the same time described nature with inimitable touches. His productions however, are not the best models, but they glow with a fire which kindles poetical sentiment. This period produced a great number of translations, particularly from the French; they are all, however, without merit as regards style, but they show the general desire and love of the age for literature. In this age the great dictionary of the Russian academy appeared, projected according to an entirely new plan, and in which the etymological order of the words is followed. This work furnishes great facilities for the study of the Russian language and literature. The Russian academy (founded October 21, 1783) has had great influence in directing the attention of authors to the pure elements of the language; several societies have likewise been formed for the improvement of the language. Finally, one man contributed greatly to the spread of literary taste, who had himself but little learning, but a good natural understanding, a love for the sciences, and withal a happy talent for illustration. This was Novikoff. He founded a typographical society, and edited a satirical journal, under the title The Painter, which at that time was very much read, and opened to Karamsin a field for the exhibition of his literary powers.—In the third period, Karamsin (q. v.) is the representative of prose, and Dmitrieff of poetry. The periodical edited by the former, after his return from his travels, effected a decided change in the Russian language. He revealed to his countrymen the secrets of happy diction, clearness, beauty and precision. The same perfection which he gave to prose, Dmitrieff gave to poetry. Karamsin's career as an author may be distinguished into three epochs. The first began with his editing the Journal of Moscow. In this publication appeared fragments of his Letters of a travelling Russian, and his tales, which were afterwards published collectively. These productions exhibit genuine taste, though they appear like the effusions of a youth. His remarks and notices of the writings of foreign countries, which appeared in that publication, excited an interest in foreign literature throughout Russia, and developed the germ of true criticism. The second epoch commenced with the publication of the European Courier. This periodical drew the attention of the public to politics, and awakened reflection. His essays upon some of the political topics of the day, and upon morals, are models in their respective kinds. His beautiful style gave to his ideas a still higher charm. The third epoch is marked by his History of Russia. This history, as a literary production, is a mine for all authors of his nation. No Russian prose writer since Karamsin has acquired a high reputation: greater purity, perhaps, prevails than did before, but his style has not been equalled. Many have wished to imitate him, but they have only shown their own inferiority. Makaroff has edited a Critical Journal; he wrote very correctly, but his style is dry. Batuschkoff has been able to give grace to his prose, and the Italian harmony to his verse. Shukoffskij was, after Karamsin, the editor of the European Courier, and wrote in it some essays in prose. These, and other authors, have each of them some peculiar merit, but they are not equal to their master. Besides, their works are unimportant, and cannot, therefore, much promote the further developement of the language. The Russian literature is very barren in original works on the subject of philosophy. In the history of the language of poetry, Dmitrieff's imitations of La Fontaine and his tales make a particular epoch. Before him Lomonosoff, and especially Derschawin, had furnished models of poetical beauty, and opened the way to bold originality. Without checking the flight of genius, Dmitrieff knew how to direct it so as not to offend against taste and sound criticism. We possess about one hundred excellent fables by him, in imitation of La Fontaine and others, many songs, which have become popular, and odes, considered classical, without having the brilliancy of Derschawin's originality and boldness. Dmitrieff has given the language of Russian poetry its permanent form. Neledinsky-Meletzsky is less pure and correct than Dmitrieff, but many of his songs are in the mouths of the common people. The true fire of passion animates his poetry. Chemnitzer is esteemed as a fabulist; his expression is natural, but very prosaic. Kriloff, a poet in the full sense of the word, is, in his department, like Derschawin, the representative of the national poetry, for his fables are almost all original. Derschawin, in his odes, described the bright side of his age; but Kriloff, in his fables, painted the absurdities and prosaic thought of his time. In expression less pure and perfect than his predecessor Dmitrieff, he, however, excels him in descriptive powers. Kriloff has much observation; his fables, which, in this respect, will bear comparison with the best in any literature, are rich in ideas and instruction; many of his verses, therefore, are now current as proverbs.—Shukoffskij has enriched the poetical language of the Russians, by describing ideas and feelings which had not been treated in their literature. His poems are a true picture of his individual character at the time in which he wrote them. They therefore possess uncommon attraction for the reader. His predilection for German poetry, which was before his time but little known to his countrymen, induced him to incorporate it with the Russian in his imitations; his poems, on this account, have a peculiar stamp, which has given a singular charm to their deep melancholy feeling and natural tone.—Batjuschkoff pleases by the charms of his diction. With a brilliant imagination he united the finest taste, and he is inimitable in the choice and harmony of his expression. We possess of his writings some amorous elegies, ingenious epistles, and attempts at lyric poetry—all excellent. Prince Wiasemskij expresses much in few words: this sometimes gives his language an air of stiffness and dryness; but his satires and epigrams are particularly happy. His prose suffers still more than his poetry from this brevity.—Wostokoff has richness of thought, power of imagination, and warmth of expression; but his style is but little refined.—Gneditsch deserves much credit for his translation of the Iliad into Russian hexameters. The general characteristic of this period is an elegance and correctness previously foreign to Russian literature. The language has acquired a more settled character; but Russian prose still wants the labor of thinking minds to perfect it. The poetical language of the Russians alone can be called rich. The latest period of Russian literature is yet in its bloom. Already it numbers one very promising poet, Alexander Puschkin, who is distinguished for his imagination and originality, and whose style is in the highest degree refined. Karamsin's historical work now opens a new field for national poetry. Russian history was previously enveloped in the obscurity of chronicles and traditions. Karamsin dissipated this obscurity, and threw light upon the darkness of the past. Poetry, by his torch, may now light her own. Among other living poets, may be mentioned Kosloff (q. v.); Gribojedoff, the author of a very amusing comedy; Glinka, a lyric poet, full of fire; baron Delwig (the editor of the Russian Almanac of the Muses, called the Flowers of the North, in 1825 and 1826); Schazykoff, Baratinskij, &c. Among the translators we may mention professor Merslä-koff of Moscow, who has translated Tasso's poem of Jerusalem Delivered. Russian prose enumerates, at the present time, but few original productions. There are many journals, but they are for the most part filled with extracts from foreign periodicals. The critical department of them cannot be important, because the national literature is poor; nevertheless, among a great number of tolerable prose writers, Gretsch has distinguished himself; his style is easy, although he sometimes offends against good taste. For many years he edited the best Russian journal. He has likewise been engaged in the composition of a Russian grammar. In connexion with this, besides the old Russian grammars of Ludolph (*Grammatica Russica et Manuductio ad Linguam Sclavonicam*, Oxford, 1696, quarto), of Gröning (Stockholm, 1750), of Lomonosoff, Rodde, Heym (Riga, 1821), that of the Russian academy (St. Petersburg, 1802), particularly that of Vater (Leipsic, 1808), and that of Tappe, on account of the happily chosen examples and practical exercises (St. Petersburg and Riga, 1810; 5th edition, 1820), deserve to be recommended, as well as Puchmayer's System of the Russian Language, in German (1820). They all, at least the modern, embrace only the common Russian. For the Sclavonian or ecclesiastical language grammatical aids are greatly needed. The grammar of the ecclesiastical Sclavian, written in the Russian language, which Peter Winogradoff published in 1811, is far surpassed in value by Dobrowsky's

Institutiones Linguæ Slawicæ Dialecti veteris (Vienna, 1822). The government itself has taken charge of grammatical education, and prohibited the sale of Lewitzkij's small Russian grammar (St. Petersburg, 1814), which was put under the interdict of the minister of instruction, in 1814, "on account of its many defects and false definitions." Concerning the dictionaries of the Russian language, by Rodde, and Heym, a German, Russian, and French pocket dictionary (Riga, 1805), and many others, see the review, by Schlözer, in the Göttingen *Gelehrten Anzeigen*, 1810, number 47. Since that, A. Oldekop has published a Russian-German and a German-Russian dictionary, in 5 vols. The present president of the Russian academy, admiral and minister Alexander Schischkoff, caused a second edition of the academy's dictionary to be published in 6 vols. quarto, in the year 1826. After having thus characterized the poets and prose writers who have had an influence upon the formation of the Russian language, we will touch more particularly on certain portions of the Russian literature, as follows: I. The old popular songs and traditions, which were formerly neglected by the Russians, have now excited their attention, on account of their similarity to the English, Spanish, and Scandinavian ballads. Like these ballads, they appear to refer to a connected series of popular traditions. In that period, however, to which these old songs belong (1015—1224), the national poetry had not freed itself from the old Sclavian mythology; and the Russian tales and popular traditions have thereby acquired a peculiar charm of a fantastical description, which is particularly remarkable in the story of Filipat and Maxim, and their valorous deeds; the marriage of Devgieiewas, and the carrying off of Stratigovnas, in the tale of Shinagrip, the czar of the Adorians. Prince Wladimir I, with his knights, is the central point of this whole series of tales, which may be compared with the stories of Charlemagne and his peers, and those of king Arthur and the Round Table. The heroes, Dobrenja Nikititsch, and Tschurilo Plenkowitsch, and others, here take the place of the well known and harmonious names of Roland, Rinaldo, and Amadis. J. Müller published the Expedition of Igor against the Polowzians (from the old Russian; Prague, 1811 and 1812), and this poem has since passed through several editions in the Russian original. Prince Wladimir and his Round Table (Leipsic, 1819) is a German imitation, drawn from a collection of old Russian songs, which were printed at the suggestion of Romänzoff. Prince Zerteloff's Spirit of Russian Poetry, or collection of old Russian songs (St. Petersburg, 1822, in 2 vols.), has excited the attention of the Russians to this portion of their literature. The ecclesiastics of that period displayed a peculiar degree of intellectual activity; and there were also laymen of considerable merit. Nestor (q. v.) has mentioned many men of rank who shared in this intellectual labor. These beginnings could not, however, be of permanent consequence, because literary institutions of a high character were wanting. The Greek teachers of the public schools at Wladimir, Smolensk, and Halitsch, did not diffuse a taste for Grecian antiquities, which might have been a permanent barrier against barbarism. The Mongolian period had a withering influence on literature. In the rich convents only, which the Mongols respected, were preserved some remains of intellectual cultivation. Thence are derived the materials for the history of that period, which alone give us some insight into it, particularly the annals in the old ecclesiastical language, composed by St. Simon, bishop of Susdal (who died in the year 1226), the *Stufenbuch* of Cyprian the metropolitan (who died in 1406), and the Chronicles of Sophia, or the Russian annals from 862 to 1534 (edited by Strojeff, Moscow, 1820—1822, quarto). These, and the lives of Alexander the Great, of the Roman emperors, of Mark Antony, and of Cleopatra, related after the manner of stories, were the only books. As the authors despised the language in common use, which, by its additions from the Tartar tongue, had acquired a foreign character, displeasing, even to the people themselves, and made use only of the old Sclavonian dialect, the taste for reading, even if we do not take into consideration the other inconveniences attending it, must necessarily have been confined to a few. As the Russians did not travel, nor learn any foreign languages, they were not connected, by intellectual bonds, with the rest of Europe. There were no schools in Great Russia. The press exercised but little influence, as it was exclusively devoted to the interest of the church, and the amusements of the people were rude. In the dramatic exhibitions which were founded on religious stories, and performed by the students of Kiev, in the principal cities, during their holydays, Judith striking off the head of Holofernes, Ahasuerus ordering Haman to be hanged, and the spectacle of the three men in the fiery furnace, excited the highest applause. The Sclavonian-Russian dramas of the monk Simeon of Polotsk (1628—1680) may be considered as an improvement on the others. These were acted in the time of Feodor III, first in the convent, and afterwards at court. Amateurs may find his Nebuchadnezzar, and his Lost Son, printed in the eighth volume of the old Russian library, and most of his other productions in manuscript, in the library of the Synod, at Moscow. The first foreign comedy translated into Russian was Molière's *Médécin malgré lui* (Physician in spite of Himself), which was performed by the czarina Sophia Alexiowna, and the ladies of her court. The Poles served as models, particularly in poetry; and the translation of the Psalms of David (Moscow, 1680), by the above-named Simeon of Polotsk, deserves to be mentioned. As early as the seventeenth century, instances of versification can be produced, which endeavored to imitate the Greek peculiarity of long and short syllables; but they had no permanent effect. Even the restriction of verses to a particular number of syllables, was considered too stiff and unnatural; and, to the present day, there remains in their poetry (which exhibits, for the most part, the national peculiarities) a free and unrestrained style, which neither requires lines equal in their number of syllables, nor assonance, nor rhyme, but rests upon certain laws of accentuation.—II. Peter the Great endeavored to advance literature by technical aids. For this purpose he patronised the press, and, in 1704, himself invented a set of written characters for the Russian language, which, being similar to the Roman characters, might make the communication and interchange of thoughts with the rest of Europe more easy. With this character the first Russian newspaper was printed, in 1705, in the ecclesiastical press at Moscow. The ukase press was established in 1711, and from it, in 1714, proceeded the first St. Petersburg gazette. Translations of foreign works, for the most part German, were intended to excite a love of reading; and he hoped, by means of the young Russians, whom he sent abroad to travel, to convince his people of the advantages of education. At his death, he left fifty-one schools for the people, fifty-six schools for the garrisons, and twenty-six other institutions for the children of the clergy, which, however, had little perceptible influence upon the great work of civilization. It was, however, less attachment to ancient usage, that opposed the effect of his labors on a people very susceptible of impressions, than the artifices of the state officers, to whom the public improvement was, frequently at least, an object of little importance. (See *Academies.*) The academy of sciences, from 1725, promoted the scientific direction which intellectual cultivation had taken, because the want of a national literature had not yet been felt. Establishments for the promotion of knowledge and education increased daily by imperial liberality, and Catharine II, by the patronage which she bestowed upon the arts and sciences, greatly contributed to the advancement of her nation. The endeavor to rival foreign countries became general, and those of the nobility and public officers who were capable of intellectual enjoyment, gave themselves up to it with such zeal that Paul I became alarmed, and ordered the communication with foreign countries to be stopped. Alexander I, in the first years of his reign, established literary institutions and popular schools, took care that the clergy should be more thoroughly educated, and patronised talent with imperial liberality. Sopikoff, in his *Essai de Bibliographie Russe* (St. Petersburg, 1813—1823, in 6 vols.), has enumerated, alphabetically, 13,249 original works and translations published in Russia, in the Sclavonian and Russian languages, from the establishment of the press (in 1553) to 1823. Since the year 1820, in which alone 3400 works appeared, among which nearly half were translations (more than 800 from the French, and 483 from the German), the annual number has very much decreased. In 1824, only 264 works were published, most of which were translations, particularly historical and geographical works, poems and romances.—III. *Poetry.* With all the imitation of the poetical forms of foreign countries, the national song has always maintained an honorable rank, and celebrates love and war, games, church festivals, and banquets. Among the older ones, those of the Cossack Semen Klimoffskij (who died in 1725) are much esteemed: a collection of such as yet enjoy a high reputation, is to be met with in Ostolopoff's Dictionary of ancient and modern Poetry (St. Petersburg, 1821), in which the names of Dmitrieff, Neledinskij-Meleczkij, Karamsin, and Shukoffskij, are distinguished above all others. Since the Russian prosody became more settled by means of Knäs Constantine Demetrius Kantemir (q. v., who died in 1744), every kind of poetry has been attempted, from the dithyrambic to the madrigal. The popular songs of the Russians, which are preserved among the common people, belong to the time of Peter the Great and the empress Elizabeth, who herself wrote verse. The lyric department has been particularly successful. We must likewise mention the philosophic odes and epistles of the prince Ivan Michailowitsch Dolgorucki (who died in the year 1823), under the title of the Existence of my Heart. Poetical tales, for which the old traditions furnish many materials, have been written by Sumarokoff, Kriloff, Batjuschkoff, Dmitrieff, and Shukoffskij. The Russian theatre was first established in 1758. In this year, there was a private theatre erected at Yaroslav, which was soon transferred to the royal residence, and, in consequence of the predilection of Catharine II for the drama, soon won the favor of the people. Sumarokoff wrote the first regular tragedy, and was succeeded by Kniäshjnin. The most distinguished dramatic writer, Wladimir Oseroff, has had the honor of having his works often translated. His Œdipus (Petersburg, 1805), his Dmitrij the Donian, his Fingal, and the Rosloff of Kniäshjnin, are considered the most important specimens of tragic literature. Kniäshjnin has also accomplished much in comedy. The genius of the Russians, so sensible to the ridiculous, and so capable of imitation, would lead us to expect a rich harvest in comedy, if the readiness with which they adopt every thing foreign did not check the productiveness of native talent. The opera in a court, which, like the Russian, delights in splendor, must naturally excite a lively interest. The first, written by Sumarokoff, was performed at St. Petersburg in 1764; and, since that time, there have continually been authors in this department of the drama. In didactic poetry, Keraskoff's Fruits of the Sciences formerly were in much repute. At the present time, the fables of Dmitrieff, Chemnitzer, and Kriloff, have gained many admirers. Of Kriloff's Russian Fables (St. Petersburg, 1826), a part has been published in the Russian language at Paris, with a French translation, by count Orloff. The minor species of poetry find a ready admission into the twenty-one Russian literary journals (which were in circulation in 1824, throughout the capital), and are very acceptable to the literary public, which is yet small.—See N. von Gretsch's *Manual of the Russian Literature, or a Collection of Specimens from poetical and prose Writers* (St. Petersburg, 1821, in 4 vols.), and Borg's *Poetical Productions of the Russians* (Riga, 1823, in 2 vols.), both in German; also Bowring's *Specimens of the Russian Poets* (2d edition, London, 1821), and Dupré de St. Maure's *Anthologie Russe* (Paris, 1823). A. Oldekop's St. Petersburg Journal is likewise to be recommended to all friends of literature, on account of the collections therein published. Among the periodicals, those which make us acquainted with the internal condition of the empire—as Bulgarin's Northern Archives; the Siberian Herald of Sspaszkij; the Son of the Country, by Gretsch; and the Promoter of Knowledge—are worthy of notice.—IV. *Prose.* Russian prose is undoubtedly inferior to the poetry of the same language. In pulpit oratory, in which its first progress was made, a bombastic rhetoric has prevailed, which is often accompanied with little intrinsic merit, as the homilies of Feofan Prokopowitsch (who died in 1736), of Gedeon, Platon, Anastasij, Georgij, Protoiereni Lewanda, Michajl the metropolitan, Filaret, and others, abundantly prove. Lately, a hypocritical rather than pious tone has passed from these homilies into political writings. The secular discourses, to which, for example, Lomonosoff owes his celebrity, are partly composed in a panegyrical style, which leads us to doubt the genuineness of the feeling which is displayed. Lomonosoff's discourse, however, on the character of Peter the Great, delivered April 26, 1755, is often mentioned as a masterpiece of eulogy. Karamsin's oration, delivered at the assembly of the Russian academy, December 5, 1818, corresponds more to the present taste. Nicholas Karamsin's name must likewise be mentioned with distinction in almost every department of description. He has given to Russia a work which may be honorably compared with the historical writings of any nation. A great number of the most distinguished literati and statesmen of Russia, have preferred, in their works, to use foreign languages rather than their own. Russia has not yet produced romances, combining originality with beauty of description, which may be worthy of being translated into foreign languages. Karamsin, Shukoffskij, and Benizkij, are the best models for the novelist. The Russian accounts of voyages and travels deserve the attention of foreigners. Since the first voyages of the Russians round the world, in the ships Nadeschda and Neva, under the command of captain Krusenstern, the American company or individuals have annually sent ships to the north-west coast of America; and Golownin's Voyages (1807—1814);

those of lieutenant von Kotzebue, at the expense of the count Romänzoff; those of lieutenant Lasareff; those of Bellingshausen and Wassiljeff; those of lieutenant Wrangel; Murawieff's travels; Broneffski's researches in Tauria, &c.—have produced very important results in a scientific point of view. Many of them exhibit traces of the improving state of the language, in passages containing much beauty of description. The Russian academicians and literati (Frähn, Krug, Schmidt, &c.) have distinguished themselves in Oriental literature. Frähn, at the expense of count Romänzoff, superintended the collection of extracts for Hammer's work, *Sur les Origines Russes, extraits de Manuscrits Orientaux*, and likewise the printing of Abulghasi's *Historia Mongolorum et Tatarorum* (Kasan, 1825). Wolkoff has been laboring upon a dictionary of the Tartar language. Senkoffski has published the text and translation of the Derbent-Nameh, and the French-Arabic lexicon of Berggren. He likewise published, in the Polish language, a Collection of ancient Accounts, in the Turkish Histories, relative to the History of Poland (Warsaw, 1824). Professor Boldyreff has likewise published, at Moscow, a Manual of the Arabic Language (1824), and a Persian Chrestomathy (in 2 vols., 1826). In 1825, eighteen journals were published in St. Petersburg, and seven in Moscow, and six almanacs. Bestucheff's and Rylejeff's Polestar, a souvenir for 1824, and the Flowers of the North, for the following years, have met with decided approbation. In 1826, there appeared at St. Petersburg only six gazettes and fifteen periodicals. To promote the knowledge of Russian literature, Von Köppen published, in 1825 and 1826, at St. Petersburg, a bibliographical paper. The society of the friends of Russian literature, established in St. Petersburg in 1816, the founders of which are N. Glinka and N. J. Gretsch, have conducted the publication of a collection of the most distinguished native productions and translations (now consisting of 16 vols.). See the *Survey of the most modern Russian Literature*, in the 7th volume of the Annals of Literature (*Jahrbücher der Literatur*), published at Vienna.

Russia, Black; formerly a subdivision of Lithuania, now forming the Russian governments of Minsk and Grodno.

Russia, Great; former name of a province comprising a large part of European Russia, extending from the Frozen ocean to about the middle of the course of the Don; now divided into nineteen governments.

Russia, Little; name of that part of Russia lying south of Great Russia; now forming the governments of Tchernigov, Cherson, Kiev, Ekaterinoslav, and Poltava.

Russia, Red; formerly an independent duchy, which belonged to Poland after 1396, and formed the palatinates of Chelm, Belcz and Lemberg. It now belongs chiefly to Austria, but partly to Russia.

Russia, White, was a part of Lithuania, which now forms the Russian governments of Smolensk, Mohilev, Vitepsk, and a small part of Minsk.

Russia Leather is prepared in Russia, chiefly from cow-hides, and is highly esteemed for its flexibility, durability, and impenetrability by water. The red leather is much used in foreign countries for book-binding, and, although it is imitated in some places, the Russian is distinguished by its peculiar odor. The best is made in Astrachan, and it forms an important article of export.

Russian Hunting Music, or Horn Music. This consists of horns, of which each produces but one tone. Twenty, thirty, or even forty performers, have each a horn. These horns vary like the pipes of an organ. One of them sounds only every C, another every D, &c., throughout the tune. The performers are, for the most part, serfs, and so well skilled, that every one sounds his note with the greatest accuracy, whenever it is necessary; and the tones of the different instruments sound as if they proceeded from a single instrument. The Russians have carried this music to such a pitch of excellence as to execute pieces of Pleyel, Haydn and Mozart, and likewise to mark the distinctions between piano and crescendo, with the greatest effect. This music is heard at a great distance, and sounds, when far off, like a harmonicon. It was invented by Narischkin. In 1763, these instruments were used, with great success, at a festival in Moscow; and they afterwards received great improvements.

Rust is the oxide of a metal, and is composed of oxygen combined with a metal. (See *Oxygen.*)

Rusty Grackle. (See *Blackbird.*)

Ruta Baga, or Swedish Turnip. (See *Turnip.*)

Rutledge, John, an eminent revolutionary patriot of South Carolina, early manifested his zeal in the cause of American liberty. He was a member of the first congress of 1774, where he was distinguished for his Demosthenian eloquence. When the temporary constitution of South Carolina was established, in March, 1776, he was appointed its president, and commander-in-chief. He continued to occupy the station until the adoption of the new constitution in 1778, which he opposed on the ground of its being too democratic, annihilating as it did the council, and reducing the legislative authority from three to two branches. In 1779, however, he was chosen governor, with authority to do whatever the public safety required, and soon took the field at the head of the militia. During the siege of Charleston, he left the city, at the request of governor Lincoln, that the executive authority might be preserved, though the capital should fall. In January, 1782, he called a general assembly, and addressed them in a speech, in which he depicted the perfidy, rapine and cruelty, which had stained the British arms. He died January 23, 1800. He was a man of eminent talents, patriotism, energy and firmness. To his government during the most calamitous scenes of the war, within the state of South Carolina, is to be attributed, in a great degree, the successful termination to which it was brought. He early perceived the superior merit of general Greene, and seconded his views with all the influence of the civil authority: his discernment was likewise manifested by his judicious promotion of Sumter, Marion and Pickens. It should also be mentioned to his honor, that, though invested with dictatorial powers, he never gave occasion for complaint.

Rutledge, Edward, one of the signers of the Declaration of Independence, was born of a respectable family at Charleston, South Carolina, in November, 1749. After a proper education, he was placed in the office of his elder brother, to prepare himself for the practice of the law. In 1769, he was sent to England to complete his legal studies, where he was entered at the Temple. On his return home, in 1773, Mr. Rutledge commenced the practice of his profession, and was rising to eminence as a lawyer, when he was elected to a seat in the first continental congress, assembled at Philadelphia, in 1774. His having been chosen at his age to so dignified a post, shows the high esteem with which he was thus early regarded by his countrymen. Owing to the strict secrecy which was preserved concerning the transactions of the congress at that time, nothing is known of his course in this new situation. He continued a member till 1777, and took an active part in the debates preceding the declaration of independence. When that decisive measure was adopted, and the political horizon of the country had become darkened by the misfortune of our army on Long Island, with other embarrassing circumstances, the British renewed their negotiations for a reconciliation. Doctor Franklin, John Adams and Mr. Rutledge, were deputed by congress to confer with lord Howe on the subject. This conference accordingly took place, but resulted in nothing of importance to either party. Mr. Rutledge used afterwards to relate an anecdote of doctor Franklin, to this effect:—When the commissioners took leave of lord Howe, his lordship had them conveyed to New York in his own barge. As they approached the wharf, the doctor began to jingle some gold and silver coin in his breeches pocket. Upon their arrival at the wharf, he offered a handful of the money to the sailors who had rowed the boat; but the commanding officer not permitting them to receive it, he replaced it in his pocket, and afterwards explained this conduct to his associates by saying, "As these people are under the impression that we have not a farthing of hard money in the country, I thought I would convince them of their mistake. I knew, at the same time, that I risked nothing by an offer which their regulations and discipline would not permit them to accept." In 1779, Mr. Rutledge was again appointed to congress; but indisposition obliged him to return home before he had taken his seat. His native state had now become the theatre of war, the scantiness of its population offering a comparatively easy conquest to the British arms. Mr. Rutledge commanded a company in a battalion of artillery, and was engaged in dislodging a party of regular troops from Port Royal island. Notwithstanding their superior discipline and their advantages of position, the British were compelled to retreat. Whilst Charleston was closely beleaguered, Mr. Rutledge endeavored to elude the vigilance of the enemy, in order to accelerate the advance of troops to its relief. In this attempt, he was taken prisoner, and sent to St. Augustine, where he remained near twelve months before he was exchanged. He afterwards resided some time in the vicinity of Philadelphia, but, as soon as possible, proceeded to the south, and, on the reëstablishment of civil government in Carolina, after the successes of the Americans there, in 1782, was one of the representatives who were convened at the village of Jacksonborough. Though he assented, as a member of this assembly to the adoption of a bill of pains and penalties, he was inclined to excuse such as were compelled, by unavoidable circumstances, to keep aloof from the standard of freedom. This intemperate convention adjourned a little previous to the evacuation of Charleston by the British, in December, 1782, when Mr. Rutledge returned home, and, soon after, resumed the practice of his profession. He was a conspicuous member of the state legislature, in which body he was opposed to any further increase of African slavery in the Southern States, and, afterwards, an unwearied advocate of the federal constitution. Mr. Rutledge was subsequently elected colonel of an artillery regiment, and supplied the place of general C. C. Pinkney in the senate, upon that gentleman's leaving his seat. He quitted the profession of the law in the year 1798, when he was elected governor of the state; but lived to complete only half the term. His weak constitution had become considerably broken by hereditary gout, which did not, however, make him relax in the execution of his official duties. While attending a session of the legislature at Columbia, his sickness increased so much as to render him desirous of returning to Charleston; but, in compliance with the requisitions of the state constitution, he remained at the seat of government until the legislature had adjourned, and, while on his return home, encountered heavy rains and cold. Soon after his arrival at Charleston, he was confined to his bed, and expired, January 23, 1800. In person, Mr. Rutledge was above the middle height, and inclining to corpulency; he had a fair complexion, with a pleasing countenance. His manners were amiable and polished, and he was an orator of a superior stamp. His eloquence was various and beautiful, rather than vehement.

Ruysch, Rachel, one of the most celebrated painters of fruit and flower pieces, was born at Amsterdam in 1664, and died in 1750. Her pictures are distinguished for truth and splendor of coloring, united with great finish.

Ruysdael, or Ruysdaal, James, one of the greatest landscape painters, was born, in 1635, at Harlem. His brother *Solomon* (born 1616, and known for the beauty of his representation of marbles, &c.) seems to have been his teacher. James died in his native city in 1681. His aim appears to have been a faithful, but poetical conception of gloomy, and sometimes wild, nature. Landscapes with dark clouds hanging over them, church-yards, or thick woods after a thunder-storm, cascades between thick foliage, lakes and rivulets surrounded by overhanging trees, &c., are his subjects, and are represented admirably. The figures in his paintings were executed by others.

Ruyter, Michael Fitz Adrian; a celebrated Dutch admiral, born at Flushing in 1607. He entered young into the naval service of his country, and rose from the situation of cabin-boy to that of captain, in 1635. He was sent, in 1641, to the assistance of the Portuguese, who had thrown off the yoke of Spain; on which occasion he was appointed rear-admiral; and, two years after, he was employed against the Barbary corsairs. In the war between the Dutch and English, which commenced in 1652, Ruyter repeatedly distinguished himself, especially in the terrible battle fought in February, 1653, near the mouth of the Channel, when Blake (q. v.) commanded the English, and Tromp (q. v.) and Ruyter the Dutch. He afterwards served against the Portuguese, the Swedes, and the Algerines, previously to the naval warfare between England and Holland, in the reign of Charles II. He commanded in the great battle fought in the Downs, in June, 1666, against prince Rupert (q. v.) and the duke of Albemarle (see *Monk*); and, in the following year, he insulted the English by his memorable expedition up the Thames, when he destroyed Upnor castle, and burnt some ships at Chatham. He was admiral of the Dutch fleet at the battle of Solebay in 1672, and signalized his skill and courage on several other occasions. He died in the port of Syracuse, April 29, 1676, in consequence of a wound received in an engagement with the French, a few days before, off Messina. His body was carried to Amsterdam, where the states-general erected a monument to his memory.

Rye (*secale cereale*); a species of grain, generally considered, in temperate climates, next in value to wheat. It is a grass, from four to six feet high, with a fibrous annual root, producing one or several slender culms, which are provided at their articulations with linear and smooth leaves; the flowers are greenish, disposed in a terminal simple compressed spike, four or five inches in length. It is supposed to have been brought originally from the Levant, but has been cultivated in Europe from a very ancient period. Of all domestic plants, it has been the least altered by cultivation, and no permanent variety has been produced. It is the only species of the genus. Rye succeeds better in cold climates than wheat, grows in a greater variety of soils, resists severe frosts better, and arrives at maturity sooner. All soils will produce rye, provided they are not too moist; and many barren lands, which are unsuitable for the cultivation of wheat, may be sown with this grain to advantage. The time of sowing is earlier than with any other grain. It does not require so much attention during its growth as wheat, and the ripening varies according as the season is more or less warm and favorable, from the first of July to the last of the month; but, in general, it precedes wheat by fifteen or twenty days. In some countries, it is customary to sow in March; but it rarely produces so well as when sown before the setting in of the winter. In many places, it is cultivated only for fodder, which is an excellent plan, as cattle are often in want of green food in the early spring. Rye is the principal sustenance in the greater part of the north of Europe, and, after wheat, nourishes the greatest portion of the population of that continent. Even in more than half of France, rye bread, either pure or mixed with wheat in equal proportions, is the only kind to be procured. Rye bread is not so nutritious as wheat, but has more flavor. The farina, or meal, differs from that of the latter in containing a much smaller proportion of gluten. In the north, the greater part of the ardent spirits is distilled from rye. The straw is long, flexible, and does not rot so easily as that of other grain: it is used by brickmakers and collar-manufacturers, and is considered an excellent material for the thatching of cottages and barns. Rye is but little cultivated in Great Britain. (For spurred rye, see *Ergot*.)

Rye House Plot. (See *Russell, Lord William*, and *Sidney, Algernon*.)

Rymer, Thomas, a critic and antiquary, studied at Cambridge and at Gray's-inn. In 1678, he published Edgar, a Tragedy, and wrote a work entitled a View of the Tragedies of the last Age. Succeeding Shadwell, in 1692, as royal historiographer, he employed the opportunities afforded him by his office, to make a collection of public treaties, which he began to publish in 1704, under the title of *Fœdera, Conventiones, et cujuscunque Generis Acta publica, inter Reges Angliæ et alios Principes* (15 vols., folio, five more being added by Robert Sanderson). Rymer died in 1713.

Rysbrach, John Michael, a statuary, was the son of a painter of Antwerp, in which city he was born in 1694. He went to England early in life, and derived considerable reputation and profit from the exercise of his art, of which Westminster abbey, and other cathedral churches, contain specimens, among which may be mentioned the monuments of sir Isaac Newton and the duke of Marlborough; while others, and especially busts, enrich the best private collections, the heads of English worthies at Stowe, and in the Hermitage at Richmond, being of the number. His death took place in 1770.

Ryswick; a village and castle situated in South Holland, a league from the Hague, where the peace of Ryswick was concluded September 20 and October 30, 1697. Louis XIV had, in 1688, attacked the German empire in order to anticipate the league of Augsburg (the object of which was to set bounds to his conquests), and, at the same time, to frustrate the design of William III, the stadtholder of Holland, to place himself on the British throne. When William landed in England (November 8, 1688), Louis declared war against Holland. He had already conquered the provinces of the Rhine, when the emperor Leopold and the states-general concluded a league against France (Vienna, May 12, 1689), to which Great Britain, Spain and Savoy acceded. The war was carried on by France on land with great success. Marshal Luxembourg conquered the Spanish Netherlands, and Cattinat was victorious in Italy. But the landing of the French in Ireland, at the instigation of the deposed James II, proved unfortunate, and the French fleet under marshal Tourville, was totally defeated by the English and Dutch, under the command of admiral Russell, near La Hogue, May 29, 1692. Since that time, the British naval power has always maintained an ascendency over the French. In the mean time, the duke of Vendome conquered Catalonia, and, August 7, 1695, also Barcelona. This, and the wish of Louis to dissolve the great European league, before the Spanish throne should become vacant, hastened the conclusion of a peace. Savoy had already concluded a separate peace with France, at Turin, August 29, 1696, and connected herself with that power. Upon this, Sweden mediated the general peace at the congress held at Ryswick, from May 9, 1697, until September 20 of the same year, when England, Spain and Holland signed a treaty of peace with France. Louis XIV restored all his conquests in Catalonia and the Spanish Netherlands, with the exception of eighty-two places, which had been taken by the process of *reunion* (see *Louis XIV*), and acknowledged William III as king of Great Britain and Ireland. The emperor and empire first signed the treaty of peace with France October 30. Louis restored all the places which he had taken possession of in Germany by the process of *reunion* (see *Louis XIV*), with the exception of those which were situated in Alsace, the sovereignty of which was conceded to him. He likewise retained the free city of Strasburg, which was taken in 1681. The clause of the fourth article of the treaty of Ryswick, according to which the Catholic religion, which had been introduced into the 1922 places now restored by the French, was to remain as it then stood, gave much dissatisfaction to the Protestants. France restored all her conquests. The navigation of the Rhine was declared free.—See *Actes et Mémoires des Négociations de la Paix de Ryswik* (in 5 vols.).

S.

S; the nineteenth letter of the English alphabet, representing the hissing sound produced by emitting the breath between the roof of the mouth and the tip of the tongue placed just above the upper teeth, so that the air is driven through the teeth. From this circumstance, *s* has sometimes been reckoned among the linguals (as the tongue is essential in its pronunciation), sometimes among the dentals (as the teeth coöperate in producing the hissing sound). It is also one of the semivowels, as it can be pronounced without the assistance of a vowel, and the sound be prolonged indefinitely, like *l*, *m*, *n*, *r*; and Missula, in Martian, does not allow it to be a letter, but only a *sibilus* (hissing). In pronouncing *s*, the breath may be driven with more or less violence over the end of the tongue; hence, in most languages, it has a twofold pronunciation—sharp, as in *sack*, *sin*, *this*, *thus*; and soft, as in *muse*, *wise*. The German *Sinn* (pronounced *zin*), and *Maus* (pronounced *mouse*), and the French *soit* and *base*, are also examples of these two sounds. In German, the *s* is soft at the beginning of a syllable, and sharp at the end or in the middle, while the contrary is usually the case in English. But in some parts of Germany (e. g. Holstein) *s* at the beginning is sharp. But the Germans have, besides, a peculiar character for the sharp *s*, being a contraction of *sz*, which, when words containing it, are printed with Roman characters, is changed into *ss*, as *Ross*, *Mass*—an inconvenient contrivance, as the *ss*, according to the common German rule, always gives the preceding vowel a short pronunciation, which is not the case with *sz*.—It is a fundamental rule of etymology, that if a word begins with two or more consonants, the last of them only belongs to the root, though the others are not always useless additions. This rule is particularly true of words beginning with *s* followed by one or more consonants; e. g. *slime*, from *lime*, Latin *limus*, in German *Lehm* and *Leim*, which, instead of *slime*, has *Schleim* (pronounced *shlime*). The German *stumm*, for the English *dumb*, which, in German (formerly also written *dumb*, now *dumm*), signifies *stupid* (one "who has not much to say for himself"), *slippery* (in German *schlüpfrig*), from the Latin *lubricus*. In both these cases, the *s* has an intensitive power, which, in fact, it has very often, and of which numberless instances are found in all languages. But it is often put before words, apparently, without this meaning; as in *Servus*, from the ancient Roman *Erus*, *Eruus*. The Greeks made *Scythians* of the *Kythi*. *Tinn* (in German *Zinn*) is of the same root with the Latin *stannum*. The Greek ὗς, ἥλιος, ὕλη and ὕδωρ became with the Latins *sus*, *sol*, *sylvia* and *sudor*. This easy addition of *s* to words is also the cause of its playing so prominent a part in the declension of substantives and verbs in many, perhaps most languages. Notwithstanding the predominance of this letter in most languages, particularly in English,* the

* If you hear two persons conversing in English at such a distance that nothing but the general sound of the discourse reaches your ear, they appear to be engaged in a continual hissing, from the frequent occurrence of the *s*. The con-

people of the South sea islands cannot pronounce it at all, and say, for instance, instead of *Ellis*, *Elliki*. The sounds of the letters *s*, *r*, *t*, *sh* and *th* (which, in fact, represents but a simple sound, though written with two characters in English, whilst the Spaniards have one, the *z*), are all produced by a very similar motion of the organs; and hence the frequent change of the *s* into the other letters. (See the articles *R* and *T*.) The sound *th* is the transition between *s* and *t*; hence the third person singular of the present tense, ending, in German, in *t*, ended formerly, in English, in *th*, and now in *s*; e. g. *has*, *hath* (Germ. *hat*); *brings*, *bringeth* (Germ. *bringet*). *S* is so nearly akin to *r*, that *Valerii*, *Furii*, *ara*, *carmen*, *lares*, and numerous other words, were originally written *Valesii*, *Fusii*, *asa*, *casmen*, *lases*. The Swedish and English *hare* is in German *Hase*. *S* often alternates with the sound *sh* (written in German *sch*); and some German tribes, particularly the Suabians, change the *s* regularly into *sch*, when it precedes another consonant: thus they say *bischt* and *hascht* (pronounced *bisht* and *hasht*) for *bist* and *hast*; and even in High German, *s*, at the beginning of a word, followed by another consonant, is generally pronounced *sh*; this, in fact, was long considered by many correct; but at present, we think, the weight of opinion is in favor of the simpler sound of *s*. It is a peculiarity of *s*, that it may be sounded before all the simple consonants—a circumstance which makes it so formidable a letter to lexicographers and encyclopædists. S signified seven, according to the verse:—

S vera septenos numeratos significabit.

Among the Greeks, σ́ signified 200, and ͵σ denoted 200,000; the sigma joined to the *tau*, i. e. ϛ, denoted 6. The samech of the Hebrew, ס, denoted 50, and with two points above, ס̈, it signified 50,000. S is the common abbreviation for *societas* and *socius* (fellow). S. S. stands for *sanctissimus*; S. D. for *salutem dixit*; S. P. D. for *salutem plurimam dixit*; S. P. Q. R. for the famous *senatus populusque Romanus*. S., in geography, stands for *south*; in music, for *solo* (alone), as T. for *tutti* (all). On French coins, *S* signifies Rheims. (See *Abbreviations*.)

Saadi. (See *Sadi*.)

Saale; the name of several German rivers, the most important of which is that which rises in the Fichtelgebirge in Bavaria, and falls into the Elbe south of Barby. Several considerable places are situated on it, as Jena, Naumburg, Merseburg, Halle, &c. It is navigable to Halle, and it is intended to make it so to Naumburg.

stant repetition of this sound produces a very bad effect in English vocal music.

Saar Louis (in the time of the French revolution called *Sarrelibre*); the Prussian fortress nearest France, on the river Sarre, belonging to the government of Treves. Including the garrison, it has 7000 inhabitants. Vauban fortified the town for Louis XIV. In 1814, it was ceded to Prussia. Lon. 6° 50′ E.; lat. 49° 20′ N.

Sabæans; the ancient name of the inhabitants of the modern Yemen, in Arabia. Their capital was Saba.

Sabæans. (See *Sabians*.)

Sabaism (from the Hebrew *Zaba*, lord, from which God is called *Zebaoth*, Lord of the heavenly hosts, because the stars or powers of heaven are called the *hosts of God*); that religion which worships the heavenly bodies, especially the sun and moon. The connexion of these with the constant changes in nature, and with the condition of men, produced the idea of their divinity; and the actual or symbolical connexion of the heavenly bodies and certain animals and plants, as well as the powers of nature, which are active in them, invested the latter also with a divine character, and made them objects of worship to the adherents of Sabaism. The sexual relations of living creatures gave rise to the fundamental idea of generation, conception and production, which predominates in the Indian mythology, and became united with the doctrines of Sabaism; and thus the latter received that character which we find it to have in the mythology of Western Asia. Egypt, Arabia, and particularly the region bounded east by the Euphrates and Tigris, west by the Mediterranean, and north by the Black sea, were the countries where Sabaism prevailed in times previous to Christianity; and even the Hebrews often showed an inclination towards it. The religious history of the Chaldæans, Assyrians, Syrians, and tribes of Asia Minor, as given in Wagner's Contributions towards a general Mythology of the ancient World, in Görres's History of Mythuses, in Creuzer's *Symbolik*, and in Baur's *Symbolik*, shows the justice of the reproaches which the prophets of the Old Testament heap on the sensual worship of these heathens.

Sabbatarians; those Christians who keep the seventh day as others do Sunday; chiefly found among Baptists. They hold that the sabbath was established by divine authority, and changed from the seventh day to the first day of the week by human authority only. (See *Sabbath.*)

SABBATH (a Hebrew word signifying *rest*) is the day appointed by the Mosaic law for a total cessation from labor, and for the service of God, in memory of the circumstance that God, having created the world in six days, rested on the seventh. Concerning the time when the Sabbath was first instituted, some Jewish writers and some fathers of the church have believed, from the language of Genesis, chap. ii. v. 2 (where it is said that God blessed and sanctified the day), that it was established from the moment of creation; but, as there is no proof, in the Old Testament, that this day was observed by the patriarchs before Moses, others have supposed that the words in Genesis mean that God intended to have the Sabbath celebrated in future; but some modern writers, particularly English and American divines, adhere to the first opinion. (For the manner in which the Jews kept it, and the awful consequences of neglecting it, we refer the reader to the Old Testament, Lev. xxvi. 34, 35; Neh. xiii. 16—18; Jer. xvii. 21; Ezek. xx. 16, 17; Numb. xv. 23—36.) A law so strictly enjoined, and whose observance is of so public a character, was naturally kept by the Pharisees with the utmost strictness, in its outward forms, so that they reproached the Founder of Christianity, who taught that religion had its seat in the heart, and that God must be worshipped in spirit, with breaking the Sabbath when he healed the sick on that day. His rebuke of their hypocrisy is contained in John v. 16, and Matthew xii. 1 et seq.—*Sabbath* also signifies, in the Bible, the eternal rest of God; also holy days in general. It likewise came to signify a week.—The explicit injunction of the celebration of the Sabbath, the enumeration of it even in the decalogue (Exodus xx. 8), had a great influence upon Christian observances; and there are many Christians to this day, especially in England and North America, who transfer all the injunctions contained in the Old Testament respecting the observance of the Sabbath, to the first day of the week, and even give this the name of Sabbath. The use of the term *Sabbath*, in this application, we believe, is confined to these two countries. In the earliest times of Christianity, the law of the Sabbath, like other parts of the Jewish faith, could not be received into the new religion, except spiritualized and refined like the sacrifices and other ceremonies. Every day, the whole life of the Christian, had become a Sabbath, destined for the service of God. St. Paul explicitly treats the reverencing of certain days as invested with a holy character by a divine ordinance, as Jewish and unchristian, and as a return to servitude of the law. The first communities assembled every day; e. g. the community of Jerusalem for common prayer, meditation on the Word, communion and love-feasts. Traces of these daily meetings are found even later. With the spread of Christianity, however, and the necessity of instructing a greater number, the appointment of a certain time for this service became necessary. This was not a departure from the spirituality of the new religion, but only an accommodation to the wants of mankind. In the same way, peculiar persons became priests, though all Christians had an equal sanctity of character, and the departure from the spirit of Christianity consisted only in assuming a peculiar spiritual character for the priests. The gradual adoption of forms and ideas from the Old Testament took place in the same way, in respect to the Sabbath, as in respect to the priesthood. When the Montanists intended to establish new fasts, assigned to fixed times, they were reminded of the Epistle to the Galatians; but Tertullian treated the censure of St. Paul as attaching only to the celebration of Jewish festivals. (Tertullian, *De Jejuniis*, c. 14.) The weekly and yearly festivals of the Christians originated from the idea of following Christ, the crucified and the arisen; hence the festival of the resurrection, and the fasts preparatory thereto. In each week, the joyous festival was on Sunday, and the preparation for it was on Wednesday and Friday, the days of the Savior's passion. This point of view is necessary for a right understanding of the early festivals. The desire of distinguishing the Christian from the Jewish observance, early gave rise to the celebration of Sunday, the first day of the week, instead of the Jewish Sabbath; the first trace of which is found in Acts xx. 7. This, however, is by no means conclusive, because the community, collected on the first day of the week, might easily have been assembled by the near departure of St. Paul; and still less can be proved from 1 Corinth. xvi. 2. Another trace is in the Apocalypse, i. 10, as here we cannot suppose that by Lord's day is meant day of judgment. In the letter of Ignatius to the Magnesians (chap. ix.), allusion is made to the

Sunday celebration, as the symbol of a new life, consecrated to the Lord, in contradistinction to the former Sabbath. Sunday was distinguished as a day of joy, so that none fasted on it; people prayed standing, and not kneeling, in allusion to Christ having raised fallen man. Neander (q. v.), a most learned and faithful inquirer into ecclesiastical history, observes,* that "the celebration of Sunday was always, like that of every festival, a human institution; far was it from the apostles to treat it as a divine command; far from them and from the first apostolic church, to transfer the laws of the Sabbath to Sunday. But perhaps as early as the end of the second century, a mistaken application of this kind had grown up, because, even then, the working on Sunday seems to have been considered sinful (as we may conclude from the words of Tertullian, *De Orat.*, chap. xxiii †). Wednesday and Friday, the latter particularly, were sacred to the memory of the Savior's passion. Jewish-Christian communities, however, retained the celebration of the Sabbath, though they adopted also that of Sunday, and thus it became customary, in the Oriental church, to distinguish this day, also, by not fasting, and by praying in a standing posture: on the other hand, in the Western, and particularly in the Roman church, in which the opposition to Judaism prevailed, the custom grew up of using the Sabbath particularly as a fast-day. (Tertullian, *De Jej.*, chap. 14.) And when, at a later period, the causes of this fasting on Saturday were lost, legends were invented to explain it, such as that Peter had fasted on this day to prepare himself for the disputation with Simon Magus. Tertullian speaks of this difference between the Oriental and Western churches with much moderation. The learned Hippolytus wrote, at the beginning of the third century, on this point of dispute." (Hieronymus, *Ep.* 72, *ad Vital.*) Constantine the Great made a law for the whole empire (321 A. D.), that Sunday should be kept as a day of rest in all cities and towns; but he allowed the country people to follow their work on that day. In the year 538 (A. D.), however, the council of Orleans prohibited country labor; but because there were still many Jews in Gaul, and the people fell into many superstitious uses in the celebration of the *new* Sabbath, in imitation of the practices of the Jews, the council declares that to hold it unlawful to travel with horses, cattle and carriages, to prepare food, or to do any thing necessary to the cleanliness and decency of houses or persons, savors more of Judaism than of Christianity.‡ The reformation, abolishing so many of the festivals, which had increased in the Roman church to an immense number, naturally elevated the character of those which it left, as Easter, Christmas, &c., and Sunday; but Sunday, though considered by the Lutherans as a proper day for religious service, was never regarded by them with that awe which was connected with its observance in the Old Testament. It is with them a day of rest and enjoyment, and many amusements are taken by Protestants on the European continent, during that day, which people there would think improper on week days appropriated for labor. Calvinism, which is altogether of a sterner character than Lutheranism, may have induced its adherents to observe Sunday more strictly; but even at Geneva, the Sunday evening is spent in various amusements, in visiting, dancing, playing foot-ball, &c., and the labors of husbandry are permitted in harvest on Sundays. The custom of calling Sunday *Sabbath* indicates the inclination to transfer the character of the Jewish Sabbath to the Christian Sunday. In fact, the Puritans, from whom it has descended, showed, in many respects, a decided inclination to the sternness of the Old Testament. (See also *Sabbatarians*.) The Puritans rejected, by degrees, the feasts of the church, as heathenish or popish, and the Sunday alone was retained, either because they considered it as, originally, of divine institution, or because, being conscious of the disadvantage of abolishing all festival days, they felt the want of a divine injunction for the one which

* General History of the Christian Religion and Church (Hamb., 1826, vol. i, part 1, p. 514).

† Solo die dominico resurrectionis non ab isto tantum (*the genuflexion*), sed omni anxietatis habitu et officio cavere debemus, differentes etiam negotia, ne quem diabolo locum demus.

‡ In the fourth volume of Blackstone's Commentaries, p. 63, the commentator says that the profanation of the Lord's day is vulgarly, but *improperly*, called *Sabbath-breaking*, and is punished by the municipal law, by a fine of three shillings and four pence; and that, by the laws of England, no fair or market is allowed to be held on any Sunday, except the *four Sundays in harvest*, on pain of forfeiting the goods exposed for sale. The law, however, does not prohibit (the commentator adds), but rather *allows*, any *innocent recreation or amusement* on the Lord's day, *after service is over*. But it prohibits *work* on that day, or exposure of goods for sale, except mackerel, milk, meat, &c., under the penalty of five shillings. He considers Sunday as a *civil institution*, to be regulated by the municipal law.

they kept. The Puritan austerity had manifested itself even in the reign of Elizabeth and Edward VI. Under both, the following injunctions were published:—"All parsons, vicars and curates shall teach and declare unto the people, that they may, with a safe and quiet conscience, after their common prayer, in time of harvest, labor upon the holy and festival days, and save that thing which God hath sent; and if, for any scrupulosity or grudge of conscience, they abstain from working upon those days, that then they shall grievously offend and displease God." But no where was Sunday kept with more rigidness and perfect abstinence from labor (prohibited even by many severe laws) than by the Puritan settlers of New England. The petitions lately presented to congress to prevent the transportation of the mail on Sundays emanate from the same spirit, and were considered by many as hostile to the principles of constitutional freedom, congress having no right to legislate on religious matters. See *Sunday Mails* (Philad., 1830).—Laws still exist in several of the U. States for enforcing the strict observance of Sunday. So much did the Puritans consider the Christian Sunday as a Jewish Sabbath, that a controversy has existed as to the time when the Christian Sabbath begins, many clergymen maintaining that it begins at sunset on Saturday; and some communities have acted on this view in their mode of observing it. Whilst in America and England, many believe it of the utmost importance, for the interests of piety and morality, that Sunday should be kept with great strictness, the opinion of the majority on the continent of Europe, may be said to be, that people whose weeks are spent in labor, should have some means of relaxation on the Sunday. The total denial of such means they consider injurious to morality, as promoting a hypocritical concealment of amusements, which, from this very cause, are apt to become immoral ones.

Sabellians. (See *Sabellius*.)

Sabellius, a Christian teacher at Ptolemais, a native of Africa, lived about 250, and is known as the founder of a sect, who considered the Son and Holy Ghost only as different revelations or manifestations of the Godhead, but not as separate persons. The Trinity, according to them, is but a threefold relation of God to the world. The *Logos* of John, called, by the church, the *Son*, was compared by Sabellius to a ray emitted from the sun, active in and through the man Jesus Christ, but by no means a separate existence from the one God. The Sabellians were suppressed in the fourth century by the orthodox church, but their views have always found adherents, and, even now, theologians exhibit conceptions of the Trinity, coinciding with that of Sabellius, in order to make it intelligible by reason.

Sabians, or Christians of St. John (likewise called *Nazoræans* and *Mendæans*); a sect which, according to tradition, has existed from the time of John the Baptist. The members at present are found chiefly in Persia, and consider their original country to have been on the Jordan, whence, they say, they were driven by the Mohammedans before the destruction of Jerusalem, and, being persecuted by the first caliphs, their temples destroyed, and their sacred books burnt, they fled to their present residence, and some also to India. Having been again persecuted, they submitted to the Nestorian bishop in Chaldæa, and allowed themselves to be called Christians, but have been separated from them for more than three hundred years. The question, whether they are really of Galilæan origin, and are derived from the disciples of John the Baptist, or whether they formed their doctrines from a mixture of the Jewish, Christian, and Persian religions, and, having chosen John as an object of meditation and reverence, afterwards supposed him to have been their founder, is difficult to decide. Tychsen has declared for the latter opinion; yet the argument seems stronger in favor of the former. In the middle of the seventeenth century, according to Ignatius a Jesu (*Narratio Originis*, &c., *Christianorum S. Joh.*, Rome, 1652), there were from twenty to twenty-five thousand families of them. Five religious books of these people are known to us: 1. The Divan, of which we have only the extracts given by Ignatius. This book is said to have been given by God to the angels several thousand years before the creation of the world, though Mohammed is alluded to in it. 2. The Book of Adam, consisting of revelations brought by angels, or æons, to Adam, and composed of eighty or ninety discourses, laudatory, didactic, hortatory and prophetic. 3. The Book of John, or Conversations of Angels. Specimens of this are given by Lorsbach. The bells and rosaries of the Christians are mentioned in it. 4. *Cholasteh*, which contains the means and conditions of salvation. 5. The Book of the Signs of the Zodiac, of an astrological character, and only known from the account of Abraham

Ecchellensis. (*Eutychii Vindic.*, i. 3.) The language and alphabet of these books are altogether peculiar; the former is an Aramæan dialect, equally resembling the Syriac and Chaldean. Their religious doctrines stand in the same relation to those of Zoroaster, that Gnosticism and Manicheism do, except that they give to John the Baptist the elevated rank which the Gnosis gives to Christ. The latter and the Holy Ghost they look upon with the same contempt with which the Gnostics regarded the God of the Old Testament. Their system is a highly complicated doctrine of emanations, on which the influence of the Jewish cabala and of Mohammedanism is perceptible. The original being (like the endless time of the Zend-Avesta) is a divine æther (Ferha) of unspeakable splendor. Next to him is a female principle (Ajar). From these two proceeds Mana (the lord of the kingdom of light). Then follow numerous æons, or angels of light, and opposite to the kingdom of light is that of darkness, under Ur, with seven chief evil spirits, which inhabit the seven planets. Their theology ends with John the Baptist (Anusch), who came to win men, by baptism, for the kingdom of light. He was produced by a single kiss of his father Zachariah, and was married, but received his children out of the Jordan, one of the first elements of light in their theology. Mohammed is the last false prophet, after whom no other will appear. They despise Mohammedans more than Christians. The best part of their doctrine is their morals, founded on the repression of sensuality, as the only condition of virtue. The elect (they allow gradations of virtue) are forbidden to enjoy sensual pleasure, singing, dancing, &c.; yet matrimony is often praised. Matrimonial fidelity, careful education of their children, respect for the first born, abstinence from usury, &c., are inculcated. Their priests are divided into three orders. The priestly dignities are hereditary, descending to the eldest son. Baptism is their most solemn rite. It is the indispensable condition of the forgiveness of sin, and is administered to new-born children and adults. The baptism of the latter takes place at least once every year, during the great feast of baptism, which lasts five days. They have also a kind of *agape*, or love-feast. Polygamy is not prohibited even to priests. Among their laws, in which we also find some resembling the Jewish, is one which prohibits mourning for the dead; but prayers are offered up, sermons delivered, and alms given Their antipathy for blue is remarkable. A pretty complete list of works relating to this sect is given in Nösselt's *Theolog. Litteratur* (§ 474). See Norberg, *De Relig. et Lingua Sabæorum*, in the 3d vol. of *Comm. Soc. Goth.* (1780); Walch, *De Sabæis* (4th vol. ibid., 1781); Norberg's *Codex Nasareus seu Liber Adami, Syriace transcriptus Latineque redditus* (t. i.—iii., 1815 and 1816); Tittman, *Meletemata Sacra* (Leipsic, 1816, p. 15 et seq.)

Sabine River and Lake. (See *Rivers, Navigable.*)

Sabines (*Sabini*); an old people of Italy, probably the descendants of the Ausonians, and related to the aborigines. This numerous people, who founded many colonies, lived in the Apennines, principally occupied with the care of herds. Horace has celebrated their honesty, modesty and simplicity of manners. Their country, to the west, was separated from Etruria by the Tiber; towards the south, by the river Anio (Teverone), from Latium; and towards the north, by the river Nar, from Umbria: towards the east dwelt the Sabine colonies of the Vestini and Marrucini, who separated it from the Adriatic sea: it therefore embraced the principal part of the mountainous country of the Apennines. The soil is very fertile, and rich in pasturage The productions are oil, fruits and wines, besides acorns in abundance.

Sabines, Rape of the. (See *Romulus.*

Sable. (See *Weasel.*)

Sacbut; a bass wind instrument, resembling the trumpet, and so contrived as to be capable of being drawn out to different lengths, according to the acuteness and gravity of the scale required. The sacbut is usually about eight feet long, and, when extended to its full length, about fifteen. There are, however, sacbuts of different sizes, to execute different parts, particularly a small one, called by the Italians *trombone piccolo*, and by the Germans *kleine Alte-Posaune*, proper for the counter-tenor. Respecting the sacbut of the ancient Hebrews, commentators have differed much. Indeed, scarce any ancient instrument has been heard of, for which the sacbut or the psaltery has not furnished a name.

Saccharine. (See *Fermentation*, and *Sugar.*)

Sacchini, Anthony Mary Gaspard, was born at Naples, in 1735, and studied music under Durante. After being employed in Rome, Venice, and several other cities of Italy, he went to London, where he composed *Montezuma*, *Perseus*, and the *Cid*. He was engaged for the opera in Paris, in 1782, where his *Œdipe à Colonne* procured him great fame at the time of the quarrel between the Gluckists and Piccinists. He died in 1786, leaving fifty operas. His bust stands in the Pantheon at Rome, next to Raphael's.

Sachem. In North America, this is the name given by some of the Indian tribes to their chiefs.—*Sagamore* is a word of similar import among the Indians.

Sacheverell, Henry, D.D., an English divine of the establishment, exalted into temporary importance by the spirit of party, was educated at Oxford. In 1705, he was appointed preacher of St. Savior's, Southwark. While in this station, he preached his two famous sermons, in 1709, the object of which was to rouse apprehensions for the safety of the church, and to excite hostility against the dissenters. Being impeached in the house of commons, he was brought to trial in February, 1710, and sentenced to be suspended from preaching for three years. This prosecution, however, excited such a spirit in the high church party, that it ultimately overthrew the ministry (see *Bolingbroke*, and *Harley*), and established the fortune of doctor Sacheverell, who, during his suspension, made a sort of triumphal progress through the kingdom. The same month that his suspension terminated, he was appointed to the valuable rectory of St. Andrew, Holborn, by queen Anne; and such was his reputation, that the copy-right of the first sermon which he afterwards was allowed to preach, sold for £100. He had also sufficient interest with the new ministry to provide handsomely for a brother. Little was heard of him after this party ebullition subsided, except by his numerous squabbles with his parishioners. His abilities, even according to writers on his own side, were contemptible; and, if we may credit doctor Swift, he was despised by the ministry whom his notoriety so much contributed to support. He died in 1724.

Sachs, Hans, the most distinguished mastersinger (q. v.) of Germany in the sixteenth century, was born at Nuremberg in 1494, and was by trade a shoemaker. He followed his business and made verses with equal assiduity. He became a Protestant, and died Jan. 19, 1576. His complete works appeared in 1570 et seq., in five folio vols., in Nuremberg; also in 1588, ibid.; and at Kempton, in five 4to vols. (1612—1616). Büsching published a selection of them in 1828 (Nuremberg, in 6 vols.). He possessed a fruitful genius, and, notwithstanding the rudeness of his language, his poems are distinguished for *naïveté*, feeling, invention, wit, and striking description.

Sachsenspiegel (*Mirror of the Saxons*); a private collection of legal precepts and legal customs, which had the force of law in the middle ages in Germany, especially in the north of Germany. A Saxon nobleman (Epko von Repkau, or Eyke von Repgow) made this collection in 1215 et seq. It enjoyed great authority even in foreign countries, as Poland, Denmark, &c., though the pope put many obstacles in its way, and though it was but a private collection. It is written in the old Saxon dialect, and is of much value, both for the lawyer and the philologist. The study of it has been revived, of late, in Germany, and Homeyer published a critical edition of it in Berlin (1827).

Sack (*secco*, Spanish; *sec*, French, *dry*); a general name for the different sorts of dry wine, more especially the Spanish, which were first extensively used in England in the sixteenth century. Thus we find the writers of that time speaking of "sherris-sack," meaning Sherry, and "Canary-sack," for the dry wines of the Canaries. Henderson gives some curious information on this point, on which there has been a good deal of confusion and dispute. (*Ancient and Modern Wines*, p. 308, seq.) The practice of putting sugar into wine, which we often find alluded to in Shakspeare and other writers, was not confined to the sacks; the English, at that time, sweetened all their wines.

Sacket's Harbor; a post village and port of entry in the township of Haunsfield, Jefferson county, New York. It is situated on the south-west side of a bay of lake Ontario, called Black River bay, and about eight miles from the lake. Lat. 43° 55′ N.; lon. 75° 57′ W. The bay and harbor are well situated for shelter and defence. The harbor is by far the best on lake Ontario for ship-building and as a naval and commercial depot. A crescent of land stretches off from the lower part of the village, forming an inner and an outer harbor. The latter has a depth of water sufficient for the largest ships of war, within two fathoms of the shore. The same depth of water extends to Black river, where there is another excellent position for ship-building. The Madison barracks, situated just above the village, were erected in 1816—17. They are built of limestone, and enclose three sides of a parallelogram, of about three acres. The side next to the lake is open. There are now laid up, at this port, a frigate of 68 guns, three ships of 28 each, four brigs, and a number of gunboats. The first settlement at this place was commenced in 1801, by Augustus Sacket. It advanced little till the commencement of the late war, when it became an important military and naval station. In 1820, it contained a population of 2020, including about 600 U. States' troops; and it seems not to have increased. Steamboats and schooners pass frequently between Sacket's Harbor, Niagara, and Ogdensburg.

Sackville, Thomas (lord Buckhurst and earl of Dorset), an accomplished statesman and poet, was the son of sir Richard Sackville, of Buckhurst, in the parish of Witham, in Sussex, where he was born about 1527. He was first of the university of Oxford, but removed to Cambridge, and afterwards became a student of the Inner Temple. At both universities he was distinguished for his performances in Latin and English poetry, and in the Temple he wrote his tragedy of Gorboduc. Of a poem intended to comprehend a view of the illustrious but unfortunate characters in English history, entitled the Mirror of Magistrates, he finished only a poetical preface, and one legend on the life of the duke of Buckingham. He was member in the two first parliaments of Elizabeth, after which he travelled. On the death of his father, in 1566, he succeeded to a large inheritance, and was soon after raised to the peerage by the title of baron Buckhurst. He was then imprisoned, owing to the influence of the favorite, Leicester, in consequence of a report in disfavor of the latter, when sent on an embassy of inquiry into his conduct in Holland. In 1598, he was joined with Burleigh in negotiations for peace with Spain, and signed the treaty which followed with the states-general. On the death of that minister, he succeeded him as lord high treasurer. In this situation he was instrumental in discovering the dangerous projects of the earl of Essex, at whose trial he presided as high steward, in which office he conducted himself with great prudence and humanity. On the accession of James I, his post of treasurer was confirmed to him, and, in 1604, he was created earl of Dorset. He died suddenly, at the council-table, in April, 1608 at an advanced age. This statesman ranks among the most prudent and able of the ministers of Elizabeth, and was a good speaker, and a still better writer. As a poet, he was the first who approached to perfection in the English heroic stanza, and gave the first example of regular tragedy in blank verse. His tragedy of Gorboduc, or, as entitled when printed in 1671, the Tragedie of Ferrex and Porrex, is a sanguinary story from early British history, composed with little pathos or attention to dramatic rules, but with considerable force of poetical conception and moral sentiment. The language is also pure and perspicuous, and free from the turgidity which soon after prevailed.

Sackville, Charles, sixth earl of Dorset and Middlesex, was born Jan. 24, 1637. He received his education under a private tutor, and, after making the tour of Italy, was chosen member of the first parliament which assembled after the restoration. He made a great figure as a speaker, but declined all public employment, being wholly engrossed with gallantry and pleasure. He, however, served as a volunteer in the first Dutch war, in 1665, and, the night before the engagement, composed his celebrated song of "To all you ladies now at land," which is esteemed one of the happiest of his productions. He succeeded to the estate of his uncle, James Cranfield, earl of Middlesex, in 1674, and, in 1675, to his title by creation. In 1677, on the death of his father, he also succeeded him in his estate and the title of Dorset. He utterly disliked and discountenanced the violent measures of James II, and early engaged for the prince of Orange, who made him lord chamberlain of the household. In 1698, on the decline of his health, he retired from public affairs, and died Jan. 19, 1705—6, leaving a son and daughter, the first of whom was created duke of Dorset in 1720. Lord Dorset wrote several small poems, which are included in Chalmers's collection; but they are not numerous enough to make a volume of themselves. He was still more celebrated as a patron of poets and of men of wit, who, in their turn, have been very copious in their panegyric; and Prior, Dryden, Congreve and Addison all bear testimony to his merit. He was a very able critic; and Butler owed it to him that the court relished his Hudibras. His own brief productions are those of a man of wit, gay and airy.

Sackville, George (viscount Sackville), was the third son of the first duke of Dorset and was born in 1716. He was educated at Trinity college, Dublin, served with reputation at the battles of Fontenoy and Dettingen, and, in 1758, had attained the rank of lieutenant-general. The following year he commanded the British cavalry at the battle of Minden, under prince Ferdinand of Brunswick, whose orders to advance with his troops during the engagement he disobeyed, either from cowardice or misapprehension. His behavior was generally attributed at home to the former cause, and he was tried by a court-martial, convicted of dereliction of duty, and sentenced to be dismissed from the service. Under the administration of lord Bute, he was restored to favor. In 1775, he was appointed colonial secretary of state, and held that office during the progress of the war with America. On relinquishing his post in 1782, he was created viscount. For a considerable part of his life, he was called lord George Germaine, having taken that name on succeeding to an estate left him by lady Elizabeth Germaine, who died in 1769. (See *Junius.*)

Saclactic Acid. (See *Mucic Acid.*)

Saco; a river which rises in the White mountains, and runs south-east into the Atlantic, below Saco, in Maine. It is 160 miles long, and has falls of 72 feet at Hiram, of 20 feet at Lymington, of 30 feet at Buxton, and of 42 feet at Saco. To Saco, six miles from its mouth, it is navigable.

Saco; a post-town and port of entry in York county, Maine, at the falls on Saco river. It is fifteen miles south-west of Portland. Population in 1830, 3219. The falls at this place carry many saw-mills, and others are constructed at the upper and middle falls. From these mills, great quantities of boards and other lumber are produced, which are shipped from Saco. The town has an active and profitable trade, and affords a great amount of water power for manufacturing purposes. Factories are now erecting at the falls, which will soon increase the population and trade.

Sacrament (Latin, *sacramentum;* the assumption of an obligation, an oath). This word received a religious sense, in the Christian church, from its having been used in the vulgate (q. v.), to translate the Greek μυστηριον. Among the early Latin ecclesiastical writers, *sacramentum*, therefore, signifies a mystery, a symbolical religious ceremony; but first acquired the peculiar sense which it now has in the Roman Catholic church, denoting seven particular religious rites. The Catholic church considers a sacrament as a visible token, ordained by Christ, by means of which an invisible grace is communicated to Christians. The seven Roman sacraments, as confirmed by the council of Trent (sess. vii.), are—1. Baptism (Matthew xxviii, 19); 2. Confirmation (Acts viii, 14—21, xix, 1—4); 3. the Eucharist (see *Lord's Supper*); 4. penance (q. v.); 5. extreme unction (James v, 14, 15); 6. orders (Acts vi, 1—7; xiii, 1—4; xiv, 20—24; and 2 Timothy i, 6 and 7); and marriage, the sacred and indissoluble nature of which is conceived to be taught in Matthew v, 31, 32; xix, 1—10; Mark x, 2—13; Luke xvi, 18; Romans vii, 2—4; 1 Corinthians vii, 10 and 11. The Greek church agrees with the Roman church in the doctrine of the sacraments. (See *Greek Church.*) The Protestants, in general, acknowledge but two sacraments, baptism and the Lord's supper, considering a sacrament to be a festival instituted by Christ, by which he who partakes of it worthily, participates in the influences of divine grace through sensible means and signs. The different views of the early reformers on the subject of the eucharist are stated in the articles *Carlstadt*, *Zuinglius*, *Lord's Supper.* (See also, *Reformed Church.*) Luther and Melanchthon at first acknowledged penance or absolution as a sacrament, but afterwards ranked it only as a preparation for the Lord's supper. The Quakers consider the sacraments as of little importance. (See *Quakers.*)

Sacrifices. (See *Offerings.*)

Sacrilege; the alienating to laymen, or common purposes, what was given to religious persons and pious uses. The idea that sacrilege is to be punished with peculiar severity, as a profanation of things sacred, or a direct indignity to God, was controverted even in the chamber of Catholic France, in the debates respecting the bill *sur le sacrilège*, in 1825. See St. Edme's work, *La Législation historique du Sacrilège chez tous les Peuples* (Paris, 1825). Church robbery, or the taking things out of a holy place, is sacrilege, and, by the common law, was punished with more severity than other thefts, for the benefit of clergy (q. v.) was denied to the offenders; but it is now put by statute on a footing with other felonies.

Sacs. (See *Indians, American.*)

Sacy, baron Antoine Isaac Silvestre de, a distinguished Orientalist, member of the academy of inscriptions, and knight of the legion of honor, was born, September 21, 1758, at Paris, where he early lost his father. He received a private education. In 1781, he was appointed counse tor of the court of the mint, and entered, in 1785, as an *associé libre*, the academy of inscriptions, of which he became a regular member in 1792. In 1791, the king made him one of the commissaries-general of the mint. From 1793 to 1796 he lived in retirement in the country. On the establishment of the national institute, he was elected a member, but did not join it, as he was unwilling to take the oath of hatred against royalty. He refused to take this oath, also, as a professor in the special school of living Oriental languages; but he was suffered to retain this office, as it was almost impossible to find a man qualified to fill his place. His uninterrupted occupation in scientific pursuits preserved him during the reign of terror. When Napoleon gave a new organization to the institute, Sacy became a member of the department of ancient literature and history. In 1808, he received the newly established professorship of the Persian language, in the *collége de France*, and was also chosen a member of the legislative body for the department of the Seine. April 3, 1814, he declared himself in favor of the deposition of Napoleon, and took an active part in the discussions of the different bills which occupied the chamber during the session. In 1813, he was made a baron. The king, in 1814, appointed him censor, and, in 1815, rector of the university of Paris, and, soon after, a member of the commission for public instruction. He has also been chosen member of many academies and learned societies. The most important writings of this first among living Orientalists are, his Arabic grammar and Anthology (published together, in 1810 and 1816, in 5 vols.), which excel all similar works (a second edition of the Arabic grammar was published in 1831); his translation of Abdollatif, which is invaluable, on account of the subjoined annotations; his *Mémoires sur diverses Antiquités de la Perse* (1793, quarto), wherein the ancient historical monuments are explained, with a deep knowledge of the language, and the whole subject; his *Mémoires d'Histoire et de Littérature Orientale* (1818, quarto); his general grammar; his little work On Carrier-Pigeons; his *Chrestomathie Arabe* (2d edition, Paris, 1826, in 2 vols.); and many others. The *Mémoires de l'Académie*, and the *Notices et Extraits*, of which latter work a number of volumes were wholly, or almost wholly, composed by him, moreover testify as much in favor of his diligence as his comprehensive knowledge. As a teacher, Sacy has done much for the diffusion of a thorough knowledge of the Arabic and Persian in Europe, and has moreover educated excellent scholars. With strict integrity he unites the most pleasing and open character, and is always ready to promote the labors and studies of others.

SADDUCEES; one of the four principal sects of the Jews, the founder of whom was Sadoc, a Jewish rabbi, who lived about 200 years B. C. The doctrines inculcated by his master, Antigonus, that we ought to practise virtue, not for the sake of reward, but solely on account of its own intrinsic excellence, led him to maintain that there would be neither rewards nor punishments in another life. His adherents, therefore, denied the resurrection and the immortality of the soul; believed neither in angels nor spirits; but were very strict in their morals; so that Christ, notwithstanding the reproach that they did not understand the Scriptures, did not censure them on account of their morals. They succeeded to the highest dignities and offices, and even to the high priesthood. This sect still exists among the Caraites. (q. v.)

SADI, or SAADI (Sheik Moslehedin Sadi el Shirazi), of Shiraz, one of the most celebrated lyric and moral poets of Persia, was born at Shiraz, in the year of the Hegira 571 (A. D. 1175), and died in the 116th year of his age (A. D. 1292). As his parents were poor, he was educated at the court of Abubeker, and received great favors from different monarchs of Persia. He spent thirty years in travelling, and did not begin to write until his ninetieth year. He completed his works, which are extensive, in the last twelve years of his life. The Persians esteem him exceedingly, on account of his golden maxims, which they consider as a treasure of true wisdom, and also on account of his pure, elegant, and simple style. Of his works, we possess, 1. a collection (Divan) of lyric poems in the Arabic and Persian languages, consisting partly of amatory poems, and partly of exhortations to partake in the joys of life, intermingled with serious reflections; 2. a moral work, under the title of *Gulistan* (the Garden of Roses), composed both of prose and verse, in eight books, with the following titles: "on the minds and morals of kings;" "on the minds and morals of dervises;" "on the quiet and happiness of contentment;" "on the importance of silence;" "on love and youth;" "on weakness and old age;" "on the education of children and good morals;" and, lastly, "on the art of associating with men:" 3. a work in verse, called *Bostan* (the Orchard), containing a collection of histories, fables and moral instructions; 4. and, lastly, a collection of moral sentences, also in verse, under the title of *Pendnahmeh*, or *Molamaat*. The complete works of Sadi have been published in Persian at Calcutta, in two large quarto volumes. Gentius has also published *Gulistan*, the finest of his poems, in Persian and Latin; and Dumoulin the same poem in Persian and English (Calcutta, 1823). Doctor Bernard Dorn has translated Three Pleasure-Walks from Saadi's Garden of Roses (Hamburg, 1827). The *Pendnahmeh* has been published separately in the East Indies and England, in the Persian and English languages. There are also translations of many of his lyric poems, by Ouseley and others; and the *Bostan* and *Gulistan* have been translated into a variety of languages. (See *Persian Literature*.) Franklin and Morier, in their travels, have described his monument, which is situated about nine miles to the north-east of Shiraz.

Safe-Conduct; a security granted by the sovereign authority, or persons delegated by it, to strangers, or other persons, to enable them to repair to, and return from a certain place undisturbed. In most of these cases, passports have now taken the place of special safe-conducts. Sometimes the safe-conduct is given to persons accused, to secure them against harm, when summoned to an examination. Thus the emperor Sigismund gave a safe-conduct to Huss, when he was cited to appear before the council at Constance (in this case, however, the safe-conduct was violated, and Huss was burnt, because the clergy persuaded the emperor that he need not keep his word towards a heretic); and Charles V gave a safe-conduct to Luther, to induce him to appear in Worms. Judges sometimes give safe-conducts to delinquents, to enable them to act in their affairs. In Germany, a safe-conduct is sometimes granted, to give a person accused an opportunity to defend himself without experiencing the usual disadvantages of a prosecution; and a safe-conduct is granted in criminal cases, "until something penal is proved against the accused;" e. g. if the accused thinks he can make out an *alibi*, or that the act with which he is charged is not punishable, &c.

Safety-Lamp. (See *Damps*.)

Saffron. The true saffron (*crocus sativus*) is a low, ornamental plant, with grass-like leaves, and large lily-shaped flowers, inhabiting the European continent and frequently cultivated for the sake of the yellow stigmas, which were formerly much employed in medicine, domestic economy and the arts: now they are used by painters and dyers; also in cookery and confectionary. The bulbs are planted in rows six inches apart, and three from bulb to bulb, in a well pulverized soil, not poor, nor a very stiff clay, and in the month of July. The flowers are collected in September, and the yellow stigmas, and part of the style, are picked out and dried on a kiln, between layers of paper, and under the pressure of a thick board, to form the mass into cakes. Two pounds of dried cake is the average crop of an acre, after the first planting, and twenty-four pounds for the two next years. After the third crop, the roots are taken up, divided, and transplanted. Other species of crocus are often cultivated in gardens, on account of the brilliancy of their flowers, and the early season at which they flower. The term *saffron* is often applied to the *carthamus tinctorius*, a large thistle-like plant, with orange-colored flowers, belonging to the family *compositæ*. The root is perennial, but the stem herbaceous. It is said to have been originally brought from the East, but is now naturalized in many parts of Europe, and is, besides, extensively cultivated. The flowers are used by the Chinese, to communicate some of the fine rose, scarlet, purple, and violet colors to their silks; for this purpose the flowers are thrown into an infusion of some alkali, and left to macerate; the colors are afterwards drawn out by the addition of lemon juice in various proportions, or of any other vegetable acid. Great quantities of these flowers are annually imported into Britain, for dyeing and painting. In Spain, they are used to color soups, olives, and other dishes. The Jews in Poland are remarkably fond of it, and mix it with their bread and most of their viands. In Germany, it is cultivated in a light soil, well pulverized, and is sown in rows about eighteen inches apart, and afterwards thinned, so as to leave three or four inches between the plants. In September the plants begin to flower, and the field is then gone over once a week for six or seven weeks, to gather the expanded florets, which are dried in a kiln, in the same manner as true saffron. The *carthamus* is sometimes used for culinary purposes, under the impression that it is the true saffron, but, if in too great quantities, communicates a purgative quality.

Saga. (See *Scandinavian Literature*.)

Sagamore. (See *Sachem*.)

Sage (*salvia*). This genus differs from

the majority of labiate plants in having but two stamens, instead of four. More than two hundred species are known which are herbaceous or shrubby, with opposite leaves, and flowers also opposite, or, more frequently, verticillate, forming spikes at the extremities of the stems and branches. The garden sage (*S. officinalis*) was formerly in great repute as a sudorific, aromatic, astringent, and antiseptic. It possesses stimulant properties in a high degree, is tonic and stomachic; the odor is strong, aromatic, and agreeable; the taste bitter, pungent, and somewhat resembling camphor, which substance, indeed, is contained in the plant. The leaves are often employed in seasoning dishes, especially in the south of Europe. The Chinese esteem this plant very highly, and use it as a tonic for strengthening the stomach, often giving it the preference to their own tea. We have several native species of *salvia* in the middle and more southern parts of the United States. Some of those species which inhabit the mountains of South America are very ornamental plants, remarkable for their long scarlet flowers.

Saghalien; a large island, or peninsula, on the eastern coast of Asia; lon. 142° to 145° east; lat. 45° to 54° north. The northern part belongs to the Chinese, the southern to the Japanese empire. It is uncertain whether it is connected with the continent by a low and narrow neck of land, or is entirely separated from it. It is inhabited by a few barbarous tribes.

Sago Palm (*sagus Rumphii*); a low species of palm, found wild in the East Indies. The trunk is upright, and is crowned at the summit with a tuft of pinnated leaves, composed of very numerous, long, narrow, pointed, smooth leaflets. The fruit is about as large as a pullet's egg, covered with shining scales, and is edible. The trunk contains a farinaceous pith, which is a very wholesome aliment: sago is made from it, as from that of most other palms. For this purpose, the pith is taken out, bruised in a mortar, and put into a cloth or strainer: it is then held over a trough, and, water being poured in, the pith is washed through the cloth into the trough below: the water being then drawn off, the sago is taken out and dried for use or transportation. It is highly esteemed as an article of food. The preparation of sago, under different forms, constitutes a principal source of employment to the inhabitants of many parts of the coast of Malabar, and of several of the East India islands. Sago is granulated in a manner somewhat similar to that adopted in the preparation of tapioca (see *Manioc*), and in this state enters into commerce.

Saguenay; a river of Canada, which flows into the St. Lawrence in lat. 48° N., lon. 69° 40′ W. Its course is south-east. At its mouth it is about a mile wide, but higher up it has two or three times that breadth, and is deep enough for the largest ships. Its length is about 350 miles, and the tide flows up about 70 miles. Its current is remarkably rapid. The harbor of Tadousac, at its mouth, is sufficient to contain twenty-five ships of the line, affords good anchorage, and is well protected.

Saguntum; a celebrated city in Hispania Tarraconensis, near the river Turius (Murviedro). It was in alliance with Rome, and therefore attacked by Hannibal, 219 years B. C., and conquered after an obstinate siege; upon which the second Punic war commenced. The city of Murviedro (*Muri veteres*) now stands upon the same spot. In the war between Spain and France, the army of Valencia, under Blake, was defeated here by Suchet, October 25, 1811; in consequence of which the fort of Saguntum capitulated.

Sahara, Zaara, or the Great Desert; an immense tract of territory situated between the states of Barbary and the countries watered by the Niger, between lat. 16° and 30° N., and lon. 29° E. and 16° W.; superficial area, 1,800,000 square miles. In its greatest length, it extends nearly across Africa, from the Atlantic to the Nile, 45 degrees of longitude, or about 3000 miles; its breadth is about 15 degrees, or 1000 miles. But the name is usually limited to the main body of the desert, which lies to the west of Fezzan and Cassina, extending through about 30 degrees of longitude. It is the largest desert on the globe. A great part of the surface consists of a dead level. In some parts it is covered with small sharp stones; in some places the surface is diversified by ravines, rocks, and eminences covered with shrubs; other parts are composed of moving sand, which, when blown by the wind, sometimes produces the most terrible effects, and whole caravans have been found buried beneath it. This vast tract is occasionally diversified by oases (q. v.) in which a supply of water affords support to a certain number of inhabitants, or, in some, merely furnishes springs, for the refreshment of travellers. These places are inhabited by nomadic Arabs. Lions, panthers, enormous serpents, ostriches and gazelles are found here. This desert is traversed, for purposes of commerce, by means of the camel, by caravans sometimes consisting of 2000 persons. (See *Africa.*) These caravans convey from Northern Africa salt, cloths, and various kinds of European goods, receiving in return gold, ivory, and slaves. The coast of Sahara, extending along the desert, is, for the most part, rocky, dangerous, and destitute of harbors. Denham, Clapperton (q. v.), and Caillié (q. v.), are among the latest travellers who have crossed this desert.

Saigon; a city of Cochin-China, on the Dongnay, 56 miles from its mouth, in lat. 10° 50′ N., lon. 106° 42′ E., with a population of 150,000 souls, of whom 10,000 are Chinese. The largest vessels can ascend the river to Saigon, which has a safe and convenient harbor. The streets are regular, but filthy, and the houses are generally low, of wood, and thatched with straw. The citadel, which contains the royal palace and barracks, is situated on an elevation sixty feet above the river, and is strongly fortified. Mr. White, who visited it in 1819, saw 250 pieces of cannon here. There are also an extensive naval arsenal, a cannon foundery, with a great number of temples, several pagodas, and a Christian church in Saigon. Previously to 1800, the commerce was monopolized by the Portuguese; but other European nations, the Chinese, and Americans, have since engaged in it. Rice, betel nut, sugar, pepper, cinnamon, silk, cotton, ivory, gold, and silver, are the chief articles of export. (See *Cochin-China.*)

Sail. (See *Ship.*)

Sailing. (See *Navigation.*)

Saint. Names of persons and places beginning with this prefix, and not given here, will be found under the head of the word following it.

Saints (from the Latin *sanctus*, holy), in its widest sense, is used by Catholics and Protestants to signify the pious, who in this world strictly obey the commands of God, or enjoy, in the eternal world, that bliss which is the reward of such a life on earth. In a narrower and more usual sense, the word *saint* signifies certain individuals, whose lives were deemed so eminently pious, that the Greek and Roman Catholic churches have authorized the rendering of public worship to them: these two churches, however, by no means acknowledge, in all cases, the same saints. The doctrine of saints, and the ideas and usages which grew out of it; their worship and invocation; the power which they are considered to possess of interceding for men with God, and of working miracles; their peculiar patronage of particular individuals, &c.,—form one of the main points of difference between the Protestants and the adherents of the above-mentioned churches. The *Dictionnaire de Théologie* (Toulouse, 1817), a work exhibiting the Catholic faith, and defending it against Protestantism, speaks in the following manner of *saints*, in the narrower sense of the word: "The name of saint is given to a person who is not only much attached to the worship of the true God, but who is exempt from every considerable vice, and who practises the Christian virtues in an exalted degree; and as the bliss of heaven is the certain reward of such a life, we often understand by *saints* those who enjoy eternal felicity. When the church is convinced that an individual has led such a holy and pure life, when God has deigned to attest it by miracles, it places him among the number of the saints by a decree of canonization, and authorizes the faithful to render him public worship. (See *Canonization.*) The church, however, does not intend to intimate thereby that such an individual has been exempt from every weakness of humanity, and that he has never sinned: human frailty does not admit of this perfection." The article from which this definition is taken treats the worship and invocation of saints, and their intercession, as something essential to the Catholic faith; while there are other Catholic writers who explicitly say, that the church has made the worship of saints, not a matter of doctrine, but simply of discipline, as the Catholic writer of the article *Heilige*, in the German Conversations-Lexicon. Without further statement of the views of Catholic writers, among whom, as may be imagined, a great many shades of opinion prevail on this subject, from the enormous absurdity—by no means unfrequently maintained—that saints are persons who have led a life so much more virtuous than was necessary to obtain happiness in another state, that this surplus of virtue is made operative by their intercession for the salvation of others, down to the view of the German writer just mentioned, we refer the reader to the decree of the council of Trent, as the acknowledged orthodox basis of the veneration of saints, images, relics, &c. It is explicitly stated there, that Jesus Christ is the only Redeemer and Savior; but that it is "good and useful suppliantly to invoke saints, and to resort to their prayers and assist ance;" that they pray for men; that their bodies are to be venerated by the faithful; and that the images of Christ, of the Virgin Mother of God, and of other saints, are to be also venerated; "not that it is believed that any divinity or power resides in them, on account of which they are to be worshipped, or that any benefit is to be sought from them, or any confidence placed in images, as was done formerly by the Gentiles, who fixed their hope in idols; but that we honor the subjects represented, when we kiss their images, or uncover our heads before them," &c. This is accompanied with the usual anathema against all who teach or profess contrary doctrines. But so much depends upon the true understanding of the decrees on these points, and so easy is it to put various interpretations on human language, that we shall give that part of the decree of the twenty-fifth session of the council of Trent, which relates to the subject of this article, in the original.* The Catholic theology has two different words for the veneration of saints, and that of God and the Mediator, the former being called *dulia*, the latter *latria*; and the church must watch that the former does not degenerate into the latter. How much the worship of saints, and the great variety of human characters which thus became objects of veneration, contributed to the diffusion of Christianity in the middle ages; how it brought Christianity into connexion with the fine arts, by affording the most copious store of religious subjects to the genius of artists; and how the worship of the Virgin Mary became a very active element in the religion of the middle ages, as it still is a prominent feature in the Roman Catholic faith—would be highly interesting to consider; but our limits will not allow it. The Catholics regard their notions on the subject of saints as supported by different parts of the Bible, e. g. Timothy ii, 12, various passages in the Apocalypse, Jeremiah xv, 1 and 5, Luke xvi, 9, and the writings of many of the early fathers, as Origen, who wrote in the third century (1 *de Orat.*, n. 11, and several other places of the same character): for the invocation of the saints, they refer chiefly to Genesis xlviii, 16, John xii, 26, xvii, 20, and many passages in early Christian writers. The Protestants object to the whole doctrine, and allege that even Christ himself said, "There is none good but one, that is God;" that not only is the idea of saints, as intercessors, no where contained in the Bible, but that it originated centuries after the establishment of Christianity; that it is against the chief doctrine of Christianity, which declares all men to be sinners, and to be saved only by Christ; that it is impious to imagine God like an earthly king, who is influenced by the suggestions of those around him; that Christ's mediation is founded either on an atonement, which is the more general opinion, or on his bringing the gospel to men; and that it can be clearly proved that many saints, now so considered, never existed, but were the offspring of ignorance, mistaking, e. g. a Greek word in a church inscription for the name of the saint to whom the church was dedicated, and that others were of a very equivocal charac-

* "Mandat sancta Synodus omnibus Episcopis, et cæteris docendi munus curamque sustinentibus, ut juxta Catholicæ et Apostolicæ Ecclesiæ usum a primævis Christianæ religionis temporibus receptum, sanctorumque Patrum consensionem, et sacrorum Conciliorum decreta, in primis de Sanctorum intercessione, invocatione, Reliquiarum honore, et legitimo imaginum usu, fideles diligenter instruant, docentes eos, Sanctos, una cum Christo regnantes, orationes suas pro hominibus Deo offerre; bonum atque utile esse suppliciter eos invocare; et ob beneficia impetranda a Deo per Filium ejus Jesum Christum Dominum nostrum, qui solus noster Redemptor et Salvator est, ad eorum orationes, opem, auxiliumque confugere: illos vero, qui negant Sanctos, æterna felicitate in cœlo fruentes, invocandos esse; aut qui asserunt, vel illos pro hominibus non orare; vel eorum, ut pro nobis etiam singulis orent, invocationem esse idololatriam, vel pugnare cum verbo Dei, adversarique honori unius mediatoris Dei et hominum Jesu Christi; vel stultum esse in cœlo regnantibus voce vel mente supplicare, impie sentire. Sanctorum quoque martyrum, et aliorum cum Christo viventium sancta corpora, quæ viva membra fuerunt Christi, et templum Spiritus sancti, ab ipso ad æternam vitam suscitanda et glorificanda, a fidelibus veneranda esse, per quæ multa beneficia a Deo hominibus præstantur: ita at affirmantes, Sanctorum Reliquiis venerationem atque honorem non deberi, vel eas, aliaque sacra monumenta a fidelibus inutiliter honorari, atque eorum opis impetrandæ causa Sanctorum memorias frustra frequentari, omnino damnandos esse, prout jampridem eos damnavit, et nunc etiam damnat Ecclesia. Imagines porro Christi, Deiparæ Virginis et aliorum Sanctorum in templis præsertim habendas, et retinendas; eisque debitum honorem et venerationem impertiendam; non quod credatur inesse aliqua in iis divinitas, vel virtus, propter quam sint colendæ; vel quod ab eis sit aliquid petendum; vel quod fiducia in imaginibus sit figenda, veluti olim fiebat a Gentibus, quæ in idolis spem suam collocabant; sed quoniam honos qui eis exhibetur, refertur ad prototypa, quæ illæ repræsentant; ita ut per imagines, quas osculamur, et coram quibus caput aperimus et procumbimus, Christum adoremus, et Sanctos, quorum illæ similitudinem gerunt, veneremur, id quod Conciliorum, præsertim vero secundæ Nicænæ Synodi, decretis contra imaginum oppugnatores est sancitum."

ters;* that fraud evidently sometimes had part in the creation of saints; and that a doctrine, which has led, for centuries, and so universally, to such gross superstitions, as Catholics themselves admit, have often arisen from the doctrine of saints, notwithstanding these superstitions are not supported by the council of Trent, must be highly dangerous; for the essential question with regard to every law and doctrine, is not For what was it intended? but How does it operate? If Protestants do not see that the Bible contains any divine command which could fairly lead to the invocation of saints, and to the supposition of their intercession for men with God, still less do they find any ground for the veneration of relics.—The doctrine of saints seems to us to have essentially originated from the virtues displayed by the martyrs. Heroism in suffering always remained the most common ground of saintship, as, in fact, is natural, since the great Prototype of Christianity became such by his sufferings. When the gospel had filled the hearts of believers with the hope of an eternal life of felicity, death soon came to be considered as affording occasion for joy rather than sorrow to the friends of the departed. Cyprian (q. v.) pronounces this opinion distinctly in his *De Mortalitate*. The anniversaries of the death of friends were celebrated by partaking of the Lord's supper, and by a gift laid on the altar, in return for which the prayer for the soul of the deceased was introduced into the prayers which preceded the communion. If this was the case with all, it was naturally still more so with the martyrs whose death was their glory. Hence the anniversaries of their suffering were called the *dies natales, natalitia martyrum*, γενεθλια των μαρτυρων. We find in Eusebius (lib. iv, 15) the report of the martyrdom of bishop Polycarp, by the community of Smyrna. They say there, in answer to the reproaches of the heathens, "They (the heathen) do not know that we can never forsake that Christ, who has suffered for all the saved, nor can worship any one besides. Him we worship, as the Son of God; but the martyrs we love, as they deserve, on account of their unparalleled love of their King and Lord," &c. They continue: "We took up his bones, which are more precious than gold and jewels, and laid them down in the proper place; and God will grant, that we may assemble there in joy and gladness, and celebrate the festival of his martyrdom, in memory of the departed champions, and to exercise and prepare those who are still awaiting the struggle." In this passage we see, already, the beginning of the veneration of relics. By degrees, the veneration of martyrs and the estimation of their relics increased; and, according to the unanimous testimony of the most distinguished fathers of the church of the fourth and fifth centuries, they were even then invoked as intercessors at the throne of God. In ages when information is transmitted chiefly by tradition, facts easily become exaggerated, without intentional violation of the truth; and soon many miracles were reported to have been wrought by their relics or intercession. At the same time, it is undeniable, that, with the diffusion of Christianity, when danger was no longer connected with its profession, and many persons came over to this religion who had but an imperfect knowledge of it, and had not abandoned entirely their former superstitions, pagan notions often became blended with the new religion; and, as many statues of pagan deities were changed into those of martyrs and other persons distinguished for piety, so some hymns, originally addressed to these deities, were now sometimes addressed to departed Christians, who had been eminent for piety; and the special protection of certain persons or things, as ships, churches, &c., was attributed to them as intercessors with God. When monarchs became Christians, and the persecution of believers ceased, so that instances of martyrdom were no longer found, the retiring from the world to the seclusion of a convent, or other great sacrifices made from religious motives, often led to investing the deceased with the character of intercessors with God. A pious bishop, who had devoted his whole life to the welfare of his flock, was looked upon as retaining his care for it in the regions of eternal bliss; so that, by degrees, many saints arose; and it naturally happened that this honor was sometimes paid to unworthy persons, and sometimes actual fraud was committed to obtain it. It was not uncommon for a person to be

* Doctor Reichlin Meldegg, Catholic *professor ordinarius* of ecclesiastical history, and temporary dean of the theological faculty at Freiburg, says, in his Proposals for Reformations in the German Catholic Church, "The old Roman breviary, crammed with fictitious or much colored anecdotes of saints, with repetitions that weary, with passages of indecorous import, &c., requires a thorough revision." In another passage he says, "Some masses are founded on stories not sufficiently proved, or palpable fictions, as the mass of the *lancea Christi*, the *inventio crucis*, &c."

long considered and invoked as a saint, when it remained doubtful whether he was so regarded by the church. Hence we find that the council at Frankfort on the Maine, in 794, prohibited the invocation of new saints; and Charlemagne again, in 805, revived the decree. The pope at last took the matter into his own hands. Pope John XV, in 993, gave the first example of a canonization by the Roman see; and Alexander III declared, in 1170, that canonization was an exclusive right of the pope, with whom it has since remained.* (See *Canonization*, and *Beatification*.) Few popes have become saints. Pius V, in 1712, was the first for almost a thousand years, and, so far, has been the last. France, Naples, and the German empire, would not acknowledge the canonization of Gregory VII, by Benedict XIII, in 1728. One of the last, if not the very last canonization, is that of cardinal J. M. Tomasi, in 1807. Countries, cities, arts, trades, orders, things, &c., have their patron saints; but the church, it seems, determines nothing in relation to them. St. Denis is the patron of France; St. George, of Russia; Olaff, of Norway; Cnut or Canute, of Denmark; Nepomuc, of Bohemia; Cecilia, of music; Hubert, of hunting; Crispin, of shoemakers, &c. The Greek church (q.v.) does not acknowledge the saints canonized after its separation from the Western Church. (See *Acta Sanctorum*.)

SAINT-FOIN (*hedysarum onobrychis*); a plant, somewhat resembling the pea, which grows wild in the countries about the Mediterranean, and is often cultivated elsewhere for fodder. The stem is about a foot and a half or two feet high; the leaves are pinnate, composed of small leaflets; the flowers are pretty large and showy, of a fine pink color, and are disposed in a short spike, upon a long axillary peduncle. Cattle are extremely fond of it. In its wild state, it is only found on dry, warm, chalky soils, where it is of great duration; and it is chiefly in such districts that it is cultivated to advantage. Its peculiar value is, that it may be grown on soils unfit for being constantly under tillage, and which would yield little undergrass. The deeper the soil is stirred previously to sowing, the better The seed is generally put in broadcast, at the rate of three or four bushels to an acre; and sometimes a little red clover is sown afterwards, to produce a crop the second season, when the saint-foin plants are but small. Saint-foin is highly nutritive, either cut green, or made into hay. The produce, on a medium of soils and cultivation, may probably be estimated at from one and a half to two tons the acre. The usual duration of this plant in a profitable state is from eight to ten years. It ordinarily attains its perfect growth in about three years. The proportion of nutritive matter in saint-foin is estimated equal to that afforded by white and red clover.

* The above-mentioned decree of the council of Trent also guards against the introduction of new miracles, new relics, &c., if not approved of by the bishop of the diocese.

ST. ALBANS (anciently Verulam); a town in Hertfordshire, England, twenty miles north-west of London; population, 3653. St. Albans owes its name to Alban (q. v.), the first martyr in Great Britain, who was buried on a hill near the town, where a monastery was dedicated to his memory. In 1455, a battle was fought here between the Yorkists and the Lancasterians; and, in 1461, another battle was fought between the same parties.

ST. ANN; a city of New Brunswick. (See *Frederickston*.)

ST. ANTHONY'S FALLS. (See *Mississippi River*, and *Anthony's Falls*.)

ST. ANTHONY'S FIRE. (See *Erysipelas*.)

ST. AUGUSTINE; a city and seaport of East Florida, on a bay of the Atlantic, two miles within the bar; about thirty miles south of the mouth of St. John's river, eighty south of St. Mary's, three hundred and ten south of Charleston; lat. 29° 45′ N., lon. 81° 40′ W. The town is built on a peninsula, is of an oblong form, and consists of four principal streets. The situation is pleasant, and has the advantages of refreshing breezes, and the fragrance of orange groves. It has a good harbor, but the bar has only eight feet of water. The houses are built of stones formed by the accretion of shells, from the island of Anastasia, near the town. A fort, twenty feet high, with walls twelve feet thick, and mounting thirty-six guns, defends the town. In 1821, when Florida was ceded to the U. States, St. Augustine contained about 2500 inhabitants; and it has not increased. The appearance of this city indicates decay, and the country around it is too low and unhealthy to sustain it.

ST. CLAIR; a river which flows from lake Huron into lake St. Clair. It is about forty miles long, one mile wide, transparent, of easy navigation, and is a pleasant and noble stream.—*Fort St. Clair* is situated at the upper end of this river.

ST. CLAIR; a lake situated between lake Huron and lake Erie, and connected with both. It is about ninety miles in circumference, and has several fine islands. Its waters are remarkably transparent. Lat. 42° 52′ N.; lon. 82° 25′ W.

St. Cyr. (See *Cyr.*)

St. Domingo. (See *Hayti.*)

St. Elias; a mountain on the western coast of North America, situated about twenty-five miles from the Pacific ocean, in lat. 60° 27′ N., lon. 140° 51′ W. It rises 17,850 feet above the ocean, and stands so separate from other mountains as to be a very important landmark. Its top is always covered with snow. This is the most elevated summit of what is sometimes called the Cordillera of New Norfolk, and is one of the highest mountains in North America.

St. Evremond. (See *Evremond.*)

St. Francis; a river which rises in Missouri, and flows into the Mississippi in Arkansas, lat. 34° 45′ N. It is a large river, and was formerly navigable 300 miles for large keel boats; but the earthquakes of 1811—12 raised its channel so much, and so irregularly, as to cause the waters to overflow the banks, and form a vast number of lakes and irreclaimable swamps along its former course. At high water, this river is still navigable about 200 miles; and there are several considerable settlements about seventy miles from its mouth. A great deal of land on its banks is fertile; its waters abound with excellent fish; and the forests through which it flows afford abundance of the finest game.

St. Gall (in German, *Sanct Gallen*); a canton of Switzerland, in the north-west part of the confederacy, bounded north by the lake Constance, east by Tyrol, south by the cantons of Schweitz and Glarus, and west by that of Thurgau; square miles 2100: population 140,000, of whom rather more than one half are Catholics. The manufactures of this canton, principally of linen and muslins, are extensive, and furnish the chief occupation of the inhabitants. St. Gall is formed from the estates of the rich Benedictine monastery of the same name, which were secularized by the French, and was admitted into the confederacy in 1803. The constitution is aristocratical, the government being conducted by a great council of one hundred and fifty members, and an executive council of thirteen, composed of members of the former. The canton sends a member to the federal diet. In 1830, St. Gall was the theatre of revolutionary movements, which were quieted by seasonable concessions. (See *Switzerland.*) The capital, St. Gall, with a population of 9000, is distinguished by the manufacturing and commercial activity of the inhabitants. It contains the old Benedictine abbey, has two libraries rich in manuscripts, and some learned societies.

St. George's Bank; a fishing bank off the coast of Massachusetts, east of cape Cod.

St. Germain. (See *Germain.*)

St. John. (See *Bolingbroke.*)

St. John's Bread, or Carob-Tree (*ceratonia siliqua*); a middling sized tree, with tortuous branches, which grows wild in the countries about the Mediterranean, and particularly abounds in Barbary and Egypt. It belongs to the *leguminosæ*, and is allied to the locust. The flowers are diœcious, small, inconspicuous, and disposed in spikes; they are succeeded by long, indehiscent, thick pods, pulpy internally, and divided by several transverse partitions. The Moors make great use of the pods as an article of food, and they have a sweetish and very agreeable flavor. It is the only species of the genus.

St. John's Wort (*hypericum perforatum*). This plant is abundantly naturalized in the U. States. The stem is straight, one or two feet high, bearing oblong and obtuse leaves, with semi-transparent dots. The flowers are in a terminal corymb, and of a bright yellow color It formerly enjoyed a high repute for medicinal purposes, but is now entirely out of use. The flowers communicate a fine purple color to spirits and oils; and the dried plant, boiled with alum, dyes wool yellow. It formerly enjoyed much celebrity among the superstitious, as a charm against witchcraft, &c. The species of *hypericum* are numerous in the U. States. They are herbaceous or shrubby, with opposite entire and dotted leaves, and are rendered conspicuous by the fine golden yellow of the flowers.

St. Louis. (See *Louis, St.*)

St. Maria de Puerto Principe; a city of Cuba, capital of the department of the Centre, on the northern coast of the island, 300 miles south-east of Havana. It has a good harbor, and contains several hospitals. The population of the city and precincts is 49,012, consisting of 32,996 whites, 6165 free persons of color, and 9851 slaves. Lat. 21° 20′ N.; lon. 77° 45′ W.

St. Mary's River, and St. Mary's Falls. (See *Mary's River, St.*)

St. Pelagie. (See *Paris.*)

St. Peter's River. (See *Peter's River.*)

St. Pierre. (See *Pierre, Saint.*)

St. Real, César Vichard, abbé de; a

historian, born at Chamberry in 1639, studied with the Jesuits at Paris, where his talents and learning gained him friends. He accompanied the duchess of Mazarin to England, and afterwards resided again in Paris, assuming the title of abbé, although without having any benefice. His writings involved him in a controversy with Arnaud, who accused him of Socinianism. He died in 1692. His principal works are his *Discours sur la Valeur ;* his *Sept Discours sur l'Usage de l'Histoire ;* and his *Histoire de la Conjuration des Espagnols contre la République de Venise*, which partakes of the romantic, and is by no means equal, in point of style, to his model, Sallust. His *Don Carlos* is well written, but is likewise of a romantic character: his translation of Cicero's letters to Atticus is of less merit. A complete edition of his works was edited by Perau in 1757 (8 vols., 12mo.).

St. Salvador. (See *Bahia.*)

St. Salvador. (See *Cat Island.*)

St. Sebastian. (See *Rio Janeiro.*)

St. Simon. (See *Simon, St.*)

St. Thomas, Christians of. (See *Christians of St. Thomas.*)

Saintonge; formerly a province in the west of France, bounded by the Atlantic, Poitou, Guienne, and Angoumois. It belonged to the English from the time of Henry II, until it was conquered by Charles V. It now forms the department of the Lower Charente. The capital, Saintes, with 10,300 inhabitants, contains some fine remnants of ancient architecture.

Saker; a name formerly used for a small species of cannon. (See *Cannon.*)

Sakhara; the necropolis of ancient Memphis (q. v.), from whose ruins it is about two miles distant, on the edge of the Libyan desert. It is remarkable for its ancient monuments, among which are thirty pyramids, besides the ruins of a great number, and numberless grottoes, sarcophagi, the ibis-catacombs, &c.

Salacine. M. Leroux, a Frenchman, extracted this principle from willow bark, and presented a memoir* on it to the French academy in 1830. He recommends it as a febrifuge instead of quinine, and cases of cures with it have since been reported. Salacine (thus called by M. Leroux) is in the form of very fine nacreous white crystals, very soluble in water and alcohol, but not in ether. It is in a high degree bitter. The process of preparing it may be found in the National Gazette (Philadelphia) of January 18, 1831.

Saladin. (See *Salaheddin.*)

Salaheddin Yuseph Ben Ayub, usually called *Saladin*, a celebrated sultan of Egypt and Syria, was born, in the year 1137, in the castle of Tecnib, of which his father, a native of Curdistan, was governor. In 1168, he was chosen to succeed his uncle Siracouh in the command of the armies of the Fatimite caliph Adhed, or rather of the sultan Noureddin, his immediate superior. He terminated the dynasty of the Fatimite caliphs of Egypt (1171), at the command of Noureddin, and subsequently endeavored to supersede the minor son of Noureddin himself, but did not succeed until after his death (1174), when he was recognised sultan of Syria and Egypt by the caliph of Bagdat. The great object both of his religion and his politics was now to expel the Christians from Palestine, and to recover the city of Jerusalem. An atrocious massacre of Mohammedan pilgrims by the French lord du Chatillon, added still more to his ardor; and his vow of revenge against the perpetrator he was enabled to make good by his famous victory on the plain of Tiberias, in 1187, where he captured Guy de Lusignan with the chieftain Chatillon (whom he cut down after the battle with his own scimetar), and many more. The fruits of this victory were the towns of Acre, Said, and Barout; after which he laid siege to Jerusalem, which yielded (1187), in a capitulation, to the articles of which Saladin faithfully adhered. He then proceeded against Tyre, but failed, in consequence of the destruction of his fleet by the Franks. The intelligence of the loss of Jerusalem, reaching Europe, produced the crusade under the emperor Frederic Barbarossa (see *Frederic*), whose death inspired the Mussulman with hopes which were soon damped by the arrival of the forces of Richard Cœur-de-Lion of England, and of Philip Augustus of France. The recovery of Acre by the two kings took place in 1191; upon which event Philip returned to France, and Richard, after twice defeating the sultan, took Cæsarea and Jaffa, and spread alarm as far as Jerusalem. At length a truce was concluded between Richard and Saladin, by the terms of which the coast from Jaffa to Tyre was ceded to the Christians, whilst the rest of Palestine remained to the sultan. The departure of Richard freed Saladin from his most formidable foe. This active and able prince soon after died at Damascus (in 1193), in the fit-

* Messrs. Gay-Lussac and Magendie reported very favorably on this memoir to the academy.

ty-sixth year of his age. Though chargeable with unjustifiable means of acquiring power, Saladin employed it, when obtained, usefully for his subjects, whose burdens he lightened, whilst he benefited them by many useful works and establishments. Magnificent in his public undertakings, he was frugal in his personal expenses. In religion he was zealous for his creed almost to fanaticism, but faithful to his engagements. A lasting proof of the terror which his name inspired, was given by the Saladin Tenth, imposed by the authority of pope Innocent X on clergy and laity, for the support of the holy war. Saladin left a family of seventeen sons and one daughter, and was the founder of the dynasty of the Ayoubites.

Salamanca; capital of a province of Spain, in the southern part of the kingdom of Leon. It is in a picturesque and agreeable situation on the Tormes, which is here crossed by a stone bridge, half of which is of Roman workmanship; lat. 41° 5′ N.; lon. 5° 10′ W.; one hundred and twelve miles north-west of Madrid; population, 13,920, exclusive of the students and religious. It is badly built, with narrow, crooked and dirty streets, but has some handsome squares, of which the *Plaza Mayor*, where bull-fights are exhibited in June, is one of the finest in Spain. There are here twenty-five parish churches and thirty-seven convents. The numerous churches, with their works of sculpture and painting, are described in Ponz's *Viage de España*. The cathedral is a magnificent Gothic edifice, begun in 1513, and completed in 1734: it presents great inequalities and disproportions. The old church, built in the twelfth century, has several interesting monuments; and in a chapel belonging to it, the mass is said according to the Mozarabic manner. The Jesuits' college, built in 1614, is one of the most splendid which the order possessed in Spain, and, since their abolition in 1798, it has been, in part, occupied as a theological seminary. The university buildings consist of two divisions separated by a street, the *escuelas menores*, and the university, properly so called, or *escuelas mayores*, in which are the theological, law, medical, philosophical, philological, &c., lecture rooms. The university was founded in the thirteenth century, by Alphonso IX of Leon; and, in 1239, Ferdinand III united with it the Castilian university of Palencia. (See Davila's *Historia de Salamanca.*) Its reputation extended through Europe, and, at the end of the sixteenth century, it had, according to Medina (*Grandezas de España*), 7000 students; but, with the decline of literature in Spain, in the seventeenth century, it sank to a very low condition. According to Hassel, the number of students, in 1827, was but 418. There are also some other institutions for education at Salamanca. The banks of the Tormes, and the country to the west of Salamanca, were the scene of an engagement between the British under Wellington, and the French under Marmont, July 22, 1812. The French had abandoned the place, on the first attack by the allied Portuguese and English forces, June 16. Meanwhile, Marmont, having received reinforcements, advanced against the English; and, after various movements, the object of which was to cut them off from Ciudad Rodrigo and Salamanca, the battle took place in the narrow space on the Tormes. The French commander had formed his plan of attack judiciously, but incautiously extended his left wing too much—an error of which Wellington promptly took advantage. Marmont himself was so severely wounded, that general Clausel took the command, and prevented the total ruin of the army. The French forces retreated to Burgos, and their communication with the body of troops under Joseph Bonaparte, in the centre of Spain, was cut off.

Salamander (*salamandra*); a genus of reptiles closely allied to the frog, from which it differs in having an elongated body, terminated by a tail, and four feet of equal length. There are no gills in the adult animal, and the tympanum is also wanting. The jaws are armed with numerous small teeth; and there are two longitudinal rows on the palate. The third eyelid is wanting. Together with the frog, this genus is included under the order *batracia*, and is easily distinguished from the lizards by having no nails on the toes, a naked skin destitute of scales, and a heart with a single auricle. The young are born in the shape of tadpoles, are provided with gills, and have their tails vertically compressed. The land salamanders inhabit the water only during the tadpole state, or during the time that they are laying their eggs: they are distinguished by a rounded tail. The aquatic species remain during life in water, and are enabled to swim with considerable briskness by means of their compressed tails: sometimes, however, they quit the water at night, and, when unable to regain it, have been found in similar situations with the terrestrial species. They are endowed with an astonishing power of reproduction; and, when mutilated, their limbs, tail, and even their eyes, are restored at the end of two, three or six months, in warm climates, or a longer period in cold ones; and no difference of organization can be discovered on dissection. They may be suffocated in the same manner as frogs, by forcibly holding open the mouth. The common salamander of Europe (*S. vulgaris*) has been celebrated from antiquity for its supposed power of braving the fiery element. It is almost unnecessary to observe that this quality has been attributed to it without the slightest foundation: still the belief is not entirely eradicated among the common people, and the salamander continues to be an object of superstition in the eyes of many. It is a sluggish, clumsy reptile, six or eight inches long, of a blackish color, with large, irregular, rounded spots of bright yellow. It is found throughout Europe in moist places, under stones or the roots of trees, near the borders of springs, in deep woods, &c., and passes its life under ground, except during rains or at night, when it comes out, but does not wander far from its place of residence. It lives on slugs, insects, worms, &c., and, when met with, seems stupid, and does not appear to shun the presence of man or other animals. The skin exudes a mucous and acrid secretion in great abundance. It is ovoviviparous. It would seem that the U. States produce a greater variety of salamanders than any other part of the globe. Our species are, however, far from being well understood; and probably more remain to be discovered. What we know of them is chiefly contained in the Journal of the Academy of Natural Sciences of Philadelphia. We shall particularize the following, among the land salamanders:—*S. subviolacea;* a large, stout species, seven inches or more in length; blackish, with two rows of large, round, whitish spots on the back, becoming single on the tail; a few similar spots on the legs. It resembles the common salamander of Europe.—*S. faciata;* green; less than the preceding; blackish, with transverse bluish-white bands on the back; found from New Jersey to South Carolina, but rare.—*S. glutinosa;* green; a more slender species, with the tail nearly twice the length of the body; blackish, sprinkled on the upper parts of the body with white specks; length about six inches. It is found in most parts of the U. States, and as far north as lat. 43°.—*S. longicauda;* green; whitish, with numerous black specks; the tail longer in proportion than in any other species; total length six inches. It is found in the Atlantic states, but is more frequently met with in the limestone caves of the west.—*S. bilineata;* green; a small, slender species; above brown, beneath yellow, with two, or sometimes three, indistinct black lines; the tail is longer than the body, and compressed towards the extremity. It inhabits New England and the Middle States, and seems to be more brisk and lively in its motions than the other terrestrial species.—*S. cirrigera*, green; a species somewhat resembling the preceding in the distribution of its colors, but remarkable for having two short, fleshy *cirri* on the snout. It was found in the vicinity of New Orleans.—*S. erythronota* (the most common species); blackish, with a broad red stripe on the back. The young are destitute of the red stripe, and in some full grown individuals a small portion only is observable, or it is even entirely wanting.—*S. symmetrica* (Harlan); reddish, with a row of bright orange ocellated spots on each side; length about three inches The skin of this animal is rough, and apparently destitute of the mucous secretion common to the other species; the back is elevated, and the tail somewhat compressed An aquatic species, resembling it precisely, except in having the color of the back browner, and the tail much more compressed, is frequently met with; and perhaps the difference is only sexual—one of our more common species.—Among the aquatic salamanders we shall particularize, *S. dorsalis* (Harlan); resembling the preceding in size and the general distribution of the colors; but the *ocelli* are irregularly elongated, and sometimes form an almost continuous line; and there is a pale line on the back: the skin is smooth; the tail very much compressed, forming a distinct edge above and below; inhabits South Carolina.—*S. maculata;* green; a stout species; whitish, with numerous round specks of a reddish brown color; tail about as long as the body, and slightly compressed; grows to the length of five inches or more.—*S. ingens;* green; by far the largest species hitherto known; nearly a foot in length. It was discovered in the vicinity of New Orleans.—This is perhaps the most appropriate place to speak of several very singular North American animals, allied to the salamander:—*Menopoma Alleghaniensis*; an animal of disgusting appearance, with a broad, flattened head, bearing a general resemblance to a salamander, but much larger than any except the *S. ingens.* It appears to be destitute of gills at all periods of its existence. It is found in the Ohio and other western rivers, and is commonly called *ground-puppet, mud-devil, young alligator,* &c.—*Menobranchus lateralis* resembles the preceding in form, but the gills persist during life; an indistinct blackish band on each side. It attains the length of one or two feet, lives in the water, and is very voracious. It is found in the Ohio and the lakes.—*Siren lacertina;* an eel-shaped animal, having external gills, and two small feet, situated at the anterior part of the body. It conceals itself in the mud, but occasionally visits both land and water. It inhabits the Southern States. Two other species of siren are found in the same districts.—*Amphiuma means;* likewise an eel-shaped animal, but it has four very small rudimentary feet, which have two toes each. It burrows in the mud, in swamps, or in the vicinity of streams, and occasionally visits the dry land. It grows to the length of three feet, and is found in the Southern States. A second species, a *tridactyla,* distinguished from the former by having three toes on each foot, has been discovered in Arkansas.

SALAMANDER. (See *Gabalis,* and *Gnome.*)

SALAMIS (now Colouri); an island (area, 80 square miles) on the eastern coast of Greece, in the gulf of Argolis, separated from Attica by a narrow channel, about half a mile wide. It is celebrated for the naval victory gained by the Greeks over the Persians (B. C. 480). (See *Themistocles,* and the article *Navy.*)

SAL AMMONIAC. (See *Ammonia.*)

SALANGANE, or HIRUNDO ESCULENTA. (See *Birds' Nests.*)

SALEM. (See *Jerusalem.*)

SALEM, a seaport, and the capital of Essex county, Massachusetts, is chiefly built on a tongue of land, formed by two inlets from the sea, called North and South rivers, over the former of which is a bridge more than 1500 feet in length, connecting Salem with Beverly; and the South river forms the harbor. Salem is 14 miles north-east from Boston, 24 south of Newburyport, 450 from Washington; lat. 42° 34′ N.; lon. 70° 54′ W.; population in 1820, 12,731; in 1830, 13,886. This town is the second in Massachusetts in respect to population, and probably in respect also to wealth; but New Bedford now surpasses it in its amount of shipping, and Lowell and some other towns greatly exceed it in manufactures. The trade of Salem is principally with the East Indies, and it employs a very large capital. In 1818, the number of vessels employed in this trade was fifty-three, carrying 14,272 tons. The harbor of Salem has good anchorage; but vessels drawing more than twelve feet of water usually lighten their cargoes at some distance from the wharves. The situation of the town is low, but pleasant and healthy. It is well built, and many of the houses have pleasant yards and gardens. The houses which have been erected within thirty years are principally of brick, and many of them are large and elegant. The town exhibits little of the bustle of business, but has the appearance of order, neatness, and the quiet enjoyment of domestic comforts. It contains a court-house, a jail, an alms-house, a market-house, an East India marine museum, and a lyceum. It has eight banks, with a total capital of $1,850,000; five insurance companies, total capital $850,000; and one mutual insurance company, and an institution for savings. There are two libraries; an athenæum containing 6000 volumes, and a mechanics' library containing 1200 volumes. Three semi-weekly and two weekly papers are published. There are two white lead factories, sixteen tanneries, eleven rope and twine factories, and a chemical laboratory. The houses for worship are, three for Calvinists, four for Unitarians, two for Baptists, and one each for Episcopalians, Methodists, Christians, Roman Catholics, Friends and Universalists, making fifteen in the whole. There are eight schools exclusively for boys, consisting of a Latin grammar school, an English high school, and six English grammar schools. There are two English grammar schools for girls, and eight primary schools, which are attended by children of both sexes. There are also two infant schools, one private, the other supported by charity; a proprietors' school for young ladies; the Salem classical school; and many others. This statement indicates, what is really true, that the people of Salem pay great attention to the education of their children. No child in the town, that is old enough, and has health to attend school, wants the means of obtaining a good education. In 1801, a society was incorporated, composed of such persons as had sailed from this port round the cape of Good Hope or cape Horn, in the capacity of masters or supercargoes of vessels. The number of such persons living in Salem, in 1824, was about 160. This East India marine society is designed to afford relief to indigent members or their families, and to promote the knowledge of navigation and trade to the East Indies. The museum belonging to it is a very extensive and interesting cabinet of curiosities, collected from all parts of the world. It is visited free of expense, on obtaining admission from any gentleman of the society. Salem is, next to Plymouth, the oldest town in the state, and was settled in 1628. Its Indian name was *Naumkeag*, or *Naumkeak*.

Salep is obtained from the tuberous roots of one or more species of orchis, and is usually imported from Turkey and other parts of the Levant; though it may be prepared in any part of Europe, from many common species of orchis, as also, in all probability, in the U. States. The process consists simply in washing the roots, and rubbing off the brown skin, when they are dried, and afterwards ground into powder. This powder, as an article of diet, is esteemed highly nutritious, containing a great quantity of farinaceous matter in a small bulk. The roots are dug up as soon as the flower stalks begin to decay, and the newly formed bulbs, which have then attained their perfect state, are separated. An ounce of this powder and an ounce of portable soup, dissolved in two quarts of boiling water, will form a jelly capable of affording sustenance to a man for a day; consequently, it is of great use in long voyages, or travels by land.

Salernum (now Salerno); a city in the province of Picenum, in Lower Italy, remarkable for the *civitas Hippocratica*, or medical institution, called also *schola Salernitana*, which flourished there in the twelfth century after Christ, and was the nursery of all the medical faculties of Europe. This was the principal source of modern practical medicine; and the dietetical precepts of this school were put into verse, and widely diffused. (See *Medicine, History of*.)

Salesian Nuns. The nuns of the order of the visitation of the Virgin Mary are so called from their founder, Francis of Sales, by whom and his friend Chanta this order was established, in 1610, at Annecy, in Savoy, originally as a refuge for widows and sick females. In process of time, however, it was enlarged, and devoted principally to spiritual exercises and the healing of the sick: the occupants were clad in black, and so numerous that, in the eighteenth century, there were 160 convents and 6600 nuns. There are still convents of the Salesian nuns in the principal cities of Italy, particularly in Venice, Trieste and Breslau They now devote themselves to the healing of the sick and the education of young girls.

Salfi, Francesco, born in 1756, at Cosenza, in Calabria, after having received the rudiments of education, became his own teacher, and acquired extensive learning. After the earthquake, in 1783, he published a work entitled an Essay on Anthropological Phenomena, which treated on the moral influence of earthquakes upon man. Some of the opinions in this work were of so bold a kind that they were near bringing him under the displeasure of the higher powers. He settled in Naples, and, in the dispute between the Neapolitan court and the pope, took the side of his sovereign, by publishing three tracts, and was rewarded by a commandery. He next produced several dramatic pieces of merit. The government suspecting him of revolutionary principles, he thought it prudent to retire to Genoa. When the French penetrated into Italy, in 1796, he went to Milan, took a part in the conducting of some of the journals, and was afterwards employed by the Cisalpine government. In 1799, he was secretary-general of the Neapolitan republic. In 1800, when the French reconquered Italy, he returned to Milan. In 1801, he was appointed inspector of the great theatres at Milan, and professor of philosophy and history at the university of Brera. In 1807, he was made professor of diplomacy, and, in 1809, of the law of nations. He now published some tracts, poems and translations, and composed his tragedy of Pausanias. On the dissolution of the kingdom of Italy, in 1814, he was recalled to his native country, and received a pension and a place in the university. He afterwards took up his residence at Paris. He has here continued Ginguené's History of Italian Literature, and, in 1817, printed a Discourse on the History of Greece. Professor Salfi was one of the contributors to the *Biographie Universelle*.

Salians, Salic Franks; a people who first appeared on the island of the Batavi, and, when they were driven thence, among the Chamari, to the south of the Meuse. As long as the Cherusci are spoken of, nothing is heard of the Salii; but as soon as the latter are noticed, the Cherusci disappear, and are no longer mentioned. The Salians probably took their name from that of a river in their former country, and first used it when they emigrated to Batavia, upon which they bordered. From the Salians originated the Salic code of laws, which was probably drawn up in Latin, before the time of Clovis, by four of their most distinguished men —Arogast, Bodogast, Salogast and Windagast. It was in force, in some degree, even as late as the eleventh and twelfth centuries. The sixty-second article of this code is very remarkable, according to which, in Salic estates,—that is, those which the Salic Franks had obtained by conquest in Gaul and modern France,—the daughters were excluded from the inheritance, and the sons alone were considered capable of succeeding to it. Notwithstanding this article had reference only to private estates, the application of it was even extended to the throne; and it is certain that, from the earliest periods of the French monarchy, no princess succeeded to the throne, except by force of some law different from the ordinary usage. The Salic law was first alleged against Edward, in the contests between Philip VI of France and Edward III of England, about the French crown, and has, since that time, remained always in force.

Salic Law. (See *Salians.*)

Salieri, Anthony, imperial chapel-master at Vienna, was born in 1750, at Legnano, a Venetian fortress. He studied at Venice and Naples, under Pescetti, Gassmann and Gluck. His opera, the Danaides, was at first considered, in Paris, to be chiefly the work of Gluck. Some of his most celebrated works are *Tarare* (introduced on the Italian stage under the title of Axur, King of Ormus), *La Passione di Gesù Cristo*, *La Scuola dei Gelosi*, *La Ciffra*, *Palmira* (1795), *Armida*, *Semiramide*, the Fair of Venice, &c. He composed thirty-nine operas, partly German, partly Italian. His death took place May 7, 1825. Hummel, Moscheles (q. v.), and others, are his pupils.—See Mosel, *On the Life and Works of Salieri* (in German, Vienna, 1827).

Salii; priests of Mars, whose name is derived from *salire* (to leap, to dance). Numa fixed their number at twelve; Tullus Hostilius increased it. Their origin is thus accounted for by the Romans: In the time of Numa, Rome was desolated by a pestilence, which ceased when the gods let fall from heaven the *ancile* (a shield of a peculiar form). The soothsayers declared that this shield was the sign of the perpetuity of the Roman power, and advised that eleven others should be made similar to it, so that the true *ancile* could not be so easily purloined. This advice was followed, and all the *ancilia* were deposited in the *curia*. On the first of March every year, when the Salii offered sacrifices to Mars, they carried them about the city, clashing them together, executing warlike dances, and singing the Salian hymns—ancient songs in praise of Mars and the other gods and of distinguished men, particularly of Mamurius, who made the eleven shields The dress of the Salii was a purple tunic embroidered with gold, and bound with a brazen belt, and a toga, with a purple border. On their head they wore a high cap, in the form of a cone, with a sword by their side, a spear or rod in their right hand, and an *ancile* in their left. None but patrician youths, whose parents were alive, could be admitted among the Salii.

Salina; a post-township of Onondaga county, New York, 130 miles west of Albany. It includes Onondaga lake, and the principal salt springs in the state. The water of the lake is salt; and wells dug on its margin, and springs flowing into it, are also salt. Very extensive salt works have been established for several years. The state of New York owns these waters, and exacts a duty of 12½ cents a bushel on all the salt manufactured from them. From 16 to 25 ounces of salt are obtained from a gallon of water. Besides the muriate of soda, small portions of the muriate of lime, sulphate of lime, oxide of iron, and Epsom salts, are contained in the water; but these are easily separated. More than half a million of bushels of salt are annually produced, and these waters are doubtless capable of yielding a very much greater quantity. Most of the salt hitherto made has been fine; probably owing to its not being allowed proper time to form into large crystals. The price is about 25 cents a bushel. The outlet of Onondaga lake communicates with Seneca river, through which is opened an extensive boat navigation. The Erie canal passes through the south part of Salina, and a side-cut connects it with the village. There are four considerable villages in the township —Salina, Liverpool, Syracuse and Geddes. The whole contained, in 1830 6920 inhabitants.

Saline; a river of Illinois, which flows into the Ohio about twenty-six miles below the Wabash. It is navigable for boats thirty miles. The U. States have extensive salt works on this river, twenty miles by the river, ten in a direct line from its mouth, and twelve miles from Shawueetown. Salt is sold here at from 50 to 100 cents a bushel.

Salisbury, Earl of. (See *Cecil.*)

Salisbury, or New Sarum; an ancient city of England, in Wiltshire, on the Avon. The cathedral is one of the finest in Europe, and is of the architecture of the thirteenth century. The whole building may be viewed as composed of the church, the tower and spire, the cloister and the chapter-house. The church consists of a nave, with two lateral aisles, a bold and lofty porch projecting on the north side, a large transept with an eastern aisle, a choir with lateral aisles, and a second or small transept with an aisle, a Lady chapel at the east end, with an intermediate vestibule or double aisle terminating the choir. On the south side of the church are a cloister, chapter-house, consistory court, and a vestry. The tower, which is built on four massive pillars in the centre of the church, is surmounted by a spire, rising to the height of 400 feet. The bishop's palace is a large irregular building, the work of different periods, the earliest part being of the same age as the cathedral. The college of matrons, for the widows of clergymen, erected by bishop Ward, is a regular building, with small but commodious gardens. There are three parish churches in the city. In Catholic times, Salisbury contained a great variety of religious establishments, the remains of a few of which may be traced; and the hospital of St. Nicholas continues still to maintain a master and twelve poor persons. There are six other hospitals in the city. Salisbury is noted for its manufacture of cutlery. Formerly it was also remarkable for its manufacture of woollens; but that branch of trade is now nearly extinct. Salisbury sends two members to parliament. Population, 8763. Twenty-one miles north-east of Southampton.

Salisbury Plain extends from Salisbury twenty-five miles east to Winchester, and twenty-eight west to Weymouth. Its breadth in some places is near thirty miles. Numerous flocks of sheep are fed here. The famous Stonehenge, and other antiquities, both British and Roman, are found in this plain.—Stonehenge consists of a great collection of stones of immense size, which, from their being some erect, some reclining, but most of them lying upon the ground, seem to have formed at one time an extensive building. They form a perfect ruin, a confused heap of standing and fallen stones, many of them squared and hewn by art. By comparing their relative situations, the shape and dimensions of the original structure can still be traced, which is supposed to have been a Druidical temple of enormous size. It is an object of great interest to the antiquary, and has excited more inquiry and speculation than any other ruin of the kind in Great Britain. But no important discoveries have been made within it; and its founders, the date of its erection, and the process by which such enormous masses of stone were conveyed to this desolate spot, and raised into their respective situations, are buried in profound obscurity. The total number of stones of which the structure was composed, appears to have been one hundred and nine.

Salisbury; a post-town, and capital of Rowan county, North Carolina, thirty-four miles south-west of Salem. It contains the county buildings, an academy and a church. Population in 1830, 1613. Near this town there is a remarkable wall of stone, laid in cement, plastered on both sides, from 12 to 14 feet in height, and twenty-two inches thick. The length of what has been discovered is about 300 feet. The top of the wall approaches within one foot of the surface of the ground. A similar wall has been discovered about six miles distant, which is from four to five feet high, and seven inches thick. No definite information exists respecting their age and use.

Saliva; the fluid which is secreted by the salivary glands into the cavity of the mouth. The secretory organ is composed of three pair of salivary glands. The saliva is continually swallowed with or without masticated food, and some is also spit out It has no color nor smell: it is tasteless, although it contains a little salt, to which the nerves of the tongue are accustomed. Its specific gravity is somewhat greater than that of water. The quantity of twelve pounds is supposed to be secreted in twelve hours. During mastication and speaking, the secretion is augmented, from the mechanical pressure of the muscles upon the salivary glands. Those who are hungry secrete a great quantity, from the sight of agreeable food. It assists the spirituous fermentation of farinaceous substances; hence barbarous nations prepare an inebriating drink from chewed roots. Saliva appears to consist; in a healthy state of the body, of water, which constitutes at least four fifths of its bulk, mucilage, albumen, and saline substances. The use of the saliva is, It It augments the taste of the food, by the evolution of sapid matter. 2. During mastication, it mixes with, dissolves, and resolves into its principles, the food, and changes it into a pultaceous mass, fit to be swallowed: hence it commences chymification. 3. It moderates thirst, by moistening the cavity of the mouth and fauces.

SALKELD, LITTLE; a hamlet of England, in Cumberland; near which is a circle of stones, seventy-seven in number, each ten feet high. At the entrance is a single one fifteen feet high. These are called by the people *Long Meg and her daughters*. They are probably a Druidical work. Within the circle are two heaps of stones, under which dead bodies are supposed to have been buried. 285 miles north of London.

SALLEE; a seaport on the western coast of Morocco, at the mouth of a river of the same name, formerly the great hold of Moorish piracy; and immense depredations were committed from it upon European commerce. The river, which formerly admitted large vessels, is now choked up with sand. Sallee has a battery of twenty-four pieces of cannon, which commands the road, and a redoubt that defends the entrance of the river. On the opposite side of the river stands Rabat, called often New Sallee. It has been chiefly frequented by Europeans, and contained once numerous factories belonging to them; but by order of the emperor, the trade has been transferred to Mogador. Lon. 6° 40′ W.; lat. 34° 3′ N.

SALLUSTIUS, Caius Crispus, was born at Amiternum, a municipal city in the territory of the Sabines, in the year of Rome 668 (86 B. C.). His gay spirits and his fiery and restless disposition led him into many youthful excesses; yet it is not improbable that he was less corrupt than has been commonly represented. We ought also to take into consideration the prevailing state of morals at that time, when we sit in judgment on his faults. His faithful and vigorous descriptions of the moral depravity of the Romans plainly show that he was accurately acquainted with it. Through the favor of Cæsar, he was appointed pretor, and sent to Numidia, where he collected great treasures. When he returned to Rome, he played a conspicuous part, and in the latter part of his life appears to have reflected on the vices of his youth, and to have lived more moderately. His death took place in the year of Rome 719 (B. C. 35). During the period of his retirement, he made the history of his country his principal study. But, unfortunately, we have only a few fragments of the copious history which described the period from the death of Sylla to the conspiracy of Catiline. Two other historical writings of his have come down to us entire; one a description of the wars of the Romans against the crafty Jugurtha, the other of the conspiracy of Catiline. These are distinguished alike for their contents and their style. Sallust appears to have taken Thucydides as a model; but, in the opinion of Quinctilian, he far surpasses him. The style of Sallust is vigorous, pure, and often very eloquent; his thoughts possess dignity, strength, truth and clearness. The principal editions of this author are those of Corte, with a copious commentary (Leipsic, 1724), and Haverkamp (Amsterdam and Utrecht, 1742).

SALLY. In the defence of a place, if particular reasons do not determine to the contrary, frequent sallies are beneficial, in order to keep the enemy at a distance; to destroy the works; to bring in, if possible, the means of subsistence from the surrounding country; to afford an easy entrance to men or arms; or to favor the operations of a friendly force without. Aided by such a force, they are often decisive against the besiegers. They are undertaken to the most advantage after midnight, in cloudy or rainy weather; but they must be so managed as to surprise the enemy, and, therefore, must be carried on with great secrecy; therefore the most resolute and faithful men are to be selected, and on going out all noise must be avoided. The object of the sally determines the number of soldiers; they are frequently accompanied by artillery and cavalry; they must in no case separate themselves too far from the fortification, to avoid being cut off, and, on their return, must neither obstruct the defence, nor occasion any confusion which may favor the attack of the enemy. By sallies with a small number of troops, the besieged often endeavor to entice the besiegers within the fire of the fortress, or to harass and exhaust them. A commander of a fortress will make use of sallies as long as he is able, as the best means of defence.

SALLYPORT; a large port on each quarter of a fireship, out of which the officers and crew make their escape into the boats as soon as the train is fired.

SALM. Previously to the French revolution, there were two counties of this name, that of Upper Salm, chiefly in Lorraine, and that of Lower Salm, chiefly in

Luxemburg. Their possessions having been annexed to France in 1802, they were indemnified from the secularisations beyond the Rhine. The elder house, Obersalm, or Upper Salm, is divided into the three branches of Salm-Salm, Salm-Kyrburg and Salm-Horstmar. The house of Niedersalm, or Salm-Reiferscheid, is divided into three branches, Salm-Krantheim, Salm-Reiferscheid, and Salm-Dyk, with domains in Suabia, the Prussian province of the Lower Rhine, and Luxemburg. All the possessions of both houses have been mediatised. (See *Mediatisation.*)

Salm-Dyk, Constantia Maria de Theis, princess of, was born at Nantes in 1767, of a noble Picard family. Her youth was devoted to study. In 1789, she was married to Pipelet, a surgeon, and went with him to Paris, where her Sappho, a lyrical tragedy, in three acts, was performed more than 100 nights with great applause. Her *Epître aux Femmes* was also received with the greatest favor. In 1803, Mad. Pipelet was married to the count of Salm-Dyk (created prince in 1816), and has since published several *Éloges* and *Discours Académiques*. Her romance *Vingt-quatre Heures d'une Femme sensible* displays great power of delineation. A collection of her poems (*Poésies de la Princesse de Salm*) appeared in 1817. The princess is a member of several learned societies and academies.

Salmasius, Claudius (the Latinized name of Claude de Saumaise), distinguished for his profound and extensive learning, was born at Sémur, in Auxois (now the department Côte-d'Or), in 1588. His father, a respectable magistrate, and a learned man, instructed him in the ancient languages, and then sent him to Paris to study philosophy. His edition of Florus, which was published in 1609, and, according to his own assertion, had already been completed several years, is a remarkable proof of his early erudition. In 1606, he went to Heidelberg, to study law, under the celebrated Gothofredus (Godefroi). The excellent university library there gave him an opportunity to gratify his literary curiosity, and to extend his reputation by the publication of his learned labors. On his return to France in 1610, he began to practise his profession, but soon withdrew from it to devote his whole time to study; and the rest of his life was occupied with critical labors and learned controversies. His mother, a Calvinist, had educated him in Protestant principles and, in 1623, he married the daughter of a respectable Protestant. Several years later, he passed some time at the country seat of his father-in-law, near Paris, where he completed his great labor on Pliny and Solinus. In 1629, his father was desirous of transferring to him his place, and the parliament of Dijon made no objection, although he openly professed Calvinism; but the keeper of the seals, Marillac, refused to sanction the step. The invitations of the universities of Padua and Bologna were declined by Salmasius; but, in 1651, he accepted the offer of the professorship, which had been held by Joseph Scaliger at the university of Leyden. His friends made several attempts to induce him to return to France, and cardinal Richelieu offered him a pension, on condition of his writing a history of his ministry. But Salmasius declined all these offers. In 1649, Charles II of England induced him to write a defence of his father (*Defensio regia pro Carolo I*), which was answered by Milton's *Defensio pro Populo Anglicano.* (See *Milton.*) The zeal with which Salmasius defended royalty in this work offended his republican patrons in Holland, and he therefore the more readily accepted the invitation of queen Christina to visit Sweden (1650). But the climate of Sweden was so unfavorable to his health, that he returned to Holland the next year, and died in 1653, at Spa, whither he had gone for his health. Although virulent in controversy, Salmasius was remarkably gentle and kind in private, and at home was entirely governed by his wife. The most important of his numerous works are his *Plinianæ Exercitationes in Solinum;* his edition of the *Scriptores Historiæ Augustæ; De Mutuo; De Modo Usurarum; De Fœnore Trapezetico; De Re militari Romanorum; De Re Hellenistica; Observationes in Jus Atticum et Romanum*, &c. All his works display a wonderful variety, extent and depth of erudition, but are less remarkable for taste or judgment. His learning was aided by a powerful memory. Besides the classical and many modern languages, he was acquainted with Hebrew, Chaldaic, Arabic, Persian, Coptic, &c He labored with great industry, but used the file sparingly.

Salmon (*salmo salar*); a celebrated fish belonging to the trout genus, which inhabits the northern seas, and ascends the rivers in spring for the purpose of depositing its spawn. The excellence of its flesh is well known, but it varies somewhat in different waters. In certain districts, the abundance of this fish forms a great source of wealth to the inhabitants, and it often forms a chief article of sustenance. The salmon inhabits the European coasts, from Spitzbergen to Western France, but is never seen in the Mediterranean. On the western shores of the Atlantic it is found from Greenland to the Hudson, but is exceedingly rare in the latter river, and never penetrates farther south. It ascends the St. Lawrence to lake Ontario, and enters the tributaries of that lake; but the fall of Niagara presents a barrier to its farther progress into the continent. In the North Pacific the salmon again makes its appearance, and frequents, in vast numbers, the rivers of North-western America, Kamtschatka, and Eastern Asia. A cold climate and clear water seem to be most congenial to its constitution. The salmon grows to the length of four, five or six feet, and usually weighs twelve or fifteen pounds. The body is elongated and compressed; the color silvery-gray, with spots; the head of moderate size, and the upper jaw rather the longest. Almost all parts of the mouth, and even the tongue, are furnished with pointed teeth, as in the other trouts, and, like them, it has an adipose fin upon the lower part of the back. All the trouts are voracious and carnivorous, and in general seek the purest water. As soon as the ice melts, the salmon enter the mouths of rivers, and, as has been ascertained, almost always of those which gave them birth. They swim usually in immense bodies, in the middle of the stream, and near the surface: their progress is slow, and they make a great noise in sporting, if the weather be fine. They are easily frightened, either by a sudden noise or floating timber, and on such occasions sometimes turn aside from their course and return to the sea. When farther advanced, they make the most determined efforts to surmount rapids and cascades, and will leap a fall of twelve or fifteen feet in perpendicular height. If alarmed, they dart away with such rapidity that the eye can scarcely follow them. The velocity of this motion has been proved to equal twenty-five to thirty miles per hour. They penetrate far into the interior of the continents, and deposit their spawn in the lakes, &c., about the head-waters of the longest rivers. When the young are about a foot in length, they descend the rivers and take refuge in the ocean. Late in the following spring or in the beginning of summer, and after the old ones have ascended, the young again enter the rivers, and are then about eighteen inches in length. They again seek the ocean on the return of frosts. At two years old, the salmon weighs six or eight pounds, and requires five or six years to attain the weight of ten or twelve. The salmon-fishery is one of the most important branches of business in the north of Europe. Immense quantities of this fish are taken every year, and form a considerable accession to the general mass of nutriment. The flesh is bright orange, but, though delicious to the taste, and very much sought after, is difficult of digestion. Formerly the New York market was supplied with fresh salmon from the Connecticut river; but, since the erection of mill-dams and other obstructions, the fish have become scarce there, and now are brought almost exclusively from the state of Maine, packed in ice. Fresh salmon are very seldom seen in Philadelphia.

Salonica, or Saloniki, or Salonichi (anciently Therma; afterwards called by Cassander Thessalonica); a city of European Turkey, in Macedonia, at the north extremity of a gulf, to which it gives name; anciently Thermaic gulf; 272 miles west of Constantinople; lon. 22° 56′ E.; lat. 40° 38′ N.; population, 70,000; 35,000 Turks, 20,000 Greeks, 12,000 Jews, and 3000 Franks. It is the residence of a pacha of three tails, and of a Greek archbishop, has an excellent commercial position, and, of the towns of European Turkey, is second only to Constantinople in point of commerce. It is pleasantly situated, being built on the declivity of a hill; and the approach to it from the sea is very imposing. The domes and minarets of mosques, together with other buildings, environed with cypresses, give it an air of splendor, but, like other Turkish towns, its interior by no means corresponds with its external magnificence. It is situated in the vicinity of a fertile district, and exports cotton, tobacco, corn, and wool. The ancient walls are nearly entire, and are five or six miles in circuit; but within them are many void spaces. Of the remains of antiquity the most remarkable are the *propylæa* of the ancient Hippodrome. The whole sculpture is in marble, and is considered among the finest pieces of art which have escaped the ravages of time. To the early Christians in this city, St. Paul addressed two epistles.

Salsafy (*tragopogon porrifolius*). This plant, which is often cultivated in gardens for culinary purposes, is sometimes called *vegetable oyster*, from a similarity in the taste of the root to the flavor of that fish. It belongs to the *compositæ*, and is allied to the endive and dandelion: the root is long, white, tapering, and fleshy; the stems upright, two or three feet high, smooth, striated, hollow, and branching; the leaves are alternate, embracing the stem, narrow, and long; the flowers are solitary and terminal, situated upon swelling peduncles; the involucre or common calyx consists of several lanceolate, very acute and equal leaflets, much longer than the corollas; the corollas are violet purple. It grows wild in the south of Europe. The roots form a light and wholesome aliment, and are cooked in various manners. The mode of cultivation is, in every respect, similar to that of the carrot. Many prefer the root of the *scorzonera Hispanica*, a plant somewhat resembling the former, but with yellow flowers. The root of this last is carrot-shaped, about as thick as one's finger, tapering gradually to a fine point, and thus bearing some resemblance to the body of a snake; hence the name of *viper's grass*. The outer rind being scraped off, the root is steeped in water in order to abstract a part of its bitter flavor, and is then boiled or stewed in the manner of carrots or parsneps. The roots are fit for use in August, and keep good till the following spring. Its culture is the same as that of the salsafy, and it is a native of the same part of the globe.

Salsette; an island on the western coast of Hindostan, formerly separated from Bombay by a strait 200 yards wide, across which, in the year 1805, a causeway was carried. It is eighteen miles long by fourteen broad, and is well adapted for the cultivation of sugar, cotton, hemp, indigo, &c.; but it has hitherto been kept in a state of nature, for the purpose of supplying Bombay with wood, charcoal, and sea salt, of which there is a considerable manufactory. Salsette is remarkably rich in mythological antiquities; and the remains of reservoirs, with flights of stone steps round them, and the ruins of temples, &c., indicate a former state of prosperity and extensive population.

Salt. This term was originally employed to denote *common salt*, but was afterwards generalized by chemists, and employed by them in a very extensive and not very definite sense. They understood by it any body which is sapid, easily melted, soluble in water, and not combustible; or a class of substances midway between earths and water. Many disputes arose concerning what bodies ought to be comprehended under the designation, and what ought to be excluded. Acids and alkalies were allowed by all to be salts; but the difficulty was, to determine respecting earths and metals; for several of the earths possess all the properties which have been ascribed to salts, and the metals are capable of entering into combinations which possess saline properties. In process of time, however, the term *salt* was restricted to three classes of bodies, viz. *acids*, *alkalies*, and the *compounds* which acids form with alkalies, earths, and metallic oxides. The two first of these classes were called *simple salts*; the salts belonging to the third class were called *compound* or *neutral*. This last appellation originated from an opinion long entertained by chemists, that acids and alkalies, of which the salts are composed, were of a contrary nature, and that they counteracted one another; so that the resulting compounds possessed neither the properties of acids nor of alkalies, but properties intermediate between the two. Chemists have lately restricted the term *salt* still more, by tacitly excluding acids and alkalies from the class of salts altogether. At present, then, it denotes only the compounds formed by the combination of acids with alkalies, earths, and metallic oxides, which are technically called *bases*. When the proportions of the constituents are so adjusted that the resulting substance does not affect the color of infusion of litmus, or red cabbage, it is then called a *neutral salt*. When the predominance of acid is evinced by the reddening of these infusions, the salt is said to be acidulous, and the prefix *super*, or *bi*, is used to indicate this excess of acid. If, on the contrary, the acid matter appears to be in defect, or short of the quantity necessary for neutralizing the alkalinity of the base, the salt is then said to be with excess of base, and the prefix *sub* is attached to its name. As almost every acid unites with every base, and sometimes in several proportions, it follows that the number of salts must be immense. Several thousands are already known, although not above thirty were believed to exist fifty years ago. The early names of the salts, so far as these bodies were known to chemists, were wholly destitute of scientific precision. At present, however, they are universally designated according to the nomenclature of Morveau. The name of each salt consists mainly of two words, one generic, the other specific. The generic word precedes the specific, and is derived from the acid; the specific comes from the base. For example, a salt consisting of *sulphuric acid* and *soda*, is spoken of generically under the name of a *sulphate*, and specifically, by adding the name of the base; thus, *sulphate of potash*. The termination *ate* corresponds with the acid whose termination is in *ic*, and the termination *ite* with the acid whose termination is in *ous*; thus *sulphuric* acid gives *sulphates; sulphurous* acid, *sulphites*. There are some acids containing less oxygen than those that terminate in *ous:* in such case, the word *hypo* is prefixed; thus we have *hypo*-sulphurous acid, *hypo*-nitrous acid, giving also salts that are called *hypo*-sulphites, and *hypo*-nitrites. When the salt is a compound of one atom, or proportional of acid with one of base, it is distinguished simply by the words denoting the acid and the base, without the addition of any prefix. If the salt contains *two* atoms of acid united to *one* atom of base, the Latin numeral adverb *bis* or *bi* is prefixed. Thus *bisulphate of potash* is a salt composed of two atoms sulphuric acid and one atom potash. Were there three, four, &c., atoms acid, the numeral adverbs *ter*, *quater*, &c., would be prefixed. Thus *quateroxalate of potash* means a compound of four atoms oxalic acid and one atom of potash. When two atoms of base are combined with one atom of acid, this is denoted by prefixing the Greek numeral adverb *dis*. Thus *diphosphate of potash* means a compound of two atoms potash with one atom phosphoric acid. The prefixes *tris*, *tetrakis*, &c., indicate three, four, &c., atoms of base with one atom of acid. Salts of this description were formerly termed *sub-salts;* at least in those instances where an alkaline reaction was produced upon test-liquors from the excess of base. We have stated above that salts are at present understood to be compounds only of acids and bases. The discoveries of sir H. Davy require us to modify, in a number of instances, this generally received definition. Many bodies, such as common salt and muriate of lime, to which the appellation of *salt* cannot be refused, have not been proved to contain either acid or alkaline matter, but must, according to the strict logic of chemistry, be regarded as compounds of chlorine with metals. Such compounds, possessing, for the most part, the properties of solubility in water, and sapidity, are to be included under the general name of salts. They are denominated *chlorides*, *iodides*, and *bromides*, of the metals, according to the particular constitution of each. Thus the compound of chlorine and calcium, formerly known as muriate of lime, is called the *chloride* of calcium. The solubility of salts in water is their most important general quality. In this menstruum they are generally crystallized; and by its agency they are purified and separated from one another, in the inverse order of their solubility. The determination of the quantity of salt which water can dissolve, is not a very difficult process. It consists in saturating the water exactly with the salt, whose solubility we wish to know, at a determinate temperature, weighing out a certain quantity of that solution, evaporating it, and weighing the saline residue. We shall give the results of some experiments upon the solubility of a few salts.

Sulphate of Soda.

Temperature.	*Salt soluble in 100 parts of water,* Anhydrous.	Crystallized.
0,00°	5,02	12,17
11,67	10,12	26,38
17,91	16,73	48,28
28,76	37,35	161,53
30,75	43,05	215,77
32,73	50,65	322,12
40,15	48,78	291,44
50,40	46,82	262,35
59,79	45,42	
70,61	44,35	
84,42	42,96	
103,17	42,65	

Hence it appears that the solubility of sulphate of soda follows a very singular law After having increased rapidly to about the temperature of 33°, where it is at its maximum, it diminishes to 103,17°; and at that point it is nearly the same as at 30,5°.

Solubility of Chloride of Potassium.

Temperature.	Salt dissolved in 100 water.
15,64°	43,50
49,31	55,63
74,89	65,51
105,48	77,89

Solubility of Chloride of Sodium (common Salt

Temperature.	Salt dissolved in 100 water.
13,89°	35,81
16,90	35,88
59,93	37,14
109,73	40,38

Solubility of Sulphate of Magnesia (Epsom Salt).

Temperature	In 100 water.
14,58°	103,69
39,86	178,34
49,08	212,61
64,35	295,13
97,03	644,44

Solubility of Nitrate of Potash (Nitre).

Temperature.	Salt dissolved in 100 water.
0,00°	13,32
5,01	16,72
11,67	22,23
17,91	29,31
24,94	38,40
35,13	54,82
45,10	74,66
54,72	97,05
65,45	125,42
79,72	169,27
97,66	236,45

(For the chemical, natural, historical, and economical history of the most important salts, see the articles upon their respective bases.)

Salt, Henry, born in Litchfield, and educated in the grammar-school of that town, was sent to London, and placed under the tuition of an artist, but had not been long with him, before lord Valentia made him an offer to take him, on his projected journey to India; and Mr. Salt accompanied him to India as his draftsman. During his travels in that country, and up the Red sea, and through Abyssinia back to England, they were gone four years; and, on their return, lord Valentia published his travels, in three volumes quarto, splendidly ornamented with plates, from the pencil of Mr. Salt. The Account of Abyssinia was written by Mr. Salt, who was employed to carry presents to the emperor of Abyssinia. Mr. Salt, on his return, published twenty-four Views taken in India, the Red Sea, Abyssinia, &c., folio (1809); and, in 1814, an account of a Voyage to Abyssinia, and Travels in the Interior of that Country, quarto. This was the narrative of a second journey which Mr. Salt made to that country, on his return from which he was appointed English consul-general in Egypt, where he engaged in active researches into the antiquities of that country. He died, near Alexandria, in 1827.

Saltpetre. (See *Potash.*)

Salt-water Baths: those which are taken in the water of the salt-springs, approach in virtue to the sea-baths. They are used chiefly in scrofulous and cutaneous disorders, inveterate gout and syphilis, lameness, rheumatism, tendency to catarrhs, &c. The daily repeated inspiration of the air near the salt-works is also beneficial in some complaints of the lungs. Even the drinking a small quantity of the brine, if not too strong, is of some use in the above mentioned complaints. These baths may be easily established wherever there are inland salt-works. There are several in Germany, much frequented. See John C. Reil, *On the Use and Application of the Brine-baths* (Halle, 1809), and Tolberg's *Experiments on the Use of Brine-baths* (Magdeburg, 1811), both in German. For *Sea-bathing*, see that article.

Salutation; the signs, which custom has rendered common, for expressing to others, in our intercourse with them, our esteem, love, submission, or good will. Greeting (in German, *gruss, grüssen*), is derived from the Low German *gröten*, to make great: thus God greet you, means, God make you great—bless you. Salutation sometimes consists of certain gestures. Sometimes an express assurance, or wish is added to these mute signs of feeling. The difference in the forms of salutation often extends so far, that one nation considers that a mark of rudeness which another esteems a mark of civility. In most German countries, it is an act of politeness to kiss the hands of ladies; but, in Italy, this is regarded as a mark of familiarity, which is permitted only to the nearest relations. On the contrary, the Russian ladies allow not only the hand to be kissed, but even the forehead, and would consider themselves insulted by the omission of this ceremony. Instead of the customary salutation in the Protestant countries of Germany,—Good morning, Your servant, &c.,—the German Catholic salutes in the manner prescribed by the pope Benedict XIII (1728),—Praised be Jesus Christ; to which the answer is, Forever, amen. The miner's salutation is, Good luck to you (*Glück auf*). The military salutations which were introduced among the Germans in the beginning of the sixteenth century, consist in touching the hat or cap, lowering the standards and the sword, or raising the musket. Vessels, when meeting, salute each other by a discharge of cannon, by striking the flag, or by the cheers of the sailors, &c. If we express our esteem for persons of distinction, by bowing, and uncovering our heads, the Russian throws himself on the ground before his master, clasps his knees, and kisses them. The Pole bows to the ground, and the Bohemian kisses at least the gown of any one for whom he wishes to express his profound respect. Mutual contact is regarded among almost all nations as the expression of friendly sentiments. The pressing of hands, embraces, and kisses, are among other nations also, as well as those of Europe, marks of esteem and love. Some nations, in saluting, touch other parts of the body. The Laplanders, for instance, press their noses firmly together. In one of the larger Cyclades, persons reciprocally moisten each other's hair; and the Franks are said to have pulled out a hair and presented it to the person saluted. The Turk crosses his hands, places them upon his breast, and bows. The salutation of the Hindoos in Bengal consists in touching the forehead with the right hand, and bending the head forwards. They first place the right hand on the breast with a profound inclination, then touch the ground, and finally the forehead with the same hand. At the same time, they call themselves the most humble slaves of him whom they salute. The inhabitants of the Manillas bend the body profoundly, place their hands upon their cheeks, raise one leg, and bend the knee. The inhabitants of Lamurzec, in the Pelew islands, seize the hand, or even the foot of the person whom they wish to salute, and rub their face with it. In the island of Sumatra, the saluting person bows, begs the left foot of him whom he addresses, kneels on the ground, and applies this foot to his crown, forehead, breast and knee: finally, he touches the ground with his head, and remains for some moments stretched out on his belly. The salutations in the East generally bear the stamp of a slavish mind. The very ancient custom of throwing one's self on the ground before persons of distinction, and repeatedly kissing their feet, has continued to the present time. At an entertainment in Persia, the host goes a considerable distance to meet his guests, bids them welcome with the most respectful compliments, then returns hastily to the door of his house, and waits their arrival to repeat the same demonstrations of respect. In China, if two persons meet on horseback, the inferior in rank dismounts from his horse before the superior, and remains standing until he has passed. Some salutations are also peculiar to men, and others to women. When acquaintances meet, they join their hands upon their breasts, or above their heads, bend their head a little, and say *Tsin, tsin*—a compliment without any particular signification. In saluting persons to whom they owe more respect, they clap their hands, then raise them, and finally let them sink down to the ground. Friends who meet after a long separation, fall repeatedly upon their knees, and bend their heads to the ground, exclaiming, at the same time, *Na fo?* (Has all passed happily?) or, *Yung fo* (Happiness is painted upon thy countenance). Women salute each other with the words *Van fo* (May all happiness be with you); but they are not allowed to salute men. Children fall on their knees before their parents, and servants before their master or mistress. In Japan, the inferior of two persons saluting takes off his sandals, puts his right hand into his left sleeve, permits his hands, thus crossed, to sink slowly upon his knee, passes the other person with short, measured steps, and a rocking motion of the body, and exclaims, with a fearful countenance, *Augh! augh!* (Do not hurt me!) In Siam, the inferior throws himself on the ground before his superior. The latter then sends one of his attendants, who are very numerous in the case of persons of distinction, to examine whether he has eaten, or carries with him any thing of an offensive smell. If this is the case, he receives a kick from the superior, and is compelled to retire immediately; if otherwise, the servant lifts him up. Women, even when advanced in age, are saluted with the names of the most beautiful and most precious objects, but not without the additional word *young*; as "young diamond," "young gold," "young heaven," "young flower," &c. If friends wish to express their mutual attachment, they scratch their hand slightly, and reciprocally suck a drop of blood from the wound. In Ceylon, when persons salute, they raise the palm of the hand to the forehead, and make a low bow. Before a superior they throw themselves upon the ground, continually repeating his name and dignity, while the superior very gravely passes on, and hardly deigns to utter a word of reply. The greeting of the common Arabian is *Salâm aleikum* (Peace be with you),—a salutation which has been long in use among the Jews. At the same time, he places his left hand upon his breast, as a sign that this wish comes from his heart. The reply is, *Aleikum essâlam* (With you be peace). But Arabians of distinction embrace each other two or three times, kiss each other's cheeks, and inquire two or three times after each other's health; at the same time, each kisses his own hand. The Arabians of the Desert shake hands six or eight times. In Yemen, persons of distinction, after a long refusal, allow their fingers to be kissed. The Abyssinians and other nations fall on their knees, and kiss the ground. Several negro nations take each other's hands, and pull the fingers till they crack. The negroes of Sierra Leone bend the right elbow, so that the hand touches the mouth; the person saluted does the same; they then put their thumb and fore-finger together, and withdraw them slowly. Other negroes snap their fingers in meeting each other, pull the comb out of their hair, and replace it. In Lower Guinea, the saluting person seizes the fingers of the saluted, brings them into a particular position, presses them, cracks them hastily, calling, *Akkio, akkio* (Thy servant, thy servant). On the Gold coast of Upper Guinea, friends embrace each other, join the fore-fingers of their right hands until they crack, bend their heads, repeating *Auzi, auzi* (Good day, good day). Persons of distinction, after cracking the fingers, exclaim, *Bere, bere* (Peace, peace). If the Mandingoes salute a female, they take her hand, raise it to their nose, and smell it twice. Mr. Snellgrave, an Englishman, with his companions, was saluted by a messenger of the king of Dahomey, attended by 500 negro soldiers, in a very novel manner. The officers of the corps approached their English guests with drawn swords, which they brandished over their heads with curious gesticulations and motions. They then placed their swords upon their bodies, and, after a repetition of these ceremonies, the messenger presented them his hand, and drank to their health. In Morocco, foreigners are saluted by the Moors, on horseback, in a manner which may well startle those not accustomed to it. The Moor rides full speed towards the stranger, as if about to run him down; he then suddenly stops, and discharges his pistol over the head of the person. Persons of equal rank salute each other nearly in the European way. They shake hands, and kiss each other's face and beard, particularly if they are friends. The Egyptians extend their hands, place them upon their breast, and bend their heads. The greatest act of politeness is to kiss their own hand, and afterwards place it upon their heads. They only kiss the hand of men of distinction, not of women. Inferior officers hold the stirrup of their superiors, mounting on horseback. In the divan, the inferior takes off the slipper of the superior, places it by his side, and receives the same salutation from the latter. In other countries of Africa, people take off their clothes, fall on their knees, bend their heads to the ground, and cover their head and shoulders with sand. The Ethiopians seize the right hand of him for whom they wish to show respect, and raise it to their mouth. They even take his sash and tie it round their waist, so that he remains for some time half naked. The salutations between the different tribes in the north-west of America are very ceremonious. If two hordes of these savages meet, they stop at the distance of twenty or thirty steps, throw themselves on the ground, and remain for some moments in this position. The two eldest of each party then advance and relate very circumstantially the dangers they have encountered. As soon as they have finished their relations, they all begin to sigh. These sighs are finally changed into a horrible yell, in which the young girls, particularly, endeavor to surpass the others of the tribe. With these affecting manifestations of sympathy both parties approach, but each sex separately. Tobacco pipes are handed about, and their affliction is soon changed into merriment. The manner in which the inhabitants of South America salute each other, is short. Their address is, *Ama re ka* (Thou); and the answer, *A* (Yes). The savage of Louisiana territory, when saluting a person of distinction, begins a loud howl. In the hut he repeats the salutation, holding his hands above his head, and howling three times. He returns thanks with another howl, when the superior invites him, with a low sigh, to sit down. In Otaheite, and particularly in the Society and Friendly islands, persons touch the ends of each other's noses. This salutation is returned by each rubbing the hand of the other on his own nose and mouth. The Otaheitan presents a person whom he chooses for a friend, sometimes with a part of his dress, sometimes with the whole. The inhabitants of New Guinea cover their heads with leaves. This action is also regarded as a sign of peace.

SALUZZO; formerly a marquisate, which, after a long dispute between France and Savoy, was finally confirmed to the latter (1601), in exchange for Bresse and Bugey. It lay between Dauphiny and Nizza, and now forms a province of tne Sardinian monarchy. The capital, of the same name, lies near the Po, and has a population of 10,150. The house of the marquises of Saluzzo was celebrated in the middle ages, and there are at present branches of it in France (Saluces), Naples, and Austria.

SALVADOR, ST., or BAYAMO; a town of Cuba, near the southern coast, 520 miles south-east of Havana, on the right bank of the river Bayamo, which forms a port at its mouth. The town is about twenty miles distant from the port. Lon. 76° 55′; lat. 20° 23′. Population, 7486; 2875 of which are whites, 3139 free persons of color, and 1472 slaves.

SALVADOR, ST. (See *Bahia*.)

Salvage; a recompense allowed by law for the saving of a ship or goods from loss at sea, either by shipwreck or other means, or by enemies or pirates. (See *Prize.*)

Salvator Rosa. (See *Rosa.*)

Salvi, Giambattista. (See *Sassoferato.*)

Salzburg; a city of Austria, on the Salza, chief place of the circle of the same name; lat. 47° 48′ N.; lon. 13° 1′ E. It contains, besides the cathedral, sixteen other churches, six hospitals, and several literary institutions. The principal article of manufacture is hardware. The cathedral is more remarkable for solidity than elegance. The university was converted (1809) into an academy. The most striking feature of the place is its romantic situation amidst lofty mountains. The citadel stands in a bold and commanding situation, and one of the gateways is cut through a solid rock, being 300 feet in length, 30 feet in height, and 24 in breadth. Population, 13,000. Sixty-three miles south-east of Munich.

Salzmann, Christian Gotthilf, a distinguished teacher at Schnepfenthal, was born, in 1744, in the territory of Erfurt, where his father was a Protestant preacher. He himself was a clergyman in Erfurt, when the works of Rousseau and Basedow directed his attention more particularly to the education of his own children. In 1778, he published Entertainments for Children, and Friends of Children, and, in 1780, his excellent *Krebsbüchlein*, in which he exposes, with keen irony, the prevalent mistakes in education. Basedow invited him, in 1781, to take part in his *Philanthropin*, an establishment for education, at Dessau. He published his Sermons, &c. at this institution, from 1781 to 1783, in 4 small vols. In 1783, he began, and in 1788 finished, his novel *Karl von Karlsberg*, or, *on Human Misery*, in 6 vols. In 1784, he established in Schnepfenthal (in Gotha), his own institution. His prudent management, and the zealous coöperation of able assistants, made it prosper. He began with his own children, and a few others; but pupils were soon sent to him, not only from all parts of Germany, but also from many foreign countries. Some of these pupils were of very high rank. In 1797, he published his Heaven on Earth, which gained him the favor of many parents. In 1803, the number of his pupils was sixty-one. In 1788, he began to publish the Thuringian Messenger, a journal which was much read. A number of books on education, by him and his associates, contributed much to the changes which took place in education. His institution was distinguished, moreover, for the health of the pupils, and the developement of their physical powers, which was owing to its salubrious situation, to the attention paid to diet, and to the gymnastics introduced there by Guts-Muths. (q. v.) Six of his associates became his sons-in-law, and two of his sons were among his associates. His daughters also taught. The wars in Europe, and the increasing number of similar institutions, reduced the number of his pupils, so that, in 1807, he had but thirty-six children under his care. Salzmann died in 1811, having effected much good as an instructer and a popular author. Clearness and simplicity, piety and practical good sense, are the prominent features of his writings. He was distinguished for firmness, sagacity, and unceasing activity, and was honored by thousands whom he had trained in the ways of virtue and wisdom. His institution continues under his son, Charles Salzmann.

Samarcand; a city of Bucharia, situated in a fertile and delightful region, 200 miles east of the city of Bucharia; lat. 39° 30′ N.; lon. 68° 50′ E. Its population is about 50,000. It is surrounded with a double wall, contains numerous fountains, 250 mosques, with 40 madrases, or religious schools (see *Mosques*), a palace, several bazars, &c. Samarcand has been, for two centuries and a half, one of the great marts of the Asiatic inland commerce. It was anciently called *Marakanda*, and was the capital of Sogdiana, which lay on the northern frontiers of the Persian empire. Alexander is thought to have pillaged it. It was taken by Gengis Khan in 1220, and, under Timour, or Tamerlane (q. v.), became the capital of one of the most extensive empires in the world. Tamerlane, towards the end of the fourteenth century, established a Mohammedan university here, and Samarcand became the seat of Asiatic learning. (See *Bucharia.*)

Samaritans. After the fall of the kingdom of Israel, the people remaining in its territory, consisting of the tribes of Ephraim and Manasseh, mingled with some Assyrian colonists, were called by the Greeks Samaritans, from the city of Samaria, around which they dwelt. When the Jews, on their return from captivity, rebuilt the temple of Jerusalem, the Samaritans desired to aid in the work; but their offers were rejected by the Jews, who looked upon them as unclean, on account of their mixture with heathens; and the Samaritans revenged themselves by hindering the building of the city and temple. Hence the hatred which prevailed between the Jews and Samaritans, which, in the time of Jesus, when the latter were confined to a narrow strip of country between Judæa and Galilee, prevented all intercourse between them, and still continues. Having never become independent, the Samaritans have shared the fate of the country which they inhabit, and have suffered so much from the oppressions of the Turks, that not only the colonies of them in Egypt (which were in a flourishing condition in the seventeenth century) are now extinct, but the number of them in Naplousa (the ancient Sichem), and in Jaffa, the only places which contain Samaritans, was, according to De Sacy, not more than 200 in 1811. In their religious opinions and usages, they resemble those Jews, particularly the Caraites, who reject the Talmud, and differ from the rabbinical Jews, in receiving only the Pentateuch and book of Joshua, and in rejecting all the other portions of the Bible, as well as the Talmud, and rabbinical traditions. In their manners, rites, and religious ceremonies, they adhere strictly to the Mosaic law. Instead of the temple at Jerusalem, they worship on mount Gerizim, in Samaria, where, in more prosperous times, they celebrated their festivals, and offered sacrifices. The worship of one God, circumcision, the purifications, and feasts (except the Purim and the feast of the dedication), they have in common with the Jews. They believe in the existence of angels, in a resurrection, and future retribution, and expect the coming of a Messiah, in whom they look only for a prophet. Their priests are of the tribe of Levi, and are treated as superiors. On account of their poverty, their only sacrifice is a lamb, on the feast of Pentecost. In the synagogue, the Aramaic Samaritan dialect is used, but they generally speak Arabic, and they are distinguished by a white turban. They support themselves by mechanical labor and by money dealings. They avoid any connexions with other sects, and marry only among their own nation. Each man is allowed two wives on his first marriage; but on the death of one of them, he cannot marry again. In case both of them die, he is suffered to have one wife. This remnant of a declining race possesses one of the oldest, if not the oldest manuscript of the Pentateuch known to be extant. (See *Bible.*)

SAMIEL. (See *Simoom.*)

SAMNITES; the inhabitants of the ancient province of Samnium, in Lower Italy, bordering on the country of the Peligni, Marsi, Campanians, Lucanians, and Apulians. In early times, they occupied the largest part of that country. They are described in Roman history as a people fond of war and of liberty, who were brought completely under the Roman yoke, after long and bloody wars, which continued, with a few interruptions, nearly 70 years. The first hostilities between the two states commenced in the year of Rome 411, when the Campanians, oppressed by the powerful Samnites, sought the aid of Rome. Valerius Corvus, the Roman consul, marched against the Samnites, and forced them to retreat, after a bloody engagement, to their own borders. At the same time, another Roman army had invaded the country of the Samnites, and, after a doubtful contest, gained the victory by the heroic decision of the young Publius Decius Mus. The vanquished nation was obliged to sue for peace; but maintained it only till they recovered from their defeat. For in the year 426 a new war broke out, more bloody than the preceding, which was prosecuted the more obstinately, as the other states in Lower Italy came to the aid of the Samnites. Though the Romans were generally victorious, yet in the year 433, their army becoming involved in a narrow pass near the city of Caudium, and being surrounded on every side by the forces of the enemy, was obliged to submit to the disgrace of passing under the yoke. The senate, however, rejected the peace concluded with the enemy by the captive consuls, delivered up the authors of it to the Samnites, and sent other commanders to prosecute the war. The valiant Papirius Cursor succeeded in revenging the disgrace which his countrymen had suffered by inflicting a similar ignominy upon the enemy. The war was still prosecuted with fury; for the Samnites were vigorously supported by their neighbors, who feared the power of Rome; and even Pyrrhus, the warlike king of Epirus, at the entreaty of the afflicted city of Tarentum, took up arms against the Romans. But the consuls, Papirius Cursor, Q. Fabius Maximus, Pub. Decius Mus, Curius Dentatus, Caius Luscinius Fabricius and others, triumphed repeatedly over the enemy, who fought with desperation; and, after the most fatal defeats, and the entire devastation of their country, the Samnites, to gether with the other nations which had assisted them, found themselves obliged to sue for peace. In 482, they obtained it. When the Italian allies of Rome revolted against her, in the time of Sylla, the Samnites once more rose against their oppressors, and fought with desperation. But Sylla entirely subdued them, and commanded that every Samnite should be put to death. Three days after the battle, he ordered 4000 of them, who had been taken prisoners, to be put to death, on the Campus Martius. The few that remained lived from that time scattered in villages. The Samnites cultivated various arts and manufactures; for the proximity of the refined Greeks in Lower Italy had a very beneficial influence upon them. Even their laws and constitution were borrowed in a great degree from the Greeks. Their form of government was democratic. At the commencement of a war they were accustomed to choose a common general.

Samogitia; a country of Europe, bounded by Courland, Prussia, and Lithuania, formerly a province of Poland, now forming the government of Wilna, in Russia. It was the first of the Polish provinces incorporated with Russia, that raised the standard of insurrection in 1831. (See *Russia.*)

Samoides. (See *Samoyedes.*)

Samoom. (See *Simoom.*)

Samos, a Grecian island in the Archipelago, opposite to the ruins of Ephesus and the promontory of Mycale, the birthplace of Pythagoras, as is generally supposed, was the most important and powerful island of the Ionians. From the reign of Polycrates, 566 B. C., this island is celebrated in history for the worship of Juno, who was born here, and was also distinguished for its skilful seamen and enterprising merchants, who even sailed as far as the mouth of the Guadalquiver through the Pillars of Hercules (now the straits of Gibraltar). The fleets of the rich Samians often made the Persians tremble. At Samos were first cast statues in bronze. Samos lost the last shadow of republican freedom under the reign of the emperor Vespasian (70 A. D.). In the middle ages, this island was alternately governed by the Arabs, Venetians, Genoese, and Turks: to the latter it finally became tributary, under an aga of the capudan pacha. It is 175 square miles in extent, very fruitful and mountainous, and besides the capital city, Cora, near which the ancient Samos and the temple of Juno (Heræum) lie in ruins (now called the *Columns*), it contains three other cities, Vahti, Carlovassi, and Fournis. During the Greek revolution, owing to the many refugees from Natolia, Scio, Ipsara, and other places, the island contained about 50,000 Greek inhabitants (where there were formerly only 12,000). Near Samos lies the island of Icaria (Nicari), inhabited by 300 Greeks. This island is celebrated as being the place near which Icarus, the son of Dædalus (q. v.), fell into the sea, and where his dead body floated on shore; whence the name. In 1821, the inhabitants of Samos took up arms at the report of the execution of the patriarch. They fortified the harbors on the Little Bogas, to guard against an attack from the coasts of Natolia, and soon collected about 10,000 men. From that time the Samians continually attacked the neighboring coasts of Asia, and Scala Nuova in particular. July 16, 1821, the island was attacked by the Turks, but without success. The Turks, in August, 1824, again made a more furious attack; but the Greek fleet, commanded by Miaulis, repulsed the Turkish.—Samos has lately been visited by an earthquake of an extraordinary nature, that produced a large opening in one of the highest mountains of the island, from which suddenly issued an enormous torrent of water, overflowing the country, and making its way to the sea. By degrees, the inundation subsided, and terminated in forming a river, which has its source at the opening formed in the mountain.

Samothrace; an island in the Ægean sea, not far from Lemnos, on the coast of Thrace, opposite the Trojan territory, and celebrated for its mysteries (q. v.), the priests of which were at first the Cabiri (q. v.), and afterwards the Dioscuri. An initiation into these mysteries was supposed to have efficacy in preserving persons from dangers by sea; and it is related of the Argonauts, that, at the suggestion of Orpheus, who was one of the initiated, they were landed at Samothrace. Over these mysteries there rests an impenetrable obscurity, which also extends to the deities that were revered. It appears certain that the Egyptian and Phœnician religious rites and ceremonies were afterwards united and mingled with those of the Greeks, and that, still later, the religious worship of the Samothracians was introduced into Etruria, although the names of the divinities were changed. Nevertheless, out of respect for its mysteries, this island enjoyed, even under the Roman dominion, a certain degree of freedom; and, even after the birth of Christ, these long celebrated mysteries still enjoyed reputation.

SAMOYEDES, or SAMOIDES; a nomadic people traversing the immense frozen deserts which extend along the ocean forming the northern boundary of European and Asiatic Russia. They extend from the river Mezen, on the European side, nearly to the Lena on the Asiatic; lon. 40 to 120 E., upwards of 2000 miles; in breadth the territory varies from 300 to 600. The population of this cold, dreary and barren country is not supposed to exceed 20,000. The Samoyedes call themselves Khasova, and are divided into three tribes—the Vanoites on the Petchora and Oby, the Tysia-Igoley on the Mezen, and the Khirutches in the interior of Siberia. They are of small stature, usually between four and five feet; have a flat, round, and broad face, thick lips, wide nose, little beard, black hair, in small quantity. They live by hunting, are extremely superstitious, and generally peaceable. As they are unacquainted with the art of writing, their traditions are imperfectly preserved only in their songs. When the victorious Russians first became acquainted with them, they had already been chased from their native seats by the Tartars, and separated from their kindred tribes. Their original country is unknown, but they appear to have come from the south. Their principal wealth consists in herds of rein-deer, which supply them with food, clothing, tents, utensils, &c.

SAMP. A word borrowed from the North American Indians, to denote maize, broken coarse, boiled, and mixed with milk.

SAMPHIRE (*crithmum maritimum*); an umbelliferous plant, remarkable for its lanceolate, fleshy leaflets, which grows wild along the sea-coast of Europe. Where it abounds, it is used by the inhabitants as a pickle, as an ingredient in salads, or as a potherb. It can be cultivated in gardens upon beds of sand and rubbish, or in pots; and it is useful to furnish the stocks with a supply of salt; for, like other maritime plants, it possesses the power of decomposing sea-water and retaining the soda. The seed is very similar to a grain of barley.

SAMSON, judge of Israel, son of Manoah, a Danite, was born, according to Usher, about 1155 B. C., and was educated, from his birth, according to the commands of an angel, a Nazarite. (q. v.) At the age of 18 years, he fell in love with a young Philistine girl, whom he married. At the wedding-feast, Samson, who had formerly torn a lion in pieces, and afterwards found a swarm of bees in the carcass, proposed a riddle to the guests, wagering thirty shirts and as many suits of clothes that they could not guess it in seven days: "Out of the eater came forth meat, and out of the strong came forth sweetness." The secret of his riddle being betrayed to them by his bride, Samson reproached them with ploughing with his heifer; but went to Askalon, killed thirty Philistines, and gave their clothes to his guests. His wife having, during his absence in his own country, married again, he caught 300 foxes, and, tying them together, tail to tail, with a fire-brand between them, let them loose in the fields of the Philistines. His own countrymen having afterwards delivered him up bound into the hands of his enemies, he snapped the cords asunder, and killed 1000 Philistines with the jaw-bone of an ass. From this period Samson was judge of Israel for twenty years. While he was on a visit to Gaza, the gates of the city were watched by the Philistines, with the intention of killing him as he went out in the morning; but he rose by night, and carried off one of the gates of the city to a distance of twenty or thirty miles. Not long after he fell in love with Delilah, to whom he foolishly revealed the secret of his strength. By cutting off his hair, which was a violation of his obligation as a Nazarite, she deprived him of his peculiar powers, and betrayed him to his enemies, who put out his eyes, and set him to work in a mill with slaves. At a great festival in honor of Dagon, Samson was brought out to furnish sport to the Philistines. But his hair had grown again; and, his vigor having returned with it, he took vengeance on his enemies by pulling down over their heads the building in which they were assembled, and under the ruins of which he also perished with them. Milton has made his death the subject of a drama—Samson Agonistes.

SAMUEL; a prophet, and the last of the judges of Israel. From his youth he was marked out as destined by God to reform the dissolute and irreligious practices of his nation. He grew up devoted to the temple service; and, sensible of the faults of his countrymen, he exhorted them, when they were hard pressed by the Philistines, to fear God, and worship him, as their only means of deliverance. His prayers and sacrifices obtained for them the victory; and the office of judge was conferred on him. He governed the people twelve years; and his administration was distinguished by the restoration of the neglected worship of Jehovah. He also gave new vigor to the theocratical institutions of Moses, by the establishment of schools of the prophets. (See *Prophets.*) In his old age, the corruption of his sons, to whom he had transmitted the office of judge, excited discontents among the Hebrews, who demanded a king. Samuel reluctantly yielded to this revolution, but at the same time anointed the king of the general choice, imposing upon him such restrictions as should preserve the old constitution, and reproving him freely when he was guilty of injustice or impiety. But when Saul attacked the priestly office and privileges, Samuel anointed a new king, David. He did not live to see the contest between David and Saul decided; but, even after his death, his spirit, evoked by the witch of Endor, threatened the latter with the divine vengeance. The books of Judges and Ruth and part of the first book of Samuel, have been attributed to him, but are probably by a later hand.

San Carlos, Joseph Michael de Carvajal, duke of, descended from the old kings of Leon, was born in Lima, in 1771, went to Spain at the age of 16, began his military career as colonel in the second regiment of Majorca infantry, of which his uncle was colonel-proprietor, was in the campaign of Catalonia, in the war of 1793, and a volunteer in the Toulon expedition. On the death of his uncle he was appointed chamberlain, and afterwards governor to the prince of Asturias, now Ferdinand VII. His system of education was, however, not suitable to the views of Godoy (q. v.), whose influence deprived the duke of that post. In 1805, he was invested with the office of major-domo to Charles IV, and in 1807 was appointed to the viceroyship of Navarre. Three months after he had taken possession of his viceroyalty, he received orders to consider himself a prisoner in the citadel. This arrest arose out of a report, that the duke had recommended to the prince to remove the queen-mother from all influence in the affairs of the kingdom, in case of the king's death, who at that time was very ill, and also to bring the prince of peace before the tribunals of his country. During the affair of the Escurial (see *Ferdinand VII*), he was subjected to various severe scrutinies; and, though liberated at the same time as prince Ferdinand, he was ordered to remove sixty leagues from Madrid, and was prohibited from fixing his residence in Navarre. He resided at Alfaro when the French armies entered Spain. In the mean time, the insurrection in Aranjuez broke out, and prince Ferdinand being placed on the throne, he immediately called the duke about his person, and appointed him grand-master of the household and member of his privy-council. He arrived in Madrid some days before the prince's departure for Bayonne, and accompanied him in that journey. The duke had several conferences with Napoleon on the subject of exchanging the crown of Spain for that of Etruria, and invariably assured him that the prince would not consent to any treaty without enjoying his liberty and being sanctioned by the cortes. The subsequent arrangements, however, which the prince was compelled to enter into, did not detach the duke from his service: he remained with him at Valençay, till, by order of Napoleon, he was called, with Escoiquiz (q. v.), to Paris. Suspicions, however, being entertained of the duke and Escoiquiz's influence over Ferdinand, they were separated from that prince; the duke being confined at Lons-le-Saulnier, and Escoiquiz at Bourges. The duke, in his retirement, cultivated his taste for botany, but above all for history, politics, and general literature. When it was determined by Napoleon to reinstate Ferdinand on the throne of his kingdom, he fixed upon the duke of San Carlos as best suited, by his counsels and knowledge of all parties in Spain, to conciliate their regards. He was therefore called to Paris in November, 1813, and afterwards went to Valençay, where long discussions ensued, which ended in the duke's setting out for Madrid, to obtain the consent of the regency to the treaty. He arrived January 16, 1814; but the arrangements made in France were not approved by the regency. In answer to applications for the return of the king to Spain, the duke of Bassano at length consented to the measure, and his majesty set out under the name of count de Barcelona. The duke was the only minister who accompanied the king. The affairs of Spain were at that time under the direction of the regency; and under these circumstances it was deemed prudent to go to Saragossa. The cortes, however, decided not to give up the reins of government, and the king and the duke proceeded to Valencia in April. May 3, San Carlos was appointed, by the king, first secretary of state; and the next day he signed the infamous decree by which a despotism was established. General Freyre, who had been nominated to the ministry of war, declined the place, and the duke accepted it, in conjunction with that of minister of the king's household: the former office he shortly after resigned to general Eguia. The duke set about introducing a system of economy into the kingdom; established a junta of ministers, over whom he presided; took measures for repairing roads, increasing the number of canals, reviving the credit of the national bank; and instituted several academies for the cultivation of the arts and sciences. Notwithstanding these benefits, his enemies were numerous; and, finding them increase in November, 1814, he demanded permission to resign, which the king granted, and don Pedro Cevallos was appointed to succeed him. He was nominated minister to Vienna, in the month of October, 1815; and in 1817 he was recalled and sent to the court of Great Britain in the same quality. In consequence of the troubles in Spain (1822—23), the duke retired to the court of Lucca, by which he was sent ambassador to Charles X, in 1825. He was subsequently named ambassador extraordinary of Spain to the same court, and continued in that station till his death, July, 1828.

Sanction, Pragmatic; 1. the ordinance of Charles VII of France, drawn up at Bourges, in 1438, conformably to the decrees of the council of Basle (q. v.), and on which rest the liberties of the Gallican church. 2. The decree of the German diet, at Mayence, in 1439, which sanctioned the same decrees of this council. Both limited the power of the pope, but were altered by subsequent concordates. 3. The instrument by which the German emperor, Charles VI, being without male issue, endeavored to secure the succession to his female descendants. He soon induced most of the monarchs of Europe to guarantee it; but the elector of Bavaria, Charles Albert, the next heir to his dominions, refused. This caused the Austrian war of succession, after the death of Charles in 1740. In the peace of Füssen, April 22, 1745, Bavaria acknowledged the pragmatic sanction. 4. Charles III of Spain, when he ceded the throne of Naples to his third son, and his posterity, in 1759, called the law of succession, which he prepared for this branch of his family, *sanctio pragmatica.*

Sand, Charles Louis, student of theology, who murdered Kotzebue (q. v.), was born October 5, 1795, at Wunsiedel, in the Fichtelgebirge, where his father held a judicial office. In 1812, Sand was sent to the gymnasium of Ratisbon. In 1814, he entered the university of Tübingen, and, in 1815, joined the Bavarian army as a volunteer against the French; but his corps was never brought into action. After peace, he continued his studies in Erlangen, where, in 1817, his most intimate friend was drowned before his eyes, without his being able to render him any assistance. In the autumn of 1817, he went to the university of Jena, where he was a member of the *Burschenschaft* (see *Universities*), but of no other secret or public society. His whole soul was animated by that love of country and liberty, which, ill defined, indeed, in some cases, was then the predominant sentiment of all the noble-minded youth of Germany. Their excitement was great, as, soon after the peace, most of the German governments had shown a decided reluctance to perform the promises which they had made of improving the political condition of their subjects. Besides this, the idea of a union of the German states, so natural to every German who reflects on the quarrels which have torn to pieces his unhappy country, took possession of the minds of the young, and especially of the students: at least, in them it was manifested more openly. The ideas of young men at a university, on the mode of effecting such political changes, must, of course, have been crude, ignorant as they were of life and of political affairs; but their desires were ardent; hundreds burned to do something towards obtaining these ends; and many were ready to sacrifice even their lives in the cause. These young men, we may be allowed to say, were inspired with as true a love of country as ever existed; but the men of mature age, who ought to have regulated their ardor and guided their efforts, were wanting to their duty, and occupied themselves merely with speculations, in which religion and politics were confusedly mingled, and which were founded on erroneous conceptions of ages gone by. At this time, some writers attacked the prevailing excitement with severe ridicule; and, among these, Kotzebue distinguished himself. In free governments, such ridicule would have been little regarded; but in this period of enthusiasm for liberty, kindled by political oppression, it was felt with bitterness. Kotzebue was discovered to be acting at the instigation of the Russian government, which, of course, added to the exasperation. Sand looked upon Kotzebue as an enemy of his country, and a criminal of the blackest dye, whom the political condition of Germany rendered it impossible to punish according to the forms of law, and who was therefore to be regarded as at open warfare with the true lovers of their country, who had a right to destroy him, as the only means left them for protecting their own rights. Having come to this conclusion, he took the deed upon himself, perfectly conscious, at the same time, that he violated the rules of social order, and willing to endure the punishment which was to be expected for such a deed. He was not, however, "made for murder," as he justly said of himself, and could not easily resolve to act on his own conclusions. He struggled for months against his own convictions, and prayed for guidance: at last he resolved that it was cowardly to defer what he deemed an act of duty. On the afternoon of March 9, 1819, he went to Kotzebue's residence in Manheim, delivered a letter to him, and, while he was reading it, pierced him with a dagger, exclaiming, "Here, thou traitor to thy country." Having given him two more blows, he went down stairs, handed a paper, inscribed "Death-blow to Augustus von Kotzebue," to a servant, went into the street, knelt down, and having cried aloud, "Long live my German fatherland!" pierced his own breast, with the words, "I thank thee, O God, for this victory." The attempt at his own destruction is the only part of the transaction which he ever regretted, and never tried to excuse. Kotzebue died soon after. Sand was executed near Manheim, May 20, 1820, aged twenty-four years, after having suffered much from the wounds which he had given himself, and from an operation which had been performed in consequence. He died with perfect calmness. The testimonies of his conduct at all periods of his life, given by his teachers, parents and friends, show that he was always strictly moral, and modest, and of uncommon purity of life. His character was mild and affectionate. He was a good scholar, although not of a rapid or penetrating understanding. His feelings were stronger than his reason. He was a warm and faithful friend, and uncommonly attached to his parents and brothers and sisters, so that his struggle, before he could resolve to commit murder, was intense. Sand's deed is a remarkable phenomenon in the moral world. As the spirit for the regeneration of Germany had manifested itself most strongly among the students and in the newly established gymnasia, on account of the many young men collected there, the latter, in many German states, were closed, and the governments, believing that Sand was merely the instrument of a secret society, commenced active inquiries to discover these secret societies; but they could not be found. It showed, moreover, a very incorrect appreciation of Sand's deed, to suppose that he was but the agent for executing an order. A comparison between him and other persons, whom history records as urged by a mistaken sense of duty to commit murder, as Ravaillac, Charlotte Corday, Staps, would be interesting.—See *Vollständige Uebersicht der gegen Sand geführten Untersuchung* (Stuttgard, 1820)—the publication was not allowed until 1823;—also *Actenauszüge aus dem Untersuchungsprocess über K. L. Sand* (Altenburg and Leipsic, 1821), and Eight more Contributions to the History of Aug. von Kotzebue and C. L. Sand (Mühlhausen, 1821).

SANDAL; a kind of covering for the feet, used among the Greeks and Romans, and which we find to be of the highest antiquity. It consisted of a thick cork sole, covered above and beneath with leather, and neatly stitched on the edge. It left the upper part of the foot bare, and was fastened on by means of straps, crossed over and wound round the ankle. In later times, sandals became articles of much luxury. The higher Catholic clergy wear a costly embroidered sock, which is called *sandal*. A kind of vessel employed in the Mediterranean sea for the purpose of unloading large ships, is also called *sandal*.

SANDAL WOOD (*santalum album*); a low tree, much resembling the privet in its leaves and flowers, but differing widely in its botanical characters. The leaves are opposite, petiolate, smooth, about two inches in length, oblong, and somewhat obtuse at each extremity: the flowers are small. This tree produces the white and yellow sandal woods of commerce, which were formerly thought to be obtained from different trees: but in India, as in a certain degree in all countries, most trees, when large and old, become colored towards the centre; and this takes place in the sandal tree, the centre of which, with age, acquires a yellow color as well as great fragrance and hardness. This is the only part of the trunk that is used, being in universal esteem for its fragrance. It is manufactured into light articles of cabinet furniture; and no insect can exist, or iron rust (it is said) within its influence. The dust of this wood is used by the Bramins to form the pigment with which they give the tilac, or frontal mark, to the god Vishnu; and the oil used in their ceremonies is obtained from the shavings, or at least scented by them. The true sandal wood grows chiefly on the coast of Malabar, and in the East Indian islands.

Sandarach; a gum resin, which oozes spontaneously from the old trunks of the common juniper (*juniperus communis*), and which is used in considerable quantities in the preparation of varnish, particularly of one kind, employed by cabinet makers and painters, called *vernix.* In its powdered form, it is known under the name of *pounce.* (See *Juniper.*)

Sandeman, Robert, in whom the sect called *Sandemanians* originated, was born at Perth, in Scotland, in 1723. He studied at Edinburgh, and afterwards engaged in the linen trade. On marrying the daughter of the reverend John Glass (founder of the Glassites), he became an elder in his congregation, and soon after published a series of letters, in which he endeavors to show that a justifying faith means nothing more than a simple assent to the divine mission of Christ. This position caused much controversy, and those who adopted it were called *Sandemanians,* and formed themselves into church order, in strict fellowship with the church of Scotland, but holding communion with no other. The chief opinions and practices in which this sect differs from others, are their weekly administration of the Lord's supper, washing each other's feet, &c. In 1764, Mr. Sandeman accepted an invitation to New England, where he died in 1771. His sect still subsists in Great Britain. He was author of some other theological tracts besides his Letters on Theron and Aspasio.

Sandemanians. (See *Sandeman.*)

Sandpiper (*tringa*); a genus of shore-birds, allied to the snipe, plover, curlew, and godwit, and included by Linnæus under the order *grallæ.* The bill is as long as the head, or longer, straight or slightly curved, rounded, slender, soft and flexible, without a cutting edge, and enlarged and obtuse at the extremity: it seems to perform many of the offices of a probe, and enables these birds to search in the soft mud for insects, small shells, or worms, which form their accustomed food. Their nostrils are linear, and situated in a groove of the bill. Their tongue is filiform and pointed. The legs are destitute of feathers for some distance above the knee, and the toes are short and incapable of grasping; hence these birds do not perch, but frequent the borders of ponds, rivers and marshes, especially in the vicinity of the ocean, and are often seen coursing rapidly along the strand, following the flux and reflux of the waves. Their wings are long, and their flight powerful. Some species prefer the interior and the vicinity of fresh water, and others almost exclusively inhabit the shores of the ocean. They build their nests in the grass, and the young at birth immediately follow their parents in search of food. At the approach of winter, they all quit the land of their birth, and migrate in flocks more or less numerous, to warmer climates. They moult twice a year, and their winter plumage is very different from the summer.

Sandrart, Joachim von, a German painter and engraver, chiefly esteemed in the latter capacity, was born in 1606, at Frankfort, and died in 1688. He wrote a work called the German Academy of Architecture, Sculpture, and Painting (1675, seq.).

Sandstone is in most cases composed chiefly of grains of quartz united by a cement, which is never very abundant, and often, indeed, is nearly or quite invisible. These grains are sometimes scarcely distinguishable by the naked eye, and sometimes are equal in size to a nut or an egg, as in those coarse sandstones called *conglomerate,* and sometimes pudding-stone or breccia. The cement is variable in quantity, and may be calcareous or marly, argillaceous or argillo-ferruginous, or even siliceous. When siliceous, the mineral often much resembles quartz. The texture of some sandstones is very close, while that of others is so loose and porous as to admit the passage of water. Sometimes, indeed, this rock is vesicular. Some varieties are so solid as to give fire with steel, while others are friable, and may be reduced to powder even by the fingers. Its fracture is always granular or earthy, although it may be at the same time conchoidal or splintery. Some sandstones have a slaty structure, arising from scattered and insulated plates of mica, and have been called *sandstone slate.* Its most common color is gray or grayish-white, sometimes with a shade of yellow-brown or green, and sometimes it is reddish or reddish-brown. In some cases, the color is uniform, in others, variegated. In addition to quartz, some sandstones embrace grains of feldspar, flint and sili ceous slate or plates of mica. The mica is sometimes in considerable quantities in those friable sandstones which accompany coal. Some sandstones are so ferruginous as to form a valuable ore of iron, containing either an oxide or the carbonate of iron. Sandstone, although decidedly a secondary rock, has been formed at different periods, under different circumstances, and is hence associated with different rocks. Red sandstone is sometimes connected with coal. Sandstone, more particularly in the older formation, sometimes contains metallic substances disseminated through the mass, or in beds or veins. Among these are sulphurets of iron, mercury, lead and copper, pyritous copper, and arsenical cobalt. Various organic remains occur in sandstone, among which are reeds, impressions of leaves, trunks of trees, and shells, both fluviatile and marine. In the U. States, sandstone is abundant in various parts. Sandstone, in some of its varieties, is very useful in the arts, and is often known by the name of *freestone*. When sufficiently solid, it is employed as a building stone. In most cases, it may be cut equally well in all directions; but some varieties naturally divide into prismatic masses. Some varieties are used as mill-stones for grinding meal, or for wearing down other minerals, preparatory to a polish. These stones, while rapidly revolving, sometimes burst with a loud and dangerous explosion. When the texture is sufficiently porous, sandstone is employed for filtering water. Some varieties are used for whetstones. Some sandstones absorb moisture, and, by exposure to the changes of the atmosphere, are gradually disintegrated; others become more solid by much exposure. Puddingstone, or conglomerate, is only a very coarse sandstone. It is composed of siliceous pebbles of quartz, flint, siliceous slate, &c., united by a cement, which is usually siliceous, sometimes both siliceous and ferruginous, and sometimes a little argillaceous. These pebbles vary in size from that of a pea to that of an egg. They are ordinarily rounded or oval; and it is, in fact, chiefly by the more or less rounded form of these pebbles that puddingstone is distinguished from breccia. It is sometimes employed for mill-stones, and some varieties receive a good polish. All true conglomerates must of course be composed of fragments of previously existing rocks. They have, however, been formed at very different periods. A breccia is an aggregate of angular fragments of the same mineral, or of different minerals, united by some cement. Sometimes, however, a few of the fragments are a little rounded.

Sandwich Islands; a cluster of islands in the North Pacific ocean, discovered by captains Cook and King in 1778, who gave them their present name in honor of the first lord of the admiralty. The group consists of ten islands, of which eight are inhabited, and extends from lat. 18° 50′ to 22° 20′ N., and from lon. 154° 53′ to 160° 15′ W., lying about one third of the distance from the western coast of Mexico to the eastern coast of China. The population of the whole group was estimated by captain King at 400,000, but, according to Ellis, does not at present exceed 150,000, the diminution being owing partly to the desolating wars of Tamehameha's reign, and partly to the ravages of a pestilence brought in by foreign vessels, which has twice prevailed in the islands. The total superficial extent is about 6000 square miles. The principal islands in extent and population are Hawaii (Owhyhee), 4000 square miles, 85,000 inhabitants; Maui (Mowee), 600 square miles, 20,000 inhabitants; Oahu (Woahoo), 520 square miles, 20,000, containing the town of Honolulu, the residence of the king, of the foreign functionaries, and twelve or fourteen merchants, chiefly Americans, with about 7000 inhabitants; Tauai (Atooi), 525 square miles, 10,000 inhabitants. The latter island and Nihau (Oneehow) are distinguished for the cultivation of the yam, and are much resorted to by ships for supplies of that article. Most of the islands are volcanic and mountainous. In some places, the volcanoes are in activity. Several of the summits are of great height. The loftiest, Mouna Roa, and Mouna Kea, are estimated at about 15,000 feet. The climate is warm, but not unhealthy, the winter being marked only by the prevalence of heavy rains between December and March. A meteorological table gives as the greatest heat during the year, 88° of Fahrenheit, as the least, 61°. The only quadrupeds originally found in these islands were a small species of hogs, dogs, and a sort of rat. There are now large herds of cattle in Hawaii, and many tame ones in the other islands, goats, sheep, and horses. There are no poisonous reptiles, excepting centipeds, which are neither large nor numerous. There are an abundance of sea-fowl on the coasts, and in the interior a species of parrot and a kind of woodpecker, with which the images of the gods were formerly adorned. The vegetable productions are taro (*arum esculentum*), yam, bread-fruit, cocoa-nut, and strawberry. Oranges, grapes, and other tropical fruits, have been introduced, and thrive well, and some culinary vegetables are cultivated for the shipping which resorts thither. The situation of the Sandwich islands renders them important to vessels navigating the Northern Pacific, partly for repairs and provisions, and partly in commercial respects. After the visit of Vancouver (1792), they were not much visited, except by traders from the U. States, who, having discovered among them the sandal wood, conveyed large quantities of it to China, where it is burnt in the temples. The independence of the Spanish colonies, and the prosecution of the whale-fishery on the coasts of Japan have greatly increased their importance. The following account of the number and tonnage of American ships which annually visit them, is from Stewart's Visit to the South Seas in 1829 and 1830 (New York,1831):—Vessels direct from the U. States for sandal wood, returning by way of China or Manilla, six (together 1800 tons); vessels bound to North-west coast,which generally winter here, five (1000 tons); vessels bound from the Spanish-American republics to China or the East Indies, eight (2500 tons); vessels owned by American residents, and trading to North-west coast, to Mexico, China, and Manilla, six (1000 tons); vessels engaged in the whale-fishery on the coast of Japan, 100 (35,000 tons); making a total of 125 vessels, and 40,000 tons. The natives are, in general, rather above the middle stature, well formed, with fine muscular limbs, and open countenances. Their hair is black or brown, and frequently curly; their complexion a kind of olive, and sometimes reddish-brown. Their language is a dialect of that spoken by the inhabitants of the Society islands. They are of a mild and gentle disposition, inquisitive and intelligent; but previously to the abolition of their idolatrous religion, the practice of sacrificing human victims prevailed among them. Since their adoption of Christianity, they have made a no less wonderful progress in the arts of civilized life than in moral character. They have many convenient and handsome houses, neat and comfortable clothing, &c. Stewart, who visited the islands in 1829, after an absence of four or five years, gives a striking description of the change which had taken place in that interval. After the visit of captain Cook, who was killed at Hawaii in 1779, the islands were involved in a series of destructive wars between several rival chiefs, for the undivided sovereignty. The result of these struggles was the ascendency of Tamehameha, chief of Hawaii, a sagacious, enterprising and ambitious prince. He built a navy, armed his guard in the European manner, fortified his palace with cannon, encouraged commerce, and introduced various mechanical arts among his subjects. On his death in 1819, he was succeeded by his son Rihoriho; and at about the same time idolatry was abolished and the idols burnt. During the last year of his reign, Tauai and Nihau, the only islands of the group not subdued by Tamehameha, submitted to his government. Rihoriho, with his queen, died in England in 1824, and his brother and successor, Kauikeaouli, is at present (1832) about 20 years of age. The regency has been in the hands of the queen-mother, Kaahumanu. In 1820, a mission was established at Hawaii by the American Board of Foreign Missions. The missionaries fortunately arrived just after the abolition of the national idolatry, and their efforts have been attended with great success. Not only have they introduced the arts, comforts and usages of civilized society to a great extent, but the Christian religion has been embraced by nearly the whole population. Printing presses have been established, books printed in the native language, an alphabet of twelve letters (five vowels and seven consonants) invented, schools established, and churches built. The Missionary Herald for Jan., 1832, states the whole number of schools in the islands to be above 900, with 50,000 learners. Missions have been established in Oahu, Hawaii, Maui, Taui; and in 1830 a band consisting of seven persons (three missionaries), and in 1831 another of nineteen persons (eight missionaries and a printer), sailed for the same destination. See Ellis, *Tour through Hawaii* (3d ed. 1827); lord Byron's *Voyage to the Sandwich Islands* (1827); Stewart's *Residence in the Sandwich Islands*.

Sandwich-Land; a barren, desert, and frozen island in the South Atlantic ocean, discovered by captain Cook in 1775; lat. 58° 35′ S.; lon. 26° 44′ W Seals, whales, and other *cetacea*, penguins and other sea-birds, are the only animals found here.

Sandy Hook; a small island on the coast of New Jersey, in the township of Middleton, seven miles south of Long Island, and 25 south of New York. It was formerly a peninsula. Sandy Hook, or Point, forms a capacious harbor. Here is a light-house on the north point of the Hook, in lat. 40° 26′ N., lon. 72° 2′ W.

SANDYS, George; second son of the archbishop of that name, born in 1577. In 1589, he was placed at Oxford. In 1610, he commenced his travels through the Levant and other parts of the Turkish empire, returning home through Italy, and staying some time at Rome. This journey occupied him upwards of two years. On his return to England, he published, in 1615, an account of the countries through which he had passed. This work was followed by several poetical productions, the first of which, a translation of Ovid's Metamorphoses, originally printed in London in 1627, with the first book of the Æneid annexed, is highly spoken of by Dryden, who styles the author "the best versifier of the last age." He also wrote a Paraphrase on the Psalms and upon the Hymns dispersed through the Old and New Testaments (London, 1636; reprinted in folio, 1638), and some other works. He died in 1643.

SANGALLO, Antonio, an eminent Italian architect of the sixteenth century, was born in the environs of Florence, and was intended for the business of a carpenter; but, happily visiting Rome, where he had two uncles who were architects, he was instructed by them in their art, his knowledge of which he perfected under Bramante, whom he succeeded as architect of the church of St. Peter. He was much employed under the popes Leo X, Clement VII, and Paul III, both in fortifying places and in the construction of public buildings, the grandeur and solidity of which have been much admired. He died in 1546.

SANGIAC (Turkish, *horsetail*) signifies, in the Turkish army, an officer who is allowed to bear only one horsetail, the pachas having two or three. The sangiac is also commonly the governor of a smaller district of country than a pachalic, thence called *sangiacat*, of which there are three or four in each pachalic. (See *Turkey*.)

SANGIACAT. (See *Sangiac*, and *Turkey*.)

SANGRAAL, or SANGREAL. (See *Round Table*, and *Romance*.)

SANGUINARINA; a vegetable alkali, discovered by Mr. A. A. Hayes, of Roxbury, in the root of the *sanguinaria Canadensis*, or blood-root. It is obtained as follows: Digest the bruised root in three parts of cold diluted sulphuric acid (water ten, acid one); after 24 hours, decant the fluid, and repeat the operations twice, using water but slightly acidulated; mix the liquors, and filter, and to the clear red liquor which passes, add a solution of ammonia, so long as it occasions precipitation; decant the fluid after subsidence, and wash the brown precipitate in cold water: it is sanguinarina combined with extractive and coloring matter, and mixed with some earths. Dissolve the soluble part in warm alcohol, and wash with the same; distil the clear fluid from a glass retort; when the solution becomes turbid by concentration, it must be decanted, while hot, into cylindrical vessels, one half filled with pure cold water: the alkali is precipitated in the form of a yellowish-white bulky powder, mingled with a substance insoluble in diluted acids, and resembling resin; by dissolving the soluble part in muriatic acid with ten of water, precipitating by ammonia, and treating as above, the alkali is obtained pure. It is a soft, white powder, destitute of odor, but having a bitter, acrid taste. It renders blue vegetable colors green; when heated, it melts into a brown, transparent and brittle substance. It dissolves in most acids, and forms along with them neutral salts of a pure scarlet-red color. The salts are soluble in water, to which they communicate their red color. They are inodorous; but their powder produces great irritation in the nostrils. They are all precipitated by infusion of galls, and are decomposed by alkalies and alkaline earths. The medicinal virtues of the salts of sanguinarina are chiefly deobstruent, acrid-narcotic, and emetic. The efficacy of the blood-root is attributable solely to the presence of this alkali.

SANHEDRIN (*Syriac*), or SYNEDRIUM (*Greek*); literally a *council*. The highest ecclesiastical and secular court of the Jews (q. v.), which was established for the decision of their internal differences, and the settlement of their affairs, was called *sanhedrin*. It consisted of seventy-one members, of the rank of priests, elders, and interpreters of the law (those skilled in biblical knowledge, or scribes), under the direction of the high-priest. Besides this high council, which had its seat in Jerusalem, there were also inferior courts in the country towns, composed of persons of the same classes. In Jerusalem there were two of these inferior courts. These national tribunals were limited, by the Roman procurators, to the affairs of religion and the settlement of questions relating to the observance of the Mosaic law; and they could not, even in such cases, inflict the punishment of death arbitrarily. After the destruction of Jerusalem by the Romans, these courts were annihilated, with the Jewish state. The great sanhedrin assembled at Paris, in 1806, by Napoleon, was only an occasional expedient, in order to regulate the civil relations of the Jews in the French empire.

San Marino. (See *Marino.*)

San Martin, José de, is a native of the Missions, on the banks of the river Parana. He made his first campaigns in the service of Spain, in the peninsula, holding the rank of captain; but he left Spain in 1811, and returned to his own country, where he rapidly rose to distinction. He received from the revolutionary government of Buenos Ayres the command of a division of the patriot army, with the commission of colonel. His first object was to improve the organization and discipline of the cavalry, in which he succeeded so well as to gain a victory over a small detachment of royalist troops at San Lorenzo, in 1813. This affair made him so conspicuous that he was appointed to the chief command in the province of Tucuman, in the hope that he might restore the patriot cause in that quarter, which was almost prostrated by the successive defeats of Belgrano. San Martin found only 570 men in Tucuman, the remnants of the patriot force. In the course of a few months, he had contrived to raise an army of 4000 men, from such slender beginnings. In 1814, he was obliged to resign his command by reason of bad health. When he resumed active service, he obtained the command in the province of Cuyo, contiguous to Chile, and devoted himself to the task of recruiting and equipping an expeditionary army, called the "army of the Andes," having for its object the liberation of Chile from the Spanish authority. The plan of the expedition was arranged in concert with O'Higgins and other Chilean exiles, who had taken refuge in Mendoza, the capital of Cuyo. Two years were consumed in the preparations necessary for this important movement. At length, at the very beginning of 1817, the patriot army of 4000 men broke up its cantonments at Mendoza, and entered the gorges of the Andes, to cross into Chile. San Martin effected the dangerous and difficult passage of the Andes in safety, and, February 12, encountering the Spanish forces posted at Chacabuco to resist his march, gained a complete and brilliant victory. Chile resumed its independence upon this event, O'Higgins becoming supreme director. Meanwhile, it was known that the viceroy of Peru was fitting out an expedition against the Chilean patriots; and preparations were made to receive it. The opposing armies met at Maypu (April 5, 1818), and again San Martin gained a complete victory, which finally accomplished the deliverance of Chile. Emboldened by these successes, he now conceived the plan of carrying his liberating arms into Peru itself, the only remaining possession of Spain in South America. Meanwhile, the republic of Buenos Ayres was distracted by one of the numberless domestic *bouleversemens* which have rendered its public administration a satire on the name of government. The faction, which happened to possess an ephemeral ascendency in the capital, called on San Martin to relinquish his splendid enterprise of liberating Peru, and to recross the Andes with his army, for the purpose of wasting its energies in the provincial broils of the republic. San Martin, and the other officers of the expeditionary army, unanimously refused obedience to the order; in consequence of which he was denounced by the government at Buenos Ayres. Hereupon he resigned his commission into the hands of the officers, and was unanimously reelected by them, thus holding his authority independent of the government. The liberating army sailed from Valparaiso Aug. 21, 1820, the land forces, under San Martin, being supported by a squadron under lord Cochrane. They landed at Pisco, and, being sustained by the Peruvians, gained possession of Lima and of most of the country, a revolutionary government being installed in the capital, and San Martin declared protector of Peru, Aug. 3, 1821. Various measures were adopted, under his auspices, for giving firmness to the new order of things, although the royalists continued in force in the interior, and still held the castles of Callao. A congress was convened at Lima, Sept. 20, 1822, by virtue of the decrees of the protector; and he immediately resigned all his authority into their hands, accepting in return only the honorary titles of generalissimo and founder of the liberty of Peru, with a pension of $20,000 per annum. He withdrew from Peru, first to Chile, and afterwards to Europe, finding little inducement, it is to be presumed, to enter into public life in Buenos Ayres, and perhaps doubting of his personal security in that country. In leaving Peru, he gave evidence of the purity and disinterestedness of his purposes, and seems entitled to the praise of good intention, if not of brilliant ability. He is still living. (Miller's *Mem.*, v. i.)

SANNAZARO, Jacopo, a distinguished Italian poet, who wrote both in Latin and Italian, was born at Naples, in 1458. He received his education in the school of Giuniano Maggo, and the academy of Pontanus, in which, according to the custom in the Italian academies, he adopted the name of Attius Sincerus. An early passion for Carmosina Bonifacia, whose praises he sung under the names of Harmosina and Phillis, unfolded his poetical talents. In the hope of conquering his love by separation, he went abroad, but, yielding to the impatience of his passion, returned to Naples, where he found his mistress dead. During his absence, he wrote his Arcadia, a series of idyls, which, although, like his other Italian poems, the work of his youth, still retains its reputation. His poetry attracted the notice of king Ferdinand and his sons Alphonso and Frederic, who made him the companion of their journeys and campaigns. Frederic, who ascended the throne in 1496, gave him the delightful villa Mergellina, with a pension of 600 ducats. But, in 1501, his benefactor was obliged to abdicate the throne, and flee to France; and Sannazaro was too faithful to desert him in his reverses. After the death of Frederic, he returned to Naples, and died there in 1533. He was buried in the church Santa Maria del Parto, which he had built at his villa. Sannazaro wrote sonnets and *canzoni* in Italian, several Latin poems, elegies, eclogues, epigrams, and a longer poem, *De Partu Virginis*, in three books. His elegance of expression, no less than the poetical beauty of his thoughts, give him a distinguished place among the modern Latin poets.

SANSCRIT, or SAMSCRIT (that is, the *perfect*), also DEVA-NAGARA (that is, the *divine*); a Brahminical language (because it is understood now by the Brahmins alone), the present dead language of the Hindoos, in which the books of their religion and laws, besides many other works of different sorts, are written. The remarkable similarity between the Sanscrit and the Greek languages reminds one of Gibbon's opinion, "that some, perhaps much, of the knowledge possessed by the Indians, originated from the Greeks of Bactriana." Francis Bopp has published a Complete System of the Sanscrit Language (Berlin, 1825, quarto). A. Langlois, also, in his *Monuments littéraires de l'Inde, ou Mélanges de Littérature Sanscrite*, &c. (Paris, 1827), has presented a popular view of the Sanscrit literature. (See also *Indian Languages*, and *Oriental Literature*.)

SANS-CULOTTES (i. e. without breeches); the name given in derision to the popular party, by the aristocratical, in the beginning of the French revolution of 1789. Like the epithet *gueux* (q. v.), bestowed on the patriot party in the Netherlands, and like that of *Methodists*, bestowed on the friends of Wesley, it was adopted by those to whom it was first applied by way of contempt. At the time when the most exaggerated principles of democracy prevailed, *sans-culottism* became a term of honor. In the French republican calendar, the *jours complémentaires* were at first called *jours sans-culottides*. (See *Calendar*.)

SAN SEBASTIANO, or RIO JANEIRO. (See *Rio Janeiro*.)

SANS-SOUCI (French, *without care*); a palace near Potsdam, where Frederic the Great was fond of residing; hence he is sometimes called the *philosopher of Sans-souci*.

SANTA AÑA, Antonio Lopez de, a Mexican general, of signal military abilities, and greatly distinguished in the political affairs of the republic, first became known extensively at the time of the second revolution (so called), when Iturbide promulgated the plan of Iguala (Feb. 24, 1821). At the head of the desultory forces of the country, Santa Ana succeeded, by a coup-de-main, in driving the royalists out of Vera Cruz, and in obtaining possession of that city, of which Iturbide appointed him governor. The castle of San Juan de Ulua, which commanded the harbor of Vera Cruz, continued to be held by the Spaniards; and in November, 1822, the emperor came to Xalapa, in the hope of effecting an accommodation with the Spanish governor of the castle. Meanwhile disputes had arisen between Santa Aña and general Echavarri, whom Iturbide had placed in command of the southern division, including Vera Cruz. The emperor summoned Santa Aña to Xalapa, to answer to the complaints made against him; and he, confident in the supposed good-will of Iturbide, whose cause he had zealously maintained, readily obeyed the summons. On his arrival, to his great surprise, he was treated harshly by Iturbide, and deprived of his command. Enraged by this unexpected treatment, Santa Aña hurried back to Vera Cruz, riding day and night, so as to reach the city in anticipation of the tidings of his disgrace. Instantly assembling his own regiment, he exhorted them to take up arms against the odious usurpation of Iturbide, and found them all ripe for the project, they having, indeed, supported the emperor only out of attachment to their immediate chief. Santa Aña accordingly unfurled the standard of the republic at Vera Cruz, and commenced hostilities against the forces of Iturbide. In this state of things, Guadalupe Vittoria left his hiding-place in the mountains, to join Santa Aña, and, being declared commander-in-chief of the insurgents, soon drew to his standard the old republican champions of independence. The fall of Iturbide, and the adoption of the federal constitution, were the well-known consequences of this movement. In the political arrangements that ensued, Santa Aña, not being duly considered, sailed from Vera Cruz (March, 1823) with six hundred men, and, landing at Tampico, advanced through the country to San Luis Potosi, where he took up his head-quarters, and declared himself protector of the federal republic. But he failed to inspire the people with confidence in his intentions, and was compelled to submit to a force sent against him from the capital. He was discharged, however, and for several years took but little part in public affairs, living the chief part of the time in seclusion on his estate near Xalapa. In 1825, an expedition against Cuba was contemplated, to be conducted by him, but was never prosecuted. But, in 1828, he again appeared on the stage, and with as decisive effects on the condition of public affairs as in 1822. When the news of Pedraza's election to the presidency, as the successor of Vittoria, reached Xalapa, Santa Aña raised his flag in favor of Guerrero; and such was his characteristic decision of purpose and execution, that the news of his rising, and of his investment and capture of the castle of Perote, reached the government almost simultaneously. Here he intrenched himself, and published a plan, having for its leading articles the annulment of the election of Pedraza, the declaring of Guerrero to be elected instead of him, and the popular object of the expulsion of the Spaniards. At length, however, Santa Aña was compelled to yield to the government troops, and fled for refuge into the mountains of Oaxaca, under sentence of outlawry, and apparently a broken and ruined man. But, in the mean time, the movement had been followed up in other parts of the republic with better success. Pedraza was compelled to flee his country, and Guerrero was recognised as president elect. Santa Aña was immediately appointed to the command of the very army sent against him, and to the government of Vera Cruz; and, on the inauguration of Guerrero into office, was made secretary of war, and commander-in-chief of the army (April, 1829). These political events a little preceded the foolish invasion of Mexico by the Spaniards, under Barradas, which afforded Santa Aña the opportunity of acquiring new laurels. Barradas landed near Tampico, July 27, 1829, and took up a position at Tamaulipas, separated from Tampico only by the river of the same name. Here, or at Altamira, in the same neighborhood, Barradas remained for about two months, when, after various engagements, he capitulated to the Mexicans under Santa Aña, who had assumed the command of the troops of the republic. Scarcely had Guerrero's administration time to enjoy this triumph, when the events of December, 1829, occurred, in consequence of which Guerrero was driven from office, with his particular friends, and the vice-president. Bustamente, assumed the direction of the government. Santa Aña was then consigned, for a while, to comparative obscurity; but is now once more in arms, and engaged in a third attempt to revolutionize the government, by driving Bustamente from power. His military talents, his activity and enterprise, and his reputation for successful intrigue, render him a dangerous enemy to the government.

Santa Cruz. (See *Cruz, Santa.*)

Santa Fé; capital of New Mexico; a territory of the Mexican republic, in the northern part of which it is situated, not far from the Rio del Norte; lat. 36° 12′ N.; lon. 109° 33′ W.; 1500 miles north-north-west of the city of Mexico. The population is between 3000 and 4000. It is the centre of a considerable overland trade between the northern part of Mexico and the western states of this Union. (See *Mexico, New*, and *Texas.*)

Santa Fé de Bogotá. (See *Bogotá.*)

Santa Fé de Guanaxuato. (See *Guanaxuato.*)

Santa Hermandad. (See *Hermandad.*)

Santa Martha. (See *Martha, Santa.*)

Santa Maura. (See *Leucadia.*)

Santander, New. (See *Mexico.*)

Santander (*S. Andero*); a small province of Spain (*Las montanas de Santander e de Burgos*), on the southern coast of the bay of Biscay, consisting of steep mountains and deep valleys. It is rich in iron of the best quality, and there are cannon founderies and manufactories of cast steel established in the mountain villages La

Cavada and Liergams. The coast has some excellent harbors. The principal town, Santander (10,000 inhabitants), has a safe and commodious and easily accessible harbor, and was formerly one of the privileged ports (*puertos habilitados*) which were allowed a free trade with South America. Its commerce with the north of Europe, to which it exports much wool, is considerable. It is the see of a bishop.

Santander, Francisco de Paula, was born at Rosario de Cucuta, in New Grenada, April 2, 1792, and received the best education which his country afforded. He commenced his studies in the place of his birth, and completed them at the college of Bogotá. During his course of study in philosophy and law, he was distinguished for his application, industry, and aptness in acquiring whatever he undertook. He received his degree in 1809, at the very time when the revolution began to agitate the country; and, like most other young men of spirit and talent, immediately embarked in the cause of independence. At first, he was merely an ensign in the militia of New Grenada; was afterwards selected as an aid by Manuel Castillo, military commandant and political chief of the province of Mariquita, and soon became attached, in the same capacity, to general Baraya. When Bolivar projected his first invasion of Venezuela, Castillo was employed to drive the Spaniards, under Correa, from the defiles of La Grita; and Santander, with two companies, was ordered to turn the defile by ascending the neighboring heights. He was successful, and, in consequence, Correa was obliged to destroy his baggage and retreat in disorder. Santander was next commissioned to defend the valley of Cucuta. He had but three hundred men. The Spaniards poured in a force ten times stronger than his own, and compelled him to evacuate Rosario, where they afterwards committed the most horrible atrocities, and succeeded in destroying Santander's little army. MacGregor was then sent to the succor of the province; and Santander commanded his vanguard. They recovered the province; and Santander, being made a colonel, was again charged with its defence. He was attacked, but repulsed the assailants; and was subsequently appointed to the more important post of Ocana. Having scarcely five hundred men under his command, he was about to be attacked by a greatly superior body of troops, but, by a bold and fortunate manœuvre, rejoined Urdaneta and Rovira, and the relics of the patriot divisions. He was now made second in command under general Serviez, who was posted at Puente Real. But the force of Murillo was overwhelming; and New Grenada became the prey of the Spaniards. Santander retired into Venezuela, and prepared to second the efforts of Bolivar. He was employed to organize the militia of the province of Casanare. To prevent this, the viceroy Samano despatched a force, under Barreiro, of 2500 men, who were harassed by the few troops under Santander, until the latter was joined by Bolivar. An engagement at Bojaca terminated in the total defeat of Barreiro. This campaign restored Bogotá to the patriots, and Santander was immediately appointed, by Bolivar, vice-president of Cundinamarca. He contributed, more than any other person, to the assembling of the congress of Cucuta; and that body elected him vice-president of Colombia. He took the oaths of office October 3, 1821. From that period, he is to be considered as the actual head of the executive; because Bolivar, the titular president, being engaged in prosecuting the war in Quito and Peru, left the administration of affairs entirely to the vice-president. Like Bolivar, he was elected to a second term of office, to commence January 1, 1827. He seems to have acted, all things considered, with judgment, prudence and ability, in the arduous task of balancing factions, giving effect to a new system, and healing the wounds of a country bleeding from a long war of the most terrible character. Until the insurrection of Paez in Venezuela, which broke out in May, 1826, Santander's success corresponded to his patriotism. During the residue of that year, he became extensively known as the great champion of that republican constitution which he was sworn to support, and, of course, became the object of unmitigated abuse, from the disorganizers and insurrectionists of Venezuela. He ended actual hostilities with Paez, and left the insurrection to be quieted by Bolivar, to whom the disaffected appealed. In 1827, Santander entered upon his second term of office, and from that time was opposed to Bolivar, and was the rallying point of the constitutional and republican party. In September, 1827, Bolivar entered upon the duties of the office of president, and, of course, the executive authority ceased to be vested in Santander, who was now regarded as the personal enemy of Bolivar; but, in fact, was hostile only to the design of the liberator to suspend or subvert the constitution, and assume the dictatorship of Colombia. This object he constantly and firmly resisted. After the dissolution of the convention of Ocaña in 1828, when the suffrages of the army placed Bolivar above the constitution, Santander sought to leave the country, but was unable to do it. At length, he was accused as an accomplice in an attempt to assassinate Bolivar. Although nothing was proved against him, except the general fact that he was the head of the republican party; and although his character and standing alone were enough to negative the presumption of his guilt; yet he was pronounced guilty, and sentenced to be banished. A fresh charge of correspondence with malcontents in Popayan occasioned his confinement in the prison of Boca Chica; but, at length, he regained his liberty, and departed from his country. After spending some time in Europe, he came to the United States in 1831, preparatory to returning to South America, where the death of Bolivar and the respect of his co-patriots have removed the obstacles to his influence. (*Revue Amér.*, No. 3, p. 450.) In May, 1832, commissioners arrived in Philadelphia to inform him that he had been elected president of Colombia.

Santee; a river of South Carolina, formed by the union of the Congaree and Wateree. It flows into the Atlantic by two mouths, twenty miles below Georgetown. It affords good navigation, at some seasons, nearly three hundred miles, to Morgantown, in North Carolina. It is connected with Cooper river by a canal. The main branch in North Carolina is called Catawba.

Santiago, the capital of Chile, is situated in a pleasant plain on the Mapocho, thirty leagues distant from the Pacific, seven from the Andes, fifty-five miles south-east of Valparaiso; lat. 33° 26′ S.; lon. 70° 44′ W. The population of the city and environs is about 40,000. Among the principal buildings are the mint, the cabildo, government-house, cathedral, and other churches, and several convents. The private houses are mostly built of clay baked in the sun; the churches and other principal buildings of brick or stone. The streets are straight and regular, and the city contains a number of handsome squares. (See *Chile.*)

Santiago, or St. Jago. (See *Jago, St.*)

Sap. (See *Plants.*)

Sap Green. This pigment is prepared by mixing the juice of the ripe berries of the buckthorn (*rhamnus catharticus*) with alum. The juice of the unripe berries has the color of saffron, and is used for staining maps or paper; and if the berries be gathered late in the autumn, the juice is purple. The buckthorn is a large shrub, with inconspicuous greenish flowers, somewhat resembling the privet when in fruit, which grows wild throughout Europe, and is naturalized in some parts of the U. States. The bark affords a beautiful yellow dye. The berries are small, globular and black, and possess purgative properties, but are chiefly employed in color-making, and sometimes in dyeing: they enter into commerce under the name of *French berries.*

Sappare (*cyanite; disthene; rhætizite*). The primary form of this mineral is a doubly-oblique prism, of which the terminations are nearly rhombs. The angles of the prism are 106° 15′ and 73° 45′; of the terminal plane on the prism, in one direction 100° 50′ and 79° 10′, and in the other 93° 15′ and 86° 45′. It ordinarily occurs in four or eight sided prisms of considerable length, and destitute of regular terminations. The cleavage is highly perfect, parallel with the broader faces of the prism, but less distinct in the direction of the narrower lateral face, and that of the terminal plane. Lustre vitreous; color generally some shade of blue, occasionally very intense berlin-blue; it is also green, gray and white; streak white, transparent or translucent; hardness not inferior to that of feldspar; on the solid angles, equal to quartz; specific gravity 3.6. The massive varieties consist of large, broad, columnar individuals; sometimes straight lamellar, often curved, variously aggregated; having their faces of composition, in most cases, irregularly streaked. Three varieties of the present species, analyzed, the first by Saussure, the second by Laugier, the third by Klaproth, have yielded,

Alumine,	54.50	55.50	55.50
Silica,	30.62	38.50	43.00
Lime,	2.02	0.50	0.00
Magnesia,	2.30	0.00	0.00
Oxide of iron,	6.00	2.75	0.50
Water,	4.56	0.75	0.00
Potash,	0.00	0.00	a trace.

It is not altered on being exposed to heat, and is infusible even in very high degrees of temperature. It is entirely soluble in borax. Some crystals exhibit positive, others negative electricity, on being rubbed. It occurs in crystals, or massive, imbedded in rocks of gneiss and mica-slate, and is frequently accompanied by staurotide

Crystals and large cleavable varieties are found at St. Gothard in Switzerland, the Zillerthal in the Tyrol, the Sau Alps in Carinthia, at Chesterfield in Massachusetts, and Litchfield, Connecticut, in the U. States. The variety of a white color in fine, interlacing prisms, called *rhætizite*, comes only from Pfitsch in the Tyrol. Thin laminæ of sappare are sometimes employed as a support in blow-pipe experiments with minerals. Blue transparent varieties are cut and polished, and then sometimes sold as an inferior kind of sapphire.

SAPPHIRE. (See *Corundum.*)

SAPPHO, a distinguished Greek poetess, was born at Mitylene, on the island of Lesbos, and flourished about 600 B. C. Alcæus, like her, a lyric poet, and a native of the same island, is said to have loved her; but his passion was not returned. The brilliant fame which she enjoyed seems to have subjected her to calumny, and even to persecution, on account of which she left Lesbos. She is particularly accused of unnatural love to her own sex; hence the expression *Sapphic love*. She must not be confounded with a later Sappho, also a native of Lesbos, the place of whose birth was Eresus, famous for having thrown herself from the Leucadian rock, in despair, on account of her unrequited love for a youth named Phaon. Ovid, however, confounds the two.—See Welker's *Sappho vindicated against a prevailing Prejudice* (Göttingen, 1816). The ancients ascribe various poems to the elder Sappho,—hymns, odes, elegies, epigrams,—of which only fragments have come down to us: these display deep feeling, glowing imagination, and a high finish. She is said to have invented several metres; at least one still bears her name, and has been used by ancient and modern poets:—

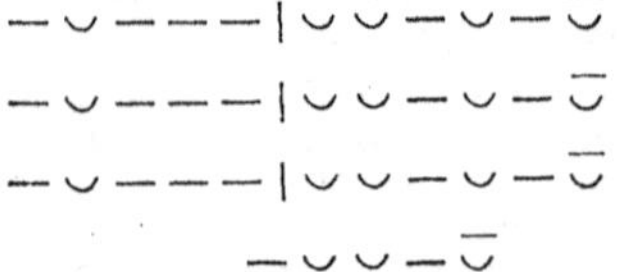

SARABAND; a dance, said to be derived from the Saracens. The tune is written in ¾ or ⅜ time, and consists of two parts. Its character is grave and expressive. It originated in Spain, where it was formerly danced to the castanets.

SARACENIC STYLE OF ARCHITECTURE. (See *Architecture*, vol. i, p. 342.)

SARACENS (*Orientals*); the name adopted by the Arabs after their settlement in Europe, as the term *Arabs* (people of the West), which indicated their geographical situation in Asia, was improper in Europe.

SARAGOSSA (in Spanish, *Zaragoza*), a city of Spain, capital of Arragon, lying in a fertile plain on the Ebro, one hundred and seventy-five miles north-east of Madrid; lon. 1° 42′ W.; lat. 41° 38′ N. It is an old town, built on the site of the ancient Roman colony Cæsar Augustus, of which the present name is a corruption. The streets, with the exception of the long and wide Cozo, and a few others, are narrow and crooked. There is a fine stone bridge, six hundred feet long, over the Ebro. Previous to 1808, it had 55,000 inhabitants, eighteen churches, and forty monasteries. Among the churches, that of Our Lady of the Pillar (*Nuestra Señora del Pilar*) is celebrated for its miraculous image of the virgin, to which pilgrimages are made from different parts of Spain. The canal of Arragon, nearly a hundred miles in length, which affords Navarre and Arragon a communication with the Mediterranean, approaches the city. The present population of the city is 45,000. Saragossa has gained celebrity by the two sieges which it sustained in 1808 and 1809. The adjoining provinces of Catalonia and Navarre were overrun by the French troops; Saragossa contained not more than two hundred and twenty regulars, and was unfortified; and the public treasury was empty. When the people were seeking for a leader, the rank of Palafox, and the favor which he was known to have enjoyed with Ferdinand, directed their choice to him, and, accordingly, May 25, 1808, he was proclaimed by them governor of Saragossa, and of all the kingdom of Arragon. He was then in his eight and twentieth year, and had but a scanty portion of military knowledge. He immediately called into service all the half-pay officers, formed several corps, composed, in part, of the students of the university, took other measures to sustain a siege, and, May 31, declared war against the French, in a proclamation remarkable for its energy. This paper was hardly issued, before a French corps of 8000 men marched to attack Saragossa. The French general was, however, met by the Spaniards, and, after a hard struggle, was compelled to retire. Palafox took advantage of this to quit the city for a while, in order to collect troops and organize the defence of the rest of the province. He returned with about 1500 men, who had retreated from Madrid, and was soon invested by the French, who had received powerful reinforcements, and a train of artillery. The besiegers carried the post of Torrero and some other exterior works, not without great loss, pushed forward their attacks against the gates of El Carmen and El Portillo, began to bombard the city, July 22, and, August 4, forced their way into the place, by the gate of Santa Engracia, and, at length, made themselves masters of nearly half of Saragossa. The French general now summoned Palafox to surrender. His summons was contained in the following laconic sentence: "Head-Quarters, St. Engracia, capitulation." With equal laconism, Palafox instantly replied, "Head-Quarters, Saragossa. War at the point of the knife." August 5, the brother of Palafox had opened a passage into the city, with 3000 regular troops. A council of war was now held, in which it was resolved that the remaining quarters of the city should be contested inch by inch, and that, should they be lost, the people should retire across the Ebro into the suburbs, destroy the bridge, and defend the suburbs to the last man. This resolution was unanimously applauded by the Saragossans. They did not, however, content themselves with resting on the defensive. They fell upon the besiegers with unequalled and irresistible fury. The struggle continued for eleven days, almost without intermission. Every day the people gained ground, till, at last, the enemy held only a narrow space within the walls. Convinced that there was no longer any hope of success, the French general abandoned the siege, which had lasted sixty-one days, and cost him several thousand men. Palafox availed himself of the breathing-time thus obtained to increase his force, and construct additional works. He was not allowed a long respite. To reduce Saragossa to submission was, on many accounts, an object of great importance to the French. In November, therefore, a large army, under marshals Mortier and Moncey, marched to recommence the siege. Palafox was defeated at Tudela, and again under the walls of Saragossa, and the place was invested. Being summoned to surrender, he replied and acted with the same energy as before. The approaches were vigorously carried on by the French, and a furious bombardment was incessantly kept up. Almost hourly combats took place between the besiegers and the besieged, in which the latter displayed a desperate valor. At length, January 27, a general assault was made, and the French established themselves on the breaches. Once more they penetrated, by degrees, into the city, and once more they met with the most obstinate and sanguinary resistance. Old men, women and children, all took a part in endeavoring to stop the progress of the besiegers. Not only street by street, but house by house, and even room by room, was contended for, like the outworks of a fortress, and frequently lost and recovered. The besiegers finally resorted to mining to win their way, their progress by open force being bought at too dear a rate. In this way they became masters of about one fourth of the surface of the city. Saragossa, however, would long have resisted all their efforts, had it not been assailed by a force more terrible than the besiegers. An epidemic fever raged in the place, and spread destruction among the ranks of the Saragossans, there being neither hospitals, nor medicines, nor even shelter for the sick. Palafox himself was attacked by it, and, February 20, was obliged to give up the command to general St. Marc, by whom the capitulation was signed on the following day. The garrison was reduced to less than 12,000 men, who, when they marched out of the city, had more the appearance of spectres than of human beings. During this second siege, 54,000 of the besieged perished, of whom a fourth were soldiers. (See *Spain.*)

SAR LOUIS. (See *Saar Louis.*)

SARATOGA; a post-township of New York, in Saratoga county, on the west side of the Hudson, thirty miles north-by-east from Albany; population in 1830, 2461. Saratoga is memorable as the place where general Burgoyne surrendered the British army, consisting of 5791 men, to general Gates, October 17, 1777. In 1819, Saratoga township was divided, and the western part was named *Saratoga Springs.*

SARATOGA SPRINGS is an incorporated village, containing celebrated mineral waters, and is situated seven miles north-east of Ballston Spa, and thirty-two north of Albany; population in 1830, 2204. Here are extensive establishments for the accommodation of the numerous invalids and people of fashion, who resort hither during the summer season. The surrounding country has very few charms. The springs are very numerous, and several of them are very large. The *Congress Spring* is the most celebrated, and great quantities of the water are bottled and sent to all parts of the union. (For the ingredients of this water, see *Congress Spring.*)

SARCOLATRÆ. (See *Apollinarians.*)

SARCOPHAGUS (from σαρξ, flesh, and φαγω, I eat); originally a species of limestone, found in the neighborhood of Assor, in Mysia, which, according to Pliny (*Hist. Natur.* ii, 96, and xxxvi, 17), had the power of destroying, within forty days, the corpses put into it, so that nothing remained entire except the teeth. Hence the name. This quality brought the stone into use for coffins, and thus the name came to be applied to all coffins of stone, though often used for a contrary purpose to that which the name expresses. The ancients, who embellished every thing, soon adorned the *sarcophagi* and often placed them upon the monuments which were originally erected over graves, to protect them against violence (*monumentum*, i. e. *munimentum*). Under the Roman emperors, this custom became more general, and rare species of stone were used. The Egyptian coffins of granite and alabaster served as models. Of the great number of *sarcophagi* which have come down to us, several are known by particular names; thus the sarcophagus of Homer, in the Besborodko gardens at St. Petersburg, and that of Alexander, in the British museum, once in the mosque of St. Athanasius at Alexandria, taken by the British from the French, during their campaign in Egypt. English archæologists have labored to prove its genuineness, and it is known that the body of Alexander was removed from the temple of Jupiter Ammon to Memphis, and afterwards to Alexandria, where Augustus and Septimius Severus (202 A. D.) saw it. The tomb, it is supposed, was so magnificent that the Christian destroyers spared it (though not the body), and changed it into a church of St. Athanasius. The sarcophagus, it is said, was used as a cistern. The statement of Chrysostom (*Opera* x, 625, ed. Montfaucon) seems to be inconsistent with this opinion, which, however, derives some support from an Oriental tradition. Clarke describes this sarcophagus, which is covered with hieroglyphics, in his Tomb of Alexander (Cambridge, 1805, 4to.). The form of these *sarcophagi* was ordinarily a parallelopipedon, or an oblong square, similar to our coffins. Sometimes the angles were rounded, thus assuming an elliptical shape. Some *sarcophagi* were not intended to contain the whole body, but only an urn.

SARD, or SARDOIN; a variety of carnelian, which exhibits, by reflected light, a dull reddish-brown color, but by transmitted light appears of a rich blood-red color.

SARDANAPALUS, or TONOSKONKOLEROS (supposed to be the Esar-Haddon of Scripture), whose name proverbially denotes effeminate softness and wantonness, was the last king of Assyria. He is said to have been a prince of great power and immense wealth, who, according to an inscription on his tombstone, built the cities of Tarsus and Anchiale in one day. Immersed in sensual gratification, he lived inactively and ingloriously, in women's clothes, among his concubines, and thereby excited against him the discontent of his subjects. Arbaces, a Median satrap, and Belesis, a Babylonian priest, together raised an army against him; whereupon Sardanapalus marched out to meet them, and overcame them in three battles. In the belief that he was perfectly secure, he returned anew to his pleasures, and prepared a splendid banquet for his victorious army. But Arbaces, aided by the Bactrians, attacked his camp by night, gained a great victory, and pursued the fugitives to the very gates of Nineveh. Here Sardanapalus defended himself for two years, while all his provinces in the mean time revolted. An inundation of the Euphrates at length destroyed a part of the city walls, and thereby rendered it impossible to continue the defence of Nineveh. In this desperate state of affairs, Sardanapalus set his palace on fire, and consumed himself, together with all his wives, servants and treasures, in the twenty-first year of his reign. His destruction is usually considered as having taken place in the year 888 B. C., but, according to Volney, it should be placed in the year 717.

SARDES, or SARDIS; the ancient capital of Lydia, on the river Pactolus, not far from the mount Tmolus. Under the Persians, it was a magnificent city, and a great market for slaves, on the commercial route from Asia to Europe. The Greeks conquered and burned it 500 B. C. An earthquake again destroyed it, but Tiberius rebuilt it. A small village stands at present on its site, and considerable ruins still attest its ancient grandeur.

SARDINIA; an island in the Mediterranean sea, having the title of kingdom, with a superficial area of 9100 square miles, and a population of 490,050. It contains nine towns, fifteen villages, and 377 hamlets, and is separated from Corsica on the north by the straits of Bonifacio The soil is fruitful, yielding corn, wine, oil, figs, and other southern fruits. There is an abundance of wood on the mountains.

but, on account of the want of good roads, the seaport towns are supplied from Corsica; on the same account Sardinia has no posts. The horses, which, in some parts, run wild, and the horned cattle, are small, but well made. The fisheries are important. Large quantities of salt and cheese are manufactured, and the latter is exported. The causes of the small population of this fertile island are to be referred to the accumulation of the landed property in a few hands, and the absence of the great proprietors (there are in Sardinia 376 fiefs, half of which belong to Spanish families), the privileges of the nobility and clergy, and the practice of private revenge (1000 murders have been committed in the space of one month). The interior exhibits an astonishing degree of barbarism; the peasants are clothed in leather or undressed skins, and the mountains are infested with banditti. The principal towns are the capital, Cagliari (q. v.), and Sassari (20,000 inhabitants). Sardinia was probably settled by Pelasgian colonies, in the time of the Heraclides, as the *noraghs*, or ancient monuments, found in the island, indicate. The number of these monuments is about 600: those which are entire are fifty feet high, with a diameter of ninety feet at base, and terminating at the summit in a cone. They are built on little hills, in a plain, of different sorts of stones, and in some cases are surrounded by a wall. The island then belonged successively to the Carthaginians, Romans, Vandals, Saracens, the popes, the German emperors, to Pisa, Genoa, and Spain. In 1720, it was ceded to the duke of Savoy, as an indemnification for the loss of Sicily. (See *Sardinian Monarchy.*) The island was mildly governed by a viceroy, and the inhabitants allowed to retain their old usages. Some dissatisfaction, however, arose towards the close of the century, and, in 1793, a rebellion broke out, which was terminated by the concessions of the government in 1796. The revenue from the island is inconsiderable. The inhabitants are Catholics, and speak several different dialects, some of which are a mixture of Spanish and Italian. The better classes speak pure Italian.—See Marmora's *Voyage en Sardaigne, de* 1819—1825 (Paris, 1826); Mimaut's *Histoire de Sardaigne* (1825); Smyth's *Present State of Sardinia* (Lond., 1828); and Petit-Radel's *Notices sur les Nuraghes de la Sardaigne* (Paris, 1826).

Sardinian Monarchy; a kingdom of the south of Europe, composed of the island of Sardinia, and of several countries of the continent. It comprises in the whole an extent of 28,000 square miles, with a population (in 1829) of 4,165,277 (300,000 French in Savoy, 3,865,077 Italians, and 3200 Jews). The population, with the exception of the Jews, and 21,900 Waldenses, is entirely Catholic. The continental parts of which the monarchy is composed are as follows. The duchy of Savoy; the duchy of Piedmont; the county of Nice or Nizza, with the principality of Monaco; the duchies of Montferrat and (Sardinian) Milan; and the duchy of Genoa (see the separate articles); which are divided, for administrative purposes, into eight provinces; Savoy, Turin, Coni, Alessandria, Novara, Aosta, Nizza and Genoa. The revenue amounts to $900,000; the expenditure to $1,050,000; debt to $2,500,000; army, 28,000 men, exclusive of 40,000 militia, on the island of Sardinia. The power of the crown is unlimited: the administration is conducted by three secretaries of state: the succession to the throne is confined to the male line. In the island of Sardinia there are estates, and in Genoa the assent of the estates is necessary for the imposition of new taxes. The nobility is numerous, but not exempt from taxation. The clergy (39 archbishops and bishops, 3996 parish priests, 293 male and 144 female convents) is not very wealthy. The papal power is limited by a concordate. There are four universities, at Turin, Genoa, Cagliari and Sassari, but education is in a low state. The reigning prince, the first of the house of Savoy Carignan, is Charles Emanuel, born 1800, married Theresa, sister of the grand-duke of Tuscany, in 1817, succeeded his uncle Charles Felix, May, 1831. He has two sons, Victor Emanuel (born in 1820), and Ferdinand (born in 1822). The royal title is king of Sardinia, Cyprus and Jerusalem, and duke of Savoy. The crown-prince is styled prince of Piedmont. Former sovereigns, Victor Amadeus II, 1713—30; Charles Emanuel III, to 1773; Victor Amadeus III, 1796; Charles Emanuel IV, abdicated 1802; Victor Emanuel I, abdicated 1821; Charles Felix, died 1831. The nucleus of this monarchy was Savoy, a fragment of several states that had crumbled to pieces (the old kingdom of Burgundy, the Frankish monarchy, the Carlovingian kingdom of Italy, and the kingdom of Arles), which became independent in the beginning of the eleventh century. Rodolph III, last king of Arles, created Berthold count of Savoy in 1016. He was probably the ancestor of the subsequent counts and dukes of Savoy. The counts of Savoy gradually extended their territories, partly by marriages, partly by their adherence to the German emperors, in the disputes between the Guelfs and Gibelines, partly by purchase, and partly by an artful policy in their connexions with the Spanish, French and Austrian courts. By the marriage of the duke Louis with Anne of Lusignan, daughter of James, king of Cyprus, and the will of the queen-dowager of Cyprus (1482), the house of Savoy obtained claims to the kingdom of Cyprus, which caused the kings of Sardinia, at a later period, to assume the title of kings of Cyprus and Jerusalem. In the history of the state we may distinguish two periods. —I. From the first settlement of the succession (1383) by the will of count Amadeus VI, which established the indivisibility of the dominions, and the descent in order of primogeniture, until the admission of the Sardinian monarchy into the European family of states, by the peace of Utrecht. In this period, among other acquisitions, the house of Savoy gained possession of the county of Nizza (1399), and count Amadeus VIII received the ducal title from the emperor Sigismund in 1416; but in the wars between the emperor Charles V and Francis I of France, it lost, in the middle of the sixteenth century, the Valais and Geneva, which put themselves under the protection of Switzerland, and the Pays de Vaud, which was taken possession of by Berne. Philibert Emanuel, who had been driven from his territories by the French, served with so much distinction as the general of Philip II of Spain, in the war against France, that by the peace of Chateau Cambresis (1559), Savoy and Piedmont were restored to him. Meanwhile Protestantism had crept into the country. At the exhortation of the pope, Philibert determined to convert the Protestants, among whom were many Waldenses, by force; but he was several times defeated by them in the mountains; on one of which occasions he lost 7000 men, and was obliged to grant them freedom of religious worship. This prince encouraged manufactures among his subjects, and laid the foundation for the present extensive culture of silk by the introduction of mulberry trees. He also began the construction of several fortresses, and built the citadel of Turin. In 1476, he acquired the principality of Oneglia by exchange, and the county of Tenda by purchase. In the war for the Spanish succession, duke Victor Amadeus II acquired possession of a part of Milan (Alessandria Val di Sesia, &c.) as an imperial fief, and of the duchy of Montferrat, which had been originally (twelfth century) a German marquisate, and which should have devolved to Piedmont by descent in 1631. The peace of Utrecht (1713) added Sicily, with the royal title; but, in 1720, the new king was obliged to receive Sardinia in lieu of that island.—II. The second period, from 1720 to the present time, embraces three distinct divisions in Sardinian history. 1. *The forty-three Years' Reign of King Charles Emanuel III* (1730—73) who was equally distinguished as a general and a ruler. By the peace of Vienna (1735), as the ally of France and Spain against Austria, he obtained a second fragment of Milan (Tortona and Novara), as an imperial fief, and by the treaty of Worms (1743), during the war for the Austrian succession, a third fragment (Anghiera, Vigevano, &c.), likewise as fiefs of the empire. In 1762, he was the mediator of the peace between France and England. By the wisdom of his government, the country was placed in a most prosperous condition; and the new code of laws (*Corpus Carolinum*), promulgated in 1770, is an honorable monument of his reign. In his disputes with the pope, Charles Emanuel maintained the rights of the state, as acknowledged by the concordate of 1726 (confirmed by Benedict XIV, in 1742), made all ecclesiastical appointments, subjected the clergy to taxation, and made his sanction requisite to give validity to the papal bulls. 2. *The unfortunate Reigns of Victor Amadeus III* (*died* 1796), *and of Charles Emanuel IV* (*abdicated* 1802). The former joined Austria against France, July 25, 1692, and was stripped of Savoy and Nizza in September of the same year. The latter entered into an alliance with France against Austria (April 5, 1797); but his territory was, nevertheless, invaded by the French directory, which made the complaints of the Sardinian people against the burden of taxes and the privileges of the nobility a pretext, and he was compelled to cede all his continental dominions (Dec. 9, 1798) to France. He retained only the island of Sardinia, whither he was obliged to retire with his family. June 4, 1802, he abdicated in favor of his brother, Victor Emanuel I, and lived as a private individual at Rome, where he died in 1819, having entered the order of Jesuits in 1817. From 1806, Piedmont with Genoa was incorporated with the French empire.—

3. *The Restoration and Extension of the Sardinian Monarchy by the Congress of Vienna.* Victor Emanuel I returned, May 20, 1814, to Turin, his continental territories having been restored by the peace of Paris. Half of Savoy was left in the hands of the French; which, however, was restored by the treaty of Paris in 1815 (November 20), together with Monaco. On the other hand, Carouge and Chesne, with 12,700 inhabitants, were ceded to Geneva (October 23, 1816). The congress of Vienna was desirous of strengthening the kings of Sardinia, as holders of the passes of the Alps, and England wished to establish a commercial intercourse with the court of Turin. Genoa, therefore, was annexed as a duchy to the Sardinian monarchy, December 14, 1814. Victor Emanuel restored, as far as was practicable, the old constitution, readmitted the Jesuits, subscribed the holy alliance, and established a rigorous censorship. In 1818, he confirmed the sales of the royal domains made by the French, and appropriated an annual sum of 400,000 lire for the indemnification of the emigrants, who had lost their estates. As an ally of England, he obtained a permanent and honorable peace with the Barbary powers, through the British admiral lord Exmouth. In March, 1821, in consequence of the troubles which resulted in the occupation of the country by the Austrians, he abdicated the crown, in favor of his brother, Charles Felix. (See *Piedmontese Revolution.*) The measures which were adopted subsequently to the suppression of the insurrection, were directed to realize the plan of the congress of Vienna in erecting Sardinia into a partition wall between Austria and France. In compliance with the terms of the convention concluded between the Sardinian general della Torre and the Austrian, Prussian and Russian ambassador, Sardinia was occupied by Austrian troops, for which Austria was to receive $1,250,000 a year, besides provisions. Rigorous measures were taken to extirpate "revolutionary principles," as they were styled. In the universities of Turin and Genoa, and other institutions of education, a strict supervision over the conduct of the students was maintained; the Jesuits were admitted into Savoy and the island of Sardinia; the royal schools were committed to their care, and, in 1823, the provincial college was put under their direction. The Jews were subjected to severe burdens and great disabilities. To protect the Genoese commerce against the Barbary corsairs, the whole navy of Sardinia (consisting of one frigate and eight smaller vessels) was ordered to sea, but effected nothing. Through the mediation of Great Britain, however, a peace was concluded in 1825, Sardinia agreeing to make certain presents to the dey of Algiers and the bey of Tunis. The congress of Verona (1822) provided for the gradual evacuation of the country by foreign troops, which was completed towards the close of 1823; but, at the same time, as apprehensions were entertained from the Piedmontese fugitives in Switzerland, such representations were made to the federal diet as not only to effect their removal, but to impose restrictions upon the Swiss press. Intercourse with Spain was broken even previously to the invasion of that country by the French; and the prince of Carignan (the present king), who had been banished from court on account of his conduct during the Piedmontese insurrection, served as a volunteer under the duke d'Angoulême. Still Sardinia embraced the Austrian politics with more cordiality than the French, both in regard to her domestic administration, and in her Italian policy in general. A royal edict, of 1825, prohibited any person learning to read or write, who had not property to the amount of 1500 lire (about $400), and any one studying at the university who had not as much more in the funds. Translations of the works of Göthe, Wieland, and Schiller, were also prohibited within the Sardinian states. Charles Felix died March 29, 1831, and was succeeded by Charles Albert, prince of Carignan. Some troubles broke out in Sardinia: the Genoese merchants offered the king a large sum of money to induce him to consent to the independence of Genoa; but the offer was rejected, and his majesty was actually besieged in Genoa, until relieved by Austrian troops.—See the articles *Italy*, and *Italy, Travels in*, with the works there referred to; see also Manno's *Storia di Sardegna* (Turin, 1825); Mimaut's *Histoire de Sardaigne* (Paris, 1825); and De la Marmora's *Voyage de Sardaigne* (1826).

SARDONYX. (See *Chalcedony.*)

SARMATIANS. The Sclavonians and other nations, who inhabited the northern parts of Europe and Asia, were called by the ancients *Sarmatians*. European Sarmatia comprehended (according to Gatterer, who, however, extended it too far) Poland from the Vistula, Prussia, Courland, Livonia, Russia, and European Tartary, together with the Crimea; Asiatic

Sarmatia embraced Asiatic Russia, Siberia and Mongolia. The Sarmatians were nomadic tribes. They were probably descendants of the Medes, and dwelt originally in Asia, between the Don, the Wolga, and mount Caucasus. They were allies of king Mithridates VI of Pontus, even at that time were settled on the west of the Don, and afterwards extended over the country between the Don and the Danube. They were, at times, formidable to the Asiatic kings. Among the most remarkable of them were the Jazyges and the Roxolani. They carried on long and bloody, but for the most part unsuccessful, wars against the Romans. A part of them, with other barbarians, entered Gaul A. D. 407; the remainder were conquered by Attila, but after his death submitted to the emperor Marcian, who assigned them a residence on the Don. Here they afterwards united themselves to the Goths, and formed with them one nation.

Sarpi, Pietro. (See *Paul of Venice.*)

Sarracenia, or Side-saddle Flower. The species of *sarracenia* are among the most singular productions of the vegetable world. They are exclusively North American, and, according to Mr. Nuttall, are not found west of the Alleghanies. The leaves have the form of a long tube or funnel, conic or swollen, often containing water, and terminated by an appendage, which varies in form in the different species. The flowers resemble, in size and form, those of the splatter-dock or yellow water-lily (*nuphar*). All inhabit marshy grounds. The *S. purpurea* is the most common species, and by far the most widely diffused, being frequently met with from Hudson's bay to Carolina: the stems are eight or ten inches high, arising from the centre of the leaves, simple, leafless, and are terminated with large flowers, of a green color mixed with reddish-brown; the leaves have a large heart-shaped appendage, smooth externally, and covered within with scattered whitish horizontal hairs. The other species are confined to the Southern States.

Sarsaparilla. The roots of the *smilax sarsaparilla*, and doubtless of other species of smilax (for all those plants closely resemble each other in their sensible properties), are very long and slender, with a wrinkled bark, brown externally and white within, and have a small woody heart. They are inodorous, and have a mucilaginous and very slightly bitter taste; they seem to possess no very active principle, although they have enjoyed a very high repute, at different times, as a specific in venereal and scrofulous diseases: they have sudorific and diuretic properties, but only in a slight degree. Sarsaparilla is one of the ingredients of the famous Rob of Laffecteur, as well as of Swaim's Panacea, and various other similar remedies. The species of smilax are very numerous in the U. States, especially in the southern parts. They are green vines, usually spiny, with scattered leaves, and are very troublesome in the woods, in certain districts, forming impenetrable thickets. They are allied, in their botanical characters, to the asparagus, but differ widely in habit; the leaves are coriaceous or membranous, entire, nerved, and usually more or less heart-shaped; the leaf-stalks are generally provided with tendrils at the base. The flowers are diœcious, chiefly disposed in little axillary umbels, and the corolla is divided into six lobes; the male flowers have six stamens; the fruit is a small globular berry, containing three seeds, or often one or two only, by reason of abortion. The *S. China* grows in China and Japan, and the roots are employed in those countries for the same purposes, and have enjoyed the same reputation as our sarsaparilla. It is, besides, used for food. The true sarsaparilla has smooth, oval, membranous, heart-shaped leaves, and grows in Mexico, Peru and Brazil: it is said, likewise, to inhabit the U. States; but it is not probable that our own is the same with the South American species.

Sarti, Joseph, a composer, was born at Faenza, in 1729, and died in 1802. He was, for a long time, master of the chapel to Catharine II, in St. Petersburg, who treated him very liberally. He composed a grand Te-Deum for the taking of Oczakow, the bass of which was accompanied by cannons of different calibre. A piece of music composed by him for Good Friday, was performed by sixty-six singers and one hundred Russian horns, besides the usual instruments.

Sarto, Andrea del (his proper name is *Andrea Vannucchi*); a celebrated painter, of the Florentine school, born at Florence, in 1488. His teachers were not of a high order, and he cultivated his talents principally by the study of great masters, such as Leonardo and Michael Angelo. Some maintain that he was deficient in invention; whence, in some of his compositions, he made use of the engravings of Albert Dürer, which had then become known. He painted many pieces for his native city. Francis I in duced him, by a considerable salary, to go to France in 1518. But his extravagant wife led him into acts of ingratitude against the prince. He soon went back to Italy, and appropriated to the use of himself and his wife large sums, which had been given him, by his royal patron, to purchase the pictures of great masters in Italy. He repented, it is true, of his faults, but could not recover the king's favor. Among other works, he painted, about this time, the beautiful Sacrifice of Abraham, which has since been placed in the gallery of Dresden. The following anecdote is related of his wonderful skill in imitation:—He copied Raphael's portrait of Leo X so exquisitely as even to deceive Giulio Romano, who had aided Raphael in the drapery. Among his most celebrated works is a Burial in the palace *Pitti*, and the Dead Savior with Mary and the Saints, in the gallery of the grand-duke; also a beautiful Madonna, in the church of *l'Annunziata*, called *Madonna del sacco*, and several others in Florence; a Charity, now in Basle; Tobias with the Angel; and several Holy Families; the History of Joseph, in two paintings, in the Paris museum. In 1529, when Florence was taken, the soldiers, on entering the refectory which contained his picture of the Last Supper, were struck with awe, and retired without committing any violence. He died of the plague, in 1530. His coloring in fresco, as well as in oil, was full of sweetness and force: his draperies are easy and graceful. The naked, in his compositions, is excellently designed, but his figures want that force and vivacity which animate the works of other great painters, though they possess correctness, truth and simplicity. Sometimes he is too anxious to produce effect. Giacomo de Pontormo was his pupil.

Sarum, Old; a rotten borough in Wiltshire, two miles north of Salisbury. It was anciently a considerable city, and by the Romans called *Sorbiodunum*, though at present reduced to some ruins and intrenchments. Two members, however, are yet returned to parliament by the proprietors, and the election takes place in the field, on the spot where the last houses of the city stood. The present proprietor of Old Sarum (lord Caledon) paid about £60,000 for the small estate on which the borough stands. It was the original situation of Salisbury, and the bishop had a castle here; but the see was removed to the present situation of Salisbury (q. v.), in the year 1219. Before the reformation in England, the most celebrated liturgy in use in that country was that styled *secundum usum Sarum*, compiled by the bishop of Salisbury, in the eleventh century.

Sassafras. (See *Laurel*.)

Sassoferato; a painter, so called from the place of his birth, a town in the duchy of Urbino, States of the Church. His true name was *Giambattista Salvi*. He was born in 1605, learned the elements of his art from his father, and afterwards studied under Domenichino, Guido and Albani. His works resemble those of the latter, and are executed with the same care. His paintings were chiefly the Madonna and Child, the latter sleeping. His heads are expressive and lovely.

Satan. (See *Devil*.)

Sate; an Egyptian goddess. (See *Hieroglyphics*, vol. vi, p. 319.)

Satin; a soft, closely-woven silk, with a glossy surface. In the manufacture of other silken stuffs, each half of the warp is raised alternately; but in weaving satin, the workman only raises the fifth or the eighth part of the warp; thus the woof is hidden beneath the warp, which, presenting an even, close and smooth surface, is the more capable of reflecting the rays of light. In this way satin acquires that lustre and brilliancy which distinguish it from most other kinds of silks. The chief seats of this branch of manufacture are Lyons in France, and Genoa and Florence in Italy. From the East Indies are imported those light stuffs called Indian or Chinese satins. They are either plain, damasked, striped, open-worked, or embroidered. Both in lustre and execution, they are far inferior to the Lyonese satins; they, however, possess this peculiar property, that, even after scouring, they retain their original gloss.

Satin-Spar; carbonate of lime, in delicate, almost compact, white fibres. (See *Lime*.)

Satire; in the widest sense of the word, pungent ridicule or cutting censure of faults, vices or weaknesses; hence the phrase a "satirical person." In a narrower sense, in which it is more commonly used, it is a poem, of which ridicule and censure are the object and chief characteristic. This species of poetry had its origin with the Romans: the name is derived from *satur* (by no means from *satyr*), and refers, originally, to the mixture of subjects treated, and of metres used, in the earlier productions of this kind. Satire is one of the latest branches of poetry cultivated, because it presupposes not merely much natural wit, but also acute observation, and much variety of life and manners to call this wit into exercise. In fact, it is only in an advanced state of society, where folly and vice force themselves on the public eye, that a taste can exist for this species of production. As the object of satire is always castigation, it is distinguished from mere wit, which may occupy itself simply with the ludicrousness of particular relations. The form of satire is very varied. It may be in the shape of epistles, tales, dialogues, dramas (as with Aristophanes), songs, epics, fables, &c. The most common form of satire, however, is that of a simply didactic composition. The ancients wrote their satires in iambic and dactylic verse. The moderns generally use the iambus, sometimes the Alexandrine (q. v.), sometimes the iambic verse of five feet, the latter sometimes with, sometimes without rhyme. The proper didactic satire originated, as we have said, with the Romans; and its inventor was Lucilius: Horace, Juvenal and Persius developed it. Vulpius, Casaubon and König have written on the Roman satire. Of the modern satirists, we may mention, among the Italians, Ariosto, Alamanni, Salvator Rosa, Menzini, Dotti, Gasparo Gozzi, Alfieri, &c.; among the Spaniards, Cervantes, Quevedo and Saavedra; among the French, Regnier, Boileau, and Voltaire, &c.; among the Germans, Seb. Brand, Ulr. Hutten, Fischart, Haller, Rabener, Lichtenberg, Falk, Wieland, &c.; among the English, Donne, Rochester, Dryden, Butler, Pope, Swift, Young, Churchill, Johnson, Peter Pindar (Wolcot), Gifford, Mathias; among the Poles, Krasiczky. The Greeks had not the proper satire. The poem of Archilochus, and that of Simonides, were more properly lampoons; and the *silli* had probably a didactic form, but were of the nature of parody. Entirely different from the satire was the *drama satyricon* of the Greeks, invented by Pratinas—a mixture of tragic, at least heroic action with comic. These dramas served as interludes and after-pieces, and had a low comic character. We possess only one—the *Cyclops* of Euripides.—See Eichstädt, *De Dramate Græcorum comico-satyrico*, &c., and Herrmann and Pinzger on the same subject.

Satraps, in the Persian empire; the governors of the provinces which were called *satrapies*. The term *satrap* is sometimes used to signify a petty despot.

Saturation. A fluid, which holds in solution as much of any substance as it can dissolve, is said to be *saturated* with it. But saturation with one substance does not deprive the fluid of its power of acting on, and dissolving some other bodies; and in many cases it increases this power. The word *saturation* is also employed in another sense. The union of two principles produces a body, the properties of which differ from those of its component parts: when the principles are in such proportion that neither predominates, they are said to be *saturated* with each other; but if otherwise, the most predominant principle is said to be *subsaturated*, and the other *supersaturated*.

Saturday (*Saturni dies*, Saturn's day), so called from the planet Saturn; the seventh day of the week; the *Sabbath* of the Jews. It is called by the Italians, *Sabbato;* by the French, *Samedi;* and by the Germans, *Sonnabend* (Sunday eve), or in High German, *Samstag*, a corruption of *Sabbathstag* (Sabbath day); and in Low German, *Saterdag*, of the same origin as the English. (See *Week.*)

Saturn; originally an old Italian divinity, who was afterwards confounded with the Kronos (Κρονος) of the Greeks. Uranus and Gæa (Terra) were the parents of the six Titans. The youngest of these Titans was Kronos (Time), who, when Uranus imprisoned his children, and thereby brought upon himself the anger of their mother, was instigated by her to vengeance, armed himself with a sharp knife, or sickle, and, as Hesiod says, cut off the privities of his father, whereupon Uranus was deprived of his sovereignty. The Titans set free their imprisoned brothers, and the government fell into the hands of Kronos. He then married Rhea, who bore him several sons and daughters. But, as he well knew that he should be dethroned by one of his sons, he devoured the children that were born to him. Jupiter alone, whom Rhea concealed in Crete, where Terra promised to educate him, was preserved. Rhea presented Kronos with a stone, in swaddling clothes, which he swallowed instead of the new born infant. By means of an emetic, administered to him by Terra and Metis, he threw up the stone, as well as all the children whom he had swallowed; by the assistance of whom, Jupiter made war upon him and the Titans, and dethroned him, after a contest of ten years. Kronos was, together with the Titans, confined in the dungeons of Tartarus: whence, however, according to the later poets, they were released: according to Pindar, Jupiter recognised Kronos as the lord of the Fortunate Island in the western ocean. The unknown Hesperia was considered as the land where Uranus, and the succeeding Titans, reigned. But when this land became more accurately known, Kronos, and the golden age, were transferred to Italy. Kronos now becoming blended with Saturn, Saturn was represented as dethroned, cast out from his kingdom, and flying before his son; and as having selected a place of refuge in Italy, and concealed himself in Latium (from *latere*). There the aged king Janus shared with him his throne, and Saturn built upon the Saturnian mount (afterwards the Capitoline hill) the city of Saturnia. His temple stood in the Roman forum, and in it were preserved the public treasures of the city. The Saturnian period was the golden age, which poets vied with each other in celebrating. At that time, the years rolled tranquilly away, and every moment offered an abundance of untroubled enjoyment. Saturn has also been made the father of Chiron, the Centaur.

SATURN. The thickness of the ring of the planet Saturn has lately been estimated by the German astronomer Bessel at $29\frac{7}{10}$ German miles (15 to a degree), $128\frac{8}{10}$ English geog. miles. (See *Planets*.)

SATURNALIA; a feast among the Romans, in commemoration of the happy period under the reign of Saturn, when freedom and equality prevailed, when truth, confidence and love, united all, and violence and oppression were unknown. It continued, at first, one day; then three; afterwards five; and finally, under the Cæsars, seven days, viz. from the 17th to the 23d of December. The festival began as soon as the woollen bands which had bound the feet of Saturn's statue through the year were removed. At the commencement of this festival, a great number of wax tapers were lighted in the temple of Saturn, as a sign that no more human victims were to be sacrificed. The slaves were freed from restraint during this season, wore caps as badges of freedom, and went about dressed in tunics, adorned with purple, and in white togas. Masters and slaves changed places; and while the servants sat and banqueted at the tables, they were waited on by their masters and their guests, who, if they did not do this, were obliged to submit to all sorts of ridiculous punishments. Jests and freedom every where prevailed; and all ceased from their various occupations. In the last days of the festival, which were added in later times, presents were sent from one to another, particularly little images of the gods, *sigilla* (seals), &c.; whence these days were sometimes called *Sigillaria*, and persons were greeted with the acclamations of "*Io Saturnalia! bona Saturnalia!*" Some prisoners were also set free, who dedicated their chains to Saturn.

SATYRS. The Greek mythology includes, under the name of *Satyrs* (σατυροι, τιτυροι), as well as under those of *Sileni*, *Fauns*, and *Pans*, a species of beings who approach, more or less, to the nature of brutes, and particularly to the form of the goat. They were, originally, Peloponnesian wood-gods. The developement of the idea of these beings is due to the Attic drama, and the *drama satyricon* in particular. The early Greeks pictured them as long-eared, bald-headed, and as having small protuberances behind their ears. Later artists made them like Pan, giving them horns and goats' feet. (See Voss's *Mythological Letters*, 2d vol. page 30.) In the representation of them by some artists, the brute characteristics, such as goats' feet, a tail, pointed ears and horns, predominate. Others mainly preserve the human form, and resemble the brutes only by their goats' ears and tails, and sometimes by the introduction of little horns, in the first stages of their growth. To this we must add, however, the general cast of the face, the cheek-bones, the beard, and the flesh hanging down upon the neck from the ears. At other times, the brute characteristics are softened into a mere clownish, rude and awkward human form. The common difference made between the Fauns and Satyrs is, that the former are represented with pointed ears and short tails; the latter, on the contrary, appear with goats' feet. The Sileni are considered to be the old Fauns. This is, however, erroneous. The Satyrs of the Greeks were, in fact, equivalent to the Fauns of the Romans. The whole race of Satyrs, Sileni, Fauns, and Pans, were generally regarded, among the ancients, as divinities of the woods and rural places, and grew up from different notions. The Satyrs and Sileni were the attendants of Bacchus, the signification of which cannot be determined, as the origin of these representations was early lost. Perhaps the idea of them arose from men dressed in the skins of beasts; or perhaps they were only symbolical, and intended to represent man in a rude state. The parents of the Satyrs were considered, by some, to be Mercury and the nymph Iphtime; but, according to others, they were Bacchus and the naiad Nicæa. They were wanton, and were extremely fond of music; and, at the festivals of Bacchus, always appear dancing and playing on musical instruments.

SAUCISSE, in the military art, is a long train of powder sewed up in a roll of pitched cloth or leather, serving to set fire to mines. To every mine there are generally two, that if one fail the other may take effect. Their length is determined by circumstances.

SAUCISSON, in fortification, a kind of fagot made of thick branches of trees, bound together, to cover the men while exposed to the enemy's fire, when on some hazardous employment. It is also used to repair breaches, stop passages, and make traverses over wet ditches.

SAUKS, or SACS. (See *Indians, American.*)

SAUL. (See *Paul.*)

SAUL; king of Israel about 1050 B. C. He was descended from an humble family of the undistinguished tribe of Benjamin, but was noted for his personal beauty and courage, and, when the people became dissatisfied with the theocratico-republican constitution, was selected by Samuel (q. v.) for their king. He was not acknowledged by the whole people until after he had gained a victory over the Ammonites. Repeated successes over the Philistines, Edomites, Moabites, Ammonites, and even over a king beyond the Euphrates, confirmed his authority. But Samuel, who had reluctantly parted with the supreme power, continued to keep up a party in the nation, and, being offended by the encroachments of the king on the privileges of the priesthood, and by his disobedience to the commands of Jehovah in a war against the Amalekites, secretly anointed David (q. v.) as king. Saul discovered his rival, and his hatred against him was increased by the reputation which the latter acquired by his warlike exploits. A civil war, which broke out between the partisans of David and those of Saul, was terminated by the death of the latter, who, after the defeat of his forces by his rival, fell upon his own sword. The history of Saul's frenzy has furnished Alfieri with the subject of one of his masterpieces—Saul, a lyric Tragedy.

SAUMAISE. (See *Salmasius.*)

SAUNDERSON, Nicholas; a celebrated blind mathematician, born in 1682. When a year old, he entirely lost his eye-sight through the small-pox. Notwithstanding this privation, he acquired a knowledge of Latin and Greek, and, having pursued his studies for some time, with the assistance of friends, he was, in 1707, sent to Cambridge. He took up his residence at Christ's college, and soon commenced giving lectures on optics. He became acquainted with sir Isaac Newton, and was chosen mathematical professor. He died 1739. His treatise on algebra was published after his death, at Cambridge (1740, 2 vols.). He left other works in an imperfect state, among which were comments on Newton's *Principia*, which were published at the end of his posthumous treatise on Fluxions (1756, 8vo.).

SAURIN, James, a French Protestant preacher, son of a lawyer at Nismes, was born in 1677. Upon the revocation of the edict of Nantes, in 1685, his father retired with his family to Geneva, where the subject of this article made a considerable progress in learning, but quitted his studies, and went into the army. When the duke of Savoy, under whom he served, made peace in 1696, he returned to Geneva, with a view to engage in the ministry. In 1700, he visited England, where he preached nearly five years to his fellow refugees in London. He subsequently became pastor to a congregation of French refugees, who assembled in a chapel belonging to the prince of Orange, at the Hague. He died in 1730, at the age of fifty-three. This eminent preacher possessed great talents, and a fine address: his voice was strong, clear and harmonious, and his style pious, unaffected and eloquent. He had the happy art of adapting his arguments, with great skill, to the understanding of the audiences before whom he spoke, and was persuasive and pathetic, or plain, clear and argumentative, as best suited his subjects or his hearers. His principles were those of moderate Calvinism. He was the author of twelve volumes of Sermons (8vo.), selections from which were translated into English, and published, between 1775 and 1784, in five volumes, by Mr. Robert Robinson (with a Memoir), a sixth being added, in 1796, by doctor Henry Hunter. Among his other works are Christianity in France (8vo.); Compendium of Christian Divinity and Morality; Discourses on the most Remarkable Events of the Old and New Testaments. Of this, his most considerable work, he nearly completed three volumes folio; to which Roques added a fourth on the Old Testament, and Beausobre two more on the New Testament.

Saussure, Horace Benedict de, a celebrated naturalist, born at Geneva in 1740, distinguished himself so much at the age of twenty-two by his proficiency in the mathematical and physical sciences, as to be appointed professor of philosophy in his native place. He continued to discharge the duties of this office, for 25 years, with reputation. The leisure which his duties left him was occupied in scientific journeys to the volcanic region of France, to the south of Italy, and to England. A favorite object of his investigations was the structure and height of mountains; and to him we are indebted for the invention of several philosophical instruments; as, for instance, an electrometer, a hygrometer, heliothermometer, &c. In 1779 he had ascended the Alps fourteen times in eight different places, and in 1787 he ascended Mont Blanc, and determined its height by barometrical measurements. Saussure died in 1799. Among his writings, his *Essais sur l'Hygrométrie*, and his *Voyages dans les Alpes* (4 vols., 1779—96), are the most valuable.

Saussurite is a massive or compact mineral, found in large masses in the Monte Rosa; in Corsica; in the Bacher mountain in Lower Stiria, and in Bayreuth. In certain varieties, traces of cleavage parallel to the sides of a prism of 124°, and to the shorter diagonal of such a figure, are observable. Fracture uneven, splintery; lustre pearly, inclining to vitreous; color white, passing into mountain-green; streak white; brittle; frangible with much difficulty; specific gravity 3.25. It consists of silex 49, alumine 24, lime 10, magnesia 3.75, oxide of iron 6.50, and soda 5.50.

Savage, Richard, an English poet of the last century, celebrated for his genius, irregularities and misfortunes, was born in London, about 1698. The singular story of Savage, adorned as it is by the pen of his intimate friend, doctor Johnson (Lives of the Poets), has acquired great celebrity; but there is reason to believe that a great part of it is utterly fictitious. Savage was probably the son of a woman who had been employed to nurse a natural son of the countess of Macclesfield by earl Rivers. That lady always asserted—and there is no good cause for doubting it—that her child died while quite young, and that Savage was an impostor. Johnson's account, taken from Savage himself, is, that no sooner did he see the light, than a most unnatural hatred took complete possession of his mother; that he was placed with a woman in the lowest state of indigence, with directions that he should be brought up in ignorance of his birth, and in the meanest condition; that the interference of his maternal grandmother, lady Mason, a little alleviated his lot; and through her kindness he was placed at a grammar school in the neighborhood of St. Alban's, during which period earl Rivers died, revoking a bequest he had made him, on being assured by the countess that her child had been some time dead; and that his mother endeavored to have him kidnapped and sent as a slave to the plantations. He was an apprentice to a shoemaker (this is true), when the woman, whom he had been taught to consider his mother, dying suddenly, some of lady Mason's letters, among her papers, discovered to him, as he pretends, the secret of his birth; or, as appears probable, suggested to him the plan of assuming to be the child of lady Macclesfield, whom his mother had nursed, and to whom these letters really related. He now became an author for the means of bodily subsistence. His first work was a pamphlet on the Bangorian controversy, which was followed by two comedies, Woman's a Riddle, and Love in a Veil, which procured him the acquaintance of sir Richard Steele and Mr. Wilkes. In 1723, his tragedy, on the subject of sir Thomas Overbury, was brought out; the author himself performed the principal character, but with little success: the profits of the piece, however, appear to have amounted to about £200. The poet was now rising in reputation, when, in 1727, in a broil in a house of ill fame, he killed a Mr. Sinclair; and, being tried for murder, a verdict of guilty was pronounced against him. Through the influence, however, of lady Hertford, the king's pardon was granted him. Soon after, lord Tyrconnel received him into his house, and allowed him two hundred pounds a year. In 1729, he published his Wanderer, a Moral Poem. A quarrel with his patron once more turned him adrift upon the world, and he now produced The Bastard, a poem of merit. A Birth-day Ode, addressed to the queen, procured him a pension of fifty pounds from her majesty, to which he was eventually mainly indebted for his support. A satire against the clergy, entitled the Progress of a Divine, caused a prosecution to be instituted against him; but the information was dismissed. From this period, he appears to have sunk into the lowest misery The death of the queen, and the loss of his pension, completed his ruin; and, although a few friends raised a subscription, with a view of enabling him to reside in Wales, the same propensity to dissipation induced him not only to squander the money advanced to him, but to incur a debt of eight pounds at Bristol; for which he was arrested, thrown into the county jail, and eventually removed to Newgate, where he died in 1743. Although Savage at one time received an allowance of fifty pounds a year from Mrs. Oldfield, and repeatedly extorted considerable sums of money from lady Macclesfield by threats of lampooning her, besides other sums from the admirers of his genius, his extravagance always kept him poor; and it is well known that he was the friend and companion of Johnson at the time when the latter was sleeping in the streets of London, houseless and pennyless. For the true character and history of Savage, see Galt's *Lives of the Players* (London, 1831, 1st vol.).

Savannah; a river which makes the north-east boundary of Georgia, and separates it from South Carolina. It is formed by the junction of the Tugalo and Kiowee, 100 miles by the course of the river above Augusta. The largest vessels come up to Five-fathom Hole, within three miles of the city of Savannah, eighteen miles from the ocean; large brigs come to the wharves; steam-boats of 150 tons ascend to Augusta, about 250 miles by water, and 127 by land; and pole-boats ascend 100 miles farther, and then 50 miles on the Tugalo branch. Boats on this branch carry from thirty to sixty bags of cotton, and return with eight or ten tons of merchandise. Tides flow up 25 miles.

Savannah; a city of Georgia, and port of entry, in Chatham county, on the south bank of Savannah river. It is built on a sandy bluff point, 40 feet high. It was laid out by general Oglethorpe in 1733. In 1829, it contained ten houses of worship, an exchange, a court house, a jail, a poor house, an hospital, a theatre, an academy, two state banks, and a branch of the U. States bank. Two of the churches are for Africans; and one of these has more than 2000 members attached to the congregation. Population in 1830, 7303; lat. 32° 2′ N.; lon. 81° 3′ W. The town is regularly laid out; the streets are wide, and ornamented with the China tree. The chief part of the exports and imports of the state are landed here. In the year ending September 30, 1826, the exports were 190,578 bags of cotton, 11,455 tierces of rice, 170 hogsheads of tobacco. Since a safe inland passage to Charleston by way of Beaufort has been discovered, some part of the exports have passed from Augusta directly to Charleston. In January, 1820, this town was burned; but it has been rebuilt in an improved style. The city abounds in benevolent institutions. Savannah was taken by the British during the revolution. (See Sherwood's *Gazetteer of Georgia.*)

Savary, René, duke of Rovigo, was born in 1774. He was Napoleon's minister of police, &c., and served with distinction, in 1789, in the line; also in 1796, under Moreau, and in 1799 under Desaix in Egypt. After Desaix's death, at Marengo, in 1800, he became Napoleon's adjutant-general, and, soon after, was intrusted with the charge of the secret police. Bold, active, and dexterous (for example, in the discovery of the conspiracy of George and Pichegru), and at the same time zealously devoted to the emperor, he soon obtained the confidence of the latter. Napoleon employed him on important missions. After the battle of Austerlitz, he was sent to the Russian and Austrian head-quarters, and, in 1808, to Ferdinand VII, at Madrid, whom he induced to come to Bayonne. On account of a brilliant charge which he successfully made at the head of his regiment at the battle of Friedland in 1807, the emperor made him duke of Rovigo (q. v.); and when Fouché fell into disgrace, he was appointed (June 3, 1810) minister of police. After Napoleon's return from Elba, Fouché was made minister of the police, and Savary was appointed general superintendent of the *gens d'armes*, and a peer of France. It is well known that the British government refused to give him permission to accompany Napoleon to St. Helena. Having been detained as a prisoner at Malta, he escaped, in April, 1816, to Smyrna. Thence he went, in 1817, to Trieste, in order to repair to Paris, to defend himself against a sentence of death passed on him December 25, 1816, by a court martial; but he was detained at Grätz until he returned to Smyrna, in June, 1818, where he engaged in mercantile business. In 1819, he went to London, and thence to Paris, where, December 27 of that year, he presented himself before the court, and was acquitted. He then lived retired, but went to Berlin in 1823, to bring before the Prussian courts of justice an action against the Prussian exchequer for indemnification (inadmissible by the peace of Paris) for the loss of his dotations in the Prussian dominions, which the king had presented to general Gneisenau. Failing in his object, he went back to Paris, and, in order to refute a passage in the *Mémorial* of count Las Cases, published a fragment from his Memoirs (*Sur la Catastrophe du Duc d'Enghien*), denying his privity to the arrest and execution of the duke, and maintaining, on the contrary, that the whole was planned and carried into execution without the previous knowledge of Napoleon, by the minister who was then at the head of foreign affairs (Talleyrand). But Talleyrand justified himself before Louis XVIII; and other publications connected with this affair, particularly those of general Hullin and Dupin, bear so hard on the duke of Rovigo, that it is difficult to believe him not to have been privy to the hurried execution of the sentence. The duke of Rovigo was thereupon banished from the court; and from that time he lived in close retirement. His *Mémoire sur la Mort de Pichegru, de Wright, de Bathurst, et sur quelques autres Circonstances de sa Vie* (Paris, 1825), has weakened the force of the charges against Savary, although the occurrences with regard to Wright and Bathurst require a further explanation. He appears to be a man of courage and adroitness, but destined by nature to follow the lead of men of more decided talent and character. His *Mémoires* were published in 1828 (8 vols. 8vo.; in English, 4 vols.). He was appointed governor of Algiers in 1832.

Savigny, Frederic Charles von, born in 1779, at Frankfort on the Maine, is one of the most distinguished professors of the civil law. After having finished his academic studies, in which Weis and Hugo were his chief guides, and having taken his degree, as doctor of laws, at Marburg, in 1800, he travelled, during several years, in Germany, France, and Upper Italy, to investigate unexplored or little known sources of the civil law, and, after his return, was appointed professor of law at Marburg. In 1803, he wrote, at this place, his Law of Possession (5th edition, Giessen, 1827). In 1808, he was appointed professor at Landshut, and, in 1810, in the university established a short time previous at Berlin, where he continues to teach. He is a member of the academy of sciences at Berlin, of the council of state, and of the court of revision, or cassation (q. v.) for the Prussian provinces on the Rhine, where the French code has remained in force. His lectures on the pandects, the institutes and the history of the Roman law, are distinguished for clearness, precision, and purity of language, and attract many students to Berlin. Savigny belongs to the historical school (so called) of German lawyers, though he cannot be termed its founder without injustice to Hugo and Schlosser. He was, however, the first to adopt this name for himself and his followers (*Zeitschrift für die geschichtliche Rechtswissenschaft*, edited by Savigny, Eichhorn, and Göschen, I, 2, Berlin, 1815), to distinguish his school from one which might, with equal reason, assume the title of the philosophical school, and call their opponents the unphilosophical, as they are far from disregarding the historical developement of law, though they endeavor to deduce law mainly from the higher principles of our nature. Savigny's views respecting the foundation of law—according to which it rests neither on positive legislation nor on the deductions of reason—are contained in a work published subsequently, in consequence of the wish expressed by other jurists, as Thibaut, Schmid, Gönner, for the introduction of a general penal and civil code, and a uniform course of procedure throughout Germany. In this work, entitled *Vom Beruf unserer Zeit für Gesetzgebung und Rechtswissenschaft* (Berlin, 1814, translated by a barrister of Lincoln's Inn, under the title, On the Aptitude of the present Age for Legislation and Jurisprudence, &c.), he endeavors to show that new codes are unnecessary and impracticable; that the codes of France, Austria and Prussia are not adapted for introduction into other countries; and that the German language is not even sufficiently matured for a code. Savigny's work, though replete with proofs of extensive erudition, and not devoid of sound views, exhibits also numerous traces of that disposition to exalt the past and the distant, at the expense of the present and the near, so often met with among the learned, who are disposed to value most highly what has cost them most labor. The fondness for ancient laws and political institutions is most common in those countries which have the least political liberty. How often does a German philologist assert that the greatest orators are those who were formed under the political institutions of antiquity, forgetting the great names who adorn the history of English eloquence! The work of Savigny cannot be called very philosophical, but it contains much matter for reflection. He has published a History of the Roman Law in the Middle Ages (4 vols., 1815—26; English, Edinb. 1829); other fruits of his researches are contained in papers read before the academy of sciences, and in articles in the periodical mentioned above. Uncommon erudition, acuteness, and elegance in the exposition of his views, are allowed him, even by those who do not belong to his school.

SAVILE, sir Henry, one of the most profound and elegant scholars of his age, was born in 1549, and, after graduating at Brazen-nose college, Oxford, removed on a fellowship to Merton college, in the same university. In his twenty-ninth year, he made a tour on the continent, for the purpose of perfecting himself in elegant literature, and, on his return, was appointed tutor in Greek and mathematics to queen Elizabeth. Seven years after, the wardenship of his college, which he held for about six-and-thirty years, the provostship of Eton being added to it in 1596, was conferred on him. In 1619, he founded two professorships, in geometry and astronomy, at Oxford, besides conferring several other valuable benefactions, both in property and books, many of the latter forming still a part of the Bodleian library. Among his works, the principal are his Commentaries on Roman Warfare; *Rerum Anglicarum post Bedam Scriptores; Prælectiones in Elementa Euclidis;* and his edition of the writings of St. Chrysostom, in eight folio volumes. Sir Henry Savile was the correspondent of J. Scaliger, Meibomius, Isaac Casaubon, and most of the learned men of his day. His death took place in 1622.

SAVILE, George, marquis of Halifax, a statesman and writer, was born in 1630. On the death of Cromwell, he distinguished himself by his exertions in favor of the absent king, and on the restoration was raised to the peerage. He was removed from the council in 1675, through the influence of the duke of York (see *James II*), in consequence of his opposition to that prince's measures in favor of the Roman Catholic religion. But when the bill for excluding the duke from the succession was in agitation, his repugnance to that measure brought him into disgrace with the party with which he had hitherto acted. In 1682, he was created marquis of Halifax, keeper of the privy seal, and president of the council, which dignities he retained in the early part of the succeeding reign, till his opposition to the proposed repeal of the test acts caused his abrupt dismissal. From this moment lord Halifax continued in opposition, till the flight of James II, when he was chosen speaker of the house of lords in the convention parliament, and contributed mainly to the elevation of William III to the throne. But, soon after the revolution, he resigned the privy seal, and, during the remainder of his life, voted against the court. A mortification in the bowels carried him off in 1695. He was the author of Advice to a Daughter, and of a variety of political tracts, the principal of which are, Maxims of State; the Character of a Trimmer; Character of King Charles II; Anatomy of an Equivalent; Letter to a Dissenter, &c.

SAVIN. (See *Juniper.*)

SAVINGS INSTITUTIONS, or, as they are often called, SAVINGS BANKS, are an institution of recent origin, but have already accomplished much good. They afford an opportunity for those who have any thing to spare, not only to deposit their savings in safety, but to receive interest for the sum so secured, against a time of sickness, or distress, or age. One of the first attempts with which we are acquainted to realize such an institution was made by Mrs. Priscilla Wakefield, at Tottenham, near London, in 1803, in which small sums were received, and interest allowed on them. The first attempt on a larger scale was made in Edinburgh, in 1814; and soon after this example was imitated in England. The Scotch banks allowing interest on mere deposits, the managers of savings institutions in that country had no difficulty in investing their funds; but in England, this not being the case, it became necessary to vest the deposits in the public funds, in some instances paying a fixed interest, in others leaving the depositors to take their chance in the fluctuations of the stocks. Such was the extent of the operations of these institutions, that from 1817 to 1828 inclusive, the commissioners for the reduction of the public debt received from the directors of savings banks, including friendly societies, the sum of £13,746,546, for which government paid four per cent. interest. By act of parliament of July 28, 1828 (to consolidate and amend the laws relating to savings banks), for the further regulation of savings banks, the rate of interest was reduced to £3 8s. 5¼d. per cent. per annum. November 20, 1830, there were 379 savings banks in England, and since that time five others have been established. The number of depositors in 369 banks, from which returns were received, was 367,812; the amount deposited, £13,080,255: of the depositors, 187,770 deposited under twenty pounds, and 102,621 under fifty pounds. In Wales, there are twenty-five institutions of this kind, with 10,404 depositors, and an amount invested of £340,721. In Ireland, there are eighty-three, returns from sixty-two of which give 34,638 depositors, and an amount invested of £945,991. (See Pratt's *History of Savings Banks.*) The first savings bank in America was opened in Philadelphia, in November, 1816. In Boston, an institution was incorporated in December of the same year; but its action did not begin until February following. Since that time, these societies have become quite numerous, and, with hardly an exception, have been exceedingly prosperous. That of New York has the largest funds: next in magnitude is the institution at Boston; then those of Philadelphia, Baltimore, Salem, New Bedford. Perhaps the number may amount to forty or fifty; for most of the northern maritime cities, and the larger manufacturing towns, afford strong encouragement to such projects. In Boston, the number of depositors exceeds ten thousand, and the amount of funds cannot be short of a million and a half of dollars.

Savonarola, Geronimo, an Italian monk, celebrated for his eloquence, and his melancholy fate, was born at Ferrara, September 21, 1452, and was designed for the medical profession. Religious enthusiasm led him, at the age of fourteen, to leave his father's house secretly, and enter the order of Dominicans. Several years later, he began to preach at Florence, but with so little success that he determined to abandon the pulpit; and, retiring to Bologna, he devoted himself to metaphysical and physical studies. The reputation of his talents and learning induced Lorenzo de' Medici to invite him to return to Florence. Here Savonarola began to preach again; and his discourses attracted such crowds that the church could not contain them. His extraordinary sanctity and his powerful eloquence gained him great influence over the minds of the Florentines, and he was emboldened to assume a prophetic tone, and to urge with vehemence, and in public, the necessity of a reform in the church. The multitude looked upon him as divinely inspired, while some ridiculed him as a fanatic, and others denounced him as an impostor. He soon broke off all connexion with his patron Lorenzo, whose character he assailed, with prophecies of his approaching fall. He refused to make the customary visit to that chief, which it was his duty to do as prior of St. Mark's, and, when Lorenzo went himself to St. Mark's, refused to see him. Although Lorenzo de' Medici was repeatedly urged to adopt severe measures against him, he refused, either from lenity, or from his respect for the character of the preacher. When Lorenzo lay on his death-bed (1492), Savonarola obtained admission to him, and spoke to the dying man with the dignity of his office. After the death of Lorenzo, and the expulsion of his son Pietro, Savonarola took the most active part in the political affairs of Florence. He put himself at the head of those who demanded a more democratical form of government, asserted that God had commissioned him to declare that the legislative power must be extended to the citizens, that he himself had been the ambassador of the Florentines to heaven, and that Christ had consented to be their king. The newly elected magistrates accordingly laid down their offices, and the legislative functions were intrusted to a council of the citizens, which chose a committee from their own number for the discharge of the duty. Dissensions, however, distracted the new republic; the aristocratical and democratical parties persecuted each other with great fury, the former consisting of the friends of the old order of things, and the latter of the devout admirers of the monk. But the zeal of Savonarola was not content with revolutionizing Florence; he meditated the reform of the Roman court, and of the irregularities of the clergy. The pontificate of Alexander VI could not fail to supply causes of complaint on both heads. He accordingly wrote, as his eulogists assure us, to the Christian princes, declaring that the church was going to ruin, and that it was their duty to convoke a general council, before which he was ready to prove that the church was without a head, and that the reigning pope was not a true bishop, had never been worthy of the title, nor even of the name of a Christian. Alexander excommunicated him, and the bull of excommunication was read in the cathedral at Florence; but Savonarola despised the thunders of the Vatican, and continued to preach. His influence was still further increased by the failure of an attempt of Pietro de' Medici to restore his family authority. But another party had, meanwhile, arisen in opposition to him. His innovations in St. Mark's and other monasteries had excited the enmity of the monks, especially of the Franciscans of the strict observance, who denounced him from the pulpit as an excommunicated heretic. Fra Domenico da Rescia, a monk of his convent, offered, in the heat of his fanatical zeal, to prove the truth of his master's doctrines, by passing through fire, if one of his opponents would undergo the same ordeal in defence of their opinions. The challenge was accepted by a Franciscan monk, and Savonarola, with his champion, appeared at the head of a large procession, chanting the Psalm lxviii, "Let God arise, and let his enemies be scattered." The Franciscan also presented himself, the fire was kindled, and Domenico was ready to enter the flames, bearing the host in his hands. But the crowd exclaimed against this sacrilege, as they termed it; and, as Domenico persisted in his determination, he thus happily escaped the ordeal for which he had offered himself. But this event was fatal to Savonarola. The people loaded him with insults, and he was finally thrown into prison. A spiritual court, under the direction of two papal commissioners, was held for his trial. His firmness and eloquence at first threw his judges into confusion, but, being examined on the rack, he confessed that he had falsely arrogated supernatural powers. He was condemned, with some of his adherents, to be first strangled, and then burnt, and the sentence was executed May 23, 1498, in presence of a large multitude, some of whom considered him as a martyr and a saint. This extraordinary man left, besides letters, a Treatise against Astrology, and several philosophical and ascetical works (*Opera*, Lyons, 1633—40, 6 vols.). His sermons (*Prediche*, Florence, 1496), though wanting in the characteristics of finished discourses, contain powerful and stirring passages. (See *Reformation.*)

Savoy (*Savoia*, Italian; *Savoie*, French); a duchy belonging to the Sardinian monarchy (see *Sardinia*), and bordering on France, Switzerland, and Piedmont, with a superficial extent of 3750 square miles, and a population of 501,165. The greatest part of the duchy consists of lofty mountains and forests, alternating with deep and narrow valleys. The Cottian and Pennine Alps belong in part to Savoy, and the Gray Alps separate it from Piedmont. (See *Alps.*) Mont Blanc (q. v.), the loftiest summit in Europe, is in Savoy. The Iseran, the Little St. Bernard, and mount Cenis, over which an artificial road leads from Savoy to Piedmont, are also in this duchy. (See *Alps, Roads over.*) Many of the summits are covered with perpetual snow and ice. Savoy is watered by the Rhone, the Isere, the Arve, which flows through the vale of Chamouni (q. v.), and the Arc. The lake of Geneva is on the borders. The smaller lakes are those of Bourget and Annecy. Near the lake of Bourget is an intermittent spring, called the Miraculous Fountain, which ceases to flow during periods varying from twenty minutes to towards three hours. The climate is very changeable, and in the course of a day the severest cold is often succeeded by a great heat. The soil is mostly rocky, and far from fertile; but where it is susceptible of being brought into cultivation, it yields corn, though insufficient to supply the inhabitants, potatoes, hemp, flax, wine, chestnuts, and orchard fruits. The forests are extensive, and the pastures good; grazing is therefore much attended to.—Game, the marmot, chamois, and ibex, are found in the mountains. Among the mineral productions are silver, copper, lead, iron, coal, and salt. The Savoyards speak a mixture of French and Italian. They are honest, faithful, frugal, and industrious, but poor. They are often compelled to quit their ungrateful soil for a subsistence (as porters, pedlars, &c.), but generally return with their earnings to their country. Chamberry, the capital, with 11,991 inhabitants, is the only considerable town. Savoy was anciently inhabited by the Allobroges. It was under the Roman dominion till 400, belonged to Burgundy till 530, to France till 879, to Arles till 1000, when it had its own counts, and, in 1416, was erected into a duchy. In 1792, it was conquered by the French, and incorporated with France, as the department of Mont Blanc. It was partly ceded to Sardinia by the first peace of Paris (1814), and by the second (1815), the remainder was given up to the Sardinian monarchy.—See Cribrario's *Notizie sopra i Principi di Savoia* (Turin, 1825).

Saw-Fish (*pristis antiquorum*); a fish of the family of sharks, remarkable for having the head prolonged in the form of a long, flat plate, having strong osseous spines implanted like teeth on each margin, the whole bearing some resemblance to a saw. This forms a powerful weapon, with which it attacks whales and other cetaceous animals, towards whom this fish seems to bear an inveterate hostility. The habits of the saw-fish are otherwise, as well as their organization, the same as those of the sharks. It grows to the length of twelve or fifteen feet. The flesh is hard, coriaceous, and ill-tasted. Several species of saw-fish are now known. They inhabit all seas, from the polar ice to the equatorial regions.

Saw-Gin. (See *Cotton.*)

Saxe, Maurice, count de, a celebrated military officer, was the natural son of Augustus, king of Poland, by the count ess of Konigsmark. He was born at Dresden in 1696, and even in childhood displayed some presages of his warlike genius. At the age of twelve, he joined the allied army under the duke of Marlborough and the prince Eugene, and was present at the sieges of Lisle and Tournay, and at the battle of Malplaquet. His father then gave him a regiment of cavalry, with which he served in Sweden, and was at the taking of Stralsund. His mother procured his marriage with a German lady of rank, when he was but fifteen; but the inconstancy of his temper occasioned a divorce after a few years. He was with prince Eugene, in Hungary, in the war with the Turks; but, after the treaties of Utrecht and Passarowitz, he withdrew to France, and was permanently attached to the service of that country by a brevet of *mareschal-de-camp*, given him in 1720, by the regent duke of Orleans. He applied himself to study at Paris, and made himself intimately acquainted with professional tactics. In 1726, he was a candidate for the duchy of Courland; and he formed various other schemes of ambition at different periods. On the death of his father, he declined the command of the Saxon army, offered him by his brother Augustus III, and joined the French on the Rhine, under the duke of Berwick. He distinguished himself at Dettingen and Philipsburg, and, in 1744, was rewarded with the staff of a marshal of France. He was employed in the war that followed the death of the emperor Charles VI, and, in 1745, gained the famous battle of Fontenoy, which was followed by the capture of Brussels, and many other places in Flanders. In 1747, he was victorious at Lafeldt, and, in the following year, took Maestricht, soon after which the peace of Aix-la-Chapelle was concluded. Marshal Saxe survived that event a little more than two years, dying November 30, 1750. He wrote a treatise entitled *Mes Rêveries*, on the art of war (2 vols., quarto). General Grimoard, in 1794, published *Lettres et Mémoires choisis parmi les Papiers originaux du M. de Saxe, depuis* 1733 *jusqu'en* 1750 (5 vols., 8vo.).

Saxe-Coburg, Saxe-Gotha, Saxe-Meiningen, Saxe-Weimar, Saxe-Altenburg, Saxe-Hilburghausen. (See the articles *Coburg*, *Gotha*, *Meiningen*, *Weimar*, *Altenburg*, *Hilburghausen*, and *Saxony*.)

Saxifrage. The species of *saxifraga* are small herbaceous plants, with leaves entire or divided, ordinarily crowded about the base of the stem; the small, delicate flowers are usually disposed in a raceme or panicle. These plants are chiefly confined to cold climates and mountainous situations: many of them contribute largely to ornament the cold and desolate regions near the verge of perpetual snow, or within the arctic circle. The species of *saxifraga* are much more common in Europe than in the U. States. More than a hundred and fifty are known, of which we have two that are common in many parts of the Union; two others, that are peculiar to the summits of some of the Alleghanies; and a third, which has been lately discovered on the White mountains of New Hampshire; the last, however, is identical with one from the north of Europe. Many of the European species have been discovered in the northern parts of Canada, and on the North-west coast; and there are some peculiar to these parts of our continent. The name is supposed to be derived from growing in the clefts of rocks. Many are of easy cultivation, and have long been favorites in the gardens; but the majority are delicate, and are liable to injury from mild and humid weather during the winter months.

Saxo Grammaticus; a learned historian, who flourished in the twelfth century. He is supposed to have been a native of Denmark, of which kingdom, and its dependencies, he compiled an elaborate history, under the auspices of Absalom, bishop of Roschild. This work, which is said to have occupied him twenty years in its composition, has gone through several editions, especially those of Paris, 1514, Basle, 1534, and Sora in Denmark, 1644, folio: of these the latter is by far the most perfect. Saxo was a priest in the cathedral of Roschild, and is said to have been deputed on a mission to Paris, in 1161, for the purpose of inducing some of the monks of that capital to visit his native country, and assist in reforming the discipline of the religious orders there. He died in 1208.

Saxons, Land of the. (See *Transylvania*.)

Saxons, Saxony. Although the Saxons are first mentioned by Ptolemy, yet it cannot be doubted that they belong to the great northern German races, whose inroads into the Roman territories rendered the name of Cimbrians and Teutones so formidable. In the third century of the Christian era, they were a numerous, warlike and piratical people, whose devastations on the British and Belgian coasts gave rise to the appointment of a particular officer (*comes littoris Saxonici*) to de fend these regions. In the middle of the fifth century, two considerable hordes of Saxons, under Hengist and Horsa, laid the foundations of the Saxon kingdoms in Britain. (See *Great Britain*, and *Anglo-Saxons.*) Those who remained in Germany, the Westphalians, Eastphalians and Engrians, occupied a great extent of country, of vague and varying limits, which bore the general name of Saxony (*Sachsen*). Charlemagne waged a thirty years' war against the Saxons, and Wittekind, their national hero, with many of his countrymen, submitted to his arms, and embraced Christianity. (See *Germany, History of.*) In 845, mention is made of a duke of Saxony; and in the new kingdom of Germany, the Saxons were the most powerful of the six German nations, viz. the Eastern Franks, Saxons, Frisians, Thuringians, Suabians and Bavarians. In 919, Henry, duke of Saxony, was elected German king (see *Henry I*), and transmitted this dignity to his son, grandson and great-grandson.—(See *Otho I*, and *Otho II.*) The duchy afterwards passed (1125) to the Bavarian branch of the Guelf family, of which Henry the Lion (q. v.), celebrated for his contest with the emperor, was a member (1146—1195). After several changes, which it is unnecessary to enumerate here, Frederic the Warrior, margrave of Meissen and landgrave of Thuringia, became (1424) duke and elector of Saxony. (See *Elector.*) The union of these three countries rendered the Saxon elector one of the most powerful princes in Germany. After the death of Frederic the Good, son of Frederic the Warrior, Ernest and Albert, sons of the former, divided the family possessions between them (1485), and founded the Ernestine and Albertine Saxon lines, which still exist. The latter received Meissen, or Misnia, and now constitutes the royal Saxon house. (See *Saxony, Kingdom of.*) The former retained the electoral dignity and Thuringia. Ernest was succeeded in the electorate by his sons Frederic the Wise (1486--1525) and John (1525--1532). The former is celebrated as the protector of Luther, the promoter of the reformation and the founder of the university of Wittenberg. But for his prudence, firmness, and personal influence with Maximilian and Charles, Luther would probably have met the fate of Huss. (See *Reformation.*) By the Wittenberg capitulation (May 19, 1547), the electoral dignity was transferred to the Albertine line, in the person of Maurice. (See the following article, and *Maurice.*) The Ernestine house is now divided into the two branches of Weimar and Gotha, the latter of which consists of the three lines of Meiningen, Altenburg and Coburg. (See the separate articles.) Towards the close of the fifteenth century, Germany was divided into circles; and the large tract of country, known vaguely by the name of Saxony, was formed into the three circles of Upper Saxony, Lower Saxony and Westphalia. (q. v.) Upper Saxony was bounded by Poland, Silesia and Lusatia on the east, and by Franconia and Bohemia on the south. It comprised the electorates of Saxony and Brandenburg, the duchy of Pomerania, and a number of small principalities. Lower Saxony had Westphalia and the Rhine to the west, and Sleswick with the Baltic to the north, and comprised the electorate of Hanover, the duchies of Mecklenburg, Brunswick and Holstein, the free cities of Hamburg, Bremen and Lübeck, with several smaller states. By the dissolution of the empire in 1806, the distinction of circles was abolished.

Saxony, Kingdom of, lying in the north-east part of Germany, is bounded on the south by Bohemia, on the east and north by Prussia (the duchy of Saxony), and on the west by the Saxon principalities and Bavaria. It is divided into five circles—Meissen, Leipsic, Erzgebirge, Neustadt and Upper Lusatia—with a superficial extent of 5800 square miles, and a population (1828) of 1,414,528. The capital, Dresden, has 56,000 inhabitants, Leipsic 40,700. Chemnitz (16,000), Freyberg (12,000) and Bautzen (11,000) are the only other places with a population exceeding 10,000 inhabitants. The face of the country is, to a great degree, mountainous. The Erzgebirge, which forms the boundary between Saxony and Bohemia, is more abrupt on the Bohemian than on the Saxon side (see *Erzgebirge*), and most of the hills are green even to their summits. The climate is as mild as that of any part of Europe in the same latitude. The soil is of moderate fertility. The mountainous districts in the south contain extensive forests, which are kept up with care, as the chief supply of fuel for the mines, coal and turf being much used for domestic fuel. In these districts, the valleys only are well cultivated; but in the level districts of the north, tillage is general. The products are wheat, barley oats, and other grain, some tobacco and hops, and, in a few favorable situations grapes. The Elbe is the only navigable river. The other rivers are the two Muldas, the two Elsters, the Queiss, &c. Saxony is rich in minerals; silver, cobalt, lead, iron, copper, zinc, arsenic and quicksilver are among the metallic productions; other minerals are topaz, chrysolites, amethysts, agates, cornelians, garnet, cinnabar, porcelain-clay, &c. The chief mining operations are carried on in the Erzgebirge, and are under excellent management. (See *Freyberg*, and *Mine*.) The value of the raw material produced is about 1,100,000 dollars, which, by the processes of industry, acquires a value of 3,000,000 dollars; 10,000 men are employed in mining, and 50,000 in the subsequent processes. Of the domestic animals, the chief attention has been bestowed on the sheep, which constitute one of the chief sources of national wealth in Saxony. The Merino breed was introduced into the country in 1765, and the native breed has been improved to a wonderful degree. The number of sheep in the kingdom is estimated at two millions, yielding annually upwards of 4,500,000 pounds of wool. Hogs are numerous, but not sufficient for domestic consumption. The inhabitants are, with the exception of 2000 Jews and 34,000 Wends, of German origin, and are distinguished for intelligence, industry and honesty. The language is intermediate between High and Low German (see *German Language*); that of the inhabitants of Dresden is the best, though it is an error to suppose that the purest German is spoken there. Saxony was the cradle of the reformation. (q. v.) The Lutherans are 1,348,100; Roman Catholics, 48,000; Greek Catholics, 100; Calvinists, 300; Herrnhutters, 1600. The royal house has been Catholic since 1697. The nobility enjoys exemptions from some taxes, tolls, &c., and some feudal rights and privileges. The peasants are some of them subject to feudal services, and in some instances are serfs. The Saxon peasant is loaded with taxes, and is not allowed to engage in the trades, which are carried on by the citizens or the inhabitants of the towns, who are not nobles. Literary men, preachers, professors and teachers likewise have particular privileges. In no country of Europe is education more attended to than in Saxony, and in no country, of equal extent, is the number of printing and book establishments so great. The university of Leipsic (q. v.) is the principal institution for education. There are common schools in all the parishes, and the lower classes are, very generally, taught to read and write; in some of the larger towns, there are also free schools for the poor. In addition to these, there are two princely schools (*Fürstenschulen*), founded from the revenues of suppressed convents, for the higher branches of education, fifteen gymnasia, two teachers' seminaries, one mining academy, one forest academy, and three military schools. There are also numerous public libraries, among which are that of the university of Leipsic, and the royal library at Dresden, with 220,000 printed books and 2700 manuscripts. The manufactures and trade are of greater extent than in most inland countries. The weaving of linen is an employment of old date, and is carried on in almost every village: woollens are also manufactured in a number of towns; but both of these branches of industry have somewhat declined. Cotton spinning and weaving increased, to a great extent, towards the close of the last century; but the conveyance of the raw material is tedious and expensive. The manufactures connected with the mines are extensive. There are cannon founderies at Freyberg and Dresden; cobalt is made into smalt; blue-dye, verdigris and green-dye are among the articles of manufacturing industry. The exports consist of wool and minerals, in a raw state, and of linen, yarn, woollens and lace. The imports are silk, flax, cotton, coffee, sugar, wine, and sometimes corn. The revenue, which is derived partly from taxes, and partly from the regalia and royal domains, amounts to 4,500,000 dollars; the debt is 12,800,000. The peace establishment of the army consists of 13,300 men; the contingent to the German confederacy of 12,000. The government of Saxony is a monarchy, limited by the privileges of the estates. The margraviate of Upper Lusatia has separate estates. Those of the hereditary lands consist of the prelates and higher nobility, the gentry and the burgesses. The estates have the power of laying taxes and advising on subjects of public importance. The higher offices of administration are intrusted to a privy cabinet, with three cabinet ministers, for foreign affairs, for the home department, and for war; the privy council, the board of finance, the military board, the department of internal administration (*Landesregierung*), the court of appeal for judicial questions, the board of taxes, and the ecclesiastical council and supreme consistory. In June, 1831, a new constitution was promised. The king of Saxony has the fourth vote in the German diet, and four votes in the *plenum*. The present king, Anthony I, born 1755, succeeded his brother in 1827. In consequence of the commotions in Dresden and Leipsic, in September, 1830, he associated his nephew Frederic Augustus (born 1797) in the government, as co-regent, the father of Frederic resigning his claims to the succession in favor of his son. His predecessor was Frederic Augustus, his brother, created king of Saxony in 1806. There are three Saxon orders; that of the Saxon crown (*Rautenkrone*), founded in 1807; that of St. Henry (1736), for military merit; and the civil order of merit (1815). We have already given a sketch of the early history of the country in the preceding article: we shall here continue the sketch from the foundation of the Albertine line, which now occupies the Saxon throne. Maurice (q. v.), grandson of Albert, was put in possession of the duchy of Saxony and the dignity of elector by Charles V. His brother Augustus (1553—86) made important accessions to the Saxon territories, and introduced many useful changes in the administration of the government. John George, his grandson (1511—56), joined Gustavus Adolphus in the thirty years' war (q. v.); and the combined Swedish and Saxon forces defeated the imperialists, under Tilly, in the battle of Breitenfeld (1631), and, under Wallenstein, in that of Lützen (1632). Misunderstandings between the elector of Saxony and the chancellor Oxenstiern (q. v.) threw the former into the arms of the emperor; and, by the treaty of Prague (May 30, 1635), Saxony obtained from Austria a cession of the two Lusatias, besides other advantages. Frederic Augustus I (1694—1733) embraced the Catholic religion (1697), to obtain the crown of Poland. But Charles XII (q. v.) conquered Poland, and occupied Saxony, subjecting it to heavy impositions; while, by the peace with Sweden, the latter country received no indemnification for its losses. (See *Northern War*.) Frederic Augustus II (1733—1763) also obtained the crown of Poland (as Augustus III, q. v.), after a war with France, and took part with Austria in the seven years' war. (q. v.) The peace of 1763 left the country, which had suffered severely during the war, loaded with a debt of more than twenty million dollars. It now became necessary for the government to renounce its ambitious schemes, and endeavor to lessen the pressure of the public burdens. Frederic Augustus III (1763—1827) reluctantly took part in the war of 1792, against France, and furnished only his contingent as a member of the empire, when war was declared by the imperial diet (1793). In 1806, 20,000 Saxons were sent to the support of Prussia; but after the battle of Jena, a peace was concluded with France, and the elector acceded to the confederation of the Rhine, with the royal title. Large additions were made to the Saxon territory, 1807 and 1809; but these acquisitions were merely temporary. In the war of 1813, Saxony was the scene of the great struggle between Napoleon and the northern powers. The battles of Lützen and Bautzen, Dresden and Leipsic (see the articles, and *Russian-German War*), stripped the king of Saxony of his newly acquired territories. The king himself was twenty months a prisoner of the allied powers, and his dominions were governed by Russian and Prussian authorities. The fate of Saxony was long a subject of discussion at the congress of Vienna. It was at first proposed to unite it with Prussia; and nothing but the jealousy of Austria seems to have saved it from this fate. Its partition was finally resolved upon, February, 1815, and the king was obliged to cede more than half of his kingdom to Prussia. This cession included the whole of Lower Lusatia, part of Upper Lusatia, the circle of Wittenberg, and parts of those of Meissen and Leipsic, the greater part of Merseburg, &c., 8160 square miles, with a population of 875,578. After the king's return to Dresden, he immediately turned his attention to a system of public credit, and to the establishment of scientific and other useful institutions. By the partition, Saxony lost all its salt works, and its finest grain districts and forests, with some valuable mining districts, but still retains the most populous manufacturing parts of the country, with the rich Freyberg mines. A prudent policy may heal the wounds she has received; but her independence is altogether precarious. (See Pölitz's *History of the Kingdom of Saxony*, and Engelhardt's *Description of Saxony*, in German.)

Saxony, the Prussian Duchy of; a province of the kingdom of Prussia, chiefly composed of the cessions made by the kingdom of Saxony to Prussia, at the congress of Vienna, in 1815, together with other territories north of Anhalt and west of the Elbe and Havel. It is divided into the three governments of Magdeburg, Merseburg and Erfurt, and comprised, in 1828, 9653 square miles, with 1,409,388 inhabitants. It is very productive.

Saxon Switzerland; a name which

has been improperly given, for about thirty years, to the eastern part of the circle of Meissen, in the kingdom of Saxony, on the Elbe. It is a group of mountains of sandstone, with valleys and rivers of the most picturesque character, extending from Liebethal to the Bohemian frontier, about twenty-four miles long, and equally wide. Some of the rocks are 1800 feet high. It is one of the most charming spots on earth, and, on account of its vicinity to Dresden, so much resorted to for its treasures of art, attracts many visitors in summer. (See Götzinger's, Hasse's and Lindau's descriptions.) The name is improper, because the region does not resemble Switzerland, even in miniature; and such comparisons lower the object compared.

Say, Jean Baptiste, a distinguished political economist, was born at Lyons in 1767, and went to Paris at an early period of the revolution, occupying himself with literature. He was subsequently one of the establishers of the *Décade* (*Revue*) *Philosophique*, with which he was, however, connected but a short time. In 1799, he was a member of the tribunate, but, being removed by Napoleon, declined subsequent offers of office from him, devoting himself entirely to his literary labors. His chief works are his *Traité d'Économie politique* (5th ed., 3 vols., 1826), translated into English by C. R. Prinsep, and his *Cours complet d'Économie politique pratique* (4 vols., 1829). (See *Political Economy.*) The third edition of his *Catéchisme d'Économie politique* appeared in 1826. One of his most ingenious works is *Le petit Volume contenant quelques Aperçus des Hommes et de la Société* (1817). His statistical treatises, *De l'Angleterre et des Anglais* (1815), and *Des Canaux de Navigation dans l'État actuel de la France*, are also esteemed.

Sbirri. In Italy, particularly in the States of the Church, there were formerly certain police officers, with a military organization, who were called by this name. They were abolished in 1809.

Scabious (*scabiosa*); an extensive genus of plants, exclusively belonging to the eastern continent, and most of the species to Europe and the countries about the Mediterranean. The stems are herbaceous, and the flowers are united in heads at the extremities of the stems and branches, and resemble compound flowers. The *S. succisa* is remarkable for having the root suddenly truncated, and as if bitten off; whence the name of *devil's bit* is applied to it.

Scævola. (See *Mucius.*)

Scaggerac (i. e. *Scagen's reef*); a sand-bank, which extends from cape Skagen, on the northern part of Denmark, a great way into the sea, on which account a large coal fire is constantly kept up there in the winter nights, as a mark for ships to avoid it. For this purpose, in the year 1753, a new tower, sixty-four feet high, was erected opposite to this sand-bank, on the spot where the former light-house stood, which had been demolished by the violence of the sea. The Scaggerac sea forms the communication between the German ocean and the Cattegat. (See *Baltic Sea.*)

Scagliola; a mixture of fine gypsum and powdered selenite (*pietra specolare*), made into a paste with glue, and serving to form paintings of a stony hardness. The process is as follows:—Upon a tablet of white stucco (consisting of this gypsum paste), the outlines of the work designed are traced with a sharp instrument, and the cavities thus made are filled up with successive layers of paste, of the same composition, but colored. The application of the different layers is continued until all the varieties and shades of color required are produced, and the surface of the whole is then polished. Scagliola work has the advantage over mosaic of being susceptible of the greatest possible variety of coloring, and, from the sameness of its material, of forming a more compact mass, so that the painting can receive a higher polish; by which means the colors are better preserved. The invention of this process is ascribed to Guido del Conte, or Fassi (1584—1649), an ingenious mason of Cari, near Correggio, in Lombardy. But we have some ancient specimens (as the Ilian tables) in white stucco; and inscriptions of the middle ages show that the art was never lost. In Bologna, such works continued to be made from ancient times, with glue prepared from parchment, like that of the ancients. Guido's scagliola is a complete imitation of marble. Annibal Griffoni, his pupil, imitated small pictures, engravings, and oil paintings, in scagliola. Giovanni Gravignani, who represented the rarest sorts of marble intersected with figures, carried the art still further. The true object of these works, however, is the imitation of marble. There are some fine specimens of scagliola in the gallery at Florence, by Paolini.

Scalds, or Skalds, like the rhapsodists of ancient Greece and the bards of the Celtic tribes, were at once the poets and historians of the Scandinavian race, the

Icelanders, Danes, Norwegians. They sang the praises of the gods, and celebrated the exploits of the national heroes. (See *Northern Mythology, Edda, Sagas,* and *Scandinavian Literature.*) The scalds were the companions and chroniclers of the chiefs, whom they accompanied to battle, and at whose court they resided in time of peace. A sacred character was attached to them, and they performed the office of ambassadors between hostile tribes. They were often richly rewarded for their songs, and even married the daughters of princes. A regular succession of the order was perpetuated, and a list of 230 of the most distinguished in the three northern kingdoms, from the reign of Ragnar Lodbrok to that of Valdemar II, is still preserved in the Icelandic language, among whom are several crowned heads and distinguished warriors of the heroic age. See Wheaton's *History of the Northmen* (Philadelphia, 1831, chap. iv.).

SCALE; a mathematical instrument, containing several lines, drawn on wood, brass, silver, &c., and variously divided, according to the purposes it is intended to serve; whence it receives various denominations, as the plain scale, diagonal scale, plotting scale, Gunter's scale, &c.

SCALE (from the Latin *scala*); the name given at first to the arrangement made by Guido of the six syllables, ut, re, mi, fa, sol, la; also called *gamut.* (q. v.) The word *scale* is likewise used to signify a series of sounds, rising or falling from any given pitch or tone, to the greatest practicable distance, through such intermediate degrees as are determined by the laws of music. (See *Tone.*)

SCALIGER, Julius Cæsar. The history of this celebrated scholar is involved in some obscurity, through his vanity. According to his own story, he was descended from the celebrated house of the Scaligers (Scalas), princes of Verona, and was born at the castle of Riva, on lake Garda, became a page of the emperor Maximilian, whom he served in war and peace for seventeen years, then received a pension from the duke of Ferrara, studied at Bologna, commanded a squadron under the French viceroy, applied himself to the study of natural law, and, in 1525, accompanied the bishop of Agen to his diocese in France, where he settled. This account found credit with some learned men, among whom was De Thou, the friend and admirer of his son Joseph; but others, even in his own day, as, for instance, Scioppius, ridiculed it, and treated it as wholly or mainly fabulous. According to Tiraboschi, Scaliger was the son of Benedetto Bordone, a Paduan, who carried on the trade of a miniature painter in Venice, and received the name *della Scala* either from the sign or the situation of his shop. Scaliger resided in Venice or Padua till his forty-second year, occupied with study and the practice of medicine, and published some works under the name of Giulio Bordone. Either some promise, or the hope of bettering his condition, induced him to remove to Agen, where he passed the rest of his days. In 1528, he appears not to have formed any such design of giving himself out as a descendant of that princely family, for he was then styled, in his act of naturalization, *Julius Cæsar della Scala di Bordone,* doctor of medicine, of Verona in Italy. He must, however, have appeared with some distinction in Agen, as, in 1530, he married a young lady of a rich and noble family there. It was from this period that he began to assert his princely descent, without furnishing any proof of the truth of his pretensions. But his name acquired celebrity by his writings, which gave him a high rank among the scholars of his age, although his arrogance made many enemies. The boldness and freedom of some of his works rendered his faith suspected; but he died a good Catholic, October 21, 1558, in the seventy-sixth year of his age. Scaliger was certainly a man of uncommon abilities; and although he was one of the late-learned, yet few men have surpassed him in erudition. He had a powerful memory, and an active mind: he thought boldly, if not always logically. Of his physical works we may mention his *Exercitationum exotericarum Liber quintus decimus de Subtilitate, ad Cardanum* (Paris, 1557), Commentaries on the Work of Hippocrates *De Insomniis* (1538), and a work upon the treatises of Theophrastus and Aristotle on Plants, and of the latter on Animals, with a translation. As a philologist, he wrote two discourses against the *Ciceronianus* of Erasmus, an excellent work on the Latin language, *De Causis Linguæ Latinæ Libri xviii* (Lyons, 1540; Geneva, 1580), the first philosophical treatise on this subject. His work *De Arte poetica Libri vii* (Lyons, 1561 and 1581) gained him much reputation, but displays more grammatical learning than poetical imagination or critical spirit. Modern critics do not accord him the same praise which Lipsius, Casaubon, Vossius, &c., bestowed on him.

SCALIGER, Joseph Justus, son of the

preceding, was born at Agen in 1540. In the eleventh year of his age, he was sent to Bordeaux, where he studied the Latin language for several years. The plague obliged him to return to his father, who required him to compose a Latin discourse daily, by which means he soon became thoroughly acquainted with that language. After the death of his father, he went, at the age of nineteen, to Paris, where he devoted himself to the study of Greek. Shutting himself up in his chamber, he read Homer and the other Greek poets and prose writers with such industry, that in the course of two years he had read them all. He next studied Hebrew and other Oriental languages, and exercised himself in poetical compositions in the classical languages, having already, in his sixteenth year, written a tragedy in Latin. He then for some time led an unsettled life, of which we have no particular account. His conversion to Protestantism doubtless prevented his advancement in France; but, in 1593, he was made professor of polite literature at Leyden, where he died in 1609. He had the character of a scholar, absorbed entirely in his books, and paying little attention to the common affairs of life, so that he was never rich; yet he refused several presents of money, sent him by distinguished men, out of respect to his talents and learning. He was never married. In regard to pride and arrogance, he was little inferior to his father, whose tales respecting the origin of his family he endeavored to confirm. He was also remarkable for his asperity and contemptuous tone towards his adversaries. He boasted that he knew thirteen languages; and he was so entirely immersed in his studies, that he would pass whole days in his chamber without eating. Of his numerous works, the treatise *De Emendatione Temporum* (Paris, 1583; Geneva, 1609) is one of the most important. In this learned work, he gave the first complete and scientific chronological system, and, for these labors, and his discovery of the Julian period, deserves to be called the founder of this science. Many errors, which were exposed by Petavius and others, he corrected in the *Thesaurus Temporum, complectens Eusebii Pamphili Chronicon* (Amsterdam, 1658). His annotations to Theocritus, Nonnus, Catullus, Tibullus, Propertius, Seneca (tragedies), Varro, Ausonius, Festus, are characterized by an excessive subtilty, and too great freedom in regard to the text of the authors. His *Poemata* have little poetical merit; his *Epistolæ* are more valuable. On the whole, Joseph Scaliger had less genius than his father, but more learning and accuracy.

Scalping; a barbarous custom, among Indian warriors, of taking off their enemies' scalps with the hair on. These are preserved as trophies of victory.

Scamander; a small stream in Asia Minor, which has acquired celebrity from the songs of Homer, according to whom it was called, by the gods, *Xanthus*. It runs through the plain of Troy, and receives the Simois, another small stream mentioned by Homer. The Homeric account, that one of its sources was warm and the other cold, has been confirmed by modern travellers.

Scammony is the inspissated juice of the root of a species of *convolvulus* (*C. scammonia*), which grows wild in Syria and other parts of the Levant. This juice is obtained, in the latter part of the spring, by making incisions in the upper part of the root, and placing shells or cups to receive the milky fluid which exudes: twice a day the portion furnished by each root is collected, and dried in the sun. The purest scammony is procured in this manner, but such is rarely exported. The scammony of commerce is merely the expressed juice of the entire roots, sometimes even mixed with that of the stems and leaves, and evaporated to the consistence of a solid extract. It is of two kinds—the Aleppo, which is the best, and the Smyrna, which is inferior; both collected respectively in the vicinity of those two cities. Scammony has been known from a very ancient period; it is mentioned by Hippocrates, and many peculiar virtues were attributed to it at that time; now it is considered only as an active purgative, and as such is still much in use. The dose varies from two to twelve grains, according to age, sex, or temperament. The root of the plant is thick, fleshy and tapering, three or four feet in length, by three or four inches in diameter; it gives out one or several slender climbing stems, provided with triangular, arrow-shaped leaves; the flowers are large, white, or slightly purplish, disposed, two or three together, upon a common axillary peduncle. Jalap is also the root of a species of *convolvulus*. (See *Jalap*.)

Scandalum Magnatum, in English law, denotes a wrong done to high personages of the land, as prelates, dukes, marquisses, earls, barons, and other nobles; and also the chancellor, treasurer, clerk of the privy seal, steward of the house, justice of one bench or other, and other great officers of the realm, by false news, or false messages, whereby debates and discord between them and the commons, or any scandal to their persons, might arise. For slanders of this kind, though such as would not be actionable in the case of common persons, redress is provided by many old statutes.

SCANDERBEG (i. e. *Alexander Bey*), prince of Albania, whose proper name was George Castriotto, son of John, prince of that country, was born in 1404. Being given by his father as a hostage to sultan Amurath II, he was educated in the Mohammedan religion, and, at the age of eighteen, was placed at the head of a body of troops, with the title of *sangiac*. After the death of his father, in 1432, he formed the design of possessing himself of his principality; and, having accompanied the Turkish army to Hungary, entered into an agreement with Hunniades to desert to the Christians. This design he put into execution; and, having ascended the throne of his fathers, he renounced the Mohammedan religion. A long warfare followed; but, although frequently obliged to retire to the fastnesses of mountains, he always renewed his assaults upon the first favorable occasion, until the sultan proposed terms of peace to him, which were accepted. The Venetians having entered into a war with Mohammed II, induced Scanderbeg to renounce his treaty with the sultan. He obtained repeated victories over the Turkish generals, and saved his own capital, although invested by an army commanded by Mohammed himself. He was at length carried off by sickness, at Lissa, in the Venetian territories, in 1467, in his sixty-third year. His death was soon followed by the submission of Albania to the Turkish dominion. When the Turks took Lissa, they dug up his bones, of which they formed amulets, to transfer his courage to themselves.

SCANDINAVIA; the ancient name of the region now comprehending the three northern kingdoms, Denmark, Sweden and Norway. The inhabitants were known to the ancient nations of the south of Europe only by vague rumor. Tacitus mentions the Suiones (Swedes) as a naval people. Pliny notices a peninsula called *Nerigon* (Norway, in Swedish, *Norrige*, Danish, *Norge*). Many suppose Iceland to be the *Thule* of the classic writers. The name *Danus* is first found in Gregory of Tours, in the sixth century of the Christian era. Sweden, Norway, Denmark and Jutland were inhabited, in the earliest times, by people of the Teutonic stock, and nomads of Finnish descent. According to Rask, Magnussen, Münter and others, the Scandinavians and the people of South Germany have a common origin with the Indian, Persian and Pelasgian tribes. B. C. 100, the natives of Jutland and Sleswick became formidable to the Romans, under the name of *Cimbri*. About A. D. 250, commence the fabulous accounts of Odin, Othin or Woden. Till the middle of the ninth century, Scandinavia was little known; but the bold expeditions of the natives into the southern and western parts of Europe, and the diffusion of Christianity among them, about the year 1000, shed light on this region. At this period, the inhabitants of Scandinavia were divided into hordes, like the Tartars. In the ninth and tenth centuries, these tribes enjoyed a golden age of piracy. By the western historians, they were spoken of under the title of *Danes* and *Normans*; in the English annals of that period, under the name of *Easterlings*; the Russians called them *Varangians*; and the Hispano-Arabic writers, *Mantchoos*. From Sweden, Norway, the Danish islands, from Jutland and Sleswick, the rude adventurers sailed to near and distant harbors within and without the Baltic, to Novgorod, Kiev and Plotzk, to England, Ireland, Holland, Germany, France, Spain and Italy; sometimes they only plundered and destroyed, and sometimes founded new states.—See Wheaton's *History of the Northmen* (Philadelphia, 1831), and the article *Normans*.

Scandinavian, or *Old Norse Literature*, includes the literature of the people of Norway, Sweden and Iceland, before their conversion to Christianity. It goes back as far as the earliest history of the north, and comes down to the period when the last traces of heathenism disappear. It is of great importance, both to Germany and England; for, as they were converted to Christianity much sooner than the Scandinavians, they retain no literary monuments of their heathen period. The old Norse literature has preserved to us not only the old versification, peculiar to all nations of Teutonic origin, and distinct from that of all the other western nations, but also a mythology which, rude as it is, approaches, in the rich invention which it displays, to the mythology of Greece. Not only the poetry and mythology, but likewise the history, the antiquities, of which the Re-nic monuments (see *Runes*) are the principal, and the existing collections of laws, afford rich materials for the knowledge of the pagan period of the northern countries. Julius Cæsar, Lucan and Tacitus furnished some slight hints on the character of the Scandinavian mythology. In the eighth century, native authors appeared, who rescued the traditions of the past from oblivion. The Lombard, Paulus Diaconus, the first of these authors remaining (about the end of the eighth century), gives us, from the traditions of his countrymen, a dialogue between the deities Woden and Frea (Odin and Freya). A war had broken out, as he relates, between the Winiles and Wandeles. The latter prayed to their god Woden for assistance and victory; Woden replied, that he would give the victory to the party which he should first see on the rising of the sun. But the leaders of the Winiles, Ibor and Ayo (Agio), who by Saxo are called Ebbo and Aggo, had an ingenious mother, named Gambara, who was related to the gods, and whose counsel was esteemed by all the people. She went to Odin's wife, Frea (Freya, or more properly Frigga), and solicited victory for her countrymen and subjects, the Winiles. Frigga advised that all the women of the Winiles should station themselves, at sunrise, with their husbands, opposite to the place whence Odin was accustomed to look to the east; and, in order that he might immediately notice them, she directed that they should draw their long hair over their faces, so as to make it resemble a thick beard. The advice was followed, and the bearded females immediately struck the eye of Woden, who suddenly exclaimed, "Who are those long-beards?" This was what Frigga expected; and, as it was an ancient custom that a person who gave a name to a child, a hero, or a nation, should give them a present, Frigga cried, "They are the Winiles; and, as you have given them another name, it is your duty to give them a present: therefore give them victory." It was agreed; and from that time, the Winiles were called *long-beards* (whence *Lombards*). That the name of the people is founded on their long beards is mentioned by early authors, as Isidorus Hispalensis, who died in the first half of the seventh century, as the general belief. Moreover, the days of the week must have been named in very early times, after the gods Tyr, Woden, Thor and Freya; for in the time of Charlemagne, their names had become so well settled, that when he gave new names to the months, he did not venture to alter the names of the days of the week. Adam of Bremen (who died in 1076), in his book *De Situ Regnorum septentrionalium*, gives an account of the Swedes, when they were yet, in part, heathens, of the temple of the gods at Upsal, and of the gods Thor, Woden and Frey (whom he calls *Fricco*). He shows how they are represented, but this is nearly all. Saxo Grammaticus, a Dane, was distinguished, in the second half of the twelfth century. His sixteen books of the *Historia Danica* are a remarkable phenomenon. Using the language of the Roman classics and skilled alike in verse and prose, he takes a course peculiar to himself. The novelty of his subjects, the obscurity of his sources, the wonderful character of his stories, the charms of his style, produce a great effect. Sǎmund Frode (died 1133), Are Frode (died about 1148), and Snorre Sturleson (murdered in 1241), are also writers of much merit. Till the invention of the art of printing, little was known of the literature of Scandinavia in the rest of Europe. The first important light shed on it was by Arngrim Jonson's discovery of a parchment manuscript of the prose Edda, that is, of the younger Edda, composed by Snorre Sturleson. In September, 1628, Jonson sent to the celebrated physician Ole Worm (Olaus Wormius) this manuscript, now preserved in the library of the university at Copenhagen, with its appendix, the Scallda. Ten years later, another Icelander, Bryngulf Svenson, discovered a second parchment manuscript of the prose Edda, and also a parchment manuscript of the poetical Edda. (See *Edda*.) Both were placed in the royal library at Copenhagen. In the year 1665, Peter Resen, or Resenius, published specimens of the poetical Edda, and the whole prose Edda. The specimens of the poetical part are entitled *Ethica Othini pars Eddæ Sæmundi vocata Haavamaal, una cum ejusdem Appendice appellata Runa Capitule a multis exoptata, nunc tandem Islandice et Latine in lucem producta est per Petrum Joh. Resenium* (Copenh., 1665); 2. *Philosophia antiquissima Norvego-Danica dicta Woluspa, quæ est pars Eddæ Sæmundi, Eddâ Snorronis non brevi antiquioris, Islandice et Latine publici Juris primum facta a Petro Joh. Resenio* (Copenh., A. D. 1665, 4 sheets, 4to.), with the variations in the text from the royal and Nolde copy, and a Latin translation, by Stephen Olai, an Icelander The prose Edda bears the following title

Edda Islandorum anno Chr. MCCXV Islandice conscripta per Snorronem Sturlæ, Islandiæ Nomophylacem, nunc primum Islandice, Danice et Latine ex antiquis codicibus MSS. Bibliothecæ Regis et aliorum in Lucem prodit opera et studio Petri Johannis Resenii, etc. (Copenhag., 1665). The text is founded chiefly on the manuscript of Stephen Stephanius, who died 1650, collated with other copies. The various readings are drawn from the royal copy and that of Worm. The Latin version is by Magnus Olai (1629), with extracts from a later and more accurate translation, by Stephen Olai, of 1646. Neither of the Latin translations, however, extends further than to the 68th *Dämisaga.* But a Latin translation from the 69th to the 78th and last *Dämisaga* (ten fables, which comprehend the German tales of the Nibelungen), was prepared afterwards by Thormod Torfäus (born 1636, died at Copenhagen, 1719). In the sixty-eight *Dämisagas* is unfolded the entire mythology of the north. The story of the characters and achievements of the gods is introduced by a fiction, relating how Gylfs, the king of Sweden, undertook a journey to the Asers (gods), to learn from their own mouths their nature and laws. He received from the eldest of the gods an account of the beginning of the world, the primitive giant Ymir, and the sons of Bőr, the origin of men, the giant Niörwi, the creation of the sun and moon, the celestial bridge of Bifröst, the building of the city of the gods, the dwarfs, the holy places of the gods, and the ash-tree of Ygdrasil, the dwellings of the gods, the origin of the wind, of summer and winter, and finally of all the Asers, and their mysterious history. But this is only the first part of this Edda. The other (*Annar partur Eddu*) treats of the names of the gods, and of all the synonyms and circumlocutions admissible in poetry, in alphabetical order, a genuine northern *Gradus ad Parnassum.* It has since appeared that there is still a third part of this Edda, containing the rules for one hundred different kinds of verse, and entitled *Háttatal, Clavis metrica.* Unfortunately (at least this was the story thirty years ago), nearly the whole edition of the work of Resen was burnt; only six copies were saved, and the library of the university of Göttingen procured one of them for 100 ducats. But, whether this account is true or not, the Edda of Resen is a great literary curiosity. Notwithstanding these rich materials, to which Thomas Bartholin made extensive additions of old Norse songs, in his work *Antiquitatum Danicarum Libri tres* (Copenh., 1689), a century elapsed before this new and wild mythology produced any considerable excitement in Scandinavia and Germany. Before the time of Resen, the lovers of northern antiquities had received from Ole Worm his Runic Monuments, in six books (1643); from Stephen Stephanius, a new edition, and full commentary on Saxo Grammaticus (1644); from Olaus Verelius, the *Hervararsaga* (1672), and the *Runographia Scandica* (1675). Scheffer's *Upsalia Antiqua* (in 1666, about the time of Resen) afforded interesting views of the doctrines and worship of the north, and Rudbeck, in his *Atlantica* (1689), excited surprise for a time. Göranson, a Swede, commenced, in 1746, a new edition of the prose Edda, and, in 1750, of the *Völuspaa.* About the same time, Gottfried Schütze, a patriotic German, wrote Apologies for the ancient Tribes of Germany and the North. The result of Gräter's researches into the manuscripts containing remains of old northern literature in the library of the university at Halle, was a collection called *Northern Flowers* (Leipsic, 1789, by Gräff). His *Bragur* stimulated the learned, particularly of Germany and Denmark, to further investigations. A new spur was given to the study of Scandinavian literature by a *rifacimento* of the *Nibelungenlied*, by Hagen, in 1807 presenting the same matter in a German and Christian form, which the long expected second part of the poetic Edda was to have given in a northern and heathen form; and the appearance, at length, of an Icelandic grammar and a dictionary by Rask. The principal subsequent publications on this subject are the commentary on the collective songs of the Edda,—*Den ældre Edda* (1821—23, 4 vols.),—by Finn Magnusen, the comprehensive examination of all the historical and poetical traditions of the north, by Erasmus Müller, in his *Sagabibliothek* (1817—20, 3 vols.), and his work On the Rise and Decay of Icelandic Historiography, with an Appendix on the Nationality of the old Norse Poems, translated by Sander (Copenh., 1815). The investigations of the Runes (q. v.) have also been of much interest. The old northern sagas, or heroic tales, which were translated into Danish, and published from the Icelandic manuscripts, by C. Chr. Rafn. secretary of the society of Scandinavian literature (Copenh., 1821—24, 3 vols.), are of four sorts—mythic, mythico-historical,

historical, and romantic. These traditions are mostly of Icelandic origin. They were composed by monks, and written on calfskin, before the sixteenth century. The learned Icelander Arne Magnusen (died 1730) collected 1554 of these manuscripts, and left by his will a large sum for their publication. This fund led professor Rafn, in connexion with doctor Brynjulfon (who died in 1827), Egilson and Gudmunsson, of Iceland, to found a society for the publication of old Norse manuscripts, which now includes 145 members. (Professor Rask is the president.) Of the amended text of the *Sagas* there have appeared three editions; one in Icelandic, one in Danish, and one in Latin: the title of the last is, *Scripta historica Islandorum de Rebus Gestis veterum Borealium.* Of this edition, three volumes had appeared in 1827, which contain the *saga* of the Norwegian king Olaf Trygveson, and other short *sagas.* (See *Northern Mythology;* also the work of Wheaton, referred to above, and an article on Icelandic Literature, in the 17th number of the Foreign Quarterly Review.)

SCANIA. (See *Schonen.*)

SCANNING, in poetry; the measuring of a verse by feet, in order to see whether the quantities be duly observed. The term is chiefly used in regard to Greek and Latin verses. Thus a hexameter verse is scanned by resolving it into six feet; a pentameter, by resolving it into five feet, &c.

SCAPE GOAT, in Jewish antiquities; the goat which was set at liberty on the day of solemn expiation, typically to bear away the sins of the people.

SCAPEMENT. (See *Watch and Clock-making.*)

SCAPOLITE. A mineral which has presented itself under a great variety of aspects, and has hence been mistaken as affording, in its varieties, the foundation of several new species; instances of which are the following: *Meionite, Dipyre, Bergmanite, Wernerite, Gabbronite, Ekebergite,* and *Nuttallite,* all of which are now recognised as coalescing with scapolite. It is often seen in well defined crystals, which are right, square prisms, terminated at one or both extremities by four-sided pyramids. The length of the prism is about double its diameter. It is sometimes truncated on its lateral edges, and thus converted into an octagonal prism; cleavage not very distinct; fracture imperfect, conchoidal, uneven; surface of the prism sometimes longitudinally streaked; lustre vitreous, inclining to resinous upon the cleavage; color various shades of white, gray and green; occasionally, also, red or purple; transparent, translucent and opaque; brittle; hardness between apatite and feldspar; specific gravity, 2.6—2.8. The massive varieties are columnar, granular, and compact. As respects some of the varieties which gave origin to the names above mentioned,—Meionite contains the purest and most transparent varieties of the species of a white color; Dipyre occurs in minute crystals, whose form is scarcely discernible, and imbedded in a steatitic rock; Bergmanite is massive, fine-grained, of a grayish, greenish or reddish white color; Wernerite is in crystals doubly terminated, of a greenish-gray color; from which Nuttallite scarcely differs, except that the crystals have a tinge of blue, and are slightly chatoyant. The following results, relative to the chemical composition of scapolite, were obtained, 1. by Stromeyer, from a variety of Meionite from Monte Somma; and, 2. by Nordenskiöld, from the scapolite of Finland:—

	(1.)	(2.)
Silex,	40.531	43.83
Alumine,	32.726	35.43
Lime,	24.245	18.96
Potash, and a little soda,	1.812	0.00
Protox. iron,	0.182	0.00
Water,	0.000	1.03

In a strong heat, before the blow-pipe, scapolite melts into a vesicular glass, and intumesces considerably; then it assumes the appearance of ice, and does not melt any longer. It is dissolved by borax, with effervescence. Meionite is met with among the minerals ejected by mount Vesuvius. The other varieties of the species are met with in primitive mountains, in beds of iron ore or limestone, and are generally accompanied by augite and hornblende. Thus it occurs at Pargas in Finland, in Greenland, and in Saxony. In the U. States, the most beautiful varieties have been found at Bolton, in Massachusetts—the white, transparent crystals, as also the Nuttallite. It is likewise found in the sienite, at Boxborough; also in Connecticut, at Canaan, where it exists in a massive state, and in mountain masses. Large crystals of scapolite are found in the highlands of New York, near West Point, and at Amity, in Orange county, of the same state.

SCAPULA, John, the author of a valuable lexicon of the Greek language, published originally in quarto, in 1583, which has since gone through a variety of editions, particularly an excellent one from the Elzevir press, and a recent one by Major (Lon don, 1820, 4to.). Henry Stephens (q. v.), while completing his *Thesaurus*, having employed Scapula to correct the press, the latter secretly abridged the work. The dictionary, thus treacherously stolen, ruined the sale of that of his employer.

Scapulary (*scapularium*); part of a monk's dress, consisting of two pieces of cloth, of which one covers the breast, the other the back. With lay-brothers, the scapulary only reaches to the knee; with the other religious, to the feet.

Scarabeus; the beetle (q. v.), which was held in great veneration by the Egyptians. The most celebrated, and that which is alone to be found represented on ancient monuments, is the *scarabeus sacer* of naturalists. This is seen on the Isiac table, and is frequent among hieroglyphics: it passed as the symbol of immortality, and as the emblem of the sun. Another species was consecrated to Isis, and indicated the moon; its two horns resembling the crescent of that planet. According to Caylus, the Egyptians gave the shape of the scarabeus to their amulets or rings. (See *Hieroglyphics*.)

Scaramouch (Ital. *scaramuccia*); one of the grotesque characters of the Italian stage, which, about 1680, took the place of the old Spanish captain, was dressed entirely in black, a color commonly worn in Naples by courtiers and magistrates. He represented the swaggerer, who is finally flogged by harlequin. The original scaramouch was a person named Tiberius Fiorelli, a native of Naples, who distinguished himself on the stage by his jests and his skill in mimicry. In France, the scaramouch was used for a greater variety of parts.

Scarborough; a market and seaport town of England, in the North Riding of Yorkshire, a place of considerable trade, and much frequented for its mineral waters, warm baths and sea-bathing. It stands in the recess of a beautiful bay, on the borders of the German ocean, and rising from the shore in the form of an amphitheatre. The town is well built; the principal streets spacious and well paved. The buildings on the cliff are striking, having in front a terrace nearly 100 feet above the level of the sands. An iron bridge of four arches, seventy-one feet span each, supported by stone pillars nearly seventy feet high, connects the terrace with a beautiful promenade, 350 yards in length, leading to the Spa, and in full view of the sea, harbor, town and castle. The plantations and public walks are agreeable; and an elegant assembly-room and a handsome theatre are open in summer evenings. The rides are also varied and romantic. Scarborough has two Episcopal churches, an Independent, Baptist, and Roman Catholic chapel, a meeting-house for Quakers, and two for Methodists. The ruins of the ancient castle form a very picturesque object, and great ornament to the town. The promontory on which they stand rises nearly 300 feet above the level of the sea. The area of the castle contains about nineteen acres. It was built about the year 1136, and became the scene of many important transactions in English history. The harbor of Scarborough is commodious, and of easy access, and has been improved by extensive works. The present prosperity of Scarborough is chiefly owing to its mineral waters, which have rendered the town a place of fashionable resort for health and pleasure. There are two wells, saline aperient, and chalybeate. It sends two members to parliament, chosen by the corporate body, consisting of forty-four persons. It was incorporated in 1181. Population in 1831, 8750. Forty miles north-east of York; lat. 54° 18′ N.; lon. 0° 23′ W.

Scarfing; a particular method of uniting two pieces of timber together by the extremities, the end of one being tapered so as to be set into the other, as in the keel-pieces. But when the ends of the two pieces are cut square and put together, they are said to *butt* to one another; and when another piece is laid on and fastened to both, as is the case in all the frame timbers, this is called *scarfing* the timbers; and half the piece which fastens the two timbers together is reckoned the length of the scarf.

Scarification, in surgery; the operation of making little cuts or punctures in the skin by means of lancets or other instruments, particularly the cupping instrument.

Scarlatti, Alessandro, chapel-master at the Neapolitan court, born at Naples, 1658, was educated at Rome under Carissimi, and, after residing some time in Germany and at Rome, passed the last years of his life at Naples, where he died, in 1728. The Italians called him the pride of art and the first of composers. Hasse says, that he was the greatest master of harmony among the Italians, and Jomelli considered his church music as the best of its kind. He composed a great number of motets, and about 200 masses. His opera *La Principessa fidele* is esteemed his masterpiece.

Scarlet Fever (*scarlatina*); a contagious fever, characterized by a scarlet-colored eruption on the skin, in patches, which, after three or four days, fall off in scales. Some have asserted that *scarlatina* never attacks the same person a second time; more extensive observation has confuted this opinion. It seizes persons of all ages; but children and young persons are most subject to it; and it appears at all seasons of the year, but is more frequently met with towards the end of autumn or beginning of winter, at which time it very often becomes a prevalent epidemic. *Scarlatina*, in its inflammatory form, is not usually attended with danger, although a considerable degree of delirium sometimes prevails for a day or two; but when it partakes much of the malignant character (*scarlatina anginosa*), or degenerates into *typhus putrida*, which it is apt to do, it often proves fatal.

Scarp, in fortification; the interior slope of the ditch with which the fortification is surrounded, and which faces the country or champaign.

Scarpa, Antonio, one of the most celebrated anatomists and surgeons of the eighteenth century, was born in Lombardy, about 1746. His work *Anatomicæ Disquisitiones de Auditu et Olfactu* appeared at Pavia in 1789; previously to which his *Anatomicæ Observationes de Structura Fenestræ rotundæ Auris* (Modena, 1772) had already attracted the notice of the learned. At the time of the revolution in Italy, he was deprived of his professorship in the university on account of his refusing to take the oath required by the Cisalpine republic. He now published his celebrated work On Aneurisms (1804). When Napoleon, after his coronation at Milan, as king of Italy, arrived at Pavia (1805), and received the officers of the university, he inquired after Scarpa. He was informed that he had long ceased to be a member of the university, and was told the reason. "What," said Napoleon, "have political opinions to do here? Scarpa is an honor to Pavia and to my dominions. Let him be honorably restored." Scarpa was the author of several other surgical works, besides those already mentioned. He died in Pavia in 1826. Most of his works have been translated into French and English.

Scarron, Paul, a comic poet and satirist, was born at Paris, in 1610. His father, a counsellor of the parliament, wished to oblige him to take orders; but the son was averse to such a step. At the age of twenty-four, he travelled into Italy, where he gave himself up, without restraint, to indulgences of every kind, and continued his excesses, after his return to Paris, in such a manner as to bring upon himself the most painful diseases. At the age of twenty-seven, having appeared during the carnival at Mans as a savage, he was pursued by the populace, and threw himself into a marsh. In consequence of this exposure, he lost the use of his limbs. Notwithstanding his sufferings, he never lost his gayety; and, settling at Paris, his wit and social powers gained him the friendship of some of the most distinguished persons in the city and at court. After the death of his father, he had a lawsuit with his mother-in-law, in which, although his whole fortune was at stake, he made a humorous defence of his claims, and lost his case. Mad. de Hautefort, his friend, touched by his misfortunes, presented him to the queen. Scarron requested permission to call himself her majesty's valetudinarian. The queen smiled; and Scarron, taking her smile as a commission, styled himself thenceforth *Scarron, par la grace de Dieu, malade indigne de la reine.* He now obtained a pension by his praises of Mazarin, whom, however, he soon after offended by his *Mazarinade* and his *Typhon*, and thus lost his pension. His marriage with Françoise d'Aubigné, afterwards wife of Louis XIV, and marchioness de Maintenon (q. v.), however much it may have increased his happiness, did not improve his fortune; and he lived with so little economy, that he soon became involved in pecuniary difficulties. The comedies, which he wrote as a means of subsistence, were borrowed from the Spanish theatre. His *Jodelet ou le Maître Valet* had great success. His *Énéide travestie*, and his *Roman comique*, particularly the latter, are among the most esteemed of his works. His works appeared at Paris (1737, 10 vols.).

Scaurus, Marcus Æmilius. There were two distinguished Romans of this name, father and son. The former was chosen consul B. C. 116, and was afterwards *princeps senatus.* He was likewise celebrated as an orator, and assumed a severity and dignity of manner which gained him great consideration, both with the senate and people, artfully cloaking his ambition and rapacity. He also celebrated a triumph, on account of his victory over the Gauls. Although he allowed himself to be bribed in the war with Jugurtha, he conducted with such caution and cunning as to secure his re-election to the consulate, and his election to the censorship.—His son was remarkable for the brilliant display which he made as *ædilis curulis*. He built a large and splendid theatre, and exhibited public games at great expense. Cicero defended him, when he was accused of being guilty of oppressions in the province of Sardinia.

SCEAUX, GARDE DES, or KEEPER OF THE SEALS. (See *Keeper of the Great Seal*.)

SCENERY; the decorations of a stage, by means of which the different places in which the action of the drama is supposed to go on, are represented. In the theatres of the ancients, the scenes were not changed during the performance; the sidewalls remained unaltered, and were decorated quite simply; perhaps, only painted with some not very bright color, adapted to any representation and every change of scene. When theatres were established in Europe, in the sixteenth century, these side-walls were not at first provided with movable scenery. When the mysteries were represented on the stage, the actors sat on particular seats along the sides. As soon as the piece commenced, the spectators saw at once all the performers. When an actor was to make his appearance in the piece, he rose from his seat, and took it again at his exit. In later times, there was a space on the side of the stage, in which some spectators were admitted, particularly the critics and wits of the day. They had servants to wait on them, who brought them pipes and tobacco; for they smoked there as well as in other parts of the house. The representation of a tragedy was indicated by black hangings round the stage, and the changes of the scene merely by inscriptions, with the names of the places represented. It was left to the imagination of the spectators to supply the local circumstances. The Italian architect Serlio (died 1540) first placed on the sides of the stage movable scenes, so as to leave intervals between them, affording a free passage. In this way, the stage could be better lighted; for hitherto two chandeliers, suspended above the stage, had been used for this purpose; but the new arrangement permitted the use of lights which were not seen by the spectators, and, besides, the brilliancy of the light could be increased or diminished, according to circumstances. In England, this mode of lighting was first introduced after Garrick's return from France. But a more important advantage of the movable sides was, that they could be varied as occasion required, so as to bring the place and circumstances of the action represented before the eye.

SCEPTICISM (from σκεπτεσθαι, to look at distant objects with the hand held above the eyes, and secondly, to survey, consider). The Greek philosophers, called *sceptics*, were also called *Pyrrhonists*, from Pyrrho of Elis; also *Aporetici*, i. e. doubters; *Ephectici*, that is, abstaining (from judging). Pyrrho (born 384 A. D.) was a man whose aim, according to Diogenes Laërtius, was uprightness of life, unconcerned about philosophical speculation, which, as then pursued, was not favorable to integrity. He wrote nothing himself; but some information respecting him is contained in the extant fragments of the writings of Timon of Phlius in Achaia. He is represented as truly virtuous, hostile to all pride of opinion, and not esteeming mankind very highly. In fact, his scepticism was essentially different from that of a later period. Ten topics of argument were used in the school of the sceptics, with this reservation, that nothing could be positively asserted concerning either the number or the force of the arguments which may be urged in favor of uncertainty. They were, 1. That, on account of the variety which takes place in the organization of different animal bodies, it is probable that the same external object presents different images to different animals, and man can have no reason for asserting that his perceptions are more conformable to the real nature of things than those of inferior animals. 2. That even among men there is a great diversity both of mind and body, which necessarily occasions a great variety of opinions; every man judging according to his particular apprehension, whilst no one is able to determine the real nature of things. 3. That the different senses give different reports of the same thing; whence bodies may have different properties from those which the senses lead us to suppose. 4. That the same thing appears differently, according to the different dispositions or circumstances of the person who perceives it; whence it is impossible for any one man to pronounce that his judgment concerning any object is agreeable to nature. 5. That things assume a different aspect, according to their distance, position, or place; and no reason can be assigned why one of these aspects should agree with the real object, rather than the rest. 6. That no object offers itself to the senses, which is not so connected and mixed with others, that it cannot be distinctly separated and examined. 7. That objects of sense appear exceedingly different, when viewed in a compound and in a decomposed state; and it is impossible to say, which appearance most truly expresses their real nature. 8. That every object being always viewed in its relation to others, it is impossible to determine what it is simply in its own nature. 9. That our judgment is liable to uncertainty, from the circumstance of frequent or rare occurrence; that which happens every day appearing to us in a very different light from that in which the same thing would appear if it were new. 10. That mankind are continually led into different conceptions concerning the same thing, through the influence of custom, law, fabulous tales, and established opinions. On all these accounts, every human judgment is liable to uncertainty; and we can only say, concerning any thing, that it seems to be, not that it is what it seems. Besides these topics, the latter sceptics made use of some others. They maintained that every proposition requires some prior proposition to support it *in infinitum*, or supposes some axiom which cannot be proved, and is therefore taken for granted without demonstration, that is, may be denied; that, in argument, the point assumed, and that which is to be proved, may often be alternately used in each other's place, both being equally uncertain; and, lastly, that nothing can be understood by itself, as appears from the endless disputes of philosophers concerning the nature of things; nor by means of something else, whilst itself remains unknown. An avoidance of all settled opinion on subjects of knowledge (ἐποχη), and a consequent tranquillity (ἀταραξια) amid all the changes of life, were the beginning and end of this system. Sextus Empiricus (q. v.), towards the end of the second century, carried out the system of scepticism with rare erudition and acuteness, and separated the reasoning of the sceptics from the negative dogmatism of the later academy (see *Plato*); and to him we are indebted for our knowledge of scientific scepticism in its maturity. Of modern sceptics, we may mention Francis Sanchez (born 1562, at Bracara, in Portugal, died 1632); Francis de la Mothe le Vayer (born 1586, died 1672; Sorbiere and Foucher were his disciples; he declared his belief in revealed knowledge); Peter Daniel Huet (born 1630, died 1721); Jos. Glanvill (died 1680); and Peter Bayle (born 1647), a man of great acuteness, and the celebrated Hume (born 1711). (See *Hume*.) A limited scepticism was recently taught by G. E. Schulze, of which the chief maxim is, that the origin of our knowledge is inexplicable.—See *History and Spirit of Scepticism*, &c., by Stäudlin (Leipsic, 1794—95, 2 vols.). It is highly necessary to distinguish between that puerile doubting which disqualifies for forming a decided opinion in individual cases, and that scepticism which, in science, is opposed to dogmatism, and is indispensable to keep the human mind within due bounds in its eternal striving for a solution of the great riddle of existence, and for a correct understanding of intellect, reality, and the power which pervades and upholds all existence.

Sceptre (from *sceptrum*, σκῆπτρον), originally a staff, the emblem of sovereign power. Some say that it was only a lance, without the metal point, to indicate the continuance of supreme power in time of peace; but in some cases it may have originated from the simple staff—with many tribes, the emblem of old age and wisdom. The *baton*, the short sceptre, has always remained a sign of distinction; as in the case of the marshals. In the Greek assemblies, a person who wished to speak received a sceptre from the herald; and the judges also bore it while in the exercise of their authority. Kings swore by the sceptre. By degrees, it became the emblem of supreme power alone. Through the Roman emperors it passed to the Western monarchs. The sceptre and ball now form the two most important emblems of royal and imperial power.

Schadow, John Gottfried, director of the royal academy of arts in Berlin, a distinguished sculptor, was born in Berlin in 1764. His parents were poor; but fortunate circumstances, aiding his energetic character, enabled him to study sculpture, and go to Italy, where he made a group in *terra cotta* for the (so called) *concorso di Palestra*, and received the prize-medal. Some of the best known works, made or modelled by him, are the statues of general Ziethen, and of prince Leopold of Dessau, in Berlin, the monument of Luther, in Wittenberg, the Victoria and the Brandenburg gate, in Berlin (which was carried to Paris, and afterwards restored), the monument of Blücher, at Rostock.—His son *Rudolf*, who died in 1822, was one of the most promising sculptors at Rome. His Sandal-binder and Spinner are celebrated, and have often been copied.—Another son, *Frederic William*, is a painter, and, since 1826, has been director of the academy of painting at Düsseldorf.

SCHÄFER, Godfrey Henry, a distinguished German philologist, was born at Leipsic in 1764, entered the university in 1781, and enjoyed the philological instructions of Ernesti, Reiz, and Beck. In 1796, appeared his edition of Athenæus, which was followed by the *Opera Moralia* of Plutarch, an edition of Herodotus, and several other works. In 1806, his *Meletemata critica in Dionysii Hal. Artem rhetoricam* procured him the privilege of lecturing. In 1808, he was appointed professor extraordinary of philosophy, and, in 1818, librarian of the university. Besides numerous classical works, Greek and Latin, the publication of which he has superintended, he has published an improved edition of Bos's Ellipses, and contributed many notes and remarks to the recent London edition of Stephens' *Thesaurus*, of which he corrected the proofs; *Ammonius de Different. Verborum Affinium* (1822); *Phalaris Epistolæ* (Leipsic, 1823); a revision of Reiske's Demosthenes (London, 1822, seq.), and an improved edition of Plutarch's Lives (1830), are among his more recent labors. In some cases he has merely given a corrected impression of standard texts, in others corrected readings, while to some of the authors he has added valuable commentaries.

SCHAFFHAUSEN; one of the smallest of the twenty-two cantons of Switzerland, in the northern part of which it lies, on the right bank of the Rhine, nearly surrounded by Baden, and separated by the Rhine from the cantons of Zürich and Thurgau, on the south. Its superficial extent is 115 square miles; population, 28,050, in seven towns and thirty-five villages, all Reformed (Calvinists), except 210 Catholics. (See *Switzerland.*) The capital, of the same name, on the right bank of the Rhine, has a population of 7000 souls. Lon. 8° 37′ E.; lat. 47° 43′ N. It has a castle, a college (*collegium humanitatis*), with nine professors, a gymnasium, a town library, theological library, town hall, &c., and manufactures of cotton, silk and leather. It is situated about a league above the celebrated cataract of the Rhine, of which the descent is seventy or eighty feet. (See *Rhine*, and *Cataract.*) The situation of the town gives it a considerable transit trade, all goods brought down the river being landed here. There is a wooden bridge here over the Rhine, 120 paces long; but the ingenious hanging bridge, which was built in 1758, was destroyed by the French in 1799.

SCHANDAU; a small town in the centre of Saxon Switzerland (q. v.), two leagues from the Bohemian frontier, with 1000 inhabitants. It is much visited in summer on account of its charming situation, the beautiful scenery in its neighborhood, and its mineral waters.

SCHARNHORST, Gebhard David von; born in 1756, at Hämelsee, in Hanover His father, in consequence of being embroiled in a lawsuit, was deprived of the means of giving him a good education, and young Scharnhorst was sent to a village school, where he remained till his fifteenth year. A few works on the seven years' war, and the Austrian war of succession, and more particularly the narratives of an invalid soldier, inspired him with a passion for the military life. To be at some future period a sergeant in command of an outpost, was at this time his ideal of felicity. At length his father gained his protracted suit, and with it an estate; and young Scharnhorst was received into the military school of count William of Schaumburg-Lippe-Bückeburg. He subsequently entered the Hanoverian service, and soon distinguished himself by several excellent military works. In 1780, he was appointed teacher in the military school at Hanover. In 1793, he was made captain of horse artillery. In 1794, he distinguished himself so much under general Hammerstein, that George III gave him a sword of honor, and made him major. The duke of Brunswick recommended him to the king of Prussia, who appointed him lieutenant-colonel. In 1804, he was made colonel; in 1807, major-general; and, in 1813, lieutenant-general. In the unfortunate battle of Auerstädt he was wounded twice; yet he took part in the battle of Eylau. (q. v.) After the peace of Tilsit, he was appointed president of the committee for the reorganization of the army, and here displayed great talents, giving the whole army a totally new constitution and spirit. He was equally practical and scientific. He infused into the army a truly national feeling. When Prussia rose *en masse*, in 1813, it was chiefly Scharnhorst who contrived, by means of the corps of volunteers, and the *landwehr* (q. v.), as well as by having previously disciplined many more men than the peace of Tilsit authorized Prussia to keep in actual service, to arm all persons capable of doing military duty. In the spring of 1813, he was chief of the staff in the army under Blücher, in Saxony. In the battle of Lützen, his leg was severely wounded; and, not allowing himself necessary rest, but setting out too soon for Vienna, to gain over the emperor of Austria to the cause of the allies, he died, June 28, 1813, at Prague. His statue stands in the King's square, in Berlin.

SCHAUENBURG, or SCHAUMBURG-LIPPE. (See *Lippe.*)

SCHEELE, Charles William, a celebrated chemist, who contributed greatly to the improvement of the science which he cultivated, born at Stralsund, in Sweden, in 1742, was apprenticed to an apothecary at Gottenburg. He became his own instructer in chemistry, went to Upsal in 1773, where his abilities introduced him to the notice of professor Bergmann, and was admitted an associate of the academy. He subsequently became director of a pharmaceutical establishment at Kioping, where he continued to the close of his life, in 1786. He discovered the fluoric acid, and the acids of tungsten and molybden; and his experiments on barytes, chlorine, various animal and vegetable acids, on the composition of water, and several other subjects, are in the highest degree important.

SCHEEREN; the rocks on the coasts of Sweden and Finland, particularly those situated before Stockholm, which extend from seventy to eighty miles into the sea. The Scheeren fleet protects the entrance into the harbor, and consists of flat vessels, able to sail in shallow water.

SCHEERERITE; a newly discovered mineral species, of a combustible nature, found in a bed of brown coal near St. Gall, in Switzerland. It exists in loosely aggregated, whitish, feebly-shining, pearly, crystalline grains and folia. It is rather heavier than water, does not feel greasy, is very friable, and destitute of taste. It melts at 36° R. into a colorless liquid, in which state it resembles a fat oil. It seems to be a mineral naphthaline.

SCHEIK. (See *Sheik.*)

SCHELDT, or SCHELDE (anciently *Scaldis*, French *Escaut*); a river which rises in the French department of the Aisne, becomes navigable at Condé, and enters the kingdom of Belgium at St. Antring. At Ghent it receives the Lys; and it is further increased by two great canals which form a communication between Ghent, Bruges, and Sas. After passing by Dendermonde, where it receives the Dender, Aupelmonde, where the Aupel, formed by the junction of the Dyle and the two Nethes, empties into it, and Antwerp, where it is 1600 feet wide, it divides, eighteen miles below the latter city, into two great branches, the East and West Scheldt. The latter takes the name of Hondt, and empties into the North sea at Flushing. Both arms are connected with the Meuse and Rhine. The principal places on the Scheldt are Cambray, Valenciennes, Condé, Tournay, Oudenarde, Ghent, Dendermonde, Antwerp, and Flushing. In 1784, the navigation of the Scheldt became a subject of dispute between Austria (then in possession of Belgium) and the Dutch republic. The subject was amicably settled by the mediation of the king of France, Austria renouncing her pretensions to the free navigation of the river, in consideration of some cessions, and the payment of a sum of money by Holland. (See *Netherlands*, Appendix to last volume.)

SCHELLING, Frederic William Joseph von, one of the most distinguished philosophers of Germany, was born at Leonberg, in Würtemberg, in 1775, studied at Leipsic and Jena, in which latter university he was a pupil of Fichte, whom he succeeded as professor there. Some years since, he was made secretary of the academy of fine arts at Munich, and was ennobled by the king of Bavaria. In 1820, he went to Erlangen, and delivered lectures at the university in that city. In 1827, he was appointed a professor in the university at Münich. His works are, On the Possibility of a Form of Philosophy in general (Tübingen, 1795); Contributions towards a Philosophy of Nature (first edition, Tübingen, 1795); Of the Soul of the World, a Hypothesis of the higher Natural Philosophy, for the Explanation of the general Organization of Things (Hamburg, 1798); First Sketch of the Philosophy of Nature (Jena, 1799); System of Transcendental Idealism (Tübingen, 1800); Lectures on the Method of Academical Study (Tübingen, second edition, 1814; first edition 1803); Bruno, or On the Divine and Natural Principle of Things (Berlin, 1802); Philosophy and Religion (Tübingen, 1804); his Complete Philosophical Writings, of which the first volume only has yet appeared (Landshut, 1809); On the I (*Ego*), as a Principle of Philosophy, or On the Unconditional in Human Knowledge (first edition, Tübingen, 1795); Philosophical Letters on Dogmatism and Criticism (in the Philosophical Journal of Niethammer, Jena, 1796); a discourse on the Relation of the Fine Arts to Nature, delivered in 1807, at the festival of the baptism of the king of Bavaria; his General Periodical, by and for Germans, of which but three numbers appeared (Nuremberg, 1813); Representation of the True Relation of the Philosophy of Nature to the improved Doctrine of Fichte (Tübingen, 1806). Of late,

Schelling has also occupied himself with mythological inquiries, a fruit of which is his Treatise on the Deities of Samothrace (Tübingen, 1816). To give a view of the philosophy of Schelling within our limits is impossible. It would require great minuteness of explanation, both of his phraseology and his ideas, and could not be made intelligible, in a limited space, to one who had not a previous knowledge of other German philosophical systems. His system, moreover, has not yet been presented to the public in a connected form, although he has promised so to exhibit it, in a work to be called the Ages of the World. The part of it as yet most developed, is the philosophy of nature; the least developed part is the ethical. His influence upon various branches of German science has been very great. Among those who have carried out his philosophy of nature, are Steffens, Troxler, Oken (q. v.), Kielmayer, Windischmann, Baader, Kieser, C. E. Schelling, Schubert, Nasse, Burdach, Creuzer, Solger, Görres, Daub, Hegel, &c. Hegel, at a later period, pursued a course of his own, and adopted a dialectic method in philosophy. Other writers have labored on other parts of Schelling's system.

SCHEMNITZ (Hungarian, *Selmecz-Banya*; Sclavonic, *Stjawnitza*); a royal free city of Hungary, in the county of Honth, eighty miles east of Presburg; lon. 18° 54′ E., lat. 48° 48′ N; population, with the suburbs, 20,211. It stands in the midst of the most picturesque scenery, a few miles from the Raab, and contains some good houses, and tolerably wide streets, though irregularly built, on account of the unevenness of the surface. The mines of Schemnitz are the most extensive in Hungary, and are hardly surpassed by any in Europe. In eighteen mines, 8000 workmen are employed. The yearly value of the products is nearly one million dollars. The chief metals are gold, silver, and lead, combined with copper and arsenic. The whole of the mining works are the property of the government. The extent of ground containing the ores is about six miles square, and includes the town, most of which is undermined.—Schemnitz has a castle, one Lutheran and four Catholic churches, a Lutheran gymnasium, and a mining academy, which has a director, five professors, and about 150 students. The course of education is completed in three years. The greatest amount of gold was produced in the year 1690, which yielded 1872 marks, or 132,428 ducats. The value of the gold and silver obtained from 1740 to 1773, was thirty million dollars.

SCHENECTADY; a city of New York, on the south-east side of the Mohawk, fifteen and a half miles from Albany. It is regularly laid out in streets and squares. The Erie canal passes through it; and it contains the county buildings, the buildings of Union college, and the usual variety of dwelling houses, school houses, houses of worship, shops and offices. Population in 1830, 4256. It is a pleasant and flourishing town, and is distinguished for the enterprise of its inhabitants. Union college, in this city, was incorporated in 1794. It is a highly respectable institution; has 10 instructers, 205 students, 5150 volumes in its library, and 8450 in the students libraries. The commencement is on the fourth Wednesday in July. The whole number of alumni in 1831 was 1373.

SCHERZO (an Italian word signifying *joke*, *jest*), in music; generally applied to a passage of a sportive character in musical pieces of some length; e. g., to symphonies, quartettos, &c. Beethoven has made it a common part of the symphony, and it has taken the place of the minuet. (q. v.)

SCHIAVONE, Andrea, an eminent painter of the Venetian school, whose true name was *Medola*, his surname (the Sclavonian being derived from his birth place, was born at Sebenico, in Dalmatia, in 1522. His parents, who were in humble circumstances, placed him with a house-painter, at Venice, where, at his leisure hours, he studied the works of Parmegiano, Giorgione, and Titian. The latter took him under his care, and soon after employed him in the library of St. Mark, where he is said to have painted three entire ceilings. He was accounted one of the finest colorists of the Venetian school. Two of his compositions are in the church of the *Padri Teatini*, at Rimini, representing the nativity and the assumption of the Virgin. His Perseus and Andromeda, and the Apostles at the Sepulchre, are in the royal collection at Windsor. He died at Venice in 1582.

SCHICHT, John Gottfried, one of the most scientific musicians and composers of sacred music, was born in 1753, near Zittau, in Saxony, and was the son of a poor weaver. In 1776, he went to the university of Leipsic to study law, but soon devoted himself entirely to music. In 1810, he was appointed to superintend the music in the two chief churches at Leipsic. He studied the theory of music with great zeal and success, and composed several beautiful pieces. Among his numerous works is his universal hymn-book, which contains 1285 melodies, including 306 of his own publication, by Härtel, at Leipsic. Several of his compositions are celebrated. He died in 1823.

SCHILL, Ferdinand von, a Prussian cavalry officer, who distinguished himself by his daring expedition against the French, was born in 1773, in Silesia. He was wounded in the battle of Auerstädt, and took refuge in Colberg (q. v.), where he essentially contributed to save this fortress—the only Prussian one which, in 1806 and 1807, escaped capture. He collected more than 1000 fugitives, and performed the boldest exploits; to reward which, the king made him a major, after the peace of Tilsit. His entry into Berlin, the next year, resembled a triumph: the inhabitants considered it an honor to quarter his soldiers in their houses. Schill burned to meet the French in the field. In 1809, when the Tyrolese rose (see *Hofer*), Dörnberg labored to excite an insurrection in Hessia; and Schill was secretly instigated (not by the king, nor the government) to rise. He marched, April 28, with his regiment, out of Berlin, as he had done on many previous days, for the purpose of exercise. But this time he did not return. He marched towards the Elbe. Here he found that he had mistaken the disposition of the Saxons. In Halle, he was informed of Napoleon's decisive victories at Tann, Abensberg, Eckmühl and Ratisbon. Dörnberg's insurrection had miscarried. Schill called his officers together, and they agreed to proceed in their enterprise. May 5, he fought at Dodendorf with the Westphalians. He strove to reach East Friesland. Ten thousand francs were offered for his head, by the king of Westphalia. He now tried to reach the Baltic, probably to obtain support from the English. After some conflicts, he took Stralsund, and fortified it in haste. May 31, Stralsund was taken by Dutch troops, after a desperate defence. Schill himself fell, with many of his brave followers, fighting for a long time in the streets. Twelve officers were taken here and at Dodendorf, and shot at Wesel: the men were sent to the French galleys. A part of his troops forced their way into the open country, and compelled the enemy to allow them a free passage to the Prussian frontier, where a Prussian court-martial broke the officers, and sent them to a fortress. Though Schill's enterprise miscarried, it had an electrifying effect on the Prussians.

SCHILLER, John Christopher Frederic von, was born Nov. 10, 1759, at Marbach, a town of Würtemberg, on the Neckar. His father, originally a surgeon in the army, was afterwards a captain, and finally superintendent of a nursery of trees attached to a castle of the duke of Würtemberg. His parents were pious and upright; and if his early education did not afford much opportunity for the developement of his genius, by intercourse with men of talents, or by a wide field of observation, it was eminently calculated to awaken that sensibility to the good and the true, which forms so essential a trait in his character; and his early acquaintance with the Bible, making him familiar with the poetical passages of the Old Testament, contributed to develope his poetical genius. The visions of Ezekiel early excited a great interest in him. When a child, he always manifested an affectionate disposition, and was devotedly attached to his parents, and his sister. He loved, at a very early period, to repeat the sermon which he had heard at church on Sunday. He would stand on a chair and preach with great zeal, never omitting the divisions which the minister had made in his discourse. His charitable disposition manifested itself early, and never left him. For a long time, he wished to study theology; although a brilliant tragedy, which he had seen performed on the stage at Stuttgard when he was nine years old, strongly attracted his attention towards the drama. His first poem is said to have been written the day before his confirmation, in 1772. He had, till this time, received instruction at a good Latin school, in order to prepare himself for the university, as his father strove to procure for him the benefits of a good education, though his own had been neglected. At this time, Charles, duke of Würtemberg, having become weary of parade and dissipation, turned his thoughts to an object of a better character, though still a whim of a petty prince, viz. the establishment of a school on a military-monastic plan, where no effort should be spared to give the pupils the best education of which he could conceive. The duke sought for pupils among the sons of his officers, and offered to take young Schiller. His father could not well refuse such an offer; and, in 1773, Schiller was received into the Charles-school, sacrificing his own inclinations to the interest of his parents. He studied jurisprudence at this institution, in which the pupils were kept so entirely separate from the world, that they were permitted to see no females, except their mothers or very young sisters, who visited them on Sundays. Thus the influences, under which Schiller's talents were developed, were precisely opposite to those which operated on Göthe. (q. v.) The plan of the school was afterwards extended, and medicine allowed to be studied in it; and the school itself was transferred to Stuttgard. Schiller now seized on the opportunity offered, and, in 1775, began to study medicine and Latin zealously. His teachers did not all consider him as possessing uncommon talents; but the duke used to say, "Let that boy alone; he will come to something." When 16 years old, he published a translation of part of Virgil's Æneid in hexameters, in a Suabian periodical; but poetry was a forbidden fruit for him and his companions, and attracted them, therefore, the more. Some poetical books found their way, by stealth, into the school—the works of Klopstock, Gerstenberg, Göthe and Lessing. In 1773, Schiller began an epic, the hero of which was Moses; but he destroyed it at a later period. Shakspeare kindled in him a passion for the drama. He undertook two dramatic compositions, which he afterwards burned. Only some passages of one were retained in the Robbers. For two years he studied medicine very ardently, and wrote a Latin treatise On the Philosophy of Physiology, which was never printed. In 1777, at the age of 18 years, he began to write his Robbers—a composition with many striking faults; but which, nevertheless, awakens a powerful interest. Schiller himself says of it, that "he dared to describe men long before he knew any thing of them within his grated cell;" but, notwithstanding this, it contains some deep views and admirable displays of character. In 1780, when he had finished his studies, he wrote a treatise, entitled Essay on the Connexion of the Animal and Intellectual Nature of Man, printed in 1821, in the *Monatschrift* of Berlin. In the same year, he was appointed physician to a regiment in Stuttgard. Whilst in the school, he had been able to compose only by stealth, and had often reported himself sick, in order to have the use of the lamp in the sick-room, while writing his Robbers, not being allowed a light in his own room. Now he enjoyed, for the first time, some degree of liberty. His Robbers was printed at his own expense, as he could not find any publisher who would take the risk; and, in 1781, he was requested to change the play in certain particulars, so as to adapt it for the stage at Manheim. In 1782, it was performed at Manheim, Schiller having willingly made changes wherever he could be convinced that they were improvements. Not being able to obtain leave of absence, to go out of the limits of the state, he left his regiment without permission, saw his piece performed, and returned with the deepest conviction of the unfitness of his present situation for his talents; particularly as the duke had asked him, after the publication of the Robbers, to show him all his poetical productions, and, upon his refusal, had prohibited him from publishing any thing more, except medical works. In 1783, the Robbers was performed again at Manheim, and he again attended the performance, but, this time, was discovered, and put under arrest. During his detention, he formed the plan of his *Cabale und Liebe*, and conceived the idea of his Conspiracy of Fiesco. He was now convinced that he must leave Stuttgard, unless he should choose to sacrifice his poetry, the charm of his life; but how could he quit the army, when he had so long enjoyed an education at the public expense? It was not probable that the duke would allow him to go. Some friends proposed to him to propitiate the duke by a panegyrical poem; but, much as he wished to gain his favor, chiefly on account of his beloved parents, he could not bring himself to use these means; besides, he knew that even if the duke should allow him to print poetry again, there was no safety in the exercise of the privilege. Schubart (q.v.) was sighing on Hohenasperg, on account of his *Fürstengruft*, in which he had painted, in strong colors, the burial-place of princes. He now thought of deserting, but the feeling of gratitude towards the duke, and the fear that his father, who, with his family, altogether depended upon the duke, would be made to suffer on his account, caused a great struggle in his mind. At last, the impossibility of living without poetry made him resolve to quit his situation. In 1782, he went, under an assumed name, to Franconia, where he was received by the mother of some gentlemen who had studied with him. He lived in great solitude, in a somewhat wild country, in a village called Bauerbach, in order to remain concealed and secure against the possible persecutions of the duke. In this situation he finished his *Fiesco* and *Cabale und Liebe*. In 1783, he went to Manheim, and conceived the idea of Don Carlos and

Maria Stuart. During this period, he also composed the Battle, the Infanticide, and poems to Laura. In Darmstadt, he won the favor of the prince by reading to him some scenes from Don Carlos. In 1785, he went to Leipsic; towards autumn to Dresden, where intercourse with men of talents, the charming scenery, the beautiful gallery, and the library, detained him until 1787. Here he became acquainted with the father of the poet Kőrner. (q. v.) This gentleman has since written a biographical sketch of Schiller. During this period, he studied all the works which he could procure, relating to the history of Philip II, to prepare himself for his Don Carlos; and these studies led to his History of the Revolt of the United Netherlands (Leipsic, 1788, vol. i). His History of the most remarkable Revolutions and Conspiracies, of which only one volume was published, was also produced at this period. Don Carlos first appeared at Leipsic, 1787. He himself has written the best and severest critique on this piece, in his Letters on Don Carlos. The Ghostseer (Leipsic, 1789) was probably caused by the tales respecting Cagliostro. (q. v.) In 1787, Schiller went to Weimar, where Wieland and Herder received him in a friendly manner. In 1788, he met Gőthe, after the return of the latter from Italy. He had seen him but once before, in his boyhood, when Gőthe, accompanied by the duke of Würtemberg, visited the academy where he was studying. He did not like him at first: partly through his influence, however, he received, in 1789, a professorship of philosophy at Jena. Schiller entered on his office with the discourse, What is universal history, and for what is it studied? He now devoted himself to history; and the few poetical productions which he wrote at this period are mostly of a historical character, though the Gods of Greece was composed at this time; and he also then formed the idea of an epic poem, the hero of which was to be Frederic the Great. He paid much attention to philosophy, particularly Kant's; and many of his philosophical and æsthetical treatises date from this period. He lectured on history, and began to publish Historical Memoirs from the twelfth Century to the most recent Times (1790); and his History of the Thirty Years' War, which appeared first in the Pocket Almanac for Ladies, from 1790 to 1793. In 1790, he married. The French republic, at the beginning of the revolution, conferred on him the rights of citizenship, and the emperor of Germany ennobled him in 1802. Incessant study, protracted far into the night, and the use of stimulants, undermined his health. In 1793, he visited his parents; on which occasion the duke took no notice of him. The periodical *Thalia* having ceased in 1793, he formed the plan of publishing, with the coöperation of the first writers of Germany, the *Horæ.* He became more intimately acquainted with Gőthe, returned with renewed ardor to poetry, and produced, particularly after 1795, the finest lyrical poems which appeared in the *Horæ*, and in his Almanac of the Muses (first number in 1796). In 1797, he produced his first ballads. In 1795, he conceived the plan of a play, to be called the Knights of Malta; but all his other projects gave way to Wallenstein (completed in 1799). Wallenstein's camp is a striking introduction to the parts which constitute the proper tragedy. From 1799, he lived in Weimar, where, in 1800 and 1801, Maria Stuart and the Maid of Orleans were produced. In 1803, appeared the Bride of Messina, and his last dramatic work, William Tell, in our opinion, much the best of his tragedies. Death prevented the completion of his Pseudo-Demetrius. He also adapted Shakspeare's Macbeth, Gozzi's Turandot, Racine's Phaedra, &c., for the stage, with which his dramatic works close. Among the numerous criticisms on his merits as a dramatist, we would refer the reader to Frederic Schlegel's Lectures on the History of ancient and modern Literature (2d vol.). After attending a representation of his own Tell at Berlin, where he was received with much honor, he died at Weimar, May 9, 1805, only 46 years old, mourned by all Germany. Gőthe well says of him:

Er wendete die Blüthe höchsten Strebens,
Das Leben selbst an dieses Bild des Lebens.

Schiller hated nothing so much as the vulgar or mean. He strove perpetually for the noble and the beautiful; hence that melancholy hue which is sometimes spread over his productions. There exist several editions of his work: a very cheap one was published, in 1822, by Cotta, in eighteen small volumes. He left a widow and several children, in narrow circumstances. His correspondence with Gőthe is interesting. The correspondence between Schiller and Will. von Humboldt (Stuttg., 1830) is, perhaps, more so; because it gives us more insight into the growth of his mind. The best account of his life is that by madame von Wolzogen, his sister-in-law (Stuttgard, 1830, 2 vols.). The second and third parts of his Wallenstein have been translated into English by Coleridge. His Don Carlos, and his Thirty Years' War, have also been translated.

SCHILLER-SPAR (from the German verb *schillern*, to exhibit a play of colors); a foliated mineral, whose primitive form is unknown. Besides the principal cleavage, there is a second one, less distinct: the inclination of the one to the other is between 135° and 140°; fracture uneven, splintery; lustre metallic, pearly, and eminent upon the perfect faces of cleavage, indistinctly vitreous upon the other faces; color olive-green and blackish-green, inclining to pinchbeck-brown upon the perfect faces of cleavage; streak grayish-white; hardness about that of fluor; specific gravity 2.69. It frequently occurs intermingled with serpentine. It consists of

Silica	62.00
Magnesia	10.00
Alumine	13.00
Oxide of iron	13.00
	98.00

When exposed to a high degree of heat, it becomes hard, and forms a porcelain-like mass. It occurs at Basta, in the forest of Hazeburg, in the Hartz. It is found in the U. States, at Blandford, Massachusetts, in serpentine.

SCHIMMELPENNINK, Rütger Jan, the last chief magistrate of the republic of the United Netherlands, or grand pensionary of the Batavian republic, was born at Deventer, in Holland, in 1761, and educated at Leyden, where he took his degree; on which occasion he published *Dissertatio de Imperio populari rite temperato.* He afterwards practised at the bar with much credit. In 1798, he was appointed ambassador to France, by the Batavian republic, in which post he acquitted himself with satisfaction to his country, and honor to himself. In 1801, he was accredited in the same character, first to the congress assembled at Amiens, and afterwards to England. The war having again broke out, Schimmelpennink resumed his embassy to France. In 1805, he was created grand-pensionary of Holland, but with different powers from those anciently attached to that character. This power, however, ceased in consequence of the elevation of Louis Bonaparte to the throne of Holland, and Schimmelpennink received, in lieu of his office, the grand-cordon of the order of Holland, about that time instituted, and became, by the change in the government, a senator of France, as well as of Holland, the two countries being united. He received also the title of count, with the appointment of grand-treasurer of the Three Fleeces. He filled these offices down to the exclusion of Napoleon from the throne of France, and voted for the creation of a provisionary government in the latter instance. April 14, 1814, he sent in his resignation, and retired into private life. He died at Amsterdam, in 1825.

SCHINKEL, Charles Frederic, one of the most distinguished architects of the present age, professor in the academy of arts at Berlin, was born in 1781, at New Ruppin. He lost his father early, and studied at the gymnasium of Berlin. He afterwards applied himself to architecture, went in 1803 to Italy and France, and returned to Germany in 1805. The disasters of Prussia in 1806 were severely felt by all architects, and Schinkel devoted himself to landscape painting, in which he succeeded remarkably well. One of his most successful attempts was to represent various historical periods in a series of pictures. When the royal family returned to Berlin, his plans for several arrangements in the royal palace were approved by the queen. In 1819, he received an appointment in the ministry of commerce, manufactures, and architecture, and, in this capacity, has done much to improve the style of building in his country. In 1821, Schinkel was ordered to rebuild the theatre at Berlin. In 1824, the French institute made him a member of their body, as did also the academy of arts at Copenhagen. Berlin has many architectural monuments by this master, and the provinces are full of churches and other edifices, public and private, planned by him. His greatest plan, that of a grand cathedral, which the king of Prussia intended to erect in Berlin, has never been executed. The new museum at Berlin, a splendid monument of art, is the last of his great works. It was finished in 1828. In 1824, he visited Italy a second time. His last and best picture represents a landscape with buildings in Greece, at the time of her highest prosperity. It was given by the city of Berlin to the princess Louisa, daughter of the king, when married to prince Frederic, son of the king of the Netherlands.

SCHIRAS; a city of Persia, capital of Farsistan; 160 miles south-east of Ispahan; lon. 52° 44′ E., lat. 29° 37′ N.; population before the earthquake of 1824, 52,000. It is situated between two mountains, on a plain of unrivalled beauty and fertility, the boast of Persia, upwards of twenty miles long, and twelve broad. The environs are laid out in magnificent gardens, the flowers and fruits of which form a favorite theme of Eastern poetry. Hafiz (q. v.) was a native of Schiras. His tomb, and that of Sadi (q. v.), are in the neighborhood of the city. The city is about six miles in circuit, but the walls have been suffered to fall to ruin. The streets are narrow, winding, and dirty, and the houses mean. The most remarkable public building is the great bazar, about a quarter of a mile long, built of yellow burnt brick, allotted to the different traders in the city. The citadel, the residence of the governor, is a fortified square of eighty yards. The royal palace within is far from being an elegant structure. Schiras carries on an extensive commerce, which consists chiefly in receiving from Bushire the spices and cotton goods of India, and transmitting them to Ispahan and Yezd. The sides of the hills that bound the plain of Schiras, produce a wine, which has the highest reputation of any in the East. Schiras is an ancient city, and has been the capital of the Persian empire, but exhibits no ruins to attest its former greatness.

Schirvan. (See *Caucasus*)

Schism (σχισμα, a fissure) is chiefly applied to separations happening through diversity of opinions among people of the same religion. In the Catholic church, the election of popes has often given rise to schisms, by the division of the Christian world in favor of rival candidates. The longest schism of this kind was the Great Schism, which began in 1378, when Urban VI and Clement VII both claimed the papacy. This was finally settled by the council of Constance, which effected the general recognition of pope Martin V, who was chosen by it in 1417. (See *Pope*.)

Schlangenbad, and Langenschwalbach; two watering places in Nassau, near the charming Rheingau. (q. v.) The water (from 79—83 Fahrenheit) contains clay and lime. It feels like soap, softens and renders pliable the fibres of the skin, and is excellent in cases of stiffness and contraction. The slime which floats on the water is used to cure old ulcers.

Schlegel; a name distinguished in German literature, chiefly as that of the two brothers Augustus William and Frederic von Schlegel. John Elias, their uncle, born in 1718, at Meissen, was the first German dramatic writer, after Gryphius, who contributed to the advancement of German belles-lettres. He died in 1749. —His brother John Adolphus, a poet and pulpit orator, was born in 1721, at Meissen. He was the author of several valuable works, and made a translation of Batteux's *Les Beaux Arts reduits à un même Principe*, which he accompanied with notes and treatises of his own (1751, 3d edition 1770). He died in 1753.—John Henry, the third brother, was born in 1724, at Meissen, and died at Copenhagen in 1780. He is the author of valuable works on Danish history, and of some translations from English poets into German. Augustus William and Frederic are the sons of John Adolphus. The first was born September 8, 1767, at Hanover; and Frederic in 1772, at the same place. The former early manifested a great ability for learning languages, as well as much poetical talent. When eighteen years old, he recited, at the lyceum of Hanover, a piece in hexameters on the birth-day of the king, in which he gave a sketch of the history of German poetry, which was justly admired. He first studied theology at Göttingen, but soon quitted it for philology. At Göttingen, he gained the friendship of Bürger, who, in the preface to the second edition of his poems (1789), consecrated him to the service of the Muses, and prophesied his immortality in one of the finest German sonnets. A. W. Schlegel contributed to Bürger's Academy of Belles-Lettres. In 1787, when in the philological seminary under Heyne, a Latin treatise by him, on the geography of Homer, obtained a prize. After leaving Göttingen, he acted as tutor for three years in the house of a banker in Amsterdam. He returned to Germany, and took part in the *Horæ*, and Schiller's Almanac of the Muses, in which his translations from Dante, with commentaries, attracted particular attention. Until 1799, he was one of the most active contributors to the General Literary Gazette. In 1797, he began his translation of Shakspeare, of which nine volumes have appeared. Tieck has undertaken the revision of them, and the addition of the pieces not yet translated, in a new edition. We know of no translation so perfect as this. It may well be called a German reproduction of the original. It has made Shakspeare a German popular poet to all intents and purposes, on the stage and in the closet. Schlegel had now become a professor at Jena, where he delivered lectures on æsthetics, and, from 1798 to 1800, was connected with his brother in the publication of the Athenæum, a critical journal, which did much to promote a more independent spirit in German literature. The first edition of his poems appeared in 1800, and Schlegel became the second father of the German sonnet. In 1800, he also published his poetic attack on Kotzebue. In 1801, appeared his Characteristics and Critiques, in two volumes; in 1802, the Almanac of the Muses, published by him and Tieck, together, which is pervaded by a mystico-symbolical spirit. Having separated from his wife, he went, in 1802, to Berlin, where he delivered lectures, published in vol. iii of *Europa*. His *Ion* appeared in 1803. He took an active part in the publication of the Paper for the Fashionable World, which was opposed by Kotzebue's *Freimüthige* (Liberal); and a paper-war began, not very honorable to the latter. In 1803, appeared vol. i. of the Spanish Theatre, containing three pieces of Calderon: vol. ii. followed in 1809. These translations fully satisfied the high expectations which the public had formed from his translation of Shakspeare. In 1804, he published his Nosegays of Italian, Spanish, and Portuguese Poetry. In 1805, he travelled with madame de Staël (q. v.), and lived with her at Copet, in Italy, France, Vienna, and Stockholm. In his elegy Rome, he celebrates his generous friend. He wrote many critiques during this time, partly in the Jena Literary Gazette, partly in the Heidelberg Annals. In 1807, he published at Paris his Comparison of the Phædra of Euripides with that of Racine, which was written in French, and attracted much attention from the French literati. In 1808, he delivered lectures on the dramatic art, in Vienna, and published them, at a later period, in three volumes, 2d edition, 1817. They have been translated into almost all the languages of Europe. In 1812, he made a new collection of his poems (2d edition, 1820). In 1813, he became a political writer in French and German, accompanied the then crown-prince of Sweden, as secretary, and received several orders, and the rank of nobility. After the fall of Napoleon, he returned to madame de Staël, after whose death, in 1818, he accepted a professorship in the university of Bonn, which had been but a short time established. His marriage with the daughter of Mr. Paulus (q. v.), in 1819, was dissolved in 1820. He now lectures chiefly upon the history of arts and sciences in ancient and modern times, and, since 1820, has published the Indian Library, a periodical for promoting the study of the Oriental languages, particularly Sanscrit. He superintends the printing of the great Sanscrit work *Ramáyana*, at the printing-office established by him at the expense of the Prussian government. In 1823, he published *Bhagavad-Gita*, an episode of the epos *Mahabharata*, with a Latin translation. His Oriental studies led him again to France, and, in 1823, to England, where he examined the manuscripts at London, Oxford, Cambridge, and Hayleybury. In the *Bibliotheca Italiana*, he wrote (in 1816) a very learned treatise, in Italian, on the bronze horses at Venice, which he declared to be Greek; another treatise (in 1817) in the *Bibliothèque Universelle*, at Geneva, on the group of Niobe, and, in the *Zeitgenossen*, a life of Necker; remarks on the Provençal language and literature, in French (1818); a historical notice of John of Fiesole; and many other pieces. In 1828, he defended himself, in a pamphlet, against the reproach of crypto-Catholicism.—His brother *Frederic von Schlegel*, born, as we mentioned above, in 1772, was intended by his father for a merchant, but was liberally educated, to leave him more freedom of choice. He became dissatisfied with the mercantile life during his apprenticeship at Leipsic, and his father withdrew him from his situation there. He was now sixteen years old, and devoted himself to philology with the greatest zeal, one year in Göttingen, and the rest in Leipsic; and could say, when he had ended his academic course, that there was no Greek or Latin author of importance whom he had not read at least once. About 1793, he first appeared as an author. He contributed to several periodicals of reputation, and, in 1797, produced his Greeks and Romans; in 1798, his Poetry of the Greeks and Romans (two vols.), a sort of continuation of the first. In Berlin, he undertook, in connexion with Schleiermacher (q. v.), the translation of Plato, but soon abandoned the project. In 1799, appeared the first volume of his Lucinda, which remained unfinished, and is reproached by many as an idealization of voluptuousness. In 1800, he settled as *privatdocent* at Jena, and appeared for the first time as a poet, publishing his productions in various periodicals. In 1802, he lived some time in Dresden, and then delivered lectures on philosophy in Paris, where he also published *Europa*, and occupied himself with the fine arts, and the languages of the south, particularly those of India. In 1808, he published a treatise on the Language and Wisdom of the

Indians; in 1804, a collection of romantic poems, of the middle ages, from printed sources and manuscripts, in two vols.; and, in 1805, Lother and Maller. We are indebted to him for illustrations of the history of Joan of Arc, drawn from the *Notices et Extraits*. He now returned to Germany, went over, with his wife, to the Catholic faith, at Cologne, and, in 1808, repaired to Vienna. In 1809, he received an appointment at the head-quarters of the archduke Charles, where he drew up several powerful proclamations. When peace was concluded, he again delivered lectures in Vienna, on modern history and the literature of all nations. They were published in 1811 and 1812. His limited views in regard to religion, after his adoption of Catholicism, appear particularly in his modern history. In 1812, he published the German Museum, and gained the confidence of prince Metternich (q. v.) by various diplomatic papers, in consequence of which he was appointed Austrian counsellor of legation, at the diet in Frankfort. In 1818, he returned to Vienna, where he lived as secretary of the court, and counsellor of legation, and published a View of the Present Political Relations, and his complete works. In 1820, he undertook a periodical, called Concordia, intended to unite the various opinions on church and state; but he did not continue it long. He also published, at a much earlier period, the Writings of Novalis (see *Hardenberg*), in conjunction with his friend Tieck, and volume I of Florentine, written by his wife. In 1807, he also published a German translation of Corinna, before the French original appeared. Since 1822, his complete works have appeared in ten volumes, with some corrections and additions. He died August 9, 1829. The two brothers always lived on the best terms, however great the difference of their views on some points. The influence which they have exercised, particularly Augustus William, on belles-lettres in general, and especially in promoting a more correct understanding of the literature of the middle ages, is very great, and extends far beyond the confines of their native country. They will be remembered in the history of literature, as two minds of uncommon vigor.

Schleiermacher, Frederic Daniel Ernest, one of the most distinguished German theologians and philologists, was born at Breslau, in 1768, and received his education at the academy of the Moravian Brethren at Niesky. In 1787, he ceased to be a member of this society, left Barby, where he had begun the study of theology, and went to Halle to continue it. In 1794, after having been employed as a teacher, he was ordained a clergyman, and appointed assistant preacher at Landsberg on the Warte. From 1796 to 1802, he was minister in the *Charité* (a great hospital) at Berlin. During this period, he translated Fawcet's Sermons (two vols.), contributed to the Athenæum, conducted by the two Schlegels (q. v.), and wrote the Discourses on Religion, and the Monologues, and Letters of a Minister out of Berlin. He soon undertook his translation of Plato. Five volumes of this work had appeared in 1828; and the whole is probably now completed. Few men have ever entered so deeply into the spirit of Plato. In 1802, he published his first collection of sermons, which has since been followed by two others. In 1802, he removed to Stolpe, where he wrote his Critical View of Ethics. In the same year, he was appointed *professor extraordinarius* of theology at Halle, and preached to the university. In 1807, when Halle was separated from Prussia, he went to Berlin, and lectured there, as well as preached, with the greatest boldness, on the existing state of things, although a hostile force under Davoust occupied the city. In 1809, he was appointed preacher at the Trinity church in Berlin, and married. In 1810, when the new university was opened in that city, he was appointed *professor ordinarius*, as he had been at Halle during the last part of his residence there. In 1811, he was elected a member of the academy of sciences, and, in 1814, secretary of the philosophical class, when he was released from the duties which he had discharged in the department of public instruction in the ministry of the interior. Since 1811, many papers by him have appeared in the Memoirs of the Academy, chiefly relating to ancient philosophy. At this period, he wrote his View of the Study of Theology. When Schmalz strove to lower the elevated feeling of the people, after the wars of 1813, '14, and '15, to a tone more convenient for an absolute government, he brought out a pungent reply, characterized by a Platonic style of reasoning. His last work is his Doctrines of the Christian Faith, of which a second edition, probably, has appeared by this time. Few men have equalled Schleiermacher in activity. He delivers lectures in various departments of theology and philosophy. He preaches every Sunday (always without notes), besides writing much, and having a wide circle of official labors. For many years his church has been crowded, and his lectures at the university are attended by large numbers of the students. He has many enthusiastic admirers; but the mystical party regard him with dislike. Schleiermacher has done much for the intellectual and religious advancement of his countrymen.

SCHLEISSHEIM; a royal palace three leagues from Munich. It has a magnificent gallery, in which above 2000 pictures are arranged, according to the schools to which they belong.

SCHLOSSER, Frederic Christopher, a distinguished historical writer, born at Jever, in 1776, early showed a strong inclination for study. In 1793, he went to Göttingen to study theology; and, after acting for several years as a private tutor, in several families, during which time he prosecuted his studies in history, philology, and philosophy, with great industry, and subsequently as a teacher in classical schools, he was made professor of history in the lyceum in Frankfort (1812), and, in 1817, in the university of Heidelberg. His Lives of Beza and Peter Martyn (1809); his Universal History; his General View of the History and Civilization of the Ancients (1806, seq.); and his History of the Eighteenth Century (2 vols., Heidelberg, 1823, all in German), display extensive acquaintance with the subjects, and much vigor and independence of thought. His History of the Eighteenth Century has been translated into French (Paris, 1825).

SCHMALKALDIC LEAGUE. (See *Smalcaldic League*.)

SCHMIDT, Michael Ignatius, a German historian, was born in 1736, at Arnstein, in Würzburg. He studied theology in the Catholic seminary at Würzburg, and became a priest. During the seven years' war, he went to Suabia, received a benefice, and, in 1771, was made librarian of the university at Würzburg. He received by degrees higher appointments in that sovereign bishopric, did much for education, and, in 1778, began the publication of his German History, to which he devoted the remainder of his life. The empress of Austria was anxious to have him in her service, and caused him to be appointed superintendent of the archives. Joseph II made him teacher of history to his nephew, the present emperor, Francis I. After a residence of fourteen years at Vienna, he died there in 1794. Schmidt was the first who wrote a proper history of the German nation: his predecessors only gave the history of the emperors, of the empire, or the estates. His chief aim was to show how the Germans became what they are; and he executed his plan with taste, judgment, and a philosophical spirit. His erudition was great. In the account of the reformation, he is not always impartial or faithful. His style is not to be imitated. This extensive work was published at Ulm, and later at Vienna. Joseph Milbiller continued Schmidt's history from his papers. The Vienna edition of the early history is in eight volumes; of the modern history, in seventeen. Dresch's History of Germany since the Confederation of the Rhine, is a continuation of the work of Schmidt and Milbiller, forming vols. 18, 19, and 20.

SCHNEEBERG; a town in the Erzgebirge, kingdom of Saxony, with 4800 inhabitants. There are important mines of silver and cobalt in the neighborhood. The inhabitants manufacture lace and similar articles in large quantities.

SCHNEEKOPF. (See *Schneekoppe*.)

SCHNEEKOPPE (*snow-summit*); the highest elevation of the Riesengebirge (q. v.), 4950 feet above the level of the sea. It is not to be confounded with Schneekopf (*snow-head*), the highest summit of the Thuringian forest, which rises 2886 feet, or, according to some, 2975 feet above the sea.

SCHNEIDER, John Gottlob. This celebrated philologist, born at Kolm, in 1752, studied under Ernesti, at Leipsic, where a wealthy relation in Dresden supported him. His first publication was Observations on Anacreon, in 1770. Soon after, he went to Göttingen, and gained the favor of Heyne, who recommended him to Brunck, whom he accompanied to Strasburg, to assist him in the publication of his *Analecta*. He lived in this place three years, and then received an invitation to the university of Frankfort on the Oder, and there, with Brunck, published Oppian. For thirty-four years Schneider was professor of ancient languages there, and published a great number of critical editions of the ancient classics. He applied himself especially to those works of antiquity which related to natural science, as Ælian's History of Beasts, and Nicander's two didactic poems on medicine, with the Greek Scholia, and the Periphrasis of Eutecnius. His *Historia Amphibiorum*, of which the two first volumes appeared in 1779, from unfavorable circumstances, was not completed. He paid much attention to ichthyology. After thirty years of labor, he published the nine remaining books of Aristotle, containing the History of Beasts (Leipsic, 1811, 4 vols.); also the physical and meteorological works of Epicurus, the *Analecta*, relating to the metallurgy of the ancients, the *Eclogæ Physicæ*, &c. His excellent Greek Lexicon, which has passed through three editions, is the basis of that of Passow, and of the English-Greek Lexicon of Donnegan, (London, 1831.) It has contributed not a little to give a new impulse to the study of the Greek language in Germany. He has also edited the political works of Aristotle; the works of Xenophon, Æsop, the Pseudo-Orpheus, the *Scriptores Rei Rusticæ*, Vitruvius, Theophrastus, and other writers. When the university was removed, in 1811, from Frankfort on the Oder to Breslau, Schneider went thither, and was made chief librarian, in addition to his other office. He died there, January 12, 1822.

SCHNEIDER, Eulogius; a German priest, vicar to the constitutional bishop of Strasburg, and afterwards public accuser before the criminal tribunal of the Lower Rhine, one of the most pernicious agents of Robespierre and his confederates. Armed with the authority of St. Just and Lebas, commissioners from the convention at Strasburg, Schneider proceeded through the department with a body of troops, and followed by the guillotine, on which he immolated citizens of every rank, sex and age, where interest or revenge furnished the slightest motive for their execution. Schneider was about to set on foot *noyades* at Strasburg, similar to those of Nantes, when he was cut short in his career. St. Just and Lebas, displeased, not by his crimes, but by his arrogance, had him arrested, December 20, 1793, and conveyed to Paris, where he was condemned by the revolutionary tribunal, and guillotined, at the age of thirty-seven.

SCHNEPFENTHAL; an institution for education, established by Salzmann, not far from Gotha, at the foot of the Thuringian forest, half a league from the town of Waltershausen. (See *Salzmann*.)

SCHNORR, Veit Julius von Karolsfeld, professor of historical painting in the royal academy of arts at Munich, one of the first living painters, was born March 26, 1794, at Leipsic, where his father was director of the royal academy of arts. Julius Schnorr early showed indications of talent. In his sixteenth year, he went with his two elder brothers to Vienna, where he supported himself by giving lessons in drawing. Michael Angelo's powerful genius at first chiefly attracted him; but by degrees he became undecided as to the style which he should adopt, and his internal struggle was so great, that he was on the point of giving up the art in despair, and becoming a mechanic, when his father's counsels encouraged him to go on. He was now attracted by the old German school—a school which has great merits, but was at that time, like many other things, of a peculiarly German character, the subject of exaggerated admiration, on account of the great incentives to patriotism furnished by the circumstances of the time. Schnorr, like many others, now thought that the ideal of painting was to be found in the simplicity and *naïveté*, but at the same time close adherence to reality, and want of elevation, which characterize this school; but a journey to Italy inspired him with juster ideas. On the way, he sketched the Marriage at Cana, which he finished for a Scotch gentleman. Soon after, the marchese Massimi engaged him to paint scenes from Ariosto, in fresco, in the centre saloon of his villa at Rome. (See *Overbeck*, *Cornelius*, and *Fresco-painting*.) After several interruptions from the Roman fever, Schnorr completed the paintings in 1825. They struck the writer as the finest among the productions of the three painters employed in adorning the villa (Overbeck and Feith are the others), breathing a truly great spirit. In 1827, king Louis of Bavaria called him to Munich, where he is employed to paint scenes from the *Nibelungenlied* (q. v.) for the king.

SCHOEN, Martin, one of the earliest and most distinguished German painters, likewise a goldsmith and engraver, was born at Colmbach, and died, in 1486, at Colmar. The Italians called him *Buon Martino*, or *Martino d'Anversa*. One hundred and twenty-one of his paintings, chiefly on scriptural subjects, are known to be still in existence. Schoen was remarkable for richness of invention, and for the life of his figures.

SCHOLASTICS. This name was given to teachers of rhetoric among the Romans. In the middle ages, a class of philosophers arose under the name of *scholastics*, or *schoolmen*, who taught a peculiar kind of philosophy, which consisted in applying the ancient dialectics to theology, and intimately uniting both. The character of this philosophy varied at different periods, and historians are not agreed as to its origin. Those who regard particularly its theological character make Augustine its founder; others consider it as having commenced in the monophysite disputes of the fifth and sixth centuries. John

Scotus Erigena (q. v.), in the ninth century, is commonly called the first scholastic, without making him, however, the proper founder of that philosophy. He was the great philosopher of his age, and his doctrines were connected with those of the New Platonic system. The name *scholastic philosophy* is derived from the circumstance that it originated in the schools instituted by and after Charlemagne, for the education of the clergy. (See *Schools*.) The philosophy therein taught consisted in a collection of logical rules and metaphysical notions, drawn from the Latin commentators on Aristotle, especially the Pseudo-Augustine and Boethius, and from the introduction of Porphyry to the writings of Aristotle. These, under the name of *dialectics*, composed the theoretical philosophy in general, and were connected with the later Alexandrian ideas of God, and of his nature and relations to the world. The original aim of the scholastic philosophy was only to establish and defend the dogmas of the church. Buhle makes three periods:—The first extends to Roscellinus in 1089, or to the contest of the Realists and Nominalists (q. v.); the second to Albertus Magnus, who died in 1280, when the metaphysical works of Aristotle were more generally known and commented on; the third to the revival of ancient learning, in the middle of the fifteenth century, and the consequent improvement in philosophy. Tiedemann explained the scholastic system as a mode of treating subjects *a priori*, in which, after a statement of the reasons, on both sides, in the form of syllogisms, the decision was made conformable to the opinions of Aristotle, and the church fathers, and the prevailing theological doctrines. According to him, its history begins with the Franciscan Alexander of Hales (a monastery in Gloucestershire), who first made a considerable use of the writings of Aristotle. He died in 1245. This Alexander of Hales was the first complete commentator on the sentences of Peter of Lombardy; was an instructer at Paris, and received the name of *doctor irrefragabilis*. He also wrote commentaries on the psychology of Aristotle. He is not an independent thinker, but decides every case on reasons drawn from other theological writers and philosophers. The second period of the schoolmen, according to Tiedemann, begins with Albert the Great (q. v.), who wrote commentaries on the physical and philosophical writings of Aristotle, and on several books of the Scriptures. Still greater is the reputation of his pupil, Thomas Aquinas (q. v.), the father of ethics, and a strict adherent of Aristotle, on whose works he left fifty-two commentaries. His opponent was the Franciscan John Duns (q. v.) Scotus, who is not to be confounded with John Scotus Erigena, before mentioned. Duns Scotus is one of the most hair-splitting logicians, and known by his scholastic or barbarous Latin. His opposition to Thomas gave rise to the parties called *Thomists* and *Scotists* (q. v.), whose controversies became peculiarly warm, when Scotus declared himself opposed to the strict Augustine doctrines of grace defended by Thomas, and which had maintained their place in the church for centuries. Another acute scholastic of this age was the Franciscan mystic Bonaventura (q. v.), the pupil of Alexander of Hales; Hervey, a general of the Dominicans; Francis Mairon, a Franciscan, pupil of Duns Scotus, and founder of the Sorbonne disputation in Paris, at which the respondent was obliged to defend the controverted positions from six o'clock in the morning to six in the evening, and was only permitted to take a short meal, without leaving the room. The third period of the scholastic philosophy some begin with William of St. Pourçain or Durandus de Sancto Porciano (who died at Meaux, in 1332); though, more properly, the third period of scholastic theology may be considered as commencing with him. From his skill in solving difficult questions, he received the name of *doctor resolutissimus*. He made a distinction between theological truth, which rests on the authority of the church, and philosophical truth, which is established, independently of the church, on private conviction, and affirmed that many things were theologically true, and yet philosophically false. Others begin the third period of the scholastics with William Ocham, or Occam (q. v., who died in 1347), a Franciscan, who revived again the nearly forgotten disputes of the Nominalists, and distinguished himself as a fearless defender of Christian liberty against the assumptions of the popes. One of the last scholastics of this period was Gabriel Biel (who died in 1495), a moderate Nominalist, and active in founding the university of Tübingen in 1477. Tennemann makes four periods of the scholastic philosophy:—I. The first, to the twelfth century, is characterized by blind Realism, and filled by detached philosophical essays on doctrinal theology. To this period belong John Scotus Erigena, Berengarius of Tours, and his opponent Lanfranc, Damianus, Hildebert of Lavardin, and the great Anselm of Canterbury.—II. Separation of Nominalism and Realism. This period extends from Roscellinus to Albertus Magnus, in the beginning of the thirteenth century, and can boast of Roscellinus, Abelard, William of Champeaux, Hugh de St. Victor, Richard de St. Victor, Gilbert Porretanus, Peter Lombard, Peter of Poitiers, Alanus Insulensis, John of Salisbury.—III. Exclusive prevalence of Realism. Complete union of the doctrines of the church and the Aristotelian philosophy, from Albertus Magnus to Occam, in the fourteenth century. To this period belong Alex. of Hales, Vincent of Beauvais, Bonaventura, Thomas Aquinas, Peter Hispanus, Henry Goethals, Rich. Middleton, Duns Scotus, Francis Mairon, St. Pourçain.—IV. A renewal of the contest between Nominalism and Realism, in which the former was victorious, and a separation of theology and philosophy gradually took place. In this period we find William Occam, Marsilius Ingenuus, Robert Holcot, Gabriel Biel, John Buridan, &c. (See Tennemann's *Sketch of a History of Philosophy*, 4th ed., or 2d rifacimento by Wendt.) On account of the excessive subtilty which prevailed in the scholastic philosophy, the expression *scholastic* has come to denote the extreme of *subtilty*. After the reformation and the revival of letters, the scholastic system gradually declined. From that time we find but few distinguished scholastics, as the Spanish Jesuit Suarez, who died in 1617. With lord Bacon and Descartes, a more enlightened and independent philosophy commences.

Scholia; explanations annexed to Greek or Latin authors, by the early grammarians, who taught the practical part of philology. The writer of such scholia is called a *scholiast*. There are many scholia to Greek authors extant, fewer to Latin. The names of the scholiasts are mostly unknown. Those, however, of Didymus, John Tzetzes, and Eustathius, the famous scholiast of Homer, have been preserved. The two last belong to the twelfth century.

Schöll, Maximilian Samson Frederic, a distinguished lawyer, author, bookseller and diplomatist, was born, in 1766, at a village in Nassáu-Saarbrück. At fifteen years of age, he entered the university of Strasburg. He afterwards became tutor to the son of a lady named Krook, and accompanied her and her family in their travels through France to Italy. He returned to Strasburg in 1790, where he devoted himself to law. The reign of terror drove him to Switzerland. After the fall of Robespierre, in 1795, he returned to his country, and, with a man named Decker, established a printing office and bookseller's shop at Basle. After the peace of Luneville, Decker sold his share in the concern, and Schöll removed the establishment to Paris. At the entrance of the allies into Paris, he was placed, by the recommendation of Alexander von Humboldt, in the cabinet of the king of Prussia, and, after the departure of the king, he remained in the Prussian legation. After many diplomatic missions, he was, in 1819, appointed a privy counsellor in Berlin, and received important employments. Of many excellent works, which he has written and published, we will mention his *Histoire de la Littérature Romaine* (1815, 4 vols.); *Histoire de la Littérature Grecque* (2d ed., Paris, 1824, 4 vols.); *Congrès de Vienne* (1815, 6th revision); *Annuaire Généalogique*; his *Recueil de Pièces officielles destinées à détromper les Français* (1814—15, 9 vols.); *Tableau des Peuples qui habitent l'Europe* (latest ed. in 1823). His continuation of Koch's *Histoire des Traités de Paix* (15 vols.) is valuable. The *Archives Politiques* (1818—19, 3 vols.) forms a supplement to it.

Schomberg, Frederic Hermann, duke of, a distinguished military officer, a native of Germany, born about 1619, was the son of count Schomberg, by the daughter of lord Dudley. He began his military career under Frederic, prince of Orange, and afterwards went to France, where he became acquainted with the prince of Condé and marshal Turenne. He was then employed in Portugal, and established the independence of that kingdom, obliging the Spaniards to recognise the claims of the house of Braganza. He commanded the French army in Catalonia in 1672, and was afterwards employed in the Netherlands, where he obliged the prince of Orange to raise the siege of Maestricht. For these services he was rewarded with the staff of a marshal of France in 1675; but on the revocation of the edict of Nantes, marshal Schomberg, who was a Protestant, quitted the French service, and went to Portugal. Being also driven from that country, on account of his religion, he retired to Holland, and subsequently engaged in the service of the elector of Brandenburg. He went to England in 1688, with William III, and, after the revolution, was created a duke, and obtained a grant of one hundred thousand pounds. He was sent to Ireland, in the following year, to oppose the partisans of James II. Being joined by king William, he was present at the battle of the Boyne, in which he lost his life, July 1, 1690, owing, it is said, to an accidental shot from his own troops, as he was passing the river to attack the enemy.

SCHÖN (German, for *beautiful*); an adjective which begins innumerable German geographical names.

SCHÖNBRUNN. (See *Vienna.*)

SCHONEN, or SCANIA (Swedish, *Skåne*); a province of Sweden, in the south of Gothland, bounded north by Halland and Smaland, east by Blekingen and the Baltic, south by the Baltic, and west by the Sound, which separates it from Denmark; 4000 square miles; population, 334,744, differing in dialect and manners from the other Swedes. This is the most level, pleasant and fertile part of Sweden, and produces plenty of rye, barley, oats, peas, buckwheat, honey, cumin-seed; likewise pit-coal, chalk, tiles, and pot-ashes. It has several rivers and lakes, all well stored with fish. The principal towns are Malmoe, Lund, Landscron, Helsinborg, and Christianstadt. It is now divided into the governments (*låne*) of Christianstadt and Malmoehus. Schonen formerly belonged to Denmark, but was ceded to Sweden with some of the neighboring districts, by the peace of Roeskild, in 1658.

SCHOODIC, or PASSAMAQUODDY. (See *Croix, St.*)

SCHOOLMEN. (See *Scholastics.*)

SCHOOLS. This momentous element of modern society is one of many instances, which show the slow progress of mankind in perfecting the most important parts of the social machine. Schools are of comparatively recent date, and their benefits are mostly confined to Europeans and their descendants. A historical sketch of their progress will be interesting, as showing how slowly and laboriously these institutions, which diffuse sound knowledge in a thousand channels, and irrigate, as it were, the whole field of society, have reached their present degree of improvement, which is far from being satisfactory. In antiquity, education and instruction were entirely a matter of domestic concern. In countries where priestly or royal despotism prevailed, schools were first established for the sons of the great and for the priests. Moses was educated in a priestly school in Egypt, Cyrus at a seminary connected with the Persian court the Indian Bramins imparted instruction in secret schools; in Palestine, those conversant with the Scriptures taught in the schools of the prophets, at later periods in the synagogues, and the schools of the rabbies, where inquiring youths assembled. The advantages of these schools were accessible to few; the means of learning were limited to conversation, reading, committing to memory, and hearing the explanation of sacred books. More was done under the Greeks. As early as 500 B. C., boys and girls, in the Greek cities, learned reading, writing and arithmetic in private schools, as the legislators, except in Sparta, left the education of children entirely to the parents; and what Lycurgus did in Sparta was much more intended for the developement of the physical powers than of the intellect. Young persons, who were eager for knowledge, resorted to the instructions of philosophers and sophists, the finest example of which are the Socratic dialogues. The country people remained in great ignorance. The same was the case with the Romans, who, from 300 B. C., had schools for boys in the cities, and from the age of Cæsar, who conferred the rights of citizenship on teachers, possessed the higher institutions of the grammarians. In these, Latin and Greek were taught scientifically, and young men of talent went from the grammarians to the rhetoricians (q. v.), who, like Quinctilian, prepared them, by exercises in declamation, for speaking in public. But a regular school system no where existed with the ancient nations. Schools were institutions confined to particular classes, or were the fruit of private enterprise. The emperor Vespasian was the first who established public professorships of grammar and rhetoric, with fixed salaries attached to them, for the education of young men for the public service; and, 150 A. D., Antoninus Pius founded imperial schools in the larger cities of the Roman empire, which may be compared to the German gymnasia. Though there was no systematic coöperation among the various professors, the imperial school at Rome, after the organization which it received, in 370, from Valentinian, resembled rather the German universities. The most celebrated place for scientific culture was Athens, to which students from all parts of Europe resorted, as late as the ninth century, and often led very dissipated lives. In the lower schools of the ancient Romans, the discipline was very severe. The rod was not spared; and

Ovid is not the only one who complained of the severity of an Orbilius. Christianity, by degrees, gave a new turn to education. In the East, it gradually came entirely into the hands of the clergy, and under their superintendence. Schools were instituted in the cities and villages for catechumens (q. v.), and in some capitals, catechetical schools for the education of clergymen, of which that in Alexandria was the most flourishing, from the second to the fourth centuries. From the fifth century, however, these higher establishments seem to have been discontinued, and the episcopal or cathedral schools to have taken their place, in which the young men, intended for the clerical profession, learned, besides theology, the seven liberal arts—grammar, logic, rhetoric (these three made the *trivium*), arithmetic, geometry, astronomy and music (*quadrivium*), from the *Encyclopædia* of the African Marcianus Capella, a poor compendium, which appeared at Rome in 470, and which remained for upwards of 1000 years the common text-book in the schools of Europe. The imperial schools declined, and became extinct, because, in the confusion which followed the irruption of the barbarians, the salaries of the professors were not paid; and the cathedral schools and parochial schools for boys and young men of all classes in the cities, were established, in which the learning of reading and writing was followed by the study of the *trivium*, which had become popular; hence they received, at a later time, the name of *trivial schools*. These schools, after the sixth century, were surpassed in importance by the conventual schools, which, at first, were only seminaries to prepare persons for the monastic life, but were soon resorted to by laymen. The Benedictine convents—those links between the civilization of ancient and modern times—flourished in Ireland, England, France and Germany, from the sixth to the eleventh century, and were the chief seats of modern European civilization. The discipline was severe and monkish; but the instruction was generally better than in other institutions, partly on account of the many distinguished literary men who embraced the monastic life, partly on account of the peculiar opportunies which they had to form considerable libraries, in consequence of the constant communications among the various convents, and the pleasure which the inmates of these took in copying; partly on account of the *esprit de corps* of the order which delighted in being able to show distinguished members or eminent men, who had been educated in its schools. There were several priests or monks, whose reputation was such as to attract pupils from great distances. The conventual schools at Armagh and Clogher, Canterbury, York and Westminster, at Tours, Rheims, Clermont, Paris, at Salzburg, of St. Emmeran at Ratisbon, Hersfeld Corvey, Fulda, Hirschau and St. Blasius on the Schwarzwald, &c., were particularly famous. The scholars who proceeded from them gave to the scholastic philosophy (q. v.) its character and name, the teachers in the conventual schools being called *scholastici*. These schools rivalled the episcopal and cathedral schools, yet were always directed more to the advantage of the priesthood than to purposes of general instruction, which was owing to a variety of causes springing from the then existing state of things. Charlemagne had in view a system of national instruction, when he issued, in 789, his decree for the improvement of the schools of his empire. Not only every bishop's see and every convent, but every parish, was to have its school, the two former for the instruction of clergymen and public officers, the latter for the lower classes. At his court, Charlemagne established an academy of distinguished scholars, to whom he himself resorted for instruction, and whom he employed to educate his children, and capable boys belonging to the nobility and other classes, in the court school (*schola palatii*). Alcuinus (q. v.) was made rector of these two schools, which accompanied the court in its changes of residence. The ladies of his court also partook in the benefits of instruction, and some nunneries, in their institutions for female education, rivalled the seminaries in the monasteries. The ladies learned Latin, which was then the common medium of communication between persons of different countries, as French is at present. Charlemagne took upon himself the superintendence of the schools in his empire, had reports sent to him, made examinations, and delivered addresses to the pupils of the school at his court. These schools often enabled him to discover the talents of young men, whom he appointed to high offices in the church or the state. It is one of the noblest traits in his character, that, in that age of gross ignorance, he labored with zeal for the instruction of the nations under his sway.—See a short article entitled Charlemagne's Life in Private and at Court, in the third volume of Raumer's Historical Pocket Book (Leipsic, 1832).—When the clergy of the cathedrals, in the ninth century, adopted the canonical life, the cathedral schools originated, which approached, in character, to the *trivial schools*, so called, whilst the episcopal schools remained seminaries for the clerical order, or for particular professions, and at a later period became transformed into universities. Mayence, Treves, Cologne, Liege, Utrecht, Bremen, Hildesheim, had, in the tenth century, celebrated cathedral schools. The encouragement which the higher authorities had afforded them, however, was soon discontinued. Charlemagne's decrees were forgotten during the disputes of his grandsons about the government, under whom, also, the above-mentioned court-school was abandoned; and his great creation declined as the school establishment of the great Alfred, in England, which was begun with equal zeal, and on an equal scale, in the ninth century, was destroyed by the invasions of the Danes, though Edward the Confessor endeavored to restore it. In the mean time, the school of the rabbis, among the Jews in Syria, Northern Africa, and even in Europe (Jewish academies existed in the seventh century, at Lunel in France, and, in the tenth and eleventh centuries, at Cordova, in Spain), preserved the remains of ancient learning; and the Arabian schools established in the ninth century in the Oriental and African caliphates, and in the Moorish kingdoms in Spain, exhibited a freer spirit and better taste. From them a knowledge of the mathematical and medical sciences was first communicated to the south of Christian Europe. In Italy, where, after the barbarism introduced by the Goths and Lombards, king Lothaire had been the first to establish schools, in the ninth century, for the large cities, as well as in Spain and France, the influence of Arabic civilization became observable, in the institution of schools for qualifying men for the different professions. At Salerno (q. v.), Montpellier and Seville, Arabic physicians taught; and the works of the Saracens on natural history and mathematics were sought for even by Christian scholars. The developement of the papal canon law gave occasion to the foundation of law schools, among which those of Bologna and Lyons acquired the greatest reputation. The academical privileges, which the former of these two received, in 1158, from the emperor Frederic I, became the foundation of the constitution of the continental universities which originated in the twelfth and thirteenth centuries. The inactivity and luxury of the clergy had led to the neglect of the cathedral and conventual schools, and they rapidly declined. The new institutions which had grown up were necessary to form new teachers and to revive the taste for science. But even these became subject to undue clerical influence, as, since the beginning of the thirteenth century, the mendicant monks not only connected popular schools with their convents, and undertook the education of the children in the cities, but also obtained entrance into the universities as teachers, where they labored to augment the importance of their various orders and the power of the pope. Thus the state of the schools, in the middle ages, was by no means so flourishing as might have been expected from the activity of former centuries and the institutions of Charlemagne. Dictating took the place of lecturing even in the higher schools; mere exercises of memory held the place of erudition; the dead letter predominated, and an intelligent investigation of the subjects studied was little practised. The pupils of the Latin or *trivial* schools wasted almost all their time in copying the manuals. In the lower parish schools, the monks would not even permit the scholars to learn to write; being desirous to confine the art, which was highly lucrative and important before the invention of printing, to the clergy (it was called the *ars clericalis*); and the privilege of establishing writing schools for the children of citizens could not be obtained by the magistrates but by special agreement with the clergy. But at length, with the increasing power of the cities (q. v.), the citizens became more independent, and the magistrates themselves began to take care of the instruction of youth, which had been so much neglected by the clergy, and to establish schools, in which reading, writing and the *trivium* were taught. For these, as well as for the cathedral and parish schools (the canons and parish priests having ceased to occupy themselves with the instruction of youth), itinerant monks and students were taken as teachers. This gave rise to a separate class of teachers, which indeed belonged to the clerical order, then in the exclusive possession of learning, but resembled the corporations of mechanics in its regular gradations, and in the unsettled life of its members, who wandered from place to place much to the detriment of their morals. The school-masters were engaged by the corporation of cities, and the parish ministers were liable to be dismissed on a year or three months' warning, and were obliged to employ assist ants, proportioned to the number of their pupils, and to pay them out of their own salaries. These assistant teachers (*locati*, because they were hired; *stampuales*, because they gave elementary instruction) were subject, as well as the head masters, to the parish ministers, who used them as writers and church servants. Sometimes the school-masters, who taught Latin, were called *rectors;* the assistant teachers, who taught singing, reading, and gave religious instruction (the latter consisting in making their pupils commit to memory the creed, the ten commandments, prayers and psalms), were called *cantors*. From this division originated, in some countries, for instance in Germany, the division of Latin and German schools, which were, however, most generally united. The elder pupils of the highest class frequently travelled from one school to another, pretending to detect hidden treasures, and practising various mummeries and fooleries; hence they were sometimes called *histriones* (because they formed the first companies of actors, as, in France, the Jongleurs and Gaillards), sometimes *vacantivi* (i. e. idlers). Generally they carried with them younger pupils, who were their slaves, to all intents and purposes, and had to procure them support, by begging and stealing, if there was no other way, and retained for themselves only such portion of their acquisitions as their tyrants were willing to let them enjoy. In the fourteenth and sixteenth centuries, these bands of vagrants, among whom there were sometimes *vacantivi* thirty years old, who were yet unable to construe a Latin author, were most numerous in Germany. As students, they were allowed to wear swords, and thus were frequently tempted to disturb the public peace. When they stopped to pursue their studies in a school, they found lodgings in the school-rooms, or about the churches, and lived upon the charity of the citizens. If there were several schools in one place, disputes often occurred between the pupils, which were decided by arms, according to the fashion of the middle ages. As late as the beginning of the sixteenth century, Luther complained that such vagrants received appointments as teachers, because, generally, these *vacantivi*, who had hardly seen a university, were the only persons who could be hired as school-masters, since the more learned youths were ambitious of clerical benefices and academical professorships. Unique in its kind, in the history of the schools of this period, was the pious fraternity of the Jeronymites. They consisted of clergymen and laymen, who lived together, occupied partly with mechanical arts, partly with the instruction of girls and boys, to whom they taught reading, writing, and useful arts. For boys of talent and diligence there were Latin classes. On the model of these schools, others were established in the Netherlands, on the Rhine, and in Northern Germany. These soon came into communication with the Greeks who had fled to Italy; and thus the study of the classics became more cultivated. Through the efforts of men like Thomas a Kempis, Hegius, Erasmus, Agricola, Reuchlin and Melanchthon, a liberal study of the remains of classic antiquity was commenced. Much was done, in and after the last half of the fourteenth century, to promote this object by Italian courts and universities, through the instrumentality of learned Greeks, and of the Platonic academy at Florence, and towards the end of the fifteenth century, through the learned Rhenish society, established by Conrad Celtes. The result, at first, was only an intellectual luxury for the great and the learned; yet many skilful teachers proceeded from Basle, Tübingen, Heidelberg and Wittenberg, which, after the time of Luther and Melanchthon, became the head-quarters of instruction for Germany. In all countries where the reformation became general, it had a decided influence upon the schools. It even had a considerable influence in several Catholic countries; but its effects were most decided in Germany. According to the advice of the reformers in that country, who, in 1529, furnished a great example of the care which government should bestow on the schools by the visitations which they made of the schools in the electorate of Saxony, the corporations of cities founded gymnasia and lyceums with permanent teachers. The property of the convents, and of the church in general, which had been confiscated by the governments, was, in most cases, applied to the use of schools. The number of these institutions was now much increased, and their character elevated, and scientific school-masters were soon formed. The newly invented art of printing assisted greatly in this work of improvement. Only the conventual cathedral and *trivial* schools of the Catholics remained restricted to the narrow limits of the seven liberal arts. Schools for girls were founded, and in the villages instructers were appointed to teach the catechism. Whilst schools were thus acquiring a systematic character in the sixteenth century, and the classical languages were even taught in the smaller towns, the Jesuit schools arose towards the end of this century among the Catholics. They soon obtained, by their better taste and more scientific spirit, a superiority over the old Catholic schools. But, though they have exercised a great influence, as has been stated in the article *Jesuits*, to which we must refer our readers, they were yet more calculated for the children of the wealthy, or those of uncommon talent among the poorer classes, than for the general education of the people. In Spain and Italy, their schools were long the best; in Hungary and Poland, they were the only ones excepting the conventual schools and the colleges of the Piarists (q. v.); and even in America and Asia, they contributed zealously, by their missions, to the diffusion of European civilization. But a variety of circumstances contributed to produce degeneracy in these latter schools as well as in those of the Protestants. The former became again confined to a fixed routine; the latter passed from the strictness of the conventual schools to licentiousness, through the influence of the privileged universities. To this was added, in Germany, the thirty years' war, in which fanaticism on both sides destroyed what had been judiciously established. Yet, about this time, some great men distinguished themselves as writers on education, as lord Bacon (q. v.), and the exiled bishop of the Moravians, Amos Comenius. (q. v.)

Considerable influence was exerted upon the system of education, towards the end of the seventeenth century, by the principles of Pietism and Quietism (q. v.), established by Fénélon and Spener, which was the basis of the instructions of A. H. Franke. (q. v.) Instructers in his spirit spread themselves, in the first half of the eighteenth century, from Halle over the whole of Northern Germany. Yet the lower schools were bad in comparison to the higher; and in these, Latin and Greek seem to have been the only thing considered essential. The idea of an education adapted to the nature and general destination of man, suggested by Bacon and Montaigne, received, about this time, a more complete developement from Locke and Rousseau; and the Philanthropinism* of Basedow and his friends introduced it, in the second half of the eighteenth century, into Germany. Schools were now instituted, in which, besides languages and history, natural history, technology, civil arithmetic, &c., were taught. They held an intermediate place between the primary schools and the gymnasia. In 1807 and 1808, the Bavarian government established, besides the gymnasia for classical education, seminaries, called *Real-Instituten*, where young persons who intend to become merchants, apothecaries, miners, manufacturers, artists, &c., are instructed in that knowledge which is of most general utility—in history, religion, modern languages, mathematics, and the natural sciences. The *trivial schools*, which continued to exist, both in the larger and smaller towns, were changed, after the end of the eighteenth century, into public schools, both common and high, and many schools were established for paupers. In fact, every where in Protestant Germany, and in some other countries, effectual steps were taken for the advancement of school instruction; but the Catholic countries took little part in this advancement. The Catholic governments trusted implicitly to the Jesuits, Piarists, Ursulines, and some other orders, unconcerned whether the instruction which they afforded did or did not correspond to the demands of the time. By the abolition of the Jesuits in 1773, moreover, a chasm was produced, which the schools of the Piarists, mostly of the *trivial* kind, were unable immediately to supply. Austria felt this abolition less than other Catholic countries, on account of her normal schools for the lower orders, intended to serve as a pattern for all the common schools in the empire. Her school system, however, was far from perfect. Under the present emperor, professorships of pedagogics (for the instruction of teachers) have been established in the universities and episcopal seminaries. Many gymnasia, common schools, Sunday schools, &c., have likewise been instituted in Austria. The normal schools were imitated by most of the Catholic states of Germany. Italy, Portugal and

* The system of Philanthropinism was directed against the prevailing faults, both of school instruction and of domestic education, against the tyranny of the rod, the stiffness of the ordinary discipline, the inconvenient and prejudicial nature of children's dress, the want of proper bodily exercise, the system of loading the memory without exercising the active faculties, &c. The object was to develope the energies of children in a more natural way, and with less constraint and hardship. Several institutions, called *Philanthropins*, were established, of which that of Salzmann (q. v.) was the only one which survived to the nineteenth century.

Spain continued inactive, as they had been for a long series of years: they left instruction to the clergy and to chance. They have only episcopal seminaries and the Piarist and conventual schools. The institutions of Leopold, in Tuscany, for popular education, after the Austrian model, were disturbed by the wars of the revolution. The French had not time to do a great deal for the education of the people; and, in fact, education had not made any great advances among themselves; and when, in Spain and Italy, the old rulers again took possession of the country, they considered education dangerous, as productive of a revolutionary spirit. The Jesuits, since their revival, have as yet been too unimportant to produce any great effect. In those countries of Europe where they have exerted an influence on instruction of late, it has been an injurious influence, intended to counteract the spirit of the time.

In France, much remains to be done for education. Before the revolution, there were, besides the episcopal seminaries and conventual schools, lyceums and colleges in the cities, where young persons were prepared, under a system of monastic discipline, for the higher seminaries. The government did nothing for the education of the people at large, and the clergy, though possessing so large a proportion of all the property in France, and having the instruction of the people under their especial care, left them in abominable ignorance; whence the horrid outrages that disfigured the early part of the revolution. Some elementary schools were supported, here and there, by religious orders, or private persons; but the instruction was scanty, and in all the institutions of education was behind the age. During the revolution, the schools were declared to be under the care of the state. It was not to be expected that a good plan could be adopted immediately. The polytechnic school (q. v.), however, was excellently arranged. Napoleon established several military schools, and others for instruction in trades and arts, and an imperial university was created, to have the supreme direction of instruction in France. But the plan was on a military principle, and as little fitted to promote the true purposes of education as the monastic narrowness of former ages. Academies (schools for the different professions) and lyceums, on an entirely military plan, were introduced. The "secondary schools" actually went into operation in but very few places, and the "primary schools" (elementary and village schools) hardly any where. The instruction in private establishments was subjected to much restriction, except in regard to mathematics and the natural sciences. The religious instruction was to be founded on the "Catechism of the Empire." This was the state in which the Bourbons found the schools in France. Changes were made by them, but not for the better. The clergy labored with them to restore a state of things which had long gone by. In 1816, elementary schools on the Lancasterian principle were introduced, which would have become a great blessing to the country; but the royalists and clergy, after a while, procured their abolition. The lower classes receive very little instruction in France, and there cannot be much doubt that a third part of the whole population of that country which considers itself the most civilized on earth, grows up without education. The whole number of individuals, subject to the conscription in 1830, was 294,975. Of these, 121,079 could read and write; 12,801 could only read; 153,635 could neither read nor write: in respect to 7460, it could not be ascertained what was the extent of their attainments.* M. Dupin, in his work, cited below, page 71, says, that "it must be acknowledged that there are no parts of Europe, except the Pyrenæan peninsula, Turkey, the south of Italy, Greece and Russia, in which education is in a more backward state than in France" For further information we refer our readers to an article, "The State of Education in France," in the Quarterly Journal of Education for July and October, 1831, containing the answers given by the *Société pour la Propagation des Connaissances Scientifiques et Industrielles* to questions put by the Society for the Diffusion of Useful Knowledge in

* The law of September 14, 1791, enacted that a system of instruction for all the people should be organized, which should be gratuitous with respect to those kinds of knowledge which are indispensable for all classes. But this law was never carried into effect. The ordinance of April, 1816, declared that every commune should be bound to provide primary instruction for all the children of the commune, giving this instruction gratuitously to indigent children. But the means of carrying this into effect have been wanting, the majority of the communes being unable to provide a salary for a primary instructer. It would seem indispensable that the state or the departments should form a common fund to pay, or to assist in paying, the teachers in the poorest communes. A law on this subject is of urgent necessity.

1830. Quite recently, professor Cousin q. v.) addressed several letters on the state of education in Germany, to the minister of public instruction in France, after careful personal examination of the subject.

In England, no general system of education for all classes of the community has ever been established. The efforts of Brougham to introduce such a system were frustrated by party spirit and ecclesiastical prejudices. Something, however, has been accomplished for the instruction of the lower classes by individual exertions, the institution of infant and Sunday schools, and the operation of the Lancasterian mode of instruction. In the middle ages, besides the two universities, the education of youth was provided for by the cathedral or episcopal schools, of which there was one in each diocese, under a *scholastic*, as the superintendent of the school was called, in which the studies were mainly intended as a preparation for the priestly office; the conventual or abbey schools in the monasteries, in which all the sciences were taught (the ecclesiastics were, at that time, lawyers and physicians), and schools in the principal towns and cities. But the great public schools of England are mostly of later origin. Winchester college was founded by bishop Wykeham, as early as the reign of Edward I (1387); Eton, with seventy king's scholars or collegers, was founded by Henry VI, in 1440; Westminster, with forty scholarships, in 1560, by Elizabeth; and Harrow free school was also instituted during her reign. The course of instruction in these high schools is not very extensive, nor judiciously conducted. At Eton, for instance, little more is taught than the Latin and Greek languages: the scholarships depend merely upon seniority, and entitle the scholars to a fellowship in King's college (Oxford), and finally to a university degree without examination. The course of reading is rather limited and injudicious, and the elementary books poor. The case is not very different at Westminster. There are numerous charitable foundations for education in England, the enormous abuses of which were exposed by the persevering and indefatigable exertions of Brougham in successive reports to the house of commons: in one instance, for example, where the funds of the charity yielded £450 per annum, only one boy was boarded and educated; and in another case, in which the revenue of the establishment was £1500 per annum, the incumbent left the care of the school to a carpenter in the village, to whom he paid £40 a year. If these abuses have been remedied, and the facilities for popular education in some degree increased, much yet remains to be accomplished in England.

In Scotland, more provision has been made for popular education. By an act of William and Mary, it is required that there shall be a school and school-master in every parish. In 1803, the limits of the salary were raised from 100 and 200 merks to 300 and 400 merks (75 to 100 dollars), with the addition of a house and one quarter of an acre of land. The proprietors of land in the parish are assessed for the latter expenses, and that of the school-house · but the salary is paid half by the proprietors and half by the tenants In a large part of the country, nearly the whole population is able to read and write; but in some parts, chiefly in the Highlands, the parishes are so extensive that there are many who have no means of education within reach, and three or four schools would be required to accommodate all the inhabitants. In some of the principal towns, the parochial schools are of a higher description, and are entitled *grammar schools*. Within the last twenty years, numerous schools have been established, under the name of *academies*, in which the higher branches are taught.

In Sweden, the schools are much on the same footing as they were in the seventeenth century among the German Protestants. The clergy, in the possession of the church property of their Catholic predecessors, show little disposition to apply a part of it to the public instruction; and the government is too poor and too jealous to admit many improvements from foreign countries.

The government of the vast Russian empire has directed its attention to a system of schools for a hundred years past, before which there were only conventual schools for the clergy, and some institutions for the sons of the great, established —almost by force—by Wladimir the Great. According to the decrees of the emperor Alexander, schools for the circles, districts and parishes, were to be instituted throughout the empire, in order to strike an effectual blow at the deep ignorance of the Russian people. The circle schools exist at present on the pattern of the German gymnasia, in most of the capital cities of the governments; the district schools are found in some towns of a middling size; the parish schools, however, in very few villages; and the greatest and best part of this plan remains, as yet, unexecuted.* Somewhat earlier, there existed, in the German provinces of Russia, good gymnasia, and some common and country schools; but the latter are still in a very low condition. The education of Catholic youth was attended to by the Jesuits, who were admitted by Catharine II into White Russia.

Poland, where, formerly, the nobility only were instructed by the members of religious orders (Lazarists, Piarists and Jesuits), had, before its partition, some gymnasia, founded towards the end of the eighteenth century, and some common and country schools, but no well arranged school system. During the existence of the grand-duchy of Poland, something was intended to be done for the education of children of both sexes; but it was not executed, and the last catastrophe, which has reduced Poland to a Russian province, must have a most injurious effect on the few means of education which the country affords.

Denmark, Holland (which has far outstripped Catholic Belgium), and Switzerland, strive to keep pace with Protestant Germany; but the improvement of Switzerland has not been so great as might have been expected, after the impulse given by Pestalozzi. Some cantons, however, have seminaries for the education of teachers; and Denmark has had them for forty years. The Danish government issued, in 1814, a school ordinance for its German provinces, which contains many wise directions. Holland distinguished itself early by institutions for philological instruction, and the society for the public welfare (founded in 1784) has given a good organization to the common schools.

In no part of the continent, however, has so much been done for schools, and education been made so much a particular branch of study by thinking men, as in Germany. Bavaria was the first of the larger states in which this subject received the particular attention of the government. Since 1806, the schools in that kingdom have been conducted systematically on a general plan. There is a particular department, in the ministry of the interior, to superintend the subject of education, whose authority extends to all the various schools and institutions. The smaller states have done much for schools, as Nassau, Lippe-Detmold, Anhalt-Dessau, and the Saxon dukedoms. Though Hanover and Brunswick established seminaries for the formation of instructers in the last century, their subsequent progress has been comparatively slow. Saxony, which took the lead in this particular after the reformation, always had its schools for instruction in philology, and also good common schools; yet it did not advance, as might have been hoped. —See Ruhkopf's *History of Schools and Education in Germany* (in German).

Out of Europe, the U. States only have an effective system of education in the various states. In the U. States, the provisions for education are made chiefly by the state authorities, and are very different in different parts of the country; but no where has popular education in general received more attention, or been carried to greater extent. Of the colleges of this country we have given some account in the article *College*. Next in rank to these seminaries are the establishments called *academies*, founded by private bequests, or public grants, in which Latin and Greek, and commonly one or more modern languages, with geography, history, the elementary portions of mathematics, and physical philosophy, are generally taught. In the grammar schools, the course of study is very different; sometimes only reading, writing, grammar and arithmetic are taught, but geography is frequently studied in them, and sometimes history. Below these, in some places, there are primary schools, kept by women for younger children, and numerous infant schools, which take the child almost from the cradle. In this way, a child may, in some instances, be educated, from the age of three or four, to that of sixteen or seventeen, without any fee for tuition. The federal government has, in the disposition of the public lands, made provisions for common schools, by reserving one section of each township for the support of schools in the township, besides making other reservations for colleges. (See *Public Lands*.) The system of free schools has been carried to the greatest perfection in the New England states, in which, though the details of the system differ much, yet the leading principles are the same. More is generally done than is required by law, by the towns in their corporate capacity, besides the great numbers of private schools, all over the country, for all ages and of all descriptions. Thus, in the city of Boston, in which the legal expenditure on the free schools would amount to but $3000 per annum, the yearly expense is actually

* See the *Statistique et Itinéraire de la Russie, par J. H Schnitzler* (Paris, 1829).

upwards of $60,000, supporting eighty schools, with 7430 pupils; besides which there are 155 private schools in the city, with 4018 pupils, making a total of 235 schools, and 11,448 pupils, in a population of less than 62,000 souls. In Massachusetts, the laws require that every town or district, containing fifty families, shall be provided with a school or schools, equivalent in time to six months for one school in a year; if containing 100 families, twelve months; 150 families, eighteen months; and the towns are required to raise the sums of money necessary for the support of the schools in the same manner as other town taxes. The state of Connecticut has a fund, derived from the sale of lands in Ohio, of $1,882,261, the income of which (upwards of $72,000) is appropriated to the support of common free schools. The number of children between four and sixteen, in 1828, was 84,899. The great principle on which the system is founded, is, that elementary education should be so free as to exclude none, and the schools so numerous as to be within the reach of all, at the same time that their management should be principally intrusted to the people themselves, in small districts, so as to excite and sustain a general interest among all classes. The tax is on property, and thus the poorer classes are saved from a burden which might otherwise be too great for them, at the same time that they pay enough to render them desirous of securing the benefit of the schools; and the rich are glad to secure the most effectual protection for order and property, in the general intelligence and morality of the people. (See the valuable paper of professor Ticknor, in the English Quarterly Journal of Education, No. IV, also reprinted in the National Gazette, Philadelphia, Jan. 17, 1832.) For the population of New England, consisting of less than 2,000,000, there are between 10,000 and 12,000 schools, 150 academies, and 11 colleges, besides great numbers of private schools and boarding schools. We have given an account of the state of schools in New York, in the article *New York*, division *Public Instruction* (vol. ix, p. 593). New Jersey has a school fund of $245,404, the income of which, with a tax of ½ per cent. on the capital stock of the banks, is distributed, in small sums, to towns which will raise an equal sum for the support of schools. In Pennsylvania, little has been done for common education. In the Report of the Society for the Promotion of Public Schools (April, 1831), it is stated that, during the preceding year, the number of children between the ages of five and fifteen, was 400,000, of which there were not 150,000 in all the schools in the state. There is no legislative provision for the support of schools. In Delaware, there is a school fund, the income of which is distributed to such towns as will raise a sum equal to that which they receive; and, in Maryland, some attempts have been made to establish a general system of primary education; but it has been only partially accomplished. The New England system of free schools has been introduced into Ohio (March, 1831); and, in Indiana, the constitution makes it the duty of the legislature to provide, by law, for a general system of education, in which tuition shall be given gratis. Similar provisions have been made in Illinois; and in Kentucky attempts have recently been made to effect the same purpose. But in the Southern and Western States generally, there is no legislative provision for the establishment of common schools, on the plan of those of New England. The Sunday schools in the U. States are, in a great measure, intended for religious instruction, and are therefore composed of the pupils of the day schools.—Further information on this subject may be found in the American Annals (Journal) of Education (1826, seq.), various numbers of the North American Review, and American Almanac (vols. ii and iii).

In Canada, education is, generally speaking, in a very low state, which is greatly owing to the population being much scattered.

In the West Indies, the schools, though improving in some parts, as in Cuba, must be subjected to very different influences before they can reach any thing like perfection; and in South America the people labor under the immense disadvantage of having been formerly under the Spanish and Portuguese governments, which did nothing for the education even of their European subjects; to which must be added that the population is scattered, and that they are under the exclusive sway of the Catholic clergy. Common schools have been established, of late, in several colonies of Europe (e. g. at the cape of Good Hope), and several schools, on the plan of mutual instruction, in the East Indies. Independent of the influence of European civilization, schools of different degrees are to be found in the East Indies, China, Japan, and the other empires of Eastern Asia, in which despots or priests give children such an education as will best fit them for their service. Persia, also, has established schools, in which boys of all classes learn to read and write. Turkey and Northern Africa alone limit instruction to the explanation of the Koran. A few schools (e. g. in Asia Minor), established by American or European missionaries, need hardly be mentioned in this general view. Missionaries from the U. States have also established schools in various parts of Greece; yet it has been found impossible to do much in the present disturbed state of that unfortunate country. We refer the reader to the chapter on education in Greece, in Mr. Anderson's Observations on the Peloponnesus, &c. (Boston, 1830).

The time in which we live is so remarkable for the important changes produced in almost all departments of human activity, by the power of science and general information, that, in most civilized countries, the urgent necessity of general education has been clearly felt, and measures have been taken (though not always the most effective, as might well be expected) to bring about this object. The changes which have taken place in science, and in the whole condition of modern nations, who are no longer dependent, like those of the middle ages, for their means of intellectual culture, on the remains of ancient civilization, necessarily make the character of school instruction very different from what it was formerly, when the whole intellectual wealth of Europe was contained in two languages; and though these noble idioms will always retain a high place in a complete system of education (see *Philology*), yet their importance is comparatively less, while that of the natural sciences, history, geography, politics, &c., has very much increased. All this has had a great influence upon schools, and will have a still greater. The importance of education, moreover, is now set in strong relief by the general conviction, entertained in free countries, that the general diffusion of knowledge is the only true security for well regulated liberty, which must rest on a just sense of what is due from man to man; and few results can be attained by the student of history and of mankind more delightful than this of the essential connexion of light and liberty; not that great learning necessarily leads to liberty; history affords many instances which disprove this; but that a general diffusion of knowledge always tends to promote a general sense and love of what is right and just, as well as to furnish the means of securing it. We see, therefore, in our age, not only a great increase in the number of schools, but also the introduction of various new kinds, as the Sunday schools (q. v.) and the infant schools: the latter we think of advantage in the case of parents who are unable to take care of their children at home, but injurious where (as it happens but too often) they induce mothers, the natural guardians of their infants, to neglect those duties which Providence has best qualified them to discharge, and thus lose those opportunities of exerting a beneficial influence on the opening character of the infant, which are fully perceived only by the keen eye of parental love.

From the circumstances which we have mentioned, a great zeal for the improvement of schools has been exhibited, in several countries, since about the year 1818, a few years after the conclusion of general peace in Europe; and we shall therefore take one more rapid view of the state of schools in Europe since that time. Prussia has done, of late, more than any other country of equal or larger size, for the improvement of schools. In addition to the nineteen seminaries for the education of instructers, which existed in 1818, nine new ones have been founded, so that, since 1825, 1500 teachers are continually educated in twenty-eight large seminaries and twenty-one of less size. The demand for teachers is great, as the country schools alone require 21,000. The expense of these seminaries for teachers is 100,000 Prussian dollars yearly, which is paid by the government. The government have also sent teachers into foreign countries to study their school systems. All the countries of Germany have seminaries for teachers, and many laws have been enacted to induce or oblige the poorest classes to send their children to school: still, however, much remains to be done, to bring the instruction of the people at large to the level of the demands of the age. The last reorganization of the Bavarian system of education took place in 1825. If much has been done in Germany for common schools, still more has been done in several states of that country for the gymnasia (q. v.), or learned schools. The great increase of aids to study, lexicographical, grammatical, metrical, critical and archæological, has given the learned schools a degree of activity and efficiency which, perhaps, twenty years ago, would have appeared unattainable. In Austria alone, the gymnasia are, as yet, circumscribed within comparatively narrow limits. In Russia, the school system has not effected what it promised. The circle schools are, as yet, confided to military directors, in most cases, and the district schools, on account of the low degree of civilization among the mass of the people, are obliged to employ themselves on the very rudiments of knowledge; and, for the parish schools, masters are yet to be formed. In the provinces on the Baltic, the schools come somewhat nearer to the German. For the army, several Lancasterian schools have been established since 1820. Sweden has, according to the decree of Dec. 16, 1820, received a new organization, which has considerably improved the learned and *trivial* schools, but the country schools very little. Seminaries for school-masters do not exist there at all. In some larger cities, Lancasterian schools have existed, since 1820, for the children of soldiers and of the poor. But the degree of information to be found among the Swedish peasants, who not unfrequently instruct their children themselves, somewhat remedies this evil. Denmark has established many Lancasterian schools. This system was first introduced into the army in 1819, and in 1822, with some modifications, was recommended by the king to all the common schools, of which above 2000 have adopted it. (See the article *Mutual Instruction.*) In 1825, a law was passed in the Netherlands, which declared the establishment of schools, public and private, dependent upon the government. In France, the ultra-montanists and the aristocratic party, after the restoration, labored, with the aid of the ministry, to bring back the system of education to the narrow limits within which it was confined by the clergy before the revolution. They broke up the Lancasterian schools, established under the influence of the constitutional party, and favored the Brethren of Christian Doctrine and the Jesuits, whose colleges not only became again institutions of education, but also had a decided influence upon others. But the French schools, generally speaking, with the exception of mathematics and the natural sciences, teach little thoroughly; skilful teachers are found only in large cities; the small towns have but very ordinary schools, and a great part of the peasants grow up without school education. There is a tax on the learning of Latin in all the colleges (q.v.) of the kingdom, amounting to fifteen francs annually for each individual, which, with other heavy taxes (some paid by the teachers themselves), goes into the treasury of the university at Paris. This explains how the schools, which are a considerable expense to other governments, yielded, in 1826, to the French government, 2,526,910 francs, and cost only 2,213,200 francs, affording therefore a surplus of 313,710 francs. All kinds of instruction in France are dependent upon the university. It was always one of the points most insisted on by the liberals, that instruction should be freed from this subjection, particularly since the amendment of the charter in 1830; and promises to this effect have even been made by the ministers; but as yet the relief has not been obtained. In the Sardinian states, where the supervision of education was restored to the Jesuits, the learning of reading and writing is prohibited, by royal decree, to all who do not possess a capital of 1500 lire, and the study of the sciences to all who have not an income of 1500 lire. The Italian schools stagnate under similar influences. Naples has not, as yet, given particular attention to this subject. In the States of the Church, Modena and Lucca, it is left to the Jesuits. In Tuscany, where a private association introduced the Lancasterian system into Florence, in 1821, education stands on nearly the same footing as in the Austrian dominions in Italy, in which it is at least established on a regular system, and is not left in the hands of the Jesuits, although it may not be more progressive than in Hungary. In Spain and Portugal, the state of education is particularly low. The activity of the university and many schools was, for a time, interrupted by the revolution. Yet the cortes had already directed their attention to education, as the ninth chapter of their constitution proves, by which, if the instrument had remained in force, a complete system of school instruction would have been established. Immediately after the revolution of 1820, the ninth chapter was carried into effect; but all that had been done was overturned in 1823. after the restoration. Many schools and other institutions ceased to teach; and where instruction continued to be given, it has been on the old scholastic system of the middle ages. Quite recently, a decree was issued, prohibiting philosophy to be taught in the universities! In many places, there is not even a school for elementary instruction. For the higher classes, there are some boarding schools, in the French style. (See an article ontitled a Brief Outline of the History of Education in Spain, in the Journal of the New York Literary Convention, in 1830.) In Portugal, dom Miguel has probably had little time to improve education. Before his usurpation, the state of things was, perhaps, a shade better, as to common schools than in Spain.

SCHOONER; a small vessel with two masts, whose mainsail and foresail are both suspended by gaffs, like a sloop's mainsail.

SCHOREEL, John, a distinguished Dutch painter, received his name from Schoreel, a village near Alkmaer, where he was born in 1495. His love of painting appeared in his boyish sports. He copied every painted window, and covered, with delicate figures, every horn-inkstand that came in his way. At the age of 14 years, he was placed with the painter Will. Cornelis. At the age of 17, he travelled to Amsterdam, and entered the establishment of Jacob Cornelis, one of the most celebrated painters and engravers on wood, of that period. Here he spent several years. He next repaired to the first of the masters then living, John of Mabuse, in Utrecht. The disorderly life of his new master disgusted the young Schoreel; and he visited, successively, many large cities, where there were painters of eminence, especially Cologne and Spire, where he studied architecture and perspective. He also visited Dürer, in Nuremberg, and was received kindly. At the age of 22, Schoreel passed through Carinthia to Venice. One of his countrymen, in a monastery there, persuaded him to undertake a pilgrimage, with him, to Palestine. For three years, he remained within the walls of Jerusalem, sketching views of the city and surrounding country; and a large painting, probably by him, is still in the church, in the place where Christ is said to have been born. On his return, he spent some time at Rhodes, which he painted, together with the surrounding country; and afterwards at Rome, among the works of Raphael, Michael Angelo and Giulio, till Adrian VI, a native of Utrecht, ascended the papal chair, in 1522, and committed to him the superintendence of the Belvedere. The death of Adrian, the following year, induced Schoreel to return home through France and Amsterdam. He now executed many splendid pieces, in Utrecht, afterwards in Harlem, and, from time to time, in other cities in the Netherlands. He died at Utrecht, Dec. 6, 1562. He has been compared with John van Eyck, whom he equalled in splendor and truth of coloring, in expression, in warmth of representation; and, at the most, was inferior to him only in the execution of particular parts. Unhappily, the rage of the fanatics, in a subsequent age, for destroying pictures, was fatal to many of his most valuable works

SCHORL. (See *Tourmaline.*)

SCHORLITE. (See *Topaz.*)

SCHREVELIUS, Cornelius, a learned critic, was born at Harlem, about 1614. His father was rector of the school of Leyden, in which office he was succeeded by Cornelius, in 1642. The latter had taken his degree in medicine; but on his promotion to the school, he turned his attention exclusively to classical pursuits, in the course of which he published several *Variorum* editions of the classics, which display more industry than taste or judgment. His name is now principally known by a Manual Greek and Latin Dictionary (1645), which has been often reprinted, in most countries of Europe. An edition, with great improvements, by Fleury-Lécluse, appeared at Paris in 1820; and it has been translated into English, with very extensive additions and improvements, by John Pickering (Boston, 3d edition, 1832). He died in 1667.

SCHUBART, Christian Frederic Daniel, a German poet of much natural talent, but of a defective education, and an irregular life, was born in 1739, at Obersontheim, in Suabia. He began the study of theology at Jena, in 1758; but his dissipation involved him in debt. For some time he supported himself by preaching; but music, for which he had much talent, drew him away from theology. In 1764, he married; and the union was an unfortunate one for his wife. In 1768, he became director of music at Ludwigsburg, near Stuttgard, but gave himself up, more and more, to dissipation, so that he was imprisoned for some time, and exiled from Würtemberg. He now lived an unsettled life, undertook various employments, which he was always obliged to resign on account of his bad life, his attacks upon the clergy, &c. His Chronicle became a popular journal. But, in 1777, he was seduced into the Würtemberg territory, and arrested on account of some things which he had written. He remained ten years in prison at Hohenasperg, was liberated at the request of Mad. Karschin (q. v.), and made director of the music of the ducal theatre at Stuttgard. He began several works, but, before they were completed, he died, in 1791. His poems, which contain much inflated and unpolished matter,—interspersed, however, with many flashes of genius,—were published at Frankfort on the Maine, in 1787, 2 vols.; another edition in 3 vols., 12mo., at the same place, with a life of him; and several short pieces in prose. His Miscellaneous Works (Zürich, 1812, 2 vols.), were published by his son.

SCHULTENS, Albert, a celebrated Orientalist, born at Gröningen, in 1686, studied theology and Arabic at that place, at Leyden and Utrecht, became a preacher in 1711, professor of the Oriental languages in 1713, and in 1717, university preacher at Franeker. His chief works, *Origines Hebrææ*, and *Institutiones ad Fundamenta Linguæ Hebraicæ* (1737), had an important influence on the study of the eastern languages.—His son *John Jacob* (1716—1778) was the author of several learned dissertations and treatises.—*Henry Albert*, son of the latter, born at Herborn, in 1749, was educated at Leyden, where he studied Arabic and Hebrew, and afterwards became a commoner in Wadham college, Oxford, and received the degree of master of arts there. On his return to Holland, he was chosen professor of the Oriental languages at Amsterdam, where he resided until the death of his father, whom he afterwards succeeded at Leyden. He died in 1793. Besides his Arabian Anthology (1772), he published an edition of Pilpay's Fables, and a supplement to the *Bibliothèque Orientale* of D'Herbelot.

SCHUMLA. (See *Choumla.*)

SCHUYLER, Philip, a distinguished American revolutionary general, was born at Albany, New York, in 1731, of an ancient and respectable family. He served as an officer in the war which commenced at lake George in 1775. When quite young, he became a member of the New York legislature, and was eminent for his intelligence and influence. To him and governor Clinton, it was chiefly owing that the province made an early and decided resistance to those British measures which terminated in the independence of the colonies. When the revolution commenced, he was appointed, June 19, 1775, a major-general, and was directed to proceed immediately from New York to Ticonderoga, to secure the lakes, and make preparations for entering Canada. Being taken sick in September, the command devolved upon Montgomery On his recovery, he devoted himself zealously to the management of the affairs in the northern departments. He gave much of his attention to the superintendence of the Indian concerns. On the approach of Burgoyne, in 1777, he made every exertion to obstruct his progress; but the evacuation of Ticonderoga by St. Clair occasioning unreasonable jealousies in regard to Schuyler, in New England, he was superseded by general Gates, in August; and an inquiry was directed by congress to be made into his conduct. He was afterwards, though not in the regular service, very useful to his country in the military transactions of New York. He was a member of the old congress; and when the present government of the U. States commenced its operation in 1789, he was appointed a senator in the national legislature. He was chosen a second time, in 1797, to the same station. In the senate of New York, he contributed, probably, more than any other man, to the code of laws adopted by the state. He died at his seat near Albany, Nov. 18, 1804, in the 73d year of his age. He possessed great strength of mind and purity of intention. In the contrivance of plans of public utility, he was wise and circumspect, and in their execution, enterprising and persevering. In his deportment, he was dignified, but courteous. He was a pleasing and instructive companion, and, in all the functions of private life, was highly exemplary.

SCHUYLKILL, a river of Pennsylvania, rises in Lucerne county, runs south-east, and unites with the Delaware, six miles below Philadelphia. It is 140 miles long, and navigable for boats 90 miles. The Tulpehocken, a navigable stream, flows into the Schuylkill a little above the town of Reading. There are falls on the river five miles above Philadelphia, and others near Norristown. A part of the valuable coal called *anthracite*, which is now so much used in Philadelphia, and exported thence to all the northern cities, is obtained from mines situated on the Schuylkill.

SCHWABACH, ARTICLES OF; a confession of faith, drawn up by Luther, for the princes and cities assembled, in October, 1529, at Schwabach. The cities of South Germany, inclining to the Swiss doctrine, refused to subscribe the above articles, on account of the doctrine of the presence of Christ in the eucharist, which is strongly expressed in them by Luther. These articles, adopted by the Smalcaldic league (q. v.), became thus a chief obstacle to a union between the party of Luther and Zuinglius.

SCHWABENSPIEGEL (i. e. *Mirror of the Suabians*); a collection of legal precepts and customs in Upper Germany, made probably between 1268 and 1282, by an unknown monk. It does not exist in its original form, as it was changed in many countries. It never acquired the same authority as the *Sachsenspiegel* (q. v.). It went out of use in the 15th and 16th centuries. It is best printed in Senkenberg's *Corp. Jur. Germ.*

SCHWARTZ, Berthold, born in the first half of the 14th century, was a Franciscan friar of Friburg, or, according to some, a monk of Cologne, and has been regarded as the inventor of gunpowder and fire-arms. He is said to have been mixing together the ingredients of gunpowder,—viz. nitre, sulphur and charcoal,—in an iron mortar, in the prosecution of some alchemical researches, when the composition exploded, from an accidental spark occasioned by the collision of the pestle and mortar. The former being driven forcibly to a distance, Berthold thence conceived the idea of forming pieces of artillery. Such is the story commonly told of the invention of gunpowder, said to have occurred in the early part of the 14th century. There is, however, much discrepancy in the accounts of this discovery; and it is certain that Roger Bacon (q. v.), who died in 1292, was acquainted with an inflammable composition similar to gunpowder, the knowledge of which Europeans appear to have derived from the Orientals. (See *Gunpowder.*)

SCHWARTZBURG, or SCHWARZBURG; a sovereign principality of Germany, in the interior of Thuringia, and bounded by Saxe-Gotha and the Prussian province of Erfurt. The house is very ancient, and is divided into two lines, Schwartzburg-Sondershausen, and Schwartzburg-Rudolstadt. In the diet, they have, with Oldenburg and Anhalt, one vote (15th), and in the *plenum* a vote each. The territories of both are hilly, interspersed with fertile valleys. The forests are extensive, and contain mines of iron, alum and cobalt; also quarries of marble, freestone and slate. The religion is Lutheran.

Schwartzburg-Rudolstadt lies further to the south, and borders on the grand-duchy of Saxe-Weimar. Rudolstadt (4000 inhabitants) is the chief town, and residence of the prince. The other principal towns are Frankenhausen and Ilmstadt. Population, 58,000, square miles, 400; revenue, 136,500 dollars; debt, 113,000. Rudolstadt has estates, but Sondershausen is an absolute government.

Schwartzburg-Sondershausen is almost surrounded by the Prussian province of Saxony. Sondershausen (3321 inhabitants) is the chief town, and residence of the prince. The other principal towns are Arnstadt, Breitenbach, and Graussen. Population, 48,106; square miles, 350; revenue, $170,000; debt, the same.

SCHWARTZENBERG, Charles Philip, prince of, Austrian field-marshal, born at Vienna, in 1771, served in the early wars of the French revolution, in which he distinguished himself on several occasions. In 1805, he was at the head of a division under general Mack, and at Ulm commanded the right wing of the Austrian forces. After the fortune of the day was decided, he forced his way through the enemy at the head of a body of cavalry. The battle of Austerlitz, at which he was present, was fought against his advice, before Bennigsen and the archduke Charles had come up. In 1808, Schwartzenberg was ambassador to the Russian court; and, in 1809, commanded the rear-guard after the battle of Wagram. In the campaign of 1812, he commanded the Austrian auxiliary corps of 30,000 men, in Galicia,—which, however, remained almost entirely inactive,—and at the close of the year, he received the marshal's staff. In 1813 he was appointed to command the army of observation in Bohemia; and after the declaration of war by Austria, prince Schwartzenberg was named generalissimo of the allied forces. (See *Dresden*, *Russian-German War*, and *Leipsic, Battle of.*) After Napoleon's return from Elba, he commanded the allied forces on the Upper Rhine; but the contest was decided at Waterloo (q. v.), without his participation. The prince died in 1820 Many of his military dispositions have been censured: and Napoleon declared that he could not command 6000 men.—See Prokesch, *Memoirs of Prince Schwartzenberg* (in German, Vienna, 1823).

SCHWARZ, or SCHWARTZ (German, *black*); an adjective which begins a great number of German geographical names.

SCHWARZWALD. (See *Black Forest.*)

SCHWEIGHÄUSER, John, one of the most distinguished German philologists, born at Strasburg, in 1742, became professor of the Greek and Oriental languages in that place in 1778. He published valuable editions of Polybius, Athenæus, Arrian, Epictetus, &c., and especially of Herodotus (6 vols., 1816). His academical writings were published in 1807 (2 vols.), and in 1824 appeared his *Lexicon Herodoteum* (2 vols.). He died in 1830.

SCHWEITZ, or SCHWYTZ; a canton of Switzerland, bounded N. W. and N. by Zug and Zürich, E. by Glarus, S. by Uri, and W. by Underwalden and Lucerne; population, 36,040, nearly all Germans, and Catholics; square miles, 336. It is surrounded by Alpine mountains, between which are a few valleys, tolerably fertile. The chief mountains are Mytten, 6300 feet high; Righi, 6000; and Pragel, 5500. The soil is better adapted to pasturage than tillage, and the wealth of the inhabitants consists in cattle. It was here that, in the beginning of the 14th century, the standard of Swiss liberty was first erected; and this petty canton had the honor of giving its name to the confederation. (See *Switzerland.*) The capital of the canton, of the same name, two miles from lake Lowerz, is situated in a fertile valley, between the mountains of Mytten and Righi; population, 5000.

SCHWERIN. (See *Mecklenburg-Schwerin.*)

SCHWERIN, Kurt Christopher, count, Prussian field-marshal, was born in 1684, in Swedish Pomerania, and, after having served in the Dutch armies, entered the Prussian service in 1720, with the rank of major-general. Frederic II, who ascended the throne in 1740, esteemed him very highly, created him field-marshal, and count, and gave him the command of his forces in the Austrian succession war (1741). In 1756, he was again placed in command of one of the Prussian armies, and fell at the head of his troops, before Prague, in 1757. (See *Seven Years' War*; consult also Frederic's *Histoire de mon Temps.*)

SCILLY ISLANDS; a group of islands, situated at the western extremity of the English channel, about thirty miles westward of the Land's End, and belonging to the county of Cornwall. The islands are numerous; but six only of them are inhabited. The views from them are picturesque. The inhabitants are chiefly engaged in agriculture, in fishing, and in the manufacture of kelp. The crops principally raised are barley, pease and oats, with a small proportion of wheat. The number of inhabitants in all the islands is about 2000, of which St. Mary's, the largest, and best cultivated of the whole group, contains 1270.

SCIO (Chios, called by the Turks *Saki-Adassi*), one of the largest and richest islands of the Grecian archipelago, contains 392 square miles. It is separated from the continent of Asia on the east by a narrow strait (*Stretto di Capo bianco*), and has a healthy climate. But little attention is paid to raising grain or keeping cattle, but it produces abundantly silk, cotton, turpentine, marble, fruits, and particularly wine (Chian wine was celebrated even in antiquity), oranges, lemons and mastic (to the amount of eighty tons a year, valued at 800,000 piasters). The beauty of the females is celebrated. On this island, remains of ancient art are still to be seen; among others, the school of Homer, the fountains of Helen, the ruins of Delphinium, Cardamissa, and a temple of Neptune. The chief city, of the same name, on the eastern coast of the island, has a harbor, spacious, but very difficult of access, and about 20,000 inhabitants. The population of the whole island was estimated, before the Greek revolution, at upwards of 120,000; mostly Greeks. When Greece revolted, in 1821, the Sciots attempted to drive away the Turkish garrison. The Turks threw themselves into the citadel, and continued the contest with the inhabitants till 1822, when a Turkish fleet landed, under the command of the capudan pacha, and a massacre began, in which, after many thousands had fallen in battle, from April 14 to 20, 40,000 persons, without distinction of age or sex, were put to the sword, and some of them cruelly tortured. The fugitives escaped to the mountain fastnesses or to the opposite continent, or, in Greek vessels, to the other islands. At length the Greek fleet attacked the Turks, and destroyed several of their vessels with fire-ships. The capudan pacha was obliged to retreat, half consumed, from his ship lying in flames, and to land upon the shore, where he had, a short time before, murdered the innocent without compunction, and where he now perished in the greatest tortures. But the Greeks were not strong enough to occupy the island, and the vengeance of the Turks now assailed the mastic villages, the people of which had remained quiet during the revolution. June 19, 1822, these villages were burnt, and 30,000 Christians murdered or sold into slavery. In March, 1823, the population of the island was only 16,000. Scio from that time has remained under the dominion of the Turks. Fabvier's attempt to reconquer Scio, in 1827, failed. A part of the unhappy Sciots fled to the ships of the French admiral De Rigny.—Before the devastation of Scio, there was a school in its chief city, and it was the see of a Greek and Roman bishop. It has been lately reported that the sultan had ordered the restoration of the property and estates of the Sciots without reservation. In 1770, a naval engagement took place between the Russians and Turks, between this island and Tschesme, which lies on the opposite coast of Natolia; a part of the Turkish fleet was burned by the Russians.

Scioto; a river of Ohio, the second in size of those which have their whole courses in this state. Its general course is south; its length about 170 miles; and it flows into the Ohio river by a mouth 150 yards wide, between Portsmouth and Alexandria. It is navigable for boats about 130 miles, and is connected with the Sandusky by a portage four miles long. The country watered by this river is known by the name of the Scioto country, and is remarkably fertile. On the eastern bank, about five miles above Columbus, is an almost inexhaustible quarry of marble, which receives a good polish, and is of a beautiful gray color.

Scipio Africanus (the elder), Publius Cornelius. The Cornelian family was rich in great men, among whom the conqueror of the formidable Hannibal is particularly distinguished. His father, who bore the same name, fought without success, but not without honor, against the Carthaginians, in the beginning of the second Punic war. In the bloody engagement on the river Ticinus, in Upper Italy, the young Scipio, hardly sixteen years old, took an active part, and is said to have saved the life of his wounded father. From the still more fatal battle of Cannæ (B. C. 216), he escaped with the remains of the conquered army. The wreck of the cavalry, having assembled at Canubium, chose him for their commander, and he led them back to Rome. Here his remarkable firmness induced a company of young men of distinction, who had resolved to flee from Italy in despair, to remain and defend their country. With his drawn sword he stepped boldly among them, and threatened to kill whoever should refuse to take the oath that he proposed. Astounded by his boldness, they did as he desired, and aided to save Rome. Such spirit met with public honor. At the age of twenty, he was made curule edile, and, a few years after, was appointed proconsul in Spain. Here he overcame the enemy, not merely by his courage and conduct, but also by his magnanimity and kindness. His first successful enterprise of importance was the conquest of New Carthage. With great boldness, he attacked the city on the side washed by the sea, which was almost defenceless, and easiest to be surmounted, with 500 of the most courageous soldiers, who waded through the low water at ebb tide, took one of the gates by storm, and, while the troops who were to assail the city on the land side were storming other parts, the enemy were so terrified that they hastened into the castle, and quickly surrendered this hold also. The Africans who were taken he sold for slaves; the Spaniards received their liberty. This treatment made a deep impression on the latter, and they separated from the Carthaginians. He gained still more esteem among the warlike Celtiberians, by restoring the beautiful bride of the young prince Allucius, who was brought to him as a prisoner, and who had made a deep impression on his heart, as soon as he heard of her being betrothed to the prince. The ransom, which her overjoyed parents urged upon the conqueror, he bestowed upon the youthful pair. Allucius, as a token of his gratitude, immediately entered the Roman service with a body of chosen troops, and rendered important service. The next year, Scipio totally defeated Asdrubal, Hannibal's brother, notwithstanding his advantageous position, and compelled him to retreat to the Pyrenees. Thus the Carthaginians lost still more adherents in Spain. A near relative of Masinissa, king of Numidia, who was among the prisoners, he liberated, and conferred on him rich presents. This kindness procured for him the favor of the Numidian monarch, and led to the advantageous alliance which Rome soon after concluded with this powerful prince. The title of *king*, which the Spaniards offered to the victorious general, he steadfastly refused. He now labored to reduce the disaffected tribes in the interior of Spain. In the mean while, the Carthaginians collected a fresh army, which was led by Mago and Hanno. Scipio attacked them, and, after a long and bloody engagement, destroyed the greater part of them. The remainder, abandoned by their commanders, were allowed to retire undisturbed, in consequence of the intercession of Masinissa. Leaving his army in Spain, he now went to Africa, to induce Syphax, king of Massæsylia, to become the ally of Rome; in which he succeeded After his return, he chastised the cities which had revolted during his absence. A short time after, he was attacked by a disease, which nearly cost him his life, and induced several Spanish tribes to revolt again from the Romans; even two legions in his own army mutinied. But Scipio recovered, and by his energy and prudence quelled the disturbances. He also obtained possession, by negotiation, of the valuable city of Gades.—Thus the Carthaginians were wholly driven from Spain, and the greatest part of that country was subjected to Rome. The general entered Rome in triumph, amid the loudest acclamations of the people. Scarcely had he arrived, before he petitioned the senate for permission to conduct an army to Africa, that he might attack the enemy in their own country. In vain did Fabius Maximus exert his influence and eloquence to frustrate the design. Scipio was empowered to go to Sicily with an army and a fleet, in order, after mature deliberation on the means of effecting a landing on the coast of Africa, to execute the plan which he had formed. He arrived successfully at the island, and despatched his friend Lælius, with a detachment of troops and of the fleet, to the enemy's country. On landing, Lælius found the country almost destitute of soldiers, took and plundered several rich cities, laid waste the fields, and gained over Masinissa to the designs of Scipio. At the approach of the hostile fleet, he returned, laden with booty, to Sicily. Scipio now labored with redoubled activity to equip the troops for his great enterprise; and then hastened to the shores of Africa. His unexpected arrival spread terror among the Carthaginians, who were without an army or a good general. But they succeeded in detaching the powerful Syphax from the Roman alliance, and he came with an army of 60,000 men to their aid. Towards winter, the Romans, were forced to retire to a distance from the city by the superiority of the enemy: the negotiations for peace produced no result. The proconsulate of Scipio in Africa, therefore, was prolonged, till the war should be terminated. The following spring, the affairs of the Romans took a more favorable turn. The camp of Syphax was assailed, and his whole army destroyed; Asdrubal suffered a similar fate. The defeat was dreadful, and none escaped but the commanders, with a few attendants. Nevertheless, the Carthaginians collected a new army with wonderful rapidity; but it was equally unable to withstand the Romans. Masinissa, associated with Lælius, had again defeated Syphax, and taken him prisoner. The beautiful Sophonisbe, the daughter of Asdrubal, by whom Syphax had been gained over to Carthage, Masinissa longed to marry. Fearing the effect of her charms, Scipio commanded her to be brought to the camp as a Roman prisoner. To avert such a disgrace, the king persuaded her to swallow poison. An armistice was now brought about between the Romans and their enemies; but the latter violated it. Hannibal had returned from Italy, to save his country, if possible; but he had now only the wreck of his once formidable army. His spies, who fell into the hands of the Romans, Scipio ordered to be led through all parts of the Roman camp, and then suffered them to return. Hannibal wished for an interview with the Roman commander; and not far from Zama, the two greatest generals of their time met (B. C. 202). They approached each other, for the first time, in the presence of their respective armies. For a long time they gazed upon each other in silence; then Hannibal advised a peace, and spoke of the fickleness of fortune. Scipio required of the Carthaginians unconditional submission; Hannibal promised to give up all the foreign possessions. This was not satisfactory to the Roman; and the generals separated and prepared for an engagement. The two armies fought with ardor; but their strength was unequal. Scipio had an excellent and well-disciplined infantry, and the numerous and valiant cavalry of Masinissa. Hannibal's troops, on the contrary, were mostly raw soldiers, or mercenaries. These fled at the first onset, and the veterans alone defended themselves with firmness. Their general stood by their side, as usual, to encourage their exertions. The Romans assailed them in vain, till Masinissa and Lælius attacked them in the rear. They now gave way, and nearly all fell victims to their perseverance. Hannibal scarcely succeeded in saving himself. He now advised a peace, which was granted on very hard conditions. Scipio's return through Italy to Rome resembled a triumphal procession; every one was eager to see the conqueror. At the gate of the city he received the congratulations of his fellow-citizens; and then followed the most magnificent triumph which Rome had ever witnessed. The spoils were immense. 120,000 pounds of silver were carried in the procession, to be deposited in the public treasury. The columns which the Romans proposed to erect in honor of Scipio he declined, but received the surname of *Africanus*. After this, he discharged, in a praiseworthy manner, the office of censor; but he lost the favor of the people, because he defended with zeal the pretensions of the senate. Afterwards he became his brother's lieutenant, when the war broke out with Antiochus, king of Syria, and went to Greece, and thence to Asia. Here he had the misfortune to see his only son fall into the hands of the enemy. As Antiochus wished for peace, he sent ambassadors to the Roman commanders, and promised the afflicted father that his son should be restored without a ransom. Scipio declared that he accepted their offer with gratitude, but warned the envoys not to imagine that he could be thus bribed to violate his duty. Nothing but complete submission could purchase peace. Soon after, Scipio was taken sick, and obliged to leave the army. As soon as Antiochus heard of it, he sent back his captive son without any conditions. With tears of joy the father embraced him, and immediately sent his thanks to Antiochus, and advised him not to encounter the Romans; but his advice was neglected. Nevertheless, he procured the defeated king (B. C. 189) tolerable conditions of peace. After his return from Asia, Scipio retired into private life. Here he experienced with grief the ingratitude of his fellow-citizens. Cato the Censor, the inveterate enemy of the Scipios, by constant accusations, procured an order for Scipio to be brought before the public tribunal, to give an account of the money which he had received. He appeared, showed the people his accounts, and then tore them in pieces in their sight. "This is the day," he exclaimed with a firm voice and a calm countenance—"This is the day when Hannibal was beaten and Carthage overcome. Why waste the time in words; the gods expect us in the capitol. Follow me, Romans, and let us offer them our thanks." The people were filled with shame, followed him directly, and left the accusers in the forum alone. Notwithstanding this, Scipio was summoned before the tribunal a second time by his enemies. He did not appear, but left the ungrateful city and retired to his villa at Linternum. As he was still persecuted, and his rural quiet disturbed, Tiberius Gracchus, the eloquent tribune of the people, at length undertook his defence, and showed the Romans the baseness and injustice of their conduct. The persecutions now ceased; but Scipio soon fell sick, and died in his retirement. He told his wife to have these words engraved upon his monument: "Ungrateful country, thou shalt never possess my bones." He died three years after he had left Rome, in the year of the city 571 (B. C. 183). The same year, Hannibal, the most dangerous enemy of the Romans, died in Bithynia.

Scipio, Publius Æmilianus, surnamed Africanus the younger, son of the famous Paulus Æmilius, who conquered the powerful Perseus, king of Macedonia, was adopted by the son of the great Scipio. He began his public career at the age of thirty, when the Roman senate was about to despatch a new army to repress the disturbances in Spain. Exasperated by the constant failure of the wars against the Spanish tribes, the people obstinately refused to serve. At this juncture, Scipio came forward, and by a spirited and powerful harangue, made such an impression on the public mind, that a multitude of Romans of all classes voluntarily enlisted. B. C. 152, he accompanied the consul, Luc. Licinius Lucullus, to Spain, as legionary tribune, and, by his disinterestedness, courage, affability and firmness, gained the love and esteem of the army. He acquired peculiar respect by conquering a gigantic Spaniard, who had long irritated the Romans by his arrogant challenges. By his magnanimity and kindness he obtained more honorable victories over the hearts of the Spaniards. But Lucullus viewed the young hero with a jealous eye, and, in order to remove him from the army, commissioned him to obtain elephants from Masinissa, in Africa. He was entertained by the king with the greatest distinction, fully accomplished the object of his mission, and returned to Spain. A few years after this, he went to Africa a second time, at the commencement of the third Punic war, in the year of Rome 605; B. C. 149. He served under the consul M. Manlius Nepos, and, by his courage and vigilance, rendered important services to the cause of the Romans. When, owing to the negligence of the consul, the Carthaginians, in this campaign, suddenly fell upon the camp, Scipio saved the army from destruction by coming unexpectedly upon the rear of the enemy and forcing them to retire. A short time subsequent to this event, the same imprudent consul attacked Asdrubal in a position unfavorable for the Romans, and was obliged to retreat. Hotly pursued by the enemy, he would have suffered a great loss, had not Scipio confronted the pursuers with a body of 300 horse, and kept them in check till the rest of the troops had passed over the river. But a few hundred of the Roman foot-soldiers were still behind. No sooner had Scipio perceived their condition, than he hastened over the river with a detachment of cavalry, took possession of a piece of rising ground, attacked the enemy, and thus enabled the Romans to escape with only a trifling loss. He returned in triumph to the Roman camp, crowned by the grateful soldiers, who owed to him their safety, with a wreath of grass, woven on the place where they were rescued. By this proof of courage and conduct, Scipio gained universal esteem and admiration. Even the severe Cato was loud in his praise, and prophesied at his death, that by him alone could the proud rival of Rome, Carthage, be destroyed. Manlius, his commander, could not forbear to recommend the young hero, in the most emphatic manner, to the senate. Hence, the next year, contrary to the usual custom, he was unanimously chosen consul, and leader of the forces against the Carthaginians. Accompanied by Lælius, the worthy son of the Lælius renowned in the second Punic war, who was the intimate friend of the elder Scipio, and by Polybius, the Greek historian, he went a second time into a hostile country. Directly after his arrival, he rescued a large body of Roman soldiers, who were surrounded, and whose destruction appeared certain. Having beaten and driven back the hostile armies, he began to make serious preparations to reduce the city, which was extremely strong, and labored to cut off all the supplies of troops and provisions, both by land and sea. But his design was frustrated by the desperate efforts of the besieged. With incredible activity, the Carthaginians excavated a new harbor, and thus opened a connexion with the troops collected without the city. And, strange as it may seem, a new fleet of fifty ships was built, which violently attacked the fleet of the Romans; and, after a protracted and stubborn contest, the Romans gained no decisive victory. An attempt which they made to storm an important rampart near the city, totally failed, as the enemy, swimming through the intervening water, set fire to the Roman machinery, and repelled the Romans themselves with fire-brands. Some time after, indeed, the consul made himself master of this rampart, and kept possession of it; but he was unable to take the city that year, and the approach of winter put a stop to military operations. The next season, he attacked the hostile army, which was strongly intrenched, with a superior force, conquered and destroyed them. He then advanced against the city, and, after twenty days, the genius of the general, and the perseverance of the devoted troops effected the reduction of Carthage (q. v.) B. C. 146. Lælius, the valiant friend of Scipio, first ascended the walls of the city with his soldiers. With unparalleled fury the Carthaginians resisted the Romans, even after they had entered the city; and much blood was spilt before the conquerors could fully reduce it. By the express command of the Roman senate, this rival of Rome, once so powerful, was demolished and burnt. This spectacle affected Scipio to tears. He was honored with a magnificent triumph at Rome, after the war was terminated, and was surnamed the *younger Africanus*. After he had lived for some time as a private citizen, he was sent with other ambassadors to Egypt, to king Ptolemy Euergetes, where he was much admired for his genuine Roman moderation, and his noble thirst for knowledge. When he returned (B. C. 142) he was elected censor. In this office he frequently urged the degenerate Romans to return to the simplicity and frugality of their fathers; he even punished severely some respectable citizens for their extravagance. B. C. 134, he entered on his second consulship, in order to put an end to the war which had long been carried on with Numantia (q. v.), a bravely defended city in Spain. On his arrival in the enemy's country, his first labor was to reduce the disorderly and enervated troops to their former state of discipline. But before he could effect this, the year was gone, and Numantia still untaken. His term of command was therefore prolonged. Reinforced by troops and elephants, which were brought to him from Numidia by the young Jugurtha, afterwards the dangerous enemy of the Romans, he commenced the siege with great energy. For his conquest of this powerful city, a triumph was decreed to Scipio, and he received the surname of *Numantinus*. He suffered, like the elder Africanus, in the last years of his life, from the ingratitude of his countrymen, and made himself many enemies among the people by opposing the agrarian law. (See the article *Agrarian Laws*.) He retired, therefore, with Lælius, his constant friend, to an estate near Naples, and lived in tranquillity. But having returned to the city, and become suspected of aspiring to the dictatorship, he was found one morning dead in his bed, with marks of having been strangled. It was generally believed that his wife, Sempronia, a sister of the Gracchi, who were the ardent supporters of the agrarian law, had a share in the deed. Papirius Carbo and C. Gracchus, the tribunes of the people, were likewise bitter enemies of his. After Scipio's death, there was found in his house only two and a half pounds of gold, and less than thirty-two of silver, so great had been his liberality and moderation. He died B. C. 129, at the age of fifty-six years. All the Romans, who knew his great virtues, lamented his death. Like the elder Scipio Africanus, he was a Roman of the highest stamp; he united courage with magnanimity, wisdom with humanity, patriotism with moderation and forecast, and benevolence with unshaken probity.

Scire Facias; a judicial writ, most commonly used to call a man to show cause to the court, whence it issues, why execution of judgment passed should not be made out.

Sciron; a celebrated robber in Attica, who plundered the inhabitants of the country, and kicked them from the rocks into the sea while washing his feet. Theseus attacked him, and treated him as he treated travellers. According to Ovid, the earth, as well as the sea, refused to receive the bones of Sciron, which remained for some time suspended in the air, till they were changed into large rocks, called *Scironia Saxa*, situated between Megara and Corinth. Böttiger thinks he was the same as Procrustes (q. v.), and Sinis, or Scinis.

Scirpus; an old Latin name for the bulrush and other plants of that tribe, which, on account of their soft flexible stems, destitute of knots, are useful for tying things together or for making baskets. It is a very numerous genus. The common bulrush is frequent in clear waters, and about the borders of rivers throughout Europe; also in North America and New South Wales. The roots are thick and stout, creeping under water in the deep mud; stems four or five feet, or more, in height; naked, smooth, round, dark green, tough, and pliant, spongy within, useful for packing and thatching, and especially for platting into the bottom of chairs, their base inverted with several sheathing scales, partly ending in leafy points.

Scirrhus; a hard tumor in any part of the body, generally proceeding from the induration of a gland, and frequently terminating in a cancer.

Scissors. (See *Cutlery*.)

Sclavonia, a kingdom under the government of the emperor of Austria, is bounded on the west by Croatia, and separated, on the three other sides, by the Drave, Save and Danube, from Hungary, Servia and Bosnia. Under the Romans, it formed a part of Pannonia. It derives its present name from the Sclavi, who settled there in the seventh century. In the tenth century, it came under the dominion of Hungary, and, in 1526, under that of the Turks; but was subjected to the house of Austria by the peace of Carlowitz, in 1699. It contains 6530 square miles, and is traversed from one extremity to the other by a chain of mountains which rise in Croatia, and run from the west to the east. It abounds in forests, which is the cause that the climate is cooler than might be expected in this latitude. In fertility of soil, Sclavonia is equal to Hungary, with the exception of the mountainous districts. Its productions are, besides poultry and the common domestic animals, venison, fish, bees, a great quantity of silk, corn (although agriculture is still very backward), melons, tobacco, and an abundance of wine. Fruit is produced in great abundance, particularly plums, of which brandy is made, and a great quantity of nuts: both articles are exported largely, particularly the plums, which form a principal article of consumption and trade. There are, likewise, considerable forests of oaks, which are used for tanning; and likewise forests of chestnuts. The mountains, most probably, contain minerals; but there is no mining carried on. Mineral springs are abundant: coals have likewise been found. The inhabitants (528,000) belong, for the most part, to the Sclavonian stock; but there are, likewise, many Magyars, Walachians, Gypsies, Germans, Greeks, Jews and Armenians. The Roman Catholic, the Greek Catholic, and the Greek non-united church, are the most numerous religious denominations. There are but few Protestants. Manufactures are almost entirely unknown amongst the inhabitants. Until 1745, the country was only divided into military districts, but since that time a beginning has been made towards giving some of them a civil constitution. These form three counties. The military district, or generalate, consists of Brod, Peterwaradin and Gradisca. It is under a military government, at the head of which is the commanding general in Sclavonia, who resides at Peterwaradin. The counties are subject to the kingdom of Hungary, and each has its governor and vice-governor. Most of the citizens of the towns, as also the peasants, are bondmen. Many of the proprietors of estates possess domains containing from 84 to 335 square miles.

SCLAVONIANS (from *slava*, fame); one of the two European families of nations which have retained their original character. Later than the Germans, the Sarmatians (q. v.) emigrated from Asia to Europe. From them descended, according to Ptolemy, the Wends, who extended themselves, in the fourth century, into the great plains along the Vistula, and contended with the Goths in the neighborhood. Jornandes, an author of the sixth century, says, that the Wends were divided into several branches, of which the most general names were *Sclavini* and *Antes*. Hence he distinguishes three tribes of one stock, by the names *Veneti*, *Antes* and *Sclavi*. The name of the chief branch, *Wends*, remained peculiar to the nations which afterwards inundated the north-eastern countries of Germany: the Sclavonians occupied the country between the southern bank of the Vistula and the Dniester; the Antes between the Dniester and Dnieper. The irruption of the Huns into Europe freed them from the yoke of the Goths, and the death of Attila from that of the Huns. They were afterwards urged by the same impulse which impelled the German tribes to the south and west, while at the same time Scythian or Mongolian-Tartar hordes came down upon them, almost uninterruptedly, from the Wolga and the Caucasus, and drove them from the northern banks of the Black sea, some to the north, and others to the west. In the sixth century, the Wends, strictly so called (afterwards the Northern Sclavonians), took possession of the regions on the Elbe, which had been deserted by the Goths and Suevi, while the proper or eastern Sclavonians occupied the banks of the Danube to the Norican and Julian Alps. But the two tribes intermingled, and there arose two great Wendish Sclavonian unions; that in Great Croatia (East Bohemia, Silesia and Lodomiria), and that in Great Servia (Misnia, West Bohemia and Moravia). Under the yoke of the Franks and the Avars, they split into various bodies, which were united, about 623, by Samo, the Frank, into a powerful empire: but after his death, it again fell to pieces, and formed numerous waywodeships, from which arose new national names before the end of the sixth century. All this rests only on tradition. In the eighth century, St. Boniface led some Sclavonic tribes into the vicinity of Fulda, Bamberg, Würzburg and Bayreuth. In Bohemia reigned Libussa, the founder of Prague, about 722, and Przemisl, first duke of the Bohemians, afterwards called Czechen. The tribe of the Liaches (probably a branch of the Antes) retired from the eastern shore of the Danube to the Vistula, and, under the name of *Polijanes*, diffused themselves abroad in modern Poland. Branches of this race, the Pomeranians and Lutitzians, advanced to the north-eastern part of Germany (Pomerania, Lower Lusatia). The Wilzians, a branch of the Wends, spread from the Oder through the Mark to the other side of the Elbe; and the Sorbians, after 640, settled in the territory deserted by the Hermunduri, on the Upper Elbe (the present Misnia, as far as to the Saale), and the Havel. The Obotrites, still later, became powerful in modern Mecklenburg. The Wends contended, on the west, with the Thuringians and Franks. Charlemagne sought the alliance of some of these tribes, and conquered others. In the war with the Avars, he subdued the southern Sclavonic territories, Carinthia, Stiria and Carniola, where he and later emperors founded German margraviates. (See *Austria*.) The Northern Wends were subsequently driven, by the Saxon kings of Germany, beyond the river Elbe; and in the tenth century were formed the margraviates of Misnia, Lusatia and Brandenburg. About the same period, the Antes, who still remained at the mouth of the Danube, were exterminated by the irruptions of the Avars, Bulgarians, Hungarians, and others, or driven to distant lands. The name of *Antes* disappeared. Probably some of this race retired to the Dnieper and to the Wolchow. On the former they built Kiev, and on the latter Novgorod, the two Sclavonic pillars of the Russian state. (See *Russia*.) The proper Sclavi maintained their position on the northern bank of the Danube, and often invaded and devastated the Roman provinces, defended their independence against the Bulgarians and Avars, received emigrants from Great Servia and Great Croatia, and, in connexion with them, founded Sclavonic settlements in Dalmatia (see *Dalmatia*, and *Illyria*), Servia, Croatia and Sclavonia. On the fall of the kingdom of Great Moravia, at the close of the ninth century, that of the Obotrites arose (in Lauenburg, Mecklenburg, &c.), under king Gottschalk (he was assassinated in 1066), and king Henry (he died 1126), till, in the twelfth century, it was conquered, partly by Saxon dukes (see *Henry the Lion*), and partly by the Danish kings. Bohemia (q. v.) retained its Sclavonic line of princes, but acknowledged the sovereignty of the German emperors till 1306. Russia and Poland (q. v.) slowly unfolded into independent states; while, on the other hand, the Sclavi on the Danube, the Sclavonians, Bosnians and Croatians, were never powerful, but almost always in subjection to the adjacent nations—the Greeks, Hungarians, Venetians and Turks. Meanwhile, centuries of emigration and war had transformed the democratic governments of the Wendish (Sclavonic) tribes into limited monarchies. Their first princes were the oldest members of the tribe; afterwards, the leaders of their armies, styled *gospodin*, or *hospodar*, *knees*, *waywode*, *ban*, *kral*, &c. The heathen priests exercised a great authority over the rulers, and the high priests at Arcon, on the island of Rűgen, governed all the Wendish tribes. The principal deity of the Sclavonians was called *Bog*, and his wife *Siwa*. They also worshipped good spirits (*Belbog*) and evil spirits (*Czernebog*). Almost every village had its divinity. At Rűgen, Swantewit was chiefly revered; the Obotrites worshipped Radegast; the Havlers, Herowit. Among the apostles of the Sclavonians, in the ninth century, Cyril (q. v.) and Methodius are worthy of notice. As the kings of the Sclavonians were hereditary monarchs, and all the nobles might be said to participate in the government, the common people became, gradually, more and more oppressed, and sunk, at length, into complete slavery. They remained, after a dreadful war, in the same condition under their German conquerors, who forcibly introduced Christianity among them in the tenth and eleventh centuries. After the fall of Henry the Lion, however, in 1180, some Wendish princes succeeded in holding their lands as immediate vassals of the emperor. Pribislaw, the son of Niklot, the last Wendish king of the Obotrites, assumed the title of prince of Mecklenburg, from the ancient capital of his country; and his posterity still reign in Schwerin and Strelitz. Thus the family of Niklot, in Mecklenburg, is the only Sclavonic (Wendish) house of princes remaining in Europe. Bogeslaw and Casimir maintained themselves as princes of the empire in the duchies of Pomerania, from the Oder to the Vistula. In Pomerania Proper, the Wendish house of princes, notwithstanding many divisions, did not become extinct till 1637. German colonists settled in the Wendish territories, which were depopulated by war; and thus their language and manners, in a great measure, disappeared (partially as early as the fifteenth century, e. g. on Rűgen); but bondage still remains. The old Wendish stock, however, has maintained its existence in several parts of Eastern Germany, as in Lusatia and Altenburg. Since the fall of the Wendish empire, the name of Sclavonians has become more general. The inhabitants of Poland, Galicia, Russia, Bohemia, Moravia, Sclavonia, Servia, Bosnia, Croatia, Illyria and Dalmatia, are still, in a great measure, Sclavonians. The whole number of them is estimated at 50,000,000. Five millions of these belong to the southern Sclavonians; and their dialect is called *Illyrian*, or *Servian*. The Servians (Rascians) are, next to the Czeches, the most civilized and powerful of all the southern Sclavonians, zealous friends of the Greek church, and brave defenders of their rights.—Surowiecki describes the Sclavonians as a nation employed wholly in agriculture and the raising of cattle, and who fight only in self-defence. The Sclavonians, in general, are courageous, lively and hospitable, attached to their national manners and national fame. Though fond of spirituous liquors, they are diligent and intelligent; but in mental cultivation they have remained, with the exception of the Bohemians and Ragusans in the middle ages, behind the Germans, because they are scattered over a wide extent of country, and have comparatively little intercourse with other nations, are engaged in frequent wars, and have unfavorable institutions of government. The Sclavonic government has been, at all times, a republican oligarchy. The different tribes were subject to chieftains (called *zupany* and *woiwody*) and independent of one another. In no Sclavonic territory have feudal laws bound the inferior lords of the soil; no where has the right of property given industry and prosperity to the great body of cultivators who have remained always vassals; no where has the Roman code, or the civilization of the West, become deeply rooted; for the Germans, on whom the Sclavonians bordered, were the objects of their mortal hatred, being always hostile neighbors, and often their oppressors. There were some cities of Sclavonic origin, which carried on an active trade; as Novgorod, Kiev, Pleskow, in Russia (Dantzic, in Pomerelia, was of Danish origin; and the existence of Wineta, the splendid commercial city of the Wends, which was situated in Pomerania, on the river Divenow, near Wollin, was destroyed by the Danes, and then sunk in the sea, is extremely doubtful, according to Gebhardi's History of the Wendish-Sclavonic states); but no one of those cities had a long duration. Julin (now Wollin), in the tenth, eleventh and twelfth centuries, was a rich and populous mart, till, in the last part of the twelfth century, it was demolished by the Danes. Ragusa, the only Sclavonic republic, maintained its existence more than 1100 years—from 656 to 1806. It was, moreover, the first nurse of Sclavonic literature. With regard to the older history of this nation, we refer the curious to Surowiecki's valuable work, On the History of the Sclavonic Tribes (in the Polish language, Warsaw, 1824), where the author shows from Procopius, Jornandes and Sidonius, that the Sclavonians are the same with the Veneti.

Sclavonic Languages. The Sclavonic language, which, both in its roots and the words formed from them, bears a strong resemblance to the Greek, Latin and Teutonic, is spoken by more than sixty nations, from the countries on the east of the Adriatic sea, to the shores of the Icy ocean, and from the Elbe to the Russian islands of the Pacific. In all of the Sclavonic dialects appear traces of an early, though imperfect, civilization, to which the race had attained in its primitive seats. The Sclavonians are thus shown to have been acquainted, not only with agriculture and mining, but with navigation; and the civilization of the whole people was promoted by the intercourse which subsisted between the different cities. The origin of the Sclavonic language must be looked for in India: the Devanagari (see *Indian Languages*) has 56 letters; the old Sclavonic alphabet consists of 46; the Bohemian of 42. The religious rites of the Sclavonians resembled those of the Hindoos; and their women, like those of the latter, were accustomed to burn themselves on the funeral pile of their husbands. The Sclavonic has even yet preserved many roots of Indian origin. The Croatian traveller Brezowski declares that he was able to understand the Hindoos as far as to Cochin-China, and to render himself intelligible to them. The Sclavonians are divided, by their dialects, into two great classes To the first belong the Russians, Illyrians, Montenegrins, Bulgarians, Servians, Bosnians, Dalmatians, Croatians, and the Wends (q. v.) in Carniola, Carinthia, Stiria, and in the county of Eisenburg. To the second belong the Bohemians (Czechen, or Tschechen), Moravians, the Slowacs of Hungary (about 4,000,000), the Upper and Lower Lusatians, the Poles and Silesians. It is a disadvantage to Sclavonic literature, that no single dialect has prevailed as the literary language; and that, owing to the great extent of country over which the Sclavonic race has spread, and the diversity of its political and religious institutions, several dialects have become written languages. It is remarkable that the Sclavonians have preserved their national character, and have flourished to such a degree, when we reflect that they have been the first to suffer from the storms which have broke over Europe, from invading hordes of barbarians. They were exposed to the first fury, not only of the Teutonic nations, but also of the Tartars, Huns and Turks. The Sclavonians of Prussia, Brandenburg, Pomerania, Saxony, Altenburg, Misnia, and Silesia, yielded up their nationality only after a long struggle, and in consequence of the severest measures. Thus Frederic of Brandenburg prohibited the teaching of the Sclavonic language under pain of death, and introduced the German by force. The Lusatians still preserve their language and manners. According to Dobrowsky, the primitive Sclavonic is extinct. It was divided into two chief dialects—the Antian, or that of the Antes, or eastern Sclavonians, and that of the western Sclavonians, or the Sclavian. To the Antian stock belong, according to this author, three branches: the Russian (divided into the Great Russian and the Little Russian), the Servian and Croatian; and to the Sclavian, the three branches of the Bohemian, the Servian and the Polish. In general, the Sclavonic is less completely developed than the other European literary languages; but the Sclavonians were the first of the European races to translate the Bible into their mother tongue. The Russian and Polish languages comprise literatures of considerable value and extent. (See *Russian Language and Literature*, and *Polish Language and Literature*, under the heads *Russia* and *Poland*.) The Servian (q.v.) or Illyrian language has recently received new cultivation. The Sclavonic dialects of Bosnia and Bulgaria differ little from the Servian. The Carinthian, or Wendish dialect, and the Slowac in Moravia, are nearly related to the Bohemian. The Wendish, in Lusatia, is a mixture of Polish and Bohemian; but in Lower Lusatia it is very different from those and from the Servian. The Bohemian has reached a high degree of cultivation. Prague is the central point of the literature. (See *Bohemian Language and Literature.*) In Schaffarick's History of the Sclavonic Language and Literature, according to its Dialects (Buda, 1826), the author adopts the following division: *A.* The South-Eastern Sclavonic, comprising first, the old Sclavonian, or ecclesiastical language; second, the Russian language and literature; third, the literature and language of the Sclavo-Servians of the Greek church; fourth, the language of the Catholic Sclavo-Servians, with the literature of Ragusa; fifth, the Wendish language and literature; principal dialect, that of Lower Carniola. *B.* The North-Western Sclavonic: first, the Bohemians, or Czeches; second, Slowacs in Hungary; third, Poles; fourth, the Sorbians, or Wends, in Lusatia.

Sclerotica, in anatomy; one of the tunics, or coats of the eye. (See *Eye.*)

Scomber. (See *Mackerel.*)

Scone; a village of Scotland, a little above Perth on the Tay. It was formerly the residence of the Scottish kings, the place of their coronation, and the scene of many historical events. There was formerly an abbey here. The remains of the palace are now incorporated with the mansion of the earl of Mansfield.

Scoresby. (See *North Polar Expeditions.*)

Scorpion (*scorpio*); a formidable insect, allied to the spider, but differing essentially in form. The body is elongated, and terminates abruptly in a jointed tail, armed at the extremity with a curved and very acute spine: under the point of this spine are two very small orifices, which serve to give passage to a poisonous fluid. The anterior pair of feet, or *palpi*, are very large, resembling those of the lobster in form, and serve to seize, and bear to the mouth of the animal, the various insects on which it feeds: the other feet do not differ essentially in form from those of the spider. At the junction of the thorax and abdomen, are two movable plates, having the form of combs, the use of which is not well understood. Several species of scorpion are known, all inhabiting the warmer parts of the globe. They shun moisture, living on the ground in places exposed to a hot sun, and hiding under stones, or in crevices, and, when disturbed, run, rapidly, with their tails curved over their backs. The species of the south of Europe are little more than an inch in length, while some of the tropical species exceed five inches. The sting of the larger ones is very much dreaded, and is said frequently to cause death. In some places, they are so numerous as to become a constant object of apprehension to the inhabitants, and even force them to abandon their habitations. The scorpions may be divided into two sections, viz. those with eight eyes, and those which have only six, like the species which inhabit the Southern States.

Scotia, Nova. (See *Nova Scotia.*)

Scotists. (See *Duns*, and *Scholastics.*)

Scotland; a country of Europe, united with England and Wales, which forms the northern division of Great Britain. It is bounded W. by the Atlantic ocean, N. by the Deu-Caledonian or North sea, E. by the German ocean, S. E. by England, S. by the Solway frith, and S. W. by that part of the Irish sea called the North channel. It is situated between 54° and 59° N. lat. (including the Shetland and Orkney islands, 61° 12′), and between 1° and 5° W. lon. Its greatest extent from north to south is 244 miles; but a direct line from Carlisle northward to the Moray frith, does not exceed 180 miles. From the Mull of Cantyre, the western coast stretches 230 miles, in a straight line, to cape Wrath. The breadth, under different parallels, is various, from 147 to 70, and even 36 miles. Area of Scotland and its isles, 29,600 square miles, or 18,944,000 English acres; of which 5,043,450 are cultivated, and 13,900,550 uncultivated lands; besides 638 square miles occupied by lakes and rivers. Population in 1821, 2,093,456. Of 447,960 families, 130,699 were employed in agriculture, and 190,264 in manufactures and commerce. The census of 1831 gave the population 2,365,700. In 1801, it was 1,599,068; in 1755, 1,265,380. Scotland is divided into the following counties, viz. Berwick, Roxburgh, Selkirk, Dumfries, Kirkcudbright, Wigton, Ayr, Renfrew, Lanark, Peebles, Haddington, Edinburgh, Linlithgow, Stirling, Dumbarton, Clackmannan, Kinross, Fife, Forfar, Perth, Argyle, Kincardine, Aberdeen, Banff, Elgin, Nairn, Inverness, Ross, Sutherland, Caithness, Cromarty, Orkney islands, and Bute. These are subdivided into 910 parishes. Scotland is of a most diversified surface. In the northern parts it is mostly mountainous and barren, while towards the south it extends into fertile plains. It has been separated into the two great divisions of the Highlands and the Lowlands, and also into the Northern, the Middle, and the Southern. The first or Northern division is cut off from the Middle by the chain of lakes which stretch from the Moray frith to Loch Linnhe. The second or Middle division is separated from the Southern by the friths of Forth and Clyde, and the Great canal. The Northern division consists generally of an assemblage of vast and dreary mountains, with some fertile valleys intervening, chiefly towards the south and east coasts. A portion of them is clothed with green herbage, more especially where sheep farming prevails; but in general they are covered with heath, vegetating above peat, rock, or gravel; and they frequently terminate in mountain caps of solid rock, or in vast heaps or cairns of bare and weather-beaten stones. The Middle division is also very mountainous, the Grampian ranges intersecting this district, and extending from the Eastern to the Western sea, and being from forty to sixty miles in breadth. The western parts of Argyleshire, which are also included in this district, are rugged, mountainous, and deeply indented by inlets of the sea. In these two divisions, which comprehend more than two thirds of Scotland, the arable ground bears but a small proportion to the mountainous regions. On the eastern coast, the proportion of the cultivated to the uncultivated land is much greater. In the Southern division we find every variety—verdant plains, well watered, and covered with cattle; gently-rising hills and bending vales, fertile in corn, waving with wood, and interspersed with meadows; lofty mountains, craggy rocks, deep narrow dells and tumbling torrents; nor are there wanting, as a contrast, barren moors and wild, uncultivated heaths. In this district are the different ranges of the Cheviot hills; the Sidlaw hills, terminating at Perth; the Ochil hills, forming the middle division; and a third, called the hills of Kilsyth and Campsey. Between the Sidlaw ridge and the Grampian mountains lies the extensive, pleasant and fruitful valley of Strathmore. Few countries in Europe display a greater extent of sea-coast. From Berwick, the coast bends north-west to the frith of Forth. The eastern part of Fife divides this frith from that of Tay. Northward, on the coast of Caithness, there is a vast bay of a triangular form, the base or eastern line of which is seventy miles. The north coast is bold, rocky and dangerous. Along the western shores are many openings or inlets, where the sea runs far inland, forming safe and commodious harbors. Scotland has numerous rivers, the chief of which are the Spey, the Dee, the North and the South Esk, the Tay, the Forth, the Clyde, the Tweed, the Southern Dee, the Annan, and the Liddal. The lakes or lochs are numerous and extensive. Scotland has no mines of the precious metals, but the lead mines contain silver. Ironstone, iron ore, and septaria ironstone, are abundant. Copper has been discovered in many places. The other metallic substances hitherto discovered are cobalt, bismuth, manganese, wolfram, plumbago, and mercury; the latter in very small quantities. Coal is abundant in the Southern and Middle districts. Limestone, freestone or sandstone, and slate, are found in every district. Marbles are also found. The Scotch pebbles are of many beautiful hues, blue and white, red and white, and frequently of all these colors, blended together in veins, and in every gradation of shade. Jasper is also found in great variety; and rock crystal, commonly denominated *cairngorm*, from the mountain of that name in Banffshire. Chalcedony is likewise found. The nature of the soil is various. There are many valleys or straths, even in the Highlands, which are exceedingly productive; and the southern and middle districts contain excellent land, and are as productive as any in the island. Scotland produces wheat, rye, barley, oats, peas, beans, hay, potatoes, turnips, &c.; flax and hemp, but in no great quantities; and, in general, all the sorts of crops which are raised in the southern part of the island. Horticulture is making rapid increase in every part Apples and other fruits are produced in abundance. Of late, many extensive tracts of waste land have been planted with wood. The *alga marina*, or sea-weed, constitutes a valuable article of commerce, from the burning of it into kelp. The climate of Scotland is extremely variable. From its insular situation, however, the cold in winter and the heat in summer are not so great as in similar latitudes on the continent. The greatest height of the thermometer that has ever yet been observed is 92° of Fahrenheit, and the lowest at Edinburgh is 3° below zero. Its ordinary range is from 84° to 8°, though it seldom maintains these extremes for any length of time. The annual average temperature may be estimated at from 45° to 47°. Like most other mountainous countries, it is subject to rain, especially on the western coasts. The general average quantity of rain that falls appears to be from 30 to 31 inches. The wild animals of Scotland are the fox, the badger, the otter, the wild-cat, the hedgehog (these are now becoming scarce), the stag, the wild roe, the hare, the rabbit, the weasel, the mole, and other small quadrupeds. The domestic animals are the same as those of England; but the native breed of black cattle and sheep is considerably different, being smaller in size, but reputed to afford more delicious meat. Of the feathered tribe, pheasants are to be found in the woods, though scarce; also that beautiful bird called the *capercailzie*, or *cock of the wood*, now become exceedingly rare; the ptarmigan, the black game, and grouse, are abundant in the heathy mountains; and in the low grounds are partridges, snipes, plovers, &c. Scotland has also most of the English singing birds, except the nightingale. The aquatic fowls are numerous in the islands. Scotland has made great advances in all the finer manufactures. Flax and hemp are manufactured into a variety of fabrics, such as sheetings, osnaburghs, bagging and canvass. The cotton manufactures have been carried, by means of machinery, to a great degree of extent and perfection. Muslins, brocades, lappets of all sorts, imitation shawls, gauzes, spidered, seeded, and numerous species of draw-loom, cambrics, shirtings, sheetings, stripes, checks, pullicates, ginghams, shawls, &c., are manufactured. Cotton is also made into thread, of which large quantities are exported. Glasgow, Paisley, and the surrounding districts, are the chief seats of the cotton manufacture, which gives employment to 150,000 persons, and of which the annual value is £6,000,000 sterling. Calico-printing is also carried to a great extent. The great iron-works established in Scotland deserve particular attention, and that at Carron, near Falkirk, is the largest manufactory in Europe. Ship-building also forms an important branch of national industry; and there are manufactories of glass for all the different sorts of bottle, window, and flint glass; also of soap, candles, and starch, salt, &c. There are tanneries, breweries, and distilleries, and almost all articles of ordinary use are manufactured in Scotland. The whole manufacturing product is estimated to exceed in value £14,000,000 sterling (including the raw material), employing nearly 300,000 persons. The different fisheries have been prosecuted with great industry and success. The whale fishery, to Davis's straits and Greenland, employs a great number of ships. The white fishery is also prosecuted with great industry along the Moray frith, Shetland, and the Western islands, and yields profitable returns. The herring fishery is carried on along the whole coast of the kingdom with great success, as is also the salmon fishery in all the different rivers. From the ports on the eastern coast of Scotland, a great trade is carried on to Holland, Norway, Sweden, and the different states on the Baltic. This trade has greatly increased of late years. The imports principally consist of flax, hemp, yarn, linen, iron, corn, wood, tallow, and other commodities produced in these countries; and, in return, colonial produce, cotton goods, and other manufactured articles, are exported. The chief shipping ports are Leith, Dundee, Arbroath, Montrose, Aberdeen, Peterhead, Banff and Inverness. The trade with Spain, Portugal, and the Mediterranean, is carried on from Leith and other ports; and the connexion with Canada extends to all the most considerable towns on the east coast of Scotland. The commerce of the west coast centres almost entirely in the Clyde, which is the grand emporium of the American, West Indian, and South American trade. Several vessels have sailed from Greenock, to carry on the trade to India, since, by the relaxation of the company's monopoly in 1814, it was partially thrown open to the merchants of this country. The principal canals—the Caledonian canal, the Forth and Clyde canal, &c.—are described in the article *Canal*, under the division *Canals of Great Britain*. (See also *Rail Roads*.) The inhabitants of Scotland may be divided into two great classes, viz. Highlanders and Lowlanders. The language, dress and customs of these two classes are very different. The language of the Highlanders is that species of the Celtic called, in Scotland, *Gaelic*, or *Erse*. The ancient dress of the Highlanders is fast giving way to a more modern costume, although it is still retained in many places, and often worn on particular occasions. (See *Highlands*.) It is formed of woollen stuff, checkered with different colors, well known by the name of *tartan*. The inhabitants of the low country more resemble the English in their dress and manners, though in the country parts some peculiarities remain. The language of the low country is English, with a mixture of the Scotch, which, however, in the ordinary dialect of the better classes more especially, is fast giving way to the English. The Presbyterian system of religion was established in Scotland by act of parliament, in 1696, and was afterwards secured in the treaty of Union. This system is founded on a parity of ecclesiastical authority among all its presbyters, excluding all preëminence of order, all its ministers being held equal in rank and power. It is also exceedingly simple in its forms, admitting of no outward splendor or ceremony, nor of any of those aids to devotion which are supposed to be derived from painting or music. There are in Scotland 910 parishes, and 938 established clergymen, who discharge the duties of the pastoral office in their several parishes. They are assisted by elders, who are selected from their congregation for the propriety of their conduct; these, with the minister, compose a kirk session, which is the lowest ecclesiastical judicature in Scotland. The ministers of several contiguous parishes constitute what is called a presbytery, which has cognizance of the conduct of the clergy, and of all ecclesiastical matters within its bounds. Synods form the next gradation in the scale of ecclesiastical judicature. They are composed of several presbyteries, and of a ruling elder from every kirk session within their bounds. They are courts of appeal, and review the procedure of the presbyteries. The general assembly, which is a representative body, consists of delegates from presbyteries, universities, and royal boroughs, in the following proportions, namely, for the presbyteries, 200 ministers and 89 elders; for royal burghs, 67 elders; and from the universities, 5 ministers or elders; in all, 361. Besides the Presbyterians (the established religion), there are numerous dissenters, namely, the Episcopalians, Burghers and Antiburghers, Quakers, Bereans, Baptists, Glassites, &c. There are Catholic churches in the principal towns; and in the northern parts of Scotland this religion has not been entirely superseded by the reformation. Members of the established church, 1,638,484; seceders (also Presbyterians), 285,000; Roman Catholics, 70,000; Episcopalians, 40,000, &c. In no country is there, perhaps, more ample provision for education than in Scotland. An act, passed in the reign of William and Mary, ordains that there shall be a school and a school-master in every parish. These establishments, in which are taught reading, writing, arithmetic, and also Latin and Greek, have been attended with the happiest effects, having spread the spirit of improvement among all classes. (See *School*.) Scotland has also four universities, namely, at Edinburgh, St. Andrews, Glasgow, and Aberdeen. The ancient constitution of Scotland was superseded at the time of the union with England. In the parliament of England, the Scots nobility are represented by sixteen peers. In the house of commons, the freeholders of the counties, amounting to about 2429, are represented by thirty commissioners or knights of the shire. The royal burghs, which are sixty-five in number, exclusive of the city of Edinburgh (which sends one member), are divided into fourteen districts, which return as many members, elected by a delegate from each burgh. (See *Parliamentary Reform*, end of last volume.) Scotland, however, still retains her own ancient laws and institutions. Civil and criminal justice is administered by the college of justice, instituted by James V, in 1532, after the model of the French parliament. It is the highest court in Scotland, and consists of a president and fourteen ordinary lords. In 1807, the court of session was formed into two divisions, the first, consisting of seven members, under the lord-president; the second division, under the lord-justice clerk, consisting of six members. In 1815, a jury court was established, under a lord chief commissioner and two other commissioners, for the trial of civil cases. The court of justiciary is the highest criminal court in Scotland. The court of exchequer has the same powers, privileges, jurisdictions and authority over the revenue of Scotland, as that of England over the revenue of England. In the high court of admiralty, there is only one judge, who is the king's lieutenant and justice-general upon the seas, and in all ports and harbors. He has a jurisdiction in all maritime causes; and, by prescription, he has acquired a jurisdiction in mercantile causes not maritime. The commissary court consists of four judges, nominated by the crown, and has an original jurisdiction in questions of marriage and divorce, and reviews the decrees of local commissary courts. Besides the above national judges, every county has a chief magistrate, called a sheriff, whose jurisdiction extends to certain criminal cases, and to all civil matters which are not, by special law or custom, appropriated to other courts. In cases of inferior importance also, the magistrates of cities and royal burghs have a jurisdiction which is subject to the review of the sheriff. (For further details, see the article *Scotland*, in Brewster's New Edinburgh Encyclopædia.) The earliest inhabitants of Scotland belonged, probably, to the great Celtic race. The Romans, who had reduced the southern part of the island of Britain fifty years before the Christian era, extended their conquests, about 130 years later, into the more northern part of the island, inhabited by the Caledonians. (See *Gaul*.) Agricola forced the natives back beyond the estuaries of the Forth and the Clyde, and the remains of Roman roads and stations still serve to trace the steps of the conquerors. Adrian (120) constructed a wall across the island, from the Tyne to the Solway, and, in the reign of Antoninus, a more northern wall was erected from the Forth to the Clyde. At a later period, the principal inhabitants of Caledonia (as the northern part of Scotland was called) were the Scots and Picts, the former of whom came from Ireland, and finally gave their name to the country; the latter were apparently of Gothic origin, but we have no knowledge of their earlier history. (See *Scots*.) Kenneth Macalpine joined in his person the crowns of the Picts and Scots, or Dalriads, as they are commonly called, and was, therefore, the first king of Scotland (843). Christianity appears to have been introduced into Scotland by Irish monks, in the sixth century. Malcolm III (1057—1093), son of Duncan (see *Macbeth*), was educated at the Saxon court, and had married a Saxon princess. The Norman conquest, also, carried many Saxon fugitives into Scotland, and a great change in the manners of the Scotch was produced by this connexion with a more civilized people. On the death of Alexander III (1284), the male line of the old race of kings became extinct, and Edward I of England began to lay schemes for extending his sway over this part of the island. Sir William Wallace (q. v.) perished on the scaffold; but Bruce (q. v.) achieved the independence of his country, by the battle of Bannockburn (1314). The Bruce male line became extinct in 1371, and the Stuart (q. v.) family ascended the Scottish throne. James I (q. v.), an accomplished prince, who endeavored to curb the power of the licentious nobles, and to promote the civilization of his dominions, was murdered by the nobles (1437). James II, his infant son, succeeded him, and pursued the plan of restraining the barons with vigor and success. James III ascended the throne at the age of seven years: his reign was not less inglorious than his end. His immoderate attachment to minions, and his tyrannical conduct towards all classes, excited a rebellion, in which he was defeated and slain. James IV (1488), a brave and able prince, whose marriage with Margaret, daughter of Henry VII, resulted in the ultimate union of the English and Scotch crowns, introduced improvements in the laws and government, and in the condition of the lower classes. He fell in the battle of Flodden (1513). James V, an infant (during whose minority the kingdom was torn by factions), by his marriage with Mary of Guise, united the Scotch court more closely with that of France; and, in addition to the troubles occasioned by the French and English interest, a new torch of discord was lighted at the flames which consumed the first reformers. Patrick Hamilton, the first who publicly embraced the doctrines of the reformation, was burnt in 1538; but the new doctrines gained adherents in spite of persecution (see *Beaton*), both among the people and the nobles, and the work was accomplished by the boldness and activity of Knox. (See *Knox*, and *Presbyterians*.) James died in 1542, and was succeeded by his daughter Mary (see *Mary Stuart*), who was betrothed to the dauphin of France, and educated in that country. Her hostility to the reformation laid the foundation of discontents, which, increased by her imprudent conduct, terminated in rebellion. Having fled for protection to England, she was beheaded at Fotheringay, in 1587. James VI (I of England; see *James I*) ascended the English throne on the death of Elizabeth, in 1603, and thus united the crowns of the two kingdoms, which were themselves united, one hundred years later (1707), into one monarchy. (See *Great Britain*.) Scotland retained a separate parliament until the act of union. The first kings of the Stuart family, on the English throne, endeavored to subvert the Presbyterian church in Scotland, and establish Episcopalianism on its ruins. These attempts gave rise to the solemn league and covenant (see *Covenant*), and contributed not a little to the fall of Charles I. (q. v.). Cromwell (q. v.) reduced Scotland to submission; but in the reign of Charles II (q. v.), new attempts to establish the Episcopalian form of church government gave rise to new troubles (1666 and 1676). Even after the revolution and union, the partisans of the Stuart dynasty twice rose in rebellion (1715 and 1745), against the house of Hanover (see *Stuart, James Edward*, and *Edward, Charles*); but since the middle of the last century, Scotland has been devoted to the arts of peace, and all kinds of industry have made a wonderful progress in that part of Great Britain.—See Buchanan's *History of Scotland*, from the Latin, with a continuation (4 vols., Glasgow, 1827); Tytler's *History of Scotland* (fourth vol., 1831, unfinished); and Scott's *History of Scotland* (2 vols.).

Scotch Language and Literature. The inhabitants of Scotland speak three different languages; the English, the Scotch, and the Gaelic. The English is spoken by all well educated persons in the kingdom, and is used in all deeds and prose works; and, although the pronunciation, and some peculiarities of dialect, generally betray the Scotch origin of the speaker, it is well known that some of the best writers and most eloquent orators in the English language during the last seventy years have been Scotchmen. The Scotch language, which is used by the lower classes in the Lowlands, and by some old persons of the higher ranks, is still employed in the national poetry. The Gaelic language is spoken in every part of the Highlands; but almost all Highlanders are acquainted with English, which is taught in their schools. (See *Highlands*, and *Ossian.*) The Scotch language has been commonly regarded as a corrupt dialect of the English; but doctor Jamieson has shown that it is a separate language, of Teutonic origin, with a strong mixture of Gaelic and French. He considers the Picts as a Teutonic race; and the fact that the topographical names in the north of Scotland, and in the Orkney islands, are of Gothic origin, strongly confirms the view. Neither has the Scotch been merely a dialect of the vulgar. It was formerly the language of a polished court, and a cultivated nation; and the earlier Scottish writings are much superior in delicacy to those of modern times. The study of polite literature was, some centuries ago, in a more advanced state in Scotland, than in many other countries, which afterwards surpassed it. Barbour, a Scottish historian and poet, prior to Chaucer, wrote in a style as pure, and with a versification as harmonious, as the latter. The poetical compositions of James I, and the work of James VI, containing precepts for writing Scottish poetry, with the numerous other productions still extant, show that much attention was paid by the court and the educated classes to the native language. The close connexion of the Scotch with the French courts introduced many of the terms of the latter. The Scottish is remarkable for its copiousness, and is well calculated to express the humorous, the plaintive, and the tender. Its power of terminations, especially in diminutives, is considerable, and it is often compared, for its simplicity, to the Doric of the Greeks. It drops final consonants, substitutes one for the other, and delights in a concourse of vowels. Apart from the peculiarly national literature of Scotland, to be found in the poetry of James I, of Douglas, Barbour, Ramsay, Burns, &c., she has contributed largely to the rich stores of English literature and science. In mathematical and physical science, the Gregorys, Maclaurin, Simpson, Black, Hutton, and Playfair, and in the practical arts, Watt, Rennie and Telford are distinguished. In history, the great names of Robertson and Hume, with those of Ferguson and Mackintosh; in philosophy, and criticism, Reid, Adam Smith, Campbell, Kames, Blair, Stewart and many others of the first eminence, show that in this provincial kingdom there has been no want of men of large views, of bold and original speculation, and of deep insight into the character of society, the workings of the human heart, and the more secret and subtile operations of the intellectual powers. In works of imagination it is only necessary to mention the names of Smollett, Mackenzie, Thomson, Armstrong, and sir W. Scott. The poems of Ossian, and the Waverley novels, have contributed to give to Scotland a romantic interest in all foreign countries, where the sorrows of the bard and the adventures of the Jacobite or Cameronian heroes are almost as familiar as on their own soil.—See Irving's *Lives of the Scottish Poets*, and Jamieson's *Dictionary of the Scottish Language* (2 vols., quarto, 1808), *Supplement* (2 vols., quarto, 1825), containing much curious matter, illustrative of the national rites, customs and institutions.

Scots. The Picts and Scots are first named in history in the fifth century. The former inhabited the eastern shores of Scotland as far south as the frith of Forth, and as far north as the island extended. The name of Picts seems to have been given them by the Romans, from their habit of staining their bodies when going to battle (*picti*, painted). They were probably of Gothic origin, though some think they were descendants of the ancient Caledonians, who were Celts mingled with Gothic settlers. The Scots, on the other hand, were of Irish origin. A colony of this people, from Ulster, settled on the coast of Argyleshire, under Fergus, about the year 503, and gradually occupied nearly the whole of the western coast of Scotland. After a long and bloody struggle between the two people, Kenneth II, king of the Scots, finally ascended the Pictish throne (843), and united the two states into one kingdom, comprising the whole country north of the wall of Antonine. (See *Scotland.*)

Scott, Michael; a celebrated Scottish philosopher, and reputed magician, of the thirteenth century. He made an early progress in the languages and the mathematics, and, after residing in France some years, repaired to Germany, and applied closely to the study of medicine and chemistry. On quitting Germany, he proceeded to England, and was received with great favor by Edward II. After his return to his native country, he received the honor of knighthood from Alexander III, by whom he was also confidentially employed. He died at an advanced age, in 1291. Michael Scott was a man of considerable learning for his time, and, being much addicted to the study of the occult sciences, passed among his contemporaries for a magician, and as such is mentioned by Boccaccio and Dante. He is supposed to have been buried in Melrose abbey, and his books were either interred in his grave, or preserved in the abbey. He is author of *De Secretis Naturæ; De Natura Solis et Lunæ;* On the Transmutation of Metals; *Mensa Philosophica*, a treatise replete with the visionary sciences of chiromancy and astrology. (See Mackenzie's *Lives.*)

Scott, Thomas, an eminent evangelical clergyman of the English church, born in 1747, in Lincolnshire, was the son of a farmer. After having acquired some acquaintance with classical learning, he was, at the age of sixteen, apprenticed to a surgeon and apothecary at Alford, in his native county. In this situation he staid only two months; and then, returning home, he was employed in his father's business. Having a strong inclination to enter into the church, he applied himself closely to study, and obtained a considerable knowledge of both the Latin and Greek languages. In 1773, he was ordained. Becoming acquainted with Mr. Newton, curate of Olney, he was converted to Calvinism, in the defence of which, both from the pulpit and the press, he greatly distinguished himself. In 1781, he removed to Olney, and, in 1785, to London, having obtained the chaplainship of the Lock chapel, near Hyde-Park corner. In 1801, he was appointed rector of Aston Sandford, in Buckinghamshire, where he died April 16, 1821. He published, in 1779, a tract, entitled the Force of Truth, 8vo., which was followed by several single sermons, and other works; but his principal productions are a Defence of Calvinism, against bishop Tomline; and a Commentary on the Bible, 6 vols. quarto.

Scott, sir Walter, bart., eldest son of Walter Scott, writer to the signet in Edinburgh, was born in that city, August 15, 1771. His mother, a friend of Burns and Allan Ramsay, was a lady of talent, and author of several small poems of considerable merit. He was educated at the high school of Edinburgh under doctor Adam, and at the university under professor Stewart. According to his own account, he had a distinguished character as a tale-teller, "at a time when the applause of his companions was his recompense for the disgraces and punishments which the future romance writer incurred for being idle himself, and keeping others idle, during hours that should have been employed on their tasks." It was the favorite amusement of his holydays to wander, with a friend of the same taste, through the solitary environs of Arthur's seat and Salisbury crags, reciting and listening to such wild stories as his own and his friend's imagination were able to devise. This truant disposition seems to have been increased by a long illness, the consequence of the rupture of a blood-vessel, at the age of fifteen, during which he was left to the indulgence of his own taste in reading, and, after having devoured all the romances, old plays, and epic poetry furnished by a considerable circulating library, his time was occupied in perusing histories, memoirs, voyages and travels. Two years spent in this manner, were followed by a residence in the country, in which he made the same use of a good library, to which he had access, that Waverley is represented to have done in a similar situation. Though lame from his birth, and early of feeble health, his health was afterwards confirmed; and, during the greater part of his life, he has been remarkable for his personal activity, and passionately fond of field sports. In 1792, having completed his preparatory studies, he was called to the bar; but his literary taste diverted his attention from the practice of his profession, which he soon abandoned for employments more agreeable to his inclinations. His patrimonial estate was also considerable, and, in 1800, he obtained the preferment of sheriff of Selkirkshire, of about £300 a year in value. In 1806, he was appointed one of the principal clerks of the session in Scotland. His first literary attempts were translations from the German ballad poetry, which first became known in Great Britain towards the close of the last century. In 1796, he published a volume containing a poetical version of Bürger's *Lenore*, and of the ballad of the Wild Huntsman (*Der Wilde Jäger*). This attempt he himself describes as a complete failure. His first original productions were several excellent ballads (Glenfinlas, the Eve of St. John, &c.), which appeared in Lewis's Tales of Wonder (1801). In 1802, appeared his Minstrelsy of the Scottish Border, a collection of ballads, ancient and modern, of the Border districts, with an introduction and notes (2 vols. 8vo.), which very much extended his reputation; to which succeeded, in 1804, Sir Tristram, a metrical Romance of the Thirteenth Century, by Thomas of Ercildoune, with a preliminary dissertation and glossary. Meanwhile, Mr. Scott had married, and taken up his residence at Ashiesteel, on the banks of the Tweed, about thirty miles from Edinburgh, "a delightful retirement," to use his own words, "in an uncommonly beautiful situation, by the side of a fine river, whose streams are favorable for angling, and surrounded by hills abounding in game." His first original work of considerable extent, was the Lay of the Last Minstrel (1805), which was received with universal applause, and was succeeded, two years after, by Marmion (1808), the appearance of which was hastened by the misfortunes of a near relation and friend. The Lady of the Lake (1810), the Vision of Don Roderick (1811), Rokeby (1812), Lord of the Isles (1814), Harold the Dauntless, and the Bridal of Triermain, the two latter of which appeared anonymously, with some other works of less merit, marked his brilliant poetical career. Upwards of 30,000 copies of the Lay were sold by the trade in England, previously to 1829, and of Marmion (for which the author received £1000), 36,000 copies were sold between 1805 and 1825; for the manuscript of Rokeby the publishers gave him £3000. If the success of his first productions is in some measure to be attributed, as the author himself modestly intimates, to the low state of poetry in Great Britain at the beginning of the present century, and to the substitution of the animated and varied octosyllabic verse, or romantic stanza, for the more cumbersome and stately heroic, yet the freshness, fire, and truth of description, the dramatic distinctness of the action and characters, the richness of the imagery, and the vivacity and poetical beauty of style which characterize them, would at any time have attracted attention, and won the admiration of the public. Mr. Scott was, during the period in which his principal poems appeared, also employed in editing the works of other authors. In his capacity of editor, he completed the Works of Dryden, with a Life of the Author, and Notes (18 vols. 8vo., 1808); Lord Somer's Tracts (12 vols., 1809 to 1812); Description and Illustration of the Lay of the Last Minstrel (1810); Sir Ralph Sadler's State Papers (2 vols. quarto, 1810); Poetical Works of Anna Seward (3 vols. 8vo., 1810); the Works of Jonathan Swift (19 vols. 8vo., 1814); and the Border Antiquities of England and Scotland, 4to. In 1811, he removed to Abbotsford, six or seven miles below his former residence, on the Tweed, where he purchased a farm of about 100 acres, for the purpose of having some more quiet out-door occupation than field sports. "The nakedness of the land," says he, "was in time hidden by woodlands; the smallest of possible cottages was progressively expanded into a sort of dream of a mansion house, whimsical in the exterior, but convenient within. Nor did I forget what is the natural pleasure of every man who has been a reader; I mean the filling the shelves of a tolerably large library." Here he has since continued to reside, exercising the most open hospitality, and receiving the homage of admiration from all parts of the world. His grounds have been very picturesquely, and, at the same time, profitably laid out, and his library amounts to about 15,000 volumes. But, in 1814, he already appeared in a new character—that of a novelist. Although the greater part of his romances were published anonymously, and he did not disclose the fact of his being the author until February, 1827, yet little doubt was previously entertained on the subject. A portion of Waverley was written as early as 1805, and announced under the title of Waverley, or 'Tis Fifty Years since. On account of the unfavorable opinion of a friend, it was thrown by and forgotten, until, about eight or nine years afterwards, the author accidentally discovered it in searching for some fishing tackle, and immediately set to work to complete it. The subsequent novels have come out in the following order: In 1815,

Guy Mannering; in 1816, the Antiquary, and Tales of My Landlord (consisting of the Black Dwarf and Old Mortality); 1818, Rob Roy, and Tales of My Landlord (2d series, consisting of the Heart of Mid Lothian); 1819, Tales of My Landlord (3d series, consisting of the Bride of Lammermuir, and the Legend of Montrose); 1820, Ivanhoe, the Monastery, and the Abbot; 1821, Kenilworth; 1822, the Pirate, and the Fortunes of Nigel; 1823, Quentin Durward, and Peveril of the Peak; 1824, St. Ronan's Well, and Redgauntlet; 1825, Tales of the Crusaders; 1826, Woodstock; 1827, Chronicles of the Canongate (1st series); 1828, Chronicles of the Canongate (2d series); 1829, Anne of Geierstein; and 1831, Tales of My Landlord (4th series). These works, rapidly as they were produced, were not only the fruits of his unaided genius, but the original manuscripts are entirely written in his own hand, excepting those of 1818 and 1819, when his illness obliged him to employ an amanuensis. Among his miscellaneous works, most of which are contained in the collection entitled Miscellaneous Prose Works of Sir W. Scott (6 vols., 1827), are Paul's Letters to his Kinsfolk (1815), giving an account of his visit to Waterloo, &c.; Essays on Chivalry, Romance, and the Drama, in the Supplement to the Encyclopædia Britannica; Lives of the Novelists; and contributions to different periodical works, &c. In 1820, he was created a baronet. In 1827, appeared his Life of Napoleon (9 vols.)—a work of partial views, and executed with too little care and research to add to the brilliant reputation of the author. The first, second, and third series of the Tales of a Grandfather, illustrative of events in Scottish history, The Letters on Demonology, and the History of Scotland (2 vols., 1830), close the long list of the works of this prolific writer. The revised editions of his poems and novels contain many interesting personal details, and sketches of his literary history, and some of them have been collected and arranged in this country, in a single volume, under the title of Autobiography of Sir Walter Scott, Bart. (Philadelphia, 1831). See likewise Peter's *Letters to his Kinsfolk*, by his son-in-law, Mr. Lockhart, from which we extract the following observations:—"His conversation is, for the most part, of such a kind, that all can take a lively part in it, although, indeed, none that I ever met with can equal himself. It does not appear as if he ever could be at a loss, for a single moment, for some new supply of that which constitutes its chief peculiarity and its chief charm; the most keen perception, the most tenacious memory, and the most brilliant imagination, having been at work throughout the whole of his busy life, in filling his mind with a store of individual traits and anecdotes, serious and comic, individual and national, such as it is probable no man ever before possessed; and such, still more certainly, as no man of original power ever before possessed, in subservience to the purposes of inventive genius. Never was any physiognomy treated with more scanty justice by the portrait painters; and yet, after all, I must confess that the physiognomy is of a kind that scarcely falls within the limits of their art. I have never seen any face which disappointed me less than this, after I had become acquainted with it fully; yet, at the first glance, I certainly saw less than, but for the vile prints, I should have looked for; and I can easily believe that the feelings of the uninitiated, the uncranioscopical observer, might be little different from those of pure disappointment. It is not that there is a deficiency of expression in any part of his face, but the expression which is most prominent is not of the kind which one who had known his works, and had heard nothing about his appearance, would be inclined to expect. The common language of his features expresses all manner of discernment and acuteness of intellect, and the utmost nerve and decision of character. He smiles frequently; and I never saw any smile which tells so eloquently the union of broad good humor with the keenest perception of the ridiculous; but all this would scarcely be enough to satisfy one in the physiognomy of Mr. Scott."

Scott, sir John. (See *Eldon.*)

Scott, sir William. (See *Stowell.*)

Scotus, Duns. (See *Duns.*)

Scotus, John. (See *Erigena.*)

Scougal, Henry, an eminent Scotch divine, born in 1650, was educated in the university of St. Andrews, where he became professor of Oriental philosophy at the age of twenty. In 1673, he was presented by his college to a living, but recalled the following year, and made professor of theology. His great exertions, both in this capacity and as a preacher, threw him into a consumption, and he died, greatly lamented, in 1678, at the early age of twenty-eight. He was the author of an eloquent and able work, entitled, The Life of God in the Soul of Man, which has run through many editions; and also of Nine Sermons, by which he acquired the reputation of being one of the most elegant writers and able divines of his country and age.

SCREW, in mechanics. (See *Mechanics.*)

SCREW PINE. The species of *pandanus* are all natives of the tropical parts of the eastern continent, and are among the most ornamental productions of the vegetable world. The *P. odoratissimus* is a large, spreading, branching shrub, with very long leaves, which are spiny on the back and margin, somewhat resembling in form those of the pine-apple, and which are disposed in three spiral rows round the extremities of the branches. It grows in all soils and situations in the tropical parts of Asia, and is much employed there for hedges. The tender white leaves of the flowers, chiefly those of the male, yield that most delightful fragrance, by far the richest and most powerful of the perfumes, for which they are so generally esteemed, and for which the plant is cultivated in Japan. The lower pulpy part of the drupe is sometimes eaten by the natives in times of scarcity, but the taste is very disagreeable; the tender white base of the leaves is also employed for food at such times. The leaves are composed of longitudinal tough fibres; and in the South Sea islands these or the leaves of some other species are used for making mats. In the Sandwich islands, the mats are handsomely worked in a variety of patterns, and stained of different colors. The plant is called *wharra* tree, at Otaheite.

SCRIBES, among the Jews, were officers of the law. There were *civil* and *ecclesiastical* scribes. The former were employed about any kind of civil writings or records. The latter studied, transcribed and explained the Holy Scriptures.

SCRIPTURE. (See *Bible*, and *Testament, Old* and *New.*)

SCROFULA, *scrophula;* (from *scrofa*, a swine; because this animal is said to be much subject to a similar disorder); a disease of children, consisting in hard tumors of the glands in various parts of the body, but particularly in the neck, behind the ears, and under the chin, which, after a time, suppurate, and degenerate into ulcers, from which, instead of pus, a white curdled matter is discharged. The first appearance of the disease is most usually between the third and seventh year of the child's age; but it may arise at any period between this and the age of puberty; after which it seldom makes its first attack. It most commonly affects children of a lax habit, with smooth, fine skins, fair hair and rosy cheeks. It likewise is apt to attack such children as show a disposition to rickets. Like this disease, it seems to be peculiar to cold and variable climates, being rarely met with in warm ones. Scrofula is by no means a contagious disease, but is of a hereditary nature, and is often entailed by parents on their children. The attacks of the disease seem much affected or influenced by the periods of the seasons. They begin usually some time in the winter and spring, and often disappear, or are greatly amended, in summer and autumn. The first appearance of the disorder is commonly in that of small oval or spherical tumors under the skin, unattended by any pain or discoloration. These appear, in general, upon the sides of the neck, below the ear or under the chin; but, in some cases, the joints of the elbows or ankles, or those of the fingers and toes, are the parts first affected. In these instances we do not, however, find small, movable swellings, but, on the contrary, a tumor almost uniformly surrounding the joint, and interrupting its motion. After some time, the tumors become larger and more fixed, the skin which covers them acquires a purple or livid color, and, being much inflamed, they at last suppurate, and break into little holes, from which, at first, a matter somewhat puriform oozes out; but this changes, by degrees, into a kind of viscid, serous discharge, much intermixed with small pieces of a white substance. The tumors subside gradually, whilst the ulcers at the same time open more, and spread unequally in various directions. After a time, some of the ulcers heal; but other tumors quickly form in different parts of the body, and proceed on, in the same slow manner as the former ones, to suppuration. In this manner the disease goes on for some years; and, appearing at last to have exhausted itself, all the ulcers heal up, without being succeeded by any fresh swellings, but leaving behind them an ugly puckering of the skin, and a scar of considerable extent. This is the most mild form under which scrofula appears. In more virulent cases, the eyes are particularly the seat of the disease, and are affected with ophthalmia, giving rise to ulcerations in the *tarsi*, and inflammation of the *tunica adnata*, terminating not unfrequently in an opacity of the transparent cornea. The joints become affected; they swell, and suffer excruciating deep-seated pain, which is increased upon the slightest motion. The swelling and pain continue to increase; the muscles of the limb become at length much wasted. Matter is soon afterwards formed, and this is discharged at small openings made by the bursting of the skin. Being, however, of a peculiarly acrimonious nature, it erodes the ligaments and cartilages, and produces a caries of the neighboring bones. By an absorption of the matter into the system, hectic fever at last arises, and, in the end, often proves fatal. The treatment consists chiefly in the use of means adapted to promote the general health, a nutritious diet, easy of digestion, a pure, dry air, gentle exercise, friction, cold bathing, especially in the sea, and strengthening medicines, as the preparations of iron, myrrh, &c. Various mineral waters, and other remedies which moderately promote the secretions, appear also to have been often useful. In irritable states of the system, hemlock has been employed with much advantage. The applications to the tumors and ulcers must vary according to the state of the parts, whether indolent or irritable; where the tumors show no disposition to enlarge, or become inflamed, it is best to interfere little with them; but their inflammation must be checked by leeches, &c., and when ulcers exist, stimulant lotions or dressings must be used, to give them a disposition to heal; but if they are in an irritable state, a cataplasm, made with hemlock or other narcotic.

Scudéri, George de, a French writer, born at Havre, in 1601, was descended from an ancient Provençal family. He was a member of the academy (1650), and died in 1667. His dramatic works (sixteen plays), sonnets, heroic poems, romances, &c., have been long forgotten.—His sister *Madeleine* was born at Havre, in 1607, and went at an early age to Paris, where, though remarkably ugly, she attracted notice by her talents and wit. Her numerous and long-winded romances depict the manners of the French court in the extraordinary taste of the time. She died in 1701. Mademoiselle Scudéri was entitled the Sappho of her time. The most distinguished scholars and wits of Europe were her friends; the academy at Padua chose her a member of their body; the French academy awarded the prize to her Dissertation on Glory. Her principal works were *Artamène, ou Le Grand Cyrus* (10 vols. 8vo.); *Clélie* (10 vols.); with 10 volumes of Conversations on different subjects, which are her best productions.

Sculpture, or the art of representing visible forms in hard masses, by means of the chisel, had its origin in the art of modelling figures in soft substances (see *Plastic Art*), as the ancient idols of all nations were formed. The more difficult art of carving figures in wood and ivory, and still more of cutting them in stone and casting in metal, were the inventions of a later period. These inventions were also the offspring of religion; at first only objects of religious worship were represented. In the earliest times, men venerated blocks and rough stones, or Bætylia, which were said to have fallen from heaven, and which are now called *aërolites*, or *meteoric stones*. Blocks of stone were also worshipped as landmarks, and were called *termini*. From the ninth to the seventh century B. C., the Greeks had much intercourse with the Phœnicians. This commercial nation worshipped the god Theut, Thoth, who had taught them the use of letters. They afterwards employed his image as their landmarks, calling it their god, and compelled the rude Autochthones to worship it. Such pillars were called *hermæ:* the god of roads and travellers was therefore called, by the Greeks, *Hermes*. They afterwards put a head upon these pillars, which is the origin of busts. The productions of sculpture are divided into insulated pieces, or such as may be viewed from all sides, whether full figures, or *Hermæ*, busts, heads, masks, vases, pedestals, &c., and works in relief. (See *Bass-relief*, and *Relievo.*) The elder sister of sculpture, in insulated forms, is architecture. The first object of sculpture was the ornamenting of temples.

History of Sculpture. We find very early indications of sculpture in the Bible. Laban, who lived in the twenty-third century B. C., had images of his domestic gods, which were called, in Hebrew, *teraphim*. In the very ancient Indian cavern and grotto temples, are found works of sculpture; for instance, in the pagoda of Elephantis, near Bombay, is a colossal statue of Brama. This deity is represented sitting, his arms crossed, with the face and figure of a man in front, and with a female face and form behind; upon his right breast is the sun; upon his left breast the moon and the stars; waters, mountains, animals and plants are exhibited upon this statue, which the Hindoos believed God to have presented to his Son, as a model, at the creation of the world. The fancy of the Hindoos was very rich, but inclined towards the symbolic and allegoric, so that they never attained to a pure style of art. Their sculpture is highly expressive, but without a feeling of beauty, and exhibits a mosaic of ideas

The Persians, who loved splendor, had many works of sculpture, as the ruins of Persepolis prove; but, as they never formed naked figures, they failed to gain a just idea of the human form. In Assyria, the art flourished under queen Semiramis. We find mention of brazen statues of Semiramis, Belus and Ninus. In the mountains of Curdistan, very ancient works of sculpture are found, which the inhabitants consider as the images of Chosroes and his beloved Shereen, and call the poet and artist Ferhad, the sculptor. The Egyptians were the first who adopted a certain style of art. The works of art produced by this nation were gloomy and grave, but full of deep sentiment, connected, by the hieroglyphics which covered them, with poetry and history, and by the mummies, with the belief of immortality. But as the kingdom of the dead seemed to them the true existence, so their art is more related to death than to life: their figures are stiff and motionless, like the mummies; even their images of Isis have this character. These are connected with the very ancient image of Diana at Ephesus, and with the most ancient Grecian art; as the use of the human form on the capitals of the columns at Dendera, the singularly extended female figures around the zodiac of that place, and the mixture of human and animal forms in the Sphinx, the Anubis, &c., are evidently related to the Indian art. If we consider the old Grecian style, we find first the abovementioned *Hermæ*, the double-headed figures which we call images of Janus, and which originally denoted the sun and the moon, numberless variations of the *Hermæ*, as the *Hermeraclæ*, *Hermathenæ*, *Hermerotæ*, &c. From these, which had neither hands nor feet, the next step was to images, formed like mummies, made of ebony or cedar wood, in which the arms were close to the body, and the feet were only indicated by an incision, the eyes and the mouth only by a slit. The artist next separated the arms from the trunk, parted the feet, and put weapons, as a shield and spear, into the hands of the idols: thus the first images of Pallas originated. Other armed idols, which belong to the Cretan family, were also called *Palladia*, as, for instance, the Taurian Diana. As they were made small, they were commonly placed upon columns. The word *statue* is derived from the Latin *statuo*, to set up, or from *sto*, to stand. In the larger statues in metal, the body of the image was merely a cylindrical pillar, as in the colossus of the Amyclean Apollo. With Dædalus (q. v.) begins a new epoch in the art, about three generations before the Trojan war. Of him, the Greeks said symbolically, that his divine genius made statues walk, see and speak. They considered him the master, or rather the inventor, of the art; he was also the symbol of the first miner hence the fable of the Dædalian labyrinth at Crete, or the horizontal passages in the first mine of that island, which abounded in metal. His disciples and imitators were called his sons: hence all artists were symbolically called *Dædalides*. The old Grecian art then became divided into three different national styles—the old Attic, the Æginetic, and the Etrurian. The arts flourished in the temples, not only by means of statues, but still more by *anathemata*, consecrated presents, thrones decorated with figures, coffers, shields, tripods, and vases. The most celebrated are, 1. the coffer of Cypselus in Olympia, made of cedar wood and inlaid with gold and ivory, and, 2. the throne of Apollo at Amyclæ, a colossal seat of a still more ancient colossus of Apollo, made by the Magnesian Bathycles, probably in the time of Solon. It contained, in twenty-eight panels outside, and fourteen panels inside, the then existing mythology of the gods and heroes. In these two pieces, a peculiar expression, united with the greatest poverty and rudeness of design and proportion, is observable; inscriptions are every where necessary for explanation, and the works are not pleasing; their character is allegory, bordering on hieroglyphics. Two temples of this epoch are memorable, as the works of the first Dædalides, Dipœnus, Rhœcus, and Scyllis:—1. the Heræum, or very ancient temple of Here (Juno) of Samos. The most ancient statue of Juno there was made by Smilis of Ægina: it was veiled and provided with supports. 2. The Artemisium at Ephesus: the most ancient statue in it was said to have fallen from heaven, and was dedicated by the Amazons. Afterwards, the black statue of Diana, in the form of a mummy with many breasts, as the goddess of nature, was carried to this temple. At that time, the statues were made of beaten brass plate; afterwards, artists began at Samos to cast them, but only in pieces, which were joined together by swallow-tailed fastenings. Several works of this primitive epoch are still preserved. Every thing in them is exaggerated: the motions are angular, the folds overcharged, the drapery stiff, the contours without regularity or precision. This early style displayed strength and energy, without expression and beauty. Under the Pisistratidæ, the art continued to flourish. But it was not until the splendid administration of Pericles, that the highest conceptions of art were formed. In this short period of twenty years, Athens produced more splendid works than Rome, the mistress of the world, produced in seven centuries. The influence of the great poets of this time, upon the art, was certainly important. It was the age of classic models and the ideal style. Phidias made two chief ideals, Minerva and Jupiter; the former for the Parthenon in Athens; the latter, the famous Olympian Jupiter at Elis. Both were wrought in ivory and gold; the god was beautifully formed, although forty feet high. His throne was splendidly adorned. The expression of Jupiter was a union of power, wisdom and benevolence; he sat at Elis as the chief judge of the contests in the Olympic games. His size is described in the words of an epigrammatist, who said, "The statue of Jupiter would have thrust off the roof of the temple like a thin shell, if it had ever risen from its golden throne." Phidias began the class of ideal forms, which, for the male figures, was afterwards divided into gods, demi-gods, and heroes; for female figures, various forms were adopted as ideals:—1. The Virgin: this is again divided into two chief branches: *a.* the Doric Cretan, short-waisted, twice-girded figure, used to represent Diana, the Amazons, Nymphs, and Bacchantes; *b.* the Attic-Ionian virgin, seen in the Muses, Canephoræ and priestesses. 2. The Matron: the highest ideal of the matronly form is in the Juno of Argos. We have also the ideal of Ceres, Cybele, and later of Nemesis, Fortuna, Pudicitia, Pietas, the Roman empresses and vestals, as well as the beautiful virgins of Herculaneum, in the cabinet of antiquities at Dresden. 3. The Hetæra was elevated to the ideal of Venus Anadyomene. 4. The female warrior was idealized in the Pallas Athene, as the perpetual Virgin, skilled in war and the arts. To the male figures belongs, also, the gymnastic and athletic class. Polycletus created the first, forming two different ideals of young men; in his Diadymenus, the mild youth, who winds the wreath of victory round his brow, and in his Doryphorus, the ardent and warlike youth, holding the lance before him, which was the famous canon, the model of all proportions. Myron created the athletic class. His athletæ are very celebrated, particularly his Discobolus, who supports his left hand on his knee, and, bending, throws the discus, with his right hand raised backwards. He completed this class by the ideal of Hercules, and formed the ideals of the whole animal kingdom. Only one hundred years after Phidias, 364 B. C., the high or ideal style gave place to the beautiful. Scopas and Praxiteles were the first in this style; they sculptured all the varieties of the dancing Bacchantes, or Thyades, in which the finest forms of beauty were joined with enthusiastic frenzy. Scopas invented the group; Praxiteles the ideals of Diana, of Venus, and of Bacchus. He was the father of a numerous family of artists. After him the beautiful style was transformed into the graceful, which gained in expression and purity what it lost in grandeur. Symmetry and proportion were most attended to. In the age of Alexander, Lysippus adopted a new style of art, by forming many portrait statues. He was the only one who was permitted to make the statue of Alexander, as Apelles alone was allowed to paint him. This last flourishing period of Grecian sculpture began 336 B. C. It contained the last class of works of the art, that of the ideal statues of kings and of warriors. Lysippus, though influenced much by Polycletus's rules of proportion, formed his bodies more slender and his heads smaller; he also bestowed particular care upon the finishing of the hair. His statues are particularly admired for their life. Through the influence of painting, sculpture acquired the expression of feeling, of which the highest perfection, in the pathetic, is the group of Laocoön. The taste for colossal statues extended itself, and contributed to the decline of the art; excess of ornament was also connected with it. After the Macedonian and Syrian wars, 200 B. C., the Romans began to carry off the statues from the conquered countries. Paulus Æmilius adorned his triumph of three days with immense treasures of Grecian statues. The *Forum Romanum* was often hung with costly carpets, and transformed into a theatre, adorned with about 3000 statues; 12,000 were placed in the capital alone. With the statues also the Grecian artists came to Rome; but the art never became naturalized there. After the time of Sylla, the love of the art was increased to a mania. The last flourishing period of the art was Adrian's age. The highest elegance, polish and perfection was its character. This taste continued under the Antonines, slightly degenerated; but it sunk entirely under Severus and his successors: before Constantine the Great, the art of the ancients was entirely lost. The early Christian works adhere to a fixed type. See the *Notizie della Scultura degli Antichi e dei varj, suoi Stili, del Abate Luigi Lanzi* (2d Italian ed., with annotations and copper-plates, in the *Poligrafia Fiesolana*, 1824). Sculpture revived in Italy in the thirteenth century. The modern artists worked also ably in metal. The greatest master of this first period of modern art was Michael Angelo Buonarotti. Through him and his disciples, sculpture raised its head in Western Europe. All the remains of art which had escaped destruction from barbarian violence, religious fanaticism, and natural causes, were now carefully preserved. We are chiefly indebted to the noble Cosmo and Lorenzo de' Medici for the restoration of a better style. Artists were honored and supported, the treasures of antiquity were collected and museums instituted. The neighboring princes vied with the Medici. Yet modern art never attained the sublimity and tranquil grandeur of the ancient. The modern artist reveals himself in his works: the ancient artist did not appear in his work. Through Buonarotti's sublime genius, the art was seduced into extravagance, and through Bernini's affected grace into mannerism and excessive ornament; the true feeling of beauty had disappeared; artists in vain endeavored to surpass the ancients, not realizing that they had sunk too low to understand them. Through the preponderating example of France, good taste in every art declined more and more; human nature itself was distorted. The folly of fashion prevailed every where. In the eighteenth century, Winckelmann was the first who lighted the torch of modern art, and opened the eyes of his contemporaries to the elevated beauty of antiquity. The cardinal Albani and Mengs supported him; thus the new dawn of the art and of beauty was ushered in. The present age can boast of several sculptors of great merit. An apparent stagnation in art was first to come, bad taste was to be destroyed, before beauty could blossom again. Canova became the founder of a new period. Thorwaldsen stands by his side, and in many respects before him; and to judge by the progress which modern sculpture has made in the last thirty years, and the noble works which have been executed in so short a time, we may hope, that it is upon a safer route than in the sixteenth century.

The most illustrious Sculptors of Antiquity.—Earliest Period.—Vulcan and Prometheus are but symbolical figures; and the ingenious Greeks denoted by the lame god and the deified man, the power and skill of art conquering matter, and the divine spirit of the mind immortalizing earthly forms. In Dædalus of Athens we behold the first great sculptor: we may place him about 1400 B. C. At the same time, Smilis, the father of statuary, lived in Ægina. Epeus is said to have made the Trojan horse. Rhœcus of Samos, 700 B. C., invented the art of moulding and casting statues in metal. Theodorus and Telecles, his sons, travelled, for the study of the art, to Egypt. The former is reported to have made the statue of the Pythian Apollo, for the temple at Samos, in two parts—one half at Ephesus, the other half at Samos—a manner of working, which was, perhaps, possible in the condition of the Egyptian art. Dibutades invented the art of making portrait figures in baked earth (*terra cotta*); his daughter Calirrhoe suggested to him this idea, by drawing the profile of her lover's shadow with coal upon the wall. Euchirus of Corinth (B. C. 663) accompanied Demaratus, the father of the elder Tarquin, to Italy, and introduced the art of modelling into Etruria. Dipœnus and Scyllis became the masters of a numerous school. Malas and his followers were among the most illustrious sculptors of that time. Canachus was the greatest master of the Sicyonian school. Perillus made the famous brazen bull (a splendid masterpiece) for Phalaris, who ruled in Sicily 564 B. C., in which the artist himself was burnt. Among the principal works in stone were those of Bathycles of Amyclæ. Callon of Ægina lived 540 B. C. Demeas of Crotona executed the statue of Milo. Iphicrates cast the brazen lioness of Leæna, who was privy to the conspiracy of Harmodius and Aristogiton against Hipparchus, and who endured the torture till death, without confessing any thing. The artist gave no tongue to the lioness, in order to express the heroic silence of Leæna. Onatas of Ægina restored the statue called the *black Ceres of Phigalea*. Ageladas of Argos is considered the master of Phidias.

Second Period.—Ideal Style.—With Phidias of Athens began the period of the high ideal style, which he created. He lived in the time of Pericles. Besides his two masterpieces, Pallas Athene and Jupiter his Pallas of brass for Athens, his Venus Urania, his Nemesis in the temple at Marathon, and his Amazon, called *Eucnemon*, from the beauty of her limbs, deserve mention. He made but a single boy from life. His favorite disciples were Alcamenes of Attica and Agoracritus of Paros. The most celebrated works of the former were his Vulcan, his Olympian conqueror, his Cupid, his Mars, and his Venus. The second was a still greater favorite of Phidias; he contended with Alcamenes in the execution of a Venus, and was adjudged to be inferior by the Athenians only out of partiality to their fellow-citizen; he transformed his Venus to a Nemesis, and sold it at Rhamnus. Varro considered this statue the finest ever executed. Polycletus of Argos made Juno, the third chief ideal figure, a companion to the Olympic Jupiter. In the Ludovisian Juno, an imitation of her head is preserved. Polycletus sculptured, besides his famous canon, all the beautiful gymnastic positions of boys, and all the sports of youth: the highest ideal of this class is his Mercury. A tender softness was peculiar to this master, as shown in his charming Canephoræ of Athens. He chiefly cast in metal. His fellow disciple and rival was Myron of Eleutheræ in Bœotia. He executed three colossuses upon one pedestal—Minerva presenting the deified Hercules to Jupiter. The fertile genius of Myron was displayed in the choice of new and bold positions. He despised the softer forms of the Ephebi, and showed his skill in the representation of the most highly finished athletic forms. His Runner, his Slinger, and his Pancratists, are celebrated. His ideal of Hercules completed this class of forms. His Heifer, and his Sea Monster, are famous among his animal forms. But one thing was wanting to this great sculptor—grace of expression: in this he was surpassed by his rival, Pythagoras of Rhegium, who adopted the undulating line as the line of beauty, and first expressed the sinews and veins with accuracy. He created the ideal of Apollo in the position of an archer who has just shot the serpent Python. The imitation of this is the most splendid statue which we possess—the Apollo Belvedere.

Third Period.—Beautiful Style.—Socrates, the sculptor of the clothed Graces, with Athenodorus and Naucydes, began this epoch. Praxiteles and Scopas brought the art to its highest perfection, since they united beauty with grace. The most celebrated works of Scopas are his furious Bacchante (the head, bending backwards, united the highest beauty with Bacchanalian frenzy), his Cupid, his Venus (probably the model of the Medicean), and his group,—the Triumph of Achilles, whom Thetis is conducting, after his death, to the happy islands, in which Scopas found an opportunity of introducing numberless Tritons, Nereids and sea monsters in the most charming combinations. Praxiteles, the most feeling of all sculptors, created the perfect ideals of Diana and of Bacchus. He formed the latter as a contrast to the Satyrs and Fauns, who express rudeness and licentiousness; it was soft and tender, without being effeminate; it was perpetual gayety personified in the victorious god, sporting with his companions. The Diana of this artist expressed virgin modesty, with bold activity. Homer's Nausicaa inspired him. He made, also, the admired statue of a Satyr (Periboetos), and the ideal of Eros, or Cupid. The god of love was never represented by the ancients as an infant; the true infantile representation was not admissible till after the Christian era. Eros always had the form of a boy approaching youth. Praxiteles first attempted to represent Venus entirely naked, and thus created the later ideal of the goddess. His most celebrated works are his Venus of Cos and of Cnidos. The former is covered from the hip downward; the latter entirely naked, holding her garment with her left hand over the bath. We possess imitations of both. The group of Niobe is also ascribed to this master. His son Cephissodorus was celebrated for his gymnastic Symplegma (two wrestlers with hands interlaced), and his Æsculapius. After his time, the art degenerated through the introduction of the most voluptuous representations. Praxiteles had already formed, for Phryne, a Group in bronze, in which he placed a laughing Hetæra opposite to a weeping matron. Hermaphrodites, groups of Satyrs and Nymphs, were formed with great perfection of art, and equal looseness of moral sentiment.

Fourth Period.—Age of Alexander the Great.—Art could only gain through grace and softness of execution, since the high ideal beauty was on the decline. Lysippus of Sicyon appeared and became the master of elevated portrait sculpture. Among the gods, Hercules was his favorite, and he perfected the ideal figure of Neptune, designed by Euphranor. He represented Alexander from his childhood to his manhood. It is affirmed that he alone made 1500 statues, some limit this number to 610; every figure of his great groups, however, is included in this estimate. The most celebrated among these groups are, Alexander hunting, and the twenty-five equestrian statues, representing the Macedonian friends, who fell in the first attack near the Granicus, at the side of Alexander. His horses are very beautiful. Euthycrates, his son, and Apollodorus and Silanion, were great sculptors of this period. Chares of Lindus cast the famous Colossus (q. v.) of Rhodes. Agesander, Athenodorus, and Polydorus, father and sons, of Rhodes, formed the celebrated group of Laocoön; Glycon of Athens, the Farnese Hercules; Apollonius and Tauriscus, the Farnese bull. The sculptors of Rome were Greeks; we only know of them, Arcesilaus, the friend of Lucius Lucullus, and Praxiteles, the greatest modeller of the age of Pompey. He wrote five books on the most celebrated works of art. Zenodorus had formed, in Gaul, a colossal Mercury in brass, and was invited by Nero to Rome, to make a colossal statue of him, 110 feet high; the casting failed. The reclining statue of the dying Cleopatra was executed in the reign of the emperor Augustus. Cleomenes, an Athenian, made the statue of Germanicus, in the time of Tiberius. The four beautiful horses of brass, above the chief entrance of the church of St. Mark at Venice, were cast during the reign of Nero. The beautiful Antinous is one of the most perfect statues of the age of Adrian.

The most Illustrious Sculptors of Modern Times.—Earlier Period.—1. *Italian Sculptors.* In the eleventh century, we find mention of a sculptor named Buono, in the twelfth, of Bonanno of Pisa. Niccolò Pisano, who died in 1270, was called the restorer of good taste in sculpture. Several works of his son Giovanni Pisani are still to be seen in Pisa. Andreas Orgagna, surnamed Buffalmaco, died in 1389. Luca della Robbia varnished his works in *terra cotta*, with great skill. Lorenzo Ghiberti, who died in 1455, was a very able master. His brazen gates at the Battisterio of Florence are celebrated. Michael Angelo declared them worthy to stand at the entrance of paradise. Donatello (born at Florence 1383, died 1466) enriched Venice, Florence, Genoa and Faenza with his works; a bald-headed old man, made by him in Florence, is celebrated. He formed, for the church of St. Mark at Florence, the brazen statues of St. Peter, St. George and St. Mark; the latter is particularly memorable for the question of Michael Angelo: "*Marco, perchè non mi parli?*" (Mark, why dost thou not speak to me?) His brother Simon made one of the brazen gates of the church of St. Peter, and the sepulchre of Martin V, in the Lateran church. Andreas Pisano was an illustrious sculptor and engraver. Lorenzo Lotto, called Lorenzetto, was the first who endeavored to restore antiques. Andreas Verrocchio, from jealousy of his pupils Perugino and Leonardo da Vinci, abandoned painting, and devoted himself to sculpture. He was the first who revived the art of modelling the busts of the deceased in soft substances. Rustici, born at Florence, in 1470, was the disciple of Verrocchio, and afterwards of Leon. da Vinci. The latter taught him the art of modelling, of cutting marble, of casting in brass, and perspective. His most celebrated works are a Europa, a Leda, a Vulcan, and a Neptune. Michael Angelo Buonarotti (q. v.), in his early youth, executed some astonishing works, as the head of an old woman, and the statue of Hercules. Particularly worthy of admiration are his Bacchus, the famous colossal statue of Julius II, for whose tomb he made three figures, among which is his famous Moses, his David, his Victory at Florence, and his statue of Night upon the tomb of Giulio de' Medici. Tatti, called after his birthplace Sansovino, born 1477, when a youth, at Rome, made a model of the Group of Laocoön, which, by Raphael's decision, obtained the prize, and was cast in bronze. He executed many works for Venice, among which the marble statues of the holy Virgin in St. Mark's, and of John the Baptist in the church at Casa Grande, are particularly celebrated. The ease of his drapery and the life of his statues are much admired. Baccio Bandinelli, born at Florence in 1487, vied with Buonarotti. He had a great knowledge of anatomy; his manner is energetic but rude. He restored the right arm of Laocoön; his bass-reliefs upon the tombs of Leo X and Clement VII, are famous. Benvenuto Cellini, born at Florence in 1500, was a sculptor, goldsmith and painter. Properzia Rossi, of Bologna, is the only celebrated female sculptor. Two angels in marble, which adorn the front of the church of St. Petronia, and several busts, were the foundation of her fame. She represented, with much skill and delicacy, the passion of Christ, and many figures of the apostles, upon peach-stones, in bass-relief. Eleven of these peach-stones are preserved in the gallery of the marchese Grassi at Bologna. She studied the rules of architecture and perspective, and was an able painter and musician. An unhappy passion caused her early death, in 1530. She sculptured the melancholy story of her feelings in marble, and this bass-relief was her masterpiece. Guglielmo della Porta, of Milan, restored several antiques in Rome; he restored also the legs of the Farnese Hercules so well, that Buonarotti did not consider the genuine legs, which he found twenty-seven years after, superior. The beautiful statue of Justice upon the tomb of Paul III, in the church of St. Peter's, is by this master, as well as the four great prophets in the niches between the columns of the first colonnade of the same church. With Bernini, born at Naples, 1598, a *second period* of Italian sculpture begins. He was a man of uncommon genius, but his boldness, his imagination, and particularly his endeavors to please, generally seduced him into irregularities; he attempted to surpass natural beauty, particularly in the dimples in the cheeks. His St. Theresa and St. Bibiana were his masterpieces. Alessandro Algardi (q. v.), born at Bologna, was the rival of Bernini. He was a disciple of Ludovico Caracci; and the painter is often discoverable in his works. He was the founder of a numerous school. Domenico Guido, Antonio Raggi, Ercole Ferrata, and Gabr. Brunelli, are distinguished among the numerous disciples of the two last masters. Gonnelli, called the blind man of Cambassi, lost his eyesight in his twentieth year, and made himself a sculptor by feeling alone. He executed a statue of Cosmo I, grand-duke of Tuscany, in *terra cotta.* Tubi, born at Rome, 1630, sculptured much for France. He made the famous group upon the tomb of Turenne. Camillo Rusconi, born at Milan in 1658, was an admirer of the ancient works of art, and imitated them in a masterly manner. His masterpiece is the tomb of Gregory XIII, in St. Peter's. The attitude of his figures is majestic and beautiful; his style is pure, full of expression, fire and life. Angelo Rossi, born at Genoa in 1671, chiefly distinguished himself by his excellent reliefs. He followed rather the taste of the ancients than the style of Algardi, not cutting so deep, but forming rather demi-reliefs. His work of this kind, for the tomb of Alexander VIII, is the finest bass-relief in St. Peter's. Gaetano Zumbo, born at Syracuse, 1656, had no other master than his own genius. He carried the working in colored wax to great perfection. He made, for the grand-duke of Tuscany, the famous representation of putrefaction, showing all its stages in five corpses, colored after nature, with so much truth as to excite horror. A Birth of the Savior, and a Descent from the Cross, are among his masterpieces.

2. *French Sculptors.*—Jean Goujon, of Paris, is the first distinguished sculptor in France; and his most celebrated work is the fountain of the Nymphs, in the market-place *des Innocents* at Paris, which he began under Francis I, and finished in 1550, under Henry II. He was also an architect and an engraver. He perished, in 1572, in the massacre of St. Bartholomew's. Germain Pilon, of Paris, had much grace, but his style was often impure. He first accurately distinguished the various materials of the drapery. The group of the three Christian Virtues, in white marble, for the church of St. Celestine, is a noble work. Jean de Boulogne was born at Douay, in 1524. He went early to Rome, and was Buonarotti's disciple. He was on the point of leaving Rome on account of his poverty, when an amateur at Florence gave him a piece of marble, out of which he formed a Venus, by which he gained celebrity. His most celebrated works are Sampson and a Philistine, at Florence, his colossal Neptune, and his Rape of the Sabine Women, in the same place, his flying Mercury, in brass, and his Jupiter Pluvius, the greatest colossus of modern art. His disciple Tacca made the horse for the statue of Henry IV, upon the Pont-neuf, and the equestrian statue of Philip IV, king of Spain, represented at full speed in *Buen Retiro.* Jacques Sarassin, born at Noyon, 1590, was educated in Rome, and united genius with taste and grace. The Caryatides, which adorn the great pavilion of the old Louvre, and the Group of Romulus and Remus in Versailles, are among his masterpieces. He founded a productive school, and died in 1660. François Anguier made the beautiful tomb of the duke of Montmorency, in the church of St. Mary at Moulins, and his brother Michael, the statues and reliefs of the Porte St. Denis. Théodon made the beautiful statue of St. John in the Lateran, and the two Groups in the garden of the Tuileries, Atlas transformed into a rock, and Phaetusa changed into a poplar tree. He died in 1680. Lerambert made several groups for Versailles. Puget, born at Marseilles, in 1622, was a painter, architect and sculptor. If he had more carefully studied the antique models, he would have surpassed all modern sculptors. His style was bold and powerful. His most

celebrated works are his two colossal Termini, in the city hall of Toulon, his statue of Milo in the park of Versailles, and his Dying Gladiator. The brothers Marsy, born in 1624 and 1628, at Cambray, made the statues of Bacchus and of Latona in bronze, at Versailles, and the famous Group of Horses at the bath of Apollo, in the same place. François Girardon, born at Troyes, in 1630, was the most celebrated sculptor of the age of Louis XIV. His equestrian statue of this king, twenty-one feet high, which stood formerly on the royal Place Vendome, was the first work of modern times, which was cast in a single piece. Most of the works of Girardon are formed after designs by Le Brun, and adorn the park of Versailles. Pierre le Gros, born at Paris, 1656, lived almost all his life in Rome, and is one of the best French artists. His most celebrated works are, a Roman Maid in the garden of the Tuileries, St. Dominic in the church of St. Peter's, the Group of St. Ignatius, and St. Theresa in the church of the Carmelites at Turin. He died in 1719, deeply mortified by the neglect of the academicians at Paris. Nicolas Coustou, born at Lyons, in 1658, had much taste and ease, but entirely a French manner. His brother Guillaume surpassed him, and finished, in bass-relief, the Passage of the Rhine, which the former had commenced. Edme Bouchardon's style was soft rather than elevated, more regular than bold. Lambert Adam, born at Nancy, in 1700, made the two statues, the Seine and Marne, eighteen feet high, at St. Cloud, and the Group of Neptune and Amphitrite at Versailles. His style is rude and wild. Lemoyne distinguished himself by his portraits: he was animated, but incorrect. René Slodz, born at Paris, in 1705, worked in a simple style of grandeur: few understood drapery better than he, yet his figures are not always correct. Baptiste Pigalle, born at Paris, 1714, owed his success entirely to his great industry. His Mercury and Venus are celebrated: the king of Prussia purchased them both. The celebrated tomb of marshal Saxe at Strasburg is his work. A Boy with a Cage, from which the bird had escaped, by its truth and expression, gained him universal approbation. He died in 1785. Etienne Falconet was invited to Petersburg, to make an equestrian statue of Peter the Great, in bronze. Mademoiselle Collot made the model of the head.

3. *German Sculptors.*—Long before Albert Dürer's time, some excellent sculptors flourished in the south of Germany, whose industry and excellence are proved by their works, which adorn the churches, city halls and fountains of Nuremberg and other places. We even find marks of still more ancient sculpture, in the numberless equestrian figures and images of saints, which, in all the minsters, and particularly in that at Cologne, cover even the smallest turrets. The names of these masters are unknown; the first probably came from Byzantium. Albert Dürer, whose genius embraced various departments of the fine arts, produced excellent works of sculpture, large and small, comprehending insulated figures, and figures in relief in wood and stone. Leonard Kern, born at Forchtenberg, in 1580, studied in Italy, and worked with much success in wood, stone and ivory. Gottfried Leygebe, born at Freistadt, in Silesia, 1630, died at Berlin, 1683, was the first who formed small equestrian figures, of cast iron. He represented the emperor Leopold I, at Copenhagen, Charles II of England, as St. George, at Dresden, and the elector Frederic William, as Bellerophon, at Berlin. Rauchmüller worked on the column of the holy Trinity at Vienna, which was finished 1693. Andreas von Schlüter, born at Hamburg, 1662, studied in Italy, chiefly the works of Buonarotti, and was invited to Berlin, where he adorned the arsenal and formed the model of the excellent equestrian statue of the elector Frederic William, which was cast, 1700, by John Jacobi. Balthasar Permoser, born in 1650, in the district of Salzburg, died, 1732, at Dresden, has left many excellent works at Berlin, Dresden and Leipsic. There are also other German sculptors of note.

4. *Dutch, English, Swedish and Russian Sculptors.*—Francis Duquesnoy, born at Brussels, in 1594, known under the name *il Fiamingo.* He had, like Algardi, a peculiar genius for representing the beauty of children, and succeeded in flying and rising figures better than any one before him. He formed an intimate friendship with Poussin, and both gave themselves, with an unlimited devotion, to art. His Andrew, twenty-two palms high, in St. Peter's at Rome, is one of the finest statues there; and his Susanna at Loretto is much admired on account of the noble attitude of the figure, its mild, pious expression, and beautiful drapery. Buyster, Slodz, Quellius and Van Obstal were Dutch sculptors of merit. Cibber made the two excellent statues at the entrance of Bedlam, in London, representing melancholy and mad

ness. Gibbons, who died at London in 1721, chiefly distinguished himself in beautifully wrought and industriously finished ornaments. His flowers and birds are exceedingly tender. Wilton and Rysbrach worked particularly in the graceful style; the female figures of the latter are highly graceful. Nollekins had good attitudes, but little correctness. Among the Swedish sculptors we ought to mention, above all, Sergel. The Russian Pawloff was a portrait sculptor of reputation. Launitz, the disciple of Thorwaldsen, is distinguished in the present time.

5. *Spanish Sculptors.*—Sculpture has flourished in Spain since the eleventh century, and Aparicio of Castile made, as early as 1033, a bass-relief in gold and ivory, representing, in twenty-two divisions, the Hunt of St. Millan, which is preserved in the convent of Yuso, and is admirable for its proportions and grace. The convents and churches gave employment to the artists. A hundred and sixty distinguished Spanish sculptors are enumerated.

Latest Period.—Cavaceppi, in Rome, makes the transition to the great sculptors of the present time. Canova (q. v.), who died in 1822, was chiefly distinguished for grace of style and perfection of execution, as the Dane Thorwaldsen, in heroic figures, is superior to his contemporaries in the grandeur of the forms, and, above all, in strength of expression. Both united, reflect much splendor on the age, and in Thorwaldsen's works especially, much truth, united with a beautiful conception of nature, and a noble composition, is visible, so that he deserves to be called one of the greatest masters of all ages. We ought also to mention the names of Dannecker in Stuttgard, whose Ariadne equals the ancient in beauty, Schadow, Rauch and Tieck in Berlin, Chaudet and Houdon in Paris, Flaxman, Chantrey and Gahagan in London. Count Cicognara has published a continuation of the works of Winckelmann and Agincourt (*Storia della Scultura dal suo Risorgimento in Italia*, &c.) until Canova (2d ed., Prato, 1824, 4 vols., with copper-plates). We shall now add a few remarks on the technical part of sculpture.

Modelling.—Before any object is executed in stone, it is the practice of sculptors to complete a representation of their design by modelling it in clay, or some other soft material. The genius of the artist is displayed altogether in the model; for the process of afterwards copying the model in stone is chiefly mechanical, and may often be executed by another person, as well as by the sculptor himself. When a clay model is taken, if the proposed figure be large, a frame of wood or iron is erected, to give support to the limbs and different parts of the figure. Upon this frame a proper quantity of wet clay is distributed and wrought into the form of the intended statue. The moulding of the clay is performed with the hands and with various instruments of wood and ivory. When the model is complete, copies may be taken from it, either by casting them in plaster, or in metal, or by chiselling them in marble. To execute a statue in marble, which shall exactly correspond to a pattern or model, is a work of mechanical, rather than of inventive skill. It is performed by finding, in the block of marble, the exact situation of numerous points, corresponding to the chief elevations and cavities in the figure to be imitated, and joining these by the proper curves and surfaces at the judgment of the eye. These points are found by measuring the height, depth, and lateral deviation of the corresponding points in the model; after which, those in the block are found by similar measurements. Sometimes the points are ascertained by placing the model horizontally under a frame, and suspending a plumb-line successively from different parts of the frame, till it reaches the parts of the figure beneath it. Sometimes an instrument is used consisting of a movable point, attached by various joints to an upright post, so that it may be carried to any part of the statue, and indicate the relative position of that part in regard to the post. Machines have also been contrived for cutting any required figure from a block, the cutting instrument being directed by a gauge, which rests upon the model in another part of the machine. Marble is wrought to the rough outline of the statue by the chisel and hammer, aided by the occasional use of drills and other perforating tools. It is then smoothed with rasps and files, and, when required, is polished with pumice stone and putty. The hair of statues is always finished with the chisel; and for this object, very sharp instruments, with different points and edges, are necessary. The ancient sculptors appear to have relied almost wholly upon the chisel, and to have used that instrument with great boldness and freedom, such as could have been justified only by consummate skill in the art. The moderns, on the contrary, approach the surface of the statue with great caution, and employ safer means for giving the last finish. Some of the most celebrated antique statues, such as the Laocoön, the Apollo Belvedere, and Venus de' Medici, are thought to have been finished with the chisel alone.—Although marble has been the common material of sculpture, both in ancient and modern times, yet other substances have been occasionally made subjects of the chisel. Statues of porphyry, granite, serpentine and alabaster, are found among the remains of antiquity. Other materials, of a less durable kind, were also employed. Some of the principal works of Phidias were made of ivory and gold, particularly his colossal statues of Jupiter Olympius and Minerva, at Athens.

Bronze Casting.—Statues intended to occupy situations in which they may be exposed to violence, are commonly made of bronze. This material resists both mechanical injuries and decay from the influence of the atmosphere. The moulds in which bronze statues are cast, are made on the pattern, out of plaster and brick dust, the latter material being added to resist the heat of the melted metal. The parts of this mould are covered on their inside with a coating of clay, as thick as the bronze is intended to be. The mould is then closed, and filled on its inside with a nucleus or core of plaster and brick dust, mixed with water. When this is done, the mould is opened, and the clay carefully removed. The mould, with its core, are then thoroughly dried, and the core secured in its central position by short bars of bronze, which pass into it through the external part of the mould. The whole is then bound with iron hoops, and, when placed in a proper situation for casting, the melted bronze is poured in through an aperture left for the purpose. Of course, the bronze fills the same cavity which was previously occupied by the clay, and forms a metallic covering to the core. This is afterwards made smooth by mechanical means.

Scuppers; certain channels cut through the water-ways and sides of a ship at proper distances, and lined with sheet-lead, in order to carry the water off the deck into the sea.

Scupper-hose; a leathern pipe or tube nailed round the outside of the scuppers of the lower decks, and which, by hanging down, prevents the water from entering when the ship inclines under a pressure of sail.

Scurvy (*scorbutus*); a disease of a putrid nature, prevalent in cold and damp climates, and which chiefly affects sailors and such as are shut up in besieged places, owing, as is supposed, to their being deprived of fresh provisions, and a due quantity of acescent food, assisted by the prevalence of cold and moisture, and by such other causes as depress the nervous energy, as indolence, confinement, want of exercise, neglect of cleanliness, much labor and fatigue, sadness, despondency &c. These debilitating causes, with the concurrence of a diet consisting principally of salted or putrescent food, will be sure to produce this disease. It seems, however, to depend more on a defect of nourishment than on a vitiated state; and the reason that salted provisions are so productive of the scurvy is, most probably, because they are drained of their nutritious juices, which are extracted and run off in brine. As the disease is apt to become general among the crew of a ship, when it has once made its appearance, it has been supposed by many to be of a contagious nature; but the conjecture seems by no means well founded. The scurvy comes on gradually, with heaviness, weariness, and unwillingness to move about, together with dejection of spirits, considerable loss of strength and debility. As it advances in its progress, the countenance becomes sallow and bloated; respiration is hurried on the least motion; the teeth become loose; the gums are spongy; the breath is very offensive; livid spots appear on different parts of the body; old wounds, which have long been healed up, break out afresh; severe wandering pains are felt, particularly by night; the skin is dry; the urine small in quantity; and the pulse is small, frequent, and, towards the last, intermitting; but the intellect, for the most part, clear and distinct. By an aggravation of the symptoms, the disease, in its last stage, exhibits a most wretched appearance. Scurvy, as usually met with on shore, or where the person has not been exposed to the influence of the remote causes before enumerated, is unattended by any violent symptoms. Slight blotches, with scaly eruptions on different parts of the body, and a sponginess of the gums, are the chief ones observed. In the cure, as well as the prevention of scurvy, more is to be done by regimen than by medicines, obviating, as far as possible, the several remote causes of the disease; but particularly providing the patient with a more wholesome diet and a large proportion of fresh vegetables; and it has been found that those articles are especially useful, which contain a native acid, as oranges, lemons, &c. Where these cannot be procured, various substitutes have been proposed, of which the best appear to be the inspissated juices of the same fruits, or the crystallized citric acid. Vinegar, sour crout, and farinaceous substances, made to undergo the acetous fermentation, have likewise been used with much advantage; also brisk fermenting liquors, as spruce-beer, cider, and the like. Mustard, horse-radish, garlic, and other substances of a stimulating character, promoting the secretions, are useful to a certain extent.

Scurvy Grass (*cochlearia*); a genus of cruciferous plants, mostly inhabiting the extreme northern parts of the globe. It consists of herbaceous plants, having alternate, and, usually, entire leaves, and their flowers disposed in terminal racemes, and ordinarily white. The horse-radish is one of them, but is much larger, and has a different aspect from the others, but resembles them in the sensible properties of the leaves and stems. The common scurvy-grass (*C. officinalis*) grows wild on the sea-shore of Greenland, Iceland, and the north of Europe: the leaves are small, angular, sinuate and sessile, and are sometimes eaten in salads: the taste is acrid and slightly bitter: they are anti-scorbutic, and stimulating to the digestive organs. About twenty species of *cochlearia* are known.

Scutari, or Iskiudar; a town of Asiatic Turkey, in Natolia, on the Bosphorus, opposite to Constantinople, called by the ancients *Chrysopolis;* population, about 33,000. It is considered a suburb of Constantinople, and serves as an emporium and rendezvous to the caravans of Asia. The Turks at Constantinople are interred at Scutari, and the burying grounds here are the handsomest in the empire. (See *Constantinople.*)

Scutari, or Iskanderie, in Albania, the capital of a pachalic, is situated at the end of a lake to which it gives its name. It was anciently the residence of the kings of Illyricum. Population, 15,000.

Scuttling; the act of cutting large holes through the bottom, sides or decks of a ship, for various occasions, particularly when she is stranded or overset, and continues to float on the surface, in order to take out the whole or part of the cargo, provisions, stores, &c.—To *scuttle a ship;* to sink her by making holes through her bottom.

Scylla; a daughter of Nisus, king of Megara, who became enamored of Minos, when that monarch besieged her father's capital. She delivered Megara into his hands, on his promising to marry her; but Minos afterwards treated her with such contempt that she threw herself from a tower into the sea; or, according to some accounts, she was changed into a lark by the gods, and her father into a hawk.—A daughter of Typhon or Phorcis, was loved by Glaucus. Scylla scorned his addresses, and the god applied to Circe. But she became enamored of him herself, and, instead of giving him assistance, attempted to make him forget Scylla, but in vain. To punish her rival, Circe poured the juice of some poisonous herbs into the waters of the fountain where Scylla bathed; and no sooner had the nymph touched the place, than she found every part of her body below the waist changed into frightful monsters like dogs, which never ceased barking. This metamorphosis so terrified her, that she threw herself into that part of the sea which separates the coast of Italy and Sicily, where she was changed into rocks, which continued to bear her name, and which were deemed very dangerous to navigators, as was also the whirlpool of Charybdis, on the coast of Sicily.

Scythians. This name was very vaguely used by ancient writers. It was sometimes applied to a particular people, and at others was extended to all the nomadic tribes which wandered over the regions to the north of the Black and the Caspian seas, and to the east of the latter. Scythia is used in the same indefinite manner, sometimes for the country of the Scythians, and sometimes for those now called Mongolia and Tartary. The Scythians may be distinguished into Asiatic and European. Among the former, the ancients included a great number of northern nations, with whose origin they were unacquainted, and who were probably of different races. The Scythians were for some time a ruling people in Asia. They are considered as the progenitors of the Turks, Tartars and Manchoos: the ancients considered the Persians, Parthians and Bactrians as their descendants. The European Scythians, in the time of Herodotus, inhabited the country from the Ister (Danube) to the sources of the Dniester and the Dnieper, in the neighborhood of the Don, and along the northern shores of the Black sea. Of this region, that portion extending from the Danube to the city of Carcinitis, was called *Old Scythia;* and the peninsula (Taurida) to the Borysthenes was called *Little Scythia,* which name, in Strabo's time, included the country as far as the Danube, formerly occupied by the Thracians, and therefore comprised *Old Scythia.*

SEA. (See *Ocean.*)

SEA-BATHING has been found very salutary in several complaints, as diseases of the glands of all kinds, and of the skin in scrofula and a scrofulous predisposition, exhausting sweats, and tendency to catarrhs, chronic nervous diseases, particularly hysteric attacks, epilepsy, St. Vitus's dance; also sometimes in chronic rheumatism. But it must not be used in the case of plethora, inclination to congestions and discharges of blood, diseases of the heart, tendency to pulmonary consumption, obstruction and induration of internal organs. The great proportion of salt and of animal substance in the sea-water, the constant motion and swell of the waves, the sea air, and the very sight of the sea, together with the excitement caused, at least in the case of timid persons, from overcoming a degree of fear, contribute to the effect of sea-bathing. Machines are sometimes used for conveying patients into the water. In these, being protected from observation, the bather can enjoy the sea perfectly undressed, which is much preferable to going into the water with a dress on.

SEA BEAR. (See *Seal.*)

SEA ELEPHANT. (See *Seal.*)

SEA HORSE. This term is often applied to the walrus, but more frequently to a small, insignificant, bony fish (*hippocampus*), the head of which bears some remote resemblance to that of the horse. The usual length of this fish is five or six inches; the body is compressed laterally, and is encased in prominent, bony, rib-like scales. The tail is much smaller than the body, destitute of a terminal fin, tapering gradually to a point, and curls up when dried; in which state it is common in museums. The mouth is small, and situated at the extremity of a long, tubular snout, as in the other pipe-fish. The species of *hippocampus* are found in almost every sea, and live on small marine insects. As some similarity has been imagined between the head of this fish and that of the horse, the dorsal fin has likewise been compared to a saddle, and the filaments on the back of the neck to a mane.

SEA-KAIL (*crambe maritima*); a cruciferous plant, growing wild in Europe, upon sandy sea-shores. The whole plant is entirely smooth and glaucous; the stems are about two feet high and branching, bearing fleshy leaves, some pinnatifid, and others sinuate, undulate, and crisped: the flowers are disposed in a terminal panicle. From time immemorial, the common people have been in the practice of watching when the young shoots and leaf-stalks begin to push through the sand, and cutting them off below the surface of the ground for boiling as greens. About eighty years ago, it was first introduced into the gardens as a culinary vegetable; and now it is very common, as such, in many parts of Europe. It is planted in a deep, sandy soil, and is blanched either by sand, ashes, litter, or by covering with flower-pots or any other opaque cover. It is forced either by taking up the roots, and planting them in a hot-bed, or in the border of a forcing house, or by surrounding them with litter in the open garden. Each plant should have a cover to keep off the dung from the young shoots, as well as to ensure their being blanched. No plant is so easily forced; and, unlike asparagus, it yields produce the first spring after raising from seed.

SEA LION. (See *Seal.*)

SEA SERPENT. The existence of an enormous marine animal of the serpent shape, and thence called *sea serpent*, or *sea snake*, is mentioned by Pontoppidan (q. v.), in his Natural History of Norway, and has since been noticed by some voyagers. The former represents it to be about 600 feet in length, with apparently about twenty-five folds on its back. Within the last twenty years, a great number of persons, among them many mariners, have asserted, in the most undoubting manner, that they have seen a similar creature on the coasts of the U. States, chiefly on those of New England. By different witnesses, the size of the animal has been differently estimated at from one hundred to forty-five feet in length; but all accounts agree in regard to the protuberances on its back, its vertical sinuosities, and its serpent-shaped head. A more particular account of the appearance and habits of this animal, as far as they have been observed, may be found in Silliman's Journal of Science for April, 1820, and in the Natural History compiled from Buffon, Cuvier, &c. (Boston, 1831, Appendix to vol. iv.).

SEA-SICKNESS (*nausea marina*); the nausea (from ναυς, a ship), retchings and vomitings experienced at sea by those unaccustomed to a sea life. The principal cause of the sickness is, doubtless, the motion of the vessel, and similar effects are sometimes produced by riding in a carriage; but it is often aggravated by the smells and effluvia of the vessel. Noxious gases are evolved by the bilge-water; and chloride of lime or ammonia have been recommended for counteracting their effects and disinfecting the ship.

SEAL. Linnæus united the seals under the genus *phoca;* but later naturalists have recognised in them a group of marine quadrupeds, composed of several natural genera, which differ exceedingly in their dentition, as well as in external characters. The form of the body bears a general resemblance to that of a fish, and the short limbs are chiefly enveloped in the common integument, the part appearing externally serving the purpose of a fin or paddle: these flippers have five toes provided with nails and united by a membrane. The tail is very short and rudimentary. The eye is large, the nostrils open or close at the will of the animal, and the external ear, when it exists, is very small. The upper lip is provided with strong whiskers. The interior structure of the seals is precisely similar to that of land quadrupeds; and atmospheric respiration is indispensable to their existence, although they are capable of remaining a long time under water. The seals live in herds more or less numerous, along the shores of the sea, and are fond of sunning themselves upon the sea-beaches, rocks, or ice-banks. Upon uninhabited coasts, they bring forth and suckle their young, and exhibit the most tender solicitude for their welfare. They are easily tamed, become strongly attached to their keepers, recognise them at a distance, and seem to be endowed with an unusual portion of intelligence; in short, they have many traits of character in common with the dog, as well as many points of external resemblance; hence their very common appellation of *sea-dogs.* They are extremely active in the water, but upon land are easily overtaken and killed. The form of their teeth and jaws shows them to be carnivorous, and their food consists of fish, crabs, and sea-birds, which they are enabled to surprise while swimming. In the Arctic regions, seals are often found under the ice, at the distance of many miles from open water, and form circular breathing holes, even though the ice be several feet in thickness; these openings are kept clear, but the surface is permitted to freeze over partially, so as to conceal them effectually, except from an experienced eye. Seals become extremely fat, and their skins and oil have now become a very important article of commerce. The oil is pure, and adapted to all the purposes for which whale-oil is used; and the skins are extensively employed in trunk-making, saddlery, by hatters, &c. Expeditions are fitted out, both in Europe and in the U. States, for the sole purpose of catching seals. Our own countrymen have particularly distinguished themselves in this branch of business, and annually visit unknown islands in the South seas in pursuit of these quadrupeds. A sealing voyage, with us, often lasts three or more years, and the crew are exposed to great hardships: they are often left in detachments upon small desert islands for months, for the purpose of hunting these quadrupeds to greater advantage; and years have sometimes elapsed before they have been enabled to obtain a release. The common seal of Europe (*phoca vitulina*) grows to the length of three feet; the color of the fur is yellowish-gray, with irregular blackish spots. It is generally considered, by American naturalists, to be identical with one that is found along the whole extent of our Atlantic coast; but we are not aware that it has been accurately compared. The *phoca lagura* is a species which inhabits Newfoundland. The size is the same as the preceding; the color silvery-gray, with blackish-brown spots; the sides and under surface almost white; the nails are strong and black; the tail woolly. Three other species of seals inhabit the Greenland seas—*P. Groenlandica*, *P. hispida*, and *P. barbata.* The latter attains the length of ten feet. It is very probable that others inhabit our coasts; but the species of seal, in general, are not well understood. The hooded seal (*stemmatopus cristatus*) is remarkable for a globular sac, susceptible of inflation, which is situated upon the summit of the head of the males. It grows to the length of seven or eight feet, and inhabits the seas about Greenland and Newfoundland. Some years since, an individual, probably a wanderer, was taken in Long Island sound. The sea-elephant (*macrorhinus proboscidea*), next to the cetacea, is one of the largest of the mammalia, attaining the length of twenty-five or thirty feet. It inhabits the Antarctic seas, and is found upon the southern coasts of Australasia, Juan Fernandez, and the neighboring parts of South America. It is remarkable for the faculty which the males possess of elongating the upper lip into a sort of proboscis: this power is only exerted at times. The canine teeth form stout tusks. The voice of these animals resembles the lowing of cattle. The sea-bear (*arctocephalus ursinus*), so named from the fur and shape of the head, inhabits the coasts of the North Pacific, and is also said to be found in the southern hemisphere. It grows to the length of five or six feet, and has small external ears. The membrane of the hinder feet is prolonged into as many lobes as there are toes; and the fore feet are placed very far back. The color of the fur is brown, and when old takes a grayish tint.—The sea-lion (*platyrhynchus leoninus*) grows to the length of from six to ten feet, and is said to inhabit both the northern and southern coasts of the Pacific. The color is yellowish-brown; and the males have a large mane upon their necks, which partly covers their head and shoulders. The nails of the fore feet are very small, and in part wanting. The voice of the males is very powerful.

SEAL, SEALING-WAX. To seal important documents is a very ancient custom. Writers on diplomatics mention, besides metals, five substances on which impressions were made, or with which letters and public acts were sealed, viz. *terra sigillata* (q. v.), cement, paste, common wax, and sealing-wax. The *terra sigillata* was used by the Egyptians, and appears to have been the first substance employed for sealing. The Romans were acquainted with sealing-earth, and used also clay and common wax, which has been employed for sealing, in Europe, since the earliest times; but writers on diplomatics are not agreed whether white or yellow wax was first used. In the course of time, it was colored. Impressions on paste or dough are of a much later origin. Proper diplomas were never sealed with wafers; but kings were accustomed to seal their letters with this paste before the invention of sealing-wax. Maltha also was used for seals. (See *Cement.*) Some writers assert that sealing-wax was invented about 1640 by a Frenchman, named Rousseau. It was called, in France, *cire d'Espagne* (Spanish wax). At the time of its invention, a kind of gum lac, that was only once melted and colored a little red, was called Portugal wax (*cire de Portugal*). That sealing-wax was either not at all or very little known in Germany, at the beginning of the sixteenth century, may be inferred from its not being mentioned either by Porta or Wecker. The French have supposed that sealing-wax was used earlier in the East Indies than in Europe; but Beckmann, in his History of Inventions, declares himself unable to decide this point. The oldest known seal, made of our common sealing-wax, is that found by Mr. Roos on a letter from London, dated August 30, 1554, and addressed to the rheingrave Philip Francis von Daun, by his agent in England, Gerard Hermann The next seal, in the order of time, is one of the year 1561, on a letter written to the council of Gőrlitz at Breslau, found in the archives of Gőrlitz. Mr. Beckmann mentions a series of other old seals. The earliest mention of sealing-wax in printed books, is probably contained in the *Aromatum et Simplicium aliquot Historia, Garcia ab Horto auctore* (Antverpiæ, 1574). It was first printed in 1563; and it appears from this that sealing-wax was then in common use with the Portuguese. The most ancient printed recipe for making sealing-wax is in a work by Samuel Zimmermann, of Augsburg, entitled *Neu Titularbuch* (1579); and it is remarkable that nothing is said of gum lac, at present the principal ingredient in sealing wax, at least in that of the best quality: the composition approaches, on the contrary, very near to that which, in diplomatics, is called *maltha*. This invention, therefore, one might conclude, was not brought from the East Indies. (For further information see vol. I. of the above mentioned *History of Inventions.*) At the time when writing was not a common accomplishment, the seal very often took the place of the name, so that we find eighty-eight seals attached to the instrument which sets forth the election of Ladislaus, by the Hungarian estates, in 1440, and 350 seals attached to the statement of grievances, sent, in 1415, by the Bohemian estates, to the council of Constance, as we find at present crosses made by Indian chiefs when they conclude treaties by written instruments. To protect seals against falsification, a counter seal (*contrasigillum*, privy seal in England) was often put on the reverse of the large seal. In Germany, this was first done under the emperor Henry III; in France, under Louis VII. These small seals were in later periods used alone in cases of minor importance. As the seal was so important, the keeper of it was always a high officer. With the Greek emperors, the keepers were the *logotheti*; with the Merovingians, the *referendarii*; with the Carlovingians, and later emperors, the chancellors. The elector of Mayence, the arch-chancellor of the German empire, was, down to the latest times of the empire, the keeper of the seals. In France, the chancellor was also, originally, the keeper of the seals; but as the office of chancellor could not be taken from him, a *garde des sceaux* was appointed if the chancellor fell into disgrace. The *garde des sceaux* had the rank, official dress and privileges of the chancellor. The seals were kept in a silver box, of which he was to carry the keys continually with him. The royal edicts and patents were sealed with green wax. Under the republic, all the royal seals were destroyed. All the impressions made with them were likewise ordered to be destroyed, and the greatest part actually were so. Napoleon adopted a seal with impressions on two sides, according to the fashion of the royal times. The chancellors in France were formerly obliged to seal the royal orders, and it was made their chief duty to attach the seal to none which were inconsistent with law or justice. In England, the office of the lord chancellor and lord keeper of the great seals have been united since the time of Elizabeth; but for the privy seal there is still a particular officer, the lord keeper of the privy seal,—generally called *lord privy seal*,—through whose hands all instruments pass before the great seal is affixed to them. The English seal has only one side, and there are two great seals, different in dignity. The most important contains the portrait of the king, the second the royal arms. From the privy seal is to be distinguished the signet, which is kept by the secretary of the cabinet. (See *Keeper*.) In Scotland, there is also a lord keeper of the great seal, a lord privy seal, and a particular officer for law papers, called *keeper of the signet*. (See *Sphragistics*.)

Seamen. It is the policy of every nation aspiring to maritime power, to increase the number of its seamen. This is one reason for promoting fisheries, as the nursery for the supply of the navy. The English laws subject men of this class to a peculiar hardship, little consonant to the spirit of the British constitution, as they are liable to be forcibly seized and detained in the naval service. The power of impressing seamen into that service has been a matter of some dispute, and submitted to with great reluctance. Sir Michael Foster has shown that impressments are of very ancient date, and have been uniformly practised for a long series of years; whence he concludes this practice to be a part of the common law. It is also recognised in many statutes, such, for instance, as exempted certain persons from impressment, though the power of impressing is not expressly granted in the acts of parliament. Sir William Blackstone says this practice is only defensible from public necessity, to which all private considerations must give way.

Seapoys. (See *Sepoys*.)

Search, Right of. (See *Prize*.)

Seasons. The year is remarkably diversified by the seasons, which depend upon the oblique position of the sun's path through the heavens, whereby this luminary rises to different heights above the horizon, making the days sometimes longer, and sometimes shorter, than the nights. When the sun rises highest at noon, its rays fall most nearly in the direction of a perpendicular, and consequently a greater number is received upon any given spot; their action, also, at the same time, continues the longest. These circumstances make the difference between summer and winter. It is true, that the sun is sometimes nearer to us by one thirtieth of his whole distance than at others. This is evident from his diameter being found, by actual measurement, to be one thirtieth larger at one time of the year than at the opposite. But the greatest proximity in the northern hemisphere takes place in winter; the sun is farthest from us in July, and nearest in January; and the difference between summer and winter temperature would undoubtedly be greater than it now is, if the sun were to remain at the same invariable distance through the year. In southern latitudes, mid-winter occurs in July, when the sun is at his greatest distance. This may be one cause of the excessive cold which prevails in high southern latitudes, as at Cape Horn and about the south pole, beyond that which belongs to similar latitudes on this side of the equator. It is found, that the sun does not rise so high in summer, or descend so low in winter, at the present time, as it did formerly: in other words, the obliquity of the ecliptic, which is half the difference between the sun's greatest and least meridian altitudes, is growing less and less continually, and the seasons are thus tending, though slowly, towards one unvaried spring. This diminution of the sun's utmost range north and south, since the time of the earliest observations, or during a period of 3000 years, amounts to nearly a fiftieth part of the whole quantity. This may be one of the causes of a melioration of winter, which seems to be so considerable in those places where there are the means of making a comparison of the degree of cold that has prevailed at different times. The year is naturally divided into four periods by the equinoxes and solstices, or those epochs when the day is equal to the night, namely, 21st of March and 23d of September, and those when there is the greatest difference, namely, 21st of June and 22d of December. Our winter, spring, summer and autumn (q. v.) have reference to these epochs, although their commencement and termination do not correspond exactly to the astronomical times above indicated. We are apt to imagine, that the four seasons are equal to each other, and that spring and summer are together just half the year. This is not the case, however, more especially with respect to the natural periods, so denominated. If, for example, we compare the time from the 21st of March to the 23d of September with the rest of the year, we shall find a difference of about one week, the former being the longer. This benefit of a long summer is confined, at present, to the northern hemisphere; but this natural distinction is not a permanent one. This longer continuance of the sun in the northern hemisphere arises from the particular position of the sun's oval orbit, or path through the heavens. We have already stated, that the sun is nearest to us in the winter season: in other words, the earth is nearest to the sun, and on this account its motion is more rapid, so that the part of the orbit from the autumnal equinox (September 23d) to the vernal (March 21st), is completed a week sooner than the other half, in which the motion is slower. (See *Equinox*, and *Precession of the Equinoxes*.) But the point of the sun's nearest approach, or perihelion, on the position of which the above-mentioned physical advantages depend, is in motion, whereby we are gradually losing the benefit of a prolonged summer, and in about 5000 years shall cease to enjoy any such privilege. In about 10,000 years the condition will be reversed, and the southern hemisphere will be the favored portion of the globe. It may be worth mentioning, that at the date fixed by chronologists for the first residence of man upon the earth, the sun's influence was equally distributed to the two hemispheres. (See *Calendar*, and *Year*.)

Sebacic Acid is obtained from tallow, and was at first called *acid of fat*, but is now known to be *benzoic acid*, contaminated with some unknown substance derived from the fat which alters some of its properties.

Sebago; a lake of Maine, about twelve miles long, which may be connected with Portland harbor by a canal—distance eighteen miles.

Sebastian, St., a saint of the Roman calendar, who, according to the legend, was born at Narbonne, and lived during the reign of Diocletian and Maximian, towards the end of the third century. He distinguished himself in the military service, and rendered great assistance to the Christians, but was finally arrested and carried before Diocletian. The emperor, finding promises and threats vain, ordered him to be shot, and he was left for dead, pierced through with a thousand arrows. A woman, who came by night to inter his body, finding signs of life in him, took him home, and nursed him till he recovered. He then presented himself before Diocletian, and remonstrated with him on his cruelty; whereupon the emperor ordered him to be beaten to death with clubs, and his body to be thrown into the common sewer. His relics were carried to Soissons, in the ninth century, whence they were dispersed through France, Spain, Germany and the Netherlands. St. Sebastian is invoked against the plague. His day is the 20th of January. There are many pictures of this saint, by the most eminent painters. He is generally represented tied to a tree, with arrows sticking in his body.

Sebastian, don, king of Portugal, posthumous son of the Infant John and of Joanna, daughter of Charles V, was born in 1554, and ascended the throne in 1557, at the death of his grandfather, John III. He showed a great love for knowledge, and was educated, unfortunately, in an injudicious way, by his guardian, Catharine of Austria, wife of John III (sister of Charles V). Fanaticism took the place of piety in his mind, and Quixotism that of bravery. In order to distinguish himself from all other princes, he assumed the title of "Most obedient king," as the king of France was styled "Most Christian king," and the king of Spain "Most Catholic king." His devotion to the church was only equalled by his aversion to unbelievers. He conversed with the Jesuits around him on nothing but the happy moment when he should shed the blood of the Moors. His adventurous spirit appeared in an expedition which he made at the age of twenty years, with 800 or 900 Portuguese, to Tangier, among the mountains of the northern coast of Africa, where he fell upon the unsuspecting inhabitants. His success on this occasion led him to undertake more daring enterprises. The nephew of the sheriff of Fez and Morocco, Muley Mohammed, was involved in an open war with his uncle, whom he aimed to deprive of the throne; and Sebastian promised him his assistance, hoping to effect something for Christianity and the fame of Portugal. He communicated his design to Philip II, who, according to some authors, earnestly dissuaded him from it; according to others, he not only encouraged him, expecting, in case of his death, to be made king of Portugal, but even promised him fifty galleys and 10,000 soldiers. In spite of the admonitions of the widowed queen, and the representations and offers of Muley Moloch, the sheriff of Morocco, who promised to cede to him four fortified places on the coast of Africa, he equipped a fleet and an army, part of which he had collected in Spain, Germany and Italy, and sailed for Africa, June 24, 1578, at the age of twenty-three years. The fleet comprised about 1000 vessels of different sizes, and had on board 9000 Portuguese, 3000 Germans, 700 Englishmen, and 2300 Spaniards. They landed safely at Alzira, and Muley Mohammed came directly with 300 Moors, to offer his son as a hostage. In the mean time, the sheriff of Morocco had collected a force of 100,000 men, and marched to the shore. He again, however, attempted to negotiate a peace, but without success. August 3, the two armies approached. "As the Portuguese is resolved upon his ruin," said Muley Moloch, "let him perish." Sebastian summoned a council of war. Some advised an attack, and others a retreat. The hostile forces were separated by a river. Sebastian's camp was distressed by want of provisions, and the enemy had taken possession of all the heights. Muley Mohammed was himself in favor of a retreat to the coast; for there the fleet was ready to receive the soldiers in case of defeat, and the sickness of his uncle Moloch made him sure of the throne in the event of his death, without unsheathing a single sword. But the king would not be persuaded. He was even unwilling to defer the attack till the afternoon, when the early approach of darkness would greatly diminish the danger of his soldiers, in case of defeat. He rode round and encouraged his men, after they were drawn up in battle array, August 4. But his adversary was not, in the mean while, inactive. The Moorish troops advanced in a large semicircle, having, in the van, the thousands who had been driven by fanaticism out of the south of Spain and on the wings 10,000 horsemen. Weak as he was, Muley Moloch left his litter, and mounted on horseback. The engagement soon became general. Sebastian was foremost in the contest, and broke through the first and second lines of the enemy. Muley Moloch was obliged to retire from the battle. He died in his litter, but his death was concealed from his troops. The ardor of the young king soon bore him into the midst of the enemy, who were already pouring on the rear of his troops. He had the alternative to die or yield. The friends who surrounded him remained faithful to him to the last extremity. Muley Mohammed was drowned in his flight. Thus fortune baffled the hopes of all three leaders. All the Portuguese troops were killed or taken. There were different reports about the fate of Sebastian. Some said he perished in the thickest of the fight, others that he was taken, but soon killed, because the Moors quarrelled about the possession of him. On the morning after the battle, Moloch's brother was proclaimed sheriff, and immediately ordered a search to be made on the field for the body of Sebastian. A valet of the Portuguese king found a corpse, which he supposed to be that of his master; but it was so disfigured with wounds that it was impossible to identify it. The consequence was, that his death remained doubtful; and after Portugal had come into the hands of Philip, four adventurers appeared successively, pretending to be Sebastian. One was the son of a stonecutter, and another the son of a brickmaker. One of these ended his life on the scaffold, and the other in the galleys. The last of the four played a most conspicuous part. He appeared, twenty years after Sebastian's defeat, at Venice, where he described particularly the mode in which he concealed himself on the battle-field among the dead and wounded, and declared that he remained in Barbary, lest he should disturb the tranquillity of Portugal. After this, he lived as a hermit in Sicily, and at length resolved to make himself known to the pope. He had been plundered by robbers, and by chance recognised by some Portuguese, and carried to Venice. This was his story. He was banished by the senate, returned, and was thrown into prison. In the examination which he underwent, he appeared so innocent and simple, that all Europe was moved with sympathy. The senate set him at liberty, but banished him from Venice. A Dominican friar, Joseph Taxera, in Paris, moved every court in Europe to take an interest in his case. In the mean time, he was apprehended again in Florence, and sent to Naples, where he was treated as a galley-slave, but persisted in his story. Finally, according to some reports, he was sent to Castile, where he died. Sebastian's enterprise destroyed the flower of the Portuguese nobility, and the treasury was exhausted in the equipment of his fleet. There were no immediate heirs to the throne, and three separate houses claimed it—Parma, Braganza, Spain. The last, under Philip II, succeeded by its superior strength. The conquest of Portugal was the last military exploit of the aged Alba.

Sebastian, San; a town of Spain, at the mouth of the Gurumea; twenty-two miles south-west of Bayonne; lon. 1° 58′ W.; lat. 43° 20′ N.; population, 12,000. It is seated at the foot of a mountain. The harbor lies within two redoubts, between which only one ship can pass at a time. Near its entrance is a fort, with a garrison. The town is surrounded with walls; besides which it is defended by bastions and half-moons; and on the mountain under which it lies is a citadel. The streets are broad, straight, and clean, the houses neat, and the churches fine. A considerable trade is carried on in this place, particularly in iron, steel and wool. San Sebastian has become celebrated for two sieges which it sustained in 1813 and 1823. After the battle of Vittoria, Wellington despatched general Graham to occupy the town, then defended by Ney. He besieged and bombarded it from the beginning of July, and on the 25th attempted to carry it by storm, but was repulsed with the loss of 2000 men, and compelled by a sally of the garrison to raise the siege. The siege was renewed after the defeat of Soult at the foot of the Pyrenees (July 30), and was continued to August 31, during which the British suffered heavy losses in repeated assaults. On that day they became masters of the most important works, at the expense of 3000 men; and the French still remained in possession of the citadel, which did not surrender till September 9. In the campaign of 1823, the French succeeded only after several assaults in getting possession of it by capitulation. They occupied it until 1828.

Sebastiani, Horace François della Porta, French minister of foreign affairs, was born in Corsica, in 1775, and, having entered the French service in 1792, rose rapidly through the different ranks to that of colonel (1799). Colonel Sebastiani took an active part in the revolution of the 18th Brumaire, and, in 1802, the first consul sent him on a mission to the Levant. After having brought about a reconciliation of the differences between the court of Sweden and the regency of Tripoli, and compelled the pacha to acknowledge the Italian republic and salute its flag, he repaired to Alexandria, and had an interview with general Stewart, in order to insist on the terms of the treaty of Amiens for the evacuation of Alexandria. To this demand the English general replied, that he had not received any orders from his court. M. Sebastiani went, therefore, to Cairo, and had many conferences with the pacha on the subject, and offered, in conformity with his orders from the first consul, to open a communication with the beys; but the offer was not accepted, the orders of the Porte being to make it a war of extermination. He afterwards went to St. Jean d'Acre, with the object of settling with the pacha a treaty of commerce, and found him pacifically inclined. In November, he set out on his return to France, having accomplished all the objects of his mission. He was, after his arrival, employed on various services, and, among the rest, in a diplomatic mission to Germany. He distinguished himself in the campaign of 1804, was wounded at the battle of Austerlitz, and obtained the rank of general of division. Napoleon entertained a high opinion of his diplomatic talents, and named him, in 1806, ambassador to the Ottoman Porte—a mission which he filled for some years, with much ability. He established, at Constantinople, a printing-office, for the Turkish and Arabic languages, and by this means contributed not a little to the French influence in that country. The English having forced the passage of the Dardanelles, and menaced Constantinople, Sebastiani immediately organized a plan of defence, marked out the batteries, and prepared for the most vigorous resistance; but the inhabitants broke out into insurrection, and he was obliged to depart for France. He was, subsequently, sent to Spain, where he distinguished himself on numerous occasions; and he served in the Russian-German war (q. v.) under Murat. July 15, 1812, he was surprised by the Russians at Drissa; but he recovered his character by his exertions at the battle of Borodino. On the invasion of France, he had a command in Champagne, and defended Châlons. April 10, M. Sebastiani sent to M. Talleyrand his adhesion to the provisional government, and, June 1, received from the king the cross of St. Louis. On the return of Napoleon, in 1815, he was elected deputy of the lower chamber, and after the second abdication of Napoleon, was one of the commissioners to treat for peace with the allies. In 1819, he was elected a member of the chamber of deputies, by the island of Corsica, and has since constantly shown himself a friend of constitutional liberty, and of national independence. His lucid and manly eloquence has been employed to throw light over all the great questions of finance, war, foreign politics and domestic administration, and has shown him to possess, at once, the talents of an orator and the knowledge of a statesman. After the revolution of 1830, general Sebastiani received the port-folio of the marine in the Guizot ministry (August), and in November that of foreign affairs under Laffitte, which he has continued to retain under Périer.

Secant. In trigonometry, the secant denotes a right line drawn from the centre of a circle, which, cutting the circumference, proceeds till it meets with a tangent to the same circle. In the higher geometry, it signifies the straight line which cuts a curve in two or more points.

Seceders, in Scotland; the Presbyterians who have withdrawn from the established church. The secession took place in 1733, when several preachers were ejected in consequence of their opposition to the law of patronage. The ejected ministers formed themselves into an ecclesiastical court, under the name of the "associated presbytery," and published an act, declaration and testimony to the doctrine, worship, government and discipline of the church of Scotland. In 1747, a division arose among the seceders respecting the legality of the burgess oath, in which burgesses profess "the true religion professed within the realm."—Those who asserted the lawfulness of the oath, were called *burghers*, those who condemned it, *antiburghers*; but a union has recently taken place between these two parties, under the name of the "united associate synod of the secession church," consisting, in 1827, of 19 presbyteries, and 333 churches. Several congregations of each party, however, refused to accede to it. (See *Presbyterians*, and *Scotland*.)

Sechelles. (See *Herault*.)

Seckendorf, Veit Louis von, a German divine and historian, was born in 1626, at Aurach, in Franconia, and received his education with the children of Ernest the Pious, duke of Saxe-Gotha, to whom he became librarian, privy-counsellor, minister, and consistorial director. In 1664, he entered into the service of the duke of Saxe-Zeitz, and, at length, into that of the elector of Brandenburg, who made him counsellor of state in 1691, and also chancellor of the university of Halle. His death took place in 1692. He was the author of a defence of Luther (in answer to Maimbourg's History of Lutheranism), which appeared in 1688 and 1692, under the title of *Commentarius historicus et apologeticus de Lutheranismo* (2 vols., folio), and a political work, entitled *Deutscher Fürstenstaat* (Hanover, 1656, 4to.)

Secker, Thomas, archbishop of Canterbury, was born of dissenting parents in 1693. Being designed by his friends for the ministry in their connexion, he early directed his attention to theological pursuits; but from scruples of conscience declined the appointment of a pastor, and went to Paris in 1719, with a view of practising in medicine, to the study of which he had devoted the three preceding years. While in this metropolis, he formed an intimacy with Talbot, son of the bishop of Durham, which eventually ripened into the sincerest friendship. By the persuasion of the latter, who promised him his father's interest in promoting his advancement, Secker became avowedly a member of the church of England. In 1722, he was ordained by bishop Talbot; and, in 1733, he received the living of St. James's, Westminster, having, in the preceding year, been appointed a king's chaplain, on which occasion he graduated as LL. D. Two years after, he was elevated to the see of Bristol, whence he was translated, in 1737, to that of Oxford, with which he held the valuable deanery of St. Paul's. In 1758, the duke of Newcastle, then at the head of the cabinet, placed bishop Secker in the primacy. As a scholar, he was elegant rather than profound, although in some of his writings, especially in his Lectures on the Catechism of the Church of England, he displays much depth of argument as well as perspicuity of style. His works, consisting of charges and sermons, have been collected and printed in twelve octavo volumes (1795), with a life by bishop Porteus, his chaplain. There was also published by him, in his life-time, a reply to Mayhew on the Charter and Conduct of the Society for propagating the Gospel, without the author's name. This controversy relates to a proposed establishment of bishops in the American colonies. Archbishop Secker died at Lambeth palace, in 1768.

SECOND. (See *Duel.*)

SECONDARY FORMATION. (See *Geology.*)

SECOND SIGHT (in Gaelic, *Taisch*); a Highland superstition, which supposes certain persons endowed with the power of seeing future or distant events as if actually present. (See *Highlands.*)

SECRETARY (from *secretus*, secret); an officer, who, by order of his superior, writes letters and other instruments. Secretaries of state in monarchical governments, are officers of the king, whose duty it is to attend to the despatch of grants, orders, &c. This term was first used in France, where the three clerks of the privy council (*clercs du secret*) received the title of *secrétaires des finances* in 1343, and in 1547, that of *secrétaires d'état.* Louis XVIII (1814) styled his ministers, *ministres secrétaires d'état.* In England, the term *secretary* was first applied to those clerks of the king, who, being always near his person, were called "clerks of the secret;" and in the reign of Henry VIII, the expression "secretary of state" first came into use. Elizabeth first admitted them to the rank of privy counsellors. There was formerly a secretary of state for North Britain, and at one time also for the American department. At present there are three *principal secretaries of state*, viz. one for the home department, one for foreign affairs, and one for the colonies, each of which has two under secretaries. The secretaries of state have the custody of the signet, and the direction of the signet-office. (See *Ministers.*) The secretary at war belongs to the war-office. In the U. States, the four heads of departments are styled *secretaries.* The department of state, created by act of congress (September 15, 1789), embraces foreign and home affairs. The secretary of state conducts treaties with foreign powers, and corresponds with the public ministers abroad, and foreign ministers to the U. States. He keeps the seal of the U. States, but cannot affix it to any commission till signed by the president, nor to any act or instrument without authority from the president. The treasury department was created by act of congress of Sept. 2, 1789. The secretary of the treasury superintends the fiscal concerns of the government. For the settlement of the public accounts, the department is divided into the office of the secretary (who has the superintendence of the whole), the offices of the two controllers, of the five auditors, of the treasurer, and of the register; to each of which is attached the necessary number of clerks. The patent office is under the control of the secretary of state, and the general land-office, in which all patents for land are made out and recorded (established April 25, 1812), is subordinate to the treasury department. The war department (created August 7, 1789) at first embraced the land and sea service; but the latter now forms a distinct department. The secretary of war superintends every branch of military affairs, and has under his direction a requisition bureau, a bounty land-office, a bureau of Indian affairs, a pension bureau, an engineer office, an ordnance office, an office for the commissary-general of subsistence, a paymaster-general's office, and a surgeon-general's office. The office of secretary of the navy was created April 30, 1798; a board of three navy commissioners is attached to the office. A *secretary of embassy* or *legation* is an officer appointed by the sovereign, and attached to an embassy, for writing of despatches, &c. He is to all intents a public minister, and as such has the same immunities as the head of the embassy himself. (See *Diplomacy*, and *Ministers, Foreign.*)

SECRETION. Many of the component parts of the animal system become, in the course of its operations, changed, and unfit for further use. For the preservation of the system, it is not less necessary that these parts should be removed, than that the constant consumption should be supplied; and in this double process the whole organic system is continually changing its ingredients, although it retains the same external form. This supply of new matter is derived from the blood, and the process itself is called *secretion.* Most animals secrete both solids and fluids. The solids are deposited by the capillary vessels at the places of their destination, and supply the continual wear of the system. The liquids are not intended to preserve the form directly, but serve to assimilate the food by promoting digestion (as, for instance, the saliva, gastric juice and bile). In these secreted fluids are contained all the component parts of the blood, slightly changed, together with an alkali. Distinguished from these are the excretions, which are produced in a similar manner, and are designed to carry off from the system useless matter.

SECTS. The term *sect* is generally applied to a party in religion or philosophy, which holds a particular body of doctrines. Thus, in ancient philosophy, there were the Ionic and Italic sects, the Epicurean, the Stoic, the Peripatetic sects. But the philosophical sects are often termed *schools*, and the word *sect* is, in its narrower sense, applied particularly to religious parties. Among the Jews, there were the sects of the Pharisees, Sadducees and Essenes, and, of a more strictly religious character, those of the Caraites, Rabbinists and Samaritans. The Mohammedans are divided into two great sects, the Sunnites and Shiites, besides numerous smaller sects, as the Ishmaelites, Wahabees, Nosairians, &c. (see the several articles, and also *Islam*, *Mohammed*, and *Koran*), who differ from each other not only in their interpretations of the Koran, but in their various views in regard to the genealogy of the prophet's family. The Hindoos are divided into the Sivaites, or those who worship Siva, and the Vishnooites, who pay particular reverence to Vishnoo. The Christian world has, from the first introduction of Christianity, been divided into an almost innumerable variety of sects. We have already given a hasty view of the earlier sects under the head of *Heretics*. The Cathari of the middle ages, who, under various names, opposed the pretensions of the papal see, and to whom the Albigenses (q. v.) and Waldenses (q. v.) mostly belonged, were, with the exception of the latter, extirpated by the inquisition and the inquisitorial tribunals of the church. (See *Cathari*, and *Paulicians*.) In the thirteenth century arose a new species of sects and schismatic fraternities, whose object was the introduction of a new spirit of sanctity among the monastic orders. (See *Fraternities*.) A party grew up among the Franciscans, which was denounced by the popes, and by their own less rigid brethren, and which insisted upon absolute poverty. They were called, in contempt, *fraticelli*, and *spiritual friars*. (See *Franciscans*.) They did not meddle with points of faith, but attacked the existing priestly government, and announced its fall. They wandered about, occupied in praying and asking alms, the excommunication which hung over them preventing them from founding monasteries. Many of the lower classes of both sexes, in France, Germany and the Netherlands, attached themselves, as a third order, to the Fraticelli, and from these Tertiarians sprang the fraternities of Beghards, Beguines (q. v.) and Lollards, whose purity of manners and benevolent institutions, for the care of the sick and the instruction of youth, rendered them more respected than their predecessors, whom they resembled in their frequent prayers, the asking alms, and their secret religious exercises. The Apostolics (q. v.), an order which arose in 1260, at Parma, but did not obtain the papal confirmation, continued to subsist in Italy, Switzerland and France, till the fourteenth century. The Brethren and Sisters of the Free Spirit, remnants of whom are discoverable during the Hussite disturbances in Moravia and Bohemia, under the names of Picards and Adamites (q. v.), aimed at restoring the state of innocence, by appearing naked in their assemblies, without regard to sex or age. Other fraternities, not acknowledged by the church, were distinguished, in the fourteenth century, for their voluntary penances and gross superstitions: such were the Flagellants (q. v.) and the Brothers of the Cross. The Wickliffites (q. v.) in England, and the Hussites in Bohemia (see *Huss*), resembled the Waldenses in their zeal for conformity with the Scriptures, and their opposition to the abuses of the papacy. These, with the Hussite sects, the Calixtins (q. v.) or Utraquists, the Horebites, the Taborites (q. v.), and the Bohemian Brethren (q. v.), preceded the reformation of the 16th century. The Protestant churches which that event created, were, with the Greek church, considered as sects by the Catholics; but by Protestant writers the word *sect* is commonly applied only to the smaller parties, disconnected with the Calvinistic and Lutheran churches. The Jansenists, Quietists and Molinists, notwithstanding the deviations on some doctrinal points, were still orthodox Catholics; the Jansenists even have distinct congregations and clergy in the Netherlands, but yet are by no means considered as forming a separate sect, since they acknowledge the supremacy of the pope, and observe all the Catholic usages, only disputing the pope's infallibility. The Appellants, Convulsionists, and Securists, Naturalists and Figurists, Discernants and Melangists, who were produced by the Jansenist controversy, merely had a short existence in France, in the beginning of the eighteenth century. (See *Jansenius*, and *Quietism*.) In the Greek church, although it has, in later times, been little addicted to religious speculations, there are some sects. These the tolerant government of Russia treats with indulgence. (See *Greek Church.*) In the fourteenth century, the Strigolnicks seceded, from aversion to the clergy, but soon became extinct. In 1666 arose the sect of the Roskolnicians (q. v.), from whom proceeded the Philippones. (q. v.) The Anabaptists, Socinians (q. v.), and Schwenkfeldians, though not Protestants in the strict sense of the word, agree with them in the rejection of the papacy. Besides the great division of the Protestants into Calvinists and Lutherans (see *Reformation*, and *Reformed Church*), the former have been much divided. Thus the different views of Calvin (q. v.) and Zuinglius (q. v.), in regard to church government, formed a ground of distinction which (notwithstanding the *consensus Tigurinus* of 1549) separated the Zuinglians, or older Swiss reformers, and their adherents in Hungary, from the Calvinists of Geneva, France, Holland, Germany and England, and the controversy concerning predestination, at the synod of Dort (1618), produced the permanent separation of the Remonstrants or Arminians (q. v.) from the strict Calvinists. The Reformed in France, under the name of Huguenots (q. v.), acquired a political importance in the sixteenth and seventeenth centuries, and the persecutions to which they were subjected produced its usual effects of religious extravagance and fanaticism. (See *Camisards.*) The English church is Calvinistic, but the majority of the clergy is Arminian. (See *England, Church of.*) Presbyterianism, which in England forms a dissenting sect, is the established religion of Scotland. (See *Presbyterians.*) From the bosom of the English church have also proceeded the Puritans, Independents, Methodists, Quakers Baptists, with other less considerable sects. (See these articles, and also *Nonconformists.*) Unitarians (q. v.) and Universalists (q. v.), who differ from the established church more widely than the sects above mentioned, on doctrinal points, are also pretty numerous in England. Seceders (q. v.), Sandemanians (q. v.), Cameronians (q. v.), &c., are among the more noted of the Scotch sects. The Herrnhutters (see *United Brethren*), and Swedenborgians, or members of the New Jerusalem church (see *Swedenborg*), have proceeded from the Lutheran church. In the U. States, where perfect religious freedom prevails, and where emigrants from all countries seek refuge, it is not strange that there should be representatives of almost all the modern sects of the Christian world, and also some sects of native origin. (See *Christians, Shakers, Tunkers.*) The following table, from the American Almanac for 1832, shows the relative numbers of the different religious denominations in the U. States:—

Denominations.	*Ministers.*	*Churches or Congregations.*	*Communicants.*	*Population.*
Baptists (Calvinistic),	2,914	4,384	304,827	2,743,453
" (Free-will),	300	400	16,000	150,000
" (Free-communion),	30		3,500	30,000
" (Seventh-day),	30	40	2,000	20,000
" (Six-principle),	25	30	1,800	20,000
" (Emancipators),	15		600	4,500
Methodist Episcopal Church,	1,777		476,000	2,600,000
Associate and other Methodists,	350		35,000	175,000
Presbyterians (General Assembly	1,801	2,253	182,000	1,800,000
" (Associate),	74	144	15,000	100,000
" (Cumberland),	50	75	8,000	100,000
Congregationalists (Orthodox),	1,000	1,270	140,000	1,260,000
" (Unitarians),	160	193		176,000
Episcopal Church,	558	700		600,000
Universalists,	150	300		500,000
Roman Catholics,				500,000
Lutherans,	205	1,200	44,000	400,000
Christians,	200	800	25,000	275,000
German Reformed,	84	400	17,400	200,000
Dutch Reformed,	159	194	17,888	125,000
Friends, or Quakers,		400		200,000
Mennonites,	200		30,000	120,000
Tunkers,	40	40	3,000	30,000
United Brethren,	23	23	2,000	7,000
Shakers, or Millennial Church,	45	15		6,000
Swedenborgians, or New Jerusalem Ch.,	30	28		5,000
Jews, and others not mentioned,		150		50,000

Besides the various sects which have formed independent religious communities, there were also, during the course of the seventeenth and eighteenth centuries, numerous theological parties and religious enthusiasts, who were united only by the bonds of common opinions, but did not form distinct ecclesiastical societies. Such were the Labadists, whose founder (1666) was Labadie, an ex-Jesuit and preacher at Middelburg, and who received the doctrines of the Reformed church, but endeavored to form a family similar to the primitive Christian societies, by acts of penance, monastic discipline, and community of goods; the Bœhmists, or followers of Böhme, also called Gichtelians, from the theosophist Gichtel (q. v.), who proposed to restore the priesthood of Melchizedek, and Angelic Brethren, from their efforts to attain angelic purity of life (see *Bœhme*); the Philadelphists, or Angelic Brethren of England, a short-lived theosophical party, collected by Jane Leade, on Bœhmistic principles, towards the close of the seventeenth century; the Dippelians, so called from their founder, Dippel, a physician, who agreed with the Gichtelians in their reverence for the writings of Böhme, but occupied themselves much with alchemy; the Pietists (see *Pietism*), and the Chiliasts or Millennarians, under their various forms. (See *Millennium.*)—See, further, the articles *Abrahamites*, *Theophilanthropists*, and *Theosophists;* and the work of Grégoire, *Histoire des Sectes Religieuses* (2 vols., 1814).

Secular Clergy; in those countries in which there are monastic orders, the clergy who do not live shut up in monasteries, and subject to monastic rules. They are so called in contradistinction to the monks, or *regular clergy* who have taken the vows, and are bound by the rules of their order.

Secular Games (*ludi sæculares*); solemn games, celebrated by the Romans about once a century (*sæculum*), in honor of Apollo and Diana. They lasted three days and three nights; and the secular ode (*carmen sæculare*), composed by Horace on one of these occasions, is yet extant.

Secularization is the act of rendering secular the property of the clergy. The first great secularization in Germany took place in 1648, on the occasion of the peace of Westphalia. The second took place after the peace of Luneville, in 1801. In England, the first great secularization was made under Henry VIII.

Secundus, Johannes. (See *Johannes Secundus.*)

Sedge (*carex*); an extensive genus of grass-like plants, mostly inhabiting the northern and temperate parts of the globe. They are easily distinguished from the grasses by having the stem destitute of joints. The flowers are monœcious, or more rarely diœcious, and are disposed in one or several dense, scaly spikes. The seeds are triangular, and are enveloped in a sort of capsule, composed of a ventricose scale, which enlarges after flowering, and often renders the spikes of these plants conspicuous. The roots are perennial and fibrous, the leaves hard, and rough on the edge. The sedges in general are but of little utility to man. They furnish coarse fodder, containing little nutriment, especially after the flowering season is over, or when dried, and which is rejected by most of the domestic quadrupeds. The roots and leaves decompose with difficulty, and, in the course of time, contribute largely to turn the soil of marshes into peat. More than three hundred species are known, of which about one third are found in the U. States. They are found in all soils, but the greater proportion are marsh plants. The *C. acuta* forms in marshes the little elevations called *tussocks*. It grows in dense tufts, and the fibrous roots interlace very closely, so as to retain a portion of the soil, which, in places subject to occasional inundation, is liable to be washed from around them. At the same time, the mass increases above by successive generation. The *C. Fraseri* is the handsomest of the genus, resembling, at a short distance, when in flower, one of the *liliaceæ*. It was discovered in the southern parts of the Alleghanies, but has not been seen in a wild state by any of our later botanists.

Sedgwick, Theodore, a judge of the supreme court of Massachusetts, was born at Hartford, Connecticut, in May, 1746. His father, a respectable merchant, died when he was about ten years of age, leaving little property; but the generosity of his eldest brother enabled him to study at Yale college. He then turned his attention to divinity, which, however, he abandoned for law; and, before he was twenty years old, in April, 1766, he was admitted to the bar. He practised in Berkshire county, Massachusetts. He embarked in the revolutionary struggle with his constitutional ardor. In 1776, he served as an aid to general Thomas, in the expedition to Canada, and subsequently made great exertions in procuring supplies for the army. At the same time, his humanity in affording protection to the tories, put his popularity in no small hazard. He represented Sheffield in the Massachusetts general court several times, before and after the revolution. In 1785 and 1786, he was a member of congress, under the old confederation. In the winter of 1787, he contributed much to the suppression of the insurrectionary spirit then pervading the state, frequently exposing himself to outrage, insult, and even death. His exertions in putting down what was called Shays's rebellion, are honorably mentioned in the history of the times. In 1788, he was a representative of Stockbridge, in the state convention that adopted the federal constitution, of which he was one of the principal advocates. In the same year, he was a member of the house of representatives of the state, and was chosen its speaker. In March, 1789, he took his seat in the lower house of congress, and was successively reëlected to it until March, 1796, when he was chosen to the senate, where he remained until March, 1799, having, during a considerable portion of one session, acted as president *pro tem.* In the latter year, he was again elected a member of the house of representatives, and chosen speaker. In 1802, he was appointed judge of the supreme court of Massachusetts, and retained that office until his death, January 24, 1813. As a statesman and jurist, Mr. Sedgwick enjoyed a high reputation. His philanthropic efforts in the cause of the emancipation of the negroes, deserve especial record. He was one of the counsel who, soon after the adoption of the constitution of Massachusetts, procured a decision, by which such a construction was given to that instrument as to abolish slavery in the state.

Sedley, sir Charles, a celebrated wit, of the age of Charles II, was the son of sir John Sedley, of Aylesford, in Kent, where he was born in 1639. At the age of seventeen he was entered at Oxford, but quitted the university without a degree, and retired to his estates till after the restoration (1660). His credit with the king was heightened by his never asking favors, although the debauchery into which he plunged soon dissipated his pecuniary resources. A fine of £500 was imposed upon him by chief-justice Hyde, for an indecent riot committed at a public house, where he harangued the mob, naked, from the balcony, in company with lord Buckhurst and sir Thomas Ogle. Being returned member of parliament for the borough of New Romney, in Kent, in 1661, he sat for that place in four successive parliaments. James II carried on an intrigue with his daughter, afterwards created by that monarch countess of Dorchester. Sir Charles was so little pleased by this elevation, that it is said to have been the principal cause of his subsequently taking a strenuous part in bringing about the revolution; and to a gentleman who taxed him with a want of loyalty, he replied that, "as the king had made his daughter a countess, the least he could do was to assist in making his majesty's daughter a queen." Sir Charles died about the commencement of the last century. He was the author of six dramatic pieces, printed with his miscellaneous poems, in 1719, in two octavo volumes. The latter consist of pastorals, prologues, songs, epilogues, and occasional pieces, which, though not free from the licentiousness of the age, are clear of much of its grossness.

Sedlitz or Seidlitz Water; a mineral water obtained from the village of Sedlitz, in Bohemia. The waters are saline and purgative, limpid, sparkling, and of a bitter and salt taste. They contain sulphates of magnesia (Epsom salt), soda (Glauber's salt), lime, and carbonates of lime and magnesia.

Seebeck, a distinguished German natural philosopher, born in 1770, at Reval, studied medicine in Berlin and Göttingen, is known by the discovery of thermomagnetism. He also partook in the discovery of the *metalloides*, discovered the *entoptic* phenomena, for which he received a prize from the French institute, and enlarged in other ways the field of optics. Since 1818, he has lived in Berlin, where he was elected a member of the academy of sciences, and died in December, 1831.

Seed; that part of organic bodies which serves to continue the species. The seeds of plants present the greatest variety of form and appearance. In shape, they are conical, round, oval, oblong, flat, kidney-shaped, &c., with smooth and shining surfaces, or rough, and provided with all sorts of appendages. They consist of an external covering, a shell or membrane, within which are the kernel and the germ. The external envelope is designed merely for the protection of the kernel, and generally consists of several membranes. When hard and woody, it is called a *nut*, or *stone*, and, in this case, the kernel is enveloped in an inner, soft, and thin covering. The kernel consists of farinaceous and mucilaginous matter of more or less hardness, and possesses the property of absorbing moisture from the earth, by means of which it is softened, swells, and affords the first nourishment to the germ. Seeds are formed of one, two, or several lobes. At the point by which the kernel was attached to the capsule or seed-vessel, a scar or mark is visible, beneath which lies the germ, which contains the future plant. Besides the wonderful provision which nature has made for the dispersion of seeds, some being wafted through the air by the light downy appendages attached to them, and others being fitted, by their form and envelope, for being carried down rivers, their vitality or dormancy is also wonderful. Seed may be kept out of the ground for a century, and still retain the power of germinating when committed to the soil. So also where seeds have been found deeply buried in the earth, or in soils not adapted for their germination, in positions in which they have lain quiescent for years, they have been known, on exposure to the air, or removal to a different soil, to exercise a vegetative power. (See *Plants.*)

Seed Lac. (See *Coccus*, end of the article.)

Seeland. (See *Zealand.*)

Seetzen, Ulric Jasper, a German traveller, a native of East Friesland, was educated at Göttingen, where he particularly studied philosophy and natural history, under professor Blumenbach. Having published some tracts on natural history, statistics, and political economy, he was appointed aulic counsellor to the czar in the principality of the Jever. He was desirous of visiting Africa and the East; and being encouraged by the dukes Ernest and Augustus of Saxe-Gotha, he set off, in August, 1802, for Constantinople. He proceeded to Syria, and remained a considerable time at Aleppo, making excursions into the neighboring territories. In 1806, he explored the course of the river Jordan and the Dead sea, travelled through Palestine, and went to Hebron and mount Sinai. His enthusiastic desire of knowledge prompted him to profess Mohammedanism, that he might undertake a pilgrimage to Mecca and Medina, which he visited in 1809 and 1810. In the month of November, 1810, he was at Mocha, whence he wrote the last letters which arrived from him in Europe. Having had his property seized by the Arabs, under the pretext of his being a magician, he proceeded towards Sana, in December, 1811, to complain to the iman of that place; and a few days after his departure, he died suddenly at Täes, probably from the effects of poison given him by order of the iman. No complete account of the researches of this unfortunate traveller ever appeared; but his letters, which he addressed to baron von Zach, were inserted in the Geographical and Astronomical Correspondence, published at Gotha, and a translation was printed in the French *Annales des Voyages* (1808—14). Extracts from his letters to Blumenbach, and others also, were published in the *Magasin Encyclopédique.*

Segars. (See *Tobacco.*)

Seguidilla; a Spanish form of versification, consisting of four lines, generally assonant lines, of seven and five syllables alternately. It usually has a close of three verses, called *estribillo*, of which the first and last lines rhyme.

Ségur; an ancient French family, which has produced several distinguished men, including the following:—*Joseph Alexander*, born at Paris in 1752, died in 1805, was the author of several comedies and operas, which still remain popular, of the *Correspondance secrète entre Ninon de l'Enclos, le Marquis de Villarceaux et Mad. de Maintenon*, and a romance *Sur les Femmes* (3 vols., translated into English). —His brother *Louis Philip*, born in 1753, died in 1830, peer of France, and member of the French academy, served in America under Rochambeau, and, after the peace of 1783, was ambassador to St. Petersburg. In 1790, he was sent to Berlin; but, after the deposition of the king, he retired from public affairs, and in 1798 published his *Théâtre de l'Hermitage*—a collection of plays which he had composed for the private theatre of the empress of Russia. In 1800, appeared his masterly *Histoire du Règne de Frédéric Guillaume II*, or *Décade historique.* In 1803, he was chosen a member of the Institute, and Napoleon appointed him one of the council of state. After the restoration, he was received into the chamber of peers. In 1824, appeared his *Œuvres Complètes* (30 vols., 2d ed., 36 vols., 1828), and, in 1825, his *Mémoires, Souvenirs et Anecdotes* (3 vols.).—His son *Paul Philip*, born 1780, served with distinction on various occasions, and executed several diplomatic missions. In 1812, he was created *maréchal de camp*, and distinguished himself in several bloody actions in 1813 and 1814. In December, 1831, he was made peer for life, being one of the thirty created for the purpose of giving ministers a majority on the question of a hereditary peerage. His *Histoire de Napoléon et de la Grande Armée pendant l'Annee* 1812, has passed through numerous editions, and given rise to several controversies, particularly one with Gourgaud, which resulted in a duel between the parties.

Seidelmann, James, professor in the academy of fine arts in Dresden, was born in 1750. He perfected himself in painting, under Mengs (q. v.), at Rome, and subsequently invented an entirely new manner of drawing in *sepia*, chiefly for the representation of the antique. His pieces, executed in this manner, and his copies in oil, are numerous, and have gained him much reputation. In his style of drawing in *sepia*, he and his wife are still unrivalled, though they have had many imitators. His wife was born in Venice, and perfected herself in miniature painting under Theresa Maron, sister to Raphael Mengs. She made the drawing of the Madonna del Sisto, from which Müller prepared his admirable engraving.

Seidlitz Water. (See *Sedlitz.*)

Seigniories, in Lower Canada; a remnant of the feudal system which prevailed in France at the time of the settlement of Canada, and many of the details of which were transferred to the Transatlantic colony. All the lands of the colony were granted under the old feudal tenure, but many modifications were successively introduced, tending to abridge the rights of the seigneur, or lord, and extend those of the tenant. On the conquest of Canada by the English, the institutions of the colony were left unchanged; but about thirty years afterwards, the tenure of free and common soccage was introduced, and all the lands not previously granted have since been considered as soccage lands. The seigneurs have no longer any jurisdiction, and the feudal services of the tenants are light. (See Bouchette's *British Dominions in North America*, vol. i, chap. xiv.)

Seiks. (See *Sikhs.*)

Seine, one of the four great rivers of France, rises in the mountains of Burgundy, flows northward, through Champagne, to Troyes, receives the Aube, and, turning to the west, is joined by the Yonne, a river from the south, and before reaching Paris, by the Marne, a larger stream flowing from the west. At Paris, the Seine varies from 300 to 500 feet in width; and it soon after receives an addition to its stream, by the influx of the Oise, when, pursuing a winding course to the northwest, it passes Rouen, and discharges itself into the sea at Havre de Grace; length of its course, 400 miles. It becomes navigable at Troyes, and large vessels can go up to Rouen.

Seine; a department in the north of France, which is, in fact, nothing more than the capital. Its district forms a tract nearly square, of which the breadth is about sixteen miles. (See *Department.*)

Seine, Lower; a department in the north of France, comprising the northeast part of Normandy. (See *Department.*)

Seine and Marne; a department in the north-east of France, occupying the western part of Champagne. (See *Department.*)

Seine and Oise; a department of the north-east of France, adjacent to that of the Oise, and to that of the Seine and Marne. (See *Department.*)

Seisin, in law, signifies *possession.*

Sejanus, the favorite of Tiberius, was the son of a Roman knight. Although he knew how to dissemble his ambition and pride before his master, yet he spared no means of gratifying his passion. He acquired the confidence of the suspicious Tiberius, so as to govern him completely; and the servile senate paid the greatest respect to the powerful favorite. The pretorian cohorts were also favorable to him, and there was no obstacle in the way of his attaining the supreme power, but Drusus, son of Tiberius, and the sons of Germanicus, the nearest of kin to the emperor. Drusus was put out of the way by poison; the latter, with their mother, were banished and thrown into prison—a step which they did not long survive. Several distinguished Romans, friends of Germanicus, were beheaded at the instigation of Sejanus; and when Tiberius finally retired from Rome, and withdrew from the government, Sejanus governed with absolute power, and the senate ordered that the statues erected in his honor should be publicly worshipped. But at the moment of his highest elevation, the suspicions of Tiberius were awakened, and his measures were taken so cautiously, that Sejanus suspected nothing, until he was openly accused by the emperor before the senate (A. D. 31). He was then imprisoned, condemned to death, and executed on the same day.

Selam. (See *Flowers, Language of.*)

Selden, John, a distinguished English scholar, was born in 1584, at Sabington, in Sussex, and received his education at Oxford. After a residence of three or four years, he repaired to Clifford's Inn, London, and about two years after removed to the Inner Temple, and, on being called to the bar, acted principally as a chamber counsel. The first object of his studies was the history and antiquities of his own county; and, in 1607, he drew up a work entitled *Analectum Anglo-Bri-*

tannicum, a treatise on the civil government of Britain before the coming of the Normans. It was succeeded, in 1610, by England's Epinomes, and *Jani Anglorum Facies altera*, a treatise on the progress of English law. In 1614, appeared his largest English work, Titles of Honor, a standard authority in regard to all that concerns the degrees of nobility and gentry in England. This was followed, in 1617, by his *De Diis Syriis*, an inquiry into the Syrian idolatry. In 1618, he entered the field of politics by his History of Tythes, the object of which was to deny their divine right. This publication highly offended James I, and the author was brought before the high-commission court, on which, without retracting his opinions, he declared his sorrow for publishing the work. In 1621, James I, in his speech to parliament, having asserted that their privileges were grants from the crown, Selden spoke so freely in opposition to this doctrine, and was so instrumental in drawing up their protestation, that on their dissolution he was committed to custody. He was discharged at the expiration of six weeks, on petition. In the following year, he was elected member of parliament for Lancaster, and was again a member in the two first parliaments of Charles I, in the second of which he was appointed to support the impeachment of the duke of Buckingham, and otherwise became a leading opposer of the arbitrary measures of the court. In 1629, he drew up his learned treatise entitled *Marmora Arundelliana*. (See *Arundelian Marbles*.) On the dissolution of the parliament, Selden was one of the eight members of the commons who were imprisoned in the tower on a charge of sedition, and who refused to give security for their good behavior. This confinement lasted two or three years; but, at length, he was admitted to bail, and finally released in the beginning of 1634. During this period, he wrote some of his treatises on Jewish antiquities, and, in 1635, published his treatise entitled *Mare Clausum*, in answer to the *Mare Liberum* of Grotius; in opposition to which he endeavors to establish the British right of dominion over the circumjacent seas. Some of the following years of his life were occupied in Hebrew studies, the result of which appeared in a work entitled *De Jure Naturali et Gentium juxta Disciplinam Ebræorum*—a valuable but not very well digested repertory of all the matter afforded by history or tradition, in relation to the subject. In 1640, memorable for the meeting of the long parliament, Selden was unanimously elected member for the university of Oxford. His name appears on several committees, appointed to inquire into abuses; but he neither concurred in the prosecution of lord Strafford, nor seemed desirous to abrogate the episcopal form of church government, although anxious to check the encroachments of ecclesiastical power. When the differences between king and parliament were manifestly tending to open hostilities, he opposed the attempts of both parties to gain possession of the sword, and, when he failed, withdrew, as much as he was able, from public business. He remained, however, with the parliament, and was one of the synod which met at Westminster for the establishment of church government. In 1643, he was appointed by the house of commons, keeper of the records in the Tower, and, the year following, subscribed the solemn league and covenant. In 1645, he was elected one of the twelve commissioners of the admiralty; and, in 1646, the parliament voted him £5000, as a reward for services. He continued to sit in parliament after the execution of the king, and employed all his influence for the protection of learning. He refused to gratify Cromwell by writing an answer to the Eikon Basilike. He died in 1654. In private life, he was universally esteemed for his goodness of heart and urbanity of manners; and, as a scholar, he must be deemed one of the most learned men of his day. His style is often labored and uncouth, although his speeches and conversation were peculiarly luminous and clear. Some opinion of the latter may be collected from his Table Talk, published, after his death, by his amanuensis. His library and museum were added to the Bodleian library. His whole works were collected in three folio volumes (usually bound in six), by doctor David Wilkins (1726), with a life of the author. (See also Aikin's *Life of Selden*.)

Selenium; a new elementary body, detected by Berzelius, in the sulphur of a sulphuric acid manufactory, at Fahlun, in Sweden. The sulphur was derived from iron pyrites, found at the copper mine of Fahlun. After the combustion of the sulphur in the acid manufactory, there remained at the bottom of the leaden chamber, a red or brownish matter, which, when heated before the blow-pipe, emitted a very strong odor, resembling that of horse-radish. The name applied to this substance comes from σελήνη, the moon, indicating its relation to *tellurium.* The purification of the selenium, as found above, is a tedious process; it being mingled with no fewer than eight foreign substances. When pure, however, it exhibits the following properties: Exposed to a heat higher than that of boiling water, it melts, and on cooling becomes solid: in this state, it has the metallic lustre, a deep brown color, and a conchoidal fracture. The powder of selenium is a deep red. In very thin slivers, it is transparent, with a ruby-red color. It crystallizes with difficulty in cubes or four-sided prisms, terminated by pyramids; specific gravity, 4.3. It is easily scratched by the knife; is brittle, and readily reduced to powder. When heated in a retort, it begins to boil at a temperature below that of a red heat, and assumes the form of a dark-yellow vapor, not so intense as the vapor of sulphur: the vapor condenses in the neck of the retort in black drops, which unite into larger drops, as in the distillation of mercury. Selenium is a very bad conductor of heat, and a non-conductor of electricity. It combines with three portions of oxygen, forming three separate compounds; viz. *oxide of selenium, selenious acid*, and *selenic acid.* The first of these is formed whenever selenium is strongly heated in the open air, and is distinguished by the smell above alluded to. It is not absorbed by water, nor is it capable of uniting with acids. *Selenious acid* may be formed by burning selenium in oxygen gas, or by heating it in contact with nitric acid, or nitro-muriatic acid. When the solution cools, the selenious acid is deposited in large prismatic crystals, longitudinally striated, and similar to those of nitrate of potash. Its vapor resembles, in color, chlorine gas. Its taste is acid, and it leaves a slightly burning sensation upon the tongue. It is very soluble in water and in alcohol. Selenious acid consists of selenium 100 and oxygen 40.43. *Selenic acid* is formed by detonating an intimate mixture of one part of selenium and three of nitre, in small quantities at a time, in a red-hot crucible. The residue, which contains seleniate of potash, is to be dissolved in water, and nitrate of lead added to the neutralized solution till all the selenic acid is thrown down in the state of seleniate of lead. This powder is carefully washed, diffused in water, and a current of sulphureted hydrogen gas passed through it till the whole lead is converted into sulphuret. The liquid being now filtered and heated to expel the sulphureted hydrogen gas, the result is an aqueous solution of selenic acid. It may be concentrated by evaporation till its temperature reaches 536°; but if the heat is raised higher, oxygen gas is given out, and the acid changed to the selenious. Its specific gravity is 2.6. It resembles sulphuric acid in its consistence, and in the heat evolved when it is mixed with water. It contains about 16 per cent. of water. The acid is composed of selenium 100 and oxygen 60.66. Thus it appears, that the selenious and selenic acids resemble sulphurous and sulphuric acid in their constitution. Chlorine and selenium appear to combine in two different proportions, and to form a *chloride* and a *bichloride;* the former of which is liquid, and the latter solid. No experiments have been made to determine the nature of the combinations of selenium with iodine and fluorine. Selenium combines with hydrogen, and forms a gaseous substance, which has been distinguished by the name of *selenieted hydrogen gas.* When selenium and potassium are fused together, a compound is formed, which dissolves in water: the liquid has the color of beer When muriatic acid is added, a considerable proportion of the selenium is precipitated, and the liquid acquires the smell of sulphureted hydrogen. When muriatic acid is poured upon this concentrated fluid in a retort, the seleniet of potassium becomes red, an effervescence takes place, and selenieted hydrogen gas is driven off. The gas is colorless, and is possessed of an odor like sulphureted hydrogen; but it speedily acts with great energy upon the organs of smell and the throat, occasioning a painful feeling, destroying the sense of smell, and producing a severe cough. It is more soluble in water than sulphureted hydrogen; the solution precipitating all the metals from their solutions. It reddens vegetable blues, and has other acid characters. When selenium is dropped into melted *phosphorus*, it dissolves rapidly, and the compound sinks through the liquid phosphorus in red streaks. When phosphorus is saturated with selenium, we obtain a very fusible compound, of a dark brown color, a good deal of lustre, and a vitreous fracture. A *sulphuret of selenium* may also be formed: it has a deep orange color; softens at 212°, and becomes liquid at a temperature a few degrees higher. Nothing is known respecting the combinations of selenium with nitrogen, carbon, boron, and silicon. Selenium is still a very scarce substance. The analogy between it and sulphur is very remarkable. We have recently found selenium in several interesting metallic combinations in the Oriental Hartz:—1. *Seleniuret of lead* is the most frequent of these. It consists of 27.7 selenium and 72.3 lead. 2. *Seleniuret of lead and cobalt.* Its constituents are

Lead,	63.92
Cobalt,	3.14
Selenium,	31.42
Iron,	0.45
Loss,	1.07
	100.00

3. *Seleniuret of lead and copper.* Of this mineral there are two varieties, composed as follows:—

Selenium,	29.96	34.26
Iron, with traces of lead,	0.44	2.08
Lead,	59.67	47.43
Iron,	0.33	
Copper,	7.86	15.45
Silver,		1.29

4. *Seleniuret of lead and mercury* contains

Selenium,	24.97
Lead,	55.84
Mercury,	16.94
Loss,	2.25
	100.00

SELEUCIA; the name of several cities in Asia, founded by Seleucus Nicator. One of the most celebrated was that which was made the capital of Babylonia, in place of Babylon, situated about thirty miles distant from the latter city. The Tigris and Euphrates flowed near its walls, and rendered it one of the richest commercial cities of ancient times. The number of its inhabitants is estimated to have been about 600,000, chiefly Greeks. It was destroyed in the time of the Roman emperor Verus.

SELEUCIDÆ. (See *Seleucus.*)

SELEUCIDES, ERA OF THE. (See *Epoch*, vol. iv, page 551.)

SELEUCUS NICATOR, or NICANOR; son of Antiochus, one of the most distinguished generals of Alexander the Great, who invested him with the government of Babylonia and Media. After the death of Alexander, Seleucus assumed the title of king of Syria, and reduced to his sway all the countries from the Hellespont to India and the Jaxartes. His descendants were called, from him, the *Seleucidæ*, and the era of the Seleucidæ dates from his reign. (See *Epoch.*) After several successful wars against Antigonus, Demetrius and Lysimachus, he was murdered in the seventy-eighth year of his age (B. C. 280), by one of his courtiers, Ptolemæus Ceraunus. Seleucus was eminent for his courage, prudence and humanity. He encouraged letters, and restored to Greece the books and monuments of art that had been carried off by Xerxes. The Athenians, from gratitude, erected a statue in honor of him at the entrance of the portico of the academy. This prince founded thirty-four cities in Asia, which he peopled with Greek colonies. He was the father and benefactor of his subjects.

SELIM III. (See *Ottoman Empire*, and *Mahmood II.*)

SELJOOKS, or SELJUKS; a Turkish dynasty, whose empire extended over Asia Minor and Syria, and whose power declined in the period of the crusades. The name was derived from *Seljuk*, a Turkman, who had been in the service of the chagan of the Chazars, and had been obliged to flee from the camp of his master. He became the leader of a horde composed of various tribes; and his grandson Togrul Beg or Bey conquered Bagdad, 1060, was made sultan by the caliph, and left the dignity of Emir el Omrah to his descendants, who held it till 1152. The most celebrated of his successors, Malek Shah, surnamed Geladeddin, died in 1092. In 1104, the empire was divided among several dynasties, of which that of Iconium (1074—1308) survived the longest. It was succeeded by that of the Ottomans.—See *Ottoman Empire;* also the work of Wilken and Raumer *CCI Emendationes in Lohmeieri et Gebhardii Tabulæ genealogicæ Dynastiarum Arabicarum et Turcicarum* (Heidelberg, 1811).

SELKIRK, Alexander. (See *Robinson Crusoe.*)

SELTZER or SELTERS WATER; a mineral water belonging to the class of acidulous waters, which is found in the village of Niederselters, near Limburg, in Nassau. It is drunk unmixed at meals, or with wine and sugar. The water is exported in great quantities, in stone bottles containing about three pints. More than one million are filled annually. On the spot, 100 bottles, pitched, &c., are sold for 11 guild. Rhenish. It is composed, according to Bergmann, of carbonic acid, 60 cubic inches; muriate of soda, 109.5 grains; carbonate of magnesia, 29; ditto of lime, 17; ditto of soda, 24; in about five pints of water. (See *Mineral Waters.*)

SEMEIOTICS, also SEMEIOLOGY (*doctrine of signs;* from the Greek σημειον), is used in medical science to denote that branch which teaches how to judge of all the symptoms in the human body, whether healthy or diseased.

SEMELE; a daughter of Cadmus by Hermione, the daughter of Mars and Venus. She was beloved by Jupiter; but Juno, jealous of her husband's amours, determined to punish this successful rival. She persuaded Semele to entreat her lover to come to her arms with the same majesty as he approached Juno. This rash request was heard with horror by Jupiter; but, as he had sworn by the Styx to grant Semele whatever she required, he came to her bed attended by lightning and thunderbolts, and Semele was instantly consumed with fire. The child, however, with which she was pregnant, was saved from the flames by Jupiter, who placed him in his thigh the rest of the time which he ought to have been in his mother's womb. This child was called Bacchus, or Διόνυσος. Semele, after death, was honored with immortality; or, according to some, remained in the infernal regions till Bacchus, her son, was permitted to bring her back.

SEMI-ARIANS. (See *Arians.*)

SEMIGALLIA. (See *Courland.*)

SEMI-METALS; a term that expresses those metallic substances not possessing ductility and malleability, these properties being deemed characteristic of real metals.

SEMINOLES. (See *Creeks;* also *Indians, American*, vol. vi, p. 571.)

SEMI-PELAGIANS. (See *Pelagians.*)

SEMIRAMIS; a queen of Assyria, whose history is enveloped in fable. Ctesias is our only authority for the early Assyrian history. Semiramis, when grown up, married Menones, the governor of Nineveh, and accompanied him to the siege of Bactra, where, by her advice, she assisted the king's operations. These services, but chiefly her uncommon beauty, endeared her to Ninus. The monarch asked her of her husband; but Menones refused to yield her, and, when Ninus had added threats to entreaties, hanged himself. Ninus resigned the crown to her, and commanded her to be proclaimed queen of Assyria. Semiramis rendered Babylon the most magnificent city in the world. She visited every part of her dominions, and left every where monuments of her greatness. She was not less distinguished as a warrior, and conquered many of the neighboring nations. Having been completely defeated on the Indus, she was either put to death or compelled to abdicate the throne, after a reign of forty-two years, by her son Ninyas. She has been accused of abandoned licentiousness. The whole history of Semiramis has the appearance of an Oriental tale; and there is nothing to indicate the date of her reign, although her existence has not been called in question.

SEMITIC LANGUAGES; one of the great families of languages. They have been divided thus: 1. Aramæan (in the north), including Eastern and Western Aramæan; the Eastern embraces (*a.*) the Assyrian, which is lost, excepting a few names of kings; (*b.*) the Babylonian, from which several dialects originated in Palestine, after the return of the Jews from the Babylonish captivity, as the Chaldaic, in which some portions of the Old Testament are written; the Syro-Chaldaic, used at and about Jerusalem; the Galilean and the Samaritan. The Western Aramæan includes (*a.*) the Syriac dialect (the common written language of the Western Syrians, of which the Syriac translation of the Bible is the oldest, to this day the ecclesiastical language of all the sects in Syria, but used as a popular idiom only in a few districts; the purest is spoken in Mesopotamia); (*b.*) the Palmyrene (see *Palmyra*), preserved only in a few inscriptions; and (*c.*) the Sabian idiom, a corrupted Syrian dialect, in which the religious works of the Sabians (q. v.) are written. 2. Canaanitish languages, or those of the earliest inhabitants of the country between the Arabian desert and the Mediterranean. This comprises (*a.*) the Phœnician language (of which remains exist only on coins and in inscriptions), with its dialect, the Punic; (*b.*) the Hebrew (see *Hebrew Language and Literature*), and the Rabbinic dialect (see *Rabbinical Language and Literature*), which grew up after the decline of Jewish science, in the middle ages, among the Spanish Jews, who chiefly sprung from the Jews of Jerusalem, whilst the Polish and German Jews were mostly Galileans. 3. The Arabic language (see *Arabian Literature*), from which originated the Ethiopian or Abyssinian (see *Abyssinia*), and, from the modern Arabic, the Maltese.

SEMLER, John Solomon, one of the most influential German theologians of the eighteenth century, was born at Saalfeld, in 1725. His father was a clergyman, and his education was good. The duke of Saalfeld and his whole court were *Pietists;* and morbid and gloomy views of religion pervaded all classes, from which Semler was at first preserved by the influence of his mother; but, after her death, he yielded to the influence of his father and brother, became desponding, and wept and prayed the whole day. He went to the university of Halle in 1742, where he became acquainted with some young men who had brighter views of life, and his gloom wore off. He became a pupil of the liberal professor Baumgarten, partook in his literary labors, and in the dissertation which he wrote on taking the degree of master of arts, defended the genuineness of some passages in the New Testament, which had been attacked by the English writer Whiston, and went, in 1750, to Coburg, where he edited the Coburg Gazette. A diplomatic paper gained him the favor of the duke, and he was appointed professor of history and poetry at Altdorf; but after the lapse of a year, he was made professor of theology at Halle, where he and professor Baumgarten were opposed to all the rest of the theological faculty. His lectures on ecclesiastical history, hermeneutics and dogmatics, were fully attended, and, in 1757, he was made head of the theological seminary, after the death of Baumgarten, whose life he published in 1758. His works are full of learning, but exhibit little elegance. He died in 1791, after having endured many severe trials, owing partly to his particular views of religion, and his hatred of all restrictions on conscience. Semler, though sometimes imprudent from want of tact, was a man of strict virtue, a most tender conscience, and a pious heart. Griesbach was his pupil. The value of Semler's labors towards illustrating the history of the sacred text, and contributing to a right understanding of the New Testament by a reference to the condition and opinions of its authors, and the fearlessness with which he proceeded in his historical method of exegetics, and thus showed the human origin of many theological dogmas (in his notes to Wetstein's Prolegomena and critical works; his Introduction to Theological Hermeneutics, and his apparatuses for a liberal interpretation of the Canon), will be long remembered, and acknowledged even by those who are opposed to some of his views.

Semlin; a Sclavonic military community, and fortified frontier city (see *Military Districts*), not far from the junction of the Save with the Danube, only a quarter of a league distant from the Turkish city of Belgrade, which lies opposite it, on the Danube. Semlin contains seven churches and chapels, one convent, 1200 houses, with 8000 inhabitants, not including the soldiers. It carries on an important commerce with Turkey. There is a daily fair on the Belgrade meadow, where, however, the Turkish merchants are separated from the Hungarian by barriers, to prevent the transmission of the plague.

Senassy. (See *Fakir.*)

Senate. This term has been applied to bodies of very different powers and constitutions in different countries. The Roman senate (*senatus*), in the early periods of the city (see *Patricians*), participated in the judicial and executive powers of the king, and even in the management of military affairs, by means of its influence with the people. Historians commonly attribute its creation to the wisdom of Romulus; but it may be asserted, without exception, that, among all the civilized nations around the Mediterranean, a senate, or select body of elder citizens, was considered no less essential and indispensable than a popular assembly. Such a council, says Aristotle, there always is, whether the constitution be aristocratical or democratical. It is also generally said that the number was increased, under Tarquinius Priscus, to 300. However this may be, it is plain that it corresponded to the tribes, the 300 houses (*gentes*), which originally composed the three tribes, being represented in the senate, each by its *decurio*, or head. At a later period, the choice (*lectio*) of the senators was connected with the censorship. Every lustre (i. e. every five years), the censor read aloud the names of the senators, the worthiest first; and the one first named was called *princeps senatus.* Those who were unworthy of the dignity were degraded by the omission of their names. The equestrian order was the nursery from which the senate was supplied. In the time of the republic, a senator was required to have property of the value of about $18,000; in the time of Augustus, of $27,000. The supreme officers of government assembled the senate, which acted on propositions laid before it by them, article by article, and decided by a majority of voices. A decree of the senate was called a *senatus consultum.* If a tribune opposed the decree, or the senate was not full, the act was called *senatus auctoritas*, and was submitted to the people. The tribunes of the people could reject every proposition before the senate by their veto. (q. v.) All matters of public administration—the choice of public officers, legislation, and questions of peace and war—were within the jurisdiction of the senate, which likewise superintended the financial concerns of the republic. The authority of the senate was styled *auctoritas;* that of the people, *potestas:* the former decreed (*decernebat*), the latter ordered (*jubebat*). Still, in those cases in which it was subject to the decisions of the people (*plebis-scita*), the authority of the senate was extensive; and in other matters its acts (*senatus consulta*) had the force of laws. Under the emperors, the senate gradually lost its political consideration; but until the time of Constantine the Great, many imperial decrees, which the senate issued by the command of the emperors, were called *senatus consulta*, and took the place of the laws enacted by the people (*leges*). It finally became so submissive, that it often decided on the propositions of the emperors, without deliberation, by acclamation.—The French senate came into existence after the revolution of the 18th Brumaire, which placed Bonaparte at the head of the government, when he caused a new (the fourth) constitution to be drawn up (Dec. 13, 1799), which, besides three consuls, the tribunate, and the legislative body, established a conservative senate (*sénat conservateur*), consisting of eighty members, of at least forty years old. The senate was to choose its own members for life, on the nomination of the first consul, the tribunate, and the legislative body; preserve the constitution, and, with this view, inspect the acts of the legislative body; choose the consuls, tribunes, and members of the legislature, from the lists presented by the departments; and supply vacancies by the choice of one of the three individuals nominated by the three other branches of government. Each senator had a yearly pension of 25,000 francs, afterwards increased (exclusive of the senatories) to 36,000. This body soon became a tool in the hands of the first consul, for the conversion of the republic into a monarchy. This took place when the senate sanctioned the decree proposed by the council of Bonaparte, for a new change in the constitution of France. The fundamental law, or *senatus-consulte*, of Aug. 15, 1801, declared the dignity of consul to be for life, and rendered the senate dependent on the first consul, by giving him the power of choosing or nominating the greater part of them, and appointing them ministers, &c. The first consul was bound to give the senate information of all treaties, before making them public. Bonaparte, as president of the senate, now caused the senators to take the oath of allegiance to him. By the *senatus-consulte* of Jan. 4, 1803, a *senatorerie* was created in each district of the courts of appeal, endowed with a palace and a yearly income of from 20,000 to 25,000 francs, from the national domains: these (thirty-two in number) the first consul conferred on the members of the senate for life. At a later period, the senate was composed of the imperial princes, the dignitaries of the empire, and 136 members. Two committees were appointed, one for personal liberty and the other for the freedom of the press, which, however, made no opposition to the wishes of the emperor. It is well known that a *senatus-consulte* of the same body which had declared Napoleon emperor (May 18, 1804), declared the throne vacant (April 3, 1814). (See *Napoleon.*) The new constitution granted by Louis XVIII (see *Charte*) substituted a hereditary chamber of peers for the imperial senate. In 1831, the peerage was limited to the life of the incumbent. (See *Peer.*)—The Russian senate is a supreme council of state, constituted by Alexander I in 1810, and consisting of thirty-two members, and four presidents, all named by the emperor. It has no power over the will of the emperor, but is merely a medium for transacting all affairs of the empire, except foreign affairs. It is divided into four departments; of legislation, justice, war, and finance.—The senate of the U. States is composed of two senators for each member of the confederacy, chosen by the states for a term of six years. (See *Congress of the United States.*) The vice-president of the U. States is the presiding officer. Besides its legislative capacity, it has, in some measure, the character of an executive council, its consent being necessary for the ratification of treaties, and for the appointment of ambassadors, other public ministers and consuls, judges of the supreme court of the U. States, heads of departments, and some other officers. (See *President.*) The senate is also a high court of impeachment.—In most of the states, the legislatures are divided into two houses, one of which is called the senate (in New Jersey, the *legislative council;* in Vermont, there is but one house), and is, in most instances, chosen for a longer term of service, and sometimes for larger districts than the more popular branch (the assembly, house of representatives, house of commons). In some states, it performs the functions of an executive council, and generally forms the high court of impeachment for the state. (See *Constitutions.*)

SENATUS CONSULT. (See *Senate*, and *Civil Law.*)

SENECA, Marcus Annæus, a rhetorician, native of Corduba, in Spain, went to Rome during the reign of Augustus, and there taught rhetoric with great success for several years. He was the author of some rhetorical works, the remaining fragments of which are often contained in editions of the works of Seneca the Philosopher, and have been published separately.—*Lucius Annæus*, his son, accompanied his father to Rome at an early age. He was born in the first year of the Christian era, and received from his father a careful education. Gifted by nature with excellent talents, and being fond of study, the young Seneca made rapid advances in knowledge. The Stoic philosophy had peculiar charms for his grave character, and he cultivated it with ardor. His reputation soon extended to the imperial court, and his various learning and practical wisdom caused him to be appointed tutor to the young Nero, and procured him several important places. His life, however, was by no means without reproach. He is accused of an excessive love of money, and of obsequiousness towards his unworthy pupil. Although he at first exerted a beneficial influence upon the government, he did not long retain it, and suffered himself to be prevailed upon by the prince to attempt a public apology for his murder of his mother. Calumniated by envious enemies, suspected by the jealous prince, whose rapacity was probably also tempted by the wealth of the philosopher, he was accused of being an accomplice in the conspiracy of Piso, and condemned to death. The only favor which the tyrant was willing to grant him, was the choice of the manner of his death. Seneca caused his veins to be opened; but, impatient at the slowness of this mode of death, he took poison, and was finally drowned in a warm bath. He died with the calmness of a Stoic philosopher, A. D. 66. We have several works under his name, partly prose and partly poetical. The former consist of letters and treatises on different subjects of philosophy; the latter of tragedies. The former are replete with just, profound and excellent remarks, conveyed in a form not entirely unworthy of them; yet they bear marks of the influence of the spirit of the age,—the inclination to the Stoic philosophy, and the style is too often artificial, antithetical, and swollen. His tragedies are much inferior to his letters and some of his philosophical works. It is by no means settled that the tragedies are actually by him; and the *Octavia* must necessarily be rejected as spurious, since the death of the heroine, which forms the subject of the piece, took place subsequently to his own. Some of them have been attributed to his father. They are formed on the Greek plan, but are far behind their models in every respect. They have so little of a dramatic character that they seem to have been composed merely to be read or declaimed. Although it is not to be denied that in these solitary remains of the tragic poetry of the Romans, there are some pleasing passages and powerful scenes, it must be allowed that they are wanting in unity of plan, truth, elevation of sentiment, dignity and strength of thought, and elegance and vigor of expression. The best editions of Seneca's philosophical works are the Elzevir (Amsterdam, 1672), Ruhkopf's (Leipsic, 1797—1811, 5 vols.), and Lemaire's, with the notes of Bouillet (Paris, 1827—28, 3 vols.). We have translations of his works by Lodge and L'Estrange, and of his Epistles by Morell. Of the ten tragedies which go under his name, the best editions are, the Gronovian (Amsterdam, 1682), that of Schröder (Delft, 1728), the Bipontine, and, more recently, that of Baden and Bothe.

SENECA; a beautiful lake of New York, about thirty-five miles long, and two and a half wide. It lies north and south, parallel to Cayuga lake, from which it is distant from six to fifteen miles. It discharges Seneca river from its north end, which runs east to the north end of Cayuga lake. The surface of Seneca lake is 431 feet above the tide-water at Albany. The town of Geneva is at the north end of this lake, and has a delightful situation.

SENECA OR GENESEE OIL. (See *Bitumen.*)

SENECA INDIANS; one of the Six Nations formerly inhabiting the state of New York. There are reservations still owned and occupied by them on Cataraugus creek and Buffalo creek, and a few reside in Ohio. Their numbers may equal 1500. (See *Iroquois.*)

SENECA ROOT. The *polygala senega* has a woody, branched, contorted root, about half an inch in diameter, and covered with ash-colored bark. It is inodorous. The taste is at first sweetish and nauseous, but, after being chewed for a moment, becomes pungent and hot, producing a very peculiar tingling sensation in the fauces. Medically, it is considered stimulating, expectorant, and diuretic, and, in large doses, emetic and cathartic. It has been celebrated as a cure for the bite of the rattle-snake, and, on a basis equally destitute of foundation, has been cried up as a remedy in pulmonary complaints. In certain stages of these complaints, however, it is not entirely destitute of utility. The plant grows to the height of about a foot, producing several herbaceous stems from the same root. The leaves are alternate, entire, oval-lanceolate, smooth and sessile. The flowers are small, white, disposed in a slender, terminal raceme, and somewhat resemble in form the blossoms of a pea. The species of *polygala* are numerous in the U. States, especially in the more southern districts. One of them (*P. polygama*) is remarkable for bearing subterraneous flowers, in addition to the ordinary ones.

Senegal; a river of Africa, the largest that flows into the sea on the western coast. It rises in a mountainous country, about lon. 7° W., lat. 11° 50′ N., about eighty miles west of the source of the Niger, and not much farther distant from the sources of the Gambia. It flows into the Atlantic in lat. 16° 5′ N., having a bar at its mouth, which prevents ships of 500 tons from entering the river. The country through which the river flows, from the coast to about sixty miles above Gallam, is a level. Above Gallam, the country becomes mountainous and broken, intersected with numerous streams, the sands of which are impregnated with gold dust. Sixty miles above Gallam is the cataract of Flau, which forms the limit of European navigation; and about forty higher is that of Govinea. A great abundance of fish, with crocodiles and hippopotamuses, are found in the river.—The *government of Senegal* is the French settlement at the mouth of the Senegal, formed in the reign of Louis XIV. The principal article of commerce is gum, called *gum Senegal*, superior to the gum Arabic. (q. v.) The quantity purchased by the French, from 1785 to 1787, amounted to 800,000 pounds. Besides gum, there were exported from the Senegal, in 1786, 2200 slaves, valued at 2,440,000 livres; gold, valued at 90,000 livres; ivory, &c., 130,000 livres. St. Louis is the capital of the settlement. The great gum fair is on a barren, desolate spot on the river, about thirty leagues above St. Louis.

Senegambia; the name applied to an extensive region on the western coast of Africa, lying chiefly between the Senegal and Gambia, in which are included many kingdoms and states. Among the principal nations are the Foulahs (q. v.), the Jaloffs or Yaloffs, and the Mandingoes. (q. v.)—Upper Senegambia, to the north of the Senegal, is inhabited by Moors, who carry on an extensive trade in gum with Europeans.—Middle Senegambia, between the Senegal and the Gambia, is inhabited by the negro tribes above mentioned, who practise agriculture, and have some manufactures. The soil is fruitful, and produces grain of all sorts, fine fruits, cotton, indigo, tobacco, pepper, &c. Elephants, lions, rhinoceroses, hippopotamuses, antelopes, and various other wild animals, are found here.—Lower Senegambia, to the south of the Gambia, has a similar soil, climate, and productions.

Seneschal (*seneschallus*); originally a steward or major-domo, whose duty it was to superintend the affairs of his lord's household; whence the name, from *senne* (house), and *schalk* (servant). (See *Steward.*) In France, the *sénéchaussée* was the jurisdiction of a *sénéschal*, as, in the course of time, that officer came to be invested with judicial functions, and the leader of the nobility within a certain district. The royal seneschal was called *grand sénéschal*, in contradistinction to the seneschals of the feudal princes, the dukes of Normandy, Brittany, Guienne, Burgundy, &c.

Senn is the name given to the cow-herds, in Switzerland, who drive the cattle high into the Alps, and remain with them during the whole summer. These herdsmen sell the milk on their own account, paying over a certain sum to the owners of the cows.—The herd is called *senne*.

Sennaar; a negro kingdom in Africa, which is generally considered as a part of Nubia, lying between the Nile and the Tacazze, and comprising the isle of Meroe. (q. v.) To the north, it borders on Turkish Nubia; to the east, on mountains which separate it from the coast of the Red sea; to the south, on Abyssinia; and to the west, on Nigritia, or Soudan. It is separated from Darfour by Kordofan; lat. 14°—17° N., lon. 31°—39° E. The soil is, for the most part, level, in some parts barren, but, on the Nile and the Tacazze, fruitful and well cultivated. Among the animals are camels, sheep, cattle, swine, and the African wild animals. Rice, grain, melons, tobacco, sugar, senna leaves, ebony, and sandal wood, and palms, are among its productions. The climate is warm; in summer, insufferably hot. The rains which follow the hot weather, render the air unhealthy. The inhabitants are negroes, who bear the name of *Shillooks*, and conquered the country from the Arabs in 1504. They are rude, ignorant Mohammedans, governed by an absolute despotism. Besides the Shillooks, there are also nomadic Arabs, and Bedouins, who are tributary, and the Daheras, or heathen Nubians, who have been purchased, or carried off from the neighboring countries. The Daheras form the main strength of the military establishment of Sennaar. 14,000 of them, armed with spears and shields, guard the capital, with 18,000 Shillooks on horseback. The manufactures of Sennaar are inconsiderable; but the commerce, carried on, by caravans, to Suakem, Jedda, Mecca, Abyssinia, Nigritia, and Egypt, is extensive. The country has been little visited by Europeans, and is but imperfectly known. Cailliaud—*Voyage à Méroë, &c.* (1824) and English—Expedition to Dongola and Sennaar (Boston, 1823)—are among the most recent travellers who have given accounts of it. The capital, Sennaar, on the Nile, has about 16,000 inhabitants. The houses are poorly built, with flat roofs. The royal palace is constructed of mud, and is surrounded with a high brick wall.

SENNE is a large heath in Westphalia, extending from Paderborn to Münster and Osnabrück. In that part of it which belongs to Lippe is the *senne-stud*, where wild horses are made fit for service.

SENNEFELDER, Aloys, inventor of lithography, born 1771, is the son of a performer at the theatre royal of Munich, and was placed, for education, in the university of Ingoldstadt, as a student of jurisprudence; but, after his father's death (1791), he attempted a theatrical career. Not succeeding in this, he became an author, though his poverty prevented him from publishing his works. He tried many plans with copper-plates and compositions, as substitutes for letter-press, in order to be his own printer. He found, in the course of his experiments, that a composition of soap, wax and lamp-black, formed a good material for writing on his plates; that, when dry it became firm and solid, and that it resisted aquafortis. Wanting facility in writing backwards on the plates, he got some pieces of Kilheim stone, as cheap materials on which he could practise after polishing their surfaces. One day, being desired, by his mother, to take an account of some linen about to be sent to be washed, and having no paper at hand, he wrote the account on a polished stone, with his composition ink, intending to copy it at his leisure. When he was afterwards about to efface this writing, it occurred to him that he might obtain impressions from it; and having eaten away the stone with acid for about the hundredth part of an inch, he found that he could charge the lines with printing ink, and take successive impressions. This new mode of printing appeared to him very important, and he persevered through all difficulties in applying his discovery to practical purposes, and in improving it. In the course of many experiments, he found that it was not necessary to have the letters raised above the surface of the stone, but that the chemical principles by which grease and water are kept from uniting, were alone sufficient for his purpose. This point obtained, lithography may be said to have been fully discovered. All that was required was the improvement of the materials, and the mode of working with them, and the construction of a proper press for taking the impressions. The perseverance with which he followed up his experiments, in order to overcome the difficulties which successively arose in his progress, was remarkable, and the more so, considering the want of method in his proceedings. Often did he waste months in surmounting a difficulty which a little knowledge, or a very little reasoning, would have enabled him to conquer immediately. The first essays to print for publication, were some pieces of music, executed in 1796: afterwards he attempted drawings and writings. The difficulty he had in writing backwards led him to the process of *transfer;* and the use of dry soap, which was found to leave permanent traces, which would give impressions, naturally led to the mode of chalk drawings. Having made considerable improvements, Mr. Sennefelder obtained, in 1799, a patent privilege for Bavaria, when he made known his process, and afterwards entered into partnership with Mr. André, of Offenbach, who proposed to establish presses, and take out patents in London, Paris and Vienna. For this purpose Sennefelder went to London with a brother of André's; and, the invention having been much spoken of, under the name of *polyautography*, most of the principal English artists made trials of it. Unfortunately, however, the art of printing from the stones was not then fully understood, and the difference between the materials of Germany and those of England, used both for the purposes of drawing and printing, caused constant failures; and the artists, in succession, abandoned the practice of it. In

August, 1800, Sennefelder, who had separated from André, went to Vienna, where, after much difficulty, a patent was obtained, and extensive preparations were made for applying his process to print cottons; but bad management, and some unfortunate circumstances, prevented his success, and he returned to Munich in 1806, leaving the establishment in other hands. Mr. Mitterer, professor of drawing at the public school of Munich, now (1806) practised lithography to multiply copies for the pupils, and is said to have invented the chalk composition in its present form, or, at least, to have improved it greatly. From this period, the practice of the art has extended and improved rapidly, and more particularly at Munich, where several establishments were formed, for the purpose of applying it to the fine arts, as well as for printing writings and official forms, for the different departments of the government. In October, 1809, Sennefelder was appointed inspector of the royal lithographic establishment at Munich, for printing, from stone, a complete map and survey of Bavaria; since which period he has devoted his time to experiments, and to writing the history of his invention. (See *Lithography*.) In 1819, Sennefelder published his Elements of Lithography (in German). In 1826, he invented a new process for taking impressions on colored sheets, so as to imitate oil-painting. This art he calls *mosaic printing*.

Senses. The internal organs of the five senses—seeing, hearing, feeling, smelling and tasting—are the nerves, small, thread-like fibres, distributed all over the body, and all connected with the brain. (See *Nerves*.) Few subjects, in comparative anatomy and physiology, have given rise to more various and contradictory opinions than the external organs of sense in some classes. Much misunderstanding on this point has arisen from the hasty application of inferences drawn from the human subject to other animals. Thus it has been supposed that those which possess a tongue must have it for the purpose of tasting, and that the sense of smell must be wanting where we are unable to trace the existence of a nose. But, in many instances, the tongue cannot, from its substance and mechanism, be considered as an organ of taste, and must be merely subservient to the ingestion and deglutition of food; while in many animals, particularly insects, an acute sense of smell seems to exist, although no part can be pointed out in the head which analogy would justify us in describing as the nose. The sense of touch appears to exist only in four classes of animals,—in most mammalia, in a few birds, in serpents, and probably in insects; and although all animals may possess that feeling which makes them sensible to the impressions of warmth and cold, very few possess, like the human subject, organs exclusively appropriated to the sense of touch, and expressly constructed for the purpose of feeling, examining and exploring the qualities of external objects. (See *Touch*.) The sense of taste, as we have above remarked, does not appear to be confined to the tongue, that member being wanting in many animals which do not seem destitute of the sense; and in many which possess it, the tongue is employed for other and different purposes. (See *Taste*.) The sense of smelling prevails much more extensively in the animal kingdom than that of taste, since it not only assists several genera in selecting their food, which they have not afterwards the power of tasting, but is also of service in finding out proper objects for the satisfaction of their sexual appetites. (See *Smell*.) We should naturally expect to find an organ of hearing in most classes of animals, when we consider the various services which this sense performs, as that of indicating the approach of danger, of conducting beasts of prey to their food, &c.; and even in those animals, in which no external organ of hearing is discoverable, the sense is evidently not wanting. (See *Ear*, and *Hearing*.) The power of vision is confined to those animals which are provided with eyes for the reception of the images of external objects. Some species, even of the higher orders, are destitute of the organ of vision, which is also entirely wanting in the lower classes of the animal creation. (See *Eye*, and *Optics*.) It is by the senses that the mysterious communication between the spiritual soul and the external world of being is kept up. The manner in which this is done, is unknown to us; we can trace the operation of outward matter, upon the organized material system, a few steps; but we soon lose sight even of these vestiges, and are obliged to acknowledge our ignorance of the workings of our own frame. We cannot give even a sketch of the speculations of philosophers on this subject, on which the history of philosophy, in fact, chiefly turns.

Sensitive Plant (*mimosa pudica*). This plant is celebrated for its apparent sensibility, shrinking and folding up its leaves on the slightest touch. These movements are doubtless mechanical. It is a native of tropical America, but is often seen in our green-houses. It is a low plant, with white flowers, disposed in heads, which are rendered somewhat conspicuous by the length of the stamens; the stem is prickly; the leaves are compound, consisting of four leaves, themselves pinnated, uniting upon a common footstalk. At the approach of night, the leaflets all fold together: the same takes place with the partial leaves; and, finally, the common footstalk bends towards the stem: at sunrise, the leaves gradually unfold, and recover their usual state: so far, this is evidently the effect of light; but the same phenomena take place on touching the plant roughly, only that it recovers itself in a short period. All these motions are independent of each other; and it is possible to touch a branch so gently that it shall shrink without the leaves being affected. Some other species of *mimosa* exhibit the same phenomena, but in a less striking degree.

Sensualism. (See *Philosophy*, division *French Philosophy*.)

Sepia, in natural history; the cuttle-fish, of which the generic character is as follows: The body is fleshy, receiving the breast in a sheath, with a tubular aperture at its base: it has eight arms beset with numerous warts or suckers, and in most species two pedunculated tentacula: the head is short; the eyes large; the mouth resembling a parrot's beak. These animals inhabit various seas, and in hot climates some of them grow to an enormous size. They are armed with a dreadful apparatus of holders, furnished with suckers, by which they fasten upon their prey and convey it to their mouths. They have the power of squirting out a black fluid resembling ink, and which is said to be an ingredient in the composition of Indian ink. The bone in the back is converted into pounce. The eggs are deposited upon sea-weed, and resemble a bunch of grapes. At the moment when the female deposits them, they are white; but the males pass over them to impregnate them, and they then become black. They are round, with a little point at the end, and in each of them is enclosed a living cuttle-fish surrounded by a gelatinous fluid. The species (*octopus*) found in the Mediterranean and Indian seas sometimes grows to a vast size: the arms are said to be eight or nine fathoms long. The Indians carry hatchets in their boats to cut off the arms, should the creature attempt to fasten upon them under the water. The arms of this species taper to a point, and are joined at the base by a membrane or web, and covered within with two rows of alternate suckers. When opened, this animal is said to exhibit so brilliant a light as to illuminate a large room.

Sepoys, or Sipoys (from *sip*, bow, or arrow, the original weapon of the Hindoo soldier); the name given in India to the forces composed of natives, disciplined after the European manner. The French were the first to see that the transportation of troops from Europe to their Indian colonies would be too expensive, and that Europeans would perish in great numbers by the exposure at sea and in the climate of India. They therefore took Hindoos into pay, and the English adopted the same policy. The East India company at present has a native force of nearly 200,000 men. There are several regiments of cavalry, and some companies of artillery composed of native troops. The pay of the sepoys is only fourteen shillings per month. Their dress is a red jacket, with a white cotton vest underneath, trowsers reaching only about half way down the thighs, and a light turban. Though not generally equal in courage and dexterity to European soldiers, they are hardy, and capable of enduring much, and very temperate in their food.

September (from the Latin *septimus*, seventh); the ninth month of our year, but the seventh of the old Roman year, which began in March. (See *Calendar*, and *Epoch*.)

Septembriseurs; the name given to the authors and agents of the horrible massacre of prisoners, in Paris, on the second and third of September, 1792. (See *France, History of*.)

Septennial Elections. The members of the British house of commons are elected for seven years, as were those of the French chamber of deputies before the revolution in July, 1830. The period of seven years was introduced into England, with a reservation of the king's right to dissolve the house at his pleasure, and order a new election, under the administration of sir Robert Walpole, in 1716; and into France in 1824, under count Villèle. This innovation was a slighter attack upon the constitution of England than of France. In England, it had always been the custom to elect the whole house of commons at the same time. In France, the fifth part of the chamber of deputies had, for many years, been renewed annually. In the former country, the existing state of things depended on a particular law; in the latter, the constitution had established the period of five years, and the partial renewal of the chamber of electors. The septennial election of the British house of commons was proposed in the house of lords, April 10, 1716, by the duke of Devonshire, on the ground that the election for three years, which had been practised till then, not only gave too frequent occasion for the great expenses of an election, but also too often produced party excitements, and afforded frequent opportunities for the intrigues of the Papists and Jacobites, who then threatened the tranquillity of the state, by means of their connexion with France, and had been with difficulty subdued, when the pretender had effected a landing in Scotland, in 1715. After a spirited debate, the bill passed in the house of lords by a majority of thirty-five votes; but thirty members signed a protest against it, on the ground that the triennial election comported with the spirit of the constitution, whereas a longer term would unduly restrict the electoral franchise, while corruption would become more frequent, and elections more expensive. In the house of commons, the bill was opposed with still more warmth; but after forty persons had spoken for and against it, it was passed by the house, 264 against 121. It deserves notice that the bill was advocated and carried by the whigs, notwithstanding the opposition of the tories. The former probably viewed it as a protection for the new dynasty against the house of Stuart, and as the most effectual means to exterminate Popery and Jesuitism, and to establish the superiority of Protestantism. In 1734, a new controversy arose about this act in the house of commons. The tories and the Jacobites (friends of the house of Stuart) proposed, in the lower house, to repeal it, and even some whigs were in favor of so doing; among them, the celebrated Pulteney, the most zealous advocate of the bill in 1716. The two parties, however, were principally actuated by the desire of power. Lord Bolingbroke wished to put down the minister Walpole. Walpole, however, triumphed by a majority of 247 votes against 184, and Bolingbroke retired to France. But the opinion that the long duration of the house of commons is injurious to the freedom of elections, and favorable to every kind of corruption, has always prevailed in England. Pitt himself, when he advocated parliamentary reform in the session of May 7, 1783, called the septennial election one of the greatest defects in the system of popular representation. His bill to restore triennial elections, in which he was supported by Fox, was rejected by a majority of only eleven. In 1824, the same subject was broached by celebrated statesmen in the French chambers. The French constitution of 1791 required an entirely new election; that of 1795, an election of a third part of the members; and that of 1799, the election of a fifth every year. The last regulation was retained in the charter of 1814, and the age required for every voter was thirty years, and for every representative forty. April 5, 1824, count de Corbière, the minister of the interior, proposed, in the house of peers, that the whole chamber of deputies should be chosen at once, and that a new election should take place every seven years. The most distinguished speakers, in both chambers, viewed the proposed measure as a violation of an essential part of the charter. Its advocates maintained that it would prove a means of promoting public peace, by diminishing the occasions of public excitement, of producing a greater uniformity in the transaction of business, and of enabling the legislators, by means of their prolonged experience, to make better laws. The bill passed the chamber of deputies June 8, 292 to 87, and was confirmed by the king on the 9th.

Septuagesima Sunday, the third Sunday before Lent (q.v.), is supposed to take its name from its being about seventy days before Easter (*septuagesimus*, seventieth).

Septuagint, the Seventy, or LXX; the Greek version of the Old Testament, which, according to the story of Aristæus, whom Josephus follows in his Jewish Antiquities, was made on the island of Pharos, near Egypt, by seventy-two learned Jews (whence the name *Septuaginta*, seventy), by command of Ptolemy Philadelphus, king of Egypt. The story further states, that although the translators were separated from each other, yet, through the operation of divine inspiration, their versions were, word for word, the same. This version is also called the Alexandrian, because it is said to have been prepared at Alexandria. (See *Alexandrian Copy*.) We probably owe it to some Alexandrian Jews, who, having lost the knowledge of the Hebrew, caused this translation to be made by some of their learned countrymen, for the use of the synagogues, about 285 B. C. At first, only the Pentateuch was translated; and the version of the remaining books of the Old Testament was accomplished gradually.

SEPULCHRE, HOLY. (See *Palestine.*)

SEPULTURE. (See *Burial*, *Burying Places*, and *Cemetery.*)

SEQUESTRATION; the act of separating a thing in controversy from the possession of both parties, till the right is determined by course of law. It is either voluntary or necessary; voluntary when it is done by consent of the parties, and necessary when it takes place by order of the official authority. The thing sequestered (*sequestrum*) cannot be claimed by either party till the dispute is decided. Persons may, in some cases, be sequestered, as well as things.

SERAGLIO, properly SERAI (q. v.); the palace of the Turkish sultan in Constantinople. It stands in a beautiful situation, on a point of land projecting into the sea. (See *Constantinople.*) Its walls embrace a circuit of about nine miles, including several mosques, spacious gardens, and buildings capable of accommodating 20,000 men, though the number of the sultan's household does not amount to above 10,000, including gardeners and menials. From the sea, it makes a fine appearance; but from the land side, the domes, the gilded cupolas, &c., are concealed by the thick and gloomy walls; and on passing by the great gate, the spectator is shocked by the sight of the heads of recently executed victims. The harem is the part of the seraglio occupied by the women of the sultan. (See *Harem.*) The principal gate of the seraglio is called *Babi Humayum* (Sublime Porte). The sultan is served by the *itch' oglans* (pages), called also *itch' agassys*, who are Asiatics of humble origin, and are divided into four chambers, according to their rank and service. The fourth and last of these chambers is called the *khasne odasshy* (treasury). The pages of this chamber are under the direction of the *kislar aga*, and are intrusted with the care of the treasures. It has been supposed that the seraglio contained treasures of great value. The sultans piqued themselves upon leaving large sums in the treasury. Whatever, therefore, the sovereign could collect during his life, was shut up at his death in his *khasne* chamber, with an inscription in letters of gold, *This is the treasure of the sultan A. B.*, which was never touched except in extreme cases. The mutes of the seraglio, about forty in number, are the court fools: they were formerly obliged to perform all the capital executions in the empire. The dwarfs are also subjects of mirth at court, and are often used as footstools for the sultan to mount his horse. The *capidgi-baschis* (see *Capi Aga*) are the door-keepers of the seraglio; and the *bostangi* (q. v.), a numerous corps who serve in the interior of the seraglio. We may here remark, that among the 5—6000 men employed in guarding the interior of the seraglio, not a single fire-arm is to be found. The *bostangi-baschi* is, after the *kislar aga*, the second person of the seraglio, and is the only individual, except the sultan, allowed to wear a beard within the palace. The *baltagis* (wood-cutters) are of the same condition as the preceding, and make a part of the household guard and servants. Besides these, the sultan has also a life-guard (*peicks* and *solacks*), who accompany him when he leaves the seraglio.

SERAI; a large building for the accommodation of travellers, common in the Eastern countries. In Turkey, these buildings are commonly called *khans* (q. v); in Persia, *caravanserais*, by corruption *caravansaries* (q. v.); but in Tartary and India, simply *serais*. The erection of them is considered a meritorious act by Hindoos as well as Mussulmans. (See *Seraglio.*)

SERAMPORE, or SERAMPOUR; a town in Bengal, belonging to the Danes, on the west bank of the Hooghly, twelve miles north of Calcutta; lon. 88° 26′ E.; lat. 22° 45′ N.; population, about 5000 It is pleasantly situated, the territory extending one mile along the river, and half a mile in breadth. The houses are built of brick and plastered, but few of them are of more than two stories, with flat roofs, balconies, and Venetian windows. It is not fortified, but has a battery with twelve pieces of cannon, and carries on a trifling trade with Europe, China, &c. This town is the head-quarters of the Baptist missionaries in India, the principal of whom are the reverend Messrs. Carey, Marshman and Ward. They commenced their establishment here in 1799, and have ever since been engaged in propagating Christianity, and translating and printing the Scriptures. (See *Missions.*) A college for the education of native preachers has also been established here.

SERAPH (in the plural, *seraphim*); the name applied, by the prophets of the Old Testament, to the highest class of angels that surround God's throne. (See *Hierarchy.*) The word is Hebrew, signi fying *nobles*, the *great*, who surround the royal throne. The Franciscans are styled the *seraphic order* (see *Francis of Assisi*); and Bonaventura (q. v.) was called the *seraphic doctor*.

SERAPIS; tutelary god of Egypt, by some considered as an old deity identical with Osiris, by others as introduced from abroad. In Alexandria he was the chief deity.

SERASKIER, with the Turks; the generalissimo of a whole army. He has very extensive power, but is under the grand vizier, and is chosen from among the pachas of two or three tails. Sometimes, also, commanders of a lower rank are called *seraskiers*.

SERENADE (Italian, *serenata*, from the Latin *serenus*, clear); properly, music performed in a clear night; hence a musical entertainment provided by a lover under the window of his mistress. It consists, generally, of instrumental music, but vocal is sometimes added. The practice existed even among the Greeks and Romans. Such music is sometimes performed merely as a mark of esteem and good will towards distinguished persons, and then is not unfrequently accompanied by long processions with torches. Hence the different character of serenades. A single singer may accompany his song with the guitar, mandoline, lute, &c.; or wind instruments may be used, as flutes, horns, clarionets, hautboys; or, as is the fashion in some of the largest cities of Northern Germany, many singers may join. Serenades are also sometimes used as concert pieces, and then, of course, experience some change of character.

SERENDIB; one of the names of Ceylon.

SERGEANT, or SERJEANT, in war, is an inferior officer in a company of foot, or troop of dragoons, armed with a halberd, and appointed to see discipline observed, to teach the soldiers the exercise of their arms, and to order, straighten and form ranks, files, &c.

SERGELL, John Tobias, a celebrated Swedish sculptor, born at Stockholm, in 1740, began his career as a stone-mason, but afterwards became a pupil of L'Archeveque, whom he accompanied to France. He subsequently went to Italy, at the expense of the king of Sweden, and acquired great celebrity. In 1778, he returned to Sweden, visiting Paris in his way, where he was nominated a member of the academy of fine arts. He then visited London, reached Stockholm in 1779, and, on the decease of his preceptor, succeeded to his place. In 1784, he accompanied Gustavus III or his travels to Italy; in 1795, was made a knight of the Pole Star and, in 1810, received letters of nobility and was appointed superintendent of the police. His works are chiefly confined to Sweden. He died February 26, 1814. Depth of thought and vigor of conception, energy and grace, are the characteristics of his style. His Cupid and Psyche; Diomedes carrying off the Palladium (in England); Mars and Venus; a Faun; Oxenstiern dictating the History of Gustavus Adolphus to the historic Muse,—are among his principal statues. Among his groups are the monument of Descartes; the Resurrection of Christ, a bass-relief; two angels over the altar in the cathedral at Carlstadt, &c. Byström is his most celebrated pupil.

SERIES, in general, denotes a continued succession of things in the same order and having the same relation or connexion with each other.

Series, in mathematics. (See *Progression.*)

Series, *Infinite*, consists of an infinite number of terms, so that, let the series be carried to any assignable length or number of terms, it can be carried yet farther without limitation.

SERINGAPATAM, or SRI-RANGA-PATANA; a city of Hindoostan, in Mysore, and, for a considerable time, the capital of the province; 215 miles south-west of Madras; lon. 76° 51′ E.; lat. 12° 26′ N. The population in 1800 was estimated at upwards of 20,000; in 1820, it was stated at less than 10,000; the diminution is owing to the removal of the court. It is situated at the upper end of an island in the Cauvery, and has existed as a fortress from a remote period. During the reigns of Hyder Aly and his son Tippoo Sultan, it rose to a degree of wealth and splendor before unknown, and was supposed to contain 150,000 inhabitants. In 1792, Seringapatam was invested by the British and allied armies, under lord Cornwallis, amounting to 400,000 men. Tippoo Sultan, terrified, relinquished half his dominions, and paid to the conquerors £3,500,000 sterling. In 1799, it was again invested by the forces of the British and Nizam, and taken by storm, May 4th, Tippoo Sultan and nearly 8000 of his men having fallen. Seringapatam afterwards became the property of the British, and is the residence of a judge, collector, &c., but has greatly declined from its former importance.

SEROUX D'AGINCOURT, Jean Baptiste, born at Beauvais in 1730, died in 1814. He passed a great part of his life in Italy.

devoted to the study of the arts. Besides his *Recueil de Fragments de Sculpture antique en Terre cuite* (4to., 1814), we have from him a very learned work, entitled *Histoire de l'Art par les Monuments, depuis sa Décadence au cinquième Siècle, jusqu'à son Renouvellement au quinzième Siècle* (3 vols., folio, 325 plates, Paris, 1810—1823).

Serpent. The serpents, or *ophidia*, form a very natural class of reptiles, in general easily distinguished by the total absence of feet, not the slightest vestige of which is discoverable on the most minute dissection. Their motion is, notwithstanding, very rapid in some species, and is accomplished by means of the sinuosities, or folds, which they form with their bodies. When in a state of repose, they usually dispose themselves in coils, with the head in the centre; and many are enabled to spring to a certain distance by the sudden unfolding of these coils. Serpents are destitute of movable eyelids, or distinct tympanums. All have teeth, but they serve only to retain their food, and are not adapted to the purpose of mastication. They are long, very sharply pointed, and incline backwards. The venomous species have the maxillaries very small and movable, and in them are implanted two teeth much longer than the rest, and traversed by a canal, for the purpose of transmitting the poison. These fangs are projected forward in the action of biting, but at other times, are disposed along the roof of the mouth, in such a manner as hardly to be discoverable at first sight. The jaws of serpents are united by ligaments in such a manner as to admit of great extension, which enables them to swallow animals of much greater diameter than their own bodies. The tongue is remarkably extensible, and terminates in two long cartilaginous points. They have only one lung. The skin, in different genera, is annulated, coriaceous or granulated, or, most frequently, covered with scales. They feed on quadrupeds, reptiles, insects, or worms, and swallow their prey entire. They do not drink, and the power of digestion is slow, one meal serving them for weeks, or even months; but when an opportunity offers, they take an enormous quantity of food. The ribs are very numerous, and surround a great portion of the trunk. The muscles, even in the smaller species, are endowed with an astonishing power of constriction; and those species which attain the enormous dimensions of thirty feet or more, are enabled to destroy the larger quadrupeds by involving them in their folds. Serpents inspire an instinctive horror in man and most animals. Their hissing, in some species, is truly startling; but, notwithstanding, most of them are perfectly harmless. In northern climates, they pass the winter in a torpid state, and change the epidermis in the spring. The eggs are rounded, and agglutinated in bead-like rows by a mucous substance, and, in the venomous species, hatch before they are excluded from the oviduct, and the young are born living. The females often take care of their young for a time, and, on the approach of danger, have been seen to receive the whole family in their throats, and, when it has passed, to restore them again to the open air. More than three hundred species are enumerated, most of which, including all the gigantic species, inhabit tropical climates. South America, in particular, abounds with them. The venomous species compose about one fifth or one sixth of the whole number; and among these are some whose bite is fatal in a few hours, and even minutes. But few species, and these mostly harmless, inhabit cold climates; and towards the poles, they seem to be entirely wanting. The venom of the European viper is neither acid nor alkaline, neither acrid nor caustic; is insipid to the taste, and harmless when taken internally; in short, possesses most of the external characters of simple mucus. It preserves its power after the death of the animal which furnished it. Its strength varies in intensity according to the warmth of the climate and season of the year, being much more dangerous in summer than in winter; as also according to the lapse of time which has intervened since the last bite, and the degree of irritation with which the action is performed. It is much more fatal to small animals than to large, and especially when they are much terrified. We have no true vipers in the U. States.—The boas or anacondas inhabit tropical America, and are, in general, easily distinguished by having the plates under the tail undivided. Some attain a gigantic size, and curl their tails about the trunks or branches of trees, and, in this position, lie in wait for the larger quadrupeds.—The pythons equal them in size, and pursue the same mode of life. They inhabit the tropical parts of the eastern continent.—The species of hydrus are small aquatic serpents, having the extremity of their tails enlarged, and very much compressed; which conformation gives them greater facility in moving through the water. They inhabit the intertropical parts of Asia, and the neighboring islands, and in some situations are very abundant. We shall now notice some of the most remarkable and best known species of the U. States.—The rattle-snakes (*crotalus*) are exclusively American, and are celebrated for the violence of their poison. They are easily distinguished by the noisy instrument at the end of the tail, composed of horny sacks loosely inserted into each other. The banded rattle-snake grows to the length of four or five feet. It inhabits the Northern and Middle States from about lat. 46°, and is also found in the Western States, and beyond the Mississippi.—The diamond rattle-snake (so called from a row of large black rhomboidal figures disposed along the back) attains larger dimensions, and inhabits the Southern States. The same, or a very similar species, is found in South America.—The ground rattle-snake (*C. miliarius*) is a small species, inhabiting the Southern as well as the Western States. It has but two or three rattles on the tail, and is much dreaded, as its small size, and the slight noise of its rattle, render it more liable to be overlooked. —The copper-head (*trigonocephalus tisiphone*) is as dangerous as the rattle-snake, which it much resembles, but is destitute of the rattle at the extremity of the tail. The color is brown, with clouded spots of a deeper hue. It is widely diffused through the U. States.—The *elaps fulvius* inhabits the southern and south-western parts of the U. States. The length is about two feet, and the tail very short. It is marked with about twenty broad black rings, alternating with about as many yellow ones. The last are speckled with brown, and are whitish on the margin. The above are our principal poisonous serpents. The following are entirely harmless:—The hog-nose snake (*heterodon*) is a remarkable reptile. The nose is slightly turned up, and flattened in front, bearing a remote resemblance to the snout of the animal whose name it bears. It possesses the power of dilating laterally the head and upper part of the neck, and, in this state, makes a formidable appearance. It is widely diffused through the U. States, but, like many others, is not found eastward of the Hudson river.—The black snake (*coluber constrictor*) is found throughout the U. States. The color is black, inclining to slate color beneath, with the throat and lips white. The scales are smooth. It grows to the length of six feet, and its motions are very rapid.—The chain snake (*C. getulus*) is a.ı allied species also, ·vith smooth scales. The colors are black and white, the black predominating. The white often forms transverse lines on the back, which unite on the sides, thus forming the semblance of a chain. The markings are, however, extremely variable; and individuals are found entirely black, thickly sprinkled with regularly oval white specks. It inhabits the Southern States, but is sometimes found as far north as New Jersey.—The coach-whip snake (*C. filiformis*) is a very long and slender species, rarely found, and only in the more southern states.—The water snake (*C. sipedon*) is found in all parts of the U. States, and is very common in the vicinity of Philadelphia. Its usual color is brown on the back, beneath pale, with indistinct dark spots; but the markings vary exceedingly, and it is often four d transversely banded with white. This variation has given rise to much confusion in the books, where it is repeatedly described under different names. The body is thick in proportion, and it attains large dimensions, sometimes growing to the length of five feet. It frequents exclusively the borders of streams, and, when disturbed, often takes refuge in them, and conceals itself at the bottom.—The striped or garter snake (*C. sirtalis*) is the most common species in most parts of the U. States. The color is brown above, with black specks, and three longitudinal lines of greenish yellow.—The collared snake (*C. Edwardsii*); a small species, of a dark leaden color on the back, having a whitish band disposed across the back of the head. It is found under the bark of trees, from lat. 43° to South Carolina.—*C. Amœnus* (Say); a still smaller species, with a remarkably small head; the color brownish above, and reddish beneath; the scales smooth. It is found, beneath stones and logs, in the vicinity of Philadelphia, but is rare.—*C. septemvittatus* (Say); with seven longitudinal blackish lines, three above, and four beneath; the general color, brown above, and yellowish beneath; a small species, inhabiting the Middle and Western States.—The scarlet snake (*C. coccineus*), beautifully marked with scarlet, black, and yellow, inhabits the Southern States.—The green snake (*C. æstivus*); a small species, entirely of a bright green color. The scales are carinated. It is found in the Southern States. —*C. vernalis;* another green snake, resembling the former, but with smooth scales, inhabiting the Northern and Middle States. —The pine snake (*C. melanoleucus*); one of our largest species, attaining the length of eight feet. The color is whitish, with large blackish spots. It is common in New

Jersey, and is found in all the more southern and western parts of the U. States, and even beyond the Mississippi. It is of a gentle disposition, and is sometimes tamed and kept about houses.—The chicken snake, or house snake (*C. guttatus*), is a beautiful species. The boby is elongated, somewhat flattened on the back, with smooth scales; the color whitish; a row of large brownish spots, bordered with black, upon the back; a second series of smaller and darker ones on each side, alternating with the former; beneath, with small, square, black specks. The abdominal plates and subcaudal scales are very numerous. It attains a large size, and inhabits all parts of the U. States, from Canada to Florida, as also the trans-Mississippi region. Although it is pretty constant in its markings, no one of our snakes has been the occasion of so much confusion among systematic writers; and it appears repeatedly in the books under a great variety of specific names. We have omitted, in the above account, several species which have been discovered, within a few years, in the region beyond the Mississippi, as also some of the Atlantic states, which are not well understood. There are probably many undescribed species in the U. States.—It may not be amiss to say a few words in this place concerning the glass snake of the Southern States. This animal is destitute of feet, and possesses many of the external characters of a serpent; but its anatomical structure shows it to belong to the family of lizards. It is excessively brittle, and is broken with the slightest blow; which circumstance has given rise to the name. (For the *Sea-serpent*, see that article.)

Serpent-Eater (*serpentarius*); a remarkable South African bird, belonging to the *rapaces*, or birds of prey, but differing from the hawks and owls in having feet incapable of grasping, and very long legs. Accordingly, it keeps constantly on the ground, in sandy and open places, and wages continual war against reptiles, especially serpents, which it pursues on foot. It runs with great rapidity. In every respect except the feet, the anatomical structure is the same with that of the eagle. When this bird attacks a serpent, it covers its breast with one wing, to protect itself from the bite, and with the other strikes violent blows, until it has stunned its prey. It then breaks the cranium with the beak, and tears the reptile in pieces, or, if small, swallows it entire. The serpent-eater is easily tamed, and is often kept in poultry-yards by the inhabitants of the cape of Good Hope, for the purpose of destroying lizards, snakes, rats, &c. It soon becomes habituated to the poultry; but care must be taken not to leave it fasting too long, for on such occasions it does not scruple to satisfy its hunger with the young chickens. The wild bird is very shy, and difficult of approach. This bird is sometimes called the *secretary*, from some long feathers on the back of the head, in allusion to the custom of placing pens behind the ear.

Serpentine; an abundant mineral, which almost invariably occurs destitute of a regular crystalline form. A few instances of crystallized serpentine, however have been observed, and the form appears to be a right rectangular prism. The massive varieties have a granular, or impalpable composition, and present red, brown, black, yellow, and gray colors, in veined, spotted, and other delineations. Fracture flat, conchoidal, or uneven; surface almost dull; lustre resinous, indistinct; streak white, acquires some lustre; translucent to opaque; sectile; hardness about that of calcareous spar; specific gravity 2.5. Serpentine is generally divided into two sub-species, the *common* and *precious* serpentine, the former of which consists of those varieties which are destitute of handsome colors, while the latter includes all such as, from the intensity and arrangement of their hues, are suited to purposes of ornament. Serpentine hardens on being exposed to the fire, and melts only (with great difficulty) on the edges. According to John, it consists of

Silica	42.50
Magnesia	38.63
Alumine	1.00
Lime	0.25
Oxide of iron	1.50
Oxide of manganese	0.62
Oxide of chrome	0.25
Water	15.20

Serpentine forms mountain masses, and beds in primitive rocks, and frequently contains crystals, grains, or compound nodules of various other species. Precious serpentine, in particular, is often mixed with granular limestone. It is met with in most European countries, and occurs abundantly in the U. States, as at Middlefield and Newbury in Massachusetts, at Newport in Rhode Island, near New Haven in Connecticut, and in the Highlands of New York. Serpentine is turned, on the lathe, into vases, and also worked into different ornaments.

Serra da Estrelha (*Mons Herminius*);

a lofty range of granite mountains in Portugal, a continuation of the Spanish chain of Guadarrama, extending into the province of Beira. Its highest summit (the Cantaro Delgado) is 8000 feet high, and is covered with snow from October to June. The ridge contains some remarkable lakes, part of which are tepid. The mountain streams Condieira and Unhaes form fine cascades over the rocks. The scenery around is highly picturesque.

Serre, Count de. (See *De Serre.*)

Sertorius, Quintus, a distinguished Roman general, born at Nursia, in Italy, at an early age served with reputation under Marius, against the Cimbri, and in Spain. As questor, in Cisalpine Gaul, he led a body of troops to the aid of his native country in the Social war (A. U. 663), and lost an eye in the war, in which he fought with his usual bravery. In the quarrel of Marius and Sylla, Sertorius at first took no part; but, in consequence of Sylla's opposition to his election as consul, he joined the party of Cinna, and thus became connected, contrary to his intention, with Marius. After the death of Marius and Cinna, Sylla again acquired the ascendency, and Sertorius was proscribed, and fled to Spain. Here his talents found a wide sphere of action. He endeavored to gain the affections of the Spaniards, and to organize a force capable of resisting Sylla, who had sent a large army for the subjugation of Spain. The means of Sertorius were unequal to the conflict, and he embarked at New Carthage, passed into Africa, and took part in a war between the king of Mauritania and his subjects, on the side of the latter. Having gained several victories, and liberated the Mauritanians, he was requested by the Lusitanians, who were threatened with war by the Roman general Annius, to take command of their forces. Sertorius eagerly seized this opportunity of encountering Sylla. Invested with unlimited powers, he appeared at the head of the Lusitanians, who placed the most implicit confidence in him. Opposed to much superior forces, he displayed the talents of a skilful general, fatiguing the enemy by hasty marches, harassing them by ambuscades, attacking them in defiles, and avoiding a general engagement where he was not sure of the victory. With 8000 men, he was thus enabled to resist four Roman generals, at the head of 120,000 foot soldiers and 6000 cavalry, and to hold nearly all Spain against them. Even Marcellus, whom Sylla finally sent against him, and constantly reinforced with new troops, could effect nothing, and suffered several severe defeats. The youthful Pompey (q. v.), who, after the death of Sylla, led an army into Spain, and acted in concert with Marcellus, met with no better success. Yet Sertorius, from love of his country, would have consented to submit, had the proscription against him been revoked. His fame even reached Mithridates, who offered him 3000 talents and forty ships of war, on condition of his forming an alliance with him. Sertorius, who fought with reluctance against Rome, and was unwilling to see the republic humbled or enfeebled, accepted the offer, on Mithridates consenting to restrict himself to the recovery of Bithynia and Cappadocia. He accordingly received the sum agreed upon, and was making preparations for pushing the war with greater vigor, when he perished by the treachery of his friends. Perpenna, who had formed a conspiracy against him, assassinated him at a feast, A. U. 682. Thus was Rome delivered from a formidable enemy, who equalled the greatest heroes of antiquity in military talents, while he surpassed most of them in the virtues of his character.

Serum. (See *Blood.*)

Servant. (See *Master and Servant.*)

Servetus, Michael, a learned Spaniard, memorable as a victim of religious intolerance, was born in 1509, at Villa Nueva, in Arragon. He was the son of a notary, who sent him to Toulouse for the study of the civil law. Excited by the discussions of the reformers in that city, he began to read the Scriptures, and conducted his researches with so free a spirit, that he printed a tract in disparagement of the orthodox doctrine of the Trinity, entitled *De Trinitatis Erroribus* (1531), which production was followed the next year by his *Dialogorum de Trinitate Libri duo.* His circumstances being depressed, he engaged for some time with the Frellons, booksellers of Lyons, as corrector of the press. He then went to Paris, where he studied physic, and carried into that science the same inquisitive spirit which distinguished him in theology He graduated at Paris, but quarrelled with the faculty, and repaired to Charlieu, near Lyons, where he practised three years, whence, at the instance of the archbishop of Vienne, he removed to the latter city. During this time he was in constant correspondence with Calvin, with whom he discussed points of controversy, consulting him in respect to his writings and Arian notions. Of this confidence Calvin subsequently made a base use, by producing his letters and manuscripts as matters of accusation against him. In 1553, Servetus published his matured theological system, without his name, under the title of *Christianismi Restitutio;* but Calvin took care that the magistrates of Vienne should be duly informed of it, and Servetus was committed to prison, whence he contrived to escape, and thereby avoided that fate from Catholic hands which he was soon after to suffer from those of the reformers. Purposing to proceed to Naples, he imprudently took his way through Geneva, where Calvin induced the magistrates to arrest him on a charge of blasphemy and heresy, advanced against him by a person who had been a servant in Calvin's family. In order to ensure his condemnation, his various writings were sifted for accusations; and, as a proof of the malignity and injustice which he encountered, it may be mentioned that one of the charges was extracted from his edition of Ptolemy's Geography, in which he asserted that Judea had been falsely extolled for its beauty and fertility, modern travellers having found it both sterile and unsightly. The magistrates of Geneva were, however, aware that many eyes were on them, in respect to this extraordinary treatment of a person who was neither a subject nor a resident, but, properly speaking, a traveller kidnapped in his passage. They thought proper, therefore, to consult the magistrates of all the Protestant Swiss cantons, who referring the matter to their divines, the latter unanimously declared for his punishment. As he refused to retract his opinions, therefore, he was condemned to the flames, which sentence was carried into execution the 27th of October, 1553, in the forty-fourth year of his age. Servetus is numbered among the anatomists who made the nearest approach to the doctrine of the circulation of the blood, as appears from a passage in his *De Restitutione Christianismi.* The life of Servetus has been written in Latin by Mosheim (Helmstädt, 1728).

Servia (Turkish, *Serf-Vilajeti*); a province of European Turkey, bordering on Walachia, Bulgaria, Macedonia, Albania, Bosnia and Hungary, from which last it is divided by the Danube. It contains 19,500, or, according to some, 21,200 square miles, and 960,000 inhabitants. This thin population is owing, partly to the desolating wars to which the country has been exposed for centuries, but principally to the oppression of the Turkish government. Servia contains immense forests; but the soil is very fertile, and cattle are raised in large numbers. Agriculture and commerce are in a very low condition. There are no manufactures except some of cotton. The country forms a part of Rumili, and is subject to a pacha, who resides at Belgrade, the capital. Besides Belgrade (q. v.), Semendra and Nissa are the most important cities. In the fortified village of Passarowitz (q. v.), July 21, 1718, a peace was concluded between Austria and the Porte, very advantageous to the former. On the plains of Cossova or the Amselfeld, on the borders of Bosnia, the Turkish sultan Amurath I, in 1389, defeated the Servians; and, Oct. 19, 1447, in the same place, Amurath II triumphed over the Hungarian and allied forces under John Hunniades, and was stabbed in his tent by Milosch Kobilitschk, a Servian. Servia is a part of ancient Illyria, which the Romans reduced under their dominion. The proper name of the province was Mœsia. Belgrade (Taurunum) belonged to Lower Pannonia. About the middle of the seventh century, Sclavonic tribes overspread all these regions. One of those tribes, the Servii (Serbi), a branch of the Sarmatians, to which the emperor Heraclius had previously assigned a portion of Macedonia, expelled or subdued the aborigines, the Illyrians, and kept possession of their country. From them it derived the name of *Servia*, which at that time included Bosnia (q. v.).—The Servians were almost incessantly involved in quarrels with the Greek emperors, Hungary, and the republic of Venice, and, notwithstanding their valor, were generally worsted. After they had been under the dominion of the Greek emperors for many years, though governed immediately by their own princes, they formed an alliance, in 1150, with Hungary, to oppose the emperor Manuel Comnenus. Manuel defeated them in 1151. A second attempt to make themselves independent was equally unsuccessful. Isaac Angelus, the Greek general, afterwards emperor, defeated them, in 1193, on the Morava. In the ninth century, Budimir, the first Christian prince, divided the country into several provinces. One of them, Bosnia, afterwards withdrew from the general government, and eventually came into subjection to Hungary, though it retained its own rulers. In the beginning of the fourteenth century, Milatin Urosch, king of Servia, was compelled by Charles I, king of Hungary, to cede a part of his territory. King Stephen Duschan (who reigned from 1336) made many successful expeditions against the Greek emperors, and subdued some of the neighboring provinces. He assumed the title of emperor, and distributed the empire of Servia into several governments; but he thus prepared the way for its fall and subsequent dissolution. During his reign, Amurath I, the Turkish sultan, as above related, defeated the Servians, June 15, 1389, on the Amselfeld. Bajazet, Amurath's successor, divided Servia between Stephen, son of Lazar, the last ruler, and his son-in-law, Wuk Brankouitsch. Both were compelled to pay tribute to him. Servia now became the chief theatre of the unhappy wars between the kings of Hungary and the Porte. After the battle on the Amselfeld in 1447, in which Amurath II conquered the Hungarians under Hunniades, Servia was completely subdued by the Turks. The successes of Eugene, indeed, procured for Austria, at the peace of Passarowitz, in 1718, the largest part of Servia, that is, the northern part, with the capital, Belgrade. But by the peace of Belgrade, in 1739, Austria again lost all this territory, and it was transferred to Turkey. The barbarity of the Turkish governors and the arrogance of the janizaries led to an insurrection in 1801. George Petrowitsch, a man of courage, known by the name of *Czerny George*, placed himself at the head of the malcontents, and fought, for eleven years, with the greatest ardor. The Servians received assistance secretly from the Russians, and their army was at length increased to 30,000 men. Czerny George, taking advantage of the weakness of Turkey, demanded that Servia, like Moldavia and Walachia, should be elevated to a principality, under a Greek hospodar. The demand was rejected. After the Servians had gained some successes over the Turks, Russia declared in their favor, and a Russian army marched into Moldavia to their aid. Supplied by the Russians with warlike stores, particularly with cannon and engineers, Czerny took Belgrade, in December, 1806, and, some time after, Shabacz and Nissa. The Servian army was now increased to 80,000 men. The Turks, occupied with other troubles in the interior of their country, and repeatedly defeated by the Servians and Russians, at length proposed an armistice, which was concluded, July 8, 1808, at Slobosje, at the Servian head-quarters. Czerny George, with the other chiefs of his nation, now prepared a constitution for Servia, under the protection of Russia. Having been before appointed chief ruler by the people, he was formally declared prince of Servia, and recognised by the Russian emperor, who, at the same time, made him lieutenant-general of the Russian army, and knight of the order of Alexander Newsky. When the war broke out again, in March, 1809, between Russia and the Porte, Czerny George, with his Servian troops, took part in it, and essentially aided the Russian arms. But the invasion of Russia by the French, in 1812, put a sudden end to the war, and led to the peace concluded at Bucharest, May 28, 1812, between Russia and the Porte. It was agreed, in the conditions of the peace, that the Porte should treat the Servians with kindness, and grant them a full amnesty. The fortresses erected by them in their country during the late war, were to be demolished, and the remainder to be put into the hands of the Turks. The administration of its internal affairs was committed to the nation. The Servians were to enjoy the same advantages with the Turkish subjects in the islands of the Archipelago and in other countries. At the end of July, 1812, the Russian troops left Servia. Many of the Servian chieftains, who were most devoted to their cause, accompanied them. The war between Servia and the Porte began anew in July, 1813, and was prosecuted with much bitterness, and with various success. After it had continued nearly four months, the Turks prevailed. Czerny George and his adherents fled to the neighboring states. The conquerors treated those who remained with the greatest cruelty. The country was made a desert. Finally, under the conduct of Milosch, the Servians concluded the treaty of December 15, 1815, which made them not so much the subjects as the dependants of the Porte. The attempt of Czerny George, in July, 1817, to kindle a new war, cost him his life. Till 1820, negotiations with the Servians were continued in Constantinople. They demanded that no Turk should possess property in Servia without the walls of Belgrade. It was granted. From that time the country has been governed by a senate, which consists of a president, Milosch, who was made prince in 1817, and four members or Servian representatives. The senate holds its sessions at Semendra, a fortified city on the Danube, containing 8000 inhabitants and an archbishop; also the residence of the hospodar Milosch Obrenowitsch, formerly a general under Czerny George. The Servians have their own judges and local magistrates, and have an agent constantly at the Porte. They pay to the Porte only the *kharadsh*, which amounts to one ducat for every father of a family, and one piaster for every other member. No Servian is permitted to reside permanently in Turkey, and no Turk in Servia. Belgrade and all the Turkish fortresses in Servia are occupied by Turkish troops. In case of a war between the Porte and any foreign power, the Servians are to furnish 12,000 men. The orders of the vizier, who remains with the Turkish garrison in Belgrade, are committed for execution to prince Milosch. This ruler, in 1825, put down, with an iron hand, a rebellion excited by his own severity, and was rewarded for it with the high office of hospodar. In the war of Russia with the Porte in 1828, the Servians were ready to rise in support of Russia.—See Ranke's *Serbische Revolution* (Hamburg, 1829).

Servian Language and Literature. The Servian language, generally called the *Illyrian*, is a Sclavonic dialect, and, among all the southern Sclavonic idioms, the most powerful. It is spoken by five millions of people, from the Culpa to the Timeck. The Sclavonic dialect, spoken in Bulgaria and Bosnia, differs little from the Servian. Recently the Servian has been more cultivated. In 1814, Wuk Stephanowitsch published, in Vienna, a Servian grammar (translated into German, with a preface by J. Grimm, and remarks by Vater, Berlin, 1824). In 1819, he published his Dictionary of the Servian Language, with German and Latin Definitions, containing above 30,000 words in common use. In the Servian poetry, the excellence of which Göthe and Grimm have acknowledged, a Sclavonic character of rude energy is united with an Oriental warmth. In 1823, Wuk Stephanowitsch published three volumes of Servian poetry, at Leipsic, which have been translated into German. Some of the songs are uncommonly fine. In 1826, he published *Danitza* (i. e. Morning Star), an annual for ladies, in Servian. The most recent publications in Servian literature are Simeon Milutinowitsch's *Serbianka*, a series of Servian heroic songs, which celebrate the insurrection of Servia, of which he was an eye-witness (4 vols., 12mo., Leipsic, 1827), and two Servian translations of Horace's *Ars poetica* (Vienna, 1827), in hexameters, and in the heroic measure of the Servians. Both are by Johannes Hadsitsch (under the name of Milosch Swetitsch). The Servian prose has produced little besides theological and religious works. In fact, the literary dialect is not yet settled: the Servian scholars are not agreed whether the artificial book language, formed after the ecclesiastical Servian, and which has been in use for almost four centuries, or the common dialect of the country, shall become the language of literature. In the former Raitsch has written his History of various Sclavonic Tribes (Vienna, 1792, 4 vols.).—See Bowring's *Servian Popular Poetry* (London, 1827).

Service Tree (*sorbus*); a pretty large European tree, closely allied to the apple and pear, but easily distinguishable by its pinnated leaves. The flowers are numerous, disposed in corymbs at the extremities of the branches, and are succeeded by very small, rounded or pear-shaped fruit. This fruit is excessively austere and astringent before perfect maturity, is little esteemed, and difficult of digestion, but, notwithstanding, is sometimes eaten when in a state of incipient decay. The tree attains the height of forty or fifty feet, but the growth is exceedingly slow, the trunk hardly acquiring the diameter of a foot in a century. The wood is very hard, compact, solid, fine-grained, and susceptible of a brilliant polish. It is in great request among turners and cabinet makers, and is very dear, especially the larger pieces. The service tree grows wild in most parts of Europe, and is, besides, occasionally cultivated. —The mountain ash is a second species of *sorbus*, often cultivated as an ornamental plant. It does not exceed the height of twenty or twenty-five feet, and is found wild in many parts of Europe. We have in the northern parts of the U. States, a species of *sorbus* (*S. Americana*), closely resembling the mountain ash, and also frequently cultivated in European gardens. It is found wild as far south as lat. 43°, and is frequent in Canada. Another species (*S. microcarpa*) inhabits the range of the Alleghany mountains.

Servile, a Spanish word of the same meaning with the English *servile*, was the name given to the opponents of the liberal changes, contemplated by the cortes, from their first session in 1808. In 1823, when the French put down the liberals, the apostolical party (so called) obtained the ascendency.

Servile Arts. (See *Arts*.)

Serving is the winding any thing round a rope to prevent it from being rubbed: the materials used for this purpose, which are called *service*, are generally spun-yarn, small lines, sennit, or ropes, sometimes leather, old canvass, &c.

SERVITES, or SERVANTS OF THE HOLY VIRGIN; a religious order, founded at Florence in 1233, which became numerous, particularly in Germany and Italy, and received the privileges of the mendicant orders, but never had much influence in the church. (See *Orders, Religious.*) The monks were also called Brethren of the Ave Maria, because they always began their conversation with the words of the angelic greeting, and Brethren of the Passion of Christ. They follow the rule of St. Augustine, and wear a black dress. Their general has the fifth place among those of the mendicant orders at Rome. They have, in recent times, lost much of their consideration. Paul Sarpi, and Ferrarius belonged to this order.

SERVITUDE (*servitus*), in the civil law, is the right to the use of a thing, without property in the same, for all or for some particular purposes. This right, by the Roman law, was not confined to any particular kind of property, but could either be limited to a particular person (*servitus personalis*), or so connected with real property (*prædium dominans*), that the owner of the same, whoever he might be, could exercise his right upon the estate subjected to the servitude (*prædium serviens*). The servitude consisted either in a right to do some act, as to gather fruit from the estate, &c. (*servitus affirmativa*), or to prevent the owner of the property from doing certain acts, as building walls beyond a certain height, blocking up a window, &c. (*servitus negativa*). The owner of a property to which a servitude was attached, could not, by the Roman law, be obliged to perform any act himself (*servitus in faciendo consistere nequit*); but this rule is not adhered to, in modern times, in those countries where the civil law prevails. Personal servitudes consist either in the full use of the property, and its products (*usus fructus*), or in a limited use (*usus*) of the same (as, for instance, merely free occupancy—*habitatio*). The usufruct was originally allowed only in regard to those things which were not consumed in the use, but was afterwards extended to such things as were consumed by use, but could be replaced by articles similar in number and quality (*quasi usus fructus*). Servitudes connected with real estate (*servitutes prædiorum*), which were divided into servitudes on tenements (*prædiorum urbanorum*), and servitudes on land (*prædiorum rusticorum*), were, by the old Roman law, required to be attached to a permanent cause (*causam perpetuam*), and to be designed for the preservation of some actual advantage. They could not, therefore, by the Roman law, be limited by conditions, or for a term of time, but were inseparable from the property, and indivisible. Servitudes being burdens upon an estate, the usufructuary must respect the rights of the owner of the same, and use his own rights *civiliter*, that is, with as little injury to the former as possible.

SERVIUS TULLIUS, the sixth king of Rome, was the son of a slave, given by Tarquin to Tanaquil, his wife. Young Servius was educated in the palace of the monarch, and raised himself to so much consequence, that Tarquin gave him his daughter in marriage. Servius became the favorite of the people and the darling of the soldiers, and was raised to the throne, on the death of his father-in-law. He defeated the Veientes and the Tuscans, established the census, beautified the city, and enlarged its boundaries by taking within its walls the hills Quirinalis, Viminalis, and Esquilinus. He also divided the Roman people into tribes, and built several temples. Servius married his two daughters to the grandsons of his father-in-law; the elder to Tarquin, and the younger to Aruns. The wife of Aruns murdered her own husband, to unite herself to Tarquin, who had likewise assassinated his wife. Servius was murdered by his own son-in-law, and his daughter Tullia ordered her chariot to be driven over the mangled body of her father (533 B. C.). Such is the history of Servius, as commonly related. But see Niebuhr's *Roman History* (3d ed., 1828), in the chapters On the Legend of Tarquinius Priscus and Servius Tullius, and Critical Examination of the History of Tarquin and Servius.

SERVUS SERVORUM (*servant of servants*); the title which the popes give themselves.

SESAMUM ORIENTALE; a plant, known from a very ancient period, and very interesting on account of the economical purposes to which it is applied. It was originally brought from India, and is said to grow wild in Ceylon, and along the coast of Malabar. It is called *semsem* in Egypt and other parts of the East, where it is cultivated extensively on account of the seeds, and an oil which they yield, not unlike or inferior to the oil of almonds. This plant was introduced into Carolina, from Africa, by the negroes, and succeeds there perfectly. It is called *bene* or *bonny*. The oil will keep many years, does not acquire any rancid smell or taste, but, on the other hand, in two years becomes quite mild, and is a good substitute for olive oil. The negroes use the seeds as an aliment. The sesamum was introduced into Jamaica by the Jews, and is now cultivated in most parts of the island. It is called *vanglo* or *oil plant;* and the seeds are frequently used in broths by many of the Europeans, but the Jews make them chiefly into cakes. In Japan, China, and Cochin-China, where they have no butter, they use the oil for frying fish, and in dressing other dishes, as a varnish, and, medicinally, as a resolvent and emollient. Pliny speaks of this oil as equally good to eat and burn. Nine pounds of the seed yield upwards of two pounds of oil. The plant grows to the height of two feet or more; the stem is upright, herbaceous, hairy, and almost cylindrical; the leaves are oval oblong, the inferior ones opposite, with long leafstalks, entire, or with some very distant teeth; the superior, much narrower, entire, acuminate, almost alternate, and nearly sessile: the flowers are solitary, axillary, and the corolla is white, and resembles, in form, that of the foxglove.—*S. indicum* is another species, cultivated in Egypt, and used for the same purposes as the preceding.

Sesostris; a king of Egypt, who by some has been deemed the Shishak of Scripture, but whom Champollion has shown to be a different person. He is called Sethos, and Sethosis, and his royal name is Ramses, or Rameses. He reigned in the fifteenth century B. C. Sesostris was a great conqueror, who overran Asia, and is said to have erected magnificent temples in all the cities of his empire, to have built a great wall on the eastern boundary of Egypt, and to have dug a number of canals from the Nile, for the purposes of commerce and irrigation.

Sessile; a botanical term, signifying without footstalks.

Session, Court of, in Scotland; the highest civil judicatory in the kingdom. The judges (lords of the session) are fifteen in number. It has extensive original jurisdiction, and its powers of review, as a court of appeal, have no limits. In 1808, it was divided into two chambers, called the first and second division; the lord president and seven judges constituting the former, and the lord justice clerk, who is head of the court of justiciary, with six judges, the latter. These divisions have independent but co-ordinate jurisdiction. The high court of justiciary or supreme criminal jurisdiction for Scotland, consists of six judges, who are lords of the session, the lord justice clerk presiding. In this court the number of the jury is fifteen, and a majority decides. The court of session is divided into the inner house and outer house, with appeal from the latter to the former, and from the former to the house of lords of the United Kingdom.

Sessions. (For the *quarter sessions*, see *Courts*, vol. iii, p. 589.)

Sestertium. (See *Sestertius.*)

Sestertius; an ancient Roman silver coin, worth two and a half *asses* (hence the name *sesquitertius*, the third half). (See *As.*) In sterling money, the sestertius was about one penny and a quarter; but it was not at all periods precisely the same. The neuter form, *sestertium*, denotes a much larger amount. It generally appears in the plural, and signifies not a real coin, but a sum of 1000 *sestertii.* If the sum amounts to 1,000,000 or more, a numeral in *ies* is connected with *sestertium* (e. g. *quadragies sestertium* is four millions of *sestertii*, i. e. *quadragies centena millia sestertiorum nummorum*). Sometimes the numeral adverb is used alone, and *decies ei dedit* signifies *decies sestertium*, i. e. *decies centena millia sestertiorum*, or a million. The *sestertius* was generally expressed by the letters L. L. S. (i. e. *libra libra semis*); and these letters were contracted into H. S. In common life, it was generally called *nummus* only. (For the manner in which the Romans expressed numerical values, see *Notation.*) As a weight, a sestertius amounted to about fifteen and three fourths French grains (about 12.91 grains Troy.)

Sestetto; a musical piece for six independent voices, whether instrumental or vocal. The former is particularly used for wind instruments, and often employed for serenades (q. v.), or *notturni*. Moscheles, Beethoven and others have composed *sestettos* for wind and stringed instruments. Vocal *sestettos* are used in operas; and that of Mozart, in the second act of Don Juan, is celebrated.

Sestina; a lyric form of versification, which comprises six strophes of six lines, and one of three lines. The verse is generally the iambic of five feet. The characteristic of the *sestina* is, that in each of the six strophes the six final words of the first are repeated in such an order that the final word of the sixth verse of the first strophe becomes the final word of the first verse of the second strophe; the other five verses of the second stropho end with the final words of the five first verses of the first strophe in an arbitrary succession. The third strophe is formed in the same way from the second as this was from the first, and so on; so that each of the six final words is once the first and once the last word in each strophe, and the last verse of the sixth strophe ends with the final word of the first verse of the first strophe. The strophe of three lines, with which the *sestina* ends, repeats the six final words again in the same order as they stand in the first strophe: each verse contains two of them, one in the middle and one at the end. There is no other rhyme in the *sestina*. Petrarca has made successful essays in this form. In general, the Italians, and next to them the Spaniards, have most cultivated it. It has been attempted, also, in German. It can be readily imagined how easily this form leads to an idle play upon words; yet it is astonishing with what skill some poets have contrived to attach different ideas and feelings to the same words.

SESTINI, Domenico, the most learned numismatist of Europe, in regard to ancient coins, as far as the knowledge of them can be acquired by inspection, was born at Florence, in 1750. After having completed his studies at the school of St. Marco, he entered the clerical order; but, in 1774, he left his native city, and visited Rome, Naples, and the Sicilies. In order to prosecute his studies with more effect, he went from Sicily, through Malta and Smyrna to Constantinople, where he prepared his observations on the plague, which then prevailed. He made short journeys from Constantinople into Asia and Europe, and lived awhile in the house of prince Ypsilanti, hospodar of Walachia. At length, he went to Vienna, and returned along the Danube and over the Black sea to Constantinople. The British ambassador at the Porte, sir Robert Ainslie, was then forming a collection of ancient coins. For sixteen years Sestini was his agent, and in the course of his travels collected the celebrated cabinet which he has described in his *Lett. e Dissertazioni numismatiche sopra alcune Medaglie rare della Collezione Ainsliana* (4 vols., 1789—90, 4to.); *Descr. Numor. vett. ex Museis Ainslie, Bellini*, etc., *necnon Animadverss. in Opus Eckhel. Doctrina Numorum vett.* (Leghorn, 1796, 4to.). To gain a thorough knowledge of ancient coins, he travelled through Germany, visited Gotha, Dresden, and Berlin, where he settled, and was appointed, by the king, superintendent of the collection there. In 1810, he went to Paris, where he was elected a corresponding member of the *Académie des Inscriptions et Belles Lettres*, and, two years later, he received the appointment of antiquary and librarian of the princess Eliza, then grand-duchess of Tuscany. When Ferdinand III ascended the throne, he confirmed him in this office, and added the title of honorary professor of the university of Pisa. In November, 1825, he was living with count Viczay at Hedervan. His principal writings are *Diss. intorno al Virgilio di Aproniano* (Flor., 1774, 4to.); *Della Peste di Constantinopoli del* 1778 (Yverdun [Flor.], 1779, 12mo.); *Lettere Odeporiche, ossia Viaggio per la Penisola di Cizico* (2 vols., Leghorn, 1785); *Viaggio di Constantinopoli a Bassora* (Yverd. [Leghorn], 1786); *Viaggio di Ritorno da Bassora a Constantinopoli* (Leghorn, 1788); *Lettere e Dissertazioni numismatiche*, which appeared at Leghorn, Rome, Berlin, Milan, Pisa, and Florence, from 1789 to 1820, in 18 vols., 4to., with many engravings; the *Descriptio Numorum veterum ex variis Museis* (Leipsic, 1796, 4to.); the *Catalogus Numorum veterum Musæi Aragoniani* (Berl., 1805, fol.); the *Descr. selectiorum Numismatum in Ære maximi Moduli Museo olim Ab. de Camps, posteaque Mareschalli d'Etrées*, etc. (Berl., 1808, 4to.); *Descr. delle Medaglie Greche e Romane del fu Benkowitz* (Berl., 1800, 4to.); *Descr. degli Stateri antichi illustr. con le Medaglie* (Flor., 1817); *Diss. sopra le Medaglie antiche relative alla Confederaz. degli Achei* (Milan, 1817, 4to.); and the *Desc. delle Medaglie Ispane appartenenti alla Lusitania Betica e alla Tarragonese del Museo Hedervariano* (Flor., 1818, 4to.). His *Classes generales seu Moneta vetus Urbium, Populorum et Regum Ordine Geographico et Chronologico descr.* (Flor., 1821, 4to., 2d ed.), may serve, in many respects, as a general index to all these works. There is but little prospect that his *Systema geographicum Numismaticum* (written by his own hand, in 16 vols., folio), the fruit of fifty years of study and investigation, will be given to the world.

SESTOS; a fortress of European Turkey, opposite to Abydos (q. v.), from which it is 2700 yards distant. The castles of the Dardanelles, sometimes called the *Sestos* and *Abydos*, are built near the sites of the ancient towns so called, famous for the loves of Leander and Hero.

SET-OFF, in law, is when the defendant acknowledges the justice of the plaintiff's demand on the one hand, but on the other sets up a demand of his own, to counterbalance that of the plaintiff, either in the whole or in part; as if the plaintiff sue for $100 due on a note of hand, the defendant may set off $90 to himself for merchandise sold to the plaintiff, or for any other demand, the amount of which is ascertained in damages.

SETTLE, Elkanah, an English poet, was born in 1648. At the age of eighteen, he entered at Oxford, but quitted the university without taking a degree, and, going to London, commenced author by profession. He wrote numerous political pamphlets, and, in reply to Dryden's poem entitled the Medal, occasioned by the whig party striking a medal to commemorate the throwing out of the bill against the earl of Shaftesbury, a piece called the Medal Reversed; and, soon after, a poem entitled Azaria and Hushai, designed as an answer to the Absalom and Achitophel. In 1685, he published a poem on the coronation of James II, and, about the same time, obtained a pension from the city, for writing an annual inauguration panegyric on lord mayor's day. Settle was, besides, an indefatigable writer for the stage, and produced fifteen dramatic pieces, none of which are now known on the boards. In the decline of life, he received a salary from the proprietor of a booth at Bartholomew fair, as a writer of "Drolls," which were generally very successful, and is said to have been, at that time, the best contriver of theatrical machinery in the kingdom. He died at the Charter-house, in 1724.

SETTLEMENT; a legal residence or establishment of a person in a particular parish or town, which entitles him to maintenance there, if a pauper. In England, the poor are supported by the parish where they have a settlement. In New England, they are supported by the town. In England, the statutes 12 Richard II and 19 Henry VII seem to be the first rudiments of parish settlements. By statutes 13 and 14 Charles II, a legal settlement is declared to be gained by birth, by inhabitancy, by apprenticeship, or by service for forty days. But the gaining of a settlement by so short a residence produced great evils, which were remedied by statute 1 James II.

SETTLEMENT, ACT OF; a name given to a statute 12 and 13 William III, cap. 2, by which the crown was limited to the present reigning house in England, and by which some new provisions were added in favor of the subject, securing his liberty and the rights of conscience.

SETUVAL, or ST. UBES; a town of Portugal, in Estremadura; fifteen miles south-east of Lisbon; lon. 8° 54′ W.; lat. 38° 29′ N.; population 14,876. It is situated in a bay of the Atlantic, at the mouth of the river Sandao, with a good harbor, capable of receiving ships of any burden, and exports lemons, olives, oil, wine, and, above all, bay salt, of which no less than 200,000 tons are annually made here. The streets are paved, and the town is fortified with a mound, a citadel, and several small forts. Setuval contains five churches, one hospital, eleven convents, and an *academia problematica*.

SEUME, John Gottlieb, known for his writings and his adventures, a man of a vigorous mind, but eccentric disposition, was born at Poserne, in 1763. He was left an orphan, but was placed, by a charitable person, at the Nicolai school in Leipsic. Here he began the study of theology; but, becoming discontented, he set off secretly for Paris. On his way, he was forced to join the Hessian troops then raising to serve in America (1781). After his return, he was obliged to enter the Prussian service, but at length studied at the university of Leipsic, and, in 1793, became secretary of the Russian general at Warsaw. He soon after returned to Leipsic, where he published several works, and was employed as a corrector of the press. In 1801, he set out on a pedestrian excursion through Austria, Italy and France, and, on his return, published an account of his tour, under the title of Walk to Syracuse (in German). In 1805, he undertook a similar expedition into Russia, Sweden, &c., which is described in My Summer of 1805 (2d ed., 1815). He died at Teplitz, in 1810. His autobiography, which he left unfinished, was completed by Clodius, and is contained in the edition of his works in twelve volumes (Leipsic, 1826, seq.).

SEVEN ISLANDS. (See *Ionian Islands.*)

SEVEN LIBERAL ARTS. (See *Arts.*)

SEVENNES. (See *Cevennes.*)

SEVEN SLEEPERS. There is an old story that Epimenides of Crete reappeared in the world, after sleeping forty years in a cave (see *Epimenides*); and all our readers are acquainted with the veracious legend of Rip Van Winkle, as related in the Sketch-Book of Geoffrey Crayon; but the slumber of the seven sleepers was of longer duration. In the time of the emperor Decius, when the Christians were persecuted, seven noble youths of Ephesus concealed themselves in a neighboring cavern, the entrance of which was closed by order of the emperor. The persecuted youths immediately fell into a deep slumber, from which they were accidentally awakened in the reign of Theodosius II, after a period of 187 years. Pressed with hunger, after their long fast, they sent one of their number to the city to purchase bread. He was astonished to see crosses erected all over the city; and his own antiquated dress and obsolete language confounded the baker, to whom he offered an old medal in payment for bread. Suspected of having found a secret treasure, he was carried before the judge, to whom he related his miraculous story. The bishop of Ephesus, the magistrates, and the emperor himself, hastened to the cave, and found the sleepers still bearing the bloom of youth. They related their story to the multitude, gave them their benediction, and expired. The church has consecrated the 27th of June to their memory. (See the *Acta Sanctorum* of the Bollandists, tom. vi, 375—397.) This legend has not been confined to the Christian world. The Koran relates the tale of the seven sleepers, to whom it assigns a dog (Al Rakim), and out of respect for whom it declares that the sun altered his course twice a day, that he might shine into the cavern. The Mohammedan and Christian story are probably both derived from the same source.

Seven Stars. (See *Pleiades.*)

Seventh Day Baptists. (See *Baptists.*)

Seven Wise Men, or Seven Sages of Greece. This name is commonly applied to seven philosophers, several of whom were legislators, of an early period of Grecian history. They were Periander of Corinth (in place of whom some give Epimenides (q. v.) of Crete), Pittacus of Mitylene, Thales (q. v.), Solon (q. v.), Bias (q. v.), Chilo, and Cleobulus (q. v.). (See *Greece*, division *Greek Literature*, p. 12).

Seven Wonders of the World; seven monuments, remarkable for their splendor or magnitude. They are the pyramids (q. v.) of Egypt (instead of which some name the Pharos (q. v.) of Alexandria), the walls and hanging gardens of Babylon (q. v.), the temple of Diana at Ephesus (q. v.), the statue of the Olympian Jupiter (see *Phidias*), the Mausoleum (see *Artemisia*, and *Mausoleum*), and the colossus of Rhodes (see *Colossus*). These are not, however, to be considered the greatest works of ancient art and taste. This group of the seven wonders originated among the Greeks in the time of Alexander. Philo the Byzantine has described them in his work *De septem Orbis Spectaculis* (late edition, Leipsic, 1816).

Seven Years' War. By the treaties of peace concluded at Breslau, July 28, 1742, and at Dresden, Dec. 25, 1745, Maria Theresa of Austria ceded to king Frederic II six principalities of Silesia and the county of Glatz. The loss of these fine territories was too painful for her not to think of recovering them. For this purpose, she concluded an alliance with Elizabeth, the empress of Russia, and personal enemy of Frederic, brought over to her cause the king of Poland and the elector of Saxony, Augustus III, and attempted to form a closer union with France, notwithstanding the enmity that had existed between that kingdom and her own for centuries. While Maria Theresa was occupied in these projects, a dispute had arisen between England and France, relating to the boundary between their possessions in America, which broke out, in 1755, into open hostilities. To protect his German states against an attack from France, the king of England concluded an alliance with Prussia; and, some months after, France made a league with the court of Vienna, promising to furnish 24,000 auxiliary troops against Prussia. But these auxiliaries were afterwards increased to 180,000; for it was rather the design of France to injure the king of England by conquering Hanover, than to aid in accomplishing the ambitious designs of the empress on Silesia. By means of Menzel, a clerk in the Saxon cabinet, all the proceedings of the Russian, Austrian and Saxon courts were discovered to Malzahn, the Prussian ambassador in Dresden, and Frederic II accordingly prepared himself for war. He demanded an explanation from the court of Vienna, received an equivocal answer, and resolved to anticipate his enemies. In August, 1756, therefore, he invaded Saxony with 60,000 men, in three divisions, invested Dresden, took possession of the documents necessary to justify his conduct, which he found in the archives of the cabinet there, and invested the Saxon army of 15,000 men in their fortified camp at Pirna. Meanwhile, field-marshal Brown advanced from Bohemia with an army to liberate Saxony. Frederic, leaving troops sufficient to maintain the siege of the Saxon camp, marched to Bohemia to meet the Austrians, and engaged them.

Oct. 1, at Lowositz. The battle, though not decisive, prevented the field-marshal from aiding the Saxons. They were forced to surrender as prisoners of war, and the inferior officers and common soldiers were compelled to enter the Prussian service; but they soon deserted, both singly and in whole regiments, because they would not fight against their own sovereign. Such was the end of the first campaign; and the Prussians remained through the winter in Saxony and Silesia. Frederic's invasion of Saxony excited a general commotion in the courts of Europe. It was pronounced to be a violation of the treaty of Westphalia, and France, as one of the guaranties of that treaty, now took part in the struggle. Sweden, too, for the same reason, and Russia, on account of her alliance with the empress, adopted a similar course. In the diet at Ratisbon, war was declared on the part of the empire against Prussia. Thus, in 1757, Austria, Russia, France, Sweden, and the German empire, were in arms against Frederic, while he had no ally but England; and, in a war by land, but little aid was to be expected from her. In order to anticipate his enemies, Frederic marched into Bohemia with four armies in April, 1757, and, May 6, a bloody battle was fought at Prague, in which the Prussians conquered, but lost their distinguished general Schwerin. The greatest part of the vanquished Austrian army threw itself into the city of Prague, to which the king immediately laid siege. Field-marshal Daun, who was stationed on the heights of Colin with 60,000 Austrians, received orders to hazard a decisive action for the relief of Prague. To prevent this, Frederic advanced to Colin (q. v.), attacked the enemy with 24,000 men, lost the battle, and 8—14,000 brave soldiers, and was forced to raise the siege of Prague, and to retreat to Saxony and Lusatia. He effected his retreat from Bohemia without further loss. Meanwhile, the French had taken possession of Wesel, the principalities of Cleve and East Friesland, the territories of Hesse-Cassel and Hanover, and laid them under contribution. The duke of Cumberland, who commanded the forces of the German states, allied with Prussia, namely, Hanover, Hesse, Brunswick, Gotha and Bückeburg, 40,000 men, to whom were opposed 100,000 French, was defeated at Hastenbeck July 26, and driven back to Stade, and concluded a capitulation, Sept. 8, at Kloster-Seven (which, however, was never carried into execution), by the terms of which all the above-mentioned troops, except those of Hanover, were to be disbanded. A French army under the prince de Soubise, with the imperial forces, 15,000 men strong, under the prince of Hildburghausen, now menaced Saxony, and the hereditary states of Frederic, who, therefore, left the duke of Bevern in Silesia, marched to Thuringia, and drove the French from Erfurt. On receiving information that an Austrian army, under Haddick, had invaded the Mark, Frederic hastened back to Torgau. But, as the Austrians soon retreated, and the French advanced anew, he marched against the latter, and fought at Rossbach (q. v.), Nov. 5, that memorable battle, in which both the French and the imperial armies were defeated, and found safety only in a hasty flight. They went into winter-quarters at a distance, and the possession of Saxony was secured to the king. Upon this, Frederic hurried back to Silesia, where Schweidnitz and Breslau had fallen into the hands of the Austrians. With a small army, fatigued by a long march, he defeated, Dec. 5, at Leuthen (q. v.), a force twice as great, under Daun. Breslau surrendered fourteen days after, with a numerous garrison, and a large quantity of stores, and, soon after, Liegnitz also. In these actions the Austrians lost upwards of 40,000 men. Silesia was again torn from them, and Frederic was now more formidable to his foes than ever. The Russians marched into Prussia, in June, 100,000 men strong, laid waste the country in a barbarous manner, maltreated the inhabitants, defeated field-marshal Lehwald, Aug. 30, at Grossjägerndorf, with his army of 24,000 men, and then returned, destroying all before them. The Swedes, in September, occupied Anklam, Demmin and Pasewalk; but, in a few weeks, they were defeated by Lehwald, and driven to Rügen. The third campaign was opened in February, 1758, by Ferdinand, duke of Brunswick (q. v.), who was now at the head of the allied armies, in the room of the duke of Cumberland, and opposed the French in Lower Saxony and Westphalia. His nephew, the hereditary prince, afterwards duke of Brunswick, Charles William Ferdinand, commanded under him. Duke Ferdinand made himself master of the Weser, expelled the French, under Clermont, from Lower Saxony and Westphalia, and defeated them, June 23, at Crefeld. He then returned over the Rhine to Hesse, where Soubise was stationed with a

French army, and whither Clermont followed him. Ferdinand, in the mean while strengthened by 12,000 English troops, forced the two hostile bodies to retire over the Maine and the Rhine, where they went into winter-quarters. In the winter of 1758, after the Austrians had been driven from Silesia, and Schweidnitz recovered, Frederic marched into Moravia, and in May commenced the siege of Olmütz; but, when Daun arrived, in July, he was forced to raise the siege, with the loss of a large stock of provisions and ammunition. The Russians, after having driven back the few Prussian troops, marched into Neumark, and Frederic hastened with a body of soldiers to protect his hereditary states. He came up with the Russian army, 50,000 men strong, who were besieging Cüstrin, attacked them at Zorndorf, Aug. 26, with 30,000 men, defeated them after a bloody engagement, and forced the Russians to retreat to Poland. After this, he again turned his attention to Saxony, where his brother prince Henry was no longer able to resist the Austrians. He encamped at Hochkirch (q. v.), where he was attacked in the night of October 14, and suffered a total defeat. Soon after, in Silesia, Frederic compelled the Austrians to raise the siege of Neisse; he then hastened to Saxony, and drove field-marshal Daun, who was besieging Dresden, back to Bohemia. At the close of the campaign, the king saw all his states, except the kingdom of Prussia, free from the enemy. In France, there was a general wish for peace; but Louis XV, and his mistress, the marchioness de Pompadour, were bent on continuing the war. A new alliance was, therefore, concluded with Austria, December 30, 1758, and the same month a treaty was also entered into between England and Prussia, in which Frederic was promised a yearly subsidy. Prince Henry marched into Bohemia, notwithstanding the severity of the winter; the hostile troops were dispersed, a corps of 2500 men was taken by general Hülsen, and an immense booty. The inactive imperial forces, in Franconia, prince Henry put to flight. Contributions were levied by the Prussians on Bamberg, Erfurt and Würzburg. Another body of Prussians invaded the duchy of Mecklenburg-Schwerin, which was compelled to furnish large quantities of military stores, besides 16,000 recruits, in the course of the war, and to pay several million dollars, in consequence of the policy of their sovereign, who first gave his vote to have Frederic II treated as an enemy of the empire. The allies, under Ferdinand of Brunswick, could effect but little at the beginning of the campaign of 1759. The French had taken Frankfort on the Maine by surprise, during the winter, and the plan for recovering this city was frustrated by the failure of the attack on Bergen, April 13. But, Aug. 1, Ferdinand gained a splendid victory at Minden over the French troops under Contades and Broglio. On the same day, the hereditary prince of Brunswick likewise defeated the French at Gohfeld, and they were driven over the Lahn on one side, and over the Rhine on the other. But general Wedel, who undertook to resist the progress of the Russians, was defeated at Kay near Züllichau, in the Neumark, by general Soltikoff, and Frederic hastened from Silesia to defend his electoral territories from the danger which hung over them. Aug. 12, he attacked the Russians at Kunersdorf (q. v.), not far from Frankfort, and had already defeated them, and even despatched messengers from the field with the news of his victory, when Laudon, who had previously joined the Russians with 18,000 Austrians, deprived him of his expected success. The Russians purchased their victory dearly, but they made no use of it. Frederic's position was extremely dangerous; indeed, he began to apprehend an unfortunate issue of the war. The Russians were victorious in his hereditary states; Daun was in Lusatia with a large army, and Saxony was overrun by the imperial troops. The Austrians and Russians wished to unite; but prince Henry deprived the former of their magazines, and thus obliged them to retreat; and Frederic anticipated the Russians in their march to Silesia, and compelled them to retire to Poland. In Saxony, the king experienced a new misfortune. General Fink, a brave commander, was forced to surrender, at Maxen, Nov. 21, with 11,000 men and a large number of cannon, to the Austrians. But, notwithstanding all these mishaps, at the close of the campaign, the enemy were nearly every where driven back; only Daun remained in Saxony, where he had occupied Dresden. The Swedes, also, who, after the battle of Kunersdorf, when Prussian Pomerania was destitute of troops, invaded that country, were driven by Manteufel and Platen under the cannon of Stralsund. The campaign of 1760 seemed, at first, to forebode ill success to Frederic. The brave general Fouquet was taken at Landshut, with 8000 Prussians; the king was forced to raise, July 30, the siege of Dresden, which he had commenced on the 14th; Glatz had gone over to the Austrians, and Frederic was obliged to march into Silesia for its protection. With 30,000 Prussians he entrenched himself at Liegnitz; the hostile troops, under Daun and Laudon, were more than 100,000 strong, and threatened an attack. But Laudon was defeated, Aug. 15, at Liegnitz, and Daun was unable to afford him any assistance. The Austrians lost 10,000 men in killed, wounded and prisoners, 23 standards and 82 pieces of cannon. Frederic's loss was 1800 killed and wounded. Meanwhile, a corps of Russians and Austrians had advanced to Berlin, and levied contributions on the people. Frederic hastened thither to cut off the enemy; but, not finding them there, he returned to Saxony, where the imperial forces were stationed, and Daun and Lascy had united. At Torgau he attacked the enemy, Nov. 3, defeated them in a bloody engagement, which was gained chiefly by the sagacity and courage of Ziethen and Möllendorf, and then went into winter-quarters in Saxony. Laudon, also, was driven back in Silesia to the county of Glatz, and the Russians were forced to raise the siege of Colberg and to retire to Poland. The allied forces, under Ferdinand of Brunswick, defeated the French, July 31, at Marburg; but the latter remained in Hesse, where they had extensive magazines. February 11, 1761, Ferdinand attacked the French in their quarters; they fled, and many of their fortifications and magazines fell into the hands of the conquerors. A corps of French and Saxon troops was defeated, February 14, at Langensalza; but the allies were obliged to raise the siege of Ziegenhain, Marburg and Cassel, with loss, and the French once more became masters of all Hesse, and had an unobstructed passage to Hanover. The people all wished for peace; but not so their rulers, except the king of Prussia. Maria Theresa would not now be satisfied merely with the restoration of Silesia. The empress Elizabeth was desirous of retaining Prussia, and the French minister Choiseul sought to revenge himself for a poetical epistle, in which Frederic had satirized him, by protracting the war. The proposals of peace, made by England and Prussia, were not accepted, and Frederic endeavored to protect Silesia against the Austrians and Russians, who had united, in August, at Striegau. The king maintained his camp at Schweidnitz against a much superior force, and the greatest part of the Russians were obliged to retire to Poland, for want of provisions. Laudon surprised Schweidnitz Oct. 1. A garrison of 3700 men, several magazines, and a large quantity of military stores, fell into the hands of the Austrians. Prince Henry, in Saxony, was also reduced to great straits by Daun. In Pomerania, detached bodies of the Prussians were defeated by the Russians, and, after a brave resistance, Dec. 16, they lost the fortress of Colberg. The Swedes, on the contrary, were driven back to Stralsund; and, July 15, Ferdinand, duke of Brunswick, gained a brilliant victory at Billingshausen over the French; but the triumph was of little importance. Frederic felt himself in a desperate condition, and, in consequence of all these misfortunes and the superior strength of his enemies, seemed to be verging to his ruin. But, January 5, 1762, Elizabeth, the empress of Russia, died; and her successor, Peter III, the personal friend and admirer of Frederic, concluded an armistice with him, March 16, 1762; which was followed, May 5, by the peace of Petersburg. Sweden, likewise, made peace with Prussia; and, as Peter's intercession with Austria was ineffectual, the Russian emperor sent a body of troops to aid the Prussians. But the emperor's early death soon broke the alliance with Frederic, and his successor, Catharine II, recalled the Russian troops, amounting to 20,000 men, from the Prussian service. Frederic, however, was delivered from one dangerous enemy, and had gained an important preponderance of strength over the rest. He now drove an Austrian corps from their entrenchments at Burkersdorf, recovered Schweidnitz in October, left the duke of Bevern with an army for the defence of Silesia, and marched to Saxony. After several successful engagements, prince Henry gained, Oct. 29, an important victory over the Austrian and the imperial troops at Freiberg, and the king now concluded an armistice with the Austrians; but it related only to Saxony and Silesia. Under duke Ferdinand and the hereditary prince of Brunswick, the allies commenced, unsuccessfully, the campaign of 1762 against the French; but the latter were defeated, June 24, at Wilhelmsthal, driven from their fortified camp at Cassel, and extremely weakened. Cassel itself was besieged, and, November 1, surrendered to the allies. Two days after this, the preliminaries of peace between England

and France were signed, and the peace itself was confirmed at Paris, Feb. 10, 1763. (See *Paris, Treaties concluded at.*) Frederic was thus exposed alone to his enemies; but he had already acquired a decided superiority. A Prussian force, under Kleist, also obliged several of the most important states of the empire to declare themselves neutral. After a short negotiation, and without the aid of foreign mediation, Frederic concluded a peace with Austria and Saxony at Hubertsburg (q. v.), Feb. 15, by which each power received again all the territories which it had possessed before the war, though in a miserable condition. The unity of purpose, which marked all the measures of Frederic, and the great supplies both of men and money, which he obtained from the conquest of Saxony, his comprehensive genius, his numerous and excellent generals, and the bravery of his troops, gave the Prussian monarch a superiority over his enemies, and brought to a happy conclusion a war which had made the Prussian kingdom more than once tremble on the brink of destruction. This war cost Europe a million lives, and exhausted all the states which took part in it, without having procured to any but England the smallest advantage.—See *Hist. de la Guerre de sept Ans*, in the posthumous works of Frederic II; *History of the Seven Years' War*, by Lloyd and Tempelhof; Ratzow's *Charakteristik der merkwürd., &c.;* the *Geständnisse eines Oestreich. Veterans* [Confessions of an Austrian Veteran], by Kuniaczo; and lord Dover's *Life of Frederic II* (London, 1832).

Seventy, The. (See *Septuagint.*)

Severians, Severites. (See *Gnostics*, and *Monophysites.*)

Severn (anciently Sabrina); a river which rises near Plinlimmon hill, North Wales, passes by Shrewsbury, Worcester, Upton, Tewksbury and Gloucester, and, entering the sea, its mouth is called *Bristol Channel.* A communication between this river and the Thames, the Trent, the Dee, and the Mersey and other rivers, has been opened by different canals; length of its course to the sea, about 200 miles.

Severus, Alexander. (See *Alexander Severus.*)

Severus, Lucius Septimius; a Roman emperor, born at Leptis, in Africa, of a noble family. He successively exercised all the offices of the state, and recommended himself to notice by an ambitious mind and a restless activity, that, for the gratification of avarice, could endure the greatest hardships. After the murder of Pertinax, Severus resolved to remove Didius Julianus, who had bought the imperial purple when exposed to sale by the pretorians (q. v.), and proclaimed himself emperor on the borders of Illyricum, where he was stationed against the barbarians. To support himself, he took, as his partner in the empire, Albinus, who was at the head of the Roman forces in Britain, and immediately marched towards Rome to crush Didius and his partisans. He was received with acclamation; and Julian was deserted by his favorites, and assassinated by his own soldiers. In professing that he had assumed the purple only to revenge the death of the virtuous Pertinax, Severus gained many adherents, and was enabled to banish the pretorians, whose insolence and avarice had become alarming, not only to the citizens, but to the emperor. But while he was victorious at Rome, Pescennius Niger was in the East, at the head of a powerful army, and with the name and ensigns of Augustus. Many obstinate battles were fought between the imperial rivals, till, on the plains of Issus, Niger was totally ruined by the loss of 20,000 men. The head of Niger was cut off and sent to the conqueror, who punished, in a most cruel manner, the partisans of his unfortunate rival. Severus afterwards pillaged Byzantium, which had shut her gates against him; and after he had conquered several nations in the East, he returned to Rome, resolved to destroy Albinus, with whom he had hitherto reluctantly shared the imperial power. He attempted to assassinate him by his emissaries; but when this had failed of success, Severus had recourse to arms, and the fate of the empire was again decided on the plains of Gaul. Albinus was defeated, and the conqueror insulted the dead body of his rival, and ordered it to be thrown into the Rhone, after he had suffered it to putrefy before the door of his tent, and to be torn by his dogs. The adherents of Albinus shared his fate; and the return of Severus to the capital exhibited the bloody triumphs of Marius and Sylla. The richest of the citizens were sacrificed, and their money became the property of the emperor. Commodus received divine honors, and his murderers were punished in the most wanton manner. Tired of the inactive life he led in Rome, Severus marched into the East with his two sons Caracalla and Geta; made himself master of Seleucia, Babylon and Ctesiphon; and advanced far into the Parthian territories. From Parthia, he marched towards the more southern provinces of Asia, and, after he had visited the tomb of Pompey the Great, entered Alexandria. The revolt of Britain recalled him from the East. After he had reduced it under his power, he built a wall across the northern parts of the island to defend it against the frequent invasions of the Caledonians. (See *Picts' Wall.*) Hitherto successful against his enemies, Severus now found the peace of his family disturbed. Caracalla attempted to murder his father, as he was concluding a treaty of peace with the Britons; and Severus, worn out with infirmities which the gout and the uneasiness of his mind increased, soon after died at York, A. D. 211, in the 66th year of his age. Severus has been so much admired for his military talents that some have called him the most warlike of the Roman emperors. As a monarch, he was cruel; and it has been observed that he never did an act of humanity or forgave a fault. In his diet, he was temperate, and he always showed himself an enemy to pomp and splendor. He loved the appellation of a man of letters, and he even composed a history of his own reign.

Severus's Wall. (See *Picts' Wall.*)

Sévigné, Marie de Rabutin, marquise de, a French woman of quality, greatly distinguished for her epistolary talents, was born in 1627. Her father, the baron of Chantal, who was the head of the house of Bussy Rabutin, left her, during infancy, his sole heiress. The graces of her person and conversation procured her many admirers; and in 1644 she married the marquis de Sévigné, who was killed in a duel in 1651, leaving her the mother of a son and daughter. She formed no second union, but devoted herself to the education of her children, and to the cultivation of her mind, by reading and literary society. She was extremely attached to her daughter, who, in 1669, married the count de Grignan, and accompanied him to his government of Provence. The absence of her daughter from the metropolis gave rise to the greater part of the Letters which have gained madame de Sévigné so much reputation. The subject of many of these epistles are so entirely domestic as to produce little interest; but others abound with court anecdotes, remarks on men and books, and the topics of the day, which are conveyed with great ease and felicity. They are models of the epistolary style, perfectly natural from their expression, lively sentiment and description, and a playfulness which gives grace and interest to trifles. In her letters to her daughter, the reader is sometimes wearied with an excess of flattery of her beauty and talents, the preservation of the former of which seems to have formed the principal object of her maternal anxiety. In fact, although endowed with abilities and penetration, she did not rise much above the level of her age in taste and principles. She was highly attached to rank and splendor, loved admiration, and felt the usual predilection of high life for manners and accomplishments in preference to solid worth. She had a strong feeling of religion, but was often inconsistent in her sense of it, and in reference to the proceedings against the French Protestants, expresses herself with bigotry and want of feeling. The most complete edition of her Letters is that which appeared at Paris in 1818 (11 vols., 8vo). An English translation was published in London about 1758. She died in 1696, at the age of seventy.

Seville, Sevilla (anciently Hispalis); a city of Spain, in Andalusia, on the Guadalquivir, capital of a province of the same name, forty-five miles north of Cadiz, 250 south-west of Madrid; lon. 5° 39′ W.; lat. 37° 24′ north; population, 94,000. It is an archiepiscopal see, and stands in a fine plain, surrounded by an old wall, built of cement, with twelve gates, and 166 turrets. The interior of the city is built in the Moorish style, the streets being often so narrow that a person can touch the houses on both sides at once; and it is badly paved. The squares are neither numerous nor spacious. There are several beautiful public walks, one, in particular, on the banks of the Guadalquivir. The city contains a cathedral, twenty-nine churches, eighty-four convents, and twenty-four hospitals. The cathedral is the largest Gothic edifice in Spain, and one of the largest churches in Europe. It was built in the fifteenth century, contains eighty-two altars, and has a tower 250 feet high, considered the finest in Spain. Other conspicuous edifices are the alcazar, or palace, a Moorish building, containing a library of 20,000 volumes, a garden, &c.; the longa or exchange, the artillery school and the mint. The houses generally cover a large space, but towards the street they have often a mean appearance, the Moors being accustomed to confine their embellishments to the interior. Seville contains an academy for the physical sciences, one for the fine arts, a medical society, and a university, founded in 1502, almost as backward as at the time of its foundation. The silk manufactures of Seville were formerly extensive. In the time of Ferdinand and Isabella, it is said there were 6000 looms. These manufactures declined in the middle and end of the seventeenth century, but revived again in the eighteenth, and between 2000 and 3000 looms are now employed. Other manufactures are coarse woollens, leather, tobacco and snuff. Vessels drawing more than ten feet of water must unload eight miles below the city, and the largest vessels stop at St. Lucar, at the mouth of the river. Seville is one of the most ancient cities of Spain; by the Romans called *Hispalis;* by the Goths *Hispalia;* by the Arabians *Ixbilla;* hence, by the Castilians *Sevilla.* It was the residence of the Gothic kings before they moved to Toledo. Ferdinand III, king of Castile, after a year's siege, forced Seville to open its gates to him. At this time it is said to have contained 600,000 inhabitants; and upon the capitulation 300,000 Moors abandoned the city. After the discovery of America, it became the centre of the commerce of the new world, and was very flourishing; but the difficulty in navigating the river, and the superior advantages of the port of Cadiz, induced the government to order the galleons to be stationed at the latter place.

Sevres; a village, with 2700 inhabitants, about half way between Paris and Versailles (two leagues from each), lying near St. Cloud, on the Seine. It is celebrated for its glass and porcelain manufactories. The porcelain of Sevres is unrivalled for brilliancy of color and delicacy of execution. The finest specimens are made for the court, and are annually exhibited at Christmas in the halls of the Louvre, with the products of the Gobelin looms. (See *Porcelain*, and *Pottery.*)

Seward, Anna, daughter of Thomas Seward, rector of Eyam, Derbyshire, and canon residentiary of Lichfield, was born at Eyam, in 1747, and in childhood exhibited a taste for poetical composition, which was rather checked than encouraged by her father. Miss Seward's first separate publication was an Elegy on the Death of Captain Cook, with an Ode to the Sun (1780, 4to.); and this was followed by a Monody on Major André, with Letters to her from Major André, written in 1769 (1781, 4to.), and Louisa, a Poetical Novel, in four Epistles (1784, 4to.). In 1799, she published a collection of sonnets; and in 1804 appeared her Life of Doctor Darwin. She died at the episcopal palace at Lichfield, in 1809. Her correspondence was published, with a biographical memoir, in 6 vols., 8vo.

Sex is the term used to designate the two divisions of all organic bodies into male and female. It is a law of nature, that all organic bodies shall be produced by their like, and each class is endowed with particular organs appropriated to this service, which constitute the distinction of sexes. In the vegetable world, the sexes are, for the most part, united in one bud; although, in many classes, they are distributed in different flowers upon the same plant, or upon different plants. Among animals, especially the more perfectly formed, the division of the sexes is complete. In general, the male sex, in comparison with the female, is stronger; the female more delicate and tender. The fundamental characters of the two sexes appear more or less distinctly in most kinds of living beings, till in man they are found in a degree of developement corresponding to his rank in creation. The muscular system of man is firmer and more powerful; his chest wider, his lungs more capacious and stronger; the outlines of his form are more distinct, and his whole frame larger and stronger. The female form is more slender; the bones are smaller and softer; the flesh less solid; the chest narrower; the lungs smaller; the heart and arterial system weaker: on the other hand, the venous and lymphatic systems predominate (thus inclining the person to delicacy and inactivity); the space between the skin and the interior parts is more loaded with fat; and thus the contour is more rounded, forming the waving line; the whole proportion, in fine, of the body smaller, and more delicate. Hence the form of man conveys the idea of strength; the form of woman, that of beauty. Man is more active, grasping distant objects; more inclined to effort, to occupy his faculties upon abstract subjects, and extensive plans. The quick and violent passions belong to the man; the quiet, the domestic. and the retiring, to the woman. The woman is confined to a smaller circle, with which, however, she is more thoroughly acquainted; and is more patient and enduring in the performance of the ordinary duties of life. Man must acquire; woman strives to keep: man strives to effect his object by force; woman by kindness or by cunning. The one is busied with the bustle of out-door life, the other is devoted to domestic quiet. Man labors in the sweat of his brow, and, exhausted by his efforts, requires deep repose; woman is always busy in a quiet activity.

SEXAGESIMALS, or SEXAGESIMAL FRACTIONS; fractions whose denominators proceed in a sexagecuple ratio; that is, a prime, or the first minute, $= \frac{1}{60}$; a second $= \frac{1}{3600}$; a third $= \frac{1}{216000}$. Anciently there were no other than sexagesimals used in astronomy; and they are still retained in many cases, though decimal arithmetic has now grown into use in astronomical calculations. In these fractions, which some call *astronomical fractions*, the denominator, being always sixty, or a multiple thereof, is usually omitted, and the numerator only written down, thus, 4° 59′ 32″ 50‴ 16⁗ is to be read, four degrees, fifty-nine minutes, thirty-two seconds, fifty thirds, sixteen fourths, &c. It is readily seen how great the advantage of the decimal division (according to which the circle has 400 degrees, each degree 100 minutes, each minute 100 seconds, &c.) is over the sexagesimal division; but as this change was one of the effects which the revolution produced in France, the sexagesimal division gained ground again under the elder line of the Bourbons. Biot often expresses the results of his calculations according to both divisions; and to show how different the expressions are, we will only state that the sun's parallax is, according to the sexagesimal division, = 8″, 8. . . . ., and according to the centesimal (less properly called *decimal*), 27″, 1. . . . .

SEXTANT; an instrument for taking altitudes and other angular distances. It is constructed on a principle similar to the quadrant (q. v.); but the arc, containing a sixth part of a circle, may be taken to 120°. Sextants are generally fitted with apparatuses for ascertaining the angular distances, &c., in lunar observations.

SEXTUS (surnamed *Empiricus*, from his belonging to the empiric school of medicine) was a celebrated sceptic, who flourished towards the close of the second century. He was probably a Greek by birth, studied at Alexandria and Athens, became a pupil of the sceptic philosopher Herodotus of Tarsus, and combined extensive learning with great acuteness. Scepticism appears in his writings in the most perfect state which it had reached in ancient times; and its object and method are more clearly developed than they had been by his predecessors. (See *Scepticism.*) He is often sophistical in the application of his sceptical principles. We have two works by him, written in the Greek language, and which are the source of our knowledge of the Greek sceptical philosophy. One of them, entitled Institutes of Pyrrhonism (in three books), explains the method of Pyrrho (q. v.); the other, entitled Against the Mathematicians, is an attempt to apply that method to all the prevailing philosophical systems, and other branches of knowledge. Fabricius edited both works (*Sexti Empirici Opera, Gr. et Lat.*, Leipsic, 1718).

SEXUAL SYSTEM. (See *Botany.*)

SEYD, or ZEID; the name of a slave of Mohammed, who was one of the first to acknowledge the divine mission of his master, was adopted by him, and received Zeinab, a cousin of Mohammed, as his wife; the prophet, however, having fallen in love with her himself, Seyd was ready to resign her. Voltaire, in his *Mahomet*, makes Seyd an innocent but blindly submissive youth, who, at the prophet's order, kills a person, who turns out to be his own father. *Seyd* is therefore sometimes used to denote a man blindly devoted to the will of another. Thus St. Just is called by Mr. Nodier the Seyd of Robespierre; and the duke of Rovigo says, in his Memoirs, that he has often been taken for the Seyd of Napoleon.

SEYFFARTH, Gustavus, professor in the university of Leipsic, made himself known by editing Spohn's explanation of the Egyptian hieroglyphics. (See *Spohn.*) He returned, in 1828, from a tour made through Italy, France and England, to try Spohn's system of deciphering. He has published Contributions to the Knowledge of the Literature, Art, Mythology and History of Ancient Egypt (first number, with four lithographic plates, 4to., Leipsic); *Rudimenta hieroglyphica; Brevis Defensio hieroglyphices inventæ a F. A. Spohn et G. Seyffarth* (4to.); *Réplique aux Objections de M. J. F. Champollion le jeune contre le Système hiéroglyphique de M. Spohn et G. Seyffarth.* (See *Hieroglyphics.*)

SEYMOUR, Edward; duke of Somerset in the reign of Edward VI, to whom he was maternal uncle, being the son of sir John Seymour, of Wolf-hall, in Wiltshire, and brother of lady Jane Seymour, the third wife of Henry VIII. He was educated at Oxford, and early devoted himself to the military profession. On the marriage of his sister with the king, in 1536, he was raised to the peerage, by the title of viscount Beauchamp, and the following year created earl of Hertford. He commanded in a maritime expedition against the Scots, in 1544, when he landed a body of troops at Leith, and set fire to the city of Edinburgh. On the death of

Henry VIII, he rose to unbounded power, both in the church and state. By the will of Henry he had been nominated one of the council of regency, during the minority of Edward VI (q. v.); but, not content with his share of power, he procured himself to be appointed governor of the king and protector of the kingdom. In 1548, he obtained the post of lord treasurer, was created duke of Somerset, and made earl marshal. The same year he headed an army, with which he invaded Scotland, and, after having gained the victory of Musselburgh, returned in triumph to England. His success excited the jealousy of the earl of Warwick and others, who procured his confinement in the Tower, in October, 1549, on the charge of arbitrary conduct and injustice; and he was deprived of his offices, and heavily fined. But he soon after obtained a full pardon from the king, was admitted at court, and ostensibly reconciled to his adversary, lord Warwick (see *Dudley, John*), whose son espoused one of his daughters. The reconciliation was probably insincere, as Warwick, who had succeeded to his influence over the young king, caused Somerset to be again arrested, in October, 1551, on the charge of treasonable designs against the lives of some of the privy counsellors. He was tried, found guilty, and beheaded on Tower-hill, in 1552.

Seymour, Jane. (See *Henry VIII.*)

Sforza; a celebrated Italian house, which played an important part in the fifteenth and sixteenth centuries, gave six sovereigns to Milan, and formed alliances with most of the princely houses of Europe. The founder of the house was a peasant of Cotignola, in Romagna, Giacomo Attendolo, whose skill and courage as a statesman and a warrior made him one of the most powerful *condottieri* of Italy. As he was one day laboring in the field, he was attracted by the sight of some mercenaries, and, throwing his axe against a tree, determined to become a soldier if it stuck in the tree, and to remain a peasant if it fell. Fate doomed him to become a soldier, and he served Joanna II, queen of Naples, who regarded him as the stay of her throne. The name of Sforza he assumed from the vigor with which he had hurled his axe. To his equally valiant son Francesco, he left, with a body of devoted followers, a power which made him formidable to any of the Italian states. Francesco became the son-in-law of Philip Maria Visconti, duke of Milan, and received the command of the Milanese forces in the war against Venice. But, after the death of his father-in-law (1447), symptoms of distrust appeared between him and the leaders of the Milanese state. He seemed to possess the power and the will to seize upon the throne, to which his wife Bianca had a hereditary claim. He accordingly concluded a treaty with Venice, advanced against Milan, and compelled the citizens by famine to surrender the city. They chose him duke in 1448, and Francesco, a fortunate and celebrated prince, became the founder of a dynasty, that did not inherit his fame nor his fortune. He died in 1466.—His son, *Galeazzo Maria*, a barbarian and a voluptuary, was murdered by some conspirators in 1476.—The son of Galeazzo, *Giovanni Galeazzo*, was deposed by his uncle Ludovico, surnamed the Moor (*il Moro*). The latter formed a connexion with Charles VIII (q. v.) of France, to whom he opened the passage through Italy to Naples (1494), and thus prevented Giovanni's father-in-law, Alphonso, king of Naples, from rendering assistance to his son. At a subsequent period, he joined the league against France, and was on that account deposed by Louis XII (1499). By the help of the Swiss, he expelled the French in the same year; but Louis again took the field against him, and prevailed upon the Swiss in his service to refuse to fight against their countrymen in the French ranks. Ludovico was afterwards betrayed by one of his Swiss mercenaries to the king, who (1500) carried him to France, where he died at Loches, in 1510.—His son, *Maximilian*, once more drove the French from his territories by the aid of the Swiss, but, in consequence of the battle of Marignano, was obliged to cede his dominions to Francis I (1515), in consideration of a pension. Francis was afterwards driven from Italy by the emperor Charles V, who invested Francesco, brother of Maximilian, with the duchy of Milan, in 1529. On the death of Francesco, in 1535, Charles V conferred the duchy on his son Philip II, king of Spain. (See *Milan.*)

S'Gravesande. (See *Gravesande.*)

Shad; a large species of herring (*clupea*), which inhabits the sea near the mouths of large rivers, and in the spring ascends them for the purpose of depositing its spawn in the shallow water about their sources. The young fry remain for a season in the waters which gave them birth, but on the approach of cold weather descend the rivers, and take refuge in the ocean. The old ones likewise return, and at this time are emaciated and unfit for food. The form of the shad is the same as that of the other herrings, very much compressed, with the abdomen gradually becoming thinner, and forming a serrated edge ; and, like them, the bones are much more numerous and more slender than in other fish. The shad which frequents our waters has not been accurately compared with the European, but is probably a different species. It usually weighs four or five pounds, but sometimes twelve: the scales are easily detached, when a row of dark spots is exposed on each side. It is found in all the rivers of our Atlantic coast, is highly esteemed for food, and is consumed in great quantities, in the fresh state, in our principal cities. During the season they are an important source of wealth to the inhabitants of the borders of the Hudson, Delaware and Chesapeake. Great quantities are salted, but are less esteemed than when eaten fresh.

SHADDOCK ; a large species of orange, attaining the diameter of seven or eight inches, with a white, thick, spongy and bitter rind, and a red or white pulp, of a sweet taste, mingled with acidity. It is a native of China and Japan, and was brought to the West Indies by a captain Shaddock, from whom it has derived its name. It is often called *pampelmoes.* (See *Orange.*)

SHADWELL, Thomas, an English dramatic poet, was born at Stanton-hall, Norfolk, a seat of his father's, about 1640, educated at Cambridge, and afterwards placed at the Middle Temple, where he studied the law for some time, and then visited the continent. On his return from his travels, he applied himself to the drama, and wrote seventeen plays. His model was Ben Jonson, whom he imitated in drawing numerous characters, chiefly in caricature, of eccentricities in the manners of the day. Although coarse, and of temporary reputation, the comedies of Shadwell are not destitute of genuine humor. At the revolution he was created poet laureate, on the recommendation of the earl of Dorset; and as he obtained it by the dispossession of Dryden, the latter exhibited the bitterest enmity towards his successor, against whom he composed his severe satire of Mac Flecknoe. He died Dec. 6, 1692, in consequence, it is supposed, of taking too large a dose of opium, to which he was attached. Besides his dramatic writings, he was author of several pieces of poetry of no great merit. The best edition of his works was printed in 1720 (4 vols., 12mo.).

SHAFTESBURY, LORD. (See *Cooper.*)

SHAGREEN, or CHAGREEN (in the Levant, *Saghir*); a kind of grained leather, of a close and solid substance, used for forming covers for cases, &c., which easily receives different colors. It is prepared by the Tartars, Russians and Tripolitans, from the skin of the Bucharian wild ass, and is also made, in some parts of Russia, and in Persia, of horse-skin. The hinder back piece of the hides of these animals is cut off just above the tail and around the loins, in the form of a crescent. The piece thus separated is soaked several days in water, till the hair drops off. It is then stretched, and the hair and epidermis are removed with a scraper. After a second soaking, the flesh side is scraped in a similar manner; the skins are then stretched on wooden frames, and the hair side is covered with the seeds of the *chenopodium album*, or goose-foot. The seeds are then trodden into the leather which, being dried, and freed from the seeds, is left full of indentations, which produce the grain of the shagreen. The dried skins are then scraped with a piece of sharp iron, till the inequalities are removed, and soaked again for twenty-four hours; the parts where the impressions of the seed were produced, are thus swollen and raised above the scraped surface. The skins are next immersed in ley, and are ready to receive their color. The most common color is sea-green (given by means of copper filings and a solution of sal ammoniac); but blue, red, black, and other colors, are also given it. Shagreen is also made of the skins of the sea-otter, seal, &c.

SHAH, or SCHAH, in Persian, signifies *king;* whence *Shahnameh* (book of kings). (See *Ferdusi*, and *Persian Literature.*)

SHAH, NADIR. (See *Nadir Shah.*)

SHAKE, in music. (See *Trill.*)

SHAKERS, or SHAKING QUAKERS; a sect which arose at Manchester, in England, about 1747, and has since been transferred to America, where it now consists of a number of thriving *families.* The founders were a number of obscure Quakers; and the Shakers still agree with the Friends in their rejection of the civil and ecclesiastical authority, and military service, in their objections to taking oaths, their neglect of the common courtesies of society, their rejection of the sacraments, and their belief in the immediate revelations of the Holy Ghost (gifts). At first, the motions from which they derive their name were of the most violent, wild and irregular nature—leaping, shouting, clapping their hands, &c.; but at present, they move in a regular, uniform dance, to the singing of a hymn, and march round the hall of worship, clapping their hands in regular time. There are at present fifteen families, as their communities, are called, in the U. States, comprising 6000 individuals. In these communities, the property is held in common, and the members are distinguished for their industry, frugality, honesty and good morals. Celibacy is enjoined, and their numbers are recruited by converts. The office of leader is bestowed by impulse or revelation on him who has the gift to assume it. The sect of Shakers was first introduced into this country by Anne Lee, who, in 1770, became their leader. She was born at Manchester, in 1736, and was the daughter of a blacksmith of Manchester, where she also, at an early age, became the wife of a blacksmith. Her first "testimony of salvation and eternal life," borne in 1770, was the injunction of celibacy as the perfection of human nature, and the holding forth herself as a divine person. She was from this time honored with the title of "mother Anne," and she styled herself "Anne the word." Having been persecuted in England, she came out to America in 1774, with several members of the society, and formed the first community at Watervliet, near Albany, where she died in 1784. Societies were soon organized at New Lebanon, in New York, and at Enfield, in Connecticut, and have gradually increased to their present number. (See the official work, *The Testimony of Christ's Second Appearance*, or the article *The Shakers*, in the 16th volume of the North American Review.)

Shakspeare, William, the greatest dramatic poet, not only of England, but of all the nations of Teutonic origin, was born in 1564, at Stratford on the Avon, a market-town in Warwickshire. The day of his birth is generally said to have been April 23, 1564. His father, according to Rowe, and most of the subsequent biographers of the poet, was a considerable dealer in wool; but according to John Aubrey (who entered himself as a student at Oxford in 1642, only twenty-six years after Shakspeare's death, and who derived his information from some of the neighbors of the family), he was a butcher; according to Malone, a glover. Malone says that William was the second of eight children. In regard to his early education, there is much uncertainty. It is probable, however, that he learned Latin in the school in his native town: the French and Italian, which he often introduces in his plays, he may have acquired afterwards by himself. Before he was sixteen years old, his father required his aid in his trade; and, in his eighteenth year, he married Anne Hathaway of Shottery, who was twenty-five years of age, and who became the mother, in 1583, of his favorite daughter Susanna, and, in 1584, of his twin children, Hamnet and Judith. It must have been soon after this event that he visited London. The time usually assigned is 1586, when he was in his twenty-second year; but the cause of his leaving his native place, as well as his connexions and prospects in London, are unknown. Rowe relates, and others have adopted the opinion, that, having fallen into bad company, he was induced more than once to assist his associates in stealing deer from the park of sir Thomas Lucy, of Charlcote, near Stratford. For this he was prosecuted by that gentleman so severely, that he at first wrote a satirical ballad on him, and afterwards fled from his home to avoid arrest. This story, however, does not rest on sufficient evidence to entitle it to credence. Without dwelling on this circumstance, or crediting another improbable story of his holding horses at the door of a theatre for his livelihood, we shall find a rational motive for his visiting London, and resorting to the theatre, by knowing that he had a relative and townsman already established there, and in some estimation. This was Thomas Green, a comedian. He became an actor, but, according to Rowe, he never rose higher than the performance of the ghost in his own Hamlet. Others, however, have endeavored to prove that he was an excellent actor. His greatest patron was a friend of Essex, the earl of Southampton, who is said to have presented him, on one occasion, with a thousand pounds. Queen Elizabeth, who was much delighted with his Falstaff in Henry IV, is said to have ordered him to write another play, in which the facetious knight might appear in love, which gave rise to the Merry Wives of Windsor. He was also favored with a letter from James I, in return, as doctor Farmer supposes, for the compliment in Macbeth. How long he acted has not been discovered; but he finally became a proprietor and manager, by license, of the Globe theatre in Southwark; and it was in this situation that he afforded Ben Jonson the opportunity of appearing as a dramatic writer. Having a sobriety and moderation in his views of life, not very common in the profession which he adopted, our great dramatist retired early, with a respectable fortune of from £200 to £300 per annum, equivalent, perhaps, to £1000 in our own day, and spent the remainder of his life in ease, retirement, and the conversation of his friends. For some years before his death, he resided at Stratford, in a house which continued in the possession of his descendants until the restoration. Garrick, Macklin, and others, were entertained, in 1742, under the mulberry-tree planted by Shakspeare. The house was afterwards sold to a clergyman of the name of Gastrel, who, being rated for the poor higher than it pleased him to pay, peevishly declared that the house should never pay again; and, from ill-will to the inhabitants of Stratford, who were benefited by the company it brought to the town, he pulled it down, and sold the materials. He had previously cut down the mulberry-tree for fuel; but a silversmith purchased the whole of it, which he manufactured into memorials of the poet. Shakspeare died on the anniversary of his birth-day, April 23, 1616, having completed his fifty-second year. He was interred in the church of Stratford. Aubrey says that Shakspeare was "a handsome, well-shaped man, verie good company, and of a verie pleasant, reddie and smooth witt." His son died at the age of twelve years. His widow survived him seven years. Susanna, who married a physician named John Hall, died aged sixty-six; and Judith, who married a Mr. Guiney, died aged seventy-seven. The children of these ladies were all without offspring; but, in 1819, mention was made of a female relation of the family of Shakspeare. In 1741, a monument was erected to him in Westminster abbey, and paid for by the proceeds of benefits at the two great theatres. In 1769, by the efforts of Garrick, a festival was celebrated in honor of the poet in his native town of Stratford. There was a splendid procession of triumphal cars, in which king Lear, Richard III, Macbeth, Romeo and Juliet, accompanied with music and the shouts of the populace, moved to a splendid temple, where speeches, oratorios and odes were combined to do honor to Shakspeare. The next year, the spectacle was exhibited at Drury lane in London, and was repeated for one hundred nights.

A. W. Schlegel has devoted to the character of Shakspeare one of the most valuable of his Lectures on the Drama, which are now translated into English. Schlegel is one of the first critics of our age; and it may not be uninteresting to our readers to know the opinions of such a man on the great English poet, whose works he has himself translated and naturalized in Germany, where they have been as much admired as in England, and perhaps more profoundly criticised by men of distinguished talent. "The ignorance or learning of the poet," says Schlegel, "has been the subject of endless controversy; and yet it is a matter very easily settled. Shakspeare was poor in dead learning, but he possessed a fulness of living and applicable knowledge. He knew Latin, and even something of Greek, though not probably enough to read Greek writers with ease in the original. With the French and Italian he had also but a superficial acquaintance. He had a very extensive knowledge of English books, original and translated. He was sufficiently intimate with mythology to employ it in the only manner he wished—as a symbolical ornament. He had formed the most correct notions of the spirit of ancient history, and more particularly of that of the Romans; and the history of his own country was familiar to him, even in detail. He was an attentive observer of nature. He knew the technical language of mechanics and artisans. He seems to have travelled much in the interior of England, and to have been a diligent inquirer of navigators respecting other countries; and he was most accurately acquainted with all the popular usages, opinions and traditions which could be of use in poetry. The proofs of his ignorance on which the greatest stress is laid, are a few geographical blunders and anachronisms. Because, in a comedy founded on a tale, he makes ships arrive in Bohemia, he has been laughed at. But, in such matters, Shakspeare is only faithful when he treats historical subjects relating to his own country. When he worked on novels, he avoided disturbing his audience, to whom they were known, by the correction of errors in secondary things. Shakspeare's anachronisms are, for the most part, committed purposely. It was frequently of importance to him to bring the subject exhibited from the background of time quite near to us: hence, in Hamlet, though avowedly an old northern story, there prevails the tone of fashionable society, and, in every respect, the costume of the most recent period. Without these circumstances, it would not have been allowable to make a philosophical inquirer of Hamlet, on which, however, the character of the whole piece depends. To me, Shakspeare appears a profound artist, and not a blind and wildly luxuriant genius. In such poets as are usually considered careless pupils of nature, I have always found, on a closer examination, when they have produced works of real excellence, a distinguished cultivation of the mental powers, practice in art, and views worthy in themselves, and maturely considered. That idea of poetic inspiration which many lyric poets have brought into vogue, as if they were not in their senses, and, like the Pythia, when possessed by the divinity, delivered oracles unintelligible to themselves, is least of all applicable to dramatic composition—one of the productions of the human mind which requires the greatest exercise of thought. It is admitted that Shakspeare reflected, and deeply reflected, on character and passion, on the progress of events and human destinies, on the human constitution, on all the things and relations of this world; so that it was only respecting the structure of his own pieces that he had no thought to spare. Shakspeare's knowledge of mankind has become proverbial: in this his superiority is so great, that he has justly been called the master of the human heart. His characters appear neither to do nor say any thing on account of the spectator; and yet the poet, by means of the exhibition itself, without any subsidiary explanation, enables us to look into the inmost recesses of their minds. How each man is constituted, Shakspeare reveals to us in the most immediate manner. He demands and obtains our belief, even for what is singular, and deviates from the ordinary course of nature. Never, perhaps, was so comprehensive a talent for characterization possessed by any other man. It not only grasps the diversities of rank, sex and age, down to the dawnings of infancy; not only do his kings and beggars, heroes and pick-pockets, sages and fools, speak and act with equal truth; not only have his human characters such depth and comprehension, that they cannot be ranged under classes, and are inexhaustible, even in conception; but he opens the gates of the magic world of spirits, calls up the midnight ghost, exhibits witches amidst their unhallowed mysteries, peoples the air with sportive fairies and sylphs; and these beings, existing only in imagination, possess such truth and consistency, that, even in the case of deformed monsters, like Caliban, he extorts the conviction that if there should be such beings, they would so conduct themselves. If the delineation of all his characters, separately taken, is inimitably correct, he surpasses even himself in so combining and contrasting them, that they serve to bring out each other. No one ever painted as he has done the facility of self-deception, the half self-conscious hypocrisy towards ourselves, with which even noble minds attempt to disguise the almost inevitable influence of selfish motives on human nature. Shakspeare's comic talent is equally wonderful with his pathetic and tragic. He is highly inventive in comic situations and motives: it will be hardly possible to show whence he has taken any of them. His comic characterization is equally true, various and profound with his serious." In regard to his diction and versification, Schlegel observes, "The language is here and there somewhat obsolete, but much less so than that of most of the writers of his day—a sufficient proof of the goodness of his choice. He drew his language immediately from life, and possessed a masterly skill in blending the element of dialogue with the highest poetical elevation. Certain critics say that Shakspeare is frequently ungrammatical. To prove this assertion, they must show that similar constructions do not occur in his contemporaries; but the direct contrary can be established In no language is every thing determined on principle: much is always left to the caprice of custom, and, because this has since changed, is the poet answerable for it? In general, Shakspeare's style yet remains the very best model, both in the vigorous and the sublime, the pleasing and the tender. The verse of all his plays is generally the rhymeless iambic of ten or eleven syllables, occasionally intermixed with rhymes but more frequently alternating with prose. No one piece is wholly written in prose; for, even in those which approach the most to the pure comedy, there is always something added which elevates them to a higher rank than belongs to this class. In the use of verse and prose, Shakspeare observes very nice distinctions, according to the rank of the speakers, but still more according to their characters and dispositions. His iambics are sometimes highly harmonious and full sounding, always varied, and suitable to the subject: they are at one time distinguished for ease and rapidity; at another they move along with mighty energy. All Shakspeare's productions bear the stamp of his original genius; but no writer was ever farther removed from a manner acquired from habit and personal peculiarities."

Forty-three dramatic pieces are ascribed to Shakspeare: eight of them, however, are considered by English commentators to be spurious, but German critics regard them as genuine. The thirty-five uncontested pieces, which were written in twenty-three years, from 1591 to 1614, Malone has attempted to reduce to the following chronological order: Love's Labor lost, King Henry VI (3 parts), the Two Gentlemen of Verona, the Winter's Tale, Midsummer Night's Dream, Romeo and Juliet, the Comedy of Errors, Hamlet, King John, King Richard II, Richard III, Henry IV (1st part), Merchant of Venice, All's well that ends well, Henry IV (2d part), Henry V, Much Ado about Nothing, As you like it, the Merry Wives of Windsor, Henry VIII, Troilus and Cressida, Measure for Measure, Cymbeline, King Lear, Macbeth, the Taming of the Shrew, Julius Cæsar, Antony and Cleopatra, Coriolanus, Timon of Athens, Othello, the Tempest, What you will. There are many objections, however, both internal and external, to this arrangement.

"The subjects of the comedies," to return to Schlegel, "are generally taken from novels: they are romantic love stories: none of them are confined exclusively to common or domestic relations: all possess poetical ornament, and some pass into the wonderful or the pathetic." The Two Gentlemen of Verona (compare Montemayor's *Diana*, book 2) paints the fickleness of love, and its infidelity towards friendship.—The Comedy of Errors (compare the *Menæchmi* of Plautus, and *A Comedy of Plautus called Monechme*, German, by Hans Sachs), the only play of Shakspeare of which the idea is borrowed from the ancients, is a piece which ought not to be played without masks. The Taming of the Shrew (compare Goulart, *Thrésor d'Histoire admirable de nostre Temps*, translated into English by Edw. Grimestone, 1607; Percy's *Reliques of ancient Poetry*, vol. i; George Gascoigne's *Supposes, a translation from Ariosto's Supvositi*; also, *The Art of Arts, or how to make a bad Woman a good one, formerly practised by an Italian Cavalier*, &c., German, Rappersdorf, 12mo.) is derived, mediately or immediately, from a piece of Ariosto. The prelude of the drunken tinker is probably from a popular tale, and the same subject has been dramatized by Holberg. These pieces are considered as productions of his youth. Love's Labor lost is referred to the same period.—All's well that ends well—the Griselda of Shakspeare (compare Boccaccio's *Decamerone, giorn.* iii, *novell.* 9; Painter's *Palace of Pleasure; Giletta of Narbon;* also the old book, *Schertz mit der Wahrheyt*)—presents in Parolles a character of rich comic humor, which would be more celebrated if it had not been thrown into the shade by Falstaff.—Much Ado about Nothing (compare Belleforest's *Timbrée de Cardonne*, &c.; Bandello's *Novelle*, Venice, 1566, vol. i; *Phœnicia, an interesting and memorable History*, &c., Magdeburg, John Franken, 1601; Ariosto, translated into English by Harrington, 1591; and particularly George Tuberville's account of this story) is the same, in its main plot, with the *Ariodante* and *Ginevra* of Ariosto.—Measure for Measure (compare G. Whetstone's *Promus and Cassandra*, 1578; Giraldo Cinthio's *Hecatomithi overo cento Novelle*, Venice, 1593, *decade* viii, *novello* 5, translated in Painter's Palace of Pleasure) is the triumph of mercy over strict justice. It contains the splendid character of Isabella.—The Merchant of Venice (compare Percy's *Reliques*, i; Giovanni Fiorentino's *Il Pecorone, nel quale si contengono* 48 *Novelle antiche belle d'Invenzione e di Stilo*, written in 1378, printed at Milan in 1554, and at Treviso in 1601; *Gesta Romanorum cum Applicationibus moralisatis ac mysticis*, Augsburg, 1489, and Strasburg, 1538; *Decamerone, giorn.* x, *nov.* 1; *The Jew*, an old English play; also *The Carnival in Venice*, an old German play) is a wonderful picture of character. It is one of Shakspeare's most perfect works. The fifth act of this play may be regarded as an afterpiece, serving to excite pleasant feelings, after the harrowing scenes exhibited in the preceding portions of the drama.—As you like it (compare Chaucer's *Coke's Tale of Gamelyn;* Thomas Lodge's *Rosalynd, or Euphues' golden Legacy*, 1590, 4to., an old pastoral romance) is a charming play, which, with its gayety, liveliness and freedom, seems to have been intended to show that nothing is wanted to call forth the poetry which has its dwelling in nature and the human mind, but to throw off all artificial constraint.—The Twelfth Night, or What you will (Bandello, t. ii, *nov.* 20), unites the entertainment of an intrigue contriv ed wit great ingenuity, to the richest fund of comic characters and situations, and the beauty of an ethereal poetry. If this was in fact Shakspeare's last work, he enjoyed to the end of his days the same youthfulness of mind, and carried all the luxuriance of his talents with him to the grave.—The Merry Wives of Windsor (compare *The Lovers of Pisa*, in Tarleton's *Newes out of Purgatorie; Il Pecorone, giorn.* i, *nov.* 2; *The Fortunate, the Deceived, and the Unfortunate Lovers; Piacevoli Notti di Straparola*, Venice, 1567, *l.* i, *notte* 4, *favola* 4) is said to have been written at the request of queen Elizabeth, because she wanted to see Falstaff in love. It is certain that it was acted in her presence (probably at Windsor, at a festival of the order of the garter). Molière's School for Women resembles it in the particular that a jealous man is made the constant confidant of the progress of his rival. Of all the pieces of Shakspeare, this approaches the nearest to pure comedy. The conclusion is made romantic by a fanciful delusion, founded on a popular superstition.—A Midsummer Night's Dream (compare Bettie's *Titania and Theseus;* Plutarch's *Theseus;* Michael Drayton's *Nymphidia, the Court of Fayrie;* Chaucer's *Knight's Tale;* Boccaccio's *Teseide; Legend of Thisbe of Babylon*); the Tempest, source unknown (compare *Twenty of the Plays of Shakspeare, being the whole Number printed in Quarto, by George Steevens, Esq.*, London, 1666, 4 vols.). These plays resemble each other in this particular, that, in both, the influence of a world of spiritual beings is interwoven with the turmoil of human passions, and the farcical adventures of folly. The former piece was written certainly earlier, and is, perhaps, the most luxuriant and fanciful of Shakspeare's productions. It unites, in Titania's amour, the extremes of the fanciful and the vulgar. The second, apparently the fruit of Shakspeare's latter years, is superior in its delineation of character. In the wise, all-directing Prospero, in the tender flame of Ferdinand and Miranda, in the masterly picture of the terrestrial monster Caliban, and the heavenly Ariel, there is a most harmonious connexion of opposite conceptions.—The Winter's Tale (compare *A Pleasant History of Dorastus and Fawnia*, by Robert Greene; Spenser's *Fairy Queen*, book v, canto 9, 15) is one of those tales which are peculiarly fitted to beguile the dreary leisure of a long winter evening, which are attractive and intelligible even to childhood, and transport even manhood back to the golden age, when it yielded to the sway of the imagination.—Cymbeline (compare Boccaccio, *giorn.* ii, *nov.* 9; Hans Sachs, *The Innocent Lady Genura; Schertz mit der Wahrheyt;* Holinshed's *Chronicles;* Dion. Cass. *Hist. Rom.*, *l*, lx, *c.* 20; Suetonius's *Caligula*, *c.* 44; Henry's *History of Great Britain*, London, 1771, quarto, vol. i, page 17) is a remarkable composition, connecting a novel of Boccaccio with ancient British traditions, from the times of the first Roman emperors. By easy transitions, the poet blends into a harmonious whole the social manners of the latest times, with the deeds of heroes, and even with appearances of the gods.—Romeo and Juliet (compare Girolamo dalla Corte's *Istoria di Verona*, 1594, vol. i; *Istoria novellamente ritrovata di due nobili Amanti, con la pietosa Morte intervenuta gia nella Citta di Verona, nel Tempo del Signor Bartolomeo della Scala;* Bandello, *l.* ii, *nov.* 1; Boisteau's *Dixhuit Histoires tragiques, mises en Langue Françoise*, 1560, 12mo.; *The Tragical Historie of Romeus and Juliet*, London, 1562; Painter's *Palace of Pleasure*, *t.* ii, *nov.* 25; see also Lope de Vega Carpio's *Castelvines y Monteses, Comedia famosa*).—Othello (compare *Giraldi Cinthio, decade* iii, *nov.* 7—translated into French by Gabriel Chapuys, 1584—Englished by Painter) is a picture of love, and its pitiable fate, in a world whose atmosphere is too rough for this tenderest blossom of human life. The sweetest and the bitterest, love and hatred, gayety and dark forebodings, tender embraces and sepulchres, the fulness of life, and self-destruction, are blended into a unity of impression in this harmonious and wonderful work. In Othello, we recognize the wild nature of the African, tamed only in appearance by the desire of fame by foreign laws of honor, and by nobler and milder manners. His jealousy is of that sensual kind which, in burning climes, has given birth to the disgraceful confinement of women, and to a thousand unnatural usages. The Moor is frank, confiding, grateful; but the force of passion puts to flight all his acquired and accustomed virtues. A more artful villain than Iago was never portrayed; cool, discontented, and morose, arrogant where he dares to be so, but humble and insinuating when it suits his purposes, he is a complete master in the art of dissimulation; accessible only to selfish emotions, he is thoroughly skilled in rousing the passions of others, and in availing himself of every opening which they give him; he is as excellent an observer of men as any one can be who is unacquainted with higher motives of action than his own experience. Desdemona is a high ideal representation of enthusiastic passion. No eloquence is capable of painting the overwhelming force of the catastrophe in Othello.—Hamlet (compare *Saxonis Grammatici Historiæ Danicæ Libri xvi*, ed. Stephanii, Soræ, 1644, *lib.* 3; Belleforest, *Avec quelle Ruse Amleth qui depuis fut Roi de Danemarc, vengea la Mort de son Père Huruondille, occis par Fengon, son Frère, et autre Occurrence de son Histoire;* English, *The Historie of Hamblet*, quarto, 1608) is unique in its kind; a tragedy of thought, inspired by continual and never satisfied meditation on human destiny, and the dark perplexity of events in this world. Hamlet is a mind of high cultivation, a prince of royal manners, endowed with the finest sense of propriety, susceptible of noble ambition, and open, in the highest degree, to enthusiasm for the excellence in which he is deficient. He acts the part of madness with inimitable superiority; but in the resolutions which he so often embraces, and always leaves unexecuted, the weakness of his volition is evident; he is a hypocrite towards himself; his far-fetched scruples are often mere pretexts to cover his want of determination—thoughts, as he says on a different occasion, which have

——but one part wisdom,
And ever three parts coward.

Hamlet has no firm belief either in himself or in any thing else; from expressions of religious confidence, he passes over to sceptical doubts. He even goes so far as to say that "there is nothing either good or bad, but thinking makes it so." The poet loses himself with him in the labyrinths of thought, in which we neither find end nor beginning.—Macbeth (compare Holinshed's and Harrison's *Chronicles of Great Britain, Scotland, and Ireland*, London, 1577, continued by Hooker and others, 1587, 3 vols., fol.—the chief source of Shakspeare's pieces relating to English history; George Buchanan's *Opera Omn.*, Edinburgh, 1715, vol. i). This is the greatest and most terrific tragedy that has appeared since the Eumenides of Æschylus. Shakspeare exhibits an ambitious, but noble hero, who yields to a deep-laid, hellish temptation. The weird sisters surprise Macbeth in the moment of intoxication after victory, when his love of glory has been gratified; they cheat his eyes by exhibiting to him as the work of fate, what can in fact be accomplished only by his own act, and gain credence for their words by the immediate fulfilment of the first prediction. The opportunity for murdering the king immediately offers itself; the wife of Macbeth conjures him not to let it slip; she urges him on with a fiery eloquence, which has all those sophisms at command that serve to throw a false lustre over the crime. Little more than the mere execution falls to the lot of Macbeth; he is driven to it, as it were, in a state of commotion in which his mind is bewildered. Repentance immediately follows, nay, even precedes the deed, and the stings of his conscience leave him no rest either night or day. Nothing can equal the power of this picture in the excitation of horror. We need only allude to the circumstances attending the murder of Duncan, the dagger that hovers before the eyes of Macbeth at the feast, and the madness of lady Macbeth.—In King Lear (compare *Shakspeare Illustrated, or the Novels and Histories on which the Plays of Shakspeare are founded*, by Miss Lenox, London, 1754, 3 vols.; Holinshed; Tyrrel's *General History of England*, London, 1700, vol. i; Percy's *Reliques*, i; the Latin Chronicle of Geoffrey of Monmouth; Sidney's *Arcadia*, Edinburgh, 1590, quarto; Spenser's *Fairy Queen*, b. ii, canto x, stanzas 27—33; and the old play *The True Chronicle History of King Leir*, London, 1605, quarto) compassion is exhausted. The principal characters in this piece are not those who act, but those who suffer. We have not in this, as in most tragedies, the picture of a calamity, in which the sudden blows of fate still seem to honor the head which they strike, in which the loss is always accompanied by some flattering consolation in the memory of the former possession; but a fall from the highest elevation into the deepest abyss of misery, where humanity is stripped of all external and internal advantages, and given up a prey to naked helplessness.—In the three Roman pieces, Coriolanus, Julius Cæsar, and Antony and Cleopatra, the moderation with which Shakspeare excludes foreign appendages and arbitrary suppositions, and yet fully satisfies the wants of the stage, is particularly deserving of admiration. Under the apparent artlessness of adhering closely to history as he found it, an uncommon degree of art is concealed.—Timon of Athens (compare Plutarch; Lucian; *Palace of Pleasure*), and Troilus and Cressida (compare *Dictys Cretensis*, and *Dares Phrygius;* Guido dalle Colonne of Messina, *Historia de Bello Trojano*, translated into Italian by Ceffi, Venice, 1481, and into German in 1489, in the parts *de sexto et septimo bello*, Lydgate,

De Boke of Troye, London, 1515, a prolix poem, modernized in 1614; Raoul de Fevre, *Recueil de Troyennes Histoires*, Englished by Caxton, 1471 and 1503; Chaucer, *The Boke of Troiles and Cresside;* Boccaccio's *Filostrate*, 1498, 8vo.; Alexander Barclay's *Ship of Fooles*, from the German of Seb. Brandt, 1570; Chapman's translation of Homer, 1581 and 1596). These pieces are not historical plays, properly speaking; and we cannot call them either tragedy or comedy. Timon, of all the works of Shakspeare, has most the character of satire, laughing satire, in the picture of flatterers and parasites, and Juvenalian satire, in the bitterness and imprecations of Timon against the ingratitude of a false world. Troilus and Cressida is the only play which Shakspeare allowed to be printed without having been previously acted. It is, throughout, a parody on the Trojan war, not as described in Homer, but in the romances of chivalry derived from Dares Phrygius.

The dramas taken from the English history are ten. The poet evidently intended them as parts of a great whole. The principal features of the events are exhibited with such fidelity, their causes, and even their secret springs, are placed in so clear a light, that we may obtain from them a knowledge of history in all its truth, while the living picture makes an impression on the imagination which can never be effaced. Eight of these plays, from Richard II to Richard III, are linked together in uninterrupted succession. According to all appearance, the four last were first written. The two other historical plays taken from the English history, are chronologically separated from this series. In King John, all the political and national motives, which play so great a part in the following pieces, are already indicated—wars and treaties with France, a usurpation, and the tyrannical actions which it draws after it, the influence of the clergy, and the factions of the nobles. Henry VIII again shows us the transition to another age;—the policy of modern Europe, a refined court life under a voluptuous monarch, the dangerous situation of favorites, who are themselves precipitated, after having effected the fall of others; in a word, despotism under milder forms, but not less unjust and cruel. In Richard II, Shakspeare exhibits to us a noble, kingly nature, at first obscured by levity, and the errors of an unbridled youth, and afterwards purified by misfortune, and rendered more highly and splendidly illustrious. The first part of Henry IV is particularly brilliant in the serious scenes, from the contrast between two young heroes, prince Henry and Percy with the characteristic name of Hotspur. Falstaff (q. v.) is the summit of Shakspeare's comic invention. King Henry V is visibly the favorite of Shakspeare in the English history. The three parts of Henry VI were much earlier composed than the preceding pieces. We do not find in this piece the whole maturity of the poet's genius, but we certainly find its whole strength. Richard III embraces the latter half of the reign of Edward IV, in the whole a period of eight years. Shakspeare intended that terror, rather than compassion, should prevail in this tragedy. Richard is the soul, or rather the demon of the whole. He fulfils the promise which he had before made of leading the murderous Macchiavel to school. Besides the uniform aversion which he inspires, he occupies us in the greatest variety of ways—by his profound skill in dissimulation, his wit, his prudence, his presence of mind, his quick activity, and his valor.—In regard to the pieces generally rejected by the English editors, Schlegel contends that Titus Andronicus is genuine, but supposes it to have been a production of Shakspeare's youth. Pericles, Prince of Tyre, he also considers as undoubtedly genuine. Of Thomas Lord Cromwell, Sir John Oldcastle, and A Yorkshire Tragedy, he says, "These three pieces are not only unquestionably Shakspeare's, but, in my opinion, they deserve to be classed among his best and maturest works." Respecting Locrine he does not express a decided opinion.

Besides his dramatic works, Shakspeare wrote one hundred and fifty-four sonnets, and two narrative poems—Venus and Adonis (printed in 1593), and the Rape of Lucretia. The former is called by Shakspeare, in the dedication to the earl of Southampton, "the first heir of his invention." In these productions, the fire and power of Shakspeare are not to be mistaken. Their luxuriant imagery, play of wit, prolixity, and inequality, are to be attributed to his youth. Shakspeare has not strictly confined himself to the ancient mythology; for instance, he makes Venus to be rejected by Adonis. The one hundred and fifty-four sonnets do not resemble, in matter or form, the productions of Petrarch. They are condensed, intellectual, and often witty. Schlegel touches upon the important aid which they may afford to some future biographer of Shakspeare, in regard to the circumstances of his private life.—For further information, we would refer the reader to the various editions of Shakspeare, by Rowe, Pope, Warburton, Johnson, Steevens, Malone, &c.; to Douce's *Illustrations of Shakspeare* (London, 1807, 2 vols., 8vo.); Drake's *Shakspeare and his Times* (London, 1817, 2 vols., 8vo.); Seymour's *Remarks on the Plays of Shakspeare* (London, 1805, 2 vols., 8vo.); Hazlitt's *Characters of Shakspeare's Plays* (London, 1817, &c., &c.). Bowdler's *Family Shakspeare* (London, 1818, 10 vols., 8vo.) is an expurgated edition. Lives of Shakspeare have been written by Rowe, Malone, and Skottowe: the last appeared in London, 1824, 2 vols., accompanied by illustrations of the poet. Numerous alterations and *rifacimentos* of the plays have been made, for the purpose of representation, by sir William D'Avenant, Dryden, Shadwell, Dennis, Colley Cibber, Garrick, Kemble, &c.—In Germany, commentaries have been written on the great dramatist by such men as A. W. Schlegel, who has translated the greater part of the plays; by Tieck, who has undertaken to complete the translation; by the poet Göthe, &c. In France, many of the plays have been adapted for the French stage by Ducis. Retzsch (q. v.), a distinguished German artist, has lately published designs illustrative of scenes from the plays of Shakspeare, which are highly commended. The first number relates to Hamlet, and was published at Leipsic in 1828.

Shamans; in Great Tartary and Mongolia, a part of China, Siberia, and Kamtschatka, priests, who are at the same time physicians, sorcerers, and conjurers. Shamanism, which contains the lowest representations of the Deity and of divine things, was probably supplanted in the southern parts of Asia by the more elevated doctrines of Confucius and Zoroaster. In its present state, in Tangut, a part of China, and in Mongolia, it is a mixture of the old heathen Shamanism with Nestorianism (see *Nestorius*), and is called *Lamaism*, or *Shigemoonism*. (See *Lama*.) It has been diffused in China, where it is the religion of the court, by the Mantchoos (q. v.), and prevails in Thibet, a part of India, in Tartary, Mongolia, and among the Calmucks. The doctrine of the metempsychosis, and the worship of the god Fo, form a part of modern Shamanism. (See *Fo*.) The principal doctrine of the primitive Shamanism was the existence of many gods, some created, some increate, existing in the form of heavenly bodies, or of animals, or of inanimate things, or arbitrarily formed by human hands. It also taught the existence of good and bad spirits After death, men continue to exist, in a melancholy condition, influenced neither by good nor bad works. The religious service of the Shamanites consists of sacrifices, prayers, &c., by which the worshippers hope to gain the favor of the good gods, and avert the wrath of the bad.

Shamo, Desert of. (See *Cobi*.)

Shampooing. The process, as practised in the East Indies, is described under *Bath*, vol. i, p. 611.

Shamrock (in the Gaelic, *seamrag*); probably, in the Irish and Gaelic languages, a generic term for trefoils.* The name is commonly given to the heraldic emblem of Ireland. It is sometimes applied to the *medicago lupulina*, or hop-trefoil, a plant very much resembling, and often confounded with, the yellow clover, from which, however, it is readily distinguished by the spiral form of the pods. It is naturalized, and, with the yellow clover, common in some parts of the U. States; but they are little relished by cattle.

Shark (*squalus* of Linnæus); a family of cartilaginous fishes, allied to the rays, and celebrated for the size and voracity of many of the species. The form of the body is elongated, and the tail thick and fleshy. The mouth is large, generally situated beneath the snout, and is armed with several rows of compressed, sharp-edged, and sometimes serrated, teeth. The water penetrates to the gills by means of several transverse openings situated on each side of the neck. The skeleton is cartilaginous. The skin is usually very rough, covered with a multitude of little osseous tubercles; and that of some species forms the substance called *shagreen*. The eggs of the sharks are few and large, in comparison with those of bony fishes; they are enveloped in a hard, horny, semi-transparent shell, terminated at the four angles with long filaments; in short, they resemble those of the rays, and are likewise frequently cast up by the waves upon the shores of the sea. The flesh of sharks is, in general, hard, coriaceous, and ill-tasted, but some are good for food. They are the most formidable and voracious of all fishes, pursue all other marine animals, and seem to care little whether their prey be living or dead. They often follow vessels for the sake of picking up any offal which may be thrown overboard; and man himself often becomes a victim

* See I. E. Bicheno's paper On the Plant intended by the Shamrock, read to the Lond. Lin Soc.; reprinted in the Nat. Gaz. (Philad.) of July 7, 1831

to their rapacity. The sharks form several natural genera, distinguished by the presence or absence of blow-holes, or of the anal fin, by the form of the head, nose and teeth, &c. &c. The teeth of sharks are movable at the will of the animal, and are usually laid down and directed backwards, but become erect at the moment the animal is seizing its prey. Shagreen, which is extensively used in the arts, is furnished by several species, and, together with their oil, forms the most important of their products. The basking shark (*selache maxima*) is by far the largest of the genus, sometimes attaining the length of forty feet; but it has none of the ferocity of the others, and the teeth are excessively small. It inhabits the northern seas, and is occasionally taken along our coasts, even as far south as New Jersey. It is sometimes called *whalebone shark*, from having in the mouth a substance resembling whalebone. The hammer-headed sharks (*zygæna*) are remarkable among fishes for having the head flattened and projecting laterally, which gives to the animal something of the form of a hammer. The eyes are placed at the extremity of these prominences. They are very voracious, and frequently attack man. One or more species are found along the coast of the U. States. The species of *squalina* differ from the other sharks in having the mouth terminal, the body flattened horizontally, and the pectoral fins large, and the eyes on the upper part of the head. One species is found in our waters. The long-tailed shark, or thresher, also frequents our coasts; it is distinguished by having the tail as long as the body. We have many other sharks, but at present they are, in general, not well understood. That some of them are sufficiently formidable we have lately had evidence; in Boston bay, a man was recently attacked in his boat, and devoured by one of these animals.

Sharp (in Italian, *maggiore;* in German, *dur*, from the Latin *durus*, hard) is a musical term applied to those keys, the basis of which is the "perfect harmonic *triad*."—*Sharp* signifies also a character, the power of which is to raise a note, before which it is placed, half a tone higher than it would be without such a prefix. The character is formed thus: ♯ (See *Flat.*)

Sharp, James, archbishop of St. Andrews in Scotland, was a native of Banffshire, born 1618, and was early destined, by his family, for the ministry. With this view, he was placed at the Marischal college in Aberdeen, but, objecting to take the "solemn league and covenant," quitted the university, and went to London. During the civil wars, he returned to his native country, and obtained a professorship in the university of St. Andrews. His eloquence and reputation caused him to be selected, by the moderate Presbyterian party in Scotland, to advocate their cause with the protector, Cromwell, against the demands of the more rigid Calvinists; and he was subsequently sent to Breda, by Monk, for the purpose of procuring the sanction of Charles II, to the proposed settlement of the ecclesiastical affairs of Scotland. He returned to Scotland, and delivered to some of the ministers of Edinburgh a letter from the king, in which the latter promised to protect the government of the church of Scotland, "as it is settled by law." The clergy, understanding this declaration in its obvious sense, were satisfied; but it subsequently appeared, that Sharp had in view to subvert the church government, which he affected to maintain, pleading to the friends of episcopacy that this letter would pledge the king to nothing, as the parliament had only to establish episcopacy, to transfer the pledge of the monarch to its support. The presbytery being accordingly overturned by parliament, Sharp was rewarded with the primacy, and appointed archbishop of St. Andrews. The wanton cruelties which followed, confirmed the horror entertained against him, and raised the fury of some of his more bigoted opponents to attempts against his life. In 1678, he narrowly escaped assassination from the hand of James Mitchell, an enthusiast, who was some time after taken and executed. A similar attempt, the following year, was more successful. His carriage, in which he was travelling in Magus Muir, about three miles from St. Andrews, on the 3d May, 1679, was met by some fanatics, headed by John Balfour of Burley, who were waiting there to intercept a servant of the archbishop's, named Carmichael. To tempers thus heated by fanaticism, the appearance of the archbishop himself was deemed a sign of the intention of Providence to substitute a more important victim; and, regardless of the tears and entreaties of his daughter, they dragged him from his carriage, and despatched him with their swords, with which they inflicted no less than twenty-two wounds.

Sharp, Granville, an English gentleman, eminent for his philanthropy and learning, born in 1734, was educated for the bar, but did not practise at it; he obtained a place in the ordnance office, which he resigned at the commencement of the American war, the principles of which he did not approve. He then took chambers in the Temple, and led a life of private study. He first became known by his defence of a poor negro named Somerset. This man, having been carried to England by his master, was turned out into the streets to die, during a fit of sickness, and when, by the charity of Mr. Sharp and others, he had been restored to health, was claimed again as property. The result of the law proceedings, on this question, not only cleared Somerset, but determined that slavery could not exist in Great Britain. Such an incident could not fail to deeply impress a benevolent mind; and slavery, in every country, became the object of his unceasing hostility. Having succeeded in the case of an individual negro, he interested himself in the condition of others, whom he found wandering in the streets of London, and, at his own expense, sent a number of them to Sierra Leone: he also, soon after, became the institutor of the society for the abolition of the slave-trade, and sought to modify the harsh practice of impressment. He was likewise led, by his political principles, to be the advocate of parliamentary reform, in support of which he published a Declaration of the People's Natural Right to a Share in the Legislature, in which he contends for a revival of the political institutions of Alfred. He died July 6, 1813.

Sharp-shooters. Formerly, there were, in several armies, a few men attached to each company of troops of the line, who, unlike the rest of the infantry, took aim at particular individuals, had better guns or rifles, and did not shoot with the mass of the troops. These were called *sharp-shooters*. The better organization of armies in modern times, and particularly the introduction of *tirailleurs* (q. v.), has caused them to be abolished.

Shastra, or Shaster. (See *Indian Literature*, division *Sacred Literature*.)

Shawls. (For the Cashmere shawls, see *Cashmere*.)

Shays's Insurrection. The war of the revolution had not only left the new states suffering under the burden of a heavy public debt, but, in consequence of the interruption of commerce and manufactures, the scarcity of money, and the depreciated state of the circulating medium, the great body of the people, in some parts of the country, were unable to meet the demands of their creditors. In the autumn of 1786, bodies of armed men interrupted the proceedings of the county courts of justice in several of the counties of Massachusetts; and at about the same time, the legislature of New Hampshire, where the same causes had produced the same spirit of disaffection, was surrounded by an armed force, which, however, was finally dispersed by the citizens of Exeter, in which town the legislature was sitting. A body of the Massachusetts insurgents, under Daniel Shays, who had been a captain in the continental army, having assembled at Springfield for the purpose of preventing the session of the courts, the government of the state despatched a detachment of militia, under the command of general Lincoln (q. v.), to suppress the insurrection. The object was successfully accomplished, with little bloodshed, by his activity and decision. Indemnity was then granted, on certain conditions, to the insurgents, 790 of whom took the benefit of this act of lenity. Fourteen persons were sentenced to death, but they were all successively pardoned. In New Hampshire, likewise, the same clemency was extended to the insurgents, and no blood was shed by the hand of the civil magistrate.—See Minot's *History of the Insurrection in Massachusetts* (1788).

Sheathing, in naval architecture; a sort of covering nailed all over the outside of a ship's bottom, to protect the planks from the pernicious effects of worms. This sheathing, in former years, consisted of thin boards; but sheets of copper having been found far preferable, these have of late been almost universally adopted, especially in long voyages.

Shechinah, in Jewish history; the name of that miraculous light, or visible glory, which was a symbol of the divine presence.

Shee, Martin Archer; a native of Ireland, distinguished as a portrait painter and as a poet. His works consist of Elements of Art, a Poem (8vo., 1800); Rhymes on Art, or the Remonstrance of a Painter (8vo., 1804); a Letter to the President of the British Institution, on the Encouragement of Historical Painting (8vo., 1809); and the Commemoration of Reynolds, and other Poems (small 8vo., 1814).

Sheep (*ovis*); a genus of ruminant quadrupeds, differing so slightly in the anatomical structure from the goat, that both genera are by some naturalists united. The principal distinctive characters consist in the absence of a beard, and the form and spiral direction of the horns

The wild sheep, or argali (*ovis ammon*), is by no means the helpless animal we are accustomed to see in a domestic state. (See *Argali.*) The sheep seems to be the most stupid of all domestic quadrupeds, and is probably the only one incapable of returning to a state of nature, even if placed in the most favorable circumstances. It neither knows how to avoid danger, nor to seek shelter from the changes of the atmosphere, nor even to procure nourishment, except in abundant pasturage. Its habits are well known. Its products are the flesh, milk, skin, and especially the wool (q. v.), which employs a vast capital in the manufacture of clothing. The time allowed for fattening them is about three months before they are sent to market, and when they have attained the age of two or three years; unless the fleece be the object, when it may be delayed to the sixth, seventh, or even the tenth year, in a district where they are long-lived. Their ordinary life does not exceed twelve or fifteen years. The fleece is shorn every year, towards the month of May. It is sometimes washed on the back of the animal; but the more usual practice is to shear it without washing, as it then contains an animal oil, which is a great preservative against insects. The sheep require particular attention afterwards, as they are more exposed to the changes of the weather. At all times they are exposed to numerous maladies. The varieties of the sheep are very numerous, differing in size, the length of their legs, the size and number of their horns; some are covered with hair instead of wool; others have enormous tails; and others, again, pendent ears. The variety most celebrated for the fineness of the wool is the Spanish Merino, as improved in Germany: all the other most approved European varieties are crosses from the Merino. The English sheep is most celebrated for the quantity of its wool. Besides the argali, there is another animal more nearly related to the goat, inhabiting the Rocky mountains, between lat. 45° and 68°. It is more numerous in the western than in the eastern parts of these mountains, and is found in large flocks, frequenting the summits in the summer, and the valleys in the winter season. It is little known, but in some parts forms the principal sustenance of the natives. It is easily obtained by the hunters, but its flesh is not esteemed, neither is a value set upon its fleece. In size it approaches the sheep, and has long hair extending beyond the wool: the horns are five inches in length and one in diameter, conical, and slightly curved backwards. An interest has lately been excited about this animal in England, and the fleece is said to be as fine as that of the shawl goat of Cashmere. It is often called the *Rocky mountain sheep.*

Sheep-Raising. Our limits will not allow us to give in detail the history of this valuable domestic animal, with the improvements which have been made in it at different periods; and we must refer the reader for more information to works which treat particularly of the subject, as Loudon's Encyclopædia of Agriculture, and the article *sheep* in Rees's Cyclopædia, to the time when it was written. In Germany, both governments and individuals have paid great attention to the improvement of the wool, and in some parts of that country it has been brought to such perfection as to surpass that of any other part of the world. Several works in German, on this subject, though referring more particularly to the country in which they were written, would afford important assistance to sheep-breeders in any country. When we look for the origin of the improvements which have been made in the breeding of this animal, which has become so important an element of national wealth, and the source of so much manufacturing and commercial industry, we are obliged to go back to the Romans. They had made such progress, that the whole system of sheep-breeding, at present in use in Spain, is essentially the same which was introduced there by the Romans. Columella, who lived under the emperor Claudius, gives us interesting information on this point. Among other things, he says that his uncle, who lived in Bœtica (which comprehends the present province of Estremadura), procured some wild African rams at Cadiz, of a coarse fleece, but of an admirable color. He put them to some fine-woolled ewes, and, the male progeny being again put to Tarentine ewes, the offspring, with their descendants, united the color of the sire with the dam's softness of fleece. Other agriculturists undoubtedly imitated him, and thus the purest white was communicated to the black or parti-colored native flocks, which, according to Pliny, were common in Spain. The Tarentine sheep were most celebrated in Italy, and the Milesian in Asia Minor. They were termed *pellitæ* and *tectæ oves*, from the coverings of skin with which they were clothed, to protect the fleece; they were also denominated *molles oves*, not only from the softness of the fleece, but also from the delicacy of their constitution. The attention paid by the ancients to the sheep was excessive, and the animal was extremely tender; so that we must account for the transition from the ancient sheep to the Merino, which is a hardy animal, thriving in almost any climate, by supposing that other agriculturists imitated Columella, and by crossing the breed imparted a stronger constitution to the fine-fleeced, but delicate sheep of ancient Italy. Strabo, indeed, describes the beginning of this improvement as having taken place in the reign of Tiberius. Fine rams were at that time sold at Truditania, part of Bœtica, for a talent, or about a thousand dollars—a price which, considering the value of money at that period, is immense. When the Roman empire was overrun, and almost all traces of civilization swept away, the Tarentine stock in Greece and Italy being very tender, and requiring the greatest care, became extinct; but the regenerated stock of Bœtica—the Merinos—being able to live in the mountains, survived the conquest of Spain by the Goths and Vandals; and from these Merinos are descended those animals which supply all the manufactories of fine cloth in Europe. Care was early taken in Spain that the improved sheep should not mix with the coarse native sheep. The government soon took this important branch of national industry under its protection, and established particular courts to have jurisdiction over all subjects connected with sheep, wool, shepherds, pastures, &c. The way in which the improved sheep is generally bred in Spain is the following:—Whilst the common sheep remains always on the spot where it was born, and is housed in winter, the fine-woolled sheep is kept the whole time in the open air, in summer chiefly in the mountainous part of Old Castile or the Montaña, and in the lordship of Molina, in Arragon, which are the highest parts of Spain, containing the finest pasture. The former affords aromatic plants, which the latter does not; these mountains are covered with oaks, beeches, birches, hazel-bushes, &c., besides producing all the plants which grow in Switzerland. When a shepherd has driven his flock to the place where they are to remain for the summer, he first gives them as much salt as they are willing to lick. The estimated consumption during the five summer months is 20 cwts. of salt for 1000 sheep (perhaps, however, this estimate is too high). Towards the end of July, the rams are admitted to the ewes, from five to six rams to one hundred ewes; before and after, they remain separated. The rams yield more wool than the ewes, but not of so fine quality; three rams or five ewes afford twenty-five pounds. In the middle of September, the sheep are marked on the thigh. Towards the end of summer, the sheep are driven in flocks comprising 10,000 individuals, divided into bodies of 1000—1200, from these mountainous districts into the southern plains of La Mancha, Andalusia, and especially Estremadura. The journey begins at the end of September, and, during its continuance, they enjoy great privileges. Sometimes they travel as much as twenty-five or thirty miles a day, in order to reach a convenient place for halting. The whole journey from the mountains to the interior of Estremadura is reckoned at about 690 miles, which occupies forty days. The shepherd conducts them to the pasture which they occupied the previous winter, and where most of the lambs were born. Here folds are constructed for the sheep, and huts made of branches for the shepherd. Shortly after their arrival in the winter pasture, the birth of the lambs takes place. The barren ewes receive the poorest pasture, the pregnant the next best, and the ewes which have lambed the best. The lambs born latest are put into the richest pastures, to acquire strength for their journey. In March, the shepherds have much to do to the lambs—cut the tails, mark the nose with a hot iron, saw off the points of the horns, and emasculate those intended for wethers. In April, they return to the summer pastures. The flock at this time shows by its restlessness its wish to migrate; some sheep escape, &c.—an interesting fact, considering the restlessness of migrating animals at certain seasons. On the first of May the shearing begins, if the weather is not cold. It is performed under cover. Before shearing, the sheep are put into a building consisting of two apartments, from 400 to 800 paces long and 100 wide. As many of the sheep as are to be sheared the next day, are taken on the evening into a narrow, long, low hut, called the *sweating-house*, where the sheep, being much crowded, perspire freely. The wool thus becomes softer, and is more easily cut. This practice was also pursued by the Romans. The wool is sorted and washed before being sent away. The sheep are carried to another place and marked, and those which have lost their teeth, are killed for mutton. There are now in Spain only about four millions of fine-woolled sheep. Sweden early imported Merinos, and greatly improved some of her sheep. In Germany, the first improvement of native flocks by Merinos took place in Saxony. In the Erzgebirge Hungarian rams had been previously introduced; but as early as 1765, above 200 Merino rams and ewes, accompanied by two Spanish shepherds, were imported into Saxony. In 1778, another importation of the finest Merinos, from the best flocks of Leon and Castile, took place, and important sheep farms were established. On that of Stolpen, the first established in Saxony, particular care has always been paid to the sheep, and it still affords extremely fine wool. It is said that Spain itself has at present no sheep equal to the stock imported in 1765; and the finest German wool brings a higher price in London than the best Spanish wool. The establishment at Stolpen has contributed greatly to the improvement of the Saxon sheep, and thereby to the promotion of industry in the country. From 1779 to 1811, more than 10,000 rams and ewes were sold there at moderate prices. The original German sheep is at present found hardly any where in Saxony, and a new, fine-woolled race has originated from the mixture with Merinos, which is called *electoral sheep*, and its wool *electoral wool*, as the present kingdom of Saxony was, before 1806, the electorate of Saxony.—See Von Ehrenfels, *On the Elector il Sheep and Electoral Wool* (Prague, 1822, in German). Besides the royal breeds, which always have been kept entirely pure, other farmers in Saxony have imported genuine Merinos. At Rochsburg, in the Erzgebirge, the sheep are fed the whole year round in stalls; and the lambs, at the age of one year, are almost full grown, and therefore yield a considerable amount of very long and strong wool. Prussia has lately made uncommon progress in the breeding of fine sheep, and some of the Prussian wool, particularly that of the Mark and Silesia, competes in the market with the electoral wool. Flocks of genuine Merinos have been imported into Prussia, and the government, some time since, undertook the establishment of a school for shepherds, where young men were to be instructed, at the public expense, in the care of sheep, in health and in sickness, made acquainted with the history of the improvements in the mode of raising them, &c. A similar school was formerly established in Sweden. The Spanish breed of sheep was first introduced into Great Britain in 1787. Some individuals of the black and spotted kinds had indeed been procured and kept in the parks of noblemen previously, but without any regard to the wool; nor was much interest awakened by the flock imported in 1787. Subsequently great attention was paid to the improvement of English wool; but it was ascertained, that though the fleece of the Merino did not much degenerate in England, it did not much improve, and the carcass, which naturally affords little weight of meat, did not improve; in consequence of which, the farmers have found it for their interest to return to the native breeds and to give up the Spanish sheep. It appears to be sufficiently established, by evidence taken before the house of lords in 1828, and other authorities, that a considerable deterioration has taken place in the quality of British wool, particularly during the last thirty years. The great object of the agriculturists has been to increase the weight of the carcass and the quantity of the wool, and it seems very difficult, if not impossible, to accomplish this without injuring the fineness of the fleece. A very great change has taken place within the present century as respects the quantity of foreign wool imported into England, and the countries from which it is obtained. Previously to 1800, the average imports did not exceed 3,000,000 lbs., brought mostly from Spain. In 1800, they amounted to near 9,000,000 lbs. They now amount to between 25,000,000 and 32,000,000, the greater part furnished by Germany. The Spanish flocks suffered severely during the campaigns in Spain, and the best Spanish wool does not now bring more than half the price of the best German wool. The breed of sheep that was carried out to New Holland and Van Diemen's land has succeeded remarkably well. The former promises, at no distant day, to be one of the principal wool-growing countries in the world. The imports into Great Britain, in 1830, amounted to 1,967,309 lbs., while those from Spain amounted only to 1,643,515. According to Mr. Luccock's estimate, which was made with great care, the total number of sheep and lambs in England and Wales, in the year 1800, was 26,148,463. (See article *England*, in the Edinburgh Encyclopædia.) The number has not probably varied much in the interim. In Scotland, it may be 3,500,000; in Ireland, it is probably under 2,000,000; so that the total number in Great Britain and Ireland may be taken at about 32,000,000. In the U. States, the first Merinos were imported (about 300 in number) in the year 1810, by general Humphreys, American minister in Portugal, and the consul, Mr. Jarvis. General Derby, of Salem, imported as many more; and, in 1825, a great number of Saxon sheep were brought into the country. These contributed to improve the American breed. But the American wool is far from competing with the Spanish or German, for which many reasons may be given, among others, that the high price of labor prevents the existence of a particular class of shepherds. The most improved flocks in the U. States are to be found in Vermont and New York. According to calculations as accurate as they could well be made, there are 20,000,000 sheep, of all kinds, in the U. States. The successful introduction of the Merino at the cape of Good Hope, New South Wales, &c., has proved that it will thrive wherever it receives proper care. In hot climates, however, particular attention is required to prevent the wool from degenerating. The sheep must not be exposed too much to the sun, nor to the dew. (For more information respecting this interesting subject, see *Wool*.)

Sheer; the longitudinal curve of a ship's decks or sides.

Sheet; a rope fastened to one or both the lower corners of a sail, to extend and retain it in a particular situation.

Sheffield, John, duke of Buckingham, a nobleman of some note as a wit and a statesman, born in 1649, was the son of the earl of Mulgrave, to whose title he succeeded in 1658. At the age of seventeen, he engaged as a volunteer in the first Dutch war. On his return, by the union of wit and spirit so agreeable to Charles II, he became a great favorite at court. On the accession of James II, he was made lord chamberlain; and his attachment to that sovereign induced him to take a seat in the ecclesiastical commission, and practise other compliances, though he opposed many of the counsels which brought ruin on his master. At the revolution, he took the part of an anticourtier, but, in 1694, became member of the cabinet. On the accession of Anne, to whom he is said once to have been a suitor, he was advanced to the dukedom of Buckingham; but jealousy of the duke of Marlborough drove him from office until the change of 1710, when he was made first steward of the household, and then president of the council under the administration of Harley. After the death of Anne, he employed his time chiefly in literary pursuits, until his death in 1720. His literary fame was mainly assisted by his rank and influence in his own day. In his Essay on Satire, he was supposed to have been assisted by Dryden; and few of his other pieces merit attention. His widow published a splendid edition of his works in 1723, in two volumes quarto; the first of which contained his poems upon various subjects, and the latter his historical memoirs, character, speeches and essays.

Sheffield; a large manufacturing town of England, in the West Riding of Yorkshire, at the confluence of the rivers Sheaf and Don: over the latter is a stone bridge of five arches, and over the former another, of one arch. The streets are regular, the houses well built, mostly of brick, but the smoke of the manufactories tends to give the town a sombre appearance. The public buildings are not remarkable for beauty. The principal are the four churches belonging to the establishment, the town-hall, cutlers'-hall, the general infirmary, the assembly-room, the music-hall, and the theatre. The town contains, besides, seven meeting-houses for Dissenters. Sheffield has been long noted for its manufactures of hardware, which comprise two great divisions, viz. those of cutlery and plated goods. The latter manufactures are wholly confined within the town; but those of cutlery goods are also carried on in all the villages and hamlets in the neighborhood, to the distance of seven miles. Besides these manufactures, there are in the town and its vicinity several extensive founderies for iron. For several centuries, its trade was inconsiderable, consisting almost entirely of sheath-knives, scissors, sickles and scythes; but since 1750, the town has advanced rapidly in population and wealth. The origin of Sheffield is unknown: it was formerly distinguished for its castle, supposed to have been built during the reign of Henry III. The population, in 1821, was 42,157. In 1831, it was, including the parish, 90,657; 36 miles south of Leeds, and 162 north-west of London.

Sheherazade. (See *Arabian Nights*.)

Sheik, or Scheikh (*Arabic*); that is to say, the *elder* or *eldest*. The chiefs of the Arabic tribes or hordes are called by this name. They are extremely proud of their long line of noble ancestors, especially the leaders of the Bedouins. Some of them also take the title of *emir*, without belonging to the race of Mohammed. The prince of Mecca is styled "sheik of Mecca," and calls himself a legitimate descendant of Mohammed, and demands presents from the caravans. The Mohammedans also call the heads of their monasteries *sheiks*, and the Turkish mufti is sometimes called *sheik ulislam* (chief of the true believers).

SHELBURNE. (See *Lansdowne*.)

SHELBY, Isaac, a distinguished American revolutionary officer, was born Dec. 11, 1750, near Hagers Town, Maryland. He received a common English education in Frederictown, and acted as a deputy sheriff in Frederic county previous to his becoming of age. He removed with his father to the western waters when twenty-one years old. In 1774, he was appointed a lieutenant in the expedition under Lewis, against the Shawanees and other Indian tribes north-west of the Ohio. In 1775, he went to Kentucky, and engaged in the business of a land surveyor. After nearly a twelve months' exposure in the cane-brakes, living without bread or salt, his health beginning to fail, he returned home. In 1776, and before his return from Kentucky, the committee of safety in Virginia appointed him captain of a minute company—a species of troops organized upon the first breaking out of the revolution—but not called into service from the extreme frontier on which he lived. In 1777, he was appointed by the governor of Virginia a commissary to supply rations for the militia posted in several garrisons to guard the back settlements, and to lay in supplies for a grand treaty, to be held at the Long Island of Holston river, with the Cherokees. These supplies were not to be obtained nearer than Staunton in Virginia, a distance of 300 miles; and to accomplish it, required the exertion of all the energy, enterprise and perseverance which marked his character. In 1778, he was still engaged in the commissary department to provide supplies for the continental army, and for a formidable expedition by the way of Pittsburg against the northwestern Indians. In 1779, he was appointed by governor Henry to furnish supplies for a campaign against the Chickamoggy Indians—a numerous banditti on the south side of the Tennessee river, under the control of a daring Cherokee chief, called *Druggon Canoe*, who, after his defeat at the Long Island of Holston, in 1776, had declared eternal war against the whites The frontiers from Georgia to Pennsylvania suffered from their depredations more than from all the other hostile tribes together. Owing to the poverty of the treasury, the government was unable to advance the necessary funds, and the whole expense of the supplies, including transportation, was sustained by his individual credit. In the spring of the same year, he was elected a member of the Virginia legislature from Washington county; and, in the autumn, was commissioned by governor Jefferson as a major in the escort of guards to the commissioners for extending the boundary between Virginia and North Carolina. After the surrender of Charleston, and the loss of the southern army in 1780, he devoted himself to the military service of his country, and, throughout the residue of the revolutionary struggle, was actively engaged in fighting her battles in the south. For his conduct in the battle of King's mountain, October 7, 1780, he received a vote of thanks and an elegant sword, from the legislature of North Carolina. In 1781, he was chosen a member of that body, and the following year was reëlected. He was also appointed one of the commissioners to settle the preëmption claims on the Cumberland river, and lay off the lands allotted to the officers and soldiers of the North Carolina line, south of where Nashville now stands. This service he performed in the winter of 1782—3. After the separation between Virginia and Kentucky, and the formation of a constitution for the latter state, by a convention, of which colonel Shelby was a member, he was chosen governor of Kentucky, in 1792. From 1796, after the expiration of his term of office, until 1812, he lived in retirement, discharging no public duty whatever, except that of elector for president and vice-president, to which he was invariably called. In the latter year he was again chosen governor, and during the war was zealous in his exertions to aid the common cause. In 1813, he marched at the head of 4000 men across the state of Ohio, to the frontier, where general Harrison commanded the American forces. In 1816, he returned to private life, and, in 1818, acted as a commissioner, in conjunction with general Jackson, in forming a treaty with the Chickasaw Indians. In 1820, he experienced a paralytic stroke, which rendered his right arm useless, and occasioned a slight lameness during the rest of his life. His death occurred suddenly, July 18, 1826, in the 76th year of his age, in consequence of a stroke of apoplexy.

SHELL. (See *Conchology*.)

SHELL, in artillery, includes bombs and grenades. (See those articles.)

SHELL-BARK HICKORY. (See *Hickory*.)

SHELLEY, Percy Bysshe, eldest son of sir Timothy Shelley, Sussex, was born at Field-place, in that county, August 4, 1792. He was sent to Eton, whence he was early removed to Oxford. This removal was owing to his eccentricity of character, which led him to neglect the studies and violate the rules of the school, and finally resulted in his expulsion from Oxford. His family, naturally offended with his conduct, and not less with his free opinions on matters of religion, was still further estranged by an ill-assorted marriage. The result was very unfortunate, for after the birth of two children, a separation took place by mutual consent; and the death of the lady soon after exposed him to much obloquy. On the decease of his first wife, he married Miss Godwin, daughter of the celebrated author of Political Justice, by Mary Wolstonecraft, and soon after retired to Marlow, in Buckinghamshire, where he wrote his Revolt of Islam. About this time, application was made by his family to deprive him of the guardianship of his two children, a boy and a girl, on the ground of his atheistical and sceptical notions, and certain dangerous opinions respecting the intercourse of the sexes. The application succeeded, principally owing to a juvenile production, called Queen Mab, written while at Oxford, and published without the consent of the author. This event caused him much uneasiness, and probably induced him to quit England, and repair, with his second wife and their children, to Italy, where he renewed an acquaintance with lord Byron, to whom he had become known during a former visit to the continent. With him and Leigh Hunt, Shelley joined in a periodical miscellany, published in London, entitled The Liberal. This publication, which contained the Vision of Judgment, by lord Byron, and other original productions, was interrupted by the untimely death of Mr. Shelley, who was drowned in his return from Leghorn to his house, on the gulf of Lerici, in the bay of Spezia, by the wreck of his sailing boat, in a sudden storm, July, 1822. A few days afterwards, the body was washed on shore near Via Reggio, and was subsequently reduced to ashes by his friends. Shelley's remains were deposited in the Protestant burial-ground at Rome. At the time of his decease, Mr. Shelley had nearly completed his thirtieth year. His principal works are The Revolt of Islam; Alastor, or the Spirit of Solitude; The Cenci, a tragedy (see *Cenci, Beatrice*); Adonais; Hellas; Prometheus Unbound; and a posthumous volume of poems.

SHELL-LAC. (See *Coccus*, end of the article.)

SHEM; one of the patriarchs, eldest son of Noah, is said in Scripture to have died at the age of 600 years. The Hebrews traced their origin to Shem, through Abraham, who was the eighth in descent from him.

SHEMITISH LANGUAGES. (See *Semitic Languages*.)

SHENANDOAH; a river of Virginia, which flows into the Potomac, after a separate course of about 200 miles, just before the Potomac bursts through the Blue Ridge. It waters a fertile country, and has good boat navigation for 100 miles.

SHENSTONE, William, was born at Hales Owen, in Shropshire, in 1714. His father was a gentleman farmer, who cultivated a moderate estate, called the *Leasowes*, which were rendered celebrated by the taste of his son. The latter was educated at Oxford, and entertained thoughts of taking his academical degrees, and proceeding to the study of some profession, but was seduced, by obtaining possession of his paternal property, to relinquish all views of an active life, and occupied himself with rural embellishments, and the cultivation of poetry. In 1737, he printed a volume of juvenile poems, which obtained little notice; and, in 1740, the Judgment of Hercules. In the following year appeared his School-mistress, the best of his poems. His great object, to render the Leasowes famous for picturesque beauty and elegance, led to expenses which he could but ill support, and he was by no means a happy inhabitant of the Eden which he had created. He died in February, 1763, in his fiftieth year. His works were collected in three volumes, octavo. The first consists of elegies, odes, songs and ballads, levities, or pieces of humor, and moral pieces; the second contains his prose works; and the third, Letters to his Friends. As a poet, he is elegant, melodious, tender, and correct in sentiment, and often pleasing and natural in description, but rather feeble. The prose works display good sense and cultivated taste, and contain just and acute observations on mankind. (See his *Life* by Johnson, and Graves's *Recollections of Shenstone.*)

Shepherd Kings. (See *Hycsos.*)

Shepherd's Dog (*canis domesticus* of Linnæus, and *le chien de berger* of Buffon) is distinguished by its upright ears and the remarkable villosity of the tail beneath, and stands at the head of the class of farm dogs. This breed of dogs is said to be preserved in the greatest purity in the northern part of Scotland, where its aid is highly necessary in managing the numerous herds of sheep bred in those extensive wilds. The same variety is diffused over most parts of Europe. The dog prevents the sheep from straggling, and conducts them from one part of the pasture to another: it will not suffer any strange sheep to mix with them. In driving a number of sheep to a distance, a well-trained dog always confines them to the road, watching every avenue that leads from it, and pursuing every straggler. At the herdsman's signal, this faithful assistant will conduct the sheep to him from a considerable distance.

Shepherd's Purse (*thlaspi bursa pastoris*); a small, insignificant, cruciferous plant, bearing diminutive white flowers, and short, triangular, compressed pods, which is now naturalized, and common in cultivated grounds, in most parts of the world. The radical leaves are pinnatifid. It is of no known utility.

Sherbet, or Sorbetto; a beverage of the Orientals, made of water, sugar, lemon-juice, rose-water, dried fruits and amber.

Shereen, or Schirin, or Sira; an Armenian princess, second wife of Chosrou or Chosroes II (q. v.), who reigned over Persia in the beginning of the seventh century. Shereen is still in Western Asia the model of female perfection, celebrated for her wit, her accomplishments, and her incomparable beauty. Her story is to be found in the *Shahnameh.* (See *Ferdusi.*) The Persian and Turkish romances represent her as the daughter of Maurice, a Byzantine emperor. They are filled with the account of her sudden passion for Chosroes, her gradual alienation from him, the love of the sculptor Ferhad, the most beautiful youth of the East, for the fascinating queen, and her melancholy fate. Her husband was murdered by his own son, and Shereen put herself to death on his tomb, to escape the importunities of the parricide. Von Hammer has drawn the materials of his *Schirin*, a Persian romantic poem (14 cantos, in German, Leipsic, 1809), from Persian and Turkish sources.

Sheridan, Thomas, son of an Irish divine, was born near Dublin, in 1721, and was sent to Westminster, where he was admitted on the foundation. He afterwards entered as a student of Trinity college, Dublin, but quitted the university for the stage, and made his first appearance in the character of Richard III (1743), in Dublin. After a visit to London, in 1744, he returned to the Irish metropolis, and became a theatrical manager. In this situation he experienced various misfortunes, and the establishment of a rival theatre completed the ruin of his affairs. He then commenced lectures on elocution, to which subject he endeavored to draw the attention of the public by means of the press. He subsequently repaired to France to avoid his creditors; and, while there, he had the misfortune to lose his wife (1767). Returning to England, after the retirement of Garrick from the stage, he became manager of Drury lane theatre, of which his son was one of the proprietors; but some disputes taking place, he retired from the office, and resumed his attention to oratory. The latest of his literary labors was an Orthoepical Dictionary of the English Language, in 1788, in which year he died.—His wife *Frances* was the author of Sidney Biddulph (3 vols)—a very interesting but sombre tale; Nourjahad, an Eastern romance, since dramatized; and two comedies, the Discovery, and the Dupe. (See the account of her life by her grand-daughter, Alicia Lefanu.)

Sheridan, Richard Brinsley, the third son of the preceding, distinguished as a statesman, wit and dramatist, was born in Dublin, Oct. 30, 1751. For the early developement of his talents, he was indebted to the instructions of his accomplished mother; and he was afterwards placed at a grammar-school at Dublin. In 1762, he was sent to Harrow school, which he left at the age of eighteen, owing to his father's embarrassments. With a view to the legal profession, he entered as a student of the Middle Temple; but the close application and industry requisite for success as a lawyer were uncongenial with his disposition, and he relinquished the bar for politics and the drama. His early marriage, also, made some more immediate means of support than the practice of a junior barrister necessary and he turned his attention to dramatic composition. His first production, the Rivals, was acted at Covent garden in 1775, with moderate success; but the Duenna, a musical entertainment, which followed, was received with general admiration; and his School for Scandal gained him the highest reputation as a comic writer. On the retirement of Garrick from the management of Drury lane theatre, Sheridan, in conjunction with doctor Forde and Mr. Linley, purchased Garrick's share of the patent. This property qualified him for a seat in parliament; and, in 1780, he was chosen member for the borough of Stafford. Lord North was then minister, and Sheridan, joining the opposition, displayed so much ability, that, on the retreat of the premier, and the conclusion of the American war, he was made under secretary of state for the war department. He resigned, with his principal, in consequence of a dispute with lord Shelburne, afterwards marquis of Lansdowne, who was at the head of the ministry. His intimate connexion with Fox brought him again into office on the coalition of that statesman with lord North, when Sheridan held the post of joint secretary of the treasury under the duke of Portland. The dissolution of that ministry threw him again into the ranks of opposition, where he remained during the whole period of the political ascendency of Mr. Pitt. He now attained distinguished celebrity as a parliamentary orator, and his talents were particularly exhibited in his opposition to the extension of the revenue laws, and on the subject of the Westminster election; but the grandest display of his eloquence occurred during the progress of the impeachment of Warren Hastings. In 1792, Mr. Sheridan lost his wife, who left one son; and, three years afterwards, he married Miss Ogle, daughter of the dean of Winchester. With this lady he had a considerable fortune, which enabled him to purchase the estate of Polesdon, in Surrey; and, as he held the office of receiver-general of the duchy of Cornwall, worth £1200 a year, and retained his interest in Drury lane theatre, he seemed to be placed beyond the reach of pecuniary distress. The political changes consequent on the death of Mr. Pitt, in 1806, occasioned the exaltation of the party with which Sheridan was connected, and he obtained the lucrative post of treasurer of the navy, and the rank of a privy counsellor. This administration being weakened by the loss of Mr. Fox, who survived his celebrated rival only a few months, new alterations took place, and Sheridan was deprived of office, to which he never returned. At the general election in 1806, he obtained a seat for Westminster, the great object of his ambition; but he was afterwards nominated for the borough of Ilchester, which he continued to represent during the remainder of his parliamentary career. The latter part of the life of this highly-talented individual was imbittered by misfortunes, principally arising from his own indolence and mismanagement, though the destruction of Drury lane theatre by fire contributed to increase his difficulties. When the affairs of that establishment were arranged, in 1811, Mr. Sheridan and his son were to have £40,000 for their share of the property; but the portion of the former was not sufficient to liquidate the debts and reserved claims to which it was liable. The dissolution of parliament, and his failure in an attempt to obtain a seat for Stafford, the borough he had formerly represented, completed his ruin. In the latter part of 1812, he had relinquished all thoughts of returning to the house of commons; and the remainder of his existence was spent in attempts to ward off the dangers to which his improvidence had exposed him. At length every resource failed, and the disappearance of his property was followed by the arrest of his person. After a few days' detention, he was released, but only to experience fresh apprehension and alarm, from which he sought a temporary relief in that unrestrained indulgence and dissipation which had occasioned his misfortunes. Intemperance had undermined his constitution, and mental anxiety completed the destruction of his health. Even on the bed of sickness he was not exempted from the terrors of being arrested for debt. His death took place July 7, 1816. Besides the plays already mentioned, Mr. Sheridan was the author of St. Patrick's Day, or the Scheming Lieutenant, a farce; a Trip to Scarborough, a comedy, altered from Vanbrugh; the Camp, a farce; the Critic, or the Tragedy rehearsed; Robinson Crusoe, or Harlequin Friday, a pantomime; and Pizarro, a play, from the German of Kotzebue. He also wrote Verses to the Memory of David Garrick (1779, 4to.); and a Comparative Statement of the two Bills for the better Government of the British Possessions in India (1788, 4to.). As a speaker, he ranks among the most finished and varied of the rhetorical school; and his speech already alluded to against Warren Hastings has been deemed one of the most striking specimens of English eloquence upon record. As a dramatist, he may be considered the head of the department of that line of comedy which exhibits the polite malice, the civil detraction, the *equivoque*, intrigue, persiflage, and lurking irony, which characterize social intercourse in the more cultivated ranks of life. Wit usually takes the lead of humor in this species of composition, with a correspondent destruction of nature and verisimilitude. The School for Scandal is a felicitous exemplification of character, and of some of the most conspicuous of the well-bred vices and follies of fashionable life. A collection of his speeches, in five volumes, was published in 1816. His Dramatic Works appeared in 1821 (2 vols., 8vo.), edited by Thomas Moore, who has since published a Life of Sheridan.

SHERIFF. The sheriff is an officer of great antiquity, and known by a corresponding name in most countries in Europe. He was called in the Danish *grävue* Swedish, *grefwe;* Anglo-Saxon, *gerefa;* German, *graf;* and, in the Latin of the middle ages, *graphio*, or *grafio.* Adelung observes that the twelve judges appointed by Odin were called *greve.* Both the officer and the name have, with some variations, been retained in Germany. The *graf* of the Germans is, for the most part, a title of dignity, answering to the *count* of the French, and the *earl* of the English; and, in some cases, it is also the title of a prince, as the *landgraf*, or *markgraf.* Among the Anglo-Saxons, the *gerefa*, or, as he is called in English, the *reeve*, was an officer of justice inferior in rank to the alderman. He was a ministerial officer, appointed to execute processes, keep the peace, and put the laws in execution. He witnessed contracts, brought offenders to justice, and delivered them to punishment, took bail of such as were to appear before the *shiregemote*, or county court, and presided at the hundred court or *folcmote.* There was a distinction both in the rank and jurisdiction of the *gerefa.* The *shire-gerefa*, *shire-reeve*, or *sheriff*, was probably distinguished by the name of the *king's gerefa*, because he more immediately executed the king's precepts, and sometimes sat in the place of the alderman in the county court. He appears, also, to have been distinguished by the title of the *heh-gerefa*, or *high-sheriff.* The *gerefa* who acted in the tithing was called the *tithing-reeve*, he who acted in the *byrig*, or burgh, a *borough-reeve*, and he who acted in the town the *tun-gerefa.* The leading duties of this officer, in England and the U. States, are the same as those performed by the Anglo-Saxon *gerefa*, namely, of an executive as distinguished from those of a judicial kind.

SHERIFFMUIR, or SHERIFF MOOR; a plain of Scotland, near the Grampian mountains, in Perthshire. Here a bloody battle was fought between the army of George I and the rebels, under the earl of Mar, in 1715. (See *Stuart, James Edward Francis.*)

SHERIFF'S TOURN. (See *Courts*, vol. iii, p. 589.)

SHERLOCK, William, an Episcopal clergyman, born in Southwark, about 1641, studied at Eton, and afterwards at Peterhouse, Cambridge, where he proceeded doctor of divinity in 1680. After the revolution, having refused to take the oath of allegiance to William III, he was suspended from the pastoral office; but, on his subsequent compliance, he was restored, and, in 1691, promoted to the deanery of St. Paul's. His death took place in 1707. Doctor Sherlock distinguished himself as a polemical divine against the Dissenters, and carried on a controversy with doctor South relative to the doctrine of the Trinity. His works on practical theology, especially his Discourses on Death and on Judgment, are much esteemed, and have passed through numerous editions.

SHERLOCK, Thomas, son of the preceding, born in London, in 1678, received his education at Catharine-hall, Cambridge, where he obtained a fellowship. In 1714, he was chosen master of Catharine-hall, and was promoted to the deanery of Chichester in 1716, after which he entered into a controversy with bishop Hoadly, in defence of the corporation and test acts. In 1725, he published Discourses on Prophecy, intended to obviate the infidel objections of Anthony Collins. Doctor Sherlock, in 1728, succeeded Hoadly in the bishopric of Bangor, and, in 1734, in that of Salisbury. He was offered the primacy on the decease of archbishop Potter, in 1747; but he refused it; and, the following year, he was translated to the see of London, where he remained till his death, 1761. Bishop Sherlock was the author of the Trial of the Witnesses of the Resurrection of Jesus; and his Sermons are among the best specimens of English pulpit eloquence extant.

SHERMAN, Roger, a signer of the Dec

laration of Independence, was born at Newton, Massachusetts, April 19, 1721. His father was a respectable farmer, but of circumstances too moderate to allow him to give his son any other education than that furnished by the village school. Roger was early apprenticed to a shoemaker; and, on the death of his father, when he was only nineteen years of age, he supported his mother and a numerous family by his labor, his older brother having, some time before, removed to New Milford, in Connecticut. Thither the whole family also removed in 1743, Roger performing the journey on foot, with his tools on his back. Soon afterwards he relinquished the shoemaking trade, and entered into partnership with his brother as a country merchant. From his earliest youth, he had always manifested an unconquerable avidity for knowledge, and, availing himself of every opportunity, became remarkable for the variety and extent of his attainments at an early age. His skill in mathematics occasioned him to be appointed, in 1745, county surveyor. In astronomy he was likewise a proficient. In 1748, and for several succeeding years, he supplied the astronomical calculations for an almanac published in the city of New York. Having devoted for some time his leisure moments to the study of the law, he was admitted, in 1754, to the bar, where he rapidly rose to distinction. In the following year, he was appointed a justice of the peace for New Milford, which town he also represented the same year in the colonial assembly. In 1759, he was appointed judge of the court of common pleas for the county of Litchfield—an office which he filled with great reputation for the two ensuing years. He then fixed his residence in New Haven, of which town he was made a justice of the peace, and often represented it in the colonial assembly. In 1765, he was made judge of the court of common pleas, and, about the same time, he was appointed treasurer of Yale college. In 1766, he was elected a member of the upper house in the general assembly of Connecticut, which station he retained for nineteen years; when, the office of judge being considered incompatible with it, he retired. His judgeship he held until his election, in 1789, to congress, under the federal constitution. His early and strenuous support of American rights caused him to be chosen a delegate to the first general congress of 1774. He was present at the opening of the session, and continued to occupy a seat in that body until his death, in 1793, a space of nineteen years. His whole congressional career was marked by indefatigable zeal, industry and fortitude. His sterling sense, integrity and firmness, gave him great influence in the assembly. The estimation in which he was held by his fellow members may be inferred from the selection of him as the associate of Adams, Franklin, Jefferson and Livingston, on the committee appointed to prepare the Declaration of Independence. While holding a seat in congress, he served the state which he represented in various other ways. During the war, he was a member of the governor's council of safety; and, from 1784 to his death, was mayor of the city of New Haven. In 1783, he was commissioned, together with Richard Law, both of whom were at the time judges of the superior court, to revise the statutes of the state—a work of great labor and difficulty, and which was executed with corresponding ability. In 1787, he was a member of the convention which formed the present constitution of the U. States; and its adoption in Connecticut was owing, in a great measure, to his influence. He appeared before the state convention, and made a plain and perspicuous explanation of the probable operation of the principles of the instrument. He was continued in his place in the house of representatives under the new government, and, at the expiration of two years, was chosen to the senate, but was obliged to retire from this station in consequence of ill health, July 23, 1793, in the seventy-third year of his age. The predominant trait of Mr. Sherman's character was his practical wisdom, or, in other words, his strong common sense. "That," said Mr. Jefferson, on one occasion, when pointing out the various members of congress to a friend, "that is Mr. Sherman, of Connecticut—*a man who never said a foolish thing in his life*." He possessed singular power in penetrating into the characters and motives of men, while the rectitude and integrity of his own nature enabled him to acquire an extraordinary influence. Though a man of naturally strong passions, he obtained a complete control over them by means of his deep religious spirit, and became habitually calm, sedate and self-possessed. As a speaker, he was slow and hesitating, and devoid of most of the graces of oratory; but the weight of his matter, and the conviction of his sincerity, caused him to be listened to with great respect and attention. His learning was extensive and profound.

Sherry; a Spanish wine, growing in the neighborhood of Xeres de la Frontera, in the province of Andalusia, near Cadiz. Many of the principal vineyards are in the hands of British and foreign settlers, to which probably is to be ascribed the improvement which of late has taken place in Sherry wines. The best soil (*albariza*) consists chiefly of carbonate of lime, with a small admixture of silex and clay, and occasionally magnesia. Red and white grapes are used indiscriminately. When ripe and gathered, they are spread on mats, and left to dry for two or three days; they are then freed from the stalks, and the rotten or unripe berries rejected. Being now introduced into vats, with a layer of burnt gypsum on the surface, they are trodden by peasants with wooden shoes. The juice is collected in casks, in which the fermentation is allowed to take place, continuing generally from October till the beginning or middle of December. The wines are then racked from the lees, and those intended for exportation receive additions of brandy, seldom more than three or four gallons to the butt. The new wine is harsh and fiery, but mellows by being allowed to remain in the wood four or five years, though fifteen or twenty years are required to perfect its flavor. Sometimes bitter almonds are infused to give the wine a nutty flavor. The dry sherry is the most esteemed. Its flavor partakes of the taste of leather (called in Spanish *olor de bota*). This is owing to the custom of bringing the wines down the country in large leather vessels, or, as the Spaniards call them, *botas*, whence we derive the term *butts*. This flavor goes off with keeping. The sherry wines are shipped, for the most part, at Cadiz, and are principally exported to England.—See Henderson's *History of Ancient and Modern Wines* (London, 1826, 1 vol., 4to.).

Shetland or Zetland Isles; the north-east division of the Scottish Northern Isles, about fifteen leagues north-east of the Orkneys. The southern promontory of the Mainland (the largest of the Shetland islands) lies in 59° 48′ 30″ of north latitude, and the northern extremity of Unst, in latitude 60° 52′ north. The meridian of London passes through this last island. The islands are about eighty-six in number, of which forty are inhabited: the others are small holms or rocky islets, used only for pasturage. The principal inhabited islands are the Mainland (with the capital, Lerwick), Yell, Unst, Whalsay, Bressay. The climate is not agreeable. The winds are tempestuous, and the rains heavy. The sea swells and rages in such a manner, that for five or six months the ports are almost inaccessible. There is great diversity of soil. The general appearance is a scene of ruggedness and sterility. Some patches of miserably cultivated soil relieve the eye of a traveller; but no tree nor shrub is to be seen. The western parts are peculiarly wild, dreary, and desolate, consisting of gray rocks, stagnant marshes and pools, broken and precipitous coasts, excavated into vast natural arches and deep caverns. There is plenty of peat and turf for fuel. Great numbers of horses are bred in Shetland, though they are of very small size. These little animals, however, are full of spirit, and bear fatigue much better, in proportion to their size, than larger horses, and evidently proceed from the Norway horse, though reduced in size, perhaps, in some degree, by scanty fare. The cattle of Shetland are also of a small size. The inhabitants are a hardy, robust, and laborious race, and hospitable. They have few manufactures. They make a coarse cloth for their own use, and a little linen. They likewise export great quantities of stockings, knit from their own wool; some of which are so fine that they equal silk in price, and can be drawn through a finger ring. Their chief trade is to Leith, London, Dublin, and Barcelona; but they also deal with the Dutch fishermen, who visit their islands. They export annually 1000 tons of cod, tusk, and ling, and 500 tons of kelp, and about £5000 worth of stockings and mittens. The whole exports may be estimated at £35,000. Population, 26,145. See Hibbert's *Description* (Edinburgh, 1821), and a full account in the article *Shetland*, in Brewster's *New Edinburgh Encyclopædia*.

Shibboleth. When Jephthah (q. v.), at the head of the Gileadites, had defeated the Ephraimites, and his troops intercepted their flight across the Jordan, they required the former to pronounce the word *Shibboleth*. The peculiar pronunciation of the Ephraimites, who, unable to give the aspirate, called it *Sibboleth*, betrayed them to their enemies. The word has thence acquired the signification of the watch-word of a party.

Shield; a piece of defensive armor, borne on the left arm, to screen the body from the blows of the enemy; afterwards superseded, in a great degree, by the use of more convenient armor. (See *Breastplate.*) Shields were composed of different materials, and were of various figures. The ancient *clypeus* was round, and of brass; the *scutum*, or ἀσπὶς, was of an oblong shape, rectangular, generally made of wood, covered with skins; the *parma* was made of skin; the *pelta* was crescent-shaped. In the centre was the *umbo*, an iron boss projecting forward, to glance off missiles, or to press the enemy. They were often highly ornamented, and the ancients esteemed it a great disgrace to leave them on the field of battle. "With it, or on it," was the exhortation of a Spartan mother to her son, giving him the buckler of his father, as he went to war. In time of peace, they were hung up in consecrated places, and those taken in war were often suspended in the temples as trophies. (Potter's *Antiquities*; Vegetius, ii, 17.) The Tartar shield is made of leather. Both in France and in England and Scotland, round leather shields were used. Many of these shields had wood wicker work or metal plates below the leather. There was a particular kind of shield used several centuries ago, called *pavois* or *tallevas*, of extraordinary dimensions, and borne by an attendant. This in sieges was interposed between the archers and the besieged. The most ancient and universal form of shields, in the earlier ages, seems to have been the triangular, vulgarly called the *heater shield.* Numerous instances of this are seen in the monuments and gems of antiquity. This was the shape of the Norman shields. The shield, though not entirely relinquished while the use of the long-bow and cross-bow continued, underwent some alteration in its form, the triangular shape gradually giving place to the circular or rectangular. They seem to have been used in affrays as late as the reigns of Elizabeth and James I. The target and broad-sword were the favorite arms of the Scotch Highlanders as late as 1746, and even later.

Shigemooni. (See *Lama.*)

Shiites (*heretics*); a name given by the Sunnites (q. v.) to all Mohammedans, who do not acknowledge the Sunna as a law. The Shiites believe that Ali, the fourth caliph after Mohammed, was his first lawful successor. The Persians are Shiites. From them the sect of Ismaelites (q. v.) separated. (See the article *Islam.*)

Shilling (Anglo-Saxon, *skylling*; Swedish, *skilling*; German, *schilling*); the name of a coin of very different value in different places (see *Coin*), the etymology of which is very uncertain. It appears to have been originally only a money of account in England, or the twentieth part of a pound; and, according to some antiquarians, the first English shillings were coined in the beginning of the sixteenth century.

Shillooks. (See *Sennaar.*)

Shingles. (See *Erysipelas.*)

Ship; a locomotive machine, adapted to transportation over rivers, seas, and oceans. As no human device is more worthy of admiration than the ship, so no investigation can be more curious than to trace, step by step, the slow progress of improvement, from the first rude attempt of incipient navigation, down to the perfection of modern times. And here, at the very threshold of the inquiry, our attention is arrested by a singular fact—the uniformity with which the human mind, prompted by the same desires, and aided by the same faculties, arrives at the same results. How small, indeed, is the difference between the canoe of the Esquimaux, framed of the bones of beasts and fishes, and covered with the skins of seals, and those in which the poets show us Dardanus fleeing before the deluge, or Charon conducting his trembling charge to the shades below; between those said to have been used in primitive times by the Egyptian, the Ethiopian, and the Arab, and the light barks of the early Britons, made of osiers and hides, which Cæsar imitated in Spain to extricate himself from the perilous situation in which he was held by the lieutenants of Pompey! In what does the canoe of our own Indian, of the islander of the south seas, and of the native African, differ from those which the savage Germans hollowed from a single tree, in the days of Pliny?

It is an old tradition, that the first idea of the canoe was suggested by a split reed, seen by some ingenious savage floating safely upon the billow. Be this as it may, there can be little doubt that the raft, as it is the most easy and obvious means of crossing the water, was likewise of most early invention. The savage who first ventured forth upon a solitary tree, that the river had brought within his reach, must have found his situation unsteady and precarious: his ingenuity suggested the idea of fastening several together, and the conveyance became at once a safe one. The earliest records which history affords on this subject, show the Egyptians traversing the Nile upon rafts. The Phœnicians also availed themselves of the invention; and we are told that many islands, even the remote ones of Sicily and Corsica, were colonized with no better assistance. This will seem less improbable, if we remember that the Peruvians still make sea voyages on their raft, called *balza*, from the spongy tree of which it is made. It consists of a number of logs tightly bound together, and strengthened transversely by beams. They are tapered at the prow, to facilitate the division of the water, whilst vertical planks, descending below the surface, prevent drift, and enable it to sail towards the wind. These *balzas* we have met in the open ocean, loaded with from ten to twenty tons of merchandise, and contending effectually with the trade wind, which prevails along the coast of Peru. This form of ship is not, however, always safe: lifted as the logs are unequally upon the waves, the thongs which bind them together, if old or neglected, sometimes break or disengage; the bark of the mariner disappears treacherously beneath him, or the logs, crashing rudely together, serve for his destruction. Yet the attempts of the uncivilized navigator do not always shun comparison with those of a maturer age. We find the native of North-western America, in his little skin-covered bark of admirable symmetry, venturing forth amid the most boisterous waves, which pass harmless over him, and outstripping the fleetest barge in his rapid course. The flying *proa* of the Ladrone islands sails towards the wind with unequalled nearness, and with a velocity far greater than civilized man has ever attained, with all the aids of philosophy.

It were a vain task to record the various fables connected with the origin and improvement of ships, though the inventors were esteemed worthy to take rank among the gods, and even the ships to be translated to the heavens, where they still shine among the constellations; how Dædalus invented the art of flying, to escape from the labyrinth of Crete—an allusion to the sails with which he eluded the pursuit of Minos; how Hercules sailed with the hide of a lion, which was only his well known garment hung up for the purpose; or how the first idea of the sail was taken from the poetic voyages of the nautilus; how Atlas contends for the invention of the oar, and how many heroes claim the honor of the rudder. These inventions all, doubtless, originated in the earliest dawnings of civilization, before there were any means of recording them; and the ascription of them to individuals may have formed the pastime of succeeding poets. It may not, however, be equally vain to inquire what was the nature of ships among those nations which made the first advances towards civilization. We find that the Egyptians, in improving upon the rafts and canoes which they first used, built vessels of stout joists of acanthus wood, which were made to lap over like tiles, and were fastened with wooden pins. The stoutness of the joist precluded the necessity of a frame, except what was formed by the benches of the rowers. The seams were tightened by introducing the leaves of the papyrus. It could not have been long before ingenuity suggested the application of a natural agent for the relief of human toil; a mast of acanthus was raised, a papyrus sail suspended from it, and the rower rested on his oar, or only used it for the direction of his bark. In ascending the Nile, when the wind was either unfavorable or too light, the vessel was drawn against the current by men on shore, as Ali Bey describes to be still the practice. In descending, a hurdle of tamarisk was often let down from the prow, which, taking a deep hold of the stream, neutralized the efforts of the strong north-east wind, which a beneficent Providence sends to check the course of the stream and increase its height, at the season of the inundation. The early Egyptians did not, however, greatly improve upon this noble invention. Their peculiar prejudices, by confining them for many centuries to the navigation of the Nile, checked the progress of improvement. They had a horror of Typhon, as they termed the sea, because it swallowed that sacred river, which, being the great source of their happiness, they worshipped as a divinity. This horror extended to those who led a sea-faring life; hence the Phœnicians were not allowed even to enter the Nile Driven to extend their voyages seaward, these mariners adapted their ships to the necessities of a more precarious navigation. Coeval with the Phœnicians, in the use of ships, were the inhabitants of China. But, situated as they are, in the neighborhood of a circumscribed sea, surrounded by islands, and, moreover, possessing, in their own resources, a supply for every want, discovery and improvement have long lain dormant there. It is believed,—and the fact is wonderful,—that the Chinese have floated down through thirty centuries in the same shapeless junk which now excites the ridicule of our seamen, and which they are yet unwilling to exchange for the improved models which daily pass them in their own seas, and continually force upon them the most humiliating comparisons. In the Chinese junk of our day we may, perhaps, see the counterpart of what the ship was in the days of the Phœnicians and of incipient navigation. Among the Phœnicians, Carthaginians, and Greeks, the earlier ships used in commerce were flat-floored, broad, and of small draught of water; the floor timbers were continuous at first, and they were without a keel, having instead a streak of wood on either side, to take the ground when stranding. Next, the keel was introduced, in order to diminish the drift with a side wind; and, to increase the strength, a keelson was soon added, overlaying the floor timbers and confining them to the keel; beams were also placed aloft, to hold the sides together and sustain the deck. The planking, which took its name, among the Greeks, from the garment which covers the human body, was firmly attached to the frame by means of iron nails, some of which passed through and were clenched within. When, however, the ancients discovered the tendency of iron to rot the wood, they substituted copper. To obviate the danger of starting the plank ends,—a danger still sometimes fatal to the mariner,—a piece of wood was let into both in the form of a dove-tail. Oak and pine, then, as now, were the woods most in favor; chestnut and cedar were also used, and to the last the Greeks gave the name of *everlasting wood*, though it was found not to hold well when nailed in the ordinary way, and to grow iron-sick; cypress, not being subject to shrink and cause leakage, was also esteemed, and elm wood was placed in such parts as were constantly under water. The Romans were very particular as to the season of felling ship timber; aware that there was much to be gained by attention to this subject, though mistaken as to the means. They would only fell between the fifteenth and twenty-third days of the moon's age, believing that when it was on the wane, the sap, which is the chief cause of early decay, descended: they were also attentive to the quarter from which the wind blew; in autumn it should be westerly, in winter north. To stop the leaking at the joints, lime and pounded shells were first applied: these being found soon to fall off, wax, rosin and pitch were advantageously substituted; flax was also driven into the seams, and leather occasionally used as a sheathing A vessel of the time of Trajan, raised, after thirteen centuries, from the bottom of a lake, was found to have a bottom of pine and cypress, still in a sound state; her seams were calked with linen smeared with pitch, then sheathed with sheet lead and copper nails. Nor were the ancient vessels without ornament: the prow was especially decorated with paint and gilding, representing the forms of the gods, taking its name from the human face, its sides were called the *cheeks*. Its foremost extremity was usually carved into the representation of men and animals, or else formed a graceful curve; where it divided the water it was called the *goose*, from the image of that animal, placed there as an omen that the vessel should never sink. The distinguishing banner stood at the bow, representing a mountain, tree, flower, or other emblem: from this the name was usually taken, and conspicuously painted on a round piece of wood called the *eye*. The stern was sometimes carved in the figure of a shield, and elaborately decorated; upon a staff there erected, ribbons were hung, distinctive of the ship, and serving, at the same time, to show the direction of the wind; there, too, stood the *tutela*, or chosen patron of the ship; prayers and sacrifices were daily offered to it, and it was held so sacred as to offer a sanctuary to those who fled to it. Family considerations, patriotic partiality, or simple expediency, determined the selection of the deity; thus merchants committed themselves to the protection of Mercury, warriors to Mars, and lovers to Cupid and Venus.

The general form and size of the ancient ships varied with the progress of improvement, and with the warlike or commercial purposes for which they were constructed. The war ships of the Greeks were at first but row boats, with which they rushed upon the enemy and decided the battle by superior force and valor; in the course of time, this grew into the galley, which, being moved chiefly by oars, was of an entirely different form from the merchant ship.* Extreme narrowness, in connexion with great length, for the accommodation of many rowers, determined the form of the first, while the latter was constructed mainly with a view to capacity; hence the length of the galley was often six or eight times its breadth, whilst that of the merchantman was but four times; and hence, too, their distinctive names of *long ships* and *round ships*. The size of the earlier ships was necessarily inconsiderable, as they were drawn on

* For a more minute description of the galley, see article *Navy*.

shore at the termination of every voyage, and had but a single mast and sail of cloth, or at first of leather, managed with ropes of the same, or of bark, broom, or hemp. When, however, the keel was added, and the size increased, stranding became no longer practicable, and the anchor and cable were invented to confine the ship at a due distance from the land. At first, this useful machine was but a large stone; it was afterwards of wood and stone combined, and lastly of iron, having teeth; the largest anchor, called the *sacred*, was only cast in extremity In the progress of enlarging their ships, there is no doubt that the ancients attained, at length, a size quite equal to the most monstrous of modern times. Even deducting much from the recorded size of the cedar ship of Sesostris, and the Isis of Ptolemy Philopator; or from the more wonderful ship which Archimedes constructed at the order of Hiero, with its wood for fifty galleys; its banqueting rooms, galleries, stables, baths, fish-ponds; its floors inlaid with scenes from Homer's Iliad; its temple of Venus, and many other wonders, the subject of a whole book;—deducting much from this as fabulous, or even rejecting the whole, there remains a testimony to the occasionally enormous size of the ancient ships, which it is impossible to evade. This is the account of the ship in which the largest of the obelisks of Heliopolis was removed to Rome. We are told that Augustus, having removed two, dared not venture upon a third, of still vaster proportions, which stood before the temple of the sun. The enterprise, which was too great for Augustus, did not deter Constantine, who ordered the enormous block to be removed to Byzantium. He died before this was done, and his son Constantius enlarged upon the idea, and undertook to convey it to Rome. In this he succeeded; for the obelisk, though weighing fifteen hundred tons, was safely erected in the circus of the Vatican, where it still stands. We read that, besides the obelisk, the vessel carried eleven hundred and thirty-eight tons of pulse; this undoubtedly was all placed towards one end of the ship, to aid the decreasing size and weight of the upper part in balancing the base. Thus we have a Roman ship laden with twenty-six hundred tons; the Santissima Trinidad could have carried no more. These enormous productions, like the obelisks themselves, owed their existence not less to the hardy genius than the despotic institutions of the times; that they were unmanageable masses, and were regarded in those times as monsters, may be gathered, not merely from their names of Cyclades or Ætna, but from the single fact that a ship of only fifty-six tons is instanced, by Cicero, for her magnitude.

Such was naval architecture in the ages prior to the Gothic invasion, which drove this art, with every other, back into barbarity. We are told that the ships in which the Saxon pirates cruised in the German ocean, and invaded Britain, were made with a wooden keel, sides and upper works of wicker, and an exterior of hides. Though they may have improved somewhat on this primitive construction, yet it is certain that much of the previous advances in ship-building, the accumulations of many centuries, was forgotten, and to be rediscovered and tested anew. The brisk trade carried on in the Mediterranean, and the naval enterprises connected with the crusades, occasioned some improvements; yet the art advanced little, if at all, beyond the condition in which the Carthaginians left it. It was not until the middle of the fourteenth century that the inconsiderable war galleys of former times began to be superseded by larger vessels, in which oars were not entirely exploded, but which were chiefly moved by sails. These were crude enough; of crooked, half-moon shape, very high at the stem and stern; the planks nailed with iron, not set edge to edge and calked, but overlapping. They had usually but one mast, never more than two, with square sails attached to yards, and were only capable of advancing with a favorable wind. What a contrast between these rude machines and the noble production now called a ship, in which art and science are exhausted, the result of the gradually accumulating improvements of many generations! Sir Walter Raleigh well says, "Whoever was the first inventor of ships, every age has added somewhat to them; and in my time they have been greatly bettered. It is not long since striking the top-masts has been devised, together with the chain pump, which taketh up twice as much water as the old one: we have now studding sails, and the weighing of anchors with the capstan, moreover, we have fallen into consideration of the length of cables, and by it we resist the malice of the greatest winds; for true it is that the length of cable is the life of the ship."

Ship-building made, indeed, but a snail-paced progress until the introduction of the compass; and the application of astronomy to nautical pursuits at once set the mariner free from dependence on the land. The discovery of America resulted from these improvements and the inspiration of a single man. Thenceforward the mariner, thrown upon the wide ocean, was brought into contact with unknown perils, and to obviate them was led to untried expedients. The art has since strode forward with giant steps. To the Italians, Catalans, and Portuguese, belong most of the advances in the earlier days of its revival; the Spaniards followed up the discovery of the new world with a rapid improvement in the form and size of their ships, some of which, taken by the cruisers of Elizabeth, carried twenty hundred tons. In modern times, to the Spaniards and French belongs the entire credit of the progress which has been made in the theory of the art. Strange as it may seem, few improvements have originated with the greatest naval power of this or any other time. We have the authority of her own authors for the singular fact, that Britain has added little to the beauty, speed and excellence of ships, the wooden walls to which she is indebted for her security. In our own country, ship-building has made unprecedented progress; with, however, little aid from theoretical principles and abstract science. And hence it may well be questioned, whether a blind attachment to arithmetical results —modified, as they must be in practice, by many causes escaping calculation—does not often serve to sanction error. The example of our builders sufficiently proves that the artist, guided by experience and a practised eye, may dispense with elaborate theories; which, after all, are but the demonstration and systematic utterance of ideas which already exist in the untutored mind, and are daily acted upon. Experiment, though it may gain something from theory, is the only infallible guide.

In order to appreciate the extent and value of modern improvements, we have only to refer to the figure of the old ships, preserved in pictures of the most famous, and which may be found engraved in Charnock's valuable work on naval architecture. There we see the Great Harry, the wonder of the sixteenth century, a most terrific looking monster. Her bow and poop are of prodigious height, the signal lantern on the latter being nearly level with the round tops. She has an immense beak, with bow and stern balconies; six round towers at the angles of the poop, gangway, and forecastle, like the turrets of a chateau; four masts, with tops literally round, like inverted cones, and abundance of streamers from every spar. Even at the beginning of the seventeenth century, a vessel constructed by the duke of Northumberland, a schemer of that day, and then esteemed a miracle of perfection, measured fifty-four feet more on deck than at the keel, and was thirty-three feet high at the bow, fifty-one at the stern, and only twenty-eight in the middle. It is true that, very shortly after, a ship, launched in England, and called the Royal Prince, was very little different from those of our day, except that she was every where encrusted with carved work and gilding. Yet this is a solitary and uncopied example, for builders still clung pertinaciously to their inequalities, excrescences, and inflections, down to a late period of the last century. Indeed, in most nations of Europe, a high poop and inflected topside are still partially continued, though no longer to the extravagant degree which characterized the fashion at its height, when it was not unusual to see a ship taper upwards to half her extreme breadth. In the U. States alone is this custom entirely abolished, experience having shown us, what theory may also demonstrate, that, it is vicious in every respect; that, while nothing can be urged in favor of *tumbling in*,—as it is well called,—but that it brings the guns nearer the centre, and hinders the smoke of the lower from incommoding the upper decks, it adds greatly to the difficulty of draughting, and the expense of timber and construction, at the same time taking from the spaciousness of the upper deck, increasing the crankness of the hull and the insecurity of the masts by allowing no spread to the shrouds which support them. The long-established custom, too, of making the deck rise into a little mountain abaft, with the sole view of accommodating the commander and other great men with better quarters, has been as little respected in our republican country. We have reduced the whole topside to one uniform, unbroken level. Hence there are no obstructions to catch the wind; and, moreover, our vessels, being lighter at the extremities, pitch and perform their vertical motions with more ease. Hence, too, they are less exposed to camber, or become broken-backed,—a bending downwards of the extremities, which takes place in all vessels, more or less, at the moment of launching, and which is promoted when at anchor by the downward pressure of the cables, and at all times by the unsustained gravitation of the extremities, from their extreme sharpness, counteracted at the centre by the accumulating pressure of the resisting fluid in an upward direction. Thus, if we compare our ships with those of the last century, it will be seen that our improvements have consisted rather in taking away than in adding; and hence the latter, being of infinitely more intricate and involved construction, would also seem more difficult to devise. But experience shows that the simplest forms are not the most obvious to discovery; the Grecian style of art, the embodied idea of simplicity, was the fruit of an age of the highest refinement. What the Parthenon, or Maison Carrée, is in civil, the American schooner—a model peculiar to ourselves—is in naval architecture. She is of the simplest form, carrying the greatest breadth before the centre; the bow is very sharp, and the draught forward inconsiderable, but increasing towards the stern, where it becomes double. With great length and breadth, furnishing stability to bear a large surface of sail, and great depth to take hold of the water and prevent drifting, the burthen and consequent displacement of the schooner are inconsiderable, a large part of the bottom consisting of mere dead wood. Above water, her form is straight, low, and unbroken, offering no obstacle to the wind; the masts are long and tapered, and the sails, like the body, adapted to approach the wind, which the schooner does within forty or forty-five degrees, just twenty degrees nearer than the best equipped frigate; and she will sail in moderate weather as fleetly by the wind as from it. Unless, indeed, in gales, when her excessive speed, in conjunction with her wedge-like form, tends constantly, as she runs over the water, to raise the bow, and, by counterpoise, to depress the stern, to the danger of being overtaken by a pooping sea, the schooner going large is also victorious. It may be possible, in smooth water, with a vessel like the flying proa, or with a double boat of capacity to bear a single man, to surpass the speed of the schooner; but not with any vessel capable of traversing the sea, whether moved by natural or artificial agents. If it be considered that, in doubling the velocity of a body moving through a fluid, that body not only impinges on twice as many particles of the fluid, but on each of them with twice its former force, so that the resistance increases as the squares of the velocity, it may well be wondered how a speed of twelve, thirteen, and even fourteen sea miles the hour, has at length been attained.

Let us now proceed to the leading object of this article—to give an idea how, in our day, a ship is built, masted, rigged, and, finally, manœuvred; premising, simply, that it is not so much our desire to suggest new notions to those who are familiar with the subject, as, in accordance with the plan of this work, to convey a plain yet palpable idea to those to whom it is yet a mystery. The nicest and most difficult operation in ship-building consists in forming the draught. This is done, in Europe, by representing the form of the proposed ship in three distinct points of view. The first is called the *sheer plan*, and gives a complete view of the side: here are represented the length, depth, rake of the stem and stern; the wales, waterlines, decks, ports, masts and channels. The *body plan* shows the breadth, having described upon it every timber composing the frame of the ship; those running from the place of greatest breadth forward being described on the right hand; those running aft, on the left. Lastly, there is the *half breadth* or *horizontal plan*, showing the whole as if seen from above. To construct these draughts is exceedingly intricate and laborious; and, when finished, they convey no very clear idea of the intended ship. Our American builders have a different mode, very easy and satisfactory. They begin by making a wooden model of the proposed construction, the thing itself in miniature. Here the length, breadth, bulk, all the dimensions, and most minute inflexions of the whole, are seen at a single glance; the eye of the architect considers and reconsiders the adaptation of his model to the proposed object, dwells minutely on every part, and is thus able to correct the faults of his future ship, at the mere expense of a few chips, and while yet in embryo. We shall now state what are the essential qualities of a good ship and how they are attained. In a ship of war, the great object is speed, connected as far as may be, with ease of movements and capacity to accommodate her crew and carry a large supply of water and provisions. One point, moreover, is especially to be looked to; this is, that the ship float sufficiently high above water to run no risk of receiving seas in her lower ports in time of action. In order to be secure of this, the constructer must make an estimate of the whole weight of the ship, including body, spars, armament, men and munitions, and must so model the bottom that it will have displaced an equal weight of water when arrived at the desired depth. But in the merchantman, of which we now particularly speak, the primary consideration is, to attain the greatest capacity to carry cargo, combined, as far as possible, with safe and easy movements and rapid sailing. Now, the only way to combine these qualities with any success, is to imitate a form which has stood successfully the test of experience. This the builder does when he forms his model, guided by a tasteful and accurate eye, accustomed to notice the forms of vessels, and to mark particularly those which have been distinguished for their good qualities. In this way the American builders have succeeded in uniting these conflicting *desiderata* in a degree heretofore deemed impossible. Our packet ships carry enormously, while, at the same time, their extreme speed has reduced, by one half, the time of passage to Europe.

Among the admitted and well established principles of construction, is the leading one, that the greatest breadth must always be before the centre, and consequently the bow be more blunt than the stern. Some of our best builders place this point only one third of the length from the stem. Abstractly, it would seem most important that the bow should be adapted to divide the water with the least possible resistance; but experience has proved that it is far more essential to facilitate the escape of the displaced water along the side of the vessel; for when once a passage is opened for the ship, the fluid tends to reunite abaft the point of greatest breadth, where, instead of offering resistance, it presses the ship forward, in its endeavor to recover its level and fill the vacuum constantly opening behind her. Without recurring to sir Isaac Newton for the demonstration by which he has shown the mathematical truth of this principle, it may be sufficient to instance the fact, familiar to every seaman, that a log tows infinitely easier by its bigger end; nor do we find a trifling concurrent testimony in the forms of the finny tribe, which an unerring nature has adapted to divide the element they move in, by a shape gradually diminishing from head to tail. As it is, then, less essential that a ship should be sharp forward than aft, there is a further advantage in having the bow full towards the edge, that it may check her in descending into the waves, not abruptly, but gently; pitching being the most dangerous to hull and spars of all a vessel's movements. Though sharpness towards the sternpost is vitally essential to fast sailing, yet care must be taken to leave the buttock full towards the surface, in order to check the stern gently in descending, and, when scudding before a gale, to lift it in timely season, on the arrival of a sea. To hit the exact mean in this respect, so as not to retard the sailing, on the one hand, nor, on the other, to endanger the safety of the ship, requires all the skill of the architect. The midship floor should be nearly flat, in order to render tne ship buoyant and stable, or capable of bearing sail. It has been suggested that, since stability is in proportion to the length, an elongation of ships might be productive of increased speed; but, though they would thus be enabled to carry more sail without an essential increase of resistance, yet it may well be questioned whether this advantage would not be more than compensated by the corresponding increase of difficulty in turning, manœuvring, and rising to escape the breakings of the sea. There must also be a loss of compactness and strength proportionate to the increase of length, so that such vessels may be only adapted to the smoothness of a lake, or to the purposes of privateers and smugglers, who are desirous to procure rapid movements at whatever sacrifice. An increase of breadth may produce equal advantage without any sacrifice; for, inasmuch as stability increases as the cubes of the breadth, by adding one quarter to the breadth you gain a double stability, and, by consequence, a capacity to bear twice as much sail, with but one fourth of increase in the resistance. If it be remembered that the pressure of the water increases in descending from the surface, and that from this cause and the augmented difficulty of displacing it, the resistance offered to a ship in advancing, is three times as great at the lower as at the upper half of the immersed section, there can be no doubt that, if the law for measuring tonnage left his dimensions optional to the builder, the excess of depth now used would be transferred to the breadth. This being the case, it is deplorable that our government should so long have retained the old rule for the measurement of tonnage. This takes only into consideration the length and breadth at a single point, and, consequently, furnishes no standard whatever to judge of the capacity: hence, the merchant may have his ship made as deep as he pleases, and carry her breadth down to the floor itself, with out any increase of tonnage; and one of three hundred tons may thus be made to carry three times as much as another of equal measurement, formed for speed and beauty. Now, as a ship's port charges are determined by her registered tonnage, this is a direct bounty for building ugly and disproportioned ships, and an equally direct tax upon every digression from the model of a bread-tray. Great detriment to the appearance, speed and safety of our freighting ships results from this absurdity. But to return to our subject: an extreme in breadth, as in length or depth, is also dangerous. All extremes are here to be equally avoided. In civil architecture, an extravagance may be an eye-sore to men of taste, and render the projector ridiculous; but in naval, it too often proves fatal to human life.

Keeping, then, all these principles in view, as far as the tonnage law and the interests of the merchant permit, the builder proceeds to form the half model of his proposed ship, making it of the usual relative dimensions (a quarter of an inch to the foot). When satisfied with his performance, he takes asunder the horizontal sections of plank of which the block was originally formed, and he has before him all the waterlines in miniature. Having marked these on the floor of the moulding loft, he has all the necessary data, and proceeds to draught the entire frame. This done, pine moulds are formed of all the different parts, and the preparatory labors are complete. The scene now changes from the moulding loft to the ship yard, and the builder turns his attention to the materials. The timber most in request is oak, pine, chestnut, locust, cedar, elm, beech, &c. In the U. States, where we have abundant supplies, our constructers confine themselves almost entirely to live oak, pine, chestnut, locust, and cedar. The felling and choice of timber is in itself an art. The tree should be taken in the second era of its growth, when it has attained maturity, without approaching the period of decay. It should be killed, by removing a ring of bark, at the beginning of winter, when the sap is down, and left to dry and harden before it be cut down. When felled, the timber should be carefully stored in some dry, airy place, not much exposed to wind and sun. Painting should not be used, as, by sealing up the moisture in the wood, it rather facilitates than prevents decay; smearing with oil or tar, when well dried, is not so open to objection. In collecting ship timber, the greatest difficulty is found in procuring the crooked sticks, of which so many are required. In countries where timber has become an object of careful cultivation, this difficulty is anticipated by bending and confining the young trees to the desired form, or by cutting their young shoots at different periods, it having been observed that pollard trees are thus naturally produced by the browsing of cattle. The timber being collected, the workmen, with each his mould, proceed to fashion the pieces of wood assigned them, a due regard being had to careful conversion, that no stick is hewn contrary to its grain, so as to impair its strength, nor a larger one ever used than is necessary for the particular purpose; and, especially, that no bad or even indifferent wood be put in an important place, whence it could be removed only with difficulty.

The frame being now ready, we proceed to put it together. And first, the blocks are placed in the slip, and the keel laid upon them, the pieces being snugly scarfed together, and bolted; the keel is also scarfed to the stem forward, and the sternpost aft, the apron being raised with the stem, and the transoms and fashion pieces with the stern, if the vessel be not large. In laying down the keel, great care must be taken to preserve its perpendicularity, for which purpose it is pinned with treenails on either side of the blocks; also in raising and propping the stem and stern, and every piece of the frame. It is only by extreme attention that the builder avoids producing a crooked ship—an artificial monster of by no means rare occurrence. The floor timbers are now let into the keel, and every other one is there firmly bolted and riveted; they are crotches of trees formed by the trunk and one of the branches. Hence, in order to have equal strength on both sides, the butts should be placed alternately to right and left. As the floor timbers are the great connecting principles of the ship, to which they bear the same relation as the ribs to the body, too much care cannot be taken in selecting and securing them. The dead wood which fills up the angles at the stem and stern being got in, the kelson is laid upon the floor timbers, which let into it, until it rests upon the keel; its pieces are scarfed together, and to the stemson and sternson, which form its prolongation up the stem and stern. A bend usually consists, besides the floor timbers, of four futtocks, and one top timber, on each side; the first, or lower futtock, descends to the keel, beside the floor timbers, to which it is either bolted or pinned with treenails; the heel of the second rests upon the head of the floor, and bolts to the side of the first; and so on up to the top timber. Towards the stem and stern, the timbers do not meet the keel at right angles, but are inclined respectively forward and aft, as well to economize timber, by adapting the sticks to the inclination of the curves, as to augment the strength of parts much exposed to shocks from waves, rocks, and icebergs. The different portions of the frame are thus raised to their places by sheers and tackles, and then carefully shored and kept to the proper breadth by cross pales; ribands are also carried round the frame and bolted, and every precaution taken to confine each separate part to its particular position. The frame, being now complete, is dubbed smoothly off within and out, preparatory to planking. Sometimes the frame is made completely solid, and calked; in this case, the interior covering of plank is dispensed with, excepting a few strengthening streaks. This method has many advantages; a little additional width to the timbers brings them in contact, when, besides their being naked, and exposed to the air within, there is no space for the generation of those destructive gases which cause dry rot. In this case, salting, which makes a ship damp and unwholesome, is also avoided.

Having advanced thus far in the construction, the next care is to proceed with the planking, which does not merely serve to exclude the water, but to protect, connect, and bind harmoniously together, and is quite as essential as the skin to the body. Though apparently the most simple part of this wonderful machine, it is yet very difficult. Just as, in draughting the frame, it is necessary to have in view all the ports and scuppers to be carried clear of the timbers, it is essential, in planking, to have a preconcerted plan of the whole. The butts must not come near the scarfs of the keel, nor beside each other within or without, nor near the port-holes, nor opposite the pumps, lest the oakum be sucked out, but must be judiciously distributed, so as to impart equal strength to every portion. It is also one of the nicest arts of the builder, so to carry up his planking as with little waste to keep his seams always fair with the waterlines. When it is necessary to bend a plank at the bow or stern, it is heated by steam, and then forced into place with screws and levers. While this is going on, the beams are erected and pillared on the inside planking; the knees, which are crotches of timber or iron, confine them to the sides, also the transoms at the angles of the stern; in like manner the breast-hooks hold the stem to the planking and cant timbers of the bow. All this being attended to—the decks, plank sheer and rails finished, pumps placed, the bits for securing the cable, the capstan for raising the anchor, or, instead of these, the windlass, which, in merchantmen, more commonly serves the double purpose, the catheads for suspending the anchors, hatchways, mast holes, and a variety of other objects, which, though too many to enumerate, must by no means be forgotten—all being complete, the carpenter makes room for the calker, who carefully stops all the seams with oakum, and smears them with pitch. The scraper follows the calker, and, water having been pumped into the hold, to ascertain whether there is any leak, the bottom is ready to be sheathed or coppered, to protect it from the worms. Sheathing with wood is practised with iron-fastened ships, because copper would cause the bolt heads to corrode, if placed against them. It consists simply in covering the bottom with pine boards, sheets of paper soaked in hot pitch being placed between. In sheathing with copper, paper is also interposed. The plates overlap each other from bow to stern, to prevent their being stripped off by the continual shock of the passing water.

Our ship is now ready to be launched. This is the triumph of the builder. It is a nice operation, and is thus performed: If there be no ways in the slip (which is always an inclined plane descending into the water), they are immediately prepared. Two parallel platforms of solid timber are laid, one on each side of the keel, at the distance of a few feet from it, and extending from the stem as far below the stern as can be reached at low water. In this position they are carefully and firmly blocked and supported throughout their length. This double platform is called the *ways*. Upon it a second system of timber is loosely laid, and well greased between. The space from these last to the ship's bottom is every where filled with wedges of soft wood fashioned to its curves. The whole is called the *cradle*. The extremities of the cradle at the bow and stern are bound tightly across the keel with chains or ropes, and it is further kept from spreading by stout mouldings, which overlap the outer edges of the ways. When the rising tide has reached well up the ways, the wedges are simultaneously driven on every side, and the ship is raised from the blocks on which she has hitherto rested, and made to repose entirely on the cradle. The shores are all removed except the two spurs planted against the counters, and when the proper moment has arrived, these are also knocked away. The vessel, now abandoned to her weight, and encouraged by the yielding of the grease, begins slowly falling along the inclined plane; her motion becomes at each moment more and more rapid; the ways smoke and ignite with the pressure and velocity of the moving mass; and, in a twinkling, the noble fabric has abandoned for ever its unworthy union with the land, and entered, careering and joyous, upon its destined element. Among the ancients, a launch was ever an occasion of great festivity. The mariners were crowned with wreaths, and the ship bedecked with streamers and garlands. Safely afloat, she was purified with a lighted torch, an egg, and brimstone, and solemnly consecrated to the god whose image she bore. In our less poetic times, there is no lack of feasting and merriment, though, instead of the torch, the egg, and the brimstone, the oldest sailor breaks a bottle of rum (unless, indeed, he may have slily substituted water as more appropriate to a christening) over the head of the emblem—still, perchance, the image of father Neptune or Apollo.

The moment the ship leaves the land, the builders cease to be competent to her control, and she passes at once to the hands of the seamen. Before launching, the sailors stationed on deck hasten to attach a small cable to some object on shore, and have it clear on deck for veering out; a small anchor, with a second cable, is also prepared to drop on the bottom. By means of this apparatus, when the velocity gained in descending the ways has declined, the ship is gradually checked, and at length drawn alongside of the wharf, which is to be the scene of her equipment. And now, while she is yet light and high out of water, is the most favorable time for shipping the rudder. The rudder is a machine placed at the stern of the ship, by means of which she is steered and turned about at pleasure; for by inclining it to one side, the passage of the water is there strongly opposed, which, checking the advance of that side, gives the other a rotatory motion around it. It consists of two or more pieces of timber, of the thickness of the sternpost, of which, when not inclined, it seems a continuation. Narrow at the water's edge, where it might be endangered by the shock of a sea, and with it the very existence of the ship, it gradually increases in width towards the keel, where, from the nearly straight line in which the water reaches it, it exerts a more direct power to turn the ship. From forty to forty-five degrees is the most favorable angle for it to make with the keel, a greater serving rather to retard velocity than to cause rotation. To ship the rudder, it is only necessary to attach weights of iron to the heel, so that they may be loosed afterwards, and then sink it behind the sternpost, guiding it with ropes to the rudder port, through which it is hoisted by means of sheers and tackle placed above. The pintals having caught the hinges or gudgeons on the sternpost, it is abandoned to their support, while a chock, placed above the upper pintal, prevents it from being un hung. A tiller, with ropes and a wheel, to turn the rudder, completes the steering apparatus. Before raising the masts, it will now be well to take in ballast, especially if the ship be sharp. In every merchant vessel, it is a good rule never to be without a small quantity of copper dross or shingle. And next, the sheers are got ready. They are two stout spars, having the large ends at the sides of the ship, the small ones being lashed firmly together, and overhanging the middle of the deck. They are lashed and rigged with guys and gantlings before being raised; the ends rest on the tafferel, and the tackle to be used in hoisting in the mast, being taken forward to the windlass, serves to raise them. If it be necessary, a small pair of sheers are used to lift the ends until the angle be sufficiently open to give power to the purchase.* When erect, they are first placed over the hole for the mizzen-mast, and, if the ship be large, the deck should be shored up, to relieve it of the weight of the sheers and mast. Overhauling your tackle down to where the mast is on the wharf, or in the water, you lash the lower block securely to the front of the mast, just above the centre of gravity. With this, and a smaller tackle or gantling to the mast-head, the mast is taken up abaft the sheers, until high enough, then lowered to its place, the step being tarred, and a piece of money thrown in for luck. The sheers are easily moved forward by their guys and tackles, the shoes in which their heels rest being greased, to slip over the deck. In this way the main and fore-masts are likewise taken in, and, the sheers being

* There is a variety of forms of rigging—ships, brigs, brigantines, schooners, sloops,—but we shall only notice the most esteemed form, called the *ship par excellence*.

drooped over the bows, lastly, the bowsprit.

There are various rules for sparring ships, all founded upon their length and breadth, which are the main elements of stability. It may be sufficient to name one simple rule for the length of the main-mast, this being the prime mover: Add the length at the load water-line to the main breadth, and take the half sum as the length of the mast. The top-mast may be three fifths of the lower mast, the main yard seven eighths of the same, and so on upwards. The fore-mast may equal seven eighths of the main, with upper masts and yards in proportion. The mizzen-mast, if stepped on the kelson, is five sixths of the main-mast. The best rules on this subject are, perhaps, found in tables accurately prepared, in which the lengths of the masts are given in fractions of the ship's breadth, and those of the yards in fractions of the length. For the rest, it will be, in most cases, necessary to modify any given rule, in all instances, with immediate reference to the particular model of the ship, and to the uses for which she is destined. A vessel of war will have spars to spread sail to the full extent of her stability, while a merchantman will be sparred with reference to the limited force of her crew. As for the disputed advantages of long or short lower-masts, we agree entirely with sir Cloudesly Shovel, who says, with equal wit and wisdom, "I mightily esteem short lower-masts; for, the shorter they are, the longer they will stand." With long top-masts you may make up an equal or even greater surface of canvass, far more advantageously spread, and more manageable, while it is procured at less expense, and with less weight aloft. It would be, moreover, an advantageous improvement in merchant ships, not sparred to the extent of their capacity, to make the fore and main-masts, in all cases, of equal dimensions. With improved appearance, they would have all the respective spars and sails, except the courses, answering equally for both masts. This would enable them to go to sea with fewer spare ones, or to derive more advantage from the usual number. In small ships, all the spars are of single sticks of pine timber, which, for equal contents, are always stronger; but, for ships above six or seven hundred tons, it is impossible to procure single trees sufficiently large; and then it becomes necessary to resort to made masts (so called), which are of oak and pine, very artificially put together, and bound with stout hoops of iron.

The spars of a ship are not abandoned to their own unsupported strength, but are sustained by what is called the *standing rigging*. This consists, for the bowsprit, of gammoning and bob-stays, confining it down to the stem, and shrouds, which sustain the immense lateral pressure which it endures when on a wind. The jib-boom and flying-jib-boom are, in like manner, supported by means of martingales and guys. The fore-mast is supported by three or four pairs of shrouds on either side, which set up to the channels, and by two stays led forward to the bowsprit. The fore-top-mast is supported by shrouds setting up in the top, back-stays descending to the channels, and stays leading to the bowsprit end. The top-gallant and royal-masts have also their shrouds setting up through the cross-trees, their back-stays descending to the channels, and their stays leading to the jib and flying-jib-booms. In like manner are the main and mizzen-masts supported, except that the main-stays set up on deck beside the heel of the bowsprit, the main-top-mast-stays at the head of the fore-mast, the main-top-gallant-stay to the fore-top-mast-head, and main-royal-stay to the fore-top-gallant-mast-head. The mizzen-stay also sets up beside the main-mast, and the same in ascending. The running rigging consists of the tacks and sheets that serve to spread the sails, the halyards, traces, lifts, clewlines, and all other ropes used in making, taking in, or manœuvring the sails.

The sails of a ship are square sails bent to the yards, and fore and aft sails traversing on stays or bent to gaffs. Let us describe an entire suit, beginning forward: On the extremity of the bowsprit is the flying-jib, a three-cornered sail, which goes from the end of its boom upward along its stay, leading to the fore-top-gallant-mast-head, and confined to the stay by rings of wood or iron, called *hanks*. It is hoisted by means of halyards, hauled down by a downhaul; and, when up, is trimmed to hold the wind by a sheet leading to the forecastle. The jib, which leads from its boom to the fore-top-mast-head, is of similar form, and so is the fore-top-mast-stay-sail, running from the bowsprit end towards the mast head. On the fore-mast we have the fore sail, bent to the fore-yard, and spread at the foot by means of tacks and sheets; above it, the fore-top-sail, bent to the top-sail-yard, by means of which it is hoisted aloft, while its lower corners are spread to the extremities of the fore-yard; next the top-gallant-sail, bent to its yard, and sheeting home to the top-sail-yard; and so with the royal and sky-sail. All these sails are turned at pleasure, to be presented to the wind, by means of braces attached to their yard-arm, and leading to the main-mast. The main-mast is furnished with a similar suit of sails, somewhat larger; the mizzen, also, though smaller than either; instead of a square-sail on the lower mast, it has a gaff-sail, hoisting up and down abaft the mast. Some ships have similar gaff-sails on the fore and main-masts, which are found of great use in gales of wind, as a substitute for storm stay-sails. Most carry, also, light stay-sails between the masts; but they are very troublesome, and worse than useless. Studding-sails, or *wings*, as they are better called by the Spaniards, spread without the square-sails when going large, and are very useful. The perfection of equipping a ship with spars, rigging and sails, consists in so disposing them, that, in a whole-sail breeze, the centre of effort of all the sails will be in the same line with the ship's centre of rotation; or that the efforts of the forward and after sails to turn the ship will be so exactly balanced as not to require any continued assistance from the rudder in either direction; for this, while it impedes her progress, does not leave the entire force of the rudder disposable, when necessary to turn. Of the two evils, however, seamen have more patience with a ship disposed to approach the wind, than with one needing the continued action of the helm to keep her from falling off. The French helmsmen well characterize these two qualities by calling a vessel which has the first *ardent*, the latter *cowardly*. Like, however, cool courage, between impetuosity and cowardice, a midship helm is still the golden mean.

Our ship is now completely equipped, and ready to receive cargo. Those articles with which a ship may be filled full are stowed with a single view to economy of space. Some, as cotton, require ballast; others, as staves, sugar and fluids, require none. When the articles are heavy and light, the heavier are placed nearest the bottom, to increase the ship's stability. When, however, all are heavy, there may be danger of making a ship too stiff; so that, not being balanced, she will roll violently, and, perchance, risk the fracture of a mast, or even spring a leak. To obviate this danger, the cargo should be raised: if iron, some should be stowed between decks; if coal or salt, it may be heaped up in the centre, taking care to secure it against shifting, should the ship be knocked down by a sea or squall. Heavy articles should never be placed towards the extremities, lest they promote pitching. In all cases, care must be taken to preserve the trim of the ship—that just proportion between her draught forward and aft, which the estimate of the builder, or, when a voyage has been made, experience itself, has determined to be most favorable to rapid sailing.

The ship, being ready for sea, is usually dropped into the stream or roadstead. There she is confined by an anchor and cable passing through the hawse-hole at the bow, and clinched round the bits or windlass. As a vessel thus anchored is free to swing round at the will of wind and tide, she is liable to wind her cable round the anchor, and thereby entangle and change the position of its flukes so as to incapacitate it for holding her. To obviate this inconvenience, it is usual to moor with two anchors, one placed in the direction of the flood, the other of the ebb tide. If there be no tides, the anchors are opposed to the prevailing winds, the heaviest being towards the most windy quarter. Should a gale occur while thus moored, by veering out the cable which holds the ship, both may be brought ahead to act in concurrence. Care must ever be taken to keep the hawse clear for thus veering, that is, to prevent the ship from twisting her cables, by turning always the same way; or, when this unavoidably occurs, the hawse must be cleared by unbinding one of the cables, and carrying it round the other beneath the bow, until the turns be removed.

When about to sail, the hatches are carefully calked down and tarpaulined, except those necessary for the ascent and descent of the crew, and the boats are stowed. You may now unmoor, preparing the first anchor for letting go before taking up the second. If tending to the tide, with the wind fair to pursue your course, the last anchor may also be taken up and stowed before making sail. If, however, as is usual, your ship lie head to wind, stop heaving in when the cable is short, and proceed to make sail. The wind being moderate, the courses, top-sails, top-gallant-sails, jib and spanker may be loosed together; the top-sails and top-gallant-sails are sheeted home and hoisted up; and the other sails hang ready to be called into action whenever necessary. The yards are now braced ready to cant the ship. If you wish her to go to the right, the head yards are braced with their right sides forward, and the after yards the contrary way. Hence the wind, striking the fore sails obliquely on the left, tends to force them to the right; and, on the contrary, the after sails, being acted upon in an opposite direction, are forced to the left; but the fore sails are forward of the centre of rotation, while the after sails are abaft it; consequently the efforts which they respectively exert will tend, the first to force the ship's head to the right hand, the others the stern to the left. The sails thus trimmed, now heave up the anchor, profiting of the trifling advance through the water to turn the ship's head still more, and make the angle of the wind with the keel more open, by the action of the rudder. As soon as the anchor trips, and the wind begins to force the ship sternward, shift the rudder to the opposite side, that, by offering an obstacle on the left of the ship, the right side may turn backward round it more rapidly. This action of the rudder, in conjunction with the sustained effort of the sails to turn the ship to the right, and, presently, the addition of the jib, will gradually make the wind more and more open on the left bow, until at length it becomes sufficiently so to fill the after sails, which have hitherto lain aback. When this is the case, the fore yards are braced full, the spanker and courses set, and the ship immediately begins advancing. This mode of weighing is practised where there are other ships or a shore to leeward; otherwise it is more common not to hoist the jib, or fill the fore sails, until the anchor is raised to the cat-head. The ship being under weigh, the time occupied in clearing the harbor is employed in stowing the anchors, unbending the cables, if the nature of the coast render it safe to do so, applying mats to the rigging and yards, to prevent chafing, and in securing the boats, water-casks, and whatever other movable objects might be in danger of starting by the pitching and rolling of the ship.

Our ship is now at sea, and it only remains to us briefly to explain the manner in which she is propelled and governed, and made obedient to her crew. There is no difficulty in conceiving how a ship may be made to move before the wind through a quiescent fluid like the sea. Let us suppose one at rest in a perfect calm, and equally pressed on every side by the gravitating action of the same fluid: she is maintained in equilibrio. But, by and by, a wind rising behind her, strikes her sails perpendicularly, and exerts a pressure in a single direction. As, however, the sails are attached to spars, and these in turn to the ship, it is evident that they cannot obey the impulse independently of the ship, but that all must move in unison; and the ship, being before pressed by the water equally, and maintained in quiescence, requires but a slight additional pressure in any direction to destroy her equilibrium. This pressure is abundantly supplied by the air of our atmosphere; for, though little more than a thousandth part the density of the sea, it may receive a velocity enabling it to strike the sails with its particles in such quick succession as to force the ship forward with great rapidity, and, if the resistance of the water check her escape before it, may even act with sufficient power to blow away the strongest sails, or even tear the masts out. Thus a beneficent Nature, in providing an element essential to our existence, by subjecting it to laws requisite for its healthy preservation, and forming a necessary link in the universal economy, has at the same time supplied an ever-active agent, which the ingenuity of man—an emanation of the same great Intelligence—has rendered subservient to the noblest purposes.

Conceiving, now, how it is possible for a ship to move freely before the wind, with a velocity determined by the force of that wind, the quantity of sail exposed to it, and the adaptation of her form to divide the sustaining fluid with the least resistance, we will now show how it is also possible for her to move in directions other than directly before the wind, and even to approach it. Let us suppose that the wind, at first dead aft, gradually veers towards the side, until it blows at an angle of forty-five degrees with the keel. If, with the wind thus blowing, I still preserve my sails braced perpendicularly to the keel, it must necessarily strike their surfaces obliquely, dividing itself into two forces, one passing off to leeward, the other exerting itself in the direction of the keel, and therefore tending to propel her forward. If, however, in order to expose my sails more fairly to the wind, I brace them forward until it becomes again perpendicular to their surfaces, the action of the wind on the sails is simple, but that of the sails on the ship is, in turn, compound, subdividing itself into two forces; one acting to drive her to leeward in a direction perpendicular to the keel; the other, forward in a line with it. If, now, the ship were of a figure to move with equal freedom in any direction—round, for instance—it is evident that she would assume a mean motion between these two forces; but, being so formed as to divide the water with infinitely greater difficulty sidewise than forwards, the force exerting itself perpendicularly to the keel is neutralized, whilst that in a line with it, encountering an inferior resistance, compels the vessel to advance. We will next suppose the wind to have drawn forward until perpendicular to the course. The sails, being trimmed forward, so as to keep full, are struck obliquely, and, if the ship were again free to move in any direction, would impel her in a course perpendicular to its surface; but the portion of this force tending to drive the ship to leeward, being again encountered by the lateral pressure, is almost balanced; while, on the contrary, she freely obeys the force tending to propel her forward. Lastly, let us consider the situation of our ship when the wind gets before the beam, so as to make an angle of less than ninety degrees with the course. It is evident that, if she still continue to advance, it must be towards the wind: this seeming paradox of a vessel approaching the wind by the very effort of that wind to drive it away, will still appear clear by the application of the same principles. To meet the emergency, let us now suppose the yards braced forward, until they make an angle of only thirty degrees with the keel; the wind, being thirty farther aft, will make an angle of sixty with the keel. In this position, the wind will strike obliquely on the after side of the sails; and though the greater part of the force passes off to leeward, there is still a partial effort to drive the sails in a direction perpendicular to their surface. This effort subdivides into two forces; one perpendicular to the keel, the other in a line with it: the first is nearly overcome by the lateral resistance; the second, encountering less, causes the ship to advance, with a velocity proportioned to the smallness of the angle of incidence, and the disadvantageous application of the propelling power.

From what has been here stated, it would seem that, in theory, the situation of the wind most favorable to propelling a ship, is when it acts perpendicularly to the sails, and they in turn to the keel; that is, when dead aft. In gales of wind, this is likewise true in practice; but in moderate weather, a ship will sail faster with the wind on the quarter, or even abeam, for then the sails do not mask each other, but all receive the wind without interruption. On this account they more than make up the disadvantages of the unfavorable angle; of having the sails transported to leeward, by reason of which that side tends to advance faster than the other, to the disordering of the steerage; of the ship's heeling, and receiving the wind obliquely in the vertical direction; and, finally, of making her sail partially on one side, instead of on an even keel, as she is designed to do. On this account our sharp schooners will sail nearly or quite as fast on a wind as off it, the sea being smooth and wind light; for whilst all their sails act advantageously, by approaching the wind, they add to its force, instead of diminishing it, as when running from it. In square-rigged ships, bracing the yards correctly is one of the nicest points of seamanship: in general, the nearer the yards approach to being perpendicular to the keel, consistently with keeping the sails full, the greater will be the velocity.

But to return to our ship: It may chance that the wind does not stop at the exact point which would enable her, close-hauled, barely to go her course, but even heads her off so far that she can no longer approach it nearer than a right angle. It is evident, now, that she is gaining nothing; but since she can sail within sixty degrees of the wind, by closing with it on the other side, she may approach within thirty degrees of the desired course. Hence it becomes essential to change sides. There are two ways of performing this evolution: the first consists in turning round towards the wind, and is called *tacking;* the second in turning before it, and is called *veering*. As the first requires the ship to turn a much smaller segment of a circle, and moreover maintains her head towards the desired course, so that all her progress during the evolution is gain, and finally, since it is performed with greater ease and expedition, it is always preferred when practicable. To tack, the crew are all stationed at the tacks, sheets, braces, and bowlines, ready to change the position of the sails. The ship being already close to the wind, the helm is gradually eased down, so that the rudder may not exert its full force until she begins to turn, nor act suddenly to check the headway, so essential to the success of the evolution; at the same time, the head sheets are flown, so as to cause the sails before the centre of rotation to shake, and lose their power of balancing the after ones. As the ship approaches the wind, the spanker is drawn gradually from the lee side towards the centre, that it may keep full, and, by its action so near the stern, continue promoting the rotation. As soon as the sails reach the direction of the wind, and cease to draw, the corners of the courses are drawn up, and the tacks and sheets overhauled, ready to swing the yards. After a while, the sails catch aback, and the fore sails, soon masking the after ones, act with a powerful lever to turn the bow. At length, having come head to wind, without loss of headway, and the evolution being certain, the after yards are swung round, ready to receive the wind on the opposite side; which operation is then more easily performed, from the sails being becalmed by the fore ones. Lastly, when the after sails are filled by the wind, the head yards are also braced round to receive its impulse, and the ship at once recovers headway. Should she gather sternway before the sails become full on the new tack, the helm is shifted, that its action in a backward direction, instead of checking, may aid the rotation. There may, however, be occasions in which it is impossible to tack, either because the wind is not of sufficient force, or else so strong as to render it dangerous; then veering is resorted to. To veer, we put the helm hard up, brail the spanker, and shiver the after sails: in this situation the pressure of the head sails, not being balanced by the after ones, tends, in conjunction with the rudder, forcibly to turn the ship. As she falls off, the after sails are still kept shivering until braced sharp on the opposite tack; when before the wind, the spanker is set to aid the after yards and helm in bringing her to; the fore sails are then squared, and gradually braced forward until the ship be by the wind again.

Thus easily is a ship manœuvred in fine weather. Not unfrequently, however, a gale comes to disturb the peaceful course of the mariner, and call forth all his exertions. Let us suppose that, whilst our ship is contending against the head wind, the misfortune is augmented by its gradual increase. Shortening sail becomes necessary, and is determined by two leading considerations—the stability of the ship, and the strength of her masts: it is to diminish the careening of the one, and avoid endangering the other, that the surface spread to the wind is reduced. In shortening sail, we always begin with the highest and lightest sails, descending gradually, and keeping pace, in an inverse ratio, with the increase of wind. The sails do not, however, come in uniformly in the direction of the length; but the after sails most rapidly; because, as the wind increases, the energy which it exerts in a forward direction upon the masts, tends, with a powerful lever, to depress the bow and raise the stern; hence the latter drifts more easily to leeward, thereby bringing the bow towards the wind; this effort is also promoted by the action of the sails passing farther to leeward, and by the ship ceasing to sail on an even keel. From all these reasons, the more the wind increases, the more she tends to come to; so, to avoid a constant recurrence to the action of the rudder, it becomes necessary to shorten sail faster aft than forward; taking in the mizzen-top-gallant-sail, and even the spanker, before the fore and main-top-gallant-sails: for the same reason, when it becomes necessary to reef, it is not unusual to begin with the mizzen-top-sail. Reefing consists in binding a portion of the sails to their respective yards, so as to reduce the surface. To reef the top-sails, we clew the yards down, haul up the sides of the sails by means of reef-tackles, and brace the yards to the wind, until the sails shiver and spill; then the men go out on the yard, and, by means of the earings and reef-points, securely bind the requisite portion. When the top-sails are double-reefed, it is time for the jib to come in to relieve the jib-boom and fore-top-mast of the pressure: to counterbalance the loss of this head sail, the mizzen-top-sail may be furled. When the top-sails are close-reefed, the main-sail is either reefed or furled. As the gale increases, furl the fore-top-sail; taking care to draw up the weather clew first, that the sail may not be in danger of shaking and blowing away. Our ship is now under reefed fore-sail, main-top-sail close-reefed, fore-top-mast-stay-sail, and storm stay-sails; these are stout triangular sails, running in the direction of the fore, main, and mizzen-stays; they are often advantageously replaced by gaff-sails, which are similar to the spanker. Should it blow still harder, it may be necessary to take in the fore sail, replace the fore-top-mast by the storm stay-sail, and even furl the main-top-sail. The ship now drifts much, and, tending to fall off, from her greater draught abaft, and consequent resistance of the water, will require the reefed spanker, and even the continued assistance of the rudder, to keep her to: the helm being kept constantly hard down, she is said to *lie to*. This is the way in which most ships make the best weather; some, however, tend so much to fall off into the trough of the sea, as to be in perpetual risk of being boarded by the waves (which wash the boats and other movables loose, sweep the crew overboard, to creep up the side again by the channels, or find a watery grave), and, if the hatches be not well secured, of having her existence fatally endangered. In this case, it may become necessary to bear up and scud. To do this with least risk, it is necessary to show the head of the fore-top-mast-stay-sail, or part of the fore-sail or fore-top-sail; taking advantage of a momentary lull and smoothness of the sea to bear away. The after sails are taken in on putting up the helm, and it may even be necessary to cut away the mizzen-mast. When before the wind, sufficient sail must be spread to keep the ship before the waves, that they may not overtake and strike her with too much force; the main-top-sail, from its height, is never becalmed by the sea, and is therefore a good sail to scud under. At such a season, special care must be taken to provide for the security of guns, boats, and other movables, liable to tear themselves loose; also that the pump-well be sounded at short intervals, to have timely notice of a leak. Too often the ship yields to the fury of the elements, disappearing for ever, with all her treasures of property and of life; oftener, however, the elements become weary with their own violence, and man remains triumphant; the gale abates; the mariners, all alacrity, send up the masts and yards which they had housed and taken down on the approach of the tempest; the reefs are all shaken out, and sail is added, to keep the ship from laboring in the still raging waves. Hope mounts with the ascending canvass: and now the wind, become less wayward, again permits us to turn the prow towards the haven whither we would arrive: the wings, whose spreading and furling are ever the signal to the mariner of joy or of sorrow, are once more wide extended; every spot is white with the bellying canvass, the sea foams beneath the bow, and we bound merrily towards the land.

And are we not justified in expressing our admiration at this great achievement of man—the production of this wonderful machine—the most complicated, most perfect, sublimest of all the works of art? If it be well said that man is the noblest work of God, it may with equal truth be asserted that the ship is the noblest work of man. Our language has indeed done well in awarding to her the honors of personification.* It were a vain task to attempt enumerating the various geometrical problems involved in her design, or the multiplied mechanical principles combined in her construction. Let us only, forgetting all we know, endeavor for a moment to realize the immeasurable distance and difficulties between the trees growing in the forest, the iron and copper buried deep in the bowels of the earth, the hemp waving in the fields, the tar sealed up in its timber, and the actual achievement of the sailing ship! Yet a very short time—a single month—suffices to transform these rude productions into the magnificent machine, which, notwithstanding its mountain form, obeys each command of the mariner; goes from the wind, towards it, halts, or redoubles its velocity, obedient to his voice; in which he launches boldly forth amid the horrors of a troubled ocean; braves them successfully, conducted by the inspirations of a sublime philosophy; attains the most distant shores; accomplishes his purpose, and returns, enriched, enlightened and triumphant, to his home. (For the sequel of this subject, see *Navigation*, and *Navy*.)

Ship of Fools. (See *Brandt*.)

Shiraz. (See *Schiraz*.)

Shire; a Saxon word, signifying *division;* the old Saxon name for the larger districts into which England was divided, and which has been, in a great measure, superseded by the Latin term *county*. (See *County*.) Hence the name *sheriff* (q. v.), given to the chief officer of the

* It is a peculiarity of the English language to apply the feminine pronouns to a vessel; in fact, the illiterate in England and America have a peculiar inclination to give the feminine gender to inanimate objects. Carpenters, moving a large piece of timber, will say, Here *she* comes; a sailor calls his watch *she*. The navy, in England, being a subject of universal interest and pride, peculiarities in the language of seamen would be more likely to come into general use, than the cant phrases of other classes. The mower calls his scythe *she;* but this was never admitted into good language. Mr. Cobbett, in his Grammar of the English Language, Letter V, says—"It is curious to observe that country laborers give the feminine appellations to those things only which are more closely identified with themselves, and by the qualities and condition of which their own efforts and their character as workmen are affected. The mower calls his scythe *she;* the plough man calls his plough *she;* but a prong, or a shovel, or a harrow, which passes promiscuously from hand to hand, and which is appropriated to no particular laborer, is called *he*," &c. The Scotch Highlanders even use the feminine pronoun for male persons, as our readers know from Scott's novels.

shire, and *shire-gemote* (Saxon, *gemote*, meeting), to the sheriff's tourn or county court. (See *Courts*.) The English county members of the house of commons are called *knights of the shire*. In the U. States, the word is little used, except in composition; as *shire-town*, the capital of the county.

SHIRLEY, James, a poet and dramatic writer, was born in London about 1594, was educated at Merchant Tailors' school, and thence removed to St. John's college, Oxford. He became a favorite with doctor Laud, who discountenanced his entry into the church, on account of a large mole upon his cheek, which he deemed a disqualification by deformity, according to the canons. On removing to Cambridge, he met with no difficulty on this score, and obtained a curacy near St. Alban's. He soon after went over to the church of Rome, and, giving up his curacy, sought to establish a grammar-school in the same town. Failing in this endeavor, he removed to London, became a writer for the stage, and acquired a reputation which caused him to be taken into the service of queen Henrietta Maria. His first comedy is dated 1629, and he wrote nine or ten between that year and 1637, when he accompanied the earl of Kildare to Ireland. He returned the following year, and when the civil war broke out, he left London, with his wife and family; and, being invited by the earl of Newcastle, he accompanied that nobleman to the wars. On the decline of the king's cause, he returned to London, and, the acting of plays being prohibited, resumed his school. In 1666, he was forced, with his wife, by the great fire, from his house in St. Giles's parish; and, being extremely affected by the loss and terror that the fire occasioned, they both died, Oct. 29, within twenty-four hours. Besides thirty-seven tragedies and comedies, he published a volume of poems, some specimens of which may be found in Ellis's Collection.

SHISHAC or SESAC; an Egyptian king, mentioned by the Hebrew writers, who made an incursion into Judea in the reign of Jeroboam, and pillaged the temple (about B. C. 791). He has been commonly supposed to be the same as Sesostris (q. v.), but Champollion has proved (*Précis du Système hiéroglyphique*, pp. 255—257) that he is the Sesonchis of the Greeks, or Sheshonk; and an inscription at Karnac represents him as carrying into captivity the king of the Jews.

SHUMLA. (See *Choumla*.)

SHOCK. (See *Choc*.)

SHORE, Jane; the wife of a rich goldsmith of London, in the fifteenth century, and mistress of Edward IV, whose favor, which she entirely possessed, she never abused to any man's hurt, but often employed to many a man's relief. After the death of Edward, in 1482, she seems to have been the paramour of lord Hastings. (See *Edward IV*.) Richard III (q. v.), partly to revive among the citizens the memory of his brother's licentiousness, and partly on account of her connexion with Hastings, whom he accused of being "the chief abettor of that witch Shore," determined to expose her to public ignominy. Laying bare his arm, all shrivelled and decayed from his birth, he declared before the council, that the incantations and witchcraft of Jane Shore and her associates had reduced him to that condition. He then had her summoned to answer against a charge of sorcery; but, unable to effect his purpose in this manner, he directed her to be tried for adultery and lewdness by the spiritual court, and she was obliged to do penance in a white sheet, at St. Paul's, before the whole people. She is supposed to have died at an advanced age in the reign of Henry VIII. Her story has been consecrated by the muse of Shakspeare (Richard III) and Rowe, and has been introduced upon the French stage, in the tragedies of Liadières (Jane Shore, 1824) and Lemercier (*Richard III et Jane Shore*).

SHORT-HAND. (See *Stenography*.)

SHORT-SIGHTEDNESS. (See *Optics*, head *Vision*.)

SHOT; a missive weapon, discharged by the force of ignited powder from a fire-arm in battle. Of these there are various kinds. Round-shot or bullets are balls or globes of iron, whose weight is in proportion to the bore of the cannon. Double-headed, or bar-shot, are formed of a bar, with a round head at each end, which fits the muzzle of the cannon. The middle is sometimes filled with a composition, and the whole covered with linen dipped in brimstone, so that the cannon, in firing, inflames the combustibles or composition of this ball, which sets fire to the sails of the enemy. One of the heads of this ball has a hole to receive a fuse, which, communicating with the charge of the cannon, sets fire to the bullet. Chain-shot consist of two balls chained together, being principally designed to annoy the enemy by cutting sails, rigging, &c. Grape-shot is a combination of balls strongly corded in canvass upon an iron bottom, so as to form a sort of cylinder, whose diameter is equal to that of the ball which is adapted to the cannon. Case-shot, or canister-shot, are composed of a great number of small bullets, put into a cylindrical tin box. They are principally used, when very near, to clear the decks of the enemy. Besides these, there are others of a more pernicious kind, used by privateers, pirates, &c.; such are langrage-shot, star-shot, fire-arrows, &c. Star-shot consist of four pieces of iron, whose bases, when separate, form the quadrant of a circle; so that the whole, being joined, forms a cylinder equal to the shot of the cannon. Each of these pieces is furnished with an iron bar, the extremity of which is attached to a sort of link, as keys are strung upon a ring. Being discharged from the gun, the four branches or arms extend every way from the link in the centre. These are chiefly intended to destroy the sails or rigging; but their flight and execution are very precarious at any considerable distance.

Shrew-Mole (*scalops*, Cuv.); head elongated and terminating in an extended and cartilaginous snout, which is very flexible; eyes exceedingly small, and entirely concealed by the hair, requiring the closest attention for their detection. The auricle is entirely wanting, and the integument of the head nearly covers the tube leading to the internal ear. The feet are very short, and five-toed; the fore feet terminate in a remarkably large hand, of which the fingers are armed with long, flat and linear nails. The hind feet are very delicate, and the toes are provided with small hooked nails. When at rest, the shrew-mole resembles a small stuffed sack. This animal is found abundantly in North America, from Canada to Virginia. He burrows with great quickness. His soft and polished fur, preventing friction, tends to facilitate his subterranean march. Numerous galleries, communicating with each other, enable the animal to travel in various directions without coming to the surface. Under ordinary circumstances, the burrows are simply oval-arched galleries, running forward, either straight or in gentle curvatures; sometimes only one to three inches deep, at other times much deeper. His favorite food is the earth-worm; and he destroys grubs and insects of various kinds in great quantities. In the winter, he burrows near streams, where the ground is not so deeply frozen. The shrew-mole is not only able to make his way rapidly under ground, but can run quite fast when on the surface. If you attempt to draw him, by his posterior extremities, out of his hole, he clings by his fore paws with great force; and, when finally dragged out, frequently inflicts a severe bite on his disturber. Shrew-moles are most active early in the morning and at mid-day. The precision with which these creatures daily come to the surface at twelve o'clock, is remarkable. The shrew-mole is covered with a bright glossy fur, about half an inch in length, and of a bright plumbeous color, very closely set, and in all parts directed backward. The whole fore arm is concealed by the skin, leaving the broadly expanded palm, with its fore nails, projecting from the fore part of the body in an awkward manner, if compared with the anterior extremity of other animals. The snout is composed of a cartilage, articulated with the premaxillary bones, and is moved in various directions, by muscles situated on the side of the head; it is naked, and of a very light flesh-color. The mouth is large, and the size of the tongue considerable. The eyes are difficult to be discovered externally, without a good glass. The eyeballs are less in size than a grain of mustard seed. The aperture of the eye-lids will about allow the passage of an ordinary sized human hair. The vision of this animal seems to be barely sufficient to give him an intimation of light, without allowing him to distinguish the figures of bodies. His whole structure seems to be studied with a view to facilitate his progress under the earth. The total length, from the point of the snout to the beginning of the tail, is five inches, and the tail is one inch long; the longest fur on the body, half an inch in length. A living specimen, kept for many weeks in a room, spent the greater part of the day in sleep, and was very active at night. He could not see in any light, as he uniformly ran his nose with some violence against every obstacle several times, before he learned to avoid those that were permanent. (See Godman's *American Natural History*, from which the above account is abridged.)

Shrewsbury; a market town and borough of England, in the county of Salop, and the chief town in the county, situated on the Severn. There is a very fine public walk, called the Quarry, along the banks of the Severn. The streets are, many of them, steep and narrow, and all indifferently paved. The public buildings deserve attention, both for their architecture and antiquity. The ruins of the castle consist of two round towers and a curtain, the work of Edward I; the walls of the inner court; and the great arch of the interior gateway. There are six churches, a Roman Catholic chapel, and meeting-houses for Presbyterians, Unitarians, Baptists, Methodists and Quakers. The charitable institutions of Shrewsbury are the infirmary, the house of industry, an hospital, &c. In the suburb called the abbey Foregate are the remains of the abbey dedicated to St. Peter, at one time a great resort of people from all parts of the kingdom, to the shrine of St. Winefrid. Besides the abbey, Shrewsbury had formerly three convents and five chapels. Shrewsbury is a place of considerable trade. Flannels used to be the staple articles, and a coarse kind of woollen cloth, made in Montgomeryshire, called *Welsh webs*. Some manufactures are also carried on in the town, viz. of linen yarn, porter, &c. It is famous for its excellent bran, which is sent to various parts of the kingdom. It sends two members to parliament. Its origin is referred to the fifth century, when the Britons are thought to have established themselves here. It was often visited by the English monarchs, and became the scene of many military events. About two miles from the town was fought the battle of Shrewsbury, in which Henry V, then prince of Wales, first distinguished himself in the field, and Hotspur was slain. At the entrance of the town is a column of freestone, to commemorate the military achievements of lord Hill. Population in 1831, 16,055. Forty miles west of Lichfield.

Shrimp (*crangon*); a small, crustaceous animal, allied to the lobster and craw-fish, which frequents shallow waters along the sea-coast. In shape, it resembles these animals, but is more elongated in proportion, and is destitute of the large anterior claws; and it is distinguished from the prawn by the absence of the long, anterior, serrated spine. The term is sometimes, but improperly, applied to the species of *gammarus*, which are much more abundant along our coasts; but these are readily distinguished by the compressed form of their bodies. The shrimp has ten feet; the tail is as long as the body, and terminated at the extremity with scale-like appendages, which unfold somewhat in the manner of a fan. During life, the body is semi-transparent, and so much resembles sea-water that the animal is distinguished with difficulty. Its ordinary motion consists of leaps. It is abundant in sandy places, and furnishes nutriment to great numbers of fishes, aquatic birds, &c. The European species is in great request for the table, and, in the summer season, is carried in vast quantities to the principal towns, even at a considerable distance in the interior. We have a species common along our Atlantic coast, from Maine to Florida, which might be usefully employed, like the European; but it is entirely neglected.

Shrouds; a range of large ropes extended from the mast-heads to both sides of a ship, to support the masts, and enable them to carry sail, &c.

Shrovetide, or Shrove Tuesday; the day before the first of Lent or Ash-Wednesday, so called because on that day it was customary for all persons to confess their sins. (See *Carnival*, and *Lent*.) After confession, at least in England, it was usual to eat pancakes. Shrove Tuesday is called in German *Fastnacht* (fast-eve), and in French *Mardi Gras* (fat Tuesday).

Shukowsskij, Wassily Andrejewitsch, a Russian poet, was born in 1784, educated at Moscow, took part in the campaign of 1812, and subsequently began his poetical career with his *Liudmilla*, a translation of Bürger's *Lenore*. He has formed himself on the model of Göthe, Goldsmith, Byron, sir Walter Scott, and Thomas Moore. His ballads, epistles and elegies are particularly esteemed. In 1824, he published the third edition of his poetical works, in four volumes. In 1824, he was made reader to the present empress, and at present directs the education of the grand prince Alexander, heir-apparent to the throne. Shukowsskij must not be confounded with prince Shakowss kij, who is considered the first comic poet of Russia.

Shumla. (See *Choumla*.)

Siam; a country in the peninsula of Farther India, or Chin-India, which is but imperfectly known to us. The Siamese empire is composed of Siam Proper, a large portion of Lao, a portion of Cambodia, and some tributary Malay states, extending from about lat. 5° to 21° N., and from lon. 97° 50′ to 105° E. Its area may be estimated at 190,000 geographical square miles, with a population of not more than 2,790,500, of which 1,260,000 are Siamese, 840,000 Laos, 195,000 Malays, 440,000 Chinese, &c. The greater proportion of the territory, although it contains some rich alluvial plains, appears to be mountainous: the soil is, much of it, fertile, the climate favorable, and the communication easy, so that the thinness of the population must be ascribed to the barbarism and bad government of the country. The capital of the empire is Bangkok (lat. 13° 50° N.), near the mouth of the Menam, the great river of Siam, the population of which Crawfurd estimates not to exceed 50,000. Ayuthia, the old capital, eighty miles from the mouth of the same river, which here becomes navigable, is the next considerable city of the empire. Siam Proper is the valley of the Menam, which, at its southern extremity, does not exceed 60 miles in breadth: its length is stated at about 360 miles, and its superficial area may amount to 20,000 square miles. The country of the Laos—a people speaking a dialect of the Siamese language—appears to be divided between the Siamese, the Chinese, and the Birmans, with which latter empires that of Siam is thus brought into contact. Subsequently to the civil war which broke out in Cambodia in 1809, that kingdom was divided between the Siamese and the Cochin-Chinese governments. The Malay states tributary to Siam are Queda, on the western coast of the peninsula, with Patani, Kalantan and Tringano on the east. The Siamese are one of the most considerable and civilized of the group of nations inhabiting the tropical regions beyond Hindoostan and China. In stature they are shorter than Europeans, averaging about five feet three inches in height. Their complexion is a light brown, rather darker than that of the Chinese. In the useful arts they have made little progress, and, in this respect, are much behind the Hindoos and Chinese. Their alphabet consists of thirty-eight consonants, and numerous vowels and diphthongs, and the characters are written from left to right. The language is destitute of inflections, and its construction depends, therefore, like the English, on juxtaposition. The literature is very meagre, consisting merely of some songs, romances and chronicles. Their sacred literature, like that of all other Buddhist countries, is in the Bali or Pali language. The Siamese are represented by travellers as servile, rapacious, slothful, disingenuous, pusillanimous and vain. The religion is Buddhism, resembling, in its morality and doctrines, that which prevails in Ceylon, but differing considerably from the Buddhism of Tartary, China and Japan. (See *Buddha*, and *Fo*.) The priests, or *talapoins*, live in monasteries, and are bound to celibacy. The earliest event of which we have any information in Siamese history, is the introduction of the religion of Buddha from Ceylon in the seventh century of the Christian era. In 1511 began the first intercourse of Europeans with this country, through the Portuguese. In 1684, the celebrated Siamese embassy was sent to Louis XIV, through the influence of Constantine Phaulcon or Falcon, a Greek adventurer, who, by a singular destiny, had become *phraklang* or foreign minister of Siam. In the middle of the last century, the country was conquered by the Birman prince Alompra (see *Birman Empire*); but it has since recovered its independence, and, during the reign of the late king (1809—1824), considerable acquisitions of territory were made.—See Crawfurd's *Journal of an Embassy to Siam and Cochin-China* (London, 1828).

Siamese Twins, two youths born in the kingdom of Siam, with bodies singularly united by a strong band at the lowest part of the sternum of each, were carried from Siam, April 1, 1829, by captain Coffin, of the American ship Sachem, and extensively exhibited in Europe and the U. States during that and the three subsequent years. "The substance by which they are connected," says doctor Warren, of Boston, who examined them, "is a mass two inches long at its upper edge, and about five at the lower. Its breadth, from above downwards, may be four inches, and its thickness, in a horizontal direction, two inches. Of course it is not a rounded cord, but thicker in the perpendicular than in the horizontal direction. At its lower edge is perceived a single umbilicus, through which passed a single umbilical cord to nourish both children in the fetal state. Placing my hand on this substance, which I will denominate the cord, I was surprised to find it extremely hard. On further examination, this hardness was found to exist at the upper part of the cord only, and to be prolonged into the breast of each boy. Tracing it upwards, I found it to be constituted by a prolongation of the ensiform cartilage of the sternum, or extremity of the breast bone. The breadth of this cartilage is an inch and a half; its thickness may be about the eighth of an inch. The cartilages proceeding from each sternum meet at an angle, and then seem to be connected by a ligament, so as to form a joint. This joint has a motion upwards and downwards, and also a lateral motion, the latter opening in such way that, when the boys turn in either direction, the edges of the cartilage are found to open and shut. The lower face of this cartilage is concave, and under it is felt a rounded cord, which may be the remains of the umbilical cord. Besides this there is nothing remarkable felt in the connecting substance. I could distinguish no pulsating vessel. The whole of this cord is covered by the skin. It is remarkably strong, and has no great sensibility; for they allow themselves to be pulled by a rope fastened to it without exhibiting uneasiness." To this we add, from the report of G. B. Bolton, esquire, read before the London royal society, April 1, 1830: "Under the cartilage, while they stand in their ordinary posture, are large hernial sacs opening into each abdomen, and into which, on coughing, congenital herniæ are forced, probably in each boy, formed by a portion of the transverse arch of the colon. Generally, however, and under ordinary circumstances, these herniæ are not apparent. Whether there is a communication between the two abdominal cavities, or a distinct peritoneal sac belonging to each hernia, is by no means obvious. When these herniæ protrude, their respective contents are pushed forwards as far as the middle of the band." If the connecting link be touched in the centre, the touch is equally felt by both; but, at half an inch from the centre, it is felt by but one. These two young persons, Eng and Chang by name, are natives of a small village, called Maklong, on the sea-coast of Siam. They were born in May, 1811, of Chinese parents. Their mother observed that she suffered no greater inconvenience at their birth than at that of her former children, as they were very small, and the head of one was presented between the legs of the other. Their parents were of the poorer class, and, until the youths left their home, they were engaged in fishing, manufacturing cocoa-nut oil, keeping poultry, &c., for the support of the family. They are about five feet two inches in height, are well made and muscular. They have been known to carry a person weighing 280 pounds a hundred feet. They are agile, can walk or run with swiftness, and can swim well. Their intellectual powers are acute: they play at chess and draughts remarkably well. Their feelings are warm and affectionate, and their conduct amiable and well regulated. They never enter into conversation with each other beyond a simple remark made by one to the other, which seems to be rationally accounted for by the fact that, their experience being all in common, they have nothing to communicate. The attempt has frequently been made to engage them in separate conversations with different individuals, but always without success, as they are invariably inclined to direct their attention to the same thing at the same time. In their movements perfect equanimity is observed, the one always concurring with the other, so that they appear as if actuated by a common mind. In their employments and amusements, they have never been known to utter an angry word towards each other. Whatever pleases or displeases one has the same effect on the other. They feel hunger and thirst at the same time, and the quantity of food taken by them is as nearly alike as possible. Both feel the desire to sleep simultaneously, and they always awake at the same moment. Upon the possibility of separating them with safety there is some difference of opinion among medical men. The majority believe it impossible. (See the *Historical Account of the Siamese Twin Brothers*, by Mr. Hale, who has the charge of them, from which the above remarks are mostly taken.)

SIBERIA; a vast country of the north of Asia, with the Altai and Caucasus mountains on the south, and the Ural mountains on the west, the Pacific on the east, and the Frozen ocean on the north. It is one of the most desolate regions on the globe. A great portion of it is included within the limits of the frozen zone; and even the southern parts, from their physical structure, are exposed to a high degree of cold. Its situation also nearly excludes it from communication with the civilized parts of the world. The rivers generally have a northern direction, flowing into the Frozen ocean, the shores of which are barred by almost perpetual ice. Of the rivers, the Oby, Enisei and Lena are among the largest on the globe; others are the Irtisch, Angara, Selinga, &c. The Ural mountains on the west, and the Altaian range in the south, form striking features of Siberia. Another characteristic feature consists in the immense steppes (q. v.), or elevated plains, covered with long rank grass and aquatic shrubs, and filled with saline lakes. The natural productions of Siberia are gold, silver, copper, lead, iron, zinc, arsenic, sulphur, plumbago, &c. In the northern districts, the prevailing animal is the rein-deer The chief fur animals are the sable, black fox, ermine, martin, &c. The ferocious animals are the bear, wolf, lynx, and wild hog. In various parts of Siberia there are found remains of extinct species of animals. (See *Organic Remains*.) The mass of the population of Siberia consists of the native tribes, who are in a degree subjected to the Russian empire. Some of the most numerous tribes are the Burats, Yakoutes, Tunguses, Samoeides and Monguls The prevailing religion is the system of Buddha, or of the Lamas. The commerce consists chiefly of two branches, one formed by the exportation of metals and furs, the other a mere transit trade, consisting in an overland intercourse carried on across Siberia with the Chinese empire. The theatre of this commerce is Kiachta. In 1825, Siberia was divided into the four governments of Tobolsk (with the province of Omsk), Tomsk, Yeniseisk and Irkutsk, with the province of Jakutsk, and the two maritime provinces of Okotsk and Kamtschatka. The population of the country is about 2,000,000, on a superficial extent of 4,280,000 square miles. Siberia was attached to the Russian dominions towards the end of the sixteenth century, and the sovereigns of Russia assumed the title of *czar of Siberia*, which they still retain. The importance of this region did not escape Peter the Great, who introduced manufactures, and settled Russian colonies in it. State criminals are also banished to Siberia. (See Martoinoff's *Voyage Pittoresque de Moscou aux Frontières de la Chine* (1819), and Cochrane's *Pedestrian Journey through Russia* (1827).

Sibyl, and Sibylline Books. Sibyl (derived by some authorities from σιος, Æolic for θεος, God, and βολη, for βουλη, counsel) signified, originally, a female inspired or counselled by God. Of these prophetic virgins, who were believed to be thrown by a god into a kind of transport or insanity, in which they were able to unveil futurity, ancient writers mention ten, among whom the Sibyl of Cumæ, in Campania, was the most celebrated. According to O. Müller, the oracle of the Sibyls, and the worship of Apollo, were carried to Cumæ from the Trojan Ida. The Sibyl of Cumæ is said to have written, in Greek verses, the collection of prophecies famous under the name of *Sibylline books*, which, according to some, she herself, according to others, an unknown old woman, offered to Tarquin for sale. When the king, on account of the high price asked, refused to buy them, the old woman threw three of the books into the fire, and, on a second refusal, three more, after which the king, alarmed, paid for the three remaining the price originally asked for the whole, and committed them, as an oracle, to be consulted on important political occasions, to the keeping of two men. The number, at a later period, was increased to ten, and by Sylla to fifteen. About that time, the temple of Jupiter, where the Sibylline books were preserved, was burned down, with the capitol. After the rebuilding of the capitol, the senate, in 677, sent delegates to all the Italian and Greek cities, especially to Erythræ, in order to collect whatever Sibylline verses they could find; and, after the rejection of those which were considered spurious, about one thousand of them were retained, and preserved in the new temple of Jupiter Capitolinus. The senate, at different times, ordered all the Sibylline books which could be found in private hands to be burned. Augustus did the same, and destroyed above two thousand such books, but caused the genuine Sibylline books to be preserved in two chests of gold under the pedestal of the Apollo Palatinus. Yet the belief in every thing which went by the name of a Sibylline prediction was so strong that, in 772, Tiberius caused an investigation of all such prophetic verses to be made, and received some of them as genuine; whereupon, in 785, one of the keepers of the sacred volumes proposed the admission of another book. In general, the Sibylline books remained longer in authority with the Romans than the oracles with the Greeks. Though they were burned a second time, in the reign of Nero, yet, in the time of Aurelian (A. D. 270), some senators were in favor of consulting the Sibylline books, respecting the event of the Marcomannic war. Yet they were then so corrupted, that Christians could find in them predictions respecting the Messiah. This collection was burned under Julian (A. D. 363); and a fourth collection was burned under Honorius (395), by Stilicho; in spite of which a fifth collection was believed to be genuine. When Belisarius, in the middle of the sixth century, was besieged in Rome by the Goths, two Sibylline verses were considered as predicting that the siege would last but five months, which, however, did not agree with the event. It may be easily imagined that the Sibylline books can have retained their authority through so many centuries only by the greatest vagueness, admitting of any interpretation, and never committing themselves. The still-existing collection of Sibylline verses, most complete in the edition of Gallæus (Amsterdam, 1689), is of a later date, and is not considered genuine. These had their origin in the second century, when there were persons called *Sibyllists* in the Christian communities, who uttered poetic oracles, and whose outpourings were collected, and also called Sibylline books, on which Theoloririus wrote a Latin essay.—See Frederic Bleek's essay on their origin and composition, in Schleiermacher's *Theolog. Zeitschrift*, vol. i, no. 1; and Angelo Maio, in the preface to his edition of a Sibylline Book (Milan, 1817).

SIBYLLINE BOOKS. (See *Sibyl.*)

SICARD, Roch Ambroise Cucurron, successor of the abbé l'Epée at the Parisian institution for the education of the deaf and dumb, was born Sept. 20, 1742, at Fousseret, near Toulouse, and entered into holy orders. He devoted himself to the instruction of persons born deaf and dumb, and became, in 1786, director of a school established for that purpose by the archbishop of Bordeaux, whence, in 1789, he removed to Paris, and was chosen successor to the abbé l'Epée, in whose system he made some important improvements. (See *Dumb and Deaf.*) In 1792, he was arrested in the midst of his pupils, by order of the commune of Paris; and, Sept. 2, was transferred to the prison of the abbey of St. Germain, where he narrowly escaped becoming a victim in the ensuing massacres. On the foundation of the normal school, in 1795, he was appointed professor of grammar; and, about the same time, he was made a member of the institute. He then became one of the conductors of the *Annales Catholiques*, on account of which he was included by the directory in the number of the journalists sentenced to be exiled to Sinamari. He concealed himself, and thus avoided deportation; but it was not till after the overthrow of the directory that he was able to return to his situation at the school of instruction for the deaf and dumb. The old age of Sicard was clouded with misfortunes arising from his improvidence; but, after the restoration, he was made a knight of the legion of honor, administrator of the hospital of the Quinze-Vingts, &c. His death took place May 10, 1822. Besides other works, he was the author of *Elémens de Grammaire générale appliquée à la Langue Française* (2 vols., 8vo.); *Cours d'Instruction d'un Sourd-muet de Naissance* (8vo.); and *Théorie des Signes pour l'Instruction des Sourds-muets* (2 vols., 8vo.).

SICILIAN VESPERS. Charles of Anjou had established himself, through the favor of the pope, in possession of Naples and Sicily. The unfortunate Conradin had perished on the scaffold, Oct. 29, 1268. But the haughty Charles ruled with an iron sceptre, and the oppressed people applied in vain for relief to the pope. Giovanni di Procida, a nobleman of Salerno, distinguished for his talents and accomplishments, determined to deliver Sicily from her sufferings. He had stood high in favor with the emperor Frederic II, and king Manfred; and had been stripped of his estates by Charles, on account of his attachment to the Suabian house. Meditating revenge, he went to Arragon, and invited king Peter, whose wife Constantia was a daughter of Manfred, to undertake the conquest of the kingdom of Sicily. Peter was disposed to embrace his proposals; but he was destitute of money and men. Procida promised to make all necessary provision. He accordingly went to Sicily in disguise, and found the public feeling favorable to his wishes. He then hastened to Constantinople, represented to the emperor Palæologus the danger which threatened him from Charles, and prevailed upon him to promise pecuniary aid to Peter. Procida next had a private audience of the pope, and found him inclined to assist in effecting the humiliation of Charles. He returned to Arragon with this account of his success, and a large supply of money; and Peter immediately began to make extensive preparations for the expedition, under pretence of an attack upon the Moors in Africa. Charles, though suspecting the truth, neglected to prepare any measures of resistance. Meanwhile pope Nicholas III, upon whom Peter chiefly relied, died, and caution became doubly necessary. He therefore embarked, with his forces, and sailed for Africa, to keep up appearances of hostilities against the Moors, while he expected some demonstrations of a rising among the Sicilians. March 30, 1282, at the hour of vespers on Easter Monday, the inhabitants of Palermo flew to arms, and fell upon the French, who were all massacred. Women and children were not spared, and even Sicilian women with child by Frenchmen were murdered. This massacre is called the *Sicilian Vespers*. The other towns of Sicily, at first, remained quiet. Before the end of April, Messina followed the example of Palermo, and the French were either murdered or driven from the city As soon as Charles, who was at Orvieto with the pope, received information of what had occurred, he hastened to Naples, and set his forces in motion. In July, he appeared before Messina, which was disposed to surrender. But when Charles required unconditional submission, the Messinese determined to resist to the last drop of blood, and conducted the defence with the most desperate valor. The women and children exposed themselves fearlessly to death; and by this universal coöperation of all classes, the efforts of superior numbers were baffled. Thus stood matters when Peter of Arragon landed at Trapani, Aug. 30, with 10,000 foot-soldiers and 800 men at arms, and entered Palermo, where he was hailed as king by the people. Charles still besieged Messina; but fearing the interruption of his connexion with Calabria, he raised the siege, and fled in haste across the straits, leaving behind him a great quantity of military stores. On the passage, he was met by Peter's brave admiral Ruggieri di Loria, who took twenty-nine of his ships, and committed great devastation on the Neapolitan shores. Oct. 2, Peter entered Messina, and was received with acclamations; whilst the pope excommunicated him and the Sicilians. In the following year, Constantia appeared in Sicily with her sons, and was received as the rightful possessor of the island. The succession was settled on her second son, James. (See *Delavigne.*)

Sicilies, The Kingdom of the Two, consisting of Naples (*Dominj al di qua del Faro*) and Sicily (*Dominj al di la del Faro*). In the most ancient times of Rome (see *Italy*), Lower Italy was inhabited by the savage Ausonians, amongst whom were the mountaineers of Lucania and Bruttii (Abruzzo), including the Samnites. The country on the eastern coast was called Apulia (Puglia); and the small peninsula at the extremity of the country, Calabria. In Lower Italy, the Greeks settled chiefly on the coasts; hence its name, *Magna Græcia.* (q. v.) The dominion of Rome over Lower Italy commenced with the conquest of Tarentum, 272 B. C. (See *Fabricius*, and *Pyrrhus II.*) After the fall of the Western Roman empire (A. D. 476), Lower Italy became subject to the Ostrogoths. About the middle of the sixth century, Naples and Sicily fell under the power of the Greek emperors. Both countries were subject to one governor, the exarch of Ravenna, who conducted the administration by means of dukes. During the contest between the exarchs and Lombards, there sprung up, in the ninth century, several independent duchies, such as Salerno, Capua and Tarento. The most powerful was the Lombard duchy of Benevento. (q. v.) Naples Amalfi and Gaeta maintained themselves as republics. About the same time, the Saracens invaded Calabria, from Sicily. They conquered Bari, and contended with the Greeks for the possession of Lower Italy, until the emperor Otho I (967) subjected Benevento to the German empire. Germans, Greeks and Arabs now struggled for the possession of this beautiful country. (See *Italy.*) This induced some warlike adventurers, Normans from France, in the eleventh century, to lend their aid to the princes in Lower Italy. They assisted the Greek duke Sergius against prince Pandorf, of Capua, and were rewarded with the tract of land on which they founded the town of Aversa. More Normans soon followed. In 1047, the twelve sons of Tancred de Hauteville, a count in Lower Normandy, came in with their followers. Among these brothers, Robert Guiscard was the boldest and most artful. He contrived to gain over the peasants, and formed out of them his best soldiers. His policy led him to hold Apulia, which he had conquered, as a papal fief (1053); and he promised, likewise, to hold, as papal fiefs, such tracts as should afterwards be subdued by the Normans, in Calabria and Sicily. He then (1060) took the title of duke of Apulia and Calabria. (See *Italy.*) His youngest brother, count Roger, conquered Sicily in 1072. After the death of count Robert and his sons, he united in his own person the whole power of the house of Hauteville, and received, in 1098, by an extraordinary bull of pope Urban II, for himself and his successors, the supreme spiritual power in his dominions on the island. His son and successor, Roger II, completed, after 1101, the conquest of all Lower Italy by subduing Capua, Amalfi and Naples, at that time celebrated commercial republics. He then received, in 1130, from pope Anacletus II, by whom he was solemnly infeoffed, the title of king of Apulia, Calabria and Sicily. The same year, he united all the countries on both sides of the straits of Messina, under the name of *the kingdom of the Two Sicilies*. This union of Naples and Sicily continued 150 years. Palermo was his residence. Each country preserved its existing laws. In Naples, however, besides the ancient Lombard laws, the French feudal law was also introduced To the pope, as lord paramount of Naples, a tribute was paid of a palfrey and a bag of ducats. When William, grandson of Roger II, died, in 1189, the race of Tancred became extinct. The German emperor, Henry VI, of the house of

Hohenstaufen, now claimed the right of succession to the throne of Naples and Sicily, as belonging to his wife, Constantia, the daughter of Roger II. The Sicilians, however, detested the German dominion, and elected Tancred, natural son of Roger, to be their king, and, after his early death, made choice of his son, William III, a minor. Henry VI then entered the kingdom a second time, with more success than during the lifetime of the brave Tancred, and, by horrid cruelties, maintained possession of it. His memory was held in abhorrence by the Sicilians; but they, nevertheless, allowed his son Frederic II, a child three years old, to succeed him, in 1197. During the reign of this distinguished emperor, Naples was made the capital. The neighborhood of the powerful imperial house was disagreeable to the popes, and pope Urban IV granted the kingdom of the Two Sicilies, on the death of Conrad IV (1254), to Charles of Anjou, brother of Louis IX of France, who caused the legitimate heir, Conradin (q. v.) of Suabia (1268), to be beheaded. Sicily, however, freed herself, in 1282, from the oppressions of the French (see *Sicilian Vespers*), by the aid of king Peter III of Arragon, whom Conradin had made his heir, and whose wife was a daughter of Manfred, natural son of the emperor Frederic II. Sicily now remained separated from Naples for 160 years. She acknowledged Peter III of Arragon as her sovereign, who left this kingdom to his younger son James. The kings of Arragon withdrew the island from the feudal sway of the pope, and Sicily was united to the Spanish monarchy until the time of the Spanish war of succession. In Naples, the house of Anjou maintained itself, and Charles bound himself to pay an annual tribute to the pope of 8000 ounces of gold, and every three years to send a white horse to Rome. His great-grandson, Charles Robert, king of Naples, was made king of Hungary by the Hungarian diet, in 1307. After the death of king Robert, in 1343, under the reign of queen Joanna I, his grand-daughter, great disturbances arose in Naples; for pope Urban VI crowned Charles of Durazzo, of the house of Anjou-Naples in Hungary, as king of Naples. He caused queen Joanna to be suffocated in 1382, and united the kingdoms of Hungary and Naples; but in the year 1386, he was assassinated in Hungary. His son Ladislaus maintained a successful struggle for the throne of Naples with Louis of Anjou, the adopted son of Joanna. He took possession of Rome, and was on the point of uniting the whole of Italy into one kingdom, when he died, in 1414. Upon this, his sister, queen Joanna II, in the year 1420, adopted king Alfonso V of Arragon and Sicily, who drove his rival, the French prince Louis III of Anjou, out of Naples in 1458. Thus arose the jealousy between France and Spain, which, towards the end of the fifteenth century, wrapt the whole of Italy in flames. Alfonso V was succeeded in Naples by his natural son Ferdinand I, whose grandson, Ferdinand II, was attacked by Charles VIII of France, the champion of the claims of the house of Anjou, and whose second son, king Frederic III, was dethroned by his cousin, Ferdinand the Catholic, king of Spain and Sicily, in conjunction with Louis XII of France. The conquerors disagreed respecting the partition of Naples, and the cunning Ferdinand the Catholic (see *Ferdinand V of Arragon*, and *Gonsalvo*) managed to maintain himself in the sole possession of the whole, by artifice and force, in 1504. During this warfare of countries and crowns, which had been carried on for centuries almost without interruption, the constitution of the cities had been developed, and the kings of the house of Anjou began to summon delegates from them to the diet, which had been done previously in Sicily; but the feudal system continued, and the barons were constantly increasing their privileges. They even acquired the right of life and death over their vassals, in return for which the kings hoped to obtain their assistance in time of war. Thus the people were plunged into the greatest misery; and at no time have the Neapolitans been able to withstand foreign arms. The aristocracy, however, remained the same under every sovereign, and the depraved manners of the court, and the example of such licentious princesses as the two Joannas, corrupted the public morals. At that period there were feudal estates, which limited the power of the kings. But in the two centuries after the peace with France in 1505, during which the kingdom of the Two Sicilies remained a part of the Spanish monarchy, the diets were no longer convened in Naples, and the viceroys consulted merely with a committee of the estates, in which the city of Naples represented the whole third estate. Thus the regal power increased, and with it the burthen of taxes. The rebellion which took place in April, 1647 (see *Massaniello*), owing to the arbitrary mode of raising the taxes, might, under more prudent management, have led to independence. Still more did the prosperity of the country decline under the oppression of the nobility and the power of the clergy. No law limited the extension of the property of the church, and, both in Naples and in Sicily, two thirds of the landed property gradually came into their possession. On the extinction of the Austro-Spanish male line, in 1700, Naples and Sicily fell into the hands of Charles V of Spain, who governed arbitrarily, without consulting the chambers. At the peace of Utrecht, through the influence of the English, who were jealous of their commerce, Naples and Sicily were divided: the former fell to Austria, the latter to Savoy. King Philip V of Spain re-conquered Sicily in 1717, at the instigation of Alberoni, but was forced to cede it to Austria in 1720; and Savoy received Sardinia in return (see *Sardinian Monarchy*), by which means the Two Sicilies became a part of the Austrian dominions; however, in the war which was occasioned by the election of a king for Poland, in 1733, Spain conquered the Two Sicilies, and retained them at the peace of Vienna (1735), for the Infant Don Carlos. In 1759, when he ascended the Spanish throne, under the name of Charles III, he conferred the kingdom of the Two Sicilies on his third son, Ferdinand, and decreed, at the same time, that it should never again be united to the Spanish monarchy. Ferdinand reigned in the Two Sicilies under the name of Ferdinand IV (see *Ferdinand I*—the title which he took after having united all his states under one kingdom of the Two Sicilies, 12th December, 1816). July 7, 1820, he was forced to establish the new Spanish constitution, in consequence of an insurrection which originated principally amongst the army. He therefore conferred the regency on his son; but Austria, Russia, and Prussia determined, at Laybach, January, 1821, in concurrence with king Ferdinand, to occupy the country with an Austrian army, and restore the old system, in which they succeeded. (See *Acton*, *Napoleon Bonaparte*, *Joseph Bonaparte*, *Murat*, and *Naples and Sicily, Revolution of*.) King Ferdinand I returned from Laybach to his capital, May 15, 1821, with the promise of giving a constitutional organization to the government. May 26, a decree was issued respecting the new constitution, providing that the government should be conducted by a council of ministers and secretaries of state, under the presidency of the king or the crown-prince (duke of Calabria), or one of the ministers; that Sicily should be governed separately from Naples, by a distinct council; that there should be two state councils (*consulte di stato*), one at and for Naples, consisting of thirty members, the other, consisting of eighteen members, at Palermo, for Sicily, to deliberate on the laws and financial measures laid before them by the council. The ultimate decision, however, was to rest entirely with the king, who was to appoint the president and members of these bodies out of the landholders and principal officers of the state, church, law, and army. These *consulte di stato* did not, however, go into operation until the year 1827, after some alterations, by the decree of 14th June, 1824, which provided that the council of Naples should not have more than sixteen members, and that of Sicily not more than eight. In matters relating to both countries, they form a general council. Both have their seat at the residence of the king. A new system of education, projected by the clergy, was introduced by the committee of instruction, to whom was likewise intrusted the examination of all foreign books. The Jesuits were reëstablished in their privileges, and received houses and money; and other orders were restored, as, for example, the Camaldulians, in 1822. Continual arrests and trials for high treason kept the people in a state of irritation. From all parts, search was made for the adherents of the revolution. A severe law against secret societies had already been passed, 3d October, 1822. Notwithstanding, the conspiracies continued. The government, in consequence of the increasing number of prisoners, prescribed to the grand criminal courts a new mode of proceeding, January, 1824. During the space of a few years, this was the fourth time that the king had adopted extraordinary measures by the way of obviating the overcrowding of the prisons. After the death of Ferdinand I, January 5, 1825, his eldest son, till then duke of Calabria, ascended the throne as Francis I. In May and June, he undertook a journey to Milan and Turin, by the way of Genoa, and effected a reduction of the Austrian army in Naples. On his return, by the decrees of 18th and 19th August, king Francis permitted all the Neapolitans, who had quitted their country through fear of political persecutions, with the exception of those who were capitally condemned, to return. In consequence of a deficiency in the revenue, amounting to ten million ducats, and to reduce the paper currency, the government contracted two loans, in 1821, with the house of Rothschild and the English banker Goodhouse, amounting together to twenty million ducats. With a view of bringing coin into the country, the minister contracted a new loan in February, 1824, with the English house of Rothschild, amounting to three million pounds sterling. The regular troops were now disbanded, in consequence of the part which they had taken in the revolution; the militia was also dissolved, and a new army was formed. The dissolution of the militia gave rise to numerous bands of robbers, for the destruction of which, the greatest part of the Austrian auxiliary army marched through the country in movable columns. A treaty was concluded at Naples, 18th October, 1821, between the emperor of Austria and the king of Naples, in reference to the occupation of the kingdom of the Two Sicilies by an Austrian auxiliary and protecting army of 55,500 men, for three years. The reduction of the forces therein stipulated was gradually executed, after the formation of the Neapolitan army was sufficiently advanced. Seventeen thousand Austrians evacuated the kingdom of the Two Sicilies, in 1823, agreeably to the treaty of Naples of 24th April, 1823. The treaty of 31st August, 1824, fixed the number of auxiliary Austrian troops, in the kingdom of the Two Sicilies, at 33,500 men, to remain till the end of May, 1826; accordingly, in the same year, 1824, 5000 Austrians left the kingdom. But as the formation of the Neapolitan army advanced but slowly, on account of the aversion of the Swiss to the Neapolitan service, it was concluded in Milan, during the presence of king Francis I, to maintain other troops in Naples and Sicily, even after the expiration of the treaty of 31st August, 1824. A reduction, however, of the auxiliary forces was then determined upon. May 28, 1825, it was stipulated that the Austrian auxiliary army should remain at the disposal of his Sicilian majesty, until the end of March, 1827; but it might be reduced to 15,000 men, and, in proportion to the augmentations of the Sicilian army, as low as 12,000 men. The troops, retiring by degrees, had all left the country in 1827. In the island of Sicily, confusion and misery of every kind existed in a far greater degree than in Naples. The deficiency in the revenue rose to 600,000 ounces, and the public debt to 1,000,000. The duty on flour was, therefore, doubled. This provoked the people to a bloody resistance. To this was added the mischief done by large bands of robbers. But the Austrian general count Wallmoden occupied the island with 12,000 Austrian troops, which traversed the country, and soon restored order. About 16,000 political offenders were arrested. A conspiracy was detected, 10th January, 1822, the object of which was to murder the governor and cardinal archbishop Gravina, and to compel general Wallmoden to sign an order for the evacuation of the fortresses of the country by the Austrians. After this, the Austrians disarmed the country people and the most turbulent citizens of Palermo. Twenty-eight conspirators were arrested, and nine of them shot. A royal ordinance abolished all guilds and corporations of tradesmen and artisans, as dangerous to the public tranquillity. Thus some time elapsed before the regular course of administration could be restored. To this was added the stagnation of all the sources of public prosperity, and further calamities. February 23, 1823, Palermo experienced a dreadful conflagration, and, March 5th, a violent earthquake; Messina, 14th May, suffered from a tremendous flood. Steam navigation was introduced, in 1824, between Palermo and Naples; a loan of a million ducats, contracted with Rothschild, in 1824, was applied to the improvement of the roads in Sicily. Francis died November 8, 1830; his son Ferdinand II succeeded.

The kingdom of the Two Sicilies contains, at present, 42,100 square miles, and 7,414,717 inhabitants. The kingdom of Naples contains 31,630 square miles, with 5,626,946 inhabitants. (Respecting the island of Sicily, see the next article.) Naples is bounded on the north by the papal dominions, east by the Adriatic, south and west by the Mediterranean. Its soil is principally volcanic, and is covered with the most luxuriant vegetation. Fertile valleys descend on both sides of the Apennines towards the sea. Separate from these lies Vesuvius, 3730 feet high. The rivers are but few, and of moderate size. The volcanic soil is often convulsed by earthquakes. The Monte Nuovo, near Puzzuoli, arose in 1538, and attained, within forty-eight hours, to the height of 2100 feet. Through the grotto of Posilippo, near Naples, you pass, on a lava road, to the Phlegræan fields (q. v.), whence the ancient poets took the imagery of the war of the giants, and of the infernal regions. Here the pozzolana earth is dug. This desert, as well as the extinct volcano of Solfatara and lake Averno, is bounded by blooming vineyards, with fruit-trees. Here you behold splendid ruins of ancient edifices, on the *Mare morto*, near the Elysian fields. In the charming environs of the capital lies the lake of Agnano, a sunken volcano, and in its neighborhood the *grotta del Cane*. (See *Naples*.) The climate is warm. In Abruzzo alone the winter is severe. The strawberry ripens in January. The summer is sultry, and brings with it the debilitating sirocco wind from the south-east. The chief productions of this beautiful country, which is, however, not even yet sufficiently cultivated, are excellent wheat, maize, fruits of various kinds, oil, hemp, and flax, cotton, the *nuces Avellanæ* of Pliny, wines (*lachrymæ Christi*), capers, saffron, &c. The Neapolitan horses, the breed of swine, in Abruzzo, the silk, wool, buffaloes, mules, poultry, quails, &c., are celebrated. Among the noxious animals are wolves, tarantulas, and scorpions. Important articles of trade are furnished by the pozzolana earth, marine and fossil salt, marble, iron, brimstone, jasper, lava, alabaster, alum, saltpetre, &c. There is, however, a deficiency of wood, so that in some places buffalo dung is used as fuel. In this warm country, however, the date-palm, the Spanish cane, the aloe, and Indian fig, thrive. The Neapolitan is lively, intelligent, and good-natured, but impoverished and exasperated by feudal oppression; the defective administration of justice often allows excesses, and the banditti are not yet rooted out. The Neapolitan dialect differs much from the Italian employed in literature. In the south, near Otranto, you still meet with villages inhabited by Arnauts and Greeks (about 40,000). Manufactures are more flourishing in Naples than in Sicily. Naples contains silk, woollen and cotton manufactories; linen is woven and metal ware made, besides articles of marble and precious stones. Mining is neglected. The maritime commerce is almost confined to exports of natural productions. The inland commerce is obstructed by the want of good roads, canals, and navigable rivers. The principal commercial towns are Naples, Palermo, and Messina. The people are extremely ignorant, being mostly unable to read and write. Among the better class, however, there are persons of distinguished talents, particularly among the Neapolitans. Antiquities are a favorite subject of study. The people are passionate lovers of music. Cicero, Horace, Ovid, Juvenal, Statius, Tasso, Thomas Aquinas, Filangieri, Galiani, and other men of eminence in the arts and sciences, were natives of Naples. Sicily is the native soil of pastoral poetry. There are universities at Naples, Salerno, Palermo and Catania, and academies at Naples and Palermo. There are schools for music, and cabinets of works of art at Naples (*Museo Borbonico*, with a particular gallery for the paintings of the Neapolitan school); the Herculaneum museum at Portici; a cabinet of medals and an observatory at Palermo. In Naples, there are four public libraries and forty-five printing-offices. The institution for the deaf and dumb deserves mention; likewise the lunatic hospital at Aversa, which is peculiarly well arranged. The kingdom of Naples (*al di qua del Faro*), in 1817, was divided into fifteen provinces—Naples, with the volcanic islands Capri, Procida, and Ischia; Abruzzo Ulteriore I and II, with Aquila, Sulmona, &c.; Abruzzo Citeriore; Terra di Lavoro, with Caserta, Gaeta, Arpino, and the volcanic island Ponza; Principato Citeriore, with Salerno, Amalfi and Pæstum; Principato Ulteriore; Capitanata; Molise; Bari; Otranto, with Lecce; Basilicata; Calabria Citeriore and Ulteriore I and II, with Reggio, Sciglio (where the rock so celebrated among the ancients, under the name of *Scylla*, projects into the strait) and Pizzo, where Murat fell, and which the king called the *most faithful town*, and declared free of taxes, on account of its fidelity. The united kingdom of the Two Sicilies forms, according to the fundamental law of 12th December, 1816, a constitutional monarchy, hereditary in the male and female line. Agreeably to this law, which, however, was never carried into effect, the king possesses supreme executive power. In the absence of the king, a governor (*luogotenente generale*) resides in Palermo, as viceroy of Sicily. This was the crown-prince until 1820. All public offices in the island are to be held by natives. The feudal system is now abolished in Sicily. It was earlier abolished in Naples. It existed at the time of the breaking out of the revolution, July 7, 1820. By the concordate concluded with the pope in 1818, the bond of feudal dependence on the papal see was totally broken, and the papal power in general limited. Nevertheless, the Jesuits were reëstablished. The duchies of Pontecorvo and Benevento were restored to the papal government. The clergy of the Two Sicilies (24 archbishops, 91 suffragan, and 21 exempt bishops, 368 abbots, 47,233 secular priests, 25,399 monks, 26,659 nuns, with 3700 parishes and 19,300 pious institutions, in the kingdom of Naples, and 3 archbishops, 7 bishops, 51 abbots and priors, and 70—80,000 clergymen of all kinds, on the island of Sicily) are in possession of nearly a third of the landed property. The inquisition was abolished in Sicily in 1782. In no country are there so many princes (120), dukes (150), marquisses (170), counts and barons, as in Naples. However, the king abolished the *fidei-commissa* (q. v.) in Sicily (1818), which threatened to bring the whole of the landed property into a few hands, and were a great impediment to moral improvement. The great abuses in the judicial administration and in the condition of the prisons (particularly in Sicily) have been gradually remedied. In consequence of the new constitution of the courts of 29th May, 1818, all the proprietary and local jurisdictions have been done away, and the royal courts of justice put on much the same footing as those of France. This system was extended to the island of Sicily, by the decree of 22d December, 1818, and a supreme court of justice established there. A new civil code was drawn up for this island in 1819. The revenue, in 1820, amounted to about twelve and a half million dollars. The new land force amounts to 30,000 men; the naval force comprises three ships of the line, five frigates, four corvettes, and a number of gun-boats. The standing army in Sicily is said not to exceed 8000 men. The orders of knights are, that of saint Januarius; the order of Constantine; the order of St. Ferdinand, and of merit; and the order *S. Giorgio della riunione.* Among the latest publications respecting this country are to be noticed the work of the Russian senator count Orloff, *Mémoires historiques, politiques et literaires sur le Royaume de Naples avec des Notes par Amaury Duval* (5 vols., Paris, 1819), and the *Costituzione del Regno di Sicilia, stabilita dal Parlamento dell' Anno* 1812 (Palermo, 1813, 2 vols.); History of the Kingdom of Naples, from 1800 to 1820 (Darmstadt, 1828), taken from the memoirs of prince Pignatelli Strangoli, and other original sources. Count Forbin's *Souvenirs de la Sicile* (Paris, 1823) present a faithful picture of the beauties of nature, and the degeneracy of society in Sicily. Captain Will. Hen. Smith's Memoir Descriptive of the Resources, Inhabitants and Hydrography of Sicily and its Islands, &c. (London, 1824, 4to.), accompanied by an accurate atlas of charts, is a work of much observation. Rich in interesting research is the work of Blunt—Vestiges of Ancient Manners and Customs, discoverable in Modern Italy and Sicily (London, 1822).—Respecting the noble remains of antiquity in the churches of Messina, Catania, Palermo, and particularly in the cathedral of Montereale, see *Architecture Moderne de la Sicile, ou Recueil des plus beaux Monumens, mesurés et dessinés par J. Hittorff et L. Zanth* (Paris, 1827, 1st *livr.*, fol.).

Sicily (anciently Trinacria and Sicilia); the largest, most fruitful, and most populous island of the Mediterranean, lies to the south of Italy, from which it is separated by the strait or *faro* of Messina, which, in the narrowest part, is only two miles wide. The surface is greatly diversified by mountains and valleys. A chain of mountains extends through the island from east to west; but the most elevated summit is the famous volcano, mount Ætna. (q. v.) The climate is warm, but pleasant, the winters mild, and the heat of summer tempered by sea breezes. Sicily has always been celebrated for its fertility, and is well watered by a great number of streams and rivulets; but the state of cultivation is very backward. The principal products are maize, wheat, other kinds of grain, flax, hemp, vines, saffron, cotton, silk, olives, and various fruits. The exports consist chiefly of silk, corn, salt, olive oil, sumac, wine and fruits. The manufactures, consisting of silk, cotton, linen, and some woollens, are confined to the three large towns of Palermo, Messina, and Catania According to the last census, Sicily contains 1,787,771 inhabitants, of whom 300,000 are ecclesiastics, or persons living on ecclesiastical revenues. There are in the island 1117 convents, containing 30,000 monks and 30,000 nuns. The nobility of this small population consists of six dukes, 217 princes, 217 marquisses, 2000 barons, and the same number of an order called gentlemen. In 1817, the island was divided into seven intendancies, which take the names of their chief towns—Palermo, Catania, Messina, Girgenti, Siragosa (Syracuse), Trapani, and Calatanisetta. To Sicily belong the groups of the Lipari (Æolian) islands on the north, and Ægades on the west, Pantellaria on the south, &c. Between the latter island (which is twenty-one leagues from the coast) and Sciacca, in Sicily, a volcanic island about one mile in circumference and 150—160 feet high, rose from the sea, in the summer of 1831, but disappeared after a few months, and again appeared in the spring of 1832. Notwithstanding the natural wealth of the island, the inhabitants are kept in a state of poverty by the great numbers of the religious and nobles (who possess almost all the land), the heavy duties upon commerce, and the want of secure communication. Sicily has been, from ancient times, a prize of war. The original inhabitants appear to have been Iberians (Niebuhr, *Roman History*, ch. On the Three Islands); but the conquests and colonies of the Greeks rendered the Greek language prevalent, and, in reality, converted Sicily into a Greek island—a character which it retained till the middle ages. The Carthaginians also founded colonies here. The island was divided between different republics, among which Syracuse was the wealthiest and most powerful, and most celebrated, in ancient history, for its princes (Gelo, Agathocles, Hiero), its wars, and the high degree of cultivation to which it carried the arts and sciences.—See Gärtner's *Views of the Greek Monuments in Sicily* (Munich, 1819). Next to Syracuse, Messana, now Messina, and Agrigentum (Girgenti), were most famous in history. In the middle of the third century B. C., the Romans became masters of Sicily, and remained in possession of it until Genseric, king of the Vandals, conquered it, in the middle of the fifth century A. D. Belisarius, Justinian's general, drove out the Vandals (535); and it remained in the hands of the Greek emperors nearly three centuries, when it was taken by the Saracens (827). The Normans, who ruled in Naples, conquered Sicily in 1072, and received it from the pope as a papal fief. Roger, a powerful Norman prince, took the title of king of Sicily (1102), and united the island with the kingdom of Naples, under the name of the kingdom of the Two Sicilies. (See *Sicilies, The Two.*) But a dislike always prevailed between the Sicilians and the Neapolitans; whence frequent attempts on the part of the former to obtain their independence. This idea was encouraged by the constitution given them by the British, and their old right to a separate parliament. This was the root of the furious outbreak of July 16—20, 1820, in Palermo. (See *Naples and Sicily, Revolution of.*) The pastoral muse has never abandoned this island; and the first notes of Italian poetry were heard in Sicily. (See *Italy*, division *Italian Poetry.*) The idyls of the Sicilian poet Giovanni Meli, published by the abbate Scopa, at Paris, 1820, unite depth of feeling and simplicity with uncommon grace and sweetness. —For the recent works on Sicily, see those mentioned at the close of the article *Sicilies, The Two*, and, likewise, Bigelow's *Travels in Sicily and Malta* (Boston, 1831).

Sickingen, Francis von, a German knight of the palatinate of the Rhine, imperial counsellor and general, one of the noblest characters of the disturbed times in which he lived, was born in 1481, at Sickingen. From early youth, he devoted himself to the military life. The protection of the oppressed was his chief occupation. He assisted many a creditor in procuring what was due him from a powerful debtor. He was the enemy of tyranny, of princes and priests. Without being a scholar, he loved science, and protected men of learning (for instance, Reuchlin, whom he defended against the monks of Cologne); and in his castle, called Ebernburg, many persecuted scholars found a safe asylum. He was a friend of the reformation, and contributed greatly to extend it in the countries which bordered on the Rhine. At last, he engaged in a quarrel with Treves, the palatinate and Hessia, which drew upon him the ban of the empire. He died in 1523, soon after the surrender of Landstuhl, one of his castles, having previously received a severe injury from a fall during a sally.

Sicyon (now Basilicon, a village with about fifty families); one of the oldest, most celebrated, and handsomest cities of ancient Greece, lying not far from the gulf of Corinth, on which it had a port. The city was occupied by the Dorians; but the Sicyonians enjoyed so much consideration, that, with the Spartans, they acted as umpires and mediators. They were not less distinguished for their superiority in the arts of peace than the Spartans for their military fame. Sicyon, although powerful by sea, was seldom engaged in wars; but was celebrated for its schools of sculpture and painting. The city, with its environs, formed a small state (Sicyonia) at a very early period; and the names of several princes, who are said to have reigned there, are given. At the time of the return of the Heraclidæ (q. v.), it formed a part of the kingdom of Argos. It afterwards became a democracy, and the supreme power was several times usurped by individuals. It maintained its independence subsequently to the period of the Persian war, but suffered much from the civil contests among the Greeks, in which it was sometimes in favor of, and sometimes in opposition to, Athens. Sicyon was induced, by the influence of Aratus (q. v.), to join the Achæan league, in which it acted an important part, and of which it finally shared the fate, and fell under the dominion of Rome.

Siddons, Mrs., daughter of Roger Kemble, the manager of an itinerant company of players, was born at Brecknock, in South Wales, in 1755. She commenced her theatrical career as a singer, but soon relinquished that line, and attempted tragedy. In her fifteenth year, she conceived a passion for a young man, who was an actor of all work in her father's company; but her parents, considering her too young to form a connexion with him, placed her, as lady's maid, with a lady in Warwickshire. In her eighteenth year, however, she was married to Siddons, with their consent; and the new-married pair entered into a strolling company. She and her husband played at Liverpool, Birmingham, and other places, gaining both reputation and profit. The theatrical character which she had acquired induced the manager of Drury lane to offer her an engagement, which she accepted. It was, however, only in secondary parts that she appeared. But in a short time she quitted the London boards, in consequence of the scurrilous attacks of a disappointed editor of a newspaper, in whose condemned after-piece she had been unlucky enough to perform. Bath was the next scene of her exertions; and, while there, she improved rapidly, and became a general favorite. The duchess of Devonshire, then in the zenith of her charms and influence, became her friend; and, through the intervention of that accomplished lady, she was again engaged at Drury lane. The re-appearance of Mrs. Siddons in London took place on the 10th of October, 1782, in the character of Isabella. Her success was complete. The public were astonished by her powers. She was acknowledged to be the first tragic actress of the English stage, and tragedy became fashionable. The manager gave her an extra benefit, and increased her salary. For that benefit she came forward as Belvidera, and at once exalted her fame, and made a considerable increase to her fortune. Such was the delight which she gave, that the gentlemen of the bar subscribed a hundred guineas as a present to her. She subsequently visited Dublin and Edinburgh with equal applause. In 1784, some calumnies circulated against her, with respect to her conduct towards an unhappy sister, occasioned her to meet with an unkind reception from a London audience, and affected her so much, that she resolved to retire from the stage; but the calumnies were speedily refuted, and her resolution was given up. For more than twenty years, she continued to astonish and enchant the lovers of the drama; and she was often invited to Buckingham house and to Windsor to read plays to their majesties. But her readings there were rather productive of honor than of profit. The fortune which she had accumulated was, however, large, and for many years she enjoyed it in the privacy of domestic life. It was not only as an actress that Mrs. Siddons displayed talents. She had considerable merit as a sculptor, in which capacity she produced, among other things, a medallion of herself, a bust of her brother, John Philip Kemble (q. v.), in the character of Coriolanus, a study of Brutus before the death of Cæsar, and a bust of president Adams. The symmetry of her person was captivating. Her face was peculiarly happy, having strength of features, but so well harmonized when quiescent, and so expressive when impassioned, that most people thought her more beautiful than she was. So great, too, was the flexibility of her countenance, that it caught the instantaneous transitions of passion with such variety and effect, as never to fatigue the eye. Her voice was plaintive, yet capable of firmness and exertion. Her eye was large; her brow capable of contracting with disdain or dilating with sympathy or pity; and her articulation clear, penetrating, and distinct. So entirely was she mistress of herself, so collected and so determined in her gestures, tone and manner, that she seldom erred, like other actors, because she doubted her own powers of comprehension: she studied her author attentively; she was sparing in action; though her acting was the result of the most refined and assiduous attention, no studied trick or start could be predicted; none of those arts in which the actress is seen, and not the character, could be found in Mrs. Siddons. What was still more delightful, she was an original; she copied no one, living or dead, but acted from nature and herself. Mrs. Siddons, having acquired an ample fortune, took her leave of the stage, in 1812, before an audience which melted into tears on the occasion. She, however, performed, in 1816, for the benefit of her brother, Mr. Charles Kemble, and a few nights in Edinburgh, to assist her daughter-in-law. Her greatest characters are well known to have been Catharine, in Henry VIII, and lady Macbeth, in which she manifested a dignity and sensibility rarely equalled. She died June 8th, 1831.—See Boaden's *Memoirs of Mrs. Siddons* (2 vols. 1827).

Sidereal Magnetism, with the believers in animal magnetism (q. v.), denotes the beneficial influence of the stars upon patients.

Sidereal Time. A sidereal day is the time during which the whole body of fixed stars appears to revolve round the earth. It is found by observing two successive passages of the same star over the meridian. The time from one passage to the other consists of twenty-four hours, each of sixty minutes, each of sixty seconds, &c. Sidereal time is not adapted to the purposes of common life (see *Solar Time*), but is particularly suitable for astronomical observations, on account of its perfect uniformity. Astronomers have sidereal clocks. The sidereal day, and of course each subdivision, is shorter than the solar day, because the sidereal day is determined simply by the rotation of the earth on its axis, and is completed as soon as this rotation is performed; but in the case of the solar day, the earth's revolution round the sun is also to be taken into the account. The earth advances in its orbit nearly a degree each day; and to bring the sun to any particular meridian, it has to make so much more than a complete rotation on its axis as will counterbalance its advance in its orbit. The average amount of this daily advance is 59′ 8″. So much, therefore, must the earth turn on its axis beyond one rotation in order to complete the solar day, which is therefore 3 minutes 56 seconds longer than a sidereal day. Hence the mean solar day is 24 hours 3 minutes 56 seconds sidereal time; or the sidereal day is 23 hours 56 minutes 4 seconds mean solar time. —See Lalande's *Abrégé d'Astronomie* (Paris, 1795); see, also, the article *Day*.

Siderismus (from σιδηρον, iron); the name given by the believers in animal magnetism (q. v.) to the effects produced by bringing metals and other inorganic bodies into a magnetic connexion with the human body. Hence we hear of *sideric* bodies and *sideric* power. The former are inorganic bodies, in contradistinction to the animated bodies, which produce somnambulism.

Siderography; the art of engraving on steel. (See *Engraving*.) The word comes from σιδηρον, iron.

Sidmouth, Lord. (See *Addington*.)

Sidney, sir Philip, an ingenious writer and accomplished statesman in the reign of queen Elizabeth, was the son of sir Henry Sidney, of Penshurst, in Kent, where he was born November 29, 1554. After studying at Christ-church, Oxford, and Trinity college, Cambridge, he set off on his travels, at the age of eighteen, visited France, Hungary and Italy, and, returning through Germany and Flanders, arrived in England in 1575. He became a favorite with the queen, who, in 1576, sent him on an embassy to Germany. Having had a quarrel with the earl of Oxford, in consequence of a dispute at a tournament, her majesty interposed her authority to prevent a duel from taking place. Sidney, displeased at the issue of the affair, retired to Wilton, in Wiltshire, 1580, and amused himself with the composition of a pastoral romance, which, in compliment to his sister, was entitled the Countess of Pembroke's Arcadia. In 1581, he again appeared at court, where he distinguished himself in the jousts and tournaments celebrated for the entertainment of the duke of Anjou; and on the return of that prince to the continent, he accompanied him to Antwerp. The prince palatine being invested with the order of the garter in 1583, Mr. Sidney was appointed his proxy, when he received the honor of knighthood. In 1585, he projected, in concert with sir Francis Drake, an expedition against the Spaniards in America; and he had gone to Plymouth to embark on the undertaking, when an express mandate from the queen recalled him to court. Her influence also was exerted to prevent him from being elected king of Poland; "refusing," as Camden says, "to further his advancement, out of fear that she should lose the jewel of her times." He was subsequently appointed governor of Flushing, and general of the cavalry under his uncle, Dudley, earl of Leicester, who commanded the forces sent to assist the Dutch against the Spaniards. September 22, 1586, being at the head of a detachment of the English troops, he fell in with a convoy of the enemy marching towards Zutphen. An engagement took place, in which his party gained the victory, dearly purchased with the life of their commander, who received a shot in his thigh, which shattered the bone. He was carried to Arnheim, where he expired, October 17. His works, besides the Arcadia, consist of the Defence of Poesy; Astrophel and Stella; a collection, entitled Songs and Sonnets; and other poetical pieces. The Defence was republished in 1752 (12mo.), and in 1831 (Boston); and a complete edition of his works appeared in three volumes, 8vo. (London, 1725). His Miscellaneous Works, with a life by W. Gray (one volume, 8vo.) appeared at Oxford (1829). The work by which sir Philip Sidney is principally known is his Arcadia, which is one of the earliest specimens of the grave or heroic romance. It is a mixture of prose and verse, the latter exhibiting various attempts to naturalize the measures of Roman poetry.—See the *Life of Sidney* by sir Fulk Greville, and Zouch's *Memoirs of the Life and Writings of Sir P. Sidney* (1808).

SIDNEY, Algernon, a celebrated English republican and martyr to liberty, was the second son of the earl of Leicester, by the daughter of the earl of Northumberland. He was born, according to some accounts, in 1617, and to others, in 1622, and educated under the inspection of his father, whom he accompanied in his embassies to Denmark and France. He was also early trained to a military life, and served with some distinction under his brother, lord Lisle, during the Irish rebellion. In 1643, both brothers returned to England, and joined the parliament. In 1645, Algernon was promoted by Fairfax to the colonelcy of a regiment of horse, and, after being present in several actions, was intrusted with the government of Chichester. He was then stationed in Ireland (1646), but soon after returned to England, where he was thanked by parliament for his services, and made governor of Dover. When the high court of justice was formed for the trial of the king (see *Charles I*), he was nominated a member, but was neither present when sentence was pronounced, nor signed the warrant for the execution. It appears, however, that he vindicated that measure, which has led to a supposition that, in withholding his signature, he only yielded to the influence of his father. A politician so inimical to the encroachments of authority was not likely to acquiesce in a usurpation; and he warmly opposed the designs of Cromwell. During the government both of the protector and his son Richard, he lived in retirement at Penshurst, where he is supposed to have composed his celebrated Discourses on Government. When the return of the long parliament gave expectations of the establishment of a republic, he assumed a public charactêr, and was nominated one of the council of state. He was soon after appointed a commissioner to mediate a peace between Denmark and Sweden, and while engaged in this embassy, the restoration took place. Conscious of the offence he had given the royal party, he refused to return, and remained an exile for seventeen years; and, although occasionally assisted by his family, he found it difficult to support himself in conformity to his birth and rank. At length, in 1677, the influence of his father obtained leave for him to return, with a pardon for all offences. At the time of his return, parliament was urging the king to a war with France; and it was feared by the opposition that Charles II would agree to it until he obtained the supplies, and would then squander them on his pleasures, or devote them to arbitrary purposes. The English patriots were therefore opposed to this war, and some of the leaders intrigued with the French ambassador, Barillon, to defeat the measure. (See *Russel, Lord William.*) It even appears, according to the Barillon papers, as given by sir John Dalrymple, that the name of Sidney was among those who received pecuniary aid from France. The testimony thus afforded against a man of high character, and whose sacrifices to principle were notorious, has led to the suspicion of fabrication and interpolation. The death of his father, soon after his return, led him openly to join in the opposition, and he consorted much with the duke of Monmouth and others who held views kindred or similar to his own. In the Rye-house plot he is named as one of a council of six, who were to organize an insurrection in conjunction with the Scottish malcontents. It was, however, for his supposed share in the subordinate conspiracy for assassinating the king, that he was arrested, with lord William Russel and others. After the sacrifice of the latter, he was tried, as the next most obnoxious person, for high treason, before the hardened tool, chief-justice Jeffreys, Nov. 21, 1683. There was no direct evidence against him, except that of the disgrace to nobility, lord Howard, while the law for high treason required two witnesses. To help this defect, the attorney-general had recourse to the expedient of producing passages from some discourses on government, found in manuscript in his closet, which maintained the lawfulness of resisting tyrants, and the preference of a free to an arbitrary government. Although there was no proof that these papers were in his own hand-writing, in defiance both of law and common sense, they were deemed equivalent to a second witness; and, in spite of his spirited defence, he was declared guilty. After his conviction, he sent, by his relation, the marquis of Halifax, a paper to be laid before the king, requesting his review of the whole matter; but it served only to delay his execution about a week. Hume acknowledges the illegality of his condemnation, for which he observes, "the jury were very blamable," but remarks, that an interference by the king might be regarded as an act "of heroic generosity, but could never be deemed an indispensable duty." Sidney was executed on Tower hill, Dec. 7, 1678, when he delivered the sheriff a paper, alleging the injustice of his condemnation, and concluding with a prayer for "the good old cause." He suffered with all the firmness and constancy belonging to his character. One of the first acts of the revolution was to reverse his attainder; and the name of Algernon Sidney has since been held in great honor by the majority of those who maintain the fundamental principles of free government. Burnet speaks of him as of extraordinary courage, steady, even to obstinacy, impatient of contradiction, and a decided enemy to monarchy and church government. His Discourses on Government were first printed in 1698, and reprinted in 1704 and 1751 in folio, and in 1772 in quarto, at the expense of Thomas Hollis, esquire, with the trial and letters prefixed. They contain much historical information, and are composed with clearness, acuteness and force.

SIDON. (See *Phœnicia.*)

SIEBENBÜRGEN. (See *Transylvania.*)

SIEBENGEBIRGE (German, *Seven Mountains*); a group on the right bank of the Rhine, near the town of Königswinter, not far from Bonn, consisting of basalt, granite, porphyry and sandstone. Seven mountains tower above the rest of the group, of which the Drachenfels, close to the Rhine, and presenting a splendid view from the river, is the most beautiful, and the Löwenberg, 1896 feet high, the highest. All of them contain ruins of ancient castles.

SIEGE. The taking of a fortified place may be attempted, 1. by surprise (*coup de main*), in case the defenders should be off their guard, or treachery should enable the assailants to enter the fortress by means of secret or unguarded passages; 2. by a sudden onset (*une affaire brusquée*), usually connected with an assault and scaling of the walls (*escalade*), if the place should not be strongly garrisoned, or not in a proper state of defence—or if the assailants have no time to lose, or are possessed of strength and means sufficient for carrying their point (of late years, this method of attack has been strongly recommended, especially if it can be seconded by an efficacious and skilful use of artillery); 3. by blockade out of gun-shot (see *Blockade*); 4. by a siege, properly so called. The fortress is first blockaded, so as to cut off all intercourse from without; it is then important to examine the nature of the fortification, to discover the strength of the garrison, as well as the means of defence, and, if possible, the weakest parts of the place, in order to mark out a proper plan of attack: after this, the cannon, together with the necessary ammunition and implements for the pioneers, are brought forward; and the other requisites (fascines, gabions, &c.) are prepared and kept in readiness. The engineer who directs the operations must accurately calculate his time, the resistance to be expected, as well as the means at his disposal, and form his plan of attack accordingly. If any detached works are situated before the fortress, their capture becomes necessary to admit the opening of the trenches, at the distance of 500—900 paces from the covered way. After they are properly marked out (*tracées*), several columns of pioneers, furnished with fascines and instruments for digging, and defended by regular troops, advance (commonly by night) towards the fortress as far as the spot designated for the trenches, and there immediately engage in opening a trench. Each laborer places his fascine before him, throws the ground over it, and thus a kind of breastwork is formed, constituting the first parallel (q. v.), where the forces directed against the fortress may be collected. The besieged, by sallies and counter operations of every kind, strive to drive off the laborers and to destroy their work, while, on the other hand, the besiegers make efforts to establish themselves more and more securely, to raise batteries, and then, by means of trenches, dug for this purpose, and new parallels which more and more closely encircle the fortress, to approach the moat, while the artillery is kept constantly playing from the batteries on the garrison as well as the works and guns of the besieged. With this the bombardment from the mortar-batteries is usually combined (see *Battery*), for the purpose of dislodging the garrison from their works, of dismantling the works themselves, and of destroying buildings, magazines, &c. From the last parallel, which approaches very near the moat of the fortress, the besiegers prepare to cross the moat, and labor to make breaches. (q. v.) Here likewise mining operations (see *Mine*) are carried on, whenever they are found advisable. The moat is crossed in saps (q. v.), or covered passages of a similar kind, and, should it be filled with water, on rafts, bridges, &c. When at last the breaches are practicable, the works of the strong-hold as much as possible demolished, the garrison and their artillery impaired, then follows the storming or scaling of the walls.—*To raise the siege* of a fortress, is to compel the enemy to retire from the place. They may be forced to this by inundations, if the situation of the place admits of them; by want of provisions, if the surrounding country has been desolated, or the convoys intended for them be captured; or, finally, by assault. If it is impossible to drive away the enemy, a temporary interruption of the siege is attempted, in order to introduce provisions or fresh troops into the fortress. This is generally done by a sudden attack on the lines of the besiegers, and forcing a way through them, with the coöperation of the besieged.

SIENITE; one of the primitive rocks, differing from granite chiefly in the substitution of hornblende for mica; but feldspar forms its most abundant ingredient, and is often red. When the quartz and hornblende are fine-grained, and the feldspar in distinctly imbedded crystals of considerable dimensions, the rock is called *porphyritic sienite*, or *sienite-porphyry*. Sienite is sometimes unstratified, though more commonly manifesting a tendency to the columnar structure. It embraces no foreign beds. It occurs in unconformable and overlying stratification, over granite, gneiss, mica-slate and clay-slate. It is equally prolific in metals as porphyry. In the island of Cyprus, it affords much copper. Many of the important silver and gold mines in Hungary are situated in sienite. In the forest of Thuringia, it affords iron. It abounds in Upper Egypt, at the city of Syene, in the Thebaid, at the cataracts of the Nile, whence it derives its name. The Romans brought it thence to Rome, for architectural purposes and for statuary.

SIENNA, or SIENA; an ancient city of Tuscany, the capital of the province of Sienna. Being built on three eminences, the streets are extremely uneven, winding and narrow, so that the chief part of the town is impassable for carriages. The only handsome public square is that in which is the town-house, and which contains a beautiful fountain. The esplanade is a fine shady avenue leading to the citadel, the ramparts of which, planted with trees, and laid out in the form of terraces, afford several interesting points of view. The cathedral of Sienna is a magnificent marble structure in the Gothic style, built in the thirteenth century, by Giovanni Pisani, and accounted inferior to none in Italy, except St. Peter's at Rome. The town-house is a large building, also in the Gothic style, and surrounded with porticoes. Adjoining is the theatre, rebuilt since 1750. There are in Sienna several family mansions, or palaces, but none of remarkable architecture. The manufactures of Sienna comprise woollen, leather, paper and hats, but all on a small scale. This town is the seat of a university. Sienna lays claim to great antiquity, but it was long a petty place. Its prosperity was greatest during the middle ages, when it enjoyed an extensive commerce, and is said to have had a population of 150,000. It long maintained itself as an independent republic; but, intestine divisions favoring the designs of foreign powers, it became successively subject to French and Spanish invaders. Population, 24,000; lon. 11° 10′ 15″ E.; lat. 43° 22′ N.

SIERRA (*Spanish*), SERRA (*Portuguese*); a chain of mountains.

SIERRA LEONE; a country of Western Africa, on the Atlantic, distinguished for the colony formed there by the British nation, rather from motives of philanthropy than from those of commercial advantage. It is traversed by a considerable river, called the Mitomba or Sierra Leone. The name is derived from a ridge of mountains, which rises near the southern bank of the river. This country equals, in fertility and populousness, any other in this part of Africa. It consists generally of one vast, almost impenetrable forest, only particular spots of which have been cleared and cultivated. Rice is raised wherever the ground is sufficiently watered for its production, and forms the constant food of the rich; but the poor content themselves with millet, yams and plantains. There is great abundance of the most delicate fruits. Elephants' teeth and civet are brought to the coast. The woods and mountains are infested with wild animals, particularly lions, from the multitude of which the country appears to have derived its name. There are swarms of insects, flies, mosquitoes, and particularly ants, the white species of which commit extraordinary devastation. The serpent species are also very numerous. The rivers, besides yielding an ample supply of fish for food, contain large alligators, and the manata or sea-cow. The natives of this country are not of so deep black a complexion as those of cape Verd, nor have they the flat nose of the negro race to such a degree. The character of the different tribes varies greatly. The Portuguese were the first who discovered and formed settlements on the river Sierra Leone. Towards the close of the eighteenth century, the British began to turn their views towards Sierra Leone, with a view to colonization, for the more effectual abolition of the slave-trade, by raising up an African colony, whither the slaves might be sent as freemen. Lord Mansfield having decided, in 1772, that a slave who sets foot in Britain becomes free, a number of blacks in England left their masters, and were wandering about in a desolate condition. Granville Sharp (q. v.) formed the plan of transporting them to Africa; and, the aid of the government having been obtained, they were landed (1787) upon a district purchased from the king of Sierra Leone. These negroes and the white females sent with them were mostly of indifferent characters, and a severe mortality ensued among them. In 1792, about 1200 negroes, who had been seduced from their masters in the United States during the revolutionary war, were also landed at Sierra Leone; and several years later the colony was increased by 550 Maroons (q. v.) from Nova Scotia. Little progress, however, had been made in the objects for which the colony was formed, and, in 1807, it was surrendered into the hands of the crown. At that period Great Britain received permission from several powers to treat as pirates such of their subjects as should be found engaged in the slave-trade north of the line; and the liberated negroes seized by her cruisers were placed at Sierra Leone. For the first six months they receive a daily allowance from the government, after which lands are assigned them, and they are left to support themselves. The number thus liberated has been about 20,000; and although their wild and improvident habits have thrown many difficulties in the way of the benevolent exertions of the British authorities, recent accounts give decided proofs of great improvements in the spirit and condition of the colonists. Freetown, the principal place of the colony, has an excellent harbor on the river Sierra Leone, about six miles from the sea (lat. 8° 32′ N.), and upwards of 6000 inhabitants. Regent's town, six miles south of Freetown, founded in 1816, has a population of 1300; and in the vicinity are several villages, with the more distant stations of Waterloo, Wellington and Hastings. Bathurst, on the Gambia, is a settlement also connected with this colony.

SIERRA MORENA. (See *Morena, Sierra.*)

SIERRA NEVADA (Spanish, *Snowy Range*); a chain of mountains in Spain, the most elevated range in the peninsula, which derives its name from the perpetual snow that covers its loftiest summits. It extends through Granada and Andalusia, from west to east, and terminates on the shores of the Mediterranean, in several promontories, of which that of Gibraltar is the most remarkable. The highest peak is Cumbre de Mulahacen, which has an elevation of nearly 14,000 feet. The principal river which descends from the Sierra Nevada is the Xenil. (See *Granada.*)

SIESTA (Spanish, for *noon*); the heat of the noon; whence it came to signify the rest or nap taken after dinner during the season of heat.

SIÈYES, Emanuel Joseph, count de, born May 3, 1748, at Fréjus, was vicar-general of the bishop of Chartres, when, in 1789, he was appointed deputy of the third estate of Paris in the estates-general. He was indebted for this appointment to his celebrated pamphlet *Qu'est-ce que le tiers État?* which gained him great favor among the people. He contributed much to the union of the three estates, and first proposed to declare the chamber of deputies of the third estate a national assembly—a measure which decided the revolution. He insisted on the removal of the troops, and advocated the celebrated oath in the tennis-court at Versailles. It was he, too, who opposed with so much warmth, August 10, the abolition of the tithes, and who uttered the famous sentiment, "You wish to be free; but you know not how to be just." He opposed the sanctioning of the royal veto, which was contended for by Mirabeau, and suggested the idea of dividing France into departments, cantons and municipalities (*communes*)—a measure which contributed not a little to give stability to the revolution. He was very active in committees, labored to frame a constitution, but rarely spoke in public; for, in 1789, he had declared himself unskilled in extempore debate, and determined not to appear in the tribune. Mirabeau then declared, in a full assembly, that the silence of Sièyes was a public calamity. In 1790, he proposed a law to the assembly for punishing offences of the press. At the same time, he proposed the admission of juries on trials for these offences. In 1791, Sièyes was made a member of the directory of the department of Paris, and, about the same time, refused the bishopric of the capital, which he was solicited to take by the electoral assembly. Amid the zeal for republicanism which then prevailed, he declared himself, in the *Moniteur*, decidedly favorable to monarchy. "I prefer monarchy," said he, "not because I am fond of ancient usages; not from any superstitious love of royalty; I prefer it because to me it seems evident, that the citizens have more real freedom in a monarchy than in a republic. But the best state is that in which all may quietly enjoy the greatest freedom possible." When he was made a member of the convention, he shunned distinction, in order to escape the storms which he saw were coming. At the time of the trial of Louis XVI, he was true to this system, and, on the occasion of the vote which decided the fate of that prince, "Yes," "No," and "Death," were the only words which were heard from his mouth. He had before maintained, without effect, that it was not proper for the assembly to unite the judicial with the legislative power. He remained comparatively in the back ground till 1795. Then he ascended the tribune, and expressed his abhorrence of the crimes of Robespierre, whom he had not dared to resist. He soon after became a member of the committee of public safety, was sent to Holland to conclude a treaty there with the new republic, and, on his return, had an important influence on the treaties with Prussia and Spain. In 1798, he went as ambassador to Berlin, and remained there till 1799, when he was made a member of the directory, in the place of Rewbel. The revolution of the 18th Brumaire was contrived by Sièyes, in conjunction with Bonaparte; and, in consequence of this, he was appointed consul provisorily, with Napoleon and Roger Ducos. On the introduction of the new constitution, he was made a member of the senate, and received the estate of Crosne; but as he did not take actual possession of it, he received an indemnification. After the restoration, he went back to the capital. On the return of Napoleon from Elba, Sièyes was made a member of the chamber of peers; but, in 1816, by the royal decree against the regicides, he was banished from France. Since that time, he has resided in Brussels.

Sigæum; a celebrated cape on the coast of Asia, with a town of the same name, not far from Troy, near which the Greeks encamped during the Trojan war. Here Achilles drew his fleet on shore, and here he was buried with his friends Patroclus and Antilochus. Large mounds of earth are still to be seen here, which have been taken for their tombs. A remarkable inscription has been found upon a block of marble at Sigæum, of which a part, written in the Æolic dialect, is thought to be prior to the time of the poet Simonides. The people in the neighborhood considered this monument as a sort of palladium; and the sick laid or seated themselves upon it, so as almost to obliterate the inscription. However, it has been copied entire, and was carried to England by lord Elgin.

Sight. (See *Eye*, and *Optics*.)

Signals; certain notices used to communicate intelligence to distant objects. At sea, they are made by firing artillery, displaying flags and pendants, lanterns, or fire-works, as rockets and false fires; and these are combined by multiplication and repetition; by which combination of preconcerted signals, the admiral conveys orders to his fleet, every squadron, every division, and ship, of which, has its particular signal. Every ship to which a signal is made, immediately answers it by hoisting some particular flag, to show that she has received and understands the order thereby conveyed. All signals at sea may be reduced to three different kinds, viz. those which are made by the sound of particular instruments, as the trumpet, horn, or fife, to which may be added striking the bell, or beating the drum; those which are made by displaying pendants, ensigns, and flags of different colors, or by lowering or altering the position of sails; and, lastly, those which are executed by rockets of different kinds, by firing cannon or small arms, by artificial fire-works, or by lanterns. All signals, to be effectual, must be simple, and composed in such a manner as to express the same signification, at whatever mast-head or yard-arm they may be displayed. They should be issued without precipitation, exposed in a conspicuous place, so as to be seen at a distance, and sufficient time should be allowed to observe and obey them. Signals are very numerous and important, and are all communicated in the instructions sent to the commander of every ship of the fleet or squadron, before their putting to sea. Few subjects have more seriously engaged the attention of nautical men. In the land forces, signals are made by the firing of cannon, or by sound of trumpet. Balloons are sometimes used for signals. (For the *Telegraph*, see that article.)

SIGNATURE; among printers, a letter or figure at the bottom of the first page of a sheet or half sheet, by which the order of the sheets is designated, so as to guide the binder. Every successive sheet has a different letter or figure; and, where letters are employed, if the sheets are more numerous than the letters of the alphabet, then a small letter is added to the capital one, as, A a, B b, &c. In large volumes, the signatures are sometimes composed of letters and figures, thus, 5 A, 5 B. It is more common, however, at present, to use only figures.

SIGNET; one of the king's seals, made use of in sealing his private letters, and all grants that pass by bill, signed under his majesty's hand. It is always in the custody of the secretaries of state. (See *Seal*.)

SIKHS, or SEIKS; a religious sect in Hindoostan, which professes the purest Deism. It is chiefly distinguished from the Hindoos by worshipping one only and invisible God. It was founded by the estimable Nanac Shah, of the caste of Cshatriyas and the Hindoo tribe of the Vedis, who was born A. D. 1469, in the village of Talwandi (now the town of Rajapoor), in the province of Lahore. When Nanac was very young, he met some fakirs, who converted him to the Nagornai worship, which consists in the adoration of one God. His lively imagination made him dissatisfied with traffic; and, to gratify his thirst for knowledge, he travelled through Hindoostan, Persia, and Arabia, visited Medina and Mecca (the Mohammedan places of pilgrimage), and the sacred sects of the Hindoos in Vatala, and the Picos (Mohammedan saints) in Moultan. Afterwards he became acquainted with the system of the Ssufi, and adopted their doctrines. He read, particularly, the works of a Mohammedan named Cabik, belonging to this sect, who enjoined, in all his writings, universal philanthropy, and, particularly, religious toleration. Nanac now renounced all worldly business, and consecrated his life to the purest devotion. He entertained the noble and benevolent idea of effecting a union between the Hindoos and Mohammedans, by introducing simplicity of faith and purity of morals. Hence he treated both religions with respect, labored to remove only what was superfluous and dissonant, and to lead the people to a practical religion, to a pure worship of God, and love to mankind. Thus he used to say, "Hundreds of thousands of Mohammeds, millions of Brahmas and Vishnoos, and hundreds of thousands of Rahmas, stand before the throne of the Almighty, and they all die. God alone is immortal. He only is a good Hindoo who is just, and a good Mohammedan whose life is pure." Nanac died about 1540, at Kirtipur, where he lies buried on the banks of the Ravee. Hence Kirtipur is deemed a sacred place by the Sikhs; and a relic of Nanac's dress is preserved in his temple there, which is shown to pilgrims. The ennobling religion established by Nanac, and the benevolence of his doctrines, corresponded to the purity of his whole life. Far from deceiving his adherents with pretended miracles, he replied to the Yogiswares (to whom a dominion over the powers of nature, procured by self-torture, is attributed in Hindoostan), when they importuned him to perform a miracle, "I have nothing worth showing. A holy teacher has no defence but the purity of his doctrines. The world may alter, but the Creator is unchangeable." As a governor and priest, he exercised, during his life, a spiritual and temporal dominion over his disciples. At his death, he transferred the power, not to his sons, but to a favorite disciple named Lehana, whom he had himself initiated into his doctrines, and dressed in the sacred garb of a fakir. Of his successors in the government of the Sikhs, Arjun gave stability to the religion, and unity to its professors, by collecting the writings of Nanac, and publishing the *A'di Grant'h*, the first sacred book of the sect. But this drew upon him the notice and the jealousy of the Mohammedan government, and he was put to death. Eager to avenge his father's death, Har Govind, the son and successor of Arjun, transformed the Sikhs from peaceful believers into valiant warriors; and, under his reign, and that of his posterity, a bloody contest was maintained between them and the Mohammedans, till the day of Behadur's execution, whose son, Guru Govind, was forced to retreat with his adherents to the Punjab, where a Hindoo chief kindly entertained him, and gave him Mekhamel, on the banks of the Setledge. Guru Govind established there the state of the Sikhs, destroying among them the Hindoo distinction of castes, and giving equal rights to the lowest Soodra and the highest Brahmin. This procured him great accessions to the numbers of his disciples, whom he excited to seek for happiness in this and the future world by destroying the tyrannical Mohammedans. From this time, in consequence of their heroic conduct during the protracted contest with their oppressors, Guru Govind's followers received the title of Sikhs or lions, which before had been confined to the Rajaputs, as the first military order among the Hindoos. This ruler, equally great as a soldier and a lawgiver, wrote the *Dasema Padshah ke Grant'h*, or the book of the tenth prince (so called because he was the tenth ruler of the Sikhs from Nanac). Besides treating of religious subjects, it contained also the history of the author's exploits. It is regarded by the sect with the same veneration as the *A'di Grant'h* of Arjun. Guru Govind directed the Sikhs, in order to distinguish them for ever from Mohammedans and Hindoos, to wear a blue dress, to let their hair grow, and to be always armed. To make his religious institutions more stable, he founded a religious order, the *acalis* (immortals), and assigned the members of it a *bonga* (monastery) by the sacred fountain at Emoilser, on the income of which they were supported. To these *acalis* he committed the care of converting and initiating new Sikhs; and in their hands still rests the supreme direction of all the religious and civil affairs. Guru Govind was the last head of the Sikhs; for a prophecy limited the number of the rulers to ten; and as he was the tenth ruler after Nanac, he said to his friends, on his death-bed, "I commit the state to God, who never dies." Hence the Sikhs suppose that their state is under the peculiar care of the Deity. Their government, therefore, is a pure theocracy. The popular faith would prove an insurmountable obstacle to any one who should attempt to subject the Sikhs to his rule. After the death of Guru Govind, the Sikhs gradually yielded to the superior power of the Mohammedans; and even Banda, one of their most heroic leaders, after a fearful struggle, was taken prisoner in the fort of Lagab, with all his followers, sent to Delhi, and put to death with the most barbarous tortures. To exterminate at length the hated sect, a price was set upon their head by the Mohammedan government, and every adherent of it, who could be taken, was put to death. But they suffered, with the greatest firmness, the pains of martyrdom, often courting, rather than fleeing from them. Nothing could induce them to renounce their faith; and a Mahommedan writer has stated that no Sikh who was taken on the pilgrimage to Amritsar (the holy place of the Sikhs) ever abjured his religion to save his life. A very small number of the Sikhs escaped to inaccessible mountains, and faithfully preserved the doctrines of their fathers, and an inextinguishable hatred towards their persecutors. After Nadir Shah's return to Persia, they ventured to leave the mountains; and, taking advantage of the confusion into which Nadir's expedition had plunged Hindoostan, they subdued all Lahore. At present, the territory of the Sikhs extends from 28° 40′ to beyond 30° north latitude, and comprehends all the Punjab, a part of Moultan, and the largest portion of the country lying between the Jumnah and the Setledge, or the north-western corner of Hindoostan, containing 69,000 square miles, and 4,000,000 inhabitants. A few chiefs, who form a diet at Amritsar, and deliberate on subjects of general interest, under the direction of the *acalis*, rule over portions of country of greater or less extent. According to the account of general Malcolm, who was in the Punjab with the British army in 1805, and to whom we are indebted for the most accurate information concerning this interesting sect (see vol. xi of the *Asiatic Researches*, containing his *Sketch of the Sikhs*, also printed separately in 1812), they are able to bring into the field 100,000 horse. Their present governor, or *maha raja*, is said to have subjected portions of Afghanistan and Cashmire to his rule. In the separate districts, subordinate chiefs, or *sirdars*, possess unlimited power. Lahore is the residence of the chief ruler, and contains 100,000 inhabitants. The city of Amritsar is the great depot of Cashmere shawls and of saffron.

Silenus; the tutor and companion of Bacchus; according to some, the son of Mercury, or of Pan, by a nymph; according to others, he sprang from the blood of Uranus. According to Pindar, his wife was the nymph Nais; according to others, a nymph of Malea, in the island of Lesbos, who bore him the Arcadian Centaur Pholus. He educated Bacchus, instructed him in the sciences, and was ever afterwards his constant companion. He loved the inspiring beverage of his pupil's invention so well, that he was generally intoxicated; and in this plight he was found by two young Satyrs, who bound him with garlands, and compelled him to sing. Midas caught him in the same condition, and entered into a philosophical conversation with him. In the war of the giants, Silenus aided the gods, and terrified their enemies by the braying of his ass. A whole race of Silenuses sprang from him. The name is often applied to old Satyrs of a cheerful, good-natured disposition. They are represented with a curly beard, a low forehead, and bald head. The chief of the race is the companion of Bacchus above described, known by the cantharus or bottle which he bears. He is often also distinguished from the other Sileni, by being mounted on an ass, or by his accompanying Bacchus, and is frequently represented holding the infant Bacchus in his arms. He sometimes also appears treading out grapes, and covered with hair. In the latter case, a caricature is intended.

Silesia (in German, *Schlesien*); formerly a duchy belonging to Bohemia, now divided, politically, between Prussia and Austria, and, geographically, into Upper and Lower Silesia. The *Prussian* province of Silesia (15,264 square miles; population, 2,396,551) borders on Posen and Poland to the east, on the Austrian territories to the south, and on Saxony and Brandenburg to the west and north. (See *Prussia.*) The southern part of the province is mountainous, being intersected by different ridges of the Sudetic chain. (q. v.) Towards Brandenburg and Posen it is level, but in part marshy and sandy, although throughout adapted to tillage. The principal river is the Oder. (q. v.) The soil of Silesia is fertile, yielding corn of all sorts, fruits, and tolerable wines. The mountainous parts are covered with wood, or afford good pasturage and meadow land. Flax is raised in large quantities, and affords an important article of manufacture and trade, and madder, hemp, hops and tobacco are among the productions of the province. The wool of Silesia is of the best sort produced in Prussia. Among the mineral productions are iron, copper, lead, some silver, sulphur, vitriol, &c., and there are mineral waters in several places. Linen is the principal article of manufacture, and owes its excellence to the inspection system, which has been introduced here. Cotton and woollen goods and leather are also manufactured to a great extent. Silesia is divided into three governments—Breslau, Liegnitz and Oppeln. The inhabitants are chiefly Lutherans and Catholics, with some Calvinists, Hussites, Herrnhutters, Jews, &c. There is a university in Breslau (q. v.), the capital of the province, with two theological faculties, one for Catholics and the other for Protestants, and numerous gymnasia, or high schools, in the large towns. The revenue is about six million dollars.—*Austrian Silesia* consists of the southern part of the old Silesian duchy, which was left to Austria by the peace of Hubertsburg, in 1763. It is divided into the circles of Teschen and Troppau, and attached to the Moravian *gubernium* of Brünn. Population, 350,000; square miles, 2500. It is mountainous, and although the soil is not in all parts favorable, it is rendered productive by the industry of the inhabitants, who are also extensively engaged in linen, cotton and woollen manufactures. In the sixth century, this country was occupied by Sclavonians, who drove out the Lygii and Quadi, and thus annexed it to Poland. It was afterwards divided into a great number of petty principalities, and in the fourteenth century, it became a dependency of Bohemia. (q. v.) Although, in consequence of its annexation to Bohemia, it came to be considered a part of Germany, it never actually formed a member of the empire. (For the more modern history of Silesia, see *Frederic II*, *Seven Years' War*, and *Prussia.*)

Silesian Poets. (See *German Poetry.*)

Silesian Wars. (See *Frederic II*, *Maria Theresa*, and *Seven Years' War.*)

Silex, or Silica. The mineral species quartz, it was mentioned under that article, consists almost exclusively of silex. It also forms a principal ingredient in nearly all the earthy minerals, and was regarded as one of the primitive earths, until after the discovery of the composition of the fixed alkalies by Davy, when it was ascertained, by this philosopher, to consist of oxygen and an unknown base, which has been called *silicon*, or *silicium*. If we ignite powdered quartz with three parts of pure potash in a silver crucible, dissolve the fused compound in water, add to the solution a quantity of muriatic acid, sufficient to saturate the alkali and evaporate to dryness, we shall obtain a fine, gritty powder, which, being well washed with hot water, and ignited, will yield pure silex. By passing the vapor of potassium over silex, in an ignited tube, we obtain boron, the basis of the earth. Thus obtained, as well as by several other methods, silicon is of a deep brown color; is a non-conductor of electricity: it stains the fingers, and adheres to every thing that comes in contact with it. Like carbon and boron, it may be exposed to a very high temperature in close vessels, without fusion; but it becomes harder, the greater the heat to which it has been subjected. By this treatment, its properties are very materially altered. Before it has been heated, it is readily combustible in the air, and burns with a very lively flame. By this combustion, about one third of it is converted into silica, while the rest is preserved by the silica formed, which prevents the unburnt portion from coming in contact with the atmosphere. Silex, or silica, is the only compound of silicon and oxygen with which we are acquainted. It is a white, tasteless powder, feeling gritty between the teeth, and having a specific gravity of 2.65. When originally formed by the combustion of silicon, it is so soluble in water, that the liquid, when concentrated, gelatinizes. But after it has been exposed to heat, it loses its solubility altogether. When silex is mixed with thrice its weight of potash, or with a quantity of carbonate of potash, containing thrice as much potash as the weight of silex employed, and the mixture is exposed to a strong heat, it fuses, and assumes, on cooling, the appearance of glass. This glass dissolves in water. If to an aqueous solution of it we add as much muriatic acid as will saturate the alkali, and concentrate the solution sufficiently, the silica assumes the form of a white translucent jelly. This characterizes silica. If we evaporate the whole to dryness, and wash off the salt of potash from the dry mass, the silica remains behind in the state of a very fine powder. Silex consists of about 48 silicon, and oxygen 52. It may be subjected to a very violent heat, without suffering any change; there is no difficulty in causing it to melt, however, before the compound blow-pipe. Though silex does not redden vegetable blues, yet it enters into definite compounds with the different bases, and forms saline compounds, which are distinguished by the name of *silicates*, and is hence called *silicic acid* by some writers on chemistry. Like other weak acids, it is capable of entering into a great variety of combinations with bases. The combinations which it forms are frequently so intimate, that no other acid is capable of removing the base and setting the silica at liberty. The different kinds of glass consist of two or more silicates melted together. Silicon burns vividly when heated in chlorine gas, and the compound formed is a colorless liquid, which is a *chloride of silicon*. It evaporates almost spontaneously, in the form of a white vapor, when exposed to the open air. It boils at a temperature below 212°. It reddens litmus paper very strongly. When dropped into water, it swims on the surface of that liquid. It is gradually dissolved in the water, but deposits, at the same time, a little silica. Silicon unites with fluorine, and forms an acid gas, which is called *fluosilicic acid*. It is easily obtained by mixing together fluor spar and glass, or quartz, both in fine powder, in a small retort, and adding a sufficient quantity of sulphuric acid, to form the whole into a semi-fluid mass. When heat is applied to this mixture, fluosilicic acid comes over in the form of a transparent invisible gas. This gas is rapidly absorbed by water, while silica is deposited in a gelatinous state. Its specific gravity is 3.6. It consists of fluoric acid 17.6, silica 27.2. When potassium is heated in it, combustion takes place, and a chocolate-colored substance is formed, which differs in its nature, according to the proportion of potassium employed. Fluosilicic acid gas combines with twice its volume of ammoniacal gas, forming a volatile salt. Silicon and carbon combine, when they come in contact in a nascent state. The *carburet* formed is a dark brown powder. *Sulphuret of silicon* is formed by heating silicon in the vapor of sulphur, and the union is attended with the phenomena of combustion. It is a white, earthy-looking substance, which is instantly converted by the action of water into sulphureted hydrogen and silica. Silicon is more allied to carbon and boron than to the metals.

SILHOUETTE is the representation of the outlines of an object filled with black color, in which the inner lines are sometimes slightly drawn in white. The name comes from Etienne de Silhouette, French minister of finance in 1759. He strove by severe economy to remedy the evils of a war which had just terminated, leaving the country in great exhaustion. At the end of nine months, he was obliged to leave his place. During this period, all the fashions in Paris took the character of parsimony. Coats without folds were worn; snuff-boxes were made of plain wood; and, instead of painted portraits, outlines only were drawn in profile, and filled with Indian ink, &c. All these fashions were called *à la Silhouette;* but the name remained only in the case of the profiles, because the ease with which they may be drawn, or cut out of black paper, makes them popular, though, considered as works of art, they have little value. Some faces—those with a marked profile—are easily taken in this way, whilst others lose their character entirely particularly those whose traits are well harmonized. In general, the extremes of expressions, as the expression of great savageness or sternness, great mildness or obstinacy, deep reflection, or great stupidity, are those most easily given in this mode. But the expression of blended imagination, thought, and goodness of disposition, is not easily conveyed in profile. On the whole, the silhouette expresses more the original disposition of the mind, than its cultivated character. These representations may be taken very well from the shadow of a person on a paper held on the wall; and in order to make the shadow more steady, it is well to rest the head on a book or the like, put between the face and the paper. The paper is then cut according to the outline of the shadow, and the outer surface pasted on black paper. The likeness can be taken still better, and of any size, by means of an instrument called a *pantograph.* A frame with a glass, on which paper slightly oiled and well dried is fastened, attached to a chair on which the person sits, whose likeness is to be taken, is also of much advantage. The invention of the silhouette, in ancient times, is said to have given rise to the art of painting. This invention is ascribed to the daughter of the potter Dibutades, who drew the outline of her lover's shadow on the wall. The time of this invention may be placed at the renewal of the Olympic games, shortly before the expulsion of the Bacchiades from Corinth, about 776 B. C. Sicyon and Corinth were the first places where painting flourished. Crato of Sicyon, Philocles of Egypt, and Cleanthes of Corinth, are mentioned as inventors of the monochromes (q. v.), they having filled the outline with colors. The silhouettes were soon applied to large objects; thus Saurias of Samos drew the shadow of his horse on a wall. The estimation of these drawings with the ancients, the beauty and delicacy with which they were executed, may still be seen from the Etruscan vases.

Silicate of Manganese; the name of a chemical family in mineralogy, which consists of two mineralogical species, viz. the *Fowlerite* and the *manganese spar*, or siliceous oxide of manganese. The *Fowlerite* occurs in feldspar-looking crystals, differing, however, in the valve of its angles, from feldspar. Its angles are 95° 0′, 121° 0′, and 113° 0′. Its hardness is the same as feldspar; specific gravity 3.5 to 3.8; color flesh-red. It is fusible with difficulty, and tinges borax red. It consists of

Silex,	29.48
Protoxide of manganese,	50.58
Peroxide of iron,	13.22
Water,	3.17

It is found in crystals of considerable size, and in foliated and granular masses, at Franklin, New Jersey, accompanied by Franklinite and magnetic iron ore. It also occurs at Cumberland in Rhode Island. The *manganese spar* occurs massive, fine, granular, and, rarely, somewhat fibrous; color rose-red; lustre intermediate between pearly and resinous; translucent; hardness but little inferior to feldspar; specific gravity, 3.5. Heated before the blow-pipe, it becomes dark-brown, and melts into a reddish globule. It tinges borax hyacinth-red. It consists of

Silex,	40.58
Protoxide of manganese,	38.92
Protoxide of iron,	13.50
Water,	3.
Carbonic acid,	3.23
	99.23

It is found in primitive districts, usually in connexion with beds of iron ore. Localities of it exist in the Hartz, in Sweden, and in Devonshire, England. It has been discovered in large quantities in Massachusetts, at Cummington, in isolated masses, from one foot to two feet in diameter. This species is sometimes wrought into articles of ornament. When polished, its color and lustre are extremely delicate.

Silius, Caius, surnamed Italicus, was born in the reign of Tiberius, about the year 15. The origin of his surname is uncertain. At Rome, he applied himself to the bar, and became a celebrated orator and advocate. He was consul at the time of Nero's death, and incurred some reproach for assisting in that tyrant's prosecutions, but acquired honor from his conduct in the proconsulate of Asia, assigned to him by Vespasian, from which he retired into private life, and collected books, statues, and busts of eminent men He finally retired to his seat in Campania, where, being seized with an incurable ulcer, he put an end to his life by starvation, in his seventy-fifth year. The only work of Silius which has reached modern times, is an epic poem on the second Punic war, in sixteen books, written with more diligence than genius. It contains, however, occasional splendid passages; and his description of the passage of Hannibal across the Alps is particularly admired. The best editions are those of Drakenborch (1717, 4to.), and of Ruperti (Göttingen, 1795—8, 2 vols., 8vo.).

SILK. According to the ancients, silk was first brought from Serica or Sereinda (China), whence the silk-worm was introduced into other countries, but not until the reign of Justinian, when two Persian monks succeeded in secretly conveying a number of the eggs to Constantinople in a hollow cane (552). From these eggs Europe and America have been supplied with their race of worms. The time of the origin of the silk manufacture is uncertain, but the Chinese ascribe the invention to the empress Si-ling-shi, wife of Hoang-ti, about 2700 years before the Christian era. However this may be, the raw material had been exported from China long before the insect which produced it, and had given employment to extensive manufactories in Persia, Tyre, &c. The invention of the celebrated Coan stuff is attributed by the Greeks to Pamphila, who is said to have taught her countrywomen of Cos to unweave the heavy silks of the East, and recompose the material into a transparent gauze, thus gaining in measure what was lost in substance. Even manufactured silk was little known in Europe before the reign of Augustus; and it is mentioned as a wanton extravagance of the prodigal Heliogabalus that he had a garment made wholly of silk. For six hundred years the culture of the silk-worm in Europe was confined to the Greek empire; but in the twelfth century, Roger, king of Sicily, introduced it into that island, whence it gradually spread to Italy, Spain, France, and other European countries. (See *Silk-Worm*, and *Mulberry*.) After the worm has enveloped itself in the cocoon, seven or eight days are permitted to elapse before the balls are gathered; the next process is to destroy the life of the chrysalides, which is done either by exposure to the sun or by the heat of an oven or of steam. The cocoons are next separated from the floss, or loose, downy substance, which envelopes the compact balls, and are then ready to be reeled. For this purpose, they are thrown into a boiler of hot water, for the purpose of dissolving the gum, and, being gently pressed with a brush, to which the threads adhere, the reeler is thus enabled to disengage them. The ends of four or more of the threads thus cleared are passed through holes in an iron bar, after which two of these compound threads are twisted together, and made fast to the reel. The length of reeled silk obtained from a single cocoon varies from 300 to 600 yards; and it has been estimated that twelve pounds of cocoons, the produce of the labors of 2800 worms, who have consumed 152 pounds of mulberry leaves, give one pound of reeled silk, which may be converted into sixteen yards of gros de Naples. Those cocoons which have been perforated cannot be reeled, but must be spun, on account of the breaks in the thread. The produce of these balls, when worked, is called *fleuret*. The raw silk, before it can be used in weaving, must be twisted or thrown, and may be converted into singles, tram, or organzine. The first is produced merely by twisting the raw silk, to give more firmness to its texture. Tram is formed by twisting together, but not very closely, two or more threads of raw silk, and usually constitutes the weft or shoot of manufactured goods. Organzine is principally used in the warp, and is formed by twisting first each individual thread, and then two or more of the threads thus twisted, with the throwing mill. The silk, when thrown, is called *hard silk*, and must be boiled in order to discharge the gum, which otherwise renders it harsh to the touch, and unfit to receive the dye. After boiling about four hours in soaped water, it is washed in clear water to discharge the soap, and is seen to have acquired that glossiness and softness of texture which forms its principal characteristic. The yarn is now ready for weaving. Velvet (Italian, *velluto*, shaggy) is one of the richest of silken fabrics, and has been made in Europe for several centuries. In addition to the warp and shoot of which the substance of plain goods is formed, it has a soft shag or pile, produced by the insertion of short pieces of silk under thread doubled under the shoot, and which stand upright on its upper surface, so crowded together as entirely to conceal the interlacings of the warp and shoot. It is this pile which gives it its characteristic appearance, and softness to the touch. The beauty of velvet results, in a great degree, from the uniform evenness of its pile; and this depends on the perfect equality of the threads of which it is composed. The pile is inserted during the operation of weaving the warp and shoot. Gauze is a very light, transparent fabric of silk, said to have derived its name from having been originally brought from Gaza, a city of Palestine. Besides brocade and damask (see the articles), there are numerous descriptions of silk goods, popularly known by distinctive names, though varying only in the thickness of the fabric or the quality of the material, and not at all differing in the arrangements of its interlacings. Thus the plainest mode of silk weaving takes the names of Persian, sarsnet, gros de Naples, ducapes, &c., of which the two first are of flimsy texture, and the two last are made of stouter and harder thrown organzine. Satin is a twill of a peculiar description, the soft and lustrous face of which is given by keeping a large proportion of the threads of the warp visible. When first taken out of the loom, satins are somewhat flossy or rough; and they are dressed by being rolled on heated cylinders, which operation gives them their brilliant lustre. Crape is a light and transparent article of plain weaving (see *Crape*); Levantine, a stout, close-made and twilled silk. Gros des Indes is formed by using different shuttles, with threads of various substances for the shoot. The process of watering silk, which gives its surface a peculiar wavy appearance, is performed by passing two pieces of silk, placed lengthwise, one on the other, between two metallic rollers: the different parts are thus subjected to different degrees of pressure, from which the wavy appearance results. Silk is embossed by passing the plain stuff between rollers, the surfaces of which contain the desired pattern, on one cylinder raised, and on the other sunk, so that the eminences of the one coincide with the depressions in the other. Silk also enters into the composition of several mixed fabrics, the most common of which is bombasin, a twilled manufacture, having its warp of silk and its shoot of worsted. Poplins and lustres are plain woven goods, with a larger proportion of silk than bombasins. The annual value of the silk manufactures in England is stated at £14,000,000, or about $62,000,000. The raw silk is imported to the amount of above 4,000,000 pounds annually, of which 1,500,000 pounds are from Bengal. In 1824, the high duty on raw silk imported was abandoned for one merely nominal; that on thrown silk was reduced nearly one half, and the admission of foreign manufactured goods was rendered legal, after July 5, 1826. In the five years preceding this change, the importation of raw and thrown silk had amounted to 10,925,646 pounds; in the five years succeeding, the total amount of the importation was 18,582,213 pounds. The admission of foreign manufactured silks has also led to a great improvement in the quality of the domestic manufactures. The value of manufactured silks, exported from France in 1824, was 100,000,000 francs. Italy supplies England and France with a large quantity of raw silk. Some attention has recently been paid in the U. States to the rearing of the silk-worm; great numbers of mulberry trees have been planted in different parts of the Union, and attempts have been made to introduce the manufacture of silks in the country. A small quantity of raw silk was exported in 1831, and a filature has been established under the direction of M. d'Homergue, for the purpose of giving instruction in the process of the manufacture. See, on this subject, a paper by Mr. Duponceau, appendix to the 17th volume of the American edition of Brewster's *Encyclopædia*. On the culture of the silk-worm and the silk manufacture, in general, see also a *Treatise on the Silk Manufacture* (15th vol. of Lardner's *Cyclopædia*); the *Manual for the Culture of Silk, prepared by Order of the Massachusetts Legislature* (Boston, 1832), and *Essays on American Silk, with Directions for raising Silk-Worms, by J. D'Homergue and P. S. Duponceau* (Philadelphia, 1830).

Silk-Worm (*bombyx mori*). This seemingly insignificant insect has now become one of the most important to man of all domestic animals. It was originally a native of China, and the neighboring parts of Asia, and was there bred and domesticated for a long time before it was known in Europe. Now, the manufacture of silk is one of the most important sources of wealth to many parts of that continent. At first, silk stuffs were sold for their weight in gold; but they are now comparatively cheap. (For the period of the introduction of silk-worms into Europe, as well as for some observations on rearing them, see *Mulberry*.)—The silk-worm is a caterpillar, which, in due time, undergoes its metamorphoses, and becomes a moth, like others of the genus. At birth, and for the first ten days, the color of the worm is blackish or obscure. As it grows, it casts its skin at stated periods, and turns whitish or bluish, and, when ready to spin, becomes yellow. It is covered with scattering hairs, and has a little fleshy tubercle on the upper part of the last ring. It feeds on the mulberry. Before spinning, it fasts for thirty-six hours, voids all its excrements, becomes soft and flaccid, and seeks a suitable place for the construction of its cocoon. Two or three days are occupied in this work; and the thread is stated by count Dandolo to be sometimes 625 yards in length. The worm then changes to a chrysalis, and, after remaining twenty days, the moth comes out, forcing its way through the cocoon. The males first appear, and are very brisk in their motions, but do not fly, at least in cold climates. They live but a few days, and the females perish also as soon as they have deposited their eggs. The eggs are attached, often to the number of five hundred, or more, by means of a gummy substance, and hatch in the ensuing spring. The successful rearing of silk-worms is a distinct art, and requires peculiar attention. They are subject to a variety of maladies. In many places, it is usual to import the eggs from some district that has acquired reputation for their production. These are packed like grain, and are chosen much in the same manner. The eggs are in many places hatched by the heat of the human body. The silk is contained, in the form of a fluid, resembling varnish, in long cylindrical sacks, many times the length of the animal, and capable of being unfolded by immersion in water. This fluid is easily forced out, and advantage is sometimes taken of this circumstance to procure threads much coarser than usual, which are extremely strong, and impermeable to water.

SILLI; Greek poems written in hexameters, belonging to the class of satire, in which the philosophers, and their doctrines in particular, were ridiculed. The *silli* were often parodies on other poems. Timon and Didymus are famous writers of *silli*.

SILLIMANITE; a newly-discovered mineral from Saybrook, in Connecticut, where it is found disseminated through gneiss. It was named by Bowen, in honor of professor Silliman, of Yale college. It is possessed of the following properties: Its crystals are long, rhombic prisms, often curved and interlaced, the primitive form of which is an oblique rhombic prism, of about 99° 30′. They possess a brilliant cleavage parallel with the longer diagonal of the prism. Hardness slightly superior to that of quartz; specific gravity 3.2; color dark gray, passing into hair brown. Before the blow-pipe, on charcoal, it is infusible, and is dissolved by borax with great difficulty. According to Bowen, it consists of

Silex,	42.666
Alumine,	54.111
Oxide of iron,	1.999
Water	.510
	99.286

Doctor Thomson, in repeating the analysis of the sillimanite, detected in its composition eighteen per cent. of zircon.

SILO; a Spanish word, signifying an excavation about fourteen feet deep, for preserving grain. It is best made in marly ground, not too dry. Over the bottom a vaulted dome is built, rising eight and a half feet, and surrounding the tube through which the corn is poured in. The walls of the excavation are lined with straw. Three hundred bushels of wheat, preserved some time in a *silo*, were found, on careful examination, to have increased in measure one bushel, while the weight of the whole was diminished two and a half per cent. The expense of preserving grain in granaries is generally estimated at ten per cent.: in the larger *silos*, however, it is only one per cent., if the grain is left shut up two years. On the farm of Mr. Ternaux, at St. Ouen, near Paris, it was found that the grain put in his *silos*, in 1819, was sound and fresh in 1824. In Hungary, the same method of preserving grain is common.

SILOA, or SILOAM; a fountain on the east side of Jerusalem, between the city and the brook Kedron, or Cedron. St. John speaks of the pool of Siloam (John ix. 7). The tower of Siloam, mentioned in Luke xiii. 4, is thought to have been near this fountain.

SILONG; a city of China, of the second rank, in Quangsi.

SILVANUS; an Italian rural deity, usually represented with a sickle in his right hand and a bough in his left, and sometimes with the horns and feet of a goat. He is described as the protector of herds and trees from wolves and lightning, the god of agriculture, or the defender of boundaries; and offerings of various kinds were made to him. He is often confounded with the Fauns, Pans and Satyrs. (See the articles.)

SILVER; a metal which appears to have been known almost as early as gold, and, without doubt, for the same reason, because it occurs very frequently in a state of purity in the earth, and requires but an ordinary heat for its fusion. Mention is made of silver in the book of Job, which is considered the oldest of the books contained in the Old Testament. The ores of silver are somewhat numerous; and we shall defer our account of them to the conclusion of the present article, commencing with the chemical history of this metal. Pure silver is of a fine white color, with a shade of yellow, without either taste or smell, and, in brilliancy is inferior to none of the metallic bodies, if we except polished steel. It is softer than copper, but harder than gold. When melted, its specific gravity is 10.47; when hammered, 10.510. It is next in malleability to gold, having been beaten out into leaves only $\frac{1}{100,000}$th of an inch in thickness. Its ductility is no less remarkable. It may be drawn out into a wire much finer than a human hair; so fine, indeed, that a single grain of silver may be extended about 400 feet in length. Its tenacity is such, that a wire of silver 0.078 of an inch in diameter is capable of supporting a weight of 187.13 pounds avoirdupois without breaking. Silver melts when heated completely red-hot; and, while in the melted state, its brilliancy is greatly augmented. If the heat be increased after the silver is melted, the liquid metal boils, and may be volatilized; but a very strong and long-continued heat is necessary. Gasto Claveas kept an ounce of silver melted in a glass-house furnace for two months, and found, by weighing it, that it had sustained a loss of one twelfth of its weight. When heated upon charcoal under the flame of the compound blow-pipe, however, the silver is volatilized with rapidity, passing off in a visible smoke. When cooled slowly, its surface exhibits the appearance of crystals; and, if the liquid part of the metal be poured out as soon as the surface congeals, pretty large crystals of silver may be obtained. Silver is not oxidized by exposure to the air: it gradually, indeed, loses its lustre, and becomes tarnished; but this is owing to a different cause. Neither is it altered by being kept under water. But, if it be kept for a long time melted in an open vessel, it gradually attracts oxygen from the atmosphere, and is converted into an oxide. When silver is dissolved in nitric acid, and an alkali dropped into the solution, a brown-colored precipitate falls in flocks, which, when washed and dried, constitutes the *oxide of silver*. Its color becomes a dark brown when dried. Its specific gravity is 7.14. When exposed to the direct rays of the sun, it gives out oxygen gas, and is converted into a black powder, the nature of which has not been examined. The oxide of silver is a compound of 93.1 silver and 6.8 oxygen. When oxide of silver is dissolved in ammonia, and the solution left exposed to the air, it is soon covered with a brilliant pellicle, which is a *suboxide of silver*. A *superoxide of silver* appears to be formed, when a platina wire from the positive extremity of a galvanic battery is plunged into a weak solution of nitrate of silver, the compound in question accumulating in iron-black octahedrons upon the wire. Silver does not burn in chlorine gas, even when heated; but it gradually absorbs the gas, and is converted into the well-known compound formerly called *horn silver*, and afterwards *muriate of silver*, though now with more propriety denominated *chloride of silver*. This chloride, however, is more easily obtained by dissolving silver in nitric acid, and mixing the solution with a solution of common salt. A copious curdy precipitate falls. When this precipitate is washed and dried, it constitutes pure chloride of silver. Its specific gravity is 5.129. It is one of the most insoluble substances known, requiring no less than 3072 parts of water for its solution. When exposed to the air, it changes from white to a purple or blackish color. It melts at 500° Fahr., and assumes, on cooling, the form of a gray-colored, semi-transparent mass, having some resemblance to horn, and for that reason called *luna cornea*. A strong heat sublimes it. When heated strongly in an earthen crucible, it passes through altogether, and is lost in the fire; but when mixed with about four times its weight of fixed alkali formed into a ball, with a little water, and melted rapidly in a crucible well lined with alkali, the silver is reduced, and obtained in a state of purity. *Chloride of silver* is composed of silver 13.75, and chlorine 4.50. A *bromide* and an *iodide of silver* may be formed simply by adding in the one case, a solution of a hydrobromate to one of nitrate of silver, and, in the other, a solution of a hydriodate. If one ounce of silver, one ounce of phosphoric glass, and two drachms of charcoal, be mixed together, and heated in a crucible, *phosphuret of silver* is formed. It is of a white color, and crystalline in its texture. It is composed of four parts of silver and one of phosphorus. Heat decomposes it by separating the phosphorus. When thin plates of silver and sulphur are laid alternately above each other in a crucible, they melt readily in a low red heat, and form *sulphuret of silver*. Its color is black, and it crystallizes in small needles. It is capable of being cut with a knife, and is more easily fused than silver. It is well known that when silver is long exposed to the air, especially in frequented places, as churches, theatres, &c., it acquires a covering of a vio-tet color, which deprives it of its lustre and malleability: this coating is sulphuret of silver. Selenium appears to enter into combination with silver in two different proportions, forming *seleniets.* Arsenic forms an alloy with silver in the proportion of sixteen of the former to one hundred of the latter; it is steel-gray, brittle, and fine granular. Silver may be alloyed with antimony by fusion. Silver and iron unite readily: the alloy has the color of silver, but it is harder, very ductile, and attracted by the magnet. When 500 parts of good Indian steel are fused along with one part of silver, the compound is greatly improved for the purposes of cutting instruments. Melted lead dissolves a great quantity of silver at a slightly red heat; the alloy is brittle and lead-colored. Silver is easily alloyed with copper by fusion: the compound is harder, and more sonorous than silver, and retains its white color, even when the proportion of copper exceeds one half: the hardness is at its maximum when the copper amounts to one fifth of the silver. The alloy of silver and tin is very brittle and hard. That of silver and mercury is formed by throwing pieces of red hot silver into mercury heated till it begins to smoke: it forms dendritical crystals, which contain eight parts of mercury, and one of silver. The most important combination among those of the acids and silver (the *nitrate of silver*) has been alluded to above, in the description of the oxide of silver. Nitric acid is the proper solvent of this metal, from which solution the other salts of silver are obtained: it dissolves more than half its weight of the metal, the solution being attended with effervescence: if the silver and the acid are pure, the solution is limpid and colorless, exceedingly heavy and caustic: it stains the skin, and all animal substances, of an indelible black color; hence it is often used to dye hair, &c.: when evaporated till a pellicle begins to form on its surface, it deposits, on cooling, transparent crystals of nitrate of silver, in the form of six-sided, four-sided, or three-sided, thin plates; but, by slow evaporation, the salt may be obtained in short, right rhombic prisms of 129° 31′: its taste is intensely bitter and metallic, and it is usually employed as a corrosive substance, under the name of *lunar caustic:* it is soluble in its own weight of cold, and in half its weight of hot, water. From the solution, the silver is thrown down in a metallic state by a great number of bodies; for example, hydrogen, sulphurous acid, sulphate of iron, proto-chloride of tin, carbon, phosphorus, volatile oils, and many of the metals. The specific gravity of lunar caustic is 3.52. When heated, it readily melts, swells up, and then remains liquid: in this state it is cast into small cylindrical moulds by apothecaries, to be employed by surgeons for the purpose of opening ulcers and destroying fungous excrescences: as an escharotic, its action is powerful, and it is greatly preferred to caustic potash also, in consequence of its not being liable to deliquesce and spread. Both the crystals and the fused salt are anhydrous, consisting of 118 parts oxide of silver, and 54 nitric acid: it detonates, when heated with combustible bodies, and with phosphorus it detonates on percussion. *Sulphate of silver* is obtained with ease by mingling together solutions of nitrate of silver and sulphate of soda: it falls in the state of a white powder, which may be dissolved in water, and crystallized: the crystals are white and brilliant, and have the form of very fine prisms: it has the peculiarly disagreeable taste of the nitrate; is anhydrous, and composed of sulphuric acid 5, and oxide of silver 14.75. *Sulphite of silver* is obtained by mixing the solutions of sulphite of ammonia and nitrate of silver. It assumes the form of small, shining, white grains: when exposed to the light, it assumes a brown color. *Phosphate of silver* is insoluble in water, and is hence precipitated when a solution of phosphate of soda is added to a solution of nitrate of silver. The *salts of silver* are decomposed by the alkalies and the earths. Prussiate of potash, when dropped into a solution of a salt of silver, occasions a white precipitate: hydro-sulphuret of potash produces a black precipitate; and an infusion of nutgalls gives a yellowish brown precipitate. A fulminating preparation of silver, similar to that of gold, but more energetic, is prepared by dissolving silver in nitrous acid, diluted with three parts of water: to the solution lime-water is added as long as any precipitation is occasioned; the precipitate is washed and dried; it is then allowed to remain for several hours in liquid ammonia, when it becomes a black powder; the liquor is decanted, and it is allowed to dry in the air: when completely dry, such is its tendency to explosion, that it cannot be touched, the slightest agitation causing it to detonate; and so violent is the detonation, that the experiment cannot be made with safety on more than a grain. The theory of its detonation is considered as similar to that of fulminating gold: it probably consists of oxide of silver and ammonia, the elements being united by affinities so nicely balanced, that the slightest external force subverts them, and causes new combinations: the oxygen of the oxide unites with the hydrogen of the ammonia, and forms watery vapor; the nitrogen must assume the elastic form, and the augmentation of elasticity in these products, by the caloric suddenly extricated, may be the cause of the detonation. A fulminating silver totally different from that above described, is frequently sold as an object of amusement: it is enclosed between the folds of a card cut in two lengthwise, the powder being placed at one end, and the other being notched, that it may be distinguished: if it be taken by the notched end, and the other be held over the flame of a candle, it soon detonates with a sharp sound and violent flame; the card is torn and changed brown, and the part in contact with the composition is covered with a slight metallic coating of a grayish-white color. This compound is formed in the following manner: Into a pint tumbler, or other glass vessel, is introduced 100 grains of dry nitrate of silver, over which is poured one ounce of alcohol, and the same quantity of smoking nitric acid. The mixture of the alcohol and nitric acid occasions much heat and effervescence in the liquid: if this is so violent as to overflow the vessel, cold alcohol is added in small portions to abate the ebullition: in a few minutes the liquor becomes turbid, and a very heavy, white, crystalline powder falls down, which is separated by the filter, and thoroughly washed with tepid water: before being fully dry, it should be separated into parcels of ten or twenty grains, which portions, when thoroughly dried at a distance from the fire, present the following properties: The substance is white and crystalline; the light changes its color to a dark brown; when heated, it explodes with great violence. It explodes also by percussion and friction, and the contact of sulphuric acid. When put into dry chlorine gas, it explodes with a loud report. So powerful is this powder in its explosions, that no persons but chemists should venture upon its manufacture, or presume to experiment with it. The most painful accidents have repeatedly occurred with it, in the hands of the inexperienced and the careless. It is composed of oxide of silver 14.75, and of a peculiar acid, called the *fulminic*, 5.25. (For some account of fulminic acid, see *Prussic Acid.*)

Silver Ores.—There are five important ores of silver, viz.—1. *Native silver*; 2. *vitreous silver* (or silver glance); 3. *black silver*; 4. *red silver*; 5. *horn silver*.—*Native silver* is occasionally found crystallized in the following shapes, viz.—the cube, octahedron, tetrahedron, rhombic dodecahedron, trapezohedron, and six-sided tables. The cube is the primitive form; but it more often occurs in dentiform, filiform, and capillary shapes; also reticulated, arborescent, and in plates; likewise in plates, formed in fissures, and in superficial coatings; cleavage none, fracture hackly; lustre metallic; color silver-white, more or less subject to tarnish; streak shining; ductile; hardness between gypsum and calcareous spar; specific gravity, 10.47. Native silver has been distinguished into *common* and *auriferous* native silver: the former consists of silver alloyed with a small proportion of antimony, arsenic, iron, &c.; the latter frequently contains fifty per cent. of gold. Native silver occurs principally in veins, traversing gneiss, clay-slate, and other primitive and transition rocks.. There are but few countries in which it is found in any considerable quantity. Among these are the mining districts of Saxony and Bohemia, also Norway and Siberia, but particularly Mexico and Peru.—*Vitreous silver* presents itself crystallized in cubes, octahedrons, and rhombic dodecahedrons. Its primitive form is the cube. It also occurs in reticulated, arborescent, dentiform and capillary shapes; also massive and impalpable; fracture imperfect, and small conchoidal, uneven; lustre metallic, subject to tarnish; color blackish lead-gray; streak shining; malleable; hardness about that of gypsum; specific gravity 7.19. It consists of silver 85.0, sulphur 15.0. It is easily fusible before the blow-pipe, and intumesces; but it gives a globule of silver by a continuation of the blast. It has been hitherto found almost exclusively in veins, along with ores of lead, antimony and zinc. It occurs in Saxony, Bohemia, Hungary, Mexico and Peru. It is an important species for the extraction of silver.—*Black silver* has for its primitive form a right rhombic prism of 100° 0′. The crystals, however, are not often observed; but it is more frequently in granular masses; fracture imperfect conchoidal, uneven; lustre metallic; color iron-black; streak unchanged; sectile; hardness about that of gypsum; specific gravity 6.2. It consists of

Silver,	65.50
Antimony,	10.00
Iron,	5.00
Sulphur,	12.00
Copper and arsenic,	.50
	93.00

Before the blow-pipe, upon charcoal, it yields a dark-colored metallic globule, which may be reduced with saltpetre. It is found in silver veins along with other ores of silver. It occurs chiefly in Saxony, Bohemia and Hungary, in Mexico and Peru. It is a valuable ore for the extraction of silver.—*Red silver*. The primitive form of this species is an obtuse rhomboid of 109° 28′. Its secondary forms are six-sided prisms, variously truncated and acuminated, and an equiangular double six-sided pyramid; cleavage parallel with the sides of the primitive form, pretty distinct; fracture conchoidal; lustre adamantine; color iron-black to cochineal-red; semi-transparent to opaque; sectile; hardness about that of gypsum; specific gravity 5.84. The crystals are very liable to occur twin-shaped. Red silver is often found massive, granular, and even impalpable. It consists of

Silver,	58.949
Antimony,	22.846
Sulphur,	16.609

It decrepitates before the blow-pipe upon charcoal, melts, and emits fumes of sulphur and antimony, after which it yields a globule of silver. Red silver is confined to a small number of localities, and occurs in veins along with other ores of silver, galena and blende. It is found in the metallic veins near Freiberg, also at Marienberg, Annaberg, Schneeberg, and Johanngeorgenstadt in Saxony; likewise in Bohemia, Hungary, Dauphiny, and Norway; but is much more abundant in Mexico and Peru. It is a valuable ore for silver.—*Horn silver* has the cube for its primitive form, in which shape it frequently occurs, as also in acicular fibres; cleavage none; fracture more or less perfect conchoidal; lustre resinous, passing into adamantine; color pearl-gray, passing into lavender-blue, and some shade of green; the color becomes brown on being exposed to light; streak shining; translucent; sectile; hardness about that of talc; specific gravity 5.5. It occurs also in crusts and granular masses. It consists of silver 76.0, oxygen 7.6, and muriatic acid 16.4. It is fusible in the flame of a candle, and emits fumes of muriatic acid. Horn silver is most frequently found in the upper parts of veins in clay-slate, but occurs also in beds, generally along with other ores of silver, or with iron-ochre. It is not abundant in European countries, but occurs in large masses in Mexico and Peru. It is used for extracting silver.—Such are the ores of silver which are properly so called, and from which silver is chiefly extracted. Besides these, however, argentiferous sulphurets of lead and copper are sometimes smelted for the small proportion of this precious metal which they contain. We have now to allude to the methods employed in obtaining the silver from its various ores. These are two in number, *smelting* and *amalgamation*. The former is founded on the great affinity of silver for lead, which, when fused with silver, acts as a solvent, and extracts it from its union with baser metals. The silver is afterwards separated from the lead by the well-known process of cupellation, which consists in exposing the alloy to a stream of atmospheric air, by which the lead is converted into an oxide or litharge, while the silver remains untouched. The latter method depends upon the property of mercury to dissolve silver without the aid of heat. The first is called the *dry*, the last, the *wet* way of treating silver ores. One or the other process is employed, according to the nature of the ores. The ores which are treated in the wet way are usually those which consist principally of argentiferous sulphuret of lead. The first thing to be done, by this method, is to pulverize and roast the ore in a furnace, to expel the sulphur. When the well or crucible is full of metal, it is tapped and run off. It is now ready for the process of refining, or cupellation. For this purpose, a reverberatory furnace is employed, the lower part of which is covered with wood ashes and clay, so as to form a cupel. On one side of the furnace there is a hole for the exit of the litharge; and on the opposite side is another for the admission of air to the surface of the metal, which is introduced through an aperture above, to which a cover is adapted. After the lead is melted and brought to a red heat, the blast of air is admitted, and the scoria, as it collects, is removed. When the litharge is formed, the heat is increased, and the quantity becomes greater, and is withdrawn through the opening in the furnace. At the same time, some lead is volatilized. Towards the end of the process, the litharge which comes off contains a small quantity of silver, and is therefore kept separate from the rest. After the whole of the litharge is removed, and the surface of the metal in the furnace becomes bright, a quantity of water is poured on it, to keep it from spirting, which it is apt to do when congealing. The metal thus obtained is subjected to a similar operation for about five hours, in a smaller furnace, and at a higher temperature, by which it is completely freed from the lead. With respect to the other method of reduction or separation—amalgamation—the following is an outline of the more important steps, of which it consists. The ores best adapted to this process are native silver and vitreous silver. The first operation that requires description is the selection of the ores to form a proper mixture, with reference to the quantity of silver and sulphur they contain. It has been observed that the amalgamation process succeeds best when the silver produce is about seventy-five ounces to the ton of ore; at the same time, regard being had to the quantity of sulphur present, which is ascertained from the quantity of sulphuret in the ore, previously learned by an assay in the crucible. The sulphur is got rid of, by adding to the mixture of raw ore ten per cent. of common salt, by which, during the furnace operation, the sulphur becomes acidified, and the acid thus formed, uniting with the base of the salt, forms sulphate of soda; whilst the muriatic acid, thus set free, combines with the silver in the ore, that was not in the metallic state, and forms muriate of silver. In this state, the ore is subjected to various mechanical operations, with riddles, mills and sieves, until it is reduced to an impalpable powder. It is then submitted to the action of mercury. This operation is performed in barrels, which are arranged so as to revolve on their axes. The mixture or charge in each barrel consists of sifted calcined ore, mercury, metallic iron, and water, in certain proportions. The ore is composed of sulphate of soda, muriate of silver, and other metals and earthy matters. By the process of amalgamation, the barrels being made to revolve during a period of sixteen or eighteen hours, the muriate of silver becomes decomposed by the action of the iron on its acid; and the silver, thus reduced to the metallic state, combines with the mercury, forming what is termed *amalgam*, whilst the sulphate of soda, the muriate of iron, and other salts, become dissolved in the water. The silver combined with mercury is then filtered, by which the surplus metal is separated, and a compound remains in the sack, consisting of six parts of mercury and one of silver This amalgam is subjected to the action of heat in a distilling furnace, by which the mercury is sublimated, and the silver remains. Silver is also sometimes separated from copper by the process of *eliquation*. The eliquation is effected by means of lead, which, possessing a greater affinity for silver than for copper, combines with the former, when brought into fusion with the alloy, and forms a new metallic compound. The argentiferous lead, thus obtained, is subjected to the usual processes of cupellation, and the coarse copper, from which the silver has been separated, is refined.—We shall now take notice of the mines of silver in different parts of the world, which furnish the silver of commerce. Those of Mexico and South America are incomparably more important than those of all the rest of the world. Mexico alone has above three thousand mines, or excavations for silver ores, which produced annually during the last ten years of the seventeenth century, about $4,000,000. The mines of Guanaxuato yielded nearly one quarter of this amount; while the single mine of Valenciana, situated in the same district, has afforded, for years together during the last thirty years, between one and two million dollars. Nor are the ores of Mexico, for the most part, rich in silver; but the rich produce of that country has depended upon their abundance, and the facility with which they have been explored. In Peru, the annual produce of this metal was formerly as great as $2,000,000; the major part of which was furnished by the mines of Tasco, of Chota, and of Huantajaya. Chile affords $150,000 per annum. Buenos Ayres contains the celebrated mines of Potosi, discovered in 1545, and which have produced, according to the estimate of Humboldt, from the time of their discovery, the enormous amount of $1,150,000,000. These mines have diminished in value of late, though they still rank next to those of Guanaxuato. The celebrated mines of Kongsberg, in Norway, once so rich in native silver, have now become in a great measure exhausted. They are estimated to have produced above $20,000,000 since they were opened in 1623. The most important silver mines of Europe at present, are those of Saxony, Hungary, and the Hartz. The annual produce of Saxony is about $250,000; while those of the Hartz and of Hungary are each about the same. Within the last sixteen years there has been a great increase in the produce of silver from the Russian mines. According to a communication from baron Humboldt, made since his return from Asia, to the editor of Poffendorf's *Annalen*, it appears that the annual produce of the mines of precious metals of Europe and Asiatic Russia amounts to 25,500 marcs of gold, and 292,000 marcs of silver; of which 76,500 of silver and 22,000 of gold are supplied from the Russian empire. The value of all this silver is about $2,353,000. The present annual produce of all the silver mines in the world is probably within $20,000,000.

Silver Fish. (See *Gold Fish.*)

Silver Tree (*leucadendron argenteum*); so called from the appearance of the leaves, which are lanceolate and silky. It is a large evergreen shrub, with handsome foliage, a native of the cape of Good Hope, together with the other species of the genus, and is a favorite in greenhouses. It belongs to the *proteaceæ*, the most remarkable family of plants in the southern hemisphere, and one which contributes largely to give peculiar features to the vegetation of that portion of the globe. More than four hundred species of these plants are known, which are arranged in numerous genera. They are usually shrubs or small trees, but some attain large dimensions: the leaves are simple, entire or serrated, in most species flat, but sometimes cylindrical or thread-shaped; the flowers are sometimes distinct, upon solitary foot-stalks, or in clusters, spikes, or corymbs, with *bracteæ* at the base; sometimes they are sessile, situated upon a common receptacle, surrounded with a many-leaved involucre, or are disposed in scaly cones; the color is green, yellow, or red: in short, the remarkable differences in the habit, foliage and flowers of these plants have given rise to the name of the order. The greater proportion of these plants inhabit New Holland, where they adorn large tracts of country; they are numerous, likewise, at the cape of Good Hope, but a few species only are found in the southern parts of South America. They are generally favorite green-house plants, and are not delicate with respect to cold; but their culture, in other respects, requires many precautions.

Silvering. The application of silver leaf is made in the same way as that of gold, for which see *Gilding*. Copper may be silvered over, by rubbing it with the following powder:—Two drachms of tartar, the same quantity of common salt, and half a drachm of alum, are mixed with fifteen or twenty grains of silver, precipitated from nitric acid by copper. The surface of the copper becomes white when rubbed with this powder, which may afterwards be brushed off and polished with leather. A cheap silvering is prepared as follows:—Half an ounce of silver that has been precipitated from aquafortis by the addition of copper, common salt, and muriate of ammonia, of each two ounces, and one drachm of corrosive muriate of mercury, are triturated together, and made into a paste with water; with this, copper utensils of every kind, that have been previously boiled with tartar and alum, are rubbed, after which they are made red-hot, and then polished. The intention of this process appears to be little more than to apply the silver in a state of minute division to the clean surface of the copper, and afterwards to fix it there by fusion; and, accordingly, this silvering may be effected by using the argentine precipitate, here mentioned, with borax or mercury, and causing it to adhere by fusion. The dial-plates of clocks, the scales of barometers, and other similar articles, are silvered by rubbing upon them a mixture of muriate of silver, sea salt, and tartar, and afterwards carefully washing off the saline matter with water. In this operation, the silver is precipitated from the muriatic acid, which unites with part of the coppery surface. It is not durable, but may be improved by heating the article, and repeating the operation till the covering seems sufficiently thick. The silvering of pins is effected by boiling them with tin filings and tartar. Holton mirrors or globes are silvered by an amalgam, consisting of one part by weight of bismuth, half a part of lead, the same quantity of pure tin, and two parts of mercury. The solid metals are to be first mixed together by fusion, and the mercury added when the mixture is almost cold. A very gentle heat is sufficient to fuse this amalgam. In this state it is poured into a clean glass globe, intended to be silvered, by means of a paper funnel, which reaches to the bottom. At a certain temperature it will stick to the glass, which by a proper motion may thus be silvered completely, and the superfluous amalgam poured out. The appearance of these toys is varied by using glass of different colors, such as yellow, blue, or green. To silver looking-glasses, the following articles are necessary:—first, a square marble table, or smooth stone, well polished, and ground extremely true, with a frame round it, or a groove cut in its edges, to keep the superfluous mercury from running off; secondly, lead weights covered with cloth, to keep them from scratching the glass, from one pound weight to twelve pounds each, according to the size of the glass laid down; thirdly, rolls of tin-foil; fourthly, mercury. The artist then proceeds as follows:—the tin-foil is cut a little larger than the glass, and laid flat upon the stone, and with a straight piece of hard wood, about three inches long, stroked every way, that there may be no creases or wrinkles in it: a little mercury is then dropped upon it, and with a piece of cotton wool, or hare's foot, it is spread all over the foil; then, the marble slab being kept nearly level with the horizon, the mercury is poured all over the foil, which is covered with a fine paper; two weights are placed near its lower end, to keep the glass steady, while the artist draws the paper from between the silver-foil and the glass. This must be done with great care, so that no air-bubbles be left. After the paper is drawn out, weights are placed upon the glass to press out the superfluous mercury, and make the foil adhere. Another method is, to slide the glass over the foil without the assistance of paper. To make *shell silver*, silver leaf is ground with gum-water, or honey: the gum, or honey, is washed away, and the powder which remains is used with gum-water, or white of eggs, laid on with a hair pencil.

Silvestre de Sacy. (See *Sacy*.)

Simeon Stylites. (See *Stylites*.)

Simois; a river of Troas, which rises in mount Ida, and falls into the Xanthus. It is celebrated by Homer, and most of the ancient poets, as many battles were fought in its neighborhood during the Trojan war. Modern travellers call it a small rivulet, and some have even disputed its existence. (See *Scamander*.)

Simon Magus, or the Magician; an impostor, mentioned in the Acts of the Apostles, a native of Samaria, who pretended to be an *æon* of an exalted nature, and called himself the supreme power of God. (See *Gnostics*.) Struck with astonishment at the miracles of the Apostles, he offered them money for their secret. (See *Simony*.) He then went about making proselytes, carrying with him a Tyrian courtesan, whom he represented as Helen, who had been the cause of the Trojan war, and sometimes as Minerva; calling her, at the same time, the first intelligence, or mother of all things. Other stories are related of him, but are not well authenticated. It has also been said that he was worshipped as a god at Rome, and that his statue was erected there, with the inscription *Simoni Deo sancto*. His followers are called *Simonians*. (See *Heretics*.)

Simon, St.; an ancient French family which claims to derive its origin, through the counts of Vermandois, from Charlemagne. Louis de Rouvroy, duke de St Simon, a peer of France, known as the author of some very curious memoirs, was born in 1675, and died in 1755. He was employed in several diplomatic missions, and was made one of the council of regency by the notorious regent, duke of Orleans (q. v.), after whose death he retired to his estates. His memoirs remained a long time in manuscript, and were afterwards published in a mutilated form, with many suppressions. The first complete edition appeared in Paris, in 1829—30 (in 21 vols., 8vo.), under the title of *Mémoires complets et authentiques du Duc de Saint Simon sur le Siècle de Louis XIV, et la Régence, publiés pour la première Fois sur le Manuscrit original entièrement écrit de la Main de l'Auteur, par M. le Marquis de Saint Simon*.—*Claude Henri, count de St. Simon*, founder of the politico-philosophical-religious sect of St. Simonians, or of the New Christianity, which has recently attracted attention in France, was born in 1760. We know little of his youth; but he appears to have been early tinctured with a spirit of enthusiasm, as we are told that he caused himself to be called, every morning, with the words, "Get up, count; you have great things to accomplish." He was attached to the French auxiliary corps, which served in this country in the last years of our revolutionary war, and, soon after his return to France, was promoted to a colonelcy. Previous to the breaking out of the French revolution, the count travelled in Holland and Spain; but he took no part in the great events of 1789. He died in 1825, the last thirty-four years of his life, if we may believe his own account, having been devoted to the objects of his mission, as the apostle of the New Christianity. His disciples are not very communicative in regard to the history of their founder, whose reputation appears not to have been always the best. In 1790, he entered into financial speculations, for the purpose, as we are told, of raising the funds necessary to aid his great projects. His partner not participating in his philanthropic views, St. Simon retired from the business at the expiration of seven years, and next applied himself to the study of the sciences. He took up his residence near the polytechnic school, formed an acquaintance with the professors, and attended their lectures. Three years were thus occupied with the study of inorganic nature, and the succeeding four years were spent in the study of organic bodies, for which purpose he lived near the medical school, conversed with the professors, heard their lectures, and kept open house and free table for men of science. A tour in Germany, England and Italy, completed his 'inventory of the philosophical treasures of Europe,' and he now felt himself master of his ideas and ready to communicate them. His fortune, however, was exhausted, and his friends had deserted him. His *Introduction aux Travaux scientifiques du 19e Siècle* (1807), contains an exposition of his philosophical views at this time. After the restoration, in 1814, his attention was turned to politics; and, partly in conjunction with his disciple and adopted son Augustus Thierry and others, he wrote several works, which show his political opinions. Among these are *De la Réorganisation de la Société Européenne* (1814); *Du Système Industriel* (1821); *Catéchisme des Industriels* (1824); *Discussions politiques, morales et philosophiques* (4 vols., 1817—18); and *Opinions littéraires, philosophiques et industrielles*. Seven years had thus been spent in obtaining pecuniary resources, seven in collecting scientific materials, ten in effecting the reformation of philosophy, and ten that of politics; and St. Simon, reduced to extreme want by the exhaustion of his resources, and to despair by neglect and ill success, attempted to shoot himself through the head. The ball grazed his forehead; but "his hour," say his pupils, after their master, "was not yet come; the philosopher and legislator becomes the prophet of a law of love; God raises him from the abyss; sheds over him a religious inspiration which animates, sanctifies and renews his whole being; a hymn of love is poured forth from that mutilated body; the divine man is manifested; the New Christianity is sent to the world; the kingdom of God is come upon earth." The *Nouveau Christianisme* (8vo., 1825) is an exposition of St. Simon's religious notions. By this new religion, the principle of antagonism is done away; a universal church, a brotherhood of peace, unites all mankind, and sanctifies all. Science is holy, industry is holy; society is formed only of priests, savans and laborers (*industriels*); government consists only of the chiefs of these three classes. The basis of the political system of the St. Simonians is a new mode of the distribution of property, by substituting the right of capacity for the right of inheritance. "Each one according to his capacity, each capacity according to its works," is the rule of this new right. All property becomes, at the death of the proprietor, the property of the church or society; all children receive a general education to a certain point till their *capacities* are ascertained, and then, *chacun à sa capacité*, each becomes a priest (or artist), savant, or *industriel*, as his talents point the way; and thus whatever he acquires is the fruit of his own industry. There is nothing, however, like a distinct system developed in the writings of St. Simon or his disciples, but abundance of crude notions and vague speculations, of which we cannot attempt to give an account. See *Doctrine de St. Simon* (3d ed., 1831), and the numbers of the *Globe* and *Organisateur*, the organs of one party, and of the *Revue Encyclopédique* (since the close of 1831), that of another party of St. Simonians. At the time of the death of the founder, this sect consisted of a small number of disciples, of whom Olinde Rodrigues was the principal, and who established the *Producteur*, a monthly journal, as the organ of their views. This, however, was discontinued for want of funds, when the revolution of July gave a new impulse to the society. A great number of converts was made, funds collected, and the *Globe*, a journal of reputation, passed into the hands of St. Simonian editors. Families were organized, churches built, schools constituted, and the hierarchy established, under Enfantin and Bazard, who were entitled *pères suprêmes* (chief fathers). But when the time came for the developement of a regular system, schisms began to appear in the society. The most important of these took place in November, 1831. Enfantin and Bazard were at the head of two parties, Rodrigues of a third, and Carnot (editor of the *Revue Encyclopédique*) belonged to a fourth. These divisions were produced partly by questions of government and partly by differences of doctrine. One of the new doctrines, in which, however, all parties seem to agree, is, that man is not, as heretofore, alone to form the political being, but that man and woman together are to form the social individual. But, on this principle, Enfantin declares that the moral law can be revealed only by the coöperation of woman; and he, therefore, awaits the appearance of the woman who shall be called to complete the *couple révélateur*. The *Globe* and *Organisateur* are in the interest of Enfantin. The French government has left the sect to itself; but the courts have decided that St. Simonianism is not a religion,—the priests of the society having claimed exemption from military duty on the ground of their religious office. (See the *Quarterly Review* for July, 1831, and the *Westminster Review* for April, 1832.)

SIMONIANS, ST. (See *Simon, St.*)

SIMONIDES; a Greek lyric poet, born in the island of Cos, about 557 B. C., went to Athens, where he became the favorite of Hipparchus, and a friend of Anacreon and Theognis. In Thessaly, he was a welcome guest of the Scopades, whose victories at the public games he celebrated in song. According to a story related by Cicero, as he was once sitting at a feast with Scopas, having recited a hymn in praise of his patron, in which he dwelt much on the merits of the Dioscuri, Scopas told him that he could pay him only half of the price promised for the hymn, and that he must get the rest from the Dioscuri, who had occupied so large a share of his praises. Soon after, some one called him out of the house, with the information that two youths wished to speak to him. On going out, he found no person, and before he could return, the hall fell in, burying the guests under its ruins. When the rubbish was removed, it being impossible to distinguish the bodies, disfigured by bruises, Simonides was enabled to determine them by recollecting the order in which they had sat. This led him to the plan of facilitating the recollection of events by certain artificial associations with places or things. (See *Mnemonics.*) Another wonderful escape of Simonides is related. Having once buried a body which he had found on the beach, as he was himself about to set sail, the spirit of the deceased warned him not to trust himself to the deceitful element. He complied with the warning, and soon after received news of the loss of the vessel, with all her crew. Simonides visited Athens several times, and is said to have conquered Æschylus, in a poetical contest, at the celebration of the victory of Marathon. During a residence in Sparta, he sang the heroic death of Leonidas, in several poems. An invitation from Hiero, king of Syracuse, induced him to go to Sicily, where he spent the rest of his days, and died, B. C. 467. Of his numerous poems, some fragments have come down to us, which are contained in Brunck's *Analecta*. The ancients celebrate the grace, ease, and simplicity of his poems; but he is accused of avarice, and of having been the first to take pay for his writings. The invention of five letters of the Greek alphabet, η, ζ, ξ, ψ, ω, is attributed to him.

SIMONY; the crime of trafficking with sacred things, particularly the corrupt presentation of any one to an ecclesiastical benefice for money or reward. Simony is also committed by buying or selling the sacrament of the Lord's supper, baptism, ordination or absolution. It is a crime severely prohibited by all Christian sects, though the theologians of the Roman *curia* do not consider the selling of certain church offices simony. The name of this offence, in which the seller and the buyer are equally guilty, is derived from the Chaldæan Magus, Simon, who, according to the Acts of the Apostles, wished to purchase from the apostles the communication of the Holy Ghost by the imposition of hands. Simony was committed in the middle ages with scandalous publicity and frequency.

SIMOOM, or SAMIEL (that is, *poison*); a noxious, hot wind, which blows at the period of the equinoxes, on the borders of Arabia, in the neighborhood of Mecca, on the Euphrates, and in Persia, and is fatal to animal life. It comes over burning deserts of sand, and its approach is indicated by terrible appearances. A dark yellow hue suddenly pervades the eastern horizon; a thick sulphureous exhalation rises from the ground, which is first hurried round in rapid gyrations, and then ascends into the air, and covers the whole heavens. Hissing and crackling noises are heard, and a hot current of air accompanied by low sounds rushes over the ground. Even the beasts manifest their terror by their howlings, and, when the burning current overtakes a caravan in the desert, bend their heads to the earth; camels plunge their nose and mouth into the sand. Travellers may have learned this means of safety from them, as they also throw themselves down with their faces to the ground, and lie immovable until the hot exhalation has passed, which it does within a half hour at the most. Persons in a stream have nothing to fear. The bodies of those who perish by it swell, and very quickly begin to putrefy. The fine dust which the wind brings penetrates into all the folds of the clothes, and even into boxes and bales. It is not improbable that these and other hot winds are overcharged with electricity.—The simoom is different from the *chamseen*, or *khamseen*, a south-west wind, which blows three or four days, between July 15 and Aug. 15, in Egypt, Arabia, and on the Persian gulf, and is accompanied by similar appearances. It is very hot and drying. In those whom it surprises in the desert, the lungs are compressed, the breathing difficult, the skin dry; the body appears as if consumed by fire. The corpses of those who have thus perished are dried up, but do not putrefy. The same means of protection are employed as against the samiel. Still different from either of these winds is the *harmattan*. (q. v.)

Simplon (Italian *Sempione*); a mountain in the Swiss canton of Valais, 10,600 feet high, belonging to the high Alpine ridge which separates Switzerland from Italy, and extends from Mont Blanc to St. Gothard. (See *Alps*.) As this ridge is traversed by a valley, which lies below the snow line, Napoleon laid out one of his most remarkable roads here. (See *Alps, Roads over*.) The Hospitium (q. v.), left unfinished by Napoleon, was sold by the government of the canton to the fathers of the Great St. Bernard in 1824, who have since completed it.

Sin. Every evil disposition, thought or action, by which the divine law (whether the positive revealed law, or the moral law, which God has implanted in the mind of man) is violated, is sin in the wider sense of the word, considered in relation to morals or religion; considered as an offence against the laws of society, an evil act is called a *crime, misdemeanor*, &c. Strictly speaking, sin can attach only to an intelligent and free agent, who has or might have a knowledge of the existence and sacredness of the law. The imputation of sin to the transgressor of the divine law is the regarding him as the author of this transgression, and as justly punishable for it. Theologians and moral philosophers distinguish several species of sins, either with reference to the nature of the law which the sinner transgresses, or to the subject against which the sin is committed, or to the sinner, or to the nature and quality of the action itself. In the first point of view, sins are divided into those of omission and commission; but this division amounts, in fact, to nothing, because, whenever a man sins, he omits something which he ought to have done, and commits something which he ought to have left undone. The same sin may fall under either class, according as we express the moral law which is violated positively or negatively. The moral relations between man and the objects of his duty are much too close to allow an essential difference between omission and commission. Sins are divided, like duties, into those towards God, our fellow-men and ourselves; but this division is little more than formal, for every sin falls, in some degree, under all three heads. As regards the sinner, sins are divided into premeditated and unpremeditated, the latter being the fruit of sudden impulse, and not of deliberate purpose. Moreover, there are internal and external sins (the former include bad appetites, evil thoughts, &c.), conditional and unconditional sins. Sin is often used also for that state of the soul which is properly called sinfulness. Lastly, sin is divided by theologians into original sin and actual sin; the former again into inherent sin (denoting that corruption of nature which is believed to have been transmitted from the first man to all his offspring), and imputed sin, denoting that liability to punishment to which all the posterity of Adam are subject by the imputation of his transgression. Actual sin is again divided by theologians into mortal and venial. Mortal sins, according to 1 John v, 16, 17, are those the commission of which is followed by spiritual death, that is, the loss of God's grace, and differ from those which may be more easily forgiven. All Christians, in early times, were of opinion that there was a difference between those sins which a Christian might fall into from the strength of natural propensity, and those which evidently showed that the offender was yet entirely in the slavery of sin, and not regenerated, such as the denial of Christianity, murder, theft, adultery, fraud, &c. But while one party (which subsequently became predominant) acted on the principle that the church was bound to receive every sinner, on condition of sincere penitence, and that absolution and communion could not be withheld from him, particularly in the hour of death, if his repentance had continued until then, there was another party which would never receive again one who had broken his baptismal vow, by committing a mortal sin, because, said they, we know of no revelation which authorizes us to do this What sins were to be regarded as mortal was not fully determined by the first fathers of the church. Augustine considered blasphemy, incontinency and murder, as falling under this class. Petrus Lombardus (*Magist. Sentent.* ii, 41, 6), following Cassianus and Gregory the Great, enumerates the following: *superbia* (pride), *avaritia* (avarice), *luxuria* (voluptuousness), *ira* (wrath), *gula* (gluttony), *invidia* (envy), *acedia* (sluggishness of heart); and, in order to facilitate the remembrance of them, invented the word *saligia*, composed of the initial letters of the several names. These are the seven mortal sins which, since the twelfth century, have been enumerated in the scholastic theology, and even now are set forth in the doctrinal works of the Catholics, particularly in Catholic catechisms for the people, though even the contemporary of Petrus Lombardus, Richard de St. Victor (*De Differentia Peccati mortalis et venalis*, Rouen, 1650), justly makes the degree of immorality in the sinner, the wrong done to others, and the contempt shown for God, the standard of mortal sin; and other schoolmen gave the name of *crying sins* to murder, sodomy, oppression of innocence, and forcible retention of well-earned wages, and, in fact, to all those sins which St. Paul mentions in Gal. v, 19—21. But many modern Catholic writers have found this number insufficient, and some of them have classed other mortal sins under some of these general heads, while others give an entirely different list; and some, again, as the writer of the article *Péché*, in the *Dictionnaire de Théologie* (Toulouse, 1817), mention none by name, and say it is extremely difficult, in some cases, to distinguish whether a sin is mortal. Many Protestants also (the Calvinists excepted) adopt the distinction between mortal sins and those which may be forgiven; but they make this difference to consist only in the degree of moral responsibility or desert of punishment; so that every intentional and well-known violation of duty is followed by the loss of God's grace. The views of the Greek church are much like those of the Roman Catholic on this point.

SINAI; a mountain of Arabia, near the head of the Red sea, celebrated in Scripture history as the spot whence the law was given to Moses. It is situated in the heart of a vast and gloomy desert, the few inhabited spots of which are occupied by hordes of Arabs, who subsist by plunder, and render the road impassable, unless for a large and well-defended caravan. At the foot of the mountain is the Greek convent of St. Catharine, founded in 1331, by William Bouldesell, which has ever since continued to afford hospitality to the pilgrims whose zeal impels them to brave the perils of this road. The monks are kept, as it were, imprisoned in this convent by the wild Arabs of the surrounding country. 150 miles south-east of Suez.

SINAMARI; a river of French Guiana, which flows into the Atlantic in lat. 5° 39′ N. To its banks were transported the victims of the 18th Fructidor. (q. v.)

SINAPISM; a poultice of mustard. These poultices are made in different ways. One is of mustard-seed and linseed or crumb of bread equal parts, vinegar a sufficient quantity; another of mustard-seed pulverized, any quantity, vinegar a sufficient quantity.

SINCAPORE, or SINGAPURA; capital of a small island at the southern extremity of Malacca, lat. 1° 15′ N.; lon. 104° E. It was ceded, with the neighboring islands within ten miles around it, to the East India company by the sultan of Johor, in 1824, who had previously, however, made a similar treaty, in consequence of which it had been occupied by sir T. S. Raffles in 1819. The climate is healthy. The interior is laid out in gardens and plantations, and its shores supply a valuable article of commerce in the agar-agar, a kind of sea-weed (*fucus saccharinus*), which is used in China for paint, glue and varnish, and the finer sorts make a sweetmeat. The town stands on a point of land near a bay affording a safe anchorage at all seasons, and commanding the navigation of the straits of Malacca. The population, which, in 1819 was 150, had increased, in 1830, to above 16,600 persons, exclusive of the garrison and the floating population. Many of the settlers are Chinese. The exports exceed £3,000,000 per annum. (See Crawfurd's *Embassy to Siam and Cochin-China.*)

SINDH. (See *Indus.*)

SINDON. (See *Byssus.*)

SINE, in mathematics; a line drawn perpendicularly from one end of an arc upon the radius, drawn to the other end. The sine of the arc is also the sine of the angle subtended by the arc. Trigonometry (q. v.) teaches that, in plain triangles, the sides are to each other as the sines of the opposite angles; in spherical triangles, however, the sines of the sides are to each other as the sines of the angles opposite to these sides. Hence it appears how important the sine is for finding certain parts of triangles, from certain given parts. To render these calculations (which occur so often) more easy, tables have been drawn up, in which the logarithms of the sines are given.—By *cosine* is understood the sine of the complement of the arc (such an arc as, if added, would make it ninety degrees).—*Versed sine* is that portion of the radius which is intercepted between the sine and the arc. (For the other important lines in trigonometry, as the *secant*, *tangent*, &c., see the respective articles.) Among the many tables, we mention only those of Vega, and the *Tables Portatives, par François Callet*, published by Didot. (See *Logarithm*.)

Sinecure (Latin, *sine cura*, without a cure); properly, an ecclesiastical term, signifying a benefice without cure of souls. (See *Abbés Commendataires*.) It has hence come to be applied to any charge or post without duties attached to it. The gross abuses which exist in England in regard to sinecures, have arisen mostly from changes in the state of society, alterations in the management of the revenue, or the administration of justice, and from the union of the three kingdoms. The offices, with their emoluments, have thus been kept up when the duties had ceased. Thus the duke of St. Alban's is master of the hawks in the royal household, with a salary of upwards of 6000 dollars. Besides the absolute sinecures, there are offices of which the duties are discharged, for a small salary, by a deputy, while the placeman pockets the principal profits. Lord Ellenborough, for instance, is clerk of the court of king's bench, with a salary of 42,000 dollars. In the departments of the army, navy, revenue, administration, &c., are numberless similar cases. The total amount of money thus paid, in great part, to noblemen, or their relations and dependants, is little short of half a million pounds sterling a year. (See *Parliamentary Reform*, at the close of the last volume.)

Singing. In the article *Music* (q. v.) we have touched upon the origin of vocal, as well as instrumental music. Singing unites, in its perfection, music with lyric poetry: we say lyric poetry, because the poetry must accord with the music, and music is, in itself, a language of feeling. The chief elements of a good singer are, 1. a voice distinguished for melody and compass; 2. skill to read notes correctly and readily, and accurate intonation; 3. a distinct utterance; and 4. adaptation of the delivery to the meaning of the words, in which the singer shows his taste and feeling. There are three chief methods, or schools of singing—the Italian, German, and French. (See *Music*, and *Italian Music*.) Formerly, the Italians only had a proper school of singing, because, with them, singing was early made a subject of scientific instruction. The Italian method is distinguished by peculiar attention to the cultivation of the vocal organs, in order to give the voice the greatest clearness and flexibility; secondly, by the soft swelling and blending of the tones, which is called *portamento di voce* (q. v.), and gives to the whole a charm and keeping similar to the effect of a perfect picture; thirdly, by a distinct utterance of the words, though in this the Italian singers are greatly aided by their melodious language. Another advantage of this school is its skill in *recitativo* (q. v.)—a musical discourse, between singing and speaking (though, even among the Italians, this latter excellence has become comparatively rare of late). The defects of this school are, that it often runs into an excess of art and ornament, which, among many other causes, is partly owing to the circumstance that, formerly, composers wrote only the fundamental notes for the singers, and left them to supply the rest. But Rossini has introduced the fashion of writing all the ornaments in full. The Italian style of singing appears to the greatest advantage in the concert, and the buffo style of the opera. The German school, or style, is more unbending, and better adapted for church music. The fugue is its triumph; firmness and steadiness its excellences. The German aims at simplicity, character, and deep meaning, and wishes to make the music a perfect expression of the feeling. Hence the German singer often neglects to make the words distinctly intelligible. Yet the Germans have adopted much from the Italians, in regard to the cultivation of the vocal organs, as well as the execution, and have treated singing most scientifically. There is a surprising similarity of character in the schools of singing and painting, in each of these two nations. The French method borders closely on declamation, and shows the proneness of the nation to conversation. The language is very unfavorable for singing, on account of its want of verbal accent, and the swallowing of the final syllables. Though the German idiom can by no means be said to be well adapted for singing, on account of its many consonants, yet the French is still less so, particularly from its many nasal sounds. The French singing is, however, truly fine in the simple national songs: these recall the time of the troubadours, and have something uncommonly charming. With the *chansons*, *vaudevilles*, and *rondelays*, the case is different: in these, the French aim chiefly at wit and point, and the song is made subservient to the words, not the words to the song. All three nations have many works for giving instruction in singing, but none so many as the Germans.

Singing Schools.—The study of singing, as an art, has been hallowed by its devotion to the service of religion, both in ancient and modern times, and it has been considered an effectual instrument in the civilization of mankind. It was a law of the Egyptians, that children should be instructed in particular branches of music and singing: we may therefore justly infer that singing schools existed in Egypt. Among the Jews, singing was connected with all their religious ceremonies. Samuel established, during the peaceful years of his rule, the celebrated schools of the prophets, in which singing, music, and poetry were taught. Under David, the chief of the Levites gave instruction in singing, and had the direction, with twenty-four assistants, of a choir of 4000 singers and musicians. Among the Chinese, also, singing schools have been established from the most remote times; two of the principal mandarins are directors of the singing schools at Pekin; eight head teachers, and sixteen under teachers, with eight subordinate mandarins, eight musicographers, and eighty scholars, compose the institution. Among the Jews, splendor, and the love of the fine arts, reached their height under Solomon, and no exhibition of modern times can be compared with the musical festival at the dedication of Solomon's temple, at which, according to tradition, were united 200,000 singers, 40,000 harps, 40,000 sistrums, and 200,000 silver trumpets. Among the Greeks, the oracles were always delivered in song. The scholars of Pythagoras were obliged, on waking in the morning, and before going to sleep in the evening, to chant songs, in order to overcome the disturbing influences of the world. The greatest variety of hymns were sung in the worship of Apollo. The singing schools of the Greeks are celebrated: at their great public games, musical contests took place, and the four most sacred festivals, the Olympic, Pythion, Nemæan, and Isthmian games, as well as the Panathenæa, thus became schools of music. Through the Etruscans and Greeks, singing was introduced among the Romans. Under the Roman emperors, the passion for music and singing reached its height; many of the emperors gave themselves up to it with ardor. But proper singing schools were not known in ancient Rome, as the most distinguished musicians were foreigners. Among the Gauls, music was taught and practised by the Druids and Bards. With the religion of the Druids, these singing schools were also introduced into Britain. From the earliest times, the singers of Scotland and Britain were celebrated; after the extinction of Druidism, they were called *minstrels*, and resided chiefly in Wales. What has been said of the Tuiscon of the Germans, is very uncertain; however, the Germans had singers, and national songs, particularly martial songs, which were transmitted from mouth to mouth. With the introduction of Christianity, the singing schools acquired a higher and nobler character. The first Christians, particularly the Therapeutæ, in Palestine and Egypt, sang hymns in alternate choirs, during their religious ceremonies. Clemens Romanus, a companion of the apostle Paul, was the first to establish the head singer, to begin the psalm, and lead the assembly; the elders of the church were also the directors of the singing. Ambrose and Chrysostom warmly promoted it. As early as the first centuries, particular singing schools were established. Cyril relates that St. Theodosius was head singer at the church, in his native place, from his earliest childhood, and St. Nicetius, archbishop of Treves, in the first half of the sixth century, resolved to have all the boys, born in his diocese, instructed in singing as soon as they could talk. Proper seminaries for spreading the knowledge of singing were first established in Rome by pope Sylvester, between 314 and 335. A singing school, belonging jointly to all the churches in the city, was instituted, and was obliged to furnish choirs for all the sacred masses and religious ceremonies conducted by the pope or presbyter. The director of this singing school, called *Primicerius*, instructed select youths in singing, reading of the Holy Scriptures, and in good manners; these scholars were called *ministrales* and *clerici*. Pope Gregory the Great (590—604) greatly extended and improved the singing schools. In the school of the Lateran, the couch was still to be seen, in the ninth century, on which Gregory reposed while he instructed the singers, as also the rod with which he threatened the boys, and his *Antiphonarium*. (See *Antiphony*.) The boys who sang well were maintained by the school, and afterwards made chamberlains to the pope. Most of the scholars were taken from the Roman orphan asylum, whence the singing school was also called *orphanotrophium.* The same pope sent Augustin or Austin as a missionary to England, accompanied by many assistants and singers. Augustus and king Alfred, at the end of the ninth century, spread the art of singing in Great Britain. Charlemagne introduced it into France and Germany. He sent singers to Rome, who were there instructed, and, on their return, founded singing schools, first at Metz and Soissons, afterwards in many other towns. Charlemagne often presided in his principal school, and directed the instruction; his daughters practised music three hours daily. All the music masters were taken from the clergy. From the time of Pepin, a royal chapel was always connected with the royal palace, under the inspection of a music master, called *menestrel.* The so called *gay science* of the Provençals embraced music as well as poetry. The troubadours diffused it from the eleventh to the fourteenth century; the schools of the minnesingers originated from them; the most flourishing period of the German minnesingers was in the thirteenth century; among them were emperors, kings, princes, and counts; but when, at a later period, the use of court fools prevailed, these noble singers became extinct at court, and the art fell into the hands of common mastersingers. (q. v.) In the middle of the fifteenth century, figurate music was already taught in the singing schools at Augsburg. French and German compositions were principally sung. The principal singing choirs of the north of Germany, sprung from the religious zeal of Luther, who advised the study of music, and the cultivation of it, as a part of the religious service. In those early times, when the custom prevailed of performing mysteries, and celebrating many other religious festivals, singing choirs often assisted in these performances. Another kind of singing school, which existed in the twelfth and thirteenth centuries, must also be mentioned. In Italy, princes and states, in the middle ages, had in their service whole companies of singers and players, who appeared in numbers at all the chief festivals. Guido of Arezzo, at the beginning of the thirteenth century, did much for the improvement of singing, and founded new schools. In the sixteenth century, a higher and purer taste for music was awakened, chiefly by Palestrina (q. v.), the famous master, of the old Roman school. The same powerful influence which he exercised over the ancient Italian school of singing, Francesco Durante (q. v.) had over the modern. At the end of the seventeenth century, the singing school of Francesco Antonio Pistochi, in Bologna, was distinguished, which was continued by his famous scholars, Ant. Bernachi and Ant. Pasi. In the eighteenth century, the following schools were celebrated: that of Brivio, in Milan; Franc. Peli, in Modena; Redi, in Florence; Amadori, in Rome; but, particularly, those of Nic. Porpora (q. v.), Leonardo Leo, and Franc. Feo, in Naples. (See *Italian Music.*) These conservatorios (q. v.), or public singing and music schools, had the greatest influence, both in Italy and France, in perfecting music.

Sinigaglia, in the papal delegation of Urbino, between Rimini and Ancona; a small fortified place with 6200 inhabitants, celebrated for its annual fair, which lasts from July 20 to August 10. During this time, *loggie* or booths are erected along the canal, which are crowded with foreign and native traders, and the place, thronged with jugglers, dancers, &c., exhibits a panorama of Italy in miniature.

Sinking Fund. The term *sinking fund* is applied to a fund appropriated by a government to the purchase or extinguishment of its own debts. Where a government merely directs its treasurer to apply moneys, accruing from permanent sources of revenue, to the payment of the public debt, the term *sinking fund* can only signify the excess of the current revenues over the current expenditures. But the term is not ordinarily applied in such a case. In England, as early as 1716, sir Robert Walpole projected the sinking fund system, which was partially applied at that time, but brought into operation more fully in 1786, by Mr. Pitt. New taxes were imposed to such an amount as, upon estimation, would leave a surplus revenue of £900,000 beyond the current annual expenditure, and the payment of interest on the public debt. Assuming that, for a given number of years, the expenditure of the government would not exceed the estimated amount, and that the resources would yield this surplus, it followed, of course, that the public debt would eventually be extinguished by the application of this surplus to this purpose. And if the revenues, and expenditures for other purposes than the payment of the interest and principal of the public debt were kept at the same amount, it would follow that a greater amount could annually be applied to the payment of the principal of the debt, since a smaller amount would be requisite for the payment of the interest, in consequence of the constant reduction of the debt. All this is quite plain, and it would be equally true whether the payments were the extinguishment of a certain portion of the debt, or the purchase of it by the commissioners, or by trustees, who should hold the amount redeemed, and receive interest upon it, like any other creditors of the government, applying the interest so received to the further purchase of stock. This latter system was adopted in Great Britain, so that, in 1813, when this system of the sinking fund had been in operation twenty-seven years, a little more than £210,000,000 sterling had been redeemed, leaving the net amount of the public debt about £575,000,000, though the nominal amount was then above £812,000,000. In 1786, the debt was about £238,000,000. When this system was adopted, it was represented that, by some mysterious operation, it would infallibly result in the extinguishment of the debt; and the system was celebrated as a grand economical discovery. But after infinite arguments and calculations, and some ridicule on the part of unbelievers, it was found that there was no advantage obtained by buying up a part of the debt, and at the same time contracting an equal or greater amount at an equivalent rate of interest. A sinking fund, in the plain and intelligible sense of being a system of provisions and guaranties for the payment of the interest and redemption of the principal of the public debt, is undoubtedly of great importance, and necessary to sustain the public credit. When no part of the debt is made redeemable, such a system can be carried into operation only by buying up the public securities. But the still continuing to call the part so bought up a portion of the public debt, and receiving interest upon it, and keeping accounts respecting it, are a mere idle ceremony. A sinking fund was early established under the government of the United States. From 1803 down to 1817, the sum of $8,000,000 annually was appropriated to that fund, and the stock bought up or paid off by the commissioners, was registered in the treasury office, to the credit of the commissioners of that fund; and the interest accruing on such stock constituted a part of the fund for the payment of the interest and redemption of the principal of the unredeemed part of the debt; and in 1814, a little more than $33,000,000 was entered in the books of the treasury to the credit of those commissioners. Certain revenues were appropriated to this fund, it being intended, like any other similar one, as a sort of pledge of the public faith and resources to the public creditors. But before the close of that war, the fund had, from time to time, been charged with the payment of amounts to which it was inadequate, so that it no longer held out sufficient security to the public creditors. Accordingly, in 1817, a larger amount of appropriations was made to the fund, and by the act of congress of the third of March of that year, it was provided that the certificates of the stock redeemed should be cancelled; that is, the commissioners of this fund did not any longer appear as the creditors of the government on the treasury books. The ordinary and plain mode of proceeding was adopted: when any part of the debt was paid, the securities were cancelled, and did not afterwards appear in the public accounts.

Sion; one of the hills on which the city of Jerusalem was built. The part of the city on mount Sion was also called the "city of David," and the lower city, on mount Acra, was called the "daughter of Sion." (See *Jerusalem*.)

Sioux, or Dahcotah Indians; a family of Indian tribes dwelling to the west of the Mississippi. (See *Indians, American*.)

Siphon; a bent tube with one leg shorter than the other, used for transferring a liquid from one vessel to another. This is effected by exhausting the siphon of the air which it contains, or at least so rarefying it that the pressure of the atmosphere on the surface of the water will force up the liquid beyond the highest point of the curve of the siphon, when it will descend by the opposite leg. The power of the siphon is limited merely to decanting, and cannot be applied to raise the liquid above its level in the original vessel; nor will it continue to act after the level of the vessel into which it is decanted becomes equal to that from which it is drawn off. Instead of exhausting the siphon of air, it may be inverted and filled with water; if both ends are then stopped, and the shorter leg immersed in the water to be drawn off, on removing the plugs, the water will flow. If the siphon is large, as is the case where it is used for carrying water over a hill, it may be filled by an orifice in the upper point of the curve, which may then be plugged; and, on removing the plugs of the ends, the water will flow, as in the case last mentioned. A Würtemberg siphon is one in which the extremities of the legs are turned upwards, and which can be kept constantly filled. (See *Hydrostatics*, and *Air*.)

Sir; a term of courtesy, now applied, without distinction of rank, to all persons, formerly confined to gentlemen (probably derived from *sieur*, *seigneur*, lord). It is also the title of honor of knights and baronets, and as such is always prefixed to the Christian name.—*Sire*, in France, is a term of respect, by which the king is addressed.

Sirach. Jesus, son of Sirach, was a Jew of Palestine, who, about B. C. 140, after his arrival in Egypt, translated into Greek, for the use of the Alexandrian Jews, the book of Proverbs, which his grandfather, of the same name, had originally composed in Hebrew. The Catholic church admits this book (Wisdom of Jesus, son of Sirach, or Ecclesiasticus) into the canon; by the Protestants it is ranked among the apocryphal books. It is written in a deep religious tone, and abounds in excellent practical rules of life.

Siren. (See *Salamander*.)

Sirens; inferior goddesses, who, by their singing, fascinated those that sailed by their island, and then destroyed them. Homer mentions but two, and represents them as young women, without informing us of their origin. Later poets, who give a different account of their persons, number, names, and place of residence, usually describe them as daughters of the Ætolian river god Achelous, by Sterope, daughter of Amythaon, or by the muse Melpomene, or Terpsichore, sometimes as having sprung from the blood which flowed to the earth from the horn of Achelous, broken in his struggle with Hercules. Euripides, in reference to the latter account, calls them the daughters of the Earth. Sophocles calls them daughters of Phorcus; and this is, perhaps, the oldest account. The author of the Orphic Argonautics places them on a projecting rock on the shore near Ætna, alluring the Argonauts by their fatal singing. But Orpheus sang a heroic song to his lute, and the Sirens flung away their flutes and lyres, and threw themselves into the sea, where they became formidable rocks. These Sirens, thus converted to stone, could not be dangerous to Ulysses, and the poet assumes others in the Tyrrhenean sea, whom he encountered. Plato feigns eight Sirens, who are borne round on the eight heavenly circles, and who make the music of the spheres, which others attribute to the nine Muses. There is likewise a story of their trial of skill in singing, with the Muses. The latter were victorious, and, plucking the feathers from the wings of the Sirens, made garlands of them. According to Hyginus, the Sirens received these wings from Ceres, after the rape of Proserpine, because, although in her train, they had not rendered her assistance.

Sirius (dogstar); the most brilliant of the fixed stars, and the largest in the constellation of the Great Dog. (See *Constellations*, and *Dogdays*.)

Sirocco; a hot, relaxing and oppressive south-east wind, which blows in Sicily and Italy. Some have supposed it to be the same as the simoom, tempered by its passage across the water.

Sismondi, John Charles Leonard Simonde de, a celebrated historian and political economist, was born at Geneva, in 1773, of a family originally from Pisa, but which had long been settled in the south of France, and in Switzerland. The father of Sismondi, a member of the old Genevan government, retired to England with his family, in consequence of the troubles in 1792. (See *Geneva*.) On his return, in 1794, he was arrested, with his son, and both were sentenced to a year's imprisonment, and a heavy fine. Having recovered his liberty after the 9th Thermidor, Sismondi went to Tuscany (1795), but was there subjected to new persecutions. The French first threw him into prison as an aristocrat; and, Geneva having been meanwhile annexed to France, the insurgent Italians next confined him as a Frenchman. In the autumn of 1800, he returned to Geneva, and soon after published his first work, *Tableau de l'Agriculture Toscane* (1801), which was soon after followed by several valuable works, particularly the treatise entitled *De la Richesse Commerciale* (2 vols., 8vo., 1803). His studies were not confined to history, politics and the sciences auxiliary to them; he also paid much attention to polite literature. His extensive knowledge of foreign literatures, particularly the German school of poetry and criticism, contributed to raise his views above the narrow conventional rules then predominant in French æsthetics; and his *Littérature du Midi de l'Europe* (2d edition, 4 vols., 1829, translated into English) forms an epoch in literary history. In the field of history, Sismondi has acquired a high reputation by his two great works, *Histoire des Républiques Italiennes du Moyen Age* (16 vols., 8vo., 3d edition, 1826), and *Histoire des Français* (yet incomplete, vols. 1—15, 1821—31). His other works are *Nouveaux Principes d'Économie politique, ou de la Richesse dans ses Rapports avec la Population* (2 vols., 2d edition, 1829); *Julia Severa* (3 vols., 1822)—a historical romance, illustrating the state of Gaul at the time of the invasion by Clovis, towards the end of the fifth century; History of the Italian Republics, being a View of the Rise, Progress and Fall of Italian Freedom (in English, 1 vol., and French, 2 vols., 8vo., 1832); and *Des Espérances et des Besoins de l'Italie* (1832). He was also a frequent contributor to the *Revue Encyclopédique* previously to its adoption of St. Simonian principles; and most of the notices of the distinguished historical personages of Italy in the *Biographie Universelle* are from his pen. In his political principles, Sismondi is aristocratico-republican; and, although he had previously appeared, if not opposed, at least indifferent, to the imperial government, yet, after Napoleon's return from Elba, he published a warm eulogium on the *acte additionnel* (*Examen de la Constitution Française*), in which he called upon all Frenchmen to rally round the emperor, in defence of the national independence. Napoleon, in consequence, named him a member of the legion of honor; but Sismondi declined receiving any mark of favor. As a historian, he is distinguished for his full and accurate narrative, drawn with great scrupulousness from original sources; and his works are replete with instruction in regard to facts, and in their pictures of the changes in the social condition. But he is sometimes prolix, and we often miss the profound views and large conclusions of the philosophical historian.

SISTINE CHAPEL (*Cappella Sistina*); a chapel in the Vatican, so called from pope Sixtus IV, who erected it, and destined it for the religious services performed during Passion Week, for which it is still chiefly used. Its dimensions are very large. The whole wall behind the altar is covered by Michael Angelo's picture of the last Judgment—a great poem in itself. On the vaulted ceiling, the same master has painted the creation of the world, and around it prophets and sibyls. The other walls contain, in twelve compartments, the productions of Signorelli, Filippi, Perugino, Roselli, &c., which relieve the mind, tasked by the gigantic and overpowering conceptions of the immortal Angelo. Words are inadequate to describe the effect of the celebration of the passion of the Savior by the pope and cardinals in this chapel during Passion Week, when grand and appropriate ceremonies, aided by incomparable music, combine with the noblest productions of the pencil, to produce the highest effect of Catholic worship.

SISTRA. (See *Indian Literature*.)

SISTRUM; a musical instrument of the ancients. The Egyptians used it in the worship of Isis, and it is still found in Egypt and Abyssinia. It consists of an oval hoop of metal with a handle. Through this hoop are bored holes, in which are metal bars, which, on agitating or beating the instrument, produce the sound. The finer the metal, and the more perfect the proportion of the holes, the more agreeable is the tone of the instrument. The German guitar has also been called *sistrum*.

SISYPHUS; king of Corinth (which, according to some, he built), and son of Æolus and Enarete. He married Merope, the daughter of Atlas. The Attic poets relate many instances of his art. Theseus, whose dominions he disturbed, slew him. Some impute his death to Jupiter, in revenge for his having informed Æsopus of the rape of his daughter. He is said to have put Death in fetters, so that, for some time, no one died. He afterwards over reached Pluto, by getting leave to visit the upper regions, whence he did not return till he had lived out the natural term of his life. In consequence of this, he was obliged to roll a heavy stone to the top of a hill in the infernal regions. The stone no sooner reached the summit than it fell back, thus rendering his punishment eternal.

SIWAH; one of the oases in the desert of Libya, to the west of Egypt, interesting from the ruins which it contains. It lies in lat. 29° 12′ N.; lon. 26° 6′ E.; 120 miles W. from the Nile, and is about six miles long by four or five wide. It is supposed to contain 8000 inhabitants, of whom 2500 are in the town of Siwah. The soil is fertile, yielding dates, pomegranates, figs, olives and grapes. Tepid springs, holding salt in solution, are numerous. This oasis is supposed to be the site of the celebrated temple of Jupiter Ammon, the ruins of which travellers think they have discovered at the distance of a league and a half from the town, covering an area of 360 feet by 300. The ruins are in the Egyptian style of archi tecture, and covered with a profusion of hieroglyphical and other sculptures in relief and painted. Nearly a mile from these ruins, in a grove of date palms, is the celebrated Fountain of the Sun, dedicated to Ammon. It is ninety feet in length by sixty, and appears to be warmer by night than by day. Close by this spring are traces of a temple supposed to be the relics of a sanctuary mentioned by Diodorus Siculus. A mountain in the neighborhood has been converted into catacombs, some of the tombs of which are on a magnificent scale, resembling the celebrated sepulchral chambers of Thebes in decoration, sculpture and painting. A succession of lakes and temples stretches into the desert towards the west, and tombs, catacombs and churches, are scattered over the waste. At a short distance from the sacred lake there is a temple of Roman or Greek construction, the architecture of which is of the Doric order—a singular circumstance in a country surrounded by immense deserts, and 400 miles distant from the ancient seats of civilization. (See Browne's *Travels in Africa and Syria.*)

SIX NATIONS. (See *Iroquois.*)

SIXTUS V, the greatest ruler and statesman among the popes of the three last centuries, was born in 1521, at Grotta a Mare, not far from the little town of Montalto, in the mark of Ancona. His proper name was Felix Peretti. He gave early indications of an aspiring spirit, and was delivered by his uncle, a Franciscan, at Montalto, from the humble labors by which his indigent parents procured their bread. In the schools of this order at Montalto, Pesaro, Fermo, Bologna, &c., Peretti, having joined the Franciscans in 1534, received the usual strict education and instruction of the monasteries. His active spirit soon made him conversant with the scholastic philosophy and theology and Roman literature. In 1544, he gave instruction in the canon law at Rimini, and, in 1546, at Sienna. In 1548, he was made priest, doctor of divinity, and superintendent of the monastic school of Sienna. He made himself famous in Rome, likewise, as an acute logician and preacher, where, in 1551, the favor of some cardinals procured him a permanent residence. Here he gained much reputation, not only by his pulpit performances, but also by his pious works, as the founding of a brotherhood for solemnly carrying the host to the sick, under the name of the society of the holy sacrament, and an asylum for indigent young girls, according to the rule of St. Clara. His work on mystical divinity, and his Golden Register, extracted from the writings of Aristotle and his commentator Averroes, were also fruits of this residence at Rome, which, however, was embittered by the vexatious controversies in which his unquiet spirit, and his aversion to the monastic life, involved him. Cardinal Capri, the protector of his order, defended him from the violence of his associates; but he was continually plunged into new difficulties by his own intolerance, and the jealousy of the monks, arising from the reputation which he had acquired as a preacher on his visits to the principal cities of Italy. His situation was not improved by his removal to Venice, where, in 1556, he was appointed superintendent of the Franciscan school, and, in 1557, inquisitor-general. He discharged these offices with great strictness, and not without some danger; for the abhorrence in which the Venetians held the inquisition compelled him several times to flee from the city. In 1560, he gladly returned to Rome, where the pope made him a counsellor of the holy office (the inquisition), and professor in the university; and his order, at the suggestion of Capri, chose him their procurator-general. He attended the papal legate to Spain, in 1565, as the theologian of the embassy. Here he became acquainted with the policy of the Spanish court, and, by his sermons, obtained the esteem of Philip II and his nobles. The cardinal of Alessandria being made pope, in 1566, under the name of Pius V, elevated his old friend Peretti to the rank of vicar-general of the Franciscans, bishop of St. Agata de' Goti, and father confessor to the pope. Peretti now labored to repress the disorders which had arisen among the Franciscans, and to improve by pastoral letters the morals of the clergy of his diocese, which he never visited but once: moreover, he generously pardoned his former enemies. In 1570, he was made a cardinal, and assumed the name of *Montalto*, because cardinals of low birth are accustomed to exchange their family name for the name of their native place. Well acquainted with the policy of his colleagues, he believed the surest way to gain the triple crown—the great object of his ambition—was to pursue a course of conduct which should not awaken the jealousy of the other cardinals. Till then, violent, ambitious, active, and strong in body, he seemed to have adopted with the purple all the opposite qualities. His influence over Pius V he used with moderation, and, after his death, avoided connecting himself with any party in the conclave.

Under Gregory XIII, he withdrew almost wholly from the court, and took part, as he pretended, very reluctantly in the improvement of the calendar, and the important political negotiations with Russia and England, in which his wisdom and experience could not be dispensed with. He treated every one with kindness and affability, and suffered injuries without seeking for revenge. Instead of permitting his poor relations to reap much advantage from his advancement, he expended his income (which was, indeed, rather small) in pious establishments, acts of benevolence, and literary enterprises, erected new monuments to forgotten saints, fed the poor, superintended an edition of the works of St. Ambrose, and presented the appearance of a sick and broken-down old man, who loved, above all things else, tranquillity and devotion. But, in the confessor's chair, where the licentious nobles confided to him their secrets, and by means of the members of his household, he secretly collected a fund of accurate information in regard to the views and characters of the most distinguished Romans; and, under the mask of pious simplicity and feeble old age, prepared himself for that high destiny for which he was born. He had deceived all about him as to his true character; and, on the death of Gregory XIII, in 1585, the majority of the cardinals were convinced that a pope like Montalto would be most easily managed. In consequence of this opinion, he was chosen to the popedom almost unanimously, and took the title of Sixtus V. As soon as he was sure of his election, he threw down, in the electoral chapel, the staff on which he had hitherto leaned, and came forward, to the astonishment of all, with a dignity and firmness indicative of that independence of spirit which he maintained during his five years' administration. At the very beginning of his reign, he showed the Romans, by the speedy execution of several criminals, how he intended to exercise justice, which had slept under his predecessors. Offences against the public peace or safety he punished generally with death, regardless of all intercession. He removed unfaithful judges, freed the States of the Church from robbers, and labored energetically to restore the public tranquillity. But he was a terror only to the wicked; oppressed innocence found in him support; the poor were fed from his storehouses, and thousands of idle hands employed in the erection of edifices, which he constructed wit[illegible]sing rapidity, for the ornament of [illegible]. The aqueduct, called *aqua felice*, the lofty obelisk in front of St. Peter's church, and the triumphal pillars of Trajan and Marcus Aurelius, which he erected at a great expense, the noble dome of St. Peter's, and the hospital on the Tiber, are monuments of his zeal for the splendor and welfare of his capital. He gained lasting honor by founding the Vatican library, for which he erected a magnificent building, with a printing-office, for the publication solely of the works of ecclesiastical authors. From this Vatican press proceeded his complete edition of the works of St. Ambrose, and the Vulgate, which he revised. At Fermo, in the States of the Church, he founded a university; at Rome, the college of St. Bonaventura, for young Franciscans; and at Bologna, the college of Montalto. His chief attention, however was directed to the government of the ecclesiastical states, and the care of its foreign relations. He endeavored to increase the trade and industry of Rome by abolishing heavy imposts, and establishing manufactures of silk and of wool for the employment of the poor. He improved the departments of the police and the finances, and accumulated a fund of three millions *scudi*, which he deposited in the castle of St. Angelo, to serve as a fund for the public wants. This was acquired by the increase and rigid collection of the public taxes, the confiscation of the property of criminals, the profits of new pawn-houses (*monti*), by an advance on the price of venal offices, and the sale of many which had never before been subjects of traffic, but principally by rigid economy. The expenses of his court he limited as much as possible. Although he was generous to his former patrons, he was moderate in his benefactions to his relatives. For the administration of the affairs of church and state, he instituted fifteen congregations, composed of cardinals and other officers. The most remarkable are the congregations for the navy, which consisted of ten galleys, for the protection of the coast, for the complaints of the people, for the continuation of the catalogue of prohibited books, for carrying into effect, and explaining, the decrees of the council of Trent, for sacred rites and ceremonies, and for the administration of justice. (See *Curia.*) Besides the establishment of several festivals in honor of saints, the reign of Sixtus V was marked by the limitation of the number of cardinals to seventy, and the obligation imposed on all Catholic bishops to visit Rome once in every three, five, or ten years, according to the distance of their sees, on pain of losing their offices—an ordinance which, though never strictly enforced, was calculated to confirm the old papal claims, and to bind the bishops more firmly to the head of the church. In theological controversies, Sixtus maintained a wise neutrality, and enjoined silence on the Jesuits, whom he never loved, when they contended with the university of Louvain. But in the political events of his time, he took a more active share. The project of restoring Germany to its former dependence on the papal see failed; but Sixtus excited the emperor Rodolph II to a violent persecution of heretics. Two Protestant sovereigns, Henry of Navarre, and Elizabeth, queen of England, he excommunicated, though it would seem only for the sake of appearances, since he sincerely esteemed them both for their intellectual vigor, and would never seriously support Spain against Henry, because he deemed the views of Philip II dangerous. He, however, aided this monarch with funds to equip the armada against England, but at the same time gave the British envoys an opportunity to see that he would not disapprove of a more energetic participation in the war for the independence of the Netherlands, in order to curtail the Spanish power. After the assassination of the Guises, he excommunicated Henry III, yet without giving direct support to the league. But while Sixtus V conducted with moderation towards all the princes of his time, he weakened one by means of another, and made them all dependent on himself. His mind was occupied with extensive plans for the enlargement of his temporal and spiritual power. He always called Naples his kingdom, and made the Spanish viceroy feel his importance on all occasions. It was his design to subject Russia to his dominion through Stephen Bathori, king of Poland, and Egypt through the grand-duke of Tuscany; but the death of these two princes frustrated his bold projects. By his numerous spies, not only his special informers, who were royally paid, but also the father confessors of the Roman Catholic church, he gained a knowledge of every thing that was passing. Hence he was always prepared for emergencies, and consulted with the cardinals only for the sake of appearance. His thorough knowledge of business, and the superiority of his bold, able and lofty mind, filled every one that approached him with respect and admiration. He was famous for humorous remarks and pithy repartees, by which he often overcame opposition and effected his objects. Plain in his exterior, and free from anxiety about a nice etiquette, he maintained his princely dignity by a majestic demeanor and strict consistency. The sternness of his deportment was rarely interrupted by displays of good nature, though this sometimes happened, as in his marks of favor to his old acquaintances of the time of his humble condition. He was reserved towards those around him, and firm even to obstinacy in all that he undertook. Though politics occupied the greatest share of his attention, yet he was wanting in nothing which became the head of the church. In no case did he abuse his power to gratify personal feelings of revenge. Though never beloved, he was universally feared. After his death, which happened August 24, 1590, the populace, irritated by the pressure of taxes, overturned the statues which the senate had erected to him in the capitol. The conjecture that his death was hastened by poison, at the instigation of the Spanish court, which he had offended by his coldness towards the league, and by the manifestation of favor towards Henry IV, is not supported by sufficient evidence. All that could be effected in so few years, by commanding talents and force of character, with the feeble means which were left to the papal see by the reformation, Sixtus accomplished; and he was the last head of the Roman Catholic church, whom kings have had reason to fear.

Skalds. (See *Scalds.*)

Skating; one of the finest gymnastic exercises, by which man, as Klopstock says, "like the Homeric gods, strides with winged feet over the sea, transmuted into solid ground." It is one of the healthiest exercises, bringing the body into action by a great variety of motions. The best skaters are found in Holland (where both men and women often skate to market, and not unfrequently ladies practise the exercise), Germany, and Russia. Skating is mentioned in the Edda, written eight hundred years ago, in which the god Uller is represented as distinguished by his beauty, arrows, and skates. Klopstock has sung its praises in several odes. Göthe, Herder, and other German poets, have celebrated it. (See Salzmann's *Gymnastics*, and Garcin's *Le vrai Patineur;* &c.)

Skeleton (from σκελλω, I dry) is the assemblage and combination of all the bones in the animal body, with a few exceptions, as the bone of the tongue (*os hyoides*), and certain other bones in certain animals. Red-blooded animals only possess a true skeleton, to which their muscles are attached, and on which the general form, as well as the greater or less flexibility of the body, depends. The skeleton is of the greatest importance, both in comparative anatomy and in the animal mechanism.—See the five first chapters of Blumenbach's *Comparative Anatomy, with Notes by Lawrence* (2d ed., by W. Coulson, London, 1827), and the numbers on *Animal Mechanism* in the *Library of Useful Knowledge;* also Arnott's *Elements of Physics* (American ed., by Isaac Hays, Philadelphia, 1 vol., 1829). See, also, Cuvier's *Leçons d'Anatomie Comparée.*

Skelton, John ; an English poet, born towards the latter part of the fifteenth century, at Oxford, where, about 1489, he received the laureateship as a degree. (See *Poet Laureate.*) He took orders in 1498, and was remarkable for his buffooneries in the pulpit. There were three objects at which he delighted to aim his satire—the mendicant friars, Lily, the grammarian, and cardinal Wolsey. His attacks on Wolsey at length roused the resentment of that prelate, and an order being issued for his apprehension, he took refuge in the sanctuary at Westminster, where the abbot afforded him protection until his death, June 21, 1529, not long before the fall of Wolsey. His works, consisting of comedies, satires, short poems, were published in 1512, and are contained in Chalmers's edition of the English poets, with the exception of a few, omitted on account of their coarseness. The whole are enumerated by Ritson.

Sketches. (See *Drawing.*)

Skiddaw ; one of the highest mountains of England, in Cumberland, distinguished for its grand and romantic scenery, as well as for the lakes in its different hollows and near its base ; height 3022 feet. It is three miles north of Keswick.

Skiff. (See *Boat.*)

Skin ; the porous organ which forms the external covering of the body, and which, besides its use as a covering, performs the functions of perspiration (q. v.) and absorption. It consists of two separate organs—the *epidermis* or scarf-skin, and the *cutis* or proper skin ; between lies the *rete mucosum.* The epidermis may be separated from the cutis by soaking in water. It is raised by the application of blisters, and, in some diseases of the skin, peels off of itself. The complexion of negroes is owing to the black color of the rete mucosum. The fat keeps the epidermis soft, and is diminished in quantity in those diseases in which the skin becomes rough. The epidermis protects the terminations of the nerves, whose sensibilities would otherwise soon become blunted. The surface of the skin is marked with very regular furrows, running parallel with each other, in which are the pores, which exhale an attenuated vapor. The proper skin forms a compact and thick membrane, which envelopes the muscles and fat. On being boiled in water, it yields a quantity of gelatinous matter, which is used for making glue. (q. v.)

Skorodite is a rare mineral, found in Saxony, Carinthia and Cornwall. It presents itself in small crystals, derived from a right rhombic prism of 120°, but which are terminated at each extremity by four-sided pyramids. It is also found massive, and in botryoidal masses, composed of crystals, diverging from a common centre. Its colors are various shades of green ; lustre vitreous ; streak white ; rather brittle ; hardness about that of fluor. Before the blow-pipe, it emits an arsenical odor, and melts into a reddish-brown scoria, which acts upon the magnetic needle. It consists of

Arsenious acid, ...	31.40
Sulphuric acid, ...	1.54
Water, ...	18.00
Protoxide of iron, with magnesia, lime, and manganese,	47.80

Skull (*cranium*) ; the bony box which contains the brain. It forms the forehead, and every part of the head, except the face. It consists of eight bones.—See the treatise on *Animal Mechanism* in the *Library of Useful Knowledge*, and Blumenbach's *Manual of Comparative Anatomy* (translated into English, 2d ed., by W. Coulson, London, 1827). See, also, the article *Phrenology.*

Skull-Cap (*scutellaria*) ; a genus of labiate plants, several species of which inhabit the U. States. They are herbaceous, with opposite leaves : and the flowers, also, opposite, and placed in the axils of the superior leaves, sometimes forming terminal spikes, from the diminished size of these leaves. The calyx is entire ; the upper lip vaulted, closing like a lid after the flowering is over. When inverted, the calyx presents the figure of a helmet with the visor raised. The flowers are much longer than the calyx, and usually of a blue color. The *S. lateriflora* has been much celebrated as a remedy for hydrophobia; but its pretensions seem to be destitute of the slightest foundation. It is the most common species in the Northern States: the stem divides from the base into numerous opposite weak branches, provided with oval acute petiolate and toothed leaves; the flowers are small and blue, situated at the summits of the branches, and usually turned to one side, by which character it is readily distinguished from the other species.

Skunk (*mephitis putorius*); a carnivorous quadruped, allied to the weasel and badger, inhabiting most parts of North America, and celebrated for the intolerable stifling stench which it discharges when threatened with danger, and which is its defence against its enemies. At other times, the animal is not at all unpleasant, and, if killed while unsuspicious of danger, the offending glands being carefully removed, the flesh may be eaten, and is said to be well flavored; in fact, it is frequently made use of, and is much relished by the Indians and hunters. The skunk is about as large as a cat. The dentition differs but slightly from that of the weasels. The upper lip is furnished with long whiskers; the fur is long and thick, composed of silky and woolly hairs intermixed; the color is white and blackish-brown, in large masses, but the respective distribution of these tints varies so greatly that no two individuals are to be found precisely alike. A second species inhabits South America, and perhaps there are others. The genus is exclusively American. The skunk is a nocturnal animal, and leaves its burrow in the twilight in search of small quadrupeds, and the young and eggs of birds, on which it feeds. When it gains access to the poultry yard, it often does much mischief. The skunk seems to be perfectly aware of its powers of defence, and takes no pains to avoid man or other animals; it seems so unsuspicious of danger as to invite attack, and strangers often pay the price of experience. Should a dog attempt to seize him, he is utterly discomfited, and runs away howling, and endeavoring to thrust his nose in the ground. The offensive fluid is ejected to a considerable distance, and is very acrimonious; the smallest drop is sufficient to render clothes detestable to the wearer and his companions for a great length of time, and without any perceptible diminution in intensity. Washing, smoking, baking, burying, in short, every process seems to be ineffectual for its removal.

Skunk-Cabbage (*symplocarpus fœtida*). Among the earliest of our spring flowers, often, indeed, before them all, appear the large, thick, purplish and spotted spathes of this plant. The leaves are later in making their appearance, are very large, and bear no inconsiderable resemblance to those of the cabbage. The whole plant has a very strong odor, singularly like that of the skunk, but not comparable to it in intensity. The skunk-cabbage is unknown in the Southern States. It belongs to the natural family *aroideæ*.

Skye. (See *Hebrides*.)

Slander. (See *Libel*.)

Slate. (See *Appendix*, end of this volume.)

Slate Clay. (See *Clay*.)

Slave Lake, or Athapesco; in North America; lat. 61° 20′ N.; lon. 115° W. It is about 200 miles in length, and fifty in breadth.

Slavery. The history of mankind shows that the empire of force gives way but slowly to the empire of reason. It is one of the most interesting and useful labors of the historian, though not the most flattering to human pride, to trace the steps by which this change takes place, as exemplified, for instance, in the history of political institutions, the relation of the wife to the husband,* and of the servant to the master. At present, we shall confine ourselves to the institution of domestic slavery. This originates in the power of the strong over the weak. Man, in the infancy of society, uses his physical power according to his own pleasure. In the case of his wife and children, natural affection restrains him, in a great measure, from the abuse of his power. But there is another class of dependants, his conduct towards whom is not restrained by such feelings—his slaves. Slaves were probably at first captives. It being considered that the victor had a right over the life of the vanquished, the latter was looked upon as altogether at the disposal of the former, who, if he chose to spare him, might subject him to any restraint that he saw fit. The principle on which slavery was thus made to rest, was only adapted to the rudest condition of society, and is

* In the article *Marriage*, it is stated that, in almost all original marriage ceremonies, the symbolic expression of buying and selling is to be found.

wholly inconsistent with the present state of morals and religion. We carry on wars, indeed, for the attainment of specific objects, and, as far as the destruction of human life is required for the attainment of those objects, we regard it as a necessary evil; but we do not consider that either individuals or governments have any right to dispose of the lives of the vanquished; nor are even criminals allowed to be made slaves in the full sense of the word. Philosophy allows of no obligation from one man to another without an equivalent; and the idea of making a man a slave, that is, of subjecting all that he has and is to the disposal of a master, who is not bound, on his part, to render any thing in return, is at war with the first principles of bodies politic. Slavery can never be a legal relation. It rests entirely on force. The slave, being treated as property, and not allowed legal rights, cannot be under legal obligations. Slavery is, also, inconsistent with the moral nature of man. Each man has an individual worth, significance and responsibility, is bound to the work of self-improvement, and to labor in a sphere for which his capacity is adapted. To give up his individual liberty, is to disqualify himself for fulfilling the great objects of his being. Hence political societies, which have made a considerable degree of advancement, do not allow any one to resign his liberty, any more than his life, to the pleasure of another. In fact, the great object of political institutions in civilized nations, is to enable man to fulfil, most perfectly, the ends of his *individual* being. Christianity, moreover, which enjoins us, while we remain in this world, to regulate our conduct with reference to a better, lays down the doctrine of brotherhood and mutual love, of "doing as we would be done by," as one of its fundamental maxims, which is wholly opposed to the idea of one man's becoming the property of another. These two principles of mutual obligation, and the worth of the individual, were beyond the comprehension of the states of antiquity, but are now at the basis of morals, politics and religion. In the most cultivated states of antiquity, the individual, as such, was little regarded. He was considered only as a citizen of a body politic. In fact, whilst we found the whole idea of the state on the prior idea of the individual, the state with them was the primitive idea, from which the individual received his significance and worth, for they did not consider the individual as a being placed on earth for the purpose of self-improvement, to promote which political societies are formed. To foreigners they gave the names of *barbarians, enemies, slaves.* Aristotle, one of the most powerful minds of antiquity, says in his politics, "With barbarians, the family consists of male and female slaves; but to the Greeks belongs dominion over the barbarians, because the former have the understanding requisite to rule, the latter the body only to obey." He calls the slave a living instrument, as the instrument is an inanimate slave. Yet he adds, "For the slave, considered simply as such, no friendship can be entertained; but it may be felt for him, as he is a man." We perceive here the nobleness of his nature struggling with the limited ideas of his age. We find several traces of a similar feeling among men of elevated character. Plutarch, for instance (in his life of Numa), expresses his belief in an early golden age, when there were neither masters nor slaves. Notwithstanding the injustice of the state of slavery, yet, when we come to the question of its abolition, the subject is often attended with numerous difficulties, of which the dangers that may accrue from the removal of restraint from men wholly unaccustomed to self-control, are among the chief; but, on the other hand, cupidity and prejudice often unnecessarily magnify the real difficulties. The abolition of slavery, and its kindred institution, villenage, and the improvement in the condition of women, are among the most important services which Western Europe has rendered to the world. The abolition of slavery in Europe was the consequence, and, in its turn, the cause, of its civilization; for slavery is the greatest bar to the progress of society. Look at Asia, so far, at one time, in advance of Europe, and now so far behind it, struggling under the burden of slavery. It is a melancholy reflection that Europe reëstablished in her colonies the hateful institution which she had overthrown at home, thereby furnishing another proof that man is capable of committing the most appalling inconsistencies, provided he finds his interest in so doing, and is at a distance from the voice of reproof We should add, that the villenage which still exists in some parts of Europe, is still more absurd than slavery, because it attempts to treat the human individual as a person and as a thing at the same time, a contradiction which appears, indeed, to some extent in all laws respecting slaves, because the rights of man cannot be altogether overlooked.

Slavery having once originated, many circumstances favored its continuance. From the heads of families who, in the infancy of society in Asia, regarded their domestic dependants in the light of property, as much as they did their flocks, originated the chiefs of the nomadic tribes, who became conquerors or priests; and from these two classes all the political institutions in Asia seem to have sprung. The conquerors established absolute despotisms, in which the persons and property of the subjects were completely at the disposal of the ruler. This is political slavery, i. e. the total absence of legal relations (i. e. mutual obligation) between sovereign and subject. Rules may, indeed, sometimes be laid down by the sovereign for the regulation of these relations; but the continuance of them depends entirely on his pleasure.* This state of political slavery furnished a great support to domestic slavery by the analogy between the rule of a king and that of a head of a family. The priests secured their power by the establishment of castes, by which society was made to form a sort of pyramid, at the top of which the priests strove to place themselves. The Greeks and Romans, by freeing themselves from the debasing institution of castes, made a great advance in civilization; but they could not elevate themselves to the idea of liberty in the domestic connexions, which lies at the basis of the political institutions of all modern civilized nations, so that the social institutions of our times are founded upon principles essentially differing from those of the ancients—a circumstance which is often overlooked. The circumscribed views of the ancients, respecting the rights and relations of men, was the reason why, in spite of their progress in civilization, they continued to treat the prisoner of war as a slave. Had they considered their enemies as equals, and not as mere barbarians, this custom would probably have been sooner abolished. If Christian nations, at later periods, also reduced prisoners of war, in some cases, to slavery,—as the Spaniards did with the Indians in America,—it was owing to the contempt which they felt for them as heathens. This made the Spaniards look upon the Indians much in the same light as the Romans did upon barbarians. Fanaticism varnished over this measure, and the disciples of the religion of love and truth pretended that the savages could be more easily converted to Christianity in slavery than in freedom.† It was this idea, also, which, as Montesquieu states, induced his most Christian majesty, Louis XIII, to sign a law, declaring the negroes in his colonies slaves. The true motive, however, in both cases, undoubtedly was cupidity; and this motive, in other instances, is proclaimed without disguise.‡ The Europeans and their descendants, in fact, have been preëminent for cupidity. Whether their greater civilization has made them more sensible of the value of money, or their superior intellectual cultivation has furnished them with more means of satisfying the universal thirst for acquisition, or whether they are naturally more prone than other races to avarice and the vices which flow from it, they are notorious for the violation of every moral and religious principle, and the commission of the most enormous inconsistencies and cruelties in the gratification of this passion. History can show no instance of such prolonged and cold-blooded cruelty as is presented in the nefarious slave-trade of the Europeans and their descendants. A historical account of the various forms of slavery in different nations, and particularly a sketch of the laws respecting slavery that have existed,

* Here we may be allowed a remark respecting the difference of absolute governments in Europe and Asia. Even the supporters of the divine right of kings in Europe, who maintain that a monarch is answerable to none but God, nevertheless admit that he is bound to rule conscientiously, and to administer justice; whilst the despotism of Asia rests simply on the idea of power, without the supposition of a higher origin. Hence the vizier who murders the reigning monarch and his family, and usurps the government, is looked upon as the lawful master of the lives of his subjects, as much as his predecessor was, while he possesses power to enforce his will.

† Arguments readily accommodate themselves to circumstances. At that time, men were to be enslaved for the good of their souls; and now, the security of the masters, as well as the happiness of the slaves themselves, require that they should be kept from all means of moral and intellectual improvement.

‡ By an act passed in Virginia in the year 1679, it was, for the better encouragement of soldiers, declared, that what Indian prisoners should be taken in a war in which the colony was then engaged, should be free purchase to the soldiers taking them. In 1682, it was declared, that all servants brought into this country (Virginia), by sea or land, not being Christians, whether Negroes, Moors, Mulattoes or Indians (except Turks and Moors in amity with Great Britain), and all Indians which should thereafter be sold by neighboring Indians, or any other trafficking with us, as slaves, should be slaves to all intents and purposes. Per judge Tucker, in the case of Hudgins *vs.* Wright. (*Henning and Munford's Reports*, 139.)

and still exist, among the more civilized nations, would be highly interesting, but would far exceed our limits.

The effects of slavery have always been most injurious to the nations which have permitted it. It is so directly opposed to the nature of man (which can as little endure absolute power as absolute subjection, without greatly degenerating), that it has always had a palsying influence on the industry and morality both of the masters and the slaves. The human mind cannot thrive without freedom. Among the evils which have originated from slavery are, the use of eunuchs, the shows of gladiators, the encouragement of the grossest sensuality and indolence, and an unparalleled disregard of human life, the corrupt character of the freedmen, and the outrages of the slave when he breaks his chains—from the horrible war in Italy, 70 B. C. (see *Spartacus*), down to the atrocities of the Haytian revolution, and the bloody insurrections on the island of Barbadoes in 1816, and several more recent ones. These are a few of the consequences of slavery, more or less conspicuous wherever it has existed, but particularly so in ancient Rome, of whose ruin slavery was the chief and most direct cause.* In Athens, slaves were treated with considerable mildness; in Sparta and Rome, with harshness. By the Roman law, if a master was killed, all the slaves who were under the same roof, or near enough to be able to hear his cry, were to be put to death. The right of the master over the life of the slave was not abolished till the time of the Antonines, in the second century A. D. If slaves were ill treated by a third person, the Aquilian law only allowed the owner of the slave to demand indemnification for the damage. In Athens, however, the perpetrator was punished sometimes even with death. Modern legislation has, in many cases, sought to protect slaves against abuses on the part of their masters, and to afford them facilities for manumission, but, as yet, with very imperfect success; nor can legislation ever protect effectually a being who is the property of another. Many legal investigations, of late years, respecting the treatment of slaves, have brought to light atrocities which most persons would have thought impossible in this age, and which would make many believe that the superiority of our race consists less in moral advancement than in refinement of manners. Examine, for instance, the facts disclosed in the proceedings instituted against Picton, the British governor of Trinidad. The laws of the Mohammedans respecting slaves, in their general spirit, and compared to the laws respecting free persons, are more humane than those enacted by Christians; one cause of which may be, that a part of their slaves are of the same color with themselves, whilst the slaves of Christian nations are all of a different color from their masters; and the color itself, from association, has become an object of disgust, peculiarly to the descendants of the English race in the U. States. The laws respecting slaves are, generally speaking, among Christians, milder in monarchical governments than in the slave-holding republics of the U. States. Thus manumission, under the Spanish and English laws, is much easier than under those of this Union. Some of the former governments allow the slave to accumulate property, by which he may eventually purchase his freedom. This is the case in the Spanish colonies; but no such right is recognised by law in the U. States. One reason of this difference undoubtedly is, that in monarchical states the government is distinct both from the master and the slave, whilst in republics like ours the masters (the interested party) are themselves the legislators, and, of course, are guided principally by their interest, in the enactment of laws: another reason is, that republics like ours, in which the executive department is intrusted with comparatively little power, must be more attentive to provide for their safety, by severe laws, than monarchical states, in which the executive has a strong military force at its disposal. Thus, whilst several English laws encourage the instruction of slaves in reading, arithmetic, and the elementary truths of religion, several slave-holding states of the Union prohibit the teaching them reading and writing, under severe penalties. Yet North America and England have done most to ameliorate the condition of this class of persons; and we believe it is generally admitted that the slave is no where better treated than in the slave-holding states of this Union. The evil of slavery was entailed on the U. States by the measures of the mother country, during the period of colonial dependence. The colonies made repeated efforts to prevent the importation of slaves into this country, but could not obtain the consent of the English government.—See Walsh's *Appeal from the Judg-*

* The late debates in the legislature of Virginia, after the insurrection in that state, in 1831, contain many highly interesting remarks on this subject.

ments of Great Britain (Philadelphia, 1819). In the ninth section of that work the subject is fully discussed. In allusion to the fact just stated, Mr. Jefferson, in his draft of the Declaration of Independence, said, "He (the king of England) has waged civil war against human nature itself, violating its most sacred rights of life and liberty, in the persons of a distant people, who never offended him; captivating, and carrying them into slavery in another hemisphere, or to incur miserable death in their transportation thither. This piratical warfare, the opprobrium of infidel powers, is the warfare of the Christian king of Great Britain: determined to keep open a market where MEN should be bought and sold, he prostituted his negative for suppressing every legislative attempt to prohibit or to restrain this execrable commerce; and, that this assemblage of horrors might want no fact of distinguished dye, he is now exciting those very people to rise in arms among us, and to purchase that liberty of which he has deprived them, by murdering the people upon whom he also obtruded them, thus paying off former crimes, committed against the liberties of one people, with crimes which he urges them to commit against the lives of another." (See the fac-simile of this draft in Jefferson's *Correspondence*.) But this passage was struck out when the Declaration of Independence was adopted; and the constitution of the U. States acknowledges slavery, by the provision that "Representatives and direct taxes shall be apportioned among the several states which may be included within this Union, according to their respective numbers, which shall be determined by adding to the whole number of free persons—including those bound to service for a term of years, and excluding Indians not taxed—three fifths of all other persons." Previous to the admission of Missouri into the Union, in 1820, a warm contest took place in congress, respecting the permission of slavery in the new state. It was finally admitted without any restrictions in regard to this point.

But, though the U. States have been unable to relieve themselves from the burden of slavery, they were the first to prohibit the prosecution of the slave-trade. In the year 1794, it was enacted that no person in the U. States should fit out any vessel there, for the purpose of carrying on any traffic in slaves to any foreign country, or for procuring from any foreign country the inhabitants thereof, to be disposed of as slaves. In 1800, it was enacted that it should be unlawful for any citizen of the U. States to have any property in any vessel employed in transporting slaves from one foreign country to another, or to serve on board any vessel so employed. Any of the commissioned vessels of the U. States were authorized to seize and take any vessel employed in the slave-trade, to be proceeded against in any of the circuit or district courts, and to be condemned for the use of the officers and crew of the vessel making the capture. In 1807, it was enacted, that after the first of January, 1808, it should not be lawful to bring into the U. States, or the territories thereof, from any foreign place, any negro, mulatto, or person of color, with intent to hold or sell him as a slave; and heavy penalties are imposed on the violators of these acts, and others of similar import. In 1820, it was enacted, that if any citizen of the U. States, belonging to the company of any foreign vessel engaged in the slave-trade, or any person whatever, belonging to the company of any vessel, owned in whole or in part by, or navigated for, any citizen of the U. States, should land on any foreign shore, to seize any negro, or mulatto, not held to service by the laws of either of the states or territories of the U. States, with intent to make him a slave, or should decoy or forcibly carry off such negro, or mulatto, or receive him on board any such vessel, with the intent aforesaid, he should be adjudged a pirate, and, on conviction, should suffer death. The same penalty was extended to those of the ship's company who should aid in confining such negro, or mulatto, on board of such vessel, or transfer him, on the sea or tide-water, to any other ship or vessel, or land him, with intent to sell, or having previously sold him.

A traffic in negroes was carried on from the beginning of the sixteenth century, by the Portuguese, and, after them, by all the Christian colonial powers, and has been continued to the latest times, in consequence of the colonial system of the European powers, and the idea that the colonial produce cannot be raised without slaves, with an atrocity at which nature revolts, and which could never have reached the height that it did, if the color of the slave had not given rise to the idea of his being by nature a degraded being. In the year 1503, slaves were carried from the Portuguese possessions in Africa to the Spanish colonies in America.* It has

*It is stated that, in 1434, a Portuguese captain, named Alonzo Gonzales, landed in Guinea, and

been generally stated, that Bartolomeo de las Casas proposed to cardinal Ximenes the regular importation of negroes, from charity towards the feeble aborigines of South America, who were treated by the Spaniards as mere beasts of burthen. But this story has been contradicted by the abbé Grégoire, in his *Apologie de B. de las Casas*, in the *Mémoires* of the French institute; also by the writer of the article *Casas*, in the *Biographie Universelle*, after an examination of all the Spanish and Portuguese historians of that period. This charge, he says, rests solely on the authority of Herrera, an elegant but inaccurate author. The Spanish government, the French under Louis XIII, and the English under queen Elizabeth, formally permitted this traffic, because the negroes were represented as delivered by it from misery or death. Yet Elizabeth declared herself against the violences used. In Spain, the slave-trade was first regularly established in 1517. Charles V granted to Lebresa, his favorite, the exclusive privilege of importing annually 4000 slaves, which the latter sold to the Genoese. These received the black slaves from the Portuguese, in whose hands, properly speaking, the traffic was. Slaves soon came to be introduced much more extensively into the plantation colonies than into the mining colonies. And thus the slavery of the negroes became, unhappily, a part of a political system. It also became a great source of profit to the petty African despots, and gave rise to interminable wars and outrages, which struck at the root of all social ties. The powerful became chiefly occupied with forcing their brethren to the market of Christian Europeans, to barter them for rum and toys. When, therefore, in consequence of the French revolution, the demand for this human merchandise had lessened, the king of Dahomy, on the Slave Coast, sent, in 1796, an embassy, consisting of his brother and son, to Lisbon, for the purpose of reviving this traffic, and concluding a treaty with Portugal against the other European powers. The most important markets for slaves in Africa were Bonny and Calabar, on the coast of Guinea; and they still remain among the principal. Here the slaves who came from the interior were and are exchanged for rum, brandy, toys, iron, salt, &c.; and the number of these beings who have been thus torn from their country during the last three centuries, is calculated to amount to above forty millions. It is estimated that at least from 15 to 20 per cent. die on the passage. The sufferings of the slaves during the passage are horrible; and the only restraint, generally speaking, on the cruelty of the traders, is such as arises from motives of interest; so that, when it interferes with humanity (for instance, if the slave labors under an infectious disease), the latter is entirely overlooked, and murder is not unfrequently committed. Since the prohibition of the slave-trade by so many nations, and the great efforts which have been made for the capture of the slave-ships, though the extent of the trade may be diminished, yet the cruelty with which it is carried on is often increased, because the slave-trader, being obliged to guard against capture by the men-of-war who are watching his movements, and, altogether, to carry on his traffic by stealth, subjects the slaves to many restraints for the purposes of concealment, which he did not find necessary while the slave-trade was legal. Notwithstanding all that has been done for its abolition, a contraband trade in slaves is still carried on to a frightful extent, and they are still imported into Cuba and many other West India islands, frequently, as is asserted, by the connivance of the public authorities. As a specimen of the cruelties committed in this nefarious trade, we will give the account of a recent traveller, whose statements are corroborated by many other authorities.*

carried away some colored lads, whom he sold advantageously to Moorish families settled in the south of Spain. Six years after, he committed a similar robbery, and many merchants imitated the practice, and built a fort to protect the traffic.

* Mr. R. Walsh, in his Notices of Brazil in 1828 and 1829 (London, 1830, and Boston, 1832), says, in describing a slave-ship, examined by the English man-of-war in which he returned from Brazil, in May, 1829, "She had taken in, on the coast of Africa, 336 males and 226 females, making in all 562, and had been out seventeen days, during which she had thrown overboard fifty-five. The slaves were all enclosed under grated hatchways, between decks. The space was so low, that they sat between each other's legs, and stowed so close together, that there was no possibility of their lying down, or at all changing their position, by night or day. As they belonged to, and were shipped on account of, different individuals, they were all branded, like sheep, with the owners' marks, of different forms. These were impressed under their breasts, or on their arms, and, as the mate informed me, with perfect indifference, "*queimados pelo ferro quento*—burnt with the red-hot iron." Over the hatchway stood a ferocious looking fellow, with a scourge of many twisted thongs in his hand, who was the slave-driver of the ship; and whenever he heard the slightest noise below, he shook it over them, and seemed eager to exercise it. As soon as the poor creatures saw us looking down at them

The first persons who liberated their slaves, and labored to effect the abolition of the slave-trade, were some Quakers in England and North America, particularly since 1727. In 1751, the Quakers entirely abolished it among themselves. Granville Sharp, in 1772, effected the acknowledgment, by the English courts, of the principle that the slave who lands in England becomes free. The principle had been earlier adopted in France. In 1783, a petition was addressed to parliament for the abolition of the trade, which Wilberforce (q. v.) eloquently supported. He labored, at the same time, to aid the cause by his pen. But the soul of all the efforts for the abolition of the slave-trade, was Thomas Clarkson. From early youth, he devoted his whole time and fortune to this object; exposed himself to hatred and outrage, even at the hazard of his life, in Liverpool and Paris made numerous journeys, and was deterred by no obstacles. He principally contributed to gain over Wilberforce, Pitt and Fox. For a full account of the protracted struggle of the friends of humanity in the British parliament against the slave-trade, and their final success, we must refer our reader to English works. It is briefly summed up in the New Edinburgh Encyclopædia. We must confine ourselves here to a short notice. The subject of the abolition of the slave-trade was introduced into the house of commons in 1788, when Pitt presented a petition against the trade. Many petitions followed, upon which the merchants immediately took the alarm. They calculated that the number of slaves in the West Indies amounted to 410,000, and that, to keep up that number, the

their dark and melancholy visages brightened up. They perceived something of sympathy and kindness in our looks, which they had not been accustomed to, and feeling, instinctively, that we were friends, they immediately began to shout and clap their hands. One or two had picked up a few Portuguese words, and cried out, "*Viva! viva!*" The women were particularly excited. They all held up their arms; and when we bent down and shook hands with them, they could not contain their delight; they endeavored to scramble upon their knees, stretching up to kiss our hands; and we understood that they knew we had come to liberate them. Some, however, hung down their heads in apparently hopeless dejection; some were greatly emaciated, and some, particularly children, seemed dying. But the circumstance which struck us most forcibly, was, how it was possible for such a number of human beings to exist, packed up and wedged together as tight as they could cram, in low cells, three feet high, the greater part of which, except that immediately under the grated hatchways, was shut out from light or air, and this when the thermometer, exposed to the open sky, was standing in the shade, on our deck, at 89°. The space between decks was divided into two compartments, three feet three inches high; the size of one was sixteen feet by eighteen, and of the other forty by twenty-one; into the first were crammed the women and girls; into the second, the men and boys: 226 fellow creatures were thus thrust into one space 288 feet square, and 336 into another space 800 feet square, giving to the whole an average of twenty-three inches, and to each of the women not more than thirteen inches, though many of them were pregnant. We also found manacles and fetters of different kinds; but it appears that they had all been taken off before we boarded. The heat of these horrid places was so great, and the odor so offensive, that it was quite impossible to enter them, even had there been room. They were measured, as above, when the slaves had left them. The officers insisted that the poor suffering creatures should be admitted on deck, to get air and water. This was opposed by the mate of the slaver, who, from a feeling that they deserved it, declared they would murder them all. The officers, however, persisted, and the poor beings were all turned up together. It is impossible to conceive the effect of this eruption—507 fellow creatures, of all ages and sexes, some children, some adults, some old men and women, all in a state of total nudity, scrambling out together to taste the luxury of a little fresh air and water. They came swarming up, like bees from the aperture of a hive, till the whole deck was crowded to suffocation, from stem to stern; so that it was impossible to imagine where they could all have come from, or how they could all have been stowed away. On looking into the places where they had been crammed, there were found some children next the sides of the ship, in the places most remote from light and air; they were lying nearly in a torpid state, after the rest had turned out. The little creatures seemed indifferent as to life or death; and when they were carried on deck, many of them could not stand. After enjoying, for a short time, the unusual luxury of air, some water was brought; it was then that the extent of their sufferings was exposed in a fearful manner. They all rushed like maniacs towards it. No entreaties, or threats, or blows, could restrain them; they shrieked and struggled, and fought with one another, for a drop of this precious liquid, as if they grew rabid at the sight of it. There is nothing which slaves, in the mid-passage, suffer from so much as want of water. It is sometimes usual to take out casks filled with sea-water as ballast, and when the slaves are received on board, to start the casks and refill them with fresh. On one occasion, a ship from Bahia neglected to change the contents of the casks, and on the mid-passage found, to their horror, that they were filled with nothing but salt water. All the slaves on board perished! We could judge of the extent of their sufferings from the afflicting sight we now saw. When the poor creatures were ordered down again, several of them came, and pressed their heads against our knees, with looks of the greatest anguish, at the prospect of returning to the horrid place of suffering below."

The English ship, however, was obliged, though with great reluctance, to release the slaver, as it could not be proved, after a strict examination, that he had exceeded the privilege allowed to Brazilian ships of procuring slaves south of the line.

annual importation of 10,000 was required; that the English bought in Africa 30,000 annually, and, therefore, could sell 20,000 to other nations; that in the prosecution of this trade, English manufactures to the amount of above £800,000 sterling were exported, and above £1,400,000 in value obtained in return; and that government received £256,000 annually by the slave-tax.* Liverpool and Bristol, which carried on the slave-trade most extensively, resisted its abolition so violently that Wilberforce, Fox, Pitt, and their friends, could effect nothing more than the institution of an inquiry into the trade, and the passage of some provisions for diminishing the hardships of the confinement on ship-board. At length, the house of commons was induced, in 1792, to pass a bill for the abolition of the slave-trade in 1795, by a majority of nineteen; the lords rejected this as well as the bill proposed by Wilberforce, in 1794, for prohibiting the English from selling slaves to other nations. In the mean time, the French national convention, February 4, 1794, had declared all the slaves in the French colonies free. Wilberforce brought in another bill, in 1796, providing that the slave-trade should be abolished for ever after March 1, 1797, and that all persons carrying on the trade after that time, should be transported to Botany bay for fourteen years. Fox and Pitt voted for the immediate abolition; but the bill did not pass. The African society, established by Wilberforce and Clarkson, now redoubled its efforts to convince the public of the horrors of this traffic. The colony at Sierra Leone (q. v.) was founded in consequence of the exertion of this society, whose object was to teach the negroes agriculture and the mechanic arts; and, from 1809, young Africans were instructed in various branches of knowledge in that colony. At length the cause of humanity triumphed. June 10, 1806, Fox moved that the house of commons should declare the slave-trade inconsistent with justice, humanity, and sound policy, and immediately take effective measures for its abolition. Generals Tarleton and Gascoyne opposed the motion in vain. It passed by 114 votes against fifteen. The abolition was resolved upon, and a petition was presented to the king, requesting him to take measures to induce the other powers of Europe and the American states to coöperate with Great Britain in the suppression of this traffic. The famous Abolition Act, as finally settled, passed February 5 and 6, 1807, when Roscoe spoke in favor of it, though he represented Liverpool, which owed a great part of its wealth to this trade. January 1, 1808, was fixed as the time when this trade, on the part of the English, should cease. On this occasion, the British papers contained, almost unanimously, the remark, that it was a melancholy yet undeniable fact, that king George III, the prince of Wales, and the whole royal family, with the exception of the duke of Gloucester, were opposed to the abolition. Another act, May 4, 1811, provided that all who knowingly participated in the slave-trade should be punished with fourteen years' transportation and hard labor. In 1824, a law for declaring the slave-trade piracy, which had been already done by the U. States, was proposed by Canning, passed the two houses, and, on March 31, received the royal assent. In Denmark, king Christian VII, in 1794, declared the slave-trade unlawful after January 1, 1804; and Frederic VI promised, at the peace of Tilsit, to prohibit his subjects from taking part in the foreign slave-trade. In France, Napoleon, when first consul, promised the continuance of their liberty to the inhabitants of St. Domingo, whilst he praised the inhabitants of Isle de France for not having freed their slaves, and promised that France would never again decree the slavery of the whites by the liberation of the negroes. After the successes of the French on St. Domingo, the slave-trade was once more established; and the counsellor of state, Bruix, said, on this occasion, *La liberté de Rome s'entourait d'esclaves. Plus douce parmi nous elle les relègue au loin!* In 1814, lord Castlereagh obtained from Louis XVIII a promise that France would abolish the slave-trade; but, by the influence of the chamber of commerce at Nantes, this traffic was permitted for five years more. Public opinion obliged lord Castlereagh to press upon the congress of Vienna the adoption of general measures for the abolition of the slave-trade; but all that he could effect was that Spain and Portugal promised to give up the slave-trade north of the line.—See the treaty between England and

* Such calculations, in which the extremest human suffering is coolly weighed against pecuniary profit, excite horror; but we should not overlook the influence of habit and circumstances, in accustoming men whose dispositions are, in general, good, to what they would otherwise abhor. The frauds practised in Prussia and some other countries, before 1806, in enlisting of soldiers, were abominable; and violence was not unfrequently used to oblige men to take the oath. (See *Soldier*.)

Portugal, Vienna, January 22, 1815. But a paper was drawn up, and signed by Castlereagh, Stewart, Wellington, Nesselrode, Löwenhielm, Gomez Labrador, Palmella, Saldanha, Lobo, Humboldt, Metternich and Talleyrand (Vienna, February 8, 1815), stating that the great powers would make arrangements to fix a term for the general abolition of the slave-trade, since public opinion condemned it as a stain on European civilization. February 6, 1815, Portugal provided for the total abolition of the slave-trade on January 21, 1823, and England promised to pay £300,000 as an indemnification to Portuguese subjects. Louis XVIII, by the treaty of Paris, November 20, 1815, consented to its immediate abolition, for which Napoleon had declared himself prepared, in April, 1815. Spain promised, by the treaty of September 30, 1817, to abolish the slave-trade entirely, October 31, 1820, in all the Spanish territories, even south of the line; and England, February 9, 1818, paid £400,000 as an indemnification to Spanish subjects. The king of the Netherlands prohibited his subjects from taking part in the slave-trade, after the provisions of the treaty of August 13, 1814, had been rendered more precise and extensive by the treaty concluded with England, at the Hague, May 4, 1818. Sweden had already done the same, according to the treaty of March 3, 1813.* The U. States engaged, in the treaty of Ghent, December 24, 1814, to do all in their power for the entire suppression of the slave-trade. November 23, 1826, a treaty was concluded, with Brazil, for the abolition of the slave-trade; and it was accordingly prohibited after March, 1830. The laws of the U. States on this subject, were mentioned in a previous part of this article. Thus England finally succeeded in her great undertaking, prompted by motives both of humanity and interest—as the abolition of the trade would pave the way for the civilization of Northern Africa, and furnish additional markets for English manufactures in that part of the globe. In spite of these treaties, the illicit slave-trade continued, and, as we have already stated, more cruelly than before. Spanish and French vessels were, and probably are still, the ones chiefly engaged in it. The latter were considered to out-number, much, all the others put together. The English, therefore, sent ships of war to Sierra Leone, in 1816, to capture the slave-ships; but they were unable to put a stop to the trade, for the slave-markets in Brazil and Cuba offered powerful temptations to unprincipled men, and some individuals in the U. States are willing to provide them with swift vessels, calculated for their disgraceful and worse than piratical traffic.† In 1832, France and England concluded a treaty, by which the two governments allow each the right of searching the other's ships, under certain circumstances, in the region of the slave-trade; and if the U. States should consent to the same arrangements, important consequences might be expected. Still more advantageous, perhaps, would it be if the U. States and Spain would conclude such a treaty, so that the vessels of the former power could search the Spanish slave-vessels in the vicinity of Cuba, which at present can be done only by the English.—The evils of slavery we have already touched on in the previous part of this article. The productiveness of slave-labor, as compared with free labor we cannot speak of at present. It is generally considered far inferior. Some, indeed, have maintained that certain kinds of work—for instance, that required on the rice and sugar plantations—could not be performed without slaves; but this is denied by others, as Bryan Edwards.‡ The numerous insurrections on the West India islands and in the U. States have shown that the abolition of slavery is highly de-

* Sweden seems altogether liberally disposed towards the negroes. In 1831, the government conferred on all the free negroes on the island of St. Bartholomew the same rights with the whites; so that, in official papers, no distinction of color is to be mentioned.

† "It should appear, then," says Mr. Walsh, in his Notices of Brazil, "that, notwithstanding the benevolent and persevering exertions of England, this horrid traffic in human flesh is nearly as extensively carried on as ever, and under circumstances, perhaps, of a more revolting character. The restriction of slavery to the south of the line, was, in fact, nugatory and evaded on all occasions. The whole number of slaves captured by our cruisers, and afterwards emancipated, for nine years, from June, 1819, to July, 1828, was 13,281, being about 1400 on an average each year. During that period, it is supposed that nearly 100,000 human beings were annually transported as slaves from different parts of the coast, of whom more than 43,000 were legally imported into one city alone. It is deeply to be regretted, therefore, that the proportion of the good to the evil is so small."

‡ The creation of free laborers, by which the mechanic arts have come to honor, is one of the greatest revolutions which have taken place in society. It is due to the cities of the middle ages (see *Cities*); and great as the effects have been, still greater remain to be produced by the cultivation and intelligence which, in consequence of it, have spread, and are spreading through all classes of society.

sirable; but the difficulty is, how to bring it about. In the U. States, a colonization society has been formed, with the view of exporting as many colored persons as possible to the colony of Liberia. Virginia has lately made an appropriation, with a provision for its increase, in aid of the colonization society. (See the articles *Colonization Society*, and *Liberia*; also the *Letters on the Colonization Society*, &c., by M. Carey, 1832.) In England, Wilberforce proposed, June 10, 1816, in parliament, that slaves should be treated as British subjects, and that the children born in future should be educated as free persons. These were the views of Burke, Fox, Pitt, Lansdowne, Howick (the present earl Grey), &c. Wyndham and others insisted that the negroes were incapable of liberty. The registering of the slaves, proposed by Wilberforce, in order to prevent the sale and importation of new slaves, as well as the reënslaving of free persons of color in the British colonies, did not then pass. At present, the registering of the slaves is established in Trinidad, St. Lucia and Mauritius (1814), which are immediately under the crown. Schools have also been established in the British colonies for the slaves. Such religious instruction as the slaves receive, is principally afforded by missionaries. In several colonies, the greatest excitement exists against Methodist missionaries, who, the planters think, not unfrequently excite the slaves to revolt; and during the recent rebellion in Jamaica, one or two of the missionaries were shot, and most of them ordered to leave the island. The Moravian missionaries are generally much preferred. In South America, with the exception of Brazil, slavery has either been abolished or is drawing to a close. In Colombia, slave children born since the revolution, are to be free on reaching their eighteenth year. Bolivar early set free all his slaves. In Mexico, president Guerrero declared all slaves free on September 15, 1829.—For the number of slaves in the various foreign countries where slavery is permitted, we must refer the reader to the articles on these countries. There are at present eleven slave-holding states in the Union, viz. Maryland, Virginia, North and South Carolina, Georgia, Alabama, Mississippi, Louisiana, Tennessee, Kentucky, Missouri. The district of Columbia, and Missouri, Arkansas and Florida territories also contain slaves. The sum total of the slaves in the U. States is 2,010,436. Of these, however, 3305 are in the state of Delaware, 2246 in New Jersey, 386 in Pennsylvania, and a few survivors of former times in New York, Connecticut and Rhode Island. The progress of the slave population in the U. States has been as follows:

Census of	Slaves.	Total pop.
1790	697,697	3,929,827
1800	896,849	5,305,925
1810	1,191,364	7,289,314
1820	1,538,064	9,638,181
1830	2,010,436	12,856,407

For information on the slavery of the blacks, see Clarkson's *History of the Abolition of the Slave-Trade*; Gregoire *On the Literature of Negroes*; Wadstrom's *Observations on the Slave-Trade, during a voyage in* 1787 *and* 1788 (London, 1789); Falconbridge's *Account of the Slave-Trade on the Coast of Africa* (London, 1788), &c. Some account of slavery among the Greeks and Romans may be found in the works of Reitemeier (History of Slavery in Greece), Walch, Œlrichs and Hurter (On the Roman Slaves), in German. (See also Comte, *Sur la Législation*.)

Slavery of the Whites, in the Barbary states; a stain on the history of the European governments, as the negro slave-trade was and is on that of the nations. It never was taken into serious consideration by the monarchs of Europe collectively (though it would have been easy for them to have destroyed those nests of piracy at once), until they met at the congress of Vienna and Aix-la-Chapelle. Piracy on the Mediterranean is as old as history; but, after the Mohammedans settled on its shores, they considered the practice of it against Christians legal. The Christian slave, in the Barbary states, was entirely at the mercy of his master. In 1815, the whole number of white slaves was computed at 49,000: in Algiers, there were 1000. As early as 1270, England and France concluded a "holy alliance" for the chastisement of the people of Barbary. Philip the Bold attacked Tunis, then their chief place, and liberated all the Christian slaves. In 1389, the English, with the French, Genoese and Venetians, forming a united force under the earl of Derby (subsequently king Henry IV), made a second attack upon Tunis with the same success. When the great Algerine state, after the downfall of the Almoravides, had fallen to pieces, Oran, Algiers, Tunis and Tripoli became petty independent republics, which, partly to revenge the expulsion of the Moors and Jews from Spain, devoted themselves, from 1494, principally to piracy. Ferdinand, Charles V, Philip V, and others, attacked them in vain. (See *Barbary States.*) Little more success attended the attempt of the English. Blake, in Cromwell's time, destroyed the greater part of the united fleet of Tunis and Algiers in 1655, and liberated many prisoners; but, in 1669 and 1670, the fleet of Charles II, in connexion with that of the Netherlands, bombarded Algiers without success. The French did the same in 1682, 1683 and 1688, with a like result. In 1683, the French admiral threw 1200 bombs into the city, and burned part of it; but the dey, Mezzo Morto, ordered the French consul Vacher to be put into a mortar and thrown towards the French. From the insufficiency of the means employed, the mutual jealousy of the European powers, the fanaticism of the Moors and Turks, and the fear inspired by the Barbary states, the humiliations which Algiers received were but momentary. In Algiers, as well as in Tunis and Tripoli, a Turkish militia, eager for pillage, were in possession of the government; and all the European governments have submitted to the degradation of purchasing peace from these barbarians by regular or extraordinary presents. France alone stood on a better footing with them; and England concluded with Algiers, Tunis and Tripoli in 1662, and with Morocco in 1721, treaties which provided that no British subject should ever be made a slave, even if he should be found as a passenger on board a hostile vessel. All English vessels furnished with passes by the admiralty were to be allowed to navigate the Mediterranean unsearched; the cargoes of wrecked vessels were not to be seized, nor their crews to be made slaves; and English men-of-war were to be permitted to enter the various Barbary ports to obtain provisions, without paying any duty. But the Barbary states kept these treaties only as long as they found it convenient. Austria, not many years since, obtained letters of protection from the Porte, without tribute, for her own ships and those of Tuscany. Russia and Prussia obtained similar firmans from the Porte. Sweden and Denmark purchased peace by the payment of tribute. Portugal, from 1795, required a contribution from the Hanse towns for protecting their vessels on her coasts. Lübeck and Bremen, as late as 1806, concluded treaties with Morocco; but they were, nevertheless, obliged at length to abandon almost entirely the navigation of the Mediterranean. The U. States protected their national honor by sending a squadron to Algiers, in 1815, under the command of Decatur, who bombarded the city, and obliged her to declare that the flag of the republic should in future be respected. (See Lyman's *Diplomacy*, and our article *Barbary States.*) Sir Sidney Smith, in 1814, soon after the general peace, founded a society at Paris, called the *Institution Anti-pirate;* but it was dissolved in 1818. The attempt of Joseph Bonaparte (q. v.) to unite England and France against these pirates at the peace of Amiens was defeated by the breaking out of war soon after the conclusion of that peace. Lord Exmouth (formerly sir Edward Pellew) concluded, April 17, 1816, a treaty with the dey of Tunis, Mahmoud Pacha, which provided that prisoners should not be treated as slaves, and should be restored at the conclusion of peace. England, at the same time, undertook to protect her allies, Naples and Sardinia, against the Barbary powers. Lord Exmouth had already appeared, March 31, 1815, before Algiers, and forced the dey to conclude a treaty with Naples and Sardinia. But the king of Naples had to pay for every captured subject 1000 piasters, and 24,000 piasters annually, besides the usual presents; and Sardinia, for every captured subject, 500 piasters. Hanover was included in the treaty with England. Tunis gave up the Sardinian prisoners without ransom, but the Neapolitans had to pay 300 piasters each. Tripoli also declared, like Algiers, that she would abolish the slavery of Christians and introduce the common laws of Europe respecting prisoners of war. May 15, 1816, lord Exmouth appeared a second time before Algiers, to force the dey also to acknowledge the European law of nations respecting prisoners of war. The dey declared that the permission of the sultan was necessary, and captain Dundas carried the Algerine minister to Constantinople, while Exmouth returned to England. In the mean time, the dey had sent orders to Oran and Bona, that all the English, and their property, on shore and on shipboard, should be seized. This order was executed most cruelly. May 23, Turkish and Moorish soldiers surprised 359 Italian vessels, which had purchased permission to fish for coral, and were lying peaceably under the English flag in the port of Bona. The English consul was ill treated, and many Christians killed; and the cruelties did not cease until a messenger arrived, whom the dey of Algiers had despatched immediately after the conclusion of the treaty with Exmouth. The news of this barbarity roused the indignation of the English. July 28, lord Exmouth sailed with six ships of the line, two frigates, two brigs, and four bomb-vessels, from Plymouth, and was joined by some more vessels at Gibraltar. The Dutch admiral Van der Capellen joined him also with six frigates. The fleet had on board 6500 men and 702 guns, and appeared, Aug. 27, off Algiers, where the dey had made preparations for an obstinate defence. 50,000 Moors and Arabians were assembled at Algiers. Lord Exmouth immediately sent the dey a written demand, stating that, as he had violated all his obligations by the cruelties at Bona, the prince regent required, 1. an immediate liberation of all Christian slaves without ransom; 2. restoration of the money which had been paid for the Sardinian and Neapolitan captives, amounting to 382,500 piasters; 3. a solemn assurance that he would in future respect the rights of humanity, like Tunis and Tripoli, and, in all future wars, treat prisoners according to the usages of European nations; 4. that he should conclude peace with the king of the Netherlands on the same terms. As no answer followed, the fleet sailed up the bay, and, at two o'clock, the admiral's vessel lay within pistol shot of the battery. The firing continued from two o'clock till nine, at which time the European cannons, 702 in number, had silenced the Algerine, amounting to about 1000; and, as the city had suffered terribly, a peace was concluded next day. An additional clause abolished all consular presents, with the exception of the personal presents; and these were never to amount to more than £500 sterling. The dey, moreover, was obliged to liberate the imprisoned consul, and pay him 3000 piasters. Respecting piracy nothing was settled, and no guarantee asked. The result, therefore, was, that the government of Algiers had declared the slavery of white captives abolished, but retained the right to make war upon any European power. This peace was concluded between Omar Pacha and England and the Netherlands, Aug. 28, 1816 on the 6th of the month of Schawal, in the year 1231 of the Hegira). The dey returned 382,500 piasters, which he had already received from Naples and Sardinia, and gave up 1211 Christian slaves to lord Exmouth. (On his first expedition to Algiers, Tunis and Tripoli, lord Exmouth had procured liberty for 1792 slaves.) The English loss in the battle amounted to 128 killed and 691 wounded: that of the Dutch to 13 killed and 52 wounded. On the other hand, 5000 janizaries and 6000 Moors were killed, besides many women and children. Of the Algerine navy, only one brig and one schooner, with some smaller vessels of war, escaped.—See the *Narrative of the Expedition to Algiers in the Year* 1816, *under the Command of Lord Exmouth* (London, 1819), by Salame, his lordship's interpreter.—The final extirpation of the band of robbers at Algiers, so long desired, was occasioned by the wish of the Polignac ministry to divert the attention of the public from the internal administration of France. (See our article *France*.) The immediate cause of the war against that state was quite trifling. Algiers had claims upon France for supplies furnished to the armies of the republic in Italy and Egypt—claims for which the dey could not obtain satisfaction. He at last wrote to the king of France himself, through the consul of a common friend. But no answer was returned; and when, at a public audience, in April, 1827, he asked the French consul the reason of this, the latter is said to have made an insolent reply; upon which the incensed dey struck him in the face with his fan. War was declared soon after against Algiers, but was carried on with no energy until the Polignac ministry sent an expedition thither in 1830, splendidly fitted out, and commanded by marshal Bourmont and admiral Duperré. It consisted of nine ships of the line, twenty-five frigates, six corvettes, twenty-five brigs and eight steam-boats, besides bomb-vessels, 400 transports, and an army, admirably equipped, and comprising 37,331 men. May 25, the ships sailed from Toulon, reunited at Palma, in Majorca, after having been separated by a storm, and reached the coast of Africa on June 13. The forces landed at Torre Chica, or Sidi Ferruch, five leagues west of Algiers, the place pointed out by Mr. Shaler, former consul of the U. States at Algiers, in his Sketches of Algiers (Boston, 1826). (See note on page 235 of our fifth volume.) No troops were stationed to defend the coast, and, on the 14th, early, the landing began. A single circumstance will show how complete had been the equipment of the expedition. The packages, sacks, barrels, &c., had been covered with a double water-proof envelope, so that, if occasion required, they might be thrown into the sea, and washed on shore by the waves uninjured. The plan was put in operation at the time when a heavy gale rendered all ordinary communication with the shore utterly impossible, and enabled the army already landed to receive supplies from the fleet. On the 29th, the field-pieces of the French arrived before Algiers, which was taken on the 4th of July. The dey was allowed to retire with his family to any place out of Africa, and the country was occupied in the name of the French. Since the revolution of the same month in France, the office of governor of the conquered country has been held by several different persons. The last is the duke of Rovigo (Savary). The French government has declared its intention to make Algiers a French colony; but the disturbed state of France has not as yet allowed this plan to receive that attention which it so much deserves.

Sleep; one of the most mysterious phenomena in the animal world. Similar appearances may also be observed in the vegetable kingdom. In sleep, the organs of sense, the power of voluntary motion, and the active powers of the soul, suspend their operation, in order to collect new strength. The vital activity, however, is in full vigor; the functions of the heart and the lungs (breathing, and the circulation of the blood) continue, but are more calm and equable than during the waking season; the nutrition of the system, the secretion and absorption of the juices, &c., are carried on more undisturbedly and perfectly. Hence sleep is not really a state of inactivity, but very partially to be compared to death. Man requires most sleep during infancy, and least during the period of active manhood. During this period, two hours before midnight, and five after it seem to be sufficient; superabundance or deficiency of sleep soon produces evil effects. It is well not to have the sleeping room occupied during the day time. It should be well ventilated, cool, quiet, without flowers or any strong odor. The bed should be hard rather than soft, and the body should be relieved from ligatures. A short slumber after dinner (*siesta*) seems to be necessary to the inhabitants of warm climates; in colder climates it is unnecessary, and frequently injurious. The dormant state of some animals presents an interesting phenomenon. (See *Dormant State*.)

Sleidanus, John (properly Philipson), born at Sleida, not far from Cologne, in 1506, was one of the most distinguished publicists of his age. He studied law at Liege, Cologne, Louvain, Paris and Orleans; was for some time in the service of king Francis I of France, and went, in 1542, to Strasburg. The princes of the Smalcaldic league (q. v.) made him its historiographer. The corporation of Strasburg employed him on important missions, and appointed him, in 1542, professor of law. The Protestants sent him, in 1545, to the king of England, and, at a later period, to the council of Trent, where he was much esteemed. He corresponded with the most distinguished and learned men of his time, and died at Strasburg, in 1556. He acquired much reputation by his work *De Statu Religionis et Reipublicæ Imper. Caroli V* (Strasburg, 1555, folio), of which professor Ranke says, in his *Zur Kritik neuerer Geschichtschreiber* (Berlin and Leipsic, 1824), "it is, throughout, documentary;" but he shows that it is necessary to weigh these documents, and the sources of the writer's statements. The best edition was published by Am Ende (Frankfort on the Maine, 1785, 3 vols.), with critical and explanatory notes; the last volume contains the life of Sleidanus, his letters, &c. Sleidanus is distinguished for knowledge of the subjects which he treats, for his smooth and elegant style, and for great impartiality, considering that he lived in the midst of the events which he describes, and was deeply interested in them. The work has been translated into several languages (into French, by P. F. le Courayer, Hague. 1767, 3 vols.). Sleidanus also wrote *De quatuor summis Imperiis Lib, iii* (Strasburg, 1556), which has been fifty-five times republished, and also continued to 1676 by Schurzfleisch; *Summa Doctrinæ Platonis de Republica et de Legibus* (Strasburg 1548); *Opuscula*, ed. Helias Putschius (Hanover, 1608). He also translated the *Mémoires de Comines* into Latin (Paris, 1545).

Sleswic (in German, *Schleswig*); a Danish duchy, in the southern part of Jutland, separated from Holstein on the south by the Eyder, and having the German ocean on the west, and the Little Belt on the east. The surface is low and level, the climate mild and healthy, and the soil productive, yielding great abundance of grain, and supporting numerous cattle and horses, which, with butter and cheese, grain and fish, are exported. Population, 323,000, on 3434 square miles. The inhabitants are Lutherans of German and Frisien descent, and, for the most part, speak Low German. Sleswic has always belonged to Denmark, and has usually been an apanage of the younger princes of the royal house. The capital, Sleswic, on the Schley or Sley, has 9000 inhabitants. Lat. 54° 32′ N.; lon. 9° 35′ E. It has some manufactures, and its commerce has been increased by a navigable canal. Near the town is the castle of Gottorp, the residence of the royal governor.

SLOANE, sir Hans, a distinguished naturalist, and founder of the British museum, was born in the north of Ireland, in 1660, and studied medicine in London, where he settled in the practice of his profession. In 1727, he became president of the royal society, of which he had previously been secretary. His Natural History of Jamaica (1707—1725) was the result of his observations in that island. George I created him a baronet in 1716, and, on the accession of George II, he was named physician in ordinary to his majesty. His death took place in 1752. (See *British Museum.*)

SLOE. (See *Plum.*)

SLOOP, in naval affairs; a small vessel furnished with one mast. Sloops of war are vessels commanded by officers of a middle rank between a lieutenant and a post-captain: these are styled *masters* and *commanders.* They carry from ten to eighteen guns, and are variously rigged, as ships, brigs, schooners, and sometimes cutters.

SLOPS; a name given to clothes for seamen.

SLOTH (*bradypus*). This name is given to two singularly constructed South American quadrupeds, remarkable for the extreme slowness of their motions, the accounts of which, however, have been somewhat exaggerated. The teeth are all cylindrical, the canines being longer and sharper than the rest. The toes are all united and enclosed under the common skin, the nails only appearing externally. These last are enormously large, compressed and curved, and when the animal is in a state of repose, are bent under along the soles of the feet. The feet are articulated obliquely upon the bones of the leg, and the outer margin only rests upon the earth: the bones of the toes are closely articulated, admitting of but little motion, and, for want of use, unite at a certain age, and form a solid piece. The fore feet or arms are much longer than the hinder; and when the sloth is upon the ground, it is obliged to draw itself along upon its elbows. The thighs are directed laterally, and the pelvis is so large, that the animal cannot bring together its knees. The internal structure is not less remarkable. The sloths are exceedingly helpless when on the ground, and seem at home only when upon trees, and, as is well observed by Waterton, when resting or moving, suspended beneath their branches. They feed on leaves. The three-toed sloth has its arms twice as long as the feet, and the body is covered with coarse hair, resembling withered grass; the color is gray, often marked on the back with brown and white. It is the only quadruped which has nine vertebræ to the neck.—The two-toed sloth differs somewhat in its anatomical characters from the preceding, and, to our eyes, seems less unfortunately constituted. The fossil bones, and sometimes the entire skeleton of a gigantic animal nearly related to the sloths, have been found in various parts of the American continent, from Buenos Ayres to the southern parts of the U. States. They show an extinct quadruped about twelve feet long and six or seven in height. It has received the name of *megatherium* (q. v.). The bones of another extinct quadruped, less than the former, but closely related to it, have been found in the limestone caves of the western country. It has received the name of *megalonyx* (q. v.), from the large size of the nails.

SLOUGH; a village of England, in Buckinghamshire, where the celebrated doctor Herschel had his residence and observatory. His son now resides there. Twenty-one miles west of London.

SMALKALDIC LEAGUE; the union, concluded in March, 1531, by nine Protestant princes and counts, and eleven free cities, for the mutual defence of their faith and political independence against Charles V and the Catholic states, at Smalkalden, in Henneberg, at first for six years. It was confirmed by the conventions at Frankfort, in July and December of the same year. It was greatly strengthened by a third convention at Smalkalden, in 1535, by the admission of new members, the extension of the term of the league to ten years, and the resolution to keep on foot an army of 12,000 men. In 1537, it received a new bond of union in the articles drawn up by Luther, and signed by the theologians present at Smalkalden. These were called the *Smalkaldic articles.* Their original object was to serve as a representation of the Protestant faith at the council of Mantua, announced by the pope. The council was never held, but the articles, which were entirely in conformity with the Augsburg confession (q. v.), were received among the symbolical

(q. v.) books of the Lutheran church. Their violence proves the embittered feelings of Luther and his party. (See *Reformation.*)

Small Pox; an eruptive fever, which, in its pustules, engenders an infectious matter, by means of which the disease may be communicated to other persons, who have not been before attacked by it. After the infection has taken place, about seven days pass before the virus operates and produces the disease. Then a feverish shivering pervades the body, which regularly lasts about three days; after which a number of red spots appear, first in the face, then over the breast, hands, and the whole body, sometimes very numerous, sometimes in a small number. This eruption also lasts about three days. From the spots rise pustules, which become inflamed and suppurate. The fever, in the mean time, continues without intermission. After the suppuration, the pustules begin to dry up, and to form a crust—a change which generally commences about the eleventh day. With us this disease never originates of itself, but only by infection. Commonly, however, the small-pox virus infects but once. A person who has had the small-pox will not have it again; nor does this virus infect at all times; on the contrary, it seems that a person must have a certain susceptibility for it; for numerous instances have occurred in small-pox epidemics of persons being spared who became infected at a later period, and even of some who have escaped during their whole life. According to some Arabic writers, this disease, as well as the measles, came first from Ethiopia to Arabia, about A. D. 572. In the first half of the seventeenth century, it passed to Egypt. The wars which were carried on in the East, and particularly the crusades in the thirteenth century, introduced it into Europe, first into Spain and France, and then into the other countries. When Maximilian I made an expedition to the Netherlands, upon the termination of which the men at arms returned to Germany through the French provinces, the small-pox was carried by them from France, for the first time, into Germany, in 1495. From Europe it was transplanted to America and Africa; from Denmark it found its way, in 1733, even to Greenland. Whenever it appears in a country for the first time, it is more fatal, and makes greater ravages, than after having prevailed for some time. As this disease is propagated only by infection, it has been thought possible to extirpate it by the strict separation of the infected from the healthy. The obstacles, however, arising from the present situation of nations and the general diffusion of the disease in all countries and climates, seem to render such a plan impracticable. The violence of the disorder, however, is lessened when it is produced artificially by inoculation with the small-pox virus. Inoculation had long been practised in Turkey, especially among females, for the preservation of the beauty of young girls, when the celebrated lady Montague introduced it into Western Europe. In Constantinople, whither she had accompanied her husband, she caused her son, six years old, to be inoculated, and after her return to England, in 1722, her daughter also. From that time inoculation became common in England, notwithstanding the opposition of many physicians, and afterwards in other countries; but never became universal, because many prejudices were entertained against it, and because the disease, although mitigated, is yet not quite without danger. More recently inoculation has been entirely superseded by vaccination, which is far more safe. (See *Vaccination.*)

Smalt. (See *Cobalt.*)

Smart, Christopher, born in 1722, at Shipbourne, in Kent, was placed at the grammar school in Durham, where his precocious talent obtained him the patronage of the duchess of Cleveland, who educated him at Pembroke college, Cambridge. A fellowship was conferred on him by his college in 1745. His marriage, in 1753, having vacated his fellowship, he settled in London, and commenced author by profession; in which capacity he became a principal contributor to the Old Woman's Magazine, and the Universal Visitor, besides publishing a volume of original poems, the Hilliad, &c. Poverty, however, overtook him; and his distresses, aided by intemperance, unsettled his intellects, and compelled his relations to place him for a while under personal restraint. His Song to David, written in a madhouse, and partly with charcoal, on the walls of his cell, bears a melancholy attestation to the strength of his mental powers, even in their derangement. A temporary recovery restored him to liberty for a few years, which was terminated by a new confinement. During the interval, he gave to the world his translations of Horace's works, in prose and verse, and of those of Phædrus, in verse. He died of a liver complaint, within the rules of the king's bench prison, May 12, 17.1.

Sme; an Egyptian goddess. (See *Hieroglyphics*, vol. vi, page 319.)

Smell. The sense of smell is that by means of which we perceive the fine effluvia which arise from bodies. The delicate mucous membrane, which lines the internal parts of the nose, and through which the olfactory nerve, descending from the brain, is distributed, is the sole organ of this sense. The air, passing through the nose, brings the effluvia, or odoriferous parts of bodies, into contact with the nerve; the nerve transmits the impression to the brain, by means of which it is perceived by the mind.' The moisture of the membrane above named is essential to the perfection of the smell. This sense is intimately connected with the respiration, and the whole life of the animal, and is most nearly related to the sense of taste; and many of the objects of the two senses are the same. The fine odoriferous effluvia of bodies are of incredible tenuity. Suppose, for instance, what daily experience teaches us is possible, that, with a portion of oil of lavender only one line square, we perfume a chamber eighteen feet long, as many broad, and ten feet high, and containing 3240 cubic feet, or 466,560 cubic lines, and suppose, moreover, that in each cubic line there are floating but four of the odoriferous particles, we shall then find that one cubic line of oil may be divided into 1,866,240 odoriferous particles. If a piece of ambergris, weighing 100 grains, is left upon a balance which is sensible to the smallest part of a grain, in an open chamber, notwithstanding there is a free draught of air from without, the chamber is filled with the odoriferous particles; and yet, at the end of five and a half days, not the smallest diminution of the ambergris is perceptible; from which the extreme fineness of the effluvia may be inferred. (See *Sense.*)

Smelt (*osmerus*); a small but delicious fish, allied to the salmon, inhabiting the salt water about the mouths of rivers. Like the trouts, all parts of the mouth are armed with long and pointed teeth, and there are four or five upon the tongue. The body is long, and somewhat compressed; the eyes large and round, and the under jaw longest. The European smelt is from three to six inches long; the head and body are semitransparent, with the most brilliant tints of green, and silvery. It has a strong odor, by many compared to that of violets. It inhabits the sea as well as the depths of those lakes which have a sandy bottom, and in the spring ascends the rivers in great multitudes, for the purpose of depositing its spawn. In certain districts, it is extremely abundant. The American smelt (*osmerus viridescens*, Les.) is considered a different species. It grows to the length of ten inches. The body is long, somewhat compressed, green on the back, and silvery-white on the sides. It inhabits the coasts of New England, and as far as the Hudson, but is unknown farther south. It is taken with the line. The flesh is highly esteemed.

Smelting. (See *Ores*, *Mine*, *Iron*, *Silver.*)

Smith, Adam, a distinguished writer on morals and politics, was the only son of Adam Smith, controller of the customs at Kirkaldy, where he was born June 5, 1723, a few months after the death of his father. He received his early education at the school of Kirkaldy, whence he was removed, at the age of fourteen, to the university of Glasgow, where he remained until 1740, when he repaired to Baliol college, Oxford, as an exhibitioner on Snell's foundation. Quitting Oxford, and all views to the church, which had led him there, in 1748 he took up his abode at Edinburgh, and read some courses on rhetoric and polite literature, under the patronage of lord Kames. In 1751, he obtained a more permanent provision by being elected professor of logic at Glasgow, and, the year following, of moral philosophy at the same university. He was now in a situation which perfectly agreed with his talents and inclination, and both in matter and manner his lectures were of the highest merit. Those on moral philosophy contained the rudiments of two of his most celebrated publications, of which the first, entitled the Theory of Moral Sentiments, appeared in 1795, and was most favorably received. His moral theory is founded upon sympathy, which he makes the source of all our sentiments on the propriety or impropriety of actions. To this work he afterwards added an Essay on the Origin of Languages; and the elegance and acuteness displayed in these treatises introduced him to several eminent persons, and, among others, to Mr. Charles Townshend, who engaged him, in 1763, to attend the duke of Buccleugh in his travels. A long residence in France with this nobleman introduced him to the acquaintance of Turgot, Quesnay, Necker, D'Alembert, Helvétius and Marmontel, to several of whom he was recommended by David Hume. He returned to Scotland in 1766, and immediately retired, with his mother, to Kirkaldy, where he led a life of strict study and retirement for ten years, the fruit of which was his celebrated Inquiry into the Nature and Causes of the Wealth of Nations (2 vols., 4to., 1776). It is unnecessary to say that this work has become a standard classic, and that it may be deemed the formal precursor of the modern science of political economy. (See *Political Economy.*) About two years after the publication of this able production, he obtained, through the patronage of the duke of Buccleugh, the lucrative place of commissioner of the customs in Scotland, in consequence of which he removed, with his mother, who attained a great age, to Edinburgh. In 1787, he was chosen rector of the university of Glasgow; and soon after his health began to decline, and he sank under a chronic disease, in July, 1790, at the age of sixty-seven. A short time before his death, he ordered all his manuscripts to be burnt, except a few detached essays. Doctor Smith was a man of much simplicity of character, subject to absence of mind in society, and better fitted for speculation than action. He was, at the same time, much beloved by his friends for his kind and benignant disposition, and died generally admired and highly respected. (See his *Life* by Dugald Stewart, and Mackintosh's *Progress of Ethical Science.*)

Smith, Charlotte, an ingenious but unfortunate English poetess and novel-writer, was born in 1749, and married, at a very early age, a West India merchant, whose imprudence, aggravated (if we are to believe the allusions of his wife in her fictitious narratives) by legal chicanery, ultimately dissipated the whole of a once handsome property, and consigned its former possessor to a prison. In this melancholy situation, his wife dedicated her talents to the support of her husband and family. Her principal novels are her Romance of Real Life; Emeline; Desmond; Marchmont; Ethelinda; Old Manor House; Celestina, &c. Much of the latter part of her life was passed in Normandy. She died in England in 1806. Besides the works already mentioned, Mrs. Smith wrote several pleasing volumes for young persons, and two volumes of sonnets.

Smith, sir William Sydney, son of a captain Smith, who served during the seven years' war, was born at Westminster, in 1764, early manifested a taste for the sea service, and was sent, very young, on board a ship of war. At the age of sixteen, he was made a lieutenant, and at nineteen, a post-captain. As at the latter period the American war was just brought to a close, he had no opportunity of acting in the navy of his own country; but, war breaking out between Russia and Sweden, captain Smith served in the navy of the latter power, and, for his conduct and bravery, was honored with the order of the sword. Since then he has been called sir Sydney Smith. A peace between Sweden and Russia (1790) again threw him out of active life, and he travelled into the south of Europe. Hearing that lord Hood had got possession of Toulon, he hastened thither, and, when it was determined to evacuate the city, the destruction of the ships of war, which could not be carried off, was intrusted to sir Sydney. He succeeded in firing ten ships of the line, the arsenal and mast-house; but much of these were saved by the exertions of the French. On his return, he was appointed to the command of a frigate, and had a small flotilla under his command, with which he did very considerable mischief to the enemy. In an attempt to cut out a ship at Havre de Grace (1796), he was taken prisoner at Toulon, and, on pretence of his having violated the law of nations, in landing assassins in France, he was detained a prisoner. After a detention of two years, he escaped by the aid of a French officer, named Phillippeaux, who accompanied him to England, and then to the East. In 1798, he sailed in the Tiger, of 80 guns, for the Mediterranean, arrived at Constantinople, and then sailed with a small squadron to Egypt. Bonaparte having marched to Syria, sir Sydney repaired to Acre, and by great exertions preserved the place, though not without an enormous loss of lives. Bonaparte having quitted Egypt, sir Sydney negotiated with general Kleber for the evacuation of the country, which, by a treaty signed at Al Arisch, was agreed to; but lord Keith would not ratify the treaty, and it cost thousands of men to drive the enemy out. In this sir Sydney assisted. At the conclusion of the war, he became, in 1802, member of parliament for the city of Rochester. As soon as the war broke out anew, he was appointed to the Antelope, of fifty guns, with the command of a flying squadron, and, in 1804, was made a colonel of marines. His squadron was engaged in protecting the British channel coast. The nature of this ser vice led him to meditate on the construction of ships capable of acting in shallow water; and the result was his invention of a vessel for that purpose. In 1805, he was raised to the rank of rear-admiral of the blue, and, in the following year, he proceeded to the Mediterranean, where he received the command of a squadron intended to harass the French in Naples, which they had recently conquered. With this force he compelled the island of Capri to surrender, and severely annoyed the enemy. In 1807, when it was supposed that the prince regent of Portugal would be compelled to act against Great Britain, sir Sydney was employed to blockade the Tagus; but, on the prince resolving to remove, with his court, to the Brazils, the British admiral despatched four sail of the line to accompany the Portuguese fleet. In 1814, he endeavored to procure, from the congress of Vienna, the abolition of the slave-trade, and a conjoint attack of the sovereigns upon the piratical states of Barbary. His laudable exertions, however, were fruitless; the congress being too busily employed in riveting the fetters of Europe, to have any time to spare for the purpose of breaking fetters in other quarters of the globe.

Smith, John, the father of Virginia, was born in the year 1579, at Willoughby, in Lincolnshire, England. From his earliest youth, he displayed a roving disposition, and was delighted with bold and adventurous feats among his companions. About the age of thirteen, he disposed of his books and satchel, and his juvenile property, in order to procure money to convey himself to sea; but the death of his father, about this period, frustrated this attempt. He was now put apprentice to a merchant at Lynn, at the age of fifteen. He had hopes, at first, that his master would send him to sea in his service; but this hope failing, he quitted the merchant, and entered the train of a young nobleman, travelling to France. He was discharged from this service at Orleans, and, with the money which had been furnished him to return to England, made his way to the Low Countries, where he enlisted as a soldier—an occupation particularly agreeable to his genius. He was subsequently persuaded, by a Scotch gentleman whom he fell in with on the continent, to pass into Scotland, with the promise of being warmly recommended to king James. His expectations from that source were, however, disappointed, and he revisited his native town; but, not finding any company there agreeable to his taste, he erected a hut in the woods, where he devoted himself to the study of military history and tactics, occasionally amusing himself with his horse and lance. Having found a companion in this exercise in the person of an Italian, a rider to the earl of Lincoln, he was induced to quit his romantic residence in the forest. He afterwards recovered a part of his patrimonial estate, and, putting himself in a better condition than before, recommenced his travels, in the winter of 1596, being then but seventeen years old. He arrived in Flanders, where he met with a Frenchman, who, pretending to be heir to a noble family, prevailed on Smith to accompany him into France. They arrived, in a dark night, at St. Valory, in Picardy, when, by the connivance of the ship-master, the Frenchman and his attendants were put on shore with Smith's baggage, while he awaited the return of the boat. When he was set ashore, both his new friends and his baggage had disappeared. He pursued them to their place of residence, but could obtain no compensation for his loss. Continuing his rambles, however, he fell in with one of the villains near Dinan, with whom he fought, and, having wounded and disarmed him, compelled him to confess his guilt before a crowd assembled around them. He now visited the seat of the earl of Ployer, with whom he was acquainted, and, receiving supplies from him, pursued his course along the French coast to Bayonne, whence he crossed to Marseilles, observing every object on his way connected with military and naval architecture. Falling in, at this place, with a company of pilgrims, he embarked with them for Italy; but the ship meeting with a tempest and contrary winds, the bigoted pilgrims attributed their misfortunes to the presence of a heretic, and threw him into the sea. He swam to the island of St. Mary, off the town of Nice, and was taken on board a ship belonging to St. Malo, the master of which entertained him kindly, and conveyed him to Alexandria, in Egypt. From this place, he coasted the Levant, and, on his return, assisted in the capture of a Venetian ship, containing a valuable cargo. He quitted this vessel at Antibes, with two thousand dollars in his possession, and, having made the tour of Italy, travelled into Stiria, the seat of Ferdinand. archduke of Austria. He was here introduced to several military officers of distinction; and the emperor being then at war with the Turks, he entered his service as a volunteer. A well conducted and successful exploit obtained for the youthful adventurer the command of a company of two hundred and fifty horse, in the regiment of count Meldrick, a nobleman of Transylvania. In this new situation, Smith distinguished himself by his talents and bravery, and his commander passing from the imperial into the Transylvanian army, he accompanied him. At the siege of Regal, the Ottomans sent a challenge, purporting that the lord Turbisha, for the diversion of the ladies, would fight any single captain of the Christian troops. The honor of meeting the barbarian was decided by lot among the Christians, and fell upon Smith, who accordingly fought and overcame him, within sight of the ladies, and bore his head in triumph to his general. A friend of the infidel, upon this, sent a particular challenge to Smith, who accepted it, and, engaging with him in the presence of the ladies, as before, slew him in like manner, and sent a message into the town to inform the ladies, if they wished for further sport, they were welcome to his head, provided their third champion could take it. Bonamalgro appeared as his antagonist, and, having unhorsed him, was near gaining the victory; but Smith remounted in a fortunate moment, and with a stroke of his falchion brought the Turk to the earth, and added his head to the former trophies of his prowess. On his return to the Christian army, he was received in the most distinguished manner; was honored with a military procession of six thousand men; was presented with a horse, elegantly caparisoned, a cimeter worth three hundred ducats, and a commission as major. When the place was captured, the prince of Transylvania gave Smith his picture set in gold, with a pension of three hundred ducats per annum, and a coat of arms bearing three Turks' heads in a shield. After this, the army in which he served was defeated by the enemy, on which occasion he was wounded, and lay among the dead. The victors, discovering him to be a person of consequence, used him well till his wounds were healed, and then sold him to a pacha, who made a present of him to his mistress at Constantinople. Smith conducted himself in so pleasing a manner as to gain the affections of the lady, who, to prevent his being ill used, sent him to her brother, a pacha on the borders of the sea of Azoph, upon the pretence that he should there learn the manners, religion, &c., of the natives. By the terms of her letter, the brother suspected the true state of the case; and in an hour after his arrival, Smith was stripped, had his head and beard shaven, and was driven to labor with the Christian slaves. An opportunity presented itself for his escape, which he took advantage of with his usual courage. Being employed in threshing, about a league from the house of his tyrant, who visited him daily, and treated him in the most abusive and cruel manner, Smith watched his opportunity, while they were together, and despatched him by a stroke with his threshing instrument. He secreted the body in the straw, and, securing a bag of grain, mounted the pacha's horse, and betook himself to the desert, where he wandered for two or three days, until he came to a post, by the marks on which he made his way into Muscovy, and in sixteen days arrived at a place on the river Don, occupied by a Russian garrison. Here he was kindly received, and furnished with letters to different governors in that region. In this manner, he traversed part of Russia and Poland, and got back to his friends in Transylvania, whose presents enabled him to journey through Germany, France and Spain, and to visit the kingdom of Morocco. Upon his quitting the latter country, he returned to England, with a thousand ducats in his purse. On his way he was engaged in another naval action. On his arrival in London, he became acquainted with captain Bartholomew Gosnold, who had, some time previous, returned from a visit to America, and was solicitous of promoting its settlement by the English. Gosnold communicated his plans to Smith. He entered with enthusiasm into the project, and letters patent were at length procured, dated April 10, 1606, dividing the territory, from thirty-four to forty-five degrees of latitude, into the southern and northern colonies of Virginia, and nominating a council for both. The southern colony was soon organized, and two ships and a barque provided for the accommodation of the colonists. The expedition sailed from Blackwall, December 19, 1606. On the voyage, Smith, having become an object of envy to the principal adventurers, was arrested on the absurd charge of an intention to murder the council, usurp the government, and make himself king of Virginia; and was kept a close prisoner during the rest of the voyage. After the planting of the colony at Jamestown, Smith was released from confinement, but excluded from the council of which he had been appointed a member, in the written instructions given for the direction of the colony. He now loudly demanded a trial; but this was refused. Meanwhile, with captain Newport and twenty men, he explored the river as high as the falls. In this expedition they paid a visit to Powhatan, the chief ruler of the country, by whom they were hospitably received. The favorableness of their reception every where among the savages, conduced to lull the English into security, while the jealousy of Wingfield, the president, whose apprehensions of conspiracy had led him to secure all the arms, and to discourage military exercises, invited hostility. While Newport and Smith were absent, a body of the natives attacked the settlement; and the inhabitants, being defenceless, would have been all destroyed had not a double-headed shot from one of the ships cut a branch from a tree, which, falling among the savages, so frightened them that they all fled. One boy on the side of the English was killed, and seventeen of the company wounded. Smith, having finally obtained a trial, was honorably acquitted of all the charges; and damages to the amount of two hundred pounds were awarded him, to be levied from president Wingfield. This money Smith generously presented for the use of the company. Smith now took his seat in the council, and, June 22, Newport embarked for England, leaving one hundred and four persons, miserably provided with the means of subsistence. Immediately after the sailing of the ships, sickness, arising from scanty and unwholesome food, made dreadful ravages among the colonists. Fifty died in one month; among them Bartholomew Gosnold. Wingfield having been expelled from the office of president for mal-conduct, John Ratcliffe was chosen to succeed him. The whole weight of the administration now devolved on Smith, Ratcliffe being confessedly incompetent to the direction of affairs. Smith made great exertions, at this time, to increase the comfort of the people, by building convenient houses. Winter at length set in, and brought with it a great supply of provisions. The rivers were covered with swarms of wild fowl, and the forests abounded in venison and turkeys. This profusion of food put a stop for a season to the complaints and dissensions of the community. Smith could not remain idle, and set out with a few men in a barge, to explore the river. Having proceeded as far up as the stream was uninterrupted, he left his barge in a bay, removed from the reach of the Indians, and enjoining the crew on no account to land, continued to follow the course of the river in a canoe, accompanied by two Englishmen and two savages. He was scarcely out of sight, however, when the boat's crew disobeyed his injunction, and went ashore at the very spot where Opechancanough, the brother of Powhatan, with a large number of his people, lay in ambush. The Indians surprised one of the men, and, after compelling him to give information of the intentions and route of his commander, cruelly murdered him, and pursued Smith in a body. Having ascended the river about twenty miles, they came upon the two Englishmen asleep by a fire in the woods, and, after despatching them, tracked Smith himself, whom they surrounded and wounded with an arrow. With remarkable presence of mind in so appalling an exigency, he immediately fastened one of his Indian guides to his left arm, as a shield against the enemy's arrows, while with his musket he killed three of the most forward assailants. In this manner he slowly retreated for his canoe, the astonished Indians keeping at a distance, when he suddenly sunk into a miry part of the swamp, whence it was impossible for him to extricate himself. The cold soon benumbed his limbs; and, being incapable of further effort, he surrendered to the Indians, who, having chafed his limbs at the fire which his two companions had kindled, marched him to their habitations. Here they furnished him with an abundant supply of food, which made him apprehend that it was their design to fatten him against some approaching festival. But they had a project, at this time, to surprise the settlement at Jamestown, with Smith's assistance. In order to divert them from this attempt, he represented to them the formidable powers of defence possessed by the colonists, and described the guns and cannon, with terrific accounts of mines, by which whole armies might be thrown into the air. That they might be convinced of the truth of his statements, he wrote on a leaf torn from his pocket-book, a list of what articles he was in need of. This he sent to the fort, with some directions to the people there how to affright the bearers. The report of these messengers, on their return, confirmed his representations, and the astonished natives relinquished their project. Smith was now brought before Powhatan, whom he found seated on a wooden throne, with two girls (his daughters) beside him. A consultation of the chief and his council took place, and it was agreed to put Smith to death, as a man whose courage and abilities were particularly dangerous to the safety of the Indians. (For the mode in which he was saved, see *Pocahontas.*) Smith was soon after set at liberty. During his captivity, a conspiracy had been formed to abandon the colony; but, by a well-timed seizure of the chiefs, he frustrated all their plans. Some time after this, Newport arrived from England, bringing with him a supply of provisions, with 120 new adventurers, and numerous presents for Powhatan. Smith soon after explored the great rivers connected with the Chesapeake bay. Upon his return to the colony, he was elected president. He remained only three days at Jamestown, but, committing the duties of the presidency to his friend Scrivener, a counsellor, he departed to prosecute his discoveries in the Chesapeake. After sailing about 3000 miles in an open boat, he returned to Jamestown (September 7, 1608), loaded with corn. September 10, Smith was reëlected president, and continued to administer affairs with vigor and success. He continued serving the colony with all the ardor and industry of which he was capable, often making excursions among the savages, to procure provisions, and as often having to combat, on his return, the mutinous spirit of some of the company. The harvest fell short, and the utmost activity was requisite to keep the colonists supplied with provisions. The Indians concealed their corn, and began to prepare for hostilities. Smith being on a visit to Powhatan to procure provisions, the savage laid a plan for entrapping him; and he was only saved by the watchful care of Pocahontas, who ventured through the woods at midnight to acquaint him with the designs of her father. Some time after this, Smith being on a visit to Pamunkey, Opechancanough made an attempt to take him prisoner, and for that purpose surrounded the house, where they had met to trade, with seven hundred Indians; but Smith, seizing him by the hair, led him into the midst of his people, who immediately laid down their arms. Opechancanough was closely confined, until the corn stipulated for his ransom was delivered, when Smith released him, and embarked for the fort. Soon afterwards, his life was attempted by poison; and while walking alone in the forest, he was attacked by the chief of Paspahey, a man of gigantic stature, whom, after a violent struggle, he secured and carried prisoner to Jamestown. From this period, the English and the Powhatans were in a state of open hostility. The vigor and activity of Smith, at length, established peace, which was followed by plenty. The colony was now in a prosperous state, when captain Argall arrived, on a trading voyage, and gave intelligence of an entire change of the charter, and the adoption of various new measures, by the company in London. The London company had formed wrong estimates, and indulged in chimerical expectations, in respect to the productiveness of the new colony, which the home returns of the infant settlement were not likely to realize; and, in consequence of their disappointment in these hopes, nine ships were sent over, in May, 1609, under the command of Newport and others, one of them bearing a captain and lieutenant-general, with an admiral, under the new charter, who were to supersede Smith in the administration of affairs. But the ship in which they embarked was separated from the fleet by a storm, and was wrecked on a rock in sight of Bermudas, which island they reached in their boats, with every thing valuable belonging to the vessel. The remainder of the squadron, except a single barque, gained the coast of Virginia. Smith was now called on to surrender his presidency; but, as the new commission was in the hands of the three governors at Bermudas, he determined, with the advice of the more reflecting and judicious portion of the original adventurers, to retain his power. The settlement immediately became divided into two parties, one of which refused to obey Smith's authority, and both prepared to have recourse to arms; but the leaders of the mutiny were apprehended and committed to prison. Some of the subordinate malcontents were despatched to form settlements at other places, for the greater convenience of procuring subsistence. Shortly after, while passing down the river, on his return to Jamestown, a bag of powder, which was in the boat, exploded by some accident, during his sleep, and burnt him in a dreadful manner. In the acuteness of his suffering, he sprung into the water, from which he was with difficulty rescued, and arrived at the fort only to meet fresh misfortunes. Finding him in a defenceless situation, the mutineers conspired to murder him, and usurp the government. Their designs were, however, discovered, and they with difficulty escaped the fury of the old adventurers. Smith now immediately embarked for England, in 1609. In 1614, he again appears on the stage of American affairs, as commanding an expedition of trade and discovery to North Virginia (now New England). He made a chart of the coast, and was honored, on his return, with the nominal but imposing title of *admiral* of the country he had visited. The following year, he obtained the command of two vessels in the service of the council of Plymouth, in order to establish colonies in America. His vessel was obliged, by stress of weather, to return to England, while her companion continued her course. He again embarked on board a small vessel with thirty men, and was met by four French men-of-war, who, pretending he was a pirate, though he exhibited his commission, detained him prisoner, but suffered his vessel to return home. They carried him to Rochelle, where he was confined on board a ship at anchor. Fortunately, a storm arose, during which he was enabled to seize the boat, when he drifted to sea, where he was near perishing. He got into Rochelle, however, and made his complaint to the admiralty, but could obtain no redress. He returned to England, and published there an account of his two last voyages; after the appearance of which, he travelled through the west of England, distributing copies to persons of note, endeavoring to engage the principal gentry in the business of colonizing his favorite America. But the disasters attendant on former adventures of this description, had damped the spirit for them, and all his efforts were fruitless. When Pocahontas was conveyed to England, he visited her at Brentford, and wrote a petition in her behalf to Queen Anne, relating the merits and services of the princess, and urging her claims upon the patronage of the English. In the year 1621, he was requested, in the name of the company, to write a history of Virginia, which he published a few years after. Smith died in London, in 1631, in the fifty-second year of his age. For all his services and hardships in the cause of the colony of Virginia, he never received the least recompense. Besides his History of Virginia, he published, at different times, several accounts of his voyages to that colony, and to New England, with a description of the latter, and some other useful tracts on the same subject. He likewise published, in a folio volume, in 1630, an account of his adventures in all the four quarters of the world, from 1593 to 1629.

Smith, James, a signer of the Declaration of Independence, was a native of Ireland, born probably between 1715 and 1720. His father was a respectable farmer, on the Susquehanna. James, the second son, was educated at the college of Philadelphia, and afterwards studied law. On being admitted to the bar, he established his residence near the present town of Shippensburg, as a lawyer and surveyor, but, some time after, removed to York, where he continued the practice of his profession during the remainder of his life. In 1774, he was a member of the meeting of delegates from all the counties of Pennsylvania, for the purpose of expressing the public sentiment on the expediency of abstaining from importing any goods from England, and assembling a general congress. In January, 1775, Mr. Smith was a member of the Pennsylvania convention, and concurred in the spirited resolution which it passed, that "if the British administration should determine by force to effect a submission to the late arbitrary acts of the British parliament, in such a situation, we hold it our indispensable duty to resist such force, and at every hazard to defend the rights and liberties of America." He was also a member of the provincial conference, which assembled on the eighteenth of the ensuing month of June, to establish a new government for Pennsylvania, in consequence of the instructions given by the general assembly to their delegates in congress, to resist every measure tending to a separation, and seconded the resolution moved by doctor Rush, to express in form the sentiments of the conference on the subject of a declaration of independence, which was carried, although the obnoxious instructions had been rescinded. Doctor Rush, Mr. Smith, and Thomas M'Kean, were the committee by whom the resolution was drafted. It was unanimously adopted, and signed by the members, and presented to congress, a few days only before the declaration of independence. In July, a convention was assembled in Philadelphia, for the purpose of forming a new constitution for Pennsylvania, of which colonel Smith was a member. On the twentieth of the month, he was elected, by the convention, a member of congress. He retained his seat in that body until November, 1778, and then resumed his professional pursuits. From these he withdrew in 1800, and died in 1806

Smith, Samuel Stanhope, president of Princeton college, and a distinguished clergyman of the Presbyterian church, was born March 16, 1750, at Pequea, in

Pennsylvania. He was educated at his father's academy; in his sixteenth year entered Princeton college; took the degree of bachelor of arts in 1769; then became an assistant in his father's school, and, soon after, tutor at Princeton. In this office, he remained two years, pursuing at the same time the study of theology. As soon as he was licensed to preach, he devoted himself to missionary labors in the western counties of Virginia. Here he became so popular and respected, that he was selected to preside over the new college, which went into operation under the name of Hampden-Sidney. In 1779, he was recalled to Princeton to be professor of moral philosophy. The war at this time had driven the president from the state, had greatly dispersed the students, and reduced the building to a state of dilapidation, and much embarrassed the funds of the institution. Mr. Smith exerted himself strenuously to revive the institution, and made considerable pecuniary sacrifices for this purpose. In 1783, he received the additional office of professor of theology, and, in 1786, that of vice-president of the college. In this latter year, he was a member of a committee, to draw up a system of government for the Presbyterian church of the U. States. In 1795, he became president of the college, in place of doctor Witherspoon, who had died the preceding year. In 1812, repeated strokes of the palsy compelled him to resign his connexion with the college. He died in August, 1819, in the seventieth year of his age, having been very infirm for several years. Doctor Smith was distinguished for his acquaintance with ancient and modern literature, for polished manners, for an elegant and perspicuous style, and for his eloquence and popularity as a preacher. His chief works are an Essay on the Variety of Complexion in the human Species; Lectures on the Evidences of the Christian Religion, and on Moral Philosophy; and a System of natural and revealed Religion. Several volumes of his sermons have also been published.

Smithfield; a square in London, in which the greatest cattle-market in England is held, as is also Bartholomew fair. The spot is still shown where heretics were formerly burnt.

Smoking Tobacco. (See *Tobacco.*)

Smolensk, Battle of. Smolensk, one of the oldest cities in the Russian empire, formerly belonging to Poland, the key to the interior of the empire, situated on the left bank of the Dnieper, contains about 1500 houses and 12,000 inhabitants. Under the walls of this city, August 8, 1812, the two main divisions of the Russian forces, under Barclay de Tolly and Bagration, united, after tiresome marches and great loss, and formed a plan to attack the French troops, whom they had hitherto avoided. But on the 16th, Napoleon appeared before Smolensk, and occupied the heights. Junot was directed to march to the right with the fifth division (the Westphalian), to cut off the Russians from the route to Moscow. Ney commanded the left wing; Poniatowski the right, and Davoust the centre. In the beginning of the year, Smolensk had been strengthened as much as possible. But Barclay de Tolly, on account of the superior force of Napoleon, was unwilling to venture a general engagement, as the French had succeeded in completely surrounding his left wing. He stationed himself, therefore, in the rear of the city, and, to make it an effectual means for covering his retreat, occupied it with two divisions, so that its capture, on the 17th, was delayed till midnight, particularly as a large body of cavalry were in possession of all the passages to the plains, and numerous foot soldiers of those to the Dnieper. On account of the strength of the walls (4000 feet in circumference, 15 feet thick, and 25 feet high), with towers at regular intervals, supporting heavy cannon, and the numbers of the garrison, 30,000 strong, the assailants suffered greatly; and when the Russians marched out, at midnight, after an eight hours' engagement, to follow the main body under Barclay, the whole city was in flames. The conflagration raged for thirty-six hours. The plan of Napoleon to take the Russian army prisoners in Smolensk, or to cut off their passage to Moscow, was frustrated. More than two thirds of the city lay in ruins. The Russians, according to their own reports, lost 4000 men; the French more than double that number; the Poles more than 5000; and owing to the devastation of the surrounding country, the scarcity in the captured city was so great, that most of the wounded and the numerous sick died in the lazarettos, and a dreadful epidemic was created. The Russians could not forgive Barclay for having sacrificed this holy city, as they used to call it, this bulwark of Moscow, without risking a general engagement. He, therefore, soon after, laid down his commission, under the pretence of ill health, and was succeeded by Kutusoff. But he had saved the army. The flames of Smolensk, and the outrages of the French soldiers, roused the Russians to revenge, and to the most obstinate resistance.

SMOLLETT, Tobias, a writer of reputation, was born at Dalquhurn, in Dumbartonshire, in 1721, and apprenticed to a surgeon at Glasgow, where he attended the medical lectures. While in this situation, he composed his tragedy of the Regicide; and, in 1741, procured the place of a surgeon's mate in a ship of the line. He was soon disgusted with the naval service, which he quitted in the West Indies, and resided some time in Jamaica. On his return, in 1746, the severities used by the king's troops in Scotland, after the battle of Culloden, induced him to write his poem entitled the Tears of Scotland. This was followed by two satires, entitled Advice, and Reproof. He soon after married a lady with whom he had become acquainted in Jamaica, but received only a small part of the fortune which he had expected, and was under the necessity of applying once more to his pen. The novel of Roderick Random, the fruit of this application, soon became highly popular. He soon after published his tragedy of the Regicide, and, in 1750, made a trip to Paris, which enabled him, in 1751, to give to the public his Adventures of Peregrine Pickle, another novel, in which, with no inconsiderable sacrifice of morality and delicacy, he exhibited strong powers of humorous invention and delineation. He next thought of settling, as a physician, at Bath, but soon found that confidence is seldom reposed in medical men who divide their attention between literature and their profession. He accordingly resumed his pen, and soon after produced his Adventures of Ferdinand Count Fathom, and a new translation of Don Quixote. In 1758, appeared his Complete History of England, in four quarto volumes, which was completed in fourteen months, and was continued by Guthrie to 1765, under the auspices of the original author. The portion from the revolution, where that of Hume ceases, is generally published as a sequel to that author. During a confinement in the king's bench, for a libel on admiral Knowles, he composed his Adventures of Sir Lancelot Greaves. When lord Bute became head of the ministry, Smollet was engaged to support him in a weekly paper called the Briton, which was encountered by the celebrated North Briton of Wilkes, that soon reduced it to silence, and dissolved a friendship which had long subsisted between the respective authors. In 1763, grief at the loss of his daughter induced him to make a tour through France and Italy, in which he spent two years; and, on his return, he published his Travels (in 2 vols., 8vo.), exhibiting a querulous disposition, for which the author is lashed by Sterne in his Sentimental Journey, under the name of Smelfungus. In 1764, he published his Adventures of an Atom, a political satire. Disease induced him to revisit Italy in 1770; but he had still sufficient vigor to compose his last, and, as many think, his best novel—the Expedition of Humphrey Clinker. In the cynical, but humane character of Matthew Bramble, the author is supposed to have had an eye to himself, whom he also more formally sketches under the name of Serle in the same work. He died near Leghorn, October 21, 1771, in the fifty-first year of his age. In his novels, he exhibits a knowledge of life and manners, and an exuberance of humor, which have seldom been excelled. At the same time, morals and decency are frequently violated. As a historian, he has little merit. (See Scott's *Lives of the Novelists*.)

SMUGGLING; the offence of importing goods without paying the duties imposed thereon. (See *Contraband*, and *Taxes*.)

SMYRNA (Turkish, *Ismir*); a city on the western coast of Natolia, situated at the bottom of a deep gulf, about fifty miles from the sea, in a delightful country; lat. 38° 28′ N.; lon. 27° 8′ E. Smyrna was probably an Ephesian colony, and was successively in the possession of the Æolians, Ionians, Lydians, and Macedonians. It was destroyed by the Lydians, and was afterwards rebuilt by Alexander. Having been received into the Ionian confederacy, it soon became the mart of Asia Minor, the seat of art, and the resort of strangers. In the thirteenth century, only the ruins of its former splendor were left; but after the Turks became masters of the country, it revived. The town rises from the shore to a hill on which is an old castle, and not far from this lies a smaller castle. The quarter inhabited by Europeans, called the Frank quarter, is the pleasantest part of the city, and lies entirely on the sea. Carriages are rare, and the streets extremely narrow; and the bustle in this great mart of the Levant is remarkable. The population is estimated at about 120,000, among which are 65,000 Turks, 25 to 30,000 Greeks, 7000 Armenians, 12,000 Jews, and some Europeans and Americans. There are Armenian, Greek, Roman Catholic, and Protestant churches, several monasteries, and three synagogues here. The bay is capacious, the anchorage excellent, and the water so deep that large ships come close to the wharfs. Smyrna has been several times destroyed by earthquakes, and frequently ravaged by the plague. In 1814, from 50,000 to 60,000 persons are said to have perished by this scourge. In the year 1831, Smyrna suffered very severely from the cholera. The principal articles of import consist of grain, furs, &c., from Odessa and Taganrog; cotton stuffs, silk and woollen goods, coffee, cochineal and dye woods, glass, &c., from Great Britain, France, Italy, the U. States, &c. The principal exports are raw silk and cotton, fruits, opium, rhubarb, drugs, oil, madder, Turkey carpets, wool, wax, &c. Smyrna is one of the places which laid claim to the honor of having given birth to Homer. (q. v.) On the banks of the Meles was shown the spot where he was brought into the world; and, in a cavern by its source, the place was pointed out where he was said to have written his poems: the coins of Smyrna bore his image, and the citizens held their assemblies under the columns of his tomb. A short distance from this place, near the baths of Diana (several fountains, which unite to form a lake), are some ruins, supposed to be the remains of a temple of Diana. The *Spectateur Oriental*, formerly published in Smyrna, was succeeded, in 1827, by the *Observateur Impartial*, which has since given place to the *Courrier de Smyrne*.

Snake. (See *Serpent*.)

Snake-root (*aristolochia serpentaria*). This plant is widely diffused through the U. States; but, as it grows solitarily in woods, and has nothing conspicuous in its flowers or foliage, and, besides, does not put forth its shoots till late in the season, it is detected with difficulty, and the root bears a high price. This last is used in *materia medica*, and is exported to Europe. The odor is aromatic; the taste warm, bitter and pungent, resembling, in some degree, that of camphor; medicinally it is stimulating, diaphoretic and tonic. The stem is eight or ten inches high, flexuous, bearing oblong, cordate, very acute leaves. The flowers are situated on radical footstalks, and consist of a swelling, curved tube, expanding at the orifice.—The *A. sipho*, or *Dutchman's pipe*, so named from the form of the flower, is a climbing vine, with very large heart-shaped leaves, which grows wild on the more southern parts of the Alleghanies. It is cultivated for ornament in gardens in other parts of the U. States, as well as in Europe.

Sneezing is a violent convulsive motion of the muscles of respiration, which is preceded by a deep inspiration, that fills the lungs, then forces the air violently through the nose, while the lower jaw is at the same time closed, and shakes the head and whole body. It is always excited by some irritation affecting the inner membrane of the nose, which, however, may be produced by very different causes. Any extraneous body brought into contact with the pituitary membrane, will excite sneezing. As a direct communication exists between the eyes and the nostrils, into which the tears are constantly passing through the lachrymal ducts, a reverse sympathy is excited in many people by irritations of the eye, so that the membrane of the nose is at the same time titillated; whence, in such persons, sneezing is immediately excited by sudden exposure to a strong light, as by passing from a shade into a bright sunshine. Irritations of the lungs, stomach and bowels, &c., have been mentioned as causes of sneezing. Sneezing, if very often repeated, may become dangerous, by an accumulation of blood in the head. If it originates only from too great irritability of the membrane of the nose, injections of tepid milk or water into the nostrils may cure it; otherwise, opiates, camphor, and other anti-spasmodics, may be necessary. Few animals, perhaps only the dog, sneeze precisely like man. The custom of blessing persons, when they sneeze, is very ancient. Aristotle professes ignorance of the origin of it. This custom is mentioned by various ancient writers. Sneezing at sacrifices was considered a good omen.

Snipe. The snipe has many of the external characters of the woodcock, but differs in having the lower part of the tibia bare of feathers, and in its habits. It keeps in marshy places, and does not frequent woods; and its flight is high, rapid, and very irregular. We have but one true snipe in the U. States, and this exceedingly resembles the European, and perhaps is not distinct. The length is eleven inches, including the bill, which is about two and a half inches. The bill is very slender, soft, destitute of a cutting edge, and enlarged at the extremity, where it is smooth during life, but shortly after death becomes dimpled like the end of a thimble. The tail is rounded, composed of sixteen feathers, all barred with black at their extremities. The snipe is found at different seasons of the year in all parts of the U. States. A few breed in Pennsylvania, but the greater portion pass on to the north and the higher regions of the interior for this purpose. In the winter they are very abundant in the rice grounds of the Southern States, and penetrate far into the tropical parts of America. They are proverbially difficult to shoot, perhaps the most so of all our birds, for they fly in sudden zigzag lines, and very rapidly.

SNORRO STURLASON. (See *Sturlason.*)

SNOW is formed in the air, when the temperature of the atmosphere sinks below the freezing point of water. The particles of moisture thus frozen form flakes, having great diversities of density, and displaying innumerable varieties of the most beautiful forms. Snow-flakes, examined by a microscope, appear to be regular crystals; and Scoresby, who has figured ninety-six varieties in his Arctic Regions, arranges them under five forms, lamellar, spicular, pyramidal, &c. Like ice, and other crystallized bodies, snow would be transparent were it not that the air which it contains renders it opaque. The regular crystals are formed only when the air is calm, and the cold intense, and do not often occur, therefore, in temperate regions. Snow has been seen in the polar regions of red, orange and salmon color. This occurs, both on the fixed and floating ice, and appears, in some cases, to result from vegetable, and in others from animal matter, suspended in the sea, and deposited upon the ice around. Snow storms sometimes present a luminous appearance, covering all objects with a sheet of fire. The electricity of snow is generally positive. Snow-water has been found, by chemical analysis, to contain more oxygen than rain or river water—a fact which accounts for its superior activity in causing iron to rust, &c. Snow answers many valuable purposes in the economy of nature. Accumulated upon high regions, it serves to feed, by its gradual melting, streams of running water, which a sudden increase of water in the form of rain would convert into destructive torrents or standing pools, and, in many countries, tempers the burning heats of summer, by cooling the breezes which pass over it. In severer climates, on the contrary, it serves as a defence against the rigors of winter, by the protection which it affords to vegetation against the frost, and the shelter which it gives to animals, who bury themselves under the snow. Even in more temperate climates, vegetation suffers from an open winter; and it has been found that Alpine plants perished in the mild winter of England, from want of their usual snowy covering. (See *Glaciers*, and *Ice.*)—The *snow-line*, or plane of perpetual snow, is the elevation at which mountains are covered with perpetual snow. The progressive diminution of temperature, as we ascend through the air, must finally conduct us to a region of perpetual snow, the elevation of which is, of course, very different in different latitudes. On the northern side of the Himalaya mountains, it is about 17,000 feet; on Chimborazo, 15,802 feet. Humboldt fixes the altitude of perpetual snows, under the equator, at 15,748 feet. Towards the pole, it is much lower. On the Alps, under 46° north latitude, it is about 8860 feet. On the Pyrenees, it is stated by Humboldt at 1400 toises, or about 8850 feet. As we recede from the equator towards the north or south, it sinks more rapidly, and, at the North cape, in latitude 71°, it is estimated at only 366 toises (about 2440 feet). In Mexico, Humboldt, from the whole of his observations made in 19° north latitude, places the elevation of the snow-line at 15,028 feet, or, at the lowest estimate, 14,708 feet. From the latitude of 19° to about 30°, we are not acquainted with the altitude of a single snowy peak. Too little is known of the range of Rocky mountains to enable us to state with accuracy their lowest plane of perpetual snow. In fact, besides the constant data of the latitude and elevation, the position of the snow-line depends so much upon variable causes, such as the form of the summits, the comparative altitude and other physical features of the surrounding country, the particular exposure of the mountains, &c., that no general rule can be given for determining the limits of perpetual snow in any given latitude, at least, with our present very imperfect information. (See *Mountains*, *Climate*, and *Temperature.*) Even the few facts which have yet been collected on this subject may stand in need of the corrections of more accurate measurements of heights; and, in addition to this, the plane of perpetual snow does not by any means maintain a constant elevation in the same latitude; but it varies with the vicissitudes of the seasons, rising during the heats of summer, and sinking by the cold of winter; changing also from one summer to another, according to the prevailing temperature of the year. (See

Alcenius *De Termino Atmosphæræ terrestris nivali* (Abo, 1823, 4to.); and the article *Meteorology*, in the *Encyclopædia Metropolitana*, in which the subject is fully treated.)

SNOW; a vessel equipped with two masts, resembling the main and foremasts of a ship, and a third small mast, just abaft the main-mast, carrying a sail nearly similar to a ship's mizzen. The foot of this mast is fixed in a block of wood, or kind of step, upon the deck, and the head is attached to the after part of the main-top.

SNOWBALL TREE, or GUELDER ROSE (*viburnum opulus*). In the wild state, the flowers of this shrub are disposed in terminal corymbs, and the outer ones are much larger than the others. They are succeeded by small red globular berries, of a disagreeable flavor. A variety which is cultivated in the gardens has all the flowers large, which gives to the corymbs the appearance of large white balls, and is a highly ornamental plant. These flowers are mostly barren. The Guelder rose is found wild in most parts of Europe; and the variety above mentioned is of easy culture, and common in gardens. We have numerous species of *viburnum* in the U. States. They are ornamental shrubs, with opposite leaves, and white flowers disposed in corymbs. The fruit of some is edible.

SNOW-BIRD (*fringilla nivalis*, Lin., *F. Hudsonia*, Wilson; *F. hiemalis*, Audubon); specific character bluish black, inclining to gray; belly and lateral tail-feathers white; length about six and a half or seven inches. This hardy and numerous species, common to both continents, pours in flocks from the northern regions into the U. States about the middle of October. At this season they migrate into the Southern States in great numbers. They collect a scanty pittance from the frozen and exposed ground, and, at length, driven by hunger, are seen about barns and outhouses and the steps of doors in towns. Before the severity of the season commences, they find their food in thickets and among fallen leaves. In the latter end of March, or the beginning of April, they reappear in flocks from the south, frequenting the orchards or the woods. Soon after, they retire mostly to the northern or remote arctic regions, to breed: many, however, according to Wilson, remain in the high ranges of the Alleghany mountains. In Europe, these birds dwell almost wholly among the Alps, the Pyrenees, and the high northern chains on the limits of the region of perpetual ice, and rarely descend in winter into the plains.—See Nuttall's *Ornithology of the United States and of Canada* (Cambridge, 1832).

SNOWDON, or PLINLIMMON; the highest mountain in Wales, 3571 feet high. (See *Wales*.)

SNOWDROP TREE (*halesia*). This ornamental genus of plants is exclusively confined to the southern parts of the U. States. The species are shrubs, or small trees, allied to the styrax and persimon, blossoming early in the season, and before the expansion of the leaves. The flowers are bell-shaped, of a pure snowy whiteness, and hang in small bunches all along the branches, lasting for two or three weeks. The calyx is very small, and four-toothed; the corolla monopetalous, swelling, and divided at the summit into four short lobes. There are twelve or sixteen stamens, which have their filaments united at the base into a tube, surrounding a single style. The fruit is a pretty large winged, juiceless drupe.

SNOW-LINE. (See *Snow*.)

SNUFF. (See *Tobacco*.)

SNYDERS, SNEYDERS, or SNYERS, Francis, an eminent painter of the Flemish school, born at Antwerp, in 1579, studied the rudiments of his art under his celebrated countryman Van Bahlen, after which he is said to have travelled through a great part of Italy; but this is denied by some writers. On his return to Flanders, he became attached to the household of the archduke Albert, and finally took up his abode at Brussels. Snyders, who is considered never to have been surpassed in his delineation of beasts, fish, hunting-parties, &c., was accustomed to work in concert with Rubens and Jordaens; and some of the most valuable paintings of that school are their joint production. Many of his choice pieces are to be found in the collections at Munich, and Dresden, and in the Escurial. His death took place in 1657.

SOANE, John; an English architect, born in 1756. His genius was fostered by Mr. Dance, and he was admitted a student of the royal academy. He obtained the prize for the best design of an original building, and, in 1777, was sent to reside in Italy at the expense of the king. While in Italy, he was elected a member of the imperial academy of Florence, and of the academy of arts at Parma. After his return to England, he speedily acquired reputation, and was employed in many important works, among others, on the bank of England. His first appearance as an architectural author, was in 1789, when he published a volume describing and delineating the works which he had executed in various parts of England. About this time, he was chosen an associate of the royal academy. In 1803, he became a royal academician, and, on the resignation of Mr. Dance, was placed in the chair of professor of architecture. The lectures which he delivered in his capacity of professor, were admired for their style and the information which they conveyed. In 1794, he was selected by a committee of the house of lords, to propose designs for the improvement of the buildings adjacent to Westminster-hall. His museum of antiquities is much resorted to.

Soap; a compound, in definite proportions, of some oil, fat or resin, with a salifiable base. When this base is potash, or soda, the soap is employed as a detergent in washing clothes; when an alkaline earth, or oxide of a common metal, as litharge, is the salifiable base, the compound is insoluble in water. Fats are composed of a solid substance, called *stearine*, and a liquid substance, called *elaïne*. When they are treated with a hot ley of potash or soda, their constituents react on one another, so as to generate the solid, pearly matter, *margaric acid*, and the fluid matter oleic acid, both of which enter into a species of saline combination with the alkali, while a third matter, the *sweet principle*, remains free. Common soap is therefore a mixture of an alkaline margarate and oleate, in proportions determined by the relative proportions of the two acids producible from the peculiar species of fat. Soap formed from vegetable oil is chiefly an *oleate*. All oils or fats do not possess, in an equal degree, the property of saponification. Those which saponify the best are the following: 1. oil of olives and of sweet almonds; 2. animal oils, as hog's lard, tallow, butter, and horse oil; 3. oil of colza, or rapeseed-oil; 4. oil of beech-mast and poppyseed, when mixed with olive-oil or tallow; 5. the several fish-oils; 6. hempseed-oil; 7. nut-oil and linseed-oil; 8. palm-oil; 9. rosin. In general, the only soaps in commerce are those of olive-oil, tallow, lard, palm-oil and rosin. A species of soap can also be formed by the union of bees-wax with alkali; but this has no detergent application, being used only for painting in encaustic. The specific gravity of soap is in general greater than that of water. Its taste is faintly alkaline. When subjected to heat, it speedily fuses, swells up, and is then decomposed. Exposed to the air, in thin slices, it soon becomes dry; but the whole combined water does not leave it, even by careful desiccation on a sand-bath. Soap is much more soluble in hot than in cold water. This solution is instantly disturbed by the greater number of acids, which, seizing the alkali, either separate the fatty principles, or unite with them in a soapy, acidulous emulsion. The solution is likewise decomposed by almost all the earthy and metallic salts, which give rise to insoluble compounds of the oleic and margaric acids, with the salifiable bases. Soap is soluble in alcohol, and in larger quantity by the aid of heat. When boiling alcohol is saturated with soap, the liquid, on cooling, forms a consistent transparent mass, of a yellow color. When it is dried, it still retains its transparency, provided the soap be a compound of tallow and soda. Marseilles white soap is composed of

Soda,	6.
Oil,	60.
Water,	34.

Castile soap of

Soda,	9.
Well-dried oily matter,	76.5
Water, with a little coloring matter,	14.5

The art of soap-making consists principally in knowing how to determine, from the appearance of the paste, and other circumstances, what kind of lixivium should be employed during each step of the operation. This is done, ordinarily, by observation and experience. The form and size of the bubbles, the color of the paste, the volume of that which is thrown out on the side of the vessel, the consistence of the matter, and its disposition to swell, as well as the appearance of the steam—all furnish criteria by which to regulate the process. It sometimes happens that the paste, though apparently very firm, yet, when set in the cold air to harden, throws out much water, and is resolved into small grains, possessing little consistency. In this case, it is evident that the ley is in excess, and must be separated by means of common salt. Frequently, also, the paste becomes greasy, and the oil appears to separate from the soda. As this, in general, proceeds from the paste not being imbued with sufficient water to keep it in combination, it is necessary to add to it a portion of water, or very weak lixivium, to remedy this defect. Potash is employed as follows, in the manufacture of hard soap: A ley of this alkali, rendered caustic by quicklime, is used in the saponification, and to the soft soap which results is added common salt, or a kelp ley, which supplies abundance of muriate of soda. The muriatic acid goes to the potash, to form muriate of potash, which dissolves in the water, and is drawn off in the spent ley, while the soda enters into combination with the fat, and forms a soap, which, on cooling, becomes solid. Two tons of tallow, properly saponified, should yield three tons of marketable white soap. The adulterations most commonly practised on soap are the following: When the soap is made, much water is added, which renders it white. Frequently, pulverized lime, gypsum, or pipe-clay, are incorporated with it. The former of these frauds is readily discovered by the rapid loss of weight which the soap suffers on exposure to a dry air. The second is as easily detected by solution in alcohol, when the earthy matters fall down.—*Soft Soaps.* The compounds of fats or oils with potash remain soft, or at least pasty. Three kinds of these are known in commerce—the soaps from rape-seed, and other oleaginous seeds, called *green soaps*, *toilet soaps*, made with hog's lard, and *common soft soap*, made with animal fat. In the manufacture of the common and green soaps, the art consists in effecting the combination of the oil with the potash, without the soap ceasing to be dissolved in the ley; while, on the contrary, in the fabrication of hard soap, it is necessary to separate the soap from the ley, even before the saturation of the oil is accomplished. It contains more alkali than is absolutely necessary for the saturation of the oil. It is, in fact, a perfect soap, dissolved in an alkaline ley. It may readily be converted into hard soap by the addition of common salt. Toilet soaps, made with hog's lard and potash, should have as small an alkaline excess as possible. The finer soaps for the toilet are made with oil of almonds, with nut-oil, palm-oil, suet or butter. They are either potash or soda soaps, as they may be preferred in the solid or pasty states.

Soap-Berry (*sapindus*). These trees somewhat resemble the hickories or walnuts in their foliage, but are widely different in their fruit and botanical characters. The fruit is globular, as large as a cherry, enclosing a nut of a shining black color when ripe. The pulp serves as a substitute for soap in washing linen, but is very apt to burn and destroy it, if used too frequently. The nuts are very hard, black, and finely polished, and are used for beads. Formerly, they were imported into Europe for waistcoat buttons, and were sometimes tipped with silver or other metals. They were very durable, as they do not wear, and seldom break. The whole plant, especially the seed-vessel, being pounded and steeped in ponds, rivulets or creeks, is observed to intoxicate and kill the fish The wood is white, and full of a gum, in odor and taste resembling copal. The flowers are disposed in terminal and branching panicles, and the berries are pendulous. A species of *sapindus* (*S. marginatus*) grows wild in the Southern States. The late Mr. Collins, of Philadelphia, had standing in his garden a stock of this species, twelve or fifteen feet in height. The other species of *sapindus* are exclusively tropical.

Soap-Stone; a species of steatite. The name is derived from its color, and from the peculiar unctuous sensation which it imparts to the feeling. (See *Steatite.*)

Sobieski, John. (See *John Sobieski.*)

Socage, or Soccage, in its most extensive signification, seems to denote a tenure by any certain and determinate service. And thus old writers constantly put it in opposition to tenure by knight-service which was uncertain. It is of two sorts; free socage, where the services are not only certain but honorable, and villein socage, where the services, though certain, are of a baser nature.

Soccatoo; the present capital of the Fellatah (q. v.) dominions; lat. 13° 4′ 52″ N.; lon. 6° 12′ E. Captain Clapperton says it appeared to him the most populous town which he visited in the interior of Africa. The inhabitants are mostly Fellatahs. (See Clapperton's *Travels.*)

Social Contract. (See *Rousseau, Jean Jacques.*)

Societies, Learned. (See *Academies.*)

Society Islands; a cluster of islands in the South Pacific ocean, discovered by captain Cook, in 1769, and lying between lat. 16° and 18° S. and lon. 149° and 152° W. Some authorities limit the name to a group composed of the six small islands of Huahine, Raiatea, Tahaa (Otaha), Bolabora, Tubai (Toobooai) and Maurua, giving the name of Georgian islands to the group comprising Tahiti (Otaheite) and Eimeo, about fifty leagues to the south-east of the former. Tahiti, the largest island of the cluster, is about 100 miles in circumference, being upwards of 30 miles long, and 20, where widest, broad. The population, estimated by Cook at 200,000, is said by Ellis not to exceed, at present, 10,000 souls, which is nearly half of that of the whole cluster. This great decrease of the population is probably in part owing to the practice of infanticide which formerly prevailed, and in part to the diseases introduced among the islanders by the licentiousness of their European visitors. The general reception of Christianity has been attended by the improvement of the moral and physical condition of the people, and the abolition of the cruel rites and debaucheries which were previously practised. The soil of these islands is generally fertile, yielding bread-fruit, cocoa-nuts, bananas, plantains, yams, jambo, arum or taro, sugar-cane, &c. The animals are swine, dogs, poultry, rats, ducks, pigeons, parroquets, and a few other birds. The inhabitants are described as tall and well made, affable and kind in disposition, and fond of music. The complexion of the islanders is olive, or reddish brown; the hair black, or dark brown, and rather coarse. The language of Tahiti was the first Polynesian language reduced to writing. This was done by the English missionaries; and there are now, besides translations of the Scriptures, numerous other works, printed in the native language, which very nearly resembles that of the Sandwich islands. A singular institution prevailing in the Society islands, previous to the prevalence of Christianity, was the *arcoi* society, many of the regulations and practices of which were of the most licentious and shocking description. The members of the society were not prohibited from marrying, but, in case they had offspring, they were required to put them to death. In 1797, eighteen missionaries from England were settled upon this island. During fifteen years, they labored with very little success. In 1814, the number of those who, in Tahiti, had voluntarily renounced idolatry, and embraced Christianity, amounted to about fifty. Since that time, the efforts of the missionaries have been attended with great success, almost the whole of the inhabitants of this and the neighboring islands having renounced idolatry and embraced Christianity. A general reformation of manners has followed: schools have been established, and the useful arts introduced.—See Ellis's *Polynesian Researches* (2 vols., 1829); Barrow's *Otaheite and Pitcairne's Island*; Stewart's *Visit to the South Seas*.

Socinians. (See *Socinus*, and *Unitarians*.)

Socinus, Lælius, of the respectable family of the Sozzini, in Sienna, was born in 1525, and abandoned the science of jurisprudence, in which his ancestors had been distinguished, and to which he had himself devoted his youth, for the study of the Holy Scriptures and theology. Doubts concerning some of the dogmas of the Roman Catholic church induced him to visit Germany and Switzerland, where he became acquainted with the leading reformers. He passed nearly three years at Wittenberg, and studied the Oriental languages. He likewise visited France, England and Poland, and in the latter country formed connexions with other individuals of similar sentiments, but taught his doctrines in secret. Having become obnoxious to suspicion, he averted the danger which threatened him only by disguising his real sentiments. His unquiet life was terminated at Zurich, in 1562; but his opinions were adopted and promulgated by his nephew *Faustus*, born in 1539. The latter had been obliged to leave Sienna, from suspicions of his entertaining heretical notions, as early as in his twentieth year, and had retired to Lyons. On the death of his uncle, he came into possession of the manuscripts of the latter, by the study of which he found his former opinions confirmed. He began to publish his views at Florence (where he lived several years at the court of the grand-duke), in anonymous writings; and he afterwards retired to Basle to avoid the persecutions of the Italian inquisition. His opinions were still more fully developed during a residence in Transylvania, and in Poland he had numerous adherents. The Unitarian societies in that country, although they agreed with him in some points of doctrine, yet differed so far on others, that they would not receive him into their communion. He formed, however, some small societies of followers there, but suffered persecution in that country, and the confiscation of his property in Italy. His death took place in Poland, in 1604. (See *Unitarians*.)

Sock (*soccus*); a sort of low shoe worn by the Greeks, and also by the Roman women, who had them highly ornamented. They were likewise worn by comic actors, the buskin (q. v.), or cothurnus, being used in tragedy. *Sock* is hence often used for *comedy*.

Socrates. In the instance of this great man, posterity has shown, in a striking manner, that true merit does not appeal to its decisions in vain He who perished in the conflict with his own age, is now venerated as a noble model of wisdom and worth in thought and action, and as the true source of the most valuable results in philosophy attained by the noblest spirits of Greece. Socrates claims our highest respect alike for the powers of his highly cultivated mind, the purity of his sentiments, the excellence of his instructions, the extent of his influence, and the end of his godlike life. He was born B. C. 470. His father, Sophroniscus, was a statuary of little reputation, and his mother, Phænarete, a midwife. As his parents were in humble circumstances, it is not improbable that his father put him in the shortest way to gain a living by teaching him his own art, although there may be no truth in the story that the three Graces, at the entrance of the Acropolis of Athens, pointed out even in the age of Pausanias, were his work. Our accounts of his youth are very imperfect; but it may be confidently asserted that, notwithstanding the poverty of his father, he received a good education, according to the notions of his age and nation, and therefore learned music and gymnastics as they were then taught, and that his divine genius early impelled him to use all the means which his age and country afforded for acquiring information on the most important subjects of human knowledge. At that time the Sophists (q. v.) were perverting the heads and corrupting the hearts of the Grecian youth, and Socrates placed himself under the instruction of the most celebrated of these blind guides; but he soon abandoned the halls of these self-styled wise men, and resolved to obtain by his own reflection what others were unable to give him, and to penetrate by patient thought to true knowledge. He was deeply impressed by the inscription on the temple of Apollo, at Delphi: Γνωθι σεαυτον. Know thyself. Agreeably to this command, he began to study himself, to reflect upon the phenomena of his own mind, and to meditate on the destiny of mankind, and determined to devote his life to instructing his fellow citizens in their highest good, and making them wise, honest and pious. Like other great men, kindled by these divine thoughts, he believed himself commissioned by the Deity, and, to the close of life, cherished the idea that he was an ambassador of God. He was about thirty years old when he formed the resolution to devote himself entirely to the pursuit of divine and human knowledge, and withstand the perverters of science and morality He now began to manifest a character entirely opposite to that of the Sophists. While they were distinguished by display and wealth, Socrates appeared in a poor cloak, which he wore at all seasons of the year, and was better dressed only at entertainments or public festivals. He even disdained the use of shoes. He was, indeed, destitute of pecuniary means for procuring the conveniences of life; but it would have been easy for him to obtain them from his friends and disciples, if he had not aimed at the completest independence; and it is certain that he refused all the offers of his rich friends, so that his most virulent enemies never ventured to impeach his disinterestedness. Socrates was first an instructer of the people. He believed himself the ambassador of God to the citizens of Athens, as he himself declares in Plato's Apology. Hence he was occupied from the dawn of day in seeking persons whom he might instruct in all that is important to mankind in general, and to the private circumstances of each. He went to the public assemblies, and the most crowded streets; or entered the work-shops of mechanics and artists, and conversed with them on religious duties, on their social and political relations, on all subjects relating to morals, and even on agriculture, war and the arts. He endeavored to remove prevailing prejudices and errors, and to substitute right principles; to awaken the better genius in the minds of his hearers; to encourage and console them; to enlighten and improve men, and to make them really happy. It is manifest that such a course must have been attended with great difficulties. But the serenity of Socrates was undisturbed; he was always perfectly cheerful in appearance and in conversation. In the market place and at home, among the people and in the society of those whom love of truth and virtue connected more closely with him, he was always the same. It cannot be doubted that a happy physical and mental temperament contributed to produce this equanimity. But it was, likewise, a fruit of self-discipline. He treated his body as a servant, and inured it to every privation, so that moderation was to him an easy virtue; and he retained in old age his youthful vigor, physical and mental. He was kind as a husband and a father, though his wife, Xanthippe, was a noted shrew. He viewed her as an excellent instrument of discipline; and we can only regret that we know nothing more of the manner in which he educated his three sons than what Xenophon, in his *Memorabilia*, has preserved of his conversation with Lamprocles, the eldest. He not only instructed his fellow citizens in their duties, but likewise set before them a perfect example. He was a zealous worshipper of the Supreme Being; and, from his care not to offend his weaker brethren, observed, with punctilious exactness, all the religious usages which antiquity and custom had consecrated. As a citizen, he discharged, with exemplary faithfulness, all his public duties. Three times he served in the army of his country; the first time when he was thirty-nine years of age, at the siege of Potidæa. Here he excelled his fellow soldiers in the ease with which he endured the hardships of a winter campaign, distinguished himself by his valor, saved the life of his friend Alcibiades, and resigned to that youth the prize of honor which was awarded to his own bravery. Seven years after this, he bore arms a second time, at Delium, and was the last to fly. 420 B. C., he marched, under Cleon, against Amphipolis. Thus, in aiming to perform all the duties of a good citizen, he did not refuse to engage in the humblest service of his country. His conduct was admirable, when, at the age of sixty-five years, he became a member of the council of five hundred. He rose also to the dignity of president, who, on the day of his holding office (no man was president but once, and that only for a single day), managed the popular assemblies, and kept the key of the citadel and of the treasury. Ten naval officers had been accused of misconduct, because, after the battle of Arginusæ, they had omitted the sacred duty of burying the slain, in consequence of a violent storm. Their enemies, finding the people disposed to acquit them, procured, by intrigue, the prorogation of several assemblies. A new assembly was held on the day when Socrates was president; and the citizens, instigated by bad men, violently demanded that sentence of death should be pronounced on all of the accused at once, contrary to law. But the menaces of violence were unable to bend the inflexible justice of Socrates; and he was able to declare, on his own trial, that ten innocent men had been saved by his influence. Socrates exerted himself particularly in leading inquisitive young men to the pursuit of truth and the formation of habits of thought. He was constantly attended by a circle of disciples, who caught from him the spirit of free inquiry, and were inspired with his zeal for the highest good, for religion, truth and virtue. The succeeding schools of philosophy in Greece are, therefore, justly traced back to him; and he is to be regarded as the master who gave philosophical investigation, among the Greeks, its highest direction. Among his most distinguished disciples were Alcibiades, Crito, Xenophon, Antisthenes, Aristippus, Phædon, Æschines, Cebes, Euclid and Plato. From the detached accounts given us by Xenophon and Plato, it appears that he instructed them in politics, rhetoric, logic, ethics, arithmetic and geometry, though not in a systematic manner; he read with them the principal poets, and pointed out their beauties; he labored to enlighten and correct their opinions on all subjects of practical prudence, and to excite them to the study of whatever is important to man. The circumstances of his being fettered by no school, and of his merely leading men to reflect for themselves, must have been of the best influence. Plato and Aristotle were more systematic; but to Socrates belongs the honor of having awakened the genius of Plato, and given philosophy its practical direction. Hence the ancients recognised a Socratic school; and the name of Socrates was esteemed, by subsequent philosophers, as one of their most venerable authorities. But his philosophy, both in form and matter, was peculiarly the fruit of his own researches. To make his instructions attractive, they were delivered, not in long lectures, but in free conversation, rendered interesting by question and answer. He did not reason before, but with his disciples, and thus exercised an irresistible power over their minds. He obliged them to think for themselves, and if there was any capacity in a man, it could not fail to be excited by his conversation. This method of question and answer is called the *Socratic method*. The fragments of his conversations, preserved by Xenophon, often leave us unsatisfied. Plato alone has transmitted to us the genuine spirit of this method; and he was, therefore, viewed by the ancients as the only fountain of the Socratic philosophy—a fact which has been too much disregarded by modern writers. The versatile genius of Socrates enabled him to adapt his instructions to the character of his hearers. If they were puffed up with their imaginary wisdom, he resorted to ingenious irony, and showed them, by their own contradictory answers, that they were destitute of true knowledge. When he entered into conversation with such men, his object often was, merely to show them their own deficiencies. Hence many of these conversations have little interest to a reader seeking after positive truth, particularly as Socrates turned against his opponents their own weapons, and often appeared as a Sophist. He proceeded very differently with persons unused to reflection, or too distrustful to rely on their own investigations. He met them with the utmost kindness, and let himself down to the humblest understandings, accommodating his instructions to their previous knowledge. He did not converse with them in pompous language, but resorted to images and arguments drawn from familiar objects. He strove to enlighten them by examples and by other means, which the resources of his comprehensive mind presented; and the more deeply the hearer penetrated into the spirit and meaning of his words, the more powerfully was he awakened and charmed. Like a spiritual midwife, as he playfully styled himself, he used to proceed with the young men, whose powers he wished to excite to action, so as to lead them inevitably to the truth; and, although he sought to effect this object by his interrogatory method, he intermingled longer discourses and explanations, into which he infused all the charms of his eloquence. Hence Alcibiades, in Plato's Banquet, bears the following testimony to his teaching: "When I heard Pericles, or any other great orator, I was entertained and delighted, and I felt that he had spoken well. But no mortal speech has ever excited in my mind such emotions as are kindled by this magician. Whenever I hear him, I am, as it were, charmed and fettered. My heart leaps like an inspired Corybant. My inmost soul is stung by his words as by the bite of a serpent; it is indignant at its own rude and ignoble character. I often weep tears of regret, and think how vain and inglorious is the life I lead. Nor am I the only one that weeps like a child, and despairs of himself; many others are affected in the same way." Socrates was, therefore, mighty in word. It is vain to seek for proofs of his eloquence in Xenophon, for the charm of oral delivery, the lofty inspiration of the moment, cannot be given to silent writing; and Xenophon does not seem to have intended to draw the true ideal of Socrates—not to say he was incapable of doing it. But in Plato we hear the genuine strains of the philosopher.—Socrates abandoned all inquiries concerning the origin of the universe and of the phenomena of nature, because he esteemed religion and practical morality more important. Astronomy and natural philosophy he by no means despised; but the want of accurate knowledge on these subjects in his age led him, perhaps, to confine their sphere within too narrow limits. He turned his attention to practical philosophy, which had been previously neglected, and, according to Aristotle, was the first to lay down general precepts of morality. In this view, it may well be said that he brought philosophy down from heaven to the abodes of men. Xenophon says, Socrates always conversed upon things relating to man's nature and condition; showed the difference between religion and impiety; explained in what the noble and ignoble, justice and injustice, reason and folly, courage and cowardice, consist; what constitutes a state, and what a statesman; spoke of the government of men, and what qualities are requisite in a governor, and other subjects, the knowledge of which he regarded important to a good man, and of which none but the mean-spirited are content to remain ignorant. All his inquiries took a practical turn, and he valued speculation and theory only as connected with practice; for the end of all knowledge, he affirmed, is virtue. Socrates was fully convinced of the existence of an all-ruling, almighty, wise, good, omniscient and invisible being. The system of nature, and especially the admirable structure of the human frame, seemed to him a positive proof of a Creator. And as man is capable of thought, the same power, he argued, must exist in a still higher degree in the author of reason. The existence of the Deity is as little to be doubted, because he is neither visible nor tangible, as the existence of powers concealed from the senses, but known from their effects. He esteemed it rash to speculate upon the substance of this lofty Being, and deemed it sufficient to set in a clear light his spiritual nature. It is evident that he worshipped one God, as the Creator of the world and the Judge of mankind, because Xenophon represents him as speaking expressly, several times, of one God only, although in other places he speaks of gods, which he seems to have regarded as subordinate to the Supreme Being. To the good providence of that God he traced all human blessings, and maintained that the omniscient and omnipresent Deity knows every thing, and observes all the secret thoughts and actions of men. For this reason, he esteemed it a sacred duty for men to wor ship him with all their powers, complying, indeed, with the forms of religious service prescribed by the customs or laws of their country, but particularly striving to do his will in all things. Hence he sacrificed and prayed at the altars of his country's gods, both at home and in public, and believed in the revelation of the Divine Being by various sensible appearances. Such revelations he supposed to be made to himself by a demon or genius, which always attended him, warning him from this or that course of conduct. But his compliance with religious usages, consecrated by age or custom, did not prevent him from raising his voice against the abuses and prejudices connected with sacrificial worship. Man, he said, could not purchase, but must merit, the favor of God; and this could be effected only by a blameless life, which is the truest and best service of the Deity. Prayer he considered a necessary part of a virtuous life, and therefore taught his disciples the following petition: "Father Jupiter, give us all good, whether we ask it or not; and avert from us all evil, though we do not pray thee so to do. Bless all our good actions, and reward them with success and happiness." Socrates entertained no less elevated ideas concerning the human soul. He considered it certain that it is of divine origin, wholly distinct from every thing material, and connected with the Deity by reason and the power of thought. He did not deny the difference between it and the divine nature, but maintained that exercise and cultivation would improve the spiritual principle in man. To this cultivation he exhorted his hearers and friends with a godlike zeal. He declared the improvement of the mind to be the highest good of which man is capable. As the chief means, he recommended self-knowledge, and he esteemed those as consummately foolish who knew every thing but themselves. Socrates distinguished, also, a sensible and a reasonable soul. Of the immortality of the soul he was firmly convinced. This doctrine he inferred from its native dignity; likewise from the supposition that the soul gives life to the body; from the phenomena of dreaming; from the opinion of former ages, and from the nature of the Divine Being from whom the soul proceeds. Hence he viewed death to the good as merely a transition to a better life, and spoke of his hopes with affecting certainty and admirable clearness. His pure soul was enraptured with the thought of meeting the virtuous men of earlier ages. He feared not to stand before the holy Judge of the world; and, in the regions of the blessed, he hoped to find unmingled happiness, with the consciousness of having labored after truth and struggled for virtue. The images and terms by which he describes the wretchedness of the vicious are terrible. Souls which have become diseased by wickedness, covered, as it were, with stains and ulcers, in consequence of their licentiousness, effeminacy, or unlawful desires, and stamped with the hateful impress of perjury and injustice, are plunged into abodes of pain, to be reformed by punishment, or to serve as examples to others. This account of the effect of vice on the substance of the soul, though all plainly symbolical, surpassed, in fearful distinctness, all that had been said on the subject. Socrates founded his morality on his religion. God wishes men to be virtuous, and, therefore, they should act well. The performance of duty is the only way to happiness. Although he did not exclude the desire of happiness from the motives to virtue, he was far from representing it as the only motive. He thus made an intimate connexion between religion and virtue. The native dignity of virtue he painted in the most delightful colors. The dominion over the senses he declared to be the highest state of freedom: he said that virtue only was true wisdom, and that vice was insanity. He exhibited no regular system of morals; but this principle may be considered as lying at the foundation of his views of morality: Do what the Deity commands thee. The true interpreter of this command he considered to be a moral sense which distinguishes between justice and injustice, magnanimity and meanness—in short, between virtue and vice. He did not entertain the idea of moral freedom. On the contrary, he maintained that every man who is acquainted with good practises it, because every one acts agreeably to his knowledge. Virtue he declared to be the striving to make one's self and others as perfect as possible. All virtue he reduced to two heads, temperance and justice; the former embracing all the duties which man owes to himself, and the latter those which he owes to his fellow men. The temperance of Socrates included dominion over every sensual impulse. This self-government he regarded as the basis of all other virtues, which, by its aid, will unfold themselves from the promptings of the moral nature, and the increasing knowledge of good. The beneficial influence of this virtue he describes with a genuine inspiration, and draws a frightful picture of excess. His representation of a just man, one who faithfully performs all his duties to God and man, is highly interesting. Injustice he held to be a great evil. He declared that justice was due even towards enemies; and that a man should never transgress the laws of his country, however unjustly they might be administered. His views of friendship, society, conjugal affection, and the pleasures of life, were excellent. He maintained in every thing the golden mean. All his precepts were equally removed from excessive rigor and pernicious laxness; and whoever follows them will be a good man. To his precepts was added his example, so superior to all reproach, that Xenophon, his friend and disciple, in his *Memorabilia*, says none ever saw him perform a vicious or unworthy action, and, at the close of his work, draws the following picture of him: "All the friends of virtue who knew Socrates are still filled with sorrow for his loss; for they found him the best guide to virtue. He was so pious that he did nothing without the advice and consent of the gods; so just that he never injured, in any way, the happiness of any man, but, on the other hand, did the most important services to those who were connected with him. He was so temperate that he never preferred the agreeable to the useful; of so clear a mind that he never erred in the distinction of good and evil, and all by his own unaided strength. He was, besides, so able in his definitions and illustrations of these subjects, in his judgment of men, in confuting error and recommending virtue and uprightness, that I esteem him the best and the happiest of mortals." Such a man has been charged by some with being guilty of a shameful passion, but it is unnecessary to refute this accusation; it is more important to explain the circumstances and grounds of his condemnation. The last part of his life fell in that unhappy period when Athens had sunk into anarchy and despotism, in consequence of the unfortunate result of the Peloponnesian war. Morality and justice are always disregarded when the government of a state is dissolved. This was the case in Athens. The dominion of the thirty tyrants had, indeed, been overthrown by Thrasybulus; but, like the ocean after a storm, Athens was still unsettled, and amid the general immorality, hatred, envy and malice found opportunities to execute their purposes. Melitus, a young tragic poet of no merit, Lycon, a public orator, and Anytus, a tanner and politician, were the accusers of Socrates, and were listened to the more readily, as he had offended the people by the freedom with which he had expressed his dislike of an ochlocracy. The charges of introducing new gods, of denying the ancient divinities of the state, and of corrupting the youth, were brought, not before the Areopagus, but before the popular tribunal in the Heliæa. The accusations were supported by perverted statements of the language of Socrates, by expressions detached from the connexion which modified them. But these, and the fact that the tyrant Critias, and the public enemy Alcibiades, were his disciples, were plainly not a valid cause for his condemnation. Socrates, conscious of his moral dignity, disdained to make a labored defence of his character. He neither feared death, nor respected his judges. Moreover, he felt confident that a long life, spent under the eye of the judges and the people, was the strongest proof of his innocence. Briefly, and with a noble dignity, he showed the groundlessness of the charges, and noticed his own deserts. Several of his blind and wicked judges took offence, and he was condemned by a majority of three voices. But, when they left him to choose the mode of punishment, and Socrates declared that, instead of deserving death, he merited a place in the Prytaneum, as a public benefactor, the furious populace, thinking themselves insulted by such a declaration, condemned him to drink poison. He consoled his afflicted friends, and reminded them that, from the day of his birth, nature had pronounced sentence of death upon him. Religious and moral feeling, and the heavenly power of a pure conscience, still triumphed within him. On the day when he was thrown into prison, the sacred galley sailed from Athens for Delos, and, in conformity with an ancient law the execution of the sentence was deferred till its return, thirty days—an important delay for the philosopher and his disciples. Every morning his friends assembled in his apartment, and he conversed with them as he had been wont to do. He encouraged them in the path of virtue, instructed them in the subjects of his investigations, and proved to them, by his own example, that obedience to his precepts produced real happiness. In his solitary hours, he composed a hymn to Apollo, and versified several of the fables of Æsop. There was a striking contrast between the resignation of Socrates and the grief of his friends, at the thought of their irreparable loss. We may well pardon them for the projects which they formed for his escape. Simmias of Thebes offered to bribe the keeper; but they could, of course, do nothing without the consent of Socrates; and, from his known principles, it was probable that he would not listen to their plan. But they determined to make the attempt. Crito, the old and tried friend of Socrates, undertook to persuade him to comply with their wishes. Early in the morning of the last day but one, he visited him for this purpose. The good man was still asleep. Crito sat down softly by his bed, and waited till he awoke. He then informed him of the unanimous request of his friends, urging every motive which the peculiar circumstances of Socrates suggested, especially the care of his family, to persuade him, if possible, to save his life. Socrates permitted his friend to finish, and thanked him for this proof of his affection, but declared that flight was wholly irreconcilable with his principles. Plato's dialogue, entitled Crito, records this conversation, and is one of the most pleasing performances of that great master. It inspires the most profound admiration of Socrates, who adhered to his lofty principles with unshaken firmness on the brink of the grave, and, notwithstanding the injustice of his condemnation, could not be persuaded to violate his duties as a citizen. At length the fatal day dawned on which Socrates was to drink the poison. His family and friends assembled early, to spend the last hours with him. Xanthippe, his wife, was much affected, and showed her grief by loud cries. Socrates made a sign to Crito to have her removed, as he wished to spend his last moments in tranquillity. He then talked with his friends first about his poem, then concerning suicide, and lastly concerning the immortality of the soul. He spent the greater part of the day in these elevated meditations. He spoke with such animation of the hopes inspired by his faith, that his friends almost viewed him as a glorified spirit. The approach of twilight at length admonished him that the appointed hour had arrived. He asked for the cup; and, when he took it in his hand, his friends were so overcome with grief, that they burst into tears and loud lamentations. Socrates alone was calm. He then drank the hemlock slowly, and consoled his friends, as he walked up and down the apartment. When it became difficult to walk, he laid down upon the couch, and, before his heart ceased to beat, exclaimed, "My friends, we owe a cock (the emblem of life) to Æsculapius." After he had said these words, he covered himself with his cloak, and expired, in the seventieth year of his age (B. C. 400). Soon after his death, the Athenians acknowledged his innocence, and regarded the misfortunes of the state as a judgment for their injustice towards him. They reversed his sentence, put Melitus to death, banished his other accusers, and caused a brazen statue to be erected to his memory by Lysippus. The person of Socrates was not prepossessing. Plato says he had the head of a Silenus; but mental grace ennobled him, and attracted the virtuous. —See Wegger's *Socrates* (Rostock, 1811, 2d edition), and Delbrück's *Socrates* (Cologne, 1816), both in German; see, also, Mitchell's introduction to his translation of Aristophanes; Cumberland's *Observer*, and Cousin's *Nouveaux Fragments Philosophiques*.

Soda; formerly called the *mineral alkali*, because, under the name of *natron*, it is found native in the mineral kingdom. It is usually obtained from the incineration of marine vegetables, of which different species afford it in different quantities and states of purity. The various kinds of *fuci* afford the impure alkaline product known in commerce by the name of *kelp* (q. v.): the genera *salsola* and *salicornia*, in particular, furnish the pure *barilla* (q. v.). These products contain much foreign matter: the soda is combined with the carbonic acid, and with that are associated muriate and sulphate of soda, a small portion of hydriodate of potash or soda, charcoal, lime, magnesia, silica and alumina. The origin of the soda in these cases is undoubtedly from the muriate of soda, with which such plants are supplied from their situation; since it has been ascertained concerning some of them, that, when transplanted to inland situations, they cease to yield soda, and only afford potash. It is usually from barilla, that soda is procured. The barilla, in powder, being lixiviated with boiling water, the solution, on evaporation, affords crystals of carbonate of soda. To remove the acid, the same process is employed as in procuring potash. The salt is dissolved in twice its weight of water, and filtered through slacked lime. The lime abstracts its carbonic acid, principally: to obtain the soda perfectly pure, however, it must be submitted to the action of alcohol. Soda hus obtained is in the state of a solid white mass. In its driest state, it contains, like potash, a portion of combined water, or is a hydrate, consisting of soda 32, and of water 9. Soda is possessed of all the alkaline properties in common with potash. It is acrid, and caustic, and abundantly soluble in water. It changes the vegetable colors to green, is powerful in neutralizing the acids, and in rendering saponaceous the animal and vegetable oils. It is acted on by sulphur and phosphorus, but does not itself act so powerfully on the metals, or the earths, as potash. It combines with the latter, however, by fusion, and forms, with silica, in particular, a very perfect glass. The basis of soda is a peculiar metal, called *sodium*, discovered by sir H. Davy, in 1807, a few days after his discovery of potassium. It may be procured in exactly the same manner as potassium, by electrical or chemical decomposition of the pure hydrate. It requires, however, a somewhat higher degree of heat, and a greater voltaic power, to decompose soda than potash. Sodium is a white metal, having a color intermediate between those of silver and lead. At the common temperature of the air, it is solid, and very malleable, and so soft that pieces of it may be welded together by strong pressure. It retains its softness and malleability at the temperature of 32°. It is an excellent conductor of electricity; specific gravity 0.972. It melts when heated to the temperature of 194°, and requires a much higher temperature to be volatilized than potassium. Its affinity for oxygen is similar to that of potassium. When exposed to the air, it speedily absorbs oxygen, and becomes converted into soda. When thrown into water, that liquid is rapidly decomposed; its hydrogen escapes in the state of gas, while its oxygen converts the sodium into soda. When projected on hot water, it burns with a yellowish flame, whereas that of potassium is reddish. Soda is composed of sodium 100 and oxygen 33.3. Another compound of sodium and oxygen is the *peroxide of sodium*. It is formed by heating sodium in oxygen gas. It is of a deep orange color, very fusible, and a non-conductor of electricity. When acted on by water, it gives off oxygen, and the water becomes a solution of soda. Only one combination of sodium and chlorine is known. This is formed when sodium is introduced into chlorine gas; the sodium takes fire, and is converted into a *chloride of sodium*. It may be formed, likewise, by passing a current of chlorine gas over soda, previously heated to redness. The soda gives out its oxygen in the state of gas, and is converted into a chloride. It is composed of chlorine 4.5 and sodium 3. It is the important substance known under the name of *common salt*, or *muriate of soda*. Vast beds of it exist in the bowels of the earth, whence it is quarried under the name of *rock salt*; and sea-water contains about 3.5 per cent. of it, from which it is easily procured by evaporation. In the latter case it is less pure than in the former, requiring some care in the evaporation, in order to separate it from the salts with which it is contaminated. In warm climates, it is obtained by spontaneous evaporation; the sea-water is admitted into shallow trenches by the sea-side, and spread over an extensive surface; as it becomes concentrated by evaporation, the liquor is removed, by sluices, from one trench to another, until at length the salt crystallizes spontaneously, and nearly pure. In colder climates, the sea-water is evaporated in large boilers by the application of heat, and the evaporation is carried so far, that the salt concretes on the surface of the boiling liquor in small crystals. As obtained by this mode, small portions of muriate of magnesia and sulphate of magnesia adhere to it, which somewhat impair its antiseptic properties, and, at the same time, render it slightly deliquescent. The same method is pursued in obtaining salt from the brine springs which are so frequent in the western parts of the U States. The annual product of the salt works at Syracuse, in New York, has been, for many years, about 50,000 bushels. Rock salt, as it comes from the mine, sometimes requires to be dissolved and evaporated, in order to free it from the oxide of iron and clay with which it is often blended. On account of these impurities, it presents, occasionally, a variety of colors, such as yellow, flesh-red, and blue. Its depositories are transition rocks which are in connexion with gypsum and sandstone. Mines of salt are found in Poland, England, Russia, Spain, and the East Indies. The most remarkable deposits, however, are those of Poland and Hungary. That at Wiliczka, near Cracow, in Poland, is supposed to contain salt enough to supply the whole world for many centuries, although it has been wrought for six or seven hundred years. It has been explored to an astonishing depth; and its subterranean regions are excavated into houses, chapels, and other ornamental forms, the roof being support ed by decorated pillars of salt. When illuminated by lamps and torches, they are described as objects of great splendor. The purity of rock salt may be seen from the following analysis by doctor Henry.—

Chloride of sodium, ...	983.35
Sulphate of lime, ...	6.50
Chloride of magnesium, ...	.19
Chloride of calcium, ...	.06
Undissolved matter, ...	10.00

Common salt, when artificially prepared, or in its state of greatest purity, has the following properties:—It is white; crystallizes in cubes (rarely in octahedrons); has a specific gravity of 2.12 to 2.25. 100 parts of water at 57° dissolve 36 of salt.

at 140	"	37	do.
at 229½	"	40.38	do.

When heated, it decrepitates, and at a red heat melts into a liquid without undergoing decomposition. In a high temperature it may be sublimed. It contains no water of crystallization.

Sodium combines readily with sulphur and phosphorus, presenting similar phenomena to those presented by potassium. The *sulphurets* and *phosphurets* of sodium are less inflammable than those of potassium. Potassium and sodium combine with great facility, and form peculiar compounds, which differ in their properties according to the proportions of the constituents. By a small quantity of sodium, potassium is rendered fluid at common temperatures. A little potassium, on the other hand, destroys the ductility of sodium, and renders it very brittle.

Salts of Soda.—In general, the salts of soda are much more soluble in water than those of potash. Many of the salts of the latter alkali contain no water of crystallization; but most of the salts of soda contain a great deal. One of the easiest methods of ascertaining whether the base of a given salt be soda, is to determine the shape of the crystals which it forms. If it does not shoot into regular crystals, separate the acid by means of sulphuric or nitric acid, and let the new-formed salt crystallize. Sulphate and nitrate of soda are easily recognised by the figure of their crystals.—*Sulphate of soda.* This salt was discovered by a German chemist, named Glauber, and for that reason is commonly known under the name of *Glauber's salt.* It may be procured by saturating soda with sulphuric acid, but is more usually obtained by decomposing common salt with sulphuric acid in order to procure muriatic acid. It crystallizes with great readiness in the form of an oblique rhombic prism; specific gravity, 2.2 to 2.3. Its taste at first resembles that of common salt, but soon becomes disagreeably bitter: 100 parts of water, at 60° Fahr., dissolve 48.6 parts of crystallized salt. When exposed to the air, it loses great part of its water, and falls into a white powder, but is not otherwise altered. In this alteration, it loses about 56 per cent. of its weight. When exposed to heat, it first undergoes the watery fusion, then its water is evaporated, it is reduced to a white powder, and in a red heat it melts. (For the solubility of Glauber's salt, see the article *Salt.*) As a purgative, the use of this salt is very general; and it has been employed to furnish soda. It has been employed also in the art of glass-making: equal parts of carbonate of lime, sand, and dried sulphate of soda, produce a clear, solid, pale-yellow glass. *Bisulphate of soda* may be obtained by dissolving sulphate of soda in dilute sulphuric acid, and, after concentrating it sufficiently, setting it aside. The crystals are oblique, four-sided prisms, resembling pretty nearly, in dimensions, those of the sulphate. They do not deliquesce in the air. Its taste is very acid. It may be exposed to a red heat without losing its excess of acid. It is more than twice as soluble as Glauber's salt.

Nitrate of soda is obtained by adding dilute nitric acid to soda, or by mixing nitrate of lime and sulphate of soda together, filtering the solution and evaporating. The crystals are transparent, and have the form of the rhombic prism. Specific gravity, 2.0. It has a cool, sharp taste, and is more bitter than nitre. One hundred parts of water, at 32° Fahr., dissolve 80 parts of this salt, whereas at 50°, only 22.7 parts are dissolved. As it attracts moisture when exposed to the air, it does not answer for the manufacture of gunpowder. It is sometimes used in fireworks, on account of its communicating a fine orange color to combustibles while burning. It contains no water of crystallization, but usually about three per cent. of water, mechanically lodged between the plates of the crystals. Its constituents are, nitric acid 6.75 and soda 4.0. An immense deposit of it, extending for many leagues, is said to exist in the desert of Atacama, in Peru. Attempts were made, some years ago, to introduce it into commerce; but they did not succeed. It might be used with advantage for the manufacture of nitric acid, and probably, also, in that of sulphuric acid.

Carbonate of soda. This salt has been

also long known, as well as common salt, above described. It is obtained from the lixiviation of marine plants, which do not afford it in purity, but associated with other salts: to separate it from these, the solution requires to be evaporated at a low heat, skimming off the crystals of common salt as they form on its surface. Of late years, large quantities of carbonate of soda have been manufactured from common salt; the consequence of which is, that it may now be obtained at one third of its former cost; and it is taking the place of potash in those manufactures that require an alkali. The process followed in Great Britain is to convert common salt into sulphate of soda by means of sulphuric acid. The sulphate of soda is heated with sawdust, or small dross of pit-coal, by which it is converted into sulphuret of sodium. Sometimes the sulphur is got rid of by means of lime, but more commonly by roasting the sulphuret, so that air from a coal fire passes through it. The sulphur is gradually dissipated, and the sodium converted into carbonate of soda. The matter thus treated is dissolved in water, and subjected to two successive crystallizations in open iron coolers. By this process beautiful crystals of carbonate of soda are obtained. They in general contain about one half per cent. of sulphate of soda. The crystals are large, frequently eight or nine inches long, and are rhombic prisms with dihedral summits. Its taste is similar to that of the carbonate of potash, but less caustic. Its specific gravity is 1.62. It dissolves in rather less than its weight of boiling water, so that, when dissolved in such water, it crystallizes as the solution cools. When exposed to the air, it very soon effloresces, and falls to powder. When heated, it undergoes the watery fusion; indeed, the soda of commerce sometimes contains so much water of crystallization, that, when once melted, it remains permanently liquid. If the heat be continued, the water gradually evaporates, and the salt becomes dry. In a red heat, it melts into a transparent liquid. A very violent heat drives off a part of the acid. It melts rather more easily than carbonate of potash, and for that reason it is preferred by glass manufacturers. Its constituents are,

Carbonic acid, ...	2.75
Soda, ...	4.00
Water, ...	11.25
	18.

The *trona*, found in the province of Sukena, near Fezzan, in Africa, and which occurs in hard, striated masses, of such firmness that the walls of Cassar, a fort now in ruins, are said to have been constructed of it, differs from the carbonate of soda in the proportions of its constituents. It is called by doctor Thomson a *sesquicarbonate of soda.* It consists of

Carbonic acid, ...	4.125
Soda, ...	4.00
Water, ...	2.25
	10.375

It may be formed artificially by exposing the common carbonate of soda to an atmosphere of carbonic acid gas, and is largely manufactured for the soda-water makers, being sold in the condition of a white powder. Its taste is alkaline, but much milder than the common carbonate: specific gravity, 1.98.

Bicarbonate of soda. This salt is obtained with ease by suspending a solution of common carbonate of soda over a brewer's fermenting tun during the fermentation of beer. It crystallizes in oblique rectangular prisms. The taste is feebly alkaline. It consists of

Carbonic acid, ...	5.5
Soda, ...	4.
Water, ...	1.125
	10.625

Phosphate of soda is prepared by saturating phosphoric acid (obtained from burned bones) with carbonate of soda, and setting the concentrated solution aside to crystallize. The crystals are oblique rhombic prisms, of about 67° 50′: taste saline and strong. It effloresces with great rapidity when exposed to the air, becoming white and opaque. It is readily soluble in water. It consists of

Phosphoric acid, ...	4.5
Soda, ...	4.
Water, ...	14.625
	23.125

As the taste of this salt is simply saline, without any thing disagreeable, it is much used as a purgative, chiefly in broth, in which it is not distinguishable from common salt. It is also employed by the chemist in assays of minerals with the blow-pipe.

Borax, or *biborate of soda.* This salt is supposed to have been known to the ancients, and to be the substance denominated *chrysocolla* by Pliny. At any rate, it is mentioned by Geber as early as the seventh century, under the name of *borax*. It is brought from the East Indies in an impure state, under the name of *tinkal*, enveloped in a kind of fatty matter, now known to be a soap, with soda for its base. When purified in Europe, it takes the name of *borax*. The purification was formerly conducted by the Dutch; of late it is done by the English, and in the U. States. When pure, it presents itself in large hexagonal or octagonal crystals, of which two sides are much broader than the others. It is white and transparent; specific gravity 1.74. It converts vegetable blues to green. Its taste is sweetish and alkaline. It is soluble in twenty times its weight of water, at the temperature of 60°, and six times its weight of boiling water. When exposed to the air, it effloresces slowly and slightly. When heated, it swells, loses about four tenths of its weight, becomes ropy, and then assumes the form of a light, porous and very friable mass, known by the name of *calcined borax:* in a strong heat, it melts into a transparent glass, still soluble in water. Borax consists of

Boracic acid,	6
Soda,	4
Water,	9
	19

Large quantities of borax are made in Great Britain from boracic acid imported from Tuscany. Borax was formerly employed in medicine as a sedative, and is still used to form a gargle. Its great utility, however, consists in its application as a flux in soldering, and in the fusion of siliceous stones for the formation of pastes, or artificial gems, and for the glazing of pottery.

Sodalite; a name originally given by doctor Thomson to a mineral discovered in West Greenland, by sir Charles Gieseke. It is crystallized in regular dodecahedrons, and also occurs massive; color green, translucent; hardness about that of feldspar; specific gravity 2.37. It was found by doctor Thomson to consist of silex 38.5, alumine 27.48, lime 2.7, oxide of iron 1., soda 25., muriatic acid 3., volatile matter 2. This mineral has since been found in transparent crystals, and crystalline masses, among the lava of Vesuvius. With the sodalite, mineralogists now associate several substances formerly believed to be distinct, but whose principal differences are confined to color and mechanical composition: these minerals are the following:—*Haüyne*, *Lapis-lazuli*, *Saphirin*, *Spinellan*, *Nosin* and *Ittnerite*.

Soemmering, Samuel Thomas von. M D., born, in 1755, at Thorn, son of a physician, was a distinguished German naturalist. He passed the last years of his life at Frankfort on the Maine, where he died, March 2, 1830. He distinguished himself by his writings—*De Basi Encephali et Originibus Nervorum Cranio egredentium* (Göttingen, 1778, 4to.); *De Corporis Humani Fabrica* (Frankfort on the Maine, 1794, 4 vols.); *Tabula Sceleti Feminini*, with descriptions (Frankfort, 1797 et seq.); and *Abbildungen des menschlichen Auges* (Frankfort, 1801 et seq.), &c. Soemmering has rendered many services to science.

Sofees, or Sophis; the professors of Sufism. (q. v.)

Soffita, in architecture; any timber ceiling, formed of cross beams, or flying cornices, the square compartments or pannels of which are enriched with sculpture, painting, or gilding.

Sofism. (See *Sufism.*)

Soho; a celebrated manufactory of Messrs. Boulton and Watt, near Birmingham, established in 1764. The construction of steam engines, and other heavy iron machinery, is here carried to great perfection. A coining mill, erected in 1788, works eight machines, and is capable of striking between 30,000 and 40,000 pieces of money in the space of an hour. The impression on both sides is received from one blow, and the machine itself disposes each piece, and removes it after it has received the stroke.

Soiling, in agriculture; the practice of supporting animals of various kinds, in the summer season, with green food of different sorts, cut daily, and given to them in racks, in the houses, stalls, or yards, instead of sending them to the fields.

Soissons; a city of France, in the department of the Aisne (Ile de France), sixty miles north-east of Paris; population, 7765. It is an episcopal see, and contains a cathedral, a royal college, twelve churches, &c. Soissons was the residence of the early Frankish kings, and before the revolution, it was the capital of a district, called *Soissonnais*. It was anciently called *Noviodunum*, and afterwards took the name of *Suessiones*, and *Augusta Suessionum*, from the people.

Solamine; a substance which M. Pelletier has procured from the *solanum mam-*

nosum of the Antilles. It is also found in the berries of the *S. nigrum*, as well as in the leaves and stems of the *S. dulcimara*. To obtain it, ammonia is poured into the filtered juice of the berries, when a grayish matter falls down, which is to be collected on a filter, washed, and treated with boiling alcohol. The solamine precipitates from this by evaporation. It is an opaque, white, somewhat pearly-looking powder; without smell; very bitter; fusible below 212 Fahrenheit; decomposable at a higher temperature; insoluble in water, ether, oil of olives, and essence of turpentine; but very soluble in alcohol. It combines with the acids, forming uncrystallizable salts. It is eminently emetic.

SOLAR (from the Latin *sol*); any thing belonging to the sun. (See the following articles.)

SOLAR DAY. (See *Solar Time*.)

SOLAR MICROSCOPE. (See *Microscope*; also *Optics*, division *Optical Instruments*.)

SOLAR PARALLAX. (See *Sun*.)

SOLAR SPOTS. (See *Sun*.)

SOLAR SYSTEM. Modern astronomy has elevated itself to the notion, that each fixed star is a sun, which we may suppose, according to the law of analogy, accompanied by a system of planets, so that each star may be the centre of a solar system. But in the narrower and most common sense of the phrase, *solar system* signifies our sun, with the planets, moons and comets that revolve round it. The planets are, Mercury, Venus, Earth, with one moon; Mars, Vesta, Juno, Ceres, Pallas, Jupiter, with four moons; Saturn, with seven; and lastly Uranus, or Herschel, with six moons already known, and probably others undiscovered. All these planets, accompanied by their moons, move, as do also the comets, in elliptical orbits, around the sun, which is situated in a focus common to all of them, and, by his mighty power of attraction, retains them in their orbits. (See *Central Forces*.) The moons also describe elliptic orbits around the primary planets, with which, at the same time, they revolve around the sun. Moreover, the planets all have a rotation on their own axes, which, together with the inclination of these axes towards the plane of the orbits, and their continuance in this situation (*parallelism*), leads to the idea that all these planets are inhabited by beings endowed with sensation, for whose use these two arrangements seem to have been established. The discoveries of astronomy (e. g. the circumstance, but lately made known by Laplace, that the moons of Jupiter are never all eclipsed at the same time, so that the nights of that planet are never entirely destitute of light) seem to confirm this idea. We can touch upon only a few of the phenomena of our solar system. One of these is the admirable regularity in the distribution of the planets in the heavens. Before the discovery of the four new planets—Ceres, Vesta, Juno and Pallas—it had been ascertained that the distances of the then known planets from the sun increase according to the following series:—4; 4+3; 4+2.3; 4+16.3; 4+32.3; 4+64.3. In this series, a member (4+8.3) was wanting between the members 4+4.3 and 4+16.3, corresponding to Mars and Jupiter, which circumstance gave rise to the supposition of the existence of an undiscovered planet at the above-mentioned distance from the sun—a supposition which has been confirmed by the discovery of the four new planets. Another remarkable circumstance, which indicates a similarity between our earth and the other planets, is the flattening (q. v.) of Jupiter at the poles. The flattening of the earth is ascribed to the original softness of the mass composing it, which yielded to the centrifugal force of rotation. As Jupiter is subject to a very quick rotation, the flattening, supposing this planet also to have consisted originally of a soft mass, would naturally be very great, which late observations have proved to be the case. (For the historical information belonging to this subject, see the articles *Copernicus*, and *Kepler*.) The following tabular view presents some of the principal points connected with our solar system:

The circumference of the earth is	25,000	miles.
" surface "	196,000,000	square miles.
" cubic contents "	170,195,852,160	cubic miles.

Planets.	Sidereal Revolution.		Rotation.			Distance from the Sun.	Cubic Contents.
	Years.	Days.	Days.	Hours.	Min.	Miles.	Earth = 1.
Sun, ...			25	14			1,300,000
Mercury, ...		88	1		5½	37,000,000	$\frac{1}{18}$
Venus,.		224¾		23	22	68,000,000	$\frac{4}{5}$
Earth, ...	1		1			96,000,000	1
Its moon, ...		27½	27⅓			From the Earth. 240,000	$\frac{1}{50}$
Mars, ...	1	322	1		39	143,000,000	$\frac{1}{5}$
Vesta, ...	3	224	Not known,			225,000,000	Very small.
Juno, ...	4	131	"	"		254,000,000	Less than Ceres.
Ceres, ...	4	220	"	"		263,000,000	Half as large as Pallas.
Pallas, ...	4	221	"	"		263,000,000	Almost as large as our moon.
Jupiter, with four moons,	11	314		9	56	490,000,000	1281
Saturn, with seven moons,	29	169		10	16	900,000,000	928
Uranus, with six moons,	84	9		7		1800,000,000	83

See Laplace's *Exposition du Système du Monde* (4th ed., Paris, 1813); Hassenfratz's *Cours de Physique Céleste ou Leçons sur l'Exposit. du Système du Monde* (Paris, 1803, with engravings). A very full tabular view of the solar system is contained in Littrow's Popular Astronomy (in German, Vienna, 1825, 2 vols., with engravings).

SOLAR TIME. The earth revolves, at the same time, on its own axis and round the sun. During one rotation on its axis, it advances about 1° in its orbit, and must, therefore, after the completion of a rotation, turn as much more as this advance, before the sun can come again to a given meridian. The time, which, in this way, passes between two successive culminations of the sun, is generally called a *solar day*. But the rapidity of the earth's advance in its orbit, is different at different times: at one period it passes through a larger portion of its orbit in a given time than at others, so that the solar days cannot be equal. Another circumstance, dependent upon the inclination of the axis of the earth to the plane of the ecliptic, is also to be taken into the account. The apparent solar time, therefore, is distinguished from mean solar time, which has reference to an imagined uniformity, in the progress of the earth round the sun, and supposes the axis of the earth to be perpendicular to the plane of the ecliptic. Sun-dials show the apparent solar time; watches and other time-pieces in common use, only the mean solar time. The difference between the two is called *equation of time*. (q. v.) The following table shows what time watches and clocks ought to indicate on the first of every month, when the sun-dial indicates twelve o'clock:

On the 1st of	January,	12	o'clock,	3′ 48″
"	February,	12	"	13′ 58″
"	March,	12	"	12′ 46″
"	April,	12	"	4′ 8″
"	May,	11	"	56′ 59″
"	June,	11	"	57′ 18″
"	July,	12	"	3′ 14″
"	August,	12	"	5′ 58″
"	September,	11	"	59′ 58″
"	October,	11	"	49′ 49″
"	November,	11	"	43′ 46″
"	December,	11	"	49′ 9″

Solar time is to be distinguished from sidereal time. (q. v.)

SOLDERS consist merely of simple or mixed metals, by which alone metallic bodies can be firmly united with each other. In this respect, it is a general rule, that the solder should always be easier of fusion than the metal intended to be soldered by it. Next to this, care must also be taken that the solder be, as far as is possible, of the same color with the metal that is to be soldered. For the simple solders, each of the metals may be used, according to the nature of that which is to be soldered. For fine steel, copper and brass work, gold and silver may be employed. In the large way, however, iron is soldered with copper, and copper and brass with tin. The most usual solders are the compound, which are distinguished into two principal classes, viz. hard and soft solders. The hard solders are ductile, will bear hammering, and are commonly prepared of the same metal with that which is to be soldered, with the addition of some other, by which a greater degree of fusibility is obtained, though the addition is not always required to be itself easier of fusion. Under this head comes the hard solder for gold, which is prepared from gold and silver, or gold and copper, or gold, silver and copper. The hard solder for silver is prepared from equal parts of silver and brass, but made easier of fusion by the admixture of one sixteenth of zinc. The hard solder for brass is obtained from brass mixed with a sixth, or an eighth, or even one half of zinc, which may also be used for the hard solder of copper. It is sold in the shops in a granulated form, under the name of *spelter solder*. The soft solders melt easily, but are partly brittle, and therefore cannot be hammered. Of this kind are the following mixtures:—tin and lead in equal parts; of still easier fusion is that consisting of bismuth, tin and lead in equal parts; one or two parts of bismuth, of tin and lead each one part. In the operation of soldering, the surfaces of the metal intended to be joined must be made very clean, and applied to each other. It is usual to secure them by a ligature of iron wire, or other similar contrivance. The solder is laid upon the joint, together with sal-ammoniac and borax, or common glass, according to the degrees of heat intended. These additions defend the metal from oxidation. Glaziers use resin; and pitch is sometimes employed. Tin foil, applied between the joints of fine brass work, first moistened with a strong solution of sal-ammoniac, makes an excellent juncture, care being taken to avoid too much heat.

SOLDIER;* originally a warrior who serves for pay, from which circumstance, as is shown in the note, the word is derived. In other languages, having corresponding words derived from the same root—for instance, in German—*soldier* is frequently used to denote more especially the modern warrior, contradistinguished to the ancient, as well as to the feudal militia, and to the mercenaries of the middle ages. The first example of mercenaries is found about 700 B. C., in Carthage, if we except the small companies of guards in the service of some kings and tyrants. Carthage, with a moderate population, and much commerce and industry, first kept an army of mercenaries on foot. Yet every citizen continued to be obliged to serve, in case of necessity. These mercenaries disturbed the peace of the city by their conspiracies, and, in most of the struggles for national independence, proved of little use. Carthage, therefore, though defended by numerous fleets and armies, was overthrown by a power of but moderate strength, but relying solely on the valor of its own citizens. The example of Carthage was followed by Syracuse and other governments of Sicily and Lower Italy, and with precisely the same result. In Egypt also, under Psammetichus and his successors, Greek mercenaries were employed (about 656 B. C., on which account the old caste of warriors emigrated to Æthiopia); but a single battle with Cambyses sufficed to overturn the throne of the Pharaohs, already shaken by the warlike hordes of Nebuchadnezzar; and another example was presented of the insufficiency of mercenaries; yet the employment of them became more general. In Persia, military service was confined to the

* One of the many words met with in all the languages of Western Europe, and though originally of Teutonic origin, yet, in its present form, borrowed from the languages of the Latin stock. *Soldier* (in German, Swedish and French, *soldat;* in Italian, *soldato*, &c.) comes from the middle Latin term *solidarius*, one who receives *sold* (German for military pay, in which sense it is also used in old English writers). This receiving pay distinguished the soldiers from the former feudal militia; and the German word *sold* came into use because the Swiss were the first hired foot-soldiers; but the term for *warrior*, derived from it, first received an Italian form, because the Italians first employed hired warriors. From them it spread to the other nations of Europe. The German word *sold* (Italian *soldo*, French *solde*, Spanish *sueldo*, always signifying the pay of troops) has been derived by some from *salt*, because salt was given to soldiers as part of their pay; but it ought rather to be derived, with *salarium*, *solvere*, and the German *zahlen*, from the ancient German word *sellen* (from which the English to *sell*), which is frequently met with in the authors of Upper Germany, and corresponds to the Swedish *sälja*. It means to *give*, to *transfer*. From this verb comes the ancient Swedish *sal*, signifying the fine paid for murder. *Söl*, in Icelandic, to this day, denotes a *present*, *gift*, *reward*—a meaning which *sold*, the pay of soldiers, probably had originally

nobler tribes: only on some extraordinary occasions, as the attempt of Xerxes against Greece, the whole nation was called to arms. With the increase of luxury among the ruling tribes, the standing armies of Persia came to be formed chiefly of barbarian and Greek mercenaries; and the consequence was that this vast empire fell to pieces when boldly attacked by the Macedonians. The flower of the army of Alexander also consisted of standing troops; but they were native Macedonians, who, elevated by the genius of their commander, fought for their national honor. In the best times of Greece, her only wars had been of a national character. The battle of Marathon, the noblest conflict recorded in Greek history, was gained by 10,000 Athenian and Platæan citizens. But when Athens and Sparta began to contend for the supremacy of Greece; when internal wars became frequent, and degeneracy increased,—then mercenaries were employed. The number of citizen-soldiers diminished, and Greece lost her liberty in the battle of Chæronea. From the time when standing armies came extensively into use, a melancholy spectacle is presented. Nations appear to await their fate passively. In all directions countries are overrun with troops, and violence prevails. Every successful army establishes an empire; every general becomes a monarch. Thus arose the thrones of the New Macedonian, the Seleucidian, Ptolemæan, and other dynasties. Even in Greece, tyrants (i. e. leaders of bands of warriors) were seen in every city, oppressing the defenceless or peaceable citizen, until, at a later period, republics again arose in Ætolia and Achaia. But the military empires which grew out of the Macedonian conquests, had no firm foundation. They fell in quick succession, when assailed by the national armies of Rome. On the other hand, the small Ætolian and Achæan leagues were conquered with greater difficulty than the wide-spreading empire of Antiochus, and their national warriors were overcome rather by cunning and treachery than by force. In Rome, until the latest times of the republic, the part of the people capable of bearing arms were bound by law to serve, when called upon by the magistrate. No pay was received until a late period; and, when it was at length introduced, on account of the protracted wars, none served for the sake of it, but merely received it as a means of support during service. Down to the times of Marius and Sylla, there were no mercenaries in the Roman armies, and the period previous to their introduction embraces the greatest triumphs of the Roman arms—the conquest of Italy, with all its difficulties and dangers, the gigantic struggle with Carthage, and the humiliation of the empires which had grown out of the conquests of Alexander. But as the avidity for conquest and plunder increased, and the people and the government became more and more corrupt, standing armies gradually came into use, and soldiers, though enlisted from the citizens, had no longer the character of citizens. Marius, contrary to the ancient laws, introduced the lowest rabble, which had been till then entirely exempt from service, into the legions, and thus changed essentially the spirit of the Roman soldiery. For now the military service became a profession, to which persons flocked, who were destitute of public spirit and true patriotism, and who became rather the soldiers of the general than of the country. Yet important victories were still gained (as those of Marius over the Cimbri and Teutones, and those of Sylla over Mithridates), and the armies retained, partially at least, a national character. It was not till the total destruction of liberty that an entire change took place in the military system. Before that time, standing troops had been kept for the defence of the frontiers, and the preservation of tranquillity in the oppressed provinces; but in Rome and Italy the army was obliged to respect the majesty of the people and the authority of the magistrate. Even the struggles, often attended with bloodshed, which took place in the *comitia*, and on other occasions, had been chiefly confined to citizens. The soldiers of Sylla were the first who shed the blood of Roman citizens without shame and without punishment. These outrages now became common, and the people were obliged to submit to the arrogance of the generals and the legions, and sometimes to the insolence of an armed rabble, until at length, after a long warfare of factions, the most successful and most artful general concentrated in himself the whole military power, and became unlimited ruler of the people and the army. From this time, there were no longer, either in Rome or the provinces, soldiers of a national character, but only tools of the monarch. The more despotic the government became, and the more the empire was assailed by barbarians, the more numerous and permanent became the standing forces. The ancient laws, obliging all citizens to serve, were forgotten, and the characters of citizen and soldier became more and more distinct. Mercenaries were now in request, who were willing to keep the citizens in subjection, for high pay and privileges of various kinds. At a still later period, when the degeneracy of the people was frightfully increased, barbarians were taken into pay, whose interest was still more opposed to that of the Roman citizens. Only in great emergencies, forced levies of the people of the country were resorted to. The emperors granted privilege after privilege, and favor after favor, to these pillars of their tyranny; and the nation was divided into two hostile classes, differing in interests, relations and rights, one of which was degraded by law, and compelled to suffer every outrage which insolence and cruelty could inflict; the other was above the law, and perpetrated with impunity every crime. But even as the people trembled before the tyrants, the tyrants themselves trembled before the pretorian guards, whom they were obliged to caress in all possible ways, and from whom they suffered many insults. The just emperors, friends to the citizens, as Pertinax, Alex. Severus, Balbinus, Probus, Gratian, &c., were killed by the soldiery, who lamented the death of monsters like Caligula and Commodus. At length, the divisions of these very soldiers, who proclaimed emperors at pleasure, shook the empire to its foundation, and the German and Scythian tribes found it easy to conquer Rome, the mistress of the world, whose sway extended over a hundred nations, and who had at her command the resources of the richest countries, and of the most experienced tactics, and whose standing army was three times as numerous as the forces with which, in former times, she had conquered the world. After the fall of Rome, the warlike spirit of the Germans spread over all Western Europe, and as far as Northern Africa. The Germans (*Germannen*, *Wehrmänner*, armed men, or men at arms), were a tribe of warriors; and war with them was generally a national affair, not the exclusive concern of one class. Hence, when the people had concluded on war, every man capable of bearing arms was obliged to march into the field. When the Germans had conquered the Roman provinces, their military constitution remained the same, though, at a later period, the obligation to perform military service was attached to a certain property. Those who possessed less than the required amount combined in greater or less numbers, to send one man into the field: thus the richer part of the nation formed the army. But political changes produced changes in the relations of the soldiers. The conquering tribe often remained in a conquered province, like an army encamped in an enemy's country separated, as it were, from the natives, who were excluded, partially or entirely, from political rights. A few unfortunate battles were always sufficient to overturn such empires as those of the Vandals, the Ostrogoths, &c.* Only when the conquered and the conquerors became mixed, or the latter were the most numerous, could permanent empires be formed, such as that of the Franks. But, by degrees, the feudal system extinguished allodial independence in the Frankish and other empires. The ancient custom of the Germans to fight not only in the wars of the whole nation, but also in the quarrels of particular leaders, gave rise to this monstrous system, which has kept Europe so long enchained, and has occasioned such an enormous expenditure of blood. Those leaders whose numerous followers had enabled them to render particular services, and those nobles who had distinguished themselves by military talent or valor, and, above all, the king, or chief leader, received large portions of the conquered country, which they again assigned to their followers as fiefs. The latter bound themselves, in return, to continual fidelity, and the performance of military service. The increasing lawlessness of those times obliged the possessors of small allodial estates to surrender them to the more powerful lords, and receive them back as fiefs. (See *Feudal System*.) Every landed estate became a fief; and this had a powerful effect on the military system. Wars were now carried on solely or chiefly for the advantage of the prince, but not for the common benefit. The old national militia gradually fell into disuse, nay, was almost forgotten. The kings and princes preferred the service of their vassals, as no resolve of the nation was necessary to call them to arms. The vassals, in their different degrees, formed a sort of standing army, ready to obey every call of the superior lord; and thus all remains of popular liberty were extinguished, and a feudal nobility, that is, nobility of a military character, dependent on the monarch, sprang up. He who was not a vassal of the crown, or of a

* The Turks in Algiers have, till lately, presented an instance of a similar government.

powerful lord, became lost in the mass of the people, who were sunk in bondage. At a later period, the spirit of feudalism changed, and so did the military service connected with it; but the oppression of the people, that is, of the mass of the people, continued, nay, became still severer. Vassals became more and more powerful; fiefs became hereditary, and the richer vassals almost independent of their feudal lord. They obeyed when it was for their interest, or when they were compelled. The only security for the existence of the governments, whose defence consisted in the feudal militia, was the state of weakness common to them all. Lawlessness and brutal tyranny now raged in each state for several centuries, until the power of the feudal aristocracy was broken by a union of the monarchs desirous of extending their authority with the third estate (deriving its origin from the growth of cities (q. v.), the great source of modern civilization), which was desirous to protect itself against the insupportable arrogance of the nobility. Then a militia, consisting of citizens, was formed in the cities—warriors who fought for their hearths and their commonwealth; and the kings (Philip Augustus of France, from 1180 to 1223, was the first) established armies of mercenaries, to protect their thrones against their vassals. The people, groaning under the oppression of the nobles and the priests, considered all the power that the throne gained as an advantage to themselves, without suspecting the pernicious consequences which were to result from the establishment of armies composed of mercenaries. Though feudal service continued, the standing troops came more and more into use; and even cities, republics and confederacies (as the Hansa, q. v.), kept armies on foot according to their means. An increase of these forces seemed necessary, on account of the increasing power of the Turks. Amurath I (from 1360 to 1389) founded the standing army of janizaries (q. v.), so peculiar in their organization, and through them obtained great advantages over the neighboring states, which were unable to oppose to him an equally strong and well-organized force. But the formation of standing armies was difficult. If they were to continue without limitation of the term of service, they must be composed of volunteers. To induce these to enlist, pay was necessary, and the troops seemed to be rather in the service of the monarch than in that of the nation, while the revenues of the former did not allow them to keep large armies on foot. In peace, therefore, only a small number of soldiers was maintained for the preservation of internal tranquillity; and, in time of war, large bodies of troops, under commanders called *condottieri* (q. v.), in Italy, were taken into pay. On the close of the war, they were dismissed, and offered their services in other quarters. This system led to great abuses. The *condottieri*, when they met, frequently spared each other, having no mutual enmity, and committed the greatest outrages against the subjects of the prince for whom they nominally fought. Their bands were schools of licentiousness and cruelty. During the same period, the princes found out a popular mode of raising taxes. The deputies of the people were assembled, and, by all kinds of influence, bribery, grants of titles, &c., were induced to assent to the taxes proposed by the princes. The nations now thought they had gained much in the important right of self-taxation. Supplies for increasing the number of troops were willingly granted, to obtain long-desired privileges; but, while the people suffered themselves to be disarmed, and furnished the means of supporting standing armies, all the barriers were overthrown, which had limited the arrogance of princes, their thirst for conquest, and the oppression of the people. In proportion as the power of the monarchs was augmented by the increase of their armies, they became able to add continually to the weight of the taxes. The kings of France, who had been the first to establish a standing army, also preceded the other princes in increasing the same, and in restricting the power of the great vassals, in the grant of considerable privileges to the communities, and the subsequent oppression of them, in the increase of taxes, and in all the measures of domestic despotism and foreign ambition. About 100 years after Philip Augustus, who had surrounded his throne with mercenaries, Philip IV, or the Fair (from 1285 to 1314), followed closely in his steps, so that the French throne became more powerful than any other. (See *Army, Standing*.) At last, the unscrupulous policy of Richelieu completed the French system of foreign aggrandizement and all restraints on the increase of the standing army were removed, as Europe learned in the pernicious wars of Louis XIV. As soon as France had completely established a military power independent of the citizens, other states did the same, some from necessity, some dazzled by her example, some merely for the gratification of the monarch. At the same time, in all countries, even in the smallest, the army became the receptacle of the idle and arrogant nobility, who, since the expiration of the feudal times, had lost their original occupation, and yet were, for the most part, too indolent and proud to follow occupations honorable to a citizen. Through a variety of misconceptions, the governments, particularly after the time of Frederic the Great, came to the monstrous conclusion that a great military state was the perfection of political society. The benefits which Europe has so long derived from the political example of Great Britain, have been peculiarly great since that period; for, notwithstanding the abuses in the English administration, the chief objects of its government have always been of a civil character, while on the continent of Europe, a military spirit came to pervade the whole system. The greater states considered their armies as the main pillar of their strength; the small ones imitated them, if from no other motive, from that of show and splendor. The sufferings arising from this state of things are much too numerous to be mentioned here: it affected society in all its ramifications: wars increased, because the instruments for war had increased; neither in the times of the allodial nor of the feudal system did such general and protracted conflicts desolate Europe as during this last period: taxes and all kinds of political burdens were fearfully augmented: the magnitude of armies and the system of military subordination had a decidedly bad effect on the citizens at large, corrupting their morals, and blunting their sensibility for justice and right: the frauds and violence employed to recruit the armies can be compared only to those employed in carrying on the negro slave-trade. If to these we add the violation of all constitutional and legal barriers, in the conduct of the governments towards the people, we shall have enumerated but a part of the evil consequences of these machines of tyranny. The invention of gunpowder, in the fourteenth century, producing a total change in the military art, had accelerated the arrival of this state of things. The long practice required to attain skill in the service of artillery, and the complicated system of tactics which had come into use since the introduction of fire-arms, seemed to make standing armies indispensable. The expensive equipment of armies demanded high taxes, and the armies compelled the nations to bow to the yoke of the Philips and Louises, to a Louvois, and even to a Pompadour. The monarch disposed of the property, and even of the children, of his subjects. Heavily did this burden press upon the continent of Europe when the French revolution began. In the wars which ensued, we all know what the national armies of France achieved against the numberless mercenaries of the other powers. The conscription (q. v.), being introduced, made every citizen liable to be drawn as a soldier. The establishment of the modern militia (of which we have spoken under the article *Militia*) is one of the most important changes in the history of national liberty, as no means so effectually oblige a monarchical government to yield to public opinion as an army of citizens. A brilliant illustration of this truth has been afforded, of late years, when some of the most powerful governments of Europe, evidently eager to make war against liberal principles, have been, hitherto at least, prevented by the well-known disinclination of their subjects. The idea of maintaining a balance of power, which has cost Europe rivers of blood, and has been made the pretext for every disturbance of peace and of the political balance, must be considered as mainly a consequence of the numerous standing armies; and if there existed no armies except those of a truly national character, men would think as little of making war upon another state to diminish its disproportioned power, as of compelling an equal division of property among individuals. It had been the policy of governments to render armies mere machines; but they found, in the wars growing out of the French revolution, that discipline and tactics are by no means the only things which ensure victory. The *morale*, that is, spirit, moral feeling, enthusiasm, fanaticism, are even more important than the physical power of an army and military skill in those who conduct it. History affords numerous instances of victories, won by troops animated by patriotism or religion, over much better organized and better commanded armies composed of mercenaries.

The class of soldiers is interesting, not only in a historical and political, but also in a legal view. Soldiers enjoy certain privileges in regard to the making of wills (see *Will*), and the acquisition of property during war (*peculium castrense*) for though the soldier may be yet under paternal power, he has the right of a *pater familias*; i. e. he may dispose of his property in any way which he may choose. In some countries, he is not allowed to be prejudiced by ignorance of law. In many countries, he is entitled to a trial on criminal charges before a particular court; in England and the U. States, however, only for military offences. What soldiers obtain by conquest is not theirs, but belongs to their government, excepting a part of the movable property, which is left to them. Public money or military stores which are taken must be given up to the public authorities. The laws of the different armies, as to military offences, are too various to be stated here, particularly as they vary much with the degree of civilization, and the character of the troops.

We shall now speak of the history of tactics. Whether an army is actuated by an enthusiastic patriotism, or any other noble feeling, or by a mere thirst for booty, it remains, to a certain degree, a machine, of which the parts must move in obedience to a directing intelligence; and in proportion as this understanding exerts a more complete sway over the great machine, composed of so many individuals, all differing morally and physically, the organization of the army approaches perfection. What we have said of the great importance of the moral character of an army, will show that we do not consider modern wars as merely the operation of two machines set against each other, and as decided simply by the skill of the commanders—a common mistake among persons ignorant of the nature of warfare. In the history of European armies and tactics we may distinguish five periods: viz. of the Roman legions, of the Teutonic feudal armies, of the invention of gunpowder, of the school of generals in the time of Louis XIV, and of the school of the French revolution.

I. The Romans were but very imperfectly acquainted with the modern system of deciding the fate of battles by preparatory movements, in which the hostile forces are sometimes occupied for months before meeting. They used neither magazines nor arsenals, nor artfully concealed their plans of operation. Cæsar, while in Gaul, made marches of thirty-seven miles in twenty-four hours. In the battles, the struggle of the line decided the victory. Till the time of Scipio Africanus, who first used foreign mercenaries as auxiliary cavalry (Numidians, Spaniards, &c.), the Roman armies consisted of Roman citizens or allies. On the *Campus Martius* the legions were formed of men both married and unmarried, from seventeen to forty-six and fifty years of age: no one was exempted except those who had made twenty campaigns. Before every war, as no standing army existed, the new legions were arranged according to their physical and moral qualities by the military tribunes. The younger and poorer were taken for *velites*, a kind of light troops (the archers and slingers were foreigners). Then the *hastati* were selected: these corresponded to the companies in the centre of our regiments of the line. Then followed the *principes*; then the *triarii*; and last the *equites*. The strength and composition of the various species of troops in the legions (q. v.) varied. Each legion constituted a small army of from 4000 to 6000 men, including all kinds of troops, workmen, utensils and ammunition. The cavalry constituted but the twentieth part of the legion, comprising only two or three hundred horsemen, who also fought on foot. The strength of armies consisted of infantry. A consular army never included more than 18,600 men, of which number 1800 were cavalry. In times of danger, several armies were united. The Roman forces at Cannæ included four such bodies as above described, since it amounted to about 80,000 men. A cohort was a company of from 400 to 600 men. The arms, defensive and offensive, differed according to the kinds of the soldiers. A Roman warrior on the march carried in arms, camp utensils, palisades, provisions for nineteen to twenty days, &c., a burthen of at least ninety pounds; hence double what the soldier now carries. Vegetius compares an army carrying 1000 palisades to a moving fortress. The physical strength of the soldier was exercised incessantly. The recruits were trained in Rome by carrying and marching in the burning sun. In the camp the soldiers worked on roads and bridges, aqueducts, &c., whereby the legions were made to diffuse Roman civilization. The Roman soldier was the best builder of walls ever known. The battle was begun by the *velites*. When they had retreated to the wings of each legion, or into the intervals, the *hastati* threw their spears when about twelve or fifteen feet distant from the enemy, and then rushed on, sword in hand. If they were repulsed, the *principes* advanced, and the former again arranged themselves in order. If the *principes* wavered, then the compact mass of *triarii* pressed forward—having till then rested on one knee, protected by their shields. If the enemy now gave way, the *velites* and cavalry assailed him, and made the rout complete. This threefold line of battle and threefold conflict gave the Roman legions an advantage over the Macedonian phalanx. (q. v.) The Roman soldier always remained in the camp, even in peace (*castra stativa*): he was always occupied, and subject to very strict discipline. This kept him strong; and there were fewer sick men to encumber the march than at present. Towards the end of the republic, the armies were much increased in number by foreigners and slaves; but their moral power decreased. Augustus was at the head of forty-nine legions and 19,000 horse; to which must be added 10,000 pretorians and the provincial troops. With the discipline, the art of war declined.

II. In the time of Honorius and Valentinian, the legions could no longer resist the irregular attacks of the Huns, Goths, Vandals, Burgundians and Franks, whose power consisted wholly in their numbers, physical strength and impetuous courage. Charlemagne gave to his armies an organization which made them superior to their brave but undisciplined enemies; but the chronicles do not afford us any particulars on this point. In the eleventh and twelfth centuries, the armies consisted of feudal militia, viz. vassals, who served under the banner of their feudal lords for three months or ninety days. For this period, every one provided himself with necessaries, and, on its expiration, went home, whether the war was at an end or not. The men at arms (horsemen in armor) were the strength of the French army; the rest consisted of infantry, badly armed and exercised, mostly bondsmen. When the arts revived in Italy, the art of war also attracted its share of attention, and was improved; but the wars were carried on by mercenaries, commanded by the *condottieri*, already mentioned. These troops, eager only for pay and booty, had no desire for each other's destruction; and this circumstance gave rise to stratagems and artificial movements, and thus, singularly enough, led to the invention of modern tactics. Choice of positions, marches and counter-marches, artificial attacks of fortresses, surprises, and avoidance of disadvantageous engagements, distinguish the wars of the famous Du Guesclin, under Charles V, king of France (1364—80). The bands of mercenaries whom he commanded, amounting to 30,000 men, were real scourges of the country when not occupied in war. After this came the struggles of the Swiss for their liberty. Their strength was in infantry. In order to withstand the men at arms, they gave to their infantry the helmet and cuirass, halberd and sword. The victories of these pike-men attracted the attention of all military nations. Louis XI of France took 6000 of them into his service; and in the Italian wars of Charles VIII, the Swiss infantry, 20,000 men strong, were the terror of the enemy, but were ready to desert the standard of their employer whenever their pay was delayed. At an earlier period, similar troops of pike-men had been in use in Germany, Spain and France. Charles VII of France, in particular, had instituted fifteen "*compagnies d'ordonnance*" (in 1444), the first standing army, and "*francs archers*" (in 1449), 16,000 infantry, and 9000 horse. Louis XI increased the army to 29,000 infantry and 19,000 cavalry. This subsequently rendered a new arrangement necessary. Francis I divided the infantry into seven legions, each of 6000 men; but regiments of from 2000 to 3000 men soon took their place. These, at a later period were again divided into battalions of from 600 to 700 men, for the sake of manœuvring with greater ease. The sharp-shooters were light troops, and fought like the *velites* of the Romans: behind them the close lines of pike-men advanced to battle.

III. Since the sixteenth century, the use of fire-arms (rifles, muskets and cannons) has made a new epoch in tactics. The famous Spanish general Pescara was victorious at Pavia, in 1525, over the French cavalry by means of fire-arms. But it was long before the use of the heavy ordnance was skilfully combined with that of the lance. This was first attempted by Puysegur, in the beginning of the reign of Louis XIV. The superiority of artillery over every other species of arms was now decided; yet the use of lances and pikes continued to the end of the seventeenth century. At this time, light cavalry substituted the carbine for the lance; but the defensive arms—helmet, cuirass, &c.—were laid aside too soon After the match-locks were changed for flint-locks, the musketry was placed in the first line, and the depth of the order of battle gradually diminished. Armies had, till then, been drawn up in lines six or eight men deep.

IV. This diminution took place chiefly after the introduction of the bayonet (q. v.), invented, in 1670, at Bayonne. Moreover, the difference between heavy and light infantry now ceased entirely, as all were armed in the same way, much to the detriment of the means of attack. The armies were burdened with a heavy park of artillery and much baggage, which greatly impeded their movements, and the disadvantage of the deep order of battle was not yet fully appreciated. But, even at this period, the infantry were placed in the centre, and the cavalry on the wings and in the reserve. (Marsin and Tallard were beaten at Blenheim (q. v.) because they had placed the cavalry in the centre.) In the time of Louis XIV, all the species of fire-arms were improved; tactics made great progress, and the art of fortification and besieging was carried to great perfection by Vauban. Frederic II of Prussia introduced greater simplicity, order and ease into the manœuvres of the infantry. The firing was performed more quickly, and on the field of battle every evolution was executed with greater precision. Among the greatest generals of that period was marshal Saxe, who knew better than any commander of his time how to adapt the art of war to the spirit of the French soldier. After the seven years' war (q. v.), the Prussian army was considered the best in Europe. Soldiers of all countries flocked to the reviews of Frederic, at Potsdam, to study in his school. But, skilful only in theory, and poor in experience, they did not perceive that the national character of the soldier properly belongs to the province of military calculation. The soldier was treated as a mere machine, and the perfection of tactics was supposed to consist in making him one, as nearly as possible, and the military service became loaded with trifling details. The French soldier, less fitted for such discipline than the native of any other country, became disgusted, and negligent of essential points of military duty. Only the French artillery retained its old reputation, because, instead of imitating it was, itself, a model. The manufacture of arms reached the highest perfection under Louis XIV. But French discipline, whose basis is honor, received the severest shock from the minister of war, count St. Germain, when he attempted to introduce the German mode of punishment, with the cane and the flat of the sword. Many unnecessary details were introduced into tactics. The mode of enlistment, too, was highly prejudicial. Vagabonds, criminals who wished to escape the laws, entered the service; and, on the other hand, the recruiting officers practised the basest frauds and violence to raise men.

V. An entire change was introduced by the French revolution; first in France. Love of country, liberty, glory, national hatred, and the hope of plunder, every thing conspired to fill the French soldier with the highest enthusiasm.* In the commencement of the wars of the French revolution, the forces of France were unsuccessful. The officers, who were all nobles, had emigrated in large numbers. Their place was supplied, in part, by inexperienced men; the old troops of the line had lost their discipline; all subordination was dissolved: France was without defenders. The people then felt the necessity of taking their own defence into their own hands; and, on the first requisition, of the unmarried men from eighteen to twenty-five, a million men entered the lines. Their school was the field of battle; their discipline enthusiasm; their tactics impetuosity. With fixed bayonets, singing songs of victory, they assaulted the batteries of the enemy. Against such courage the fire of cannon was of little avail. When the first enthusiasm had in some measure subsided, the aid of the guillotine† was resorted to; but the national pride and enthusiasm for liberty still remained the great moving power. The French generals again employed artillery; and it often decided the victory. In the time of Louis XIV, an army of 90,000 men had but 40 cannons: in the seven years' war, an army equally large had 190—200; at the battles of Austerlitz, Jena, Friedland, Wagram, Dresden, Leipsic, about 1200 cannons were brought into action. The mixture of the old

* During the siege of Mahon, wine was cheap; the French soldiers intoxicated themselves; the service suffered, and severe punishments were of little avail. At last the duke of Richelieu gave orders, that whoever should be found intoxicated, should never have the honor of sharing in the assault. No soldier was seen intoxicated again in the camp. A regiment of dragoons had suffered very severely in the battle of Marengo, and Bonaparte, at the review after the battle, promised them good quarters. "No," cried the brave dragoons, "let us have the honor of the first attack to-morrow." With such soldiers good generals could do wonders.

† When, after the loss of the lines of Weissenburg (October 13, 1793), a want of generals existed, St. Just and Lebas, the commissioners of the convention, called upon every soldier who felt the talent for command, to put himself at the head of the army, but threatened him with the indignation of the people, if he should allow himself to be deceived by his vanity. Only eleven officers accepted this offer, with the obligation to conquer or die: among them were Kleber, Pichegru, Desaix, Hoche.

troops of the line with the citizen-soldiers required the new distribution of troops into divisions, brigades, half brigades (2400 men, or three battalions). But the new system of managing and supporting the troops caused too much writing. In the train of the army was found a multitude of commissioners and agents, often detrimental both to the conquered country and the army. Great advantage was derived from the *tirailleur* system (see *Tirailleurs*), which originated in North America during the war of the American revolution, and was perfected by the French. The light troops were increased and organized anew, and the infantry of the line were taught to perform the service of the light infantry, so that the French *tirailleurs* soon became much dreaded. In order to march quickly, and to execute movements with large masses easily, the use of baggage-wagons was abolished, and pack-horses substituted. Light artillery, which had been introduced by Frederic II, was carried to great perfection by the French. In the battle of Dresden (August 26 and 27, 1813), 60 batteries of mounted artillery, comprising, perhaps, 240 pieces, in the course of three hours, silenced the cannon of the enemy. A fault was committed in arranging together in regiments this species of force, which is intended to act sometimes in small divisions, sometimes in large masses. Napoleon at length assigned a regiment of artillery to each corps of troops of the line. It is singular that a truly military character was not given to the camp equipage till 1793. This important improvement was soon generally imitated, most perfectly in Russia. On account of the size of the armies, it was necessary to dispense with tents and barracks; and the system of bivouacking was introduced, which, at first, gave the French great advantages, but soon weakened their troops greatly, by the diseases which it occasioned.

Sole (*solea*). The soles are distinguished from the flounders by having the mouth turned in an opposite direction with respect to the eyes, seemingly deformed, with teeth only on one side, and the front of the head almost always projecting. The common sole of Europe usually weighs about four pounds, but occasionally six or eight. The flesh is tender and delicious. Several other species are found in the European and Mediterranean seas. The New York sole (*S. mollis*, Mitch.) is a small, ugly, forbidding fish six or seven inches in length and destitute of pectoral fins. The back is banded with five or more transverse, entire, black lines. It is a soft, mucous fish, of an oval shape, and destitute of spines or prickles, which is brought to the New York market.—The *S. plagusia* is also destitute of pectoral fins, but is pointed behind, the dorsal, anal and caudal fins all uniting. The upper side is grayish. It is found along the coasts of Carolina.—The fishes of the *pleuronectes* family are remarkable, among vertebral animals, for the want of symmetry between the two sides of the body—a character entirely unique, and which destroys many a beautiful theory conjured up by the ingenuity of physiologists. The head is remarkably distorted, both the eyes being placed on the side which is turned upwards when the animal is in the water. The other, or blind side, is always flat and whitish. Sometimes individuals are found with the eyes placed in a reversed position from the rest of the species; others have both sides colored alike, and are called *double*. This happens most commonly to the brown side, but sometimes to the white also. They are all destitute of a swimming bladder, and rarely leave the bottom. A singular method of taking flounders from the shore is practised at Boston with great success. Two rods are selected; a hook is attached to the extremity of one, and the sole of a shoe at right angles to that of the other; the latter is vibrated in the water, and attracts the attention of the fish, which, as they rise to visit it, are caught by a sudden jerk of the hook held in the other hand. The season when this mode is practised is when the ice is partially melted.

Solebay, or Southwold Bay; a bay of the German ocean, on the coast of Suffolk, noted as the scene of a sanguinary naval engagement, in 1672, between the combined fleets of England and France, consisting of 101 sail, and that of the Dutch of 91 sail. In 1666, a famous sea fight also took place here between the English and Dutch, in which the latter lost seventy vessels.

Solecism (from the Latin *solœcismus*; Greek σολοικισμος); the violation of the rules of a language in speaking or writing, so called from the town of Soli, in the eastern part of Cilicia, in Asia Minor, the inhabitants of which spoke the Greek language very badly. The Romans included even awkward gestures on the stage under this name. The ancients distinguished *solecism* from *barbarism*, and designated by the latter the faulty use of single words, by the former, every violation of syntax. (*Quinctilian*, lib. i. ch. 5.) Modern grammarians have retained the words, yet not with precisely the same distinction; nor do they all agree in the distinction which they make.

SOLEURE (in German, *Solothurn*); a canton of Switzerland, bounded north by France and the canton of Basle, east by Basle and Zurich, south and west by Berne; square miles, 275; population, 54,330 of German origin, 4310 Calvinists, the remainder Catholics. The Jura mountains occupy a part of the canton; the rest of it is level and fertile. The ground is partly arable, and partly adapted to pasture; and the cattle of this canton are considered the best in Switzerland. Soleure was received into the confederacy in 1481. The capital, of the same name (4471 inhabitants), stands at the foot of mount Jura, is divided by the Aar into two parts, fortified with walls and bastions, and, though irregular and built in a bad taste, has several good edifices. It contains three churches, five convents, an hospital, a lyceum with five professors, and a town library of 8000 volumes. The environs are pleasant and picturesque. The town is very ancient, and several Roman antiquities are found here. (See *Switzerland*.)

SOLFAING signifies, originally, to exercise the voice upon the syllables ut, re, mi, fa, sol, la (solmization), adopted by Guido of Arezzo to designate the notes. To these, at a later period, the French added the syllable *si*, in order to complete the octave. It is applied also to the singing and reading of notes without text, in which the tones only are named. Pieces without text, intended for this sort of exercise, are called *solfeggi*. Sometimes this word is applied also to instrumental music (e. g. on the piano) and then those pieces are meant, which are merely intended to exercise the learner in reading notes and hitting intervals. Solfaing, according to the above-named syllables, had reference to the system of twenty-two diatonic tones (from g to $\overline{\overline{e}}$), divided into seven hexachords, established by Guido of Arezzo. If the music went beyond the sixth, the syllables were changed, in order to bring the *mi*, *fa*, which designated the transition from the third to the fourth degree of the hexachord, to its proper place again, for which certain rules were given. With the extension of the system of tones by the enharmonic and chromatic genera, the difficulty of singing after these syllables increased, on which account the Germans and Dutch gave up this way of designating them. (See *Ut*, *Re*, *Mi*.)

SOLFATARA; a height near Naples (see *Naples*); also a lake near Rome. (See *Campagna di Roma*.)

SOLFEGGI. (See *Solfaing*.)

SOLICITOR, SOLICITOR GENERAL. (See the articles *Advocates*, and *Advocate of the Crown*.)

SOLID, in philosophy; a body whose parts are so connected together as not to give way or slip from each other upon the smallest impression; in which sense *solid* stands opposed to *fluid*. Geometricians define a solid to be the third species of magnitude, or that which has three dimensions, viz. length, breadth, and thickness or depth. A solid may be conceived to be formed by the revolution, or direct motion, of a superficies of any figure whatever, and is always terminated or contained under one or more planes or surfaces, as a surface is under one or more lines.

SOLID ANGLE is that formed by three or more plane angles meeting in a point; like an angle of a die, or the point of a diamond well cut. Or, more generally, it may be defined the inclination of several plane surfaces, or one or more curved surfaces.

SOLIDS. (See *Animal Matter*.)

SOLILOQUY, or MONOLOGUE, in the drama, or a work of dramatic character; the expression of the thoughts or feelings, in language not addressed to a second person; it is therefore opposed to the *dialogue*. Dramatic writers have recourse to soliloquy for the purpose of exhibiting more distinctly the real character of the persons of the action, their secret motives, and the manner in which they are affected by important events, and thus show the hidden springs of the action. It has been objected that soliloquy is unnatural, and that, in real life, persons alone never express their feelings aloud, except under a strong excitement and in a few words. Even if this criticism is just, the monologue cannot be dispensed with in the drama; but good taste requires that it should be used sparingly, and only when the same object cannot be effected by means of the dialogue.

SOLIMAN II. (See *Solyman II*.)

SOLINGEN; a town in the Prussian province of Juliers-Cleves-Berg, noted for its manufactures of iron and steel ware, and silk stuffs. The population of the town and parish exceeds 9000; twenty miles north-east of Cologne.

SOLIS, Antonio de; a Spanish poet and

historian, born at Placenza, in Old Castile, in 1610. His inclination for dramatic poetry procured him the acquaintance of Calderon, for some of whose pieces he wrote the preludes (*loas*). He is principally known at present as a historical writer. Having been appointed historiographer of the Indies, he drew up a work entitled *Historia de la Conquista de Mejico*, which passed through many editions, and of which an English translation was published in 1724 (folio). He took orders in the church in the latter part of his life, and died at an advanced age, in 1686. An edition of the History of the Conquest of Mexico, in the original Spanish, was printed in London in 1809 (3 vols., 8vo.).

Solitaire (French, *solitary*) is used also as a substantive. One of the meanings is a diamond set alone, without other stones round it.

Solmization. (See *Solfaing*.)

Solms; a German family of counts and princes, in Wetteravia, sprung from the stock of Conrad the Salian. Since 1432, it has consisted of two lines, Solms-Braunfels and Solms-Lich, the latter of which is divided into the branch of Lich and Hohensolms and that of Laubach. The line of Braunfels received the dignity of prince of the empire in 1742, and the branch of Lich and Hohensolms in 1792. In 1806, the possessions of the family were mediatised, and are now subject to Hesse-Darmstadt and Prussia.

Solo is a piece of music, or a passage, in which a single voice or instrument performs quite alone (i. e. without accompaniment), or is distinguished above the other voices. Thus there are violin solos, solos for the pianoforte, &c., pieces for the violin or the piano only; but a solo for the violin also signifies a passage in which the violin part is the principal. A solo, also, in a piece of music for several instruments or voices, denotes a passage which is to be executed by one of the instruments separately. And *tutti* signifies that all the voices or instruments are to commence again after the solo has been played. *Soli*, in the plural, denotes that two or more voices or instruments are to execute a passage in the same manner, distinctly from the other instruments or voices. (See *Obligato*.) Peculiar freedom, ease, distinctness, and power of execution, is required to perform the solo with correctness, taste and feeling.

Solomon; son of David by Bathsheba, through whose influence he inherited the Jewish throne, in preference to his elder brothers. During a long and peaceful reign, from B. C. 1015 to 975, he enjoyed the fruits of his father's labors. A youth surrounded with royal splendors inspired him with a sense of dignity, and he carried with him to the throne, which he ascended, while young, with the cruelty of an Eastern monarch, the wisdom which he had derived from the lessons of his father and his father's counsellors. To confirm his power, he caused his brother Adonijah, and some discontented nobles, to be put to death, and formed alliances with foreign rulers. His remarkable judicial decisions, and his completion of the political institutions of David, showed a superiority of genius, which gained him the respect of the people. By the building of the temple, which, in magnitude, splendor and beauty, exceeded any former work of architecture, he gave to the Hebrew worship a magnificence which bound the people more closely to their national rites. The wealth of Solomon accumulated by a prudent use of the treasures inherited from his father by successful commerce, through which he first made the Hebrews acquainted with navigation; by a careful administration of the royal revenues, which he caused to be collected by twelve governors; and by an increase of taxes,—enabled him to meet the expense of erecting the temple, building palaces, cities and fortifications, and of supporting the extravagance of a luxurious court. But while, on the one hand, the prosperity of the people was promoted, and the arts and civilization were improved, on the other, an example of pernicious luxury, and of a gradual relaxation of the severity of the Mosaic religion, was exhibited. Admiration of Solomon's wisdom and regal magnificence, which brought crowds of foreigners to his capital, and, among the rest, a queen of Sheba, easily drowned the few voices of discontent. His justice gained him the respect of his subjects; and an army stood at his command, consisting of 12,000 horsemen, armed in the Egyptian manner, and 1400 war-chariots, to overawe the Gentile tribes, which had been subjugated by David to the Jewish yoke, and were now forced to labor in the service of Solomon. Fortune long seemed to favor this great king; and Israel, in the fulness of its prosperity, scarcely perceived that he was continually becoming more despotic. Contrary to the laws of Moses, Solomon admitted foreign women into his numerous harem of 700 wives and 300 concubines; and, from love to these women, he was weak enough, in his old age, to permit them the free practice of their idolatrous worship, and even to take part in it himself. Still his adversaries, who, towards the close of his life, aimed at his throne, could effect nothing; but, after his death, the discontent of the people broke out into open rebellion, and his feeble son, Rehoboam, could not prevent the division of the kingdom. (See *Hebrews.*) The forty years' reign of Solomon, the last years of which were less glorious than the first, is still, however, celebrated among the Jews for its splendor and its happy tranquillity, as one of the brightest periods of their history. Throughout the East it is considered as a golden age. In fact, Solomon belonged more to the East, in general, than to his own nation. His mode of thinking was freer than beseemed a Hebrew. The writings contained under his name in the Bible, though they may have been collected and arranged at a later period, are substantially the work of Solomon. They breathe a philosophical spirit, elevated above the prejudices of his nation. His Proverbs are rich in ingenious and sagacious observations. His Ecclesiastes, or Preacher, savors of the philosophy which men of the world, sated with a long course of pleasure, form from the results of their own experience. It teaches that nothing is permanent, and therefore we should hasten to enjoy present good, and that God is the source of all wisdom. (For the Canticles, see *Solomon's Song.*) The book entitled the Wisdom of Solomon, though received into the canon by the Roman Catholic church, is rejected, as apocryphal, by Protestants. Solomon's wisdom and happiness have become proverbial; and the fables of the rabbins, and the heroic and erotic poems of the Persians and Arabians speak of him, as the romantic traditions of the Normans and Britons do of king Arthur, as a fabulous monarch, whose natural science (mentioned even in the Bible), whose wise sayings and dark riddles, whose power and magnificence, are attributed to magic. According to these fictions, Solomon's ring was the talisman of his wisdom and power, and, like the temple of Solomon, in the mysteries of the free-masons and rosicrucians, has a deep, symbolical meaning.

Solomon's Seal (*polygonatum*); a genus of plants, allied to the asparagus, which it resembles in the flowers and fruit, but the form of the leaves is very different. These last are entire, more or less oval or lanceolate. In most of the species, the leaves are alternate, and all directed upwards, while the flowers are pendulous, and, to the number of two or more, are disposed upon a common foot-stalk, which arises from the axil of each of the leaves. The calyx is wanting; the corolla monopetalous, cylindrical, divided at the summit into six obtuse lobes; the capsule is a rounded berry, containing three cells. We have two species or more in the U. States. The name is said to be derived from the roots, which, in the common European species, are full of knots; and a transverse section of them shows characters which have been thought by the superstitious to represent the impress of the famous seal of Solomon.

Solomon's Song, or the Canticles, or the Song of Songs; one of the books of the Old Testament, commonly attributed to Solomon. The manner, tone and coloring of this book bear marks of the voluptuousness, splendor and luxury of the age of Solomon; but on account of the traces of the Aramæan dialect, which it contains, it has been assigned by Eichhorn, Jahn and others, to a later period. The scenes and incidents depicted in it form a connected whole, which has more of the idyllic or pastoral than of the dramatic character. Whether we consider it as the work of Solomon or of some later Hebrew poet, we must view it as a love song, entirely destitute of religious allusions: its subject is the passion of the bridegroom and the bride. From the time of Origen to the seventeenth century, critics ascribed an allegorical religious meaning to this book; and, for above 1200 years, it was interpreted to describe the union of the faithful with God, Christ being signified under the emblem of the bridegroom, and his church under that of the bride. The older Jewish rabbis, however, permitted the reading of the song to no one under thirty years of age, and did not allow it to be read and explained publicly. Erasmus was the first theologian who endeavored to expose the error of giving an allegorical interpretation to this poem. Bossuet considered it Solomon's epithalamium. Lowth represents it as a sacred drama. Mr. Good, who has given a metrical version of it in English, considers it a collection of Hebrew idyls; to which division of poetry sir William Jones had previously referred it.

Solon, one of the seven wise men of Greece, and the legislator of Athens, flourished about B. C. 600. He was descended from the ancient kings of Athens, and from Codrus. but was in such narrow circumstances as to be obliged to get his living by commerce. He possessed poetical talents, and had acquired extensive knowledge by his travels. His manners were affable and pleasing: he was a friend to reasonable enjoyment, not indifferent to riches, but free from avarice: universally esteemed by his fellow-citizens, he exercised an important influence in public affairs. It was by his means that the inhabitants of Cirrha were punished for a violation of the temple at Delphi; that those persons who had, contrary to their promise, murdered the adherents of Cyron (who attempted to make himself master of Athens) on sacred ground, were arraigned and condemned; and that Epimenides was sent for from Crete, to purify the city, and to soften the fierceness of the Athenians by religious influences. Plutarch says, that Solon made use of the services of Epimenides in the promulgation of his laws. As an instance of his patriotism, we may mention his venturing to propose the recovery of Salamis, at the hazard of his life. That island had been conquered by the Megarensians; and all the attempts of the Athenians to reduce it had been without success. It had therefore been forbidden, under pain of death, to propose the renewal of the attempt. Solon, discontented with this state of things, composed an elegy, reproaching the Athenians for their weakness, and, feigning himself mad, recited the poem with the greatest warmth before the people. The impression which he produced was heightened by the exhortations of Pisistratus, who mingled with the crowd: a new war was resolved upon, and the command of the expedition was given to Solon and Pisistratus. By the courage and prudence of the commanders, Salamis was recovered; and it would now have been easy for Solon to have made himself tyrant of Athens; but he rejected all proposals of that nature, convinced that the happiness of his fellow-citizens, and the introduction of a new and salutary form of government, would bring him a more permanent reputation. Draco's bloody laws had effected no reform in the internal condition of the state: Athens was divided into factions: the common people were entirely in the power of the rich and noble, and were cruelly oppressed by them. The rich compelled their poor debtors either to cultivate their grounds as serfs, or to sell their children, or to give themselves up as slaves; and many citizens, on this account, abandoned their country. The public treasury and the temples were likewise plundered. A new constitution was the general wish, and even many of the rich saw the necessity of it. In the third year of the forty-sixth Olympiad (B. C. 594), all parties united in choosing Solon archon, and in investing him with full powers as a lawgiver. He immediately abolished most of the cruel laws of Draco, raised the nominal value of money, entirely abrogated the debts, or reduced them so that they should not be burdensome to the debtors; and although, at first, neither party was satisfied with these measures, the poor being desirous of an equal division of the lands, yet they were afterwards convinced of their expediency and wisdom. At the same time, it was made a standing law, that no citizen should give up his own person or his children to his creditors, in satisfaction of his debts. The constitution of Solon was founded on the principle that the supreme power resided in the whole people, and that in the popular assemblies lay the prerogatives of declaring war and making peace, contracting and abrogating alliances, choosing and removing magistrates, repealing and passing laws. The judicial power was divided between the people and the judicial tribunals, already in existence. Public offences were tried before the Areopagus and the other courts; private suits were prosecuted before new tribunals, the members of which were chosen by lot from the whole people. The citizens were divided into four classes, three of which were determined by the amount of property, the fourth being composed of all those who had no property: this class was excluded from all public offices, but was admitted into the general assemblies of the people. This arrangement had the effect to encourage industry among the lowest class, by rendering it an object of ambition to them to raise themselves above the operation of the exclusion; and it was the policy of Solon to encourage arts and industry, upon which the prosperity of Athens depended. It also tended to place the most worthy and enlightened citizens in offices of trust. By making the choice of magistrates dependent not on lot, but on the votes of the citizens, a proper degree of influence was secured to the most respectable portion of the people. The only reward of public officers was the honor attached to their offices, no salary being connected with them. Still further to excite industry among the poor, the Areopagus was empowered to punish vagabonds; and the son was released from the obligation of supporting his parents, if they had taught him no trade. The great counterpoise to the power of the people consisted in the organization of the Areopagus and the institution of a council. The Areopagus not only judged in capital cases, but kept up a rigorous inspection into the morals and lives of the citizens, watched over the faithful observance of the laws, and possessed many of the privileges of archons. In cases of emergency, it seems to have exercised all powers, like the Roman dictators. The new senate of 400 (chosen from each *phyle*) had still more extensive powers, and was directed by an executive committee (*prytanis*), chosen from its own number. Solon attempted to give stability to his constitution, by a law, that no decree contrary to existing laws should be valid, and that whoever repealed an old law, should propose a new one in place of it; and to prevent the increase of a needy populace, he made it difficult for a foreigner to acquire the right of citizenship in Athens. Prodigal, extravagant or otherwise immoral citizens were not permitted to speak in the popular assemblies, and were thereby excluded from all public offices. Bribery was punished by death, or a fine of ten times the amount of the bribe, or by infamy, both parties being treated as equally guilty. Adulterers, seducers of a free person, and procurers, were punished with death. A woman guilty of adultery was to be divorced, and could not appear at the public festivals. The hours for the public instruction of youth were fixed with the greatest exactness; and foreigners were forbidden all access to the gymnasia. The education of boys, youths and men was regulated by particular laws; and public officers were appointed to superintend the conduct of masters and pupils. Whoever could not afford to send his children to a gymnasium, was required to have them taught agriculture or a trade. Solon left religion unchanged, but gave to the Areopagus the supreme direction of religious matters, and built several temples, among which was one to Venus Pandemos (the priestesses of which were public strumpets). When Solon had completed his laws (see *Petiti Leges Atticæ*, Paris, 1635), he caused them to be engraved on wooden cylinders, and bound the Athenians by an oath not to make any changes in his code for ten years. He himself left the country, to avoid being obliged to make any alterations in them, and visited Egypt, Crete, Cyprus, Lydia (see *Crœsus*), Miletus, where he met Thales (q. v.), and several cities of Greece proper. Returning to Athens, after an absence of ten years, he found the state torn by the old party hate; but he was received with general esteem, and all parties submitted their demands to his decision. Among the leaders, at this time, was Pisistratus, who was at the head of the popular party. Although a friend and favorite of Solon, he found an opponent in him, when his purpose of obtaining the sovereignty became obvious. Solon left Athens for ever, and died soon after; but when and where his death took place is uncertain. He is generally represented to have died in his eightieth year, in the second year of the fifty-fifth Olympiad. Of his poems and other writings we have some fragments, which are contained in Glandorf's *Gnomicorum Poetarum Opera* (Leipsic, 1776, 2d vol.). The letters to Pisistratus, and to some of the seven wise men, attributed to him, are spurious.

SOLOTHURN. (See *Soleure*.)

SOLSTICE, in astronomy; that time when the sun is in one of the solstitial points; that is, when he is at his greatest distance from the equator, and is so called because he then appears to stand still, and not to change his distance from the equator for some time—an appearance owing to the obliquity of our sphere, and which those living under the equator are strangers to. The solstices are two in each year, the estival or summer solstice, and the hyemal or winter solstice. The summer solstice is when the sun seems to describe the tropic of Cancer, which is on June 22, when he makes the longest day: the winter solstice is when the sun enters the first degree, or seems to describe the tropic of Capricorn, which is on Dec. 22, when he makes the shortest day. This is to be understood of our northern hemisphere; for, in the southern, the sun's entrance into Capricorn makes the summer solstice, and that into Cancer the winter solstice. The two points of the ecliptic, wherein the sun's greatest ascent above the equator, and his descent below it, are terminated, are called the *solstitial* points; and a circle, supposed to pass through the poles of the world and these points, is called the *solstitial colure*. The summer solstitial point is in the beginning of the first degree of Cancer, and is called the *æstival* or *summer* point; and the winter solstitial point is in the beginning of the first degree of Capricorn, and is called the *winter* point. These two points are diametrically opposite to each other.

SOLUTION. (See *Cohesion*.)

SOLYMAN II (called the *Lawgiver* by his own subjects, and the *Magnificent* by the Christians) was the only son of Selim I, whom he succeeded in 1520. Three days previous to the death of his father, and at the same time when Charles V was crowned at Aix-la-Chapelle, he was proclaimed sultan. He had not been educated in the usual manner of the Ottoman princes, but, on the contrary, had been initiated in all the secrets of state policy. His love of justice appeared at the very commencement of his reign, when he returned the property which his father had taken from individuals. He restored the authority of the courts of justice, which had been entirely destroyed, and selected governors and other officers from persons who possessed property and were honest. "I intend," said he, "that they should resemble the rivers which fertilize the countries through which they flow, not the streams which break down all they meet." Gazeli Beg, the governor of Syria, had at first declared against Solyman, and involved a part of Egypt in his revolt; but he was overcome by the generals of Solyman, who also destroyed the Mamelukes in Egypt, and concluded an armistice with Persia. Having thus secured himself from disturbance on the side of Syria and Egypt, he besieged and took Belgrade in 1521. In 1522, he resolved to besiege the island of Rhodes, which had been in the possession of the knights of St. John for 212 years. He wrote a haughty letter to the knights, in which he called on them to surrender, unless they wished to be put to the sword. The siege of Rhodes cost him many men; but, at length, the town, being reduced to extremity, was forced to surrender, Dec. 26, 1522. The conqueror now turned his arms against Hungary, where he gained the battle of Mohatz, in 1526. He afterwards took Buda (1529), advanced to Vienna, and, in twenty days, made as many assaults upon this city, but was finally forced to raise the siege, with the loss of 80,000 men. In 1534, he marched towards the East, took possession of Tauria, but was defeated by Shah-Thamas; and, in 1565, his army met with the same fate before Malta as formerly before Vienna. In 1566, he took possession of the island of Scio, and ended his life, Aug. 30 of the same year, at the siege of Sigeth, in Hungary, in the seventy-sixth year of his age, and four days before the taking of the fortress by the Turks. His victorious arms made him equally dreaded in Europe and in Asia. His empire extended from Algiers to the Euphrates, and from the extremity of the Black sea to the farthest limits of Greece and Epirus. His abilities were equally great for the conduct of affairs in peace and in war As a general, he possessed a wonderful activity: his word was held sacred: he was a firm friend to justice, although his love for the sultana Roxalana, and her persuasions, prevailed upon him to put to death all his children by another sultana, to secure the succession to Selim her son. His cruelty tarnished his fame. After the siege of Mohatz, by his orders, 1500 of the most distinguished prisoners were placed in a circle, and beheaded, in presence of the victorious army. Solyman thought nothing impossible to be done which he commanded. When one of his generals sent him word that his orders to build a bridge over the Drave could not be executed, Solyman sent him a linen cord, with this answer: "The sultan, thy master, commands thee, without consideration of the difficulties, to complete the bridge over the Drave: if thou doest it not, on his arrival, he will have thee strangled with this cord, which announces to thee his supreme will." Solyman used his unlimited power to establish order and security in his dominions. He divided them into districts, of which each was compelled to furnish a certain number of soldiers. The produce of a certain division of country in every province was reserved for the support of the troops; and he provided for every thing connected with military discipline, and the equipment of soldiers, with the greatest care. He introduced a system for the regulation of the finances in his empire; and, that the taxes might not be too oppressive, he was very exact in his expenses. He was the greatest of all the Ottoman emperors, and extended his power widely, by force of arms, in Asia and Europe. Under his government the Turks attained their highest glory; but this was gradually lost under his successors, who seldom appeared at the head of their armies. He was in the highest degree ambitious, active, and fond of power; and every year of his reign was distinguished by some great enterprise. A faithful observer of his religion, he was less vicious, and much better educated, than his predecessor. He loved mathematics, and particularly the study of history. He wanted but few qualities to make him a great prince, but many to make him a good one. Those who reckon the emperors of Turkey from the conquest of Constantinople, call him Solyman I

SOMERS, lord John, a distinguished lawyer and statesman, was the son of an attorney at Worcester, where he was born in 1652. He was entered a gentleman commoner at Trinity college, Oxford, and, being destined for the legal profession, passed some time as clerk to a barrister, and, when called to the bar himself, evinced talents of a high order. His principles led him to oppose the measures of Charles II; and, on the accession of James II, he continued a firm opposer of the court, and acquired great credit as one of the council for the seven bishops. He heartily concurred in the revolution, and sat, as one of the representatives for Worcester, in the convention parliament, summoned by the prince of Orange, and was one of the managers appointed by the commons to confer with the lords on the word *abdicate*. In 1689, he was knighted, and made solicitor-general; in 1692, attorney-general, and lord-keeper of the great seal the following year, in which capacity he displayed equal ability, integrity and gentleness. He was one of the first patrons of Addison, for whom he procured an allowance, to enable him to make the tour of Italy. In 1695, he was made lord high chancellor of England, and was raised to the peerage by the title of lord Somers, baron Evesham. Being now regarded as the head of the whigs, he made great exertions to moderate the zeal of that party. After the death of William, lord Somers spent his time in literary retirement, and was chosen president of the royal society. In 1706, he drew up a plan for effecting a union between England and Scotland, which was so much approved, that queen Anne appointed him one of the commissioners to carry it into execution. Upon a change of ministry, in 1708, he was nominated president of the council, but was again dismissed in 1710, and, in April, 1716, was carried off by an apoplectic fit, at the age of sixty-four. He was a patron of men of letters, and one of those who redeemed Milton's Paradise Lost from the obscurity in which party prejudice had involved it. Besides the many speeches and political tracts attributed to him, he translated some of Ovid's Epistles, and Plutarch's Life of Alcibiades. He also made a collection of scarce tracts, of which there has been published a selection, in four parts, each consisting of four volumes (4to.; new edition, 1809—1812, 12 vols., 4to., edited by sir Walter Scott). His collection of original papers and letters was destroyed by a fire at Lincoln's Inn.

SOMERS' ISLANDS. (See *Bermudas' Islands.*)

SOMERSET, EARL OF. (See *Overbury.*)

SOMERSET, DUKE OF. (See *Seymour.*)

SOMERVILE, William, a minor poet, was born in Warwickshire, in 1692, and educated at Oxford. He early cultivated his talent for poetry, and inherited a considerable paternal estate, on which he chiefly lived, mingling an ardent attachment to the sports of the field with the studies of a man of letters. He was courteous, hospitable, convivial; but carelessness in pecuniary matters, by involving him in embarrassments, preyed on his mind, and produced habits which shortened his life. He died in 1742. As a poet, Somervile is chiefly known by his Chase, a poem in blank verse, which maintains a respectable rank in the didactic and descriptive class. Another piece, connected with the same subject, is entitled Field Sports. His Hobbinol, or Rural Games, is a kind of mock heroic. His other pieces are not fitted to increase his reputation. (See Johnson's *Lives of the Poets.*)

SOMME. (See *Department.*)

SOMNAMBULISM designates the well known phenomena of sleep-walking. It is also used for a certain state of a person under the influence of animal magnetism. (q. v.) The phenomena of sleep-walking are very singular, the person affected performing many voluntary actions, implying a certain degree of perception of the presence of external objects. This affection is commonly considered as an imperfect degree of sleep. "In the case of the somnambuli," says Dugald Stewart, "the mind retains its power over the limbs, but possesses no influence over its own thoughts, and scarcely any over the body, excepting those particular members of it which are employed in walking." Sleep-walking is not unfrequently connected with the changes of the moon; when people will rise, walk about, do certain things, and go to bed again. The placing of a wet cloth by the side of the bed of such a person, so as to wake him immediately when he steps on it, is recommended as a means of curing this habit. The subject is very obscure, the cases not having been philosophically studied to a sufficient extent. As to somnambulism in animal magnetism, the votaries of this science believe that the brain—the peculiar seat of the higher faculties—rests during somnambulism, but that the vital power of the nervous system of the abdomen is heightened so much, that it can supply, in a degree, the place of the brain, and afford the means of perception. Hence a letter placed on the stomach of a person in the state of somnambulism can be read by him! We must refer the reader to the works mentioned in the article *Magnetism, Animal*, viz. those of Wolfarth, Kieser, &c.

SOMNUS (Latin, *sleep*), or HYPNOS (ὕπνος); in ancient mythology, the god of sleep, son of Nox (Night), and twin brother of Mors (Death). He dwelt at the western extremity of the world, where the imagination of early poets placed all awful beings. The Orphic hymn (84) calls Lethe (Oblivion) his sister. His power is great, and both mortals and gods are subject to him. Some of the later poets describe him as a handsome youth, some as a dull and lazy god, whose dark abode no ray of Phœbus enters. (*Ovid.*) He is sometimes represented with a wreath of poppies; sometimes with a horn, in which he carries dreams. According to some poets, he produces sleep by the motion of his wings; according to others, he sprinkles drops of Lethe on the eyes of mortals. Ovid gives him a thousand children, but mentions only Morpheus, Icelos, Phobetor and Phantasos. (See *Morpheus.*)

SON (in the Tartar languages, *river*); a syllable which appears in many geographical names, as *Karason* (black river), *Akson* (white river).

SONATA (*sonata*, or *suonata*, Italian, from *sonare*, to sound) is a simple piece of instrumental music, intended to express various feelings in different passages, according to the character of the instrument used. It was originally designed for one instrument only, principally for the violin; afterwards for the piano almost exclusively. Subsequently, sonatas were composed, in which the piano or harpsichord is accompanied by other instruments; for instance, the violin or flute, horn, clarionet. But these latter were also called *trios*. The union, however, is not pleasing, as the tone of the harpsichord is too weak, and the pianoforte does not harmonize well with any other instrument. The expression of the sonata is to be determined by the character of the instrument—a circumstance which modern composers have not sufficiently observed. In sonatas for several instruments, the principal instrument is either only assisted (as is the case, for instance, with many sonatas for the pianoforte accompanied by the violoncello), or the instruments alternate, so as to make the sonata a dialogue of instruments. Formerly the sonata usually began with a lively passage, followed by an andante or adagio; then came a minuet with a trio (afterwards a scherzo); and lastly a rondo or presto: instead of the second, third or last division, variations are also made use of. The old arrangement, however, is no longer adhered to, and sonatas are now written in two, three, or four divisions. But still it is a complete musical piece, in which the passages are connected by a common character. An easy or short sonata is called *sonatina.* The most distinguished composers of sonatas are Bach, Haydn, Beethoven, Clementi, Cramer, Hummel, Weber, Moscheles, Kalkbrenner, Field.

SONNET (Italian *sonetto*); a species of poetic composition, consisting of fourteen lines of equal length—the most ancient form of Italian poetry. It was used at an earlier period among the Provençals (q. v.); and, in the thirteenth century, count Thibaut de Champagne mentions it as a species of poetry universally used and known. A Provençal sonnet, written in 1321, and entirely conformable to the rules for this species of poem, in which William de Almarichi congratulates king Robert of Naples, is to be found in Nostradamus, from whom Crescembeni borrowed it in his *Storia della volgar Poesia* (t. i.). In Italy, the sonnet was naturalized about the middle of the thirteenth century, when Italian poetry became imbued with the spirit of the Provençal. Fra Guittone, of Arezzo (died 1295), the first Italian poet of note, was also the first who gave to the sonnet, at least in Italy, that regular form which Petrarca (died 1374) carried to perfection, and made a model. In France, the sonnet was not cultivated after the extinction of the Provençal poetry, until the sixteenth century; but the *bouts rimés* (q. v.) reduced it to a mere play on words. In Germany, it first came into use in the first half of the seventeenth century. It has been of late much cultivated there, but is not adapted for the language, on account of its poverty in rhymes. In fact, the strict rules of the rhyme often compel the poet to accommodate the ideas to the expression, even in languages which, like the Italian, have a great number of rhymes for al most every final syllable; and in German, in which many final syllables have very few rhymes, there are many words which almost always are made to rhyme with certain others; so that the occurrence of one of them in a sonnet inevitably suggests to the reader what words are to follow. so as to destroy the great pleasure of rhyme. A sonnet may produce a good effect when the subject is well chosen, and naturally accommodates itself to the divisions of the poem; but it requires much skill to make it pleasing; and Petrarca himself sometimes becomes tame, from the constraints to which he is subjected. Göthe wrote but few; and their subject is the difficulties of the form, and the pleasure of overcoming them. The sonnet is often attempted by persons who find it easier to furnish rhymes than ideas; and the number of insipid sonnets in Italian and Spanish is immense. In English, also, there is an abundance of them.—The sonnet properly consists of fourteen iambic verses of eleven syllables, and is divided into two chief parts: the first consists of two divisions, each of four lines (*quadernario, quadrain*); the second of two divisions of three lines each (*terzina*). The quadrains have two rhymes, each of which is repeated four times, and, according to the Italian usage, either so that the first, fourth, fifth and eighth verses rhyme, and, again, the verses between them the second, third, sixth, seventh (*rima chiusa*); or, which is rarer, the rhymes alternate (*rima alternata*); or, what is still rarer, the first quadrain is written in the first way, and the second in the second. In the two terzine there are either three rhymes, each twice repeated, or two rhymes, thrice repeated, in all positions. The Italians, who use hardly any form for lyrical poetry but the sonnet and canzone, have invented varieties of it, such as the Anacreontic sonnets, with lines of eight syllables, and those with a *coda*. The sonnet generally contains one principal idea, pursued through the various antitheses of the different strophes, and adorned with the charm of rhyme.

SONNITES. (See *Sunnites*.)

SONORA; one of the states of the Mexican confederacy (see *Mexico*), lying on the Pacific ocean, on which it has a seacoast of 900 miles, with several good ports. It is generally hilly, a large portion of it lying on the table land. It abounds in mineral wealth: gold is found in washings and mines, and the silver mines are rich and numerous. The soil is also fertile. The capital of the state is Arispe, with a population of 7600 souls. Cinaloa (9500), Sonora (6400), and Culiacan (10,800), are among the principal towns.

SONTAG, Henrietta, a very distinguished singer of our time, was born in 1808, at Coblentz. Her parents were players. When five years old, she appeared on the stage at the Frankfort theatre. In Prague she received instruction at the excellent conservatory. (q. v.) For some time she held an appointment in the Italian opera at Vienna. In 1824, with her mother and her younger sister, she performed in Berlin, where she became a great favorite. In 1826, she went to Paris, where she attracted equal admiration, and became, in 1827, a performer at the Italian opera. In 1828, she visited London. She has lately left the stage, and married a count. Purity, clearness, agreeableness and flexibility are united, in an uncommon degree, in her voice. Her expression is masterly; her person and her acting fine; her manners accomplished; her reputation unstained, and her disposition benevolent. These qualities combined to make her one of the most popular singers who ever appeared in Europe. She excels in the sentimental, the humorous and the graceful, and in Italian songs. Her chief parts were Agathe, in *Der Freischütz;* Donna Anna, in Mozart's *Don Juan;* Euryanthe, in the Princess of Navarre; Helene, in *Donna del Lago;* Cinderella; Rosina, in Rossini's Barber of Seville; Caroline, in *Matrimonio Segreto;* &c.

SOODRAS. (See *Hindoos*.)

SOOT. (See *Lamp-Black*, and *Manure*.)

SOPHI; a professor of Sufism. (q. v.)

SOPHIA, CHURCH OF ST. The foundation of this magnificent temple in Constantinople was laid in the sixth century, in the reign of Justinian; and the work was completed by Anthemius Tralles, the most celebrated architect of his age, with the aid of Isidorus of Miletus. Anthemius was the first who undertook to erect a dome on four arcades: he chose for this purpose the form of a Greek cross. Twenty years after its dedication, in 558, the dome was shattered by an earthquake. Another Isidorus, nephew of the former, restored it, but raised it twenty feet higher than before, giving it an elliptical instead of a spherical form. The curvature of the dome is so slight, that the depth is equal to only one sixth of the diameter, which is 115 feet; the crescent, which has supplanted the cross on the centre, however, is 180 feet from the ground. This flattened form of the dome has a fine effect; and if the architect attempted to imitate the arch of the heavens, Dalaway pronounces the attempt more happily accomplished in the mosque of St. Sophia than in St. Peter's at Rome. The ceiling of the dome over the twenty-four windows is ornamented with mosaic work, in the form of small cubes, of a vitreous substance, which Vitruvius calls *smaltum.* Besides containing four colossal figures, which represent seraphim, the ceiling is gilt all over, but defaced by time. The arrangement of the capitals is not conformable to rule ; they belong to no particular style, and have no entablature. With the principal dome are connected two half domes and six smaller ones, which add to the general effect. The form of the building is a Greek cross, inscribed in a quadrangle ; but the interior area from east to west forms an ellipse. The mass of the edifice is of brick, but it is overlaid with marble : the floor is of mosaic work, composed of porphyry and verd antique. The great pillars, which support the dome, consist of square blocks of stone, bound with hoops of iron. The gallery round about is formed by sixty-seven columns, eight of which are porphyry (from Aurelian's temple of the sun, at Rome). Eight others, of green jasper, were taken from the temple of Diana, at Ephesus. The vestibule has nine bronze doors, ornamented with basso-relievos. The interior of the mosque is 243 feet in width, from north to south, and 269 in length, from east to west. The exterior of St. Sophia has many defects and incongruous additions ; among others, four minarets, made since it became the chief mosque of the Turks (1453), have given it the appearance of an irregular mass.—See Gibbon's *Decline and Fall of the Roman Empire* (ch. 40 and 68). Grélot, *Voyage de Constantinople* (with engravings) ; Banduris, *Imper. Orient.* (Paris, 1711, 2 vols., folio) ; and Mouradgea d'Ohsson's *Tableau Général de l'Empire Ottoman* contain representations of it.

Sophism ; a fallacy in reasoning. (See *Sophists.*) Sophisms are usually divided by logicians into those in the words (*in dictione*), and those in the matter (*extra dictionem*). Whately divides them into those in which the conclusion does not follow from the premises, and in which the reasoning is, therefore, false, or logical fallacies ; and those in which the conclusion does follow from the premises, or material fallacies. For the various kinds of sophisms—*petitio principii*, *ignoratio elenchi*, paralogism, &c.—we must refer the reader to treatises on logic.

Sophists. This name of a peculiar class of teachers of eloquence, philosophy and politics, which flourished in Greece in the fifth century before the Christian era, signifies properly wise men (σοφος, wise), and was assumed by them out of learned pride. But as the later sophists strangely perverted the science which they taught, made themselves ridiculous by their arrogance, and drew upon themselves the hatred and contempt of reasonable men, by the pernicious and corrupt principles which they advocated with the utmost shamelessness, the title became a term of reproach, and was applied to men who seek to confound the understanding by vain subtleties and false axioms, to shake the force of the pure precepts of religion and morals. We find the names of a considerable number of sophists, mentioned in Grecian history, differing not less in the kind and degree of their knowledge than in the places of their birth. The most celebrated are Gorgias of Leontium, in Sicily, Protagoras of Abdera, Hippias of Elis, Prodicus of Cos, Thrasymachus of Chalcedon, in Asia Minor. All these were contemporary with Pericles and Socrates, and resembled each other in being teachers of natural philosophy, geometry and arithmetic, astronomy, music, theology, morals, logic and eloquence. This variety of subjects, which they taught among a people of the highest refinement, proves that they had cultivated their powers to a certain degree ; and, in fact, they rendered important services to learning, as they were the first cultivators of rhetoric as well as of grammar and morals. They taught all these sciences in attractive language, both orally and in writing, and were every where received with admiration. Besides, they often distinguished themselves in the service of their country. At least, it is certain that Gorgias, Prodicus and Hippias were employed in difficult negotiations. But brilliant as the sophists appear when viewed as men acquainted with all the learning of their age, and successfully extending its limits, it is not to be denied, that, when viewed on the dark side, they are deserving of abhorrence. The unblushing effrontery with which they set themselves up for the sole possessors of all wisdom, human and divine, shows them to have been impostors or conceited pretenders. In the next place, they abused knowledge to gratify the basest of passions—avarice ; and, finally, they preached irreligion and immorality, and attacked whatever was held dear and sacred by the people They denied the existence of the gods, attributed every thing to chance, and all religious ideas to the invention of some artful individual, who, after men had long dwelt in the woods like wild beasts, inspired his barbarous brethren, by the fiction of avenging gods, with fear, and compelled them to submit to a better state of things. They maintained that the right of the strongest was the only law of nature, and that all actions were indifferent—neither good nor bad. This distinction was first made by positive laws; and hence different nations form different estimates of the morality or immorality of the same actions. It is folly, they asserted, to point out what is good or just; for such a course of conduct would be connected with so many disadvantages that no man of common sense would adopt it. Proceeding on these principles, they declared every species of fraud, robbery and violence, innocent. They maintained that moderation and self-denial were marks of a weak mind, and that man's true happiness consists in the gratification of all his desires. Such were the infamous doctrines of the Sophists; and they appear still more hateful, when we remember that they were adopted merely for the purpose of attracting followers, and satisfying their own love of gain. For the same men, who so shamelessly preached up vice, were equally eloquent in praise of virtue, when they were afraid of offending their hearers or losing their wealthy disciples. If money was to be got by sound precepts of morality, they made the most florid speeches in praise of virtue. An example of this is the beautiful story of Prodicus, called the Choice of Hercules, one of the most elegant and ingenious fictions of antiquity. It is preserved by Xenophon, in his Memorabilia of Socrates (book ii, chap. 1). From the Sophists, likewise, proceeded the pernicious art of defending the most contradictory opinions, and of making the most evident truths appear uncertain, and the most extravagant absurdities probable. They effected this by false reasonings and captious questions, by which they confused their opponents. This art was the more dangerous in the hands of these corrupters of learning, as it enabled them to pass themselves off on inexperienced young men as possessors of universal knowledge, and to persuade them that they knew all the secrets of heaven and earth. Many of their arguments and conclusions were extremely absurd; but at first sight they surprised and astonished the hearer. Thus Gorgias, in a treatise on nature, proved, 1. that there is nothing real; 2. if there were any thing real, it could not be known; and, 3. if it were capable of being known, it could not be communicated by words. Prodicus of Cos proved, in a discourse cited by Æschines, that life is not a desirable gift, and attempted to remove the fear of death by declaring death a nonentity; it does not concern the living, for they have nothing to do with it; nor the dead, because they are no more. By similar sophistry, Protagoras destroyed the distinction between truth and falsehood. He maintained, that man is the measure of all things, and that nothing really exists but what he conceives, and in the way in which he conceives it; and as every assertion may be met by another, it is folly to dispute, and refutation is absolutely impossible. These notions relate to important subjects; but among the host of disciples, who followed the Sophists, there was a multitude who endeavored to make themselves conspicuous by the most absurd and ridiculous assertions. Plato has drawn one of these characters in his Dialogue of Euthydemus, which, in the persons of Euthydemus and Dionysodorus, describes the whole tribe, and holds them up to contempt. A single example will suffice. Dionysodorus says, "Tell me, Ctesippus, have you a bitch?" *C.* "Yes, and a very bad one too." *D.* "Has she young?" *C.* "Yes; just like herself." *D.* "Is not a dog their father?" *C.* "Yes; I saw them couple myself." *D.* "Is he not your dog?" *C.* "Certainly." *D.* "Then he is your father! So your father is a dog, and the puppies are your brothers!" On such miserable verbal quibbles did these learned disputants lay claim to the title of profound and subtle inquirers. But however little intrinsic value their teachings had, they served to set the mind at work; and we cannot help regretting the total loss of their writings, as we can now only judge of their tenets and practice from the accounts of others. These accounts, however, are so full and consistent that we should probably find no cause for changing our opinions, if we had their own works. The most flourishing period of the Sophists was from the Persian war, 490 B. C., to the death of Socrates, ninety years later. A rapid glance at the causes of the rise and success of such a class of men in Greece, is necessary. It is, in fact, however, not more wonderful than that a Socrates should flourish there: the versatile genius of the Greeks exerted itself in every form imaginable. Besides, the state of scientific and religious knowledge among the Greeks, at that time, will sufficiently account for the appearance of the Sophists. Learning was in its infancy; science was but just beginning to flourish; morals and theology had never yet been made the subject of deep and critical examination. These great services were first performed by the Socratic school; and it is not strange that selfish and superficial men erred so egregiously respecting those lofty subjects, particularly where the Eleatic school denied the reality of experience and the evidence of the senses, and perverted logic into dialectics. Considering also the democratical constitution of the states of Greece, which allowed unlimited freedom of investigation, it will appear not less natural for Sophists to have sprung up among the Greeks, than impossible for them to have arisen among the Hebrews or Romans.

Sophocles. This immortal poet, who carried the Greek drama to perfection, was probably about twenty-five years younger than Æschylus, and fifteen years older than Euripides, whom, however, he survived. They both died in the third year of the 93d Olympiad. The second year of the 71st Olympiad (B. C. 495) is assigned as the period of his birth. He was descended from a rich and noble family in Athens (or rather in Colonos, a village belonging to Athens). The advantages of a fine person (though nature had denied him a good voice) and his brilliant genius contributed to open a splendid career before him. Though the fame of Sophocles, as a poet, has eclipsed his reputation as a statesman, yet he is mentioned in the history of Athens as an archon, with Pericles and Thucydides, in the war against Samos; and his name is recorded among the priests of the city. His death, which happened in his ninety-fifth year, is so enveloped in obscurity, that, by some, he is said to have expired from excessive joy, in consequence of the unexpected success of one of his dramas at the Olympic games; and by others, to have closed his life during the recitation of his *Antigone*, then just completed. In his eightieth year, an ungrateful son charged him before a judicial tribunal with being incompetent, from age, to manage his domestic affairs; but, on his reading to the judges his Œdipus at Colonos, which he had just written, the complaint was dismissed, and he was carried to his house in triumph. On his tomb was erected a marble statue of Bacchus, with the tragic mask of Antigone in his hand. Sophocles began his career as a lyric poet; but, at the age of twenty, he devoted himself to the drama, and became the rival of Æschylus, whom he surpassed in the popular favor. The first victory which he gained over his predecessor was brilliant: the first prize was awarded to him nineteen times; the second still oftener, but never the third. His reputation soon spread to foreign countries, and several princes invited him to their courts. But he remained faithful to his country. The Greek drama is seen in its perfection in his productions. Of his numerous plays, which some have estimated at 130, only seven have come down to us; but these are all complete and masterly performances: 1. the Ajax; 2. Electra; 3. Antigone; 4. King Œdipus; 5. Œdipus at Colonos; 6. the Trachinians; 7. Philoctetes. We will give a short sketch of their contents, remarking, by the way, that we can distinguish no trilogies and tetralogies, as in Æschylus; and that, according to the Scholiasts, he introduced the practice of contending for the prize with a single piece; so that the distribution of the tragic part into trilogies (three parts or distinct pieces), to which a satirical piece was often appended (the whole being styled a *tetralogy*), almost wholly went out of use. Sophocles also first introduced a third actor, and limited the lyrical element or chorus, which Æschylus frequently made the chief part of the tragedy. In the Ajax, we see that hero, wounded in his honor by Ulysses, in the contest for the armor of Achilles, seized with frenzy: on recovering from which, as if blinded by the dreadful discovery, he destroyed his own life. The Electra belongs to the tragic scenes of the family of Pelops. It contains the murder of Clytemnestra (who, with her lover, Ægisthus, had assassinated her husband Agamemnon) by the hand of her son Orestes, under the direction of his sister Electra. By the art of the poet, Electra, who would naturally appear as a subordinate character, is made the heroine of the action. In Antigone, we see the highest triumph of female tenderness. Antigone, the wretched daughter of the wretched Œdipus, and guilty of no crime but that of attaching her own fate to that of her father, is the only being in Thebes who does not submit to Creon, the new sovereign. Her heroism is of the highest and most feminine character. Her brother Polynices, who was slain before Thebes, in a single combat with his brother Eteocles, in which both fell, and whose burial had been prohibited by Creon, owed a grave to his sister. After performing this last office of affection with the tenderness of a woman, but an unshaken firmness, she goes her sad and solitary way to the cold, stony bed prepared for her. According to Solger, the point of the tragedy consists, not in the elevation of the heroine, but in the conflict of divine and human laws. The King Œdipus, and Œdipus at Colonos, are parts of one story; and the tragic points in the history of Œdipus are thus exhibited in a terrific double picture. These tragedies are founded on the principle that man cannot escape his destiny, and that the profoundest wisdom only draws the cords of fate more tightly, till that almighty Power is appeased by voluntary penance and humiliation. In the former, a dreadful mystery is suddenly revealed, while the wretched victim trembles to behold the unwelcome light. The unconscious patricide, and husband of his mother, as one veil after another falls away, hurries back to the darkness, which has been removed from around him, by tearing out his eyes, and flees into miserable exile. The counterpart of this moving picture is drawn in the Œdipus at Colonos, weighed down by guilt and age. The darker lines of the horrible event are now softened by time. His crime has been expiated by long sufferings. In the grove of the avenging goddesses, by whom the whole dreadful tissue had been woven, his wretched wanderings end. Œdipus finds at Colonos, near the walls of Athens, in the solitary abode of the Furies, rest and a grave. The Trachinians is founded on the history of Hercules; Dejanira, in the excess of her love, becomes the murderer of the hero who is taken, as it were, in the snares of fate itself, like Agamemnon, only that, in the latter case, the victim is more innocent than Hercules, and, in the former, the murderer is more guiltless than Clytemnestra. Philoctetes, the heir of the weapons of Hercules, languished for years on the desolate Lemnos, where he had been deserted by the ungrateful Greeks during a magic slumber, which, after every attack of pain, gave him some relief. But fate at length pities him, and compels his enemies to search for him, as it was decreed that, without the bow of Hercules, Troy could not be taken. This exposes him to new sufferings. Neoptolemus, the generous and worthy son of Achilles, is appointed to rob him of his quiver, and thus compel the defenceless Philoctetes to go against Troy But the frank and honest Neoptolemus is incapable of carrying on such a design; and Hercules now appears bringing reconciliation, promising health, and persuading Philoctetes to pardon the ingratitude of the Greeks, and to comply with their request. The distinguishing characteristic of the Greek drama is simplicity. Thence its precision and perfection of form; thence its little external ornament, the accuracy with which the characters are defined, the finish of the coloring, the keeping of the whole, and the perfection of the versification. The unities of time and place are strictly observed; the plot is seldom intricate, but is skilfully contrived, and the diction is lofty and pure. The beautiful rather than the strange and awful, as in Æschylus, than the tender, as in Euripides, is its predominant feature. (See *Drama*.) In all these qualities, Sophocles excelled, and was therefore the finest model of Grecian poetry. The characters of Sophocles are undoubtedly the most perfect, distinct and individual that can be drawn, and, at the same time, arrayed in all the charms of ideal representation. His choruses have always been celebrated as the finest productions of dramatic poetry. No tragic poet, in ancient or modern days, has written with so much elevation and purity of style. The versification of Sophocles stands alone in dignity and elegance, and his iambics are acknowledged to be the purest and most regular. Of the modern editions of his tragedies, the best are those of Brunck (Strasburg, 1786, 2 vols., 4to., and 4 vols., 8vo.; 1789, 3 vols.), and Erfurdt (a small edition, continued by Hermann, Leipsic, 1809—25, 7 vols., and a larger, 1802, 6 vols.). The tragedies have been translated into English by Francklin and Potter.—See Lessing's *Leben des Sophocles;* Jacob's *Character of Sophocles*, in the *Nachträge zu Solger*, 4th vol.; and Solger's *Nachlass* (1828).

Sophonisba. (See *Masinissa.*)

Soprano, in Italian (*discantus*, Latin *le dessus*, in French), in music, denotes the highest vocal part, which is only sung by boys, women and castrates (q. v.) hence the name of *sopranos*, or *sopranists*, applied to the last of the three. There is a great difference in the voices of these three descriptions of singers. That of boys has sometimes quite a peculiar and affecting charm. According to the compass of the tones, the descant is divided into a higher and lower *soprano;* second descant is equivalent to *alto;* but the tones of descant are sharper, lighter, finer. The compass of a common descant is from $\bar{c}$ to $\bar{\bar{c}}$, and is quite sufficient for a voice of the chorus. A high descant, necessary for the bravura song, can reach as high as $\bar{\bar{\bar{f}}}$ $\bar{\bar{\bar{g}}}$; the lower descant, also called *mezzo soprano*, reaches from $\underline{g}$ or a to $\bar{\bar{g}}$ or $\bar{\bar{a}}$. Seldom, however, will there be found a complete compass, with complete equality of the tones from g to $\bar{\bar{c}}$. Generally, the grace of the more important middle tones is lost by the violent exertion to produce the higher tones. To the soprano belongs the melody. It is also capable of variegated ornaments and runs, since the higher tones are by nature more appropriate to these. Since high tones depend on quick vibrations, high voices are able to speak and sing quicker than deep voices. For this reason, and in this view, the soprano is the chief or leading part, to which the composer must pay particular attention. Hence it is highly important for him to understand thoroughly the nature and capacity of the soprano voice, in order to know what it can perform with ease, and, without unfavorable exertion, what are the natural divisions of the voice, &c. The same knowledge is necessary for the singer. The violin clef is now almost universally used instead of the descant clef.

Sorb Apple; the fruit of the service tree. (See *Service Tree*.)

Sorbonne; originally a college for the education of secular clergymen at the university of Paris, so called after Robert of Sorbon, in Champagne, a theologian of Paris, who founded it during the reign of St. Louis, about 1250, and endowed it with an income which was subsequently much increased. This institution, the teachers in which were always doctors and professors of theology, acquired so much fame that its name was extended to the whole theological faculty of the university of Paris, which was called, till the end of the eighteenth century, *Sorbonne*. Its opinions and decrees had a decided influence upon the character of Catholicism in France. The kings seldom took any steps affecting religion or the church without having asked the opinion of the Sorbonne; and, even without the limits of France, its opinions were often esteemed more highly than those of other academies. Not less inimical to the Jesuits than to the reformation, the Sorbonne steadfastly maintained the liberties of the Gallican church (q. v.), opposed the bull *Unigenitus* (q. v.); and, in the Jansenistic disputes, though it could not be said to take part with the society of Port-Royal, yet was always opposed to the Jesuits. In later times, the Sorbonne devoted itself much more to the defence of the rights of the church than the perfection of its doctrines and practice. Its spirit often degenerated into pedantic obstinacy, and not unfrequently into blind zeal for the letter of ancient doctrine; so that it formed a striking contrast to the acute philosophers, *beaux esprits* and freethinkers of the eighteenth century; and its condemnation of the writings of Helvetius, Rousseau and Marmontel, subjected it to much derision. The Sorbonne, therefore, had long outlived its fame, when the revolution put an end to its existence. The candidates for the degree of doctor in the Sorbonne were subjected to a severe trial of their patience. They were obliged to defend their theses from six o'clock in the morning to six in the evening uninterruptedly, and were merely allowed a slight refreshment in their desk.

Sordino (*Ital.*); a small instrument of copper or silver, applied to the bridge of a violin, or violoncello, to render the sound fainter, by intercepting the vibrations of the body of the instrument.

Sorelle, or Sorel; a river of Canada, which flows from lake Champlain into the river St. Lawrence, forty-five miles below Montreal. It is sixty-nine miles long.

Sorites, in logic; a string of syllogisms in an abridged form, in which the predicate of the first proposition is made the subject of the next, and so on to any length, till finally the predicate of the last of the premises is predicated of the subject of the first. A sorites (from σωρος, a heap) has as many middle terms as there are intermediate propositions between the first and the last; and consequently it may be drawn out into as many syllogisms.

Sorrel. The true sorrel (*rumex acetosa*) has long been cultivated in Europe for its leaves, as spinage and salad. They have an acid and slightly astringent taste, are cooling, and possess antiscorbutic properties. They are often put in refreshing drinks, and administered in cases of fever, &c.; but their most general use is for culinary purposes. The stems are upright, a foot and a half or two feet high, provided with a few petiolate, oblong, arrow-shaped leaves on the inferior part of the stem, and lanceolate, sessile ones above. The flowers are reddish or whitish, and are disposed in branching, upright racemes.—The sheep's-sorrel (*R. acetosella*) is abundantly naturalized in the U. States, growing in barren, gravelly lands, and is often found at a considerable distance from habitations: it is less than the preceding, but resembles it in habit, as well as in its sensible properties. The leaves are hastate. All domestic cattle are fond of the species of sorrel.

Sorrel Tree (*andromeda arborea*). This tree sometimes attains the height of fifty feet, with a trunk twelve or fifteen inches in diameter. These dimensions are remarkable in a genus otherwise consisting entirely of shrubs. It inhabits, exclusively, the range of the Alleghanies from Virginia to Georgia. The leaves are four or five inches long; oval-accuminate, and finely toothed; downy in the spring, but becoming smooth as they attain their growth. The flowers are small, white, disposed in long spikes, which are united in groups, and render the tree highly ornamental. The corolla is monopetalous, ovate, and downy. The name has been applied on account of the acidity of the leaves. These last, in drying, become black, and are sometimes used for imparting this color to wool, when sumac cannot be procured. The wood is of a pale rose color, very soft, burns with difficulty, and is wholly rejected in the arts. This tree is well adapted for an ornamental plant, as it is capable of enduring a cold climate, and the flowers begin to show themselves when it is only five or six feet high. We have numerous species of this beautiful genus of shrubs in the U. States.

Soubise, Charles de Rohan, prince de, marshal of France, born in 1715, was, at the beginning of the seven years' war, perhaps the richest nobleman in France; and, without military talents, but merely as the favorite of Pompadour, received the command of a separate division, which, however, was subordinate to the main army under marshal d'Estrées—a circumstance which deeply wounded his pride. In the summer of 1757, at which time he was lieutenant-general, he therefore separated from the main army, and joined the imperial forces, with the purpose of delivering Saxony from the Prussians. Having reached Gotha, he allowed himself to be surprised by the Prussian general, who occupied the place intended for Soubise, at a feast in the ducal palace. Confiding in his superior numbers, Soubise next attempted to surround Frederic in his camp at Rossbach, but was suddenly attacked on the flank, and his troops were entirely routed. The loss of this battle, and the general ridicule which followed it, did not prevent his being again placed in command, in 1758, when he was more successful, by the aid of the duke of Broglio, who was associated with him. He received the marshal's staff in reward for his services. After the peace, he continued for some time in the cabinet, and died in 1787.

Soubrette; a name given, in the French theatre, to the ladies' waiting maids; hence it is used for a subaltern and intriguing female in general.

Soudan. (See *Nigritia.*)

Soul. What is the soul? The explanation of the soul is involved in this great difficulty, that the thinking, by which we arrive at our results concerning its nature, is an act of the soul itself; and can a single function show the nature of the power from which it proceeds? Impossible as this seems, the human mind has at all times drawn a picture of the soul, and ascribed properties to it which distinguish it from every thing divisible and transitory. Hence, with the exception of inquirers like Democritus and Epicurus, who considered every thing as composed of original atoms, or strove to explain every thing from the changes of physical organization, men have always attributed to the soul the qualities of simplicity, volition, immateriality and immortality. Plato proposed to himself the double question, What was the state of the soul before its union with the body? and what will it be after death? It was a noble conception of this philosopher, that the soul, before its temporal existence, was imbued with the pure ideas of truth, beauty and virtue (*Platonic præexistence*), which, though impaired in this world of sensible phenomena, still remain in a degree, and may be freed by effort from the influence of disturbing causes. As the ideas of truth, beauty and virtue are infinite, and each of them forms a characteristic of the human soul, and strives to elevate it above every thing finite and concrete, we may conclude that the soul itself must be infinite. But connected with the quality of infinity are those of immateriality, freedom and immortality. The original faculties of the soul afford further assurance of its elevated nature. Conscience, faith, the deep longing for higher good, seem inconsistent with a finite nature. The Stoics and Plato conceived the soul to partake both of a ma terial, or sensual, and an intellectual, or rational nature.

SOULT, Jean-de-Dieu, duke of Dalmatia, marshal and peer of France, was born in 1769, at St. Amand, entered early into the army as a private soldier, and became a subaltern in 1790. He was adjutant in the division of Lefebvre, on the Moselle, in the campaigns of 1794 and 1795, and was a warm partisan of the revolutionary measures of that epoch. He was appointed general of brigade in 1796, and was subsequently raised to the rank of general of division: as such he served with the army of Italy, and was intrusted with the military command of Turin. He afterwards made the campaign of 1799, with the army destined to combat the Austro-Russian forces, and was shut up, with Massena, in Genoa, where he was wounded and made prisoner in a sortie. The battle of Marengo gave him an opportunity of returning home. On the elevation of Bonaparte to the chief consulate, the proofs of courage and ability which Soult had shown, occasioned his being appointed to command a corps of observation in the kingdom of Naples. In 1803, he was named commandant of the corps at St. Omers, and afterwards marshal of France, on the establishment of the imperial dignity. In 1805, he commanded one of the divisions of the grand army destined to act in Austria. At the battle of Austerlitz, he commanded the centre of the army, and contributed, by a very vigorous attack, to the success of that day. He distinguished himself, also, at the battles of Jena and Eylau. On the peace of Tilsit, he was appointed to a command in Spain; and, on the 10th of November, 1808, he attacked the army of Estremadura, put the Spaniards to route, and seized on Burgos and Santander. He was charged to observe the movements of sir John Moore, at Salamanca; and he pursued the English to Corunna. Marshal Soult was afterwards sent into Portugal, where, at first, he obtained some success; but was compelled to make a precipitate retreat, with the loss of his artillery and baggage. Joseph Bonaparte having lost the battle of Talavera, marshal Soult marched, in conjunction with Ney and Mortier, to his succor; and on their approach lord Wellington retired into Portugal. At this time, he was appointed major-general of the French armies in Spain; and it was under his advice and direction that Joseph Bonaparte gained the battle of Ocaña, on the 19th of November, 1809. (See *Spain*, and *Wellington.*) He was next charged with the conquest of Andalusia, and, in consequence, forced the passages of the Sierra Morena, and marched on Seville, of which he took possession. After the battle of Salamanca, he evacuated Andalusia; and the French armies, with the exception of that of marshal Suchet, were concentrated at Burgos. Soult was now recalled, in order to be sent into Germany; he was, however, soon summoned back. The loss of the battle of Vittoria having exposed the frontiers of France, the marshal was sent to Bayonne to take the command of the remnant of the routed French corps. He speedily organized a formidable force, with which he twice endeavored to deliver Pampeluna; but the allies advanced into the French territory, and Soult was obliged to retire upon Tarbes, in order to cover Toulouse. At this time, he published a proclamation, in which he discovered great zeal in the cause of Napoleon. Arrived at Toulouse, a bloody battle ensued, which led to the surrender of that city to the allies. On the restoration of the Bourbons, the king confided to Soult the command of the thirteenth military division, in the government of Britanny. In December, 1814, he was made minister of war. On the landing of Napoleon, the suspicions of the court obliged him to retire from his post; but it was not till commanded by the emperor, that he presented himself at the Tuileries. He was then raised to the peerage, and appointed to high military command. He fought at Fleurus and Waterloo, and, on the entrance of the allies into the capital of France, retired with the army beyond the Loire, and was comprised in the ordonnance of the 24th of July. On his banishment, he published a memoir, with the view of refuting the charge of treason, brought against him for adhering to Napoleon on his return. In 1819, he was included in the amnesty, and his military distinctions were restored in 1821. Marshal Soult was not recalled to the chamber of peers until 1827, when he was one of seventy-six created by the ordinance of November 5. As this creation was declared null, after the revolution of 1830, he was again named peer by the new king; and, in November of that year, was created minister of war, which post he has continued to retain during several changes of ministry. Soult is distinguished for his energy, activity, and great military and political capacity Napoleon said of him. "Soult is an excellent minis ter of war, and an invaluable major-general."

SOUND. (See *Acoustics*, and *Ear*.)

SOUND (properly *Oresound*, or *Oeresound*); the strait between the Danish island of Zealand and the Swedish province of Schonen, which forms the usual passage from the North sea into the Baltic. The narrowest part, at Elsinore, is about 2½ miles wide, and is commanded by the Danish fortress of Cronburg on Zeeland. The crown of Denmark has, from time immemorial, commanded not only the passage through the sound, but also through the two other straits connecting the North sea and the Baltic, the Great and Little Belt, and imposes a toll upon all vessels passing in and out, which is paid at Elsinore. French, English, Dutch and Swedish vessels pay one per cent. on the value of their cargoes; those of other nations, and even Danish vessels, pay 1¼ per cent. The Dutch ships are only required to show their papers; other ships must submit to a search. The annual amount of this toll is about $600,000. The number of ships, up and down, in 1827, was 13,016; of which 5199 were English.

SOUNDING; the operation of trying the depth of the water, and the quality of the ground, by means of a plummet sunk from a ship to the bottom. Two plummets are used, one called the *hand lead*, weighing about eight or nine pounds; and the other, the *deep-sea lead*, weighing from twenty-five to thirty pounds: both are shaped like the frustum of a cone or pyramid. The former is used in shallow waters, and the latter at a great distance from the shore, particularly on approaching the land after a sea-voyage. The lines employed are called the *deep-sea lead* and the *hand-lead line*. The hand-lead line, which is generally twenty fathoms in length, is marked at every two or three fathoms, so that the depth of water may be ascertained either in the day or night. Sounding with the hand lead, called *heaving the lead* by seamen, is generally performed by a man who stands in the main-chains, to windward. Having the line all ready to run out without interruption, he holds it nearly at the distance of a fathom from the plummet, and having swung the latter backwards and forwards three or four times, in order to acquire the greater velocity, he swings it round his head, and thence as far forward as is necessary; so that, by the lead's sinking while the ship advances, the line may be almost perpendicular when it reaches the bottom. The deep-sea lead is marked with two knots at twenty fathoms, three at forty, four at fifty, and so on to the end. It is also marked with a single knot in the middle of each interval, as at twenty-five, thirty-five, forty-five fathoms, &c. To use this lead more effectually at sea, or in deep water on the sea-coast, it is usual previously to bring-to the ship, in order to retard her course; the lead is then thrown as far as possible from the ship on the line of her drift, so that, as it sinks, the ship drives more perpendicularly over it. —*In soundings* implies the being so near the land, that a deep-sea lead will attain the bottom, which is seldom practicable in the ocean.—*Soundings* is also a name given to the specimen of the ground: a piece of tallow, being stuck upon the base of the deep-sea lead, brings up distinguishing marks of the bottom, as sand, shells, ooze, &c., which adhere to it. The soundings, i. e. the depth of the water and the nature of the ground, are carefully marked in the log-book, as well to determine the distance of the place from the shore, as to correct the observations of former pilots.

SOUP; a kind of pottage, made of bread, broth, or the juice of flesh, with various other ingredients.—*Portable soup* is a kind of cake, formed of concentrated broth, which, being freed from all fat, and, by long boiling, having the most putrescent parts of the meat evaporated, is reduced to the consistence of glue, and will keep sound for many years. In long voyages, this has been found to be a most valuable article of food.

SOUR GUM. (See *Tupelo*.)

SOUTH, Robert, a celebrated divine of the church of England, the son of a London merchant, was born at Hackney, in 1633, and educated at Westminster school and Christ-church, Oxford. In 1654, he addressed a copy of Latin verses to Cromwell, on the conclusion of peace with the Dutch; and the following year produced a poem entitled *Musica Incantans*. In 1660, he was chosen public orator of the university of Oxford; and soon after was nominated domestic chaplain to lord Clarendon, then lord chancellor. In 1663, he became a prebendary of Westminster, was admitted DD., and obtained a living in Wales. On the disgrace of his patron, he was made chaplain to the duke of York. In 1670, he was installed canon of Christ-church; and, in 1676, he went to Poland, as chaplain to the English ambassador, Lawrence Hyde. On his return home in 1678, he was presented to the rectory of Islip, in Oxfordshire. In the latter part of the seventeenth century, doctor South commenced a controversy with doctor Sherlock, relative to the doctrine of the Trinity. Both disputants professed to be orthodox sons of the church, their difference relating to the mode of explaining the doctrine in question. Doctor South died in 1716. He possessed an abundant share of wit and humor, which he not unfrequently displayed in his most serious compositions. His Sermons, which have been much admired, were published in 11 vols., 8vo. He also wrote an account of his journey to Poland, and other works.

South America; the southern half of the new world, forms a triangle, extending from lat. 12° N. to 52° 30′, or, including the archipelago of Terra del Fuego, to 55° 58′ S., and from 35° to 80° W. lon. It is connected by the isthmus of Panama (q. v.) with North America. Its extreme length from the gulf of Maracaybo to the straits of Magellan is 4600 miles; its greatest breadth from cape St. Roque to cape Blanco, in lat. 4° S., 3500; superficial area, about 7,400,000 square miles. (See *America.*) The surface rises gradually from the shores of the Atlantic ocean to the summit of the great mountain chain, which extends along the western coast, no where more than 80 miles from the Pacific ocean. This chain, called the Andes or Cordilleras (see the articles), stretches north and south through South America from capes Froward and Pilares, on the straits of Magellan, to the isthmus of Panama, where it sinks somewhat. It is volcanic almost throughout; in many parts there are volcanoes in activity. The lofty valley of Quito (q. v.) is often desolated by earthquakes. On the Pichincha, Humboldt counted eighteen shocks in less than thirty minutes. To the south, towards the Rio de la Plata, are extensive plains covered with saltpetre and salt, in which the springs and rivers are also saline. From the gulf of Arica, on the western coast, to cape St. Roque, runs the mountain chain Chiquitos, separating the basins of the Amazons and of the Plata. At the foot of this ridge lie two immense plains, the pampas of the Plata (see *Pampas*), and the plains of the Amazons, the former covered with grass, the latter with wood. To the north is the detached chain of Guyana, in the western part of which, called the Mei, the Orinoco rises; the eastern part of the chain is called Tamucaraque. Still further north, on the coast of the Caribbean sea, is the chain of Caracas, or the sierra of Santa Martha, in which is the Silla, 8500 feet high. This chain bounds tne great basin of the Orinoco, 1,000,000 square miles in extent. To complete the view of the natural divisions of South America, it is necessary to distinguish the valleys of the three great rivers, which drain nearly the whole continent, and are striking features in its geography. The Orinoco, the Amazons and the Plata have been described in separate articles. Besides these, the principal rivers are San Francesco in Brazil, the Colorado in Buenos Ayres, and the Magdalena in Colombia, flowing north into the Caribbean sea. The vicinity of the Andes to the western coast renders the streams which flow into the Pacific, little more than mountain torrents. The lakes are neither so numerous nor extensive as those of North America. Maracaybo in the north, Titicaca in the west, and Patos in the south-east, are the most considerable. In the great plains, temporary lakes are formed during the rainy season, by the overflowing of the rivers, which have sometimes been marked on the maps. The elevated plains or plateaus of South America are inferior in extent to those of the northern division of the continent, not exceeding 100 miles in circuit; but they are higher (from 8500 to 9000 feet), and are separated by deeper valleys. The lowest plain, however, the Llanos, (q. v.), extends over a space of 250,000 square miles, from the mountains of Caracas to the forests of Guyana, and to the delta of the Orinoco. In some parts, it is covered with woods, standing under water; in others, it is destitute of trees and fountains, or bears a few scattered palms. In the dry season, the parched grass falls to powder, the ground cracks, and whirlwinds raise clouds of dust, which resemble the waterspouts of the ocean. Even the alligator and the boa lie immovable in the dried clay, till they are revived by the first rains. Then the plain is suddenly covered with a rich carpet of grass. The climate of South America is colder throughout than in other regions under the same latitude. Even under the line, the heat is not excessive, owing to the height of the surface and the narrowness of the continent in this part. Many of the summits in the torrid zone are covered with perpetual snow. Humboldt fixes the snow-line under the equator at 15,000 feet. (See *Snow-Line.*) On the cordilleras of Grenada and Peru, it rains almost the whole year; on their coasts, it never rains nor thunders at all. In other parts, the heat is tempered by the great marshy lowlands, or by frequent rains. In some of the countries on the Amazons, it rains during ten months of the year. Guyana is thus rendered extremely unhealthy. In Patagonia, the air is raw, the skies are rarely clear, and the coasts are covered with almost perpetual fogs, and subject to violent storms. In Terra del Fuego, the valleys on the northern side are in the vicinity of high, bare mountains, covered with snow in midsummer. The peculiarities of the soil and climate, of course, have an effect upon the natural productions. The wonders of the tropical vegetation are exhibited in the great work of Bonpland and Humboldt—*Nova Genera et Species Plantarum, quas in Peregrinatione ad Plagam æquinoctialem Orbis Novi collegerunt* (fol., Paris, 1816). The potato (*solanum tuberosum*) is a native of the Andes, and, according to Pavon (*Flora Peruviana*), grows wild around Lima, in Chile, and in other places. The natives cultivate it, and call it *papas*. There are fourteen species of the cinchona or quinquina known. (See *Bark, Peruvian.*) Great quantities of the bark are collected between lat. 2° and 6° south. Cacao, vanilla and maize are also native plants, and the soil yields a great number of medicinal plants and dye-stuffs, and resinous trees. Particularly remarkable are the aracatscha (q. v.), from the root of which a farinaceous substance of an agreeable flavor is obtained, and the wax palm, which grows to the height of 160—180 feet. In America alone there are 87 species of palms known, which are equally distinguished for their beauty and size, and for their various uses, furnishing wine, oil, wax, flour, sugar and salt. Of the *orchideæ*, the chief ornament of the tropical vegetation, 244 species are counted in America. Around the cataracts of Tequendama, formed near Santa Fé by the Bogotá, nature appears to have scattered various species of unknown plants and strange animals, as from her horn of plenty. The forests are so thickly filled with bushes, trees and plants, as to be impenetrable except in some places where the wild beasts have made a path to the water. Chile abounds in medicinal plants, frankincense, the cocoa-palms, &c. In the Brazilian forests there are more than eighty species of wood useful for carpentry or dyeing. In the low lands of the Orinoco, and on the coasts, the valuable guaiacum (q. v.) and caoutchouc (q. v.) exude from the trees. The plantations in Guyana yield all the productions of the West Indies without manure or ploughing. Cayenne produces spices, and Brazil, matte, or tea. In the animal kingdom, the lama, the guanaco and the vicugna, of the sheep kind, and the tapir and the peccary of the hog kind, are peculiar to the countries on the Andes. The American tiger, or jaguar (q. v.), and the puma (q. v.), are the principal beasts of prey. The alligator (q. v.), or cayman, attains to a length of fifteen feet and more. The birds are not numerous in the higher parts of the country, but of great variety of colors and size, from the colibri to the condor. The low lands abound in birds and fishes. The whale fishery on the coasts of Brazil is important, and the manati, or sea-cows, are numerous in the rivers of Guyana. The alco, or wild dog, and the tuyu, or American ostrich, which inhabits the pampas, the electric eel, and the penguin, are also found in this part of the continent. In the great grassy plains between the arms of the Plata and the Madeira, roam numberless herds of wild horses and cattle, sprung from those brought to the country by Europeans. In the Brazilian province of Rio Grande and on the Plata, the latter are so numerous that they are killed merely for their hides. In the high lands are found some of the most venomous and dangerous of the serpent tribe; for example, the rattlesnake, the enormous boa (q. v.), &c. Centipedes, scorpions, frogs (for instance, the rana pipa of the Orinoco) and lizards are also found. In Guyana, the air is filled with butterflies of the most various colors. The lantern flies light the traveller by night with their shining heads. The mineral kingdom abounds in the most precious productions. In Brazil, diamonds are found of the largest size and in the greatest number; but they are inferior to the Oriental diamonds. (See *Diamond*, and *Diamond District*.) In some parts of Brazil, there are gold mines; but the greatest quantity of gold is obtained from the sands of rivers. Other minerals, as iron, tin, lead, quicksilver, salt, &c., although abundant, are little sought after. Gold mines are found in Grenada and Peru; platina (q. v.) is found in the mines of Choco and Barbacoas; silver is plentiful only in the colder Peruvian provinces, and the silver mines of Potosi are less productive than formerly. (See *Mine*.) In Chile, there is scarcely a mountain without gold, or a river without golden sands. Copper and tin are exported. (See *South America, Geology of* in the Appendix, end of this volume.) South America, formerly almost entirely in the possession of two effete monarchies of Europe, is now, with the exception of

Guyana, entirely independent of European rulers. It is divided into the empire of Brazil, the republics of Colombia, Venezuela, Ecuador, Peru, Bolivia, Chile, Buenos Ayres, or the United Provinces of La Plata, and the Banda Oriental, or Uraguay; Guyana, Paraguay, or the dominions of Francia, and Patagonia, with the Terra del Fuego, in possession of the native tribes. The whole population is estimated at between 13 and 14,000,000. The history and geographical details of each of these divisions will be found under the separate heads. (See, also, *America, Columbus, Americus, Cabot, Pizarro,* &c., for the earlier history; *Bolivar, Francia, Pedro I, San Martin, Sucre, Santander, Paez,* &c., for more recent events; for the commerce of South America, see the article *Commerce of the World*, and the articles on the separate countries.) The population of South America is composed of whites, Indians and Negroes, and of various mixed races descended from two or all three of the pure varieties. The whites are mostly Creoles (q. v.), or native born descendants of Europeans, the number of the latter being very small. The native tribes are, in some parts of the country, still entirely independent, and, in others, have long been subdued, and converted to the Catholic religion. (See *Indians, American.*) The Negroes are Africans, or of African descent, and are not very numerous. Slavery has been abolished in the South American republics. Mestizoes (q. v.) form a large class of the population. Peace and order, which can only be secured by the stability of the governments and the intelligence of the people, are yet wanting to render the possession of liberty a blessing to these new states, and to heal the wounds which the bad policy of the parent states, civil wars, and domestic factions, have inflicted on that part of our continent.

South American Revolutions. (See the articles on the different countries of South America.)

South Carolina. (See *Carolina.*)

South Polar Islands. Cook sailed south as far as lat. 60° S. (See *Sandwich Land.*) In 1819, the Russian captain Bellinghausen advanced to 70°, and, several years later, captain Weddel reached the parallel of 74° 15′; and the whale and seal fishery is carried on in the Antarctic ocean from the U. States. Still the south pole has not been approached so nearly as the north pole, nor have these waters been carefully examined. It was for a long time supposed that there was a great southern continent; but later voyages render it probable that the Southern ocean does not contain any great masses of land. The islands which have been visited here are: New or South Georgia (lon. 37° W.; lat. 54° 30′ S.), inaccessible during a great part of the year on account of the ice; it was discovered by La Roche, in 1675: Sandwich Land, visited by captain Bellinghausen, in 1819; he found it to consist of small islands, surrounded with icebergs, and enveloped in fog: New South Shetland, discovered in 1819, by captain Williams (lat. 61°—63° S.; lon. 70°—81° W.); the captain explored the coast for 200 miles, went on shore, and found the island covered with snow, and uninhabited; the coast abounded with whales and seals: Alexander and Peter's island (lat. 69½° S.), discovered by Bellinghausen, in 1821; it is the most southern land yet discovered: the Austral or Southern Orkneys, discovered by captain Weddel, in 1822 (lat. 60° 45′ S.; lon. 50° W.), and described as a mass of naked rocks.—See Weddel's *Voyage towards the South Pole* (1825).

South Sea. (See *Pacific Ocean.*)

South Sea Islands. (See *Australia.*)

South Wales, New. (See *New South Wales.*

Southern Lights, or Aurora Australis. (See *Aurora Borealis.*)

Southcott, Johanna; a singular fanatic, whose extravagant pretensions attracted a numerous band of converts in London and its vicinity, said to have, at one period, amounted to upwards of a hundred thousand. She was born in the west of England, about the year 1750, of parents in very humble life, and, being carried away by a heated imagination, gave herself out as the woman spoken of in the book of Revelation. In this capacity, although in the highest degree illiterate, she scribbled much unintelligible nonsense, and, for a while, carried on a lucrative trade in the sale of seals, which were, under certain conditions, to secure the salvation of the purchasers. A disorder subsequently giving her the outward appearance of pregnancy, after she had passed her grand climacteric, she announced herself as the mother of the promised Shiloh, whose speedy advent she predicted. The faith of her followers, among whom were several clergymen of the established church, rose to enthusiasm. A cradle of the most expensive materials, and highly decorated, was prepared by her expectant votaries at a fashionable upholsterer's, and every preparation made for the reception of the miraculous babe that superstition and credulity could induce. About the close of the year 1814, however, the prophetess began to have her misgivings during some comparatively lucid intervals, in which she declared that, "if she was deceived, she had, at all events, been the sport of some spirit, either good or evil;" and, Dec. 27 in that year, death put an end to both her hopes and fears. With her followers, however, it was otherwise; and though for a time confounded by her decease, which they could scarcely believe to be real, her speedy resurrection was confidently anticipated. In this persuasion many lived and died; nor is her sect yet extinct; but, within a short period, several families of her disciples were living together in the neighborhood of Chatham, in Kent, remarkable for the length of their beards and the general singularity of their appearance. The body of Johanna underwent an anatomical investigation after her death, when the extraordinary appearance of her shape was accounted for upon medical principles; and her remains were conveyed for interment, under a fictitious name, to the burying-ground attached to the chapel in St. John's Wood.

Southern, Thomas, a dramatic poet, was born at Dublin, in 1660, and educated there at Trinity college. In 1678, he went to London, with the view of making the law his profession, and entered himself of the Middle Temple, but soon abandoned the study, and dedicated his time to the cultivation of his muse. His first dramatic effort was a tragedy, entitled the Persian Prince, or the Loyal Brother, founded on the story of Shah Thamas. It was first performed in 1682, and, besides raising the author's reputation, procured him the favor of the duke of York, to whom he had paid his court in it. On the accession of James to the throne, Southern went into the army, and rose to the command of a company, in which he served during Monmouth's rebellion. Another of his tragedies, the Spartan Dame, written in 1687, was acted in 1721. From this period, he continued to produce occasionally comedies as well as tragedies: in the former style of composition, however, he was far from being successful; but two of his tragedies yet keep possession of the stage. These are his Oronooko, founded, it is said, on a true story, which forms the ground-work of one of Mrs. Behn's novels; and Innocent Adultery, which, under its modern name, Isabella, or the Fatal Marriage, is one of the most pathetic dramas in the language. The latter part of his days was passed in ease and affluence. His death took place in 1746, when he had attained the advanced age of eighty-six. His works have gone through several editions.

Southey, Robert, poet laureate, was born at Bristol, in 1774, where his father was a wholesale linen draper. He received his education at Westminster school, where he took part in a rebellion against the master. In 1792, he became a student at Baliol college, Oxford, being designed for the ministry; but his Unitarian principles and the French revolution inspired him with other thoughts. Mr. Southey had imbibed republican principles with such zeal that he and his friends (Lovell and Coleridge) formed a plan of settling on the Susquehanna river, and establishing a community (pantisocracy), in which all things should be in common. They had not, however, the money to put their plan in execution. In 1795, Mr. Southey first came forward as an author, by publishing, in conjunction with his friend Mr. Lovell, a volume of poems; and about the same time produced his republican drama of Wat Tyler, in which he advocated the principles of liberty and equality with a fervor which exceeded that of any writer of his time. In the same year, he married Miss Fricker (see *Coleridge*), and accompanied to Portugal his uncle, who was chaplain of the English factory at Lisbon. On his return to England, he devoted himself to literature, and in 1797 gave to the world his epic poem of Joan of Arc, which was written in the short space of six weeks. The second edition was, however, almost entirely re-written. In 1798, he published his Letters from Spain and Portugal, the result of his observations in those countries. His next work was the Annual Anthology, a collection of original poetry by various authors, a volume of which was designed to make its appearance annually; but it expired in 1800, at the second volume. His own minor poems he collected in 1797 and 1799. In 1801, he obtained the appointment of secretary to Mr. Corry, chancellor of the exchequer of Ireland; but this appointment did not last. Mr. Southey, however, had a pension of £200 a year granted to him, as a reward for his services during the short time he was in office. He seems now to have been entirely converted from his republican principles, and, on his retiring from office, went to reside near Keswick, in Cumberland, with his wife and her two sisters, one of whom was then married to his friend Mr. Coleridge, and the other was the widow of his friend Mr. Lovell. From that time, he appears to have been almost wholly employed in writing for the booksellers, and has been a most fertile author. He has since produced Amadis de Gaul, from the Spanish version (4 vols. 12mo., 1803); the Works of Chatterton (3 vols.); Thalaba, the Destroyer (2 vols., 1803); Metrical Tales, and other Poems (1804); Madoc, a Poem (4to., 1805); Specimens of later English Poets, with Notes (3 vols., 1807); Palmerin of England, from the Portuguese (1807); Letters from England, written under the fictitious name of Espriella (3 vols., 1807); the Remains of Henry Kirk White, with his Life (2 vols., 1807), to which he has since added another volume; the Chronicle of the Cid, from the Spanish (4to., 1808); the History of Brazil (4to., 1810), completed in three volumes; Omniana (2 vols., 1812); the Curse of Kehama (2 vols., 1813); Life of Lord Nelson (2 vols., 1813); Carmen Triumphale (1814); Odes to the Prince Regent, the Emperor of Russia, and the King of France (4to., 1814); Roderic, the last of the Goths (2 vols., 1814); a Poet's Pilgrimage to Waterloo (1815); a reprint of the Byrth, Lyf and Actes of King Arthur, with an Introduction and Notes (2 vols., 4to., 1817); the Life of John Wesley (2 vols., 1820); the Vision of Judgment, a Poem (1821); Book of the Church (3d ed., 1825); a History of the War in Spain and Portugal (6 vols., 1828); Select Works of British Poets, from Chaucer to Johnson (1831); Colloquies on the Progress and Prospects of Society (1st and 2d series), &c. In the Quarterly Review, to which he has been one of the principal contributors, Mr. Southey has attacked the reformers with all the bitterness of apostasy. He has not only waged war against principles, but has assailed, with acrimony, his former associates in politics, and every friend of liberal principles. In his religious and political principles, Mr. Southey displays the most narrow and illiberal spirit, vehemently opposing every measure of reform in church and state. In his controversial writings, he assumes a fierce and acrimonious tone, and conveys his partial and prejudiced views with all the heat and blindness of a zealot. His prose works are remarkable for the purity and beauty of the style, and his poems are characterized by great splendor of diction, dignity of language and metre (not, however, always sustained), and a rich and brilliant imagination.

Southwark. (See *London.*)

Souza Botelho, Joseph Maria, baron de, a Portuguese nobleman, distinguished as a diplomatist and man of letters, born at Oporto, in 1758, studied at Coimbra, entered the army, and served from 1778 to 1791. He was successively Portuguese ambassador at Stockholm, Copenhagen and Paris, till 1805, and spent the rest of his days in literary retirement. His leisure was devoted to the preparation of an edition of the Lusiad of Camoens, with a memoir. This magnificent work, printed by Didot at Paris, in folio, with engravings by Gerard, appeared in 1817. In 1824, he published a translation, in his native language, of the *Lettres Portugaises,* with the French on the opposite pages, and prefatory observations. His death took place in 1825. After the death of his first wife, he married, at Paris, in 1802, the countess de Flahault, widow of the count de Flahault, guillotined in 1792. This lady is well known in the literary world as the authoress of *Emilie et Alphonse; Adèle de Sénanges; Charles et Marie;* and other popular works of fiction.

Sovereign, in politics; a word of various meanings. In the widest sense, it denotes that political person, or body of persons, from whom all legal power is considered to emanate. Thus, where the monarch is regarded as the original fountain of all legal power, he is called the sovereign: in an aristocracy, such as that of Venice was, the body of the nobles is the sovereign; and in a democratic republic, like ours, the people themselves, as the source of power, are the sovereign. The historical origin of sovereignty is viewed by some as of great importance. others think it of little moment. The inquiries of the first class have led them to diverse results. Some of them say that the power which the divine law confers on the father over his family, gradually gave rise to chief priests and monarchs. They acknowledge no true sovereignty but that vested in a monarch. Others derive sovereignty from the right of the strongest. The husband has a right, they say, to exercise authority over his wife, because he has the power to do so; and the authority of the monarch rests on the same foundation. Strangely enough, this very theory, which, in fact, justifies all kinds of revolutions, and is the principle whence spring the violences which continually convulse the despotisms of Asia (see the beginning of the article *Slavery*), has been preached of late, with great zeal, by many of the apostles of divine right and absolutism. (See *Haller, Louis von.*) Others, again, have traced the origin of sovereignty to the social compact, representing a number of men as uniting to form a state, and as delegating certain powers to certain individuals or bodies of men, either expressly or tacitly (in the latter case, the delegation being proved by the resumption of the delegated power at the pleasure of the majority). The advocates of this opinion rely upon the fact, that in many instances we find such contracts actually made in the case of civilized nations, as well as of tribes in their infancy, who easily remove a chief if he is disagreeable to the majority; and where no contract is found recorded, they say that the monarch's power rests on the consent of the people, because they have the power to remove him, if they choose; and we often find him, in fact, driven from his throne by a revolution of his subjects. The doctrine of divine right, they contend, is quite unnecessary to account for a people's submission to a particular man, because there are abundance of other causes to account for the fact of a people or an army supporting one man in authority rather than another.

Others, we have said, consider the historical origin of sovereignty of little importance in determining the true source of sovereign power. Its principles, they say, can be well settled without ascertaining this point, just as we can settle the true principles of language, music, architecture, the useful arts, &c., although we may be unable to trace out their origin. The great question is not, How did governments originate? but, What is the principle which lies at the basis of them all, and becomes more distinctly developed with the progress of political society? The principle which supports the organization of a tree remains the same whether it be raised from a seed or a cutting; and the inquirer would learn but little of its nature from determining to which of these its origin is to be referred. If we investigate the nature of man and of governments, we cannot but see that the fundamental principle of all the latter is the sovereignty resting in the collective body of the individuals comprising a political society, often disguised in various ways, sometimes to the benefit, sometimes to the disadvantage, of the people. This theory has rapidly gained ground of late, and, in fact, was, to a great degree, always acted upon in Europe until the last century, when the monarchs of the continent strove to establish systematic despotisms. Never would so much have been said about the sovereignty of the people, had not the monarchs and the supporters of absolute governments started such absurd theories respecting the nature of sovereignty. What we have said refers immediately to the internal organization of states. The external sovereignty, i. e. the entire independence of one government upon others, and the acknowledgment of this independence by other governments, are intimately connected with its internal constitution. A sovereign state, therefore, may adopt whatever laws it pleases for the regulation of its domestic concerns, and, as to its external relations, is not bound to acknowledge any superior. It may, therefore, appeal to arms or to arbitration if differences arise between it and another state. The princes of the German empire (while that empire existed) were called *états mi-souverains*, because they stood, in certain respects, under the emperor, and were not entirely free in their foreign relations. The states forming the confederacy of the U. States, call themselves sovereign; but they are not so in the sense in which this word has always been taken, because they have given up to the general government many of the rights of sovereignty; i. e. such as can be exercised only by the supreme power of the state, or in the name of the whole state. The rights of sovereignty embrace the power of making laws, and of providing for the administration of justice, even by capital punishments; the power of making war and peace, and of conducting the foreign relations of the country; of raising and supporting armies, levying taxes, of coining money, &c. The various states of the Union have ceded the following powers to congress—the power to declare war, maintain armies and navies, and make peace; to regulate all foreign relations; to raise taxes; to coin money, and provide for matters connected with it; jurisdiction in certain cases (see *Courts*) and the power of legislation necessary for carrying into execution the delegated powers. (See also *Constitution.*)—*Sovereign* also means, in a narrower sense, the monarch, even if he is acknowledged to share his power with other branches, as in England, where the king by no means unites in himself the whole sovereign power. (See *Political Institutions*, *Estates*, and *Legitimacy.*)

SOVEREIGN; an English coin. (See *Coins.*)

SOY; a dark-colored sauce, prepared

by the Chinese from the seeds of a sort of bean (*dolichos soja*). The plant has an upright and hairy stem, erect bunches of flowers, and pendulous, bristly pods, each containing about two seeds. The common story that soy is made from cockroaches or beetles, has probably originated from the form and color of these seeds. The process of preparing soy consists in boiling the seeds until they become soft, and mixing with them an equal weight of wheat or barley meal, coarsely ground. This mixture is fermented, and, a certain proportion of salt and water being added, the whole is allowed to stand for two or three months, care being taken to stir it daily: at the end of this time it is ready for use. The seeds are, besides, employed in China and Japan as food: they are made into a kind of jelly or curd, which is esteemed very nutritious, and is rendered palatable by seasoning of different kinds. In Japan, they are put into soups, and are the most common dish of the country, being frequently eaten three times a day. Soy is chiefly imported from China and Japan, and that from the latter country is the most highly esteemed. The quantity annually sold in England, at the East India company's sales, is from 800 to 2000 gallons.

Spa, or Spaa; a celebrated watering-place in the Belgian province of Liege, situated in a romantic valley, surrounded by heights covered with woods, about seven leagues from Aix-la-Chapelle; population, 3100. Spa has been long famous for its medicinal springs, which are mentioned by Pliny, and are six or seven in number. The principal ones are Pouhon, Geronstère, Sauvenière, and Tonnelet. The waters are all chalybeate, and those of Pouhon, being the most strongly impregnated, are bottled for exportation. (See *Mineral Waters*.) Their effect is diuretic and exhilarating; useful in cases of relaxation, obstructions of the liver, &c. They are visited in the warm season, lasting about four months. The company is composed, in a great measure, of men of rank from Germany, France, Russia, Netherlands, and England. Spa is provided with various amusements, and has good accommodations. The new Vauxhall is one of the finest buildings of the kind on the continent. The town, on account of its being resorted to from various parts of Europe, has been allowed neutrality during the hottest wars. The promenades are the four o'clock walk (*la prairie de quatre heures*), and the seven o'clock walk (*la prairie de sept heures*), so called from the hours at which they are respectively visited. The inhabitants manufacture various little ornamental articles of varnished wood, as boxes, &c., called Spa work (*ouvrage de Spaa*).

Spagnoletto, a celebrated painter, whose true name was Joseph Ribera, or Ribeira, was born at Xativa, in Valencia, in 1588, but educated at Naples, and probably takes the name by which he is usually known from the country of his birth. He was at first a pupil of Caravaggio, but afterwards improved himself by the study of the works of Raphael and Correggio, at Rome and Parma. After his return to Naples, he was appointed court painter to the viceroy, the duke of Ossuña (q. v.), and overseer of all the royal works, in which post he conducted with great haughtiness towards the artists, and is said to have shown a particular jealousy of Domenichino. It has been said that Ribeira concealed himself, out of chagrin, occasioned by an amour of don John of Austria, natural son of Philip IV, with one of his daughters, and that nothing more was heard of him; but, according to Bermudez, he died, in good circumstances, at Naples, in 1656. Ribeira excelled in the representation of terrible scenes, such, for example, as the flaying of St. Bartholomew. He executed such subjects with a minute accuracy that excites horror, and was very skilful in delineating the separate parts of the body—hair, wrinkles, skin, &c. There are works of his in Naples, Paris, Vienna and Dresden.

Spagnuolo. (See *Crespi*.)

Spahis, or Sipahis; a part of the Turkish cavalry, which is said to have been organized by Amurath I, the founder of the janizaries. (See *Janizaries*.) Their number is estimated at 20,000 men. They are paid by the sultan. The lowest rate of pay is twelve aspers a day; but those who have performed especial services, or have the advantage of favor, receive higher pay. When the sultan takes the field in person, each spahi receives a present of money; and the janizaries enjoyed the same privilege. The spahis are composed of two classes: the *spahaoglari*, who have red, and the *silhatari*, who have yellow banners. The latter, who pretend to have been instituted by Ali, the pupil of Mohammed, were formerly the most important; but the former have now become superior. The usual arms of the spahis are a sabre, a lance, a jereed (a dart about two feet long, which they hurl with great strength and skill), and a second sabre, or rather broad sword, attached to the saddle. Some of them have bows and arrows, and also pistols and carbines; but they make little use of fire-arms. In war, the spahis form a tumultuous mob, without discipline or organization. Their first charge is formidable; but if they are unable to make an impression on the enemy's line after three attempts, they flee in confusion.

SPAIN (*España*). The physical features of the Spanish peninsula have exercised a most important influence on the character and history of its inhabitants. The whole surface of the peninsula comprises 225,600 square miles, of which 187,110 belong to Spain, and the rest to Portugal and the republic of Andorra (110 square miles). It is separated from France and the rest of Europe by the Pyrenean chain of mountains, and is surrounded by three seas, the Mediterranean, the Atlantic, and the bay of Biscay. Spain lies between lat. 36° and 43° 47′ N., and between lon. 9° 13′ W. and 3° 15′ E., and is the sixth in extent of territory among the European powers. The bay of Biscay gives great facilities for northern commerce; the gulfs of Alicant and Rosas offer secure harbors and roads to the merchants of Italy, the Levant, and Northern Africa, whilst the bays of Corunna and Cadiz open to her mariners the path to the Indies. One hundred passages lead over the Pyrenees to France; but only three of these are passable for carriages. (See *Pyrenees.*) From this frontier ridge rise the Cantabrian mountains, which traverse Asturia and Galicia, and terminate at cape Finisterre. To the south-east extends the Sierra d'Occa, five ridges of which, running nearly east and west, separate the basins of the Minho, Douro, Tagus, Guadiana and Guadalquivir; and two others, to the south-west, form the southern point of Spain, the island Tarifa. The valleys of the Xucar and the Ebro have a southerly direction. These sierras, among which the Somo Sierra, the Guadarrama, the Sierra Morena, the Alpuxarras, the Sierra Nevada, and the Sierra de Ronda, are the principal, surround the plains of Castile and La Mancha (the highest of such extent in Europe) with strong bulwarks, and even constitute distinct moral divisions of the inhabitants. The whole country thus appears to be formed of several great intrenched camps, and is admirably adapted for a war of posts, and particularly for guerilla warfare. Although Spain contains 150 considerable streams, very few of which, however, are navigable, there is a deficiency of water. Except the Albufera, in Valencia, there is no lake of much extent; and there are no marshes except in the valley of the Guadiana. The marshy islands in the Guadalquivir have been drained and planted since 1819. The dry and pure mountain air renders the inhabitants vigorous and healthy: the sea breezes have the same effect upon the coasts; but in the southern parts the scorching solano, from the shores of Africa, is felt during some seasons. Snow lies upon the summits of some of the mountains till July; and the capital is situated in a region fifteen times more elevated than the site of Paris. The fertile soil, wherever it is well watered, produces abundance of plants with little cultivation. The finest wines are exported in great quantities (Alicant, Sherry, Malaga), and other kinds are consumed at home. Since the expulsion of the Moors, agriculture has been in a low state, in spite of the patriotic exertions of numerous societies; hardly two thirds of the productive soil is under cultivation. Wheat, in Valencia, yields from twenty to forty fold. The Andalusian wheat commands a higher price in the Spanish market than the northern. Among the principal productions are olives, saffron, anise, cumin, cork, esparto or Spanish broom, soda, &c. In the warmer parts of the country, the sugar-cane and the banana thrive; and even the heaths, or *landas*, are covered with fragrant herbs and shrubs. But neither the wood (except in the maritime districts), which is sold by weight in Madrid, nor the corn (with the exception of barley), is produced in sufficient quantity to supply the wants of the inhabitants. The breeding of Merinos is profitable for the *mesta* (a society composed of owners of the flocks), but is injurious to agriculture. The whole number of migrating sheep is about ten millions; that of the stationary flocks, about eight millions. Valencia produces much silk: Andalusia breeds excellent horses; but the Andalusian studs have lost their importance. The mules are also of excellent quality. The gold mines of Spain have long ceased to be worked: but iron, copper, tin and lead are obtained. Silver mines are worked on the Sierra Morena, and the quicksilver mines of Almaden, in La Mancha, are rich, but do not yield enough for the mining operations of America. Sea and mineral salt are abundant, and there are mineral springs at Salcedon and other places. The Spanish people are descended from

Iberian Celts, mixed with Carthaginian and Roman colonists, with a strong infusion, at later periods, of Teutonic (Gothic) and Moorish blood. The population of Spain was estimated by Minaño, in 1826, at about 13,900,000; and that of the Spanish colonies at 4,088,000, making the total population of the monarchy 17,988,000. The kingdom is politically divided into fourteen principal parts, each of which has its separate authorities and administration, and several of which are subdivided into smaller provinces, forming, in all, forty-one provinces. The division into fifty-one provinces by the cortes, in 1822, was abolished on the restoration of absolute power. The general divisions are as follows: 1. the kingdom of Navarre; 2. the Vascongades, or Biscay; 3. the principality of the Asturias; 4. the kingdom of Galicia; 5. the kingdom of Arragon; 6. the principality of Catalonia; 7. the kingdom of Leon; 8. Old Castile; 9. Estremadura; 10. New Castile; 11. the kingdom of Valencia; 12. Andalusia (including the kingdoms of Cordova, Seville, and Grenada); 13. the kingdom of Murcia; 14. the Balearic isles. The Spaniard is, in general, temperate, persevering, reserved, honest and pious. The Spanish gravity is more observable in the higher than in the lower classes, or among women. The Spaniard of the lower order has more gayety, wit, vivacity, and, though frugal, is so indifferent to outward goods, that, were he less courteous and good-humored, he might pass for a practical philosopher of the school of Diogenes. His pride of birth, rank and faith appears, however, on every occasion; and he is suspicious, irritable and vindictive. This pride also manifests itself in the contempt with which the northern Spaniard, the inhabitant of Biscay or the Asturias, looks down upon the native of the south, whose darker complexion and smaller frame betray his Moorish blood. The nobles are distinguished into the *titulados*, grandees who have the right to cover themselves in presence of the king (in 1787, their number was 129), marquises, counts, and viscounts (in 1787, their number was 535); and the lower nobility, *cavalleros*, *escuderos*, and *hidalgos* (q. v.), the number of whom, in 1797, was 484,131. Music, singing and dancing are national amusements. The two former are simple, often monotonous, but full of feeling; the latter is extremely voluptuous. The *bolero* is popular on the stage: the *fandango* and *seguidilla* are favorite dances in the open air, and in the family, the latter is danced by four couple, to the music of the cithern, which the player accompanies with his voice. Athletic sports, as the *barra* (throwing an iron bar at a mark) and balloon (a game at ball) are common. The favorite popular amusement is the bull-fights (q. v.), which was prohibited in 1805, but has been revived by Ferdinand VII. The Spaniard, in general, is of the middle size, and well built, with an expressive countenance, brilliant eyes, white teeth and black hair. The men of the higher classes are much less robust than those of the lower. The Spanish women are distinguished for beauty of person and dignity of manner. Their complexion is neither white nor delicate, but healthy: they dress with taste, and move with ease and grace: they are unaffected, and have often, particularly among the lower classes, a ready vein of wit. In general, they are characterized by intelligence, deep feeling, fidelity and constancy; but they are almost entirely uneducated. Their courage and patriotism have often been displayed even in the field of battle. The strictness with which the female sex was formerly treated, and the formal stiffness which prevailed in society, have been much diminished; and the Oriental Moorish traits are gradually disappearing. The most important element in Spanish society is religion: the ecclesiastics form the most privileged order, and every family endeavors to find a place in the church for some of its members. Religion, however, consists merely in the outward observances of the church, in the practice of penances, and in the reverence of priests and monks. The apostle James is the tutelary saint of the kingdom; but he has lost reputation, since Charles III, with the estates, in 1760, took an oath of their belief in the immaculate conception of the virgin Mary, who was declared the patroness of the Spanish monarchy. The invocation of the virgin is, therefore, the chief act of divine service; and there are saints for all orders and degrees, whose festivals occupy a great portion of the time. The clergy, particularly the inquisition, has hitherto usurped the direction of education and literature; and the Spanish church has thus obtained possession of the supreme power, although it has had the prudence to conceal its exercise of it. The most enlightened ecclesiastical college is that of the chapter of San Isidoro, which has been exposed to persecution on a charge of Jansenism

The edict of March 2d, 1819, divided the prohibited books into two classes: 1. books which are forbidden even to those who have received a license from the Holy Office for reading prohibited books in general; and 2. books which contain revolutionary principles, are directed against the inquisition, the clergy, true religion, the king and monarchical power, or which ridicule the sacrament of marriage, or jealous men. The importation of Spanish books, printed out of the country, is punished by four years' confinement to the galleys. (See *Inquisition.*) The number of the clergy, before the wars with France, was 256,000; in 1826, 146,696, among whom were sixty-one archbishops and bishops, 61,327 monks, and 31,400 nuns. According to an estimate of a member of the cortes, the income of the clergy and convents in Spain, in 1808, from their real estate alone, was $51,000,000; and, according to the statement of Arguelles, minister of finance in the time of the cortes, the property of the church exceeded, by one third, the domains of the state. The inaction of the Spaniard arises less from indolence than from his frugality and fondness for religious festivals, the fertility of the soil, and the ease with which his few wants are supplied. The system of taxation—founded not upon the land, but upon production—and the privileges and monopolies of particular classes and societies, also contribute to discourage industry. The greatest activity prevails in the maritime towns and provinces, where industry is sure of its reward. The woollen manufactures are the most important; but they do not furnish more than one twentieth of the consumption. The best stuffs are made at Segovia and Guadalaxara. There are silk manufactures at Talavera, Madrid, Segovia, Toledo, Valencia, &c.; but less flourishing than in the fifteenth and sixteenth centuries. Iron and steel wares are exported from Biscay, blankets from Valencia, and fine handkerchiefs from Barcelona. The black Cordovan leather, from Cordova, is of excellent quality. The manufacture of hats at Valencia. Segovia, &c., and of sailcloth, is on the increase. The glass and mirror works at San Ildefonso produce good articles, but at a high price. The porcelain of Madrid is much inferior to that of other countries. The principal tobacco works are in Seville. The esparto, or Spanish broom, is a peculiar product of Spain, and is spun and woven into forty different articles. The commerce has undergone an entire change since the loss of the American colonies, from which the mother country received $35,000,000 yearly in gold and silver and $20,000,000 in cochineal, cacao, vanilla, sugar, tobacco, hides, cotton, vicugna wool, cinchona, dye-woods, ipecacuanha, sarsaparilla, &c. The commerce with the colonies was closed against all foreign nations, but, since they have become independent, is carried on by the North Americans, the English and Dutch. Internal commerce suffers from the heavy tolls, and the want of means of communication. Among the five canals, none of which are completed, the imperial canal, or the canal of Arragon, is the most important. The form of government is monarchical. The king, who bears the title of *Catholic majesty*, is absolute in Castile, Arragon, and in the islands; but the three northern provinces of Biscay, Guipuzcoa, and Alava, have maintained their privileges; and they consented to pay the extraordinary taxes of 1816, only on condition of the confirmation of these privileges, and the removal of the troops stationed among them. The Cortes forms an important element in Spanish history. (See *Cortes.*) The crown is hereditary, both in the male and female line. The crown-prince has the title of *prince of Asturias*; the other children of the king are called *infantes* and *infantas*. The king is grand master of the orders of the golden fleece, of St. Jago (St. James), of Calatrava, of Alcantara, of Montesa, and of Charles III. The order of Maria Louisa was founded in 1792, for sixty ladies of the high nobility. The reigning king, Ferdinand VII (q. v.), was born in 1784, and ascended the throne in 1814. His three first wives died without children; his fourth wife, Mary Christina, sister of Ferdinand, king of the Two Sicilies (born 1806, married 1829), has borne him a daughter, who is heiress apparent to the Spanish throne; to which don Carlos, his brother, born in 1788, is next heir. The predecessors of Ferdinand have been, 1. of the Austrian dynasty: Philip I, husband of Joanna of Castile; Charles I of Spain (V, as emperor of Germany), resigned the crown 1556; Philip II (died 1598); Philip III (1621); Philip IV (1665) Charles II (1700): 2. of the Anjou (Bourbon) dynasty; Philip V (abdicated in 1724, but his successor, Louis, dying the same year, he resumed the crown, and died 1746); Ferdinand VI (died 1759); Charles III (1798); Charles IV (resigned 1808). Of the Bonaparte dynasty, Joseph (expelled 1813). The colonial possessions of Spain are, in Asia, the Philippine islands and the Carolinas; in Africa, the *presidios* (towns on the coast) of Ceuta, &c., remnants of her former conquests in Northern Africa; the Canaries, and the three islands on the coast of Guinea, Annaboa, Fernando Po, and Prince's island: in America, Cuba and Porto Rico are the sole relics of the magnificent colonial empire of Spain. The administration is conducted partly by five ministers, who have a seat and voice in the council, and partly by the provincial councils, of which the most distinguished, the council of Castile, existed as early as 1246. Justice is administered in the towns and villages by *alcaldes*, of whom there are five classes. The *alcaldes mayores*, or superior *alcaldes*, are also called *corregidores*. An appeal lies from them to the royal courts (*audiencias*), of which there are twelve at Valladolid, Grenada, &c., and to each of which is attached a chamber of criminal jurisdiction. The laws, the judiciary, and the legal process, all stand in need of a thorough reform. The public revenue is about $20,000,000; the expenditure is much greater, and the public debt is stated at nearly $800,000,000. In 1817, the conscription was introduced; at the close of 1827, the forces consisted of 91,000 men, including the militia, and of 350,000 royal volunteers. The naval force is composed of ten ships of the line, sixteen frigates, and thirty other vessels, with 14,000 men.—See, for the geographical and statistical accounts of Spain, the works of Bourgoing, Townsend, Laborde, Bory de St. Vincent, and Miñano's *Diccionario de España y Portugal*. The fourth edition of Laborde's *Itinéraire de l'Espagne* (5 vols., and an atlas) appeared in 1827.—For descriptions of the life, manners and character of the Spaniards, see Southey's *Letters written in Spain and Portugal;* Doblado's (Blanco White) *Letters from Spain; A Year in Spain*, by a young American; and Inglis's *Year in Spain* (London, 1831, 2 vols., 8vo.).

The *ancient history* of Spain embraces the period previous to the great irruption of the northern tribes into the Roman empire. As early as the third century before the Christian era, the two rivals, Rome and Carthage, contended for the possession of this important peninsula. The determined spirit of the people is shown by the resistance of Saguntum to Hannibal (B. C. 219), of Xativa (A. D. 1707) and Barcelona (A. D. 1714) to Philip V, and of Saragossa (1808 and 1809) to Napoleon. More than one Roman army found its grave in Spain. The Lusitanian Viriathus, at the head of his countrymen, withstood the Roman power till he fell by assassination (B. C. 140). For fourteen years, the Romans attempted, without success, to subjugate the Numantines, till Scipio (B. C. 133) triumphed over the ashes of the city, whose inhabitants had destroyed themselves. Afterwards, this land, which is possessed of much natural strength, afforded refuge to several of the popular leaders of Rome, on their fall from power. Thus Sertorius, an adherent of Marius, lived in Lusitania (B. C. 72), and the sons of Pompey fought against Cæsar in Hispania Bætica, where Cneius fell. After a struggle of 200 years, when Agrippa, the general of Augustus, conquered the Cantabrians, Spain was first completely subjected to the Roman power. Augustus himself founded the colony of Cæsar Augusta (Saragossa) and Augusta Emerita (Merida). For 400 years, the Roman manners and language took root in the Spanish provinces, which, in Cæsar's time, had a population of 40,000,000. Merida supported a garrison of 90,000 men; Tarragona had 2,500,000 inhabitants. In the arts of war and peace, the peninsula rivalled Rome. Pomponius Mela, Seneca, Lucan, Trajan, and Theodosius the Great, were natives of Spain The Celtic language continued only in Cantabria, and is still understood in Biscay, as William von Humboldt's investigations have shown. See his *Attempts to ascertain the original Inhabitants of Spain by Means of the Basque Language* (Berlin, 1821).—The *Middle Ages* of Spain include the times of the Goths and Arabians from the irruption of the barbarians into the Roman empire to the fall of Grenada, the last Moorish kingdom in Spain (1492). At the commencement of the fifth century, the Vandals, Suevi and Alans spread themselves over the peninsula. About 419, the brave Wallia founded the kingdom of the Visigoths in Spain. The Vandals, from whom Andalusia received its name, could not withstand him, and withdrew into Africa in 428. From 467 to 484, the great Euric extended the kingdom of the Visigoths by the expulsion of the Romans, and gave them their first written laws. At length Leowigild, in 585, overthrew the kingdom of the Suevi, in Galicia. Under his successor, Reccared I, the introduction of the Catholic faith, in 586, gave the corrupt Latin language the predominance over the Gothic; and, after that time, the unity of the Spanish nation was maintained by the

Catholic religion and the political influence of the clergy. But, after 125 years, Alaric's family, from revenge at being passed by in the choice of a king, recalled the Arabians, who had passed over into Africa. King Roderic fell in the seven days' battle against Tarik, at Xeres de la Frontera, in Andalusia, in 711. After that, the greatest part of Spain became a province of the caliphs of Bagdad. Forty years later, in 756, Abdorrhaman I, the last of the Ommiades, made himself master of Spain, overthrowing the government of the Abassides, and establishing a separate caliphate at Cordova; which, however, after 1038, fell to pieces, the different governors becoming independent, and assuming the title of kings. Thus Arabian princes reigned at Saragossa, Toledo, Valencia and Seville. In these places, the Moorish language and customs were almost universal. Yet the Christians were allowed the free exercise of their religion. The Arabians likewise permitted their new subjects (called *Mozarabians*, that is, spurious Arabians) to retain their language, laws and magistrates. At this time, the Jews spread over Spain. Meanwhile, the Visigoths, under their hero Pelayo and his successors, maintained their freedom in the mountains of Asturia and Galicia. The Moorish governments being weakened by changes of dynasties, and by internal dissensions, the Christian kings wrested from the Arabians one portion of the country after another, till, after the great victory, which the united Christian princes obtained over the Almohades, in 1220, at Tolosa, in Sierra Morena, there remained to the Arabians only the kingdom of Grenada, which was likewise obliged to acknowledge the Castilian supremacy in 1246, and was finally conquered by Ferdinand and Isabella in 1491. During the period of Arabian power, agriculture, commerce, the arts and sciences, flourished in Spain. The population was considerable. In Tarragona, there were 80,000 families, or 350,000 inhabitants. The rich city of Grenada contained 70,000 houses, 250,000 inhabitants, and 50,000 men able to bear arms. The Ommiades had connexions with the Byzantine emperors. The universities and libraries at Cordova and other places were resorted to by Christians, as the seat of the Greco-Arabic literature and the Aristotelian philosophy. From these institutions, Europe received the knowledge of the present arithmetical characters, of gunpowder, and of paper made from rags. Among the Gothic Spaniards, the blending of the chivalrous and religious spirit gave occasion to the foundation of several military orders. The great Cid (q. v.), or don Rodrigo Diaz de Vivar el Campeador, the hero without an equal, has been celebrated since the end of the eleventh century as the hero of his age. The romantic elevation of national feeling, which found its support in the religious faith and national church, preserved the Christian Gothic states Navarre, Arragon and Asturia, from many internal and external dangers. The county of Castile, at first called *Burgos*, became, in 1028, a separate kingdom. Ferdinand I, by his marriage in 1035, united with it Leon and Asturia. For him the great Cid conquered a part of Portugal. The kingdom of Navarre has existed since the ninth century. It formed a part of the Spanish territory of Charlemagne, south of the Pyrenees, obtained by conquest from the Arabians, and extending as far as the Ebro. Here, in the county of Barcelona, now the principality of Catalonia, powerful vassals ruled, till one of them, Raymond V, became, by marriage, king of Arragon, in 1135. His descendants in the male line reigned there 258 years. Alphonso VI (died 1109), king of Leon, Castile and Galicia, together with Portugal, as far as Montego, conquered the Moorish kingdom of Toledo, or New Castile; but he gave up Portugal (q. v.) to his son-in-law Henry of Burgundy. Ferdinand III did more: he conquered Cordova, Murcia, Jaen, Seville, Cadiz, and subjected Grenada to a feudal dependence on him. He became, in 1252, the true founder of the kingdom of Castile, by establishing the rule of indivisibility and primogeniture in the succession. Still the whole was as yet but an imperfect confederation. The privileges granted to the Jews in Spain, in the middle ages, had an injurious influence on the government and the public welfare. They were placed nearly on a level with the nobles; they were appointed ministers of finance, farmers of the public revenues, and stewards to the great: thus they obtained possession of all the money in the country, and, by their excessive usury, at length excited a universal outcry against them; and, in 1492, they were banished for ever, to the number of 800,000, from Spain. The improvement of the country was much retarded by the defects in the public administration, particularly in regard to the taxes, by powerful vassals, bad kings, and family disputes, so that the third estate was not formed in Castile till 1325, 200 years later than that of Arragon, and with inferior privileges. Meanwhile, the Cortes, consisting of the estates of the kingdom, namely, the clergy, the high nobility, the orders of knights, and eighteen great cities, restricted the royal power, without, however, bringing about a state of legal order. But, in Arragon (a kingdom since 1035), of which Alphonso I, since the conquest of Saragossa, in 1115, had been in complete possession, the third estate was formed before the middle of the twelfth century, sooner than in any other European country, and a well-settled political order ensued. Disputes between the king and this estate, or of the members of this estate among themselves, were decided by a supreme judge, called *justitia.* (See Mariana, *Teoria de las Cortes*, Madrid, 1812.) From these circumstances, and the wisdom of the kings, the country flourished. Arragon comprehended, besides Catalonia and Cerdagne, already united to it, in 1135, the counties of Roussillon, Montpelier, the Baleares, or Majorca, from 1220 (where, however, from 1276 to 1344, a collateral line reigned), also Valencia, from 1238, Sicily from the Sicilian Vespers, in 1282, and Sardinia from 1326. But, by the provisions of James II, in 1319, the states of Arragon, Catalonia and Valencia only were indissolubly united, each with its own constitution. At length the marriage of prince Ferdinand of Arragon (see *Ferdinand V the Catholic*), with Isabella, heiress of Castile, in 1469, laid the foundation of the union of the crowns of Castile and Arragon. This followed on Ferdinand's accession to the throne in 1479.—See Murphy's splendid work upon the Arabian Antiquities of Spain (London, 1816); and the *Introduction to the History of the Mohammedan Empire in Spain;* and particularly Conde's *History of the Dominion of the Moors in Spain* (Spanish, Madrid, 1820), with the *History of the Visigoths*, by Joseph Aschbach (Frankfort on the Maine, 1827); and doctor E. A. Schmidt's *History of Arragon in the Middle Ages* (Leipsic, 1828; the two last in German).—With this union, with the entire subjugation of the Moors, and the discovery of America, a new period in the history of Spain begins. The young monarchy advanced immediately to the first place among the European governments; but, exhausted by political and spiritual oppression, it quickly declined in consequence, till the Spanish branch of the Hapsburg race became extinct in 1700. Spain now became a power of the second rank, under the kings of the house of Bourbon. These reigned without a cortes, and brought Spain into a close political connexion with France. At length they sunk before the power of Napoleon, and the revolt of Spanish America followed. The state of Spain since the restoration of the Bourbons will be treated in the sequel.—*From* 1479 *to* 1700. Spain had, when Ferdinand and Isabella founded the monarchy, a population of about 14,000,000, which, however, was much divided by difference of customs and laws. To unite the discordant parts into one powerful nation, was the great object which occupied for forty-three years Isabella, Ferdinand and cardinal Ximenes. (q. v.) By a severe administration of justice, and by the institution of the Hermandad (q. v.), order was established through the country. The royal power was particularly strengthened and extended by the introduction of the inquisition, and by the union with the crown of the office of grand master of the three great military orders of Castile. Grenada was conquered in 1491, after a ten years' war. Soon after began the cruel persecution of the Jews and Moors, so injurious to Spain. They were obliged to be baptized, or to leave the country. Till then toleration had prevailed in Spain. Princes and nobles at one time even fought for the Albigenses; and, in the thirteenth century the kings of Arragon braved the papal excommunication. But by this system of persecution the peace and prosperity of the country were deeply shaken. The discovery of America, in 1492, by Christopher Columbus, under the patronage of Isabella, withdrew much of the activity of the nation from the improvement of the mother country; and avarice, united with fanaticism, established in the West Indies an unwise colonial system. In general, the politics of Spain, under Ferdinand the Catholic, were characterized by cunning and desire of foreign aggrandizement, as appears from the acquisition of Naples, the league of Cambray, and the conquest of Navarre, south of the Pyrenees, though the warlike fame of the nation was maintained by one of the greatest commanders of his time, Gonsalvo Fernandez of Cordova, and by the expedition of the great Ximenes into the north of Africa. After Charles I (as emperor of Germany, Charles V, q. v.), son of the Infanta Joanna and Philip of Burgundy, had succeeded his father in the government of the Netherlands, his maternal grandfather (1516) in that of Spain, and his paternal grandfather in that of the Austrian dominions (1519); and after he had repressed, with the help of the nobles, insurrections in Valencia and Majorca, and particularly in Castile (1520), where the third estate demanded a freer constitution; and after he had annihilated the principal part of the liberties of the nation by the separation of the deliberative estates,—Spain became the first military and political power in Europe, during the four wars which Charles carried on with Francis I of France, and by which he obtained Milan. The victory of the Spaniards at Pavia (Feb. 24, 1525), which made Francis I the prisoner of Charles, in Madrid, till the peace of Madrid (Jan. 14, 1526), and the expedition of Charles into the north of Africa, extended the fame of the Spanish arms throughout Europe. The wealth which flowed in from Mexico, conquered by Cortez, in 1518, and from Peru and Chile, conquered by Pizarro and Almagro, in 1528, was not sufficient to supply the demands of the royal treasury; so that the revenues of the crown were exhausted, the taxes increased, and debts contracted. The thirty-five years' union of Germany with Spain promoted the intercourse between the two countries. But the strength of the powerful monarchy was exhausted by the forty-two years' tyranny of Philip II. (q. v.) Oppression and religious intolerance, war and insurrections, occasioned the loss of the Netherlands, and depopulated the rest of the monarchy; and the conquest of Portugal, which remained united with Spain from 1581 to 1640, could not prevent its decay. England and Holland triumphed over the naval force of Spain, and destroyed her commerce; and Philip died in 1598, a bankrupt. Under his weak successors, Philip III (died 1621), Philip IV (died 1665), and Charles II (died 1700), the abuses in the administration increased. An incurable wound was inflicted upon the country by the expulsion of 600,000 Moriscoes in 1609. On the whole, the persecutions of the Arabians cost Spain about 2,000,000 of souls, and the expulsion of the Jews about 800,000. The southern coasts, likewise, were depopulated by the continual incursions of the pirates of Northern Africa. Favorites, such as Lerma and the count Olivarez, wasted the resources of the kingdom. Olivarez (q. v.) wished to employ harsh measures; insurrections were excited; and Mazarin (q. v.) compelled Spain to acknowledge the superiority of France, in the peace of the Pyrenees (1659). By the peace of Aix-la-Chapelle, in 1668, by that of Nimeguen, in 1678, and by the *reunions* of Louis XIV, Spain lost many places in the Netherlands and Franche Comté. But after the death of Charles II (1700), the monarchy sunk entirely from its ancient elevation, in consequence of the wars respecting the Spanish succession; and the population, which, in 1688, amounted to about 11,000,000, had diminished, in the first fourteen years of the 18th century, to about 8,000,000.—*From* 1700 *to* 1808. Charles II, the last Spanish sovereign of the race of Hapsburg, in his second will, made Philip of Anjou, a grandson of his sister, the consort of Louis XIV, and second son of the dauphin, sole heir of his dominions, in order to prevent the division of the Spanish monarchy, which had been resolved on in a treaty between England, Holland and France. Louis XIV acknowledged his grandson king, according to the testament. The emperor Leopold I, of the race of Hapsburg, laid claim to the throne, whilst William III, king of England and stadtholder of Holland, was in favor of a division of the monarchy, for the sake of preserving the balance of power in Europe. The measures of Louis XIV at length brought on a war with England. Thus began the war of the Spanish succession (see *Eugene*, *Marlborough*, *Utrecht*, *Peace of*), in which the Bourbon, Philip V, after many changes of fortune, by the victories of Berwick and Vendome, maintained himself on the Spanish throne in opposition to Charles of Austria (afterwards the emperor Charles VI). But by the peace of Utrecht, in 1713, he was obliged to resign the Spanish dependencies in Europe—Naples, Sardinia, Parma, Milan and the Netherlands to Austria, and Sicily to Savoy. England likewise retained Gibraltar and Minorca. Under the Bourbons, the nation lost its last constitutional rights; for Arragon, Catalonia and Valencia were treated by Philip as conquered countries. The last diet held in Castile was in 1713, and in Saragossa in 1720. Biscay and Navarre alone retained some of their privileges. The ambition of cardinal Alberoni (q. v.), in 1717 et seq., involved Europe for a short time in confusion. Spain, in 1735, again obtained possession of the Two Sicilies, for the Infant Carlos, and, in 1748, of Parma, for the Infant Philip. Naples and Sicily were ceded to a Spanish Bourbon. Under the reign of Charles III, 1759—88, the Bourbon family compact of 1761 involved Spain, to its injury, in the war between the French and English. The expeditions against Algiers likewise miscarried; as did the siege of Gibraltar, in the war of 1779—83. Yet this did not disturb the course of the internal administration, to the improvement of which, men like Aranda, Campomanes, Olavides and Florida Blanca (q. v.) devoted themselves. They provided particularly for the advancement of agriculture, the useful arts, and commerce. The population consequently increased. According to the census of 1768, it amounted to 9,300,000, and in 1798, to 10,061,000 men. The power of the inquisition was restricted, and the secret opposition of the Jesuits annihilated at a blow, by the pragmatic sanction of April 2, 1767, which banished them from all the Spanish dominions, and confiscated their property. But the imagination of the nation was employed upon the mystery of the immaculate conception, and the sinless purity of the virgin Mary. The pope, at the desire of Charles III, declared the whole Spanish monarchy, together with the colonies, under the protecting influence of the immaculate conception. The king established some orders with the device of a female figure dressed in white and blue, in allusion to this doctrine; and every Spaniard, who wished to receive a degree from a university, or to belong to a corporation, and even mechanics, on joining the associations of their trades, were obliged to take an oath of their firm belief in the immaculate conception. The progress in improvement, even during the reign of Charles IV, 1788—1808, was obvious; so that Florida Blanca was able to quiet the wish of the people for the reassembling of the ancient cortes. But he was superseded, in 1792, by Godoy (q. v.), whose administration was as void of plan as it was injurious to the state, and greatly exasperated the nation; so that the fall of the most fortunate and proudest favorite of modern times, was immediately followed by that of the royal house. Spain, at first, entered with zeal into the war against the French republic (the voluntary contributions of the nation to the expenses of the war amounted to 73,000,000 francs); but the favorite, who wished to conduct the war from his palace, ruined all, and hastened to conclude the discreditable peace of Basle, by which Spain resigned half of St. Domingo; on which occasion Godoy received the title of "prince of peace." He then concluded with the republic, the leaders of which deluded him with the prospect of placing a Spanish prince on the throne of France, the important offensive and defensive alliance of St. Ildefonso, in 1796, and declared war against England; but being defeated at sea, Spain lost Trinidad, by the peace of Amiens, in 1802. In consequence of the entire interruption of the colonial trade, taxes and debts increased, whilst the credit of the nation sunk. The prince withdrew from the conduct of affairs, but his relation Cevallos (q. v.), after the banishment of the able Urquijo, became prime minister in 1800. The prince retained his influence, and rose to high dignities. He leaned to the politics of Napoleon, and commenced military operations, in 1801, against Portugal, which was obliged to cede Olivença to Spain, at the peace of Badajoz; whilst France took possession of Parma, and made its duke king of Etruria in 1801; in consequence of which, Spain ceded Louisiana to Napoleon, who, in 1803, sold it to the U States. Charles IV, in the war between England and France, in 1803, having purchased permission to remain neutral, by a monthly tribute of 1,000,000 piasters to Napoleon, the English seized the Spanish frigates, which were carrying the products of the American mines to Cadiz (October, 1804); and Spain, though suffering under great exhaustion, famine, and the yellow fever, was compelled to declare war against England. The victory of the English at Trafalgar, Oct. 21, 1805 (q. v.), destroyed its naval power; the bold Miranda (q. v.) excited the desire for independence in Spanish America, in 1806, and Napoleon overthrew the throne of the Bourbons in Naples.—See the works of Desormeau, *Chronological Abridgment of the History of Spain* (in French); and of W. Coxe, *Memoirs of the Kings of Spain of the House of Bourbon* (1700—1788, 2d edition, London, 1815).

III. *Spain from* 1808. The prince of peace (Oct. 3, 1806) called on the nation to arm against "the common enemy;" and Napoleon, therefore, sent a Spanish army, under Romana, to Denmark, and another, under O'Farill, to Tuscany. Oct. 27, 1807, he concluded a secret treaty at Fontainebleau, respecting the division of Portugal, mentioned in the article *Napoleon.* 28,000 French soldiers, maintained by Spain, marched over the Pyrenees, and were joined by 11,000 Spaniards. The family quarrels of the royal family favored the plans of the French ruler on Spain. The prince of Asturias (Ferdinand) had refused to marry the sister-in-law of the prince of peace; and, to secure himself against the vengeance of the offended favorite (see *Godoy*), he wrote, by the advice of Escoiquiz, his former teacher (Oct. 11, 1807), to Napoleon for protection, and requested the hand of one of his nieces. The emperor did not answer this letter till April 16, 1808, when the prince was on his way to Bayonne. At the time of his writing to Napoleon, the prince had addressed a letter to his father, exposing the mistakes and abuses of the administration, and requesting to be allowed some participation in the government. The queen was enraged, and the prince, Escoiquiz and the duke of Infantado were arrested. Charles IV, at the instigation of Godoy, now wrote to Napoleon, stating that the prince of Asturias had intended to dethrone him, and to deprive his mother of life, so that he ought to be excluded from the succession. The junta, however, which was convened for that purpose, unanimously acquitted the prince and the other prisoners; but Godoy induced Ferdinand to ask pardon of the king and queen; on which the king caused the letter to be published in the Gazette of Madrid, and issued a decree granting pardon to the prince on account of his repentance. The other prisoners were banished. Thus ended, in November, 1807, the process of the Escurial. In the mean while, French troops had entered Spain. Charles IV received them as allies; but, on a sudden, the court prepared to leave Aranjuez for Seville. It was rumored that the royal family intended to go to Mexico. A violent commotion now took place in Madrid, and multitudes flocked to Aranjuez. March 18, 1808, the people and the soldiers broke out into fury against the prince of peace, who was only saved by the promise of the prince of Asturias, that he should be brought to justice. In other parts of the country, also, the people showed their bitter hatred of this unworthy favorite. Charles IV, on the same day, took the command of the army and fleet, the prince of peace being dismissed. But on the 19th, he resigned the crown in favor of his son, of which he informed Napoleon, as he had done of the former step. Ferdinand VII, on March 24, made a public entry into Madrid, which had been occupied by Murat, grand-duke of Berg, and commander of the French troops, the day previous. Ferdinand informed Napoleon of his assumption of the royal power; but the emperor caused the whole family to be conveyed to Bayonne, where he himself arrived, April 15. Charles IV had secretly retracted his resignation, on March 21; and on the same day the queen had written to Murat, to obtain protection for the prince of peace. Charles IV informed Napoleon of his having retracted his resignation; and, in short, the affairs of the royal family were most wretchedly embroiled. (For an account of the proceedings at Bayonne, see the article *Joseph Bonaparte.*) During the meeting at Bayonne, a commotion, attended with bloodshed, took place, on May 2, at Madrid. The Spaniards had been excited by the arrogance of the French, and attacked them. Many were killed on both sides. This event is thought to have hastened the steps taken at Bayonne. But though the most enlightened part of the Spaniards were in favor of Joseph and all the ministers of Ferdinand VII entered Madrid with him (July 20), some parts of the country would not acknowledge him so easily, in many cases instigated by the priests and monks, who had every thing to fear from a more enlightened government. It could not, however, be expected that any country should change dynasties so suddenly without a struggle; yet this struggle would have, at length, ceased, had it not been kept up, in the sequel, by the support of England. The people in Asturia first took up arms; Arragon, Seville and Badajoz followed. Palafox carried from Bayonne to Saragossa the order of the prince of Asturias, that the people should arm; and the supreme junta received permission to assemble the cortes. Revolution broke out every where, which the French were too weak to resist. Moncey retreated to Valencia; and generals Dupont and Wedel were beaten at Baylen, July 19 and 20, 1808. The badge adopted by the Spanish soldier was a red ribbon, with the inscription *Vencer o morir por patria y por Fernando VII.* June 6, the junta at Seville had issued a proclamation of war. The French squadron at Cadiz surrendered, June 14, to the Spaniards. Six days later an insurrection broke out in Portugal. July 4, the alliance of Great Britain with the Spanish nation was proclaimed, and a struggle began, which, whatever opinion may be entertained respecting the conduct of Napoleon, every one will admit to have led, as far as respected Spain, to nothing but evil. Marshal Bessières was successful in the battle at Medina del Rio Secco, July 14, over general Cuesta; but the affair at Baylen, above mentioned, decided the retreat of the French from Madrid, and, August 23, Castaños entered the city. General Romana had secretly embarked his troops at Fühnen, and landed in Spain, and Wellesley was victorious over the French under Junot, August 21, at Vimeira, on which the French general capitulated the day after at Cintra, and soon after evacuated Portugal. A central junta had been formed September 25, 1808, but unity did not prevail in it. Napoleon advanced with a new army, November 6, as far as the Ebro. On the 10th, Soult defeated the centre of the great Spanish army. Victor and Lefebvre's victory on the 11th, at Espinosa, opened the way to Asturia and the northern coast; and, in consequence of the success of Lannes, at Todela, November 22, many fugitives took refuge in Saragossa. (See *Saragossa.*) The mountain pass of Somo Sierra was taken by assault, by the French and Poles, November 30, under Napoleon and Bessières; and, December 2, the French army appeared before Madrid, which surrendered on the 4th. The central junta now retired to Badajoz, and afterwards to Seville. The Spaniards believed that the success of the French was owing to treachery, and more than one of their generals was assassinated in consequence of this suspicion. The French gained many victories and took many fortresses; but the conquerors remained masters only of the places which they occupied. The guerillas surrounded and harassed them every where.* No line of communication was safe for the French: their means of support failed. In vain did Napoleon, December 4, 1808, abolish the feudal privileges, and the inquisition; in vain did Joseph try every means to win the love of the people; nothing could avail against the fanaticism of the monks. Austria now declared war. Napoleon was obliged, in January, 1809, to leave the conduct of the war to his marshals; and the Spaniards considered his departure as a victory. During the following five years, the French generals did all that talent and courage could do; but the charm of Napoleon's presence was wanting, and Wellington (q. v.) finally triumphed over them. The situation of Joseph became extremely unpleasant, even as regarded his relations with France, as has been stated in the article *Joseph Bonaparte.* Many of his adherents began to waver when the rumor was spread that Napoleon intended to separate some provinces from Spain; against which, however, Joseph declared himself explicitly. The struggle continued during six bloody campaigns, from May 2, 1808, to the battle of Toulouse, April 10, 1814. Every where, and almost daily, blood was shed, from Cadiz to Pampeluna, and from Grenada to Salamanca. No mercy was shown. Spanish women tortured and murdered the prisoners. Seven hundred French prisoners were drowned in the Minho. In Oporto and Coimbra, the French sick and wounded were murdered in the hospitals. Even non-combatant officers were killed. The supreme junta created armies with restless activity. Napoleon's exertions were also great. The French forces in the peninsula, when most numerous, viz. when Masséna marched with 80,000 men to Portugal, amounted to 200,000 infantry and 30,000 cavalry; and, in 1813, when Madrid and Valladolid were evacuated by them, to 130,000 infantry and 20,000 cavalry. The non-combatant officers, besides, were extremely numerous. In the French lines, the sword and dagger, plague and want, were active in the work of destruction. De Pradt estimates the loss which France suffered in the actual expenses of the war, during six years, at 230,000,000 of francs, without reckoning the loss occasioned by the interruption of commerce. Two objects chiefly occupied the French generals in 1809 and 1810—the re-conquest of Portugal, and the march over the Sierra Morena to Cadiz. As the British had become masters of Portugal, and the northern coasts of Spain, including Ferrol and Corunna, were again open to their ships, the re-conquest of Asturia was not effected by Ney and Kellermann until May 14—20, 1809. In the mean time, sir Arthur Wellesley (subsequently duke of Wellington) advanced from Lisbon, by the way of Alcantara, up the Tagus, and Cuesta joined him near Truxillo, whilst the English general Wilson advanced over Placenzia, and the Spaniard Venegas, from the Sierra Morena, towards Madrid. This bold plan of attack was frustrated by the battle of Talavera (July 27 and 28). The English, indeed, were victorious over

* According to Carnicero, the system of the guerillas was principally organized by Romana. General Juan Martin, surnamed the *Empecinado,* collected a body of them in the neighborhood of Madrid. Among the other guerilla leaders, Mina and Porlier were distinguished. This system preserved the energy and the confidence of the nation unbroken. After every reverse, the Spaniard consoled himself with the well-known *non importa.*

Joseph, Victor and Jourdan; but, not being sufficiently supported by the Spaniards, and being threatened by Soult and Ney advancing on their flank, they were obliged to retire to the frontiers of Portugal; after which Venegas also began to retreat, and was defeated by Joseph at Almonacid, August 11, as was Wilson by Ney, in the passes of Baros. Madrid thus escaped a siege. August 18, the Spanish orders of monks were abolished; but this measure was far from popular, and the sufferings of Spain, which the people, as usual, attributed to the existing government, tended greatly to aggravate the excitement of the mass of the nation against their French sovereign. The central junta at Seville now resolved to yield to the universal wish, to assemble the cortes and to nominate a regency. New armies were created. Arezaga advanced with 55,000 men as far as Ocaña, where, however, he was entirely defeated by Mortier, November 18. Madrid, therefore, was again saved; but in Catalonia, Arragon and Biscay, the bloodiest struggle was carried on with the bands of the insurgents. The Empecinado's troop advanced even to the vicinity of Madrid. In Old Castile, the troops of Barrioluchio, Couvillas, Rodrigues and Jacobe, in Navarre, the troops of Mina, were a terror to the enemy. The largest company of them, 4500 men, under the dreaded Marquesito, formerly a colonel in the army, encountered several French generals in the open field. In vain did the French establish fortresses on their lines of communication, and endeavor to protect their rear by movable columns. Yet their plan against Andalusia succeeded. With 22,000 men, the rash Arezaga thought he could maintain the line on the Sierra Morena, fifteen leagues long, intrenched and mined, and having in its centre the fortified pass of Perapero, against 60,000 troops commanded by the best generals of Europe. Dessolles and Gazan, on January 20, 1810, took the pass of Despenna-Peras; Sebastiani stormed the defile of St. Estevan, and took the bridges over the Guadalquivir; and, January 21, Joseph entered Baylen. Jaen was conquered; Cordova submitted. Sebastiani occupied Grenada January 28, Malaga February 6, and Joseph entered Seville February 1, from which the junta had fled to Cadiz. This place, the only one which remained in the hands of the Spaniards, defended by 16,000 men under Albuquerque, and 4000 English soldiers under Graham, and the combined British and Spanish fleets, was besieged February 6; but all the efforts and offers of the French were in vain. The war in Catalonia and Arragon continued. In Leon, the French conquered Astorga, April 22, and now directed their arms against Portugal. In this country, to the north of the Tagus, Wellington commanded a British army of 30,000 men, and Beresford a Portuguese army of 59,500 men, besides 52,800 militia. The right wing of Wellington, at Badajoz, was joined by 20,000 Spaniards under Romana, and 8000 under Ballesteros. The main body of the allied force was posted on the heights of Lisbon, which had been rendered impregnable. Wellington's plan, therefore, was defensive. Masséna began his undertaking in June, by the siege of Ciudad-Rodrigo, which surrendered July 10, and Ney entered Portugal, over the river Coa, July 24; but Almeida, which was defended by Coxe, detained Masséna until August 27, when it was obliged to capitulate. Wellington ordered the whole country, through which Masséna could follow him, to be laid waste; and the latter was obliged to take measures for the support of his army during four weeks, before he could proceed. At last, Masséna advanced, September 18, over the Mondeja, to Coimbra. On this march, he was beaten, on the 27th, at Busaco, but, nevertheless, was able to occupy the heights of Sardico, which opened to him the plains of Lisbon. Wellington now entered the strong position of Torres-Vedras, which consisted of two lines on the heights of Lisbon, defended by 170 well-placed works and 444 cannons. Masséna found this position unassailable, and retreated, after several engagements of little importance, November 14, to Santarem. Here he remained till March, 1811, when he was compelled, by want of provisions, to evacuate Portugal entirely. He hardly succeeded, by the battle of Fuentes d'Onoro, of two days' continuance, in effecting a union with the garrison of Almeida, which blew up the works, and fought its way to him under Brenier. But the French were victorious at other points. Suchet, January 2, 1811, took the important fortress of Tortosa, in Catalonia, and, June 28, after a murderous assault of five days, the fortress of Tarragona: Soult took the frontier fortresses towards Portugal, Olivença and Badajoz, March 10; and Victor defeated the English general Graham, who wished to deliver Cadiz, March 3, at Chiclana. In the autumn, Suchet marched against Valencia. After having beaten the army under general

Blake, Saguntum fell, October 26, and Valencia surrendered, January 9, 1812. Wellington now again entered Spain. Jan. 19, he took Ciudad-Rodrigo, and, April 7, Badajoz. (q. v.) But he was ill supported by the cortes and the regency, consisting of general Blake* and the naval officers Agar and Ciscar. Marmont was now at the head of the army in Portugal. But the loss of the decisive battle of Salamanca, July 22, 1812, obliged him to give up the defence of Madrid. Wellington entered the city Aug. 12. The French retired from before Cadiz Aug. 25, 1812: they withdrew their forces from the south of Spain, and concentrated it in the eastern and northern parts. After the occupation of Madrid, Wellington followed the enemy to Burgos; but the siege of the castle of Burgos, after several unsuccessful assaults, occupied him from Sept. 19 to Oct. 20, when he gave it up, as the Spaniards afforded him insufficient support, and the French had received succors. He retreated to the Duero. After several engagements, he transferred his head-quarters to Freynada, on the frontier of Portugal, Nov. 24, and the French again entered Madrid. Thus ended the year 1812, in which 134 members of the cortes had drawn up a new constitution for the monarchy, and signed it, March 18, at Cadiz. March 20, the regency took the oath to maintain it. This constitution was acknowledged by the allies of Spain—Great Britain, Sweden Denmark, Prussia, &c.—also by Russia, in the treaty of alliance concluded with Spain, at Welicki-Lucki, July 20, 1812. It perhaps gave too much power to the cortes for a monarchical government, and a people so little accustomed to the exercise of civil rights. At length, Napoleon's disasters in Russia decided the fate of the peninsula. Soult was recalled in the beginning of 1813, with 30,000 men, from Spain. Suchet left Valencia in July, but delivered Tarragona, which was besieged by Bentinck, in August, and withstood Clinton on the Lobregat. But Joseph had been obliged to leave Madrid again, May 27, and Wellington had occupied Salamanca, May 26. The French army, commanded by Joseph and Jourdan, retreated to Vittoria. Here Wellington overtook the enemy, and gained the splendid victory of Vittoria, June 21; after which the French army, pursued by Graham and Hill, retreated in disorder over the Pyrenees to Bayonne. It lost all its baggage. The victors immediately invested Pampeluna. Count Abisbal occupied the pass of Pancorbo. Graham besieged St. Sebastian, and Wellington entered France July 9. In the mean time (July 1), Napoleon, then in Dresden, had appointed marshal Soult his lieutenand and commander-in-chief of his armies in Spain. He united the beaten corps, and opposed a considerable force to the victor. July 24, the struggle began in the Pyrenees, and was maintained until Aug. 1, on every point. Wellington, on Aug. 31, took St. Sebastian by assault, after having several times repulsed the enemy, who approached to deliver the garrison. It was not, however, till Oct. 7, that he left the Pyrenees, and passed the Bidassoa. After Pampeluna had fallen (Oct. 31), no French soldier was left on the Spanish territory, except in Barcelona and some other places in Catalonia. Wellington now attacked the enemy on the fortified banks of the Niville (Nov. 10), and Soult retreated into the camp of Bayonne. But, until Wellington had passed the Nive (Dec. 9 and 10), and had repulsed several attacks, which continued to the 13th, it was not possible for him to obtain a secure footing in the hostile territory. His head-quarters were at St. Jean de Luz. Thence he repulsed, in 1814, Suchet's attacks on the Garve. Feb. 26, he fought a battle with Soult at Orthies, by which the latter was driven from his strong position, and obliged to retreat, in great disorder, to the Upper Garonne. Wellington followed the French, under Soult, to Toulouse, where the bloody battle of April 10, and the occupation of the place, put an end to the war. The cortes had already held its first session (Jan. 15, 1814), and had resolved that Ferdinand VII should swear to preserve the constitution, before he should be recognised as king. The treaty of Valençay, between Ferdinand and Napoleon (Dec. 11, 1813), was made void by declaring all the acts of the king during his captivity null. Ferdinand arrived at Valencia, where he received the deputies of the cortes, April 16. In reply to their question, when he would swear to maintain the constitution, he answered coldly, "I have not thought about it;" and, on the 4th of May, he issued a proclamation, declaring it invalid. May 14, he entered Madrid, after having caused the principal members of the regency, and sixty-four members of the cortes, to be arrested. The people, dissatisfied with the new direct taxes which had been imposed by the cortes, received him with acclama

* In 1813, the cardinal of Bourbon, archbishop of Toledo, took Blake's place.

tions. The friends of the cortes and of Joseph were persecuted with the greatest rigor. All officers above the rank of captain, who had served under Joseph, were condemned to perpetual banishment, with their wives and children, and many civil officers received the same sentence. Freemasonry was abolished, and the inquisition was revived; the conventual estates were restored, and the Jesuits recalled, and reinstated in all the rights and property of which they had been deprived since 1767. And, although the king had solemnly promised a new constitution, founded on liberal principles, in place of that of the cortes, declared his abhorrence of despotism, and promised security of property and person, liberty of the press, &c., none of these promises was fulfilled. The persecutions for political offences produced disturbances and conspiracies in different parts of the country. A great number of officers, who had aided in the restoration of Ferdinand, were executed as conspirators, on account of their opposition to the domineering pretensions of the monks. The army was in the highest degree disaffected to these proceedings, and guerillas, or bands of soldiers, infested the interior. Even the lower classes, though averse from liberal principles, were discontented with the severity of the government, while the better classes were divided into the hostile factions of the serviles and the liberals. Those counsellors who ventured to remonstrate with the king, as the Empecinado, Ballesteros, &c., were banished or thrown into prison. For six years, Ferdinand reigned with absolute power (1814—1820). The dispute with the court of Brazil, which had occupied the Banda Oriental (q. v.), while Spain refused to give up Olivenza to Portugal, would have resulted in the invasion of Portugal, but for the interference of the English. In 1820, Spain ceded Florida to the U. States, for the sum of $5,000,000. Preparations were meanwhile making against the American insurgents, who were declared rebels by the king, and required to submit themselves unconditionally. These preparations served only to exhaust the resources of the state; and the insurgent privateers captured Spanish vessels in sight of the coast, while the Spanish officers were literally dying of hunger. Cadiz at length obtained permission to fit out frigates, at its own expense, for the protection of its trade. The people were oppressed with extraordinary taxes, and recourse was had to loans. The sentence of the arrested members of the cortes was finally pronounced by the king, after repeated dissolutions of the commissions named for that purpose, on account of their mild proceedings. They were condemned to imprisonment in the fortresses and African *presidios*, or banished to the convents, or obliged to enter the army. From 1814 to 1819, there were twenty-five changes in the ministry, mostly sudden, and attended with severities. They were produced by the influence of the *camarilla*, or persons in the personal service of the king. Every attempt to save the state was frustrated by such counsellors, and the overthrow of this ancient monarchy was accelerated by the loss of the American colonies. The army was the instrument of its fall: several conspiracies had been organized by the officers for the restoration of the constitution of the cortes, and Porlier, Mina (q. v.), Lacy and Vidal, were successively the leaders of the conspirators. Mina had been obliged to save himself by flight: the others had been executed, and their friends had suffered on the rack, or been thrown into prison. The army was indisposed to the American service, for which it was destined, and the officers favorable to the constitution of the cortes, took advantage of this state of feeling to effect their own purposes: whole regiments had determined not to embark, and the commander himself, O'Donnel, count del Abisbal, was in the secret. But, finding his ambitious project of becoming dictator of the monarchy frustrated by the civil authority, he caused a division of troops which had given the signal of insurrection to be disarmed (July 8, 1819), and the officers, 123 in number, to be arrested. The embarkation of the troops was fixed for January; but, on the first day of the month, four battalions, under Riego (q. v.), proclaimed the constitution of 1812, surrounded the head-quarters of general Callejo, who had succeeded O'Donnel in the command, took possession of the town of Isla de Leon, and delivered the officers arrested in July, among whom was Quiroga. (q. v.) The insurgents were unsuccessful in their attack on Cadiz, but occupied La Caracca, where the naval arsenal, a ship of the line, and other vessels of war, with some transports, fell into their hands. Quiroga declared, in the name of the army of the nation—the title assumed by the insurgents—that it was their purpose to obtain from the king the acceptance of the constitution. All attempts to engage the people of Cadiz in the cause were frustrated by the influence of the bishop of Cienfuegos. Meanwhile, the troops in Seville had put generel Freyre in command; and the king had confirmed him in the post, on account of his popularity among the soldiers. Freyre endeavored, without success, to detach the insurgents from their leaders by promises of amnesty; but he did not venture to attack them, from fears of the fidelity of his own soldiers. Riego, at the head of a troop of 2500 men, now occupied Algesiras, entered Malaga, and, after some fighting with O'Donnel, advanced through Ecija and Cordova to Antequera, while the national army, under Quiroga, in addresses to the king and to the nation, declared their only object was to save their country by the restoration of the constitution, which had already been accepted by the nation. Risings now took place in all quarters in favor of the constitution of the cortes; the royal forces joined the insurgents; Freyre himself was obliged to proclaim the constitution in Seville; and Ferdinand, abandoned by his own troops, was compelled to yield to the general cry, and, by proclamation of March 8, declared himself ready to summon the cortes of 1812, and accept the constitution of that year. On the same day, a general amnesty was proclaimed. On the 9th, a provisory junta of eleven members was named, to conduct affairs till the meeting of the cortes; and Ferdinand swore to observe the constitution in presence of this body, and of the municipal authorities of Madrid. The inquisition was abolished on the 10th, as inconsistent with the constitution, and obnoxious ministers, &c., were succeeded by others favorable to constitutional principles. In place of the council of Castile, and that of the Indies, a supreme judicial tribunal, with appropriate subordinate courts, was established, national guards were organized in the provinces, the municipal authorities were made to conform to the constitution, and the cortes finally assembled, July 9. It was composed of 149 deputies for the peninsula, and, in place of regular deputies from America, of 30 delegates of the Americans in Spain. In a session of four months, this body endeavored to moderate the violence of the liberals, to restore the *afrancesados* (q. v.) to their rights, to counteract the machinations of the *serviles*, and to heal the wounds of the country. But the abolition of many of the convents, and of the *majorates* (q. v.), the banishment of the non-juring clergy, and some other of their measures, excited discontents. An apostolical junta established itself on the frontiers of Portugal, and, in several provinces, bands of peasants, monks and guerilla soldiers were formed, for the purpose of restoring the privileges of the crown and the clergy. On the other hand, some parts of the country were disturbed by popular excesses. In March, 1821, began the second session of the cortes, which, in April, declared the whole country in danger, and in a state of siege. The command of the armed force was now given to Morillo (q. v.), and quiet was in some measure restored. But the ultra-liberals, or *exaltados*, as they were called, were not a little excited by the events in Naples and Piedmont, in 1821; and the kingdom was in so disturbed a state that an extraordinary cortes was summoned in September. In the summer, Catalonia was desolated by a yellow fever, which, since 1800, had prevailed almost every year in the southern parts of Spain. At the same time, Mexico declared itself independent; Lima was occupied by the Chileans, under San Martin; and the Spanish part of the island of St. Domingo was lost by its union with Hayti. Under these circumstances, the government wished to temporize; but the *comuneros*, or the party of the adherents of the constitution, at the head of whom were don Romero Alpuente and don Diaz de Morales, made complaints of the weakness and mistakes of the ministers, and the cortes, in December, 1821, requested the king to appoint an abler ministry. He at last yielded, in 1822: on the other hand, the cortes passed several laws by which the *descamisados*, who were in favor of a republic, were disarmed. The *absolutistas* alone, though beaten every where by the troops of the government, could not be entirely suppressed; the cortes declared themselves ready, at the same time (January, 1822), to acknowledge America as a kingdom independent of Spain, but united with her under a common sovereign, Ferdinand VII; but the deputies sent to America could effect nothing on these conditions. The session of the extraordinary cortes was concluded Feb. 14, 1822. In the third session of the cortes, from March 1 to June 20, 1822 (during the firs month under the presidency of general Riego), the moderate liberal party prevailed at the outset, and tranquillity was gradually e-stored to the internal affairs of the coun try, when it began to be threatened from without. The strong sanitary cordon ot

French troops along the Pyrenees, and the intrigues of the exiles, led the government to suspect that the disturbances excited among the peasants in Navarre and Catalonia, by priests and monks, were instigated by the French government. Bands of *soldiers of the faith*, so called, who, under political pretences, frequently committed robbery on the highways, infested other parts of the country. The cortes therefore armed the volunteer national guards. They were every where victorious; but the pecuniary resources were chiefly in the hands of the supporters of despotism. Most of the educated classes belonged to the *comuneros*. The freemasons formed also a powerful party, and were in possession of most of the offices, while the friends of absolute power instigated the democrats, particularly the *zurriagists*, so called from the gazette termed *Zurriago* (a whip), to excesses which they hoped would disgust the moderate party with constitutional liberty. The Landaburu club, in which terrorism was recommended, became important. Discontent was kindled against the ministry, which attached itself particularly to the freemasons; and, in July, 1822, the friends of absolute government dared to attempt the overthrow of the constitution, with the assistance of the royal guards; but the national guards frustrated their project. The royal guards, in spite of the opposition of Murillo, their commander, entered Madrid July 7; but Ballesteros, at the head of the national guards, defeated them, and they fled into the royal palace; but the king, who favored them originally, now showed himself irresolute. They were unable to resist the popular force, but would have been allowed to retire, if they had not again fired on the national guards, who then fell upon them, and killed or wounded the greater part of them. On the 8th, every thing appeared calm. The *anilleros*, or moderate party, who had been in favor of a chamber of peers, and the extension of the royal power, now joined the popular party (the *comuneros*). All the ministers resigned, as the king had offended them by keeping them confined in separate rooms in his palace during the insurrection of the guards. The new ministers acted in conformity with the views of the *comuneros;* and the king, whose authority had sunk entirely since July 7, approved of every thing which they proposed. Many persons of rank, including some bishops, were banished. General Elio was executed; but the guards were treated with much mildness. The king again declared his adherence to the constitution; but the apostolical troops in Biscay, Navarre and Catalonia, continued their revolting cruelties. Under the marquis Mataflorida a regency of the friends of absolute government was established at Seo d'Urgel, near the French frontier, in August, 1822. It issued orders, in the name of the "imprisoned" king, for the restoration of every thing to the state in which it had been before March 7, 1820. The troops of the apostolical party, after much bloodshed, were beaten by Mina and Milans. Generals Espinosa, Torrijos and Jaureguy, called *El Pastor*, distinguished themselves against Quesada, a Trappist, and others. The regency fled to France in November, 1822; and it was obvious that its cause was not that of the nation. No troops of the line nor national guards, no important cities nor individuals, went over to them. Some companies of "soldiers of the faith" still continued in Spain, particularly those of Bessières, Ullmann, &c. An extraordinary cortes was again convened, which, from Oct. 7, 1822, to Feb. 19, 1823, was occupied with raising and equipping an army, and with the care of the foreign relations. The pope refused to receive the Spanish ambassador Villanueva, and the papal nuncio in Madrid left the city in January, 1823. England received an indemnification of 20,000,000 francs for damage done to English vessels by Spanish privateers in the American waters. France threatened war, and the royalists of that country assisted the apostolical party in Spain. At last, the French government aided the equipment of apostolical soldiers on French territory; and, in November, 1822, France acceded, at the congress of Verona, to the principle of armed intervention (q. v.), pronounced by Austria, Russia and Prussia, in relation to Spain. The French ambassador at Madrid, La Garde, received orders to advise a change in the constitution, as the condition on which the continuance of peace between France and Spain must depend; and, in order to enable Ferdinand VII to make such changes freely, he must first of all be restored to the full enjoyment of sovereign power. The same demand, and even in bolder terms, was made by the ministers of Prussia, Austria and Russia, while England advised the cortes to yield, and offered her mediation. The Spanish government answered the notes of the foreign ministers in a circular, of Jan. 9, 1823, addressed to its foreign ministers, and repelled with indignation the interference of the foreign powers. The remarkable sessions of the cortes (Jan. 9 and 11) showed that all parties among them felt alike on this point. The threatened discontinuance of diplomatic intercourse on the part of the foreign powers now took place. The French ambassador was recalled, after the Russian, Prussian and Austrian ministers had left Madrid. 100,000 French soldiers were assembled with the *feotas* (soldiers of the faith) at Perpignan and Bayonne, and the cortes summoned the national guards to serve with the troops of the line; but the attempts to raise an army were unsuccessful, because the bands of the *feotas* gave full employment to the troops of the line and the national guards in various quarters. Feb. 19, the ministers were dismissed; but disturbances in Madrid obliged the king to reinstate them. The king now remained, in general, passive. The seat of government was transferred to Seville. April 2, the duke of Angoulême issued a proclamation to the Spaniards, declaring that the object of the French was only to aid them, and that France desired nothing but the deliverance of Spain from the evils of revolution; and, without a declaration of war, the French army passed the Bidassoa, April 7, and marshal Moncey entered Catalonia towards the end of April: with him entered the *feotas*, or *afrancesados*, under Quesada and Eroles. The duke of Angoulême established a junta, consisting of Eguia, Calderon and Erro, who formed a provisional government, declaring the king the sole depositary of sovereign power, and that no change in the government should be recognised but such as the king should make of his own free choice. All the decrees of the cortes were declared void. The cortes had no ally. The relations of Portugal to Great Britain did not allow her to conclude a defensive treaty with Spain. The treaty made March 8, 1823, between the two countries, only provides for the exchange of deserters, criminals and rebels; and the fourth article contains a remarkable stipulation, allowing each of the governments to pass the frontiers of the other in the pursuit of rebels, and to carry on such pursuit either by itself or by the aid of the military power of the other. England remained neutral, though Canning, in parliament, called the attempt of the French unjust, and wished the arms of the cortes success. Her government, however, allowed the exportation of arms and ammunition to Spain; and, in return, the ports of the new world were opened to her ships. April 23, the king of Spain formally declared war on France. The cortes were deceived respecting the state of the nation, and hoped that England would take part with them in the war; but a memorandum, sent by the duke of Wellington to Madrid, in which he earnestly recommended a change of the constitution, was not heeded, and England remained neutral. The adherents of the constitution were confined to the educated class, the army, and the people of the cities: the country people were under the influence of the priesthood. April 11, the king arrived in Seville. April 27, the cortes passed a law respecting the registering of all rights on personal service or real property, which rendered the great landholders unfriendly towards the constitution; and in vain did Ferdinand VII call on the nation by a proclamation, May 1, 1823, to support the constitution. The French army consisted of 91,800 men, including the Spanish division. The French government provided, at an immense expense, for the support of the army; every thing was well paid for in ready money; discipline was strictly maintained, and no one was persecuted by the French for his political opinions or former conduct, while the Spanish troops gave themselves up to the greatest excesses of party hatred. The French were received, by the clergy and the lower orders of the people, as "good Christians." The Spanish army amounted to about 120,000 men, in four divisions, commanded by Ballesteros, Mina, L'Abisbal and Morillo. San Sebastian and Pampeluna, Santona and Santander, made a good defence, but were obliged to surrender, Santona on the 11th, Pampeluna on the 17th, and San Sebastian on the 27th of September. The French corps not employed in the siege of these places marched, without difficulty, into the interior. Only at Logrono an engagement took place, April 18, in which the French were defeated. Upper Catalonia, Biscay, Arragon and Castile were occupied by the French, with hardly any resistance. A guerilla warfare now commenced in Lower Catalonia, where Mina occupied the enemy for a considerable time. The royalists every where conducted in the most outrageous manner The duke of Angoulême, commander-in-chief, marched by the way of Aranda and Buitrago, the duke of Reggio by the way of Burgos and Valladolid, to Madrid.

Abisbal became suspected by the cortes, and fled to France. May 24, the duke of Angoulême entered Madrid, with a great show of rejoicings on the part of the people. He nominated a regency, consisting of the duke of Infantado, the duke of Montemar, the bishop of Osma, the baron d'Eroles, and don Ant. Gomez Calderon (May 26). The majority of the people demanded the "absolute king," and the regency put every thing on the same footing as before March 7, 1820, except that they confided the ministry of foreign affairs to the confessor of the king, D. Victor Saez. The regency had no pecuniary resources, and no power, if they had the will, to prevent the furious eruptions of party hatred. The theatre of the war was now transferred to Andalusia and Estremadura. The cortes had in vain tried to excite a general guerilla war. On account of the want of money, they decreed the seizure of all the property of persons of the opposite party, a forced loan of 200,000,000 of reals, and the coining of the superfluous church plate, by which measures the hatred of the people was still more increased. Yet the ministers did not dare to propose to the cortes the mediation offered by England, through sir W. A'Court, the British minister. The king refused to go to Cadiz; and a regency of three members, with royal powers, was appointed, because the case of moral incapacity on the part of the king, provided for by the constitution, had occurred. On the 12th of June, the cortes and the king, with the regency, departed for Cadiz; but the people showed themselves so furious against the constitutionalists that the authorities called in the aid of the French; but general Bourmont could not enter until June 21. The king had arrived at Cadiz, June 15, and the regency had again ceased. The regency in Madrid declared all the members of the cortes who had participated in the session of the 11th, when the king was declared morally incapable, to be traitors; but more it could not do: it was so destitute of resources that it was even supported by French money. The kings of France, Prussia, and the emperor of Austria, sent ministers to the regency in Madrid. Morillo declared himself, on June 26, against the cortes. In vain did Quiroga, in Corunna, where sir Robert Wilson (q. v.) also was, collect a troop of constitutionalists, with whom he continued the struggle. The heights of Corunna were taken, July 15th, by general Bourck, after a bloody contest, five hours in length. Quiroga (q. v.) then left Corunna, which was bravely defended by Novella until August 13th, when it was surrendered; and the war in Galicia was soon after terminated. Mina, with not more than 6000 men, sustained a partisan warfare, in Catalonia, for two and a half months, unequalled in the boldness and skill with which it was carried on. June 26, he took up his head-quarters near Barcelona. Donnadieu and Curial advanced upon Barcelona, July 8, while Milans and Llanera gradually fell back, disputing the ground before them. General Sarsfield, at this time, abandoned the cause of the constitutionalists, and offered his services to marshal Moncey; the garrison of Cordova planted the standard of Ferdinand, and Barcelona was blockaded by sea. Meanwhile, Molitor had compelled Ballesteros to evacuate Valencia, and gained several advantages over him, which resulted in his capitulation, August 4, and the termination of the campaign. July 23, the regency issued a decree, removing from office all volunteers and members of secret societies; and such was the violence practised towards the friends of the constitution, that the French generalissimo published an ordinance forbidding arbitrary imprisonments, and commanding the release of persons illegally confined for political offences; notwithstanding which the outrages were continued. The duke of Angoulême presented himself, August 16, before Cadiz, which had been previously invested by generals Bordesalle and Bourmont, and took possession of the city on the 4th of October. An act of the cortes, September 28, had already reinvested the king with absolute power, and requested him to retire to the French camp. On the first of October, the king and his family had been received by the duke, in form, at Puerto-Santa-Maria, with cries of *Viva el rey! Viva la religion! Muera la nacion* (Death to the nation)! *Mueran los negros!* The first measure of Ferdinand was to declare all the acts of the constitutional government, from March 7, 1820, to October 1, 1823, void, on the ground that during that time the king was acting under compulsion. The war, which still continued in Catalonia, where Riego had been wounded and made prisoner, September 15, was brought to a close in the beginning of November; and, on the 22d, the duke of Angoulême took his leave of the army of the Pyrenees, which had so successfully accomplished the military objects of its mission. See Pecchio's *Journal of Military and Political Events* *in Spain*, translated by Blaquière (London, 1824). The political objects of the expedition, to secure a system of mildness and moderation, were frustrated by the bad faith of the Spanish government. (See *France*.) In direct violation of the terms of the military capitulations, a persecuting and vindictive policy was adopted towards the former partisans of the constitution. Among the crowds of fugitives were Mina (q. v.), the count del Abisbal, Morillo, &c. Riego was executed, at Madrid, Nov. 6, and on the 13th the king made his entry into the capital on a triumphal car 25 feet high, drawn by 100 men, and amidst the rejoicings of the people. In addition to the evils caused by the excesses of political and religious bigotry, the bad credit of the government rendered it impossible to raise a loan; and it became necessary to have recourse to the former system of indirect taxes, and even to revive the income tax (*frutos civiles*). To restrain the violence of party fury, a treaty was concluded with France, stipulating for the maintenance of a French force of 45,000 men in the country, until the Spanish army could be organized; and the debt due to France for the expenses of the French expedition was fixed at 34,000,000 francs. At the same time, the Spanish government invited the great powers to hold a congress in Paris, on the subject of the Spanish American colonies; but the opposition of England prevented the execution of this project. February 9, 1824, Spain, therefore, opened the ports of her American colonies, as she continued to call them, to the subjects of all friendly powers. The personal moderation of the king towards the constitutionalists led to the formation of a plot by the absolutists, to compel him to abdicate, and to raise don Carlos to the throne (thence their name of *Carlistas*). The introduction of the inquisition was successfully resisted by the moderate party, supported by the French, and was pronounced inexpedient and impolitic even by the pope. The decree of amnesty finally appeared, May 1, 1824, but contained so many exceptions that those who were to enjoy its benefits seemed rather to form the exception than the rule. The year 1825 was disturbed by several insurrections of the Carlists, which were attended with numerous executions; and the frequent changes of ministry which occurred at this period show the weakness of the government. The independence of the colonies was acknowledged by foreign powers, and the general interruption of commerce and industry, with the flight of many persons of property, occasioned much distress. The disturbances continued during the subsequent years, attended with the same marks of feebleness on the part of the government, and a continuance of the general distress. In 1827, Spanish subjects were permitted to trade with the Spanish American republics, but under foreign flags; and in the following year Spain was evacuated by the French troops. The fort of St. Juan de Ulloa, near Vera Cruz, was lost November 22, 1825, and Callao, near Lima—the last post on the American continent in the possession of Spain—January 22, 1826. The foolish and ill-concerted expedition against Mexico was terminated by the surrender of Barradas to Santa Aña (q. v.), in September, 1829. The French revolution of 1830, although it excited some Spanish patriots in exile* to attempt to awaken their countrymen to a struggle for more liberal institutions, had little effect on the people at large. There is, in fact, no liberal party left in Spain: the sword, the scaffold, exile, and the dungeon, have devoured or dispersed the unhappy constitutionalists; and the troubles of which we have spoken above, were produced by the struggles of the more or less absolute of the absolutists, the former having been favored by the views of don Carlos, then heir presumptive to the throne, and the latter by the king. The birth of a royal princess, in 1830, has—in consequence of a royal decree of March 29, 1830, rendering the crown hereditary in the female line, in default of male heirs—changed the relation of the prince to the throne.—For the history of Spain, see Mariana's *Historia General de España* (to 1612); Bossi's *Storia della Spagna Antica e Moderna* (Milan, 1822, seq.); Robertson's *Charles V*; Watson's *Lives of Philip II and Philip III*; Sempère's *Considérations sur la Grandeur et la Décadence de la Monarchie Espagnole* (Paris, 1826), &c.; Southey's *History of the War in the Peninsula*; Napier's work on the same subject; Foy's *Hist. de la Guerre de la Peninsule* (Paris, 1827); *History of Spain and Portugal*, in Lardner's *Cabinet Cyclopædia* (London, 1831).

Spanish Language, Poetry, Literature and Art. To understand these subjects, it will be necessary to say a few words respecting the character and situation of the Spaniard. Nature has given him a beau-

* One of the most distinguished of these was general Torrijos, who entered Spain, with a few companions, for the purpose of stirring up the people, but failed, was taken, and executed.

tiful country, the excellences of which were acknowledged even by the Romans. Claudian says, *Dives equis, frugum facilis, pretiosa metallis.* On account of the situation of Spain, separated from the rest of Europe, the character of the people developed itself, in a great degree, independently of the influences of other nations—a case the reverse of that which has prevailed in Italy, lying, like Spain, beneath a southern sun, but always visited by all the nations of Europe. Gravity, fire, national pride, originality, became characteristic traits of the Spaniards, whose peculiarities were heightened at a later period by their mixture with the Moors—a gallant and chivalrous people—and by a struggle of 700 years against the Crescent, whence originated their peculiar mixture of romantic spirit and religious fervor, not unfrequently rising to fanaticism. The Spaniard is brave, provided his soul is in his cause; but when he becomes excited, he is also cruel, and shows the untamed spirit of the African. The conquest of America affords a dreadful example of what he is capable under the influence of religious hatred, pride and avarice. The deep earnestness of the Spanish character made it capable of carrying chivalry to the highest degree of developement; and, with all his pride and exquisite sense of honor, the Spaniard has been famous for unconditional submission to the fair, the church, and the king, and could even endure the horrid fetters of the inquisition. The ease of obtaining the necessaries of life in a country so highly favored by nature, and the wretched government under which it has laoored for a long series of years, are the reasons why industry is much neglected, so that thousands suffer from want. The government is extremely poor, and the country very thinly peopled, compared with other countries in the south of Europe. The Spaniard dislikes to adopt foreign manners, and fights with obstinacy if his national pride is offended. The ancient Celts, before the times of the Romans, carried on wars with the Phœnicians and Carthaginians. The Romans then colonized the country. The Visigoths conquered it in the fifth century. The unfortunate struggle of their descendants against the Moors, in the eighth century, obliged them to retire into the mountains and to the sea-shore, where, however, they soon acquired new strength, until, after a contest of seven hundred years, they again delivered their country. —The oldest language of the country was that of the ancient Cantabrians, which may yet exist in the Basque language, spoken by the people of the Pyrenees. This, perhaps already enriched by Phœnician and Carthaginian words, was followed by the Latin during the Roman sway; and Spain gave to Rome herself her best writer on eloquence—Quinctilian. Under the Visigoths, however there grew up in Spain a *romanzo* or *romance* dialect, yet without extinguishing the Latin before the invasion of the Moors, and without having an opportunity to develope itself much. When the Moors conquered most of Spain, they treated the inhabitants generously; and the Moorish dialect, then already a fine one, and much cultivated for the purposes of poetry, was soon adopted by the people, and within a short time was fluently spoken every where. But in the small kingdoms which originated during the struggle with the Moors, in the mountainous districts and on the sea-shore, the *romanzo* again gained ground with the victories of the people. The descendants of the Visigoths had retired before the Moors, leaving them in possession of the greatest part of the country, and confining themselves to the shores of the Atlantic ocean, to the mountains of the regions subsequently called Asturia, Galicia and Biscay, to the chain of the Pyrenees, and the territories of Navarre and Arragon; and a number of small principalities were formed, all united against the Moors, but, from jealousy and other causes, often at war with each other when not contending against the common enemy. The kingdom of Leon, originally including the whole of what was afterwards called Portugal, became very powerful, and Arragon was the centre of the most vigorous resistance to the Moors. Between the two lay Old and New Castile, Navarre, Catalonia, Valencia, &c. Among the latter, Castile, including the greatest part of the north-west of Spain, having become independent, attained to the highest power, and surpassed even Arragon, with which, after the expulsion of the Moors in the fifteenth century, under Ferdinand, it was permanently united by his marriage with Isabella. This division of Spain naturally had an effect on the Spanish language; and, during the period of the struggle with the Moors, we find as many dialects of the Spanish *romanzo* as Spanish kingdoms. These dialects, however, became blended with each other, on the gradual union of these kingdoms. The *romanzo* became developed at an early period, peculiarly on the coasts of Murcia, Valencia, Catalonia, and Portugal as far as Galicia, where it even took the name of *Galician* language. The Galician language, at a later period, developed itself into the Portuguese—an idiom which vies with the Castilian. The Catalonian dialect flourished in the time of the Troubadours, and continued, after having spread to the kingdom of Arragon, as long as Provençal poetry existed in Spain. But it was entirely superseded by its neighbor, the Castilian dialect, when Arragon and Castile were united under one sceptre. In the heart of Spain, the provinces of Asturia and Leon, which were subjected to the new sceptre, now gave rise, during the struggle against the Moors, to a kingdom which was destined, by its situation, to exercise a commanding influence in the peninsula, viz. the kingdom of the two Castiles. The mountains of Castile were inhabited by a valiant race, among whom the Spanish character was most developed. Here the Castilian poetry and language grew up, and soon obtained the predominance over the poetry and language of the neighboring Catalonia, which was at last united to Castile. But the Portuguese dialect remained, because Portugal, as early as the twelfth century, formed a separate kingdom. The Castilian language came to be considered as the standard Spanish, and became the idiom of the court and the learned, whilst the other languages sunk into mere dialects of the common people. Thus we find, at last, but three chief divisions in the Spanish *romanzo*, of which, however, the third—the Catalonian—has not come down to us; and we may confine ourselves, therefore, at present, to the consideration of the Castilian. Every romance language is a mixture of Germanic languages with the Latin, and each of them received a peculiar character from the nature of the country and of the conquering tribes, from political relations and other circumstances. The dialect of Spain became deeply imbued with the Oriental element, in consequence of the influence of the Moors, who were much more cultivated than the conquered people. The Castilian idiom originated in the mountains of the interior of Spain, and, like that of the Doric mountaineers among the Greeks, was characterized by deep and open tones, which now distinguish the Spanish from the Portuguese. The latter we may compare to the Ionic dialect in the Greek language. The Spanish abounds in full-sounding vowels, and every discourse is filled with assonances. Its rhyme is the most natural and most perfect to be found in the modern European languages. The Spanish gutturals indicate, perhaps, the Teutonic and Moorish elements. The language is peculiarly fitted to express the dignified and the pathetic. Not unfrequently its solemn dignity seduces the Spaniard into bombast. The poetry, the fine arts and general literature of a nation bear the stamp of its peculiarities. Few are the nations among whom these have flourished equally. The Spanish people is decidedly poetical. In works of eloquence, both religious and secular, no language is so poor as the Spanish, though, in some respects, finely adapted for them. As to architecture, Spain may, perhaps, have exercised an important influence, in consequence of the contact into which the Moorish and Gothic architecture were brought in this country. Gothic architecture, indeed, has sprung from the whole spirit of the modern Christian nations, and belongs much more to Germany than to Spain, Italy and England; but it is very probable that what is called the new Gothic architecture developed itself with more beauty and grace in the neighborhood of the light, splendid and rich architecture of the Moors. The innumerable churches of Spain are in the Gothic taste, like the old buildings of Germany and England; and among them are many fine edifices, but not to be compared with the minster of Strasburg, St. Stephen's church at Vienna, or Westminster abbey. One of the most remarkable monuments of Spanish architecture and Spanish greatness is the famous Escurial. (q. v.)—Music, dancing and painting could not be wanting in so poetical a nation. Music was used to accompany their songs and ballads, and every shepherd still knows how to play on his instrument. The dance, so natural to southern nations, acquired a national character in Spain, and, to this day, the Spaniard has many an almost allegorical dance, borrowed from the Moors. Painting and sculpture were used to ornament the churches (Seville, Toledo) and palaces. Madrid has even an *Academia de las tres nobles artes, pintura, escultura y architectura,* and the royal palace of that city and the Escurial have galleries; but there is no proper Spanish school of reputation in either of these arts. Yet we cannot pass by the names of the painters Velasquez, Murillo, Zusbaran, L. de Vargas. The art of dramatic representation never reached a high degree of perfection in Spain. We therefore proceed to the poetry. In general, it may be observed that the spirit of the Spanish poetry is found, likewise, in the Portuguese. Both are the representatives of a peculiar species of romantic poetry. The time when Spanish poetry began to flourish coincides with the origin of the Italian epic, being just at the period when the Provençal poetry expired, in the middle of the fourteenth century. If we consider the time of the Troubadours as the infancy of the modern poetry of Southern Europe, the Spanish poetry, and the Italian, which begins with Dante, form the adult age. The age of the Provençal poetry could not last long in Spain. The life of the Spaniard, filled with battle and toil, was too grave to allow him to be satisfied with poetry of so gay, and often trifling a character. Only at the court of Arragon, and for a short time at that of the king of Castile, there were courts of love and wandering minstrels. The more Castile extended its power from the centre of Spain, the more did the Provençal poetry retire from Arragon, Catalonia and Valencia to France. Castilian poetry began with the ballad, passed over to the romance, and reached its highest point in the drama, and in each of these departments always remained of a decidedly romantic character. Spanish poetry differs from the Italian by a peculiar mixture of romantic fervor, frequently of an Oriental kind, with deep gravity. The Moors may have added to this spirit, besides having introduced into Spanish fiction the fairy world of the East. Spanish poetry proceeds always with a solemn pace. Its plays of wit are heavy, and its fondness for allegory excessive. The perfection of the intrigue is one of the great merits of Spanish writers, and they have served as models to the rest of Europe. A great peculiarity of Spanish versification is found in the *redondillas*, which became not only the standing metre of the ballad, but also of the drama, and in the assonances, which the Spaniards carried to the highest perfection. *Redondillas*, in their later form, are strophes of four lines in trochaic verses, mostly of four feet, and are peculiarly adapted for Spanish poetry. In the Spanish sonnets, prior to the connexion with Italy, they assumed the most popular character. The rhyme alone did not satisfy the writers, but the assonance was carried through whole lines. The song was the natural growth of the warlike period of Spain, and served to commemorate martial exploits. No language has such a store of ballads as the Spanish; but they are, particularly the earlier ones, little more than simple, childlike relations of chivalrous deeds. They may be properly divided into the chivalrous (derived especially from the fabulous history of Charlemagne, in which are mingled also tales of Moorish and Spanish heroes—as don Gayferos, the Moorish Calaynos, count Alarcos, &c.) and the historical: of the latter kind, an endless number originated during the struggle with the Moors. After those which belong to the early times of these conflicts, in the ninth and tenth centuries, there arose the brilliant ballads relating to the Cid (q. v.), the hero of the first Castilian king, Ferdinand. Their nature is fully exhibited to us in probably the earliest poem of length relating to this subject which has been preserved, *El Poema de Cid*—a story whose simplicity and poetic coloring are very striking. It is nothing more, and, in this early childhood of Spanish poetry, could be nothing more, than a long historical Spanish ballad, without any plot. The language is often very old Castilian, and the verse, which is considered by many as Alexandrine, though it cannot properly be so called, on account of its great want of precision, is truly iambic. It belongs, according to all conjecture, to the twelfth century, and is much superior to the *Poema de Alexandro Magno*, which is of nearly equal antiquity, and to the rhymed prayers, legends, and rules of religious orders, by the Benedictine monk Gonzalo Berceo. In connexion with these ballads should be read those which are taken from the history of the Moors, of which many are found in the *Historia de los Vandos de los Zegris y Abencerrages*, which is itself a sort of romantic chronicle of the Moorish heroes. There are also a number of Spanish ballads, founded on various popular stories. Little different from the ballad was the song; and perhaps the whole difference, especially in the thirteenth and fourteenth centuries, consisted in this, that the song was divided into couplets or small strophes. Subsequently the song became more lyrical; and then arose the *canciones*, properly so called (in twelve lines, similar to the madrigal and the epigram), the kindred species of *villancicos* (stanzas of seven lines), and the poetical paraphrases of known songs and ballads, in which the old songs were interwoven, line by line, with the words unchanged. Spain is distinguished above other countries for having united the greatest part of her ballads and songs in large collections, and thus preserved them to posterity; and the only thing to be regretted is, that the date and the author are not generally given. Thus there is a great collection of ballads made in the sixteenth century, called *Romancero general* (by Miguel de Madrigal, 1604, and Petro de Flores, 1614), and an older one, *Cancionero de Romances*, &c. (Antwerp, 1555). The songs are to be found in the *Cancionero general* of Fernando del Castillo, which belongs to the commencement of the sixteenth century, and was preceded by a *Cancionero de Poetas Antiguos*, in the reign of John II. Here we should mention the *Silva de Romances viejos, publicada par Jac. Grimm* (Vienna, 1815), and Collections of the best old Spanish historical, chivalrous and Moorish Ballads, arranged with notes, by Depping (Altenb. and Leipsic, 1817). Spain, in the sixteenth and seventeenth centuries, reached its greatest elevation; and when the grandson of Ferdinand the Catholic, Charles V, united the German imperial throne with the Spanish, and was powerful in Italy, Spain became so flourishing that his successor Philip could lavish, without restraint, the resources of his kingdom, which yet were not consumed until about the end of the seventeenth century, when, after the death of the weak Charles, the Bourbon family ascended the throne. With the prosperity of the monarchy, poetry also flourished. Crowned heads, as Alphonso X, in the thirteenth century, and the Castilian prince don Juan Manuel (who died in 1362), had tried their powers in verse and prose; and Manuel's work, the Count Lucanor, a collection of important rules for the lives of princes, remains a beautiful monument of Spanish refinement in the fourteenth century. The knights themselves, and not, as in other lands, merely monks, had employed themselves in writing chronicles; and the Spanish historical style has hence become more dignified and noble. The pursuits of active life and of literature have been so intimately connected in Spain, that its greatest warriors have been also the most intellectually cultivated, and not unfrequently were distinguished poets. Thus we find, in the fifteenth century, at the court of John II, celebrated as a patron of poetry, the marquis Henry de Villena, who has left the oldest Spanish Art of Poetry, under the title of *La gaya Ciencia* (the gay science), and, from his knowledge of natural philosophy, almost acquired the reputation of a magician; and his yet more celebrated pupil, don Iñigo Lopez de Mendoza, marquis of Santillana, author, among other works, of the *Doctrinal de Privados* (Manual of Favorites), in which the favorite of John II, don Alvaro de Luna, who was executed, relates his transgressions, and enjoins moral truths on the turbulent Castilians. Santillana's letter upon the oldest Spanish poetry is very celebrated. Several others, for instance, Juan de Mena (the Spanish Ennius), who died in 1456, author of the allegoric-historical-didactic poem *Las Trecentas* (The 300 Stanzas), and Rodriguez del Padron, who, in his songs of love, exchanged his French idiom for the Castilian, received distinguished favors from the above-mentioned king. Attempts were now made in all branches of the art. During the reign of John II, and his celebrated daughter Isabella, the dramatic spirit first prevailed. Yet before the time of Juan de la Enzina, who, about the end of the fifteenth century, composed pastoral dramas (also the author of the *Disparates*, which is in the ballad form), the marquis de Villena encouraged the writing of allegorical plays, and an unknown author produced the celebrated satirical pastoral dialogue *Mingo Rebulgo*. Then followed the dramatic romance of Callistus and Melibœa, which was also called a tragi-comedy. Some historical and biographical works of importance appeared at the same time. The Chronicles of the poet Perez de Guzman, and of the high chancellor of Castile, Pedro Lopez de Ayala, have been reprinted in modern times, by the academy of history at Madrid. The History of the Count Pedro Nino de Buelna, by Gutierre Diaz de Games; the History of Alvaro de Luna, by an unknown friend; and the *Claros Varones* of Fernando de Pulgar, still preserve their reputation. Then commences the period when the whole monarchy was permanently united under Ferdinand the Catholic. Spain and Italy were brought into connexion by the conquest of Naples, under the great captain (*el gran capitan*) Gonsalvo Fernandez de Cordova; the inquisition, which, restraining the faith of the Spaniards, left freer room to its fancy, was established, and America discovered. Boscan (about the year 1526), nourished by Italian genius, gave Castilian poetry a classic character, by judiciously incorporating in it the excellences of his Italian models. He confined himself to sonnets and songs; but his friend Garcilaso de la Vega (q. v.)

became the author of very popular pastoral poems, to which, in later times, the Portuguese Saa de Miranda and Montemayor gave a more elevated character; the latter, in his pastoral romance Diana. More imbued with the spirit of Horace and Aristotle was the distinguished statesman Diego de Mendoza, the dreaded minister of Charles V, in Italy, and author of the comic romance *Lazarillo de Tormes*, who composed, upon the model of Sallust and Tacitus, his History of the Rebellion in Grenada. He wrote various songs, poetical epistles, and satirical pieces. In odes, in the new style, Herrera and Luis de Leon met with much success. The witty Castillejo was particularly inimical to this classic Italian school. All attempts to imitate the romantic epic of the Italians in Spanish literature failed; and, in fact, even the later attempts of the Spaniards in the epic have been unsuccessful, if we except the *Araucana* of Alonzo de Ercilla y Zuñiga (about 1556), which celebrates the conquest of a brave tribe of American Indians. But the fairest flower of the Spanish Parnassus now opened. We mean its drama. The history of this, henceforth, embraces nearly all the history of Spanish poetry. The drama of Spain first became independent in the time of John II. It originally proceeded from the religious spectacles; and a great part of its productions has always remained of a religious character. In connexion with the Spanish drama, the old Art of Poetry of Juan de Cueva is particularly deserving of attention. This drama does not recognise the Grecian distinction of comedy and tragedy, but its peculiar divisions are the *comedias divinas* and *comedias humanas*. The former have been divided, since Lope de Vega, into histories of the lives of the saints (*vidas de santos*), and *autos sacramentales*, plays which were performed upon Corpus Christi days, and had for their object the commemoration of the sacrament. The *comedias humanas* consist of three classes:—1. The heroic, more properly historical in their nature; 2. pieces of the cloak and the sword (*comedias de capa y espada*), drawn from high life, and full of the most complicated intrigue; 3. the *comedias de figuron*, in which vain adventurers or ladies play the chief parts. With these arose, too, the preludes (*loas*), and the interludes, mostly comic (*entremeses*), and usually accompanied with music and dancing (*saynetes*). If we estimate the modern dramatic art according to its true romantic character, we soon see that two nations have reached the highest excellence in it, each in its own way—the English in their Shakspeare, and the Spanish in their Lope de Vega and Calderon. The religious comedy is peculiar to the Spaniards; and Calderon's Devotion to the Cross proves of what elevation it is capable. This grave people, too, has produced the most original comedies; and its theatre has become a fund of comic intrigues for the writers of the rest of Europe. In the first half of the sixteenth century, after a learned party had attempted, without success, to imitate the Grecian and Roman drama, Torres Naharro appeared, and laid the foundation of true Spanish comedy; and Lope de Rueda, called, by Cervantes, the *great*, followed, with pieces in prose. The theatres of Spain at that time consisted, according to Cervantes, of some boards and benches; and the wardrobe of the actors, with the decorations, could be packed into a bag. From rude beginnings, among which we must not omit the two tragedies on the history of Ines de Castro, by the Dominican Bermudez, the drama unfolded itself, until the time of Cervantes, the rival of Lope de Vega. Lope de Vega (born 1562) held the highest rank before the appearance of Calderon. In all the above-mentioned kinds of Spanish comedy, he obtained unbounded applause; and his celebrated plays, with the exception of the *autos*, and the preludes and interludes, fill alone twenty-five volumes. He possessed an inexhaustible power of inventing complicated intrigues, but wanted the highest kind of refinement. A crowd of imitators surrounded him (among whom we may mention Mira de Mescua); but the drama was carried to its highest perfection by the immortal Pedro Calderon de la Barca, who was born in 1600. He was the friend and poet of Philip IV, who had a great fondness for the stage, and wrote himself for it. (See *Calderon*.) His example also allured a swarm of imitators; but Solis, Moreto, Molina, Roxas de Castro, and others, should be mentioned with respect. With the monarchy sank the poetic standard. With the French race of sovereigns the French taste also was introduced into the Spanish theatre; and it was not till the second half of the eighteenth century that Vincente Garcia de la Huerta attempted to revive the old Spanish theatre. He published his *Teatro Español* (16 vols.) in 1785—a collection of the best old plays of Spain. Among the late tragic poets are De Mora-tin and Quintana; among the comic, Ramon de la Cerucycano and Commella. In one of the finest departments of works of fiction—the romance—Spain has accomplished much. The romance of chivalry early received a peculiar character in the *Amadis* (probably by Vasco Lobeira, in the fourteenth century), and flourished for a long time. Its principal productions we may best learn from the judgment passed on them by the curate and barber in Don Quixote. Diego de Mendoza, in his *Lazarillo de Tormes*, furnished the model of the romances of low life (*del gusto picaresco*), which afterwards became so numerous, and of which *Don Guzman de Alfarache*, by Mattheo Aleman (1599), is one of the most distinguished. A flood of other tales appeared about the same time, among which must be mentioned those of Timoneda and Perez de Montalvan. But the immortal Miguel de Cervantes Saavedra (born in 1547), in his Don Quixote, surpasses all his predecessors and followers. In this, Spanish prose found its perfection; and the work makes an epoch in the history of romance—a circumstance which would not have been so much overlooked had it not been customary to consider the knight of La Mancha only as a subject of jest, and to put out of sight the fact that the work affords the most vivid picture of human life. With the addition of the other works of Cervantes, the circle of poetic creation in Spain may be said to be completed. The continual decline of Spanish literature, with the decline of the state, has been already mentioned. The brothers Argensola, with the title of the Spanish Horaces, many writers of epic, pastoral and lyric poetry, of moderate merit, Espinel, Morales, the Figueroas, Sousa, Virues, Montalvan, can scarcely be distinguished above the increasing deluge. The usual appearances of a declining poetry and literature are observed here. The ingenious, but affected, Louis de Gongora de Argote (after 1600) soon carried a bombastic and strained mode of writing to a great height, and found many followers both in poetry and prose. Spain had, likewise, at this time, as Italy at an earlier period, her Marinists, or concettists, and a peculiar class, called *culturists*, who veiled their want of genius in turgidity and affectation. They were not, indeed, without opponents. The celebrated satirist Francis de Quevedo Villegas (at the beginning of the seventeenth century) bitterly assailed the Marinists; and he, as well as the Spanish Anacreon, Stephen Manuel de Villegas, upheld, in some measure, the old Spanish simplicity. But the time of decline had come; and the introduction of the French style, under the Bourbons, could only add to the degradation. In the department of criticism, we must mention the *Poetica* of Ignatius de Luzan (1737, folio), the founder of the French school. In philosophy, theology, &c., nothing of importance is to be found; but the prose style has not been neglected. On the contrary, it has been cultivated in a peculiar manner in works relating to the history of the nation. The learned theologian Perez de Oliva, who died in 1533, much improved didactic prose; and his scholar and nephew, Ambrosio de Morales, the historiographer of Philip II, pursued the same course. Diego de Mendoza wrote, as we have already mentioned, a History of the War in Grenada, and Geronymo Zurita *Anales de la Corona de Arragon*. Antonio de Solis wrote, in the seventeenth century, an excellent work upon the conquest of Mexico; yet the Jesuit Mariana deserves, perhaps, to be called the most industrious Spanish historian. Lorenzo and Balthasar Gracian, the latter of whom, by his *Arte de Ingenio*, had an important influence on the Spanish literature of the seventeenth century, contributed to the introduction of Gongora's defects into the prose style. The *Real Academia Española*, at Madrid, founded in 1713, deserves great praise for its *Diccionario de la real Academia** (in 6 vols., folio), by which the Castilian dialect became the established language. Candamo, Zamora, Cañizares, and the Mexican nun Inez de la Cruz, and some others, were distinguished as lyric poets in the eighteenth century. Jos. Lopez compiled a *Parnaso Español*, in 1768, drawn from the old lyric poets. Lately, Llorente has appeared as a historical and political writer; but his works have been produced out of his own country. The first historical romance that has come from the pen of a Spaniard, is in English, namely, Gomez Arias, or the Moors of Alpujarras, by Telesforo de Trueba y Cosio (3 vols., London, 1828). Anaya's Essay on Spanish Literature (London, 1818) gives a short account of Spanish literature. See, also, Bouterwek's *History of Spanish Literature*, which is contained in his *History of Modern Poetry and Eloquence*, and has been translat-

* The most complete Spanish dictionary, for foreign students of the language, is the *Dictionnaire Espagnol-François et François-Espagnol*, by Nuñez de Taboada (2 vols., Paris)

ed into Spanish, French and English. The events of the reigns of Charles IV and Ferdinand VII have created an excitement beneficial to Spanish literature. Jovellanos has written, with talent and elegance, on legislation and political economy; Capmany has distinguished himself in philology; Antillon in geography; Llorente in the history of his country; Conde in Oriental literature; the canon Moralez in mathematics and general literature; and various others might be mentioned. Juan Melendez Valdez has been called the Spanish Anacreon. Badia is known for his Travels in the East, under the name of Ali Bey. We have mentioned, in the course of this article, *Coleccion de las mas celebres Romances antiguos Españoles historicos y caballerescos* (edited by Depping, Leipsic, and by a Spaniard, London, 1825, 2 vols.; the Leipsic edition contains the Moorish ballads, which the London does not); there is also a *Coleccion de las Piezas dramaticas de los Autores Españoles:* the first six volumes (Madrid, 1826) contain the best pieces of Calderon, Moreto, Tirso de Molina, Ruiz de Alarcon, and Perez de Montalban. Spain has now, besides the seminaries, fifteen universities. In these there were, in 1826, 9867 students, and in the seminaries 3810.

Spallanzani, Lazarus, an eminent naturalist, born at Scandiano, in Italy, in 1729, studied at Reggio and at Bologna, under Laura Bassi, the celebrated female professor of physics in that place. Being nominated professor of natural philosophy at Pavia, he devoted himself to experimental researches, which he pursued for many years with assiduity, and published, in Italian, various works on physiology, which made his name known through Europe. In 1779, he travelled through the Swiss cantons; in 1785, he made a voyage to Constantinople, Corfu and Cerigo, and, in 1788, journeyed through the Two Sicilies, and part of the Apennines, to collect volcanic products for the museum at Pavia. This celebrated natural philosopher died of apoplexy in 1799. Among the numerous writings of Spallanzani are Experiments on animal Reproduction; On infusory Animalcules; On the Phenomena of Circulation; On animal and vegetable Physics; Travels in the Two Sicilies; On the Transpiration of Plants.

Spandau; a fortified town in Prussia, on the Havel, at its union with the Spree; eight miles west of Berlin; lon. 13° 11′ E.; lat. 52° 33′ N.; population, 4303. It is well fortified, and contains a large work house and a manufactory of arms.

Spangenberg, Augustus Gottlieb, a Moravian bishop, was born at Klettenberg, in Germany, in 1704, became a student of law at Jena, and, in 1726, doctor of philosophy. The following year he formed an acquaintance with count Zinzendorff, founder of the sect of Moravians or Herrnhutters, of whom he became a follower, and was sent on a mission to the West Indies and North America (1735—1739). Having established a colony of the United Brethren (q. v.) in Georgia, and visited Pennsylvania, he returned to Europe. In 1744, he was elected bishop of the Moravians, and sent again to America as superintendent of all the establishments of the brethren among the English and savage nations. He returned from this mission in 1749, and in 1751 crossed the Atlantic a third time. On the death of Zinzendorff (q. v.), in 1760, he was called to the supreme council of the Herrnhutters, and, in 1764, was appointed general inspector of the establishments in Upper Lusatia. He took up his residence at Zeitz, whence, in 1769, he removed to Herrnhut, devoting his time especially to the seminaries for the education of foreign missionaries. In 1789, he became president of the general directory, and died at Berthelsdorf, near Herrnhut, in 1792. Among his works are the Life of Zinzendorff (in German, 1772—75, 8 vols., 8vo.); and *Idea Fidei Fratrum*, or a Summary of the Christian Doctrine of the Evangelical Community of the Brethren (1779, 8vo.), translated into English by Latrobe.

Spanheim, Ezekiel, a distinguished numismatist and philologian, son of Frederic Spanheim, a professor of divinity at Geneva and Leyden, was born at Geneva, in 1629, accompanied his father to Leyden in 1642, and, although at that period the animosity between Heinsius and Salmasius was at its height, succeeded, by his modesty and abilities, in obtaining the esteem of both those scholars. In 1651, he accepted a professorship of rhetoric in his native city; but, his reputation inducing the elector palatine to select him as superintendent of his son's studies, he entered the service of that prince, and soon after published a tract in support of his patron's pretensions to the grand vicarship of the empire. That prince despatched him as his envoy to Rome, where he became personally acquainted with his father's patroness, queen Christina, who afterwards employed him in diplomatic missions to the states-general, Breda, and London. Circumstances induced him to enter the service of the elector of Brandenburg, afterwards king of Prussia, who raised him to the order of nobility, while ambassador extraordinary at Paris. In 1702, he proceeded in the same capacity to London, where he died in 1710. His principal works are a Dissertation on the Excellence and Use of the Medals of the Ancients (folio, 2 vols.); Letters and Essays on Medals; a Commentary on the Writings of Aristophanes and Callimachus; an edition of the writings of the emperor Julian, in Greek and Latin, and a French translation of the same work, illustrated by medals.—*Frederic Spanheim*, brother of Ezekiel, was born in 1631, at Geneva, studied at Leyden, and succeeded to the divinity chair at Heidelberg, in 1665, which he exchanged for that at Leyden in 1670. He was a voluminous writer, principally on theological subjects, and compiled an elaborate history of the Christian church. His death took place in 1701.

Spaniel (*canis extrarius*, L.). The spaniel has the hair very long in parts; it is generally white, with large, brown, liver-colored or black spots, of irregular shape and size; the nose is sometimes cleft; the ears are very long and pendulous, and covered with long hair. This race came originally from Spain, whence its name. The setter is sometimes called the *English spaniel*. It corresponds, in every point, with the true spaniel, but is trained more particularly for field sports. The Alpine or St. Bernard's variety of the spaniel breed exceeds all others in size and beauty. It is generally two feet high at the shoulders, and full six feet from the nose to the end of the tail. These dogs are sent out in couples to scour the mountain in search of lost or wearied travellers. They have frequently been of great use in this way.—The smaller spaniel, king Charles's dog (*canis brevipilis*, L.), is a small variety of the spaniel, used as a lap dog. It is sometimes found entirely black, and is then called, in England, *king Charles's dog*, from the liking of Charles II for this variety.—The Maltese dog and the lion dog (*canus leoninus*, L.) are small species of spaniel. The first is supposed to have sprung from the intercourse of the little spaniel with the smaller water dog. It has the hair, all over the body, very long and silky, and generally pure white. The other has long silky hair about the head, neck, shoulders, and extremity of the tail; but, on the other part, short, giving the little animal a leonine appearance. It is probably bred between the little spaniel and one of the naked varieties.—The great water spaniel (*canis aquaticus*, L.) is supposed to be the offspring of the great water dog and the little spaniel. It is very much like the former animal, but the curly hair is more silky, and like that of the land spaniel There is also a useful variety of this breed between the water spaniel and the shepherd's dog. These animals are used to find water-fowl, shot over water.

Spanish Æra. (See *Epoch.*)

Spanish Fly. (See *Cantharides.*)

Spanish Main; the Atlantic ocean and coast along the north part of South America, from the Leeward islands to the isthmus of Darien.

Spanish Succession, War of the. (See *Spain*, and *Utrecht.*)

Spar. (See *Barytes*, *Corundum*, *Fluor*, and *Lime.*)

Sparrman, Andrew, a Swedish naturalist and traveller, born about 1747, studied medicine at Upsal; and his attention to natural history attracted the notice of Linnæus. In 1765, he made a voyage to China. On his return, he described the animals and vegetables which he had discovered; and, to continue his researches, went to the cape of Good Hope in 1772. Doctor Forster and his son visiting the cape with captain Cook, he joined them in the voyage round the world, and returned, in 1775, to Africa, undertook a journey into the interior; and, after penetrating to the distance of 350 leagues from the cape, he returned to that settlement in April, 1776, bringing a copious collection of African plants and animals. The same year he returned to his native country. In 1787, he engaged in an abortive attempt to explore the interior of Africa, and returned home in 1788. He died at Stockholm, July 20, 1820. He was the author of several works, among which is an Account of his Voyage to the Cape of Good Hope, and Travels in Africa, written in Swedish, and published in German at Berlin, and in English at London, 1785 (2 vols., 4to.).

Sparrow. (See *Appendix*, end of this volume.)

Sparrow-Hawk, American (*falco sparverius*, L.). This beautifully marked bird appears to reside principally in the warmer parts of the U. States. It is particularly abundant, in the winter, throughout South Carolina, Alabama, Georgia and Florida, whither the birds assemble from the remote interior of the Northern

States, wandering, in summer, as far as the Rocky mountains. They do not seem to visit the maritime districts of New England. They are found in the West Indies, also south of the equator, even in Cayenne and Paraguay. The nest is built in a hollow, shattered or decayed tree, at a considerable elevation. The eggs are said to be four or five, of a light brownish-yellow, and spotted with brown. The food of this bird is sparrows and other small birds, also mice, grasshoppers and lizards. The female is eleven inches long; the stretch of the wings twenty-three inches. The male is about nine and a half or ten inches long. The cere and legs are yellow; the head bluish-ash; crown rufous. The upper parts are reddish-bay, striped transversely with dusky brown; the lower parts pale yellowish-white, marked with longitudinal spots of brown; the claws black.—The European sparrow-hawk is a short-winged hawk, which destroys many pigeons and partridges.

Sparry Iron. (See *Iron, Ores of.*)

Sparta, or Lacedæmon, one of the most powerful states of ancient Greece, called also *Laconia*, lay to the east of Messenia (q. v.), in the Peloponnesus. The Eurotas here empties into the gulf of Laconia, the western shore of which terminates in cape Tænarus (Matapan). Here, near the town of Tænarus (q. v.), was pointed out a cave, which was said to be the entrance to the regions of Pluto. At Amyclæ, near Sparta, stood one of the most celebrated temples of Apollo. According to fable, Lacedæmon, son of Jupiter, and of the nymph Taygeta, married Sparta, daughter of Eurotas, king of the Leleges, succeeded his father-in-law on the throne, and gave the country his own name, calling the city by that of his wife. He was probably a Hellenic prince, and one of the leaders of the Achæan colony, which Archander and Architeles led into Laconia, after their expulsion from Phthiotis. Here Lacedæmon, having persuaded the natives to receive the colony, gave his own name to the united people. Among the most celebrated of the early kings was Tyndarus, with whose sons Castor (q. v.) and Pollux the male line of Lacedæmon became extinct. Menelaus, between whom and Lacedæmon five kings had reigned, married Helen (q. v.), the daughter of Tyndarus, and thus acquired the throne. Orestes, son of Agamemnon, who had married Hermione, the daughter of Menelaus, united Argos and Mycenæ with Lacedæmon. In the reign of his son and successor Tisamenes, it was conquered by the Heraclidæ (q. v.) about 1080, who established a dyarchy or double dynasty of two kings in Sparta. For, as neither the mother nor the Delphic oracle could decide which of the twin sons of Aristodemus, Eurysthenes and Procles, was first born, the province of Laconia was assigned to them in common; and it was determined that the descendants of both should succeed them. The Lacedæmonians, however, had little cause to rejoice at the arrival of the foreigners, whose fierce disputes, under seven rulers of both houses, distracted the country with civil feuds, while it was, at the same time, involved in constant wars with its neighbors, particularly the Argives. The royal authority was continually becoming feebler, and the popular power was increased by these divisions, until the government ended in an ochlocracy. At this time, Lycurgus was born, for the healing of the troubles. He was the only man in whom all parties confided; and, under the auspices of the gods, whose oracle he consulted, he established a new constitution of government in Sparta (about 880 B. C.), and thus became the savior of his country. (See *Lycurgus.*) Lacedæmon now acquired new vigor, which was manifested in her wars against her neighbors, particularly in the two long Messenian wars, which resulted in the subjugation of the Messenians (B. C. 668). The battle of Thermopylæ (B. C. 480), in which the Spartan king Leonidas (q. v.) successfully resisted the Persian forces at the head of a small body of his countrymen, gave Sparta so much distinction among the Grecian states, that even Athens consented to yield the command of the confederated forces, by land and sea, to the Spartans. Pausanias (q. v.) guardian of the infant son of Leonidas, gained the celebrated victory of Platææ (q. v.) over the Persians (B. C. 479), at the head of the allies. On the same day, the Grecian army and fleet, under the command of the Spartan king Leotychides, and the Athenian general Xanthippus, defeated the Persians, by land and sea, near Mycale. With the rise of the political importance of Sparta, the social organization of the nation was developed. The power of the kings was gradually limited, while that of the ephori was increased. After the Persians had been victoriously repelled, the Grecian states, having acquired warlike habits, carried on hostilities against each other. The jealousy of Sparta towards Athens rose to such a height that the Lacedæmonians, under pretence that the Persians, in case of a renewal of the war, would find a tenable position in Athens, opposed the rebuilding of its walls, and the fortification of the Piræus. Themistocles (q. v.), discerning the real grounds of this proceeding, baffled the designs of Sparta by a stratagem, and thus contributed to increase the ill will of that state towards Athens. The tyrannical conduct of Pausanias alienated the other allies from Sparta; and most of them submitted to the command of Athens. But, while Sparta was learning moderation, Athens became so arrogant towards the confederates, that they again attached themselves to the former power, which now began to make preparations in secret for a new struggle. The Athenians, however, formally renounced the friendship of Sparta, and began hostilities (B. C. 431). This war, the Peloponnesian (q. v.), ended in the ascendency of Sparta, and the entire humiliation of her rival (405). The rivalry of the Spartan general Lysander and the king Pausanias soon after produced a revolution, which delivered the Athenians from the Spartan yoke. The Spartans next became involved in a war with Persia, by joining Cyrus the Younger in his rebellion against his brother Artaxerxes Mnemon. The Persian throne was shaken by the victories of Agesilaus; but Athens, Thebes, Corinth, and some of the Peloponnesian states, were instigated by Persian gold to declare war against the Lacedæmonians, who found it necessary to recall Agesilaus. The latter defeated the Thebans at Coronæa; but, on the other hand, the Athenian commander, Conon, gained a victory over the Spartan fleet at Cnidus, and took fifty galleys. This war, known as the Bœotian or Corinthian war, lasted eight years, and increased the reputation and power of Athens, by the successes of her admiral, Conon, and her fortunate expeditions against the Spartan coasts and the islands of the Ægean. The arrogance of Athens again involved her in hostilities with Persia; and Antalcidas (B. C. 388) concluded the peace which bears his name, and which, though highly advantageous to Persia, delivered Sparta from her enemies. The ambitious designs of Sparta in concluding this peace soon became apparent: she continued to oppress her allies, and to sow dissensions in every quarter, that she might have an opportunity of acting as umpire. Besides other outrages, she occupied, without provocation, the city of Thebes, and introduced an aristocratical constitution there. Pelopidas delivered Thebes, and the celebrated Theban war followed, in which Athens took part, at first against Sparta, but afterwards in her favor. The latter was so much enfeebled by the war, that she thenceforward ceased to act a distinguished part in Greece. No state was strong enough to take the lead, and the Macedonian king Philip at last made himself master of all Greece. Agis, king of Sparta, one of the bravest and noblest of its princes, ventured to maintain a struggle for the liberties of Greece; but he lost his life in the battle of Megalopolis against Antipater. Archidamus IV was attacked by Demetrius Poliorcetes, and Sparta was saved with difficulty. New troubles soon arose: Cleonymus, nephew of the king Areus, invited Pyrrhus into the country in aid of his ambitious projects, which were frustrated, partly by the negligence of Pyrrhus, and partly by the courage of the Spartans. Luxury and licentiousness were continually growing more and more prevalent, and, though several succeeding kings attempted to restore the constitution of Lycurgus, and restrain the power of the ephori, it was without success. Cleomenes, indeed, accomplished a reform; but it was not permanent. After an obstinate and unfortunate war against the Achæans and Antigonus, king of Macedonia, Cleomenes fled to Egypt, where he died. The state remained three years without a head, and was then ruled by the tyrants Machanidas and Nabis (q. v), by the latter of whom the most atrocious cruelties were committed. The Romans and the Achæan league effected the final fall of the state, which had been upheld for a short time by Nabis. Sparta was obliged to join the Achæan league, with which it afterwards passed under the dominion of the Romans. Sparta, or Lacedæmon, the capital of Laconia and of the Spartan state, lay on the west bank of the river Eurotas, and embraced a circuit of forty-eight stadia, or six miles. The ruins are still seen nearly a league to the east of Misitra, and are known by the name of *Palæopolis* (Ancient City). Sparta was irregularly built, and consisted of five separate quarters, which, as late as the 120th Olympiad, were not enclosed by any common wall. Among other remarkable objects enumerated by Pausanias are the following: the market-place (ἀγορα), containing the public buildings, in which the most distinguished magistrates held their meetings, and the principal or nament of which was the *Persice*, a celebrated colonnade, built from the spoils taken from the Persians; its roof was supported by statues of Persians: the *chorus*, or place in which the ephebi executed their dances, in the gymnopædia, adorned with statues of Apollo, Diana and Latona: the *Baroneta*, or residence of the kings of the family of Eurysthenes, in the street Aphetai, so called because the people bought it of the widow of Polydorus for a herd of cattle: the *Leschai*, or halls in which the popular assemblies were held, and of which there were two, the *Lesche* of the Crotanes, near the tombs of the Agides, and the *Lesche Pœcile:* the temple of Minerva Poliouchos (Chalciœca), on the Acropolis, &c. The Spartans were distinguished among the people of Greece by their manners, customs and constitution. Their kings ruled only through the popular will, as they had no other privileges than those of giving their opinion first in the popular assemblies, acting as umpires in disputes, and of commanding the army: their only other advantages were a considerable landed estate, a large share of the spoils, and the chief seat in assemblies and at meals. The Spartans, that is, the descendants of the Dorians, who acquired possession of Laconia under the Heraclidæ, were occupied only with war and the chase, and left the agricultural labors to the Helots (q. v.); but the Lacedæmonians, or Periœci (the ancient inhabitants of the country), engaged in commerce, navigation and manufactures. Although the Spartan conquerors were superior in refinement and cultivation to the Lacedæmonians, the arts of industry flourished only among the latter. They gradually intermingled with the Spartans, whom they exceeded in number, and formed one people. Herodotus states the number of Spartans at only 8000. Both people constituted one state, with a national assembly, to which the towns sent deputies. The military contributions in money and troops formed the principal tribute of the free Lacedæmonians to the Spartans (Dorians). The former were sometimes divided by jealousy from the latter, and, in the Theban war, several towns withdrew their troops from the Spartans, and joined Epaminondas. The distinguishing traits of the Spartans were severity, resolution and perseverance. Defeat and reverse never discouraged them. But they were faithless and crafty, as appears from their conduct in the Messenian wars, in which they not only bribed the Arcadian king, Aristocrates, to the basest treachery towards the Messenians, but also corrupted the Delphic oracle, of which they made use to the prejudice of the Messenians. The age at which marriage might be contracted was fixed by Lycurgus at thirty for men and twenty for women. When a Spartan woman was pregnant, it was required that pictures of the handsomest young men should be hung up in her chamber, for the purpose of producing a favorable effect on the fruit of her womb. The child was brought forth, it is said, upon a shield, and, if a male, was laid, without swaddling clothes (to leave him the free use of his limbs), in a shield, with the words Α ταν ἀ επι ταν (Either with this or upon this). The other Greeks washed the new-born infants with water, and afterwards rubbed them over with oil; but the Spartans bathed them in wine, to try the strength of their constitution. They had a notion that a wine bath produced convulsions or even death in weakly children, but confirmed the health of the strong. If the infant proved vigorous and sound, the state received it into the number of citizens; otherwise it was thrown into a cave on mount Taygetus. In the other Grecian states, the exposition of children was a matter of custom: in Sparta it was forbidden by law. If we may trust to Homer, it was, at an early period, a custom among the Spartan women to employ nurses in order to preserve the beauty of their breasts. The nurses were treated as part of the family. The Spartan children were early inured to hardship and accustomed to freedom. Stays, which were in use among the other Grecians, were unknown to the Spartans. To accustom the children to endure hunger, they gave them but little food; and, if they stood in need of more, they were obliged to steal it; and, if discovered, they were severely punished, not for the theft, but for their awkwardness. Every ten days, they were required to present themselves before the ephori, and whoever was found to be too fat, received a flogging. Wine was not generally given to girls in Greece, but was commonly allowed to boys from earliest childhood. In Sparta, the boys were obliged to wear the hair short, until they attained the age of manhood, when it was suffered to grow They usually ran naked, and were generally dirty, as they did not bathe and anoint themselves, like the other Greeks. They took pride in having the body covered with marks of bruises and wounds. They wore no outer garment, except in bad weather, and no shoes at any time. They were obliged to make their beds of rushes from the Eurotas. Till the seventh year, the child was kept in the gynæceum, under the care of the women; from that age to the eighteenth year, they were called *boys* (πρωτηρες), and thence to the age of thirty, *youths* (ἐφηβοι). In the thirtieth year the Spartan entered the period of manhood, and enjoyed the full rights of a citizen. At the age of seven, the boy was withdrawn from the paternal care, and educated under the public eye, in company with others of the same age, without distinction of rank or fortune. If any person withheld his son from the care of the state, he forfeited his civil rights. The principal object of attention, during the periods of boyhood and youth, was the physical education, which consisted in the practice of various gymnastic exercises—running, leaping, throwing the discus, wrestling, boxing, the chase and the *pancratium*. (q. v.) These exercises were performed naked, in certain buildings called *gymnasia*. Besides gymnastics, dancing and the military exercises were practised. A singular custom was the flogging of boys (*diamastigosis*) on the annual festival of Diana Orthia, for the purpose of inuring them to bear pain with firmness: the priestess stood by with a small, light, wooden image of Diana, and if she observed that any boy was spared, she called out that the image of the goddess was so heavy, that she could not support it, and the blows were then redoubled. The men who were present exhorted their sons to fortitude, while the boys endeavored to surpass each other in firmness. Whoever uttered the least cry during the scourging, which was so severe as sometimes to prove fatal, was considered as disgraced, while he who bore it without shrinking was crowned, and received the praises of the whole city. According to some, this usage was established by Lycurgus; others refer it to the period of the battle of Platææ. (q. v.) To teach the youth cunning, vigilance and activity, they were encouraged, as has been already mentioned, to practise theft in certain cases; but if detected, they were flogged, or obliged to go without food, or compelled to dance round an altar, singing songs in ridicule of themselves. The fear of the shame of being discovered sometimes led to the most extraordinary acts. Thus it is related that a boy who had stolen a young fox, and concealed it under his clothes, suffered it to gnaw out his bowels, rather than reveal the theft by suffering the fox to escape. Swimming was considered among the Spartans to be so indispensable, that it was a proverb among them, to intimate that a man was good for nothing—He cannot even swim. Modesty of deportment was also particularly attended to; and conciseness of language was so much studied, that the term *laconic* is employed to signify a short, pithy manner of speaking. The Spartans were the only people of Greece who avowedly despised learning, and excluded it from the education of youth. Their whole instruction consisted in learning obedience to their superiors, the endurance of all hardships, and to conquer or die in war. The youth were, however, carefully instructed in a knowledge of the laws, which, not being reduced to writing, were taught orally. The education of the females was entirely different from that of the Athenians. Instead of remaining at home, as in Athens, spinning, &c., they danced in public, wrestled with each other, ran on the course, threw the discus, &c. This was not only done in public, but in a half-naked state. The object of this training of the women was to give a vigorous constitution to their children.—See Müller's *History and Antiquities of the Doric Race*, translated, with additions, from the German (London, 1830). The Mainots have been supposed to be the descendants of the ancient Spartans. (See *Mainots*.)

Spartacus; a Thracian gladiator, the instigator of the servile war or revolt of the slaves in Italy. He had been compelled, like other barbarians, to serve in the Roman army, from which he had deserted, and, at the head of a body of chosen companions, had carried on a partisan war against the conquerors. Being made prisoner, Spartacus was sold as a slave; and his strength and size caused him to be reserved as a gladiator. He was placed in a gladiatorial school at Capua, with two hundred other Thracian, German and Gaulish slaves, among whom a conspiracy was formed (B. C. 71) for effecting their escape. Their plot was discovered; but a small body, under Spartacus, broke out, and, having procured arms, and gained some advantages over the Roman forces sent against them, they were soon joined by the slaves and peasantry of the neighborhood, and their numbers amounted to 10,000 men. By the courage and skill of Spartacus, several considerable battles were gained; but his authority was insufficient to restrain the ferocity and licentiousness of his follow ers, and the cities of the south of Italy were pillaged with the most revolting atrocities. In a few months, Spartacus found himself at the head of 60,000 men; and the consuls were now sent, with two legions, against the revolted slaves. Mutual jealousies divided the leaders of the latter, and the Gauls and Germans formed a separate body under their own leaders, while the Thracians and Lucanians adhered to Spartacus. The former were defeated; but Spartacus skilfully covered their retreat, and successively defeated the two consuls. Flushed with success, his followers demanded to be led against Rome; and the city trembled before the servile forces. In this crisis, Licinius Crassus, who was afterwards a triumvir, was placed at the head of the army. His lieutenant, Mummius, whom he despatched with two legions to watch the motions of the enemy, was defeated by a superior force, and slain. Crassus, after having made an example of the defeated legions, by executing every tenth man, surrounded Spartacus, near Rhegium, with a ditch six miles in length. Spartacus broke through the enemy by night; but Crassus, who did not doubt that he would march upon Rome, pursued him, and defeated a considerable part of his forces, who had abandoned their general from disaffection. Spartacus now retreated; but his followers compelled him to lead them against the Romans. His soldiers fought with a courage deserving success; but they were overcome, after an obstinate conflict, and Spartacus himself fell fighting on his knees, upon a heap of his slain enemies. According to the Roman statements, 60,000 rebels fell in this battle (A. D. 71). 6000 were made prisoners, and crucified on the Appian way. A considerable number escaped, and continued the war, but were finally destroyed by Pompey.

Spasmodic Cholera. With a view of giving more complete information on the subject of this disorder than can be obtained at present, we have thought it best to defer the account of it till we arrive at the end of the concluding volume.

Spawning of Fish. In the oviparous fishes, with distinct sexes, the eggs are impregnated externally, and arrive at maturity without the aid of the mother. The spawn being deposited by the female, the male then pours upon it the impregnating fluid. In the ovoviviparous fishes, sexual intercourse takes place, and the eggs are hatched in the uterus. In the oviparous fishes, which are hermaphrodite, the spawn is impregnated previous to deposition by the same individual which deposits the eggs. Fishes exhibit a great variety in regard to the number of their eggs. In some, the number is small; while in the spawn of a codfish 3,686,760 eggs have been found; in that of the flounder, 1,357,400, and in that of the mackerel, 546,681. The season of spawning varies according to the species and even the habits of the individual. In general, before spawning, fish forsake the deep water, and approach the shore, that, the roe, being placed in shallow water, may be vivified by the influence of the solar ray. At that season, some fish forsake the salt water, and ascend the rivers, and, after spawning, return again to the ocean. The eggs of various species of fish are used as articles of food, sometimes in a recent state, and sometimes salted, as in the well-known article of trade, caviar. (q. v.)

Speaker. The lord-chancellor is, *ex officio*, the speaker of the British house of lords, and may, if a lord of parliament, as in practice is always the case, give his opinion and argue any question before the house. The speaker of the house of commons is a member of the house, elected by a majority of the votes, to act as chairman or president in putting questions, reading briefs or bills, keeping order, reprimanding the refractory, adjourning the house, &c. The first thing done by the commons, upon the meeting of a parliament, is to choose a speaker, who is to be approved of by the king, and who, upon his admission, begs his majesty that the commons, during their sitting, may have free access to his majesty, freedom of speech in their own house, and security from arrests. The speaker is not allowed to persuade or dissuade in passing a bill, except in committee, but only to make a short and plain narrative; nor to vote, unless the house be equally divided, when he has a casting vote. He receives a salary of £6000 a year. (See *Parliament*.) The presiding officer of the French chamber of deputies is styled *président*, and is chosen by the chamber itself. The chancellor of France presides in the house of peers. In the senate of the U. States, the presiding officer is styled *president*; and the constitution (i. 3.) provides that the vice-president shall be president of the senate, and shall have no vote, unless the votes of the senators are equally divided. In his absence, or in case he exercises the office of president of the U. States, the senate chooses a president *pro tempore*. The speaker of the house of representatives is chosen (*Const.* i. 2.) by the house itself.

Specific Gravity. (See *Gravity.*)

Specifics, in medicine; such articles in the *materia medica* as have the special power of curing particular diseases in all persons and under all circumstances. Multitudes of such medicines are continually announced by quacks; but men of science and sense do not now believe in the existence of any specific, in the full sense of the word. Peruvian bark was formerly supposed to be a certain cure for intermittents and agues; but it is now known to fail in many cases, and not to be more efficacious than some other tonic medicines. The two medicines which approach nearest the character of specifics, are sulphur as an antidote to the itch, and mercury to venereal poison. Yet there are cases of disease not distinguishable from lues venerea, which are cured without the aid of mercury; and the power of sulphur in curing the itch is considerably augmented by the addition of other substances.

Spectacles are of two sorts, according as they are intended to assist short-sighted or far-sighted persons. In the former case they must be concave, in the latter convex; concave to diminish the excessive refraction of the rays of light by the humors of the eye, convex to increase the refraction. In both cases care should be taken to adapt the degree of concavity or convexity to the condition of the eye; for since the eye gradually accustoms itself to glasses continually used, the defect in the vision will be increased by the use of such as are too powerful, while it may be diminished, or, at least, prevented from increasing, by those of an opposite character. In addition to this, it ought to be considered, that, with most persons, the field of vision in one eye is greater than that in the other. But if a person, in the selection of spectacles, suffers himself to be guided merely by the first impression, he will commonly choose glasses that are too powerful, and seldom be able to adapt them to both eyes. Opticians have a contrivance for determining the degree of short or far sightedness, and the glasses are numbered according to their degree of convexity or concavity, so that suitable ones may be more readily selected. Those persons who are far-sighted should refrain, as long as they conveniently can, from increasing the power of the glasses. To afford the means of seeing distinctly, and to be used without injury, spectacles should be regularly formed; that is to say, the concavity or convexity should be uniform. Moreover, the glasses should be perfectly transparent, and entirely destitute of color. Green spectacles are to be recommended only to such persons as have very sensitive eyes, or to such as are exposed for a long time to a glittering white surface (for instance, snow in bright sunshine). Spectacles are also used to cure squinting. These have no glasses, but consist merely of a thin plate of some substance. In the middle, opposite the axis of the eye, there is a small opening, to which the pupil must turn, in order to see any thing. In this way it gradually becomes accustomed to the proper direction. The ancient Greeks and Romans were entirely unacquainted with the use of spectacles. In the twelfth century, we find a discovery mentioned by an Arabic writer, Alhazen, which might have led to the invention of spectacles. At the close of the thirteenth century, Roger Bacon speaks of them. The common spectacles must have been invented early (1280—1311). In Germany, a kind of spectacles were known in 1270. (For further information, see the article *Optics*, section *Vision.*)

Spectrum, Prismatic. (See *Colors, Doctrine of;* also *Optics.*)

Speech, Organs of. (See *Voice.*)

Spelman, sir Henry, a celebrated English antiquary and philologist, born in 1562, was sent, at the age of fifteen, to Trinity college, Cambridge, and entered as a law student at Lincoln's Inn; but he seems to have paid little attention to legal science at this period, and within three years he settled on his estate in the country. At length embarrassments, partly arising from a numerous family, aroused him to the exertion of his talents. He went to Ireland in 1607, as member of a board of commissioners for settling the titles to lands and manors in that kingdom; and he was afterwards employed to investigate the subject of the exaction of fees by the civil and ecclesiastical courts. On this occasion, he drew up his treatise *De Sepultura*, in which he demonstrates the flagrant abuses which had occurred to his notice. His services were rewarded with the honor of knighthood. In 1612, he settled in London, devoting his leisure to the study of the juridical antiquities of his native country. Having purchased the lands which had belonged to two suppressed monasteries, and meeting with obstacles to the quiet enjoyment of the property, he began to entertain scruples of conscience relative to the alienation of church lands, and wrote on the subject his work entitled *De non temerandis Ecclesiis.* On the revival of the society of antiquaries in 1614, sir H. Spelman became a member, and produced a Discourse concerning the Original of the four Law-terms of the Year. In his researches into legal archæology, he found it necessary to study the Saxon language; and this led to the composition of his great work, the Archæological Glossary. He printed a specimen in 1621, and in 1626 appeared the first part, entitled *Archæologus in Modum Glossarii ad Rem antiquam posteriorem* (folio). Before he had completed the glossary, he engaged in preparing a History of English Councils, of which the first part, to the Norman conquest, appeared in 1639; and two additional volumes were subsequently published, partly from the papers of Spelman, by sir W. Dugdale. In 1639, likewise, appeared his last work, entitled the History of Tenures by Knights' Service in England. His death took place in 1641, and his body was interred in Westminster abbey. Besides the works already noticed, he was the author of a History of the Civil Affairs of the Kingdom from the Conquest to the Grant of the Magna Charta; a Treatise concerning Tithes; a History of Sacrilege; Aspilogia; &c. His English works were published, collectively in a folio volume, in 1727.

Spelter. (See *Solder.*)

Spence, Joseph, a critic, born in 1698, received his education at Oxford, where he obtained a fellowship. In 1727 appeared his Essay on Pope's Translation of the Odyssey, which led to an intimate friendship with the poet. In 1728, he was elected professor of poetry at Oxford; and he afterwards travelled abroad with the earl of Lincoln. On his return, he obtained a living in Buckinghamshire, and, in 1754, was promoted to a prebendal stall in Durham cathedral. After the death of his friend, Mr. Rudge, in 1763, he resided much with the widow of that gentleman, who usually spent the summer months at Weybridge, in Surrey. On the morning of Aug. 20, 1768, Mr. Spence was found, by a servant, lying on his face in a shallow piece of water, into which it appeared that he had fallen, and, being unable to extricate himself, he was unfortunately drowned. His principal work is entitled *Polymetis*, or an Enquiry into the Agreement between the Works of the Roman Poets and the Remains of ancient Artists (1747, fol.). In 1819 appeared Anecdotes, and Characters of Books and Men, collected from the Conversation of Mr. Pope, and of other Persons, from a manuscript of Mr. Spence, with his life, &c. by S. W. Singer (8vo.).

Spencer, George John, earl, is of the second branch of the Spencer family, the elder possessing the title of duke of Marlborough. His father, in 1761, was created baron Spencer, and, in 1764, viscount Althorpe and earl Spencer. The present earl was born in 1758, and was educated at Harrow, and afterwards had for his tutor the celebrated sir William Jones. From Harrow he removed to Trinity college, Cambridge. When he had completed his education, he travelled, and on his return was elected member of parliament for the county of Northampton. In 1789, by his father's death, he became earl Spencer. In the house of lords, he voted with the whigs, till the period of the French revolution, when, with some others of the party, he joined the administration, and held the place of first lord of the admiralty. In 1801, he retired with Mr. Pitt, but afterwards again joined his old friends, and, when they came into place, in 1805, he was appointed secretary of state for the home department. Earl Spencer is one of the principal members of the Roxburghe (q. v.) club, and has the largest and richest private library in the world: the foundation of it was laid in 1789, by the purchase of count Rewiczki's collection, for an annuity of £500 sterling. This he increased, at a great expense, by collecting books in all parts of Europe. The greater part of the library is at his seat, Althorp, in Northamptonshire, and consists of 45,000 volumes: the rest is at London. A catalogue of the rarest and most costly works of the collection has been prepared by Dibdin—*Bibliotheca Spenceriana*, or a descriptive Catalogue of the Books printed in the fifteenth Century, and of many valuable first Editions (4 vols., 1814). It contains engravings, wood cuts and fac similes illustrative of 1004 incunabula.—Earl Spencer's eldest son, John Charles, known as viscount Althorp, chancellor of the exchequer, and therefore ministerial leader in the house of commons, was born in 1782, educated at Cambridge, entered parliament in 1803, was one of the lords of the treasury during Fox's short administration (1806), and was soon after returned for Northamptonshire which he has since continued to represent. His services and exertions in favor of the reform bill have gained him much reputation, as well as great popularity.

Spener, Philip Jacob, a celebrated divine of the Lutheran church in the seventeenth century, was born in 1635, at Rappolsweiler, in Upper Alsace. His piety was early awakened by his patroness, the countess of Rappolstein, and was confirmed by witnessing, at the age of fourteen years, her preparation for death. In 1651, he commenced his theological studies at Strasburg, became, in 1654, tutor of the princes of the Palatinate, and delivered lectures on philosophy and history. From 1659 to 1662, he travelled in Germany, Switzerland and France, where he became acquainted with the Jesuit Menestrier, celebrated for his knowledge of heraldry, and, having been thus led to study this science, wrote several works on heraldry, still much esteemed. In 1664, he was made doctor of theology at Strasburg, and, in 1666, he received the first place among the clergy at Frankfort on the Maine. His practical sermons, which deviated entirely from the dogmatico-polemic method then universal, were received with much applause. In 1670, he instituted his celebrated *collegia pietatis*, which, against his will, became the origin of *pietism*. (q. v.) From this time, Spener's history is wholly connected with this remarkable change in the religious state of Protestant Germany, as it was chiefly owing to his example and the spirit of his writings. The Lutheran church, at that time, was fast sinking into a lifeless dogmatism. Doctrines, forms and polemics were confounded with a religious life. Spener, in his *Pia Desideria* and other treatises, exposed the evils of this state of things, and showed how the important office of the ministry had become alienated from its proper purpose—that of instructing the people in true religion, correcting their faults, and alleviating their afflictions. He was violently opposed by the clergy, who reproached him with not making any difference between practical and theoretical theology. But posterity acknowledges his services in the restoration of catechetical instruction, which had been almost entirely forgotten. From 1686 to 1691, he was preacher to the court in Dresden, and even then occupied himself with the religious teaching of children. A representation which he made to the elector in writing, respecting his faults, brought him into disgrace. He went, in 1691, to Berlin, where he took an active part in the foundation of the university of Halle. In 1698, the court of Dresden invited him to return; but he preferred to remain in Berlin, where he was in the possession of high appointments. He died in that city, in 1705. In his letters, reports, opinions, &c., a truly Christian benevolence and zeal for the cause of goodness is perceptible. Spener may be compared with Fenelon.

Spenser, Edmund, a celebrated English poet, was born in London, near the Tower, about 1553. It is not known where he received his early education, but he was admitted as a sizar of Pembroke hall, Cambridge, in 1569, and graduated M. A. in 1576. On leaving the university, he took up his residence with some relations in the north of England, probably as a tutor, where he unsuccessfully wooed a lady, whom he records in his Shepherd's Calendar, under the name of Rosaline, which was his first publication, and appeared in 1576. The year preceding, he had been advised by his friend Gabriel Harvey to remove to London, where he was introduced to sir Philip Sidney, to whom he dedicated the Shepherd's Calendar. In 1580, he accompanied lord Grey de Wilton, lord lieutenant of Ireland, as his secretary. He returned, in 1582, with lord Grey, who, in conjunction with the earl of Leicester and sir Philip Sidney, procured for him, in 1586, a grant of 3028 acres in the county of Cork, out of the forfeited lands of the earl of Desmond; on which, however, by the terms of the gift, he was obliged to become resident. He accordingly fixed his residence at Kilcolman, in the county of Cork, where he was visited by sir Walter Raleigh, who became his patron in lieu of sir Philip Sidney, then deceased, and whom he celebrates under the title of the Shepherd of the Ocean. He was then engaged in the composition of the Faery Queen, of which he had written the first three books. With these he accompanied Raleigh, the next year, to England, where they were published, with a dedication to queen Elizabeth, and an introductory letter to Raleigh, explaining the nature of the poem. Raleigh also gained him the favor of the queen, who rewarded his poetry and dedication with a pension of fifty pounds per annum. In 1591, he returned to Ireland; and, the succeeding year, his rising reputation induced his bookseller to collect and print his smaller pieces. He then passed an interval of two or three years in Ireland, where, in 1594, he married, being then in his forty-first year. His happiness was disquieted by the disturbances excited by the earl of Tyrone which were probably the cause of his revisiting England the following year. Here he printed some poems, and drew up his View of the State of Ireland; which, in consequence, it is supposed, of the severity of some of its suggestions, lay in MS. until printed, in 1633, by sir James Ware, who bestows much applause on the information and judgment displayed in it. In 1596, he published a new edition of his Faery Queen, with three additional books. Of the remaining six, which were to complete the original design, two imperfect cantos of Mutabilitie only have been recovered, which were introduced into the folio edition of 1609, as a part of the lost book, entitled the Legend of Constancy. There has been much controversy in respect to the presumed loss of the remainder of these six books on the poet's flight from Ireland: the most probable conclusion, from the investigation, is, that they were never finished, but that some parts of them were lost on that melancholy occasion. In 1597, he returned to Ireland, and, in September, 1598, was recommended to be sheriff of Cork. The rebellion of Tyrone, however, took place in October, and with such fury as to compel Spenser and his family to quit Kilcolman in so much confusion that an infant child was left behind, and burnt with his house. The unfortunate poet arrived in England with a heart broken by these misfortunes, and died the 16th of the following January, 1599, in the forty-sixth year of his age. It is asserted that he terminated his life in great distress; but it has been contended that the poverty referred to by Camden and several of his poetical contemporaries, applies rather to his loss of property generally than to absolute personal suffering. This inference seems the more probable, as he was interred in Westminster abbey at the expense of the earl of Essex, who would scarcely have allowed the man to starve whom he thus honored. A monument was afterwards erected over his remains by the celebrated Anne, countess of Dorset. Of the personal character of Spenser there is no direct testimony; but the friendships which he formed are favorable to its respectability, which is also to be implied from the purity, devotion, and exalted morality of his writings. Neither, although he paid assiduous court to the great, was he guilty of the mean adulation so common in his time, except, indeed, to queen Elizabeth, by whom, both as a sovereign and a woman, it was levied as a kind of tax. As a poet, although his minor works contain many beauties, Spenser will be judged chiefly from the Faery Queen, the predominant excellences of which are imagery, feeling, and melody of versification. With all its defects, it furnishes admirable examples of the noblest graces of poetry, sublimity, pathos, unrivalled fertility of conception, and exquisite vividness of description. Its great length and want of interest, as a fable, added to the real and affected obsoleteness of the language, may, indeed, deter readers in general from a complete perusal; but it will always be resorted to by the genuine lovers of poetry as a rich store-house of invention. The stanza which Spenser has adopted in the Faery Queen, is usually called the *Spenserian*, either because he invented it, or was the first to apply it to extensive use. It consists of a strophe of eight decasyllabic verses, and an Alexandrine, and has a three-fold rhyme—the first and third verses forming one, the second, fourth, fifth and seventh another, and the sixth, eighth and ninth the third. It is susceptible of great variety of expression, and admits equally of the most different kinds of composition—the droll or pathetic, descriptive or sentimental, tender or satirical. The best editions of Spenser's works are those of Hughes and Todd (8 vols., 8vo., 1805, with notes and a life).—See Warton's *Observations on the Faery Queen.*

SPERMACETI, SPERM OIL. (See *Fat*, and *Whale*.)

SPESSART; a woody, mountainous chain of Germany, in the Bavarian circle of the Lower Maine, extending along the right bank of the Maine, by which it is nearly surrounded. The highest summit is Geyersberg, 2000 feet high. There are about 300,000 acres (*morgen*) of forest, belonging principally to the crown of Bavaria, and consisting chiefly of oak and beech. Cobalt, copper and iron are obtained in the Spessart. Aschaffenburg, on the south-western edge, is the principal place.

SPEYER, or SPEIER. (See *Spire*.)

SPEZIALE, member of the junta of government, instituted in 1799, at Naples, was the son of a peasant of Borgetto, not far from Palermo. His servile deportment procured him a place in the *corte pretoriana e capitanale* at Palermo. When the court of Naples fled to Sicily, he showed a bitter hatred towards the French, and violently persecuted the suspected, so that the chevalier Acton (q. v.) appointed him to try the persons accused of having taken part in the revolution. Even before the French had left Naples, he began to exercise his office on the island of Procida, which was protected by Nelson. He surrounded himself with gibbets and executioners, and every day was marked with executions. The cruelty of his character now became manifest. No sex, age or class was spared. No defence was allowed. Hardly was the cardinal Ruffo in possession of the capital, when Speziale received orders to transfer his bloody court thither. He even deceived his own friends, and allured them to their destruction. This monster followed the court to Palermo in 1806, became insane soon after, and died distracted, in 1813, loaded with the curses of the nation.

Spezzia. (See *Hydra.*)

Sphagnum. (See *Appendix*, end of this volume.)

Sphere; a solid, every point of the surface of which is equally distant from a certain point within the same, called its *centre*. It is generated by the rotation of a circle upon one of its diameters as an axis. Any circle described on the sphere, and whose centre is that of the sphere, is called a *great circle*. The solid contents of a sphere are to those of a cylinder (q. v.) of equal base and altitude (the diameter of the base of the cylinder being equal to that of the sphere) in the proportion of two to three; to those of a cone of equal base and altitude as two to one. These proportions were discovered by Archimedes. Nature, from the egg of the smallest worm, and from the drop of dew to the largest body in the universe, strives after the form of the sphere. Therefore, in antiquity, when the spiritual was represented by the sensible, many philosophers conceived of God under the form of a sphere.

Spheroid; a solid, generated by the entire rotation of a semi-ellipse, or other curve not differing much from it, upon its axis. As our earth has the form of a sphere, flattened at the poles, it belongs to the spheroids. Telescopes show a similar form in Jupiter and Saturn; and there are sufficient grounds for ascribing the same form to all the heavenly bodies which have a rotation on their axis. (See *Earth.*)

Sphinx; a fabulous monster, which figures both in the Grecian and Egyptian mythologies, and was probably of Egyptian origin. The sphinx of the Greeks is distinguished for cruelty as well as wisdom. Juno, says the fable, provoked with the Thebans, sent the sphinx, the daughter of Typhon and Echidna, to punish them. It laid this part of Bœotia under continual alarms by proposing enigmas, and devouring the inhabitants if unable to explain them. The Thebans were told by the oracle that the sphinx would destroy herself as soon as one of the enigmas she proposed was explained. In this enigma, the question proposed was, what animal walked on four legs in the morning, two at noon, and three in the evening. Upon this, Creon, king of Thebes, promised his crown and his sister Jocasta in marriage to him who should deliver his country from the monster by a successful explanation of the enigma. It was, at last, happily explained by Œdipus, who observed that man walked on his hands and feet when young, or in the morning of life; at the noon of life he walked erect; and in the evening of his days, he supported his infirmities upon a stick. (See *Œdipus.*) The sphinx no sooner heard this explanation than she threw herself from a rock, and immediately expired.—The Egyptian sphinx does not appear to have been distinguished by the same traits of character. It is formed with a human head on the body of a lion; is always in a recumbent posture, with the fore-paws stretched forward, and a head-dress resembling an old-fashioned wig. The features are like those of the ancient Egyptians, found in the ancient ruins. The colossal sphinx, near the group of pyramids at Gize, has recently been uncovered by Caviglia. It is about 150 feet long and sixty-three feet high: the body is monolithic; but the paws, which are thrown out fifty feet in front, are constructed of masonry. The sphinx of Sais, formed of a block of red granite twenty-two feet long, is now in the Egyptian museum in the Louvre. There has been much speculation concerning the signification of these figures. Winckelmann observes that they have the head of a female, and the other parts of a male, which has led to the conjecture that they are intended as emblems of the genera tive powers of nature, which the old mythologies are accustomed to indicate by the mystic union of the two sexes in one individual.

Sphragistics (from σφραγις, a seal); a branch of diplomatics (q. v.) which teaches the history of seals and the means which they afford of determining the genuineness of the documents to which they are attached. Originally, only persons of rank, churches, convents, or corporations, had the right to use seals. The old seals represented the persons to whom they belonged either on foot (*sigilla pedestria*) or on horseback (*sigilla equestria*), or had figures emblematical of their dignity. They are round or oval, impressed in gold, silver, lead, but generally in wax of various colors. The difference in the color of the wax indicated different degrees of dignity, &c. In the sixteenth century, sealing-wax came into use. (See *Seal.*) Sphragistics, as a science, dates from the great work of Heineccius on seals, in 1709 (new ed. 1719, folio, Leipsic).—See also Ficoroni's *I Piombi Antichi* (Rome, 1740, 4to.); Manni's *Osservazioni istoriche sopra i Sigilli antichi de' Secoli Bassi* (Florence, 1739—86, 30 vols., 4to.); and Ph. W. Gercken's *Anmerkungen über die Siegel zum Nutzen der Diplomatik* (Augsburg, 1781; Stend., 1786).

Spice Islands. (See *Moluccas.*)

Spider. (See *Appendix*, end of this vol.)

Spinage. (See *Appendix*, end of this vol.)

Spine (from *spina*, thorn, so called from the shape of the processes of the vertebræ), in anatomy, the vertebral or spinal column, the *back-bone* in common language, is the articulated bony pillar at the back of the trunk, forming the foundation or basis of support and connexion to all the other parts of the frame. It is placed perpendicularly in the body, supporting the head on its upper extremity, while the lower end rests on the pelvis. The bones of the chest, to which the upper extremities are attached, are fixed to its sides, while the *ossa innominata*, or the great bones to which the lower limbs are articulated, are immovably united to it below. It is the point of attachment and support in front for the viscera of the thorax and abdomen, and for the great trunks of the blood-vessels. We may thus regard it as the central and most essential piece of the skeleton, as the centre of motion for the head and limbs, and the basis of support for all the great internal organs. Again, the bones which compose it give attachment to the principal muscles moving the head, the shoulders and the arms, to those which act on the trunk, and to some part of the abdominal muscles, and of those which move the lower limbs. Further, it constitutes a canal, which receives and protects the spinal marrow, and gives issue to the various nerves proceeding from that organ to the trunk and limbs. The importance of the spine is so great that it modifies all the details of the organization of the animals which possess it. It is formed of twenty-nine pieces of bone, strongly articulated into each other, and placed in succession from above downwards. The twenty-four upper ones are called *vertebræ.*

Distortions of the Spine are the unnatural inflections of the spine, which give a more or less deformed figure to the trunk, and even to the limbs; hence wry neck, high shoulders, humpback, uneven hips, lameness, &c., are very frequent among the higher classes of our time, particularly among females, and generally owing to want of care or judgment in those who have charge of children, or to the injudicious habits of the persons afflicted, and frequently aggravated or made permanent by improper means used for remedying them. The beauty of the whole body depends chiefly upon the natural formation of the spine. This column of vertebræ ought not permanently to deviate from the straight line to the right or left; but it has naturally some slight curvatures forwards and backwards. In the region of the loins, it is bent a little forward; in the region of the chest, a little backward, and, at the neck, again, somewhat forward. This regular formation of the spine is produced by the character of the vertebræ, the cartilages which unite them, and the muscles of the back, which support and move them. If the vertebræ themselves suffer from disease, as, for instance, in case of rickets, the spine is not capable of supporting the head and keeping the body straight, it becomes curved, and, if remedies are not applied in season, this unnatural curvature increases daily, and permanent distortion at length takes place. If the cartilages and ligatures suffer relaxation, as in case of a debilitated state of the body, the spine cannot, after every motion, resume its proper position, and it may easily happen that some vertebræ become partially dislocated, and thus a disposition to distortion takes place, because the part of the spine over these vertebræ is deprived of its proper support, and must incline to one side. The muscles of the back, situated on both sides of the spine, equal in number and form, and destined not only to execute the manifold movements of the trunk, but also to maintain, by the equilibrium of their power, the straight direction of the spine, frequently occasion distortions, by losing their vigor; for the spine, in this case, wanting its natural support, inclines sideways or backwards. The same effect may be produced by too frequent or too continued use of one set of muscles in a particular way; for the spine becomes at last permanently fixed in the posture which it has been compelled to assume during the exercise. This survey shows us the various causes of distortions, and the proper means for preventing them. The causes may be reduced to diseases and injudicious habits. The diseases of children which may occasion distortions of the spine are chiefly scrofula and rickets, so often connected with it, and general debility. These diseases may be best prevented by the use of food easily digestible by pure air, hard beds not too warm, frequent exercise, great cleanliness, frequent bathing, washing and rubbing the skin, and similar requisites of a good physical education. The muscles of the back are often debilitated by compelling children, particularly weakly ones, to sit up in a constrained posture, which distresses the spine, and produces a sinking and bending in search of relief, or by allowing children too little free movement and exercise, and obliging them continually to sit still and read—the surest mode of producing physical and intellectual cripples. The use of corsets also contributes much to the weakness of the dorsal muscles, and consequently to distortion of the spine. If the shoulders are continually supported artificially by a corset, the dorsal muscles, destined by nature to keep the spine straight, remain inactive, and lose their power, the body becomes unable to support itself without the corset, and a sinking and bending take place as soon as it is removed. If to this is added the continual command, perhaps accompanied by threats, to sit straight, which has become actually impossible to the child, its exertions result in nothing but a curvature of the spine, which is therefore so frequent in girls of the higher classes, but in boys of the same families, who are neither tormented with corsets, nor admonished so repeatedly to sit straight, is much rarer. The second cause of distortions—injudicious habits—deserves particular attention, because much may be done to prevent them. The habit of many nurses to carry children always on the same arm, accustoms the child to incline always towards one side, and to sleep in one position, from which a distortion of the spine naturally arises in the course of time. The bad position of the body in some amusements and occupations; for instance, the manner in which young people sit in writing, reading, drawing, sewing, embroidering playing on the flute, violin, harp and guitar, the habit of crossing the feet in standing, or of standing on one foot; the habit of lying crooked in bed, and even the habit of girls to spend a long time in a constrained position dressing their own hair,—may occasion distortion of the spine. Every one-sided motion, often repeated, may produce a tendency to such distortion, and, the tendency once existing, the evil increases every day. This distortion, besides disfiguring the body, and unfitting the subject for certain avocations, also tends to produce inflammation of the lungs, dropsy of the chest, pulmonary consumption and apoplexy, a general disturbance of the health, and early death. With women, it often gives rise to painful labors, and sometimes makes a natural delivery impossible. The proper means of guarding against distortion we have already suggested in the directions respecting food, air, exercise and cleanliness, the prevention of ill habits on the part of nurses, and of the children themselves, and in the important rule, not to compel a straight carriage of the body by the wearing of corsets, nor by the continual injunction to stand and sit straight, as both tend directly to produce the evil intended to be prevented. It is important to detect a distortion of the spine as early as possible. It is therefore the duty of mothers and governesses to examine often the body of children. The child should be undressed, and placed in such a way (not lying down) that the entire back may be seen. The head must be held straight, the face directed forwards; the arms must hang down, and the whole position must be as easy as possible. Then the vertebræ must be struck slightly with the hand, to discover if there is a prominence or a sensation of pain in any place. The examiner should then proceed to the parts of the body on each side of the spine, which ought to be perfectly equal. The neck, the shoulders, and the hips, are to be looked at: if the latter are uneven, the hip joints and feet must be also tried. The examiner should also see whether the breast-bone is precisely in the middle of the breast, and whether it forms a straight line, whether the clavicles are uniform, whether the ribs lie even. With grown girls, the unevenness of the breasts often furnishes the earliest sign of distortion of the spine. These examinations ought to be made once or twice a week, and in the case of girls, even after they have arrived at maturity, because the years immediately succeeding the period of puberty are those in which distortions are most frequently manifested in the female sex, and because a cure can be hardly expected much after the twentieth year Attention to distortion ought not to be delayed until a high shoulder or hip shows itself these are only proofs of a distortion which has already long existed. If, however, any thing like distortion is perceived, do not resort to the means so often recommended of suspension by the arms, or the use of plasters, which can avail nothing, and do not expect that the dancing-master can remedy the evil, which will only increase under his lessons. Assistance can be rendered only by a physician familiar with these deformities, and who has made himself acquainted with the general state of body of his patient by a careful examination. The cure must not be expected too soon; and the orders of the physician must be scrupulously obeyed. Too much reliance is not to be placed on machines.—See Wenzel, *On the Diseases of the Spine* (with engravings, Bamberg, 1824, folio); see, also, *Orthopædic Institutes*.

SPINELLAN. (See *Sodalite*.)

SPINELLE (*Spinelle Ruby* and *Pleonaste*). The primary form of this species is the regular octahedron; and this is the figure under which it generally occurs. It is rarely modified by the truncation or the bevelment of its edges, and sometimes presents itself in hemitrope crystals. Its crystals vary in dimensions, though they are usually not above the size of a pea. Their cleavage is very difficult; fracture conchoidal; lustre vitreous; color red, passing into blue and green, also into yellow, brown and black; transparent to opaque; hardness above that of quartz; specific gravity 3.5. The red varieties of spinelle are called, by jewellers, *spinelle ruby*, while those possessed of a darker color are called *Ceylonite* or *Pleonaste*. The following analyses—the first of which is by Berzelius, the second by Klaproth, and the third by Descotils—exhibit the chemical composition of the species:

	1. Blue Spinelle.	2. Spinelle Ruby.	3. Pleonaste.
Alumine,	72.25	74.50	68.00
Silex, . .	5.45	15.50	2.00
Magnesia, .	14.63	8.25	12.00
Oxide of iron,	4.26	1.50	16.00
Lime, . . .	0.00	0.75	0.00
	96.59	100.50	98.00

The red varieties, exposed to the heat of the blow-pipe, become black and opaque; on cooling, they appear first green, then almost colorless, and at last re-assume their red color. They are with difficulty fused with the aid of borax—melting, however, a little more easily with salt of phosphorus. Pleonaste yields a deep green color to the globule. The original depositories of this species are white limestone and a drusy volcanic rock. It is often found, however, in more recent deposits, formed by diluvial or alluvial action, along with crystals of corundum and zircon. The isolated crystals chiefly come from Ceylon. In Südermannland, in Sweden, bluish and pearl-gray varieties occur, imbedded in granular limestone. Crystals of a green color are found imbedded in the drusy cavities of rocks ejected by Vesuvius. But the U. States surpass the rest of the world, both as to the number of the localities of spinelle, and the dimensions of its crystals. It abounds particularly in the towns of Amity and Edenville, in Orange county, New York; at which places it occurs in a highly crystalline, white limestone, and likewise loose in the soil, in crystals varying from the size of a pea and under, to those whose smallest diameter is four inches. Their colors are either black, or dark greenish, or bluish black, though it is rarely of a pale pink, or reddish-brown. These crystals are associated with hornblende, mica, augite, idocrase and scapolite. Spinelle of a rich green color is also found in the neighboring county of Sussex, New Jersey, at Franklin, near the iron works in that place. The crystals from this spot are highly modified in their figure, and are sometimes nearly transparent. Green and blue spinelle is also found in Massachusetts, in the lime quarries of Bolton, Boxborough and Chelmsford. Clear and finely-colored red varieties of the present species are highly prized as ornamental stones in jewelry. They go generally by the name of *spinelle ruby*, or *balas ruby*.

SPINET; a stringed instrument, formerly much in use, but now superseded by the pianoforte, somewhat similar to the harpsichord, and, like that, consisting of a case, sounding-board, keys, jacks, and a bridge. The difference between the spinet and the harpsichord is, that the latter is larger, and contains two or three sets of jacks and strings, so disposed and tuned as to admit of a variety of stops, while the former has only one set of jacks and strings, and consequently only one stop. When the spinet was first brought into use, though its invention was certainly anterior to that of the harpsichord, is not exactly known. But that it is derived from the harp is evident, from its character as well as construction, internal and external; and, indeed, it was originally called the *couched harp*, though since denominated *spinet*, from its quills, which resemble thorns, called, in Latin, *spinæ*.

Spinning. When the fibres of cotton, wool, or flax, are intended to be woven, they are reduced to fine threads, of uniform size, by the well-known process of spinning. Previously to the middle of the last century, this process was performed by hand, with the aid of the common spinning-wheel. Locks of cotton or wool, previously carded, were attached to a rapidly revolving spindle, driven by a large wheel, and were stretched or drawn out by the hand, at the same time that they were twisted by the spindle, upon which they were afterwards wound. Flax, the fibres of which are longer and more parallel, was loosely wound upon a distaff, from which the fibres were selected and drawn out by the thumb and finger, and at the same time were twisted by flyers, and wound upon a bobbin, which revolved with a velocity somewhat less than that of the flyers. The manufacture of flexible stuffs by means of machinery, operating on a large scale, is an invention of the last century. Although of recent date, it has given birth to some of the most elaborate and wonderful combinations of mechanism, and already constitutes, especially in England and in this country, an important source of national wealth and prosperity. The character of the machinery which has been applied to the manufacture of cotton, at different times, has been various. There are, however, several leading inventions, upon which most of the essential processes are founded, and which have given to their authors a greater share of celebrity than the rest. These are, 1. The *spinning jenny*. This machine was invented by Richard Hargreaves, in 1767, and, in its simplest form, resembled a number of spindles turned by a common wheel, or cylinder, which was worked by hand. It stretched out the threads as in common spinning of carded cotton. 2. The *water spinning frame*, invented by Richard Arkwright, in 1769. The essential and most important feature in this invention consists in the drawing out or elongating of the cotton, by causing it to pass between successive pairs of rollers, which revolve with different velocities, and which act as substitutes for the finger and thumb, as applied in common spinning. These rollers are combined with the spindle and flyers of the common flax wheel. 3. The *mule*. This was invented by Samuel Crompton, in 1779. It combines the principles of the two preceding inventions, and produces finer yarn than that which is spun in either of the other machines. It has now nearly superseded the jenny 4. The *power loom* for weaving by water or steam power, which was introduced about the end of the eighteenth century, and has received various modifications. The foregoing fundamental machines are used in the same or different establishments, and for different purposes. But, besides these, various auxiliary machines are necessary to perform intermediate operations, and to prepare the material as it passes from one stage of the manufacture to another. The number of these machines, and the changes and improvements which have been made in their construction from time to time, render it impossible to convey, in a work like the present, any accurate idea of their formation in detail. We have already given, in the article *Cotton Manufacture*, a brief view of the principal changes which the raw material undergoes preparatory to spinning in a modern cotton factory, founded and improved upon the general principles of Arkwright. The roving being, as there described, transferred to the spinning frame, it is once more drawn out by rollers and twisted by flyers, so that the spinning is little more than a repetition of the process gone through in making the roving, except that the cotton is now twisted into a strong thread, and cannot any longer be extended by drawing. The flyers of the spinning frame are driven by bands, which receive their motion in some cases from a horizontal fly wheel, and in others from a longitudinal cylinder. As the thread is sufficiently strong not to break with a slight force, the resistance of the bobbins by friction is relied on to wind it up, instead of having the spindles geared together and turned with an exact velocity, as they are in the common double speeder. In the spinning frame the heart motion is retained to regulate the rise and fall of the rail, and in those frames which spin the woof, or filling, it is applied by a progressive sort of cone, the section of which is heart-shaped, and which acts remotely to distribute the thread in conical layers upon the bobbins, that it may unwind more easily when placed in the shuttle. (See *Mule Spinning*, *Weaving*, and *Woollen Manufacture*; also Bigelow's *Technology*.)

Spinola, Ambrose, marquis of, one of the most distinguished generals of his age, was born at Genoa, in 1569. His brother Frederic, who had been appointed to the command of the Spanish fleet on the coast of the Netherlands, induced him to join the Spanish forces in the Low Countries, with 9000 Italian and Spanish veterans. After the manner of the old Italian *condottieri*, or leaders, who collected forces on their own account, and then served at their head in the pay of the Italian states, he was permitted to pay his troops himself, and to receive his compensation from the Spanish treasury. This circumstance, at a time when the conduct of wars depended so much upon the troops being paid regularly, and the best concerted expeditions failed for want of money, assured him of the success which soon rendered him so celebrated. While mutiny and insubordination prevailed in the rest of the army, his 9000 Walloons were models of discipline and order. The archduke Albert of Austria, whom Philip II had appointed governor of the Netherlands, employed Spinola in the capture of Ostend, which had been so long besieged by the Spanish troops, that Albert despaired of reducing it. Spinola was more successful: it fell into his hands in 1604, after having sustained a siege of three years and two months. He obtained possession of a mere heap of ruins, but his reputation was at once spread over all Europe, in which every eye was fixed upon this siege. Spinola hastened to Madrid, to give the feeble Philip information of the state of his troops, and received full powers to suppress their disorders. He was named commander-in-chief of all the Spanish and Italian forces in the Netherlands. On his way back to the theatre of war, he had a conversation with Henry IV, at Paris, who inquired of him his plan for the next campaign. Spinola explained to him all his designs without reserve; but Henry, supposing that this was a mere feint, and that he would follow exactly a contrary course, communicated his suspicions to prince Maurice, and both of them were thus completely duped. "Others," said Henry, "deceive their enemies by falsehood, Spinola by the truth." Maurice at length discerned the artifice, but was able to gain no decisive advantage over his adversary. The two generals ably availed themselves of the fortresses and the nature of the ground, to keep each other in check. A decisive naval action near Gibraltar, in which the whole Spanish fleet was destroyed by the Dutch admiral Heemskerk (1607), induced the Spanish court to propose an armistice, which was concluded between Spinola and Maurice for twelve years (1609). The neighborhood of Juliers-Cleves-Berg had tempted the Dutch to take part in the dispute concerning the succession to that duchy, (see *League*), and Spain, instigated by hatred of Protestantism, by her connexion with the house of Austria, and the hope of recovering her lost dominion over Holland, entered into the war (1621). Cleves fell into the hands of Spinola, Breda was invested by the Spanish forces, and Maurice perished in his efforts to compel the enemy to raise the siege. Spinola himself was made sick by the noxious air of the marshy soil; but the gates were finally opened to him after a ten months' siege (May, 1625). This was his last achievement; his health obliged him to resign the command, although he once more appeared in the field, in Italy (1630). But chagrin at the ill treatment of the Spanish court hastened his death, which took place in 1630, too soon for Spain, but not too soon for his fame, which, perhaps, like that of Tilly, would have suffered, had he lived to encounter Gustavus Adolphus. His rival, Maurice, when asked who was the greatest captain of the age, said, "Spinola is the second."

SPINOZA. (See *Appendix* to this vol.)

SPIRAL. Geometry usually considers two curves, under the name of *spirals*—the logarithmic and that of Archimedes. (q. v.) The latter is generally defined to be a curve of the circular kind, which in its progress recedes from its centre. But it is easily perceived that this definition is not mathematically satisfactory. The spiral may be imagined to be thus generated: If a right line has one end fixed, while the other describes the periphery of a circle, and at the same time a point is conceived to advance continually on the right line from the fixed towards the movable end, this point, with its double motion, will describe a spiral curve. The spiral spring of a watch gives a good idea of this curve.

SPIRE, or SPEYER (anciently *Noviomagus*, and *Nemetes*); a city of Bavaria, capital of the circle of the Rhine, formerly the capital of a bishopric of the same name; 12 miles south-west of Heidelberg; lon. 8° 26′ E.; lat. 49° 19′ N.; population, 7700, chiefly Lutherans. It contains an old cathedral, in the Lombard or Byzantine style of architecture, begun by Conrad in 1030, and finished by Henry IV in 1061, and a gymnasium. It was frequently the seat of the German diet, and it was in the diet held here in 1529, that a *protest*, entered against certain pro ceedings of the emperor, procured for the reformers the name of *Protestants*. The bishopric of Spire, in the circle of the Upper Rhine, contained about 55,000 inhabitants, on 594 square miles. Much of it is mountainous and covered with forests. It was secularized in 1802, and now belongs partly to Bavaria and partly to Baden.

SPIRITUALES; the officers who superintended the observance of piety and good morals in the seminaries of the Catholic bishops, and direct the religious exercises; also a branch of the Franciscans.

SPIRITUALISM; that hypothesis in philosophy, according to which, 1. every thing is spirit; 2. the physical proceeds from the spiritual, and can be explained from it; 3. the human soul, in particular, is opposed to matter, or the physical phenomena can be explained from the soul. Spiritualism is opposed to materialism, and therefore may be called *immaterialism*. (See *Matter*.) The system of Des Cartes had the character of spiritualism.

SPIRITUOUS LIQUORS. (See the article *Temperance*.)

SPITHEAD; a noted roadstead for shipping in the English channel, situated between Portsmouth and the Isle of Wight, directly facing Portsmouth harbor. It is about twenty miles in extent, and is said to be capable of holding 1000 vessels in great security.

SPITTLE. (See *Saliva*.)

SPITTLER, Louis Timothy, baron von, a distinguished German historian, was born at Stuttgart, in 1752. He showed, at a very early age, a disposition for historical and critical research. From 1771 to 1775 he studied at Tübingen. In 1777, he was an instructer in the theological seminary at Tübingen. Here he produced his Critical Inquiry into the 60th Laodicean Canon (Bremen, 1777); History of the Cup in the Lord's Supper; History of the Canon Law to the Times of the spurious Isidore (Halle, 1778), all in German; and was appointed *professor ordinarius* of philosophy at Göttingen. In 1797, he was made a privy counsellor in his native country. In 1806, he was appointed a minister of the Würtemberg government, and curator of the university of Tübingen. He died in 1810. His chief works are Sketch of the History of the Christian Church; History of Würtemberg under the Counts and Dukes (Göttingen, 1782); History of Würtemberg (ibid., 1783); History of the Principality of Hanover (1786); and Outlines of the History of the European States (3d ed., 1823), continued by Sartorius. He also wrote a History of the Danish Revolution of 1660 (1796), and many articles in the Göttingen Historical Magazine, which he edited in connexion with Meiners. (q. v.) All his works are in German. They are full of research, erudition, and just reflection, concise, yet complete. He never colors; the facts speak for themselves. His style is not free from negligence. His complete works were published by Wächter (Stuttgart, 1827). Plank, Heeren, Hugo and Woltmann have borne testimony to his merit.

SPITZBERGEN, or EAST GREENLAND; a group of islands, in the Frozen sea, supposed to have been first discovered by sir Hugh Willoughby, in the year 1553. They received their name from their mountainous and rocky appearance. The sun never sets for three months—June, July and August: for the rest of the year, it is hardly seen, light being chiefly produced by the Aurora Borealis. In the month of June it freezes; in July the heat is violent; the cold returns in August. On the coasts are found whales, sea-dogs, sea-cows and sea-lions, with other marine and amphibious animals. These islands are uninhabited. Eight English sailors, accidentally left there by a whale-fishing ship, survived the winter, and were brought home the next season. The Dutch attempted to settle a colony there, but the settlers perished. Schmeerenburg is the best harbor (in lon. 9° 51′ E.; lat. 79° 44′ N.) in the later season of the whale fishery. Lon. 6° to 16° E.; lat. 76° 30′ to 79° 40′ N. (See the article *North Polar Expeditions*; and Scoresby's work on the *Arctic Regions*.)

SPIX, John Baptist von, a distinguished German naturalist, was born at Höchstadt, in Bavaria, in 1781, and, after devoting two years to the study of theology, was led, by his taste for natural science, to apply himself to medicine. In 1808, the Bavarian government provided him with the means of visiting Paris for the purpose of studying comparative anatomy, and soon after his return appeared his History of all Zoölogical Systems, from the time of Aristotle (in German). In 1815, he published his *Cephalogenesis, seu Capitis ossei Structura per omnes Animalium Classes*, &c., tracing the human head, in its gradual developement, from those of insects, up through all classes of animals. In 1817, doctor Spix was appointed by the government, with doctor Martius, to make a scientific expedition to

Brazil. The travellers landed at Rio de Janeiro, July 14, and, after exploring the eastern parts of the empire, embarked on the Amazons, July, 1819, which they ascended, and returned to Europe in 1820. Doctor Spix died in 1826. The results of the expedition to Brazil have been given in the following works; Travels in Brazil (from the German, London, 1824); Spix's *Simiæ, Serpentes, Testudines et Ranæ, Aves, Lacertæ Brasilienses;* and Martius's *Genera et Species Plantarum,* &c. (Munich, 1824—26), *Nova Genera et Species Plantarum,* &c. (3d vol., folio, 1829), and *Icones selectæ Plantarum cryptogamicarum Brasiliensium* (1829, folio).

Splanchnology (from σπλαγχνον, an intestine); a branch of anatomy, which treats of the viscera, including not only the viscera of the abdomen, but all the organs contained in the other cavities of the body, as the brain, lungs, &c.

Spleen, or Milt (Greek σπλην, Latin *lien*); a spongy viscus, varying much in form and size, situated on the left side, between the eleventh and twelfth false ribs, and covered with a simple, firm membrane, arising from the peritonæum. (See *Stomach.*) It is of an oval form, and about one fifth smaller than the liver. Its upper surface is connected with the diaphragm, and its interior with the stomach. It is convex towards the ribs, and concave internally, and of a livid color. The splenic artery is very large in proportion to the size of the organ, and is divided into numerous small branches penetrating the substance of the spleen. The splenic vein is larger than the artery in the proportion of five to one, and, by its junction with the mesenteric, constitutes the trunk of the *vena portæ*, which carries the blood into the substance of the liver. From this splenic artery, several branches (called *vasa brevia*) go off to the stomach, which they supply with blood. The uses of the spleen are entirely unknown; but they appear to have some connexion with the process of digestion. The spleen is subject to inflammation (*splenitis*), and, as often happens after agues, the inflammation sometimes becomes chronic. The tumor is then commonly called the *ague-cake*, though that name is also given to a tumor of the liver succeeding intermittents. It is also in some cases too feeble in its action, and then the digestion suffers. Spleen is also sometimes used to signify the *hypochondriasis.* (q. v.)

Splicing, among seamen, to join the two ends of a rope together, or to unite the end of a rope to any part thereof, by interweaving the strands in a regular manner. There are several methods of splicing, according to the services for which it is intended; all of which are distinguished by particular epithets. The term is also used in architecture. (See vol. i, page 338.)

Splinters; the pieces of a ship's side, masts, decks, &c., which, being knocked off by a shot, acquire great velocity, and frequently do more damage among the men than the shot itself.

Splinter-Netting; sinnet made into nets, and nailed upon the inner part of the ship's sides, to lessen the effect of the splinters.

Spodumene is a mineral found massive, in large cleavable individuals, whose primary form is an oblique rhombic prism of 93°. Its cleavage, parallel with the lateral planes of this figure, is easily effected; but its terminal cleavages are obscure; lustre pearly; color various shades of grayish-green, passing into greenish-white; streak white; translucent; brittle; hardness nearly equal to that of quartz; specific gravity 3.17. It consists of

Silex, ...	66.40
Alumine, ...	25.30
Lithia, ...	8.85
Oxide of iron, ...	1.45
	102.00

If exposed to a red heat, it loses its transparency and color. Before the blow-pipe, it exfoliates, intumesces, and then melts into a nearly colorless, transparent glass. It occurs in primitive rocks, usually associated with quartz and feldspar. It was first discovered in Sweden, at Utoe, afterwards at Sterzingen, in the Tyrol, and was considered a rare mineral until within a few years, during which period it has been found in the greatest abundance in Massachusetts, in the towns of Goshen, Chesterfield and Sterling.

Spohn, Frederic Augustus William, a distinguished German philologer, was born at Dortmund, in 1792, studied at Wittenberg, and became professor of the Greek and Latin languages at Leipsic in 1819. Notwithstanding his early death in 1824, he had published several works, which show his learning and industry. Among them are a dissertation *De Agro Trojano* (1814); *Commentarius de extrema Odysseæ Parte; Nicephori Blemmidæ duo Opuscula geographica; Lectiones Theocriteæ* (1822 and 1823). The last years of his life were devoted to Egyptian studies; and an account of his system of hieroglyphics will be found under that head. His friend Seyffarth (q. v.) has edited some of his papers on this subject.

SPOHR, Louis, a distinguished violin-player and composer, was born in 1783, at Seesen, in Brunswick, visited Russia, and, in 1805, was appointed concert-master at Gotha, where he composed many musical pieces, mostly instrumental, also songs, an oratorio (the Last Judgment), and an opera (the Duel of the Lovers). He is probably at present the most perfect performer on the violin in Germany. In 1813, he received an appointment in Vienna. Here he wrote his Faust (1814), his first great symphony, and the oratorio Germany Delivered. In 1817, he went to Italy, where he met with great applause. In 1819, he went to London, and at present is chapel-master in Cassel. He has produced many works besides those above mentioned; for instance, the operas of Zemire and Azor, Jessonda, and Peter of Apone. His oratorio "The End of Things" is somewhat in Mozart's style. Spohr is one of the greatest harmonists. His compositions have been blamed for an excess of modulation.

SPOLETO; a delegation, formerly a duchy, of the ecclesiastical states, comprising the great part of ancient Umbria; population, 102,053.

SPOLETO, the capital of the delegation, with a population of 6000, is a bishop's see, and lies fifty-three miles north of Rome; lon. 12° 36′ E.; lat. 42° 45′ N.; on an eminence near the small river Mareggia. It was once the residence of some of the Gothic kings. It contains twenty-two churches, twenty-one convents, and seventeen hermitages, and several ruins of Roman antiquities, the chief of which are a triumphal arch, an aqueduct, and an amphitheatre. The cathedral is built almost entirely of marble, and contains some good pictures.

SPONDEE, in prosody; a foot consisting of two long syllables, as *omnes*. (See *Rhythm*.)

SPONGE. (See *Appendix*, end of this vol.)

SPONSOR. (See *Godfather*.) To the remarks contained in that article we will only add that, when the person baptized is an adult, the sponsor answers for his religious belief. Some suppose that sponsors came into use in the first centuries of Christianity when the assurance of a Christian of known character, that those who presented themselves for baptism were worthy of it, was considered requisite. This surety was also to answer for their further instruction. But Neander, in his excellent General History of the Christian Religion and Church (Hamburg, 1826, vol. i, part 2), says that sponsors were probably introduced with the baptism of infants, in order to make a profession of the Christian faith in their name, and to guaranty their religious education. Tertullian, who opposed the baptism of infants, mentions the case of the sponsors as one of the objections, because they must take upon themselves an obligation, which they may be prevented from fulfilling by death or the sinfulness of the godchild. The Roman and Greek Catholic churches consider the relation of the sponsor to the godchild a kind of adoption, and therefore forbid marriage between them. Between the sponsors themselves, they do not allow marriage to take place. The Catholics sometimes take a sponsor for confirmation.

SPONTANEOUS COMBUSTION. The phenomenon of combustion, it is well known, is often produced by friction, fermentation, and other causes, without the application of fire. Forests have sometimes been set on fire by the friction of dry wood; and it is well known that moist wool, hay, corn, madder, meal, malt, hemp and flax, and linseed-oil, and other animal and vegetable substances, take fire of themselves. In the latter case, the combustion is the result of a chemical action, being produced by the decomposition of the substance inflamed, and a new combination of its component parts, or by some other chemical change, attended with the evolution of heat. (See *Combustion*, and *Oxygen*.) A similar phenomenon is exhibited on sprinkling new-burnt lime with water, which is rapidly absorbed with the evolution of heat and light. The heat, in this instance, proceeds from the consolidation of the liquid water into the lime, and the consequent developement of the latent caloric which always attends the conversion of a liquid into a solid. (See *Caloric*.) There have also been instances of spontaneous combustion taking place in living bodies, by which they have been reduced to ashes. It has been observed that persons who have suffered in this way were addicted to the excessive use of ardent spirits.

SPONTINI, Gasparo, one of the most distinguished theatrical composers now living, since 1819 master of the chapel of the king of Prussia, was born in 1778, at Cesi, a small city in the States of the Church. He studied music at Bologna, at Rome and at Naples. At the age of seventeen, he composed the *opera buffa*, *I Puntigli delle Donne*, which was received with great applause. The next year he went to Rome, then to Venice, but soon returned to Rome, and afterwards went to Naples. Here he lived with Cimarosa five years, after which he went to Florence and Palermo. After having produced fourteen operas, eleven comic and three serious, for the best theatres in Italy, he resolved to go to Paris. Here he was first made known by his *Finta Filosofa*, which was brought out in 1804. His opera of Milton attracted general admiration. His great opera is the Vestal. In 1809, his Ferdinand Cortez appeared at the imperial opera; but it seems not to have maintained the fame acquired by the Vestal: it is, however, a work full of spirit and energy, and the contrast in it between the heathen Mexicans and the Christian Spaniards is excellently represented. In December, 1819, his opera of Olympia was brought upon the stage in Paris. It is supposed that its lukewarm reception, and the fact that the composer did not receive the direction of the grand opera there, induced him to accept the office of master of the chapel at Berlin. His later operas, particularly in Berlin, have been objected to as depending too much on the aid of stage effect.

Sporades; the general name for nineteen islands in the Archipelago (q. v.), lying to the east of the Cyclades. The principal are Scio, or Chios, Samos, Cos, Rhodes and Lesbos (see the articles). Patmos, or Pathmos, a small rocky island of the Sporades, is celebrated as the place of St. John's exile. The grotto in which he is said to have written the Apocalypse is still shown, and a monastery, called the *monastery of the Apocalypse*, has been erected in commemoration of the event. The name *Sporades* is derived from the Greek σπειρειν, to sow, indicating the scattered position of the islands: hence the medical phrase *sporadic diseases*, in opposition to *epidemic*, signifying those which seize a few persons at any time or season.

Sports. The national amusements and pastimes of a people form an important feature in the national character. Taking their tone from the manners, habits and condition of the age or country in which they prevail, they lead us behind the scene on which the great drama of public life is exhibited, to the daily and familiar customs and events of popular life. The sports of a nation are of a religious or martial spirit, gay and mild, or dark and fierce, rude or refined, bodily or intellectual, as they are tinged by its habits and character, on which they reciprocally exercise a powerful influence. Besides numerous local holydays and sports, such as the harvest-home, in honor of Ceres and Bacchus, the panthenæa (q. v.), celebrated in honor of Minerva by all the people of Attica, &c., there were four great national festivals among the Greeks, open to all people of the Grecian name. The Olympic, Pythian, Nemæan and Isthmian games (see the articles), were great public festivals, which inspired that polished people with a love of the arts, and imbued them with the spirit of social life. In these games, which were at once religious festivals and commercial fairs, the gymnastic and musical contests were exhibited in union (see *Music*); and the productions of genius, poems and histories, were rehearsed before all that was choice and learned of Greece, surrounded by the masterpieces of statuary, painting and architecture. The public amusements of the Romans were of a fierce and sanguinary, or of a coarse and rude character. Their triumphs, their gladiatorial fights, their combats of wild beasts, their religious festivities, which were scenes of boisterous revelry, showed how much behind the Greeks they were in refinement and taste. (See *Circus*, *Gladiators*, and *Triumph*.) In the middle ages, religion and war were the chief elements of the social life, and the amusements were chiefly of a religious or military character. (See *Festivals*, *Chivalry*, and *Tournament*.) Many of the modern popular sports originated from religious festivals: such are morris-dances (q. v.), theatrical shows (see *Mysteries*, and *Moralities*), &c. Bull-fights (q. v.) continue to form the national amusement of the Spaniards, though the baiting of beasts has nearly gone out of use in England. Cock-fighting, horse-racing, and boxing, national dances, and the field sports of hunting, hawking or archery, are the favorite amusements of some people. But, in some countries, the progress of industry, the habits of domestic life, and the general diffusion of books have in a great measure superseded the pastimes which were formerly so universal. (See Strutt's *Sports and Pastimes of the People of England*; Brand's *Popular Antiquities*; and Smith's *Festivals, Games and Amusements*.) Among the amusements of most nations, games of chance hold an important place, and are undoubtedly of very ancient origin. Those in which the fingers are the instruments, as in the Italian *mora* (q. v.), are probably the oldest. The invention of dice (q. v.) is attributed to the Greek Palamedes; that of chess (q. v.) to the people of India. Both games were known to the Greeks and Romans. The games of mixed chance and skill are also of early origin. These were known to the Romans, but they were principally attached to games of chance (*aleæ*), although they were prohibited by law, and the players reputed infamous. The ancient Germans, according to the description of Tacitus, were passionately devoted to gaming. "They addict themselves," says he, "to dice when sober, and as a serious employment, with such a mad desire of winning or losing, that, when stripped of every thing else, they will at last stake their liberty and their very selves. The loser suffers himself to be bound and sold." Cards (q. v.) are of modern invention; and the games at cards are some of them purely games of chance, others of chance and skill combined. The laws of some countries, as of England and many of the U. States, prohibit gaming: those of France, and some other countries of Europe, license gaming houses. Henry VIII of England issued a proclamation against unlawful games, in consequence of which dice, cards, tables and bowls, were seized and destroyed in many places, though he himself was a great gambler; and we read of his losing much of the plunder of the suppressed abbeys at games of chance. Suspected gamesters, in England, may be brought before magistrates, and required to find sureties not to play or bet during twelve months, to the amount of twenty shillings, and, in default of sureties, may be imprisoned.

Sports, Unlawful. (See *Sports*.)

Spotted Fever. (See *Appendix*.)

Sprat, Thomas, bishop of Rochester, was born in 1636, and received his academical education at Wadham college, Oxford, of which he was elected a fellow in 1657. Upon the death of Cromwell, he composed an Ode to the Memory of the late Lord Protector, abounding with the most high-flown adulation, and of the irregular class then termed *Pindaric*. Another, On the Plague of Athens, followed in the same style. On the restoration, he showed an equal excess in the contrary direction, and, taking orders, was recommended by Cowley to the duke of Buckingham, who made him his chaplain, and whom he assisted in the composition of the Rehearsal. Being introduced by that nobleman to the king, the latter nominated him one of his chaplains. His intimacy with bishop Wilkins caused him to be chosen one of the fellows of the new royal society, of which, in 1667, he wrote the history. In 1668, he edited the Latin poems of Cowley, to which he added a life of the author. His reputation and talents for society rapidly advanced him in the career of preferment, and he became, in 1686, bishop of Rochester, probably as a reward for drawing up an account of the Rye-house plot. The manner in which he accomplished this task, undertaken, as he asserts, at the king's command, rendered it expedient for him, after the revolution, to print an apology. He was nominated by James II one of the commissioners for ecclesiastical affairs, in the execution of which office he exhibited compliances, in expectation, it is said, of the archbishopric of York, which produced general censure, that was only partially alleviated by his withdrawing from the commission, in 1688. When James retired, Sprat spoke in his favor in the great conference on the vacancy of the crown, but submitted to the new government, and was left unmolested. In 1692, he was involved, with Sancroft, Marlborough, and others, in a pretended conspiracy. He detected the infamous practices of the informers, and cleared himself from the charge, but was so affected by the danger, that he commemorated his deliverance by an annual thanksgiving. He died in 1713. His writings are little esteemed at present.

Sprat; a small fish. (See *Appendix*, end of this volume.)

Spree, a river of Germany, which rises in Upper Lusatia, intersects the Spree forest, in Lower Lusatia, with more than a hundred arms, becomes navigable at Kossenblatt, forms, at Berlin, an island, on which lies Kőln (see *Berlin*), and fall below Spandau, into the Havel.

Sprengel, Kurt, a distinguished German naturalist and medical writer, was born in 1766, at Boldekow, near Anklam, where his father was pastor, who instructed him in the languages, even in some Oriental idioms, also in the natural sciences, &c. In his fourteenth year, he wrote an Introduction to Botany for Females, intended for the use of his sister. Even before he went to the university, he was examined by the consistory of Greifswald (then in Swedish Pomerania), as he intended to study theology and medicine at the same time, and he was found to be so well informed that he received a license to preach at that time. At the age of 19 years, after having been for some time tutor, he went to the university of Halle, where he soon gave up theology, and confined his attention to medicine. In 1787, he wrote his inaugural dissertation—*Rudimenta Nosologiæ Dynamicæ*—and was graduated. He soon resolved to confine himself to the theoretical part of medicine, and to exert himself as an author only. He contributed much to a periodical,—the Literary News for Physicians, Surgeons, and Naturalists,—and edited it himself from 1787 to 1789, when it ceased. In 1789, he was appointed *professor extraordinarius*, having lectured some time previous on forensic medicine and the history of medicine. In 1795, he was appointed *professor ordinarius*, with 50 Prussian dollars salary !* In 1797, he also received the professorship of botany, and his salary was raised to 400 Prussian dollars. He now received many offers of appointments, and his salary was accordingly put upon a more liberal scale. Meusel gives the list of the numerous works of this distinguished man, who soon became an ornament of his country and Europe. They are distinguished by great erudition, research, and grasp of mind. His Pathology; his History of Medicine (third edition, Halle, 1821, 5th and last volume 1828), translated into several languages; his *Institutiones Medicæ*, reprinted in Milan; his *Historia Rei Herbariæ ;* his translation of Theophrastus; and his edition of Linnæus's *Systema Vegetabilium* (sixteenth edition), deserve to be particularly mentioned. He is a member of nearly seventy learned societies, including the French academy; and the king of Sweden, as well as his own king, has conferred on him an order of knighthood. His eldest son, William, is professor of surgery at Greifswald, and is also known as an author. The character of Kurt Sprengel is very amiable. He is beloved by his pupils, who accompany him on his botanical excursions, and in the evenings assemble at his house. He intends to crown his literary labors by an edition of Dioscorides.

Spring. This season begins when the sun, in its ascent, crosses the equator, and ends when it reaches its highest position in the heavens at mid-day. With us, the beginning of spring is ascertained by the sun's entrance into Aries; and its entrance into Cancer forms the end. The former happens March 22, and the latter June 21. In the southern hemisphere, the astronomical spring begins September 23, and ends December 21; thus it falls at the time of our autumn. Under the equator, and, in general, in the torrid zone, the seasons of the year are not divided in the same manner as in the temperate. They are distinguished into the dry and wet seasons. (See *Seasons.*)

* A Prussian dollar is about 68 cents.

Spring, among sailors, implies a crack running transversely or obliquely through any part of a mast or yard, so as to render it unsafe to carry the usual quantity of sail thereon.—*Spring* is also a rope passed out of a ship's stern, and attached to a cable proceeding from her bow, when she lies at anchor. It is usually employed to bring the ship's broadside, or battery of cannon, to bear upon some object, as another ship, a fortress, &c. When a ship rides by anchors which are only attached to one end, she will move according to the direction of the wind or tide. Now, if a rope be extended from the other end to the same anchor, it is evident that, by slackening one of these ropes, and keeping the other fast, her side will lie more or less obliquely to the wind or tide, as occasion may require, so as to be opposed to any distant object to the right or left.—*Spring* is likewise a rope extending diagonally from the stern of one ship to the head of another which lies abreast of her at a short distance, and is used to make one of the ships sheer off to a greater distance from the other. Springs of this kind are occasionally applied to a wharf or pier for the same purposes.—*To spring a mast, yard,* &c. is to crack it transversely or obliquely.

Spring Tide; the periodical excess of the elevation and depression of the tide, which happens soon after the new and full moon. (See *Tide.*)

Springfield; the shire town of Hampden county, Massachusetts, on the east side of Connecticut river, 97 miles southwest of Boston, 18 south of Northampton, 28 north of Hartford. The houses are very well built, and the town has the appearance of great industry and wealth. Many new and elegant buildings have lately been erected, and five meeting-houses have been built within a few years. It contains the county buildings, and is united with West Springfield by an elegant bridge Population in 1830, 6784. On Mill river, which flows into the Connecticut, there are very extensive mills and factories of various kinds. These give to Springfield a very active business It has easy communication by the river with the large towns of Connecticut, as well as those above it in Massachusetts. Great attention is paid to the common schools, and the people generally are intelligent and enterprising. There is in this town, belonging to the U. States, a very extensive establishment for the manufacture of arms. The arsenal is situated on an elevated plain, about half a mile east of the village. The buildings are finely arranged around a level square of 20 acres, and make an elegant appearance. One of the buildings is 204 feet by 32, and two stories high; another is 100 by 40; a third is 60 by 32; and there are several smaller ones, and about 20 dwelling-houses. Great quantities of arms are manufactured annually, and preserved for public use, or sent to the several states. The people of this town suffered much annoyance by the party of rebellious opponents to the state government, who collected here in 1786, and continued till January, 1787. They were commanded by Shays. (See *Shays's Insurrection.*)

SPRINGS. The origin of the numerous springs that break forth from beneath the earth's surface cannot be referred to one exclusive cause. The internal reservoirs by which they are supplied are, in many cases, derived from the water which the earth absorbs from rains and melted snow; from these reservoirs, wherever there is uneven or mountainous ground, the water flows out by minute fissures in the sides of the hills. But when we see springs rising up in plains, it is evident that they must have ascended, that is, travelled in a direction contrary to that produced by the force of gravity, in order to reach the surface. This, no doubt, is sometimes to be attributed to water flowing under ground from distant elevations, and to the natural tendency of a liquid to find its level. But the rising up of springs in plains cannot always be accounted for in this manner; and it has, therefore, been supposed, that the earth contains capillary tubes. (q. v.) It is also evident that such springs as suffer no diminution even from the longest continued dry weather, must be derived from a source quite independent of rains, and other external means of supply. They must, therefore, proceed from some vast body of water within the earth; and it has, with apparent reason, been concluded, that many springs arise from the ocean, filtering through the pores of the earth, the salt particles being lost in the passage. Springs which have their waters combined with mineral substances, and are, from that circumstance, called *mineral*, are very numerous, and of various kinds. (See *Mineral Waters.*) Warm and hot springs are also common, especially in volcanic countries, where they are sometimes distinguished by violent ebullitions. Iceland is noted for these curious phenomena: its celebrated boiling fountain, the great Geyser, frequently throws out its contents to the height of more than a hundred feet; sometimes to twice that elevation. Periodical or intermittent springs are those which differ periodically in the quantity of water which they deliver; or even cease to flow entirely for a time. The spring of Fonsanche, near Nismes, flows daily for a little more than seven hours, and ceases five hours; that of Colmars, in Provence, ceases to flow every seven minutes. In 1755, the great earthquake which destroyed Lisbon rendered it a perpetual fountain; but in 1763, it again became intermittent. This phenomenon is explained with much probability by the supposition, that there are cavities or basins under the earth, filled from above, and emptied by siphons. These empty the basin to the level of the point where the legs meet, then cease to flow until the leg connected with the basin is again filled to its highest point. (See *Siphon.*) If the siphon conducts the water to a distance, it may flow in dry weather and cease in wet.

SPRIT; a small boom, or pole, which crosses the sail of a boat diagonally from the mast to the upper aftmost corner, which it is used to extend and elevate. These sails are accordingly called *spritsails.*—*Spritsail* is also a sail attached to a yard which hangs under the bowsprit.

SPRUCE. (See *Appendix*, end of this vol.)

SPUNGE; an instrument used to clean the cannon after firing, and to extinguish any sparks that may remain behind. They are sometimes made of bristles, resembling a round brush, but more generally of sheep-skin, with the wool outwards, nailed upon a block of wood nearly as large as the calibre of the piece. The block is either fixed upon a long wooden staff, or upon a thick piece of rope, well stiffened by serving it with spun-yarn. This latter is much more convenient on board of ships, on account of its flexibility, and generally has a block at the upper end, to use as a rammer.—*To spunge a gun* is to clean it out with the spunge.

SPUNGE. (For the substance so called, see *Appendix*, end of this volume.)

SPUN-YARN; a small line, or cord, form

ed of two, three, or more rope-yarns, twisted together by a winch; the yarns are usually drawn out of the strands of old cables, and knotted together. Spun-yarn is used for various purposes, as serving ropes, weaving mats, &c.

SPURRED RYE. (See *Ergot.*)

SPURZHEIM, Gaspard, doctor, a celebrated physiologist, was born near Treves, in 1776, and received his medical education at Vienna, where he became acquainted with doctor Gall, the founder of the science of craniology. (See *Phrenology.*) To this science Spurzheim became exceedingly partial; and he soon joined doctor Gall in making inquiries into the anatomy of the brain. They quitted Vienna, in 1805, to travel, and went, in 1807, to Paris. Since 1814, doctor Spurzheim has travelled and lectured in England, Scotland and Ireland, and, in conjunction with doctor Gall, published the result of his inquiries into the Anatomy and Physiology of the Nervous System; Inquiry into the Nervous System in general, and that of the Brain in particular; Physiognomical System of Doctors Gall and Spurzheim, &c.; an Examination of the Objections urged, in England, against the Doctrines of Gall and Spurzheim; Observations, &c. &c. on Mental Derangements; and Observations on Phrenology (of which a fourth edition is now preparing). He has, from time to time, resided in Paris, where he has published some phrenological works in French. An account of his system will be found in the article *Phrenology.*

SQUARE, in geometry; a quadrilateral figure, both equilateral and equiangular, or, in other words, a figure with four equal sides and equal angles, which geometry proves must be right angles. It holds the first place among the parallelograms. The height and width of a square are equal: all squares are geometrically similar, and the diagonal line, or the line through two opposite vertices, divides the square into two equal and similar triangles. On account of its perfect regularity, the square is of great importance both in pure and applied mathematics. In the measurement of surfaces, it is the form to which all others are reduced. From the rules for calculating the superficial contents of parallelograms in general (to multiply the base by the perpendicular height), and from the nature of the square, it appears that it is only necessary to multiply one side by itself to have the area of the square, because each of the sides may be considered as the basis, or as the perpendicular height. Thus a square, the sides of which measure four feet, is equal to sixteen square feet; i. e. sixteen squares each a foot high and a foot long. The area of countries is generally given in square miles. Sometimes a great mistake is made by using square miles for miles square: 300 square miles is an area of 300 squares, each of which measures one mile in length and breadth, whilst 300 miles square is a square each side of which measures 300 miles—hence the whole square contains 90,000 square miles. To square a figure (e. g. a polygon) is to reduce the surface to a square by mathematical means. It has often been attempted to square the circle, but as yet without success. (See *Circle.*) To obtain the square of a number, the number is multiplied by itself (see *Power*); and to extract the square root of a number is to find that magnitude which, multiplied by itself, gives the magnitude from which we have to extract the root. (See *Root.*)

Square, in tactics, is the figure formed by infantry to resist most effectually an attack of cavalry in the open field. It can be formed in different ways; and it was once customary to spend much time in drilling troops to execute all the varieties of squares and other figures having the same object; but experience has shown that the so called solid square is the best, on account of its movability and simplicity, as well as its power of resistance, though it is, perhaps more exposed to the effects of artillery. In some armies (e. g. the Prussian), all other squares are abandoned. A column, being of a square shape, can be thrown into a solid square immediately by making the men face to each of the four sides. (See the article *Column.*) If a solid square is broken, the parts again form squares by facing to the four sides.

Magic Squares are square tables with divisions, like a chess board, filled with numbers in the natural series, or any other arithmetical progression, in such a way that the numbers in the horizontal and vertical lines, and sometimes, also, those in the diagonal lines, yield equal sums if added together; for instance,

1	15	14	4
12	6	7	9
8	10	11	5
13	3	2	16

Euler, Kircher, Franklin and others have

made investigations respecting this subject.—See, among other works, Mollweide's *Commentat. de Quadratis Magicis* (Leipsic, 1816). In India, in which country these tables were probably invented, they are used as talismans.

Square-rigged vessels are contradistinguished to all whose sails are extended by stays, lateen, or lug-sail yards, or by gaffs and booms, the usual situation of which is nearly in a plane with the keel.

Square-Sail is any sail extended to a yard suspended by the middle, and hanging parallel to the horizon, as distinguished from sails extended obliquely.

SQUATTERS. (See *Public Lands.*)

SQUILL. (See *Appendix*, end of this vol.)

SQUINTING. (See *Optics*, head *Vision.*)

SQUIRREL. (See *Appendix* to this vol.)

STAAL, madame de, an ingenious French writer, first known as mademoiselle de Launai, was the daughter of a painter of Paris, where she was born, towards the close of the seventeenth century. Her father, being obliged to quit the kingdom, left her in great indigence; but some female recommendation procured her a good education at a priory in Rouen. Her patroness dying, she was compelled to hire herself as bed-chamber woman to the duchess of Maine. Unfit, however, for the duties of such an office, she was about to quit it, when a singular event rescued her from obscurity. A beautiful girl of Paris, named Tétard, was induced by her mother to counterfeit being possessed; and all Paris, including the court, flocking to witness this wonder, mademoiselle de Launai wrote a very witty letter on the occasion to M. de Fontenelle, which was universally admired. The duchess of Maine, having discovered the writer in the person of her waiting-woman, employed her, from that time, in all her entertainments given at Sceaux, and treated her as a *confidante*. Thus encouraged, she wrote verses for some of the pieces acted at Sceaux, drew up the plans of others, and was consulted in all. She was involved in the disgrace incurred by the duchess, her patroness, during the regency, and was kept two years a prisoner in the Bastile. On her release, the duchess found her a husband in M. de Staal, lieutenant in the Swiss guard, having previously refused the learned, but then too aged, Dacier. She died in 1750; and some Memoirs of her Life, written by herself, were soon after published in 3 vols., 12mo. They contain nothing of much importance, but are composed in a pure and elegant style, and are very entertaining. A fourth volume has since appeared, consisting of two comedies acted at Sceaux, entitled *L'Engouement*, and *La Mode*. This lady, who, even by her own description, did not abound in personal attractions, was, nevertheless, engaged in various gallantries or amours more or less sentimental. Being asked how she would treat such matters in her Life, "I will paint myself *en buste*," was the reply. Her Memoirs have been poorly translated into English.

STABAT MATER; a celebrated Latin church song, in terzines, which is sung in the Catholic church, particularly on the festival of the Seven Sorrows of Mary, and generally during the services in Lent. Some consider one of the popes (John XXII, or one of the Gregories) as its author; but, according to the most probable opinion, it was written by the Minorite Jacobus de Benedictis, generally called Jacoponus, who lived in the thirteenth century, a learned jurist, whom the death of his wife induced to enter, in 1268, the order of the Tertiarii, and to give himself up to the severest penances, which terminated in insanity. He died in 1306. The words have received several changes. The best composers of church music have employed their talents upon it. The best compositions are those of Palestrina (for eight voices), of Pergolesi (for two voices, with an accompaniment) and Astorga. Among the later composers of this beautiful piece are Haydn, Winter, Neukomm, and Stunz (a very excellent composition). The *Stabat Mater* is one of those Latin songs of the early church which breathe a truly poetical and sacred enthusiasm, and cannot be generally known in this country. We, therefore, give it at length, as we have done the *Dies Iræ*.

Stabat mater dolorosa,
Juxta crucem lacrymosa,
  Dum pendebat filius;
Cujus animam gementem,
Contristatam et dolentem
  Pertransivit gladius.

O! quam tristis et afflicta,
Fuit illa benedicta
  Mater Unigeniti.
Quæ mœrebat et dolebat
Et tremebat, cum videbat
  Nati pœnas inclyti.

Quis est homo qui non fleret
Christi matrem si videret,
  In tanto supplicio?
Quis posset non contristari,
Piam matrem contemplari
  Dolentem cum filio.

Pro peccatis suæ gentis,
Videt Jesum in tormentis,
Et flagellis subditum;
Vidit suum dulcem natum,
Morientem, desolatum,
Dum emisit spiritum.

Eia mater, fons amoris!
Me sentire vim doloris
Fac, ut tecum lugeam.
Fac ut ardeat cor meum
In amando Christum Deum
Ut illi complaceam.

Sancta mater! istud agas,
Crucifixi fige plagas
Cordi meo valide.
Tui nati vulnerati,
Tam dignati pro me pati,
Pœnas mecum divide.

Fac me vere tecum flere,
Crucifixo condolere,
Donec ego vixero.
Juxta crucem tecum stare,
Te libenter sociare,
In planctu desidero.

Virgo virginum præclara!
Mihi jam non sis amara,
Fac me tecum plangere;
Fac ut portem Christi mortem,
Passionis ejus sortem,
Et plagas recolere.

Fac me plagis vulnerari,
Cruce hac inebriari,
Ob amorem filii.
Inflammatus et accensus,
Per te, virgo! sim defensus
In die judicii.

Fac me cruce custodiri,
Morte Christi præmuniri,
Confoveri gratia.
Quando corpus morietur,
Fac ut animæ donetur,
Paradisi gloria.

STABIÆ. (See *Herculaneum*.)

STACCATO (Italian, *separated*), in music, is designated by a few small dots or dashes over the notes, which are then to be played more or less abruptly, and unconnected with each other.

STADIUM; an ancient measure of length, about equal to a furlong, or the eighth of a mile. It was six hundred feet in length; but, as the foot was different, the stadium, also, differed exceedingly. The most known measures of this name were the little stadium of Aristotle, of 19½; the stadium of Cleomedes, of 13.91; the Pythian or Delphian, of 12.79: the stadium of Eratosthenes, of 11.64; that of Herodotus, or the nautical or Persian stadium, of 11.12; the Olympic, of 10.1; the Phileterian, of 9; and the great stadium (called, also, the Alexandrian or the Egyptian), of 8.35 to a geographical mile.—The race-course of a gymnasium was, originally called *stadium*, and was of a certain length, whence was derived the name of the measure. It consisted of an oblong causeway, open at one end, and terminated at the other by a semicircle. The two sides, running parallel with each other, were, likewise, enclosed; and from these three enclosed sides the seats of the spectators rose step-wise.

STADT; the German word for *town* and *city:* hence many geographical names are compounds of this word or *stad*.

STADTHOLDER, in the republic of the United Netherlands; the commander-in-chief of the military forces (Dutch, *stadhouder*, governor). The title was derived from the period when Spain and Burgundy had dominion in that country. The United Netherlands were then under a governor-general, and the separate provinces had particular governors. After becoming independent, the republic retained the office of stadtholder, partly from gratitude to the house of Nassau-Orange, but chiefly to secure the obedience of the people, which would not have been rendered to the states while their authority was new, and not yet confirmed. Philip II, on leaving the Netherlands, had intrusted the government of Holland, Zealand and Utrecht, to William I, prince of Orange; but, when the duke of Alva arrived in the Netherlands, in 1567, at the head of the Spanish forces, with the purpose of spreading the Catholic faith by fire and sword, William retired to Germany to escape the threatening danger. But, being proceeded against during his absence, he took up arms to deliver the Netherlands from the tyranny of Alva. The first attempt failed; but, after the capture of Briel, in 1572, by the Gueux (q. v.), fortune favored the Dutch arms. Most of the cities of Holland and Zealand joined the prince against the Spaniards, and he was once more acknowledged royal stadtholder in Holland, Zealand and Utrecht. Two years afterwards, the two first of these provinces committed the government to him during the war. But the powers of this government were extremely indefinite: orders were issued at one time in the name of the king of Spain; at another, in that of the gentry and cities; sometimes in the name of the prince of Orange and of the gentry and cities; and sometimes in the name of the prince alone. This fluctuation continued even after the accession of Utrecht (1579), till the authority of the king of Spain was wholly shaken off, in 1581. In 1582, the powers previously intrusted to the prince were renewed without restriction, and all public decrees and ordinances were issued in his name alone. At length, Holland and Zealand were on the point of formally investing him with the supreme authority, when he was assassinated, at the instigation of the Spaniards, in 1584. After the death of William, the states-general declared the earl of Leicester (who was sent with a body of troops by Elizabeth, queen of England, to aid them against the Spaniards) stadtholder. The states of Holland and Zealand, however, had conferred the government of their provinces on prince Maurice, second son of the murdered prince of Orange; and he was the first stadtholder who had been appointed by the separate provinces. When Leicester resigned the stadtholderate, Maurice was chosen, in 1590, stadtholder of Guelders, Utrecht and Overyssel. He was succeeded by his brother Frederic Henry and his son William II, in the government of the five above-mentioned provinces. William Louis, count of Nassau, a son of the count of Nassau-Dillenburg, the younger brother of William I, was stadtholder of Friesland, and afterwards of Gröningen. He was succeeded in Friesland, after his death, by his brother Ernest Casimir, count of Nassau-Dietz; but Gröningen, and the province of Drenthe, elected prince Maurice, so that he was now governor of six provinces. After his decease, count Ernest Casimir was also elected by Gröningen and Drenthe. The next stadtholder in Friesland and Gröningen was his son Henry Casimir; and, after his decease, Frederic Henry, prince of Orange, attempted to unite the stadtholderate of these provinces with that of Holland, Zealand, Utrecht, Overyssel and Guelders, which he already enjoyed. But he only acquired Gröningen, to which his son William II succeeded. In Friesland, William Frederic, brother of count Henry Casimir, was made stadtholder; and, on the early death of William II, prince of Orange, he was likewise elected stadtholder of Gröningen. The government of both these provinces thenceforward devolved on the male posterity of William Frederic. In the five remaining provinces—Guelders, Holland, Zealand, Utrecht and Overyssel—after the death of William II, the stadtholderate ceased. By his disputes with the states of Holland, he had made himself many enemies; and, by the artifices of John de Witt, grand pensionary of Holland, his son William III was excluded from the stadtholderate by the act of exclusion agreed to by the province of Holland, in a treaty with Cromwell, in 1654, and in 1667 by the *perpetual edict*, as it was called. But, in 1672, when Louis XIV attacked the United Netherlands, the magistrates of the Dutch cities were forced, by popular insurrections, to repeal the perpetual edict, and to declare William III, prince of Orange, stadtholder The same scene was acted over again in Zealand, Guelders, Utrecht and Overyssel; and, in these five provinces, the stadtholdership was declared to be hereditary in the male line of William III. He retained this authority after he was made king of England, in 1688. But, as he died without children, in 1702, the place was vacant for many years. In 1722, William Charles Henry Friso (a son of John William Friso, prince of Nassau and Orange, and stadtholder of Friesland and Gröningen) was elected stadtholder by the province of Guelders. Holland, Zealand, Utrecht and Overyssel retained their former government till 1747, when France invaded the lands of the generalty. The states of Zealand and Holland were now compelled, by a general insurrection, to appoint the above-named prince, William Charles Henry Friso, stadtholder, and Friesland and Overyssel soon followed the example. William IV was thus the first stadtholder of all the seven provinces. The dignity was declared hereditary both in the male and female lines; but kings and electors, and all persons out of the pale of the Reformed church, were excluded, whether male or female. In case the stadtholderate should devolve upon a minor, the mother was to preside, under the title of *governess*, as long as she remained a widow and a resident of the states; and, in case of war, she was to have the privilege of nominating a general to the states. If the mother were absent, or not living, the states were to have the right of electing a guardian. On the death of William IV, he was succeeded by his son William V, then three years old, under the guardianship of his mother, a daughter of George II of England, who, on the day of her husband's death, assumed the office of governess. She died in 1759, and Louis, prince of Brunswick, who had been, from 1750, field-marshal-general in the Dutch service, was chosen guardian of the young prince; and, in 1766, at the age of eighteen years, William took upon himself the discharge of his office. The authority of the stadtholder was not the same in all the pr inces; for he was appointed by each province separately, and received from them more or fewer privileges. With the general stadtholderate was connected the dignity of captain-general and admiral of the state; and his authority consisted in the exercise of sundry high privileges with regard to the affairs of government, and the military and naval forces. In regard to the former, he might appoint from a certain number of persons nominated by the states of a province various judicial and other officers, and could appoint and remove the magistrates of some cities, according to circumstances. This right he exercised, particularly in the provinces of Utrecht, Guelders and Overyssel, because they were excluded from the union in 1672, on account of their feeble opposition to the French, and, in 1674, were readmitted only on condition that the civil magistrates should be appointed by the stadtholder. In Holland, he had the right of advising in regard to the persons proper to be appointed to office. He presided, by virtue of his office, over the states-general and provincial assemblies, and had an important influence on the legislation. He administered, likewise, those parts of the executive government which most concerned the general interests. He had the right of pardoning criminals not guilty of murder or any heinous crime. By the terms of the union of Utrecht, he was also made umpire of all disputes between the provinces. It was his duty to defend the rights and immunities of the provinces and cities, to execute the laws and ordinances of the states, and to maintain peace and good order in the provinces. The military force was under his direction; for, as captain-general, he was commander-in-chief of the troops; and they were required to swear allegiance to the stadtholder as well as to the states-general and the provincial estates. He appointed all officers up to the colonel, and, from a list presented to him, selected the governors of the forts. When at the head of the army, he might often appoint a general absolutely; but he could not undertake any campaign, or other military enterprise, without the consent of the states-general; and they often sent commissioners to the army, whose assent was requisite to every movement. He could station the troops, however, in the provinces and fortifications, wherever he pleased. As high-admiral, he commanded the naval force of the state, and presided over the college of admiralty, where he nominated his deputies, and performed many duties connected with the naval service. The tenth part of the spoil gained in naval actions belonged to his office; and, formerly, this was exceedingly valuable. These important rights, which, in many respects, amounted to sovereignty, were made still greater in 1747, by the institution of the general hereditary stadtholdership. In 1748, William IV was appointed by the states-general captain-general and admiral of the lands of the generalty. The East India company elected him their president—an office which no stadtholder had ever before enjoyed; and the West India company soon after chose him to a similar office. This gave him great influence in both, and the authority of the stadtholder became greater than ever before. His revenue was derived from numerous sources, and was very great: his court exhibited a royal splendor. In the war between France and England, in 1778 (the American war), in which the republic of the Netherlands became involved, the people grew dissatisfied with William V; and he was accused of not protecting the Dutch ships from the violences of the British, of neglecting to use the navy of the republic to the best advantage during the war, and of encouraging and promoting its inactivity. The party which opposed him, and was made up of merchants and magistrates, attributed his conduct to the restrictions of the stadtholder's power. As William V had married a niece of Frederic the Great, the court of Berlin advocated the rights of the stadtholder with the greatest zeal, and the Prussian ambassador at the Hague was instructed to provide expressly against their diminution. But the states, notwithstanding, stripped the stadtholder of his authority in the Hague, and suspended him from his office as captain-general By the aid of Prussian troops, the contest at length turned in favor of the stadtholder. He recovered the rights and privileges which had been taken from him, and obtained the power of making such changes in the governments of the Dutch cities as secured him a majority. In 1788, the stadtholderate, with all its rights, was declared to be an essential part of the government of each province, and of the whole republic of the Netherlands. The stadtholder and his wife took advantage to the utmost of the power thus put into their hands, and declared the brightest ornaments of the opposite party, the *patriots* (so called), incapable of holding any office. These measures induced many to leave the country, and filled those that remained with dissatisfaction. At the period of the revolution, France profited by this state of things. It declared war, not against the republic, but against the stadtholder; and, in 1794, after a slight resistance, Holland was occupied by the French, under Pichegru, and the hereditary dignity of general-stadtholder was abolished for ever. By the decree of the imperial deputation, in 1803, the hereditary stadtholder received indemnification in Germany; but, by the war of 1806 and 1807, he lost it again, and lived as a private man till 1813, when he was recalled, and, by a decree of the congress of Vienna, received the title of king. (See *Nassau*, and *Netherlands*.)

STAEL-HOLSTEIN, Anna Louisa Germaine Necker, baroness de, a highly gifted woman, who has been called the greatest female writer of all ages and countries, and who was certainly the most distinguished for talents among the women of her age. Since Rousseau and Voltaire, no French writer has displayed equal power. The favorable circumstances of her early life gave full developement to her powers. She was born at Paris, in 1766, and the elevation of her father (see *Necker*) to the ministry of finance, in 1777, brought him into close connexion with the most brilliant circles of the capital. Her mother, the daughter of a Swiss clergyman, a pious and sensible woman, somewhat given to metaphysical speculations, and rather stiff in her manners, directed at first the education of the lively girl, who early acquired habits of diligent application, and was accustomed to hear conversations above the comprehension of her age. Necker's house was the resort of the most distinguished men of the capital; and, like other ladies of the day, who made pretensions to literary taste, Mad. Necker assembled around her celebrated scholars, e. g., Raynal, Marmontel and Thomas. The encouragement to converse, which the young girl received in this society, and the various excitements which it furnished to her faculties, had an important influence on the formation of her mind. To these she owed that rare conversational power for which she was so remarkable, and her taste for intellectual contests, with an inclination to ingenious, brilliant and striking theories, which appears in her earlier works. Her lively spirit found much more satisfaction in the society of her father than in that of her mother. His character, in fact, was much more like her own, and he better understood how to act on her mind. His affection for her was mingled with a father's pride, and she was enthusiastically fond of him, while her respect for him bordered on veneration. Necker, however, never encouraged her to write, as he disliked female writers, and had forbidden his wife to occupy herself in that way, because the idea of disturbing her pursuits when he entered her chamber was disagreeable to him. To escape a similar prohibition, his daughter who early began to write, accustomed herself to bear interruptions without impatience, and to write standing, so that she might not appear to be disturbed in a serious occupation by his approach. When her father's *compte rendu* was published, in 1781, she wrote him an anonymous letter on the subject, which he recognised, by the style of thought, to be hers. In her fifteenth year, she made abstracts from Montesquieu's Spirit of Laws, accompanied with remarks; and at this time Raynal wished her to furnish a treatise on the revocation of the edict of Nantes, for his work on the Colonies and Commerce of the Europeans in the two Indies. Her earliest productions were Sophia, a comedy, written in 1786, and two tragedies, Lady Jane Grey, and Montmorency. Her *Lettres sur les Ouvrages et le Caractère de J. J. Rousseau*, which were printed in 1788, first attracted the public notice. In 1786, she was married to the baron de Staël-Holstein, Swedish ambassador at the French court, a man much older than herself, whose suit was favored by Mad. Necker's desire that her daughter should marry a Protestant, and by the promise of his king to continue him in his post several years. Her heart, however, appears to have been given to the viscount de Montmorency, with whom she maintained a friendship during her life. The breaking out of the revolution (1789) necessarily exercised a powerful influence, both on her mind and fate. She was early accustomed to take an interest in public affairs. Her youth was passed amid great events, which, although occurring in another hemisphere, hastened the crisis of the European states. The first period of her father's service in the ministry (1777—81) brought his family into connexion with the great world and public affairs, and political topics formed the chief subjects of conversation, even in the coteries of the ladies. Familiar with the views of her father, and with the liberal principles of several of the most distinguished French writers of the day, she was inspired with an enthusiastic love of liberty, and had expressed her feelings in her work upon Rousseau. "Neither her disposition nor her situation," says Mad. Necker de Saussure, a near relation and intimate friend of Mad. de Staël, "would allow her to be indifferent to the general agitation; since she was placed in the focus of its influence. She admired the constitution of England, as much as she loved France; and the thought of seeing Frenchmen as free as Englishmen, equal in all that was necessary to secure the rights and maintain the dignity of men, was her ardent wish; and with these views was connected the hope that her father would aid in this great work, and earn gratitude for his services; so that we need not wonder at her enthusiasm." She has related at length her share in the events of the time, in her posthumous work. Her father's banishment, in 1787, and his triumphant return, in 1788, deeply affected her; and when the storm became too fierce for him, and he was obliged to retire from public life, she saw with grief all her hopes disappointed. During Robespierre's ascendency, she exerted herself, even at the hazard of her life, to save the victims, and published a powerful and eloquent Defence of the Queen, who had always shown a dislike to her. After the insurrection of Aug. 10, she delayed her departure from day to day, unwilling to provide merely for her own safety, while so many of her friends were in danger. On Sept. 2, when the tocsin called the populace to riot and murder, she attempted to leave Paris, but was detained, and escaped the popular fury only by a remarkable concurrence of circumstances. She arrived safely at her father's house, which now became the refuge of the unhappy fugitives from the tyranny which preyed upon France. When Sweden recognised the French republic, her husband was again sent as ambassador to Paris, whither she also returned, in 1795. The quiet which was restored with the government of the directory, gave her an opportunity of effecting the recall of some of the emigrants. Barras became her friend; and she acquired so much influence, that, on Talleyrand's return from America, in 1796, she obtained, through Barras, his appointment to the ministry of foreign affairs. To this period also belong two political pamphlets, *Sur la Paix*, and *Sur la Paix intérieure*, which contain her views respecting the situation of France in 1795, and express the remarkable opinion that France could arrive at limited monarchy only through military despotism. In 1796 appeared her work *De l'Influence des Passions sur le Bonheur des Individus et des Nations* (1796), which, though characterized by deep thought and enlightened views, does not contain any complete exposition of the subject. Her domestic relations at this time were not happy. Her connexion with her husband, whose tastes were different, and whose talents were inferior to her own, had been, from the first, marked by coldness; and, when she became desirous of securing the property of their children from the effects of his lavish habits, a separation took place; but, his infirmities rendering the services of his friends necessary to him, she again joined him. He died in 1798, while on the way, in company with her, to her father's residence. The man who exercised so fatal an influence upon the rest of her life—Bonaparte—she had seen, for the first time, in 1797, on his return to Paris, after the peace of Campo-Formio. His brilliant reputation, which had inflamed the lively imagination of the French, also excited her admiration; but this sentiment soon gave way to fear and aversion. She formed the design of gaining him over to the cause of Swiss independence, when an invasion of Switzerland was in contemplation, for the purpose of raising money for the Egyptian expedition; but she soon saw that her plan could not succeed. The danger which threatened Switzerland led her to Coppet, where a French guard under Suchet was posted; but when Geneva was incorporated with France, she hastened back to Paris, to cause her father's name to be struck from the list of emigrants. Necker now seemed likely to pass the remainder of his life undisturbed. Bonaparte visited him before his passage over the Great St. Bernard, and made a favorable impression upon him during a long interview, in which he spoke of his future plans. But some observations of Necker in his *Dernières Vues de Politique et des Finances* (1802), in which he spoke with freedom of the consular constitution, and mentioned Bonaparte's design of establishing a monarchy, and surrounding himself with a new nobility, offended the first consul, who had no wish to see his plans prematurely announced, and therefore caused the work to be attacked in the journals. By his direction, the consul Lebrun wrote a sharp letter to Necker, advising him not to meddle any more with public affairs. Mad. de Staël was banished from Paris, under pretence that she had given her father false information of the state of France. During her banishment, she lived with her father at Coppet, but spent much time in travelling, and once (in 1806) passed some days secretly in Paris. Her literary reputation was meanwhile increased by her *De la Littérature considérée dans ses Rapports avec les Institutions sociales* (2 vols., Paris, 1802), and her *Delphine* (1802). The former work attracted many assailants, among whom Fontanes was the ablest and acutest. She had, indeed, over-estimated the influence of literature upon the character and happiness of men, and pronounced too confidently upon its history and prospects. Her romance *Delphine* contained a faithful picture of herself, as she was in her youth—a creature separated from the multitude by genius and sensibility, and struggling against the restraints of custom and her sex. Mad. de Staël, who never otherwise reverted to her earlier writings, found herself obliged to defend the moral tendency of *Delphine*, in a particular essay. In 1803, she made a visit to Germany, whence her father's sickness recalled her to Switzerland; but he died before she reached home. She always retained the greatest attachment and veneration for his memory. His death rendered her religious feelings more lively, and in this state of mind she wrote an admirable account of his domestic life, (prefixed to the *Manuscrits de M. Necker publiés par sa Fille*, 1805), which gives us much insight into her own character. To dissipate her grief, Mad. de Staël paid a visit to Italy in 1805; and from that time A. W. Schlegel, with whom she had become acquainted in Berlin, was her constant companion. (See *Schlegel.*) The fruit of her journey to Italy was *Corinne ou l'Italie* (1807), the most perfect and brilliant of her works, combining in a happy manner the charms of romance with a faithful picture of Italy. In 1810, she went to Vienna to collect materials for a work upon the manners, literature and philosophy of Germany, which she had planned on her first visit to that country. Many passages had been struck out from the manuscript of this work by the censors of the press; and no sooner was the impression completed, than the whole edition was seized by Savary, minister of police. It first appeared entire at London, in 1813, and was printed at Paris in 1814. This work is rich in acute and ingenious ideas, but has been justly criticised as containing many erroneous views. Mad. de Staël was now persecuted with more bitterness, and her exile from Paris was extended to banishment from France. During her residence on her father's estate, she formed a new connexion about this time, which strongly illustrates the peculiarity of her character. A young officer from the south of France, by the name of de Rocca, who had distinguished himself by his bravery in Spain, rendered infirm by his wounds, came to reside at Geneva. Some expressions of sympathy which fell from Mad. de Staël made a deep impression upon him, and inflamed his heart and his imagination. "I will love her so passionately," said he, "that she will marry me at last." Circumstances favored his wishes; Mad. de Staël, in the midst of her sufferings, had cherished the hope of consolation in a new union, and accepted the hand of the officer. The marriage, however, remained a secret till her death. While she wished to leave a place where she feared to involve others in her fate, she saw the dangers and difficulties of a flight, watched by spies and informers, and was reluctant to abandon the graves of her parents and her second country, and wander, like a criminal, by land and sea. But in the spring of 1812, the last moment when flight was possible, she resolved upon departure, having been already threatened with imprisonment if she left her residence for a day. She hastened through Vienna to Moscow, and, on the approach of the French army, went to Petersburg, and soon after, in the autumn of 1812, to Stockholm. Here appeared her work on suicide (*Reflexions sur le Suicide*), which she had just completed, and which points out to the unhappy the aids of religion and morality. In the beginning of the next year, she went to England, where she was received with the most flattering attention. After a long exile, the sufferings of which she has described in her *Dix Années d'Exil*, she landed at Calais, in 1814. The allied princes treated her with great distinction, and her influence contributed not a little to hasten the removal of the foreign troops from France. On the return of Napoleon, in 1815, she retired to Coppet. It is said that Napoleon invited her to return to Paris, that she might assist in the preparation of the new constitution, but that she refused, adding, "He has dispensed with the constitution and me for twelve years, and now he loves neither of us." After the restoration, she received from the government public stock to the amount of two millions of francs, the sum which her father had left in the royal treasury at the time of his dismission from office. Surrounded by a happy domestic circle—a beloved husband, an excellent son, and an amiable and highly accomplished daughter, who was united to a man of distinguished merit, the duke de Broglio (see *Broglio*)—esteemed and courted by the most eminent men of the capital, and cheered with the hope of seeing her country's wounds healed by a free constitution, she lived in Paris, with the exception of a short absence, till her death. Until her last sickness, she was employed on her *Mémoires et Considérations sur les principaux Événements de la Révolution Française* (Paris, 1819, 3 vols.). Few persons were more favorably situated than Mad. de Staël for appreciating the importance of the events of which she treated. She had three principal objects in this work—the justification of her father's public life, a faithful delineation of the course and character of the revolution, and a developement of the political principles, consonant to the spirit of the age. See the remarks on it in Bailleul's *Examen* (2 vols., 1819). The completion of this work was interrupted by her death. She had suffered much since the beginning of 1817, and in the summer of that year her disease took a decided character. Although reluctant to leave her friends, and dreading, as she said to her physician, the thought of the dissolution of her body, she was not afraid to die. To the last moment she retained her tranquillity, and expressed her hope of again meeting her father. "I think," she said one day, as if awaking from a dream, "I think I know what the passage from life to death is, and I am convinced that the goodness of God makes it easy; our thoughts become confused, and the pain is not great." In the morning of July 14, 1817, she replied to the question of her nurse, whether she had slept, "Soundly and deeply." These were her last words. Her body was embalmed, and deposited in the family vault at Coppet.—See the *Notice sur le Caractère et les Écrits de Mad. de Staël*, by Mad. Necker de Saussure, prefixed to the complete edition of her works, published at Paris, in 1821, in 17 vols.; and Schlosser's *Parallel between Mad. de Staël and Mad. Roland* (in German and French, 1830). The taste of Mad. de Staël is not altogether correct; her style is irregular, and has too much pretension; her attempts at effect and her occasional tendency to exaggeration sometimes mislead her judgment, and cause her to give a false coloring to facts. But in all her works we find original and profound thought, great acuteness, a lively imagination, a philosophical insight into the human heart, and into the truths of politics and literature.—Her son *Augustus*, baron de Staël, born 1789, died 1827, is favorably known by his *Notice sur M. Necker* (1820), and his valuable *Lettres sur l'Angleterre*. He left a son, the only descendant of Mad. de Staël.

Staff (from the staff formerly borne by officers in high command), in military affairs, means generally the officers whose command extends over several bodies of troops, of which each has its particular officers. Thus the general staff (in French, *état majeur général*) is composed of the general, the chief and the officers of the staff, the commanders of artillery, and of the corps of engineers, and the heads of the different departments of military administration. The staff of a division comprises a lieutenant-general, major-generals, and the officers of the staff, of the artillery, engineers and administration. The staff of a regiment comprises the colonel, the superior officers, adjutant-majors, quarter-masters, &c. In England, the chaplain and surgeon of the regiment also belong to it. The military divisions, fortified places, &c., have their staffs composed in a similar manner to those of the armies. Under the French empire, the staff of the emperor had quite a peculiar organization, originating in his always commanding in person, and directing, in time of peace, the whole military machine personally. In Prussia, the staff is employed in preparing the maps of the kingdom, and in similar duties. In time of peace, the officers of the staff are attached in part to the various divisions of the army. In Austria, the staff is employed in the military topography of the empire; trigonometrical and geodesical operations; the military, geographical and statistical description of the provinces; in fortifications; in the care of the archives, &c. The English army has a very good staff, which has produced an excellent military map of the part of England along the coast from Portsmouth to the Thames. The corps is under the command of the quarter-master-general of the British forces. The officers employed in it are examined, and go through a course of studies. (See *Force Militaire de la Grande Bretagne*, by Charles Dupin.)

STAFF, BISHOP'S. (See *Crosier.*)

STAFFA; a small island of the Hebrides, celebrated for its basaltic pillars and its natural caverns, particularly the cave of Fingal; nine miles north of Iona, fifteen west of Mull. It is of an oval form, one and a half miles in circuit, presenting an uneven table-land, terminating nearly all round by cliffs of variable height. The greatest elevation is 144 feet. The surface is covered by a rich soil and luxuriant grass, affording excellent pasture for a herd of black cattle; but there is no house on the island. A considerable portion of the precipitous face of Staffa is in a columnar form: the highest point of this face is 112 feet above high-water mark. There are several remarkable caves, as Great cave, 224 feet long; Boat cave, 150 feet long; Mackinmon's, or the Scart, or Cormorant's cave; and, above all, Fingal's cave, which is celebrated, by those who have visited it, in terms of high admiration. (See *Fingal's Cave.*)

STAG. (See *Deer.*)

STAGGERS. (See *Stomach Staggers*, and *Sturdy.*)

STAHL, George Ernest, a German physician and chemist, born at Anspach, in 1660, studied, at Jena, under Wedelius; and, in 1687, became physician to the duke of Saxe-Weimar. In 1691, he was chosen second professor of medicine at Halle, and rendered his name famous over all Germany by his academical prelections and his publications. He was, in 1700, elected a member of the *Academia Curiosorum Naturæ.* His fame procured him the appointment of physician to the king of Prussia, in 1716; and, going to Berlin, he died there, in 1734. Stahl was one of the most illustrious medical philosophers of his age: his name marks the commencement of a new era in chemistry. He was the author of the doctrine which explains the principal chemical phenomena by the agency of phlogiston; and though his system was, in a great measure, overturned by the discoveries of Priestley, Lavoisier and others, it nevertheless displays powerfully the genius of the inventor. This theory maintained its ground for more than half a century, and was received and supported by some of the most eminent men which Europe had produced. (See *Chemistry*, and *Oxygen.*) He was also the proposer of a theory of medicine, founded on the principle of the dependence of the state of the body on the mind; in consequence of which he affirmed that every action of the muscles is a voluntary effort of the mind, whether attended with consciousness or not. His principal works are *Experimenta et Observationes Chymicæ et Physicæ* (1731, 8vo.); *Disputationes Medicæ* (2 vols., 4to.); *Theoria Medica vera* (1737); *Fundamenta Chymiæ dogmaticæ et experimentalis* (3 vols., 4to.).

STAINER, or STEINER, Jacob; a famous maker of stringed instruments, near Hall, in Tyrol, about the middle of the seventeenth century, and a pupil of the famous violin maker Amati of Cremona. He made, principally, violins. They are rare, and bring 300 ducats apiece. He became insane towards the end of his life. He died in or before 1684.

STALACTITES. (See *Appendix.*)

STALL. (See *Prebend.*)

STAMBOL. (See *Constantinople.*)

STAMMERING. (See *Stuttering.*)

STAMP ACT. (See *United States.*)

STAMPED PAPER, for the purpose of raising a tax, is a Dutch invention. De Basville, or Baville, in his *Mémoires pour servir a l'Histoire de Languedoc*, affirms that stamped paper was introduced as early as the year 537, by the emperor Justinian; but Beckmann, in his History of Inventions, shows this opinion to be erroneous. The states of the United Provinces promised a reward for the invention of a new tax, which would press lightly on the subjects, and yet yield much to the government; and stamped paper was proposed. It was legally introduced, Aug. 13, 1624, by the states, and was gradually imitated by other governments. In the year 1831, the stamps produced to the English government £6,484,580.

STANDARD, or FLAG; originally, a signal, erected on a pole, spear or lance. Such signals were used for different purposes, and were known among the Hebrews as early as the time of Moses, and adorned with emblems. Ephraim carried a steer; Benjamin a wolf, &c. We find something similar among the Greeks: the Athenians had an owl, the Thebans a sphinx, on their standards, by the raising or lowering of which they gave the signal for attack or retreat. The standard of Romulus was a bundle of hay tied on a pole. In place of this, a hand, and, finally, an eagle, were substituted. The real standards came first into use under the Roman emperors, who retained the eagle: they were also ornamented with dragons and silver balls. The standard of the cavalry consisted of a square piece of purple cloth, decorated with gold, on which the figure of a dragon was afterwards represented. The Germans fastened a stream er to a lance, which the duke carried in front of the army. From *band*, the name which this bore, comes our English word *banner* (*bandum*, *banderium*, *bandiera*). Afterwards, a large cloth was used, ornamented with emblems and inscriptions. The imperial French armies, in imitation of the Romans, had an eagle for an ensign, but of a different shape from the Roman eagle. (See *Eagle*.)

Standard of Money; the degree of the purity or fineness of the metal contained in the coins of a particular country, and the quantity or weight of such metal contained in these coins. We have given a comparative view of the standard of money, in different countries, in the table contained in the article *Coins*, to which, and to the article *Circulating Medium*, we refer the reader. The alloy in coins is reckoned of no value: it is allowed to save the trouble and expense of refining the metals to the highest degree of purity, and to render the coins harder, and, therefore, less liable to be worn or rubbed. The standard is sometimes arbitrarily changed by governments, as a means of raising money, either by simply altering the denomination of the coins, without changing their weight or purity, or by issuing coins of baser metal, or by reducing the weight of the coin. But experience has taught that such changes are not only frauds upon the public creditor, and a source of confusion and distress to the people at large, but that they afford only a temporary relief to the public treasury, at the expense of new embarrassments. The present standard of the English coins has remained unchanged since the conquest, except for a period of sixteen years, from thirty-fourth of Henry VIII to second of Elizabeth. That of the gold coins was changed in the eighteenth of Henry VIII; previously to which the standard had been twenty-three carats three and a half grains fine, and one half grain alloy.* It was then fixed at twenty-two carats fine and two carats alloy. The former was called the old standard, the latter the new standard or crown gold, because crowns were first coined of it. The practice of making gold coins of both these standards was continued, however, till 1633, since which all the gold coined has been of the new standard. The coins of the old standard remained in circulation until 1732, when they were withdrawn. But the standard has been degraded by the reduction of the weight of the coin, so that a pound weight of silver, which, at the time of the conquest, was coined into twenty shillings, was, in 1601, coined into sixty-two, and, in 1816, into sixty-six shillings. In other countries, the degradation of the coin has been still greater. But it would far exceed our limits to give a detailed statement of the facts, which are, however, of great importance to readers of history.

* The purity of gold is estimated by an Abyssinian weight called a *carat* (bean), which is subdivided into four parts, called *grains*. Gold of the highest purity is said to be twenty-four carats fine.

Stanhope, James, first earl, was born in Herefordshire, in 1673, and accompanied his father, who was sent envoy extraordinary to the court of Spain early in William's reign. He continued in Spain some years, made the tour of France and Italy, served as a volunteer in Flanders, and received the commission of colonel at the age of twenty-two. He served as brigadier-general under the earl of Peterborough at the capture of Barcelona. In 1708, he was made major-general and commander-in-chief in Spain, and, the same year, he reduced the island of Minorca. In a subsequent campaign, in 1711, he was made prisoner, but was exchanged the following year. On the accession of George I, he was appointed one of the secretaries of state. In 1716, he attended the king to Hanover, where he was principally concerned in the formation of the alliance concluded with France and the states-general, which removed the pretender beyond the Alps. The next year, he was appointed first lord of the treasury and chancellor of the exchequer. In 1718, he became secretary of state, and was created earl Stanhope. He died in 1721.

Stanhope, Philip Dormer. (See *Chesterfield*.)

Stanhope, Charles, the third earl, was born in 1753. He received the early part of his education at Eton, and finished it at Geneva, where his genius led him to pay a close attention to the mathematics; and such was his progress that he obtained a prize from the society of Stockholm for a memoir on the pendulum. In 1774, he stood candidate for Westminster without success; but was introduced, by the earl of Shelburne, into parliament as a member for the borough of Wycombe, which he represented until 1786, when the death of his father called him to the house of peers. He was one of the many English politicians who regarded with pleasure the dawn of the French revolution: but, what was much more extraordinary in a peer by birth, he openly avowed republican sentiments, and went so far as to lay by the external ornaments of the peerage. He was also a frequent speaker against the war; and, although singular in many of his opinions, a strong vein of sense and humor often qualified his statements of peculiar views. As a man of science, he ranked high, both as an inventor and patron, and, among other things, was the author of a method for securing buildings from fire, an arithmetical machine, a new printing press, a monochord for tuning musical instruments, and a vessel to sail against wind and tide. He was twice married; first, to lady Hester Pitt, daughter of the first earl of Chatham, by whom he had three daughters; and, secondly, to Miss Grenville, by whom he had three sons. This scientific, ingenious, but eccentric nobleman published several philosophical and a few political tracts. He died December 14, 1816.

Stanhope, Henry Philip, the present earl, son of Charles, earl Stanhope, was born in the year 1781, and professed principles diametrically opposite to those of his father, against whom he even carried on a suit in equity. On the opening of parliament, in 1818, he made a speech, in which he recommended that France should be dismembered, to prevent her from troubling, in future, the tranquillity of Europe. In the investigation, with respect to the conduct of the late queen Caroline, his lordship voted against the bill of pains and penalties. His eldest son, known as viscount Mahon, is the author of a life of Belisarius, and of a History of the War for the Spanish Succession (1832).

Stanhope, lady Hester; an English lady, a niece of Pitt, famous for her singular mode of life. She has resided in Syria for about twenty years, and, in 1827, was living about eight miles from Sidon, at a villa of her own construction, called D'Joun. It is situated on a solitary mountain, remote from any village. Doctor Madden, who went to see her in 1827, gives the following account of his visit:—"Every thing without was wild and barbarous, and all within confessed the hand of taste. I was led from the court into a little garden, at the extremity of which there was a sort of kiosk, consisting of two rooms—a sitting room and a bed room—furnished, in the European style, with chairs and tables. The room into which I was ushered was in the Arab style; and at the farther corner I perceived a tall figure, in the male attire of the country, which was lady Hester herself. For seven hours there never was a pause in the conversation. Every subject connected with Oriental learning was discussed, and every observation of her ladyship's evinced a degree of genius that astonished me, and was couched in such forcible and energetic language as to impress me with the idea that I was conversing with a woman of no ordinary intellect. The peculiarity of her opinions in no wise detracted from the general profundity of her reflections; and, though I could not assent to many of her notions regarding astral influence and astrological science, I had no reason to alter my opinion of her exalted talents, though they were unfortunately directed to very speculative studies. Nothing is more difficult than to ascertain the point where eccentricity terminates and insanity begins: at all events, I am sure that whatever may be the eccentricity of lady Hester Stanhope, her mind is unimpaired, and that few women can boast of more real genius, and none of more active benevolence." Lady Hester showed doctor Madden a horse which she said was of the race of Solomon's favorite steed, saddled by the hand of God (there was an indentation in the back, resembling a Turkish saddle). The rich presents which she made to the Turkish pachas gave her a great influence over them for a time; but at the time of doctor Madden's visit, this was greatly diminished. The Bedouins, however, or wild Arabs, whom her wisdom and kindness had won, still continued to look up to her, not only as a benefactor, but as a being of a superior order. Her belief in magic and astrology may also have contributed to extend her influence. She is a woman of great personal bravery as well as moral courage, and has encountered the robbers of the desert at the head of her servants, sword in hand.

Stanislaus I, king of Poland, was born at Lemberg, in 1677. His family name was Leczinski, or Lesczinski, and his father held the important post of grand treasurer to the crown. He very early displayed indications of an amiable and estimable character, and at the age of twenty-two was intrusted with an embassy to the Ottoman court. In 1704, being then palatine of Posnania, and general of Great Poland, he was deputed by the assembly of the states at Warsaw to wait upon Charles XII of Sweden, who had invaded the kingdom, with a view of dethroning Augustus of Saxony. (See *Augustus II.*) In a conference with the

Swedish monarch, he so rapidly acquired his esteem, that Charles immediately resolved to raise him to the throne of Poland, which he effected at an election held, in the presence of the Swedish general, on the 27th July, 1704, Stanislaus being then in his twenty-seventh year. He was, however, soon after driven from Warsaw by his rival Augustus; but another change brought him back to that capital, where he was crowned, with his wife, in October, 1705; and the next year Augustus was compelled solemnly to abdicate. (See *Charles XII.*) The fatal defeat of his patron Charles XII, at Pultowa, in 1709, again obliged him to retreat into Sweden, where he endeavored to join Charles XII, at Bender, in disguise; but, being detected, he was held captive in that town until 1714. Being then suffered to depart, he repaired to Deux-Ponts, where he was joined by his family, and remained until the death of Charles XII, in 1719, when the court of France afforded him a retreat at Weissemburg, in Alsace. He remained in obscurity until 1725, when his daughter, the princess Mary, was unexpectedly selected as a wife by Louis XV (q. v.), king of France. On the death of Augustus, in 1733, an attempt was made by the French court to replace Stanislaus on the throne of Poland; but, although he had a party who supported him and proclaimed him king, his competitor, the electoral prince of Saxony, being aided by the emperors of Germany and Russia, he was obliged to retire. (See *Poland*, and *Augustus III.*) He endured this, like every other reverse of fortune, with great resignation, and, at the peace of 1736, formally abdicated his claim to the kingdom of Poland, on condition of retaining the title of king, and being put in possession for life of the duchies of Lorraine and Bar. Thenceforward he lived as the sovereign of a small country, which he rendered happy by the exercise of virtues which acquired him the appellation of "Stanislaus the Beneficent." He not only relieved his people from excessive imposts, but, by strict economy, was able to found many useful charitable establishments, and to patronise the arts and sciences. He was himself fond of literature, and wrote some treatises on philosophy, morals and politics, which were published under the title of *Œuvres du Philosophe bienfaisant* (4 vols., 8vo., 1765). He died in 1766.

Stanislaus II, Poniatowski, king of Poland. (See *Poniatowski, Stanislaus.*)

Stanitza (*village, place of encampment*); a word found in numerous Russian geographical names belonging to the regions inhabited by the Cossacs.

Stannaries, Court of. (See *Courts.*)

Stanza (Italian, a *stand*); a strophe or number of verses connected with each other, terminating with a full point or pause, and forming one of the regular divisions of a poem. It was formerly sometimes used to denote an entire lyric poem of one strophe. Thus Dante speaks in his work *De vulgari Eloquentia* (book ii. chap. 3 et seq.) of *cantiones* (*canzoni*) and of *stantii* (*stanze*). Stanzas are said to have been first introduced from the Italian into French poetry, about the year 1580, and thence passed into English. The principal Italian stanza—the *ottava rima*—originated in Sicily, where poets made use of it even in the thirteenth century: thence it passed into Italy, and there received, in the fourteenth century, from Boccaccio, that regular form which it has ever since retained, as the standing division of the Italian epic. Boccaccio first made use of it in his *Theseide*. Politian improved it further. Trissino, in the sixteenth century, wrote a narrative poem in blank verse, but had no imitators. The *ottava rima*, or stanza of Boccaccio (as we may call it, in contradistinction to the Sicilian, which forms a continued chain of alternate rhymes, without the double rhyme in the two last lines), consists of eight iambic verses of eleven syllables each, with female rhymes (q. v.), of which the six first are alternate, but the two last are successive, and thus give to the whole an agreeable conclusion. These two last lines, however, easily seduce the poet into attempts at pointed expression, unbecoming a serious epic, and from which even Tasso is not always free. Boiardo, and particularly Ariosto and Tasso, are the great masters of the *ottava rima*. Göthe, Schlegel, Tieck and others have used it with great success in German, with the change required by the genius of the German language, viz. that they employ male and female rhymes in the first six lines, but the two last always end with female rhymes. (For the *Spenserian* stanza, see *Spenser.*)

Stanze. (See *Raphael*, and *Vatican.*)

Staple; a public market, whither merchants are obliged to carry their good for sale. Various derivations have been suggested; as, 1. staples, found in the Ripuarian laws, and signifying a place where justice is administered; 2 the German *stapelen*, to put in a heap; 3. *stabile emporium* used in the civil law style of former times, and signifying a fixed post. Formerly the merchants of England were obliged to carry their wool, cloth, lead, and other like staple commodities, to particular places, in order to utter the same by wholesale. *Merchants of the staple* was the denomination of the most ancient commercial society of England, from their exporting the staple wares of the kingdom. It is said to have originated in 1248. In 1336, the staple of wool was fixed in Brabant; in 1341, at Bruges; and, in 1348, at Calais. In 1353, it was removed from Bruges to several English and Irish towns. Calais, however, still remained a staple. In the staple towns courts of law-merchant were established for determining all mercantile disputes and for punishing offenders.

Stapss, Frederic, born March 14, 1792, son of a Protestant clergyman at Naumburg, in Thuringia, undertook to assassinate the emperor Napoleon, because he supposed him to be the author of the misfortunes of Germany. With this design he went to Vienna, remained ten days, and on Oct. 23, 1809, travelled to Schönbrunn, where Napoleon was reviewing his forces. The emperor stood between Berthier and Rapp, when the youth advanced, and desired to speak with Napoleon. Rapp directed him to wait till after the muster. But, being struck with the look, the voice and the bearing of Stapss, he ordered him to be imprisoned in the castle. Here a large case-knife was found upon him, and the portrait of a young female. Rapp, who spoke German, asked him his name, and why he carried a knife. "I can tell no one but Napoleon himself." "Do you intend to murder him with it?" "Yes, sir." "For what reason?" "I can answer this question to none but himself." The emperor then commanded the young man to be brought before him. Bernadotte, Berthier, Savary, Duroc and Rapp were present. With an air of calmness, and his hands bound behind his back, the youth came into the presence of the emperor, and respectfully bowed to him. Napoleon asked him, through Rapp, the following questions: "What is your place of residence?" "Naumburg." "Who is your father?" "A Protestant clergyman." "How old are you?" "Eighteen years." "What did you intend to do with your knife?" "To kill you." "You are beside yourself, young man: you are an Illumine." "I am not beside myself; I do not know what an Illumine is." "You are sick, then." "No, I am not; I am perfectly well." "Why did you mean to kill me?" "Because you have injured my country." "Have I ever wronged you?" "You have injured me in common with all the Germans." "Who sent you? Who urged you to this crime?" "No one: the conviction that I should do a great service to my country and to all Europe by putting you to death, was my motive." With the same calmness, Stapss replied to all the emperor's interrogatories. Corvisart, Napoleon's physician, was called to feel the pulse of the young man. "Is it not true, sir, that I am not sick?" "The young man is well," said Corvisart, addressing the emperor. "I said so," observed the youth. "Your head is disordered," continued the emperor; "you will make your family unhappy. I will spare your life, if you acknowledge your crime and ask my pardon." "I wish for no pardon. I deeply regret the failure of my plan." "Whose was the portrait found on you?" "It was that of a young person, whom I love." "She will be greatly afflicted by your enterprise." "She will be pained at its ill success. She hates you as much as I do." "If I pardon you, will you thank me for it?" "It shall not prevent my killing you, if an opportunity offers." Stapss was led away, and general Lauer appointed to question him further, to discover whether he had any associates. The youth firmly maintained that no one was acquainted with his undertaking. He was shot, Oct. 27, at 7 o'clock in the morning. He had taken no nourishment since the 24th. Food was offered him, but he refused to eat. He said that he was strong enough to go to the place of execution. (See Rapp's *Memoirs*.)

Star. (See *Fixed Stars*, *Constellations*, and *Planets*.)

Star, Falling or Shooting. (See *Falling Stars*, *Fireballs*, and *Meteors*.)

Star of Bethlehem. (See *Appendix*.)

Star-Chamber (*camera stellata*); a room in the house of lords, so called from having its ceiling adorned with gilded stars, or, according to some, because it was originally the place of deposit of the Jewish starrs (*starra*) or covenants. The despotic tribunal, which sat here, was also called the *star-chamber*. It was under the direction of the chancellor, and had jurisdiction of forgery, perjury, riots, maintenance, fraud, libel and conspiracy, and, in general, of every misdemeanor, especially those of public importance, for which the law had provided no sufficient punishment. It was this criminal jurisdiction (its civil having gone into disuse) that made it so powerful and odious an auxiliary of a despotic administration. Its process was summary, and often iniquitous, and the punishment which it inflicted, often arbitrary and cruel. It became particularly violent in the reign of Charles I; and it was abolished, with the no less hateful high commission court, by the long parliament, in 1641. Its fall was an important step in the progress of English liberty.

STARBOARD; the right side of a ship, when the eye is directed forward.

STARCH is a white, insipid, vegetable substance, insoluble in cold water, but forming a jelly with boiling water. It exists chiefly in the white and brittle parts of vegetables, particularly in tuberose roots, and the seeds of gramineous plants. It may be extracted by pounding these parts, and agitating them in cold water, when the fibrous parts will first subside, after which the starch will gradually precipitate itself in a fine white powder; or the pounded or grated substance (as the roots of arum, potatoes, acorns, or horse-chestnuts, for instance) may be put into a hair-sieve, and the starch washed through with cold water, leaving the grosser matters behind. Farinaceous seeds may be ground and treated in a similar manner. Oily seeds require to have the oil expressed from them before the farina is extracted. In starch-making, the farina ferments and becomes sour; but the starch that does not undergo fermentation is rendered more pure by this process. Some water, already soured, is mixed with the flour and water, which regulates the fermentation, and presents the mixture from becoming putrid; and in this state it is left about ten days in summer, and fifteen in winter, before the scum is removed and the water poured off. The starch is then washed out from the bran, and dried, first in the open air, and finally in an oven. When starch is triturated with iodine, it forms combinations of various colors. When the proportions of iodine are small, these compounds are violet; when somewhat greater, blue; and when still greater, black. We can always obtain the finest blue color by treating starch with an excess of iodine, dissolving the compound in liquid potash, and precipitating by a vegetable acid. The color is manifested even at the instant of pouring water of iodine into a liquid which contains starch diffused through it. Hence iodine becomes an excellent test for detecting starch, and starch for detecting iodine. Starch is convertible into sugar by dilute sulphuric acid. To produce this change, we must take 2000 parts of starch, diffuse them in 8000 parts of water, containing 40 parts of strong sulphuric acid, and boil the mixture for thirty-six hours in a basin of silver or lead, taking care to stir the materials with a wooden rod, during the first hour of ebullition. At the end of this time, the mass, having become liquid, does not require to be stirred, except at intervals. In proportion as the water evaporates, it ought to be replaced. When the liquor has been sufficiently boiled, chalk and animal charcoal are added, and it is clarified with white of egg. The whole is then filtered through a flock of wool, and the clear liquid is concentrated, till it has acquired a sirupy consistence. After this, the basin is removed from the fire, in order, that, by cooling, its sulphate of lime may be precipitated. The pure sirup is now decanted, and evaporated to the proper dryness. It is found, also, that sugar may be obtained from starch without the use of sulphuric acid. It is obtained by leaving the starch, first brought to the pulpy state, to itself, either with or without the contact of the air, or by mixing it with dried gluten. At the same time, however, other products are obtained; viz. 1. a gum like that from roasted starch; 2. amydine, a body whose properties are intermediate between those of starch and gum; and, 3. an insoluble substance, like ligneous matter. Twelve parts of boiling water and one of starch, fermented by dry gluten, yielded,

	Without contact of air.	With contact of air.
Sugar,	47.4	49.7
Gum,	23.0	9.7
Amydine,	8.9	5.2
Amylaceous lignin,	10.3	9.2
Lignin with charcoal,	a trace	0.3
Undecomposed starch,	4.0	3.8

Potato starch differs considerably from that of wheat. It is more friable, is composed of much larger sized grains, forms a jelly with water at a lower temperature, and is less readily decomposed by spontaneous fermentation. Starch is composed of carbon 43.48, oxygen 49.45, hydrogen 7.06. Doctor Prout considers starch as sugar partly organized; for it has the same essential composition, but differs in containing minute portions of other matter, which, we may presume, prevent its constituent particles from arranging them selves in the crystalline form, and thus cause it to assume totally different sensible properties. When starch is roasted at a moderate heat in an oven, it is converted into a species of gum, employed by calico printers: potato starch answers best for this purpose. *Salop* is composed of a little gum, very little starch, and much of a kind of gum called *Bassorine*. *Sago* is an uniform substance, soluble in cold water, more so in hot, precipitated blue by iodine, and differing from common starch only in the first mentioned property. *Tapioca* seems to be identical with sago. *Arrow root* is nearly pure starch, agreeing in all respects with the starch of potato, which may be converted by heat into something similar to sago and tapioca.

Stark, John, a brigadier-general in the American revolutionary war, was born at Londonderry, New Hampshire, on the 17th of August, 1728. At the age of twenty-one years, while hunting, he was captured by the Indians, by whom he was detained a prisoner four months He commanded a provincial company of rangers in the French war of 1755, and accompanied the British general, lord Howe, at the assault on the French lines, in July, 1758, when that officer was killed. This war being concluded, he retired with reputation, and when the report of the battle of Lexington reached him, was engaged at work in his saw-mill. Instantly seizing his musket, he repaired to the camp of his countrymen, at Cambridge, where he received a colonel's commission, and was enabled, by his own popularity, added to the spirit of the times, to levy eight hundred men in two hours. In the battle of Breed's hill, colonel Stark fought at the head of his New Hampshire troops, and evinced much zeal and bravery. Upon the evacuation of Boston, he joined the northern army in its retreat from Canada, and commanded a party employed in fortifying mount Independence. In December, 1776, he served with distinction under general Washington, in the brilliant stroke at Trenton. He also shared in the affair at Princeton soon after. The achievement, however, on which Stark's fame principally rests, was performed at Bennington, in Vermont, at one of the most lowery periods in the revolutionary struggle. After his successes in the northern colonies of the confederacy, and while his army was triumphantly marching towards Albany, general Burgoyne formed a project for capturing a quantity of stores collected by the Americans at Bennington. With this design, he despatched colonel Baum, a German officer, at the head of fifteen hundred Hessians and tories, with one hundred savage auxiliaries and two field-pieces. Colonel Baum commenced his march on the 14th of August, and, having proceeded twelve or thirteen miles, halted. Fortunately Stark was at or near Bennington, with about fourteen hundred New England militia, part of whom, from the New Hampshire grants, were denominated *Green mountain boys*. Advancing to reconnoitre the position of the Germans, skirmishing ensued, with some loss to the latter, when their commander became alarmed, and sent to Burgoyne for a reinforcement. The 15th was a wet day, and no operations of moment took place; but on the 16th, Stark, having made the proper arrangements, assaulted the enemy, when a severe and long conflict ensued. Notwithstanding the superior force of Baum, with the advantage of breast-works, his efforts at resistance were ineffectual: the Americans demolished his defences with the muzzles of their guns, and compelled his detachment to surrender at discretion. The victory was complete on the American side, they taking possession of two pieces of brass cannon, a number of prisoners, baggage, &c. Scarcely was this affair finished, the troops under general Stark being scattered in the performance of various duties, when a body of one thousand German troops, with two field-pieces, commanded by colonel Breyman, arrived to assist their defeated countrymen. Being joined at this moment by a fresh regiment under colonel Warner, Stark rallied his own wearied and hungry soldiers, and proceeded to attack this new enemy. He ordered a field-piece, which had been taken from Baum, to be brought forward; but his men had never seen such a thing before, and he dismounted himself to instruct them in the management of it. In the action which followed, both parties fought with determined courage; but, on the approach of night, the Germans were entirely routed, and retreated under cover of the darkness. The loss of the enemy was nine hundred and thirty four, of whom one hundred and fifty-seven were tories: six hundred and fifty-four were made prisoners. One thousand stand of arms, four brass field-pieces, two hundred and fifty dragoon swords, eight loads of baggage, and twenty horses, were added to the numerous trophies taken by the conquerors. Colonel Baum soon after died of a wound received in the action. The loss of the Americans did not exceed one hundred. Congress passed a resolve of thanks to general Stark and his men, for their conduct in this action, and appointed him a brigadier-general in the army of the U. States. He volunteered his services under general Gates previously to the capitulation of Burgoyne, and was one of the council that arranged the terms of that officer's surrender. In 1778, he conducted the defence of the northern frontier, and served in different quarters till the conclusion of the war. In person, general Stark was of the middle size. He was an excellent soldier, and a citizen of unblemished character. He lived to see his country grow and flourish under the benign system which he had fought to establish; and, having attained the venerable age of ninety-three years and eight months, he was gathered to his departed compatriots on the 8th of May, 1822.

STARLING. (See *Appendix*, end of this volume.)

STAROSTS, in Poland; those noblemen who were reckoned among the dignitaries of the land (*dignitarii terrarum*), and who received a castle or landed estate from the crown domains (*mensa regia*). The starosty was granted only for the life of the occupant, on whose death, however, the king was obliged to grant it anew. Some of the starosts had civil and criminal jurisdiction over a certain district (*grod*); others (*tentuarii*) merely enjoyed the revenues of the starosty.

STATE (*respublica, civitas, societas civilis*); a body politic; an association of men for political ends, the object of which is well expressed in the term *commonwealth* (i. e. common good). Experience, as well as reason, shows that the isolated individual can attain but very imperfectly the ends of his being, and instinct early led men to form unions, for promoting the good of each by the power of all. Such a union is a state, and may be called the natural condition of man, because essential to the full developement of his faculties. Separated from society, he remains a brute. So true is the ancient definition of man as being a political animal, though it may have been taken, when first used, in too narrow a sense. (See the beginning of the article *Slavery*.) The right of men to form states being thus obvious from their nature, the next questions which arise are, What is the historical origin of states? and what is the best state, or best government? History shows, that states have been formed in a great variety of ways, by the violence of one or many, by artifice, by contract, &c. (See the articles ***Political Institutions***, ***Sovereignty Estate***, ***Legitimacy***; also ***Communities***, ***Cities***, ***Corporations***, ***Land***, ***property in***.) As to the other question, that state is the best, which is best adapted to promote the general good; so that the organization of such a state may, and must, differ according to circumstances. This fact is overlooked by those who treat the organization of a state merely as a matter of abstract speculation, and, on the other hand, is often used as a pretext for retaining abuses diametrically opposed to the true objects of political society. It should never be forgotten, that the form of government, important as it is, is merely a means of obtaining the great objects of the state; and the first objects to be provided for are security and good order, to which all forms must be made to yield. These terms include much more than the mere protection of individuals against violence on the part of each other—a sense to which none but despotic governments would limit the words.

STATE ADVOCATE. (See *Advocate of the Crown*.)

STATEN ISLAND is situated south of the city of New York, the centre of it being distant from the city eleven miles. It constitutes the county of Richmond, and is the most southern land belonging to New York. Its length is fourteen miles, and its greatest breadth eight miles. Its southern extremity is in lat. 40° 29′ N.; its western extremity is 18′ west longitude from New York; population in 1830, 7084.

STATES-GENERAL. (See *Netherlands*.)

STATES OF THE CHURCH. (See *Church, States of the*.)

STATICS. (See *Dynamics*, and *Mechanics*.)

STATISTICS. The past, in all its extension, belongs to history; the present to geography and statistics. Schlözer (q. v.) said with much truth, "History is statistics in a state of progression; statistics is history at a stand." The subject of statistics is the investigation and exposition of the actual condition of states and nations, in regard to their internal organization and foreign relations. The description of the face of the country belongs to geography. Statistics is often considered in too confined a view, as if it had to treat only of those particulars in the condition of a country which can be reduced to numerical calculation, and exhibited in tables, such as the number, employments and wealth of the people. The frequent reference to "statistical tables," and the frequent use of the phrase, may be in part the occasion of this. A full, statistical view of the actual condition of a people requires the exhibition, 1. of the physical character of the country and the parts composing it, in regard to situation, boundaries, extent and soil, mountains, woods, rivers, climate; also of the numbers and national diversities of the people; their extraction, languages, &c.; the classes into which they are divided (nobility, free proprietors, bondsmen, slaves, officers, merchants, manufacturers, farmers, mechanics, soldiers, &c.); and their religious differences (the various sects, &c.): 2. of the degree of civilization shown in the state of the useful arts and occupations (agriculture, mechanical and manufacturing industry, commerce); in the institutions for the promotion of the fine arts; in the schools, universities, scientific academies, sale of books, &c.; in the manners of the people, and their conduct in all their important relations, moral, political and religious: 3. of the form of government, whether monarchical or republican, despotic or limited; whether there be a popular representation or an assembly of the estates (q. v.); whether the representation is in one or two chambers; whether the representatives take part in legislation, or merely in the imposition of taxes; whether there is a responsibility of the ministers, and none of the monarch, &c; also of the relations of church and state (whether any exist, and, if so, whether the hierarchical or territorial (q. v.) system prevails; whether there are concordates (q. v.) with Rome); likewise of the family of the monarch, where one exists, the age, religion, &c., of the members, the family laws of the ruling house, the court, and the laws relating to it, the military orders, &c.: 4. of the administration of the state (including all the temporal and spiritual authorities, &c., in particular the departments of justice, police, finances, the army and navy). In treating of the foreign relations of the state, this science shows, 1. the standing of the particular state (if it be in Europe) as to the other members of the European family, whether it be a power of first, second, third or fourth rank, and particularly its relations to its immediate neighbors (thus, in treating of German states, it would show their relations to the whole confederacy; so likewise with the Helvetic cantons and the American states): 2. the reciprocal influence of its domestic and foreign politics: 3. of the existing treaties with foreign states, indicating the sources of information respecting them, their most important points, and their beneficial or injurious consequences. According to the example of some distinguished statistical writers (e. g. Hassel, in the statistics of Austria and Russia; Stein, in those of Prussia, and others), a view of the gradual increase or decrease of the state, in respect to extent, population, &c., may be given advantageously. Statistics differ from geography in this respect, that, though many particular facts belong equally to both, yet geography arranges them always on the principle of locality, but statistics with reference to their effect on the general condition of the nation. Thus geography mentions the mountains, rivers, woods, in describing the districts where they are found, or speaks of their distribution, to give a view of the face of the country: statistics treats of them collectively, with a view to their political importance, as affecting the productiveness of the country, favoring or obstructing communication, &c. In a military description, the same subjects would be treated with particular reference to their military importance. Geography treats also of manufactures, commerce, trade, public authorities, universities, schools, seminaries, museums, &c., in describing the places in which they are situated; but statistics combines them, with a view to arrive at scientific results. Statistics, in modern times, has often been mixed with geography, in some cases advantageously to the immediate purpose in view, but in many to the disadvantage of science and sound knowledge. Statistics was first scientifically treated in Germany: Achenwall (q. v.) gave it, in 1749, its name and systematic form. Since his time, it has become more and more separated from geography and history, and has been cultivated independently of them; but even before him, authors had scientifically combined statistical materials; for instance, some Italians, as Sansovino Botero; some Frenchmen, as d'Avity; and particularly Germans, as Conring, Oldenburger, who died in 1678, at Geneva, the author of *Thesaurus Rerum publicarum* (4 vols., Geneva, 1675); Gastel, in his *De Statu publico Europæ novissimo* (Nuremberg, 1675, folio); Von Zech, in his European Herald (3 vols., Leipsic, 1705, folio, in German), and several others; Dutchmen, as De Luca, in his *Descriptio Orbis*, &c. (Leyden, 1655); and Everhard Otto, in his

Primæ Lineæ Notitiæ Europæ Rerum publicarum (Utrecht, 1762). Following Conring's example, Achenwall delivered university lectures on statistics. His *Staatsverfassung der Europäischen Reiche im Grundrisse*, passed through seven editions. Several other manuals appeared. To the department of the theory and history of statistics belong Gatterer's Idea of Universal Statistics (Göttingen, 1773); Schlözer's unfinished Theory of Statistics (Göttingen, 1804); Niemann's Sketch of Statistics (Altona, 1807); and a vast number of other works. Among the statistical manuals are Hassel's Complete Manual of the most recent Geography and Statistics, and Stein's Manual of Geography and Statistics (4th ed., 1819). Among the living statistical writers of Italy are Balbi, Quadri and Melch. Gioja. The statistics of crime have been most attended to in France and England. The French writers have paid particular attention to comparative statistics; for example, baron Dupin, a statistical writer of the first order; also the Italian Gioja, in his *Filosofia della Statistica* (2 vols., 4to., Milan, 1826 et seq.). Meusel published a Literature of Statistics (2d edition, 2 vols., in German). Statistical tables may lead, and have led, to incorrect notions, when the bare results are considered, without reference to the causes and accompanying circumstances, but, when used with due caution, they are of the highest importance. The influence of the study of statistics has been incalculable: it is the test and the basis of the principles of political economy, and has mainly contributed to that knowledge of the condition and interests of nations which distinguishes our time. Every nation will find its interests essentially promoted by cultivating and making public its own statistics; and writers like Dupin are public benefactors. Among the best statistical works are Hassel's Statistical Sketches of all the European States (1805, 2 vols.); his Statistical Tables, comprising a view of all the European States, and some others; his General Geographico-Statistical Lexicon (Weimar, 1827); and his Genealogical, Historical and Statistical Almanac (an annual); Crome's works; Stäudlin's Ecclesiastical Geography and Statistics (2 vols., Tüb., 1804); Herbin and Peuchet's *Statistique de la France* (7 vols., Paris, 1803); Dupin's *Forces productives et commerciales de la France* (Paris, 2d vol., 4to., 1832); Colquhoun's Treatise on the Wealth, Power and Resources of the British Empire (London, 1814, 4to.); Dupin's *Voyages dans la Grande-Bretagne* (1820); Wichmann and Hassel's works on Russia; and J. H. Schnitzler's *Statistique et Itinéraire de la Russie* (Paris and Petersburg, 1829); Von Hammer and Lindner's works on Turkey; Bisinger's, Hassel's, Demian's, André's, on Austria; Schwartner's, on Hungary; Mirabeau's, Krug's, Demian's, Stein's, on Prussia; Thaarup's work on Denmark; Pölitz's, on Saxony. There is no complete statistical view of the present condition of the U. States, though such a one would be highly desirable, in order to give other nations correct notions respecting this country. Much valuable information is contained in Warden's Statistical, Political and Historical Account of the United States (3 vols., 8vo., Edinburgh, 1819); Timothy Pitkin's Statistical View of the Commerce of the United States (8vo., New York, 1817); Adam Seybert's Statistical Annals of the U. States (Philadelphia, 1818); William Darby's Historical, Geographical and Statistical View of the United States (Philadelphia, 1828); Watterston and Van Zandt's Tabular Statistical Views of the United States (Washington, 1829); Ouseley's Political Institutions of the United States (1832); and the American Atlas (3d edition, Philadelphia, 1827).

STATIUS, Publius Papinius; a Roman epic poet, born at Naples, in the reign of the emperor Domitian (A. D. 61), and educated by his father, a rhetorician. His principal productions are two epic poems, the *Thebais*, in twelve books, and the *Achilleis*, in two books. The last is unfinished. These works are both dedicated to Domitian, whom the adulatory bard ranks among the gods. The style of Statius is bombastic and affected, often exhibiting the art of the declaimer rather than that of the poet; but he attracted general admiration in his own time, and even some modern critics have considered him as inferior only to Virgil. He wrote some shorter poems, called *Sylvæ*, which have been distributed into four books; and some of these compositions are eminently beautiful. Statius is supposed to have been destitute of fortune, as he is said to have supported himself by writing for the stage; but none of his dramatic compositions are extant. He died about the hundredth year of the Christian era. Among the best editions of the works of Statius are those of Barthius (1664, 2 vols., 4to.), and the Variorum, Lugd. Bat. (1671, 8vo.); of the *Thebais* separately, that of Warrington (1778, 2 vols., 12mo.), and of the *Sylvæ*, that of Markland (London, 1728, 4to.).

STATUE (from the Latin *statua*). Statues are divided into ideal and portrait statues (*statua iconica:* this term also signified a statue of the natural size). The former, in respect to invention, are much superior, and reach the highest point of the art, when, as in Greek antiquity, they represent divine beings, serene, and superior to all sensual impulses. The latter have all the qualities of portraits (q. v.) except coloring. In Greece, such statues were given to those who had been thrice victorious in the Olympic games. Portrait statues seem to have been first set up in Athens to the memory of Harmodius and Aristogiton, the avengers of liberty and destroyers of the Pisistratidæ. At first, the Greeks seem to have made no statues but those of the gods; but, in later times, and especially during the decline of the Roman republic, when servility and adulation became more and more common, a great number of portrait statues were produced. Gods and monarchs were originally represented of a colossal size; and, in general, the size of the statues, with the ancients, had a symbolical meaning. Originally, statues were colored. The Romans called statues in Greek costume, *statuæ palliatæ;* in Roman costume, *togatæ*, &c. There were *statuæ pedestres* (on foot), *sedentes* (sitting), *equestres* (on horseback), and *curules* (driving; and these, again, *bigatæ*, *quadrigatæ*, in which way many deities and triumphant generals were represented). Sometimes whole groups were and are exhibited, as the Laocoön; but, in these, the figures were generally distinct, except in those which represented figures intertwined with each other (*symplegmata*, as in the case of groups of wrestlers). Statues were often used by the ancients to ornament buildings, &c. (As to the material employed, see *Plastics*, and *Sculpture*.) The most celebrated statues are mentioned in the article *Sculpture*.

STATUTE; an act of the legislature of a state; a positive law. *Statute* is commonly applied to the acts of legislative bodies, consisting of representatives. In monarchies not having representative bodies, the acts of the sovereign are called *edicts*, *decrees*, *ordinances*, *rescripts*. Statutes are distinguished from common law. The latter owes its force to the principles of justice, to long use, and the consent of a nation; the former to a positive command, or declaration of the supreme power. (For the forms of the passage of bills through the English parliament and the congress of the U. States, see *Parliament*, and *Congress of the United States*.)

STAUBBACH, FALLS OF. (See *Cataract*.)

STÄUDLIN, Charles Frederic, doctor and professor of theology at Göttingen, was born in 1761, at Stuttgart, and early began his History and Spirit of Scepticism, particularly in respect to Morality and Religion (which appeared at Leipsic, 1794). He travelled in Switzerland, France and England, and was appointed *professor extraordinarius* at Göttingen, in 1790, where he became doctor of theology in 1792. His writings are very numerous, and the latter ones have been charged with the faults often attending too great fertility. He died in 1826. His works are a Manual of the Extent, Method and History of Theological Sciences (Hanover, 1821); Ecclesiastical Geography and Statistics (Tubingen, 1804); Contributions to the Elucidation of the Prophets of the Old Testament (Stuttgart, 1786); continuation of the same (Göttingen, 1791); Origin, Contents and Construction of Solomon's Song, in Paulus's *Memor;* Essay towards a Criticism of the System of the Christian Religion (1791); Sketch of Academical Lectures on Morals and Dogmatics for future Teachers of the Christian Religion (2 vols., 1798—1800); Text-Book of Dogmatics, and the History of Dogmas (3d edition, 1809); Outlines of Philosophical and Biblical Morals (an academical text-book, 1805); New Text-Book of Morals for Theologians, with Introductions to the History of Morals and moral Dogmas (1813); Practical Introduction to the Books of the Sacred Scriptures (1826); a History of the Ideas which have been entertained respecting the Morality of Theatres, the Doctrine of Suicide, Conscience, Oaths (1824), and Friendship (1826); a History of Rationalism (1826); a History of the Ethics of Jesus (4 vols., 1799—1823); Outlines of a History of Philosophical, Hebrew and Christian Morals (Hanover, 1806); General History of the Christian Church (3d edition, 1823); History of Christian Morals since the Revival of Learning (1808); General Ecclesiastical History of Great Britain (Göttingen, 1819); History of Moral Philosophy (Hanover, 1822); History of the Theological Sciences (2 vols., 1811); History and Literature of Ecclesiastical History (edited by Hemsen, 1827). He edited several periodicals himself, as the Göttingen Library of the latest Theological Literature

(1794—1800); Contributions to the Philosophy and History of Religion and Ethics in general, and of the various Creeds and Churches (1797—99); Magazine for the History of Religion, Morals and the Church (1801—6); Archives of ancient and modern Ecclesiastical History (1813—20); Archives of Ecclesiastical History, in conjunction with Tzschirner and Vater (vol. i., Halle, 1823). He also wrote a great number of occasional treatises.

Staufen. (See *Hohenstaufen.*)

Staunton, sir George Leonard, a traveller and diplomatist, was a native of the county of Galway, in Ireland. He was destined for the medical profession, with a view to which he studied at the university of Montpellier, and took the degree of doctor of physic. About the year 1762, he established himself in practice in the island of Grenada, in the West Indies, where he obtained the patronage of the governor, lord Macartney, who made him his secretary; and he likewise held the office of attorney-general of Grenada, till the taking of that island by the French. His lordship, being appointed governor of Madras, took Mr. Staunton with him to the East Indies, where he was employed in the arrest of general Stuart, who had opposed the authority of the governor. He also induced the French admiral Suffren to suspend hostilities before Gondelour, previously to the official announcement of the peace in 1714; and he negotiated a treaty with Tippoo Saib. Returning to England, the East India company repaid his services with a pension of £500 a year; the king created him a baronet, and the university of Oxford bestowed on him the diploma of doctor of laws. When lord Macartney (q. v.) went as ambassador to China, sir George accompanied him as secretary of legation, with the provisional title of envoy extraordinary and minister plenipotentiary. Of that mission, and of the empire and people of China, he published an Account in 1797 (2 vols., 4to.), which was translated into French and German. He died in London, in January, 1801.

Staunton, sir George Thomas, baronet; only son of the preceding, sir George Leonard Staunton, who, having only one child, paid uncommon attention to his education; and the youth was introduced to a knowledge both of the dead and living languages, and of botany, chemistry, &c., much earlier than usual. He was born in 1781, and was only twelve years old when his father was appointed to go to China. Sir George, with his son, instantly set off for Rome, where he engaged two native Chinese, of the Propaganda, to return with them to their native country. From these men young Staunton, in the course of the voyage, learned Chinese. On his arrival, he was presented to the emperor, who, seeing so young a man acquainted with his own language, looked on him with surprise, and made him a handsome present. On the return of the embassy, sir George had interest enough with the court of directors to get his son appointed a writer in the factory at Canton and Macao, for which young Mr. Staunton embarked, and resided there many years. During that period, he translated into the Chinese language the History and Progress of Vaccination, which practice has been successfully diffused through that empire. The knowledge of the Chinese language, it had been supposed, would produce to young Staunton great pecuniary advantages; but it was with difficulty the court of directors could be induced to add £500 to his salary as secretary of the Chinese language. Sir George published, in 1810, the Fundamental Laws and Penal Code of China, with an Appendix and Notes. He had risen almost to the head of the Chinese factory, when he returned to England, and then determined not to go any more to China. Sir George has also published the Narrative of the Chinese Embassy to the Khan of the Tourgouth Tartars in 1712—15 (1821), a translation from the Chinese; and Miscellaneous Notices relating to China, and the British Commercial Intercourse with that Country (1822). He has also written an Account of Lord Amherst's Embassy to China; and Memoirs of Sir G. L. Staunton, which have been printed, but not published. He has been several times returned to parliament, where he has voted with the tories.

Staurotide; a mineral species, so called from σταυρος, a cross, in allusion to the regular crossing of its crystals, which so frequently takes place. The primitive form of the crystal is a right rhombic prism of 129° 30′, which is rarely modified at its extremities, though its acute lateral edges are usually truncated, converting the crystals into six-sided prisms. The cruciform crystals of this species are of two kinds: in the first, the crystals cross each other at right angles; in the second, at angles of 60° and 120°. Fracture uneven or conchoidal; lustre vitreous, inclining to resinous; color reddish-brown, or brownish-red, very dark; streak white; translucent; hardness a little superior to that of quartz; specific gravity 3.3 to 3.9. According to an analysis, by Vaquelin, of the variety from Brittany, and another by Klaproth, of the variety from St. Gothard, staurotide consists of

Silex,	33.00	37.50
Alumine,	44.00	41.00
Lime,	3.84	0.00
Magnesia,	0.00	0.50
Oxide of iron,	13.00	18.25
Oxide of manganese,	1.00	0.50

It assumes a dark color before the blowpipe, but does not melt. Staurotide occurs, for the most part, in mica slate, and is often accompanied by garnet and cyanite. It is found in single crystals on St. Gothard, in Switzerland, and on the Greiner mountain, in Zillerthal, in the Tyrol. It is an abundant substance in the U. States, particularly in the states of Maine, New Hampshire and Massachusetts.

Stay; a large, strong rope, employed to support the mast on the fore part, by extending from its upper end towards the stem of the ship, as the shrouds are extended on each side.

Stays. (See *Corset.*)

Stealing. (See *Larceny.*)

Steam. When water is exposed to the action of heat, it expands, and assumes the gaseous state called *steam.* In this condition, it is extremely light and expansible, like air, and, like it, capable of being easily reduced into less space by external pressure, and resisting, like it, the force which thus compresses it. If we introduce a tea-spoonful of water into a large glass globe capable of holding several gallons, and exhausted of its air, and afterwards apply heat to the globe, the water will gradually disappear, so that the vessel will appear perfectly empty; yet it is completely filled with the water, now existing in the state of vapor or steam. By increasing the heat, we augment the expansive force of the vapor; and it may easily be increased so as to shatter the globe to pieces. Water is converted into vapor at all temperatures, even at 32°, or lower; but the elasticity at low temperatures is low; and it increases as the temperature increases, till, at 212°, it is equal to that of the atmosphere, or capable of supporting a column of mercury 30 inches in height. In this condition, it occupies 1689 times the bulk of the water from which it was formed, and has a density expressed by 0.625, that of air being 1. Attempts have been made to represent the increase in the elasticity of steam at increasing temperatures; but they are not esteemed accurate for elevated temperatures. The elasticity of steam at 419° is 1050 times greater than that of air; so that it exerts a force equivalent to 14,700 lbs upon every square inch of the inside of the vessel in which it is confined—a pressure so enormous that few vessels can be made strong enough to withstand it. It is obvious that the specific gravity of the vapor of water is proportional to its elasticity: consequently, if we know this specific gravity at any one temperature, we may, from our knowledge of the elasticity, determine the specific gravity at any other. The following table exhibits the specific gravity of vapor at various temperatures:—

Temperature.	Specific Gravity.	Weight of 100 Cubic Inches in Grains.
32°	0.004166	0.12974825
36	0.0048828125	0.15206406
56	0.009765628	0.304128125
78	0.01953125	0.60825625
100	0.0390625	1.2165125
150	0.15625	4.86625
212	0.625	19.465
250	1.25	39.93
293.4	2.5	79.86
343.4	5.	159.72
419.	21.875	681.3

Hence we see that, at the temperature of 419°, water, when converted into steam, expands only thirty-seven times. When such steam comes into the air, it would expand thirty-five times. This would prodigiously increase its specific heat, and of course diminish its temperature. It is probable that, at a temperature not much higher than 500°, the steam of water would not much exceed double the bulk of the water from which it was generated. The expansive force of such steam would be amazing. When issued into the atmosphere, it would undergo an expansion of 650 times its original bulk. We do not know at what temperature water would become vapor without any increase of volume. It would then support a column of mercury 3243 feet in height, and exert a force of 19,459 lbs. upon every square inch of the vessel containing it. Such are some of the principal phenomena of the conversion of water into steam, which has been proved by doctor Black to be owing to the very same cause as the conversion of solids into liquids, namely, to the combination of a certain amount of caloric with that liquid, without any increase of temperature. The truth of this very important point is shown by the following experiments: 1. When a vessel of water is put upon the fire, the water gradually becomes hotter till it reaches 212°; afterwards its temperature is not increased. Now, heat must be constantly entering from the fire and combining with the water. But as the water does not become hotter, the heat must combine with that part of it which flies off in the form of steam; but the temperature of the steam is only 212°; therefore this additional heat does not increase its temperature. We must conclude, then, that the change of water to steam is owing to the combination of this heat; for it produces no other change. Doctor Black put some water in a tin plate vessel upon a red hot iron. The water was of the temperature 50°; in four minutes it began to boil, and in twenty minutes it was all boiled off. During the first four minutes, it had received 162°, or 40½° per minute. If we suppose that it received as much per minute during the whole time of boiling, the caloric which entered into the water, and converted it into steam, would amount to $40\frac{1}{2}\times20=810°$. This heat is not indicated by the thermometer, for the temperature of steam is only 212°; therefore doctor Black called it *latent heat*. 2. Water may be heated in a Papin's digester—a cylindrical copper vessel, having a lid nicely fitted to it, and kept fast by screws—to 400° without boiling; because the steam is forcibly compressed, and prevented from making its escape. If the mouth of the vessel be suddenly opened while things are in this state, part of the water rushes out in the form of steam, but the greater part still remains in the form of water, and its temperature instantly sinks to 212°; consequently 188° of heat have suddenly disappeared. This heat must have been carried off by the steam. Now, as only about one fifth of the water is converted into steam, that steam must contain, not only its own 188°, but also the 188° lost by each of the other four parts; i. e. it must contain 188×5, or about 940°. Steam, therefore, is water combined with at least 940° of heat, the presence of which is not indicated by the thermometer. 3. If one part of steam, at 212°, be mixed with nine parts, by weight, of water at 62°, the steam instantly assumes the form of water, and the temperature, after mixture, is 178.6°; consequently, each of the nine parts of water has received 116.6° of caloric, and the steam has lost $9\times116.6°=1049.4°$ of caloric. But as the temperature of the steam is diminished by 33.4°, we must substract this sum. There will remain rather more than 1000°, which is the quantity of heat that existed in the steam without increasing its temperature. This experiment is made by passing a given weight of steam through a metallic worm surrounded by a given weight of water. The heat acquired by the water indicates the heat which the steam gives out during its condensation. The latent heat of steam, as determined by different philosophers, is as follows:

950°	by	Watt.
945°	"	Southern.
1000°	"	Lavoisier.
1040.8°	"	Rumford.
955.8°	"	Despretz.

The number 978, which is the mean of these estimates, cannot be very far from the truth, though doctor Thomson is of opinion that the true number cannot fall below 1000°.

Before we describe the application of steam in the steam-engine, we shall briefly allude to some other useful purposes to which it has been subjected. It has been ascertained that one cubic foot of boiler will heat about 2000 feet of space, in a cotton mill, to an average heat of about 70° or 80° Fahr. It has also been proved that one square foot of surface of steam-pipe is adequate to the warming of 200 cubic feet of space. This quantity is adapted to a well finished, ordinary brick or stone building. Cast-iron pipes are preferable to all others for the diffusion of heat, the pipes being distributed within a few inches of the floor. Steam is also used extensively for drying muslin and calicoes. Large cylinders are filled with it, which, diffusing in the apartment a temperature of 100° or 130°, rapidly dry the suspended cloth. Experience has shown that bright dyed yarns, like scarlet, dried in a common stove heat of 128°, have their color darkened, and acquire a harsh feel; while similar hanks, laid on a steam-pipe heated up to 165°, retain the shade and lustre they possessed in the moist state. Besides, the people who work in steam-drying rooms are healthy, while those who were formerly employed in the stove-heated apartments, became, in a short time, sickly and emaciated. The heating, by steam, of large quantities of water or other liquids, either for baths or manufactures, may be effected in two ways: The steam-pipe may be plunged, with an open end, into the water cistern; or the steam may be diffused around the liquid in the interval between the wooden vessel and the interior metallic case. The second mode is of universal applicability. Cooking food for man and cattle is another useful application of steam; for it is the most effectual carrier of heat that can be conceived, depositing it only on such bodies as are colder than boiling water. Chambers filled with steam, heated to about 125° Fahr., have been introduced, with advantage, into medicine, under the name of *vapor baths*. But the most splendid application of steam remains to be described.

As steam possesses the elasticity of air, and as it may be immediately condensed by the application of cold, it is obvious that it may be applied as a moving force, and that it must possess unlimited power. The medium in which it is so applied is called the *steam-engine*, and constitutes the finest present ever made by science to the arts. It is admitted to have been invented by the marquis of Worcester, though it does not appear that he was ever able to interest the public in his invention, or that he attempted to apply it to any useful purpose. It was reinvented by captain Savary, who took out a patent towards the end of the seventeenth century, and published an account of it, in the year 1696, in a book entitled the Miner's Friend. In Savary's machine, the elasticity of steam was applied directly to force water up a pipe. The waste of steam was so enormous, and the quantity of fuel necessary so great, that it does not appear ever to have been attempted to apply it directly for the purpose of draining water out of mines, which was the object that Savary had in view when he took out his patent. In 1705, a new patent was taken out jointly by captain Savary, Newcommen (q. v.), a blacksmith, at Dartmouth, in Devonshire, and Mr. Crawley, a glazier in the same place. The merit of the machine has been universally ascribed to Newcommen, under whose name it went. It consisted essentially of a metallic cylinder, in which a piston, made air-tight, was capable of moving from the top to the bottom. The top of the cylinder was open, the bottom close. The piston was attached to the piston-rod or chain, which connected it with the end of the working-beam. The working-beam was supported on a gudgeon, and the end opposite to that to which the piston-rod was attached was loaded, and, of course, the pump-rod attached to it was at the bottom of the well from which the water was to be pumped. The cylinder is filled with steam till all the air is driven out. The piston was at the top of the cylinder. The steam in the cylinder is condensed by means of a jet of cold water. A vacuum is produced in the cylinder. The atmosphere presses upon the top of the piston, and forces it to the bottom of the cylinder. The pump-rod, at the other end of the working-beam, is drawn up. It makes a stroke, and a quantity of water is pumped out of the well or mine. Steam is again introduced below the piston in the cylinder; the vacuum is removed, and the piston rises to the top in consequence of the load at the other extremity of the working-beam. The cylinder is filled with steam, as before: this steam is condensed, the piston is forced down, more water is pumped up, and thus the machine continues to act as long as it is supplied with steam.

The great improvement in the steam engine was made by Mr. Watt, a native of Glasgow, who, accidentally having had his attention directed to the construction of the steam-engine, discovered that water, when confined in a close vessel, and heated considerably beyond the boiling point, would, when the steam was permitted to escape, cool, rapidly, down to the boiling temperature; which suggested an idea that the amount of steam issuing from any vessel was simply in proportion to the amount of heat applied, and that the economizing of fuel could only be obtained by the economizing of steam. He also noticed the great change which took place in the temperature of the cylinder when the cold water was injected to condense the steam, and concluded that, as the coldness of the cylinder would remain after the necessary condensation had been effected, a wasteful condensation of the newly introduced steam must take place. By experiment, he found that the quantity of steam thus wasted was no less than thrice the contents of the cylinder, or three times the quantity which was required for producing the effect sought. The modes to which he had recourse to remedy this defect were, first, the substitution of a wooden cylinder, which, upon repeated trials, he was compelled to abandon, on account of the roughnesses produced by wet and the changes of temperature; secondly, the enclosing of the cylinder with wood, and filling the intermediate space with powdered charcoal, which, afterwards, was superseded by the introduction of an extra cylinder, that enclosed the working cylinder, and permitted steam to flow around it, which maintained it at a regular temperature. This outer cylinder is termed a *jacket*. In the year 1763, he made the capital improvement of effecting the condensation of the steam in a separate vessel, communicating only by a pipe with the cylinder. Such was the importance of this alteration in the mode of construction, that one half the quantity of fuel, consumed in an engine of the former construction, was saved. Still, however, the machine was not complete: the piston required to have water upon its upper surface to keep it air-tight; and as this, in its descent, cooled the cylinder considerably, it was productive of a loss in the operation of the engine. Mr. Watt conceived the idea of closing the top of the cylinder, and of causing the piston-rod to work through a close collar, stuffed with hemp and grease; and, instead of using water to make the piston air-tight, to employ oil or fat; and, instead of causing it to descend by the pressure of the atmosphere, of employing steam of an expansive force equal to that pressure. In Watt and Bolton's engine, therefore (as it is called), steam from the boiler lifts the piston, and steam let in above depresses it—condensation of the steam taking place at the same time by communication with a cold vacuum connected with an air-pump—and thus the stroke and condensation are alternate; the cylinder is kept constantly hot, and the condenser cold by water pumped in by the working machinery from below: the hot water formed from the condensed steam is returned to the boiler by the operation of the machinery, the atmosphere not operating except on the horizontal section of the piston-rod. In what is called the *high pressure engine*, there is no condensation of the steam, but it is driven out alternately above and below the piston against the atmosphere. As this engine works simply by the dead lift of expansive steam, it requires great strength in the machinery. The principal advantage is in economy of machinery and room.

The steam-engine is now applied to almost every species of manufacturing industry as a substitute for the labor of men and animals. In its earliest forms, it was used to raise water, although very early efforts were made to adapt it to the propulsion of vessels. Savary proposed to make the water, raised by his engine, turn a water-wheel within a vessel which should carry paddle-wheels acting on the outside; and Watt is stated to have said in conversation, that, had he not been prevented by the pressure of other business, he would have attempted the invention of the steam-boat. To the U. States, however, belongs the honor, notwithstanding the many rival claims which have been set up, from time to time, by foreigners, of originating the first successful steam-boat. Rumsey and Fitch were contemporaneous in their researches. Both attempted to construct steam-boats as early as the year 1783; and models of both of their contrivances were exhibited, in 1784, to general Washington. Fitch's apparatus was a system of paddles; Rumsey, at first, used a pump, which drew in water at the bow and forced it out at the stern of the boat. The latter afterwards employed poles, set in motion by cranks on the axis of the fly-wheel of his engine, which were intended to be pressed against the bottom of the river. About the date of these experiments, Fitch sent drawings of his apparatus to Watt and Bolton, for the purpose of obtaining an English patent; and, in 1789, Rumsey visited England upon the same errand. The former was not successful in obtaining patronage; but the latter, by the aid of some enterprising individuals, procured the means to build a vessel on the Thames, which, however, was not set in motion until after his death, in 1793. Fitch's boat was propelled through the water at the rate of four miles per hour; but that of Rumsey proved unsuccessful. John Stevens, of Hoboken, commenced his experiments on steam-navigation in 1791. He invented the first tubular boiler. His first attempts were made with a rotary engine, for which, however, he speedily substituted one of Watt's. With various forms of vessels, and different modifications of propelling apparatus, he impelled boats at the rate of five or six miles per hour. In the year 1797, chancellor Livingston built a steam-boat on the Hudson river. In the full confidence of success, Livingston applied to the legislature of New York for an exclusive privilege, which was granted on condition that he should, within a year, produce a vessel impelled by steam at the rate of three miles per hour. This he was unable to effect, and the project was dropped for the time. In the year 1800, however, Livingston and Stevens united their efforts, and were aided by Mr. Nicholas Roosevelt. Their apparatus was a system of paddles resembling a horizontal chain-pump, and set in motion by an engine of Watt's construction. The joint proceedings of these persons were interrupted by the appointment of chan cellor Livingston to represent the American government in France; but neither he nor Stevens was yet discouraged: the latter continued to pursue his experiments at Hoboken, while the former carried to Europe high-raised expectations of success. About this time, an attempt was made at steam-navigation under the patronage of lord Dundas of Kerse. The attempt was made by Symington as engineer, who limited himself to the drawing of boats upon a canal. The experiment was made upon the Forth and Clyde canal; but the boats were drawn at the rate of no more than three and a half miles per hour; which not answering the expectations of his patron, the attempt was abandoned. During this enterprise, Symington asserts that he was visited by Fulton, who stated to him the great value such an invention would have in America, and, by his account, took full and ample notes. In the attempt he thus makes to claim for himself the merit of Fulton's subsequent success, he is defeated by the clear and conclusive evidence, that Fulton exhibited in a court of law, of his having submitted a plan analogous to that he afterwards carried into effect, to lord Stanhope, in 1795, six years prior to the experiment of Symington. Fulton, after having occupied himself at Paris, along with Livingston, in the investigation of the capabilities of different apparatus for propulsion, was finally led to the conviction, that, of all methods proposed, the paddle-wheels possessed the greatest advantages. He next planned a mode of attaching wheels to the engine of Watt, ingenious in itself, but complicated, and which he afterwards simplified extremely. Up to this time, the relation of the force of the engine to the velocity of the wheels, and the resistance of the water to the motion of the vessel, had never been made a matter of preliminary calculation. Aware, however, that upon a proper combination of these elements all positive hopes of success must depend, he had recourse to the recorded experiments of the society of arts, and, limiting his proposed speed to four miles per hour, planned his machinery and boat in conformity. The vessel was then constructed at Paris, and, being launched upon the Seine, performed its task in exact conformity to his anticipations. This experiment was performed in 1803. The trial having proved successful, it was resolved to take immediate measures to have a boat of large size constructed in the U. States; but as, at that time, the workshops in America were incapable of furnishing a steam-engine, it became necessary to order one from Watt and Bolton. This was done, and Fulton proceeded to England to superintend its construction. In the mean time, Livingston was sufficiently fortunate to obtain a renewal of the exclusive grant from the state of New York. The engine reached New York towards the close of the year 1806, and the vessel built to receive it was set in motion in the summer of 1807. The success that attended it is well known. In the mean time, Livingston's former associate, the elder Stevens, had persevered in his attempts to construct steam-boats. In his enterprise he now received the aid of his son; and his prospects of success had become so flattering, that he refused to renew his partnership with Livingston, and resolved to trust to his own exertions. Fulton's boat, however, was first ready, and secured the grant of the exclusive privilege of the state of New York. The Stevenses were but a few days later in moving a boat with the required velocity, and, as their experiments were conducted separately, have an equal right to the honor of invention with Fulton. Being shut out of the waters of the state of New York, by the monopoly of Livingston and Fulton, Stevens conceived the bold design of conveying his boat to the Delaware by sea; and this boat, which was so near reaping the honor of first success, was the first to navigate the ocean by the power of steam. From that time until the death of Fulton, the steam-boats of the Atlantic coast were gradually improved, until their speed amounted to eight or nine miles per hour. When the exclusive grant of the state of New York to Livingston and Fulton was set aside, the younger Stevens prepared a boat for the navigation of the Hudson, which performed its voyages at the rate of thirteen and a half miles per hour. Steam-boats were not introduced into Great Britain until 1812, five years later than the successful voyage of Fulton. Bell built the first boat upon the river Clyde, at Glasgow. In March, 1816, the first steam-boat crossed the British channel from Brighton to Havre. Since that period, their use has been much extended, and their structure improved; but no European steam-boat is at present known to possess a speed above nine miles per hour. In 1815, steam-boats, previously constructed by Fulton for the purpose, commenced to run as packets between New York and Providence, a part of which passage is performed in the open sea. One of these vessels had been intended to make a voyage to Russia; but the greatness of the expense deterred the proprietors from undertaking it. This voyage was performed in 1817, by the Savannah; and, in 1818, a steam-ship plied from New York to New Orleans, as a packet, touching at Charleston and the Havana. In 1815, also, a steam-boat made a passage from Glasgow to London, under the direction of Mr. George Dodd; but it was not until 1820 that steam-packets were established between Holyhead and Dublin. In 1825, a passage was made, by the steam-ship Enterprise, from London to Calcutta. All doubts, therefore, in respect to the practicability of navigating the ocean by steam may be considered as settled. In point of economy, however, it can never compete with sails, and hence, probably, can only be used to advantage for conveying passengers, or for purposes of war. In the steam-boats of the Ohio and Mississippi, high pressure engines are now in the most general use: the boilers are generally cylindrical, with internal flues, and the position of the cylinder is horizontal. In France, steam-navigation has been of more recent introduction than in England. Five years elapsed from the time of Fulton's successful voyage until Bell navigated the Clyde; four more passed before a boat built in England crossed the channel, and proceeded up the Seine to Paris.

As steam-navigation took its rise on the Hudson, so the steam-boats navigating that river have uniformly been before all others in point of speed. Two vessels on this river have a speed of thirteen and a half miles per hour; and many others have approached this so nearly that the difference of passage has not been many minutes in the distance of 150 miles. The wheels of the New Philadelphia are stated to average twenty-five and a half revolutions in a minute; and the piston to move with a velocity of 405 feet per second.

Steam is also employed to move carriages upon the land. For this purpose, the wheels of the carriage are set in motion by the engine, in the same manner that the paddle-wheels of a steam-boat are caused to turn: the friction which they experience upon their track causes them to move forward, unless they meet a resistance to their progressive motion equal to this friction. The tire of wheels is made of iron, and steam-carriages usually run upon tracks, also of iron, forming what is called a *rail-road*. Railroads are parallel bars of iron, laid either level, or with a gentle and uniform slope; and steam has, as yet, only been usefully applied to locomotion upon roads of this character. The workmanship of locomotive engines has been regularly improving for several years past. The latest calculations seem to admit, that a locomotive engine will drag after it, in carriages furnished with wheels equal in diameter to its own, at least seven times its own weight. (See *Rail-Ways.*)

We shall conclude this article with some remarks relating to the explosions of steam-boilers, and the statistics of steam-boats in the U. States. The chief precautions to prevent steam-boat explosions are the following: 1. Cylindrical boilers, without any return flue, either without or within, are safer than any others. 2. Internal flues should be avoided whenever it is possible; and especially the chimney, or vertical flue, should never be permitted to pass through the boiler. 3. Every boiler should be furnished, in addition to the safety-valve, with one not under the control of the fire man. 4. All boilers should be furnished with gauge cocks, or other apparatus, to show the level of the water; and these should be so placed in steam-boats that no error in their indication can take place when the vessel heels or rolls. 5. Plates of fusible metal should be provided, having such a degree of fusibility as to melt at a temperature so low as to let off the steam before it could acquire a dangerous degree of heat. 6. A thermometer should be introduced into the boiler, whose indications may be seen from without. 7. Self acting feeders should be adapted to the boiler, by which water will enter, and keep the fluid within at a constant temperature. 8. The chimney should be provided with a damper, by which the draught of the flues may be suddenly checked; and doors should, if possible, be placed upon the ash-pit. 9. The proof of the boiler should be conducted with the greatest care, first with water, at a pressure five or six times as great as the boiler is intended to carry, and afterwards with steam of twice the proposed tension. The water-proof should be repeated from time to time, and every part carefully examined, to ascertain that all the safety apparatus is in working order.

From a neglect to employ the above precautions, a great number of explosions have occurred in the U. States. The whole number of lives which have been lost by these accidents already amounts to at least 300. The amount of steam-boat business in the U. States has been increasing immensely since 1824. In that year, but one steam-boat ran in the waters of the Connecticut, and but two from New York eastward. At present, there are from sixteen to twenty in full activity in that direction. One boat on the Hudson, built in 1825, has carried near 200,000 passengers; and there are now about twenty plying on that river. So late as the commencement of the year 1817, the whole number of steam-boats which had been built on the western waters was ten; and in that year the feat of performing a passage from New Orleans to the falls of the Ohio in twenty-five days, was celebrated by public rejoicings: at present, only ten days are required for a steamer to ascend from New Orleans to Cincinnati. The whole number of steam-boats which had been built in 1830, upon the western waters, was about 375. Some of them are of 500 tons burthen, and from that down to 100, —their average tonnage not exceeding 200 tons. The number of boats now in commission is above 200; the annual expense of which for fuel is estimated at $1,180,000, and their other expenses at $1,300,000,—making an aggregate of nearly $2,500,000. Thus the Mississippi and its innumerable branches, separated from the Atlantic coast by ridges of barren mountains, and almost inaccessible from the gulf of Mexico by either sails or oars, has become the seat of flourishing settlements, and is enabled to vie in commerce with the maritime regions of the U. States. We know of no important art whose history is more interesting than that of the application of steam to useful purposes, especially in its subserviency to utility in the steam-engine. Feeble and imperfect in its first beginnings, and limited, for nearly a century after its introduction, to a single, and by no means important object, it became, in the hands of Watt, an instrument of universal application. It is now equally subservient to those purposes which require the greatest delicacy of manipulation, and those which demand the most intense exertions of power. Its introduction and gradual improvement have put in action inventive talents of the highest order; in its uses we see realized the fables of romance; it has already changed the state of the world, and altered the relations of civilized society; and in its farther progress seems destined to perform even more important services.

Steam-Gun. As early as 1805, the French general Chasseloup is said to have shown the possibility of preparing steam-artillery. In 1814, a French engineer constructed ordnance of this sort. The generator supplied at once six pieces of artillery with steam. The turning of a cock supplied all the pieces at once with balls and steam. This machine could make 150 discharges in a minute. The steam artillery invented by Jacob Perkins is thus described by him, in a letter to doctor Jones, editor of the Franklin Journal, dated March 8, 1827:—"I am now engaged in building steam artillery, as well as musketry, for the French government. The piece of ordnance is to throw sixty balls, of four pounds each, in a minute, with the correctness of the rifled musket, and to a proportionate distance. A musket is also attached to the same generator, for throwing a stream of lead from the bastion of a fort, and is made so far portable as to be capable of being moved from one bastion to another. The musket is to throw from one hundred to one thousand bullets per minute, as occasion may require, and that for any given length of time. I am within the truth when I say that, if the discharges are rapid, one pound of coals will throw as many balls as four pounds of powder."

Stearine. (See *Fat*, and *Soap*.)

Steatite (*soapstone*). All the varieties of steatite are so soft that they may be easily cut by a knife, and in most cases scratched by the nail. Its powder and surface are soft, and more or less unctuous to the touch. It is seldom translucent except at the edges. Its fracture is, in general, splintery, earthy or slaty, with little or no lustre. By friction it communicates to sealing-wax negative electricity. Exposed to heat, it becomes much harder, but is almost infusible by the blow-pipe. It is a compound of silica, magnesia, alumina, oxide of iron, and water. It is sometimes much mixed with talc, asbestus, &c. It is very common in Cornwall and Germany. Common steatite is usually solid, and its texture compact: sometimes it is almost friable, and its texture earthy. Its surface is often like soap to the touch. Its color is usually gray or white, seldom pure, but variously mixed with green, yellow or red, and is sometimes a pale yellow, red or green, of different shades. The colors sometimes appear in spots, veins, &c. Its specific gravity is usually between 2.38 and 2.66. When solid, it is somewhat difficult to break. It sometimes presents pseudomorphous crystals. It agrees with talc in its composition. Common steatite occurs in masses or veins, or small beds, in primitive and transition rocks, more particularly in serpentine. The variety of steatite called *potstone* is in hardness nearly the same as common steatite, but is more tenacious. The substance employed in the arts under the name of *soapstone*, usually belongs to steatite, but sometimes to lamellar or indurated talc. The soapstone of Springfield, in Massachusetts, and Francistown, in New Hampshire, appears to be composed chiefly of talc. Steatite is not susceptible of a good polish; but its softness and tenacity, in consequence of which it may be cut or turned into various forms, and its property of becoming hard by heat, render it a useful mineral in the arts. It is employed for the hearths of furnaces, the sides of fire-places and stoves, &c. The potstone has received its name from having been manufactured into culinary vessels. The common steatite has even been employed for the purpose of engraving; for, being easily cut when soft, it may be made to assume any desired form, and afterwards rendered hard by heat. It then becomes susceptible of a polish, and may be variously colored by metallic solutions. Steatite is used in England in the manufacture of porcelain. It has a great affinity for glass. It is also employed in the manner of paste, reduced to a fine powder, and mixed with coloring matters, for painting on this substance. Tailors and embroiderers prefer it to chalk for marking silk. It possesses the property of uniting with oils and fat bodies, and enters into the composition of the greater number of the balls which are employed for cleaning silks and woollen cloths. It also forms the basis of some preparations of paints. It is used to give lustre to marble, serpentine and gypseous stones. Mixed with oil, it serves to polish mirrors of metal and crystal. When leather, recently prepared, is sprinkled with steatite to give it color, and afterwards, when dry, is rubbed several times with a piece of horn, it assumes a very beautiful polish. Steatite is also used in the preparation of glazed paper. It facilitates the action of screws, and, from its unctuosity, may be employed with much advantage for diminishing the friction of the parts of machines which are made of metal.

Steel is a compound of iron and carbon. Its discovery was antecedent to the origin of authentic history. The Greeks distinguished it by the name of *στομωμα*; by the Romans it was called *acies*. Pliny says that, in his time, the best steel came from China, and the next best from Parthia. A manufacture of it existed in Sweden as early as 1340; but it is the general opinion that the process for converting iron into steel, called *cementation*, originated in England. The furnace in which iron is converted into steel, has the form of a large oven, or arch, terminating in a vent at the top. The floor of this oven is flat and level. Immediately under it there is a large arched fire-place, with grates, which runs quite across from one side to the other, so as to have two doors for putting in the fuel from the outside of the building. A number of vents, or flues, pass from the fire-place to different parts of the floor of the oven, and throw up their flame into it, so as to heat all parts of it equally. In the oven itself, there are two large and long cases or boxes, built of good fire stone; and in these boxes the bars of iron are regularly stratified with charcoal powder, ten or twelve tons of iron being put in at once, and the box is covered on the top with a bed of sand. The heat is kept up, so that the boxes and all their contents are red hot for eight or ten days. A bar is then drawn out and examined; and if it be found then sufficiently converted into steel, the fire is withdrawn and the oven allowed to cool. This process is called *cementation*. The bars of steel formed in this way are raised, in many parts, into small blisters, obviously by a gas evolved in the interior of the bar, which had pushed up, by its elasticity, a film of the metal. On this account, the steel made by this process is usually called *blistered steel*. The bars of blistered steel are heated to redness, and drawn out into smaller bars by means of a hammer, driven by water or steam, and striking with great rapidity. This hammer is called a *tilting hammer*, on which account, the small bars formed by it are called *tilted steel*. When the bars are broken in pieces and welded repeatedly, and then drawn out into bars, they acquire the name of *German* or *shear steel*. Steel of cementation, however carefully made, is never quite equable in its texture; but it is rendered quite so by fusing it in a crucible, and then casting it into bars. Thus treated, it is called *cast steel*, and sells at a much higher price than common steel. The process was contrived at Sheffield, in England, in 1750, and for a long time kept secret. When steel is to be cast, it is made by cementation in the usual way, only the process is carried somewhat farther, so as to give the steel a whiter color. It is then broken into small pieces, and put into a crucible of excellent fire clay, after which the mouth of the crucible is filled up with vitrefiable sand, to prevent the steel from being oxidized by the action of the air. The crucible is exposed for five or six hours to the most intense heat that can be raised, by which the steel is brought into a state of perfect fusion. It is then cast into parallelopipeds about a foot and a half in length. To fuse one ton of steel, about twenty tons of coals are expended; which accounts for the high price of cast-steel, when compared with that of iron, or even of common steel. Every time that cast-steel is melted, it loses some of its characteristic properties; and two or three fusions render it quite useless for the purposes for which it is intended. It has recently been proved that the steel of which the Damascus blades were made, and which was steel from Golconda, owed the peculiarity which these blades have of showing a curious waving texture on the surface, when treated with a dilute acid, to their consisting of two different compounds of iron and carbon, which have separated during the cooling. It is cast-steel in which the process is carried farther than usual, and which is cooled slowly; both common steel and cast-steel are formed, which separate during the slow cooling. The steel is rendered black by the acid, while the cast-iron remains white. This kind of steel can only be hammered at a heat above that of cherry-red. The specific gravity of good blistered steel is 7.823. When this steel is heated to redness, and suddenly plunged into cold water, its specific gravity is reduced to 7.747. The specific gravity of a piece of cast-steel, while soft, is 7.82; but when hardened by heating it red-hot, and plunging it into cold water, it is reduced to 7.7532. Hence it appears, that when steel is hardened, its bulk increases. The color of steel is whiter than that of iron. Its texture is granular, and not hackly, like that of iron. The fracture is whitish-gray, and much smoother than the fracture of iron. It is much harder and more rigid than iron; nor can it be so much softened by heat without losing its tenacity and flying in pieces under the hammer. It requires more attention to forge it well, than to forge iron; yet it is by its toughness and capability of being drawn out into bars, that good steel is distinguished from bad. Steel is more readily broken by bending it than iron. If it be heated to redness, and then plunged into cold water, it becomes exceedingly hard, so as to be able to cut or make an impression upon most other bodies. But, when iron is treated in the same way, its hardness is not in the least increased. When a drop of nitric acid is let fall upon a smooth surface of steel, and allowed to remain on it for a few minutes, and then washed off with water, it leaves a black spot; whereas the spot left by nitric acid on iron, is whitish-green. Steel is not so easily converted into a magnet as iron; but, when once converted, it retains its magnetic properties much longer.

Numerous investigations have, at different periods, been made concerning the composition of steel. In an elaborate dissertation by Monge, Berthollet and Vandermonde, it is asserted that good hammered iron consists of *iron* free from all heterogeneous matter; that steel is a combination of iron and carbon; and that cast-iron is a combination of iron with carbon, in which the proportion of carbon is greater, and the iron not wholly free from oxygen. Doctor Thomson gives the following as the composition of cast-steel:

Iron, ...	99
Carbon, with some silicon, ...	1
	100

It is a very desirable thing to combine the extreme hardness of steel with the toughness and tenacity of iron. This is done by welding them together. It is in this way that edge tools are made. A bit of steel is welded to the iron on that side of the plate or bar which is to be worked into an edge; or the surface of a piece of iron is converted into steel by cementation, and the process is stopped before the carbon penetrates so far as to convert the whole piece into steel. This is called *case-hardening*. The piece of work, when nearly finished, is covered with a paste made of combustible matter. Certain animal substances, as horns and hoofs, chopped hair, bone, shavings, &c., are made up into a paste. The iron is covered with it, and the whole wrapped up in clay. This is first dried and hardened before the fire, and then put into a forge, and kept in a low red heat for an hour or two. When taken out, the surface is converted into steel. In this way almost all the parts of gun-locks are treated. Besides the superficial hardness that they thus acquire, it is well known that they have much less friction than while in the state of iron, and they are much less liable to rust. Every kind of iron is not suited to the manufacture of steel. English iron does not answer at all. The iron which answers best is made at Danemora, in Sweden, from the magnetic iron ore. (See *Iron.*) The whole of the yearly produce of the Danemora mines, amounting to 8000 tons, is imported into Britain, and converted into steel. A single house in Hull monopolizes the whole of this iron, under a contract, by which the parties in Sweden are to forfeit £10,000 sterling if they sell to anybody else. There is also one Russian forge, which yields a good iron for steel.

The *natural steel*, or *German steel*, is an impure and variable kind of steel, procured from cast-iron, or obtained at once from the ore. It is much cheaper than the cementation steel. It has also the property of being easily welded, either to iron or to itself. Its grain is unequally granular, sometimes even fibrous; its color is usually blue; it is easily forged; it requires a strong heat to temper it, and it then acquires only a middling hardness. When forged repeatedly, it does not pass into iron so easily as the other kinds. The natural steel yielded by cast-iron, manufactured in the refining houses, is known by the general name of *furnace steel;* and that which has only been once treated with a refining furnace, is particularly called *rough steel*, and is frequently very unequally converted into steel. The best cast-iron for the purpose of making natural steel, is that obtained from the brown hæmatite, or from the sparry iron ore. (See *Iron, Ores of.*) If it contains manganese, this is thought to be an advantage. It should be of a gray color. White cast-iron does not yield steel, unless its charge of carbon is increased, either by stirring the melted metal with a long pole, and keeping it melted a long time, that it may absorb charcoal from the lining of the furnace, or by melting it with dark-colored iron. Black cast-iron yields a bad, brittle steel, unless the excess of carbon that it contains is either burnt away, or it is mixed with finery cinder. The cast-iron to be converted into steel is then melted in blast furnaces, and treated nearly the same as if it were to be refined into bar-iron, only the blast is weaker; the tewyre, instead of being directed so as to throw the wind upon the surface of the melted metal, is placed nearly horizontally; the melted metal is kept covered with slag, and is not disturbed by stirring. When the iron is judged to be sufficiently refined, and is grown solid, it is withdrawn from the furnace and forged. The natural steel made directly from the abovementioned ores, in small blast furnaces, is a good steel for ploughs and similar machines: the best of it is excellent for saws and cutlery. The most esteemed steel of this kind comes from Germany, and is made in Stiria. It is usually sold in chests or barrels, two and a half or three feet long. It is only within a short time, that the manufacture of steel has commenced in the U. States. At present, we have fourteen steel furnaces, in the following places: viz. Pittsburg, two; Baltimore, one; Philadelphia, three; New York, three; York county, Pa., one; Troy, one, New Jersey, two; Boston, one. These furnaces are said to be capable of affording more than 1600 tons of steel annually —an amount equal to the whole importation of steel, of every kind. The American steel is employed for common agricultural purposes; and it has excluded the common British blister steel altogether. Its principal use is in the fabrication of plough-shares, shovels, scythes, crosscut and mill saws. One factory devoted to this kind of manufacture, in Philadelphia, requires a ton and a half of this steel *per diem.* The English still continue to supply us, however, with the best quality of blister steel, made from Danemora iron, as well as with shear steel and cast steel. (See the treatise on iron and steel in Lardner's Cabinet Cyclopædia.)

Steele, sir Richard, was born at Dublin, in 1671, of a family of English extraction. He was educated at the charter-house, whence he removed to Oxford. He left the university without taking a degree, and (a thing not unusual at that time with needy young men of good connexions), for some time, rode as a private trooper in the dragoon guards. His frank and generous temper soon, however, gained him friends, and he obtained an ensigncy in the foot guards. Being led into many irregularities, he drew up and published a little treatise as a testimony against himself, entitled the Christian Hero, the seriousness of which excited much ridicule among his companions, his conduct falling far short of his theory. For this reason, as he himself observed, to enliven his character, he wrote his first comedy, entitled the Funeral, or Grief à-la-mode, which was acted in 1702, with considerable success. Through the recommendation of Addison, he was appointed, in the beginning of the reign of Anne, to the post of writer of the London

Gazette. His comedy of the Tender Husband appeared in 1703, and his Lying Lover in 1704. In 1709, he began the periodical paper so celebrated under the title of the Tatler, which included a portion of the information of a common newspaper, but, in raciness of humor, and vivacity and urbanity of tone, was not, perhaps, exceeded by the most celebrated of its successors. As it sided with the existing ministry, and was extensively circulated, its projector was appointed one of the commissioners of the stamp duties. In 1711, the Tatler was succeeded by the still more celebrated Spectator, in which the assistance of Addison and other eminent writers was more regular than in its predecessor, although Steele, as before, supported the chief burden. The Spectator terminating, he commenced the Guardian, in 1713, and also produced a political periodical, called the Englishman, with several other political pieces of temporary celebrity. His object was now to obtain a seat in parliament, for which purpose he resigned his place in the stamp office, and a pension. He was accordingly elected for Stockbridge, but was soon after expelled the house for an alleged libel in the last number of the Englishman, and in another paper, called the Crisis. His expulsion being purely the result of ministerial resentment, he regained favor on the accession of George I, and received the appointments of surveyor of the royal stables, and governor of the king's comedians, and was knighted. He also again entered the house of commons as member for Boroughbridge, and received £500 from sir Robert Walpole, for special services. On the suppression of the rebellion of 1715, he was appointed one of the commissioners for the forfeited estates in Scotland, when he busied himself in an abortive scheme for a union between the churches of England and Scotland. Devoid of all prudential attention to economy, although he married two wives successively with respectable fortunes, he was uniformly embarrassed in his circumstances. Always engaged in some scheme or other, few or none of which succeeded, he wasted his regular income in the anticipation of a greater, until absolute distress was the consequence. A scheme for bringing fish to market alive, in particular, involved him in much embarrassment, which was heightened by the loss of his theatrical patent, in consequence of his opposition to the peerage bill. He appealed to the public, in a paper called the Theatre, and, in 1720, honorably distinguished himself against the famous South sea scheme. He was restored, the following year, to his authority over Drury-lane theatre, and soon after wrote his comedy of the Conscious Lovers, on a hint from Terence, first acted in 1722, and dedicated to the king, who rewarded the author with £500. His pecuniary difficulties, however, increasing, he retired to a seat in Wales, where a paralytic stroke impaired his understanding, and finally terminated his life, in 1729. Besides the works already mentioned, sir Richard Steele published two periodical papers, called the Lover, and the Reader, as well as numerous political pieces.

STEELYARD; a kind of balance, called also the Roman balance, by means of which the gravities of different bodies are found, by a single weight being placed on the lever or beam, so as to secure an equilibrium, the notches and figures marked on it denoting the number of pounds.

STEEN, Jan, a distinguished painter, was born at Leyden, in 1636. He studied under Brouwer and Van Goyen, and married the daughter of the latter. Being imprudent and intemperate in his habits, he neglected all the advantages which lay in his way, until finally reduced to paint for a mere subsistence. He had a strong, manly style of execution, the result of native talent rather than of application, which, together with a fine feeling of humor, conducted him to a high degree of professional excellence. Among his capital pictures are a Mountebank surrounded with Spectators, a Quaker's Funeral, and a Marriage Contract. His works did not obtain an extraordinary price during his life; but, after his death, being far from numerous, they so rose in value as to become some of the highest priced of his peculiar school. His death is generally dated in 1689, but by Houbraken eleven years earlier.

STEENKERKE, or STEINKIRCHE, or STEENKERQUE; a village of Belgium, in Hainaut, thirteen miles north of Mons. Here a bloody battle was fought between the allies, commanded by William III (q. v.), king of England, and the French, under the duke of Luxembourg (q. v.), the 24th of July, 1692, in which the latter were victorious.

STEERAGE; an apartment before the great cabin, from which it is separated by a partition or bulk-head. In merchant ships, it is generally the habitation of the inferior officers and crew; but in ships of war, it serves only as a hall or ante-cham ber to the great or captain's cabin.—*Steerage* is also used to express the effort of the helm.—*Steerage-way* implies a sufficient degree of motion communicated to a ship for her to become susceptible of the effects of the helm in governing her course.

STEERING. (See *Helm.*)

STEEVENS, George, a dramatic critic and biographer, was born at Stepney, where his father, an East India director, resided, and educated at Cambridge. In 1766, he published twenty of the plays of Shakspeare, with notes, in 4 vols., 8vo. The skill which he displayed as a commentator induced doctor Johnson to take him as a coadjutor in his edition of the works of the great dramatist (1773, 10 vols., 8vo.). A new edition of the Shakspeare of Johnson and Steevens appeared in 1785; and, in 1793, Mr. Steevens produced an enlarged and improved edition of the same work, in 15 vols., 8vo. He was one of the contributors to Nichols's Biographical Anecdotes of Hogarth; and he also assisted in the *Biographia Dramatica.* His death took place at Hampstead, Jan. 22, 1800. Mr. Steevens left a valuable library of dramatic and other English literature, of which a catalogue appeared after his decease.

STEFFENS, Henry, a distinguished German philosopher, combines, in his writings, much knowledge of natural history with what many would call mysticism. He was born in Stavanger, in Norway, in 1773. In 1790, he entered the university. Having studied natural history, and travelled to accomplish himself in this science, he went, in 1794, to Germany. In 1796, he went to Kiel, and subsequently to Jena, where, having been excited to investigation by the writings of Spinoza, he studied Schelling's (q. v.) philosophy. In Freyberg, he studied under Werner, and wrote his Contributions to the Natural History of the Interior of the Earth. In 1802, he lectured in Copenhagen with great applause. In 1804, he was appointed professor in Halle; but the battle of Jena put an end to his labors in that place. In 1806, he published his Outlines of Philosophical Natural Science. In 1811, he received an appointment at Breslau. In 1813, he fought against the French, and, after the war, returned to his professorship. His works, besides those already mentioned, are a Manual of Oryctognosy; a treatise on False Theology and True Faith (1824); Anthropology (1822); besides some political writings and some novels Walseth and Leith, 1827. and the Four Norwegians, 1828). He is at present *professor ordinarius* of physics and natural philosophy at Breslau.

STEGANOGRAPHY. (See *Cryptography.*)

STEIERMARK, or STEYERMARK. (See *Stiria.*)

STEIN, John Andrew, a distinguished organ and piano-forte maker, was born, in 1728, in the Palatinate, and died in 1792. He invented several musical instruments. His piano-fortes were sent all over Europe.

STEIN, Charles baron von, Prussian minister, was born, in 1757, at Nassau on the Lahn. When about thirty years old, he entered the service of the Prussian government. He distinguished himself much by his acquaintance with political economy, and was in favor of unrestrained liberty of trade. His activity was very great. He was minister before 1806, and followed the court to Königsberg, where, in 1807, he was ungraciously dismissed from office on account of disputes in the cabinet. After the peace of Tilsit, however, he was recalled, and, in 1808, became prime minister. He soon began to make secret preparations for the deliverance of Germany from the French. Napoleon, learning this fact by means of an intercepted letter, declared him outlawed. Stein, therefore, left Prussia, and repaired, in 1809, to Austria, where he lived until 1812, when he went to Russia. He subsequently took part in political affairs during the stormy period which preceded the first peace of Paris; but being dissatisfied with the course taken on that occasion, he retired again. He was present only for a few days at the congress of Vienna. He afterwards occupied himself with the plan of making a collection of the sources of German history, and through his agency chiefly the *Societas aperiendis Fontibus Rerum Germanicarum Medii Ævi* was established, in 1819. It has its chief seat in Frankfort. The society is patronised by various governments, and has already published some valuable works. In 1827, Stein was appointed a member of the council of state. He now lives on his estates. In 1828, he was the marshal of the provincial diet of Westphalia, and published something respecting it. Whilst he was minister, he established the Prussian *Städteordnung*, an ordinance to regulate the government of the Prussian cities. (See *Prussia*, vol. x., page 391, note.) Bourrienne, in his Life of Napoleon, makes some insinuations against him, which have been proved to be utterly false. Stein seems to incline, in his political views, to the principles of times gone by, which dazzle at a distance with false splendor. (His family can trace their line up to the year 1000.) He is acknowledged, by all parties, to be thoroughly honest; but many consider him as obstinate and severe.

STEINKOPF, John Frederic, professor and court painter at Stuttgart, died in 1825, ninety-four years old. Many of his paintings, particularly horses, are in the royal castles.

STELLIONATE, in Roman law; the deceiving others to their pecuniary disadvantage. The Romans frequently used *stellionatus* to express all kinds of deceits that had no proper names.

STEM; a circular piece of timber, into which the two sides of a ship are united at the fore end: the lower end of it is scarfed to the keel, and the bowsprit rests upon its upper end; the ends of the wales and planks of the sides and bottom are let into a groove or channel cut in the middle of its surface from top to bottom. The outside of the stem is usually marked with a scale of feet answering to a perpendicular from the keel. The use of this scale is to ascertain the draught of water. *From stem to stern;* from one end of the ship to the other.

STEM, in botany. (See *Plants.*)

STEMMATA, in the history of insects, are three smooth, hemispheric dots, placed generally on the top of the head, as in most of the *hymenoptera* and other classes.

STENOGRAPHY (from στενος, narrow, and γραφω, I write); the art of writing in abbreviations and with many arbitrary signs to denote whole syllables, words and phrases, so that the writing may occupy but little room, and be executed with much more rapidity than is possible in the common mode. *Tachygraphy* (from ταχυ, quickly, and γραφω) signifies the same art, as far as its object is expedition; and as this is generally the chief thing aimed at, and the use of abbreviations is only the means, *tachygraphy* would be the preferable name, yet *stenography*, or *short-hand*, has been generally adopted. Even the Greeks and Romans made use of this art, though in an imperfect state, for the sake of taking down oral discourses. Their stenography consisted of a number of arbitrary signs, not reduced to rules, which, of course, rendered the learning of it very difficult. In the eighteenth century, professor Taylor of Oxford reduced stenography to rules, and Bertin, in France, simplified it still more. In 1824 appeared, in Paris, the fourth edition of Conen de Perpéan's *Sténographie*, and the second edition of Grosselin's *Vocabulaire Sténographique*, with a theory. William Harding's Universal Stenography, on Taylor's principles (London, 1825), is the most complete work on this subject, on which nearly 100 works have appeared in England during the two last centuries.*

STENTOR; a warrior of the Greek army before Troy, of whom Homer tells us that his voice was equal to that of fifty others; hence the phrase a *Stentorian* voice. Juno assumed his form, and encouraged the Greeks to fight valiantly against the Trojans.

STENWYCK, or STEENWYCH, Henry, the elder, born at Steenwych, in Flanders, in 1550, was the disciple of John de Vries; and, following the steps of his master, he became celebrated for his delineation of the insides of convents and churches of Gothic architecture, viewed by the light of torches or lustres, to which his perfect knowledge of *chiaro-scuro*, and the lightness and delicacy of his pencil, gave a surprising effect. His pictures are very rare, and bear a high price. He died in 1603.—*Henry Stenwyck*, the younger, son and pupil of the preceding, copied his father's manner, and was thought frequently to equal him. He was introduced by Vandyke to the court of Charles I; and he painted many pictures in England, where he died, in what year is unknown.

STEPHEN. Besides the first martyr of the Christian church, who was stoned to death (Acts vi. 9—15, and vii. 53—60), there are two saints of this name—Stephen I, a pope and martyr of the third century, and Stephen I, king of Hungary, who, towards the end of the tenth century, introduced the Christian religion into his dominions, and was therefore canonized. His successors received from the pope the title of apostolic majesty, which is still borne by the emperor of Austria, as king of Hungary.

STEPHEN, king of England, son of Stephen count of Blois, by Adela, fourth daughter of William the Conqueror, was born in 1104, and invited, when young, into England by his uncle Henry I, who gave him the earldom of Mortaigne, in Normandy, and large estates in England. He likewise procured for him in marriage the heiress of Eustace, count of

* It ought, however, to be remarked that the reporters of the parliamentary debates for the English newspapers do not make much use of stenography, because the manuscript would be difficult for the printer to decipher. (See *Newspapers.*)

Boulogne. For these favors Stephen professed the most grateful attachment to the king, and was most zealous in taking the oath for securing the succession to Henry's daughter, the empress Matilda or Maud. No sooner, however, did that monarch's death take place than he hastened from France to England, and laid claim to the crown for himself. (See *Henry I.*) Having ingratiated himself with both nobles and people, he was at once received as king in London; and the concurrence of the clergy was obtained by Stephen's brother, the bishop of Winchester, aided by the oath of a nobleman of the late king's, testifying his intentions in favor of his nephew, while on his death bed. David, the king of Scotland, marched an army into England, and Carlisle and the county of Cumberland formed the price which Stephen was obliged to pay for peace. He was, however, able to subdue the opposition of the nobles of England, and was also invited by the barons to take possession of the duchy of Normandy. Another war with Scotland followed, which was terminated by the battle of the Standard, in which the Scots were entirely defeated by the northern barons. The empress Matilda landed in England, with her brother, the earl of Gloucester, and, being joined by several powerful barons, a civil war ensued, which proved one of the most calamitous in the English annals. Stephen performed his part with vigor and courage, but, being taken prisoner in 1141, his party was broken up, and Matilda was acknowledged queen. The haughty conduct of the new sovereign excited an insurrection against her government; and, being invested in Winchester castle, she escaped with difficulty, while the earl of Gloucester was taken prisoner. Stephen was exchanged for the earl, and the war was renewed. Matilda was induced, by the death of the earl, to retire to Normandy; and the contest was carried on by her son, Henry Plantagenet, who, in 1153, landed an army in England, and was joined by the barons of his mother's party. An armistice, however, took place, and it was agreed that Stephen should reign during his life, that Henry should succeed him, leaving to William, the son of Stephen, his father's patrimonial estates. On the death of the king, the following year, Henry quietly ascended the throne. (See *Henry II.*) Stephen died in the fiftieth year of his age, and the nineteenth of his uneasy reign. Had he succeeded fairly to the throne, he possessed talents which would have enabled him to fill it with honor. His resistance to the encroachments of the clergy and the see of Rome were spirited and creditable; and he was active and able both in the cabinet and the field.

STEPHEN BATHORI, one of the most distinguished kings of Poland, was descended of a noble family in Transylvania, where he was born in 1532. His prudence and courage had already (1571) raised him, through the suffrages of his countrymen, to the dignity of prince of Transylvania (q. v.), when, on the death of Sigismund, a powerful party in Poland, under count Zamoyski, called him to the Polish throne. Another party had chosen the emperor Maximilian II; but Stephen was gradually joined by the whole nation, and the death of Maximilian left him without a competitor. He maintained the royal dignity with vigor and defended the kingdom successfully from foreign enemies. After three successful campaigns against the Russians, who had invaded Livonia, he forced the czar Ivan II (1582) to restore all his conquests in that province; he obliged the Cossacks to submit to the Polish laws, and established three supreme tribunals of justice for the whole kingdom. His toleration was shown in his mildness towards his Protestant subjects, and, when urged to extirpate heresy in his dominions, he replied, that there were three things which God only could do—to make something of nothing, to foresee the future, and to command consciences. He died Dec. 12, 1586, after a reign of ten years, and in the 54th year of his age, probably of poison.

STEPHENS, or STEPHANUS (the English and Latin forms of Estienne); the name of two distinguished scholars and printers. *Robert*, born in 1503, at Paris, devoted himself to learned studies. He possessed a profound knowledge of Latin, Greek and Hebrew, as the works edited by him in those languages evince. After his father's death, he was for several years connected with Simon de Collines, and superintended an edition of the New Testament, which was more correct and of a more convenient form than any which had yet appeared. The rapid sale of this edition disturbed the doctors of the Sorbonne, who only wished for a pretence to forbid the dissemination of a book, from which the adherents of the new doctrines, which Stephens embraced, drew all their arguments. Robert soon after married Petronella, the daughter of the printer Jodocus Badius Ascensius, who was so well acquainted with Latin, that she taught it to her children and servants; and there was no person in the house who did not speak Latin fluently. About 1526, Stephens erected a press in his own name, from which proceeded a series of the most valuable works. Most of his editions of the Greek and Roman classics were enriched with notes and valuable preliminary treatises. He endeavored to attain the greatest possible correctness, and for this purpose hung up his proof-sheets publicly, and offered a reward for the discovery of errors. At first he printed with the types of his father and Simon de Collines; but about 1532 he had a handsomer type cast, with which he printed the elegant Latin Bible, dated that year. This drew upon him new persecutions, which, however, were averted by the protection of king Francis I, and by his promising to print nothing more without the consent of the Sorbonne. In 1531, he published the first edition of his excellent *Thesaurus Linguæ Latinæ*, which he improved in every successive impression, and which Gessner has since taken as the basis of his. In 1539, he was appointed printer of Latin and Hebrew to the king. At his request, Francis I caused the beautiful types to be cast, which are still in possession of the royal press at Paris. The new attacks which he suffered, in consequence of his Bible of 1545, were rendered harmless for a time by the favor of the king; but after his death they were renewed with increased violence, and Stephens was at length forced to abandon France. In 1552, he went to Geneva, where, in connexion with his brother-in-law, he printed the New Testament in French, and established a new press of his own, from which several valuable works were issued. He died in 1559. His Hebrew Bibles (4 vols., 4to., and 8 vols., 16mo.); the Latin Bible (folio, 1538—40); the New Testament (folio, 1550), which was formerly regarded as the most beautiful Greek book ever printed; his *Historiæ Ecclesiasticæ Scriptores; Eusebii Preparatio et Demonstratio Evangelica;* his Dionysius of Halicarnassus; Dio Cassius (first complete edition); and his Terence, Cicero, Plautus, &c., are highly esteemed. —Equally celebrated is the son, *Henry*, born at Paris, in 1528. He was distinguished for his talents, and devoted himself particularly to the study of Greek. The celebrated Peter Danes was his instructer. He also enjoyed the teaching of one Tusanus Turnebus, and in a short time became one of the most able Hellenists of his age. His rapid progress in the Latin language is shown by his annotations on Horace, published at the age of twenty years. He likewise studied the mathematical sciences with zeal. In 1547, he went to Italy, to avail himself of the treasures contained in the libraries at Florence, Rome, Naples, and Venice, and brought away several valuable copies of the classics. He also visited England and the Netherlands, and returned to Paris in 1552, just as his father was on the point of setting out for Geneva. He perhaps accompanied him thither; but, in 1554, he was in Paris again, where, in consequence of the privilege granted to his father by Francis I, he applied for permission to establish a press. The same year he again visited Italy, to collate the manuscripts of Xenophon and Diogenes Laërtius; and, at the beginning of 1557, he commenced the publication, from his own press in Paris, of some of the works which he had procured with so much labor and care. He would, however, have been unable to meet the expense, had he not been assisted by Ulrich Fugger, out of gratitude to whom he called himself, till the death of his patron, Fugger's printer. The death of his father, in 1559, filled him with grief; but his marriage roused him to fresh exertions. In consequence of his attachment to the new doctrines, his peace was often disturbed, and his labors interrupted. In 1566, he republished Valla's Latin translation of Herodotus, with a preface, in which he defended the father of history from the reproach of credulity. Robert Stephens had already begun to collect materials for a Greek dictionary; Henry pursued the arduous work, and, in 1572, produced his still unrivalled *Thesaurus* of the Greek Language, which is a treasure of learning and criticism, and would alone suffice to secure its author permanent fame. An edition of the *Thesaurus* has lately been published in London (1816—26), with the additions of several philologists; and new editions have recently been announced (1830) by Hase (q. v.), at Paris, and, with the additions of Dindorf, at Leipsic. The high price of this work, and the abridgment published by Scapula (q. v.), soon after its appearance, made the sale extremely slow; and the author became greatly embarrassed. He then went to Germany, either for the purpose of recreation, or to seek new means of support. Henry III granted him, on account of his work *De la Précellence du Langage François*, a reward of 3000 livres, and a pension of 300 livres, to enable him to continue his examination of ancient manuscripts, and treated him with great distinction; but this money was probably never paid him. At any rate, Stephens continued in embarrassed circumstances, and finally retired from court, in order to occupy himself more advantageously, and lived at Orleans, Paris, Frankfort, Geneva and Lyons. On a journey to the latter place, he fell sick, and died in the hospital, in 1598, apparently deranged. Such was the end of one of the most learned and indefatigable scholars, who is preëminent for the services which he rendered to the cause of ancient literature. His impressions are not so handsome as those of his father, but they are equally valuable in correctness and matter, and exceed them in number. His editions of the classics have served as the basis of the text of almost all subsequent ones; and the charge that he tampered with the text of authors arbitrarily, is without foundation. He made Latin verses with great facility. He was lively and affectionate in his feelings, fond of gayety and wit, but impatient of contradiction; he indulged himself in caustic epigrams upon his opponents. Among his numerous editions, the principal are, *Poetæ Græci, Principes Heroici Carminis* (1566, folio); *Pindari et cæterorum octo Lyricorum Carmina* (1560, 1566, 1586, 24mo.); also editions of Maximus Tyrius, Diodorus, Xenophon, Thucydides, Herodotus, Sophocles, Æschylus, Diogenes Laërtius, Plutarch, Apollonius Rhodius, Callimachus, Plato, Herodian, and Appian, Horace, Virgil, Pliny the younger, Gellius, Macrobius, the collection of Roman historians, &c. He translated many Greek authors into Latin. He also produced numerous other valuable works.

Stephen's, St. The commons of Great Britain hold their assemblies in St. Stephen's chapel, in Westminster, built by king Stephen, and dedicated to his namesake, the protomartyr. It was rebuilt by Edward III, in 1347, and has been applied to its present use since the reign of Edward VI. The interior has been plainly fitted up, with more regard to convenience than ornament. It is too small, especially since the admission of the Irish members. There are galleries on each side, but they are for the use of the members: the gallery at the end of the house, opposite the speaker's chair, is the only place for strangers, who gain admittance by orders from the members, or by a present to the door-keeper. Not more than 130 strangers can be accommodated at a time. The galleries are supported by slender iron pillars, crowned with gilt Corinthian capitals; and the walls are wainscoted to the ceiling. The speaker's chair stands at some distance from the wall, and is highly ornamented with gilding, having the royal arms at the top. Before the chair is a table, at which sit the clerks, who take minutes of the proceedings, read the title of bills, &c. In the centre of the room, between the table and the bar, is a capacious area. The seats for the members occupy each side and both ends of the room, with the exception of the passages. There are five rows of seats, rising in gradation above each other, with short backs, and green morocco cushions. The seat on the floor, on the right hand of the speaker, is called the *treasury bench*, because there many of the members of administration usually sit. The side immediately opposite is occupied by the leading members of the *opposition*. There are coffee rooms attached to the house, for the accommodation of the members. They communicate directly with the house, and are for the use of members only, many of whom dine there during a long debate; and so near is the spot to the chief chamber, that the voice of a speaker who talks in a high tone, or cheering, may be distinctly heard. Strangers from the gallery may get sandwiches, &c. at the bar, as a favor; but they are not permitted to enter the rooms. The whole is under the superintendence of the housekeeper. Should the bell ring, to announce that a division is about to take place, and to direct the messengers and officers to lock all the doors leading to the house or its lobby, an amusing spectacle is beheld: members are seen running in all directions, with the utmost haste, to get into the house before the fatal key is turned.

Steppe (from the Russian *step*, a desert; also a dry plain). The steppes of Russia, which are not unlike the *landes* of Guienne, in France, and the heaths of Northern Germany, are in part susceptible of cultivation; and they afford pasturage for the numerous herds of the nomadic tribes. In the extensive steppes of Astrachan, between the Volga and the Ural, the Calmucs and Nogay Tartars rove with their cattle. They produce several sorts of flowers, herbs, and are frequented by wild goats and birds.

Stère. (See *French Decimal System*, vol. v., p. 205.)

Stereographic Projection. (See *Projection of the Sphere.*)

Stereometry (from στερεος, solid, and μετρον, measure); literally, the measure of solids; a branch of geometry, the name of which would make it applicable to the measurement of all solids, but which, in fact, is limited, by elementary geometry, to a certain number, and is made to embrace other qualities in addition to their solid contents. The solids of which it treats, are those inscribed within plane surfaces, and a few inscribed within curved surfaces, viz. the cylinder, cone and sphere: all the others it leaves to the higher geometry. A solid, in geometry, is that which has length, breadth, and thickness. If the body in question is a prism (q. v.), its height indicates how many layers, each equal to its base, must be laid one above the other, in order to form the solid figure; in other words, the contents of the prism are equal to the product of the height multiplied by the base. The same is the case, as will be readily seen, with the cylinder. (q. v.) A prism of three sides may be divided, as is easily shown by actual cutting, into three pyramids (q. v.), each of three sides, of the same height and base with the prism. A prism of many sides, and a pyramid of many sides, may be divided into as many three-sided prisms or pyramids as the base has sides; hence the contents of every pyramid are equal to a third of the product of the height multiplied by the base. The same is the case with the cone (q. v.), which has a circle for its base, i. e. a polygon of innumerable sides, and, therefore, can be considered as a pyramid. A sphere (q. v.) may be considered as composed of an infinite number of pyramids, all of which have their vertices in the centre of the sphere: its contents, therefore, are equal to a third of the product of its surface (which makes the sum of the bases of all these pyramids) and its radius. These are the chief points of stereometry; but it also teaches how to compare the various solids with each other, and to ascertain their superficial contents.—See Hossfeld's *Lower and Higher Practical Stereometry* (1812, 4to.); see, also, the article *Stereometry* in the fourth volume of Klügel's Mathem. Dictionary (in German), by Molweide (Leipsic, 1823).

Stereotype Printing. (See *Printing.*)

Sterling; an epithet of English money of account. It is by some derived from *easterling*, a name by which the Hanseatics were called in some of the western countries of Europe; others derive it from the Anglo-Saxon *steore* (rule, or law). (See *Coins.*)

Stern; the posterior part of a ship, or that part which is presented to the view of a spectator, placed on the continuation of the keel, behind.

Stern-Post; a long, straight piece of timber, erected on the extremity of the keel, to sustain the rudder and terminate the ship behind. It is usually marked, like the stem, with a scale of feet, from the keel upwards, in order to ascertain the draught of water abaft.

Sterne, Lawrence, a divine, and an original writer, the son of a lieutenant in the army, was born at Clonmell, in Ireland, in November, 1713, and was put to school at Halifax, in Yorkshire, in 1722, whence he removed to Cambridge, and studied for the church. He took his degree of master of arts in 1740, before which he was advanced; and, by the interest of doctor Sterne, his uncle, a prebendary of Durham, he obtained the living of Sutton, a prebend of York, and, subsequently, by the interest of his wife, whom he married in 1741, the living of Stillington, at which, and at Sutton, he performed the clerical duties for nearly twenty years. During this period, he appears to have amused himself with books, painting, music, and shooting, but was little known beyond his vicinity, the only production of his pen being his humorous satire upon a greedy church dignitary of York, entitled the History of a Watch Coat. In 1759, following, appeared the two first volumes of his celebrated Tristram Shandy, which drew upon him praise and censure of every kind, and became so popular that a bookseller engaged for its continuance on very lucrative terms. Accordingly a third and fourth volume appeared in 1761, a fifth and sixth in 1762, a seventh and eighth in 1764, and a ninth, singly, in 1766. If, in the groundwork of this extraordinary production, a resemblance may be traced to the ridicule of pedantry and false philosophy in Scriblerus, the style and filling up are chiefly his own, although he borrowed entire passages from Burton's Anatomy of Melancholy, and the works of bishop Hall and others. In 1768, he produced his Sentimental Journey (in 2 vols., 12mo.), which, by a number of pathetic incidents, and vivid strokes of national and characteristic delineation, is rendered extremely entertaining, and acquired a more general reputation than even its predecessor. In 1760 appeared two volumes of Ser-of Mr. Yorick, to which he added two additional volumes in 1766, with his own name. He died of pulmonary consumption, in March, 1768, leaving a widow and one daughter. The latter, who was married to a French gentleman, published a collection of her father's letters, in three volumes, 12mo., to which were prefixed memoirs of his life and family. In the same year, an anonymous editor published Letters between Yorick and Eliza, which were regarded as the authentic correspondence, in a strain of high sentimental friendship, between Sterne and Mrs. Draper, an accomplished East Indian lady. His private character was by no means honorable to his genius, affording another proof that the power of expressing and conceiving strong feelings by no means implies that they will influence the conduct.

STERNHOLD, Thomas; the principal author of the metrical version of the Psalms long used in public worship in our churches, and not yet entirely discontinued. He was a native of Hampshire, and educated at Oxford, and became groom of the robes to Henry VIII, who left him a legacy of 100 marks. He held a similar office under Edward VI, in whose reign he died, in August, 1549. The principal coadjutor of Sternhold, in his versification of the Psalter, was John Hopkins; and the names of these persons have become a proverbial designation of bad poets. Sternhold also produced Certayne Chapters of the Proverbs of Solomon, drawen into Metre, which were published after his death.

STERNUTATION. (See *Sneezing*.)

STESICHORUS; a Greek lyric poet, born at Himera, in Sicily, about B. C. 612. He composed a number of works, which were highly esteemed by the ancients. Horace speaks of *Stesichori graves camœnæ;* and Dionysius Halicarnassus says, that he had all the graces of Pindar and Simonides, while he surpassed them both in the grandeur of his subjects. He was the first who introduced into the ode the triple division of strophe, antistrophe, and epode; and he is said to have thence derived his name, which was before Tisias. A few fragments of his works, to the amount of fifty or sixty lines, alone remain.—See Kleine's *Stesichori Fragmenta* (Berlin, 1828), with a preliminary treatise.

STETHOSCOPE (from *στηθος,* chest); an instrument consisting of a short tube, widening towards one end, with which physicians have, for some years, been accustomed to examine the internal state of the human body (e. g. in diseases of the lungs and other internal organs, also in hernia, and the condition of women in pregnancy, &c.), by applying the stethoscope to the chest or abdomen, and putting the ear to the narrower end. Many disorders may be distinguished very clearly in this way; and the instrument has proved, in the hands of many physicians, a useful invention.—See Laennec, *Auscultation Médiate* (Paris, 1819).

STETTIN; a town of Prussia, capital of Pomerania, and of a government and circle of the same name, situated on the Oder, about 60 miles from the Baltic, 80 miles north-east of Berlin; lon. 14° 46′ E.; lat. 53° 20′ N. It stands on an eminence on the left bank of the Oder, and has three suburbs, five gates, and several squares. The principal public buildings are the castle, government house, arsenal, barracks, hospitals, exchange, theatre, and public library. It has five Lutheran churches, an academical gymnasium, college, &c. Population, 32,191. Stettin is a place of extensive trade, the great outlet of the manufactures of Silesia, and the depot of colonial goods and foreign fabrics required by that province, as well as by Berlin, and other towns in Brandenburg. The number of vessels entered here, in 1814, was 1534; cleared, 1180. Vessels drawing more than seven feet water stop at Swinemunde. (See *Oder*.) The leading articles of export are linen, corn, and timber; of imports, coffee, sugar cotton, dye-woods, and wine. The man ufactures are very various.

APPENDIX.

Rhythm, in general, means a measured division of time. The rhythm, in dancing, is made manifest to the eyes by steps, and, in music and language, to the ears by tones. (See the beginning of the article *Dancing*.) We must refer the fondness for rhythm, in the human mind, to its love of order, harmony, symmetry, which lies at the basis of all the arts. As song, music and dancing sprung from the same sources, and, in the earliest periods of nations, are actually united, the rhythm of all three has much in common. The rhythm of poetry is susceptible of the same exact divisions of time as the rhythm of dancing and music; but rhetorical rhythm is satisfied with a pleasing cadence of syllables—an approximation to the rhythm of verse, particularly at the beginning and end of periods. The orator or eloquent prose writer arranges his words in an expressive and pleasing succession, but he does not follow precise rules, like the versifier. The poetical rhythm, like every species of rhythm, requires a succession of motions of regular duration, which, variously interrupted, must yet be obvious, and combined according to the rules of beauty and grace, so as to form a harmonious whole. In order to make rhythm please, its constituent parts must excite the feeling of variety in harmony or unity. The various parts must form a whole, and exhibit a beginning, middle and end, by a measured rise and fall. Those parts which receive the *ictus*, the stress, of the rhythm are called *arsis* (elevation), the other parts *thesis* (*positio*, depression). To denote the arsis, the common acute accent is used (′), e. g.

Síngula quǽque locúm teneánt sortíta decénter.

The arsis must by no means be confounded with the long syllable, nor the thesis with the short syllable. As the short syllable is the smallest constituent part of a verse, it is considered as the original unit for the measure of time in the rhythm, and is called a *time*, or *mora*. The absolute duration of this unit depends upon the quickness or slowness with which the rhythmical composition is uttered. The smallest rhythmical magnitude is the foot by which every union of arsis and thesis is understood. A single word may constitute a foot; or the beginning and end of the foot may be in the middle of words, as in the following verse:

Contém-nit, ár-tibús-que ví-vit dé-ditúm turpís-si-mís.

Rhythm can be imagined without words, and may be indicated by notes, or other signs of long and short syllables. Hence the rhythm may also be divided differently from the words, as we have just seen; and the division of the words should not agree with the rhythmical feet, except where a rhythmical series is concluded, or the pausing of a part of the same requires a break in the text. In all other cases, the divisions of the rhythm ought to separate the parts of words as much as possible, which is called *cæsura*. (q. v.) The Greeks distinguished the feet according to the number of units of time contained in them. The Romans divided them, according to the number of syllables, into four of two syllables. eight of three syllables, and sixteen of four syllables, and called them, with the Greeks, thus:

1. *Feet of two Syllables.*

◡◡ Pyrrhichĭus.
— — Spondēus.
— ◡ Chorēus, or Trochæus.
◡ Iambus.

2. *Feet of three Syllables.*

⏑ ⏑ ⏑ Tribrachys.
– – – Molossus.
– ⏑ ⏑ Dactylus.
⏑ ⏑ – Anapæstus.
⏑ – ⏑ Amphibrăchys.
– ⏑ – Amphimăcer.
⏑ – – Bacchēus.
– – ⏑ Palimbachēus, or Antibachēus.

3. *Feet of four Syllables.*

⏑ ⏑ ⏑ ⏑ Proceleasmatĭcus (Dipyrrhichĭus.)
– – – – Dispondēus.
– ⏑ – ⏑ Dichorēus, or Ditrochæus.
⏑ – ⏑ – Dijambus.
– ⏑ ⏑ – Choriambus.
⏑ – – ⏑ Antispastus.
⏑ ⏑ – – Ionĭcus a minore.
– ⏑ ⏑ Ionĭcus a majore.
⏑ ⏑ ⏑ Pæon primus.
– ⏑ ⏑ Pæon secundus.
⏑ – ⏑ Pæon tertius.
⏑ ⏑ ⏑ – Pæon quartus.
⏑ – – – Epitrĭtus primus.
⏑ – – Epitrĭtus secundus.
– – ⏑ – Epitrĭtus tertius.
– – – ⏑ Epitrĭtus quartus.

These feet are simple or compound, redundant or retrenched. The first consist of but one arsis and thesis, as ⏑́ ⏑, ⏑́ ⏑ ⏑, ⏑́ ⏑ ⏑ ⏑, ⊥ ⏑, ⊥ ⏑ ⏑, &c. The second consist of two of each sort, of which one arsis and thesis, taken together, is considered as a single arsis or thesis, as ⏑́ ⏑ ⏑́ ⏑, ⊥ ⏑ ⊥ ⏑, ⏑ ⊥ ⏑ ⊥, ⊥ – ⊥ – or – ⊥ – ⊥. The third are such as contain, besides a simple foot, a short prefix or affix, or in which feet of unlike quantity are connected with each other, as ⏑ ⊥ ⏑, ⏑ ⊥ ⏑ ⏑, ⏑ ⏑ ⊥ ⏑; ⏑ ⊥ – ⊥, ⊥ ⏑ ⊥ –, – ⊥ ⏑ ⊥, ⊥ – ⊥ ⏑. The fourth sort are feet which, with two arsises, have but one thesis, or have two arsises immediately succeeding each other without a thesis between, e. g. ⊥ ⏑ ⊥, ⊥ ⏑ ⏑ ⊥, ⊥ ⏑ ⏑́ ⏑ or ⏑́ ⏑ ⏑ ⊥, ⊥ – –; ⊥ ⊥ ⏑, ⏑ ⊥ ⊥, ⏑́ ⏑ ⊥ ⏑, ⏑ ⊥ ⏑́ ⏑, ⏑ ⊥ ⊥ ⏑; ⊥ ⊥ ⏑ ⏑, ⏑ ⏑ ⊥ ⊥, ⊥ ⊥ –, – ⊥ ⊥. Of the simple feet, those only which have a long syllable in the arsis, and a short syllable in the thesis, afford natural variety, as ⊥ ⏑, ⊥ ⏑ ⏑, ⏑ ⊥, ⏑ ⏑ ⊥. The trochee and dactyle, therefore, the iambus and anapest, are considered as the fundamental feet of all rhythm, with which the other feet can be brought into connexion by resolving a long syllable into two short ones, or by contracting two short into one long. (For more information, see *Verse*.)

SLATE. *Clay slate* (*Thon Schiefer* of the Germans) and *argillite*. By the early English geologists, this rock was called *argillaceous schistus*, and it is denominated *phyllade* by the modern French writers. The structure of slate is eminently foliated or schistose, separating, in some of its varieties (as in the roofing slate, for example), into laminæ as thin as pasteboard. Prevailing color gray of various shades: it is also bluish, reddish and greenish; opaque and dull; yields to the knife, but varies considerably, as respects hardness, in its different varieties; fissile; specific gravity 2.7. When moistened, it emits an argillaceous odor. The common roofing slate appears to consist very nearly of the following ingredients:—

Silex,	48.00
Alumine,	25.50
Oxide of iron,	11.30
Potash,	4.70
Magnesia,	1.60
Carbon,	.30
Water,	7.60

But slate varies exceedingly in its chemical constitution, as might very naturally be expected, since it is a mixed rock, consisting of very minute individuals of quartz, feldspar and mica, to which are occasionally added scales of talc, and particles of carbonaceous matter. Those slates which contain a large proportion of quartz, are called *whet-slate*. In these, the mechanical composition is impalpable, and the fracture splintery *in the small*, though slaty *in the large*. They are translucent, and of a greenish-white color. When magnesia enters largely into the composition of slate rocks, they are distinguished by their green color, and by their unctuous feel. These are the slates which, for the most part, have talc as an ingredient, and are often called *talc*, or *chlorite* slates. When carbonaceous matter prevails to the proportion of eight or ten per cent., the slate soils more or less, and even writes. It is then called *drawing slate*, or *black chalk*. This variety is softer than the preceding kinds, and sometimes possesses the property of adhering to the tongue. Its specific gravity is only 2.18. A variety of slate called *adhesive* slate, from its property of adhering to the tongue, deserves to be mentioned, although it is very remote in its properties from the roofing slate, which may be considered as the type of the present rock. Fracture in the large slaty; in the fine earthy; color light gray; specific gravity 2.08; easily broken; absorbs water with a hissing noise. It consists of

Silex,	62.50
Magnesia,	8.00
Oxide of iron,	4.00
Alumine,	0.25
Carbon,	0.75
Water,	22.00

Still another argillaceous aggregate, which has been treated of along with the slates, is the *polishing* slate. It differs from adhesive slate in not adhering forcibly to the tongue, in being very soft, and in having a low specific gravity, namely, 0.50 to 0.60.—Slate, in varieties approaching roofing slate, occurs in vast strata in primitive countries, and is often observed graduating into mica slate. Wherever its strata are contiguous to granite, gneiss or mica slate, it is noticeable that it has a more shining lustre: as it recedes, however, from the primary rocks, its texture is more earthy. It is commonly divided into beds of various degrees of thickness, which are generally much elevated; and, from the natural divisions of the rock, they often form peaked and serrated mountains. The cleavage of these beds is in a transverse direction, making with the slope of the bed an angle of about 60°. The finest variety which is used for roof slate seldom forms entire mountains, but is generally imbedded in slate rocks of a coarser kind. Those kinds are selected for the covering of buildings which have the smoothest surface, and split into the thinnest plates. Quarries of slate of this description are worked extensively in Westmoreland, Yorkshire, Leicestershire, North Wales, Cornwall and Devonshire. Excellent deposits of roofing slate occur at several places in Vermont, one of which is situated near Brattleborough, upon the Connecticut river; also in Massachusetts, in Worcester county, where it is associated with the peculiar mica slate that contains anthracite coal. Excavations of considerable extent have been made in Harvard and Pepperell; and the slate obtained has been employed both as a roofing slate and for grave-stones. *Whet* slate is found in beds between strata of common slate in transition formations. The use of this variety for hones and whet-stones is well known. The most valuable kinds come from Sonnenberg, in Meiningen, and from Saalfeld. They are likewise brought from the Levant. It has been discovered, within a few years, in great perfection, over a very large extent of country in North Carolina. An inferior variety occurs extensively in the vicinity of Boston, at Charlestown, Quincy and Malden. Talcose and chlorite slates are found abundantly in various parts of New England, and afford the gangue for the most part of the native gold of the Southern States. The drawing slate, which is used as a drawing material, comes from Italy, Spain, and Bayreuth in Thuringia. It has been observed also at several places in Rhode Island, and in the neighborhood of coal measures generally in the U. States. Adhesive slate occurs only at Menil, Montant and Montmartre, near Paris. Polishing slate, which is believed to have been formed from the ashes of burnt coal, occurs at Planitz, near Zwickau, and near Bilin, in Bohemia. It is used as a polisher of metals.

South American Geology. The equatorial regions of America exhibit the same composition of rock that we meet with in other parts of the globe. The only formations which Humboldt could not discover in his travels were those of chalk, roe-stone, gray-wacke, the topaz-rock of Werner, and the compound of serpentine with granular limestone, which occurs in Asia Minor. Granite, in South America, constitutes the great basis which supports the other formations: above it lies gneiss: next comes micaceous schist, and then primitive schist. Granular limestone, chlorite schist, and primitive trap, often form subordinate beds in the gneiss and micaceous schist, which is very abundant, and sometimes alternates with serpentine and sienite. The high ridge of the Andes is every where covered with formations of porphyry, basalt, phonolite, and green-stone; and these, being often divided into columns, that appear from a distance like ruined castles, produce a very striking and picturesque effect. At the bottom of these huge mountains occur two different kinds of limestone; the one with a silicious base, enclosing primitive masses, and sometimes cinnabar and coal; the other with a calcareous base, and cementing secondary rocks together.—Plains of more than 600,000 square miles are covered with an ancient deposit of limestone, containing fossil wood and brown iron ore: on this rests the limestone of the higher Alps, presenting marine petrifactions at a vast elevation. Next appears a lamellar gypsum, impregnated with sulphur and salt; and, still higher, another calcareous formation, whitish and homogeneous, but sometimes cavernous. Again occurs calcareous sand-stone, then lamellar gypsum mixed with clay; and the series terminates with calcareous masses, involving flints and hornstone. But what may perplex some geologists, is the singular fact noticed by Humboldt, that the secondary formations in the new world have a most enormous thickness and elevation. Beds of coal are found in the neighborhood of Santa Fé, 8650 feet above the level of the sea, and even at the height of 14,700, near Guanuco, in Peru. The plains of Bogota are covered with sandstone, gypsum, shell-limestone, and, in some parts, with rock-salt. Fossil shells, which, in the old continent, have not been discovered higher than the summits of the Pyrenees, or 11,700 feet above the sea, were observed in Peru, near Micuipampa, at the height of 12,800; and again at that of 14,120; besides at Guancavelica, where sandstone also appears. The basalt of Pichincha, near the city of Quito, has an elevation of 15,500 feet; while the top of the Schneekoppe, in Silesia, is only 4950 feet above the sea, the highest point in Germany where that species of rock occurs. On the other hand, granite, which in Europe crowns the loftiest mountains, is not found in the American continent above the height of 11,500 feet. It is scarcely known at all in the provinces of Quito and Peru. The frozen summits of Chimborazo, Cayambe and Antisana, consist entirely of porphyry, which, on the flanks of the Andes, forms a mass of ten or twelve thousand feet in depth. The sandstone near Cuença has a thickness of 5000 feet; and the stupendous mass of pure quartz, on the west of Caxamarca, measures, perpendicularly, 9600 feet. It is likewise a remarkable fact, that the porphyry of those mountains very frequently contains hornblende, but never quartz, and seldom mica.—The Andes of Chile have a distinct nature from those three chains called the *Maritime* mountains, which have been successively formed by the waters of the ocean. This great interior structure appears to be coeval with the creation of the world. It rises abruptly, and forms but a small angle with its base; its general shape being that of a pyramid, crowned at intervals with conical, and, as it were, crystallized elevations. It is composed of primitive rocks of quartz, of an enormous size and almost uniform configuration, containing no marine substances, which abound in the secondary mountains. From the Cordillera of this part of the Andes are obtained blocks of crystal of a size sufficient for columns of six or seven feet in length. The central Andes are rich beyond conception in all the metals, lead only excepted. One of the most curious ores found in the bowels of those mountains is the pacos, a compound of clay, oxide of iron, and muriate of silver, with native silver. The mines of Mexico and Peru, hitherto worked with remarkable success, so far from being exhausted, promise, under a liberal and improved system, to become more productive than ever. Nature has, however, blended with those hidden treasures the active aliments of destruction. The whole chain of the Andes is subject to the most terrible earthquakes. From Cotopaxi to the South sea, no fewer than forty volcanoes are constantly burning, some of them, especially the lower ones, ejecting lava, and others the muriate of ammonia, scorified basalt, and porphyry, enormous quantities of water and *moya*, or clay, mixed with sulphur and carbonaceous matter. (See, further, the articles *Mines*, *Diamond District*, *Peru*, *Potosi*, *Brazil*, &c.)

Sparrow, or Finch (*fringilla*). The common European sparrow is almost domesticated in that portion of the globe, frequenting the habitations of man, even in the midst of populous cities, and nestling under the eaves of houses, in holes in the walls, in pots placed for their use, &c. It is of a robust form, and has a stouter bill than the majority of the finches. It is found almost throughout the Eastern continent, supporting equally well severe cold and extreme heats. It is inconveniently familiar, and its incessant and monotonous note is fatiguing to the ear. In many districts it is so numerous as to do great injury to the grain fields. Its voracity is extreme; neither can its flesh or plumage be applied to any useful purpose. Fortunately, we are free from this pest on this side of the Atlantic. We have, in its place, the chipping sparrow, a delicate bird, almost as familiar, but nowise obtrusive. We have, besides, numerous species of finch in the U. States. They are readily distinguished from other small birds, by the short, conical bill, with cutting edges, which seems peculiarly adapted to the purpose of freeing seeds of the hulls—an operation which these birds accomplish with great adroitness. Though granivorous, they feed their young on worms and soft insects only.

Sphagnum; a very natural genus of mosses, easily recognised when once known, and remarkable for the whitish color of the leaves. These plants are soft, flaccid, and, when moistened, absorb water like a sponge, but become friable in drying. They grow in moist places, and are usually saturated with water, often occupying, exclusively, considerable tracts of marshy ground. The formation of peat, in such situations, is often owing, in a great measure, to the presence of these plants. They are found in all parts of the globe, from the equator to the polar regions, and to the summits of the highest mountains. They are excellent for enveloping the roots of plants intended for distant transportation.

SPIDER (*aranea*). These well-known animals are among the most interesting of the insect world, from their habits and mode of life. They differ essentially, in their internal structure, from insects proper, and their external form is so peculiar that they are easily recognised. The body is composed of two pieces only, the head being united with the thorax; and the feet are always eight in number; the jaws consist of two cylindrical, horny pieces, each having a palp, or feeler, at base, and terminated by a movable hook; the eyes are six or eight, variously disposed in the different genera, but always simple. They do not undergo metamorphoses: all envelope their eggs in a cocoon of silk, varying, however, in form and texture. The spiders are now arranged under numerous genera, differing, not only in anatomical characters, but very generally in their habits and the form of the web which they construct. The most familiar form of web is that of a wheel, perpendicular or slightly inclined, having its radii or spokes crossed by numerous concentric circles: in the centre of this the spider remains immovable, or more frequently in a little cell, at some distance from the web, but connected with it by threads. The struggles of an entangled insect communicate an undulatory motion to the whole web, which gives notice to the spider, who immediately sallies forth, and, if his victim be small, seizes it at once, and immediately sucks its blood: if, however, it be too large to be thus disposed of, the spider rolls it with his hinder feet, encircling it with a new thread at every turn, until, sometimes, the insect is completely coated, when it may be devoured at pleasure. Other spiders spin an irregular web, consisting of threads intersecting each other at every angle. Others, again, make a horizontal, closely-matted web, having a funnel-shaped retreat, into which they convey their prey. Others make only a retreat by binding a few leaves together, from which they sally forth and seize insects which approach them. Some of these seem to be extremely venomous; for it is observed that no insect that has been once bitten by them, ever recovers, even though it be many times larger and more powerful than its adversary. Some are aquatic, and spin a cup-like web, which answers the purpose of a diving-bell, under which they disengage the air they bring down from the surface, and pass their lives feeding on aquatic insects. Some spiders spin no web, but take their prey by running; others, by approaching quietly till within a certain distance, when they suddenly leap upon their prey. Other spiders form cylindrical and perpendicular holes in the ground, into which they retreat on the approach of danger.

SPINAGE (*spinacia oleracea*). This plant is a native of Persia, and has been cultivated in Europe, as an esculent, for about two centuries. The root is annual; the stem herbaceous, smooth, upright, a foot or more high, and somewhat branching; the leaves alternate, petiolate and arrow-shaped; the flowers small and greenish, disposed in several little bunches, in the axils of the superior leaves, and diœcious: in short, the whole plant much resembles some of the species of goose-foot (*chenopodium*), to which genus it is allied in its botanical characters. It is eaten sometimes in salads, but more frequently, cooked in various manners. It is a wholesome and agreeable aliment, but contains little nutriment, and is not suitable for delicate stomachs. The plant is of the easiest culture, and may be procured nearly all the year round, by sowing at intervals of time. It requires a rich soil, and frequent watering in dry weather.

SPINOZA, Baruch, or, as he translated his name, Benedict, was born, in 1632, at Amsterdam, of a Jewish-Portuguese family, and early gave proof of a reflecting mind and an independent spirit, which a scanty education only excited to new efforts. He was early dissatisfied with the instructions of the rabbins, and determined to examine for himself. The goodness of his disposition could not preserve him from persecution when his mode of thinking was discovered. He was calumniated and accused before the synagogue. He refuted the accusations with calmness, in spite of menaces on one hand, and zealous attempts to convert him on the other, but was at length excommunicated. He received the sentence with equanimity, and thenceforth joined no particular religious denomina tion. After this event, Spinoza learned Latin and Greek of Van den Ende, a Dutch physician, and fell in love with his daughter; but a rival succeeded in winning her affections, and Spinoza remained unmarried. The Jews still persecuted him, and even attempted to assassinate him. Meanwhile, he continued his investigations, at first following the doctrines of Descartes, as his Principles of the Cartesian Philosophy show, and, for support, employed himself in grinding optical glasses.—See Siegwart, *On the Connexion of Spinozism with the Cartesian Philosophy* (Tüb., 1816); and Ritter, *On the Influence of the Philosophy of Descartes* (Leipsic, 1816). Through the intrigues of the Jews, he was banished from Amsterdam by the magistrates for several months, and retired quietly to the house of a friend. He then went to Rynsburg, in the vicinity of Leyden, and to Voorburg, near the Hague, where he devoted himself, for three or four years, to philosophical investigations; and at length, in compliance with the solicitations of several friends, he settled permanently at the Hague. Here he published his two principal works. Even his enemies allow that he was very temperate, regular and frugal: in the intercourse of life, he was kind and gentle, always affable and equable, patient, diligently employed in writing or making telescopes, so that he would remain at home for three months together, seeking his chief recreation in a pipe of tobacco, or in observing the contests of flies with spiders. His disinterestedness appears from the circumstance that he refused a gift of 2000 florins and a valuable legacy from his friend Van Vries, who then bequeathed to him an annuity of 500 florins, which Spinoza reduced again to 300. To his avaricious sisters he gave up all his patrimony, which was legally adjudged to him, except a single bed, that he might assert his right. He had many distinguished friends with whom he corresponded. The prince of Condé invited him to visit him, in 1672, at Utrecht, and sent him a passport. Spinoza accepted the invitation, but missed seeing the prince, who had been obliged by business to leave the city. The elector palatine was anxious to draw him to Heidelberg as professor of philosophy, with liberty to lecture as he should see fit; but Spinoza refused For more than twenty years he had a tendency to consumption, and for this reason he observed the strictest temperance; but owing to the clearness of his mind, and the usual kindness of nature to those who labor under this disease, he was calm and cheerful. He died in 1677. Several different authors have written his life, especially Diez (Dessau, 1783) and Philipson (Brunswick, 1790). His works in the Latin language are, 1. the Principles of the Philosophy of Descartes, with an appendix, containing metaphysical opinions (Amsterdam, 1663, 4to.); 2. a Treatise, political and theological, in which it is shown not only that freedom of thought can exist without endangering the public peace and virtue, but that it must necessarily stand or fall with them (1670, 4to.); 3. Posthumous Works (Amsterdam, 1677, 4to.); to wit, *a*. Ethics, demonstrated geometrically; *b*. a Treatise on Politics; *c*. an unfinished work on the Improvement of the Mind; *d*. an unfinished Hebrew Grammar; and *e*. Letters. H. E. G. Paulus published these works of Spinoza in two volumes (Jena, 1802--3). His system is principally laid down in his Ethics, although valuable information is also to be obtained respecting it from his letters. Spinoza felt, like every other philosopher, the longing to elevate himself to a point at which the struggle between matter and mind, liberty and necessity, &c., is done away, and all discord ceases. This led him to the idea of an original substance embracing all existence. Substance, of course, in this sense, means something very different from what we usually understand by the word. (See *Substance.*) This original substance, in which all contradictions cease, and all subjects of finite consciousness disappear, he called God; by which he understood that which has an independent existence, and the understanding of which requires not the idea of any thing else. This substance, according to him, is infinite, and nought else exists; it is incapable of creating any thing material or intellectual, for all matter and mind are comprehended in itself; its attributes are infinite thought and infinite extension. God, this all-embracing being, can act only in accordance with the established order, for otherwise we must suppose him capable of a change of nature, or that there exists a nature different from his own. Thought and extension, spirit and matter, the finite and infinite, motion and repose, good and evil, causes and effects, are attributes of this sole substance, which produces nothing but modifications of itself. All that exists is only a necessary succession of modes of being in a substance for ever the same. It is impossible to give, in a work like the present, a satisfactory sketch of this system, which is very liable to be misunderstood, as it often has been. We can only refer the reader to the works mentioned below. The morality of Spinoza is founded mainly on force and utility.—See Jacobi's work, *The Doctrines of Spinoza, in Letters to Mendelssohn* (Berlin, 1785; 2d ed., 1789); Moses Mendelssohn's *Morning Hours* (Berlin, 2d ed. 1786); and *To the Friends of Lessing, an Appendix to the Correspondence of Jacobi* (Berlin, 1786); also *God and Nature, according to the System of Spinoza*, by G. K. Heydenreich (Leipsic, 1789), with his *Animadversiones in Mosis Mendelii Filii Refutationem, etc.* (Leipsic, 1786); also Franke *On the modern Fate of Spinozism, and its Influence on Philosophy generally* (Sleswic, 1812).

SPONGE (*spongia*); a marine production, generally to be met with in the shops in pieces only. Its texture is cavernous and porous. Its great elasticity, and its property of imbibing, and as readily parting with, a large quantity of water, render it useful. Sponge is to be chosen as light as possible, perfectly clean, and free from stone, of as pale a color as may be, with small holes, and fine, and soft to the touch. It grows in the Archipelago, at considerable depths, on the rocks, about some of the islands there; and multitudes of people make a trade of diving for it. It is also common in the Mediterranean and many other seas, though in general browner or yellower, and not so fine as that of the Archipelago. It adheres in large masses to rocks and stones, sometimes to large shells, and is either round, flat, or hollow, like a funnel. There has been much dispute among naturalists concerning the real nature of the sponge; nor is it yet satisfactorily decided whether it belongs to the animal or vegetable kingdom. But it appears to be destitute of irritability as well as of any locomotive power; and some recent writers have maintained that it is during a part of its existence a vegetable, and during the rest an animal. The opinion that sponge is, like coral, the work of a polype, is erroneous.

SPOTTED FEVER. (See page 600.)

SPRAT, or SARDINE (*clupea sprattus*); a small fish, hardly distinguishable, at first sight, from the herring, but smaller and more slender. It is found in the North Atlantic and Mediterranean, and keeps usually in the depths of the ocean; but during the autumn approaches the shore in vast numbers, for the purpose of depositing its spawn. The fishery is very lucrative, and has become an important branch of commerce in many parts of Europe. Sprats are taken in the same manner as herrings, except that the nets have smaller meshes; but it is necessary to salt them before bringing them to land.

SPRUCE (*abies*). The spruces are more strictly confined to the north than the pines, and their deep, gloomy forests form a striking feature in the vegetation of the colder parts of North America, Asia and Europe. In the U. States, they become rare south of the forty-second parallel of latitude, and are altogether wanting beyond the fortieth, except on the mountains, while in the upper parts of Maine, New Hampshire and Vermont, they constitute the greater portion of the entire forest. They are, however, successfully cultivated for ornament much farther south. They are distinguished from the pines by their habit, and by their solitary evergreen leaves, deprived of a sheath at the base.—The black or double spruce (*A. nigra*) is very abundant in Lower Canada, Newfoundland, New Brunswick, Nova Scotia, Maine, and the upper parts of New Hampshire and Vermont. It grows to the height of seventy or eighty feet, with a trunk a foot or a foot and a half in diameter; and, as the summit has a regular pyramidal form, a solitary tree makes a beautiful appearance. The timber is distinguished for lightness, strength and elasticity, and furnishes most of the spars used for vessels in the U. States. These spars are exported to the West Indies and to Britain, where they are preferred to those of the Norway spruce; but they are not sufficiently large for the yards of ships of war. Knees for vessels, made from the base of the trunk and one of the principal roots, are much used in Maine, and sometimes also at Boston. The timber is, besides, extensively sawed into boards, which are sold one fourth cheaper than those of the white pine, and are exported to the West Indies and to England.—The red spruce is a mere variety of this timber, produced by a difference in soil. It is chiefly with the young branches of this species that the wholesome drink called *spruce beer* is prepared. —The white or single spruce (*A. alba*) inhabits the same districts, but is less abundant. It is a smaller tree, rarely exceeding fifty feet in height, and twelve or sixteen inches in diameter at the base of the trunk. The wood is employed for the same purposes as the preceding, but is inferior in quality. The fibres of the roots are very flexible and tough, and after maceration in water are used in Canada to stitch together the birch-bark canoes. It is distinguished from the preceding by its less crowded leaves, and their pale green color, and the longer and more cylindrical form of its cones. It is much esteemed in Europe as an ornamental tree, and is frequently cultivated in parks and gardens.—The American silver fir (*A. balsamea*) is still less than the white spruce, and rarely exceeds forty feet in height. It is a beautiful tree, having the leaves longer than those of the black spruce, and silvery beneath. The cones are four or five inches in length, cylindrical, obtuse and violaceous. The wood is light, but slightly resinous, and is little used. A few bottles of the turpentine are collected and sold under the improper name of *balm of Gilead;* and this remedy has acquired some celebrity, in England, in certain stages of the pulmonary consumption. This is a favorite ornamental tree in many parts of the U. States.—The hemlock spruce (*A. Canadensis*) is readily distinguished by having the leaves distichous, or disposed in two ranks, and the cones terminal. It is one of our most beautiful trees, and is particularly valuable for the properties of the bark. (See *Hemlock Spruce.*)—The European firs are more lofty than our own, but the properties of the timber are analogous: that of the Norway spruce (*A. communis*) is called *white deal* in England.

Spunge. (See *Sponge*, on page 597.)

Squill. The officinal squill (*scilla maritima* of Linnæus) is now referred to the genus *ornithogalum.* This plant is allied to the onion, which it somewhat resembles: there are six stamens and a single style; the calyx is wanting, and the corolla is deeply divided into six segments: the root is a bulb almost as large as a man's head, and similar in form and structure to that of the onion; the stem upright, cylindrical, terminated by a long raceme of white flowers: the leaves appear after the flowers, and are all radical, very large, oval-lanceolate and fleshy. It grows on the sandy coasts of the Mediterranean. The bulb has a nauseous, bitter and acrid taste, but is destitute of any perceptible odor. It is poisonous to several animals, and, if much handled, produces ulcers on the skin. In large doses, it occasions vomiting, strangury, inflammation of the stomach and bowels, &c.; but in small doses, acts simply as an expectorant and diuretic. It has been much esteemed from antiquity, and its various preparations are much used in medicine.

Squirrel (*sciurus*); a genus of quadrupeds, belonging to the *rodentia*, or gnawers, distinguished from most animals of the tribe by the compressed form of the lower incisors. The upper lip is cleft; the fur soft and silky; the molar teeth are four on each side of the lower jaw, and five in the upper, the first of which is only a small tubercle, often shed with age; the incisors are two in each jaw; the toes are armed with hooked nails, by means of which these animals are enabled to climb trees, among the branches of which they pass their lives, feeding on the fruit. Their light and graceful motions, their beauty, and extreme neatness, have made them general favorites. When on the ground, they move by successive leaps, with the tail extended and undulating; but the forest is their home, and they display wonderful activity in leaping from branch to branch, sometimes stopping to listen, sitting erect upon their hinder limbs, with the tail elevated like a plume. In the same posture they take their food, using their fore-feet like hands. The hardest nuts serve them for nutriment, and the facility with which they cut through the shell is remarkable. They build nests of sticks and leaves, in the tops of trees, or sometimes in hollow trunks. Previous to the approach of winter, they lay up large hoards of nuts and grain for future use. When in captivity, they permit themselves to be handled, without ever appearing to distinguish the person who takes care of them, or experiencing any real attachment for him. The species are numerous in the U. States, but at present are not very well understood. In some districts, they multiply so exceedingly as to become a pest to the farmers, literally laying waste the cornfields: the woods and fields seem then to be alive with them, and sometimes they make partial migrations, during which, vast numbers are drowned in crossing rivers.—The fox squirrel (*S. vulpinus*) inhabits, exclusively, the pine forests of the Southern States, and is our largest species. The body is fourteen inches in length, and the tail sixteen. The color is gray and black, or mottled, &c.—*S. capistratus* is a variety having the nose white.—The cat squirrel (*S. cinereus*) is found in the Northern and Middle States, and is distinguished by its size and by the fur being less coarse in its texture. The length of the body is twelve inches, and of the tail fourteen; the color cinereous above, and white beneath; the tail is less distichous than in the others, and striped with black. There are four molar teeth only on each side of the upper jaw.—The gray squirrel (*S. Carolinensis*) is still very common in most parts of the U. States, especially in oak, hickory and chestnut forests. Formerly, it was so abundant in many districts as to become a scourge to the inhabitants. It is remarkable for its beauty and activity, and, when kept in confinement, is exceedingly playful and mischievous. It is much smaller than the two preceding; the color is usually fine bluish-gray, mixed with a slight tinge of orange, and the tail is edged with white. These three species often occur entirely black, and in this state have been described as a distinct species.—The great-tailed squirrel (*S. macrourus*) is the most common species on the Missouri. It is a large species, of a ferruginous color, and has the tail larger than the others.—The red squirrel, chick-a-ree, or Hudson's bay squirrel (*S. Hudsonius*), is a beautiful species, very common in the Northern States. The ears are distinctly tufted; the color is reddish-brown above, pale beneath, with a pretty distinct black line on each flank. It is smaller than the gray squirrel.—*S. quadrivittatus* is a very small species, inhabiting the vicinity of the Rocky mountains, about the head waters of the Platte and Arkansas. The general color is reddish above, mixed with black, and whitish beneath, with four broad white lines on the back. It has not been observed to ascend trees, but nestles in holes, or on the edges of rocks; and the nest is composed of a most extraordinary quantity of different vegetable substances, sometimes sufficient to fill a cart. Its principal food seems to consist of the seeds of the pine.—The ground squirrel (*tamias lysteri*) has been separated from *sciurus*, on account of the presence of cheek-pouches; it differs also, somewhat, in its habits, as it makes a burrow, generally, about the roots of trees, or along fences and walls, often of considerable extent, and having several branches, and always two openings. It is one of the most familiar animals in the U. States, and is usually seen running along fences and walls; but it occasionally ascends trees. On the back are five longitudinal black bands, separated on each side by two white ones. It is a very pretty and lively animal.—The common flying squirrel (*pteromys volucella*) differs from *sciurus* in having the skin on the sides very loose, and capable of being spread out when the limbs are extended, with the assistance of an additional bone articulated with the wrist. By means of this structure, the flying squirrels are enabled to make surprising leaps: taking advantage of the wind, they launch into the air, buoyed up as by a parachute, and sail swiftly and obliquely downwards. It is an exceedingly beautiful animal, very common in many parts of the U. States. Another and larger species is found in Canada and about the Rocky mountains. The squirrels of North America are far from being well understood, and, probably, more will be discovered, especially about the Rocky mountains and in the region beyond. It is much to be regretted, that the author of the Fauna of British North America, while waiting at New York for a passage to England, did not avail himself of the opportunity to visit the Philadelphia museum; as much of the confusion respecting the animals brought by the expedition of Lewis and Clarke might then have been removed. Lewis's squirrel (*sciurus Lewisii* of Hamilton Smith) (see Griffith's *Translation of Cuvier*) is a marmot (*spermophilus*, probably the *S. Franklinii*); Clarke's squirrel of the same author, is also a *spermophilus;* the nails of these animals are too straight to permit them to ascend trees. There exists, however, in the collection brought by those enterprising travellers, a specimen, apparently a true squirrel, which seems to have escaped the prying eyes of naturalists: it is about as large as the chick-a-ree, and has pretty much the same distribution of colors, except that there is less of the reddish tint, and a considerable portion of the tail is entirely black.

Stalactites are formed by the filtration of water, containing calcareous particles, through pores or fissures in the roofs of those caverns which are frequent in limestone. The water, having percolated through the roofs, remains suspended in drops. Evaporation commences at the exterior of the drop, and the calcareous particles are deposited on the roof of the cavern in the form of a little ring, which extends by degrees till a small tube is produced. The bore of this tube is, in most cases, diminished by successive deposits, till it becomes entirely closed; and the stalactite then increases by concentric layers applied to the exterior. Thus cylinders or cones are produced, and sometimes so enlarged that they unite with each other. While the stalactite is forming, a part of the water drops from it on the floor of the cavern, or trickles down the sides, and thus produces those calcareous concretions called *stalagmites.* When large, they are called *alabaster.* On the floor, they often form large masses, sometimes rising till they meet the stalactites pendent from the roof, and extending in all directions. A great variety of imitative forms are produced; hence a lively imagination will perceive, in these caverns, representations of the most diverse objects, especially by the light of a candle. The color of stalactites is seldom pure white; it more frequently presents shades of yellow, red, or brown. Among the more remarkable foreign localities of stalactites are the grotto of Antiparos, in the Archipelago; Baumann's cave, in the Hartz; Pool's hole, in Derbyshire; the caves of La Balme, in Savoy; and of Auxelle, in Franche Comté. Fine specimens of alabaster are found in Spain, near Grenada, &c., in Italy, Sicily and Sardinia. The most beautiful alabaster employed by the ancients, is supposed to have been found in Egypt, in mountains west of the Red sea. In the U. States are many caverns containing stalactites.

STAR OF BETHLEHEM (*ornithogalum umbellatum*). This plant is sometimes called *eleven o'clock,* from the circumstance of the flowers opening at about that time in the morning. It is allied to, and somewhat resembles, the onion. The root is a bulb; the leaves are linear, and all radical; the stem six or eight inches high, and terminated by a corymb of six or eight white and star-like flowers: these last are very evanescent, and close four or five hours after expansion. The plant grows wild in Europe, and is sometimes cultivated in our gardens for ornament; it is, besides, naturalized in some parts of the U. States.

STARLING (*sturnus*). The common European starling, in size and in its habits, somewhat resembles the red-winged blackbird of the U. States. The color is blackish, with blue, purplish, or cupreous reflections, and each feather is marked at the extremity with a whitish speck. The beak is long, straight, entire, somewhat flattened and obtuse at the extremity; the tail shorter than in our blackbirds. It is found in almost all parts of the eastern continent, and, except in the breeding season, lives in numerous flocks, retiring in the evening to marshes, to pass the night among the reeds. The flight of these birds is peculiar: they form a sort of vortex while advancing. During the day time, they disperse throughout the fields, and seem particularly fond of the company of cattle. They are often kept in cages, and learn to whistle some tunes, and even to pronounce words and sentences. The meadow-lark of the U. States is a species of *sturnus*, but it differs widely, in its habits and appearance, from the European starling; the bill however, is similar in form.

SPOTTED FEVER. An epidemic disease, now generally recognised by the name of *spotted fever*, prevailed extensively in many parts of New England, and in some parts of several of the other American states, at different times between the years 1806 and 1815. A few cases of the disease occurred in Medfield, Massachusetts, about thirty miles south-west of Boston, in March, 1806. The number was small, however, not exceeding twenty, and the disease did not extend itself so as to attract general attention until the following year. In March and April, 1807, it appeared in Hartford, Connecticut, and in several other places on the Connecticut river; and also in Williamstown, in the north-western part of Massachusetts, on the Green mountain range. It disappeared during the summer, but returned the following winter, visiting, in some instances, the same places, besides many others in the same neighborhoods and similar situations, and also attacking other and detached parts of New England. The disease followed a similar course for several succeeding years. It disappeared during the summer, and recurred with the return of winter; and for several years, until 1813, it became, each year, more extensive and more destructive. In some of these years, it also prevailed extensively in the interior of the states of New York and Pennsylvania. In 1812, the troops of the U. States' army suffered by it severely at various places in New York and Vermont. After 1813, the disease rapidly diminished, although it still remained destructive, especially in some parts of Maine. It finally ceased in the spring of 1815. The last place visited by it, so far as our information extends, was Berwick, in Maine. There have, indeed, been occasional reports of the prevalence of a similar disease, at different times since that period; but it may well be doubted whether any of them actually refer to the true spotted fever as it prevailed from 1807 to 1815. This concise sketch of the progress of the epidemic shows that it prevailed much less in summer than in winter. In fact, it was only during a part of the colder season of the year that the disease raged the most severely. Unlike the ordinary typhus fever of our climate, it was much less frequent through the autumn and the early part of winter than during the later months of winter and the first months of spring.

It is worthy of remark, that the disease, in a great measure, avoided the large towns on the sea-coast. Although it pervaded, at different times, almost the whole of the interior of New England, Boston and the other large towns were only slightly visited by it. In the interior also, the epidemic was not more prevalent, perhaps even less so, in the larger and more crowded villages, than among the more scattered population. This is the more remarkable since those persons whose modes of life render them peculiarly susceptible to disease of every kind are more frequently collected in the larger towns and villages. But this epidemic seemed scarcely to regard peculiar susceptibilities of any kind. The man whose constitution was exhausted by excesses, undoubtedly yielded more readily if attacked, and fell a more certain victim, than the man of temperate and regular habits. But it does not appear that such were more frequently attacked than others. On the contrary, the disease seemed rather to select the healthy and vigorous. Although its range embraced persons in every period of life, from childhood to old age, yet the proportion of cases and of deaths was much greater among adults of mature age, of firm health, and of habits every way calculated to resist ordinary disease. In many an agricultural town in New England, the correct, virtuous, middle-aged heads of families were swept off in such numbers as to leave an impression on the general aspect of the community which is even now observable, after the space of twenty years, in the absence of old men from their congregations when assembled for their weekly public worship.

Of the extent of the mortality produced by the spotted fever, there are no means of obtaining accurate knowledge. Except in the larger towns, no returns are preserved of the number of deaths, or their causes. There are, therefore, no data upon which to found an estimate of the destruction of life caused by this epidemic. It was, however, very great, and, from the character and relative station of many of its victims, peculiarly afflicting. The visitation, too, was sudden, and, therefore, produced the greater alarm and distress. In some instances, the disease visited a place twice, or even three times. But, in general, its work was accomplished in a single visitation of a few weeks duration. Dr. Gallup remarks of the epidemic in Vermont, that "There are but few towns whose surviving inhabitants will not long, with grief, remember the winter of 1812—13, for the loss of twenty, forty or eighty of their most valuable citizens—most valuable to society on account of their being adult persons, and at the acme of human life."*

Of the causes of spotted fever, no satisfactory account can be given. There was nothing in the habits of the disease, or the manner in which it proceeded from place to place, to countenance the supposition of contagion; and such an opinion, we believe, has never been suggested. It is difficult to reconcile the phenomena of this disease to any of the other theories by which the progress of epidemics has been explained. If we attribute it to some secret atmospheric influence, it is not easy to account for the irregular and fitful manner in which it lighted upon detached and distant places almost at the same moment, while intermediate places were passed by for the time, only to be the subjects of a future visitation. It is still more improbable that exhalations from the surface of the earth could have been the cause, for the favorite season of the disease was when the whole surface of the earth was fast locked up by the frost. For a time, many physicians were inclined to suppose that ergot in the rye, which is much used in New England, might have contributed to produce the disease. But it has never been shown that ergot was more abundant in those years in which the epidemic prevailed, than in others; and what is still more conclusive, the disease was not confined to those districts in which rye was used for bread. We must, therefore, regard the peculiar causes of spotted fever as altogether unknown.

In the description of the disease, we must necessarily be very brief. There were two leading forms of it. One was a simple fever of a peculiar character. The other was complicated by local inflammation, but still retaining the same general character as the other. The more simple form began, like most other fevers, with coldness, not generally with distinct shivering; pain in the head and back, and especially in the limbs; prostration of strength, &c. In the milder cases, this was followed, as in other fevers, with some degree of reaction, manifested by heat, and afterwards by sweating; but,

* Epidemics of Vermont.

unless aided by proper remedies, the reaction was very imperfect; the coldness soon returned, with a peculiar want of action over the whole system. The surface of the body lost its peculiar elasticity, and had, in its stead, a torpid, half-œdematous, doughy feeling. Near the close of life, it was covered with a profuse perspiration. The stomach early became irritable, and rejected whatever was put into it, though without much vomiting of any thing else. The prostration increased, and was accompanied by violent pains in the back or limbs, which frequently changed from place to place, but without spasms of any kind. In many cases delirium came on very early. In most, as the strength of the patient failed, the mind became obscured, and he died comatose. In the more severe form of the disease, this comatose state followed the first attack, without any intervention of a stage of reaction: the patient became insensible, and died in a few hours. It was generally in this severe form that the spots, or *petechiæ*, appeared, which gave the name of *spotted* fever to the epidemic. They were not, however, confined to the more violent, or to the fatal cases, but were occasionally found in those which were comparatively mild. Neither, on the other hand, were they, by any means, general in the severer cases. In the earlier periods of the epidemic, they were much more common than towards the close of its progress. When they did appear, the spots were generally small blotches, caused by blood extravasated into the cellular membrane under the skin, of a dark purple color. In many other cases there was a slight eruption of a very different character, which seemed to be caused by the excited state of the skin, where the diaphoretic and stimulating mode of treatment was carried to a great extent.

About the beginning of the year 1812, the spotted fever first began to assume a new form, in many cases, by becoming complicated with some local inflammation. This inflammation was sometimes in the throat, producing a species of cynanche; but its more common seat was some one or more of the textures of the lungs. The fever, however, still retained the same general character as before; and in most of the places where this form of the disease prevailed, frequent cases of the more simple form were intermingled with it. The cases with inflammation were ushered in, rather more frequently than the others, with a distinct chill; and this was oftener, perhaps, followed by a distinct reaction; but the general disease did not in these, any more than in the others, retain an inflammatory character. On the contrary, it ran speedily into a state of great depression; and when death ensued, it seemed to be less from the influence of the pulmonic symptoms, than from the violence of the general disease. There was pain in the chest, cough, and bloody expectoration; but these symptoms, although sometimes severe in the commencement of the disease, rarely retained their prominence so long as to appear to exert a very important influence upon the course of the disease, or to demand much consideration in the treatment, beyond what was necessary to give relief to the symptoms themselves. There were many other varieties in the modifications of the spotted fever, which the limits of this sketch will not permit us to notice; for it assumed a greater diversity of forms and appearances than most diseases. It was not always sudden and abrupt in its attack, as we have here described it, but sometimes crept on silently, slowly converting a slight indisposition into a severe and often fatal disorder. In whatever form it appeared, however, it preserved the same general character of great prostration and debility.

Little is known of its pathological character, except what is learned by inferences from its description and history. Only a few examinations after death were made. The state of the public feeling throughout the interior of New England was much less favorable to such examinations, twenty years ago, than it is now; and the medical profession were then much less accustomed to press the importance of this mode of investigation than at present. Such examinations as were made, have done little to enlighten us in regard to the essential character of the disease. And had they been much more numerous, the result would probably have been no more conclusive, than that of similar observations, in respect to the nature of fever in general. The blood was found to remain fluid for some hours after death. It consequently flowed to the depending parts, giving a dark color to the skin in those parts, which was often mistaken by careless observers for putrefaction. But putrefaction did not begin early after death. The vessels of the brain, as might be expected from the comatose state which preceded most of the deaths, were found to be turgid with blood, and there was more or less effusion of serum into the ventricles, and sometimes of lymph under the arachnoid. In the chest, the heart sometimes exhibited marks of disease; its vessels being peculiarly injected with blood. The lungs, in the cases of simple spotted fever, were healthy. We have seen few accounts of dissections in the pneumonic form of the disease. In some cases, ulcerations, of a peculiar character, with black, gangrenous edges, were found in the pleura of the lungs, extending deep into the substance of the organ. This appearance can hardly have existed except in the severest form of pneumonic affection. But we do not remember any description of marks of inflammation in the lungs, which did not involve the serous membrane, although, from the symptoms, it can hardly be doubted that many such cases existed. The abdominal viscera were generally healthy. The gall bladder and the urinary bladder were filled with their appropriate fluids, showing that the secretions had been carried on until death. The result of our pathological observations is, that this disease was a fever, having a peculiar tendency to run rapidly into a state of great prostration and debility, and often more or less complicated with local inflammation of an erysipelatous character.

The practice which had previously been applied to ordinary fevers, was so entirely unsuccessful in the treatment of spotted fever, that many of the practitioners on whom the management of the disease at first devolved, seem early to have lost all confidence, not only in such a course of practice, but also in the resources of professional skill and science, and for a time to have abandoned themselves and their patients to empirical experiments. A respectable writer gives the credit to a worthy matron, of the first discovery of a successful treatment. This consisted in exciting a profuse perspiration, by drinking large quantities of a decoction of the leaves and twigs of the ground hemlock, or dwarf yew, aided by a rude sort of vapor bath, made by boiling billets of wood (of the hemlock, if to be obtained), and laying them, wrapped in cloths, into bed with the patient, who was, at the same time, to be kept highly stimulated with brandy, and other diffusible stimulants. But the more judicious and scientific part of the profession were not long in adapting their treatment to the true state of the disease. Adopting a hint, perhaps, from the effects of the empirical sweating and stimulating, which soon became common, they were able to pursue a course of diaphoretics and stimulants, which, while it avoided the dangers of empirical excess, was eminently successful in arresting the fatal tendency of the disease. Such diaphoretics were selected, as, while they act promptly and surely, have the least tendency to induce debility. A moist heat, applied externally, added much to the efficacy of internal diaphoretics. A combination of ipecacuanha, opium, and camphor, sometimes with the addition of calomel, was much used, and with the best effects. It was necessary that a gentle diaphoresis should be constantly preserved, always with great care avoiding profuse sweating. The true measure of the use of stimulants, was the preservation of a healthful temperature and an equable pulse. In some cases, the tendency to coldness and prostration was so great, that large quantities of the most powerful kind were necessary—brandy, in hot water, tincture of cinnamon, tincture of opium, with tinctures of peppermint and lavender, were among the best; and these must be used, not so much in reference to the quantities given, as to the effects produced. Very early in the disease, almost as soon as a diaphoresis was established, tonics of a more permanent character were employed. The cinchona, in its different modes of administration, was chiefly relied upon. A favorite mode of using it, by many physicians, was in a fermented decoction, with orange peel and serpentaria. A nutritious and rather stimulating liquid diet was directed also quite early in the disease. Emetics were avoided, or used only when there were manifest symptoms of decided derangement of the stomach; and cathartics were only used to remove costiveness, and then none but the mildest laxatives were admissible. In the pulmonic form of the disease, blisters and expectorants were added to the other means. It was sometimes necessary, on account of the cough, &c., to defer a little the use of the cinchona and other tonics; but this did not often happen, and it never appeared safe to wait for a decided convalescence before resorting to them.

This is a mere outline of the treatment adopted by a large proportion of the most successful practitioners in this singular and formidable disease. It of course admitted and required great diversity in its application to the many varieties of form and symptoms which the disease assumed in different places and in the several cases

There were a few physicians, however, who objected to such a stimulating practice, and insisted upon the necessity of blood-letting and other evacuants, and who still contend, that an anti-phlogistic course of treatment was the most successful. It may be said, indeed, that the prostration and debility must have been produced by some active disease, and if that disease could be arrested by early bleeding, and other means, much of the prostration would be prevented. But, however true this may be in general, in the present instance, the good effects which generally followed a judicious course of stimulants, sufficiently showed that no such disorganization was produced by the disease, which was supposed to cause the debility, as to render it unsafe to trust to them to remove it. If the bleeding recommended had failed to prevent the sinking by arresting the disease, it must have increased the exhaustion, and consequently added to the difficulty of the cure; and to perceive accurately when it would be liable to do this, would have required a nicety of discrimination greater than belongs to most practitioners of medicine, if, indeed, it can ever be attained.

The results of the treatment were very various in different places. In many places, the disease, though violent and severe, yielded to remedies with a docility truly remarkable. At the same time, it required unceasing vigilance and care to prevent fatal relapses. In such places, most of the deaths *seemed* to result more from accidental imprudences or neglect, than from the incurable nature of the disease itself. In other places, the disease was speedily fatal to a large proportion of those attacked. In some small districts, twenty or thirty died in rapid succession, before any recovered. Much of this inequality is doubtless to be attributed to differences in the virulence of the epidemic itself. But there are many facts which go to show, that something must be ascribed to diversities of treatment. The comparison here intended, is not between the diaphoretic and stimulating practice on the one hand, and the anti-phlogistic on the other, so much as between either of these and an awkward attempt to engraft either upon a routine of earlier days, which many men found it difficult to abandon. To our minds, the stimulating treatment, properly regulated, was incomparably preferable in its effects to the bleeding; but either was immeasurably better than the hesitating, inefficient practice to which we have alluded. If it were proper to go into details, many examples might be adduced, in which a change of practice was followed by a change of results, in the same neighborhood, and often in the same families, so immediate and so striking, as to render it difficult to attribute the difference to any thing but the change of treatment.—The principal treatises on spotted fever, besides various papers in the several medical journals of the time, are North on Spotted Fever; Strong on do.; a Report of a Committee of the Massachusetts Medical Society, published in the second volume of that society's communications; Gallup on the Epidemics of Vermont; and Hale on the Spotted Fever in Gardiner.

CONTENTS.

www.ingramcontent.com/pod-product-compliance
Lightning Source LLC
LaVergne TN
LVHW021103110826
845150LV00001B/157